D1080062

CHILDREN'S
ILLUSTRATED
ENCYCLOPEDIA

REVISED EDITION

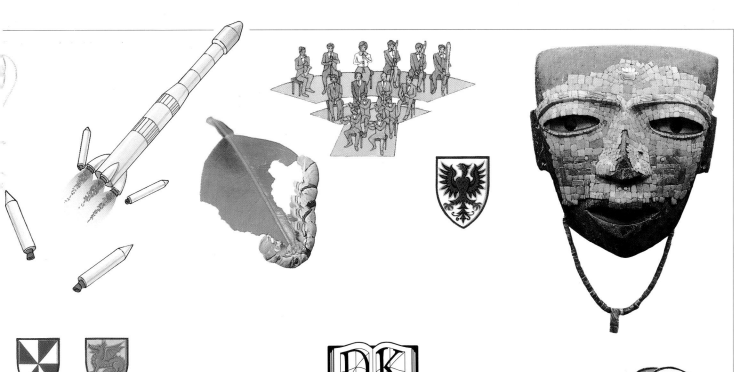

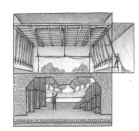

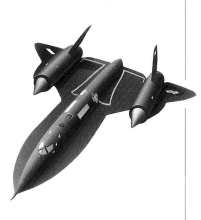

DK

CHILDREN'S ILLUSTRATED ENCYCLOPEDIA

REVISED EDITION

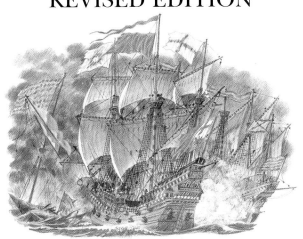

DK

DORLING KINDERSLEY

London • New York • Moscow • Sydney

www.dk.com

A DORLING KINDERSLEY BOOK
www.dk.com

Senior Editor Ann Kramer
Senior Art Editor Miranda Kennedy
Editors
Christiane Gunzi, Susan McKeever, Richard Platt, Clifford Rosney
Art Editors
Muffy Dodson, Debra Lee, Christian Sévigny, Val Wright
Picture Research Anne Lyons
Additional Research Anna Kunst, Deborah Murrell
Picture Manager Kate Fox
Production Manager Teresa Solomon
Editorial Director Sue Unstead

Contributors
Simon Adams, Neil Ardley, Norman Barrett, Judy Clark, Chris Cooper,
John Farndon, Adrian Gilbert, Barbara Gilgallon, Peter Lafferty, Margaret Lincoln,
Antony Mason, Rupert Matthews, Steve Parker, Steve Peak, Sue Seddon,
Marilyn Tolhurst, Frances Williams, Tim Wood

Advisors and Consultants

CHEMISTRY AND PHYSICS
Ian M. Kennedy BSc
Jeff Odell BSc, MSc, PhD

CULTURE AND SOCIETY
Iris Barry
Margaret Cowan
John Denny B.Mus.Hons
Dr. Peter Drewett BSc, PhD, FSA, MIFA
Dr. Jamal, Islamic Cultural Centre
Mlles Smith-Morris
Brian Williams BA
The Buddhist Society

EARTH RESOURCES
April Arden Dip.M
Hedda Bird BSc
Conservation Papers Ltd.
Peter Nolan, British Gas Plc
Stephen Webster BSc M.Phil
Earth Conservation Data Centre

EARTH SCIENCES
Erica Brissenden
Alan Heward PhD
Keith Lye BA, FRGS
Rodney Miskin MIPR, MAIE
Shell UK Ltd.
Christine Woodward
The Geological Museum, London
Meteorological Office

ENGINEERING
Karen Barratt
Jim Lloyd, Otis Plc
Alban Wincott
Mark Woodward MSc, DICC.Eng, MICE

HISTORY
Dr. Anne Millard BA, Dip Ed, Dip Arch, PhD
Ray Smith
The Indian High Commission
Campaign for Nuclear Disarmament

MEDICINE AND THE HUMAN BODY
Dr.T. Kramer MB, BS (London), MRCS, LRCP
Dr. Frances Williams MB BChir, MRCP

NATURAL HISTORY
Wendy Ladd and staff of Natural History Museum
London Zoo

SPACE SCIENCE
NASA
Neil MacIntyre MA, PhD, FRGS
John Randall BSc, PGCE
Christian Ripley BSc, MSc,
Carole Stott BA, FRAS

SPORT
Brian Aldred
David Barber
Lance Cone
John Jelley BA
International Olympic Committee

TECHNOLOGY
Jeremy Hazzard BISC
Paul Macarthy BSc, MSc,
Cosson Electronics Ltd.
Robert Stone BSc, MSc,
C. Psychol, AFBsF, M. ErgS,
Advanced Robotic Research Ltd.
Stuart Wickes B. Eng,
British Broadcasting Corporation

TRANSPORT
Doug Lloyd,
Westland Helicopters Ltd.
John Pimlott BA PhD
Tony Robinson
Wing Commander Spilsbury,
Royal Air Force
M.J. Whitty GI Sore.E

First published in Great Britain in 1991
by Dorling Kindersley Limited,
9 Henrietta Street, London WC2E 8PS
Reprinted 1991, 1992 (twice), 1993
Reprinted with revisions 1992
Second edition 1993
Third edition 1995
Fourth edition 1996, reprinted 1997
Updated and revised 1999

2 4 6 8 10 9 7 5 3
Copyright © 1991, 1993, 1995, 1996 Dorling Kindersley Limited, London

A CIP catalogue record for this book is available from the British Library.

ISBN 0 7513 5770 7

Reproduced by Colourscan, Singapore
Printed and bound in Slovakia by Neografia

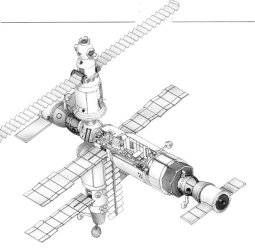

CONTENTS

HOW TO USE THIS BOOK

IT'S EASY TO FIND what you're looking for in *The Dorling Kindersley Children's Illustrated Encyclopedia*. The next three pages will show you how. Main entries are in alphabetical order, beginning with Aboriginal Australians and ending with Zoos. Each main entry has either one or two pages to itself. A large heading at the top of the page tells you what the entry is about.

Just look through the headings alphabetically for the topic you want to learn about. If you can't find it, that means it is not a main entry and does not have its own page. In that case, turn to the index at the back; it will tell you what page to look at for information about your topic.

ENTRY HEADING
Entry headings describe the main entries. This is the main entry on the Bronze Age.

MAPS
Many pages include a map to show the location of a certain area in the world. For example, this map shows the location of Mesopotamia, where one of the first Bronze Age civilizations began.

INTRODUCTION
Each entry begins with an introduction which explains the subject. The introduction provides basic facts you need to know before reading on.

MEASUREMENTS AND ABBREVIATIONS

SIZE COMPARISONS
Occasionally you will find this girl and boy. They stand about 1.2 m (4 ft) tall and they are there to give you an idea of the size of different things, such as a rocket or a dinosaur.

ABBREVIATIONS
Some words are abbreviated, or shortened, in the encyclopedia. The list below explains what the abbreviations stand for:

°C = degrees Celsius
°F = degrees Fahrenheit
mm = millimetre
cm = centimetre
m = metre
km = kilometre
sq km = square kilometre
km/h = kilometres per hour
in = inch
ft = foot
yd = yard
sq mile = square mile
mph = miles per hour
g = gram
kg = kilogram
oz = ounce
lb = pound
l = litre
c. before a date = "about"
B.C. = before Christ.
A.D. = anno Domini, which refers to any time after the birth of Christ.

PHOTOGRAPHS
There are all kinds of photographs in the encyclopedia showing people, places, machines, and objects. This photograph of the Standard of Ur shows you what Bronze Age charioteers looked like.

This photograph of a Bronze Age chariot mount was specially photographed in a museum.

SUB-ENTRIES
You will find more topics under these large headings. They are sub-entries or additional entries and they occur on nearly every page in the encyclopedia. This sub-entry, for example, tells you about Sumer, a place in Mesopotamia where many Bronze Age developments took place.

ILLUSTRATIONS
Many pages in the encyclopedia are illustrated with detailed drawings. For example, this illustration of a Sumerian village shows what daily life was like in the Bronze Age.

BRITTLESTAR *see* STARFISH AND SEA URCHINS

BRONZE AGE

ABOUT 8,000 YEARS AGO, humans discovered how to work with metal. At first, people made things from naturally occurring copper and gold nuggets, hammering them into shape with hard stones. But gradually craftsworkers learned how to work these metals by heating them until they were liquid, then pouring the liquid metal into molds. The advantages of metal were obvious. It could be cast into complicated shapes to make tools, weapons, and other objects and, if broken, could be melted down and remade. People probably first discovered bronze by accidentally mixing a little tin with copper. They soon realized that bronze was harder and longer lasting than other metals, and could be given a sharper edge. Bronze weapons and tools could also be resharpened. Gradually the Bronze Age began as people worked with bronze in workshops and villages. One of the first places to produce bronze was Sumer, in Mesopotamia, where the first cities developed.

MESOPOTAMIA
One of the first Bronze Age civilizations began in Sumer, in Mesopotamia. Mesopotamia was a plain lying between the Tigris and Euphrates rivers. Its fertile land was farmed by the Sumerians.

WRITING AND THE WHEEL
The earliest form of writing, called cuneiform emerged during the Bronze Age. It was invented by the Sumerians, who also made the first wheels, which they used on wagons and war chariots and to make pottery. Wild asses pulled the chariots into battle, shown in the Standard of Ur, above.

HORSES
Horses came into widespread use during the late Bronze Age. Aristocratic horsemen often had elaborate bronze mounts on their chariots, such as this one with a red enamel pattern, found in Norfolk, England.

SUMER
The Sumerian plains were fertile but dry. The farmers dug ditches and canals to control the water from the rivers and irrigate the land. They could produce huge harvests, sometimes twice a year.

BRICKMAKING
Like many places in Bronze Age Middle East, there was no stone and little wood in Sumer. Large buildings, such as temples and palaces, were made from bricks. Sumerians mixed mud with chopped straw and poured the mixture into molds. The bricks dried quickly in the hot sun.

Plowing the land with oxen

Pouring mud mixture into molds

Digging up mud to make the brick mixture

The Sumerians left their bricks to dry in the hot sun.

78

CAPTIONS AND EXPLANATIONS
Every picture has a caption that explains and describes the illustration, such as this one about bricklaying (above). Many important and interesting details within an illustration or photograph are also explained nearby. A line usually connects each detail to its explanation.

RUNNING INDEX

Subjects appear in main entries only if there is a full page or more devoted to them. To help you find other subjects, there is a running index at the top of most pages. For instance, there is no full-page entry on "Brittle star", but the running index tells you to turn to the main entry "Starfish and Sea Urchins", where you will find a picture and information about the brittle star. Like main entries, the running index is also alphabetical.

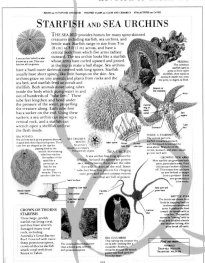

INDEX

There is a 15-page index at the back of the book where you can find any subject mentioned in the encyclopedia. The numbers in the index refer to page numbers.
• Numbers in **bold** type refer to main A to Z entries.
• Numbers in *italic* type refer to pages in the Fact Finder, the reference section at the back of the encyclopedia.
• Numbers in normal type refer to general references within the encyclopedia.

The number 77 tells you that there is a main entry about bridges on page 77.

Brian Boru, King 287
bricks 78, 456
bridges **77**, 221, *623*
Brisbane 52
Britain *see* United Kingdom
British Empire 571
British Isles 285
British Raj 278
brittle stars 515

The number 623 tells you that there is more information about bridges in the Fact Finder.

The number 515 tells you that brittle stars are mentioned on page 515.

TIME LINE

Many entries include a time line, which is like a calendar of history on a scroll. Time lines give you all the dates you need, at a glance. This time line guides you through the Bronze Age from its beginning to the time when iron replaced bronze as the main metal that people used.

4500 B.C. First plough used in Mesopotamia. Sails first used on boats sailing on the Tigris and Euphrates rivers.

The date comes first, followed by a brief description of the event.

ASSYRIANS

TWO THOUSAND YEARS AGO, a mighty empire rose to power in the Middle East where Iraq is today. This was the Assyrian Empire.

CELTS

TWO THOUSAND YEARS AGO, much of western Europe was inhabited by a fierce, proud, artistic people known as the Celts.

PREHISTORIC PEOPLES

COMPARED WITH the rest of life on Earth, human beings arrived quite recently, after the dinosaur age and the age of mammals.

Find out more

ASSYRIANS
BABYLONIANS
CELTS
GREECE, ANCIENT
PREHISTORIC PEOPLES

The "find out more" box at the bottom of each new entry will send you to yet more entries so that from Bronze Age you can get to Prehistoric Life and beyond.

FIND OUT MORE

You will see a "find out more" box at the bottom right-hand corner of each entry page. This box directs you to other main entries that are related to the one you are reading. Turn to any of the entries listed in the "find out more" box and you will learn more about your subject.

For example, the Bronze Age "find out more" box lists five related entries: Assyrians, Babylonians, Celts, Ancient Greece, and Prehistoric Peoples. By turning to these you will discover more about the Bronze Age and "find out more" about other subjects.

PREHISTORIC LIFE

WHEN PLANET EARTH FORMED more than 4.5 billion years ago, there was no life.

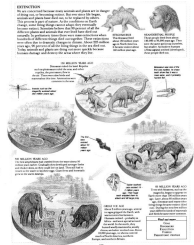

MAPS

All the continents and major countries of the world have special map pages. On each map page you will find lots of information about that country. The map itself shows all the main regions, physical features, major cities, and some historical sites. Every map page has a fact box containing flags, information about the region, and photographs of important places.

On all map pages (except for those showing whole continents) you will find the flag of every country in the area shown.

A fact box alongside each map gives important statistics of the region such as land area, population, religion, and currency.

Each map page includes photographs to give you an idea of what the country and its people look like.

If there are any major islands that are too small to see on the main map, they are shown enlarged in a box.

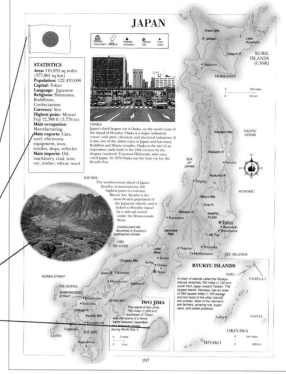

JAPAN

SYMBOLS
Each map has symbols which indicate the following features:

★ *Capital city of the country*

● *Major cities and largest towns*

▲ *Tallest mountain or highest point in the country*

Major volcanoes, including those that are no longer active

▥ *Ancient monument or place of historical importance*

There is a scale on each map so that you can work out distances.

0 — 100 miles
0 — 200 km

A compass rose shows you where the directions of north, south, east, and west lie on the map.

FACT FINDER
At the back of the encyclopedia is the Fact Finder, an illustrated reference section with information on history, science, geography, and nature. The Fact Finder provides instant information that will help you with homework and school projects, all clearly arranged in charts and tables.

HISTORY
The history section summarizes the history of the world from prehistory to the present day, with each page concentrating on one continent.

A time line runs across the top of all six pages so you can compare what was happening in each continent on a certain date.

You will also find lists of the world's greatest writers, artists, and composers.

Charts list the world's tallest buildings, longest bridges, largest islands, and highest mountains.

NATURE
The nature section includes a comprehensive chart classifying plants and animals, a list of endangered species, and many other facts about the natural world.

SCIENCE
The science section contains measurement conversion charts, mathematical formulas, star maps, and the periodic table.

THE WORLD AROUND US
The section on the world around us features a map of the world, a graph of world population growth, and tables giving information about the world's people and places.

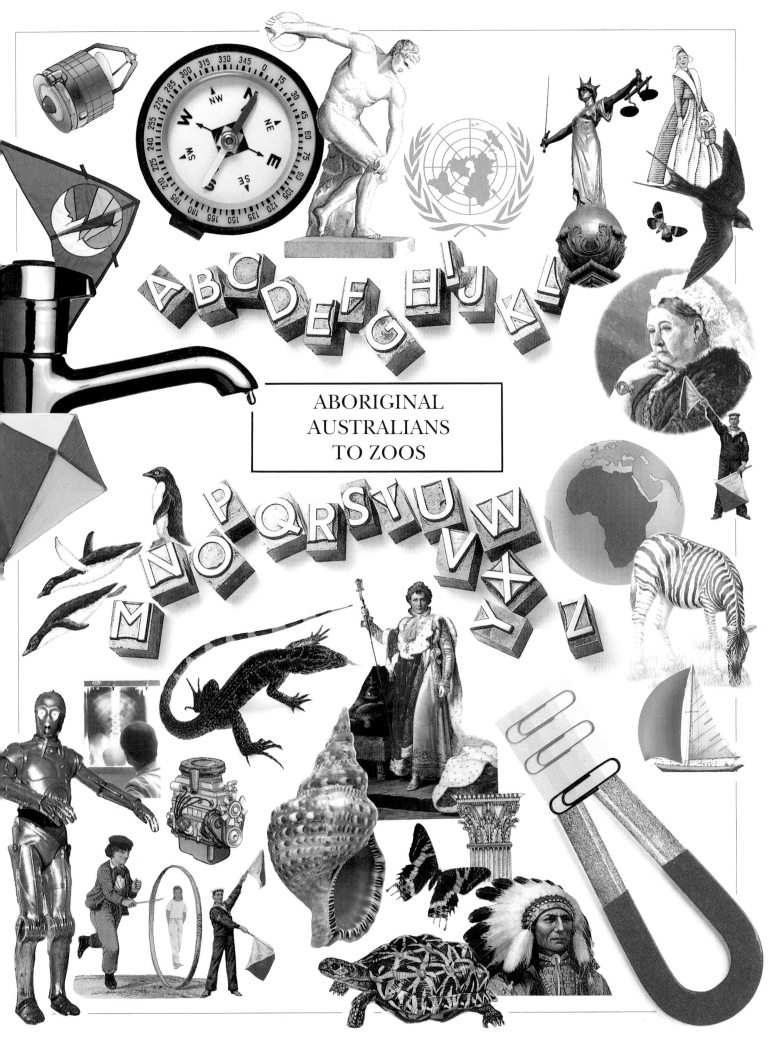

ABORIGINAL
AUSTRALIANS
TO ZOOS

ABORIGINAL AUSTRALIANS

THE FIRST INHABITANTS of Australia were nomadic (wandering) people who reached the continent from Southeast Asia about 40,000 years ago. When Europeans settled in Australia at the end of the 18th century, they called these native inhabitants "aboriginals", meaning people who had lived there since the earliest times. Today there are about 160,000 aboriginals in Australia. Most live in cities, but a few thousand still try to follow a traditional way of life. They travel through the bush, hunting with spears and boomerangs (throwing sticks) and searching for food such as plants, grubs, and insects. They have few possessions and make everything they need from natural materials. This way of life does not change or harm the fragile environment of the Australian outback (the interior). The well-being of the land, and its plants and animals are vital and sacred to the aboriginal people.

ART
Aboriginal art is mostly about Dreamtime and is made as part of the ceremonies celebrating Dreamtime. Paintings of the people, spirits, and animals of Dreamtime cover sacred cliffs and rocks in tribal territories. The pictures are made in red and yellow ochre and white clay, and some are thousands of years old.

Private ceremonies and secret rituals are an important part of aboriginal life. Through dancing, singing, and chanting, young aboriginal people learn about Dreamtime.

Dancers, singers, and musicians paint their bodies with elaborate patterns.

The didjeridu, a wooden wind instrument, is used to play basic rhythms in aboriginal music.

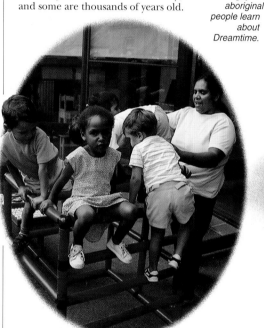

DREAMTIME
Aboriginal Australians believe that they have animal, plant, and human ancestors who created the world and everything in it. This process of creation is called Dreamtime. There are many songs and myths about Dreamtime, which generations of aboriginal people have passed down to their children.

URBAN LIFE
The majority of aboriginal Australians live in cities and towns. Some have benefitted from government education and aid programmes and have careers as teachers, doctors, and lawyers. Many, though, are poor and isolated from white society. They have lost touch with traditional aboriginal tribal ways, and because they do not fit neatly into white Australian society, they cannot share its benefits. However, there are now campaigns among urban aboriginal people to revive interest in the tribal culture of their ancestors.

LAND CLAIMS
When British settlers arrived in Australia, they seized sacred sites and other land which belonged to aboriginal people. With the help of aboriginal lawyers, aboriginal Australians campaigned to get the land back. In 1976, the Australian government agreed that aboriginal people have rights to their tribal territories, and some land was returned.

The curved returning boomerang is used only for sport.

BOOMERANGS

As well as the curved returning boomerang, aboriginal Australians use a straight, non-returning boomerang as a weapon for fighting and for hunting mammals such as kangaroos.

Find out more
AUSTRALIA
AUSTRALIA, HISTORY OF
AUSTRALIAN WILDLIFE
FESTIVALS AND FEASTS
MYTHS AND LEGENDS

ADVERTISING

GIANT HOARDINGS by the side of the road serve the same purpose as tiny classified newspaper advertisements. They tell us what products are available, and try to persuade us to choose one brand instead of another. Today's television commercials reach millions of people, but the first forms of advertising were much more local. Market traders shouted out what they had for sale, and shops displayed large signs to indicate their trade. Modern advertising began about 150 years ago when factories first produced goods in large quantities. Newspapers carried advertisements for everything from hats to patent medicine. Nowadays advertising forms part of the business of marketing, which also includes product design, competitive pricing, packaging, and shop displays. Advertisements appear everywhere, not just on television and radio. They are also broadcast through in-store music, and painted on vehicle sides and in smoke trails in the sky. These advertising messages often amuse us, but not all advertisements are welcome. Strict laws protect the shopper from misleading advertising, and there are restrictions on the advertising of certain harmful products, such as tobacco and alcohol.

Market research questionnaire

Sample packaging

COCA-COLA

Successful advertising makes a product so familiar that shoppers ask for it by name. Well-known goods are called brands. Some brands are sold worldwide. Coca-Cola is one of the most famous brand names. It was invented in the United States in 1886. From the beginning the makers of Coca-Cola advertised the drink widely, using a distinctive symbol, or trademark, of elegantly interlocking red letters. Within 10 years people in every state drank Coca-Cola. Today, the trademark is so well-known that it is recognizable in any alphabet.

LAUNCHING NEW PRODUCTS

Advertising is very expensive, so before launching a new bar, the chocolate company must be sure that it has created an appealing product that people will want to buy.

Storyboard

STORYBOARDS

Before filming a commercial, a designer must draw the action on paper scene by scene, like a comic strip. A copywriter makes up the script and slogans to go with the pictures.

MARKET RESEARCH

Hundreds of people taste the chocolate bar before it goes on sale, and answer questions about it. This process is called market research. They give their opinions on price, name, and size of the bar, and may look at plans for the wrapper.

CAMPAIGNS

No manufacturer has an unlimited budget, so most advertising is concentrated into campaigns – short, intense bursts of advertising. During the campaign, advertisements appear in very carefully chosen spots. For example, commercials for a chocolate bar might appear during children's television programmes, not late at night. Similarly, press ads might appear in magazines aimed at young people.

PROPAGANDA

Government advertisements which inform or advise the public are called propaganda. This poster, for instance, encourages Chinese people to work for a better society. Other campaigns persuade people to stop smoking, or to drive safely.

团结起来,争取更大的胜利!

Press advertisement

Displays in shops are called point-of-sale advertising.

Television advertising is very costly, but reaches the biggest audience.

Catchy tunes feature in much radio advertising.

Find out more

SHOPS AND SHOPPING
TELEVISION AND VIDEO
TRADE AND INDUSTRY

AFRICA

FEW REGIONS OF THE WORLD are as varied as Africa. On this vast continent there are 53 independent nations and many times this number of peoples and ancient cultures. There are mountains, valleys, plains, and swamps on a scale not seen elsewhere. The northern coast is rich and fertile; below it lies the dry Sahara Desert. South of the Sahara, lush rain forest grows. Most of southern and eastern Africa is savanna, or scrub, a form of dry plain dotted with trees and bushes. The nations of Africa are generally poor, though some, such as Nigeria, have rich natural resources. Many governments are unstable, and rebellions and civil wars are common. There are very few large cities; most are near the coast. The rest of the continent is open countryside where people follow traditional life styles.

Africa is roughly triangular. The Atlantic Ocean is to the west and the Indian Ocean to the east. In the northwest only a few kilometres of sea separate Africa from Europe.

Schools in African towns are much like schools anywhere, though pupils sometimes walk many kilometres to the schoolhouse.

The Tuareg peoples, who inhabit the Sahara, keep large herds of camels and goats.

The Ashanti of West Africa live in dense forests.

The tall Masai of Kenya herd cattle on the open plains.

Few pygmies are taller than 5 ft (1.5 m) They live in the dense Zairean Congo rain forest.

PEOPLE

In the African countryside many people live in tribal villages. Some, such as the Kikuyu of East Africa, are descended from tribes which have lived in the same place for many centuries. Others, such as the North African Arabs, are recent immigrants from other parts of Africa or from other continents. Borders between countries take little account of these varied cultures. People of one culture may live in two different countries, and in one nation may be found more than a dozen different tribal groupings.

The towers of mosques dominate Cairo's skyline.

The Bushmen roam the deserts of southern Africa and gather wild food from the harsh environment.

CAIRO
Cairo, the capital city of Egypt, is the largest city in Africa, with a population of nearly nine million. It sits on the River Nile near the head of the river's delta. The older part of the city contains narrow, winding streets. The new city has wider streets and many modern office buildings and flats. The people of Cairo come from all over North Africa, as well as from Europe and the Middle East.

KILIMANJARO
The tallest and most beautiful mountain in Africa is Kilimanjaro, in Tanzania. Its highest peak, which rises 5,895 m (19,340 ft), is an extinct volcano. Although the mountain is only a few kilometres from the equator, the top is always covered in snow. A footpath leads to the top, which can be reached in three days from the nearest road. Many people live on the lower slopes, where they farm tropical fruit.

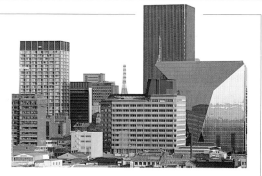

REPUBLIC OF SOUTH AFRICA

Vast mineral deposits, including gold, platinum, and diamonds, have enabled South Africans to develop an advanced industrial society, the richest in the continent. South Africa produces 40 per cent of the world's gold. But wealth is divided unevenly. The past "apartheid" laws have, however, left most of the wealth in the hands of the minority whites.

WAR AND FAMINE

Civil wars and famines are common in Africa. Although many are caused by political disagreements, some are the result of tribal conflicts. In Chad a civil war lasting many years was fought between the desert Tuaregs, backed by Libya, and the farmers of the wetter areas. In Zimbabwe fighting between the Matabele and the Shona tribes has led to thousands of deaths. Other misery is caused by famine. Food production has not kept pace with Africa's growing population. Traditionally, most people have grown just enough food each year to last until the next harvest. If crops do not grow properly thousands of people may starve to death within a few months.

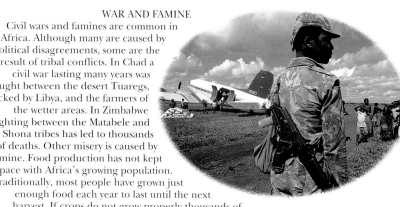

RURAL LIFE

Most Africans live in the countryside. They grow their own food and only rarely have a surplus to sell or exchange for other goods. Most tribes have farmed the same land for generations, living in simple villages with all of their relatives. Sometimes the young men go to live in cities for a few years to earn money in mines or factories. Then they return to the village to marry and settle down. The types of crops grown vary widely. Yams, cassava, and bananas are produced in the lush tropical regions; farmers in drier areas concentrate on cattle and corn.

SAHARA DESERT

The Sahara is the largest desert in the world and covers nearly one third of Africa. In recent years the desert has spread, destroying farmland and causing famine. In some areas irrigation has stopped the spread of the desert, but long-term irrigation can make the soil salty and infertile.

Road building in Nigeria

In West Africa, drumming is a highly developed art. People once used drum beats to pass on messages.

MUSIC AND CULTURE

Africa has a rich and varied culture. North Africa shares the Islamic traditions of the Middle East, producing beautiful mosques and palaces. West African music has a strong rhythm, and there are many interesting dances. The area is also home to a flourishing wood-carving industry. Eastern and southern Africa have become famous for beautiful beadwork and colourful festive costumes.

DEVELOPMENT

A lack of basic resources such as roads, railways, and a reliable electricity supply holds back the growth of many African nations. A few countries sell enough goods abroad to pay for these vital facilities. But many more rely on gifts and loans from Western governments to pay for their development programmes.

Find out more
AFRICA, HISTORY OF
AFRICAN WILDLIFE
ARABS
DESERT WILDLIFE
EGYPT, ANCIENT

AFRICA

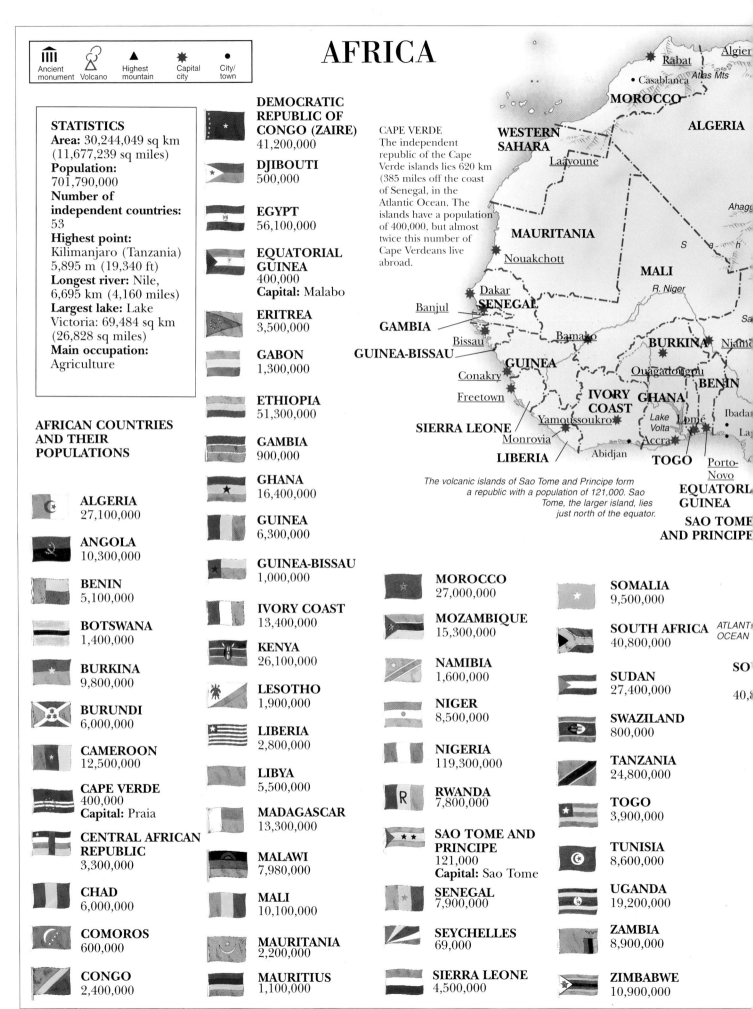

Legend:
- Ancient monument
- Volcano
- Highest mountain
- Capital city
- City/town

STATISTICS
Area: 30,244,049 sq km (11,677,239 sq miles)
Population: 701,790,000
Number of independent countries: 53
Highest point: Kilimanjaro (Tanzania) 5,895 m (19,340 ft)
Longest river: Nile, 6,695 km (4,160 miles)
Largest lake: Lake Victoria: 69,484 sq km (26,828 sq miles)
Main occupation: Agriculture

AFRICAN COUNTRIES AND THEIR POPULATIONS

ALGERIA 27,100,000

ANGOLA 10,300,000

BENIN 5,100,000

BOTSWANA 1,400,000

BURKINA 9,800,000

BURUNDI 6,000,000

CAMEROON 12,500,000

CAPE VERDE 400,000 **Capital:** Praia

CENTRAL AFRICAN REPUBLIC 3,300,000

CHAD 6,000,000

COMOROS 600,000

CONGO 2,400,000

DEMOCRATIC REPUBLIC OF CONGO (ZAIRE) 41,200,000

DJIBOUTI 500,000

EGYPT 56,100,000

EQUATORIAL GUINEA 400,000 **Capital:** Malabo

ERITREA 3,500,000

GABON 1,300,000

ETHIOPIA 51,300,000

GAMBIA 900,000

GHANA 16,400,000

GUINEA 6,300,000

GUINEA-BISSAU 1,000,000

IVORY COAST 13,400,000

KENYA 26,100,000

LESOTHO 1,900,000

LIBERIA 2,800,000

LIBYA 5,500,000

MADAGASCAR 13,300,000

MALAWI 7,980,000

MALI 10,100,000

MAURITANIA 2,200,000

MAURITIUS 1,100,000

MOROCCO 27,000,000

MOZAMBIQUE 15,300,000

NAMIBIA 1,600,000

NIGER 8,500,000

NIGERIA 119,300,000

RWANDA 7,800,000

SAO TOME AND PRINCIPE 121,000 **Capital:** Sao Tome

SENEGAL 7,900,000

SEYCHELLES 69,000

SIERRA LEONE 4,500,000

SOMALIA 9,500,000

SOUTH AFRICA 40,800,000

SUDAN 27,400,000

SWAZILAND 800,000

TANZANIA 24,800,000

TOGO 3,900,000

TUNISIA 8,600,000

UGANDA 19,200,000

ZAMBIA 8,900,000

ZIMBABWE 10,900,000

CAPE VERDE
The independent republic of the Cape Verde islands lies 620 km (385 miles off the coast of Senegal, in the Atlantic Ocean. The islands have a population of 400,000, but almost twice this number of Cape Verdeans live abroad.

The volcanic islands of Sao Tome and Principe form a republic with a population of 121,000. Sao Tome, the larger island, lies just north of the equator.

Map labels: Algier, Rabat, Casablanca, Atlas Mts, MOROCCO, ALGERIA, WESTERN SAHARA, Laâyoune, MAURITANIA, Nouakchott, MALI, R. Niger, Ahagg, S a h a, Dakar, SENEGAL, Banjul, GAMBIA, Bissau, GUINEA-BISSAU, Bamako, BURKINA, Niam, Conakry, GUINEA, Ouagadougou, BENIN, Freetown, IVORY COAST, GHANA, Ibada, SIERRA LEONE, Yamoussoukro, Lake Volta, Lomé, La, Monrovia, Accra, TOGO, Porto-Novo, LIBERIA, Abidjan, EQUATORIAL GUINEA, SAO TOME AND PRINCIPE, ATLANTIC OCEAN, SO

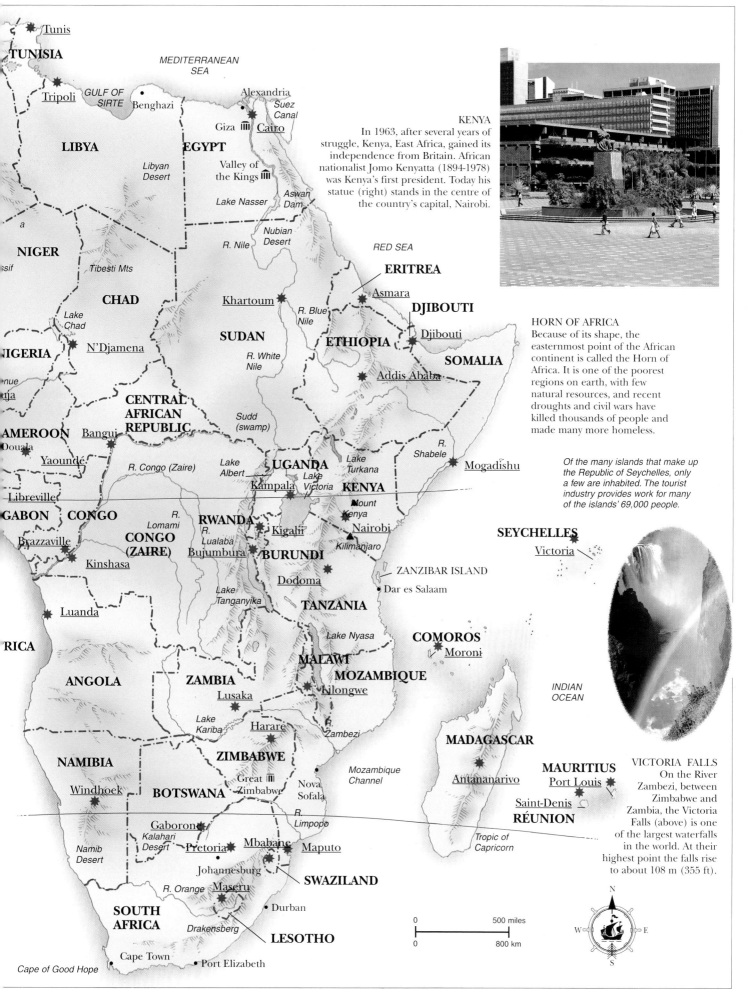

Tunis
TUNISIA

MEDITERRANEAN
SEA

Tripoli
GULF OF
SIRTE
Benghazi

Alexandria
Suez
Canal

Giza 🏛 Cairo

LIBYA
EGYPT

Libyan
Desert

Valley of
the Kings 🏛

Lake Nasser

Aswan
Dam

a

NIGER

ssif

Tibesti Mts

Nubian
Desert

R. Nile

RED SEA

ERITREA

Asmara

DJIBOUTI

CHAD

Lake
Chad

Khartoum

R. Blue
Nile

Djibouti

NIGERIA
N'Djamena

SUDAN

ETHIOPIA

SOMALIA

nue

uja

R. White
Nile

Addis Ababa

CAMEROON
Bangui

CENTRAL
AFRICAN
REPUBLIC

Sudd
(swamp)

R.
Shabele

Douala

Yaoundé

R. Congo (Zaire)

Lake
Albert

UGANDA
Lake
Victoria

Lake
Turkana

Mogadishu

Libreville

GABON
CONGO

Kampala

R.
Lomami

RWANDA
R.
Lualaba

Kigali

KENYA

Mount
Kenya

Nairobi

SEYCHELLES

Victoria

Brazzaville

CONGO
(ZAIRE)

Bujumbura

BURUNDI

Kilimanjaro

Kinshasa

Dodoma

ZANZIBAR ISLAND
Dar es Salaam

Luanda

Lake
Tanganyika

TANZANIA

RICA

Lake Nyasa

COMOROS
Moroni

INDIAN
OCEAN

ANGOLA

ZAMBIA

MALAWI
MOZAMBIQUE
Lilongwe

Lusaka

Lake
Kariba

Harare

R.
Zambezi

MADAGASCAR

NAMIBIA

Windhoek

ZIMBABWE

BOTSWANA

Great 🏛
Zimbabwe

Nova
Sofala

Mozambique
Channel

Antananarivo

MAURITIUS
Port Louis

Saint-Denis
RÉUNION

Gaborone

Kalahari
Desert

Pretoria

Mbabane
Maputo

R.
Limpopo

Tropic of
Capricorn

Namib
Desert

Johannesburg

SWAZILAND

SOUTH
AFRICA

R. Orange

Maseru

Durban

Drakensberg

LESOTHO

Cape of Good Hope

Cape Town

Port Elizabeth

KENYA
In 1963, after several years of struggle, Kenya, East Africa, gained its independence from Britain. African nationalist Jomo Kenyatta (1894-1978) was Kenya's first president. Today his statue (right) stands in the centre of the country's capital, Nairobi.

HORN OF AFRICA
Because of its shape, the easternmost point of the African continent is called the Horn of Africa. It is one of the poorest regions on earth, with few natural resources, and recent droughts and civil wars have killed thousands of people and made many more homeless.

Of the many islands that make up the Republic of Seychelles, only a few are inhabited. The tourist industry provides work for many of the islands' 69,000 people.

VICTORIA FALLS
On the River Zambezi, between Zimbabwe and Zambia, the Victoria Falls (above) is one of the largest waterfalls in the world. At their highest point the falls rise to about 108 m (355 ft).

0   500 miles

0   800 km

N
W   E
S

HISTORY OF
AFRICA

FOR MUCH OF ITS HISTORY, Africa has been hidden from outsiders' eyes. The Sahara Desert cuts off communication from north to south for all but the hardiest traveller. The peoples of Africa have therefore developed largely by themselves. By about 1200 B.C., rich and powerful empires such as Ancient Egypt had arisen. The empires have disappeared, but they left behind buildings and other clues to their existence. Other African peoples left records of their history in songs that have been passed down from parent to child through countless generations. Europeans remained ignorant of this rich history until, during the 1400s, they explored the west coast. Soon they were shipping thousands of Africans to Europe and the Americas as slaves, a "trade" that destroyed many traditional societies. During the late 1800s, Europeans penetrated the interior of Africa and, within 20 years, had carved up the continent between them. Almost all of Africa remained under European control until the 1950s, when the colonies began to gain their independence. Today, the peoples of Africa are free of foreign control.

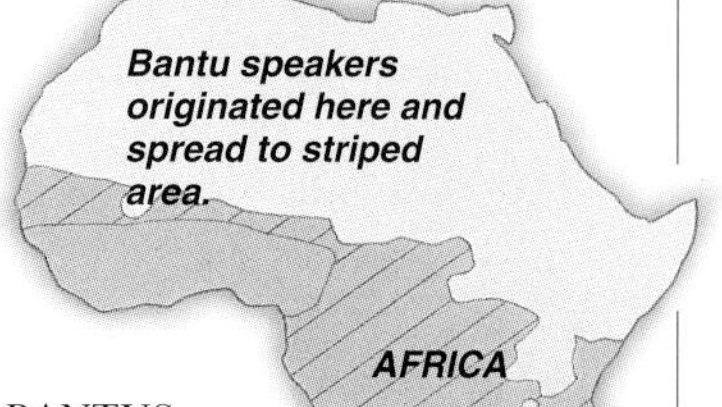

Bantu speakers originated here and spread to striped area.

AFRICA

BANTUS
Most of the peoples of southern Africa are related to the Bantus, who originated in the western part of the continent between 3000 and 2000 B.C. They had moved south by A.D. 400.

Ivory traders

GREAT ZIMBABWE
The stone city of Great Zimbabwe was a major religious, political, and trading centre in southern Africa during the 14th century. It grew rich on the proceeds of herding cattle and mining gold, copper, and iron. The peoples of Great Zimbabwe exported their produce to the coastal port of Sofala in what is now Mozambique, and then up the coast of Africa to Arabia.

Great enclosure at Great Zimbabwe

Men armed with spears and shields guarded the city's walls.

Thatched buildings

City's walls were made from huge granite slabs.

Cattle herder

BENIN
The West African kingdom of Benin reached the height of its power between the 14th and 17th centuries. Its people traded ivory, pepper, palm oil, and slaves with the Portuguese. They also excelled in casting realistic figures in bronze. On the left is a Benin bronze mask.

SOAPSTONE BIRDS
Soapstone carvings of birds on columns stood in an enclosure outside Great Zimbabwe. One of these birds has been the national symbol of Zimbabwe since the country gained its independence in 1980.

SCRAMBLE FOR AFRICA

Until the 1880s, European conquest in Africa was restricted to the coastal regions and the main river valleys. But European powers wanted overseas colonies (settlements). Throughout the 1880s and 1890s, European nations competed for land in Africa. By 1900, almost all of Africa was in European hands. The only independent states left were the ancient kingdom of Ethiopia in the east, and the free slave state of Liberia in the west. The cartoon (left) shows Germany as a bird "swooping" onto Africa.

ON THE SWOOP!

ZULU WARS
Some African peoples managed to resist the Europeans for a time. After 1838, the Zulus of southern Africa fought first the Boers (Dutch settlers) and then the British. In 1879, however, Britain finally defeated the Zulus. In 1887, Zululand became a British colony. Above is a picture of the British trying to break through Zulu lines.

INDEPENDENCE
The coming of independence to much of Africa after 1956 did not always bring peace or prosperity to the new nations. Many were weakened by famines and droughts or torn apart by civil wars. Few have managed to maintain civilian governments without periods of military dictatorships. In 1964 Malawi (formerly Nyasaland) became Africa's 35th independent state. Above is the celebration scene.

AFRICA

700-1200 Kingdom of Ghana in West Africa grows rich on cross-Saharan trade with the Arabs.

c. 800-1800 Kanem-Bornu kingdom.

1200s Trading cities flourish on east coast.

1235-1500 Kingdom of Mali.

1300-1600 Kingdom of Benin.

1300s Great Zimbabwe flourishes.

1350-1591 Kingdom of Songhai.

1500-1800s Europeans take Africans as slaves to America.

1838-79 Zulus fight against Boers and British.

1880s Europeans take almost total control of Africa.

1957-75 Most of Africa independent.

1990 Namibia independent.

APARTHEID

In 1948 the National Party came to power in South Africa. Years of segregation, known as apartheid, followed. This policy gave white people power but denied black people many rights, including the vote. In 1990 the African National Congress (ANC), a banned black nationalist movement led by Nelson Mandela, was legalized, and the apartheid laws began to be dismantled. In 1994, the first-ever free elections were held.

ORGANIZATION OF AFRICAN UNITY
Despite the many political differences that exist between the individual African states, they all share problems of poverty, poor health, and lack of schools. In 1963, the Organization of African Unity (OAU) was founded to promote unity in the continent and to co-ordinate economic, health, and other policies among its 51 member nations. Above are two members of the OAU medical unit treating civil war victims.

NELSON MANDELA
In 1994, Nelson Mandela (left), a leader of the ANC, became the President of South Africa.

Find out more
AFRICA
EGYPT, ANCIENT
PREHISTORIC PEOPLES
SLAVERY

AFRICAN WILDLIFE

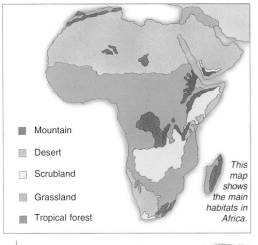

Mountain

Desert

Scrubland

Grassland

Tropical forest

This map shows the main habitats in Africa.

AFRICA HAS AN INCREDIBLE variety of wildlife. The cheetah, the world's fastest runner, lives in Africa, sprinting after its prey in the scrubland. The huge Nile crocodile lurks in the River Nile. Vast herds of wildebeest, zebra, and buffalo wander the grassy plains, together with the biggest land animal, the elephant, and the largest bird, the ostrich. In Africa's central rain forests are gorillas and chimpanzees. In the Kalahari and Namib deserts, which are among the driest areas on Earth, sand skinks shelter in the shade of giant euphorbia plants, watching out for the poisonous Namibian sidewinder snake. Although humans have turned many regions into farmland, there are still plenty of wild places in Africa.

NATIONAL PARKS
Many wild places in Africa are being destroyed for timber, firewood, and farmland. The Korup National Park in Cameroon is one of Africa's least spoiled rain forest areas. It is now protected as a national reserve.

GIRAFFE
The giraffe is the tallest animal on Earth. A large male can measure 5 m (17 ft) to its horn tips. Its long legs and long neck enable it to reach higher into the trees to feed than any other creature. The giraffe's long tail, with its coarse hairs, is an effective fly swatter to flick away flies and other insects.

SAVANNA
The grassy African plains are called savannas. They are home to many spectacular large mammals, including elephants, rhinoceroses, zebras, and lions. The African savannas cover almost a quarter of Africa, mainly in the east and south.

Egyptian vulture has a bald head and neck. It feeds on carrion (remains of dead animals).

The secretary bird is a snake killer found in grassland areas.

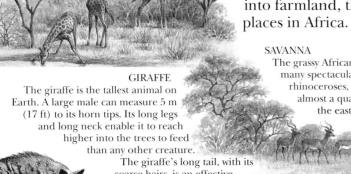

HYENA
This hunter-scavenger hunts at night and consumes whatever it can, including goats and other mammals, birds, snakes, fruit, and the remains of other animals' prey. Despite its dog-like shape, the hyena is more closely related to the mongoose family.

MEERKAT
The meerkat is a kind of mongoose. It forages for insects, lizards, and other small creatures, then moves to a new area as the food supply decreases. Meerkats live in groups and dig burrows for shelter and for raising young.

AFRICAN WETLANDS
The African wetlands consist of swamps and lakes and are inhabited by a great number of herons, pelicans, flamingos, and other water birds, as well as lungfishes and huge shoals of cichlids and other fish. In the Kalahari Desert, crocodiles and hippopotamuses live in the water among vast beds of papyrus stems in the Okovango Basin – the largest oasis on Earth.

Two male hippos fighting each other for their territory

HIPPOPOTAMUS
An adult hippopotamus can weigh more than 2.7 tons (2.7 tonnes), making it one of the heaviest animals on land. During the day, hippopotamuses wallow in mud or bathe in rivers and lakes, almost submerged, with only their ears, eyes, and nostrils showing. At night they come onto land to feed on grass near the riverbank.

Meerkats sit upright near the burrow entrances to watch for predators.

PANGOLIN
There are seven kinds of pangolins in Africa and in Asia. They live in savanna and forest areas, where they lick up ants and termites with their long, sticky tongues. A pangolin can roll itself into a ball for defence; its overlapping scales help protect it against predators.

Countless beetles and other creatures scavenge and recycle nutrients in the soil.

Find out more
ELEPHANTS
LIONS, TIGERS, and other big cats
MARSH AND SWAMP WILDLIFE

AIR

A MIXTURE OF GASES makes up the air that all plants and animals need for life. When air moves, it presses against everything in its path, rustling leaves and lifting kites high above the treetops. We give the name wind to pressure caused by moving air. Still air presses too. There is a blanket of air roughly 640 km (400 miles)deep that surrounds the Earth. Although air is light, this layer of air is so thick that it presses down on everything at ground level with a force equal to 10.4 m (34 ft) of water. We do not notice the weight of air pressing down on us, because it presses equally from all sides and because the liquids in our body press outwards against the pressure of the air. Atmospheric pressure is lower at high altitudes; in an aeroplane at a height of about 16,000 m (52,000 ft) above the ground, air pressure is only one tenth the pressure on the ground.

78 per cent of the air is nitrogen. Nitrogen is a very stable gas; it does not readily react, or combine, with other substances.

GASES IN THE AIR
Most of the gases in the air are colourless and have no smell.

21 per cent of the air is oxygen. This gas is vital for human and animal life.

The air contains very tiny amounts of the gases carbon dioxide, methane, helium, hydrogen, krypton, neon, ozone, and xenon.

A gas called argon makes up about 1 per cent of the air.

PARACHUTE
By gathering air in its canopy, a parachute increases air resistance so that the parachutist falls slowly and safely to the ground. Skydivers also use air resistance to control their speed before opening the parachute. They spread their arms and legs to slow the fall.

AIR RESISTANCE
When a car moves along, it has to push the air out of the way. This produces a force called air resistance, or drag, which slows down the car. Modern vehicles are designed with sleek, streamlined shapes to reduce drag. New designs are tested in wind tunnels which blow air at high speed over a model of the car.

AIR PRESSURE

Air pressure can help with everyday tasks. For example, a siphon uses the push of atmospheric pressure to empty a fish tank that is too heavy to lift when full. Many machines work using air pressure. Pumping air under pressure into car tyres keeps them solid yet flexible, cushioning passengers from bumps in the road. Many tools, such as screwdrivers and pneumatic drills, are powered by air at high pressure which is produced by mechanical pumps.

Large propellers provide propulsion and steering.

Fan sucks air downwards into the flexible rubber skirt.

HOVERCRAFT
A layer of pressurized air keeps a hovercraft, or air-cushion vehicle, floating a little distance off the ground and distributes the vehicle's weight evenly. This means the hovercraft can travel over swamps, deep snow, or water without sinking in. A large fan creates the cushion of air which lifts the craft off the ground.

SUCTION
Differences in air pressure provide a useful way of moving liquids and solid objects. For example, when you suck on a drinking straw, you use your lungs as a pump to reduce the air pressure above the liquid in the straw. The higher pressure of the air outside the straw pushes the drink up the straw and into your mouth.

_____ *Find out more* _____
ATMOSPHERE
EARTH
OXYGEN
POLLUTION
WEATHER

AIR FORCES

Before the
invention of
aeroplanes, armies
used balloons and
kites to watch and
attack their
enemies. The first
air force pilots flew
in aircraft made of
wood, canvas, and
wire. They fought
with machine guns
and dropped small
bombs out of the
cockpit by hand.

HELICOPTERS, JET FIGHTERS, AND BOMBERS play a vital
role in modern warfare. As part of an air force, these aircraft
support and defend armies and navies. They can also attack
targets that are impossible to approach by land or sea. Armies
first used aeroplanes in battle during World War I (1914-18),
and by World War II (1939-45) modern air forces had been
established. People serving in the air force perform a variety
of jobs. The crew of an aircraft includes a pilot, a navigator,
and a gunner to operate the weapons. Many more people
work on the ground. Radar crews find out where enemy and
friendly aircraft are flying. Surface-to-air missile crews try to
shoot down enemy aircraft. Rescue crews go to the aid of
pilots whose aircraft have crashed in the sea or on land.

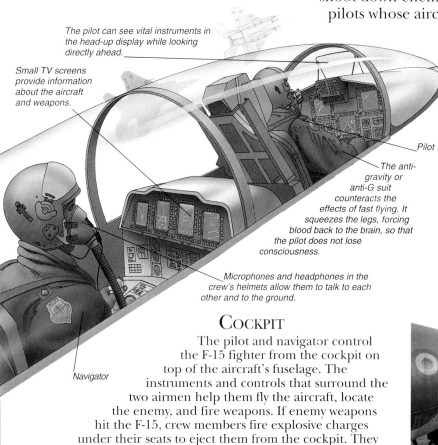

The pilot can see vital instruments in
the head-up display while looking
directly ahead.

Small TV screens
provide information
about the aircraft
and weapons.

Pilot

The anti-
gravity or
anti-G suit
counteracts the
effects of fast flying. It
squeezes the legs, forcing
blood back to the brain, so that
the pilot does not lose
consciousness.

Microphones and headphones in the
crew's helmets allow them to talk to each
other and to the ground.

Navigator

COCKPIT
The pilot and navigator control
the F-15 fighter from the cockpit on
top of the aircraft's fuselage. The
instruments and controls that surround the
two airmen help them fly the aircraft, locate
the enemy, and fire weapons. If enemy weapons
hit the F-15, crew members fire explosive charges
under their seats to eject them from the cockpit. They
land by parachute.

AIRCRAFT
Modern air forces
use different types
of aircraft for
different tasks.
Large bombers carry lots of
fuel to reach distant targets.
Transport aeroplanes and
helicopters carry stores and
personnel. Fighters shoot
down other aircraft and attack
small targets. Helicopter
gunships help ground troops.

Bomber

Transport aircraft

Fighter

Transport helicopter

Helicopter gunship

RELIEF SUPPLIES
In peacetime air forces
do not fight. Instead
they patrol the air to
monitor other air forces
and discourage them
from attacking. During
emergencies such as
famines and
earthquakes, transport
planes carry food and
supplies to the victims.

AIRCREW
Personnel who
fly in aircraft are
called the
aircrew. They
include pilots,
navigators, who
tell the pilot which
course to fly, and
loaders, who work
in transport planes.

GROUND CREW
People who work on
the ground are called
the ground crew. They
maintain and repair
the aircraft. Armourers
ensure that fighter
planes always have
enough ammunition
and bombs on board.

Pilots carry
flight plans in
pads on their
knees.

Women aircrew
do not usually
fly aircraft in
battle.

Ground crew uses
hand signals to
show pilots where to
park their aircraft.

Engineers check
aircraft carefully
after every flight.

Find out more
AIRCRAFT
BALLOONS AND AIRSHIPS
HELICOPTERS
NAVIGATION
RADAR
WORLD WAR I
WORLD WAR II

AIRCRAFT

LESS THAN 100 years ago, even the fastest ship took more than a week to cross the Atlantic Ocean. Today most jet airliners (large passenger planes) can make this 4,800-km (3,000-mile) journey in less than seven hours. Aircraft are the fastest way to travel because they can soar straight over obstacles such as mountains and oceans. Powerful jet engines enable the fastest combat aircraft to reach speeds of 3,200 km/h (2,000 mph) – three times faster than sound. Even ordinary jet airliners fly at more than 850 km/h (530 mph). Modern aircraft are packed with advanced technology to help them fly safely and economically at great speed. Sophisticated electronic control and navigation systems keep the aeroplane on course. Computer-designed wings help cut fuel costs. And airframes (aircraft bodies) are made of metal alloys and plastic composites that are lightweight and strong.

JET AIRLINER
Like all jet airliners, the *Boeing 747-400* flies high above the clouds to avoid bad weather. Its airtight cabin is pressurized – supplied with air at normal atmospheric pressure. This protects passengers and crew from the drop in air pressure and lack of oxygen at high altitudes.

The undercarriage (landing wheels) folds up inside the aeroplane during flight to reduce drag (air resistance).

The Boeing 747-400 airliner can carry 412 people and fly nonstop for more than 13,600 km (8,470 miles). Seats are arranged on two decks.

The aircraft's radar shows the crew the weather conditions up to 320 km (200 miles) ahead so that they can avoid storms.

FLIGHT DECK
The captain and crew control the aircraft from the flight deck. In the past, the flight deck of an aeroplane was a mass of dials and switches. New jet airliners are packed with electronics, and computer screens have replaced the dials. Other new features include computer-controlled autopilot systems that enable the plane to take off and land when bad weather obscures the pilot's vision.

FLYING AN AEROPLANE
Every aeroplane has three main controls: the throttle to control speed; rudder pedals for steering to the left or right (yawing); and a control column that tilts the aircraft to either side (rolling), or up and down (pitching). The pilot usually operates all three to guide the plane through the air.

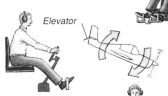

To roll, the pilot moves the control column to the left or right, which raises the ailerons on one wing and lowers them on the other.

Aileron

Elevator

To pitch up or down, the pilot pushes or pulls on the control column, raising or lowering the elevator flaps on the tail wing.

To yaw left or right, the pilot's feet swivel the rudder bar, turning the upright rudder on the tail of the aeroplane.

Rudder

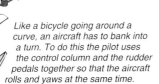

Like a bicycle going around a curve, an aircraft has to bank into a turn. To do this the pilot uses the control column and the rudder pedals together so that the aircraft rolls and yaws at the same time.

AEROPLANES
Aeroplanes are powered aircraft that have wings. The word *aircraft* describes all flying machines including helicopters, gliders, hang gliders, and aeroplanes. Most large airliners and combat aeroplanes have jet engines enabling them to fly fast and high. But jets are expensive and use a lot of fuel, so many smaller planes are driven by propeller, just like the first aeroplanes.

OBSERVATION PLANES
Specially designed aircraft give a clear view of everything from traffic jams to diseased crops.

JET AIRCRAFT
Each year jet airliners enable billions of people to take long journeys. A jet engine called a turbofan drives most jet airliners. Turbofans are powerful and relatively quiet.

SEAPLANES
Aircraft are ideal for getting in and out of remote places. Seaplanes have floats instead of landing wheels to land and take off on water.

CONCORDE
The airliner *Concorde* is supersonic, which means it can fly faster than sound. Indeed, it streaks over the Atlantic in less than four hours, twice as fast as any other airliner. But its engines are noisy and use a lot of fuel.

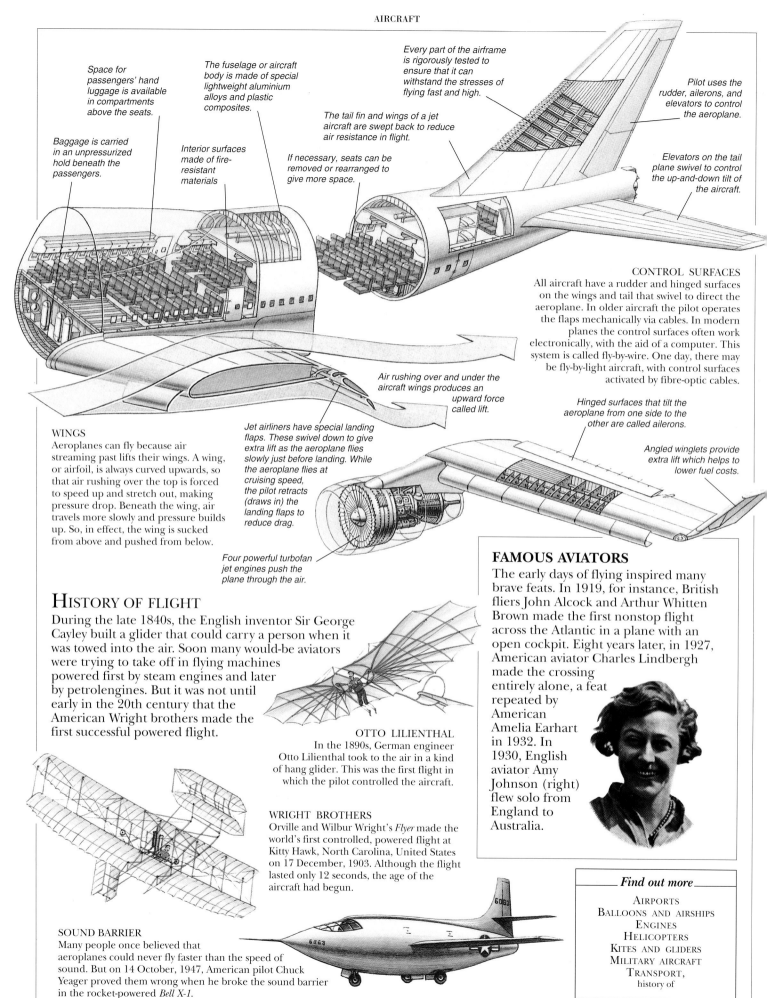

Space for passengers' hand luggage is available in compartments above the seats.

The fuselage or aircraft body is made of special lightweight aluminium alloys and plastic composites.

Every part of the airframe is rigorously tested to ensure that it can withstand the stresses of flying fast and high.

Pilot uses the rudder, ailerons, and elevators to control the aeroplane.

Baggage is carried in an unpressurized hold beneath the passengers.

Interior surfaces made of fire-resistant materials

The tail fin and wings of a jet aircraft are swept back to reduce air resistance in flight.

If necessary, seats can be removed or rearranged to give more space.

Elevators on the tail plane swivel to control the up-and-down tilt of the aircraft.

CONTROL SURFACES

All aircraft have a rudder and hinged surfaces on the wings and tail that swivel to direct the aeroplane. In older aircraft the pilot operates the flaps mechanically via cables. In modern planes the control surfaces often work electronically, with the aid of a computer. This system is called fly-by-wire. One day, there may be fly-by-light aircraft, with control surfaces activated by fibre-optic cables.

Air rushing over and under the aircraft wings produces an upward force called lift.

Hinged surfaces that tilt the aeroplane from one side to the other are called ailerons.

Angled winglets provide extra lift which helps to lower fuel costs.

WINGS

Aeroplanes can fly because air streaming past lifts their wings. A wing, or airfoil, is always curved upwards, so that air rushing over the top is forced to speed up and stretch out, making pressure drop. Beneath the wing, air travels more slowly and pressure builds up. So, in effect, the wing is sucked from above and pushed from below.

Jet airliners have special landing flaps. These swivel down to give extra lift as the aeroplane flies slowly just before landing. While the aeroplane flies at cruising speed, the pilot retracts (draws in) the landing flaps to reduce drag.

Four powerful turbofan jet engines push the plane through the air.

HISTORY OF FLIGHT

During the late 1840s, the English inventor Sir George Cayley built a glider that could carry a person when it was towed into the air. Soon many would-be aviators were trying to take off in flying machines powered first by steam engines and later by petrol engines. But it was not until early in the 20th century that the American Wright brothers made the first successful powered flight.

OTTO LILIENTHAL
In the 1890s, German engineer Otto Lilienthal took to the air in a kind of hang glider. This was the first flight in which the pilot controlled the aircraft.

WRIGHT BROTHERS
Orville and Wilbur Wright's *Flyer* made the world's first controlled, powered flight at Kitty Hawk, North Carolina, United States on 17 December, 1903. Although the flight lasted only 12 seconds, the age of the aircraft had begun.

FAMOUS AVIATORS

The early days of flying inspired many brave feats. In 1919, for instance, British fliers John Alcock and Arthur Whitten Brown made the first nonstop flight across the Atlantic in a plane with an open cockpit. Eight years later, in 1927, American aviator Charles Lindbergh made the crossing entirely alone, a feat repeated by American Amelia Earhart in 1932. In 1930, English aviator Amy Johnson (right) flew solo from England to Australia.

SOUND BARRIER
Many people once believed that aeroplanes could never fly faster than the speed of sound. But on 14 October, 1947, American pilot Chuck Yeager proved them wrong when he broke the sound barrier in the rocket-powered *Bell X-1*.

Find out more

AIRPORTS
BALLOONS AND AIRSHIPS
ENGINES
HELICOPTERS
KITES AND GLIDERS
MILITARY AIRCRAFT
TRANSPORT,
history of

AIRPORTS

EVERY YEAR MORE than 100 million people pass through the world's airports. Freight terminals handle the millions of tonnes of cargo carried by aircraft. Whenever people or goods travel by air, they must pass through an airport. Some airports are extremely large. At John F. Kennedy International Airport in New York City, in the United States, nearly 1,000 aeroplanes take off every day. Some huge international aircraft fly thousands of kilometres to other continents. Smaller planes make internal flights, taking passengers to other parts of the country. They may land at tiny airports which serve towns or islands. All airports have runways for aircraft to pick up speed and take off. They also have facilities for refuelling and making repairs. In larger airports there are restaurants and lounges where passengers can wait to board their flights.

PASSPORTS
International travellers use passports to prove their identity. Officials at the airport often stamp the passport to show that the traveller entered the country legally. The use of passports began in the 16th century but has only become widespread in the last 50 years.

The whole airport can be seen from the control tower.

Ground crew refuels the aircraft from tankers or hydrants.

Catering staff supplies food and drink to the galleys, or kitchens.

Cleaners vacuum the cabin and remove rubbish.

Engineers make careful checks on all the aeroplane's functions.

Fire fighters stand by while the aircraft refuels.

Ramp for boarding

PASSENGER TERMINAL

A large modern airport employs thousands of people. As soon as an aircraft lands, air traffic controllers direct it towards a disembarkation point, where it stops. Passengers leave the aircraft by means of a ramp or steps from the aircraft to the ground. Baggage handlers remove the suitcases from the aircraft and take them to the terminal for collection. When passengers have their luggage they go through customs, then take connecting flights or travel onwards by bus, car, or train.

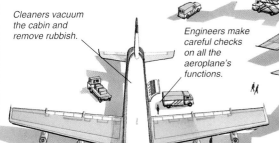

Smugglers hide drugs in hollow ornaments and other objects.

CUSTOMS
Passengers on incoming flights pass through customs. Officials there search baggage and clothing for drugs and other illegal substances, and check for goods on which travellers should pay import or export tax. Smugglers try to trick customs officers by hiding illegal or taxable goods.

SECURITY
Airport authorities carry out security checks to protect aircraft from bombs and armed terrorists. X-ray machines scan hand luggage for bombs and guns. Passengers walk through an arch that detects metal; a heavy lump of metal such as a gun triggers an alarm.

AIR TRAFFIC CONTROL
At a busy airport, as many as 50 aircraft take off and land every hour. Air traffic controllers in the control tower decide when each plane can take off. They also radio instructions to the aircraft that are circling in the sky above, waiting to land.

Find out more
AIR FORCES
AIRCRAFT
TRANSPORT, HISTORY OF
X-RAYS

ALEXANDER THE GREAT

ALEXANDER
As a young man Alexander (356-323 B.C.) was brave and intelligent. He was taught by the Greek philosopher Aristotle, from whom he developed a lifelong interest in Greek culture.

BY 323 B.C. ONE MAN had conquered most of the known world and set up an empire that extended from Asia Minor (now Turkey) to India. The name of the general was Alexander, today known as Alexander the Great. He was the son of King Philip II, ruler of Macedonia, a small but powerful Greek kingdom. In 336 B.C. Philip was murdered and Alexander became king, although he was only 20 years old. Alexander was an ambitious and brilliant general. In 334 he invaded the great Persian Empire ruled by Darius III. By a series of remarkable victories, Alexander then went on to conquer a vast empire running from Egypt in the west to India in the east. When Alexander died, aged only 33, he had led his armies at least 19,312 km (12,000 miles) and had encouraged the spread of Greek culture throughout the known world. After he died, his empire was divided. But he is still considered one of the greatest generals who ever lived.

PHALANX
The army that Alexander led into Persia (Iran) consisted mostly of infantry, or foot soldiers, armed with long spears. The infantry fought in a formation called a phalanx. The men were packed closely together with their spears pointing towards the enemy.

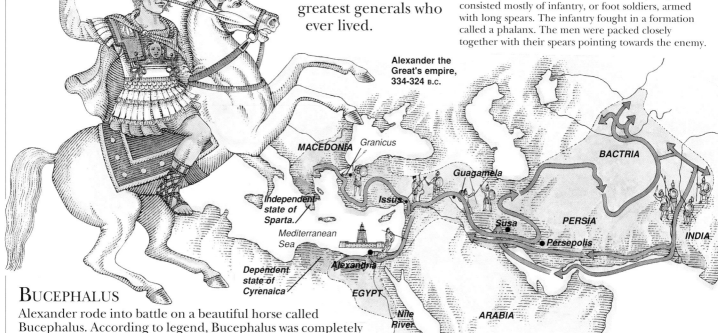

Alexander the Great's empire, 334-324 B.C.

MACEDONIA
Granicus
Independent state of Sparta.
Mediterranean Sea
Issus
Guagamela
Dependent state of Cyrenaica
Alexandria
Susa
Persepolis
PERSIA
BACTRIA
INDIA
EGYPT
Nile River
ARABIA

BUCEPHALUS

Alexander rode into battle on a beautiful horse called Bucephalus. According to legend, Bucephalus was completely wild and responded only to Alexander. When Bucephalus died, Alexander built a monument and town, called Bucephala, in honor of him. The city still exists in India today.

BATTLES
Alexander fought many battles. Usually he had fewer men than his enemy, but he won because his men were well trained and equipped. At the Battle of Issus in 333 B.C. Alexander, with 36,000 men, defeated Darius and his 110,000 troops. Two years later, with a force of 45,000 men, Alexander again overwhelmed Darius and his 100,000 soldiers at the Battle of Gaugamela.

ALEXANDRIA

In 332 B.C. Alexander founded the city of Alexandria (named after himself) on the Mediterranean coast. It soon became a great port and a centre of Greek culture and learning, attracting poets and scientists from all over the world. Today Alexandria is the second largest city in Egypt.

THE ALEXANDRIAN LIBRARY
After Alexander's death, Ptolemy Soter, commander of Egypt, created a huge library at Alexandria. It was said to have contained more than 500,000 books; today only ruins remain.

Find out more
ARMIES
GREECE, ANCIENT

ALPHABETS

WHEN PEOPLE FIRST began to write, they did not use an alphabet. Instead they drew small pictures to represent the objects they were writing about. This is called picture writing, and it was very slow because there was a different picture for every word. An alphabet does not contain pictures. Instead, it is a collection of letters or symbols which represent sounds. Each sound is just part of one word. Joining the letters together forms a whole word. The human voice can make about 35 different sounds in speech. So alphabets need at most 35 letters to write any word, and most alphabets manage with fewer. The Phoenicians, who lived about 3,000 years ago in the Middle Eastern country now called Syria, developed the first modern alphabet. The ancient Greeks adapted the Phoenician alphabet, and later the Romans improved it. The Roman alphabet is now used widely throughout the world.

The ancient Romans used the letters of the alphabet for numbers. For example, C is 100.

abcdefghi jklmnopqr stuvwxyz

CAPITAL AND SMALL LETTERS
The first Roman alphabet used only capital letters. Small letters started to appear after the 8th century. In English, capital letters are used at the beginning of a sentence, and for the first letter of a name. Capital letters are also used when words are abbreviated, or shortened, to their first letters, such as UN for United Nations.

In every alphabet, letters have a special order that does not change. Dictionaries, phone books, and many other books are arranged in alphabetical order so that it is easy to find a word or a name.

SYMBOLS AND ACCENTS
In addition to letters, writers use punctuation marks such as a full stop to show where a sentence ends. Some languages, such as French, also use accents – marks which show how to speak the word. The sloping acute accent over the *e* in *café* makes it sound like the *a* in *day*.

In traditional printing, raised lead letters are used to print the words on paper.

The Romans did not have the letter W. For J they used I, and for U they used V.

ROMAN ALPHABET
The alphabet used in English and other European languages is based on the Roman alphabet, which has 26 letters. This alphabet is also used in some Far Eastern languages, such as Vietnamese and Indonesian.

АБВГДЕЁЖЗИЙКЛМНОПРСТУФХЦЧШЩЪЫЬЭЮЯ
Cyrillic (Russian)

Α Β Γ Δ Ε Ζ Η Θ Ι Κ Λ Μ Ν Ξ Ο Π Ρ Σ Τ Υ Φ Χ Ψ Ω
Greek

अ आ इ ई उ ऊ ऋ ए ऐ ओ औ क ख ग घ ङ च छ ज झ ञ ट ठ ड ढ ण त थ द ध न प फ ब भ म य र ल व श ष स ह
Hindi (India)

MODERN ALPHABETS
The Roman alphabet is only one of the world's alphabets. Many other languages use different symbols to represent similar sounds, and the words may be written and read quite differently from the Roman alphabet. Japanese readers start on the right side of the page and read to the left, or start at the top and read down the page.

ROSETTA STONE
The ancient Egyptians used a system of picture writing called hieroglyphics. The meaning of this writing was forgotten 1,600 years ago, so nobody was able to read Egyptian documents until 1799 when some French soldiers made a remarkable discovery. Near Alexandria, Egypt, they found a stone with an inscription on it. The words were carved in hieroglyphics and in Greek. Using their knowledge of Greek, scholars were able to discover what the hieroglyphics meant.

CUNEIFORM
About 5,000 years ago in Mesopotamia (now part of Iraq) a form of writing called cuneiform developed. It started off as picture writing, but later letters began to represent sounds. The Mesopotamians did not have paper; instead they wrote on damp clay using wedge-shaped pens. Cuneiform means "wedge-shaped."

CHINESE PICTOGRAMS
In traditional Chinese writing, symbols called pictograms are used to represent ideas. There is a different character for every word.

Bird

Horse

Tree

Sun

Find out more
BABYLONIANS
BRONZE AGE
EGYPT, ANCIENT
LANGUAGES
PHOENICIANS

ANIMAL SENSES

ALL ANIMALS ARE AWARE of their surroundings. Touch, smell, taste, sight, and hearing are the five senses that animals and humans use to detect what is happening around them. Animals, however, have a much more complex array of senses than humans. A dog's nose is so sensitive to odours that it "sees" the world as a pattern of scents and smells, in the same way that we see light and colour with our eyes. Many creatures, particularly fish, can determine where they are by picking up the tiny amounts of bio-electricity produced by other living things around them. A fish also detects vibrations in the water using a row of sense organs down each side of its body, called the lateral line.

An animal's senses, like its body shape, are a result of evolution and suit the animal's needs. Eyes would be of little use to a creature such as the cave fish, which lives in endless darkness. Instead, these creatures rely on other senses such as smell and touch. Some senses are extremely specialized. Long, feathery antennae enable a male emperor moth to "smell" the odour of a female moth 5 km (3 miles) away.

HUNTING SENSES
A shark can smell blood in the water hundreds of metres away. As this shark closes in for the attack, it makes use of its keen eyesight and electricity-sensing organs.

The otter's scenting organs can detect many scents in the air. These special organs lie inside the nose in the roof of the nasal cavity.

A clear lens at the front of the eye focuses rays of light into the back of the eye to produce a sharp image.

Lips detect sharp pieces of shell in food, then spit them out.

Whiskers are sensitive to touch. They also respond to vibrations, so they are useful in murky water.

The skin and hair roots bear sensors that detect vibrations, light touch, heavy pressure, and heat and cold.

The otter hears by sensing vibrations when they strike its eardrums. To help the otter balance, tiny fluid-filled canals inside the ear work like miniature levels to register gravity.

Sensitive forepaws manipulate food. The otter also uses its paws to crack open shellfish.

Taste buds on the otter's tongue, cheeks, and upper throat sense different flavours in food.

Claws and soles of feet are sensitive to touch.

OTTER

While the sea otter floats on its back in the water, eating a shellfish, its sense organs continuously send information about its surroundings to the brain. The organs include the eyes, ears, nose, tongue, whiskers, fur, skin, and balance sensors. Stretch receptors in the joints and muscles also convey information about the otter's body position. The smell of a poisoned shellfish or the ripples from a shark's fin instantly alert the otter to possible danger.

BLOODHOUND

Bloodhounds have been specially bred as tracker dogs. Their sense of smell may be as much as one million times sharper than a human's sense of smell. Bloodhounds can even detect the microscopic pieces of skin that are shed from a moving person's body.

Floppy ears hang down to the ground, funnelling the scent into the bloodhound's nose.

Dog follows scent with nose very close to ground.

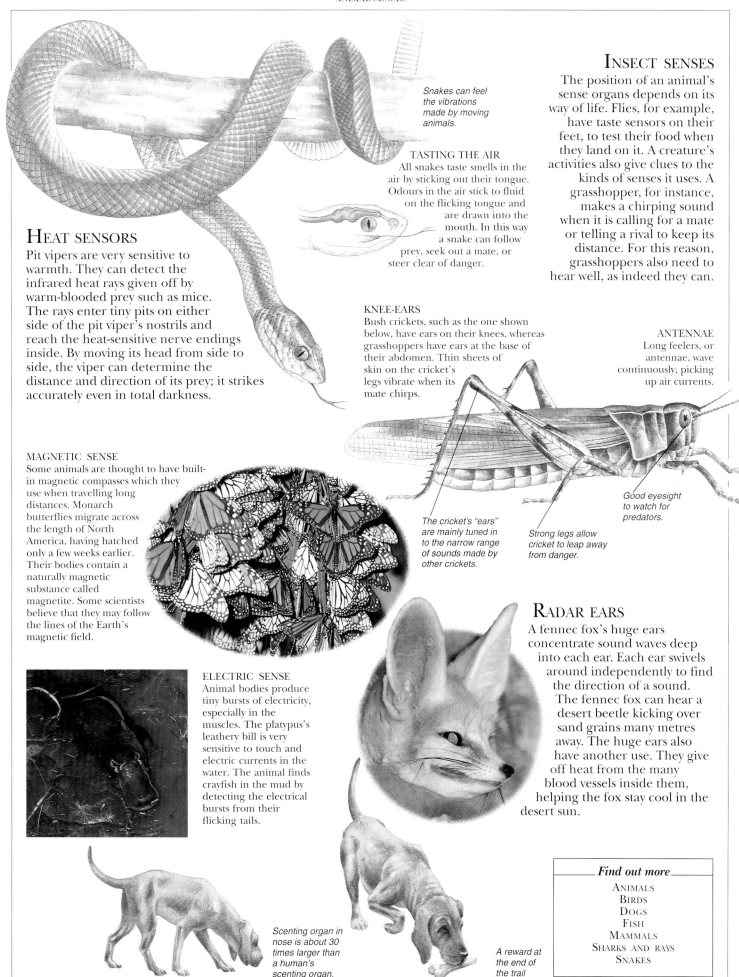

Snakes can feel the vibrations made by moving animals.

HEAT SENSORS

Pit vipers are very sensitive to warmth. They can detect the infrared heat rays given off by warm-blooded prey such as mice. The rays enter tiny pits on either side of the pit viper's nostrils and reach the heat-sensitive nerve endings inside. By moving its head from side to side, the viper can determine the distance and direction of its prey; it strikes accurately even in total darkness.

TASTING THE AIR

All snakes taste smells in the air by sticking out their tongue. Odours in the air stick to fluid on the flicking tongue and are drawn into the mouth. In this way a snake can follow prey, seek out a mate, or steer clear of danger.

INSECT SENSES

The position of an animal's sense organs depends on its way of life. Flies, for example, have taste sensors on their feet, to test their food when they land on it. A creature's activities also give clues to the kinds of senses it uses. A grasshopper, for instance, makes a chirping sound when it is calling for a mate or telling a rival to keep its distance. For this reason, grasshoppers also need to hear well, as indeed they can.

KNEE-EARS

Bush crickets, such as the one shown below, have ears on their knees, whereas grasshoppers have ears at the base of their abdomen. Thin sheets of skin on the cricket's legs vibrate when its mate chirps.

ANTENNAE

Long feelers, or antennae, wave continuously, picking up air currents.

MAGNETIC SENSE

Some animals are thought to have built-in magnetic compasses which they use when travelling long distances. Monarch butterflies migrate across the length of North America, having hatched only a few weeks earlier. Their bodies contain a naturally magnetic substance called magnetite. Some scientists believe that they may follow the lines of the Earth's magnetic field.

Good eyesight to watch for predators.

The cricket's "ears" are mainly tuned in to the narrow range of sounds made by other crickets.

Strong legs allow cricket to leap away from danger.

ELECTRIC SENSE

Animal bodies produce tiny bursts of electricity, especially in the muscles. The platypus's leathery bill is very sensitive to touch and electric currents in the water. The animal finds crayfish in the mud by detecting the electrical bursts from their flicking tails.

RADAR EARS

A fennec fox's huge ears concentrate sound waves deep into each ear. Each ear swivels around independently to find the direction of a sound. The fennec fox can hear a desert beetle kicking over sand grains many metres away. The huge ears also have another use. They give off heat from the many blood vessels inside them, helping the fox stay cool in the desert sun.

Scenting organ in nose is about 30 times larger than a human's scenting organ.

A reward at the end of the trail

ANIMALS

THE ANIMAL KINGDOM is one of the largest groups of living things; scientists believe that there are about 10 million species. Animals range from tiny, simple creatures that look like blobs of jelly, to gigantic blue whales. The huge animal kingdom is divided into many groups. A hedgehog, for example, belongs to the order of insectivores because it eats insects. It also belongs to the class of placental mammals. All mammals belong to the group known as vertebrates (animals with backbones).

An animal is a living creature that feeds, moves, and breeds. It senses its surroundings by smell, touch, sight, hearing, and taste. During its life cycle, an animal is born, grows, matures, reproduces, and eventually dies. It ingests (takes in) food to build and develop its body. Food provides the animal with the energy to move around. A few kinds of animals do not move at all; the sponge, for example, spends its life anchored to a rock. Only a fraction of the animals that have ever lived on Earth are alive today. All kinds of animals from dinosaurs to dodos have become extinct; many others, including elephants and tigers, may soon disappear forever.

FROG
Like all animals, the common green frog is aware of its surroundings and able to move, feed, and reproduce. Frogs belong to the class of animals called amphibians. All amphibians spend part of their lives in or near water.

INTERNAL SKELETONS
The animal world can be divided into vertebrate animals and invertebrate animals. Vertebrates have an internal skeleton with a vertebral column or backbone. In most cases, this is made of bone. Some sea-dwelling vertebrates, such as sharks, have a backbone made of tough, rubbery gristle called cartilage.

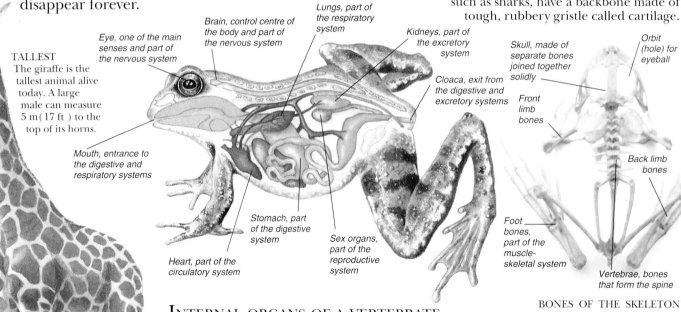

TALLEST
The giraffe is the tallest animal alive today. A large male can measure 5 m (17 ft) to the top of its horns.

Eye, one of the main senses and part of the nervous system

Brain, control centre of the body and part of the nervous system

Lungs, part of the respiratory system

Kidneys, part of the excretory system

Mouth, entrance to the digestive and respiratory systems

Cloaca, exit from the digestive and excretory systems

Heart, part of the circulatory system

Stomach, part of the digestive system

Sex organs, part of the reproductive system

Skull, made of separate bones joined together solidly

Orbit (hole) for eyeball

Front limb bones

Back limb bones

Foot bones, part of the muscle-skeletal system

Vertebrae, bones that form the spine

INTERNAL ORGANS OF A VERTEBRATE
Inside an animal such as the frog above are many different parts called organs. Organs are all shapes and sizes. Each one has a job to do. Several organs are grouped together to form a body system, such as the digestive system, the circulatory system, and the reproductive system. The nervous system and the hormonal system control and co-ordinate all the internal systems.

The smallest animals are single-celled creatures called protozoa – so tiny they can hardly be seen by the human eye. The tiniest mammals are the bumblebee bat and Savi's pygmy shrew. This pygmy shrew measures only 6 cm (2.3 in) including its tail.

BONES OF THE SKELETON
Each vertebrate animal has a different skeletal design, depending on its size and way of life. A frog, for example, has long, strong back legs for leaping. There are similarities, however: all vertebrates have a skull that contains the brain and the main sense organs. All vertebrates also have two pairs of limbs. Some bones, such as the skull bones, are fixed firmly together; others are linked by flexible joints, as in the limbs.

VERTEBRATES

Fishes, amphibians, reptiles, birds, and mammals are the largest groups of vertebrate animals. Birds and mammals are warm-blooded. Their bodies generate heat so they can stay active in cold conditions. Fishes, reptiles, and amphibians are called cold-blooded because they cannot regulate their body temperature.

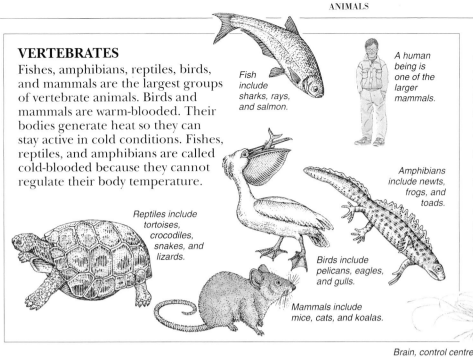

Fish include sharks, rays, and salmon.

A human being is one of the larger mammals.

Reptiles include tortoises, crocodiles, snakes, and lizards.

Amphibians include newts, frogs, and toads.

Birds include pelicans, eagles, and gulls.

Mammals include mice, cats, and koalas.

EXTERNAL SKELETONS

Many invertebrate animals, such as insects and spiders, have an outer skeleton. It forms an exoskeleton – a tough outer casing around the body. The exoskeleton has flexible joints, and muscles pull on it from the inside, so that the animal can move. It also supports and protects the internal organs. The exoskeleton is hard and cannot grow larger. As the animal grows, it sheds or casts off the old skeleton to reveal a new one underneath.

The prawn is a crustacean, a relative of shrimps, crabs, and lobsters.

INTERNAL ORGANS OF AN INVERTEBRATE

A complicated invertebrate such as a prawn (right) has internal organs similar to a vertebrate. Prawns, together with insects and spiders, belong to a huge group of joint-limbed creatures known as arthropods. When a prawn sheds its skeleton, even the delicate coverings of its feelers and eyes are cast off.

Brain, control centre of body and part of nervous system

Heart, part of circulatory system

Abdominal muscles, part of muscle-skeletal system

Antenna (large feeler)

Antennule (small feeler)

Pincer on first walking leg

One of five pairs of jointed walking legs

Uropod (tail fan)

Pleopods (swimmerets)

Intestine, part of digestive system

Bladder, part of excretory system

Image-forming eye

INVERTEBRATES

Some invertebrates, such as snails, have fleshy bodies protected by shells. Others, such as jellyfish, have soft, unprotected bodies. Insects are the largest single group of invertebrates. There are more than one million kinds of insects. The smallest invertebrates are visible only under a microscope. The largest is the giant squid, with a total length of 20 m (60 ft).

Crustaceans include crabs, lobsters, and barnacles.

Cnidarians include jellyfish, corals, and sea anemones.

Bryozoans include sea mats and moss animals.

Echinoderms include starfish, sea urchins, and sea cucumbers.

Arachnids include spiders, scorpions, and mites.

Insects include beetles, flies, and fleas.

Sponges

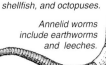

Molluscs include snails, shellfish, and octopuses.

Nematode worms include roundworms and hookworms.

Flatworms include tapeworms and flukes.

Annelid worms include earthworms and leeches.

Centipedes

Millipedes

Find out more

BIRDS
FROGS
and other amphibians
INSECTS
MAMMALS
REPTILES

ANTARCTICA
AND THE ARCTIC

AT OPPOSITE ENDS of the world there are waste-lands of snow and ice. Antarctica and the Arctic are the names given to the cold polar regions – the areas at the far south and north of the globe. In these places the sun never rises for half of each year – and then, for the next six months, it never sets. When it does shine, the sun's rays are weak, so both regions are very cold all or part of the time. Antarctica, the southern polar region, is the coldest place on Earth. It is a vast ice-covered continent, larger than the United States of America. In places the ice is 2,000m (6,500 ft) thick. The whole of the continent is surrounded by oceans which, in winter, also turn to ice. Even in summer, the air temperature hardly rises above freezing. About 4,000 scientists and visitors live there.

The Arctic is not a continent; it is a vast ocean surrounded by land. Much of the ocean is frozen throughout the year, but the fringes of the Arctic have a more varied climate. In some places the weather is warm enough for plants to grow. And since prehistoric times Eskimo people have lived there.

ANTARCTICA
Situated at the southernmost point of the world, Antarctica covers an area of about 14 million sq km (5.5 million square miles) The nearest land masses are Africa, South America, and Australia. The highest point is Vinson Massif, which rises to 5,140 m (16,864 ft).

ARCTIC
The most northern part of the earth is the Arctic region. It takes in the polar icecap and parts of Norway, Sweden, Finland, the Russian Federation, Greenland, Alaska, and Canada. Drifting ice covers large areas of the Arctic Ocean, and there is a permanent icecap on Greenland.

Radio transmitters allow scientists to track the movements of penguins.

POLAR TEMPERATURES

2°C/-28°F Sea water freezes. On the Antarctic coast, summer temperatures are only a degree or so warmer than this.

-25°C/-13°F Steel crystallizes and becomes brittle.

-40°C/-40°F Synthetic rubber becomes brittle, and exposed flesh freezes rapidly.

-89°C/-128.6°F Lowest temperature ever recorded, at Vostok research station, Antarctica, 1983.

ANTARCTICA
There is more fresh water in Antarctica, locked up in the form of ice, than in the whole of the rest of the world. Yet very little rain falls there, and only 10 to 15 cm (4 to 6 in) of new snow coats the continent each year. Hurricane-force winds often blow, making Antarctica a hostile place for people and animals. The largest land creature is a tiny insect, though penguins and other birds live on offshore islands. For travelling on land, scientists in Antarctica use special tracked vehicles. Despite the savage cold, several countries have claimed sections of Antarctica. There may be valuable minerals beneath the ice, but an international treaty now prevents mining.

Platinum

Iron

Gold

MINERAL WEALTH
Both regions have deposits of minerals, such as gold, copper, uranium, and nickel. However, extracting them may damage the fragile polar environment.

ARCTIC
Much of the Arctic fringe is tundra – low, swampy grass plains. Here nomadic tribes such as the Sami graze reindeer. People also live in the more northerly areas, which are largely covered by ice; the Inuit of northern Canada, for example, live by fishing and hunting. However, traditional ways of life are changing. Immigrants, attracted by the valuable Arctic natural resources, bring with them new cultures and technologies.

Umanak, on Greenland's western coast

ANTS AND TERMITES

IMAGINE HOW MANY millions of ants and termites live on this planet. There are at least 14,000 different kinds of ants and 2,250 kinds of termites. These tiny creatures are among the most fascinating animals on Earth. Both ants and termites are social insects, living in large groups called colonies where each individual has a specific job to do. The queen (the main female) mates with a male, then spends her life laying eggs. The hordes of workers do such jobs as gathering food and rearing the young. Soldiers and guards protect the nest and the foraging workers. Ants eat a variety of food, including caterpillars, leaves, and fungi. Termites feed mostly on plant matter, and they are among nature's most valuable recyclers.

ANT HEAD
The Asian tree-living ant has simple jaws for feeding on soft insects. Other ants and termites have strong jaws for chewing wood and hard plant stems.

TERMITE MOUND

Many termites make small nests in dead trees or underground. A few kinds of termites build a mound which contains a termite city – a home for many millions of termites. In hot areas the mounds have tunnels and ventilation holes, and may be more than 6 m (20 ft) high. The mounds are often occupied for more than 50 years, and the thick walls help to keep out anteaters and other predators. The queen and king termites live in a royal chamber deep inside the mound.

Termite mound

Cooling chimney lets air in and out of the termite mound.

ANT HILL
Most of the passages of an ant hill are underground. Eggs, larvae (grubs), and pupae are kept in separate parts of the nest. Large-jawed sentries guard the entrances. A large ant nest may contain 100,000 ants.

Courtier worker

Queen termite

Soldier termite

Front leg

Antenna can bend like an elbow joint.

Eye

Jaws

Middle leg

Abdomen

Head

Claw

Rear leg

Termite mound has many tunnels.

Fungus grows on the termites' dung (waste matter) inside the termite mound. These areas are called fungus gardens. Termites feed on the fungus.

Nursery for termite larvae

Queen lays 20,000 or more eggs daily in royal chamber.

King termite

Young female termite

Ant squirts formic acid from rear of body in self-defence.

Thorax

Worker ant

WORKER ANT

All worker ants are female. Their long, claw-tipped legs allow them to run fast and climb well. Workers collect food, regurgitate it to feed the other ants, look after eggs and larvae, and clean the nest. They lack wings, unlike the queen and male ants.

Workers regurgitate (spit out) food for queen, king, and soldier termites. Courtier workers feed and clean queen and king.

TERMITES
The queen and male termites have wings. They take flight and mate, then the queen returns to the nest. The queen does not leave the nest again, and is cared for by the courtier workers. The main male, or king, is larger than the workers and remains with the queen.

ARMY ANTS
A few ants, such as these army ants of South America, live on the move instead of making permanent nests. As the colony marches through the forests, the workers forage for insects and other creatures. Even goats and other large animals may be eaten alive.

LEAF-CUTTING ANTS
Ants can lift objects that weigh more than they do. Leaf-cutting ants bite off pieces of leaves and carry them back to a huge underground nest. Here they chew the leaves and mix them with saliva to make a kind of compost. Fungus – the leaf-cutting ant's only food – grows on this compost.

Find out more
AFRICAN WILDLIFE
ANIMALS
ECOLOGY AND FOOD WEBS
INSECTS

ARABS

STRETCHING 8,000 km (5,000 miles) from the Atlantic Ocean to the Arabian Sea, the Arab world is the home of 206 million people. All these people share the Arabic language and a distinct Arab culture. But in every other way Arabs are very different from one another. They are not one nationality: they live in many countries. They can range from dark-skinned to light-skinned in appearance. And though most Arabs are Muslims (followers of the Islam religion), many are Christians. Their ways of life vary widely too. A few Arabs are nomads (wanderers). Some, called Marsh Arabs, live in southern Iraq's marshes; some are mountain shepherds; and others live in towns and cities. Before the 20th century the different beliefs and aims of these peoples seemed more important than their common Arab identity. But the Arab people have become increasingly united. Together, they have a louder voice in world politics and are better able to resist domination by more powerful nations.

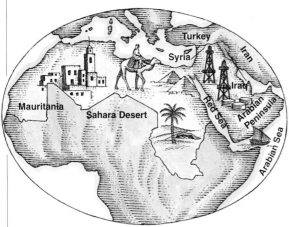

ARAB WORLD
The countries of the Arab world are situated in north Africa and the Middle East. The Atlantic coast of Mauritania is the most western point. The Sahara Desert marks the southern boundary. In the east, the Arabian peninsula is bordered by the Persian Gulf, the Red Sea, and the Arabian Sea. And in the north, Syria and Iraq meet Turkey and Iran.

AGRICULTURE
The climate of most Arab countries is very dry, so irrigation is vital for productive farming. The careful management of water has brought enormous benefits. Saudi Arabia, which once imported almost all its wheat, is now self-sufficient and has a surplus to export. The Saudis grow grain on land that was once desert.

Larger dhows are equipped with engines as well as sails, and are capable of making long ocean voyages.

Shipping
Huge oil tankers and small dhows (traditional Arab sailing boats) tie up at berths in Arab ports. Shipping is a major industry, and Arabs are expert sailors. They sailed the sheltered waters of the Mediterranean and the Persian Gulf many centuries ago. The legendary Arab sailor Sinbad is said to have set sail from Oman (on the Arabian Peninsula) on one of his great voyages.

Under the laws of Islam, every woman must wear a black cloak that hides her entire body.

YASSER ARAFAT
The Palestine Liberation Organization (PLO) was formed in 1964 to represent the Arabs of Palestine who lost their land when the Jewish state of Israel was created in 1948. Yasser Arafat became chairman of the organization in 1969.
In 1994 the Israeli government granted the Palestinians limited autonomy in the Gaza Strip.

ISLAMIC FUNDAMENTALISM
Muslim Arabs follow the codes of behaviour set down in the Koran, the holy book of Islam. Some interpret these codes less strictly than others, but there is a growing trend towards a return to strict Islamic law. This is termed Islamic fundamentalism.

Find out more
ARABS, HISTORY OF
ISLAM
ISRAEL
JEWS, HISTORY OF
MIDDLE EAST
RELIGIONS

HISTORY OF THE
ARABS

DURING THE SEVENTH century A.D., a great force arose in the world. Inspired by the prophet Muhammad, founder of the Islamic religion, Arab peoples created a great empire. The Arabs were originally wandering tribespeople who lived around the Arabian peninsula. After Muhammad died, a series of powerful caliphs (successors) took over the leadership of Islam. Under the caliphs the Arabs grew in strength and expanded their lands. Their culture flourished and they grew rich through trading around the Mediterranean and with Africa and India.

The Arab empire was soon divided, particularly between Shi'ite Arabs, who supported only direct descendants of Muhammad, and Sunni Arabs, who did not. Different dynasties ruled different regions. In the 13th century the Mongols, and in the 16th century, the Ottoman Turks, invaded and took over parts of the old Arab empire. During the 19th century, Europeans began occupying Arab territories. Since the 1920s, however, Arabs have been throwing off European control.

ARAB EMPIRE
By about 750 the Arab empire stretched from the Atlantic Ocean in the west to the frontier of India in the east. It included Persia (Iran), Turkestan, North Africa, Spain, and part of France.

ARABS
c. A.D. 570 Prophet Muhammad born in Mecca.

632 Death of Muhammad; rule of caliphs.

c.750 Arab empire reaches greatest extent.

1258 Mongols take Baghdad.

1517 Ottoman Turks conquer most of Arab empire.

1918 End of Ottoman Empire.

1945 Arab League founded to further co-operation between Arab states.

1948 State of Israel created. First Arab-Israeli war.

1956 Egypt seizes Suez Canal; leads to Israeli invasion and British-French occupation of canal.

1979 Peace agreement between Egypt and Israel.

1980-88 Iran-Iraq War.

1990 Iraq invades Kuwait.

1991 Gulf War

Mosque (Islamic place of worship)

Craftworkers traded their wares in the centre of Baghdad.

Carpet trader

BAGHDAD
In 762, the city of Baghdad became the capital of the Arab empire. Under the great caliph Harun ar-Rashid (ruled 786-809), Baghdad became a world centre for art and learning. In 1258, the Mongols overran Baghdad and the city declined.

SCIENCE
Arabic learning has had a powerful influence on the rest of the world. During the 8th century, Arab scholars studied the knowledge of Ancient Greece but also made great advances in astronomy, mathematics, and medical science. The Arabs understood the circulation of the blood centuries before European scientists. Arab sailors developed the astrolabe (right), an instrument to help them navigate the oceans away from the sight of land. In 971, the world's first university was founded in Cairo, Egypt.

NASSER
In 1958, Gamal Abdel Nasser (above left), president of Egypt from 1956 to 1970, set up the United Arab Republic (UAR) between Syria and Egypt but the union failed. Nasser is seen here a year after he led a revolt that overthrew King Faruk (1920-65), the last king of Egypt, and established a republic.

Find out more
ARABS
BYZANTINE EMPIRE
CRUSADES
ISLAM
MIDDLE EAST
OTTOMAN EMPIRE

ARCHAEOLOGY

FOR AN ARCHAEOLOGIST, brushing away the soil that hides a broken pot is like brushing away time. Every tiny fragment helps create a more complete picture of the past. Archaeology is the study of the remains of past human societies, but it is not the same as history. Historians use written records as their starting point, whereas archaeologists use objects. They excavate, or dig, in the ground or under water for bones, pots, and anything else created by our ancestors. They also look for seeds, field boundaries, and other signs of how long-dead people made use of the landscape. But archaeology is not just concerned with dead people and buried objects. It also helps us understand what may happen to our own society in the future. Archaeology has shown that human actions and changes in the climate or environment can destroy whole communities.

HEINRICH SCHLIEMANN
In 1870 the pioneer German archaeologist Heinrich Schliemann (1822-1890) discovered the site of Troy in Turkey. He also set out basic rules for excavation, such as careful recordkeeping. He did not always follow his own rules. His impatient hunt for treasure sometimes destroyed the objects he was seeking.

A grid pattern divides the site into squares so that archaeologists can quickly record in which square they made each find.

In photographs of the site, the stripes painted on poles make it easy to judge the size of objects.

By sketching objects, archaeologists can sometimes record more detail than a camera can.

ANALYSIS
The position and location of the objects uncovered in a dig can provide important information. So archaeologists measure, examine, record, and analyze everything they find, and preserve it if possible. Scientific methods such as radioactive dating enable archaeologists to find out the exact age of objects made thousands of years ago.

Archaeologists sieve the soil they remove to check for objects they may have overlooked.

A soft brush removes dry soil without damaging the object.

Small trowels allow archaeologists to remove soil carefully.

EXCAVATION
Archaeologists gather much of their information about the past by carrying out excavations, or digs. They decide where to dig by looking at aerial photographs, old pictures, maps, documents, or marks on the ground. Then they carefully remove layers of soil, often using trowels and other small tools. The archaeologists keep digging until they reach undisturbed soil with no trace of human occupation.

STRATIFICATION
Archaeologists on a dig determine the relative age of each object they find from where it is buried, using the principle of stratification. This principle says that older objects are usually buried deeper in the ground than newer objects.

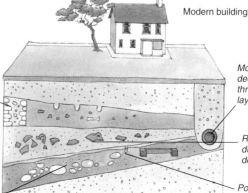

Modern building

Remains of 19th-century wall

Modern sewer in deep trench cuts through several layers.

Archaeologists know that ax and arrow heads are from the Bronze Age because of their position between older Stone Age and newer Iron Age layers of earth.

Remains of 15th-century rubbish dump lie below more recent deposits.

Bronze Age tools

Posthole from Iron Age building is above Bronze Age objects.

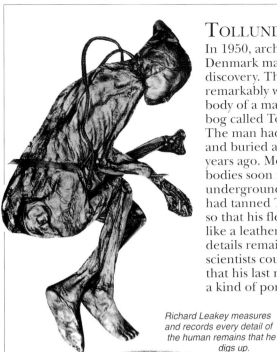

TOLLUND MAN

In 1950, archaeologists in Denmark made a dramatic discovery. They found the remarkably well preserved body of a man in a peat bog called Tollund Mose. The man had been hanged and buried about 2,000 years ago. Most dead bodies soon rot underground, but the peat had tanned Tollund man so that his flesh was hard like a leather shoe. Many details remained, and scientists could even tell that his last meal had been a kind of porridge.

AERIAL PHOTOGRAPHY

Photography of the ground from aeroplanes began in the 1920s. It made archaeology easier because the high viewpoint reveals traces of buildings, roads, and fields that are invisible from the ground.

Richard Leakey measures and records every detail of the human remains that he digs up.

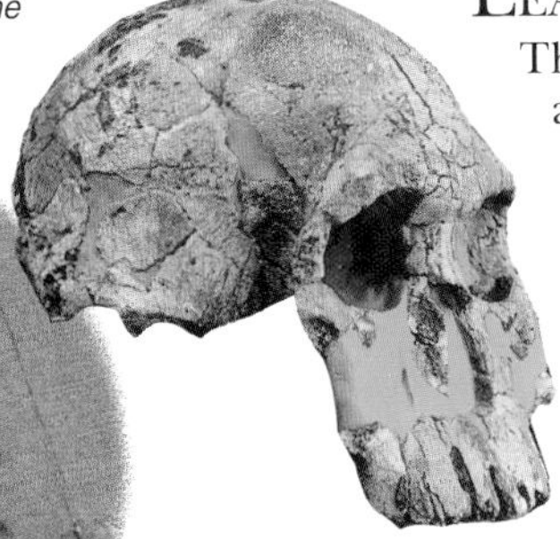

LEAKEY

The Leakey family has made major discoveries about the origins of human beings. Louis and his wife, Mary, began to work in the Olduvai Gorge in Tanzania (Africa) in the 1930s. There they showed that human life existed 1,750,000 years ago. They found that human evolution began in Africa, not – as people once thought – in Asia. Since the 1960s their son Richard has continued their research, and now believes that the human race may be more than two million years old.

Among the objects found in the tomb of Tutankhamun was a pectoral, or brooch, in the shape of a scarab beetle.

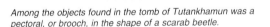

Archaeologists excavating the wreck of the Slava Rossi found Russian icons (religious paintings).

SHIPWRECKS

The development of lightweight diving equipment over the last 50 years has enabled archaeologists to excavate sites under water. They use many of the same methods that are used on land. Most underwater archaeologists look for shipwrecks, but the sea sometimes covers landscapes, buildings, and even towns.

TUTANKHAMUN

The discovery of the tomb of Tutankhamun was one of the most sensational moments in the history of archaeology. Tutankhamun was a boy-king who ruled in Egypt 3,500 years ago. In 1922, the British archaeologist Howard Carter (1873-1939) found Tutankhamun's fabulously rich burial place in the Valley of the Kings. Near the boy-king's remains lay gold treasure and beautiful furniture.

Howard Carter (left) found the sarcophagus, or coffin, of Tutankhamun. It was remarkably well preserved.

Find out more

BRONZE AGE
EGYPT, ANCIENT
EVOLUTION
FOSSILS
GEOLOGY
IRON AGE
PREHISTORIC PEOPLES

ARCHITECTURE

EVERY BUILDING you see – home, school, airport – has been planned by an architect. The word *architect* is Greek for "builder" or "craftworker" and architects aim to design and construct buildings that are attractive, functional, and comfortable. Architecture means designing a building; it also refers to the building style. Styles of architecture have changed over the centuries and differ from culture to culture, so architecture can tell us a lot about people. The Ancient Greeks, for example, produced simple, balanced buildings that showed their disciplined approach to life. Architects are artists who create buildings. But unlike other artists, they must sell their ideas before they are able to produce their buildings.

Built around 200 B.C., this Indian stupa, or dome, was originally a mound covering a site or an object sacred to Buddha.

In 447 B.C., the Greek architects Ictinus and Callicrates designed the Parthenon, a temple to the goddess Athena, in Athens, Greece. With its graceful columns, it is a perfect example of classical architecture.

CLASSICAL ARCHITECTURE

The Ancient Greeks and Romans developed a style that we call classical architecture. Most Greek buildings consisted of columns supporting a triangular roof. The types of columns varied according to the particular classical "order" (style) that was used. Everything was simple and perfectly even. The Romans, who came after the Greeks, developed the arch, dome, and vault.

Elegantly curving skyward in several tiers, pagodas were built as shrines to Buddha. On the right is the pagoda of Yakushi-ji Temple, Japan. Each element in the building's design originally had a religious meaning.

Milan Cathedral in Italy (right) is an example of late Gothic architecture.

GOTHIC ARCHITECTURE

With their multitudes of pointed arches, finely carved stonework, and intricate windows, Gothic buildings are the opposite of simple classical ones. The Gothic style of architecture began in western Europe in the 12th century. It was used mainly in building cathedrals and churches. Although most Gothic buildings were huge, their thin walls, pointed arches, and large areas of stained-glass windows made them seem light and delicate.

FRANK LLOYD WRIGHT

American architect Frank Lloyd Wright (1869-1959) influenced many other architects. He tried to blend buildings into their natural surroundings and create a feeling of space, with few walls, so that rooms could "flow" into one other. At Bear Run, Pennsylvania, he built Falling Water, a house over a waterfall.

Following the client's brief, the architect presents a drawing (below) to the client to show how the finished building will look.

ARCHITECTS

If you wanted to build a house, you would approach an architect, giving clear and precise details of what you required (a brief). An architect must know from a client what the building is to be used for, how many people will use it, what materials it should be built from, and how much money is available. A good architect will make sure that the new design fits in with existing buildings around it. The architect then presents drawings and plans to the client. When the plans are approved, work on the building can begin.

Doric column

Ionic column

Corinthian column

Barrel vault

Groin vault

Rib vault

Dome

EXTRAORDINARY ARCHITECTURE

Some architects design weird and wonderful buildings which really stand out from the rest. A new town was built outside Paris, France, called Marne-la-Vallée. It has many extraordinary buildings, designed by various adventurous architects. The apartment complex, left, is like a monument that people can live in. Two circular buildings face each other across a central courtyard. It was designed by a Spaniard named Manolo Nunez-Yanowsky.

Jean Louis Charles Garnier was the architect of the Paris Opera House (built 1861-75). It is neobaroque – a 19th-century revival of the baroque style.

The American Chrysler Building, a New York City skyscraper, was completed in 1929.

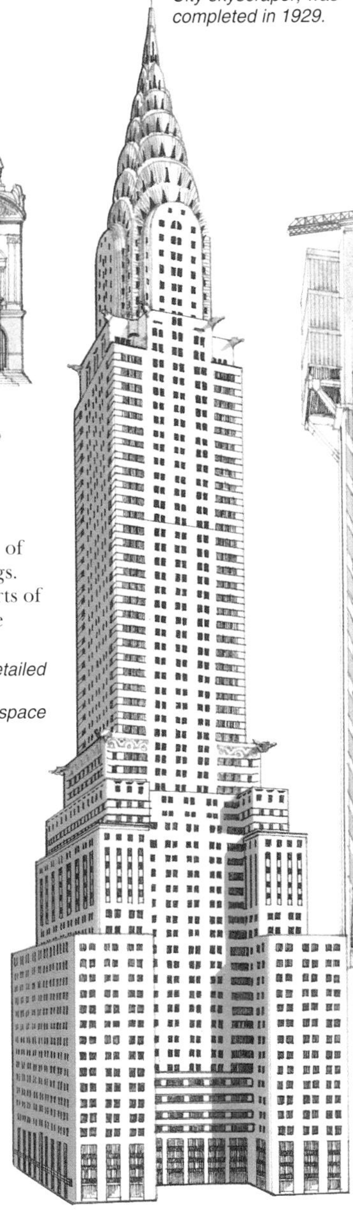

Designed by the British architect Richard Rogers, the Lloyds office building in London, England has all its services, such as plumbing, on the outside. This means they can be easily replaced.

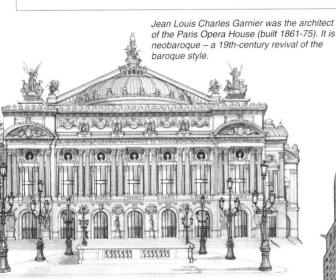

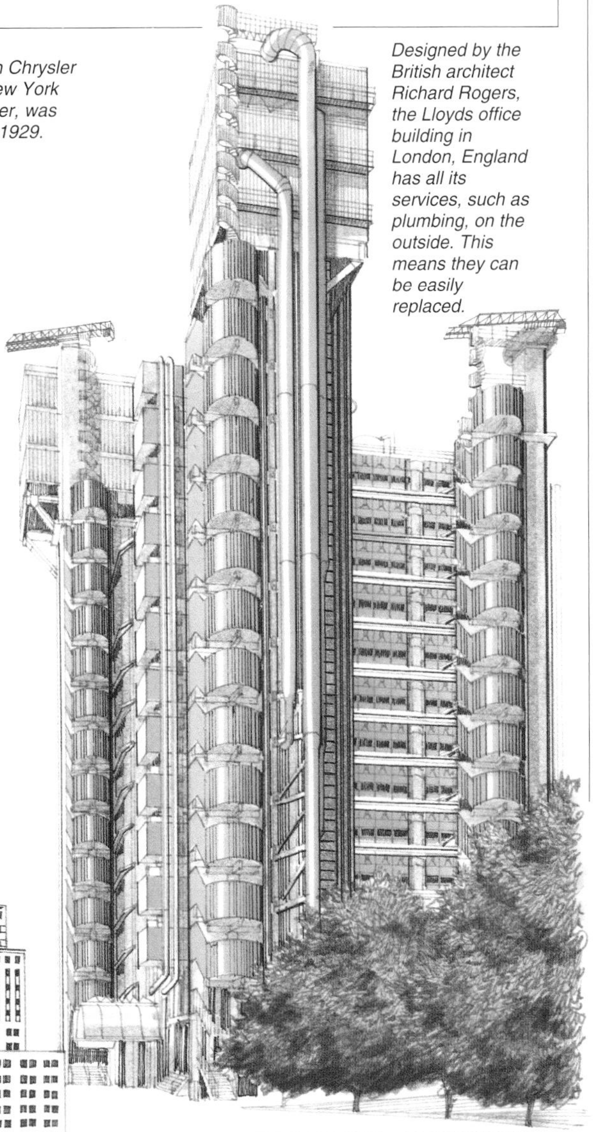

BAROQUE ARCHITECTURE

During the 1500s in Rome, architects wanted to break the classical rules of simplicity and evenness and build more exciting, dramatic buildings. So they added domes, clusters of statues, and ornate decoration and carving to their buildings. This style, known as baroque, spread from Italy to other parts of Europe. Many churches and grand palaces were built in the baroque style.

The architect draws up detailed plans of the inside of the building to show how the space will be used.

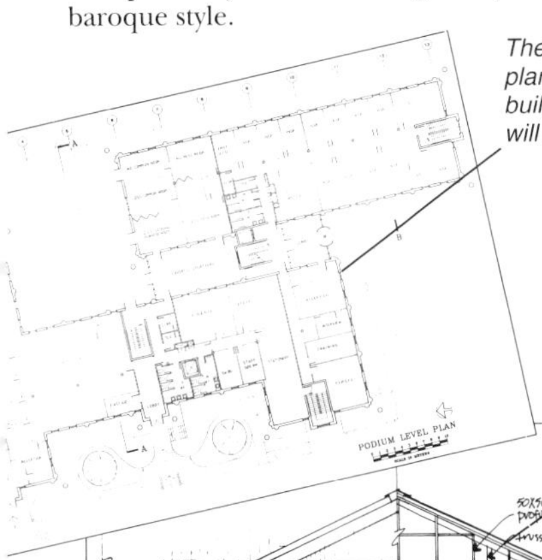

Working drawings contain exact measurements, materials, and structures, down to the tiniest detail.

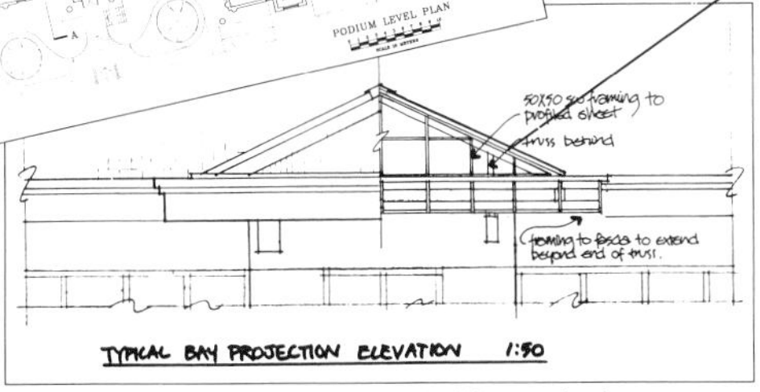

PODIUM LEVEL PLAN

TYPICAL BAY PROJECTION ELEVATION 1:50

The builder works from working drawings (above) when constructing the building.

CONTEMPORARY ARCHITECTURE

Glass, steel, and concrete are the building materials of today's architecture. There is little decoration, because a building's purpose is considered more important than its shape or form. The "international" style – glass and concrete suspended on a steel framework – is seen almost everywhere in the world.

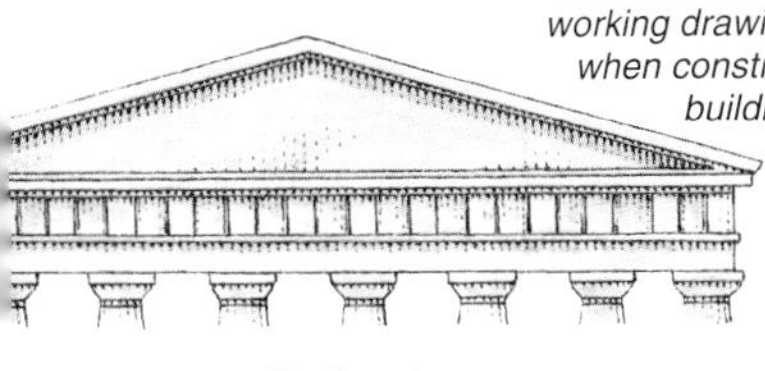

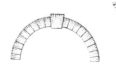

Pediment

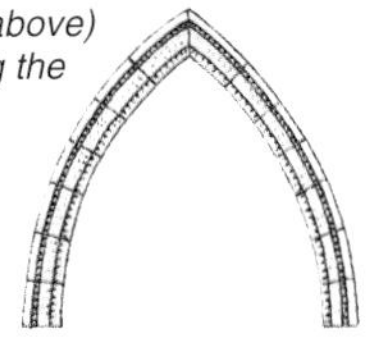

Gothic arch

Romanesque arch

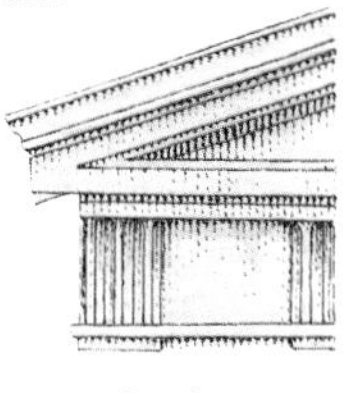

Cornice

> ### Find out more
> BUILDING
> CHURCHES AND CATHEDRALS
> CITIES
> HOUSES
> SCULPTURE

ARMIES

EVER SINCE THE ASSYRIAN armies swept across the ancient region of Mesopotamia more than 2,000 years ago, the purpose of armies has been the same: to conquer enemy territory and to defend their country. In Europe, there were no modern-style armies until the 16th century; instead sections of the population were called to arms whenever the country was at war. Today, however, most nations have a full-time army consisting of highly trained soldiers. Armies vary in size but most modern armies contain not only personnel but also the latest technology, including helicopters, guided missiles, and tanks. Technology has changed the role of the army. Previously soldiers engaged in hand-to-hand combat; today most armies rely on long-range weaponry.

RECRUITMENT

In 1917 Uncle Sam, symbol of the United States, called on young men to enlist, or volunteer for fighting, in World War I. Some countries recruit volunteers during peacetime but have conscription – compulsory military service – during wartime.

I WANT YOU FOR U.S. ARMY
NEAREST RECRUITING STATION

Pouches on webbing, or harness, hold small equipment.

Mask protects against gas attack.

Helmet with protective padding

Mess kit for cooking and eating

TRAINING

Soldiers such as these Israeli women are fighters trained for combat on land. In the army men and women learn the techniques of fighting and how to care for their weapons, and they exercise to become fit. They also learn confidence, discipline, and the importance of obeying orders so that they will fight well.

Uniform fabric is coloured to look like foliage, so that soldiers are hard to see in battle.

Heavy boots for marching

UNIFORM

A soldier's fighting uniform must be practical. Strong, heavy clothes and boots provide protection against weather. Uniforms are also designed to provide camouflage so that the soldier can hide from the enemy.

Australia   China

United Kingdom   United States

UNIFORMS OF THE WORLD
Soldiers of each nation have ceremonial uniforms which they wear when they are not fighting. Badges show the rank of the soldier and the regiment or group he or she belongs to.

GUERRILLA ARMIES

In 1808 France invaded and defeated Spain. But Spanish farmers formed small groups and continued the war. They made surprise attacks on French patrols and supply depots. The Spanish called the campaign *guerrilla*, meaning "little war"; this term is still used today to describe similar methods of fighting wars.

Modern guerrillas, such as these in Africa, usually belong to a group of people fighting for religious, national, or political beliefs.

Find out more

GUNS
NAPOLEONIC WARS
ROCKETS AND MISSILES
VIETNAM WAR
WEAPONS
WORLD WAR I
WORLD WAR II

ARMOUR

ANCIENT WARRIORS quickly realized that they would survive in battle if they could protect themselves against their enemies. So they made armour – special clothing which was tough enough to stop weapons from injuring the wearer. Prehistoric armour was simple. It was made of leather but was strong enough to provide protection against crude spears and swords. As weapons became sharper, armour too had to improve. A thousand years ago the Roman Empire employed many armourers who made excellent metal armour. But after the fall of Rome in the 5th century, blacksmiths began to make armour and its quality fell. In the 14th century, specially trained armourers invented plate armour to withstand lances, arrows, and swords. But even the thickest armour cannot stop a bullet, so armour became less useful when guns were invented. Today no one uses traditional armour, but people in combat still wear protective clothing made out of modern plastics and tough metals.

ANIMAL ARMOUR
Soldiers have used animals in warfare, such as dogs for attack and horses for riding into battle. Armour protected these animals when they fought. The most elaborate animal armour was the elephant armour of 17th-century India.

Arrows bounced off the curves of the helmet. Knights often wore mail or padding beneath the helmet.

The breastplate was flared so that sword strokes bounced off.

The vambrace was a cylindrical piece to protect the upper arm.

The cowter protected the elbow, but allowed it to move freely.

The gauntlet was made up of many small pieces so that the hand could move freely.

The cuisse protected only the front of the leg.

Poleyns had to bend easily when the knight rode a horse.

Greaves were among the earliest pieces of body armour to be made of sheet metal.

SUIT OF ARMOUR
Late 15th-century armour provided a knight with a protective metal shell. The armour was very strong, and cleverly jointed so that the knight could move easily. However, the metal suit weighed up to 30 kg (70 lb), so that running, for example, was impossible.

HELMETS
A single heavy blow to the head can kill a person, so helmets, or armoured hats, were among the first pieces of armour to be made. They are still widely used today. Different shapes gave protection against different types of weapon.

Bronze Age helmets protected against swords more than 3,000 years ago.

Pikemen of the 16th century

Twelfth-century helm.

Modern helmets give protection against shrapnel (metal fragments from bombs).

BULLETPROOF VEST
Modern police and security forces sometimes wear bulletproof vests to protect themselves from attack by criminals and terrorists. The vests are made of many layers of tough materials such as nylon and are capable of stopping a bullet.

CHAIN MAIL
Chain mail was easier and cheaper for a blacksmith to make than a complicated suit of plate armour. Mail was very common between the 6th and 13th centuries. It was made of a large number of interlocking rings of steel. It allowed the wearer to move easily, but did not give good protection against heavy swords and axes.

Find out more
JAPAN, HISTORY OF
KNIGHTS AND HERALDRY
MIDDLE AGES
ROMAN EMPIRE
WEAPONS

ASIA

THE LARGEST OF THE SEVEN CONTINENTS, Asia occupies one third of the world's total land area. Much of the continent is uninhabited. The north is a cold land of tundra. Parched deserts and towering mountains take up large areas of the central region. Yet Asia is the home of well over half of the world's population, most of whom live around the outer rim. China alone has more than 1,205 million people, and India has nearly 896 million. Altogether, Asia is an extraordinary variety of 48 nations, and many times this number of peoples, languages, and cultures.

Asia has five main zones. In the north is the Russian Federation. Part of this is in Europe, but the vast eastern region, from the Ural Mountains to the Pacific Ocean, is in Asia. The Pacific coast, which includes China, Korea, and Japan, is known as the Far East. To the south of this lie the warmer, more humid countries of Southeast Asia. India and Pakistan are the main countries of the Indian subcontinent in south Asia. One of the world's first civilizations began here, in the Indus Valley. To the west is the Middle East, bordered by the Mediterranean and Arabian seas.

The Ural Mountains divide Asia and Europe. The Suez Canal and the Red Sea separate Asia from Africa. The Bering Strait, only 88 km (55 miles) wide, marks the gap between Asia and North America. Australia lies to the southeast.

MIDDLE EAST

The hot, dry lands of the Middle East occupy the southwest corner of Asia. Almost the entire Arabian peninsula, between the Red Sea and the Persian Gulf, is desert. To the north, in Iraq and Syria, lie the fertile valleys of the rivers Tigris and Euphrates. Most of the people of the Middle East are Arabs, and speak Arabic.

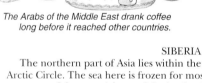

The Arabs of the Middle East drank coffee long before it reached other countries.

Siberian scientists looking for minerals in north Asia have to work in subzero temperatures, and the cold can freeze their breath.

SIBERIA

The northern part of Asia lies within the Arctic Circle. The sea here is frozen for most of the year. A layer of the land, called permafrost, is also always frozen. This area is part of the vast region of the Russian Federation called Siberia. Despite the cold, Russian people travel to work in Siberia because the region is rich in timber, coal, oil, and natural gas.

TROPICAL RAIN FORESTS

The warm, damp climate of much of Southeast Asia provides the perfect conditions for tropical rain forests, which thrive in countries such as Burma (Myanmar) and Malaysia. The forests are the habitat for a huge variety of wildlife, and are home to tribes of people whose way of life has not changed for a thousand years. But because many of the forest trees are beautiful hardwoods, the logging industry is now cutting down the forests at an alarming rate to harvest the valuable timber.

Sunlight breaks through the dense foliage of the rain forest only where rivers have cut trails through the trees.

SILK ROAD

Even 2,000 years ago, there was trade between the Far East and Europe. Traders carried silk, spices, gems, and pottery. They followed routes across India and Pakistan, past the Karakoram mountains (above). These trade routes were known as the Silk Road; they are still used today.

PROSPERITY

Some Asian countries, such as Japan and Singapore, are among the world's most prosperous nations. The discovery of oil in a number of other countries, such as Saudi Arabia in the Middle East, and Brunei in Southeast Asia, has made them very wealthy.

Brunei's vast oil wealth has enabled the sultan (ruler) to build a magnificent new palace.

"Floating markets" are a common sight on the busy waterways of the Far East.

Vanilla vines grow well in the warm climate of Indonesia, and women harvest the pods by hand.

FAR EAST

East Asia is often called the Far East. In the 19th century, European traders and travellers used this name to distinguish east Asia from the Middle East. The Far East includes China, Japan, and Korea.

KOREA

The Korean peninsula juts out from northern China towards Japan. The two Korean nations were at war between 1950 and 1953. They have lived in constant mistrust of each other since the war ended, but are now trying to mend the divisions between them. South Korea has a booming economy and is heavily supported by the United States. North Korea is Communist and poorer. The climate favours rice growing, with warm summers and icy winters.

Construction work is a common sight in South Korea, as new offices and factories are built for the country's expanding industries.

SOUTHEAST ASIA

Many different people live in the warm, tropical southeastern corner of Asia. There are ten independent countries in the region. Some of them – Burma (Myanmar), Thailand, Cambodia (or Kampuchea), and Vietnam – are on the mainland attached to the rest of Asia. Further south lie Malaysia and the tiny island nation of Singapore. Indonesia stretches across the foot of the region. It is a scattered nation of more than 13,000 islands. The islands of the Philippines are to the east. Although some of these countries are very poor, Southeast Asia as a whole has one of the most rapidly developing economies in the world.

Hundreds of different languages are spoken in the Indian subcontinent, but Indian schools teach pupils to read and write Hindi, which is the country's official language.

INDIAN SUBCONTINENT

The triangular landmass of south Asia extends south from the Himalaya Mountains to the warm waters of the Indian Ocean. This region is also known as the Indian subcontinent. It includes not only India but also Pakistan, Nepal, Bangladesh, and Bhutan. At the very southern tip of India lies the island nation of Sri Lanka.

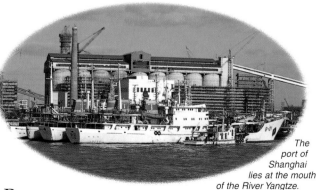

The port of Shanghai lies at the mouth of the River Yangtze.

RIVER YANGTZE

The Yangtze Kiang (or Chang Jiang), the world's third longest river, flows 6,379 km (3,964 miles) through the middle of China, from its source in Tibet to the sea at Shanghai. In 1997, the first stage was completed on the Three Gorges Dam, China's largest construction project since the building of the Great Wall.

Find out more

CHINA
INDIA
JAPAN
RELIGIONS
RUSSIAN FEDERATION
SOUTHEAST ASIA

ASIA

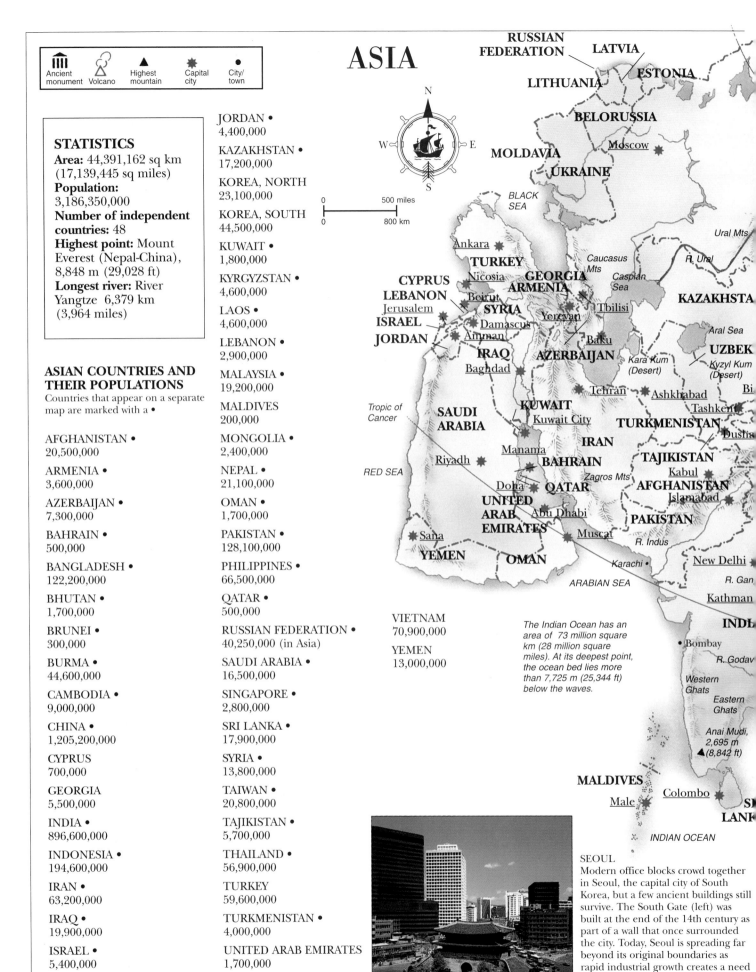

STATISTICS
Area: 44,391,162 sq km
(17,139,445 sq miles)
Population:
3,186,350,000
**Number of independent
countries:** 48
Highest point: Mount
Everest (Nepal-China),
8,848 m (29,028 ft)
Longest river: River
Yangtze 6,379 km
(3,964 miles)

ASIAN COUNTRIES AND THEIR POPULATIONS
Countries that appear on a separate
map are marked with a ●

AFGHANISTAN ●
20,500,000

ARMENIA ●
3,600,000

AZERBAIJAN ●
7,300,000

BAHRAIN ●
500,000

BANGLADESH ●
122,200,000

BHUTAN ●
1,700,000

BRUNEI ●
300,000

BURMA ●
44,600,000

CAMBODIA ●
9,000,000

CHINA ●
1,205,200,000

CYPRUS
700,000

GEORGIA
5,500,000

INDIA ●
896,600,000

INDONESIA ●
194,600,000

IRAN ●
63,200,000

IRAQ ●
19,900,000

ISRAEL ●
5,400,000

JAPAN ●
125,000,000

JORDAN ●
4,400,000

KAZAKHSTAN ●
17,200,000

KOREA, NORTH ●
23,100,000

KOREA, SOUTH ●
44,500,000

KUWAIT ●
1,800,000

KYRGYZSTAN ●
4,600,000

LAOS ●
4,600,000

LEBANON ●
2,900,000

MALAYSIA ●
19,200,000

MALDIVES ●
200,000

MONGOLIA ●
2,400,000

NEPAL ●
21,100,000

OMAN ●
1,700,000

PAKISTAN ●
128,100,000

PHILIPPINES ●
66,500,000

QATAR ●
500,000

RUSSIAN FEDERATION ●
40,250,000 (in Asia)

SAUDI ARABIA ●
16,500,000

SINGAPORE ●
2,800,000

SRI LANKA ●
17,900,000

SYRIA ●
13,800,000

TAIWAN ●
20,800,000

TAJIKISTAN ●
5,700,000

THAILAND ●
56,900,000

TURKEY
59,600,000

TURKMENISTAN ●
4,000,000

UNITED ARAB EMIRATES
1,700,000

UZBEKISTAN ●
21,900,000

VIETNAM
70,900,000

YEMEN
13,000,000

The Indian Ocean has an
area of 73 million square
km (28 million square
miles). At its deepest point,
the ocean bed lies more
than 7,725 m (25,344 ft)
below the waves.

SEOUL
Modern office blocks crowd together
in Seoul, the capital city of South
Korea, but a few ancient buildings still
survive. The South Gate (left) was
built at the end of the 14th century as
part of a wall that once surrounded
the city. Today, Seoul is spreading far
beyond its original boundaries as
rapid industrial growth creates a need
for more offices, factories, and
homes.

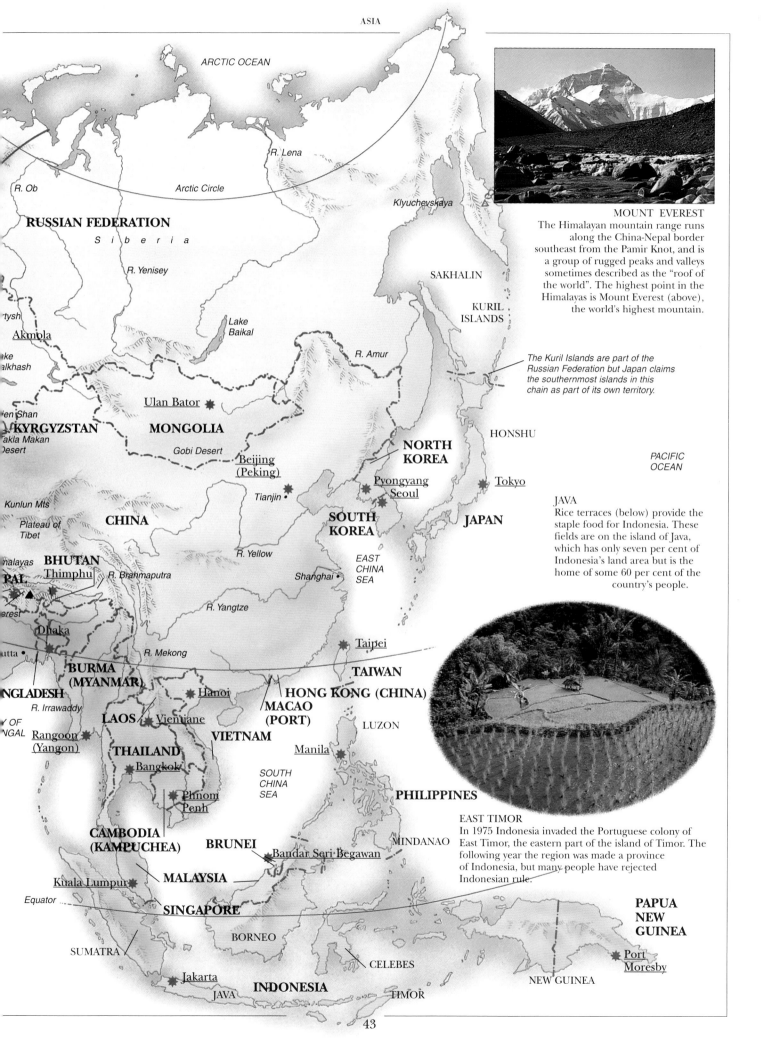

ARCTIC OCEAN

R. Lena

Arctic Circle

R. Ob

tysh

RUSSIAN FEDERATION

S i b e r i a

R. Yenisey

Klyuchevskaya

SAKHALIN

KURIL
ISLANDS

Akmola

ake
alkhash

Lake
Baikal

R. Amur

ien Shan

KYRGYZSTAN

akla Makan
Desert

Gobi Desert

Ulan Bator ✴

MONGOLIA

**NORTH
KOREA**

HONSHU

Beijing
(Peking)

Tianjin •

Pyongyang
Seoul

✴ Tokyo

PACIFIC
OCEAN

Kunlun Mts

CHINA

Plateau of
Tibet

**SOUTH
KOREA**

JAPAN

R. Yellow

EAST
CHINA
SEA

halayas

BHUTAN

Thimphu

R. Brahmaputra

Shanghai •

PAL

erest ▲

R. Yangtze

Dhaka

utta •

R. Mekong

Taipei ✴

**BURMA
(MYANMAR)**

TAIWAN

NGLADESH

R. Irrawaddy

Hanoi ✴

HONG KONG (CHINA)

**MACAO
(PORT)**

LUZON

Y OF
NGAL

Rangoon
(Yangon) ✴

LAOS

Vientiane ✴

VIETNAM

THAILAND

Bangkok

Manila

SOUTH
CHINA
SEA

Phnom
Penh

PHILIPPINES

**CAMBODIA
(KAMPUCHEA)**

BRUNEI

MINDANAO

Bandar Seri Begawan

Kuala Lumpur ✴

MALAYSIA

Equator

SINGAPORE

**PAPUA
NEW
GUINEA**

BORNEO

SUMATRA

CELEBES

Port
Moresby ✴

Jakarta ✴

INDONESIA

NEW GUINEA

JAVA

TIMOR

MOUNT EVEREST
The Himalayan mountain range runs along the China-Nepal border southeast from the Pamir Knot, and is a group of rugged peaks and valleys sometimes described as the "roof of the world". The highest point in the Himalayas is Mount Everest (above), the world's highest mountain.

The Kuril Islands are part of the Russian Federation but Japan claims the southernmost islands in this chain as part of its own territory.

JAVA
Rice terraces (below) provide the staple food for Indonesia. These fields are on the island of Java, which has only seven per cent of Indonesia's land area but is the home of some 60 per cent of the country's people.

EAST TIMOR
In 1975 Indonesia invaded the Portuguese colony of East Timor, the eastern part of the island of Timor. The following year the region was made a province of Indonesia, but many people have rejected Indonesian rule.

ASSYRIANS

ABOUT THREE THOUSAND YEARS ago, a mighty empire rose to power in the Middle East where Iraq is today. This was the Assyrian Empire. It lasted for more than 300 years and spread all over the surrounding area from the River Nile to Mesopotamia. Under King Shalmaneser I (1273-1244 B.C.) the Assyrians conquered Babylon and many other independent states, and eventually united the region into one empire. With an enormous army, armoured horses, fast two-wheeled chariots, and huge battering rams, the Assyrians were highly skilled, successful fighters, ruthless in battle. The Assyrian Empire grew quickly with a series of warlike kings, including Ashurbanipal II and Sennacherib. Great wealth and excellent trading links enabled the Assyrians to rebuild the cities of Nimrud and Nineveh (which became the capital), and to create a new city at Khorsabad. Assyria was a rich, well-organized society, but by the 7th century B.C. the empire had grown too large to protect itself well. In about 612 B.C., the Babylonian and Medes peoples destroyed Nineveh, and the Assyrian Empire collapsed.

WARRIORS
The Assyrians were famed and feared for their strength in battle and for torturing their victims. They developed the chariot and fought with swords, shields, slings, and bows.

Men armed with spears and swords accompanied the king on lion hunts.

ASSYRIAN EMPIRE
In the 7th century B.C. the Assyrian Empire reached its greatest extent. It stretched down to the Persian Gulf in the south and the Mediterranean coast in the west, and included Babylon.

LION HUNT
Hunting and killing lions was a favourite pastime of the Assyrian kings. Lions represented the wild strength of nature. It was considered a noble challenge to seek them out and kill them, although captive lions were also kept to be hunted. Only the king was allowed to kill a lion.

ROYAL LIFE
Stone reliefs tell us much about the lives of the Assyrian royalty. This relief sculpture shows King Ashurbanipal II (668-633 B.C.) drinking wine in his garden with his queen. It looks like a quiet, domestic scene, but on another section of this sculpture there is a head hanging from a tree. It is the head of Teumann, the king of the Elamites, whose defeat the king and queen are celebrating.

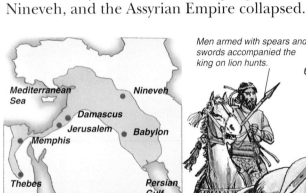

WINGED BULLS
Massive stone sculptures (right) of winged bulls with human heads were placed on each side of important doors and gateways.

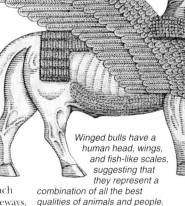

Winged bulls have a human head, wings, and fish-like scales, suggesting that they represent a combination of all the best qualities of animals and people.

Assyrian slaves had to drag the massive sculptures to the palace.

> **Find out more**
> BABYLONIANS
> MIDDLE EAST

ASTRONAUTS

The astronaut wears a special undergarment with tubes that water flows through, keeping the astronaut's body cool.

The different parts of the suit, such as the gloves and helmet, are locked in position.

WORKING IN SPACE
Getting dressed for work outside a spacecraft is a complicated task. An astronaut must put on a spacesuit and, sometimes, a rocket-powered backpack called a manoeuvering unit.

ON 12 APRIL 1961, the world watched in wonder as Russian Yuri Gagarin blasted off from Earth aboard a huge rocket and entered space. He was the first cosmonaut – the Russian word for astronaut – a person trained to work in space. Eight years later Neil Armstrong walked on the moon and became the first human being to step onto another world away from our planet. Since then, a few hundred other astronauts, both men and women, have voyaged into space. Astronauts have jobs to do during their missions. They perform scientific experiments under the weightless conditions of space, venture from the spacecraft to repair damaged satellites, and photograph distant planets and stars. Today astronauts are preparing for the next major landmark in space exploration: to visit other planets in the solar system.

Main tanks provide oxygen for the astronaut to breathe.

There is no air in space to carry sound waves, so astronauts communicate by radio.

Control panel allows the astronaut to adjust the temperature and oxygen flow in the suit.

Urine-collection device worn by the astronaut is like a big nappy.

Layers of different plastics make the suit strong yet flexible.

Battery provides power for spacesuit systems.

The manoeuvering unit enables the astronaut to move around outside the spacecraft. Thrusters in the unit fire jets of nitrogen gas, moving the astronaut in different directions.

Reserve oxygen tanks provide emergency oxygen supply.

SPACESUIT

Space is a perilous place for a human being. There is no air to breathe, and without a spacesuit for protection, an astronaut would explode. This is because the human body is built to function under the constant pressure of the Earth's atmosphere, which is not present in space.

TRAINING
People have to undergo long training programmes to become astronauts. They also must be very fit. These cosmonauts are practising working under weightless conditions using a life-size model of a *Salyut* spacecraft inside a huge water tank.

WEIGHTLESSNESS

We have weight because of the pull of Earth's gravity. In space, gravity holds the astronauts and their spacecraft in orbit around the Earth. But there is no force holding the astronauts to their spaceship, so they float around inside it. This is called weightlessness.

Food and drinks come in special packs that do not spill. There is an oven to heat food.

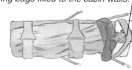

On some spacecraft, astronauts sleep in sleeping bags fixed to the cabin walls.

Special exercise machines help the astronauts keep fit.

LIVING IN SPACE
While on board a spacecraft, astronauts consume the same kind of food and drink as they do on Earth. There is usually no bath or shower; astronauts wash with damp cloths instead. Regular exercise is essential, because living in weightless conditions can weaken bones and muscles.

Find out more
GRAVITY
ROCKETS AND MISSILES
SPACE FLIGHT
U.S.S.R., HISTORY OF

ASTRONOMY

OBSERVATORY
Astronomers study space from observatories (right) that are often at the top of a mountain where there is a clear view of the sky. This photograph took several hours to make. The stars trace circles because the rotation of the Earth makes them appear to move across the sky.

THERE ARE AMAZING sights to be seen in the heavens – other worlds different from our own, great glowing clouds of gas where stars are born and immense explosions in which stars end their lives. Astronomers are scientists who study all the objects in the universe, such as planets, moons, comets, stars, and galaxies. Astronomy is an ancient science. The early Arabs and Greeks looked up to the sky and tried to understand the moons, stars, and planets. However, most of these objects were too distant for early astronomers to see in any detail. It was only after the invention of the telescope in the 17th century that people really began to learn about the universe. Today astronomy makes use of a vast array of equipment to explore space. Astronomers look through ground-based telescopes of many kinds, launch space probes that visit the other planets in the solar system, and send up satellites to study the universe from high above the Earth's surface.

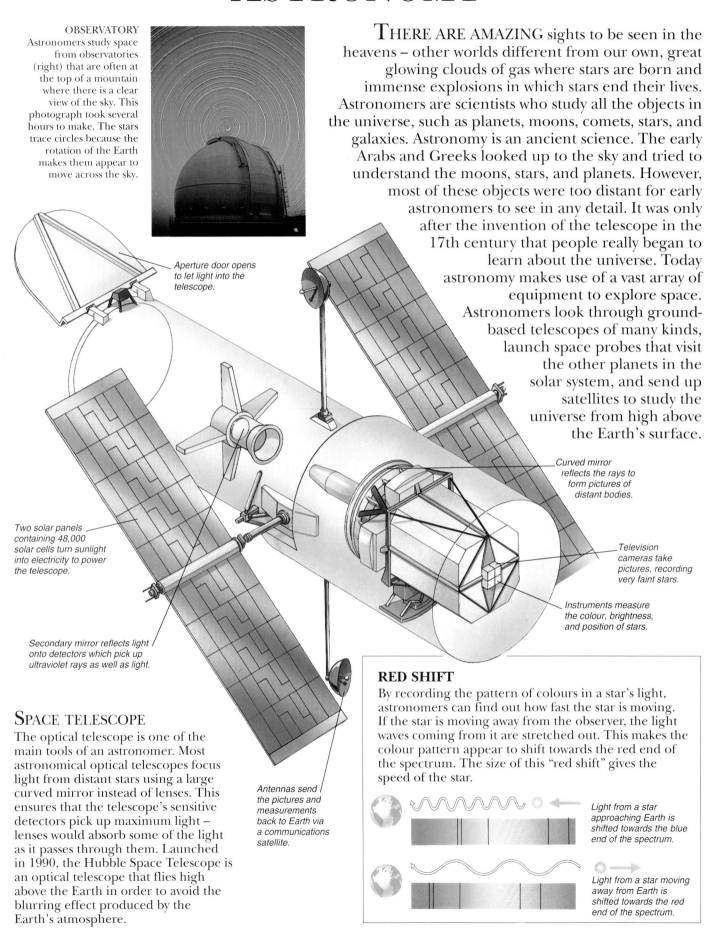

Aperture door opens to let light into the telescope.

Curved mirror reflects the rays to form pictures of distant bodies.

Two solar panels containing 48,000 solar cells turn sunlight into electricity to power the telescope.

Television cameras take pictures, recording very faint stars.

Instruments measure the colour, brightness, and position of stars.

Secondary mirror reflects light onto detectors which pick up ultraviolet rays as well as light.

Antennas send the pictures and measurements back to Earth via a communications satellite.

SPACE TELESCOPE
The optical telescope is one of the main tools of an astronomer. Most astronomical optical telescopes focus light from distant stars using a large curved mirror instead of lenses. This ensures that the telescope's sensitive detectors pick up maximum light – lenses would absorb some of the light as it passes through them. Launched in 1990, the Hubble Space Telescope is an optical telescope that flies high above the Earth in order to avoid the blurring effect produced by the Earth's atmosphere.

RED SHIFT
By recording the pattern of colours in a star's light, astronomers can find out how fast the star is moving. If the star is moving away from the observer, the light waves coming from it are stretched out. This makes the colour pattern appear to shift towards the red end of the spectrum. The size of this "red shift" gives the speed of the star.

Light from a star approaching Earth is shifted towards the blue end of the spectrum.

Light from a star moving away from Earth is shifted towards the red end of the spectrum.

EXPLORING THE UNIVERSE

Stars and other objects in the universe produce streams of tiny particles and many kinds of waves, such as radio waves. Except for light, these waves and particles are all invisible, but astronomers can study them to provide information about the universe. The atmosphere blocks many of the rays, so detectors are mounted on satellites that orbit above the Earth's atmosphere.

INFRA-RED RAYS

Objects in space can also send out infra-red (heat) rays. Satellites and ground-based telescopes pick up these rays. They can reveal the centres of galaxies, and gas clouds called nebulae (right), where stars are forming.

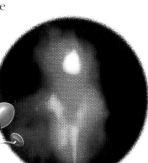

ULTRAVIOLET RAYS

Astronomers can learn about the substances in stars by analysing ultraviolet (short wavelength) rays that come from them. A computer-generated picture produced by detecting ultraviolet rays (left) gives the composition and speed of gases that circle around in the outer atmosphere of a star.

X-RAYS

Special satellites carry detectors that pick up x-rays. These satellites have discovered black holes, which give out x-rays as they suck in gases from nearby stars. This is an x-ray image of a supernova, which is an exploding star.

GAMMA RAYS

Some satellites detect gamma rays, which are waves of very high energy. Gamma rays come from many objects, including pulsars, which are the remains of exploded stars. This is a gamma ray map of our own galaxy.

RADAR SIGNALS

Astronomers produce radar maps of planets and moons by bouncing radio waves off their surfaces. The radar map of Venus (left) was recorded by the United States *Pioneer* space probe. The map is colour-coded to represent plains and mountains on the planet's surface.

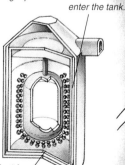

Radio image of a quasar. Quasars are thought to be distant galaxies.

RADIO WAVES

Many bodies produce their own radio waves, which are picked up by the large dishes of radio telescopes. Objects called pulsars, quasars, and radio galaxies were discovered in this way.

VISIBLE LIGHT

Telescopes on the ground and on satellites detect the light rays that come from planets, comets, stars, and galaxies. Earth's atmosphere distorts light rays, making pictures slightly fuzzy. However, new computer-controlled telescopes are able to reduce this distortion.

A supernova as seen through an optical telescope.

NEUTRINOS

Tiny particles called neutrinos come from stars. Most neutrinos pass right through the Earth, but special detectors lying deep underground can detect a few of them. By studying neutrinos, astronomers can find out about the sun and exploding stars.

An array of sensitive light detectors pick up flashes of light produced when neutrinos enter the tank.

Neutrino detectors consist of large tanks of water, in which flashes of light occur as the neutrinos pass through.

HISTORY OF ASTRONOMY

In the third century B.C., the Greek scientist Aristarchus suggested that the Earth and planets move around the sun. The telescope, first used to observe the heavens by Italian scientist Galileo, proved this to be true and led to many other discoveries. In the 1920s, the astronomer Edwin Hubble found that stars exist in huge groups called galaxies and that the universe is expanding in size.

The ancient observatory at Jaipur, India, contains stone structures that astronomers built to measure the positions of the sun, moon, planets, and stars.

Find out more

MOON
PLANETS
SATELLITES
SPACE FLIGHT
STARS
SUN
TELESCOPES
UNIVERSE

ATMOSPHERE

WITHOUT THE ATMOSPHERE, it would be impossible to live on Earth. The atmosphere forms a layer, like a blanket around the Earth, protecting us from dangerous rays from the sun and from the cold of outer space. It contains the air that we breathe, together with water vapour and tiny pieces of dust. Air contains the gases oxygen, carbon dioxide, and nitrogen, which are necessary for life; water vapour forms the clouds that bring rain. The atmosphere is held by the pull of the Earth's gravity and spreads out to about 2,000 km (1,250 miles) above the Earth. Three quarters of the air in the atmosphere lies beneath 10,700 m (35,000 ft) because the air gets thinner higher up. The air at the top of Mount Everest is only one third as thick as it is at sea level. That is why mountain climbers carry an air supply and why high-flying aircraft are sealed and have air pumped into them.

There is no definite upper limit to the atmosphere. The final layer before outer space is called the exosphere; it contains hardly any air at all.

A layer of very thin air called the thermosphere extends from about 80 to 480 km (50 to 300 miles) above the ground. It contains the ionosphere – layers of electrically charged particles, from which radio waves can be bounced around the world.

The mesosphere extends from 50 to 80 km (30 to 50 miles) above the Earth. If meteors fall into this layer, they burn up, causing shooting stars.

Above the troposphere lies the stratosphere. It extends from 11 to 50 km (7 to 30 miles) up. The stratosphere is a calm region. Airliners fly here to avoid the winds and weather lower down.

Although it is the narrowest layer, the troposphere contains most of the gas in the atmosphere. It reaches about 11 km (7 miles) above the ground, but this varies around the globe and from season to season. Most weather occurs in the troposphere.

LAYERS OF THE ATMOSPHERE

The Earth's atmosphere is divided into several layers. The main layers, from the bottom upwards, are called the troposphere, the stratosphere, the mesosphere, the thermosphere, and the exosphere.

OZONE LAYER

Within the stratosphere, there is a thin layer of the gas ozone. Ozone is a form of oxygen that absorbs ultraviolet rays from the sun. Without the ozone layer, these rays would reach the ground and kill all living creatures. Pollution and the use of certain chemicals are destroying the ozone layer.

Compared to the size of the Earth, the atmosphere forms a very narrow band – approximately equivalent to the skin around an orange.

SKY AND SUNSET

When rays of light travel through the atmosphere, they hit pollen, dust, and other tiny particles. This causes the rays to scatter, or bounce off in all directions. Some colours of light are scattered more than others.

BLUE SKY
The atmosphere scatters mainly blue light; this is why the sky looks blue. The other colours of light are scattered much less than blue so that they come to Earth directly. This causes the area of sky around the sun to look yellow.

SUNSET AND SUNRISE
At sunset and sunrise, when the sun is below the horizon, the light travels through much more of the atmosphere before we see it. The blue light is scattered so much that it is absorbed, or soaked up, by the atmosphere. Only red light reaches us, so the sky looks red.

OTHER ATMOSPHERES

Other planets' atmospheres are very different from Earth's. On Neptune (above), the atmosphere is mainly methane gas. Jupiter and Saturn have thick, cloudy atmospheres of hydrogen. None of these planets can support life.

___*Find out more*___
AIR
CLIMATES
OXYGEN
PLANETS
WEATHER

ATOMS AND MOLECULES

LOOK AROUND YOU. THERE ARE countless millions of different substances, from metals and plastics to people and plants. All of these are made from about 100 different kinds of "building blocks" joined together in different ways. These building blocks are tiny particles called atoms. Atoms are so small that even the tiniest speck of dust contains more than one million million atoms. Some substances, such as iron, are made of just one kind of atom; other substances, such as water, contain molecules – atoms joined together in groups. Such molecules may be very simple or very complex. Each water molecule contains two hydrogen atoms and one oxygen atom; plastics are made of molecules which often contain millions of atoms. An atom itself is made up of a dense centre called a nucleus. Particles that carry electricity, called electrons, move around the nucleus. Scientists have discovered how to split the nucleus, releasing enormous energy which is used in nuclear power stations and nuclear bombs.

A drop of water contains about 3,000 million million million molecules.

A molecule of water contains three atoms – two hydrogen atoms and one oxygen atom.

Protons and neutrons are made up of quarks.

Electrons whiz around the nucleus. An atom of oxygen has eight electrons.

There is a lot of empty space in an atom. If the nucleus were the size of a tennis ball, the nearest electron would be 1 km (about half a mile) away.

The nucleus of an oxygen atom has eight protons and eight neutrons. The nucleus is held together by powerful forces.

PROTONS AND NEUTRONS

The nucleus of an atom contains particles called protons and neutrons. These contain even smaller particles called quarks. Protons carry electricity. However, they carry a different kind of electricity from electrons. They have a "positive charge", whereas electrons have a "negative charge". Neutrons have no electric charge.

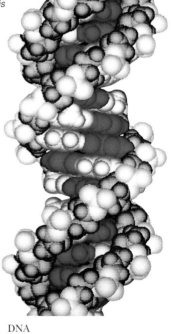

DNA
All plants and animals contain molecules of DNA (deoxyribonucleic acid). DNA carries the blueprint for life: coded information in DNA molecules determines the characteristics of each living thing and its offspring. A DNA molecule consists of millions of atoms arranged in a twisted spiral shape.

DISCOVERING THE ATOM

About 2,400 years ago, the Greek philosopher Democritus believed that everything was made up of tiny particles. It was not until 1808 that English scientist John Dalton proved that atoms exist. Around 1909, New Zealand scientist Ernest Rutherford (above) discovered the nucleus.

IMMORTAL ATOMS

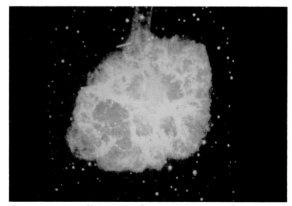

Atoms never disappear but are constantly journeying through the universe as part of different substances. But all atoms originated with the formation of the universe around 15,000 million years ago. In the same way, atoms from an exploding star such as the crab nebula (above) may drift through space and eventually form part of animals and plants on Earth.

Find out more
CHEMISTRY
OXYGEN
PHYSICS
PLASTICS
REPRODUCTION

AUSTRALIA

THE COUNTRY OF AUSTRALIA is remote and vast. The nation's distance from its neighbours has forced the Australian people to be self-reliant. And their huge country has provided Australians with the natural resources they needed to live independently. Australians have a healthy, outdoor lifestyle and enjoy a high standard of living. Most of the country's 17.8 million people live in the fertile strip of land on the east and southeast coast. Many of them live in Melbourne and Sydney, Australia's two largest cities, and in the nation's capital, Canberra, all of which lie in this strip. The region also contains four of Australia's six states and two territories. Inland lies the outback – the flat, hot, barren interior of the continent. Today few people live in the outback, though the original inhabitants of Australia, the aborigines, learned to survive the harsh conditions there. Some of Australia's 228,000 aborigines still live a traditional life in the outback. However, many have now moved to cities. Most other Australians are descendants of settlers from Britain and other European nations, and from Southeast Asia.

Australia lies southeast of Asia, with the Pacific Ocean to the east and the Indian Ocean to the west. It is the only country that is also a continent. Together with several nearby islands, Australia covers a total area of 7.68 million sq km (2.96 million square miles).

SURFING
Surfing is a favourite Australian sport. Surfing carnivals are held regularly in many towns. Polynesian people invented the sport hundreds of years ago; recently it has expanded to include windsurfing, trick surfing, and long-distance surfing. Because of the warm sunny climate many Australians spend hours on the beach at the weekend.

At a surfing carnival lifeguards give demonstrations of lifesaving, and there are surfing competitions.

During the celebrations of Australia's 200th anniversary, ocean-going sailing ships gathered in Sydney's famous harbour.

SYDNEY
The city of Sydney is the oldest and largest city in Australia. Sydney was founded in 1788 as a British prison colony with about 1,500 prisoners and their guards; today it is home to more than 3.6 million people. The city stands around Port Jackson, a huge natural bay spanned by Sydney Harbour Bridge. Sydney is a busy industrial centre and tourist resort.

Australia's currency is the Australian dollar. On one side the coins feature a portrait of the queen of England, who is the head of state.

FILMMAKING
The Australian film industry produces a number of important films each year. Some, such as *Picnic at Hanging Rock* (1975), which tells of the mysterious disappearance of a group of Australian schoolgirls, have received international acclaim.

TASMANIA

The island of Tasmania lies off the southeast coast of Australia and is a state in itself with a population of nearly half a million. The island has a cooler, damper climate than the rest of the country and is famous for its fruit, vegetables, and sheep. Tin, silver, and other products are mined. Much of western Tasmania is unpopulated and covered in dense forest where native wildlife, such as the Tasmanian devil, below, survives in large numbers.

GREAT DIVIDING RANGE

Running along the eastern coast of the continent from Cape York to Ballarat is a 3,700 km (2,300 mile) mountain chain called the Great Dividing Range. The tallest mountain is Kosciusko, at 2,228 m (7,310 ft). Other peaks are much lower. The mountains divide the fertile coastal plains from the dry interior. The steep hills were once a major barrier to travel; even today only a few roads and railways cross from east to west.

The Three Sisters mountains in New South Wales form part of the Great Dividing Range.

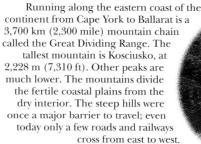

OUTBACK

Very few people live in Australia's interior, called the outback. The dry land is good only for raising sheep or cattle. Some ranches, called stations, cover hundreds of square kilometres. Because of the great distances, outback Australians live isolated lives and communicate by radio.

Ancient rock and bark paintings show that aboriginal culture flourished nearly 40,000 years before European settlers arrived.

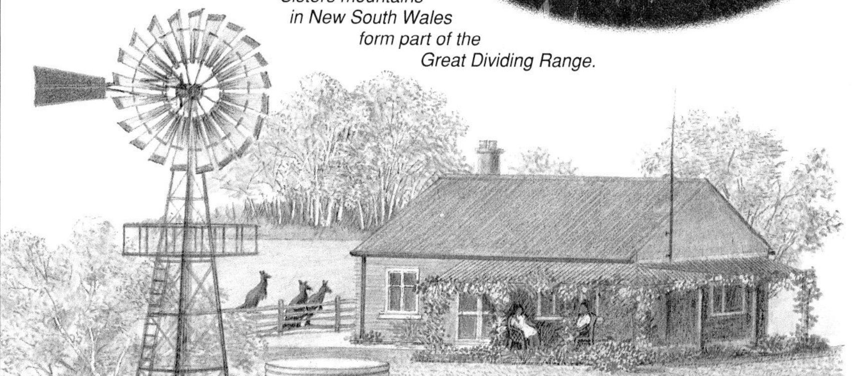

Outback ranchers ride motorbikes or horses to round up cattle and sheep.

AYERS ROCK

One of the most impressive natural sights in Australia is Ayers Rock. This huge mass of sandstone stands in the middle of a wide, flat desert and reaches a height of 335 m (1,142 ft). Although it lies hundreds of kilometres from the nearest town, Ayers Rock is a major tourist attraction with its own hotel. The rock is particularly beautiful at sunset, when it seems to change colour.

STRIP MINING

The country has huge mineral wealth, and mining is an important industry. Australia produces one third of the world's uranium, which is essential for nuclear power. In recent years iron ore has been excavated in large strip mines where giant digging machines remove entire hills.

Find out more

ABORIGINAL AUSTRALIANS
AUSTRALIA, HISTORY OF
AUSTRALIAN WILDLIFE

AUSTRALIA

| Ancient monument | Volcano | ▲ Highest mountain | ✳ Capital city | • City/town |

STATISTICS

Area: 7,686,848 sq km (2,967,207 sq miles)
Population: 17,800,000
Capital: Canberra
Language: English
Religions: Protestant, Roman Catholic
Currency: Australian dollar
Highest point: Mount Kosciusko 2,228 m (7,310 ft)
Longest river: Murray-Darling 3,717 km (2,310 miles)
Main occupation: Wholesale and retail trading
Main exports: Wool, metal ores, coal, non-ferrous metals
Main imports: Vehicles, manufactured goods

MELBOURNE
The capital city of Victoria and the second largest city in Australia, Melbourne (above) displays a dramatic mixture of old and new. Melbourne was founded in 1835 by an Australian farmer, John Batman. Nearly 20 years later, gold was discovered in Victoria and Melbourne's population climbed sharply. Today, Melbourne is a leading seaport, and the commercial and industrial centre of Victoria.

INDIAN OCEAN

```
0                    300 miles
|--------------------|
0                    500 km
```

•Port Hedland

•Dampier

Hamersley Range

R. Ashburton

R. Gascoyne

WESTERN AUSTRALIA

R. Murchison

Lake Barlee

• Geraldton

Kalgoorl

Fremantle • •Perth

Darling Range

Bunbury •

Cape Leeuwin

•Albany

PERTH
Founded in 1829, Perth (above) is the state capital of Western Australia and its financial and commercial heart. Most Australian people live in cities, and the population of Perth reflects the European ancestry of a large percentage of today's Australians.

DRY LAKES
Many of Australia's vast desert "lakes" contain no water. Lake Eyre, for example, fills with water rarely and was completely dry for a century until 1950.

BRISBANE

The state capital of Queensland and its largest city, Brisbane (left) is a bustling seaport lying above the mouth of the River Brisbane at Moreton Bay. In this way, it is similar to Australia's other state capitals, all of which were founded near rivers close to ocean harbours. Like other state capitals, Brisbane too is the commercial centre of its state, with its main business district situated near the waterfront.

MELVILLE I.

Darwin

Arnhem Land

R. Daly

GROOTE EYLANDT

GULF OF CARPENTARIA

Cape York

CORAL SEA

Kimberley Plateau

R. Ord

R. Victoria

R. Roper

MORNINGTON I.

R. Mitchell

R. Gilbert

PACIFIC OCEAN

Great Barrier Reef, the world's largest coral reef. It is 2,028 km (1,260 miles) long.

NORTHERN TERRITORY

R. Flinders

Townsville

Great Sandy Desert

Great Dividing Range

Macdonnell Ranges

R. Fitzroy

QUEENSLAND

Tropic of Capricorn

Gibson Desert

Alice Springs

Great Artesian Basin

Great Dividing Range

R. Dawson

Ayers Rock ▲

Simpson Desert

Great Victoria Desert

Musgrave Ranges

SOUTH AUSTRALIA

Lake Eyre

Brisbane •

Gold Coast

Grafton •

Lake Torrens

R. Darling

NEW SOUTH WALES

Nullarbor Plain

Lake Gairdner

Flinders Ranges

Maitland •
Newcastle •

R. Lachlan

GREAT AUSTRALIAN BIGHT

Iron Knob •

• Port Pirie

• Sydney
• Wollongong

NULLARBOR PLAIN
The Nullarbor Plain was given its name because it is completely treeless: in the Latin language, *null* means nothing, and *arbor*, tree.

Spencer Gulf

• Adelaide

R. Murray

R. Murrumbidgee

Canberra

KANGAROO I.

VICTORIA

Mount Kosciusko 2,228 m (7,310 ft) ▲

Australian Alps

AUSTRALIAN CAPITAL TERRITORY

• Bendigo

Ballarat •

• Melbourne

Geelong •

KING I.

FLINDERS I.

DESERT
Few people live in Australia's huge interior, which is covered mainly by desert. The four largest deserts are the Simpson, Gibson, Great Sandy, and Great Victoria deserts. Most are vast areas of swirling sand that drifts into giant sand dunes.

TASMANIA

• Hobart

HISTORY OF
AUSTRALIA

As RECENTLY AS 1600, the only people that knew about Australia were the aboriginal peoples who had lived there for more than 40,000 years. The rest of the world had no idea that the continent existed. In 1606, the Dutch explorer William Jansz landed in northern Australia. Although he did not know it, he was the first European to see the country. Further exploration of the coastline by Dutch and British explorers revealed that Australia was an island. In 1770 the British captain James Cook claimed the east coast of Australia for Britain and named it New South Wales. The British sent convicts to their new colony, forming the basis of Sydney, today the country's largest city. Throughout the 19th century, the population of Australia grew as more convicts arrived, followed by immigrants. For many of them life was tough, but the British colony grew richer when gold was discovered in 1851. Farming also became established. In 1901, Australia became an independent commonwealth, although it remained close to Britain for many years and Australian troops fought in both world wars on the side of Britain. More recently, Australia has branched away from Britain and set up links with other countries.

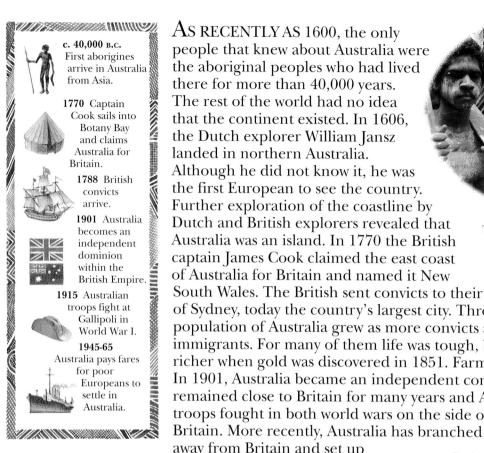

ABORIGINES
The first aboriginal peoples probably arrived in Australia from the islands of Southeast Asia about 40,000 years ago. In 1770, there were about 300,000 aborigines in Australia.

Convict ships in the bay

Chopping wood to make timber huts

The convicts carried supplies onto the shore.

At first, the convicts (prisoners) were miserable and hungry.

The first British settlement in Australia was at Port Jackson in Sydney Harbour, next to the location of the present-day Sydney Opera House.

BOTANY BAY
In 1770, the English explorer James Cook dropped anchor in Botany Bay, south of what is now the city of Sydney. In 1788, the first 750 British settlers arrived in Australia. These people were convicts – guarded by 250 soldiers – who had been transported abroad to relieve the overcrowded British prisons. They lived in a prison camp set up on the shores of Sydney Harbour. The colonists came close to starvation, but gradually their lives improved. The tents they lived in were replaced by brick and timber huts, and eventually the colony began to prosper. In 1868, the transportation of convicts ended, leaving more than 160,000 convicts living in Australia.

EXPLORATION

The first explorers of Australia mapped out the coastline but left the interior largely untouched. In 1606 the Dutch navigator William Jansz briefly visited northeastern Australia. Between 1829 and 1830, the English explorer Charles Sturt explored the rivers in the south but failed to find the inland sea that many people assumed existed in the centre of Australia. In 1840, Edward Eyre, from England, discovered the vast, dry salt lakes in South Australia before walking along its southern coast. In 1860 and 1861, the Irishman Robert O'Hara Burke and Englishman William Wills became the first people to cross Australia from south to north. It was not until the 1930s that Australia was completely surveyed.

- Burke and Wills
- Sturt
- Eyre
- Cook
- Jansz

Alice Springs
Perth
Brisbane
Sydney
Adelaide
Melbourne

Map showing the routes of the different explorers of Australia

BURKE AND WILLS
In 1860 and 1861, Burke and Wills succeeded in crossing Australia from south to north. However, both of them died of starvation on the return journey south.

GOLD RUSH
In 1851, gold was discovered in New South Wales and Victoria. Thousands of prospectors rushed from all over the world, including China, to make their fortunes in Australia. The national population rose from 400,000 in 1850 to 1,100,000 by 1860. Conditions were tough for the gold miners, and in 1854 a group of miners at Eureka Stockade at Ballarat, near Melbourne, refused to pay the licence fee required to mine for gold. The government sent in troops; 24 miners and six soldiers were killed in the battle that followed.

OVERCOMING ABORIGINES
During the 19th century, the European settlers disrupted the aboriginal way of life. Many aboriginal languages and customs died out as their land was taken. Children were taken away from their parents to be educated in the European way. As a result, the total aborigine population fell from 300,000 in 1770 to about 60,000 by 1900.

The aborigines were amazed to see the crowds of white people landing in their territory.

IMMIGRATION
In 1880, there were only two million people on the vast Australian continent. A century later, almost 15 million people lived there. Most had come to Australia from Britain, Italy, and Greece. In a deliberate attempt to boost the population after 1945, the Australian government offered to pay part of the passage for poor Europeans. About two million people took advantage of the scheme, which ended in 1965, with one million coming from Britain alone. Asians and other non-white peoples were denied entry until the 1960s. Many children travelled on their own. The group of immigrants (left) are on their way to a farm school in Western Australia from Waterloo Station, London, England.

URANIUM MINING
Australia is rich in minerals such as uranium, the raw material used to fuel nuclear power stations and produce nuclear bombs. Although uranium mining increased dramatically during the 1970s, many Australians opposed it because of the dangers of radiation from uranium. In addition, many of the uranium deposits lie within aboriginal tribal lands. Protests have therefore regularly occurred to prevent the exploitation of this dangerous mineral.

Find out more

ABORIGINAL AUSTRALIANS
AUSTRALIA
COOK, JAMES
NUCLEAR AGE

AUSTRALIAN WILDLIFE

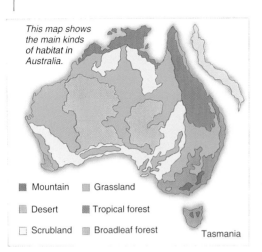

This map shows the main kinds of habitat in Australia.

■ Mountain ■ Grassland
■ Desert ■ Tropical forest
□ Scrubland ■ Broadleaf forest

Tasmania

OF ALL THE CONTINENTS, Australia has the most unusual assortment of animals and plants. Almost half of the world's 266 kinds of marsupials (pouched mammals) are found only in Australia. Marsupials include kangaroos, koalas, possums, gliders, and bandicoots. The platypus and echidna – the only mammals that lay eggs – also live in Australia. The Australian landscape is very varied. In the northeast are steamy tropical rain forests and swamps which are home to crocodiles and wading birds. In the central part of Australia there are vast hot deserts made up of sand and rocks. Australia has more desert than any other continent, and there is sometimes no rainfall in these areas for several years. In the south, where the climate is milder, eucalyptus trees grow on rolling grasslands and shrubby bushland.

FUNNEL-WEB SPIDER
The large, hairy funnel-web spider is so-named because it builds a funnel-shaped web to catch its prey. These spiders are feared by humans because their bite is extremely poisonous.

EUCALYPTUS
There are about 500 different kinds of eucalyptus trees in the world. Almost all of them came originally from Australia. The koala depends mainly on the leaves of the eucalyptus trees for food.

KOALA
The koala is found only in the eucalyptus forests of Australia. It spends most of its life in the trees, feeding at night and sleeping for up to 18 hours each day.

Kangaroos are herbivores (plant eaters); they feed mostly on grasses and leaves.

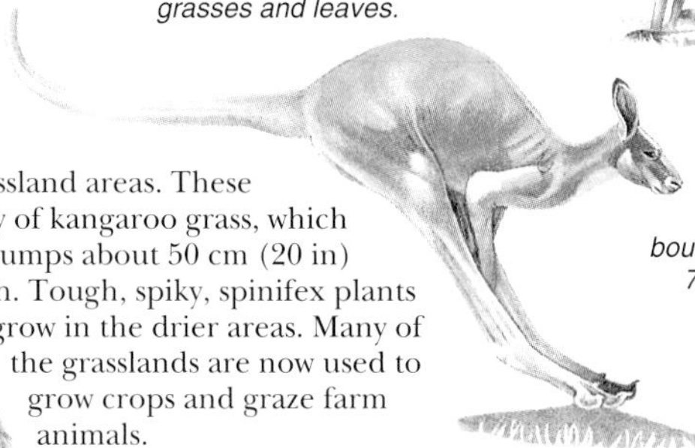

GRASSLAND
Kangaroos live in grassland areas. These areas consist mainly of kangaroo grass, which grows in clumps about 50 cm (20 in) high. Tough, spiky, spinifex plants grow in the drier areas. Many of the grasslands are now used to grow crops and graze farm animals.

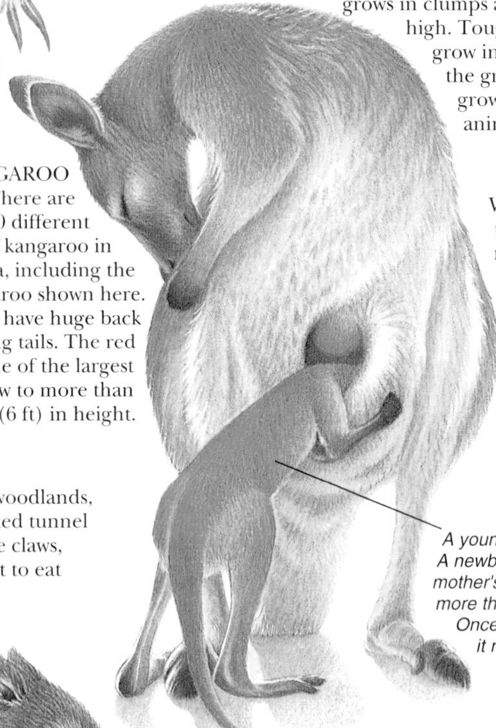

Strong back legs are well adapted for jumping. A kangaroo can bound along at about 70 km/h (40 mph).

KANGAROO
There are about 50 different kinds of kangaroo in Australia, including the red kangaroo shown here. Kangaroos have huge back legs and strong tails. The red kangaroo is one of the largest – a male can grow to more than 2 m (6 ft) in height.

RED-NECKED WALLABY
Wallabies are smaller members of the kangaroo family. The red-necked wallaby shown here is nicknamed the brusher because it prefers brush and scrubland areas rather than open countryside. It is also called the red wallaby, Eastern brush wallaby, and Bennett's wallaby.

WOMBAT
Wombats live in grassland areas, dry woodlands, and shrublands. They dig a complicated tunnel system with their strong legs and large claws, and come out of their burrow at night to eat plants such as spear grass.

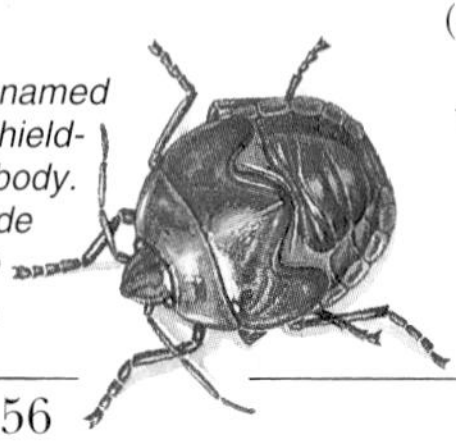

A young kangaroo is called a joey. A newborn joey crawls into its mother's pouch, where it stays for more than 30 weeks, suckling milk. Once the joey has left its mother, it returns only to feed.

WEDGE-TAILED EAGLE
With a wingspan of 2.5 m (8 ft), the wedge-tailed eagle is one of the world's largest eagles. It soars over bush and desert areas of Australia searching for rabbits and similar prey.

Shield bugs are so-named because they have a shield-shaped plate on the body. They feed on the sap inside plants and are also known as sap suckers.

RAIN FOREST
Tropical rain forests grow along a strip of Australia's northeast and north coast, together with luxurious palms, bunya-bunya pines, tree ferns, and colourful orchids. There are many other forests, including subtropical rain forests of kauri pine and scrub box near the mid-eastern coast of Australia, and cooler temperate rain forests of Antarctic beech in parts of the southeast and on the island of Tasmania.

BOWERBIRD
In the warmer forests, male bowerbirds build small structures called bowers to attract a female. They use twigs, leaves, stems, and petals to make the bower. Each kind of bowerbird makes its own kind of bower, sometimes using bottle caps and other shiny pieces of rubbish.

Satin bowerbird

ORCHID
More than 600 kinds of orchids grow in Australia. Some orchids grow high in the forks of tree branches and are also called air plants because they obtain all their nourishment from the air and do not need soil in order to grow.

The desert scorpion catches its food of insects and worms with its pincers, using its sting-tipped tail mainly in defence.

LORIKEET
There are seven different kinds of lorikeet in Australia; the one shown here is the rainbow lorikeet. Lorikeets are colourful, noisy relatives of parrots, and gather together in large flocks. They have brushlike tongues for sipping nectar from orchids and other flowers.

STRANGLER FIG
Many tangled vines grow among the rain forest branches. The strangler fig twines around a tree trunk for support as it grows. Its thick stems may choke the tree to death.

DESERT
Australia has many poisonous animals, including snakes, spiders, and scorpions. Many poisonous animals live in the vast deserts in the centre of the country. Dry scrubland and desert cover more than half of Australia. One of the most common trees is the mulga, a shrublike acacia that provides some food and shelter in the burning heat.

POSSUM
Possums, gliders, and ringtails are active at night. They live in wooded areas and eat mainly food from plants, particularly nectar from the large, massed flowers of the evergreen banksia shrubs.

The honey possum's brushlike tongue laps up nectar from the banksia flower. The possum helps the banksia reproduce by carrying its pollen to the next plant.

NATIONAL PARKS
Australia has more than 2,000 national parks and wildlife reserves, which cover 80 million hectares (197 million acres). These parks include Seal Rock in New South Wales and Lamington National Park, shown here.

Australia is home to many kinds of snakes, including the Eastern brown snake.

DESERT PEA
The Sturt's desert pea is named after the British explorer Charles Sturt (1795-1869). It grows in sandy deserts and blooms only after rainfall. Its seeds may lie in the soil for many years, waiting until the next rainstorm before they can develop.

Barking spiders make a noise by rubbing their mouthparts together. They catch frogs, insects, and small reptiles.

DINGO
Australia's wild dog – the dingo – probably first came to Australia about 40,000 years ago with the aboriginal settlers. Dingoes eat a variety of food, including rabbits, birds, reptiles, and wallabies. They also kill sheep, which makes them unpopular with farmers.

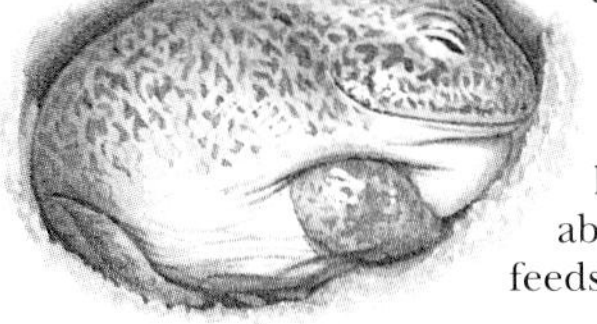

WATER-HOLDING FROG
During the dry season this Australian frog burrows about 50 cm (20 in) below the surface of the soil and forms a bubble-like layer of skin around its body. Only its nostrils are uncovered. After it rains the frog wakes, rubs off the cocoon, and digs its way out. It lays its eggs in the puddles, absorbs water through its skin, feeds, then burrows again.

Find out more
AUSTRALIA
AUSTRALIA, HISTORY OF
FOREST WILDLIFE
MAMMALS
SPIDERS AND SCORPIONS

AZTECS

MORE THAN SEVEN HUNDRED YEARS AGO a civilization was born in what is now Mexico. The Aztecs, founders of this civilization, were the last native American rulers of Mexico. They were a wandering tribe who arrived in the Mexican valley during the 13th century. The Toltec and Olmec Indians had already established civilizations in this area, and influenced the Aztecs. Over the next 200 years the Aztecs set up a mighty empire of some 12 million people. The Aztecs believed that the world would come to an end unless they sacrificed people to their sun god, Huitzilopochtli. They built pyramids and temples where they sacrificed prisoners from the cities they had conquered. In 1519 Spanish conquistadors (adventurers) arrived in Mexico and defeated the Aztecs. Montezuma II, last of the Aztec emperors, was captured and killed by his own people, and the Aztec empire collapsed.

Victim being sacrificed on top of the temple.

Preaching priest

Aztec pyramid with temple at top

The bodies of sacrificed victims were thrown to the ground.

Causeway

Temple precinct at Tenochtitlán

TENOCHTITLÁN

The Aztec capital, called Tenochtitlán, was a "floating city", built in Lake Texcoco, on one natural and many artificial islands. To reach the mainland, the Aztecs built causeways (raised roads) and canals between the islands. Today Mexico City stands on the site.

AZTEC ARTISTS
The Aztecs made beautiful jewellery using gold, turquoise, pearls, shells, and feathers. They also used other valuable stones, such as obsidian and jade.

Ceremonial jade mask

HUMAN SACRIFICES
Aztec priests used knives with stone blades to kill up to 1,000 people each week, offering the hearts to their sun god, Huitzilopochtli.

TRIBUTES
The Aztecs became very rich by collecting tributes (payments) from conquered tribes. Cloth, maize (a type of corn), pottery, and luxury goods were brought to Tenochtitlán from the conquered cities by porters, and exchanged in four huge markets. Officials made lists of all the tributes in picture writing. The Aztecs declared war on any tribe that refused to pay tribute.

Find out more

CONQUISTADORS
SOUTH AMERICA,
history of

BABYLONIANS

ONE OF THE FIRST CIVILIZATIONS developed about 6,000 years ago in the Middle East, between the Tigris and Euphrates rivers. This region was known as Mesopotamia, meaning "land between rivers". The land was fertile, and farming methods were highly refined. The people were among the first to develop a system of writing, use the wheel, and build cities. One of these cities was Babylon, founded in about 2000 B.C. It became the capital city of Babylonia (now part of Iraq). Babylon was an important trading centre. It was also a religious centre and the site of many splendid temples. Its people were strong and prosperous under the great king Hammurabi, who united the different areas into one empire. Babylon became even more magnificent later, under King Nebuchadnezzar II. In 538 B.C., the Persian king Cyrus the Great conquered Babylon; Alexander the Great conquered it again in 331 B.C. When the Romans eventually captured Babylon, the capital city lost its importance, fell into ruins, and became part of the Roman Empire.

CYLINDER SEAL
The Babylonians wrote using cylinder seals. These seals were often made of semiprecious stone and were very delicately carved. To sign or stamp a document, a person rolled a cylinder seal over damp clay. This seal shows clearly the god Shamash, the goddess Ishtar (with wings), and the god, Ea.

Ziggurat

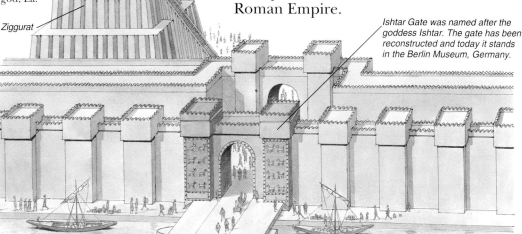

Ishtar Gate was named after the goddess Ishtar. The gate has been reconstructed and today it stands in the Berlin Museum, Germany.

BABYLONIAN EMPIRE
Babylon was one of several important cities in Mesopotamia. For about 2,000 years, its fortunes rose and fell. At its height, under King Hammurabi, and later King Nebuchadnezzar II, the Babylonian empire controlled the entire southern area of Mesopotamia.

BABYLON
The city of Babylon was rebuilt many times before its final destruction. It reached the height of its glory in about 600 B.C. It was an impressive city, with massive walls and elaborate religious buildings, including a pyramid-like ziggurat. Babylon also had a fabulous Hanging Garden – one of the Seven Wonders of the Ancient World.

RUINS OF BABYLON
About 90 km (55 miles) south of Baghdad, Iraq, lie the ruins of ancient Babylon. Although the ruins are sparse, it is still possible to see where the palaces and ziggurat once stood. During the 19th century, archeologists excavated the site. Today, various parts of the ancient city wall have been rebuilt, as shown above.

HAMMURABI
Under King Hammurabi (1792-1750 B.C.), Babylon gained control of a large part of Mesopotamia. Hammurabi is famous for the laws he introduced, which are carved on a stela, or pillar, of stone. The stone shows a portrait of Hammurabi standing before Shamash, the god of justice. Beneath this are the laws of Babylon, carved in cuneiform (wedge-shaped) writing. They deal with all aspects of life and show that Babylon was a sophisticated civilization.

NEBUCHADNEZZAR
Nebuchadnezzar II (605-562 B.C.) was one of the most famous kings of Babylonia. Among other conquests, he captured Jerusalem and forced thousands of its people to live there in captivity. This story is told in the Bible, in the Book of Daniel. Nebuchadnezzar is said to have gone mad at the end of his reign, as shown in this picture of Nebuchadnezzar by the English artist William Blake (1757-1827).

Find out more
ALPHABETS
ASSYRIANS
PHOENICIANS
WONDERS OF THE
ancient world

BADGERS AND SKUNKS

Muscular body

Tough, wiry fur

Small ears

Small eyes and poor eyesight

Short, thick legs

Keen sense of smell

Long, strong claws

SETTS

Badgers live in family groups in a system of tunnels called a sett, which they often build on a bank, or among tree roots. Over the years the badgers extend the sett. A large sett may be 100 years old and have more than 20 entrances; it may house up to 15 badgers. The badgers regularly bring fresh bedding of grass, leaves, and moss to their rest chambers, dragging out the old lining and leaving it near the entrance.

DAWN AND DUSK are the favourite hunting times for badgers and skunks, which prowl at night in search of food. Badgers and skunks are members of the weasel family, found in Europe, North America, Asia, and Africa. Badgers are heavy, sturdy animals, with broad, muscular bodies. They use their strong claws for digging under-ground homes called setts, where they rest by day. Their thick fur is black, white, and brown. Like badgers, skunks have black and white markings, but their tails are large and bushy. Skunks live in open woodland areas of North and South America. There are three kinds – striped, spotted, and hog-nosed. Striped and hog-nosed skunks live in underground burrows; the spotted skunk lives in trees. Badgers and skunks have an effective way of fending off enemies. They have scent glands on their bodies which produce a very unpleasant-smelling spray when the animal is threatened.

HONEY BADGER

The African ratel feeds on honey and is also called the honey badger. The badger relies on a bird called the honey guide bird to lead it to bee and wasp nests, which the badger then breaks into with its strong claws. The thick fur and loose skin of the honey badger seem to shrug off any stings from the bees and wasps.

Badgers are easily recognized by the vivid black and white markings or "badges" on their faces.

Boar (male badger)

Sow (female badger) with cubs (young)

Chinese ferret badger

American badger

SKUNK

The striking black and white pattern on the striped or common skunk warns other animals to keep away. The skunk is famous for spraying enemies with a stinking substance from glands near its anus. If the spray touches the eyes of another animal, it can cause temporary blindness. There are 13 different kinds of skunks. They eat small animals, insects, birds' eggs, and fruits.

Skunk stamps its front feet to warn others it is about to spray.

BADGER CUBS

Two or three cubs are born in late winter or early spring. They play outside the sett entrances during the summer months.

STRIPES

Many badgers and skunks have stripes on their faces or along the sides of their bodies. These stripes provide camouflage by helping to break up the animal's outline in twilight. No two faces are exactly the same, so the stripes may also enable the animals to recognize one another.

Find out more

ANIMALS
MAMMALS
NESTS AND BURROWS

BALL GAMES

IN MANY SPORTS AND GAMES, players kick, bowl, or throw a ball around a playing area. They sometimes use bats, rackets, cues, and clubs – as well as their hands, feet, and heads – to roll or drive the ball. The balls vary in shape and size. Most are round, either solid and hard as in billiards and baseball, or hollow as in tennis. Football players use a round ball made of pigskin. In badminton the "ball", called a shuttlecock or bird, has feathers.

Ball games began in prehistoric times. At first they were part of religious ceremonies. People believed ball games would prolong the summer or direct the winds. The Ancient Greeks were among the first to play a ball game for pleasure. Ball games were a vital part of life for the Mayas and Aztecs of Central America. Today, popular ball games range from racket sports such as tennis and squash, to team games such as soccer and baseball.

JAI ALAI
Jai alai, a Spanish game, is also called pelota. Players use a curved scoop called a cesta to hurl a ball (the pelota) at the front wall of the court.

Pool balls are numbered from 1 to 15.

The leather cover of an English football protects an inflated rubber inner lining.

Three fingerholes enable players to grip a bowling ball.

In Ping Pong the "racket" is a solid paddle.

TEAM GAMES

Most of the world's major team sports are ball games, including baseball, basketball, and football. Team games move very fast. Team members need individual skills, such as the ability to run fast, but team skills such as passing the ball are equally important. Team games encourage friendship, discipline, and the ability to work with others.

RACKET GAMES
In racket games such as squash, players use a racket to propel the ball over a net or against a wall. The racket is usually a mesh of strings stretched on a frame. Players compete individually (singles) or in pairs (doubles). Some racket sports do not need a racket: handball players use a glove or the hand as their racket.

GOLF
Golf players use clubs to aim the small ball at a hole in the ground. Other ball games require careful aim too. In bowling, the object is to knock down ten or five pins with one ball. Bowls players aim their balls close to a target ball, or jack. In pool and billiards, players aim balls at pockets around a table.

TENNIS
Tennis evolved from a curious game called real, or royal, tennis, which is still played today in a few countries. Real tennis began in France nearly a thousand years ago; its court has open windows, doors, and sloping roofs. Modern tennis is called lawn tennis. It is sometimes played on a grass lawn but usually on a hard surface such as clay. The top international tennis competitions are held in Wimbledon, England, the United States, Australia, and France. Leading tennis players earn huge sums from prize money and equipment sponsorship.

BASEBALL AND CRICKET
Baseball is the national sport of the United States. Winners of the National and American league pennants (championships) compete in the World Series each year. A gentler version, softball, is a popular amateur sport. Cricket players use a wooden bat and a hard ball. Cricket is popular in England, Australia, the West Indies, and India.

___ *Find out more* ___

AZTECS
FOOTBALL
SPORTS

BALLET

The tips of female dancers' toe shoes are stiffened to allow them to dance on tiptoe without hurting their feet.

MUSIC, DANCE, and mime combine in ballet to tell a story. Ballet began as entertainment for the royal families of Europe more than 300 years ago, and classical ballet style has developed gradually since then. The original French names for steps and jumps are still used. In the 19th century "romantic" ballet became popular. Dancers in floating white dresses performed *La Sylphide* and *Giselle*. In the early 20th century the Russian Sergei Diaghilev founded the Ballets Russes, one of the greatest of all ballet companies which performed all over the world. In ballet each step and movement is planned in advance. This is called choreography. Great choreographers such as the Russian Fokine (1880-1942) arranged dances for the Ballets Russes.

Most ballet dancers begin training at an early age. Ballet dancing is hard work and requires hours of practice.

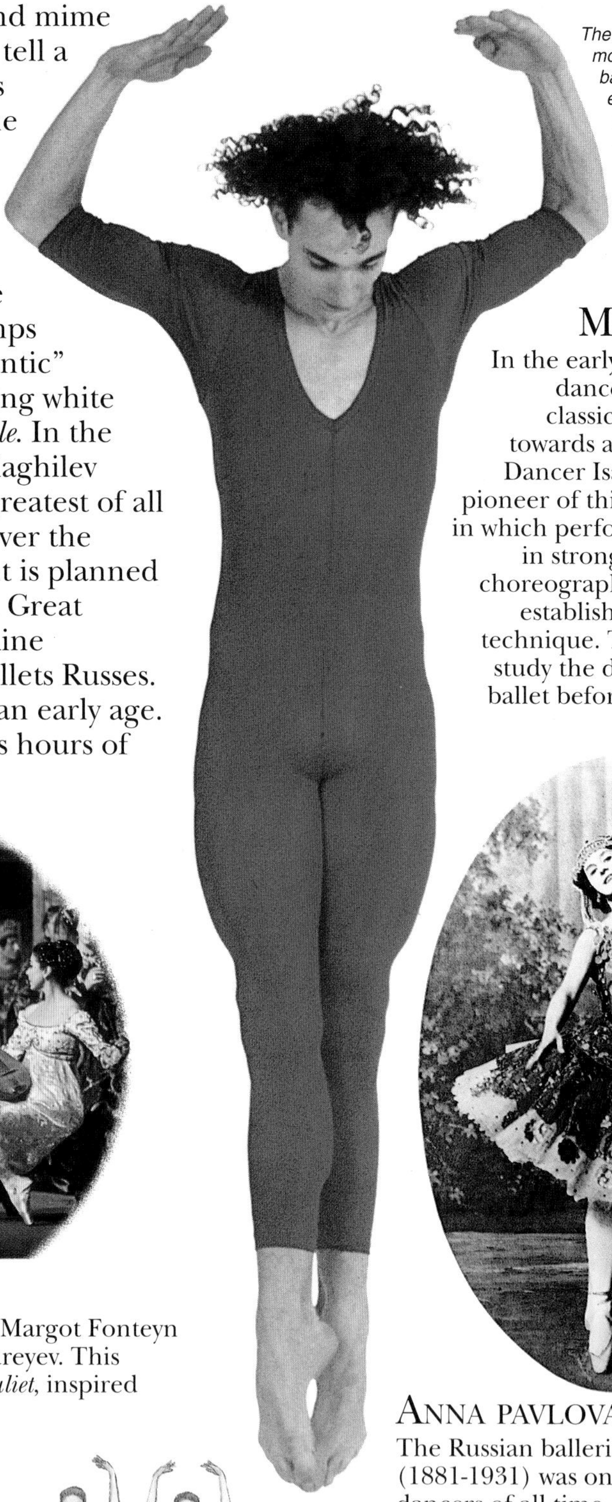

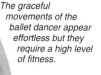

The graceful movements of the ballet dancer appear effortless but they require a high level of fitness.

MODERN BALLET

In the early 20th century some dancers broke away from classical ballet and moved towards a freer sort of dance. Dancer Isadora Duncan was a pioneer of this more natural style in which performers express ideas in strong movements. Later, choreographer Martha Graham established a modern dance technique. Today dancers often study the discipline of classical ballet before adopting modern styles.

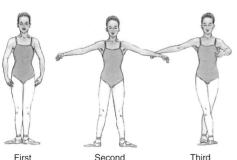

FONTEYN AND NUREYEV

Towards the end of her career, British ballerina Margot Fonteyn began dancing with a young Russian, Rudolf Nureyev. This famous partnership, shown here in *Romeo and Juliet*, inspired them both and delighted their audiences.

ANNA PAVLOVA

The Russian ballerina Anna Pavlova (1881-1931) was one of the greatest dancers of all time. She worked from the age of 10 to perfect her dancing. Her most famous solo was *Dying Swan*, which was created for her by Fokine.

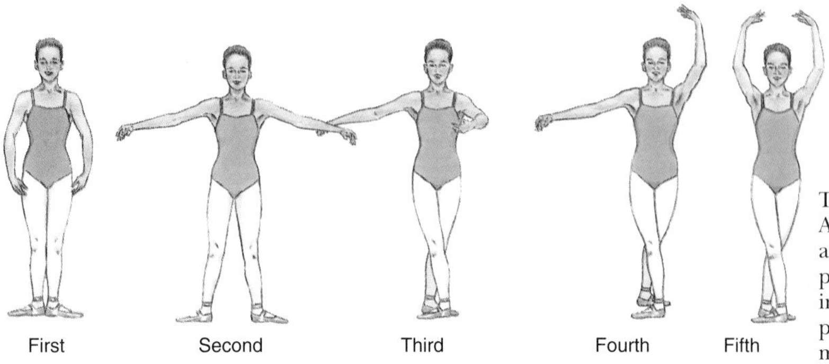

First   Second   Third   Fourth   Fifth

THE FIVE POSITIONS
All ballet movements begin and end with one of the five positions; they were created in the 18th century to provide balance and to make the feet look elegant.

Find out more
COMPOSERS
DANCE
MUSIC
THEATRE

BALLOONS AND AIRSHIPS

HAVE YOU EVER watched bubbles rise as water boils? That is how balloons and airships fly. They do not need wings to lift them into the air; instead they use a huge, bubble-like bag that floats up because it contains a gas that is lighter than the air around it. In the early days the gas was usually hydrogen, which was explosive and dangerous. Today most balloons use hot air, and airships use helium gas. The main difference between balloons and airships is that balloons go where the wind takes them; airships have engines and can fly wherever the pilot chooses. People flew in balloons and airships long before aeroplanes were invented. But in the 1930s, aeroplane design improved, and airships and balloons were gradually forgotten. In recent years, however, ballooning has become popular again, and new airships are being built.

MONTGOLFIER BROTHERS
The French brothers Joseph and Jacques Montgolfier built the first balloon that carried people into the air. It made its first free flight in Paris, France, on 21 November 1783, 120 years before the Wright brothers built the first aeroplane.

HINDENBURG DISASTER
The airships of the 1930s were huge, and the German *Hindenburg* was the largest, with a length of more than 244 m (800 ft). The *Hindenburg* was filled with flammable hydrogen; in 1937 it burst into flame and was destroyed.

Envelope is not rigidly constructed, but is held in shape by the pressure of the gas inside it.

In order to save helium, some airships have special air bags, called ballonets, inside the envelope (the large gasbag). Air is let out instead of helium as the ship goes up, then sucked back in as the airship goes down.

Air let out from ballonet

Propeller fans allow the airship to take off and land vertically and manoeuver in the air with great precision.

The gondola carries water ballast (weight to stabilize the craft) which can be let out to help gain height quickly.

Gondola made of Kevlar, a light, extremely strong plastic.

Air let out from ballonet

AIRSHIP
Airship engines can propel the craft in any direction. This airship has swivelling propeller fans that drive it up, down, or forward. It can fly at a speed of more than 90 km/h (55 mph).

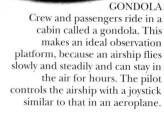

GONDOLA
Crew and passengers ride in a cabin called a gondola. This makes an ideal observation platform, because an airship flies slowly and steadily and can stay in the air for hours. The pilot controls the airship with a joystick similar to that in an aeroplane.

HOT-AIR BALLOONS
Hot-air balloons consist of a wicker basket and a bright, colourful envelope made of nylon. The envelope can be made in almost any shape, from a camel to a castle. Filling the envelope takes a lot of hot air. The heat from burning propane gas produces the hot air. The propane gas is stored as a liquid in metal cylinders carried in the basket.

Balloons sometimes carry sand as ballast which can be thrown out of the basket in order to gain height rapidly.

Before each balloon flight, the envelope is laid on the ground and held open, and the propane burner is lit to inflate the envelope with hot air.

As the balloon fills up with hot air, it gradually rises. When there is enough hot air to lift the basket, the flight can begin.

Once in flight, an occasional blast of hot air from the propane burner is enough to keep the balloon at a steady height.

Find out more
AIR
AIRCRAFT
GAS
PLASTICS
TRANSPORT, HISTORY OF

BARBARIANS

BY THE FOURTH CENTURY A.D., the once-great Roman Empire was in decline. A great threat came from tribal groups living outside the boundaries of the empire. The Romans despised these tribes. They thought they were uncivilized because they did not live in cities. Today we often call these tribes barbarians. But in fact they were superb metalworkers, farmers, and great warriors, with well-organized laws and customs. Around A.D. 370 hordes of one particular tribe, the Huns, moved from central Asia and pushed other tribes further westwards and through the frontiers of the Roman Empire. Some of the tribes nearest the empire asked the Romans for shelter. But in 406 hordes of Alans and Vandals swept into Gaul (modern France); in 410 the Visigoths, under Alaric, attacked and captured Rome, and barbarians flooded the Roman Empire. In 1452 the Huns, led by Attila, attacked northern Italy. The Empire was constantly under attack by many Barbarian tribes. Each tribe ruled the area it conquered in its own way.

ATTILA THE HUN
The nomadic Huns were jointly ruled by Attila (434-453) and his brother Bleda. In 452, after killing Bleda, Attila invaded Italy.

SACK OF ROME
In 410 Alaric, king of the Visigoths, captured and looted the great city of Rome which had been unconquered for 800 years. The sacking of Rome shocked the civilized world, but the empire itself did not collapse until 476.

CRAFTWORK
Each barbarian tribe had its own culture, laws, and customs. Even before 500 many barbarians had lived inside the Roman Empire, and many eventually became Christians. The barbarians were not just warriors. Their metalwork and jewellery were particularly beautiful.

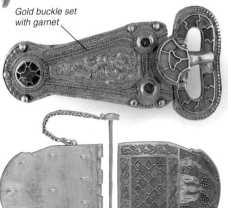

Gold buckle set with garnet

This gold and enamelled fibula was used to fasten a barbarian man's cloak.

BARBARIAN INVASIONS
By A.D. 500 barbarian tribes had overrun the Western Roman Empire. They divided their territory into separate kingdoms. As time passed, the invaders adopted some Roman ways, such as Roman laws and some Latin words. This map shows the routes of the barbarian invasions in the fifth century.

Find out more

CHARLEMAGNE
ROMAN EMPIRE
VIKINGS

BATS

Bats sleep upside down in a nesting place called a roost.

WHEN MOST other creatures return to their homes for the night, bats take to the air. Bats are the only mammals capable of flight. They are night-time creatures with leather-like wings that enable them to swoop and glide through the darkness catching moths and other airborne insects. Although most bats are insectivores (insect eaters), some feed on fruit, nectar, pollen, fish, small mammals, and reptiles. Most bats give birth to one or two young each year. The young are left in a nursery roost, clustered together for warmth, while the mother flies off to feed. There are nearly 1,000 different kinds of bats, including red bats, brown bats, and dog-faced bats. They make up one quarter of all mammal species, yet few people have ever seen one. Today, many kinds of bats are becoming rare as their roosts are destroyed and their feeding areas are taken over for farming and building. In Britain, all bats and their roosts are protected by law.

VAMPIRE BAT
The vampire bats of South America bite mammals and birds to feed on their blood, but they do not usually attack humans.

Bat's wings are supported during flight by long, thin arm and finger bones. When resting, the bat hangs in its roost by its clawed back feet.

FISHING BAT
The South American fishing bat has long legs and sharp claws for catching fish. It uses echolocation to detect ripples on the water's surface, then flies low with its feet dangling in the water. When the bat hooks a fish, its legs pull the slippery prey up to its mouth, where sharp teeth hold the fish securely.

At the top of each wing is a claw which the bat uses to cling on to rocks as it clambers about in the caves where it lives.

HORSESHOE BAT
There are more than 60 different kinds of horseshoe bats. Their name comes from the fleshy, curved flaps on their noses, which help with echolocation. The greater European horseshoe bat has a wingspan of more than 30 cm (12 in).

FRUIT BAT
The fruit bat is the largest bat; some measure almost 2 m (7 ft) from one wing tip to the other. It is also called the flying fox because it has a fox-like face. Fruit bats roost in trees or caves and fly out at dawn and dusk to feed on fruit, flowers, and leaves. Fruit bats are found in Africa, southern Asia, and Australia. In areas where they live in large numbers, fruit bats cause great damage by eating farm crops.

ECHOLOCATION
Bats find their way in the dark by making squeaks and clicks, which are so high-pitched that most humans cannot hear them. This is called echolocation. The sounds made by the bat bounce off a nearby object such as a tree or a moth. The bat can detect the returning echoes with its large, forward-pointing ears, and in a split second it has worked out the size, distance, and direction of the object.

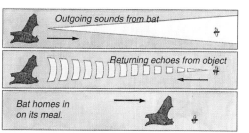

Outgoing sounds from bat

Returning echoes from object

Bat homes in on its meal.

Find out more
ANIMAL SENSES
ANIMALS
FLIGHT IN ANIMALS
MAMMALS
WHALES AND DOLPHINS

BEARS AND PANDAS

Small ears

Large head

Small eyes with poor eyesight

Short muzzle

Keen sense of smell

Huge, powerful paws

ALTHOUGH BEARS are often portrayed as cuddly, they are among the most dangerous of all creatures. There are seven kinds of bears. The largest is the polar bear. It stands nearly 3 m (10 ft) tall and weighs more than half a tonne. The smallest bear is the sun bear from Southeast Asia, which measures about 1.2 m (4 ft) from head to tail. Other bears include the grizzly and the sloth bear. Bears are heavily built, carnivorous (flesh eating) mammals. Giant pandas, which eat mostly bamboo shoots, are related to bears. The giant panda is a large black and white creature that weighs as much as 135 kg (300 lb). Today they are very rare. The red panda, which is much smaller, is more closely related to the raccoon. All bears and the giant panda have poor eyesight, so they find their food mainly by smell.

DANCING BEAR
Although bears are dangerous, people sometimes teach them to perform.

BLACK BEAR

There are two kinds of black bear – one from North America and the other from Southeast Asia. Not all American black bears are completely black. Some are dark brown or reddish brown. Black bears are skilful tree climbers and run fast – up to 40 km/h (25 mph). American black bears inhabit the forests of North America, and many live in national parks.

PAWS
A bear's paws are large, broad, and powerful, with tough, thick claws for grasping food, digging, and defending their young. One blow from a polar bear's huge paw can kill a person.

GIANT PANDA

The giant panda is also called the panda bear. Giant pandas live in central and western China and eat mostly bamboo shoots. There are only a few hundred giant pandas left in the wild, and they have become a worldwide symbol of conservation.

GRIZZLY BEAR

The huge grizzly bear has no enemies apart from humans. Grizzly bears live in North America, Europe, and Asia. The grizzly is also called the brown bear, or Kodiak bear. A female grizzly bear gives birth to two or three cubs in a winter den. Grizzly bears eat almost anything, including spring shoots, autumn fruits, animal flesh, and honey taken from bees' nests.

RACCOON
There are 15 kinds of raccoons; all are found in the Americas. They are fast, agile creatures related to bears. Raccoons are active mainly at night, when they feed on rubbish dumps, farm crops, and livestock.

In autumn, grizzly bears scoop up salmon that have swum upriver to spawn (lay their eggs).

Find out more

ANIMALS
CONSERVATION
and endangered species
MAMMALS
NORTH AMERICAN WILDLIFE
POLAR WILDLIFE

BEAVERS

THERE ARE TWO KINDS of beavers – the European and the North American. Both are rodents, a group of animals that includes rats, mice, and squirrels. Like other rodents, beavers have long, sharp front teeth for gnawing at plants and trees. Beavers are excellent builders. They use their teeth like chisels to bite through branches, which they drag away to build dams and lodges in rivers and streams. Although beavers go on land to find food, they are aquatic animals and spend most of their time in or near water. They are good swimmers, using their webbed back feet for speed. A beaver can dive and hold its breath underwater for several minutes. The beaver has a flat, scaly tail which it uses for steering and also for extra speed, thrusting the tail up and down in the water like a powerful paddle. Beavers also use their tails to warn others of danger by slapping the tail on the surface of the water. During the 18th and 19th centuries, beavers were hunted for their thick fur, which was used to make coats and hats. In some parts of North America beavers almost died out completely. Today, however, trapping beavers for their fur is controlled and these animals are no longer in danger of becoming extinct.

TEETH
The beaver's huge front incisor teeth can cut through bark and wood to fell small trees for food and for dam building.

DAMS
Using sticks, stones, and mud, beavers build a dam at a suitable place across a stream. The water around the dam spreads out to form a lake, which is where the beavers build their lodge.

Beaver can hold and manipulate small items with its front paws, such as twigs and stones for the dam.

Beaver uses its flat tail as a rudder when it is swimming underwater.

WOOD FOR DAMS
As wood becomes scarce, beavers may have to travel greater distances to find more. They dig canals and float tree branches along them to add to the dam.

Some lodges are more than 3 m (10 ft) high.

Adult beaver brings leafy twigs home to food store.

FEEDING
Beavers are herbivores (plant eaters). Their food varies according to the season. In autumn and winter beavers feed on bark and soft wood, particularly aspen and willow. They store twigs and branches underwater in the lake or river where they live. Even when the surface of the water is frozen hard in winter, beavers can swim from the underwater entrance of their home to bring back stored food. In spring and summer beavers feed on grass, leaves, and water plants.

BREEDING
Young beavers are called kits. They are born in spring and can swim a day or two after birth.

Underwater entrances help keep kits safe from predators.

UNDERWATER ENTRANCE
The lodge has several underwater entrances. Inside the lodge the beavers are safe from predators such as wolves, which cannot dig through the strong walls or swim down through the entrances.

LODGE
A beaver family lives in a structure called a lodge, built from tree branches and mud. Inside the lodge, the beavers hollow out a dry chamber above the water level. This is where they rest and sleep. In autumn the adults coat the outside of the lodge with a layer of mud. The mud freezes in winter and gives protection against predators.

Find out more
ANIMALS
CONSERVATION
and endangered species
MAMMALS
MICE, RATS, AND SQUIRRELS

BEES AND WASPS

HONEYBEES, BUMBLEBEES, and common wasps are a familiar sight to many of us, but there are thousands more, such as carpenter bees, stingless bees, mud wasps, and potter wasps. Bees and wasps first existed millions of years ago and live in almost every part of the world. These insects fly well, and the movement of their powerful wings makes the buzzing sound. Many bees and wasps are solitary, living in a nest in the ground or in a hollow plant stem. Some, such as bumblebees and honeybees, live in large groups, or colonies, in trees, roofs, and rocks. In a bumblebee colony the queen resembles her workers and shares many of their jobs. In a honeybee colony, however, the queen does not share these jobs and spends most of her life laying eggs. A honeybee colony may contain 50,000 bees.

Honey is a food that bees produce and store inside the hive. The bees feed on honey through winter.

Queen honeybee lays 1,500 eggs every day during summer.

Eggs hatch into larvae after a few days. The larvae become pupae, then adult bees.

Workers gather food, care for young, and clean and protect the hive.

Drone (male) mates with queen bee then dies.

BEEHIVE
Beekeepers provide hives where the honeybees raise their young and store their food of honey. Inside the hive are rows of wax combs full of eggs, growing larvae (grubs) and pupae, the queen with her drones (males) and workers, and cells of stored pollen and honey. In a hive there may be about 40,000 worker bees, a few hundred drones, and one queen.

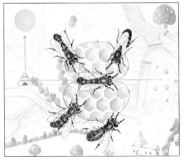

PARASITIC WASPS
These wasps paralyze spiders and insects, then lay eggs on their victim. These eggs hatch into larvae that eat the animal alive.

Wasp eggs develop into larvae inside the nest.

WASP'S NEST
After the winter hibernation, the queen wasp builds a papery nest. The queen scrapes up and chews wood, mixes it with saliva to make a pulp, then builds the nest with the pulp. The queen wasp lays eggs in hexagonal (six-sided) cells inside the papery nest, then catches and chews up insects to feed to the growing larvae. The larvae develop into worker adults who continue to enlarge and reinforce the nest. The males and the new queen are produced later in the season. A big nest may contain 5,000 workers. They fly out to feed on plant sap, fruit, and nectar.

Shaft of wasp's sting

COMMON WASP
Yellow and black markings warn other animals of the wasp's venomous sting. Some wasps use the sting as a defense against predators and to kill or subdue prey. Bees sting only if they are provoked.

Only female wasps (the queen and workers) sting.

BEE DANCE
When a honeybee finds a good source of food, it informs other bees in the hive by "dancing" in a figure of eight pattern. The bee dance shows the other bees where the source of nectar or pollen is in relation to the position of the sun.

Find out more

ANIMALS
FLOWERS AND HERBS
INSECTS
MONASTERIES

BEETLES

WHIRLIGIG BEETLES, CLICK BEETLES, and deathwatch beetles belong to the largest group of animals in the world. Of all the animals known to science, one in three belongs to the group of insects called beetles. Many beetles can fly, and have hard, often colourful wing cases. These wing cases fold over the insect's back when the beetle is not in flight, and they protect the wings beneath. During flight, the front wing cases are usually raised to allow the main wings to beat. Some beetles are active predators; the long-legged tiger beetle, for example, hunts down and eats smaller insects. Others, such as the Colorado beetle, eat only plant material. A few beetles are a nuisance to humans; Colorado beetles destroy potato crops, and elm bark beetles spread Dutch elm disease, destroying thousands of elm trees. But many kinds of beetles help to recycle dead leaves, dead animals, and other plant and animal material. Beetles are among only a few creatures that can break down dead wood.

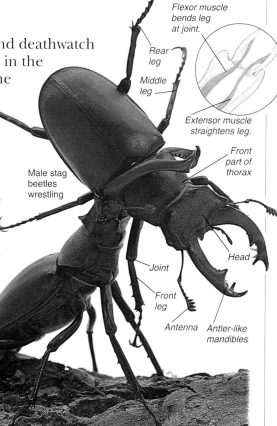

Flexor muscle bends leg at joint.

Rear leg

Middle leg

Extensor muscle straightens leg.

Male stag beetles wrestling

Front part of thorax

Head

Joint

Front leg

Antenna

Antler-like mandibles

GLOW-WORM
The glow-worm is a beetle. It has organs on the underside of its tail which produce a pale green glowing or flashing light. The light is used by the female to attract a mate or, in some species, a meal.

Tiger beetle

Wasp beetle

Two-lined collops beetle

Weevil

DUNG BEETLE
Dung beetles are so named because they feed on, and lay eggs in, animal droppings. The larvae (grubs) hatch and feed on the droppings before developing into pupae (chrysalises). Some dung beetles shape a lump of dung into a ball and roll it into their burrow before laying eggs in it.

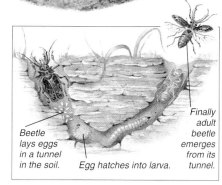

Some dung beetles are also called scarab beetles. The Ancient Egyptians believed they were sacred.

STAG BEETLE

Stag beetles take their name from their antler-like mandibles (jaws). Enlarged mandibles are found only on the male, and are so heavy that the beetle cannot give a strong bite. The huge mandibles are mainly for show, as when males threaten and wrestle with each other in order to mate with a female.

LADYBIRD
The bright colours of ladybirds warn predators not to attack them because they taste bad. Many ladybirds feed on greenfly and other aphids that damage garden plants. This makes ladybirds popular insects with humans.

COCKCHAFER BEETLE

The cockchafer beetle is a slow, awkward flier. It is attracted to light and often crashes into windows. The larvae, called white grubs, live in soil where they eat the roots of grasses and other plants. Adult cockchafer beetles are sometimes called may bugs or june bugs.

Finally adult beetle emerges from its tunnel.

Beetle lays eggs in a tunnel in the soil.

Egg hatches into larva.

LIFE CYCLE OF A WOOD-BORING BEETLE
A beetle starts life as an egg, then hatches into a larva (grub). The larvae of some beetles, such as the longhorn, eat wood and make tunnels in wooden furniture. During its life inside the wood, a larva changes into a pupa, then into an adult. As it leaves the wood, the adult woodborer beetle makes an exit hole. Old furniture sometimes contains hundreds of these tiny holes, which are nicknamed woodworm.

Find out more
ANIMALS
FLIGHT IN ANIMALS
INSECTS
MOUNTAIN WILDLIFE

BICYCLES AND MOTORCYCLES

APART FROM WALKING, there is no simpler and cheaper way to travel than on a bicycle. Bicycles were invented in Europe little more than 200 years ago; today they are popular the world over, not only because they are less expensive than cars but also because they do not produce pollution. Motorcycles are not as simple or cheap. Like bicycles, though, they are small and manoeuvrable, which makes them ideal for nipping in and out of city traffic. Specially built off-road motorcycles can be ridden in places no car can reach. When you first ride a bicycle, it is hard to believe you will stay up. At slow speeds, staying up depends on your sense of balance. But once a bicycle is going fast enough, it stays up by itself. This is because the frame is a special shape that makes a bicycle very stable.

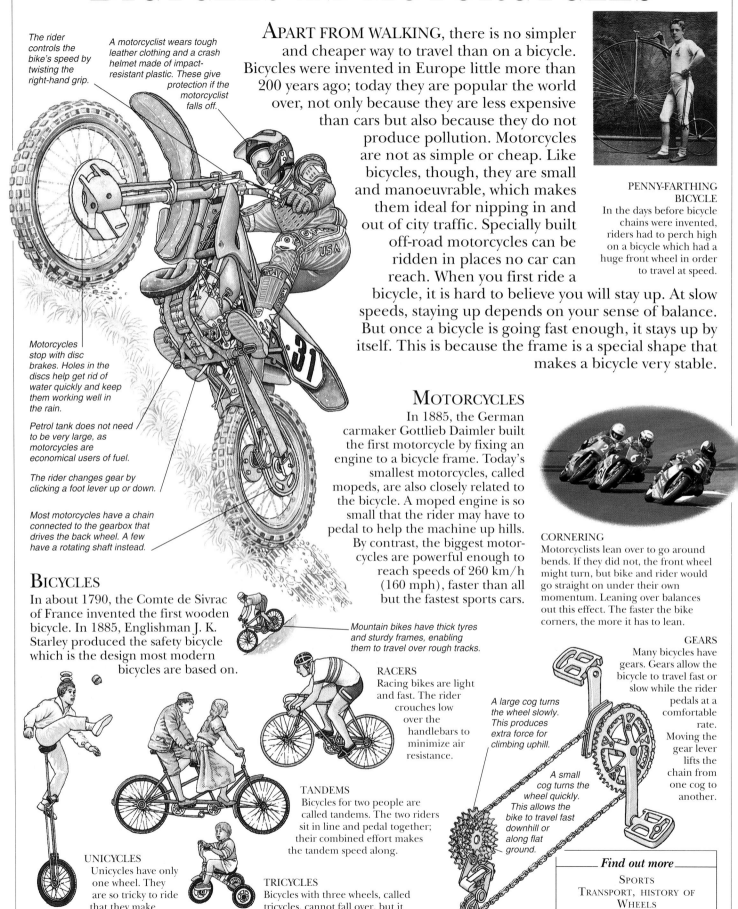

The rider controls the bike's speed by twisting the right-hand grip.

A motorcyclist wears tough leather clothing and a crash helmet made of impact-resistant plastic. These give protection if the motorcyclist falls off.

Motorcycles stop with disc brakes. Holes in the discs help get rid of water quickly and keep them working well in the rain.

Petrol tank does not need to be very large, as motorcycles are economical users of fuel.

The rider changes gear by clicking a foot lever up or down.

Most motorcycles have a chain connected to the gearbox that drives the back wheel. A few have a rotating shaft instead.

PENNY-FARTHING BICYCLE
In the days before bicycle chains were invented, riders had to perch high on a bicycle which had a huge front wheel in order to travel at speed.

MOTORCYCLES
In 1885, the German carmaker Gottlieb Daimler built the first motorcycle by fixing an engine to a bicycle frame. Today's smallest motorcycles, called mopeds, are also closely related to the bicycle. A moped engine is so small that the rider may have to pedal to help the machine up hills. By contrast, the biggest motorcycles are powerful enough to reach speeds of 260 km/h (160 mph), faster than all but the fastest sports cars.

CORNERING
Motorcyclists lean over to go around bends. If they did not, the front wheel might turn, but bike and rider would go straight on under their own momentum. Leaning over balances out this effect. The faster the bike corners, the more it has to lean.

BICYCLES
In about 1790, the Comte de Sivrac of France invented the first wooden bicycle. In 1885, Englishman J. K. Starley produced the safety bicycle which is the design most modern bicycles are based on.

Mountain bikes have thick tyres and sturdy frames, enabling them to travel over rough tracks.

RACERS
Racing bikes are light and fast. The rider crouches low over the handlebars to minimize air resistance.

GEARS
Many bicycles have gears. Gears allow the bicycle to travel fast or slow while the rider pedals at a comfortable rate. Moving the gear lever lifts the chain from one cog to another.

A large cog turns the wheel slowly. This produces extra force for climbing uphill.

A small cog turns the wheel quickly. This allows the bike to travel fast downhill or along flat ground.

TANDEMS
Bicycles for two people are called tandems. The two riders sit in line and pedal together; their combined effort makes the tandem speed along.

UNICYCLES
Unicycles have only one wheel. They are so tricky to ride that they make good circus acts.

TRICYCLES
Bicycles with three wheels, called tricycles, cannot fall over, but it takes more effort to pedal them.

Find out more
SPORTS
TRANSPORT, HISTORY OF
WHEELS

BIOLOGY

THE NATURAL WORLD is full of marvels and mysteries: the beautiful colours of a flower, the magnificent display of a peacock, the magic of new life when a child is born. Biology is the science of all living things, from the tiniest microscopic organisms (living things) to the largest whales in the sea; it is the study of all plants and animals and their environments, or surroundings. Biologists study how living things grow, feed, and move, how they reproduce, and how they evolve (change) over long periods of time. Biology covers an enormous range of topics and deals with millions of species (kinds) of animals and plants. Because of this, biology is divided into different specialized branches such as anatomy, which deals with the structure of living things, and physiology, which is concerned with the way animals and plants function. Biology is important in other sciences and professions that deal with living things, such as agriculture, forestry, and medicine.

LABORATORY
A biologist works in a specially equipped room called a laboratory. Biologists use a variety of techniques to study animals and plants. They may dissect (cut up) specimens, or use powerful microscopes to probe into the structure of tiny microscopic organisms, such as cells and bacteria.

BOTANY
The study of plants and flowers is called botany. It is one of the two main branches of biology.

Stamen of flower

Cross-section of stamen

Botanists study the structure of plants and how they reproduce.

ZOOLOGY
Zoology, the other main branch of biology, is the scientific study of animals.

Clump of a frog's newly laid eggs, called frogspawn

Zoologists study the life and growth of animals.

EVERYDAY BIOLOGY
There are biological processes going on all around us. For example, bread dough rises when it is left in a warm place. This is because live yeast in the dough gives off gas bubbles that make the dough expand, a process called fermentation.

Yeast is made up of single-celled living organisms. Yeast cells obtain their energy from the dough mixture and give off carbon dioxide gas in the process.

Once the bread is cooked, it is full of little holes made by the gas bubbles.

Carbon dioxide gas makes the dough rise.

HISTORY OF BIOLOGY
The Greek philosopher Aristotle was one of the first biologists. He studied birds and animals in about 350 B.C. During the 17th century, the English scientist Robert Hooke discovered living cells through the newly invented microscope. In 1953, English scientist Francis Crick and American scientist James Watson discovered the structure of deoxyribonucleic acid (DNA), the chemical that controls all cells and life patterns.

Francis Crick (left) and James Watson

Tiger pierid butterfly of Central and South America

Hairstreak butterfly of South America

TAXONOMY
Biologists classify plants and animals into different groups so they can understand the relationships between them. This is called taxonomy. For instance, butterflies and moths belong to the same taxonomic group, called lepidoptera.

HUMAN BIOLOGY
Human biology is the study of the human body and how it works. Human biology is concerned with all the different systems of the human body. These include the digestive system, the circulatory system, the nervous system, and the muscular and skeletal systems.

> ### *Find out more*
> ATOMS AND MOLECULES
> CHEMISTRY
> EVOLUTION
> HUMAN BODY
> PLANTS
> REPRODUCTION

BIRDS

IN THE ENTIRE ANIMAL world, birds are the only creatures with feathers. They are also warm-blooded, like mammals. There are about 9,000 different kinds of birds, living in all parts of the world. They include exotic, colourful birds such as parrots, garden birds such as robins and thrushes, sea birds such as puffins and penguins, and many more. Most birds are well adapted for flying and have large, powerful chest muscles to allow them to flap their wings. Their bones are light, with tiny honeycombed holes to save weight when they are flying. Feathers are light too. They protect the bird's body and keep it warm. Wing feathers fit together to form a smooth, airtight surface for gliding. Tail feathers provide balance and help the bird steer in midair. A few birds, however, cannot fly. Flightless or nearly flightless birds include ostriches, penguins, and the rare kakapo, a kind of parrot from New Zealand. Birds do not have teeth, which would be too heavy; instead they have a strong, light bill, or beak. Most birds, particularly eagles and other birds of prey, have good eyesight and hearing. Their sense of smell, however, is poor.

Outer feathers produce lift for flight.

Short, strong beak for cracking open seeds.

Brightly coloured plumage attracts a female in the breeding season.

Male chaffinch in flight

Long tail feathers act as a rudder, to help with steering during flight.

PLUMAGE

A bird's feathers are called its plumage. Some birds, such as the wren and the sparrow, have brown plumage for camouflage. Other birds have bright plumage with dazzling colours and patterns. The colours help them recognize and choose a mate in the breeding season, and help the members of a flock keep together.

Skeleton of a pigeon

Humerus (upper arm bone)

Skull

Radius and ulna (forearm bones)

Mandibles (jaws)

Keel on breast bone

Spine (backbone)

Ribs

Sternum (breast bone)

Femur (thigh bone)

Pelvis (hip bone)

Pygostyle (tail bone)

Tibia (shin bone)

Tarsus (ankle bone)

Internal system of a starling

Beak (bill)

Lungs

Gullet

Kidney

Crop

Heart

Liver

Gizzard

Cloaca

Intestine

THE BIGGEST AND SMALLEST BIRDS
The tiny bee hummingbird is one of the world's smallest birds. It measures about 5 cm (2 in) from beak to tail, and is so light that 17 bee hummingbirds would weigh only 28 gm (1 oz). The ostrich, which is more than 2.5 m (8 ft) tall, is the world's largest bird, but it cannot fly at all.

BIRD BONES

Most of the bones in a bird's skeleton are hollow, to save body weight. Wings are controlled by powerful muscles attached to the keel, which is a ridge along the edge of the breastbone.

INSIDE A BIRD

Most of a bird's body is taken up by the muscles, heart, lungs, and digestive system. Birds have two stomachs, as in the starling shown here. The first stomach, the crop, stores food; the second, the gizzard, grinds it to a pulp.

This ostrich head looks huge in comparison to a tiny bee hummingbird.

A bee hummingbird is so small that it can fit in the palm of your hand.

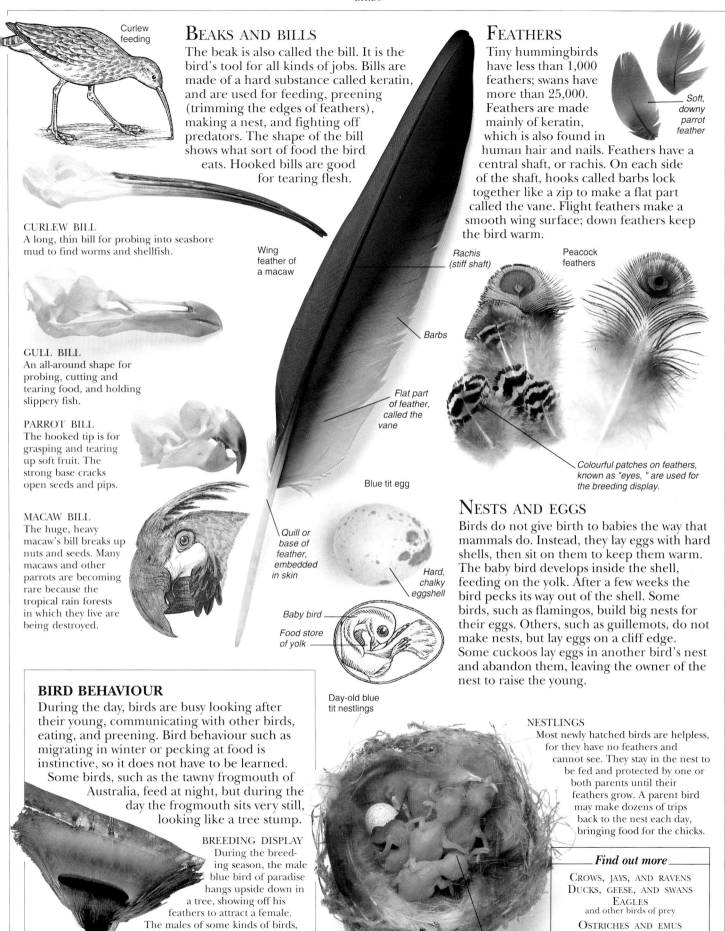

BEAKS AND BILLS

The beak is also called the bill. It is the bird's tool for all kinds of jobs. Bills are made of a hard substance called keratin, and are used for feeding, preening (trimming the edges of feathers), making a nest, and fighting off predators. The shape of the bill shows what sort of food the bird eats. Hooked bills are good for tearing flesh.

Curlew feeding

CURLEW BILL
A long, thin bill for probing into seashore mud to find worms and shellfish.

GULL BILL
An all-around shape for probing, cutting and tearing food, and holding slippery fish.

PARROT BILL
The hooked tip is for grasping and tearing up soft fruit. The strong base cracks open seeds and pips.

MACAW BILL
The huge, heavy macaw's bill breaks up nuts and seeds. Many macaws and other parrots are becoming rare because the tropical rain forests in which they live are being destroyed.

Wing feather of a macaw

Barbs

Flat part of feather, called the vane

Quill or base of feather, embedded in skin

FEATHERS

Tiny hummingbirds have less than 1,000 feathers; swans have more than 25,000. Feathers are made mainly of keratin, which is also found in human hair and nails. Feathers have a central shaft, or rachis. On each side of the shaft, hooks called barbs lock together like a zip to make a flat part called the vane. Flight feathers make a smooth wing surface; down feathers keep the bird warm.

Soft, downy parrot feather

Rachis (stiff shaft)

Peacock feathers

Colourful patches on feathers, known as "eyes," are used for the breeding display.

NESTS AND EGGS

Birds do not give birth to babies the way that mammals do. Instead, they lay eggs with hard shells, then sit on them to keep them warm. The baby bird develops inside the shell, feeding on the yolk. After a few weeks the bird pecks its way out of the shell. Some birds, such as flamingos, build big nests for their eggs. Others, such as guillemots, do not make nests, but lay eggs on a cliff edge. Some cuckoos lay eggs in another bird's nest and abandon them, leaving the owner of the nest to raise the young.

Blue tit egg

Hard, chalky eggshell

Baby bird

Food store of yolk

Day-old blue tit nestlings

NESTLINGS
Most newly hatched birds are helpless, for they have no feathers and cannot see. They stay in the nest to be fed and protected by one or both parents until their feathers grow. A parent bird may make dozens of trips back to the nest each day, bringing food for the chicks.

BIRD BEHAVIOUR

During the day, birds are busy looking after their young, communicating with other birds, eating, and preening. Bird behaviour such as migrating in winter or pecking at food is instinctive, so it does not have to be learned. Some birds, such as the tawny frogmouth of Australia, feed at night, but during the day the frogmouth sits very still, looking like a tree stump.

BREEDING DISPLAY
During the breeding season, the male blue bird of paradise hangs upside down in a tree, showing off his feathers to attract a female. The males of some kinds of birds, such as the grouse, fight over a patch of ground called a territory. Without a territory, no females will come to mate.

Blue bird of paradise

Eyelids still joined together

Find out more

CROWS, JAYS, AND RAVENS
DUCKS, GEESE, AND SWANS
EAGLES
and other birds of prey
OSTRICHES AND EMUS
OWLS
SEA BIRDS
SONGBIRDS

BLACK DEATH

Map showing how the plague spread in waves across Europe

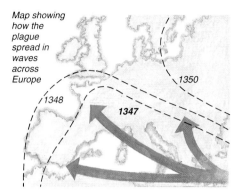

THE MEDITERRANEAN ISLAND OF SICILY was a terrifying place in 1347. Everywhere people were dying of a mysterious disease. Those who caught it usually had violent stomach cramps and boils under their arms. Dark patches covered their bodies, and death followed within three days. The disease became known as the Black Death because of the dark patches; today we know it was bubonic plague. It spread into Italy and France. By the end of 1348 millions had died – about one third of the population of Europe. There was panic as the Black Death advanced. People avoided each other, fearful that they might catch the plague. Many townspeople fled into the countryside carrying the disease with them. There was a shortage of food because there were fewer people to farm the land. Fields were filled with rotting animal bodies.

SPREAD OF PLAGUE
The Black Death began in Asia. It spread through Turkey, then arrived on ships at Sicily in October 1347, and reached Britain near the end of 1348. The plague reappeared every few years until the early 18th century; outbreaks were even reported in the early 19th century.

Large plague grave where victims were buried

15th-century illumination

THE BLACK DEATH
Death came to rich and poor alike. Some, thinking the plague was a punishment from God, whipped themselves and prayed to be saved.

CROSS OF DEATH
Crosses were painted on the doors of plague-ridden houses. Criminals and volunteers put the dead bodies on carts and buried them in large graves.

BUBONIC PLAGUE

Fleas living on black rats carried the bubonic plague. The fleas passed on the disease when they bit people. A more infectious form of the plague – pneumonic plague – was spread by coughing.

TREATMENT OF PLAGUE

Doctors used herbs or cut open people's veins to let out "bad" blood. But these methods failed. Many people refused to go near sufferers, even sick members of their own family.

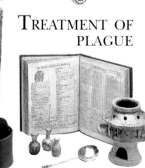

PEASANT REVOLT
The Black Death killed so many people that there was a shortage of workers. The survivors demanded higher wages and organized revolts in France and England against high taxes and strict, out-of-date laws.

_____ **Find out more** _____
DISEASE
MIDDLE AGES

BOOKS

LINDISFARNE GOSPELS
Monasteries were centres of learning throughout the Middle Ages in Europe (5th-15th centuries). They preserved the skills of writing and bookmaking. Monks in England wrote the Lindisfarne Gospels 1,300 years ago. It is a copy of part of the Bible, handwritten and beautifully illuminated (decorated with pictures).

NEARLY ALL THE IDEAS and discoveries that have been made through the ages can be found in books. The book is one of humankind's great inventions, and it is very adaptable. There are many kinds of books, from fiction or storybooks to nonfiction (information) books, such as how-to books, dictionaries, and encyclopedias like the book you are reading. Egyptians made the first books 5,000 years ago. They wrote them on scrolls of papyrus – paper made from reeds. The Romans invented the book as we know it today, using treated animal skin called parchment for pages. For hundreds of years all books were handwritten. They were rare and precious. The Chinese invented printing in the 9th century; it arrived in Europe during the 15th century. Printing made it possible to produce more than one book at a time, so as books became cheaper, more people began to read them and knowledge was spread more widely.

AUTHORS AND EDITORS
The author writes the book and submits it to the editor, who checks for errors and prepares the manuscript for the printer.

MAKING A BOOK
To make modern books, printers use computers to set the type (arrange the words on the page) and cameras to make the printing plates. Machines print, fold, stitch, and bind the books in a single operation.

Cardboard stiffens the cover.

Gluing cloth onto cardboard makes a "case".

Fitting the pages into the spine is called casing-in.

Spine cloth is glued on to reinforce the sewn ends.

Pages are folded into sections of 16 and sewn together.

Glued endpapers hold the pages on the case.

PAPERBACKS
Books with soft paper covers first appeared in the 19th century. They were cheaper to produce than hardcover books, so more people could afford to buy and read them.

THE PUBLISHER
Thousands of new books are published every year. A publisher decides which books to print and pays the costs of book production. Publishers also advertise books and distribute them through bookshops.

LIBRARIES
A library is a collection of books. There are private libraries and public lending libraries. The librarian arranges books by authors' names, and in subject order. Fiction and nonfiction books are kept on different shelves.

Find out more
LITERATURE
MAGAZINES
PRINTING
WRITERS AND POETS

BRAIN AND NERVES

EVERY THOUGHT and movement that we make is controlled by the brain. The brain is more complex than any computer ever invented. It enables us to think, speak, hear, see, feel, and move. It works nonstop, day and night. The brain consists of billions of living units called neurons or nerve cells. Neurons carry millions of messages to the brain along the spinal cord, which runs down the back and links the brain to the rest of the body. When these messages, or nerve signals, reach the brain, it sorts them out and sends instructions to the rest of the body along the nerves. Nerves are like wires, made of bundles of nerve cells. Sensory nerves take signals from the eyes, ears, and skin to the brain; motor nerves take signals from the brain to the muscles, telling them when to move the body. The average adult human brain weighs about 1.4 kg (3 lb) and has a texture like jelly. It is protected inside the head by the skull.

SLEEP
When we sleep, the body rests but the brain is still busy, controlling our breathing and heartbeat. We remember some of our night thoughts as dreams.

CEREBRAL HEMISPHERES
The largest parts of the brain are the two folded cerebral hemispheres. Our thoughts are based in these hemispheres. The outer layer of the brain is called the grey matter. It is rich in nerve cells. The inner layer is called the white matter. It consists mainly of nerve fibres. If the two hemispheres were spread out, they would cover an area the size of a pillowcase.

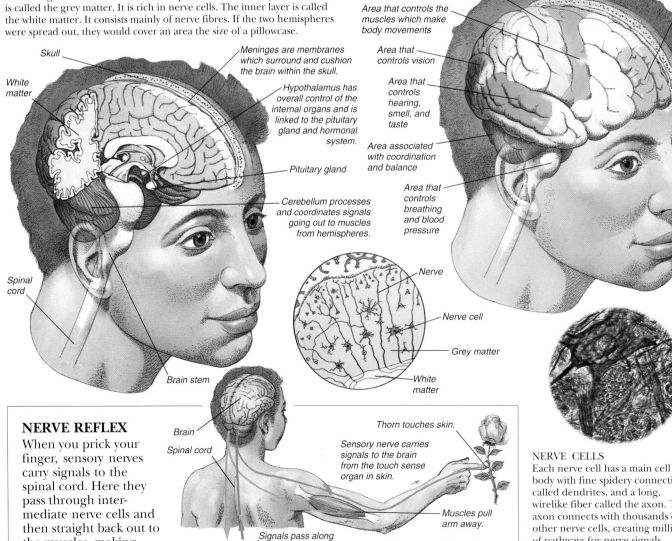

Skull

White matter

Meninges are membranes which surround and cushion the brain within the skull.

Hypothalamus has overall control of the internal organs and is linked to the pituitary gland and hormonal system.

Pituitary gland

Cerebellum processes and coordinates signals going out to muscles from hemispheres.

Spinal cord

Brain stem

Area associated with touch

Area that controls the muscles which make body movements

Area that controls vision

Area that controls hearing, smell, and taste

Area associated with coordination and balance

Area that controls breathing and blood pressure

Area involved with consciousness, creativity, and personality

Nerve

Nerve cell

Grey matter

White matter

NERVE REFLEX
When you prick your finger, sensory nerves carry signals to the spinal cord. Here they pass through intermediate nerve cells and then straight back out to the muscles, making them pull the finger away. This is called a reflex – an automatic reaction that we make without thinking.

Brain

Spinal cord

Thorn touches skin.

Sensory nerve carries signals to the brain from the touch sense organ in skin.

Muscles pull arm away.

Pain receptor in hand

Signals pass along arm to spinal cord.

Nerve cell

Motor nerve carries signals to muscles in arm.

NERVE CELLS
Each nerve cell has a main cell body with fine spidery connections called dendrites, and a long, wirelike fiber called the axon. The axon connects with thousands of other nerve cells, creating millions of pathways for nerve signals.

Find out more
HEART AND BLOOD
HUMAN BODY
MUSCLES AND MOVEMENT

BRIDGES

TRAVEL ON LAND is easier, safer, and more direct with bridges. Motor vehicles and trains can speed over lakes, rivers, and deep valleys. Bridges raise busy roads over others so that the roads do not meet. Major roads and railways enter cities on long bridges sometimes called viaducts. Footbridges allow people to cross roads, rivers, and railways safely.

The first bridges were made by placing tree trunks across rivers, and laying flat stones on rocks in shallow streams. Later, people made rope bridges by weaving plants together, and built stone bridges with strong arches. Similar kinds of bridges are built today with concrete and other strong, modern materials instead of natural materials. Steel beams and cables are used as supports. The world's longest bridge crosses Lake Pontchartrain in the United States. It is almost 39 km (24 miles) long. Land cannot be seen from its centre.

SUSPENSION BRIDGE
A pair of long steel cables fixed to high towers suspends the roadway. Suspension bridges can span the longest distances because they are lightweight.

ARCH BRIDGE
A curved arch firmly fixed to the banks supports the bridge. Arches are very strong structures.

CANTILEVER BRIDGE
Each half of the bridge is balanced on a support in the river. Where the two halves meet, there may be a short central span.

CABLE-STAYED BRIDGE
Sets of straight steel cables attached to towers hold up the bridge from above.

BASCULE BRIDGE
Sections of the bridge tilt like a drawbridge, allowing ships into port.

BEAM BRIDGE
Several columns in the riverbed or the ground support the bridge from beneath. Sometimes the bridge is made of a hollow girder through which cars and trains can run.

BUILDING A BRIDGE
The supports and ends of the bridge are built first, firmly fixed in the ground or the riverbed and banks. The deck of the bridge carrying the road or railway is then built out from the ends and supports, or lifted onto them.

SUSPENDING THE CABLES
The towers of a suspension bridge are built first. Steel ropes are then placed over the towers. A machine moves along the ropes, spinning long lengths of wire into strong steel cables.

RAISING THE DECK
Long lengths of cable, called hangers, are fixed to the suspending cables. The deck of the bridge is made in sections elsewhere. The sections are taken to the bridge, lifted into position, and attached to the hangers.

THE LONGEST SPANS
The Akashi-Kaikyo Bridge in Japan, has the longest single span of any bridge. The central span is 1,990 m (6,530 ft) long. The bridge was completed in 1997. The Humber Bridge, England, (left) has the next longest single span, at 1,410 m (4,626 ft).

KINDS OF BRIDGES
There are various ways of building bridges to span rivers and other barriers. Most bridges rest on solid supports. Pontoon bridges, which are found on some lakes, float on the surface of the water.

TACOMA BRIDGE DISASTER
The Tacoma Narrows Bridge in Washington, United States, failed in 1940. The wind made the bridge twist back and forth until the deck gave way. Nobody was hurt.

AQUEDUCTS

Bridges that carry water are called aqueducts. The aqueduct may be part of a canal, or it may bring a water supply to a town or city. The Romans built many aqueducts with high stone arches, several of which survive today.

Find out more
ARCHITECTURE
BUILDING
ROMAN EMPIRE

BRONZE AGE

ABOUT 8,000 YEARS AGO, humans discovered how to work with metal. At first, people made things from naturally occurring copper and gold nuggets, hammering them into shape with hard stones. But gradually craftworkers learned how to work these metals by heating them until they were liquid, then pouring the liquid metal into moulds. The advantages of metal were obvious. It could be cast into complicated shapes to make tools, weapons, and other objects and, if broken, could be melted down and remade. People probably first discovered bronze by accidentally mixing a little tin with copper. They soon realized that bronze was harder and longer lasting than other metals, and could be given a sharper edge. Bronze weapons and tools could also be resharpened. Gradually the Bronze Age began as people worked with bronze in workshops and villages. One of the first places to produce bronze was Sumer, in Mesopotamia, where the first cities developed.

MESOPOTAMIA
One of the first Bronze Age civilizations began in Sumer, in Mesopotamia. Mesopotamia was a plain lying between the Tigris and Euphrates rivers. Its fertile land was farmed by the Sumerians.

BRONZE AGE
6000 B.C. Early people experiment with copper. A few small objects are made in the Middle East.

5500 B.C. First irrigation systems appear in Mesopotamia.

4500 B.C. First plough used in Mesopotamia. Sails first used on boats sailing on the Tigris and Euphrates rivers.

3500 B.C. First cities built in Mesopotamia. People begin to use bronze in Mesopotamia – beginning of Bronze Age in the Middle East.

3250 B.C. First picture writing develops in Mesopotamia.

2800 B.C. Rise of Bronze Age culture of the Indus Valley, an agriculturally based civilization in India.

2500 B.C. Use of bronze spreads across Europe.

2100 B.C. Sumerian city of Ur reaches height of its power.

c. 1600 B.C. Bronze Age begins in China. Manufacture of magnificent bronze ceremonial vessels.

c. 1200 B.C. Rise of Assyria.

1000 B.C. Iron begins to replace bronze as main metal.

WRITING AND THE WHEEL
The earliest form of writing, called cuneiform, emerged during the Bronze Age. It was invented by the Sumerians, who also made the first wheels, which they used on wagons and war chariots and to make pottery. Wild asses pulled the chariots into battle, shown in the Standard of Ur, above.

HORSES
Horses came into widespread use during the late Bronze Age. Aristocratic horsemen often had elaborate bronze mounts on their chariots, such as this one with a red enamel pattern, found in Norfolk, England.

SUMER
The Sumerian plains were fertile but dry. The farmers dug ditches and canals to control the water from the rivers and irrigate the land. They could produce huge harvests, sometimes twice a year.

BRICKMAKING
Like many places in Bronze Age Middle East, there was no stone and little wood in Sumer. Large buildings, such as temples and palaces, were made from bricks. Sumerians mixed mud with chopped straw and poured the mixture into moulds. The bricks dried quickly in the hot sun.

Ploughing the land with oxen

Pouring mud mixture into moulds

Digging up mud to make the brick mixture

The Sumerians left their bricks to dry in the hot sun.

FARMING AND FISHING
Sumerians tied reeds from the riverbanks into bundles to make fishing boats and pens for their animals. All Sumerians were governed by, and paid taxes to, both their gods and their rulers, who represented the gods on Earth.

Find out more
ASSYRIANS
BABYLONIANS
CELTS
GREECE, ANCIENT
PREHISTORIC PEOPLES

BUDDHISM

ONE OF THE WORLD'S great religions, Buddhism, began in India about 2,500 years ago. It grew and spread, and today there are more than 300 million Buddhists, mainly in Asia. All Buddhists follow the teachings of Buddha, a name which means "Enlightened One". Buddha himself was born in about 563 B.C. He was originally called Siddhartha Gautama, and was a wealthy prince who became horrified at the suffering in the world. He left his wealth and family and began travelling and meditating (thinking deeply). After three years he achieved enlightenment, or complete understanding, became a monk, and began to pass his ideas on to others.

Buddhists believe that everyone is reborn after their old body has died. The quality of their new life depends on their karma. Karma is the total of all the good and bad deeds they did in the life they have just left. Buddhists aim to achieve absolute peace – a state they call nirvana. Buddha taught that nirvana could be reached by following the Eightfold Path: rightness of views, intention, speech, action, livelihood, effort, mindfulness, and concentration.

GOLDEN PAGODA
Buddhist temples usually contain relics of Buddha such as robes or a sandal. Some, such as the Golden Pavilion in Kyoto, Japan, are magnificent buildings inlaid with gold and decorated with diamonds.

BUDDHAS
Although they vary greatly in size, images of the Buddha all look similar. They represent Buddha sitting on a lotus flower. In the home a small Buddha forms part of a shrine. The image reminds followers of the goodness of Buddha and helps them meditate and pray.

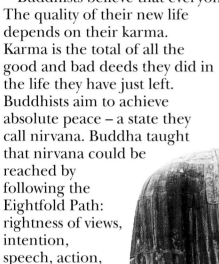

Buddhists burn incense at the shrine and leave offerings of flowers.

FESTIVALS
Bodhi Day – the day Gautama became the Buddha.

Parinirvana – passing of the Buddha into nirvana.

Wesak or Vesakha Puja – a three-day festival to celebrate the main events of Buddha's life.

Dharmacakra Day – when Buddha gave his first sermon.

MONKS

Buddhist monks give up most possessions. They keep only their saffron yellow robes, a needle, a razor, a water strainer, and a begging bowl. Monks spend their time praying, teaching, and meditating. Each day they go out to beg for food. In some Buddhist countries, boys spend a short time at a monastery as part of their schooling.

WHEEL OF LIFE
Buddhists share with Hindus a belief in the Wheel of Life, also called the Wheel of the Law. This is the continuous cycle of birth and rebirth that traps people who have not yet achieved nirvana. The spokes of the wheel remind the Buddhist of the Eightfold Path.

Find out more
ASIA
FESTIVALS AND FEASTS
HINDUISM
RELIGIONS

BUILDING

CRANE
The crane grows as the building rises. It may also be fixed on top of the building.

The frame is constructed of beams made of steel or concrete.

A hoist fixed to the side of the building carries workers to the top.

SKYSCRAPERS TOWER above the streets in many cities. The tallest free-standing building, the CN Tower in Toronto, Canada, reaches 553 m (1,815 ft) into the sky. The highest office building is the Sears Tower in Chicago, United States, at 443 m (1,454 ft). How are such enormous buildings constructed so that they stay up?

A house has walls built of wood, stone, or brick. They hold up the house, supporting themselves as well as the floors and roof. A skyscraper built like this would fall down. The walls could not support the heavy weight of such a high building. So hidden inside a skyscraper is a frame made of steel or concrete. The frame supports the floors and walls, which are often made of glass. Also hidden are the foundations beneath the skyscraper, which support the weight of the building.

A powerful pump carries liquid concrete from the ground to the upper floors of the building.

REINFORCED CONCRETE
Liquid concrete is pumped into moulds crossed with steel rods. It sets hard, producing a very strong material called reinforced concrete.

MOBILE MIXER
A truck with a revolving drum brings concrete to the site. As the drum turns, it keeps mixing the concrete so that it does not set.

PILES
Beams of steel or concrete, called piles, support the building's base. A huge mechanical hammer, called a pile driver, forces the piles into the ground.

BUILDING SITE

Workers on a building site always wear hard hats to protect their heads. They use many machines to construct a tall building such as a skyscraper. Parts of the building, such as steel beams and concrete slabs, are made elsewhere and brought to the site. Cranes lift the parts into position, and workers fit them together.

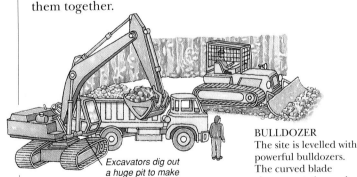

Excavators dig out a huge pit to make the foundation of the building.

BULLDOZER
The site is levelled with powerful bulldozers. The curved blade clears vegetation and piles up the soil.

SCAFFOLDING
Builders erect scaffolding made of steel tubes so that they can get to any part of a building. In the Far East, strong scaffolding is often made from lengths of bamboo tied together.

EXCAVATOR
Trenches and holes are dug with excavators. The bucket digs out soil and dumps it into waiting trucks.

FOUNDATIONS
Every building is supported by a foundation. This usually consists of a huge pit which contains a base made of reinforced concrete. The frame is built on top of the base, which supports the huge weight of the building.

BUILDING MATERIALS

Since early times, people have built with wood and stone. Bricks are made from clay. Stone blocks and bricks are laid in rows and joined together with sand and cement. Wood is cut into parts and assembled into structures. Concrete, made by mixing sand, stones, cement, and water, can be moulded to form any structure.

Find out more

ARCHITECTURE
ESCALATORS AND LIFTS
HOUSES

BUSES

THE WORD *BUS* comes from the Latin word *omnibus*, which means "for all". This is an apt description, for buses were the first kind of public transport, and are still usually the cheapest. The first buses date from the early 19th century when cities grew tremendously during the Industrial Revolution, and working people had to travel further to get to work. Before this time, only people who owned horses and carriages were able to travel long distances. Today, there are buses in cities and villages throughout the world. In most big cities, buses usually run regularly on an organized network of routes, and pick up people at special bus stops. In more remote places, the bus may be just a truck that passes through once in a while and stops wherever there are passengers.

CITY BUS
In busy English cities, where the streets are crowded and there are plenty of passengers, some buses, such as this London bus, have two decks.

ROAD BUS
Away from cities, buses can be longer to provide space for both passengers and luggage. Some road buses, such as this one from Iraq, may be articulated (hinged) to manoeuvre around hairpin bends on mountain roads.

SCHOOL BUS
Many children's first bus ride is on a school bus which takes them to school in the morning and brings them home safely in the afternoon. In comparison to other road vehicles, buses have a very good safety record.

INTERCITY BUS
Long-distance buses and coaches such as those of the American Greyhound line have comfortable reclining seats, toilets, coffee machines, and videos.

COUNTRY BUS
In less industrialized parts of the world, there are often no railways and most people cannot afford a car, so the bus is the only way to travel. Buses bounce along dusty roads, packed inside and out with people and all their luggage, including chickens, dogs, and other animals.

TRAMS AND TROLLEY BUSES

In some cities, such as Amsterdam in the Netherlands, you can catch a tram or a trolley bus instead of a bus. Trams glide along rails laid in the road and run on electric power picked up from overhead cables through rods on the roof. Trolley buses are powered in the same way, but they run on ordinary wheels rather than a track.

BUSES

In the richer countries of the world, buses are becoming increasingly sophisticated. Many city buses have electronic ticket machines and doors that open and shut automatically, and some buses have computers to guide them along the route. In poorer countries, people frequently crowd into battered vans and pickup trucks, all of which serve the same function as buses.

Find out more
CARS
TRANSPORT, history of
TRUCKS

BUTTERFLIES AND MOTHS

Wings and body are covered with scales.

Butterflies often have slim, nonfurry bodies.

Most butterflies have thin antennae with clubbed ends.

AS BRILLIANT IN COLOUR as many exotic flowers, butterflies are among the most beautiful of all creatures. Butterflies are more familiar to us than moths because they are active by day, whereas moths are active mainly by night. However, there are more than 250,000 different kinds of moths compared to about 15,000 kinds of butterflies. Together these creatures make up the insect group called Lepidoptera. Moths and butterflies have a life cycle in four stages – egg, caterpillar (larva), pupa (chrysalis), and imago (adult). The change in form between one stage and the next is called metamorphosis. All butterflies and moths are plant eaters and live wherever plants grow, except in extremely cold regions. Some, such as red admiral butterflies, hibernate (sleep) during winter. Others, such as bogong moths, migrate long distances to find food. A few butterflies and moths are pests to humans. Cabbage white caterpillars devour garden vegetables, and clothes moth caterpillars eat the natural fibres in clothing.

SILKWORM
The silkworm is the caterpillar of a moth. It spins a cocoon of silky thread around its body, then changes into a pupa inside the cocoon. People produce silk thread from silkworm cocoons.

MORPHO BUTTERFLY
Butterflies, particularly those living in tropical regions, are often more brightly coloured than moths. The blue morpho shown above is found in South America.

Forewing

Hind wing

The owl butterfly lays its eggs in batches. The eggs become darker as the time for hatching approaches. Their actual size is only about 1 mm (1/20th in).

Swallowtail butterfly

MOTH
Moths usually fly at night. Their wings are often but not always dull in colour. When the moth is at rest, it holds its wings to the side of its body. A moth's body is usually plump and hairy, and the antennae are feathery or fernlike. This *brahmaeid* moth from Southeast Asia has fernlike antennae.

EGG TO CATERPILLAR
After mating, a female moth lays eggs on or near a suitable source of food for the caterpillars to eat when they hatch. The eggs of some kinds of moths hatch only when the weather becomes warmer after a cold spell. This usually means that spring has arrived; the plants are beginning to grow again, and they provide food for the hungry caterpillars.

Egg

Caterpillar cuts open egg with its strong jaws and emerges from egg head first.

Hairy head waves around as the pink-striped body struggles to escape from the shell.

Oak silkmoth caterpillar eats a leaf.

Caterpillar eats the eggshell, which contains important nutrients.

Legs

In a few minutes the leaf is almost gone.

FEEDING
Each type of caterpillar feeds on a certain kind of vegetation. It spends almost all its time eating; as a result caterpillars can cause great damage to plants and farm crops. Caterpillars stop eating only to molt, or discard their skin when it has become too tight. The caterpillar expands in size before the new skin hardens.

Large, powerful jaws rapidly snip off and chew small pieces of food.

Not all moths are dull in colour – many are beautiful, including the moths shown here.

Caterpillar works along leaf blade between veins.

Jaws are hardened with a substance called chitin.

Caterpillar is attached to twig by silken thread.

Caterpillar spins silk girdle around its body, then skin of caterpillar begins to split.

Silk girdle is finished. The pupa is starting to form inside.

New skin of pupa

Caterpillar of the citrus swallowtail butterfly attaches its body to a twig and prepares to change into a pupa (chrysalis).

Spinnerets produce silken thread.

Empty skin and legs of caterpillar

CATERPILLAR TO CHRYSALIS

Before its final moult, a caterpillar stops feeding and may change colour. It finds a safe place to pupate (change into a pupa, or chrysalis). It anchors itself to a stem with silk thread from spinnerets at its rear end. Many moth caterpillars spin a silken cocoon around themselves for protection. Leafroller caterpillars curl leaves around their bodies and, using their mandibles (mouthparts), stitch them together with silk.

PUPA TO BUTTERFLY

The pupa stage is often called the resting stage. But inside its hard skin the creature is undergoing an amazing transformation, controlled by its chemical hormones. After several weeks, the skin of the pupa splits and the adult butterfly or moth emerges. Its damp, crumpled wings soon spread and dry.

SCALES

Tiny overlapping scales cover the wings of moths and butterflies. The colours and arrangement of the scales create the beautiful pattern of the whole wing.

With folded wings, the Indian leaf butterfly looks just like a dead leaf.

Adult blue morpho butterfly with wings closed

CAMOUFLAGE

Seen alone, a butterfly or moth may look so colourful that it would easily be noticed. But in many species the wing colours and patterns are designed to blend in with the natural surroundings. The shape of the wing may also closely resemble a natural object such as a leaf or a fruit.

Resting pupa of blue morpho butterfly disguised as a leaf

Butterfly begins to emerge.

Blood pumps into wing veins to expand them. Wings gradually dry and harden.

Indian leaf butterfly with wings open

CONSERVATION

Hundreds of species of moths and butterflies are in danger of extinction. They are threatened because the areas where they live are cleared for farms and homes. Butterflies and moths are also killed and sold to collectors because of their great beauty.

The Taenaris macrops butterfly from New Guinea feeds on ripe bananas.

When the wings are open, the eyespots flash like the eyes of a predator.

Spanish moon moth is now a protected species.

Queen Alexandra's birdwing butterfly is in danger because the forests where it lives are being cut down.

Large blue butterflies were extinct in Britain, but have now been reintroduced.

EYESPOTS

The eyespots on a butterfly's wings look like the eyes of a predator such as the owl above.

Find out more
ANIMALS
CAMOUFLAGE
FLIGHT IN ANIMALS
INSECTS

BYZANTINE EMPIRE

AS THE ROMAN EMPIRE began to decline in the 3rd century A.D., the Byzantine Empire began to emerge. In 330, the Roman Emperor Constantine moved the capital of the Roman Empire from Rome to Byzantium in Turkey. He renamed the capital Constantinople (now Istanbul), and it became the centre of the new Byzantine Empire. At first the empire, named after Byzantium, consisted only of the eastern part of the Roman Empire. But after the Western Roman Empire collapsed, the Byzantine Empire began to expand. Christianity became the state religion, and Constantinople became a Christian centre. Artists and scholars from all over Europe and the Middle East came there to study. Under Emperor Justinian I, the Byzantine Empire regained much of the territory of the old Roman Empire. Trade, art, and architecture thrived. But the empire suffered many attacks. By 642 Muslim Arabs had overrun Byzantine territories in North Africa and the Middle East. Gradually the empire lost its lands in Asia Minor (Turkey) and southeast Europe. In 1453 the Ottomans captured Constantinople, and the Byzantine Empire ended.

BYZANTINE EMPIRE
In 565 A.D., the Byzantine Empire stretched from Spain in the west to Syria in the east. By 1350, the empire had shrunk to a fragment of its former area.

Central dome measures 31 m (100 ft) across.

Marble floors

HAGIA SOPHIA
Justinian I (483-565) built the Hagia Sophia (Church of Holy Wisdom) in the centre of Constantinople. It was the largest Christian church in the Eastern world and was intended to provide a spiritual centre for the Byzantine Empire. After 1453, the church became a mosque (Muslim house of worship). Today the Hagia Sophia is a museum.

BYZANTINE EMPIRE

395 Roman Empire splits into East and West, with Constantinople as the capital of the Eastern Empire.

476 The Western Roman Empire collapses; the Byzantine or Eastern Empire takes over the whole Roman Empire.

527-65 During the reign of Justinian I, the Byzantine Empire reconquers much of the old Roman Empire.

635-42 Byzantine Empire loses control of the Middle East and North Africa to the Arabs.

1071 Byzantine Empire loses Asia Minor to the Turks. Calls in help from Europe.

1333 Ottoman Turks gain a foothold in Europe and begin to encircle Constantinople.

1453 Constantinople falls to the Ottoman Turks; the Byzantine Empire comes to an end.

CONSTANTINE THE GREAT
In 314, Constantine the Great (288-337) became Roman emperor. At that time Christianity was forbidden, but in about 312, Constantine himself was converted, some say by the sight of a cross in the sky. Christianity became the official religion of the Byzantine Empire and is now known as the Eastern Orthodox Church.

SIEGE OF CONSTANTINOPLE
By 1453, the Ottoman Turks had overrun the entire Byzantine Empire and reached the gates of Constantinople. Under the leadership of Sultan Muhammad II, the Ottomans besieged the city and captured it after two months. The Christian inhabitants of Constantinople were allowed to remain in the city, which became the capital of the Muslim empire.

Find out more
CHRISTIANITY
OTTOMAN EMPIRE
ROMAN EMPIRE

JULIUS
CAESAR

IN 49 B.C. A BRILLIANT MILITARY COMMANDER and politician named Julius Caesar became head of the Roman Republic. Caesar made himself popular with people by paying for magnificent public games in Rome. After holding various public offices, including that of consul, he was given command of an army and extended the boundaries of the Roman Republic by conquering Gaul (modern France, Belgium, and Switzerland). He also invaded Britain twice. The senate, a group of elected representatives who ruled Rome, feared he might make himself king, so they ordered Caesar to surrender his army, but instead he marched towards Rome. Pompey the Great, Caesar's son-in-law, headed the senate's troops. In 48 B.C. Pompey was murdered; and in 45 B.C. Caesar was elected dictator. But a year later he was violently assassinated.

100 B.C. Born in Rome.
65 B.C. Elected public games organizer.
62 B.C. Elected praetor, a law official.
60 B.C. Forms First Triumvirate.
59 B.C. Elected consul.
58 B.C. Begins Gaul campaign.
55 B.C. Invades Britain.
49 B.C. Fights civil war. Becomes dictator.
48 B.C. Defeats Pompey.
46 B.C. Defeats Pompey's supporters.
45 B.C. Made dictator for life.
44 B.C. Assassinated

As Caesar wondered whether or not to cross the River Rubicon, legend has it that a vision of a larger-than-life man appeared, playing a trumpet, luring him across the river. Caesar took it to be a sign from the gods, and gave the order for his troops to proceed.

THE TRIUMVIRATE

In 60 B.C. Caesar, wanting to be elected consul, allied his fortunes with Pompey (above) and Crassus, another leading politician, to form a three-man group (a triumvirate) which was the most powerful political group in Rome.

CROSSING THE RUBICON

Caesar's victories in Gaul made him very popular with many Romans. However, others feared and distrusted him. In 49 B.C. the senate ordered him to give up his army. Caesar refused and crossed the River Rubicon to invade Italy and begin the civil war.

Each army unit, or legion, carried its own standard, shaped like an eagle.

CAESAR'S DEATH

Many politicians in Rome thought that Caesar had too much power. Led by Marcus Brutus and Gaius Cassius, a number of Pompey's supporters plotted against Caesar and decided to kill him. On 15 March (the Ides of March), 44 B.C., the plotters attacked Caesar in the senate and stabbed him to death. Civil war raged after his death; finally his adopted son Octavian emerged as victor, and the Roman Empire was born.

LAUREL CROWN
Victorious Roman military commanders often wore laurel wreaths to symbolize their power. Later, emperors would wear a crown of gold olive leaves after a great victory.

Find out more
ROMAN EMPIRE

CAMELS AND LLAMAS

A CAMEL IS MORE SUITED TO life in the desert than almost any other beast. With a hump full of fat on its back as a permanent store of fluids, the camel is able to travel great distances without eating or drinking. Then, when food is plentiful, the camel's enormous stomach can hold huge amounts of grass and water. There are two kinds of camels – the dromedary and the Bactrian. The llama of South America is closely related to the camel, but it has no hump; other members of the camel family include the alpaca, guanaco, and vicuna, also from South America. Both camels and llamas have long, sturdy legs and are good runners. They have long necks, and their eyes, ears, and nostrils are set high on the head so they can detect danger from a distance. Camels, llamas, and alpacas have been used as beasts of burden for thousands of years. Most dromedary camels are domesticated and kept for meat and other products; Bactrian camels still live wild in the Gobi Desert, in northern Asia.

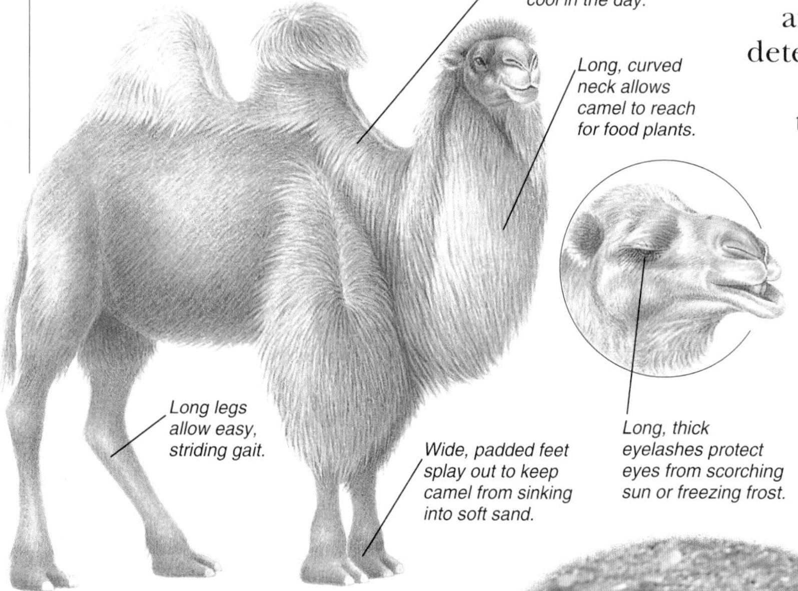

Thick fur keeps Bactrian camel warm at night and cool in the day.

Long, curved neck allows camel to reach for food plants.

In a sandstorm the camel kneels down on its thick kneepads, presses its ears flat, shuts its long-lashed eyes, seals its mouth, and closes its nostrils almost completely. In this way the camel avoids breathing in too much of the sand and dust whipped up by the storm.

Long legs allow easy, striding gait.

Wide, padded feet splay out to keep camel from sinking into soft sand.

Long, thick eyelashes protect eyes from scorching sun or freezing frost.

SHIP OF THE DESERT

Famous for carrying people across the hot lands of North Africa and the Middle East, the camel is often called "the ship of the desert". Camels provide people with milk and meat, and their hair and hides are used to make tents, rugs, and clothes. Camels have tough lips that can grip thorny plant food. They seldom need to drink, but when water is plentiful they can drink 114 litres (25 gallons) at one time.

LLAMA

Weighing about 140 kg (300 lb), an average llama is almost 1.2 m (4 ft) tall at the shoulder. Llamas were first tamed by people more than 4,000 years ago. Cars, lorries, and trains have largely replaced them, but llamas are still used in South America for transport. Both llamas and alpacas are killed for meat and for their hides. These llamas are carrying goods in Peru.

GUANACO
The graceful guanaco shown here lives wild in the foothills of the Andes Mountains, in South America. Vicunas live wild too, higher up on the Andean mountain pastures. The vicuna is an officially protected species, but both vicunas and guanacos are still hunted for their meat, hides, and wool.

Almost all the 14 million camels in the world are dromedaries.

The Bactrian, or Asian camel, has long, shaggy fur.

CAMEL HUMPS

The dromedary or Arabian camel has one hump; the Bactrian or Asian camel has two. An adult camel is about 2.1 m (7 ft) tall at the hump and weighs 500 kg (1,100 lb).

Find out more
AFRICA
ANIMALS
DESERT WILDLIFE

CAMERAS

ALTHOUGH THE FIRST photograph was taken little more than 150 years ago, cameras are much, much older. Around 1500 B.C., the Chinese found that light entering a dark room through a pinhole would project a fuzzy image of the world outside onto the opposite wall. Many years later, in Europe, a room like this was called a camera obscura, which is Latin for "darkened room". In the 17th century some artists drew sketches with the aid of a camera obscura which had a lens instead of a pinhole to make the image sharper and brighter. The discovery of chemicals that darkened when exposed to light finally made it possible to fix the image permanently.

Today, thanks to materials such as plastics and aluminium, cameras are generally compact and easy to carry. The sophisticated electronic technology in many cameras ensures that each picture gets the right amount of light (autoexposure) and is perfectly sharp (autofocus). But all cameras still work on the same basic principle as the camera obscura of old.

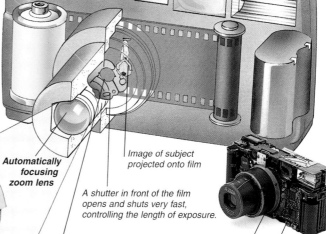

An invisible infrared beam automatically measures how far away the subject is. A motor then adjusts the lens for sharp focus.

The viewfinder shows how much of the subject will appear in the picture.

Electronic flash gives a brief but brilliant light when it is otherwise too dark for a picture.

Automatically focusing zoom lens

Image of subject projected onto film

A shutter in front of the film opens and shuts very fast, controlling the length of exposure.

The aperture, a round opening, changes width to adjust the brightness of the light entering the camera. In this camera the shutter and aperture are combined as one unit.

A motor winds the film across the camera after each picture has been taken.

Electronic circuits control autofocus and autoexposure.

KINDS OF CAMERAS

Most cameras get their name from the film they use. Tiny 110 cameras use film 11 mm (0.4 in) wide. The popular 35 mm camera takes a roll 35 mm (1.4 in) wide. Large-format cameras take huge sheets of film up to 255 mm (10 in) wide. Advanced Photo System (APS) cameras feature drop-in film loading. Digital cameras do not use film at all, but capture images on a computer chip for sending over the Internet.

AUTOFOCUS CAMERA

A camera is essentially a lightproof box with a lens at the front to project the image onto the film. But inside most modern cameras are intricate electric circuit boards which control functions such as exposure and focus.

SINGLE-LENS REFLEX CAMERA
The single-lens reflex (SLR) camera is popular with professional and amateur photographers because it is handy and versatile. A mirror and a special prism in the viewfinder allow the photographer to see exactly the same view that will appear on the film. The lens can be interchanged with others to give a wide view or to magnify the subject.

POLAROID CAMERA
The Polaroid "instant-picture" camera uses slim envelopes of plastic instead of a roll of film. Inside is a sheet of film and a pod of chemicals that bursts to process the picture in just 90 seconds.

MOVIE CAMERAS
The movement we see in the cinema is an illusion. A movie (cinema) film is really a series of still pictures projected on the screen in such quick succession that they seem to merge into one another. If the subject is in a slightly different place in each picture it looks as if it is moving. Most movie cameras take 24 pictures, or frames, every second, on a very long strip of film wound steadily through the camera. The film stops while each picture is taken, then advances quickly, ready for the next picture.

LARGE-FORMAT CAMERA
In early cameras, the lens was focused by moving a bellows – a concertina-like cloth tunnel – in and out. Many photographers still use large-format bellows cameras for high-quality studio work.

Find out more
FILMS
LIGHT
PHOTOGRAPHY
TELESCOPE
TELEVISION AND VIDEO

CAMOUFLAGE

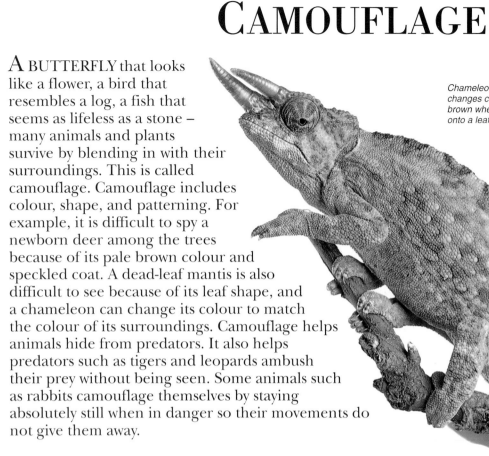

A BUTTERFLY that looks like a flower, a bird that resembles a log, a fish that seems as lifeless as a stone – many animals and plants survive by blending in with their surroundings. This is called camouflage. Camouflage includes colour, shape, and patterning. For example, it is difficult to spy a newborn deer among the trees because of its pale brown colour and speckled coat. A dead-leaf mantis is also difficult to see because of its leaf shape, and a chameleon can change its colour to match the colour of its surroundings. Camouflage helps animals hide from predators. It also helps predators such as tigers and leopards ambush their prey without being seen. Some animals such as rabbits camouflage themselves by staying absolutely still when in danger so their movements do not give them away.

Chameleon quickly changes colour to brown when it moves onto a leafless branch.

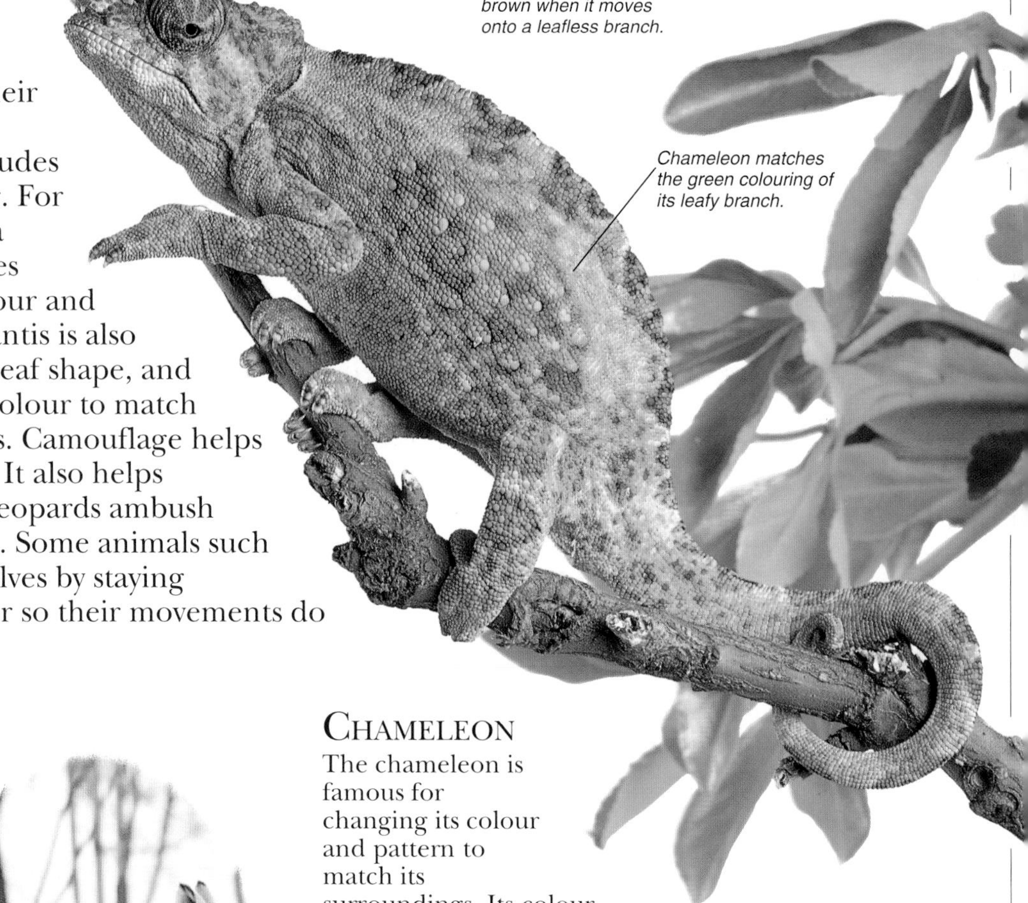

Chameleon matches the green colouring of its leafy branch.

ARCTIC HARE

The Arctic hare is brown in summer to match its surroundings of soil and shrubs. In autumn it sheds its fur and grows a new white coat, for camouflage in the winter snow. The Arctic fox preys on the Arctic hare. In winter the Arctic fox also has a white coat for camouflage.

CHAMELEON

The chameleon is famous for changing its colour and pattern to match its surroundings. Its colour alters when cells in the skin change size, moving their grains of colour nearer the surface or deeper into the skin. When the Jackson's chameleon shown here was taken off its branch, its colour changed from green and yellow to mottled brown in about five minutes.

STICK INSECT
The spindly stick insect is very difficult to recognize among twigs and branches because of its shape and colour. It can fold its thin legs alongside its body and look even more like a twig. When danger threatens, it stays absolutely still – like a stick.

TIGER STRIPES
The tiger is camouflaged by its stripes, which match the light and dark patterns of sunlit grasses. The tiger hunts mainly by ambush, creeping stealthily towards its prey in the undergrowth, then charging over the last few metres.

___*Find out more*___

ANIMALS
BIRDS
FISH
INSECTS
LIONS, TIGERS,
and other big cats
RABBITS AND HARES

CANADA

THE SECOND LARGEST COUNTRY in the world is also one of the emptiest. Much of Canada is virtually uninhabited. The northern part of the country is a hostile wasteland of snow and ice for much of the year. Few people live among the high Rocky Mountains in the west. And even in the huge wheat-growing plains in the centre there are few people. Most of Canada's 27.8 million inhabitants live in the southeast, close to the border with the United States.

Most Canadians speak English, but for some, particularly those in the province of Quebec, French is the first language. This is because they are descendants of the French who settled in Canada in the 16th century. The languages of the native North American and Inuit inhabitants are rarely heard today. Much of Canada's trade is with its neighbour, the United States. However, Canada has close links with many European, Asian, and African nations.

Canada occupies the northern half of North America, stretching from the Pacific to the Atlantic oceans. Part of the country lies within the Arctic Circle. At 6,416 km (3,987 miles) the Canadian-U.S. border is the world's longest continuous frontier between two nations.

TORONTO

More than three million people live in the city of Toronto. It is Canada's business centre and capital of the province of Ontario. Toronto has many skyscrapers, including the 553 m (1,815 ft) high Canadian National Tower.

Timber and maple syrup are just two of the products extracted from Canada's vast forests.

SPORTS AND LEISURE

Winter sports such as skiing, skating, and ice hockey are popular in Canada because winters are long and there is plenty of snow and ice. Modern ice hockey was invented in Canada in the 1870s and is now played nearly everywhere in the world. During the summer, sailing, canoeing, and field hockey are also popular.

Ice hockey is the Canadian national sport.

NATURAL RESOURCES

Canada is rich in minerals such as copper and iron ore and has huge reserves of oil, coal, and natural gas. Many Canadians are employed in manufacturing, forestry and agriculture. Most Canadian exports are sent south to the United States; the two countries have formed a free-trade zone, which means that exports or imports between them are not taxed.

ROCKY MOUNTAINS

Western Canada is dominated by the Rocky Mountains, which stretch from the United States border in the south to Alaska in the north. The mountains are covered in trees and are a haven for bears and other wildlife.

LAW AND ORDER

The nickname of the Royal Canadian Mounted Police – the national police force – is the Mounties. They boast that they "always get their man".

Find out more

CANADA, HISTORY OF
ESKIMOS
INDIANS, NORTH AMERICAN

CANADA

YUKON TERRITORY
Few people live in the Yukon Territory in northwestern Canada but the region is rich in silver, zinc, lead, and gold. During the 1890s it was the site of the Klondike gold rush. Prospectors and adventurers who came to the Yukon hoping to strike gold founded Whitehorse, which became the territorial capital in 1952. Winters in the Yukon are long and cold, but in summer the weather becomes warm, with temperatures reaching 16°C (60°F). This allows the growth of many kinds of vegetation which take on a rich variety of colours in the autumn. Moose, caribou, beavers, and bears are common in the Yukon.

STATISTICS
Area: 9,970,610 sq km (3,849,656 sq miles)
Population: 27,800,000
Capital: Ottawa
Languages: English, French
Religions: Roman Catholic, Protestant
Currency: Canadian dollar
Main occupation: Service industries
Main exports: Cars, tractors, newsprint, wood pulp, timber
Main imports: Cars, chemicals, machinery, computers

PROVINCES
showing date of joining the Confederation of Canada

ALBERTA 1905
Area: 661,190 sq km (255,286 sq miles)
Population: 2,565,200
Capital: Edmonton

BRITISH COLUMBIA 1871
Area: 947,800 sq km (365,946 sq miles)
Population: 3,282,061
Capital: Victoria

MANITOBA 1870
Area: 649,950 sq km (250,946 sq miles)
Population: 1,091,940
Capital: Winnipeg

NEW BRUNSWICK 1867
Area: 73,440 sq km (28,355 sq miles)
Population: 728,500
Capital: Fredericton

NEWFOUNDLAND AND LABRADOR 1949
Area: 404,720 sq km (156,649 sq miles)
Population: 568,474
Capital: St. John's

NOVA SCOTIA 1867
Area: 55,490 sq km (21,425 sq miles)
Population: 899,942
Capital: Halifax

ONTARIO 1867
Area: 1,068,630 sq km (412,298 sq miles)
Population: 9,906,400
Capital: Toronto

PRINCE EDWARD ISLAND 1873
Area: 5,660 sq km (2,185 sq miles)
Population: 129,765
Capital: Charlottetown

QUEBEC 1867
Area: 1,540,680 sq km (594,857 sq miles)
Population: 6,895,963
Capital: Quebec

SASKATCHEWAN 1905
Area: 652,330 sq km (251,865 sq miles)
Population: 998,928
Capital: Regina

TERRITORIES
showing date of joining the Confederation of Canada

NORTHWEST TERRITORIES 1870
Area: 3,426,320 sq km (1,322,903 sq miles)
Population: 57,649
Capital: Yellowknife

YUKON TERRITORY 1898
Area: 483,450 sq km (186,660 sq miles)
Population: 27,797
Capital: Whitehorse

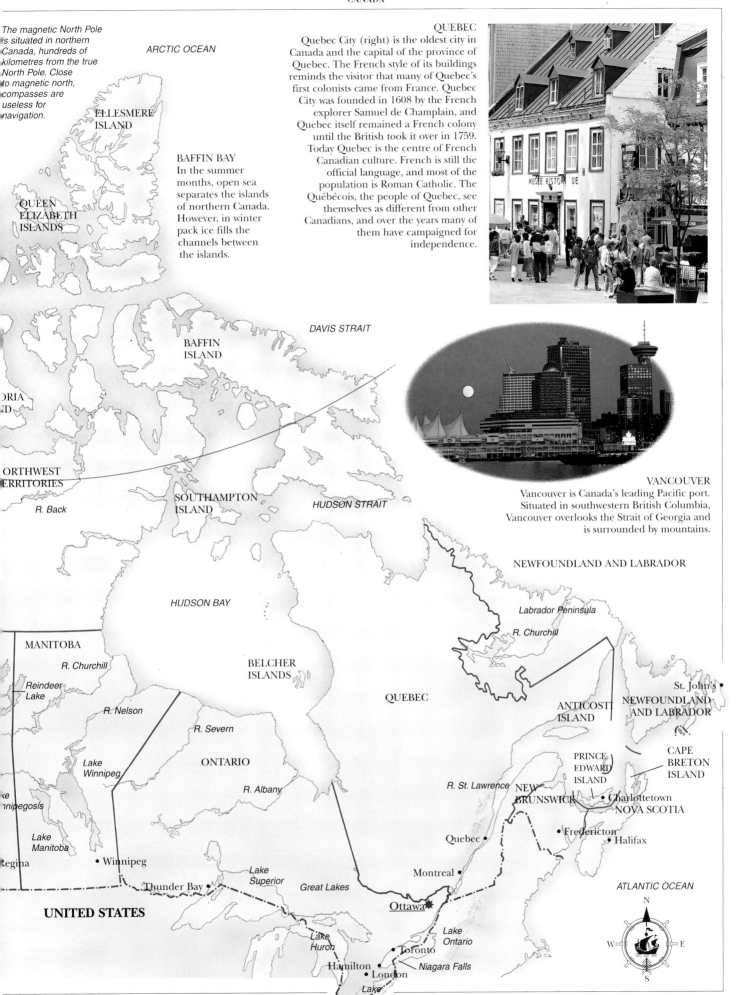

The magnetic North Pole is situated in northern Canada, hundreds of kilometres from the true North Pole. Close to magnetic north, compasses are useless for navigation.

ARCTIC OCEAN

ELLESMERE ISLAND

QUEEN ELIZABETH ISLANDS

BAFFIN BAY
In the summer months, open sea separates the islands of northern Canada. However, in winter pack ice fills the channels between the islands.

QUEBEC
Quebec City (right) is the oldest city in Canada and the capital of the province of Quebec. The French style of its buildings reminds the visitor that many of Quebec's first colonists came from France. Quebec City was founded in 1608 by the French explorer Samuel de Champlain, and Quebec itself remained a French colony until the British took it over in 1759. Today Quebec is the centre of French Canadian culture. French is still the official language, and most of the population is Roman Catholic. The Québécois, the people of Quebec, see themselves as different from other Canadians, and over the years many of them have campaigned for independence.

DAVIS STRAIT

BAFFIN ISLAND

ORIA ND

NORTHWEST TERRITORIES

R. Back

SOUTHAMPTON ISLAND

HUDSON STRAIT

VANCOUVER
Vancouver is Canada's leading Pacific port. Situated in southwestern British Columbia, Vancouver overlooks the Strait of Georgia and is surrounded by mountains.

NEWFOUNDLAND AND LABRADOR

HUDSON BAY

Labrador Peninsula

R. Churchill

MANITOBA

R. Churchill

BELCHER ISLANDS

Reindeer Lake

R. Nelson

R. Severn

QUEBEC

St. John's •

ANTICOSTI ISLAND

NEWFOUNDLAND AND LABRADOR

Lake Winnipeg

ONTARIO

R. Albany

PRINCE EDWARD ISLAND

CAPE BRETON ISLAND

ke nipegosis

R. St. Lawrence

NEW BRUNSWICK

Charlottetown

NOVA SCOTIA

Lake Manitoba

Regina

• Winnipeg

Quebec •

• Fredericton

• Halifax

Lake Superior

Great Lakes

Montreal •

ATLANTIC OCEAN

Thunder Bay •

UNITED STATES

Ottawa ★

Lake Huron

Lake Ontario

• Toronto

N

Hamilton •

• London

Niagara Falls

W   E

Lake Erie

S

Windsor •

HISTORY OF
CANADA

Canada's most popular emblem is the leaf of the local tree, the red maple.

ABOUT TWENTY-FIVE THOUSAND YEARS AGO Canada's first people walked across the land that then existed between Siberia and Alaska. Fishing people from Europe began to explore the rich coast of Canada about 1,000 years ago, and the original North American Indian inhabitants of the country lost control when British and French settlers began to establish trading posts for fur during the 17th century. Britain and France fought each other for the land, and in 1759 Britain won control of the whole country. A century later, Canada became independent of British rule but remained a British dominion (territory). After World War II, Canada became very prosperous and developed a close business relationship with the United States. During the 1970s French Canadians demanded more power and threatened to make the province of Quebec independent. However, Canada is still united.

Indians were the first inhabitants of Canada.

Snowshoes

Wood cabin

European traders exchanged goods with Indians who trapped wild animals for their valuable furs.

Traders travelled by canoe to trading posts. Transport by canoe also opened the way to missionaries and explorers in Canada.

HUDSON'S BAY COMPANY

Both the British and French set up companies in the 17th century to trade in valuable Canadian furs. These companies grew wealthy and powerful and acted like independent governments. The British Hudson's Bay Company ruled much of northern Canada until 1869 when its lands were made part of the Dominion of Canada.

PIERRE TRUDEAU

Since the 1960s Canada has become increasingly independent of Britain. A new flag was adopted in 1965 and two years later a world fair – Expo '67 – was held to show off Canadian skills in the centenary year of independence. In 1968 Pierre Trudeau (right) was elected as prime minister. A great intellectual, he was a strong supporter of a unified Canada.

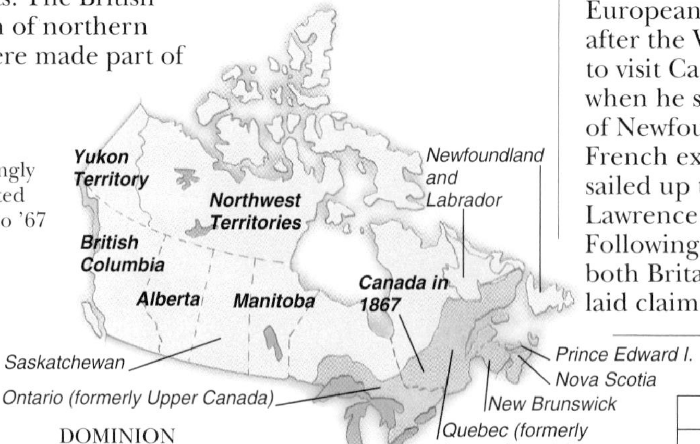

CABOT AND CARTIER

John Cabot

The Italian explorer John Cabot, sailing for England, was the first European, after the Vikings, to visit Canada when he sailed along the coast of Newfoundland in 1497. The French explorer Jacques Cartier sailed up the mouth of the St. Lawrence River in 1534. Following these voyages, both Britain and France laid claim to Canada.

Yukon Territory

Northwest Territories

British Columbia

Alberta

Manitoba

Saskatchewan

Ontario (formerly Upper Canada)

Canada in 1867

Newfoundland and Labrador

Prince Edward I.

Nova Scotia

New Brunswick

Quebec (formerly Lower Canada)

DOMINION

In 1867, the four British colonies of Nova Scotia, New Brunswick, and Upper and Lower Canada formed the self-governing Dominion of Canada. Six more colonies joined after 1867. Newfoundland, which controlled Labrador, came last in 1949.

Find out more

CANADA
COOK, JAMES
ESKIMOS
VIKINGS

CARIBBEAN

STRUNG OUT LIKE a rope of pearls is a long row of tropical islands curving for more than 3,200 km (2000 miles) between Mexico and Venezuela. Together they are usually called the Caribbean islands, sometimes the West Indies. Some are tiny, uninhabited rocks or coral reefs; others are much larger islands with thriving populations. On Martinique, for instance, 400,000 people live around the wooded slopes of several volcanoes which tower hundreds of metres above the sea.

There are 13 countries and 12 other territories in the Caribbean. Cuba, with a population of 10.9 million people, is the biggest nation. Although each country has its own distinctive culture, many have connections with other countries. These links are left over from the 18th and 19th centuries, when the whole region was controlled by European kingdoms. The ruling nations brought African slaves to the Caribbean to harvest sugar cane. Today, descendants of the slaves dominate the island populations.

The Caribbean Sea is about 1,943,000 sq km (750,193 square miles) in area. It is enclosed on three sides by Central America, South America, and the Caribbean Islands.

TOURISM
The Caribbean islands are very beautiful, with lush trees, colourful birds, long sandy beaches, and months of sunshine. The region attracts tourists from all over the world. This has created many new jobs, particularly in the towns. Tourism is now the main source of income for several islands.

ARAWAKS AND CARIBS
In 1492, the Italian explorer Christopher Columbus (1451-1506) became the first European to land on a Caribbean island. Several of the islands were inhabited by tribes of American Indians – the Arawaks, Tainos, and Caribs. More Europeans arrived and made the Indians slaves; those who refused to become slaves were killed. Today only two small Carib communities remain, on Dominica and St. Vincent.

African slaves cutting sugar cane

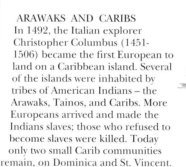

AGRICULTURE
More than half the people of the Caribbean earn a living from agriculture. Many work for a landowner, producing crops such as sugar and coffee. They may also rent or own a small plot of land. On this land they grow food to feed their families or to sell in local markets.

BASTILLE DAY
The islands of Guadeloupe and Martinique are part of France so the people have strong links with this country. They speak the French language, use the French franc for money, fly the French flag, and celebrate French holidays such as Bastille Day. Other islands depend on Britain, the Netherlands, or the United States for political and financial help.

ARCHITECTURE
Brilliant colours enhance the traditional shapes of Caribbean architecture. Similarly, Caribbean music, literature, art, and food are a unique mixture of European and African styles.

Find out more

CENTRAL AMERICA
COLUMBUS, CHRISTOPHER
SLAVERY

CARIBBEAN

Ancient monument | Volcano | Highest mountain | Capital city | City/town

ANGUILLA (UK)
Area: 91 sq km
(35 sq miles)
Population: 8,960
Capital: The Valley

ANTIGUA AND BARBUDA
Area: 442 sq km (171 sq miles)
Population: 81,000
Capital: St. John's

ARUBA (Neth)
Area: 193 sq km
(75 sq miles)
Population: 70,415
Capital: Oranjestad

THE BAHAMAS
Area: 13,935 sq km
(5,380 sq miles)
Population: 300,000
Capital: Nassau

BARBADOS
Area: 431 sq km
(166 sq miles)
Population: 260,000
Capital: Bridgetown

BERMUDA (UK)
Area: 54 sq km
(21 sq miles)
Population: 58,000
Capital: Hamilton

CAYMAN ISLANDS (UK)
Area: 259 sq km
(100 sq miles)
Population: 27,200
Capital: George Town

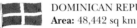
CUBA
Area: 114,524 sq km
(44,218 sq miles)
Population: 10,900,000
Capital: Havana

DOMINICA
Area: 751 sq km
(290 sq miles)
Population: 72,000
Capital: Roseau

DOMINICAN REPUBLIC
Area: 48,442 sq km
(18,704 sq miles)
Population: 7,600,000
Capital: Santo Domingo

GRENADA
Area: 344 sq km
(133 sq miles)
Population: 91,000
Capital: Saint George's

GUADELOUPE (Fr)
Area: 1,779 sq km
(687 sq miles)
Population: 400,000
Capital: Basse-Terre

HAITI
Area: 27,750 sq km
(10,714 sq miles)
Population: 6,900,000
Capital: Port-au-Prince

JAMAICA
Area: 10,991 sq km
(4,244 sq miles)
Population: 2,500,000
Capital: Kingston

MARTINIQUE (Fr)
Area: 1,101 sq km
(425 sq miles)
Population: 400,000
Capital: Fort-de-France

MONTSERRAT (UK)
Area: 101 sq km
(38 sq miles)
Population: 11,852
Capital: Plymouth

NETHERLANDS ANTILLES (Neth)
Area: 992 sq km (385 sq miles)
Population: 194,000
Capital: Willemstad

PUERTO RICO (US)
Area: 8,897 sq km
(3,435 sq miles)
Population: 3,600,000
Capital: San Juan

ST. KITTS AND NEVIS
Area: 269 sq km (104 sq miles)
Population: 42,000
Capital: Basseterre

ST. LUCIA
Area: 616 sq km
(238 sq miles)
Population: 156,000
Capital: Castries

ST. VINCENT AND THE GRENADINES
Area: 388 sq km (150 sq miles)
Population: 109,000
Capital: Kingstown

TRINIDAD AND TOBAGO
Area: 5,128 sq km (1,980 sq miles)
Population: 1,300,000
Capital: Port-of-Spain

TURKS AND CAICOS ISLANDS (UK)
Area: 500 sq km (193 sq miles)
Population: 12,350
Capital: Cockburn Town

VIRGIN ISLANDS (US)
Area: 352 sq km
(136 sq miles)
Population: 101,809
Capital: Charlotte Amalie

VIRGIN ISLANDS, BRITISH (UK)
Area: 153 sq km (59 sq miles)
Population: 16,644
Capital: Road Town

0 6 miles
0 10 km

UNITED STATES

BERMUDA (UK)

MARTINIQUE
Martinique is the largest of the Windward Islands in the eastern Caribbean. It is a volcanic island, the highest point being Mont Pelée (right) which is 1,397 m (4,583 ft) high; it erupted in 1902, killing about 30,000 people. The island climate is warm; bananas are the chief crop.

FLORIDA

THE BAHAMAS

 Nassau

STRAITS OF FLORIDA

Tropic of Cancer

Havana

CUBA

Santa Clara

Camagüey

Santiago de Cuba

CAYMAN ISLANDS (UK)

GREATER ANTILLES

DOMINICAN REPUBLIC

Santiago

HAITI

Pico Duarte 3,175 m (10,417 ft)

Port-au-Prince

Santo Domingo

CARIBBEAN SEA

TURKS AND CAICOS ISLANDS (UK)

BRITISH VIRGIN ISLANDS (UK)

San Juan

PUERTO RICO (US)

VIRGIN ISLANDS (US)

ST. KITTS AND NEVIS

MONTSERRAT (UK)

ANGUILLA (UK)

ANTIGUA AND BARBUDA

GUADELOUPE (FRANCE)

DOMINICA

MARTINIQUE (FRANCE)

LESSER ANTILLES

ST. LUCIA

ST. VINCENT AND THE GRENADINES

BARBADOS

GRENADA

TRINIDAD AND TOBAGO

JAMAICA Kingston

0 200 miles
0 300 km

N
W E
S

ISLAND GROUPS
The larger islands of the Caribbean between Cuba and Puerto Rico are often called the Greater Antilles, to distinguish them from the Lesser Antilles to the east. The small islands from the Virgin Islands to Dominica are sometimes called the Leeward Islands; and the islands to the south (Martinique to Grenada), the Windward Islands.

NETHERLANDS ANTILLES (NETH)

ARUBA (NETH)

CARS

IF YOU COULD line up all the world's cars end to end, they would form a traffic jam stretching all the way to the moon; and the line is getting longer, because a new car is made every second. Most cars are family cars, used for trips to school, work, and shops, to see friends and take holidays. But there are also a number of special-purpose cars, including taxis, sports cars, police patrol cars, and ambulances.

Petrol or diesel engines power modern cars, just as they did the first cars of the 19th century. But the cars of today are very different from cars even 30 years ago. The latest cars have low, sleek shapes that are attractive and also reduce drag, or air resistance. Other features include powerful brakes for stopping quickly and electronic engine control systems that allow cars to travel faster and use less fuel.

HOW A CAR WORKS

In most cars, the engine is at the front and drives the back or front wheels (or all four wheels) through a series of shafts and gears. There are usually four or five different gears; they alter the speed at which the engine turns the wheels. In low gear, the wheels turn slowly and produce extra force for starting and climbing hills. In high gear, the wheels turn fast for travelling at speed.

The steering wheel turns the steering gear via a long shaft.

A car radiator is full of water. A pump keeps water flowing around the engine to keep it cool. As the car moves forward, cold air rushes through the radiator, cooling the water before its next circuit around the engine.

Turning the steering wheel inside the car turns a system of gears that point the front wheels towards the left or right.

Tread, or grooves on the tyres, improve traction (grip) in the rain.

This car has a manual gearbox, which means the driver uses the gear lever to change gear. In other cars, gear changes are automatic.

The exhaust pipe carries waste gases from the engine safely out behind the car. Some cars have special filters, called catalytic converters, fitted to the exhaust system. These filters remove poisonous gases that damage the environment.

Suspension springs and shock absorbers soften a bumpy ride for the passengers and keep the wheels firmly on the ground as the car travels over uneven surfaces.

Pressing on the brake pedal pushes a special liquid down tubes, which in turn push on pistons at each wheel. These pistons squeeze the brake pads against steel discs or drums attached to the wheels, slowing down the wheels and stopping the car.

TYPES OF CARS

Cars have numerous uses, and there are many different kinds of cars available to suit almost any task. Most family cars combine a large interior with speed and fuel economy. However, for other, more specialized vehicles, speed, luxury, or power may be the most important design feature.

CRASH PROTECTION

Driver and passengers are cocooned in a strong steel cage to protect them in a crash. But the rest of the car is designed to crumple easily and absorb some of the impact. Wearing seat belts can protect car passengers from injury in a crash.

SPORTS CAR

With its large engine, sleek design, and usually seating for only two people, a sports car is designed purely for speed. Some can travel at about 300 km/h (190 mph).

LUXURY CAR

Large, carefully crafted cars such as the world-famous Rolls-Royce are among the most beautiful and expensive automobiles in the world.

OFF-ROAD VEHICLE

Rugged vehicles built specially for driving across country have powerful engines, four-wheel drive, and heavy ridged tyres for extra grip.

HISTORY OF THE CAR

People laughed at the first rickety "horseless carriages" of the 1880s. But rapid technical progress soon made it clear that cars were here to stay. In 1903, cars could already reach speeds of more than 110 km/h (70 mph). But they were expensive and often broke down. Since then cars have become steadily cheaper and more reliable. Now they are everyday transport for millions of people throughout the world.

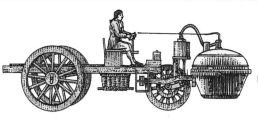

NICOLAS CUGNOT

The first road vehicles were powered by steam. In 1769, Nicolas Cugnot, a French soldier, built a steam carriage for dragging cannon. It travelled about 5 km/h (3 mph) and had to stop about every 10 minutes to build up steam.

DAIMLER AND BENZ

In the 1880s, German engineers Karl Benz and Gottlieb Daimler worked independently to produce the first petrol engine. In 1885, Karl Benz built his flimsy motorized tricycle (left), the first petrol-powered car.

PANHARD AND LEVASSOR

In the 1890s, two Frenchmen, René Panhard and Emile Levassor, built the first car with the engine in the front, the arrangement found in most cars to this day.

The production line for the Ford Model T

FORD MODEL T

Early cars were handmade and cost so much money that only the rich could afford them. In 1908, Henry Ford opened a factory to produce large numbers of the Model T (above). This was the first car cheap enough to be purchased by ordinary people.

Rear airfoil

Wide tyres, called slicks, are smooth to minimize rolling resistance, but wide to give a good grip on the track.

Powerful disc brakes can slow the car from 290 km/h to 65 km/h (180 mph to 40 mph) in less than three seconds.

The light aluminium body shell is carefully shaped to keep drag to a minimum.

The body frame is made from ultralight carbon-fibrecomposites.

NEW DESIGNS

Prototypes (test models) of new cars are packed with electronics and computers that can do anything from parking the car automatically to finding the best route through town. Many parts of these cars are made from plastics and other new materials; some new engine designs contain ceramic components instead of metal ones.

Enormously powerful engine with 8 or 10 cylinders drives the car along at speeds up to about 400 km/h (250 mph).

A computer continually adjusts the suspension to make sure the wheels do not bounce up from the track.

Aerofoils at the front and back work like upside-down airplane wings. Air rushing over them pushes the car firmly onto the track, which improves traction.

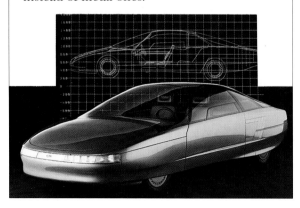

RACING CAR

Grand Prix racing cars are designed for speed alone, so they are built very differently from road cars. They have big, powerful engines and are made of special light materials. Their ultra-low shape allows them to slice through the air easily so they can travel as fast as possible. Indeed, the driver has to lie almost flat to fit in.

Find out more
BUSES
ENGINES
POLLUTION
ROADS AND MOTORWAYS
TRANSPORT, history of
TRUCKS
WHEELS

CARTOONS

TUMBLING AND SPINNING

on the TV screen, cartoon characters make impossible feats look easy. But the process of creating a cartoon is slow and requires great patience. An artist must make 12 drawings of the figure to produce just one second of movement. This kind of film, called an animated cartoon, first appeared on the cinema screen about 100 years ago. But it was the American Walt Disney who made cartoons famous. In 1928 Disney created the immortal Mickey Mouse and in 1937 produced his first feature-length film, *Snow White and the Seven Dwarfs*. An animated film is just one example of a cartoon. Originally the word meant the paper pattern an artist made for a painting; today a cartoon usually means a funny drawing. Political cartoons criticize politicians and other public figures, and the imaginary characters in comic strip cartoons help us laugh at ourselves when life gets us down.

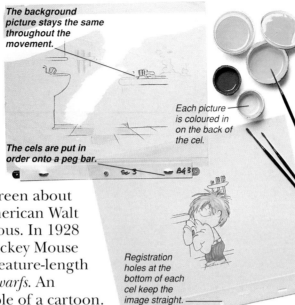

The background picture stays the same throughout the movement.

The cels are put in order onto a peg bar.

Each picture is coloured in on the back of the cel.

Registration holes at the bottom of each cel keep the image straight.

CARTOON FILM

Nine separate drawings follow each other rapidly to create a smooth-flowing sequence of a boy pulling his sweater over his head.

ANIMATION

To make an animated film, artists draw each stage of every movement on clear plastic pages called cels. The background is painted on a separate cel, and shows through the clear cels. Photographing the cels in the correct sequence makes the figures move. Artists may produce a million drawings for one feature-length film.

HISTORICAL CARTOONS

Cartoons can help politicians attack their opponents. Daumier, a 19th-century French artist, was a harsh critic of the French government. In this cartoon Daumier balances a figure representing Europe on the tip of a bayonet, to show how unstable European politics had become.

© 1987 United Feature Syndicate, Inc.

4-13

COMIC STRIP

The comic strip tells a story in a series of pictures. Sometimes the meaning is clear from the pictures alone; sometimes speech balloons put words in the characters' mouths. Characters such as Superman and Snoopy (above) have amused generations of children, and many adults follow their adventures.

© Alexander Wolf

To suggest world peace, the cartoonist drew the world as the egg of a dove, a bird that symbolizes peace.

POLITICAL CARTOONS

Political cartoons have a serious purpose. They can be funny or savage, but their aim is to make brief, visual comments on political events. Cartoonists often show their disapproval of a famous person using exaggerated portraits called caricatures.

Find out more
DRAWING
FILMS
MAGAZINES
NEWSPAPERS

CASTLES

THE MASSIVE WALLS AND TOWERS of a castle were designed to make it impossible for enemy soldiers to destroy it. Inside was a whole world in miniature – lords and ladies, government officials, soldiers, servants, animals, gardens, treasure stores, and dungeons where prisoners could be tortured. The best site for a castle was on a hill surrounded by water. If there were no natural features, the builders made an artificial hill or dug a deep ditch and filled it with water to make a moat. A well-built castle with a good military commander in charge could withstand an enemy siege for many months. Most castles were built between the 9th century and the 16th century, when many countries were almost constantly at war. Early castles were small and made of wood; the later stone buildings housed town-sized populations, and many are still standing today. The invention of gunpowder at the end of the 13th century made castles hard to defend. As times grew more peaceful, kings and lords moved into comfortable country houses.

LOOPHOLES
Archers fired through loopholes – narrow slits in the walls which were wider on the inside to make aiming easier. The inner walls were often higher than the outer walls, so archers could fire at the attackers over the heads of their own soldiers.

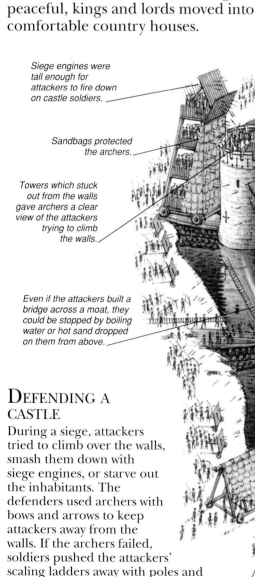

Siege engines were tall enough for attackers to fire down on castle soldiers.

Sandbags protected the archers.

Towers which stuck out from the walls gave archers a clear view of the attackers trying to climb the walls.

Even if the attackers built a bridge across a moat, they could be stopped by boiling water or hot sand dropped on them from above.

DEFENDING A CASTLE

During a siege, attackers tried to climb over the walls, smash them down with siege engines, or starve out the inhabitants. The defenders used archers with bows and arrows to keep attackers away from the walls. If the archers failed, soldiers pushed the attackers' scaling ladders away with poles and poured tubs full of boiling water or hot sand onto the enemy below. Deep moats or solid rock foundations stopped the attackers from digging under the walls.

Attackers used a battering ram to break down drawbridge.

Deep moats surrounded castle walls.

HOW CASTLES DEVELOPED

International wars, especially the Crusades in the Middle East, led to bigger armies, more powerful weapons, and stronger, more sophisticated defences. These wars speeded up castle building.

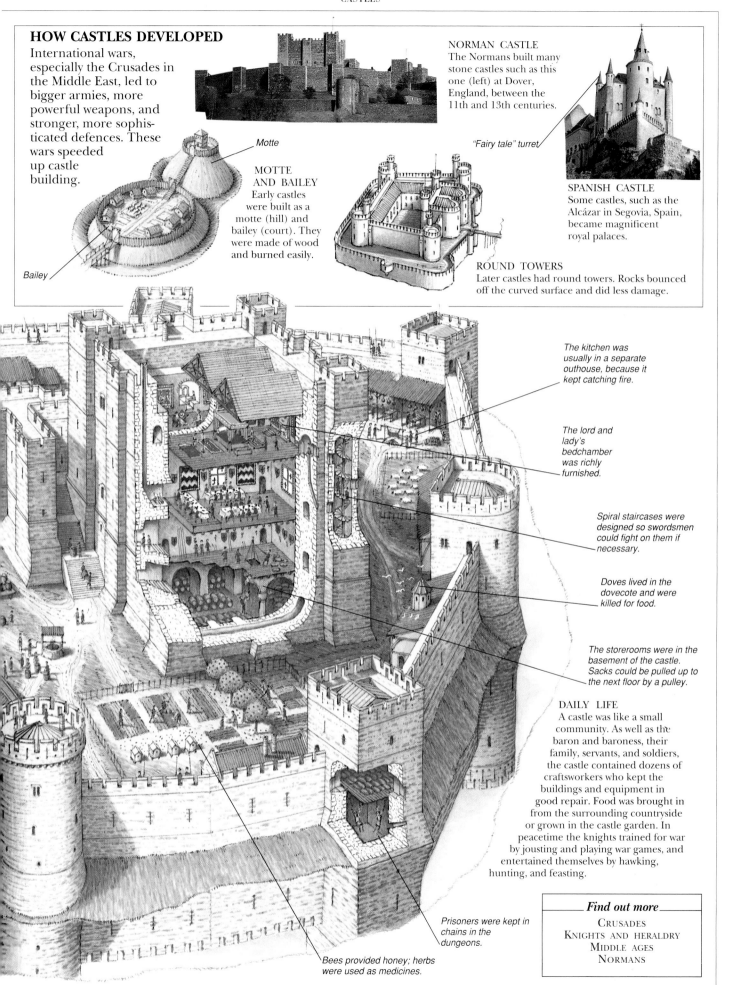

Motte

Bailey

MOTTE AND BAILEY
Early castles were built as a motte (hill) and bailey (court). They were made of wood and burned easily.

NORMAN CASTLE
The Normans built many stone castles such as this one (left) at Dover, England, between the 11th and 13th centuries.

"Fairy tale" turret

SPANISH CASTLE
Some castles, such as the Alcázar in Segovia, Spain, became magnificent royal palaces.

ROUND TOWERS
Later castles had round towers. Rocks bounced off the curved surface and did less damage.

The kitchen was usually in a separate outhouse, because it kept catching fire.

The lord and lady's bedchamber was richly furnished.

Spiral staircases were designed so swordsmen could fight on them if necessary.

Doves lived in the dovecote and were killed for food.

The storerooms were in the basement of the castle. Sacks could be pulled up to the next floor by a pulley.

DAILY LIFE
A castle was like a small community. As well as the baron and baroness, their family, servants, and soldiers, the castle contained dozens of craftsworkers who kept the buildings and equipment in good repair. Food was brought in from the surrounding countryside or grown in the castle garden. In peacetime the knights trained for war by jousting and playing war games, and entertained themselves by hawking, hunting, and feasting.

Prisoners were kept in chains in the dungeons.

Bees provided honey; herbs were used as medicines.

Find out more
CRUSADES
KNIGHTS AND HERALDRY
MIDDLE AGES
NORMANS

CATS

WHEN YOU WATCH a cat stalking a bird, it is easy to see how cats are related to lions and tigers. All cats are excellent hunters. They have acute senses and sharp teeth and claws, and they are strong and agile. Cats do most of their hunting at night, and have evolved excellent eyesight in dim conditions. Even a domestic cat, or house cat, could survive in the wild by catching mice, small birds, insects, and other creatures. Many exotic pedigree (purebred) cats, however, might not be able to live for long in the wild, since most are used to a pampered lifestyle indoors.

The ancestor of our domestic cats is a wild tabby-coloured cat that has existed for about one million years – the African wild cat. This small wild cat spread through Africa, Asia, and Europe, until it was gradually tamed by people in Africa, where it helped protect food stores from rats and mice. Since then, domestic cats have been bred by people into many different types, from striped tabbies and Persian longhairs to the tailless Manx cat. Three thousand years ago, domestic cats were a common sight in Egypt, where they were held in great esteem. Today there are more than 500 million domestic cats around the world.

WILD CATS
The African wild cat looks similar to the domestic tabby cat, but it has a heavier build and a larger head. African wild cats have black stripes on their legs and tail.

AGILITY
Cats have exceptional balance and often climb trees, walls, and fences when they are hunting or exploring. Cats also have extremely quick reflexes in case of a fall. As a cat drops, the balance organs inside its ears tell it at once which way is up. The cat rights its head, followed by its body, then lands safely on all four paws.

Cat suddenly falls.

Head twists around first.

BLACK CATS
For thousands of years, black cats have been associated with magic and witchcraft. They are still believed by some people to bring both good and bad luck.

Long flexible tail helps cat balance on narrow ledges.

Large ears can pick up faint sounds.

Touch-sensitive whiskers for feeling in the dark

Claws retracted in sheaths to keep them sharp

Pupils open wide in dim light to let in more light.

Pupils are narrow in bright light to let in less light.

EYES
In dim conditions, a cat's pupils open wide to let the maximum amount of light into the eye. The tapetum, a mirror-like layer inside the eye, reflects the light at the back of the eye. This is why a cat's eyes shine in the dark.

Body follows head around.

Legs stretch out for landing.

DOMESTIC CAT

There are more than 100 official breeds of domestic cat, and many more unofficial breeds. Cat experts are continually creating new varieties by selective breeding. The Bombay cat (left) is a new breed which was developed in the United States in the 1970s. It was bred by mating a Burmese with an American Black Shorthair. Although the Bombay has very short, dense hair, it still shows all the main features of a typical cat.

KITTENS

Young cats are called kittens. They spend hours chasing their tails, springing on each other, and having mock fights. Their play has a serious purpose. It helps them develop hunting skills, quick reactions, and strength and suppleness for those times when they have to fend for themselves.

GROOMING
Cats are famous for their cleanliness. Every day they spend at least an hour washing their fur with saliva and licking it with their rough-surfaced tongues. This makes the fur smooth and glossy. It also helps keep body heat in, removes pests, and stimulates the skin's blood flow.

SLEEPING
The average cat sleeps 16 hours each day, usually in short intervals called cat naps. A cat's body is designed for quick bursts of action, with much rest between.

BEHAVIOUR

Domestic cats resemble their wild ancestors in several ways. Although most domestic cats do not have to catch their own food, they show many signs of hunting behaviour such as being particularly active at dawn and dusk, and stalking and pouncing on pretend prey. Much of this behaviour is instinctive, or inborn, and does not have to be learned. A cat that is brought up away from all other cats still behaves in this way.

HUNTING
A cat's sensitive nose easily picks up the scent of a mouse. As the cat nears its victim, its eyes and ears also come into use. After stalking up silently and slowly, the cat leaps forward with bared claws and grabs the prey, often biting it on the back of the head to break its neck.

LEAPING
Long, supple legs, with strong muscles and flexible joints, give cats great jumping ability. A cat usually looks before it leaps, moving its head from side to side so that it can judge the distance accurately. If the jump is too big, the cat may try to find another route.

During lactation (milk-feeding), the kittens suckle milk from teats on their mother's abdomen.

The mother cat guards her young until they are able to fend for themselves.

HAIRLESS CAT
The sphynx breed of cat was developed in the 1960s from a kitten that was born without fur. The sphynx has bare skin except for a few fine, dark, downy hairs on its face, paws, and tail tip. It is unlikely that a hairless cat such as this one could survive in the wild for long.

BREEDING

Female cats, or queens, are pregnant for about nine weeks. They give birth to between one and 10 kittens, but two to five kittens is average. A family of young kittens is called a litter. Newborn kittens are helpless. Their eyes are closed for the first week or more, and they do not begin to crawl for about two weeks. They feed on their mother's milk at first. After about eight weeks they gradually stop taking milk and begin to eat solid foods. This process is called weaning. About four weeks later, the mother cat is ready to mate again.

Ancient Egyptians kept domestic cats to guard grain stores. Cats became so celebrated that some were worshipped as gods, and statues such as the one shown here were made.

Find out more

ANIMAL SENSES
ANIMALS
EGYPT, ANCIENT
LIONS, TIGERS,
and other big cats
MAMMALS

CAVES

BENEATH THE SURFACE of the Earth lies a secret world. Caves run through the rock, opening out into huge chambers decorated with slender stone columns. Underground rivers wind through deep passages, and waterfalls crash down on hidden lakes. Caves such as these are many thousands of years old; they were formed as water slowly dissolved limestone rocks. But not all caves are underground. Sea cliffs contain caves that have been eroded by the waves. Caves also develop inside glaciers and within the solidified lava around volcanoes.

Caves are damp, dark places. Some are only large enough to contain one person; others, such as the network of caves in Mammoth Cave National Park, United States, stretch for hundreds of kilometres. One of the world's deepest caves, in France, lies almost 1.6 km (1 mile) below the ground. Prehistoric peoples used caves for shelter. Caves at Lascaux, France, contain wall paintings and ancient tools that are perhaps 20,000 years old. Even today there are still a few cave dwellers in parts of Africa and Asia.

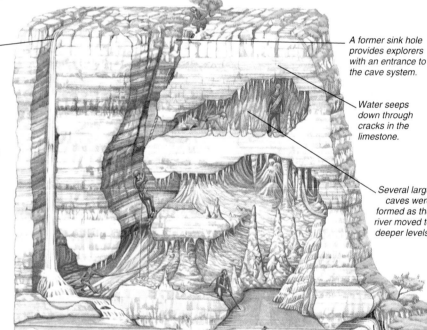

Stalactites and stalagmites take thousands of years to grow.

STALACTITES
Slender stalactites often hang from a cave roof. Drops of water seeping down from above dissolve a white mineral called calcite from the rock. As the water dries, small amounts of calcite are left behind. These build up to form stalactites. This process is usually very slow; stalactites grow only about 2.5 cm (1 in) in 500 years.

Water drop falls from tip of stalactite.

STALAGMITES
Water dripping from the roof or from a stalactite falls to the cave floor, leaving layers of calcite on the floor. In this way a pillar called a stalagmite slowly builds upwards.

HOW CAVES FORM
Large cave systems lie beneath the ground in regions made of limestone rock. For thousands of years, rainwater, which is naturally acidic, dissolved away the limestone. Small cracks formed, slowly widening to create deep holes which became underground caves and rivers as water continued to erode the rock.

A stream plunges down a deep hole, called a sink hole or swallow hole, to feed an underground river.

A former sink hole provides explorers with an entrance to the cave system.

Water seeps down through cracks in the limestone.

Several large caves were formed as the river moved to deeper levels.

A stalactite and stalagmite may grow and meet to form a column from floor to roof.

Creatures adapted to the dark, such as blind fish and bats, live in the depths of the cave.

In search of a new cave, a cave diver attempts to swim under a barrier in the river. Cave diving is a very dangerous sport.

The river emerges after flowing underground.

Potholers marvel at the fascinating rock formations around an underground lake at the mouth of a cave in France.

POTHOLING
The sport of exploring caves is called potholing. Clambering about in caves is a dirty and often wet pastime, so potholers wear tough clothing. Other important equipment includes nylon ropes, a helmet with a light, and ladders made of steel cables. Potholers work in teams and may stay in a cave for several days. Potholing can be dangerous; rain can cause flooding, and potholers can be trapped by sudden rockfalls.

Find out more
BATS
GEOLOGY
PREHISTORIC PEOPLES
ROCKS AND MINERALS
VOLCANOES

CELTS

TWO THOUSAND YEARS AGO, much of western Europe was inhabited by a fierce, proud, artistic people known as the Celts. They were skilled warriors, farmers, and metalworkers. For several hundred years their art and culture dominated northwest Europe. All Celts shared a similar way of life, but they were not a single group of people. They included many different tribes such as the Atrebates of southern Britain and the Parisii of northern France. Most Celts lived in villages or hill forts, some of which developed into small towns. But the Celts never formed a unified nation. Between 3000 B.C. and A.D. 100 they were absorbed into the Roman Empire. Today Celtic-speaking people can still be found in parts of Britain, Ireland, and France.

BOUDICCA
In A.D. 61 Boudicca (or Boadicea), queen of the Iceni, a Celtic tribe in Britain, led a massive revolt against Roman oppression. The Britons, however, were no match for the well-organized Romans, and the revolt was suppressed.

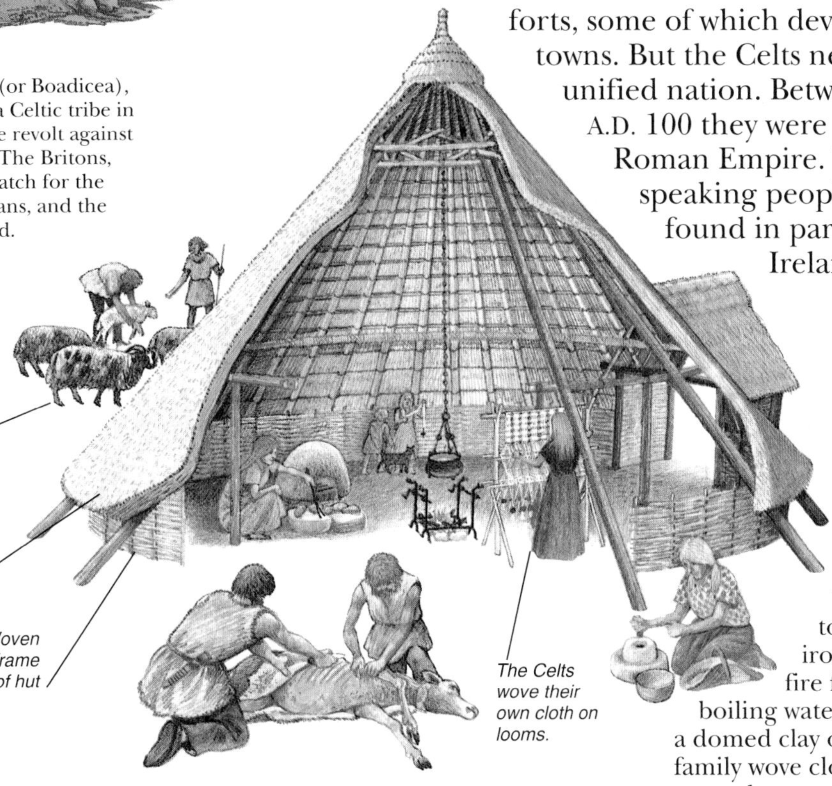

Livestock were kept for food and dairy produce.

Huts were covered in clay and thatch to protect them from bad weather.

Woven wooden frame of hut

The Celts wove their own cloth on looms.

THE HOME
Celtic families lived together in one large hut. Some huts were made of stone; others of wattle and daub – wood-framed huts covered in clay to make a hard wall. Thatch was often used to keep the rain out. An iron caldron hung over a fire for cooking meat or boiling water. Bread was cooked in a domed clay oven. Members of the family wove cloth, worked as farmers, or made pots.

DRUIDS
Druids, a very important group in Celtic society, were priests who led religious ceremonies, acted as judges and advisers, and were responsible for teaching the sons of chiefs. Druidism involved the worship of many gods. Oak trees and mistletoe were also sacred to Druids.

METALWORKING
The Celts worked with many different metals including iron, bronze, copper, gold, and silver. Farm tools, weapons, shields, chariots, and helmets were made from metal, and many were beautifully decorated with distinctive plants and animals, as shown on the border around this page.

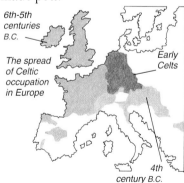

6th-5th centuries B.C.

The spread of Celtic occupation in Europe

Early Celts

4th century B.C.

CELTIC LANDS
The earliest Celts lived in central Europe, in what is now southern Germany. By about 500 B.C. Celts had spread out to cover much of Europe, from Ireland to the Black Sea.

Find out more

IRON AGE

CENTIPEDES
AND MILLIPEDES

WITH MORE LEGS than most other creatures, the centipede is a speedy predator. This active hunter runs swiftly after insects and other small prey, and sometimes chases millipedes, too. Centipedes and their slower-moving relatives, the millipedes, belong to the larger animal group called arthropods, which means "jointed feet". They may have as many as 180 pairs of legs – centipedes have one pair on each body segment; millipedes have two pairs on each segment. There are about 3,000 kinds of centipedes and 10,000 kinds of millipedes. Both kinds of creatures are found in dark, moist woodland areas, in soil, in leaf litter, and in rotten wood. Most centipedes lay their eggs in the soil, leaving the young to hatch and fend for themselves. Millipedes lay eggs in batches of between 30 and 100. Some millipedes leave the eggs in the soil; others make a nest from hardened excrement or spin a silk cocoon for protection. Millipedes are mainly plant eaters. They are important recyclers of dead leaves and wood, chewing them up and returning the nutrients to the soil in their droppings.

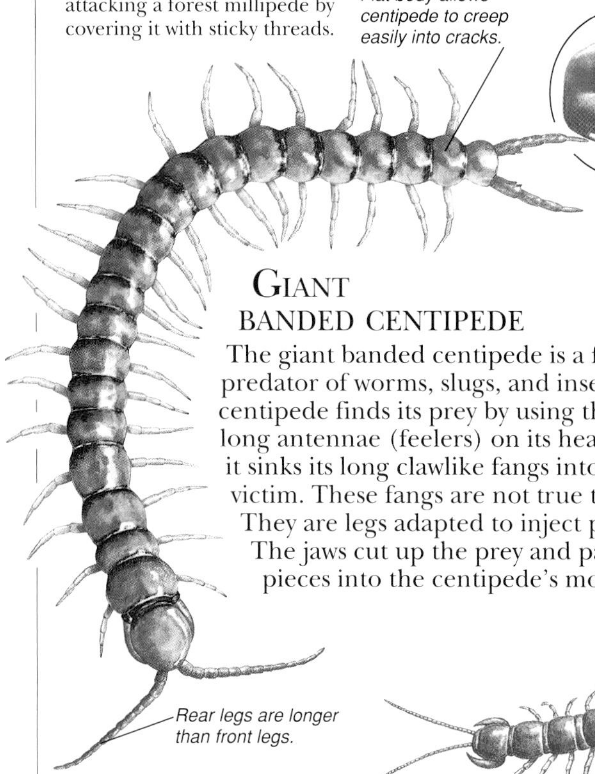

VELVET WORM
The wormlike peripatus, or velvet worm, has many legs and is similar in shape to centipedes and millipedes. This picture shows a peripatus attacking a forest millipede by covering it with sticky threads.

Flat body allows centipede to creep easily into cracks.

Antennae (feelers) sense the movement and scent of prey.

GIANT BANDED CENTIPEDE
The giant banded centipede is a fearsome predator of worms, slugs, and insects. A centipede finds its prey by using the two long antennae (feelers) on its head. Then it sinks its long clawlike fangs into the victim. These fangs are not true teeth. They are legs adapted to inject poison. The jaws cut up the prey and pass the pieces into the centipede's mouth.

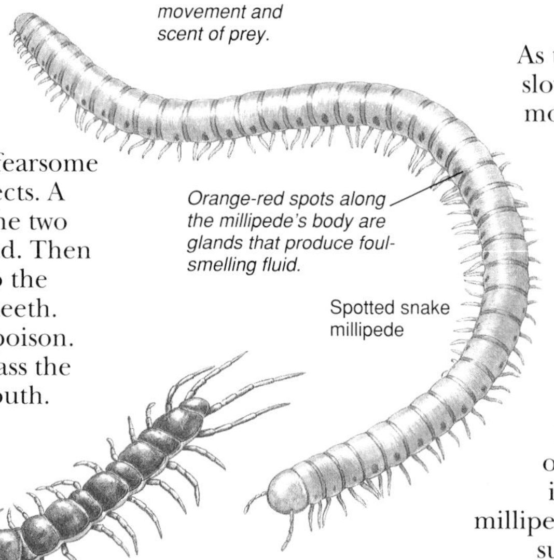

Orange-red spots along the millipede's body are glands that produce foul-smelling fluid.

Spotted snake millipede

Rear legs are longer than front legs.

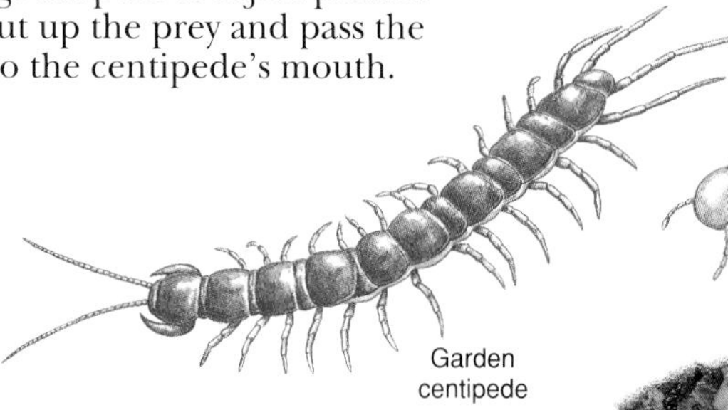

Garden centipede

GARDEN CENTIPEDE
The common garden centipede attacks any animal of its own size, including other centipedes. Garden centipedes have 15 pairs of legs and are found mainly in damp places under logs, stones, bark, and leaves.

POISONOUS CENTIPEDE
Some centipedes are huge, such as the long scolopendra centipedes of Africa, Asia, and the Americas. They grow to about 30 cm (12 in) long. These giant centipedes sometimes wander into houses, where they feed on household pests. Their poisonous bite can be dangerous, so these centipedes are best avoided.

MILLIPEDE
As the millipede pushes its way slowly through the soil, its legs move in waves, 10 to 20 legs at a time. The millipede's mouthparts are specialized for scraping and chewing plant material. Most millipedes feed on decomposing plant matter; others eat plant roots and are pests on farm crops. A few millipedes live in rocky habitats and caves and prey on animals. Most millipedes, including this spotted snake millipede, produce a foul-smelling substance to deter predators.

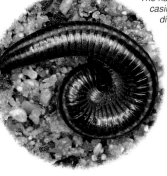

The hard exoskeleton, or outer casing, on a millipede's body is divided into many segments. These segments overlap and allow the millipede to curl its body up in self-defence when threatened.

These creatures are well named – centipede means "a hundred legs", and millipede means "a thousand legs".

Millipede's legs move together in waves when it is walking.

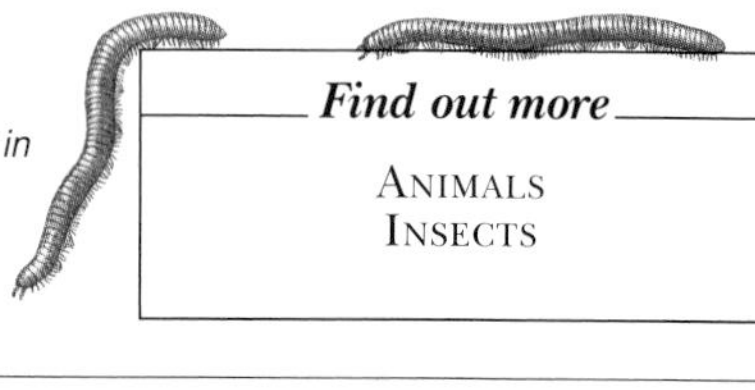

Find out more
ANIMALS
INSECTS

CENTRAL AMERICA

LIKE LINKS IN A CHAIN, the seven Central American countries seem to tie together the continents of North and South America. The climate is hot and steamy; trees, plants, and jungle animals thrive around the marshy coasts and on the high mountains. More than 2,500 years ago Native Americans made Central America their home. Some of the people who live there today are direct descendants of these early inhabitants. Many, though, are mestizos: people with both Native Americans and European ancestors. European people first came to Central America in about 1500, and the Spanish empire ruled the area for more than three centuries. By 1823 most of the countries had gained independence, but this did not bring peace and prosperity to their people. Most Central Americans are still very poor and have no land. There are too few jobs and not enough food. Governments in the region have been unable to solve these problems, and wars and revolutions are common.

Central America forms an isthmus, or narrow land bridge, between Mexico to the north and Colombia to the south.

There are many active volcanoes in Central America. The largest is Tajumulco in Guatemala.

The soil in the valleys is very fertile.

Jungle covers the eastern coastal plain and many mountains.

MAYAS

Between A.D. 250 and 900 Native Americans people called Mayas lived in Central America, where they created a vast empire. They built great cities at Palenque and Tikal (in present-day Mexico and Guatemala) and constructed huge stone temples and palaces in the shape of pyramids. To feed the people in the cities, the Mayas became skilled at cultivating food. They used clever farming methods to grow plentiful crops on the small areas of suitable land.

PEOPLE

More than 31 million people live in Central America, mostly in the countryside and in small towns. The biggest city is Guatemala City, which has a population of 2 million. Most people speak either Spanish or one of the local Native American languages. In Belize, many people speak English. Many Central Americans are Christians, and the Roman Catholic Church is an important influence in everyday life and culture.

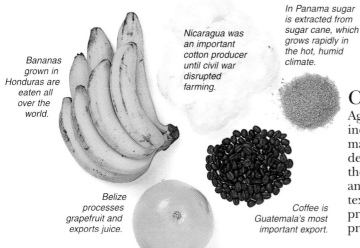

EDUCATION

Civil wars and other armed conflicts have disrupted normal life in Central America. One result is that many people are illiterate, but in Nicaragua there is a major campaign to teach people to read.

Bananas grown in Honduras are eaten all over the world.

Nicaragua was an important cotton producer until civil war disrupted farming.

In Panama sugar is extracted from sugar cane, which grows rapidly in the hot, humid climate.

Belize processes grapefruit and exports juice.

Coffee is Guatemala's most important export.

CROPS

Agriculture is the major industry in Central America; many of the countries depend on only one crop for their income. Both Belize and El Salvador also make textiles and light industrial products. Guatemala produces oil for export.

Find out more
AZTECS
CARIBBEAN
CONQUISTADORS
MEXICO

CENTRAL AMERICA

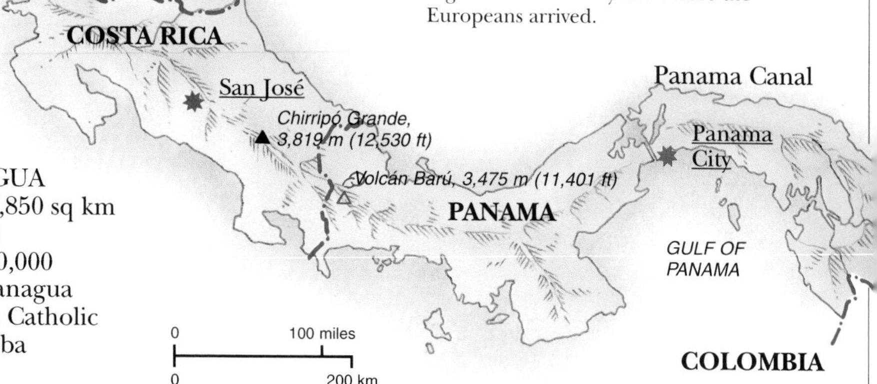

MEXICO

Tikal 🏛

R. Belize

• Belmopan

BELIZE

GULF OF
HONDURAS

STATISTICS
Area: 521,367 sq km (201,300 sq miles)
Population: 31,300,000
Number of independent countries: 7
Languages: Spanish, English, Local
Main occupation: Agriculture

GUATEMALA

Lake Izabal

R. Motagua

△ Volcán
Tajumulco,
4,220 m
(13,845 ft)

• San Pedro Sula

R. Ulúa

R. Patuca

HONDURAS

EL SALVADOR

Tegucigalpa

San Salvador

R. Lempa

Cordillera Isabelia

Rio Grande

NICARAGUA

N
W   E
S

Lake Managua

PACIFIC
OCEAN

Managua

Lake Nicaragua

R. San Juan

CARIBBEAN
SEA

GUATEMALA
Guatemala is the most heavily populated
country in Central America. Many of its
people, such as the woman shown here, are
of Native American origin, descendants of the
Mayas whose civilization flourished in the
region hundreds of years before the
Europeans arrived.

Panama Canal

COSTA RICA

San José

Chirripó Grande,
▲ 3,819 m (12,530 ft)

Volcán Barú, 3,475 m (11,401 ft)
△

Panama
City

PANAMA

GULF OF
PANAMA

COLOMBIA

BELIZE
Area: 22,965 sq km
(8,867 sq miles)
Population: 200,000
Capital: Belmopan
Religion: Roman Catholic
Currency: Belizean dollar

COSTA RICA
Area: 51,100 sq km
(19,730 sq miles)
Population: 3,300,000
Capital: San José
Religion: Roman Catholic
Currency: Colón

EL SALVADOR
Area: 21,393 sq km
(8,260 sq miles)
Population: 5,500,000
Capital: San Salvador
Religion: Roman Catholic
Currency: Colón

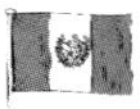

GUATEMALA
Area: 108,889 sq km
(42,042 sq miles)
Population: 10,000,000
Capital: Guatemala City
Religion: Roman Catholic
Currency: Quetzal

HONDURAS
Area: 112,088 sq km
(43,277 sq miles)
Population: 5,600,000
Capital: Tegucigalpa
Religion: Roman Catholic
Currency: Lempira

NICARAGUA
Area: 127,850 sq km
(49,363 sq miles)
Population: 4,100,000
Capital: Managua
Religion: Roman Catholic
Currency: Córdoba

PANAMA
Area: 77,082 sq km
(29,761 sq miles)
Population: 2,600,000
Capital: Panama City
Religion: Roman Catholic
Currency: Balboa

0   100 miles
0   200 km

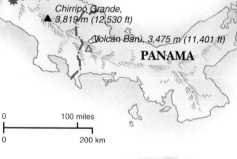

PACIFIC COASTAL STRIP
Half the population of Central
America lives on the western slopes,
which are higher and drier than the
lowlands that border the Caribbean
coast. Most people in the west work as
farmers, producing coffee, bananas,
sugar cane, and cotton.

COSTA RICA
More than half of Costa Rica's people live on a broad,
fertile plateau surrounded by volcanic ranges (above).
Small farms dot the area; coffee, corn, rice, and sugar
are grown on the hillsides. Unlike other Central
American countries, Costa Rica enjoys political stability.

🏛   △   ▲   ✴   •
Ancient   Volcano   Highest   Capital   City/
monument   mountain   city   town

CHARLEMAGNE

ELEVEN CENTURIES AGO one man ruled most of western Europe. Charlemagne could hardly read or write, yet he built up a vast empire. Charlemagne was a Frank, one of the peoples who had invaded the Roman Empire when it collapsed in the 5th century, and who then settled in northern France. He was a great warrior. When he became king in A.D.768, his territory was small, and threatened by its French neighbours. Charlemagne soon overcame them all and then invaded northern Italy. He fought the people of Hungary, and the Saxons in Germany. He also invaded Spain and stopped the Muslims who lived there from threatening the rest of Europe. Charlemagne's aim was not just to rule more countries; he wanted to convert the inhabitants to Christianity. To achieve this Charlemagne was ruthless with those who opposed him. However, Charlemagne was not an especially cruel ruler. He reformed the countries he conquered, and, perhaps because he was not an educated man, he encouraged learning and set up many schools. The pope, who was head of the Christian Church, rewarded Charlemagne by crowning him Emperor of the Romans in 800, for Charlemagne's European empire was the first to be formed since the fall of Rome. When he died 14 years later, Charlemagne was the most powerful ruler in Europe.

THRONE
Charlemagne was a very powerful ruler, but his marble throne was plain and undecorated. The throne was a copy of the one described in the Bible from which King Solomon ruled his kingdom of Israel. Charlemagne built a chapel in his palace to house his throne. The chapel survives today as part of Aachen cathedral, in Germany.

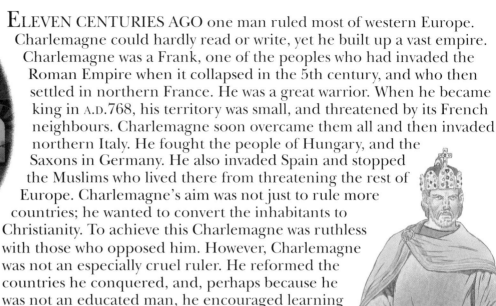

WHAT HE LOOKED LIKE
There are few known portraits of Charlemagne, but those that remain show a tall, bearded, blond-haired man.

CORONATION
Pope Leo III crowned Charlemagne Emperor of the Romans on Christmas Day in 800, at St. Peter's Basilica in Rome. Charlemagne became the first Roman emperor for more than three centuries. Although he accepted the title, he believed that it had little value.

HOLY ROMAN EMPIRE
Charlemagne's domain (coloured purple here) covered most of Europe. Though his empire was split up after his death, what remained later became known as the Holy Roman Empire (coloured green). The last emperor, Francis II, resigned the title in 1806. Some say he abolished the empire to stop Napoleon Bonaparte, emperor of France, from taking the title. Others say Napoleon ended it because he didn't want a rival emperor in Europe.

Holy Roman Empire

Charlemagne's empire

Part of both empires

ROYAL TOMB
Scenes from Charlemagne's life cover his tomb in Aachen cathedral. One panel shows his armies besieging the town of Pamplona in Spain. The tomb is richly decorated with gold, and set with precious stones.

Find out more

BARBARIANS
MIDDLE AGES
NAPOLEON BONAPARTE

CHEMISTRY

HAVE YOU EVER WONDERED why cooking changes raw, tough food into a tasty meal? Cooking is just one example of a chemical reaction that converts raw materials into new substances. Chemists use chemical reactions to make plastics, medicines, dyes, and many other materials that are important in everyday life. They also study what substances are made of and how they can be combined to make new materials. Chemicals are the raw materials used by a chemist. About 4 million different chemicals have been made by chemists; there are about 35,000 chemicals in common

Chemists use special flasks and jars to mix chemicals, together with equipment that is electronic and automated.

use. These chemicals can be made by combining simple substances called elements into more complicated substances called compounds. Early chemists thought that there were four elements: fire, water, air, and earth. Today we know there are 92 that occur in nature, and a few others that can be made in laboratories. The most common element in the universe is hydrogen, which is the main component of stars.

CHEMICAL REACTIONS
When different substances combine together to form new materials, a chemical reaction occurs. Some reactions need heat to start them off; others produce heat as the reaction proceeds.

Chlorine is a poisonous yellow-green gas.

Sodium is a soft, silvery metal.

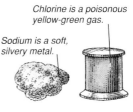

Sodium chloride is a non-poisonous white powder.

$$H_2O$$

Chemists use a shorthand to describe chemicals. This is the symbol for water which says that each water molecule contains two hydrogen atoms and one oxygen atom.

ELEMENTS AND COMPOUNDS
Elements are substances which are made of a single kind of atom. When different elements combine, their atoms join to produce molecules of a new substance, which is called a compound. For example, common salt is a compound called sodium chloride. It is made by combining the element sodium and the element chlorine. When the two elements combine, they form a compound which is entirely different from either of the elements used to produce it.

HISTORY OF CHEMISTRY
The Egyptians were the first chemists. The word *chemistry* comes from *Chem*, the name for Ancient Egypt. Modern chemistry began around 1790 when a Frenchman, Antoine Lavoisier, explained how chemical reactions work. In 1808 an English scientist, John Dalton, showed that substances were made from atoms. By 1871, a Russian teacher, Dimitri Mendeleyev, had produced the periodic table, which classifies elements according to their properties and is the cornerstone of chemistry.

ALCHEMY
Early chemistry, called alchemy, was a mixture of magic and guesswork. From about A.D. 300, alchemists tried to make gold from lead, mercury, and other cheap metals. They also tried to find an elixir, or preparation, to prolong life. Although the alchemists did not succeed in these aims, they found ways of separating substances and making them pure. They also discovered many new substances.

Find out more
ATOMS AND MOLECULES
EGYPT, ANCIENT
HEAT
PHYSICS
SCIENTISTS AND INVENTORS

CHINA

TO DESCRIBE CHINA you need to use enormous numbers. The country is vast, covering more than 9.5 million sq km (3.7 million square miles). China's written history stretches back 3,500 years – longer than any other nation's. 1,205 million people live there, and one fifth of the world's population is Chinese. In such a large country, there are many variations, including four major language families. The land, too, is tremendously varied. The east and southeast, where most people live, is green and fertile. Other parts of the country are barren deserts of sand and rock. Organizing and feeding the huge and varied Chinese population is a mammoth task. Since 1949 China has been ruled by a Communist government that has tried to provide adequate food, education, and health care to every part of the nation. During the late 1970s, Communist party moderates embraced economic reforms that lifted government controls and encouraged private enterprise. Consequently, China became the world's third-largest economy in the mid 1990s. China's human rights record, however, is still criticized because of political oppression at home and in Tibet.

China is the third largest country in the world. It is situated in eastern Asia between the Russian Federation to its north, and Southeast Asia and the Indian subcontinent to its south and west. The East China Sea lies to its east.

Private cars are almost unknown in China. The bicycle is the main method of transport for people and luggage.

Chinese farmers make use of every suitable piece of land, carving steps or terraces in the hillsides to grow rice and other crops.

Rice is grown in flooded fields called paddies.

FAMILY LIFE

The family is the most important institution in Chinese life. Children respect their parents and look after them in their old age. China's population is growing, and the government now rewards parents who limit their families to just one child.

AGRICULTURE AND LAND USE

Most Chinese people are crowded together in just 15 per cent of the total land area, mainly in river valleys in the east. One in five live in huge cities; the rest live in the countryside. There they grow rice and wheat and raise pigs and other livestock. Much of the rest of the country is mountainous and wild. The Takla Makan Desert in the east is dry and cold, and few people live there.

Tiananmen Square, Beijing

BEIJING

The capital city of China is Beijing, formerly Peking. Modern Beijing spreads out around the older central area. To the north and west are houses and Beijing University. The industrial area is to the east of the centre. At the heart lies Tiananmen (Gate of Heavenly Peace) Square. Here parades and celebrations take place on national holidays. In 1989, the government forcibly disbanded a pro-democracy student demonstration here, killing hundreds.

CHINA

Ancient monument | Volcano | Highest mountain | Capital city | City/town

STATISTICS

Area: 9,560,990 sq km (3,691,502 sq miles)
Population: 1,205,200,000
Capital: Beijing (Peking)
Languages: Mandarin and Cantonese Chinese, local languages and dialects
Religions: Buddhism, Confucianism, Taoism, Islam
Currency: Yuan
Main occupations: Agriculture, industry
Main exports: Chemicals, electrical goods, agricultural products, mineral fuels
Main imports: Machinery, grain, iron

HAN CHINESE
The Han Chinese people make up about 90 per cent of the population of China. Their ancestors may have come east from Turkestan, part of which is now in western China, and part in Central Asia and Afghanistan. However, it is possible that Han Chinese people descended from Mongolian tribes who moved south.

KAZAKHSTAN

Altai Mts

Ürümqi

Tien Shan Range

KYRGYZSTAN

R. Tarim

Turfan Depression

Pamirs

XINJIANG

Takla Makan Desert

(K2) Mount Godwin Austen

Kunlun Mts

QINGHAI

Administered by China but claimed by India

TIBET (XIZANG)

INDIA

Himalayas

R. Salween

R. Brahmaputra

Lhasa

NEPAL

Mount Everest, 8,848 m (29,028 ft)

BHUTAN

IN

Mount Everest, on the border between China and Nepal, is the highest mountain in the world.

SHANGHAI
The largest city in China, Shanghai (above) is one of the world's biggest seaports. For centuries China was closed to the west, but in 1842 the Treaty of Nanking, between China and Britain, opened the port to western trade. Since then Shanghai has been the leading commercial and industrial centre in China. Today, about half of China's foreign business passes through the city.

TAIWAN
Taiwan is ruled by the Chinese Nationalists who lost power in mainland China in 1949.
Area: 36,180 sq km (13,969 sq miles)
Population: 20,800,000
Capital: Taipei
Language: Chinese
Religions: Buddhism, Taoism, Christianity
Currency: Taiwan dollar

HONG KONG
Area: 1,071 sq km (413 sq miles)
Population: 5,800,000
Capital: Victoria
Languages: English, Cantonese Chinese
Religions: Buddhism, Christianity, Taoism
Currency: Hong Kong dollar

MACAO (PORTUGAL)
Area: 16 sq km (6 sq miles)
Population: 487,000
Capital: Macao
Languages: Portuguese, Cantonese Chinese
Religions: Buddhism, Christianity, Taoism
Currency: Pataca

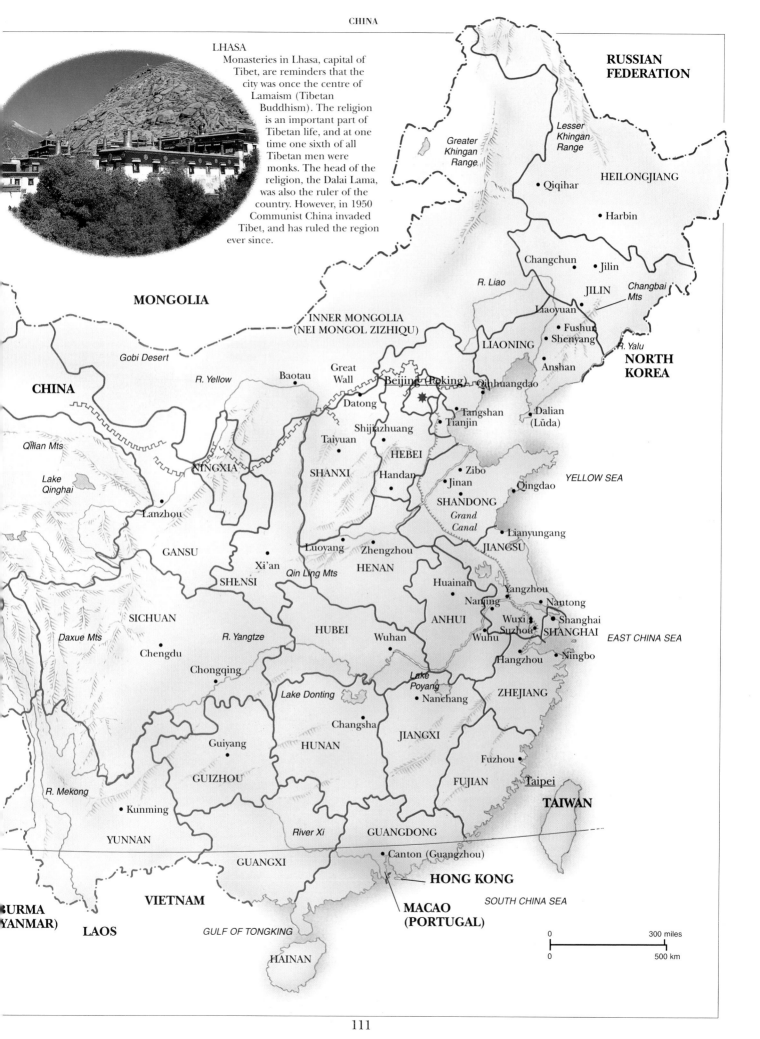

LHASA
Monasteries in Lhasa, capital of Tibet, are reminders that the city was once the centre of Lamaism (Tibetan Buddhism). The religion is an important part of Tibetan life, and at one time one sixth of all Tibetan men were monks. The head of the religion, the Dalai Lama, was also the ruler of the country. However, in 1950 Communist China invaded Tibet, and has ruled the region ever since.

RUSSIAN FEDERATION

Greater Khingan Range

Lesser Khingan Range

HEILONGJIANG

• Qiqihar

• Harbin

MONGOLIA

INNER MONGOLIA (NEI MONGOL ZIZHIQU)

Changchun

• Jilin

R. Liao

JILIN

Changbai Mts

Liaoyuan

• Fushun

LIAONING

Shenyang

NORTH KOREA

Anshan

R. Yalu

Gobi Desert

CHINA

Qilian Mts

R. Yellow

Baotau

Great Wall

Beijing (Peking)

Qinhuangdao

Datong

• Tangshan

Dalian (Lüda)

Taiyuan

Tianjin

Shijiazhuang

HEBEI

Lake Qinghai

NINGXIA

SHANXI

Handan

• Zibo

YELLOW SEA

• Jinan

Qingdao

SHANDONG

Lanzhou

Grand Canal

Luoyang

Zhengzhou

Lianyungang

GANSU

JIANGSU

Xi'an

HENAN

Huainan

Yangzhou

SHENSI

Qin Ling Mts

Nanjing

• Nantong

SICHUAN

HUBEI

Wuhan

ANHUI

Wuxi

Shanghai

Daxue Mts

R. Yangtze

Wuhu

Suzhou

SHANGHAI

EAST CHINA SEA

• Chengdu

Hangzhou

• Ningbo

Chongqing

Lake Poyang

ZHEJIANG

Lake Donting

• Nanchang

Changsha

JIANGXI

Guiyang

HUNAN

Fuzhou

GUIZHOU

FUJIAN

Taipei

R. Mekong

TAIWAN

• Kunming

River Xi

GUANGDONG

YUNNAN

GUANGXI

Canton (Guangzhou)

VIETNAM

HONG KONG

BURMA (MYANMAR)

MACAO (PORTUGAL)

LAOS

GULF OF TONGKING

SOUTH CHINA SEA

0   300 miles

0   500 km

HAINAN

MEDICINE

Medicine in China is a mixture of East and West. Modern surgical and drug techniques are borrowed from Europe and the United States. However, doctors still use traditional cures that have been popular for thousands of years, including herbs and other natural remedies. To relieve pain Chinese doctors sometimes use acupuncture, a technique in which fine needles are inserted into specially-chosen parts of the body. "Barefoot doctors", or locally-trained healers, keep people healthy in the countryside, with natural remedies.

Acupuncture charts show the positions of meridians, or lines of energy, where the acupuncturist inserts needles.

A Chinese apothecary or chemist makes use of a wide range of natural plant and animal cures.

INDUSTRY

Chinese factories have been modernized since 1949 but in comparison with the factories of Japan or the United States, they are still old-fashioned. But China is the world's leading manufacturer of television sets and produces other electrical goods, farm machinery, machine tools, and textiles. With such a huge population, there is no shortage of workers.

FOOD

Rice is one of the main ingredients of Chinese food, as are noodles and many vegetables. Dried foods, soybeans, fish, and meat are also used in Chinese cooking, which varies considerably in the different regions of China.

The Chinese eat with chopsticks. They hold both sticks in one hand, and pinch the tips together to pick up food.

Buddhist monks in Tibet, southwest China, spend much time studying and writing.

HONG KONG AND TAIWAN

The tiny, prosperous colony of Hong Kong (above) in south China was British, but from July 1997 China took control. From 1999, China will also control the nearby Portuguese colony of Macao. The island of Taiwan is ruled by supporters of the old Chinese government, deposed in 1949.

CHINESE LANGUAGE

Northern or Mandarin Chinese, the official language of China, is spoken in all but the southeast coastal areas. There, Cantonese and other Chinese languages are spoken. Within each language there are many dialects, or regional variations. Although each vocabulary is different, all the variations are written in the same script.

Chinese writing consists of thousands of symbols, each one representing a different word or idea.

The Peking Opera performs traditional and new works, mainly with political themes.

CULTURE

China has a rich and ancient culture: paintings found in some Chinese tombs are more than 6,000 years old. Today, artistic traditions continue in the form of folk dancing and music; films, opera, and theatre are all very popular. Artists are encouraged to produce works that depict the achievements of the Chinese people.

兒童百科全書

Find out more

ASIA
CHINA, HISTORY OF
COMMUNISM
MAO ZEDONG
MONGOL EMPIRE

HISTORY OF
CHINA

CHINA HAS A LONGER continuous civilization than any other country in the world, and its civilization has often been far more advanced. People have lived in China for about 500,000 years. They built cities about 5,500 years ago, long before cities existed in Africa, the Americas, or Europe. The Chinese invented paper, ink, writing, silk fabric, printing, and gunpowder. Until this century, China's vast empire was ruled by emperors who came from different dynasties, or royal families. They kept China practically isolated from the rest of the world until the 19th century. But, in 1911 the Chinese people forced the last emperor off the throne. A republic was established, but it was weakened by civil war and Japanese invasion. In 1949, the Communist party took power and began to transform China into a major industrial nation. Since the late 1970s, the Party has encouraged free enterprize.

TERRACOTTA ARMY

In 221 B.C. Shih Huang Ti became the first emperor of all China. His vast army helped him unite rival Chinese kingdoms. When Shih Huang Ti died in 210 B.C., a life-size copy of his army was made by 700,000 slaves and craftsworkers. More than 8,000 terracotta clay archers, soldiers, chariots, and horses were buried in silent rows to guard his tomb.

The bodies of the figures were hollow for lightness.

CH'IN DYNASTY
China gets its name from the Ch'in dynasty of Shih Huang Ti, which ruled China between 221 and 206 B.C. The dynasty was ruthless and its army was invincible. Army officers often rode in light wooden chariots and could be recognized by their special headgear and armour.

The weapons were real. When the tomb was discovered in the early 1970s, some weapons were still sharp enough to cut hair.

GREAT WALL
The Great Wall of China is the longest wall in the world. It is 3,460 km (2,150 miles) long, 12 m (39 ft) high, and between 6 m (20 ft) and 15 m (49 ft) wide. The wall was built during the reign of Shih Huang Ti to defend China's northern borders against hostile tribes from central Asia.

CONFUCIUS
Confucius (551-479 B.C.) was a wise teacher. His ideas greatly influenced the Chinese. He taught that people should be courteous, loyal, and unselfish.

Figures were made in separate pieces.

T'ANG DYNASTY
China was powerful and rich during the T'ang dynasty (A.D. 618-906). Craftworkers made beautiful pottery and sculptures, and artists painted superb watercolours on silk. The T'ang empress Wu Tse-t'ien allowed women to take examinations for government posts. The golden bowl below shows the wealth of the dynasty.

HAN DYNASTY
The Han dynasty ruled China from 206 B.C. to A.D. 220. It was a peaceful era, during which China greatly expanded its territory. Schools were built and learning was encouraged. Paper and ink were invented at this time. Artists created many beautiful objects, such as the bronze "horse of heaven" (above), made nearly 2,000 years ago.

MING DYNASTY
The Forbidden City in Beijing (above) was built during the Ming dynasty (1368-1644). The Ming emperors and their families lived in a palace in the city. Ordinary people were forbidden to enter.

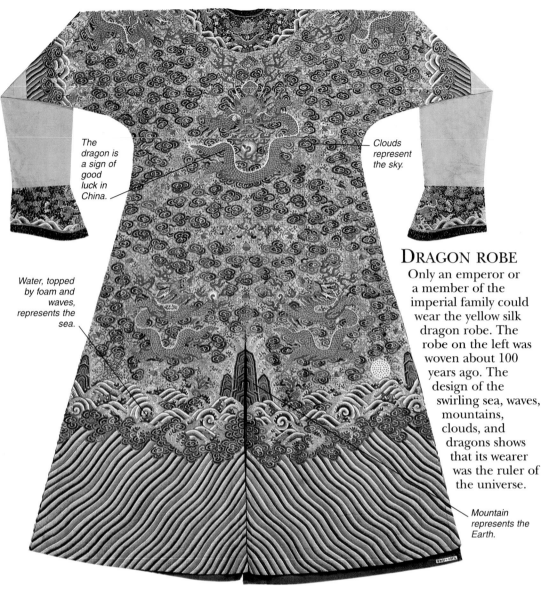

The dragon is a sign of good luck in China.

Clouds represent the sky.

Water, topped by foam and waves, represents the sea.

DRAGON ROBE

Only an emperor or a member of the imperial family could wear the yellow silk dragon robe. The robe on the left was woven about 100 years ago. The design of the swirling sea, waves, mountains, clouds, and dragons shows that its wearer was the ruler of the universe.

Mountain represents the Earth.

SUN YAT-SEN

In 1911, a rebellion broke out against the corrupt and inefficient Manchu dynasty, and in 1912 a republic was declared. The first president of China was Sun Yat-sen (1866-1925; right). He founded the Kuomintang (Chinese National Party). He tried to modernize the country but his authority was disputed and he soon resigned. However, Sun continued to dominate Chinese politics until his death.

COLLAPSE OF THE EMPIRE

During the 19th century, many foreign countries forced China to grant them trading rights and allow their citizens to ignore Chinese law. The cartoon above shows Britain, Germany, Russia, Italy, and Japan sharing the Chinese "cake" among them. But the Chinese resented this interference in their affairs and rebelled against the hated foreigners.

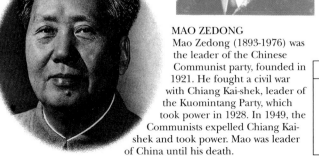

MAO ZEDONG

Mao Zedong (1893-1976) was the leader of the Chinese Communist party, founded in 1921. He fought a civil war with Chiang Kai-shek, leader of the Kuomintang Party, which took power in 1928. In 1949, the Communists expelled Chiang Kai-shek and took power. Mao was leader of China until his death.

Find out more
CHINA
COMMUNISM
JAPAN, HISTORY OF
MAO ZEDONG
MONGOL EMPIRE

CHRISTIANITY

Church windows tell Bible stories in pictures made from stained glass.

FROM VERY HUMBLE ORIGINS, Christianity has grown to be the largest of all world religions. Christians are the followers of Jesus Christ, a Jew who lived almost 2,000 years ago in the land that is now Israel. Jesus was a teacher and a prophet, but Christians believe that he was also the Son of God and that he came into the world to save people from sin, or doing wrong. Jesus was killed by his enemies, but his disciples (group of followers) taught that he rose from the dead and rejoined his father in heaven, a basic Christian belief called the Resurrection. After Jesus' death, his followers began to spread his teaching. Christianity grew, but it was against the law in most lands, and many early Christians died for their beliefs. Today more than 1,600 million people throughout the world practise Christianity. There are different divisions within Christianity; the three most prominent are Protestantism, the Roman Catholic Church, and the Eastern Orthodox Church. Each has its own way of worshipping. But despite their differences, all Christian groups share a belief in the teachings of Jesus Christ. Most Christians worship by meeting in groups called congregations. They pray together and sing hymns (sacred songs).

In New Testament stories Jesus compares God to a good shepherd, caring for his "flock" of believers.

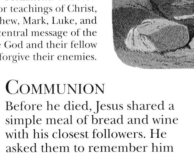

BIBLE

The Bible is sacred to both Christians and Jews, who believe it contains the word of God. It consists of two parts – the Old and New Testament. Both Jews and Christians accept the Old Testament, but only Christians accept the New Testament. The New Testament includes the gospels, or teachings of Christ, as told by his followers – Matthew, Mark, Luke, and John. Christians try to follow the central message of the New Testament, which is to love God and their fellow humans and to forgive their enemies.

COMMUNION

Before he died, Jesus shared a simple meal of bread and wine with his closest followers. He asked them to remember him in this special way. Today the ceremony of Holy Communion, in which worshippers receive bread and wine, is a reminder of Christ's Last Supper and helps Christians feel closer to God. Roman Catholic and Eastern Orthodox churches celebrate communion daily in the form of Mass.

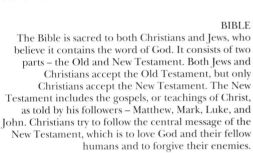

FEASTS AND HOLY DAYS

Advent Preparation for Christmas.

Christmas December 25; birth of Jesus.

The birth of Jesus is remembered at Christmas. This feast is popular with many non-Christians as well, who enjoy the atmosphere of festive goodwill.

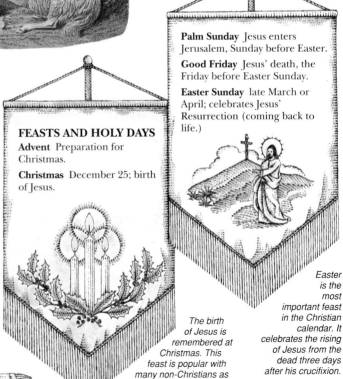

Palm Sunday Jesus enters Jerusalem, Sunday before Easter.

Good Friday Jesus' death, the Friday before Easter Sunday.

Easter Sunday late March or April; celebrates Jesus' Resurrection (coming back to life.)

Easter is the most important feast in the Christian calendar. It celebrates the rising of Jesus from the dead three days after his crucifixion.

ROMAN CATHOLICISM

Roman Catholics make up the largest Christian group. They believe that the pope, the head of the Catholic Church, is God's representative on Earth. His authority on religious matters is always obeyed. The pope lives in a tiny independent state in Rome called Vatican City. The Roman Catholic Church is spread worldwide and is the main religion of many countries, including Spain, Ireland, and France. Catholics try to attend Mass on Sundays and to regularly confess their sins to a priest. They pray to God and have special regard for Mary, the mother of Jesus. They also pray to the Christian saints, deeply religious people, some of whom died for their faith.

ROSARY
Catholics use a rosary – a symbolic string of beads – to help them pray. They say a prayer for each bead in the chain.

ORTHODOX CHURCH
At first Christianity was "catholic", meaning that it was spread all over the world. In A.D. 1054, however, the Christian church divided. The pope in Rome and the patriarch, head of the church of Constantinople (now Istanbul, Turkey), disagreed about the leadership of the Christian world. As a result the Church in Rome and the Eastern Church separated. Roman Catholics and members of Eastern Orthodox churches such as those of Russia and Greece share many beliefs. However, Orthodox Christians do not accept the authority of the pope. Many Christians in Eastern Europe and western Asia belong to Orthodox churches. In their churches religious portraits called icons are considered sacred.

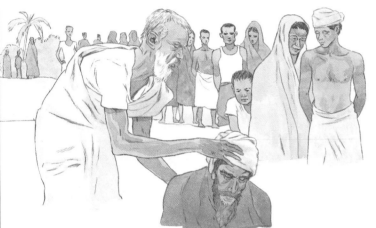

BAPTISM

Adults and children enter the Christian church through baptism, a ceremony in which they are sprinkled with water or immersed in it. Baptism washes away a person's sins. Children are often named, or christened, at their baptism. Parents promise to raise them as good Christians. In some countries baptism takes place outdoors in lakes or rivers. Jesus was baptized in the Jordan River in the Middle East.

Most of the Christians who worship in the United States are members of Protestant churches.

PROTESTANTISM
In the early 16th century some Christians felt that the Roman Catholic Church was no longer correctly following the teachings of Christ. Martin Luther, a German monk, led the protests. Others who agreed with him broke away and formed protest groups in a movement that became known as the Reformation. Today most Christians who are not members of the Roman Catholic or Orthodox churches are called Protestants. Some Protestant churches, called Evangelist churches, are among the fastest growing christian groups in the world. They have mainly Afro-Caribbean congregations.

MOTHER TERESA

Christians believe it is their duty to help relieve the suffering of the poor and sick. Mother Teresa, founder of the Missionaries of Charity, is famous for her work among the homeless and dying in India. In 1979 she was awarded the Nobel Peace Prize.

Mother Teresa was born in Albania in 1910, but became an Indian citizen. All the nuns in her missions wear a flowing Indian dress called a sari.

Find out more

CHURCHES AND CATHEDRALS
JESUS CHRIST
REFORMATION
RELIGIONS

CHURCHES AND CATHEDRALS

SHINING WHITE TOWERS, ugly stone faces, and golden domes decorate churches and cathedrals in Christian countries. Churches everywhere are constructed according to local customs, so they look very different from one another, but all serve the same purpose: a church is a building for Christian worship and prayer. Its name comes from a Greek word meaning "God's house." An old church is often the most magnificent building in a town. The people who built it believed that a glorious church was a symbol of God's glory. So they made the church as beautiful and long-lasting as they could. A cathedral is a church in which a bishop presides and organizes the worship of a whole region, including many smaller churches. Many cathedrals are ancient and decorated with vast stained-glass windows. Other religions also have special buildings for worship, but they are not called churches. Many Jewish synagogues, Buddhist temples, and Islamic mosques are as magnificent as the world's finest cathedrals.

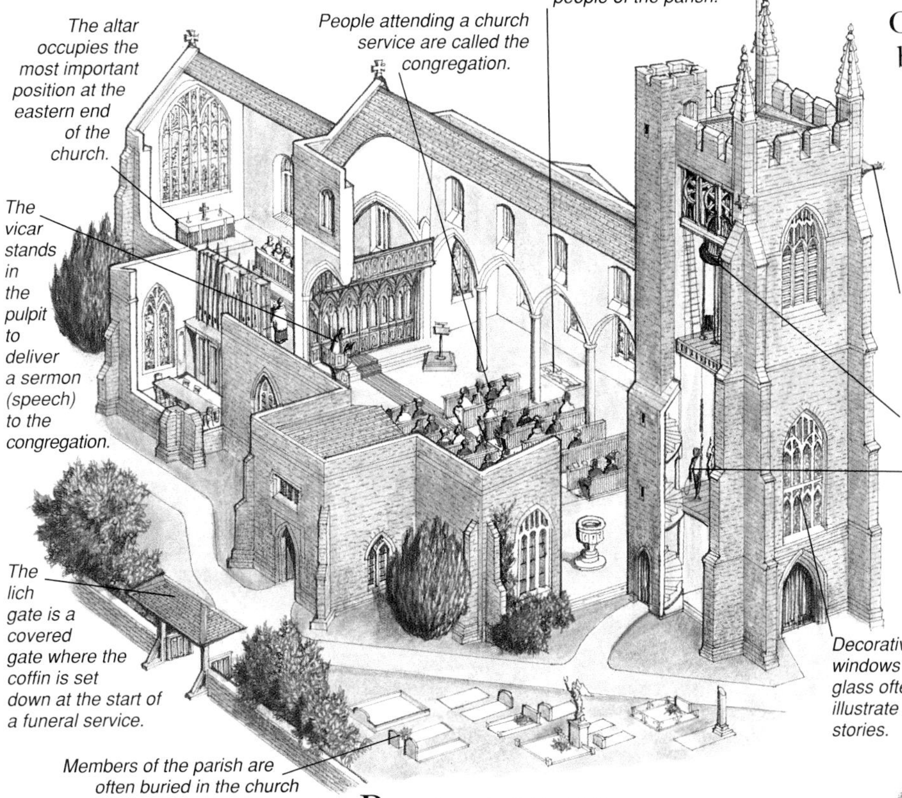

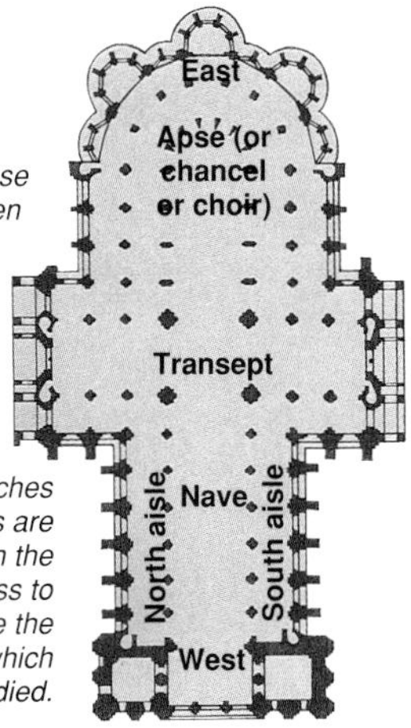

EARLY CHURCHES
The first churches were built from local materials. Some early Norwegian churches, such as the one shown here, are made entirely of wood and have steep roofs to stop the snow from piling up.

The altar occupies the most important position at the eastern end of the church.

People attending a church service are called the congregation.

Carved tombs were built inside the church for important people of the parish.

The vicar stands in the pulpit to deliver a sermon (speech) to the congregation.

Elaborate spouts called gargoyles carry rain water away from the building. These ugly faces are said to frighten away devils.

Each bell in the tower has a different note.

Bell ringers pull on ropes to ring the bells.

The lich gate is a covered gate where the coffin is set down at the start of a funeral service.

Many churches and cathedrals are laid out in the shape of a cross to symbolize the cross on which Christ died.

East
Apse (or chancel or choir)
Transept
North aisle
Nave
South aisle
West

Decorative windows of stained glass often illustrate Bible stories.

Members of the parish are often buried in the church graveyard.

PARISH CHURCH
In many Christian countries, the land is divided into different areas called parishes, each of which has a church with its own priest or vicar. In the past, the parish church was the centre of village activities. Here people were baptized as babies, married as adults, and buried when they died.

CATHEDRAL
From a cathedral, the bishop controls a whole diocese, or group of parishes. Cathedrals get their name from the bishop's cathedra, or throne, which is kept in the cathedral. Many individual cathedrals – and some churches – are named after Christian saints.

St. Mark's Basilica in Venice, Italy, was built between the 11th and 15th centuries.

MODERN CHURCHES
New churches are still being built today. Some architects follow traditional patterns of church architecture, but many use modern building materials and techniques to produce new and startling effects (left).

___Find out more___
ARCHITECTURE
CHRISTIANITY
MIDDLE AGES
RELIGIONS

SIR WINSTON
CHURCHILL

IN 1940 BRITAIN badly needed a strong leader. The country was at war with Germany and faced the danger of invasion. Winston Churchill's appointment as prime minister provided the leadership that the British people wanted. He went on to guide the country through the worst war the world had ever experienced. In his underground headquarters he formed the plans which helped to win the war. Churchill's wartime glory came at a surprising time. He was 66 and held no important government post at the time. He had been almost alone in urging a strong army and navy to oppose the German threat. Working people remembered how he helped crush the general strike of 1926 and cut their wages. But when victory came in World War II, all of this was forgotten, and everyone cheered Churchill as one of the greatest politicians of the age.

1874 Born at Blenheim Palace, Oxfordshire, England.

1893 Enters the Royal Military College at Sandhurst.

1899 Taken prisoner during Boer War in South Africa, but escapes.

1900 Elected Member of Parliament.

1906-15 Holds cabinet posts.

1919 Appointed secretary of state for war.

1940-45 As prime minister, leads Britain in World War II.

1951-55 Prime minister.

1965 Dies.

YOUNG WINSTON
As a young soldier and newspaper reporter in India and Africa, Churchill had many adventures. He became world famous when he escaped from a Boer prison in 1899.

HOLDING THE LINE!

BRITISH BULLDOG
Churchill's famous British determination was often portrayed in cartoons and posters. This 1942 American poster shows him as a bulldog.

WARTIME PRIME MINISTER
As wartime leader, Churchill travelled the country visiting bombed cities and raising people's spirits. His simple "V for Victory" sign seemed to sum up British determination to win the war. His most important work took place behind the scenes, where he directed the British war effort. He met the leaders of the then Soviet Union and the United States to draw up plans for fighting the war and for the postwar peace settlement. Above he is seen giving the "V" sign to American sailors.

PAINTING
Churchill was an enthusiastic amateur painter. He also wrote many books about history. These hobbies kept him busy after 1945 when he lost his post as prime minister in a disastrous election. He did not return to power until 1951.

BROADCASTS
During World War II, Churchill made many radio broadcasts, which inspired the nation. Churchill always explained the situation clearly and listed the dreadful problems which lay ahead, yet he left no doubt that the enemy would eventually be defeated.

Find out more
UNITED KINGDOM, HISTORY OF
WORLD WAR I
WORLD WAR II

CIRCUSES

EARLY CIRCUS ACTS such as tumbling and bull-leaping go back to very ancient times. But the circus that we know today was not developed until 1768, when the Englishman Philip Astley started a trick riding show in London. He soon added other acts such as tightrope walkers and strong men, and in 1793 John Ricketts set up similar circuses in the United States. These early circuses took place indoors in special buildings; later, travelling tented circuses such as Barnum and Bailey were developed. They moved from town to town, taking the show and its spectacular acts to the audience. Today the circus combines tightrope acts, juggling, clowns, bareback riders, and animal acts and is one of the most popular forms of family entertainment. Circus work is highly skilled. Venice, Florida, United States, is home to the world's only clown college.

FLYING TRAPEZE
Trapeze artists rely on split-second timing as they perform their midair somersaults. This daring act was invented by the French-man Jules Léotard in 1859.

THE BIG TOP
Some circuses take place in a huge tent called the big top. It must be very strong to resist high winds and to support lighting and rigging for aerial acts. The performers and circus animals live in caravans and trailers.

THE CIRCUS RING
Philip Astley discovered that the perfect area for bareback riding was a circle measuring 12.8 m (42 ft) in diameter. This has become the standard circus ring size.

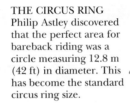

CLOWNS
Every clown is unique. With their funny clothes and makeup, clowns are a special part of every circus. Making people laugh is a serious business, and clowns learn many skills. They may be musicians or acrobats, mimes or comedians. The first real clown, Joseph Grimaldi, was a stage clown in the 19th century, and circus clowns take their nickname, Joey, and their white faces from him. British clowns "register" their makeup by drawing the design on an egg.

Joseph Grimaldi

Clowns' painted egg heads

THE CIRCUS PARADE
Marching through the street, the parade lets everyone know the circus is in town. Highly-trained horses are part of circus tradition, but many people now think that it is cruel to tame wild animals such as lions and tigers in the ring.

RINGMASTER
At the beginning of each performance the ringmaster strides into the ring, carrying a whip to show that he is in charge. The ringmaster has many responsibilities. Before introducing each act he makes sure that the clothes and equipment are ready. He keeps the mischievous clowns in order and makes sure the show runs smoothly.

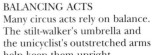
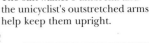

BALANCING ACTS
Many circus acts rely on balance. The stilt-walker's umbrella and the unicyclist's outstretched arms help keep them upright.

Find out more
THEATRE

CITIES

ONE THIRD OF all the world's people live in cities. The world's largest city, Tokyo, Japan, has a population of more than 18 million. But not all cities are vast, because the word *city* can mean different things. In many places, a city is any large town. In Europe, it is a town with a cathedral. And in some places, like the United States, "city" is the name given to an urban area with definite boundaries.

City people need many services: water, power, sanitation, transport, schools, and shops are all essential. Providing these services requires a lot of organization. Badly run cities are unpleasant and unhealthy, with problems such as poor housing, traffic congestion, and pollution. The first cities developed as trading centres in Asia and the Middle East about 7,000 years ago. Rich cities such as Alexandria in Egypt became the centres of government and power. Like today's cities, they had markets, banks, hotels, factories, and places of entertainment.

CAPITAL CITIES
The most important town of any country is called the capital. It is usually the place where the government is based, but it may not be the biggest city in the country. Some capital cities, such as Brasilia, have been specially built in modern times.

Brasilia was built to replace Rio de Janeiro as the capital of Brazil.

Factories require a lot of space, so they are built in the outer parts of cities. They need easy access to roads and railways so they can send their goods to other parts of the country.

The city centre usually contains the most stylish shops. Shopping precincts are built close to residential areas on the outskirts of town.

Land is expensive in the city centre, so office developments grow upwards rather than outwards.

Cities must have a good public transport system of buses and underground railways, or traffic will block the streets.

Quiet parks and other recreation areas provide a restful break from the busy city streets.

MODERN CITY
The oldest part of the city often forms the centre. Further out are the industrial zones and the areas where people live, all connected by a network of roads.

Some families live in homes close to the city centre. More live a few kilometres from the centre in less crowded areas called suburbs.

PLANNING
Many cities grow up around their historical centres with no overall plan. However, some cities, such as Washington, D.C., have been carefully planned from the start. Streets and squares, transport, sewers, business centres, and sports facilities are all carefully mapped out before any building starts.

Swiss-French architect Le Corbusier (1887-1965) planned this city for three million people.

The city streets follow a grid pattern.

Find out more

ARCHITECTURE
INDUSTRIAL REVOLUTION
ROADS AND MOTORWAYS

AMERICAN CIVIL WAR

Free states

Slave states

Territories

Oregon

Territories

California

Free states

Slave states

THE DIVIDED NATION
In 1860 the free states and slave states were divided as shown on the map above.

ONLY 80 YEARS AFTER the states of America had united and won their independence from England, a bitter conflict threatened to destroy the Union. Between 1861 and 1865, civil war raged as the nation fought over several issues, one of which was slavery. Slavery was legal in the South but had been outlawed in the North. The immediate cause of the war was the election in November 1860 of Abraham Lincoln as president. Lincoln wanted to stop the spread of slavery, and he hoped it would die out in the South. The southern states disagreed, and one by one they left the Union to form their own alliance, called the Confederacy, with Jefferson Davis as president. Fighting broke out in April 1861. General Robert E. Lee, an able military leader, led the Confederate armies. However, the Union army was larger, and the North had many industries which supplied the army, whereas the South's main business was agriculture. The war was brutal, and by the time the Confederacy was defeated in 1865, much of the South was devastated. The Union victory led to the abolition of slavery throughout the United States, but the country remained split between North and South for many years.

A MODERN WAR

The American Civil War was the first conflict in which railways and iron warships played an important part. It was also the first war to be widely photographed and reported in the world's newspapers.

THE END OF THE WAR

On 9 April 1865, Confederate general Robert E. Lee surrendered to Union general Ulysses S. Grant at Appomattox, Virginia, United States. More than half a million Americans were killed in the war, and many more were injured.

Union   Confederacy

TROOPS
Most of the American Civil War troops were infantrymen (foot soldiers). Three million people fought in the two opposing armies.

EVENTS IN CIVIL WAR

1860 Abraham Lincoln is elected president.

1860-1861 Eleven southern states leave the Union and join the Confederacy.

1861 Confederates attack Fort Sumter. Civil War begins.

1861 Confederate victory at Bull Run.

1862 Stalemate for months.

1862 Confederate victory at Fredericksburg.

1862 Naval battle between battleships *Monitor* and *Merrimack*.

1862 Battle of Shiloh, Tenn.

1863 Lincoln's Emancipation Proclamation proclaims freedom of slaves in Confederacy.

1863 Confederate victory at Chancellorsville.

1863 Confederate defeat at

Gettysburg, during invasion of the Union marks turning point in war.

1863 Confederate defeats at Vicksburg and Chattanooga.

1864 Union general W.T. Sherman captures Atlanta, Georgia, and begins "march to the sea".

1865 Confederate general Robert E. Lee surrenders to Union general Ulysses S. Grant; war ends.

1865 Slavery abolished in U.S.

Find out more

LINCOLN, ABRAHAM
SLAVERY
UNITED STATES OF AMERICA,
history of

ENGLISH
CIVIL WAR

IN 1649 CHARLES I, king of England, was put on trial for treason and executed. His death marked the climax of the English Civil War, also called the English Revolution, a fierce struggle between king and Parliament (the law-making assembly) over the issue of who should govern England. The struggle had begun many years before. Charles I believed that kings were appointed by God and should rule alone; Parliament believed that it should have greater power. When the king called upon Parliament for funds to fight the Scots, they refused to cooperate, and in 1642 civil war broke out. England was divided into two factions – the Royalists (also called Cavaliers), who supported Charles, and the Roundheads, who supported Parliament. Charles was a poor leader, and the Roundheads had the support of the navy and were led by two great generals – Lord Fairfax and Oliver Cromwell. By 1649 Cromwell had defeated Charles and declared England a republic. Despite various reforms, Cromwell's rule was unpopular. In 1660 the army asked Charles's son, Charles II, to take the throne and the monarchy was restored.

CHARLES I
King Charles I (reigned 1625-49) was the only English monarch to be executed. He ruled alone, ignoring Parliament, from 1629 to 1640. After a disagreement with Parliament in 1642, Charles raised an army and began the civil war which ended his reign.

Parliamentary (New Model) army

Royalist cavalry

Royalist officers wore wide-brimmed hats.

Pikeman

Musketeer reloading his musket

BATTLE OF NASEBY
At the Battle of Naseby in 1645 the heavily armed and well-organized pikemen and musketeers of Cromwell's "New Model Army" crushed the Royalists.

OLIVER CROMWELL
The English Republic (1649-60) was mainly organized and ruled by lord protector Oliver Cromwell (1599-1658). Cromwell was an honest, moderate man and a brilliant army leader. But his attempts to enforce extreme purity upon England made him unpopular with many.

DIGGERS
During the turbulent years new political groups emerged. Some, such as the Diggers, were very radical. They believed that ordinary people should have a say in government and wanted to end private property.

RUMP PARLIAMENT
At the end of the English Civil War, all that was left of King Charles's parliament was a "rump" parliament, whose members refused to leave. In 1653 Cromwell, determined to get rid of any remnant of the king, dismissed Parliament. He pointed at the mace, the speaker's symbol of office, and laughingly called it a bauble (left).

Find out more
UNITED KINGDOM,
history of

CLIMATES

SOME PARTS OF THE WORLD such as the tropical rain forests of South America, are hot and damp throughout the year. Other regions, such as the Arctic, have long, freezing winters. Conditions such as these are known as the climate of an area. Climate is not the same as weather. Weather can change within minutes; climate describes a region's weather conditions over a long period of time. Every region has its own climate. This depends on how near it is to the equator, which governs how much heat it gets from the sun. Landscape also influences climate; high mountain regions, such as the Himalayas, are cooler than nearby low-lying places. The ocean can prevent a coastal region from getting very hot or very cold, while the weather in the centre of a continent is more extreme. The climate of a region affects landscape and life – clothing, crops, and housing. But climate can change. Today climatologists, people who study climates, believe that the world's climate is gradually warming up.

THE FREEZING ANTARCTIC
Only hardy creatures, such as penguins, can survive amid the ice and snow of the Antarctic.

The cool forest climate exists only in the northern half of the world.

The treeless landscape of the polar regions is called the tundra.

POLAR CLIMATE
It is cold all year, and ice and snow always cover the ground. No crops grow, and the few people who live there hunt animals for food.

In temperate climates, trees shed their leaves in winter.

TROPICAL CLIMATE
It is hot all year round in tropical regions, and torrents of rain usually fall every afternoon. Rain forest covers much of the land. In regions where wet and dry seasons occur, tropical grasslands grow.

The Sahara is the largest desert in the world.

WORLD CLIMATES
The different climates of the world run in broad zones around the Earth on either side of the equator. They range from hot and rainy climates at the equator to cold climates at the poles. There are five main climatic zones, each of which is shown on this map by a different colour.

DESERT CLIMATE
In the dry, barren deserts, cold, clear nights usually follow burning-hot days. However, high mountain deserts may have cold, dry winters.

TEMPERATE CLIMATE
Warm summers and cool winters feature in warm temperate climates. Rain may fall all year, or the summer can be dry and sunny, as in Mediterranean regions.

COOL FOREST CLIMATE
Summers are cool and short, and winters are long and cold. Pines and other conifers grow in huge forests which cover much of the land.

Away from the equator, the sun's rays are spread over a wide area.

Sun's rays — *Escaping heat* — *Trapped heat*

GREENHOUSE EFFECT
The atmosphere works like a greenhouse, trapping the sun's heat and warming the Earth. Pollution in the air traps more heat, making the Earth warmer. Unless pollution is reduced, the Earth's climate could be upset.

CLIMATIC CHANGES
Great climatic changes, such as ice ages, come and go during thousands of years. But severe changes in climate can also occur suddenly or within a few years. Dust from volcanic eruptions can obscure the sun, making a climate cooler. Changes in winds can cause rainfall to shift from a region, bringing drought. Human activities, such as pollution, affect climate.

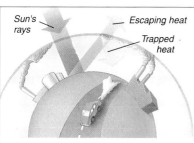

SAHARA DESERT
The Tuareg nomads are one of the few peoples that live in the punishing climate of the Sahara Desert, coping with the searing heat of the day and the freezing temperatures at night.

SUN AND CLIMATE
The sun's rays warm the equator directly from above, making the tropics hot. Away from the equator, the sun's rays are less direct, making climates cooler.

Find out more
ATMOSPHERE
DESERTS
EARTH
GLACIERS AND ICECAPS
WEATHER

CLOCKS AND WATCHES

HAVE YOU EVER COUNTED how many times you look at a clock in one day? Time rules everyday life. To catch a bus, get to school, or meet a friend, you need to be on time. Clocks and watches make this possible. Clocks are timekeeping devices too large to be carried; watches are portable. Some tell the time with hands moving around a dial; others with numbers. All clocks and watches use a controlling device, such as clockwork, that steadily keeps the time.

Early people relied on the passing of days, nights, and seasons to indicate time. Later, they used other methods, such as sundials, water clocks, and candles with marks on them. Mechanical timepieces were developed between the 15th and 17th centuries with the invention of clockwork and the pendulum. Springs or falling weights moved gearwheels to drive the clocks. These clocks had hands and a dial, and could be made small enough to allow the invention of the watch. Today many clocks and watches are electronic and rely on the regular vibrations of a quartz crystal to keep time accurately.

SUNDIAL
The sun's shadow moves slowly around a dial marked off in hours. As the shadow moves, it indicates the time. The sundial, which was invented more than 5,000 years ago in Egypt, was one of the earliest methods of measuring time.

ASTRONOMICAL CLOCK
This beautiful clock in Prague, Czechoslovakia, not only shows the hours and minutes but also the signs of the zodiac and the phases of the moon.

WATER CLOCK
Water flows in and out of bowls so that changing levels of water, or a moving float, indicate the passing time. This Chinese water clock dates back to the 14th century.

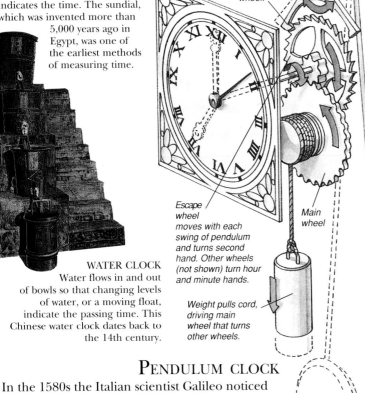

Ends of anchor engage teeth of escape wheel.

Anchor

Escape wheel moves with each swing of pendulum and turns second hand. Other wheels (not shown) turn hour and minute hands.

Main wheel

Weight pulls cord, driving main wheel that turns other wheels.

Swinging pendulum rocks anchor.

PENDULUM CLOCK

In the 1580s the Italian scientist Galileo noticed that each swing of a suspended weight, or pendulum, takes a fixed time. He suggested that this regular movement could be used to control a clock. But it was another 70 years before the first pendulum clock was built.

MECHANICAL WATCHES
A spring powers a mechanical watch, which otherwise operates like a pendulum clock. The first watch was invented in Germany in about 1500.

This 19th-century fob watch was worn on the end of a small chain.

ATOMIC CLOCK
If it were to run for more than one million years, this atomic clock would be less than one second off! The atomic clock is the most accurate of all clocks. It is controlled by vibrating atoms and is used in science to measure intervals of time with extraordinary accuracy.

Watch unit and strap

Cover and display window

LCD (liquid crystal display)

Quartz crystal

Microchip

Battery

DIGITAL WATCH

A battery powers a digital watch, and a tiny quartz crystal regulates its speed. Electricity from the battery makes the crystal vibrate thousands of times each second. The microchip uses these regular vibrations to make the numbers on the display change every second, so the watch shows the time very precisely.

Find out more
ELECTRONICS
ROCKS AND MINERALS
TIME

CLOTHES

ELEGANT SILK or a practical working outfit: the clothes people wear reflect how they live. The first clothes were animal skins which kept out the cold and rain. Clothes still give protection against the weather, but society and customs also dictate their shape – a business suit looks out of place on a beach, and nobody goes to the office in a bathing suit.

Many people wear fashionable clothes. Fashion means the style of every new product, and clothing fashions change often. This year's summer clothes will be "out of fashion" next summer. Fashion started as a way to display wealth. When clothes were expensive, only rich people could afford to dress fashionably. Through the centuries fashion has evolved as lifestyles changed. For instance, when women had few rights, fashionable dresses restricted movement, just as society restricted what women could do. But as women gained greater freedom, loose trousers became fashionable, and women could move around more easily.

COLD CLIMATE
Traditionally, clothes for a cold climate are made from animal skins. The fur, worn inside, traps a layer of air which resists the flow of heat from the body. Modern jackets and trousers are made of closely woven nylon and are wind- and waterproof. Down padding traps air between the feathers to keep heat in.

THE VEIL
Under the religious laws of Islam women must dress modestly. So many Muslim women (followers of Islam) cover their heads and faces with a black veil or mask when they go out.

FUNCTIONAL CLOTHES
Sometimes the function of clothes – the job they have to do – is the most important influence on their design. For example, the function of bad-weather clothes is to keep out cold, wind, and rain; appearance or colour is not so important. Functional garments are also worn for religious reasons, for different types of work, and for sports. Sports clothes must be lightweight, easy to move in, and machine-washable.

FACTORY CLOTHES
Work clothes must have pockets for tools, be easy to wash, and not restrict movement or get caught in machinery.

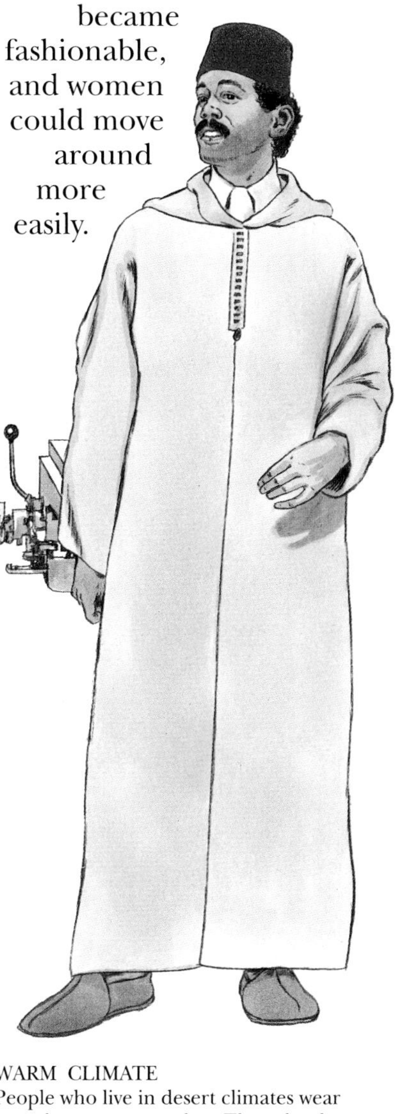

MAKING CLOTHES
Today most people in Europe and North America buy mass-produced clothes in shops. But homemade clothes are still popular among people who want original clothes in the fabric of their choice, or who cannot afford clothes sold in shops. Paper patterns show how to cut each piece of fabric. Pinning the cut pieces of fabric holds them together to make sewing easier.

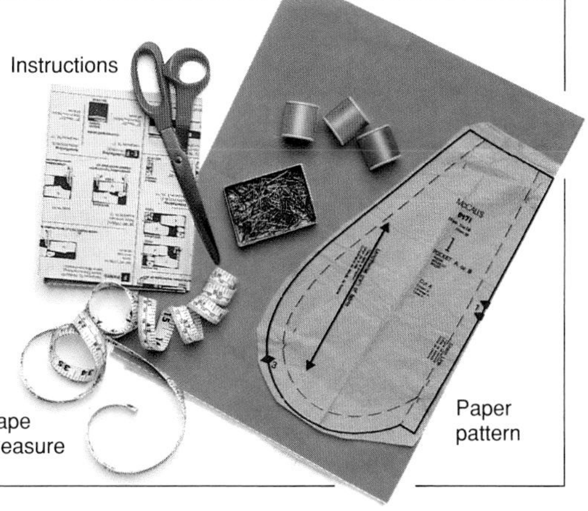

Instructions

Tape measure

Paper pattern

WARM CLIMATE
People who live in desert climates wear long, loose, cotton robes. The robes have a double function: they protect the skin from the harmful rays of the sun and keep the body cool by trapping layers of air between the folds of cloth. The garment shown here is called a djellabah and is worn mostly in North Africa.

BUSTLE

Past fashions can look strange or ridiculous. In the late 19th century the bustle was popular. It made a dress stick out at the back.

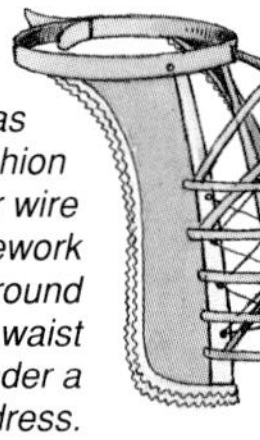

The bustle was a cushion or wire framework tied around the waist under a dress.

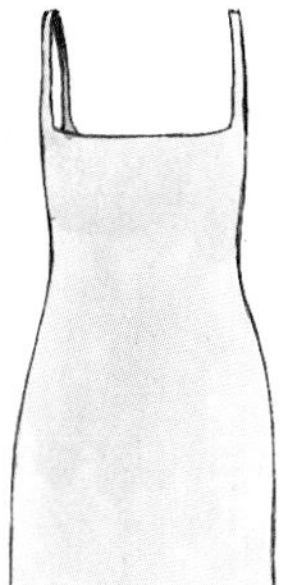

DRESSES

Clothing has changed through the ages. Ancient Greek dresses were pieces of cloth draped around the body. In 14th-century Europe dresses were tailored to fit. In the 16th century women's vests were stiffened with whalebone. Tight boning went on to the end of the 19th century. The 1920s saw a sudden change: skirts were short for the first time.

When fashions changed, the simple, loose-fitting slip replaced the awkward bustle under women's dresses.

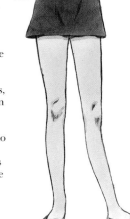

MINISKIRT

In the 1960s young people had more independence than ever before. Women expressed their freedom by wearing very short skirts.

SHIFT

Fashionable dresses of the 1930s, called shifts, gave women enough freedom of movement to enjoy the spontaneous dances of the era, such as the Charleston.

FASHION HOUSES

The most fashionable clothes come from *haute couture* (high fashion) designers. Their companies are called fashion houses. Models show off the designers' new creations at fashion shows called collections. Designer Coco Chanel (1883-1971) revolutionized women's clothing when she created simple and comfortable dresses, suits, and sweaters from jersey, a knitted fabric which stretches as the wearer moves.

Coco Chanel's clothes were the first fashionable garments that were uncluttered and easy to wear.

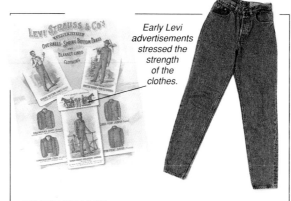

Early Levi advertisements stressed the strength of the clothes.

BLUE JEANS

Inexpensive, easily washed, and hardwearing, blue jeans first appeared in the United States in 1850. A miner digging for gold in the California gold rush asked tailor Levi Strauss to make him a sturdy pair of trousers, because ordinary fabric wore out so quickly. Jeans are made of denim, a tough cotton fabric coloured with the natural blue indigo dye.

UNIFORMS

People who belong to the same group or organization often wear similar garments so that they can be easily identified. These standard clothes are called uniforms. Uniforms promote a sense of team spirit and companionship, so many people are proud of their uniforms. Some, such as nurses' uniforms, are very functional and protect the wearer while at work.

School uniforms

Nurse   Soccer player   Policeman

PROTECTIVE CLOTHING

Workers such as fire fighters and nuclear power workers need clothes which protect them while they are at work. As protection from bees, the beekeeper shown here wears long, tight sleeves, a hat, and a veil. Bees always crawl upwards, so the beekeeper sometimes tucks trousers into boots.

Find out more

DESIGN
TEXTILES

COAL

A lump of anthracite, a type of hard black coal

PEOPLE HAVE used coal for cooking and heating for thousands of years. During the 19th century, coal was the world's most important fuel. It powered the steam engines that made the Industrial Revolution possible. Today coal is still used in vast amounts. Most coal is burned at power stations to produce electricity, and burning coal meets much of the world's energy needs. Coal is also an essential raw material for making many products, the most important of which are iron and steel. Coal is often called a fossil fuel because it is formed from the fossilized remains of plants that are millions of years old. Sometimes a piece of coal bears the imprint of a prehistoric plant or insect. The Earth contains reserves of coal which, with careful use, may last for hundreds of years. But many people are concerned that coal burning adds to global pollution.

FORMATION OF COAL

1 PREHISTORIC SWAMP
Coal began to form in swamps as long ago as 300 million years. Dying trees and other plants fell into the water, and their remains became covered in mud.

2 PEAT
The plant remains slowly dried out under the mud, forming layers of peat, a fuel that can be dug from the ground.

3 LIGNITE
Layers of peat became buried. Heat and pressure turned the peat into lignite, or brown coal. Lignite is dug from shallow pits called strip mines.

4 BLACK COAL
Intense heat and pressure turned deeper layers of peat into a soft black coal called bituminous coal, and anthracite.

Pumps suck fresh air through the mine.

COAL MINERS

For centuries, miners had to cut coal by hand. Now there are drills and computer-controlled cutting machines to help them.

MINING

Mine shafts are dug down to seams (layers) of coal far below the surface. Miners dig a network of tunnels to remove coal from the seams. In addition to coal, many other useful minerals, such as copper, are mined. The deepest mine is a gold mine in South Africa nearly 4 km (2.5 miles) deep.

Air shaft

Miners' cage carries miners up and down mine.

Skip (shuttle car) lifts coal to surface.

Railway takes miners to the coal faces.

Miners use cutting machine to dig out coal at coal face.

Miners have lamps on their helmets to help them see.

USES OF COAL

A few steam-powered trains still burn coal, and some homes have open fires or coal-fired heating systems. The main use for coal is in the production of electricity. Heating coal without air produces coke, which is used to make steel, and coal gas, which may be burned as a fuel. Another product is coal-tar pitch, which is used in road making. Coal is also treated to make chemicals which are used to produce drugs, plastics, dyes, and many other products.

A large coal-fired power station in Berlin, Germany

Conveyor belts take coal to shaft.

Supports hold roof and sides of tunnels in place.

Find out more
ELECTRICITY
FIRE
INDUSTRIAL REVOLUTION
IRON AND STEEL
PREHISTORIC LIFE
TRAINS

COLD WAR

POTSDAM
In 1945, British Prime Minister Winston Churchill, U.S. President Harry Truman, and Premier Joseph Stalin of the Soviet Union (left to right) met at Potsdam, Germany to decide the future of the Western world. But serious disagreements arose because Stalin was not prepared to release the countries of Eastern Europe from Communist control. This greatly worried the Western leaders.

WHEN WORLD WAR II ENDED in 1945, Europe was in ruins. The United States, and what was then the Soviet Union, had emerged as the world's two most powerful countries or "superpowers". By 1949, two new power blocs of countries had formed. The Eastern bloc, led by the Soviet Union, was Communist; the Western bloc, headed by the United States, was Capitalist. Over the next 40 years the two superpowers opposed each other in what became known as the Cold War. Each bloc attempted to become the most powerful by building up stocks of weapons. The Cold War was a time of great tension but during the 1980's the rivalry eased. Both sides began to disarm, and in 1990 the United States and the Soviet Union declared the Cold War over.

THE IRON CURTAIN IN 1949
Immediately after World War II ended, Stalin shut the borders of Eastern Europe. In a famous speech made in 1946, Winston Churchill declared that "an iron curtain has descended across the continent" of Europe. The Communists seized control of the countries behind the imaginary Iron Curtain. The Soviet secret police rounded up opponents of Communism. The countries became Soviet satellites – nations controlled by the Soviet Union. What was then Yugoslavia broke away in 1948, East Germany was added in 1949.

U.S.S.R.

East Germany

West Germany

Czechoslovakia

Albania

The NATO symbol

NATO
In 1949, the United States and several European countries formed the North Atlantic Treaty Organization (NATO). A military organization, its aim was to prevent a Soviet invasion of Europe. In response to this the Soviet Union formed an alliance of Communist states called the Warsaw Pact.

BERLIN AIRLIFT
In 1945, Britain, France, the United States, and the Soviet Union divided Berlin between them. In 1948, Stalin blocked all traffic to West Berlin. But in the Berlin airlift, the Western allies flew in supplies, and Stalin lifted the blockade.

INF TREATY
Since the 1960s relations between the two superpowers have improved. In 1987, President Ronald Reagan and Soviet General Secretary Mikhail Gorbachev signed the Soviet-American Intermediate-Range Nuclear Forces (INF) Treaty. The INF treaty cut numbers of nuclear weapons and was a major breakthrough in the Cold War.

KOREAN WAR
In 1950, Communist North Korea, equipped with Soviet weapons, invaded South Korea. The United States led a United Nations force to drive the Communists out. When the United Nations troops invaded North Korea, China sent soldiers to fight them. It was the first time the United States had fought a "hot war" against communism.

Find out more
COMMUNISM
NUCLEAR AGE
UNITED NATIONS
U.S.S.R., HISTORY OF
VIETNAM WAR
WORLD WAR II

COLOUR

A WORLD WITHOUT colour would be a dull place. It would also be difficult to live in. Imagine how hard it would be to tell if traffic lights meant stop or go if there were no red or green. Nature has colour signals too: the bright colours of a tree frog warn other animals that it is poisonous, and the beautiful colours of a flower attract bees to its nectar.

Not every creature sees colours in the same way; some animals, such as guinea pigs and squirrels, are colour blind and cannot distinguish between different colours at all. Colour is really the way our eyes interpret different kinds of light. Light is made up of tiny, invisible waves, and each wave has a particular size or wavelength. Each coloured light is composed of different wavelengths which our eyes are able to detect. White light, such as light from the sun, is actually a combination of light of all the colours of the rainbow.

PRISM
A triangular chunk of glass called a prism separates all the colours in white light. When light goes through a prism, it is refracted, or bent, because glass slows it down. But every colour goes through at a different speed, and is bent to a different degree. So the colours spread out when they leave the prism.

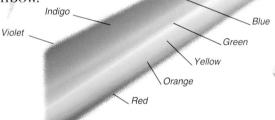

Indigo
Violet
Blue
Green
Yellow
Orange
Red

SPECTRUM
When a prism splits white light into colours, they always come out in the same order, with red at one end and violet at the other. This is called the spectrum. When sunlight is reflected by raindrops, a rainbow is produced which contains all the colours of the spectrum.

MIXING COLOURS
Red, green, and blue are called the primary colours of light. This is because you can mix red, green, and blue light in different proportions to make any colour in the spectrum. In printing there is a different set of primary colours: cyan (green-blue), magenta (blue-red), and yellow. These too can be mixed to give any colour except white.

Mixing any two primary colours produces secondary colours.

PAINT PRIMARIES
Mixing together the three primary colours of paint in the correct amounts gives black. Artists mix paints to make hundreds of different shades and colours.

LIGHT PRIMARIES
When the three primary colours of light are mixed together in the correct proportions they make white. During rock concerts and theatre performances, lighting technicians produce a wide range of colours on the stage by mixing different coloured spotlights.

COLOURED OBJECTS
Objects look coloured because of the way they reflect the light that hits them. When white light falls on any surface, some colours are absorbed, or taken in, and some bounce off. When we look at the surface, we see only the colours that bounce off. It is this coloured light that produces the colour we perceive the object to be.

RED SHOES
When daylight hits a pair of red shoes, they look red because they reflect only red light and absorb all the other colours.

BLACK SHOES?
In blue light, red shoes look black because all the blue light is absorbed, and no light is reflected.

Find out more
CAMOUFLAGE
EYES
LIGHT
PRINTING
RAIN AND SNOW

CHRISTOPHER
COLUMBUS

IN 1492 THREE SMALL SAILING SHIPS named the *Niña*, the *Piñta*, and the *Santa Maria* left Spain on a daring voyage. Their aim was to find a new sea route to the East in search of spices and treasure. In command was Christopher Columbus, an Italian sailor from Genoa. Unlike other explorers of the time, who were sailing east, Columbus believed that if he sailed west he would reach India and its luxuries within a few months. The Spanish were eager to profit from trade with India and the rest of Asia, and Columbus persuaded Queen Isabella of Spain to pay for his expedition. He set sail in August and two months later sighted land which he believed was Asia. In fact Columbus had arrived in the Caribbean Islands. He did not realize what he had found, but his journey paved the way for later European settlement in the Americas.

THE FIRST VOYAGE
Columbus's voyage from Spain to the Caribbean lasted four months. He made three more voyages but did not find the mainland.

Landed on San Salvador 12 Oct 1492.

Set sail from Spain 3 Aug. 1492.

Cuba

Began homeward voyage 19 Jan. 1493.

Hispaniola

PTOLEMY'S WORLD MAP
The map used by Columbus had been produced by the Greek mapmaker Ptolemy in the 2nd century. The world it showed did not include the American continents, Australia, or the Pacific.

EXPLORING THE CARIBBEAN
When Columbus arrived in the Caribbean he was welcomed by the Carib and Arawak people. Native Americans became known as Indians because the early explorers thought they were in India.

Food and other supplies were stored here.

THE *SANTA MARIA*
Columbus's flagship was a slow, clumsy, wooden cargo ship, no larger than a modern fishing trawler. The ship relied on wind power, and conditions on board were cramped and difficult.

Spare canvas for mending sails

THE CREW
The *Santa Maria* carried a crew of 40. The main risk of such a long voyage was running out of food and water.

Find out more

CARIBBEAN
CONQUISTADORS
EXPLORERS

COMETS AND METEORS

ON A CLEAR NIGHT you may see several shooting stars in the space of an hour. A shooting star, or meteor, looks like a point of light which suddenly darts across the sky and disappears. A meteor occurs when a piece of dust from space, called a meteoroid, burns up as it enters the Earth's atmosphere. As the meteor plummets to Earth at a speed of about 240,000 km/h (150,000 mph), friction with the air produces intense heat which leaves a bright glow in the sky. Meteors usually burn up about 90 km (56 miles) from the Earth's surface.

Many meteoroids are fragments left over from comets which orbit the sun. A comet appears as a faint starlike point of light that moves across the sky for a few nights. As it nears the sun, the comet grows a "tail". Then it swings past the sun and travels away, becoming smaller and fainter. Comets often reappear at regular intervals (every few years) as they travel past Earth on their orbits.

COMET TAIL
As a comet approaches Earth, the heat of the sun turns the ice into gas. The gas escapes, along with dust, and forms one or more tails (the gas and dust usually form separate tails). The tails always point away from the sun. They get shorter as the comet moves away from the sun.

Dust tail can be up to about 1 million km (600,000 miles) long. It glows white because the particles of dust reflect sunlight.

Gas tail can be up to 100 million km (62 million miles) long. The gas tail has a bluish glow. This is because the heat of the sun makes the gas molecules emit blue-coloured light.

The size of a comet's nucleus can range from a few hundred metres across to more than 10 kms (about 6 miles) across.

The solar wind – a blast of charged particles that stream from the sun – blows the comet's tails away from the sun. When the comet approaches the sun, its tails follow. The tails lead when the comet moves away from the sun.

COMETS
A comet consists of a central core, or nucleus, of dust and ice; a cloud of gas and dust around the nucleus, called the coma; and one or more tails. Astronomers have observed hundreds of comets and believe that about one million million other comets orbit the sun unseen, far beyond the most distant planet.

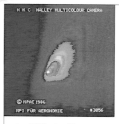

H M C HALLEY MULTICOLOUR CAMERA
© MPAE 1986.
MPI FÜR AERONOMIE   #3056

In 1986, the Giotto space probe flew past Halley's Comet. Giotto sent back many pictures, including this false-colour image.

Chinese astronomers probably observed Halley's Comet more than 2,200 years ago. The comet also appears in the 11th-century Bayeux tapestry, which shows the Norman Conquest of England.

HALLEY'S COMET
The English astronomer Edmund Halley (1656-1742) first realized that some comets appear regularly. In 1705 he showed that the comet now called Halley's Comet returns every 75 or 76 years.

METEORITES
Huge lumps of rock called meteorites pass through the Earth's atmosphere without burning up completely. About 25,000 years ago, a meteorite that weighed about 900,000 tonnes (more than 890,000 tons) caused a crater in Arizona, United States, (above) 1,200 m (4,000 ft) across. Some scientists believe that the impact of a huge meteorite about 65 million years ago may have destroyed many animal species.

METEORS
There are two types of meteors: those that occur individually and those that occur in showers. This spectacular meteor shower (left) occurred in 1833. Similar impressive displays occur every 33 years during November. At this time the Earth passes through a swarm of meteors, called the Leonids, that spread out along the orbit of a comet.

Find out more

ASTRONOMY
EARTH
PLANETS
ROCKS AND MINERALS
SUN

COMMUNISM

AFTER 1917, A NEW WORD came into popular use – Communism. For it was then that Russia set up the world's first Communist government. By 1950, nearly one-third of the world's population lived under Communist rule. The word communism comes from the Latin word *communis*, meaning "belonging to all". More than 2,000 years ago, the Greek writer, Plato, put forward the earliest ideas about communism in his book *The Republic*. Much later the Russian revolutionary, Vladimir Lenin, developed modern Communism from the writings of the German philosopher Karl Marx. Unlike Capitalists, who believe in private ownership, Communists believe that the people should own a country's wealth and industry, and wealth should be shared according to need. In Communist countries, the Communist party is all-powerful and controls every aspect of daily life. During the 20th century, Communism was a major political force. Increasingly, people in Communist countries resented economic hardship and their lack of freedom. From the late 1980s, various countries, including the former Soviet Union, rejected Communist rule.

CHAINS AROUND THE WORLD
"The workers have nothing to lose . . . but their chains. They have a world to gain," wrote Marx in his *Communist Manifesto*. On this magazine cover, a worker strikes down "chains" that bind the world.

KARL MARX
Communism is based on ideas written down in the 1800s by Karl Marx (1818-83). His major work, *Das Kapital*, became the Communist "bible". He believed that all history is a struggle between the rich rulers and the poor workers, and that the workers will eventually overthrow their rulers in a revolution. Marx died in exile in London, England.

SPREAD OF COMMUNISM
After 1917, Communism spread from Russia to many countries elsewhere in the world (shown in red above). Most of these countries had large populations, ruled, often badly, by a small number of very rich people. For the masses, their only hope for a better future lay in joining the revolution.

CAPITALISM
Owner   Worker

Under capitalism, a few people own all the factories. Working people are paid wages but do not share the profits.

COMMUNISM
Worker   Worker

Under communism, the factories are owned by the people that work in them; the workers share the profits equally.

CHINA
In 1949, China became a Communist state under Mao Zedong (1893-1976). China has the largest communist party in the world, with 49 million members. The lives of the poor peasants have been improved by communism, but they have little freedom. The Chinese Communist Party directs the lives of its people through education. The party encourages people to take part in group sports, such as tai chi, shown left.

FIDEL CASTRO
In 1959, Fidel Castro (left), a Cuban lawyer, led a revolution against Cuba's dictator, President Batista. Castro became head of government, and Cuba became a Communist state. Castro seized all American property and promised freedom to the Cuban people. Since then Castro has encouraged and supported the growth of communism throughout Central and South America.

Find out more

CHINA, HISTORY OF
COLD WAR
MAO ZEDONG
RUSSIAN REVOLUTION
SOUTH AMERICA, HISTORY OF
U.S.S.R., HISTORY OF

COMPOSERS

AN AUTHOR CREATING A STORY has a choice of more than a hundred thousand words made up from the 26 letters of the alphabet. With only the 12 notes of the chromatic scale – the notes on the piano from any C to the next C above – a composer can make an infinite variety of music of many different styles. These can include jazz, folk, popular, or what is known as classical music.

Composers learn their craft through writing exercises in harmony and counterpoint. Harmony is placing the main tune on the top line with chords (three or more notes sounding together) in support; counterpoint is placing the principal theme in any position with other tunes weaving around it. Composers also discover what instruments can or cannot do, what they sound like, and how to explore their capabilities. The best way to learn all this is to study the music of many composers. Great composers move audiences to tears of joy or sadness with their talent for expressing emotion through music.

In the 15th century beautiful coloured pictures decorated the margins of composers' work.

Many composers like to write music sitting at the piano, so that they can play the themes as they work on them.

PURCELL
English composer Henry Purcell (1659-1695) sang in the king's chapel in London (above) when he was a boy. At the age of 20 he became the organist at Westminster Abbey, London. He composed beautiful chamber music and dramatic operas such as *Dido and Aeneas*.

Each member of the orchestra uses a line of the score showing only the music for his or her individual instrument.

Composers of orchestral music write a complete score which includes the instrumental parts played by every section of the orchestra.

HOW COMPOSERS WORK
Most composers begin by either inventing themes or melodies that are developed for one or more instruments, or by setting words for one or more voices. Sometimes, as with operas and choral works, both voices and instruments are used. Blending them together so that all are heard clearly is a skilled job. The music is written out in a score. As a symphony can last up to an hour, or an opera up to three hours, composing can be seen to be hard work.

BAROQUE MUSIC
The music of the 17th and early 18th centuries was called Baroque, after the elaborate architectural styles popular in the same period. It is complex music in which the instruments weave their melodies in and out like threads in a rich, colourful tapestry.

BACH
The greatest of the Baroque composers was Johann Sebastian Bach (1685-1750) of Germany. The *Brandenburg Concertos*, which he completed in 1721, are among his best-known works.

HANDEL
George Frideric Handel (1685-1759) was born in Germany and moved to England in 1712. He composed music for the English royal family and wrote many famous choral works.

Handel wrote one of his most famous pieces of music to accompany a royal fireworks display in 1749.

CLASSICAL ERA

Serious music is often called classical to distinguish it from popular music. However, for musicians, classical music is the music composed in the late 18th and early 19th centuries. Classical composers extended the harmony and forms of the Baroque era. The symphony developed in this period. Joseph Haydn (1732-1809) composed 104 symphonies.

MOZART

Wolfgang Amadeus Mozart (1756-1791) of Austria was a talented composer and performer by the age of five. He went on to write chamber music, symphonies, and concertos, as well as great operas such as *The Magic Flute*.

Mozart performed all over Europe when he was only six.

BEETHOVEN

The German composer Ludwig van Beethoven (1770-1827; above) was completely deaf for the last 10 years of his life but continued to compose some of the greatest music in the world. His late works moved towards the Romantic movement.

ROMANTIC MOVEMENT

From about 1820 composers began to experiment with new harmonies and forms, achieving a much wider emotional range. For composers such as Tchaikovsky, formal rules were less important than creating drama, painting pictures in sound, or telling stories.

TCHAIKOVSKY

The Russian composer Peter Ilyich Tchaikovsky (1840-1893) was unhappy in his personal life, which brought great emotional depth to his music. He wrote many well-known ballets and symphonies, including the famous *1812 Overture*.

Stravinsky's ballet The Firebird *caused a sensation at its first performance in Paris in 1910.*

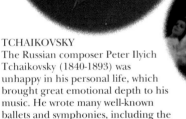

Playing a tune on an electric piano adds the notes to the score on the screen.

COMPUTER COMPOSITION

Computers can help composers to write music. The composer can use an electronic instrument to enter the melodies into the computer, where they can be stored, altered, and printed out.

MODERN MUSIC

In the 20th century there have been great changes in serious music. Russian-born composer Igor Stravinsky (1882-1971) experimented with new harmonies, creating sounds that his audiences sometimes found difficult to understand. Today, modern composers such as the German Karlheinz Stockhausen still challenge listeners' ideas about music. In *Zyklus*, for example, Stockhausen tells the percussionist to start on any page of the score and play to the end before starting again at the beginning.

COMPOSERS

800s Composers begin to write down their music for the first time. At the same time, monks develop a form of chant, called plainsong, for singing church services.

1300-1600 Composers of the late Medieval and Renaissance period start to develop harmony by combining different voices together, producing a richer sound called polyphony.

1597 Jacopo Peri (1561-1633) of Italy composes *Dafne*, the first opera.

1600s Baroque music begins, and composers gradually make their music more complicated and elaborate.

1750-1820 The rise of classical music introduces simpler, popular tunes that more people could enjoy.

1817-23 Beethoven composes the *Choral* symphony, the first symphony to use a choir.

1820s The romantic era begins, and composers start to look for new ways to make their music appeal to the listeners' emotions.

1850s Composers in eastern and northern Europe begin to write nationalistic music, based on traditional songs and stories from their countries.

1865 Richard Wagner's (1813-83) opera *Tristan and Isolde* points towards Modern music.

1888 Russian nationalist composer Nikolai Rimsky-Korsakov composes his *Scheherazade*, based on the *Thousand and One Nights*.

1900s The modern era in music begins. Composers of the impressionist movement write music that creates atmosphere, movement, and color in sound.

1905 French impressionist composer Claude Debussy (1862-1918) writes *La Mer* (The Sea).

1924 George Gershwin composes *Rhapsody in Blue* for jazz orchestra and piano.

1959 German composer Karlheinz Stockhausen (born 1928) writes *Zyklus* for one percussion player.

Find out more

MUSIC
MUSICAL INSTRUMENTS
OPERA AND SINGING
ORCHESTRAS
RENAISSANCE

COMPUTERS

ACCURATE WEATHER forecasting, safe air travel, reliable medical technology – in today's world we take these things for granted, but they would be impossible without computers. A computer is a special kind of machine. Although it cannot "think" for itself in the same way as a person, a computer works like an electronic brain that can do many tasks and interpret data (information) very quickly. The huge computer in an airport air traffic control system, for instance, can keep track of hundreds of aircraft at the same time and indicates where they should fly to avoid collisions. A computer consists of thousands of tiny electronic circuits. Before a computer can work, it must be given a set of instructions, called a program, that tells the computer how to do a particular job. Once the program is running, the computer can perform its task, which involves processing some kind of information. For example, the program in a computer game asks a player questions and throws images onto the screen according to information contained in the player's answers.

MICROCOMPUTERS

Many homes, schools, and offices use micro-computers – small computers designed for one person. A microcomputer consists of four basic units: a keyboard, to type in information; a memory, to store information and programs; a processing unit, to carry out the instructions contained in the program; and a screen, for seeing the results of the computer's work.

HIDDEN COMPUTERS People usually think of computers as having a screen and a keyboard, but this is not always the case. Many devices, such as washing machines, cars, and cameras, contain tiny computers that are specially programmed to control the machine.

Pictures, charts, text, and all kinds of other information appear on the monitor screen.

The memory of a computer consists of microchips. There are two types: ROM (read-only memory) contains permanent instructions; RAM (random access memory) holds programs and information as they are needed. The microchips store information in the form of electric charges.

The part of the computer that does calculations and other similar tasks is a microchip called the CPU (central processing unit), or microprocessor.

The CPU receives data and instructions from programs held in the computer's memory. It processes the data according to the instruction in the program to produce a result, such as the answer to a calculation.

The mouse ball is connected to two slotted wheels. As each wheel turns, it interrupts a beam of light. From the changes in the light beam, the computer detects where the mouse has moved.

Light detector

Mouse ball

Lamp

Information that has to be kept for long periods is stored on magnetic disks (or tape). There are many types of disks, including hard disks, which store vast quantities of data, and floppy disks, which store less information but are removable and can be used to carry data from one computer to another. CD-ROMS (compact disc read-only memory), which hold 650 times as much information as a floppy disk, are the most popular format for multimedia programs.

Moving a device called a mouse moves an arrow in the same direction on the screen. It is an easy way to feed information and instructions into the computer.

When a key is pressed, its letter or number appears on the screen.

The keyboard has keys just like a typewriter. Pressing the keys feeds information such as names and numbers into the computer.

A hard disc consists of several magnetic discs. An electromagnet "writes" information onto them and "reads" data from them.

A floppy disc is contained in an oblong plastic cover. An electromagnet moves across the disc, aligning the magnetic particles in the disc so that they represent data.

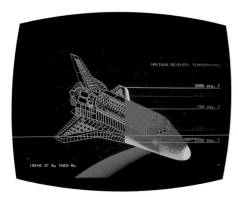

HARDWARE

The computer machinery that people use is called hardware. There are many different kinds of hardware: microcomputers, small portable computers, and large mainframe computers at which many people can work simultaneously. Hardware also includes monitor screens, printers, and similar computer equipment.

Image scanner, for transferring pictures from paper into the computer

Printer, for producing a permanent copy of the material that is shown on the screen

SOFTWARE

The programs that make the computer perform different tasks are called software. A computer can perform many different jobs simply by using different software, from computer games and word processing programs to painting programs and scientific programs that do complex calculations.

This pattern is called a fractal. It is produced by a supercomputer which generates numbers according to a strict rule, which it then plots onto the screen, producing the pattern. Such calculations are so complex that only the most powerful supercomputers can do them.

SUPERCOMPUTERS

The most powerful computers are called supercomputers. They can do difficult calculations very quickly and are therefore used in science and engineering. Supercomputers help engineers design cars and aircraft, and weather forecasters predict the weather.

HOW COMPUTERS WORK

A computer changes everything it handles, such as letters of the alphabet, into numbers. The numbers are stored in the computer in the form of electric signals. The computer does all its different tasks, such as inserting a word into a sentence, by doing rapid calculations with these numbers. Once it has finished its job, the computer changes the numbers into words and pictures that we can understand.

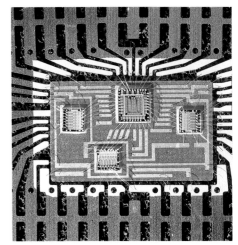

All computers contain a set of microchips (right). Inside a microchip are thousands of tiny electronic parts that store and process electric signals.

HISTORY OF COMPUTERS

In 1834, English inventor Charles Babbage designed the first programmable mechanical computer. However, he never made the machine because it was too complex for the techniques of the day. In 1946, the first fully electronic computer, ENIAC, was built in the US. In the 1980s, transistors and microchips enabled computers to become smaller and more powerful. In the early 1990s, web browsers opened up the Internet to millions of private individuals.

BILL GATES

In 1975, American Bill Gates (born 1955) founded the Microsoft company. In the 1980s, Microsoft's easy-to-use software programs fuelled the home-computer revolution. By the late 1990s, Microsoft was supplying over half the world's software needs.

Binary number 01000001

Binary number 01000010

Binary number 01000011

This series of electrical signals is the binary representation of the letter A.

Computer representation of the letter B.

Computer representation of the letter C.

BINARY CODE

A computer stores all information (including programs) as electric signals in which "on" stands for 1 and "off" stands for 0. All numbers, letters, and pictures are represented by sequences of 1s and 0s. This is called binary code.

Find out more
ELECTRONICS
MACHINES
MATHEMATICS
ROBOTS
TECHNOLOGY

CONQUISTADORS

AT THE BEGINNING OF THE 16TH CENTURY the first Spanish adventurers followed Christopher Columbus to the Caribbean and South and Central America. These conquistadors (the Spanish word for conquerors) were soldiers, hungry for gold, silver, and land. They took priests with them, sent by the Catholic Church to convert the Native Americans. The two most famous conquistadors were the Spaniards Hernando Cortés (1485-1547), who conquered the Aztecs of Mexico, and Francisco Pizarro (1470-1541), who conquered the Incas of Peru. Although the conquistadors took only small numbers of soldiers along, they were successful partly because they had guns, horses, and steel weapons. The conquistadors also accidentally brought European diseases such as smallpox and measles, against which the Native Americans had no resistance. These diseases wiped out more than 70 million Native Americans and destroyed their civilizations. By seizing the land, the conquistadors prepared the way for a huge Spanish empire in the Americas that was to last until the 19th century.

EL DORADO
The first conquistadors heard legends of a golden kingdom ruled by "El Dorado", the golden man. They kept searching for this amazing place but never found it. Most of the beautiful goldwork they took to Europe was melted down and reused.

Hernando Cortés

Montezuma

HERNANDO CORTÉS
In 1519 Cortés set out from Cuba to conquer Mexico, against the governor Velázquez's wishes. Velázquez believed that Cortés was too ambitious. From an early age Cortés had sought adventure and wealth. Eventually his wish was fulfilled and he controlled the whole of Mexico.

NEW SPAIN
The Spanish quickly settled the conquered areas and created the empire of New Spain. The wealth from its silver mines and ranches became the envy of Europe.

Aztecs

Incas

MONTEZUMA MEETS CORTÉS
When the Aztec emperor Montezuma met Cortés in Tenochtitlán, he believed that Cortés was the pale-skinned, bearded god Quetzalcoatl, who was prophesied to return from the east. He welcomed Cortés with gifts and a ceremony. But Cortés captured him and took over the Aztec empire.

FRANCISCO PIZARRO
In 1532, Pizarro marched into Peru with 200 soldiers. He seized the Inca emperor, Atahualpa, ransomed him for a roomful of gold, then had him killed. The leaderless Inca empire crumbled.

NATIVE AMERICANS
After conquest the Native Americans were treated cruelly and forced to work for the Spanish. Many slaved in the gold mines. It was not long before their old way of life disappeared forever.

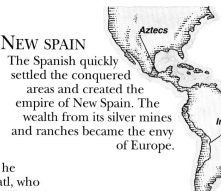

_____ *Find out more* _____

AZTECS
COLUMBUS, CHRISTOPHER
EXPLORERS
INCAS
SOUTH AMERICA,
history of

CONSERVATION
AND ENDANGERED SPECIES

ANIMALS AND PLANTS ARE DYING OUT at a greater rate than ever
before. Living things have become extinct throughout the Earth's history
– often due to dramatic changes in the climate – but today humans are the
greatest threat. Thousands of animals and plants are endangered (in danger
of extinction) because we cut down forests and drain wetlands to farm or
build on the land where they live. We change the environment so much that
animals and plants cannot survive. This is called habitat loss. Another great
threat is hunting. People hunt animals for their fur, hide, horns, and meat,
and sometimes simply because the animals are a nuisance. Pollution is yet
another serious threat, damaging many oceans, rivers, and forests. Conservation
is the management and protection of wildlife. It includes sheltering and trying
to save wild animals and plants from destruction
by humans. People are more aware of these
threats to wildlife than ever before, and there
are conservation organizations in many
parts of the world. They work to protect
endangered creatures by setting
aside areas in the wild where
animals and plants can live
in safety.

GREENPEACE
International organizations
such as Greenpeace work
in various ways to save
endangered polar wildlife,
particularly whales and
seals. Here, a Greenpeace
worker is spraying a seal
pup with harmless red dye
so that seal hunters will not
want to kill the pup for its
beautiful fur.

CONSERVING NATURE
Conservation involves studying wild
places, identifying the animals and
plants that live there, and watching
what happens to them. The
International Union for the
Conservation of Nature and
Natural Resources (IUCN)
collects scientific data and works
on conservation in many
countries, together with
organizations such as the
United Nations Environment
Programme (UNEP).

CACTUS
The Mexican
neogomesia cactus
and dozens of
other cacti are very
rare because plant
collectors have
taken them from
the wild.

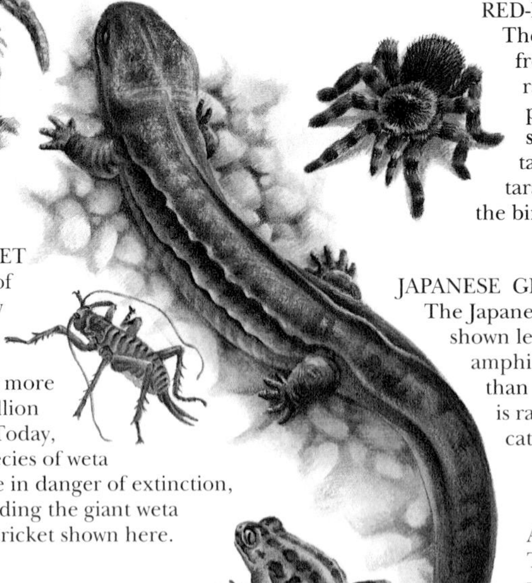

Neogomesia cactus

Siamese crocodile

SIAMESE CROCODILE
Many crocodiles and alligators have been
killed for their skins, to be made into leather
bags, shoes, and belts. Today, about 20
members of the crocodile family are in
danger of extinction, including the Siamese
crocodile and the Orinoco crocodile.

GREY BAT
Many kinds of bats are
threatened because of the loss of
their forest homes for farmland,
and because of the increasing
use of insecticides on the food
they eat. The American grey bat
shown below is endangered.

RED-KNEED TARANTULA
The red-kneed tarantula
from Mexico (left) is
rare because many
people keep exotic
spiders as pets. This
tarantula is not a true
tarantula but a member of
the bird-eating spider group.

GIANT WETA CRICKET
There are many kinds of
weta crickets in New
Zealand. Fossils
have been
found that are more
than 180 million
years old. Today,
several species of weta
cricket are in danger of extinction,
including the giant weta
cricket shown here.

JAPANESE GIANT SALAMANDER
The Japanese giant salamander,
shown left, is the world's largest
amphibian, growing to more
than 1.5 m (5 ft) long. Today it
is rare. Sometimes people
catch it for its meat.

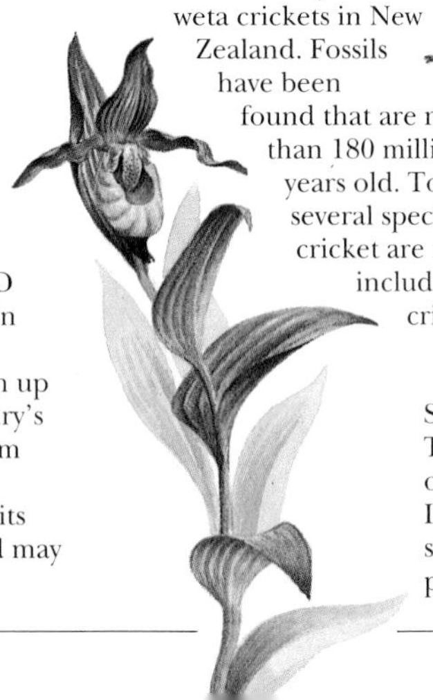

SLIPPER ORCHID
Many orchids are in
danger because
collectors dig them up
from the wild. Drury's
slipper orchid, from
India, has almost
disappeared from its
natural region and may
soon be extinct.

SPADEFOOT TOAD
There are many kinds
of spadefoot toad. The
Italian spadefoot toad
shown here is
particularly endangered.

AFRICAN VIOLET
The African violet is a
well-known houseplant,
but it has almost
disappeared from its
natural habitat –
tropical mountain
forests in Tanzania,
Africa.

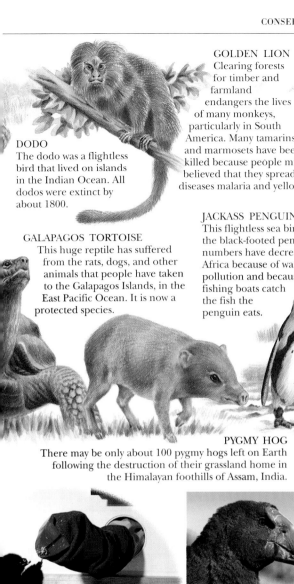

DODO
The dodo was a flightless bird that lived on islands in the Indian Ocean. All dodos were extinct by about 1800.

GALAPAGOS TORTOISE
This huge reptile has suffered from the rats, dogs, and other animals that people have taken to the Galapagos Islands, in the East Pacific Ocean. It is now a protected species.

GOLDEN LION TAMARIN
Clearing forests for timber and farmland endangers the lives of many monkeys, particularly in South America. Many tamarins and marmosets have been killed because people mistakenly believed that they spread the diseases malaria and yellow fever.

JACKASS PENGUIN
This flightless sea bird is also called the black-footed penguin. Its numbers have decreased in South Africa because of water pollution and because fishing boats catch the fish the penguin eats.

PYGMY HOG
There may be only about 100 pygmy hogs left on Earth following the destruction of their grassland home in the Himalayan foothills of Assam, India.

MONK SEAL
Nature reserves have been set up for the Mediterranean monk seal so that it would not be disturbed by tourists on the coasts where it breeds.

VICTORIA'S BIRDWING BUTTERFLY
The Victoria's birdwing butterfly was first collected by scientists in 1855, when they shot it with guns. Today this butterfly and many other kinds of butterflies are endangered because collectors kill them.

SUMATRAN RHINOCEROS
Rhinoceroses are in great danger of extinction, but poachers (illegal hunters) still kill them and sell their horns. The horns are carved into dagger handles or powdered into fake medicine. There are only a few hundred Sumatran rhinoceroses left, in Sumatra and mainland Southeast Asia.

HABITAT LOSS
Tropical rain forests are being destroyed at an alarming rate. Trees are burned or sold for timber, and the land is farmed or used for roads and buildings. Scientists believe that many rain forests contain kinds of animals and plants that we have never seen. For every plant or creature that is threatened or extinct, there may be 100 that we do not know about.

CAPTIVE BREEDING
One way to help an endangered species recover its numbers is by breeding it in captivity. Experts capture a few animals from the wild, raise them carefully, and encourage them to breed in captivity. Later they release, or reintroduce, the offspring into a suitable area. The notornis is a flightless bird that scientists believed to be extinct until it was rediscovered in 1948. Eggs from its nests are hatched in an incubator, and the chicks are kept warm with tiny electric blankets. They are fed by someone wearing a puppet-like glove that resembles the parent bird.

CONTROLLING TRADE
Some animals and plants are taken from the wild for their skins and other products. Elephants die for their ivory tusks. Colourful flowers are made into pulp to make dyes. The Convention on International Trade in Endangered Species (CITES) has lists of hundreds of species, or kinds, of plants and animals. Selling or exporting these animals or their products is illegal without a special licence. All whales, dolphins, and porpoises are on this list; so are all monkeys, apes, and lemurs.

SNAKE SKIN
The brightly coloured objects shown here were once the skins of snakes and lizards. The skins are dyed different colours, then made into all sorts of leather goods, including bags and shoes.

SNOW LEOPARD
The snow leopard lives high in the mountains of the Himalayas and Central Asia. In winter its fur becomes thicker to keep out the bitter cold. In the past, the snow leopard's winter coat was much prized by fur traders. Today, the snow leopard and many other big cats are protected by the CITES agreement, but they are still hunted illegally in some remote areas.

Find out more
ANIMALS
ECOLOGY AND FOOD WEBS
FOREST WILDLIFE
PLANTS
POLLUTION

CONTINENTS

ALMOST A THIRD of the surface of the Earth is land. There are seven vast pieces of land, called continents, which make up most of this area. The rest consists of islands which are much smaller land masses completely surrounded by water. The seven continents are crowded into almost one half of the globe; the huge Pacific Ocean occupies most of the other half. The largest continent is Asia, which has an area of more than 44 million square km (17 million square miles).

Most scientists now agree that, about 200 million years ago, the continents were joined together in one huge land mass. Over millions of years they drifted around and changed shape, and they are still moving today. The continents lie on vast pieces of solid rock, called plates, which collide and move against one another. These movements cause volcanoes and earthquakes, push up mountains, and create huge trenches in the Earth's crust.

3 THE WORLD TODAY
The Americas have moved away from the other continents and joined together, and India has joined Asia. Australia and Antarctica have drifted apart.

Europe
Asia
North America
Africa
South America
Australia
Antarctica

The continents are made of many smaller pieces of land which have been pushed together.

1 PANGAEA
The continents were joined in one supercontinent, called Pangaea, which began to break apart about 200 million years ago.

North America
Asia
Europe
India
Australia
Pangaea
South America
Africa
Antarctica

Asia
North America
Laurasia
Africa
Europe
India
South America
Gondwanaland
Australia
Antarctica

2 BREAK-UP
About 135 million years ago, Pangaea split up into two areas – Gondwanaland and Laurasia.

CONTINENTAL DRIFT
A glance at the globe shows that the eastern sides of North and South America and the western sides of Europe and Africa follow a similar line. In 1912, Alfred Wegener, a German meteorologist, suggested that the continents once fitted together like pieces of a jigsaw. This huge piece of land then broke up, and the continents drifted apart.

PLATE TECTONICS
The continents and oceans lie on top of several huge plates of rock about 100 km (60 miles) deep. These plates float on the hot, molten rock in the mantle underneath. Heat from the Earth's interior makes the plates move, carrying the continents with them. Mountains and undersea ridges, deep trenches, and huge valleys form at the edges of the plates as they move and collide.

Pacific Ocean
Atlantic Ocean
Trench
South America
Mountains and volcanoes
American plate
Undersea ridge
Africa
Nazca plate
Molten rock from Nazca plate forces its way up, forming volcanoes along edge of continent.
Nazca plate moves under American plate, forming trench in ocean floor.
Hot rock rises from below, pushing the American and African plates apart and forming an undersea ridge.
Mantle
African plate
Indian plate
Indian Ocean

SAN ANDREAS FAULT
The San Andreas fault in the United States is at the border between two plates. They slide against one another, causing severe earthquakes.

MOVING PLATES
The plates move about 2.5 cm (1 inch) every year – about as fast as your finger-nails grow. The Atlantic Ocean is widening at this speed as the Americas drift apart from Europe and Africa.

Find out more
EARTH
EARTHQUAKES
GEOLOGY
MOUNTAINS
OCEANS AND SEAS
VOLCANOES

JAMES COOK

IN THE LATE SUMMER OF 1768, a small sailing ship left Plymouth, England, on an expedition to the Pacific Ocean. In charge of the ship was Lieutenant James Cook, who was to become one of the greatest explorers the world has ever known. The voyage lasted three years. Cook was an outstanding navigator. He was also a fine captain. He insisted that his sailors eat sauerkraut (pickled cabbage) and fresh fruit, and so became the first captain to save his crew from scurvy, a disease caused by lack of vitamin C. On his return to England, Cook was sent on two more voyages: one to the Antarctic, the other to the Arctic. On these voyages he became the first European to visit a number of Pacific islands, sailed further south than any other European, and added many lands, including Australia and New Zealand, to the British Empire.

1728 Born in Yorkshire, England.

1741 Signs on as ship's boy on the coal ship *Freelove*.

1759 Charts St. Lawrence River in Canada.

1772-75 Voyage to discover "southern continent", a land that scientists thought must exist. Circles Antarctica.

1775 Promoted to captain.

1776-79 Voyage to discover a northwest passage around North America.

1779 Killed in Sandwich Islands (Hawaii).

The Endeavour *was 30 m (98 ft) long, weighed 360 tonnes and carried 112 sailors and five scientists.*

ENDEAVOUR

Cook's ship, the *Endeavour*, was originally a coal ship. Cook chose this ship because it was sturdy, spacious, and easy to handle. On the *Endeavour* voyage, Cook added many new lands to the British Empire.

Cook purified the air in the ship once a week by burning vinegar and gunpowder.

Cook stocked up with fresh fruit at every landing.

KEEPING RECORDS

Cook made many maps, took regular measurements, and recorded every event of the voyages in minute detail. The scientists on board collected botanical specimens from the lands they visited. In an age before cameras, artists on board made drawings of the people, plants, and wildlife they saw to show to people at home. They collected so many specimens in one bay in Australia that they named it Botany Bay. It later became a dreaded prison colony.

Sydney Parkinson was the ship's artist on board the Endeavour. *He drew this plant, Banksia serrata, 1, in around 1760.*

FIRST VOYAGE

The British Royal Navy sent Cook on his first voyage to observe the planet Venus passing between the Earth and the sun. He also had secret orders from the government to sail into uncharted regions to prove the existence of a southern continent, which they wanted to add to their empire. He did not succeed, but in the attempt he became the first European to visit New Zealand and the east coast of Australia.

Sandwich islands (Hawaii)

North America

Asia

Pacific Ocean

Africa

Australia

South America

Islanders killed Captain Cook here on 14 February 1779.

Find out more

AUSTRALIA, HISTORY OF
EXPLORERS
NEW ZEALAND, HISTORY OF

COOKING

MANY FOODS NEED to be cooked before we can eat them. Cooking usually means heating the food to make it easier to digest and to improve its flavour. But it can also mean the preparation of uncooked food. Some people cook as a hobby, others as a necessity; a few think cooking is an art form. Different countries have developed their own style of cooking, or cuisine, by combining local ingredients and producing distinctive dishes. In the past, cuisine varied from season to season according to the food available. Now that it is easy to preserve food and transport it quickly, fresh, frozen, and tinned ingredients are available all year round. Electrical appliances such as mixers and blenders have speeded up food preparation, and convenience foods have become popular in Western countries because people have less time for cooking. Though these instant meals cut down on the need for lengthy cooking, many people think fresh food is healthier.

MEDIEVAL COOKING
Cooking methods in the Middle Ages were simpler than those in use today. Food was often stewed in a caldron hung from a pothook. Meat went bad quickly, so it was often heavily spiced to disguise the taste.

THE CLOSED RANGE
A physicist named Benjamin Thompson invented the closed range below in 1795. For the first time people could regulate cooking temperature.

COOKING WITH ELECTRICITY
Electric ovens became common early in this century. They were safe, clean, and economical and rapidly became the most popular form of oven.

FLAMES FOR COOKING
Open-fire cookery is the oldest method of cooking. Meat was roasted on the spit, and food was boiled in pots hung overhead.

COOKING IN THE PAST
Prehistoric people probably discovered by accident that food tasted better when heated over the fire. Roasting was the first method, followed by stewing or boiling. Cooking bread on a hot stone gradually led to baking in clay ovens.

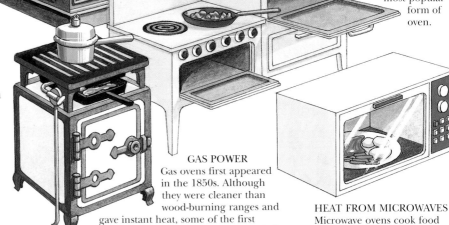

GAS POWER
Gas ovens first appeared in the 1850s. Although they were cleaner than wood-burning ranges and gave instant heat, some of the first models leaked gas, and others exploded!

HEAT FROM MICROWAVES
Microwave ovens cook food quickly from the inside out by heating the water molecules in the food.

NATIONAL CUISINE
Each country has developed its own ways of cooking based on local crops and animals. Religious and other customs and the amount of fuel available also play a part.

Fast stir-fry cooking in a wok developed in China because of a good supply of fresh food and a shortage of timber for fuel.

APICIUS
The world's first known cookery writer was Apicius, a Roman, whose recipes included snails in milk and stuffed mice!

FEASTS
Holy days, weddings, and special occasions are celebrated everywhere with a feast.

Find out more

FESTIVALS AND FEASTS
FOOD AND DIGESTION
HOUSEHOLD APPLIANCES

CORALS
ANEMONES, AND JELLYFISH

Tentacles trail more than 15.2 m (50 ft) from a man-of-war's body.

IN THE WARM, TROPICAL seas surrounding coral islands are some of the most fascinating sea creatures. Despite being so different in appearance, corals, jellyfish, and anemones belong to the same family. The fabulous corals that make up coral reefs are created by little animals called polyps, which look like miniature sea anemones. Every polyp builds a cup-shaped skeleton around itself, and as the polyps grow and die, their skeletons mass together to create a coral reef. Unlike coral-building polyps, jellyfish can move around freely, trailing their long tentacles below their soft bodies as they swim. Some jellyfish float on the surface and are pushed along with the current. Anemones are anchored to rocks by their stalks, where they wait for a fish to swim through their tentacles.

Sea wasp

JELLYFISH
The sea wasp jellyfish uses its tentacles to sting fish. Tentacles contain venom which is painful to humans and can cause death.

CLOWN FISH
These fish live in harmony with sea anemones. The thick, slimy mucus on their bodies keeps them safe from the stinging cells. Clown fish keep anemones clean by feeding on particles of food among their waving tentacles.

Carijoa coral

Clown fish

MAN-OF-WAR
The Portuguese man-of-war is not one jellyfish. It is a floating colony of hundreds of jellyfish-like creatures known as polyps. Some polyps form the float, which drifts on the water; others bear stinging tentacles for paralysing prey; still others digest the prey and pass the nutrients through the body.

CORAL SHAPES
The shape of a coral depends on the arrangement and growing pattern of the tiny polyps that build it. Corals can be dazzling in colour and extraordinary in shape, resembling all sorts of objects. This Carijoa coral looks like a branching tree.

Whip thrown out

Stinging tip

Stinging cell body

Coiled whip

STINGING CELLS
Each jellyfish tentacle is armed with deadly weapons. If a fish touches a tentacle, stinging cells containing tiny coiled-up threads are triggered into action. They shoot out a hollow whip like a harpoon, injecting paralysing poison into the prey.

Common sea anemone

Anemone slowly digests a trapped fish.

ANEMONE
As a fish stops struggling, the anemone's tentacles shorten and pull it into the mouth, through to the stomach chamber in the "body" of the anemone. Any undigested remains pass out later.

HOW CORAL REEFS ARE FORMED

Corals grow in shallow water around an island.

Coral reef builds up as island sinks.

Island disappears, leaving an atoll.

HYDRA
The tiny hydra is a freshwater polyp that lives in ponds. It may be green, brown, or grey in colour. Hydras feed on other tiny water creatures which they catch with their tentacles. Each tentacle has stinging cells that contain poison to paralyse the prey. Hydras reproduce by growing "buds" on their "stalk." The buds break off to form new hydras. This is a form of asexual reproduction.

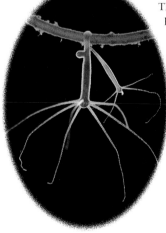

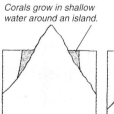

Some corals live in shallow water around an island where bright sunlight makes them grow. As movements in the Earth's surface make the island sink, corals form a reef. Finally the island disappears, leaving a ring of reefs called an atoll.

Find out more
ANIMALS
DEEP-SEA WILDLIFE
OCEAN WILDLIFE

COWBOYS

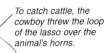

To catch cattle, the cowboy threw the loop of the lasso over the animal's horns.

A slip knot pulled the loop tight.

When the cowboy had pulled the cow to the ground, he tied it up so it could be marked with the owner's special sign or brand.

IN WESTERN MOVIES cowboys live exciting lives and perform heroic deeds. But in reality, the job of a cowboy was dirty, dull, and dangerous. Between 1860 and 1895, cowboys rounded up the wild cattle that roamed the range, or grasslands, west of the Mississippi River. They drove the herds northeast to towns where the cattle were sold for meat. Cowboys spent hours in the saddle each day and faced the perils of heat, cold, storms, stampedes, rustlers, and Indians. But by 1900, the range was fenced to create ranches, and the growing railway network made transporting cattle easier. Cowboys were no longer needed in such numbers, but they live on in songs, books, and films.

RANCHING

There are still a few cowboys in the United States and in South America, where they are called gauchos. They work on cattle stations – huge cattle ranches which produce beef. Some ranches are so big that it would take a cowboy many days to ride around the boundary on horseback, so modern cowboys sometimes use helicopters or pickup trucks to reach the animals in their care.

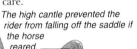

The cowboy anchored one end of the rope to the horn while roping cattle.

The high cantle prevented the rider from falling off the saddle if the horse reared.

A cowboy's saddle was his prized possession. It had to be comfortable because the cowboy might be on horseback 12 hours a day.

The fender protected the rider's leg from the horse's sweat.

A good felt hat kept off the sun and rain and could be used as a bucket to hold water.

The cotton bandanna or scarf absorbed sweat. Tied over the mouth, it kept out dust.

Boots with heels gave a good grip in stirrups and on the ground when roping cattle.

To rope cattle, the cowboy carried a lasso or lariat of hemp or rawhide.

SADDLES AND EQUIPMENT

Ropes, spurs, branding irons, and a saddle were the cowboy's tools. The cowboy heated the branding iron in a fire and used it to burn the owner's mark on the hide of the cattle. Some cowboys did not own their horses, but rode cow ponies which their employers supplied.

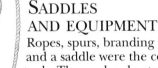

Leather chaps worn over trousers gave protection against thorns and cacti.

CALAMITY JANE

Martha Canary, also known as Martha Burke, was born in about 1852 and appeared as a cowgirl in Wild West shows. She was a colourful character: she wore men's clothes, carried a gun, and could drink more alcohol than most men. She died in 1903.

Spurs helped control horses.

Tight, streamlined trousers stayed up without suspenders, which might have got in the way.

RODEOS

At the spring and autumn roundups cowboys found time to compete against each other. These skill tests grew into rodeos and have continued ever since. The five main rodeo events are calf roping, bull riding, steer wrestling, saddle bronc (unbroken horse) riding, and bareback bronc riding. There are also races and trick riding contests.

Find out more

UNITED STATES OF AMERICA, history of
WILD WEST

Cows
CATTLE, AND BUFFALOES

EVERY TIME WE EAT ice cream or drink milk, we should thank the dairy cow. Each year cows, or dairy cattle, provide us with millions of litres of milk to make many different dairy products. The dairy cow is just one member of the much larger family of animals called cattle. Humans first domesticated cattle about 5,000 years ago. Today cattle are bred on every continent for their meat, milk, and hides. There are many different kinds of cattle – all have horns and distinctive split (two-toed) hooves and live in herds. As a group they are often described as ruminants or cud chewers because of the way in which they digest food. Wild cattle include the water buffalo of central and Southeast Asia and the rare anoa, found in the rain forest of Celebes, in Indonesia.

SACRED COW
In parts of Asia, cattle are sacred and must not be harmed. Here the Hindu goddess Pravati is shown with a sacred cow.

Horns can be used in defence, but they are sometimes removed by cattle breeders.

Ears can swivel to locate the direction from which a sound comes.

Milk comes from cow's udder.

Tail is used as a fly whisk.

Guernsey cow and calf

Split (two-toed) hoof

CHEWING THE CUD
Cattle have large, four-chambered stomachs. They eat grass and other plants, which they swallow and partly digest in the rumen (the first chamber of the stomach). Later, the cow regurgitates, or brings up the coarse, fibrous parts of the food as small masses called cud. The cow chews the cud then swallows it again, and it goes into the reticulum (the second chamber). The food then passes into the omasum and finally into the abomasum, where digestion takes place. This complex method means that the cow can extract all the nutrients from the food.

Small intestine

Rumen

Reticulum

Omasum

Abomasum

Large intestine

Food takes more than three days to pass through the entire digestive system.

CATTLE
There are about 12 billion domestic or farm cattle around the world. Their ancestors were wild cattle called aurochs; the last auroch died out in 1627. Over many years, breeders have developed various types of domestic cattle. Each is suited to a particular climate and produces mainly meat, milk, or hides for leather. Jersey, Guernsey, Ayrshire, and Holstein are dairy (milk-giving) breeds; Hereford, Angus, Charolais, and Brahman are beef (meat-giving) breeds.

BISON
Herds of bison, sometimes mistakenly called buffalo, once roamed the North American plains by the millions. A century ago, however, so many had been killed by settlers that only 500 were left alive. Today, there are about 50,000 bison in America, living in protected wildlife parks. The smaller European bison has also been saved from extinction by being bred in captivity, then released into the wild.

North American bison

BUFFALO
There are about 130 million domestic water buffaloes in Asia, Europe, North Africa, and South America. They pull farm equipment and provide meat and milk. With their wide hooves and thickset legs, water buffalo can walk easily in mud along riverbanks and lakesides. They are often used to farm flooded rice paddies.

Find out more
ANIMALS
FARM ANIMALS
FARMING
MAMMALS
NORTH AMERICAN WILDLIFE

CRABS
AND OTHER CRUSTACEANS

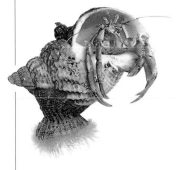

THOUSANDS OF DIFFERENT kinds of crabs scuttle over our sandy shores and skulk in rock pools. They range from tiny parasitic crabs living inside mussels to the giant Japanese spider crab, whose legs can be more than 3 m (10 ft) long. Crabs breathe underwater using gills, but some can also survive out of water for a long time. All crabs are protected by strong, hard shells like a suit of armour on the outside of their bodies. Crabs, along with lobsters and crayfish, belong to the animal group called crustaceans. Their bodies are divided into sections, with jointed limbs and two pairs of antennae on the head. A crab begins life as an egg, which develops into a larva, then into a crab. Each time the crab reaches another growing stage, it sheds the outer layer of its shell, revealing a new layer beneath.

HERMIT CRAB
The hermit crab often makes its home in the empty shell of a whelk, which protects it from predators such as gulls.

EDIBLE CRAB
The so-called edible crab is only one of many kinds of crustaceans that are caught, cooked, and eaten by people around the world.

Three sets of mouthparts for sorting food

Antenna

Eye on stalk

Fiddler crab

Huge claw for defence

Carapace (shell)

Eight walking legs

LOBSTER

The lobster scavenges on the sea bed for dead fish and other animal remains. One claw has blunt knobs for crushing; the other has sharp "teeth" for cutting. The biggest lobsters are 60 cm (2 ft) long and can live as long as people – up to 70 years.

Antenna

Crushing claw

Carapace over front part of body

Four pairs of walking limbs

Eye

Telson (tailpiece)

Six segments on abdomen

SHRIMPS AND PRAWNS
These little sea creatures are good scavengers. During the day they dig into the sand and hide. At night they emerge to hunt for food using their long feelers. When in danger, prawns and shrimps escape by scooting backwards with a flick of their tail fan.

Long antenna (feeler)

Shrimp

Tail fan

Feeding claw

Tail fan

Prawn

Feeding claw

Short antenna (feeler)

BARNACLES

These sea crustaceans have no heads. Their long, feathery legs beat the water, collecting tiny food particles. Acorn barnacles live in volcano-shaped shells cemented on to rocks. Goose barnacles attach themselves to driftwood by their stalks.

Goose barnacles

Acorn barnacles

WHERE CRUSTACEANS LIVE
Some crustaceans such as the yabby (a freshwater shrimp) and the water flea live in rivers and lakes. A few crustaceans live on land. The woodlouse, for example, can be found under dead leaves and in damp woodland areas.

Woodlouse

Water flea

Yabby

Find out more

ANIMALS
OCEAN WILDLIFE
SEASHORE WILDLIFE

CROCODILES AND ALLIGATORS

LYING LOW IN THE WATER looking like an old log, but ready to snap up almost any animal, the crocodile seems like a survivor from the prehistoric age, and it is. One hundred million years ago, crocodiles were prowling through the swamps with the dinosaurs. Crocodiles and alligators belong to the reptile group called crocodilians. This group includes 14 kinds of crocodiles, seven kinds of alligators (five of which are commonly called caimans), and one kind of gavial. Crocodilians are carnivorous (meat-eating) reptiles; they lurk in rivers, lakes, and swamps, grabbing whatever prey they can. Crocodiles and alligators eat fish and frogs whole. They drag larger prey such as deer under the water, where they grip the animal in their jaws and spin rapidly, tearing off chunks of flesh. Crocodiles and alligators occasionally eat humans.

Nile crocodiles measure up to 6 m (20 ft) long and weigh more than 1 tonne.

Female carries the young in her mouth.

CROCODILE
The fourth tooth on each side of the crocodile's lower jaw is visible when the mouth is closed.

ALLIGATOR
Unlike crocodiles, no lower teeth are visible when the alligator's mouth is closed.

CAIMAN
The caiman has a broad mouth for eating a variety of prey.

GAVIAL
The gavial has a long, slender mouth with sharp teeth for catching fish.

NILE CROCODILE
The Nile crocodile is found in many watery parts of Africa. Like most reptiles, the female lays eggs, which she looks after until they hatch. The newly hatched young listen for their mother's footsteps and call to her. She gently gathers them into her mouth in batches and carries them to the safety of the water.

YOUNG
After about three months, the young crocodiles hatch out of the eggs. The mother guards them closely because they are in danger of becoming food for large lizards and foxes.

CROCODILE SMILE
Crocodiles often bask in the sun with their mouths wide open. Blood vessels inside the mouth absorb the sun's warmth. This raises the animal's body temperature and gives the crocodile the energy to hunt for its prey in the evening.

ALLIGATOR
There are two kinds of true alligators – the Chinese and the American alligators. Today the Chinese alligator is in great danger of extinction – only a few hundred survive. The American alligator lives in rivers and swamps across the southeastern United States, where it eats fish, water birds, and anything else it can catch. In more populated areas, the American alligator also grabs unwary farm animals.

Long tail swishes back and forth for rapid swimming.

Sharp teeth grip land animals such as deer and drag them under the water to drown.

Eyes and nostrils are high on head, so alligator can see and breathe when body is almost submerged in water.

American alligator

Legs fold along body when alligator is swimming.

Find out more
ANIMALS
LIZARDS
PREHISTORIC LIFE

CROWS, JAYS, AND RAVENS

THE MEMBERS OF THE CROW FAMILY are among the best known of all birds because of their large size, bold habits, and noisy "crowing" calls. There are 116 kinds of crows. They include carrion crows, jays, magpies, ravens, and rooks. Many crows in Europe, North America, Africa, and Australia live in open countryside and are pests to farmers because they eat seeds and grains. In Asia and South America, however, some jays and magpies live in dense forests and are seldom seen. Crows have varied diets. Apart from seeds, they eat fruits, insects, small mammals, and dead animals, as well as birds' eggs and nestlings. They are good mimics and can imitate the sounds of other birds, animals, and human speech. In bird intelligence tests, members of the crow family, particularly jackdaws and ravens, score higher than any other birds.

ROOKERIES
Rooks breed in colonies high in the treetops. They build big nests of sticks and twigs early in spring.

COMMON CROW
Crows can be a nuisance to farmers because they spoil their crops. These clever birds are rarely fooled for long by a scarecrow standing in the field.

Crows often feed on newly planted seeds

MAGPIE
The magpie is famous as a bird thief. It makes off with coins, jewellery, and other bright, shiny objects, then hides or buries them. Magpies live in Europe, North America, North Africa, and Asia.

JAY
The brightly coloured European jay lives mainly in woodlands, where it feeds on acorns, beechnuts, fruits, and berries. The blue jay is beautifully patterned in blue and black, and lives among the trees in parks and gardens of central and eastern North America. There are also colourful jays in Asia.

Leg feathers puffed out

Head feathers fluffed out

RAVEN
The raven is the largest of the crow family, with a wingspan of 2 m (6 ft). Ravens were once thought to bring bad luck, probably because they fed on the dead bodies of criminals left hanging on the gallows.

CROW COURTSHIP
Many crows perform elaborate dances and displays in the breeding season, when the male courts the female. Here a male raven puffs out his feathers and bows to his partner while making *kaaa*-ing sounds.

Male raven performing bowing ceremony

JACKDAW
Tree holes and chimney tops provide nesting places for the European jackdaw. It builds a nest of twigs lined with grass, hair, fur, and wool plucked from the backs of sheep. Like magpies, jackdaws are attracted to shiny objects.

Find out more
BIRDS
FLIGHT IN ANIMALS

CRUSADES

NINE CENTURIES AGO the pope appealed to Christians to recapture the holy city of Jerusalem from the Turkish Muslims who had seized it. Thousands of European Christians – knights, princes, pilgrims, and peasants – responded to the call and set out on a long warring pilgrimage, called a crusade, from western Europe to Palestine (now Israel). Four years later, after battles, starvation, and disease, the surviving crusaders captured the city of Jerusalem. The crusaders set up a Christian kingdom on the shores of Palestine that lasted nearly a century. But in 1187 Saladin recaptured Jerusalem. At least seven more crusades set out. None was successful, but links between Europe and the Middle East were established that continue today.

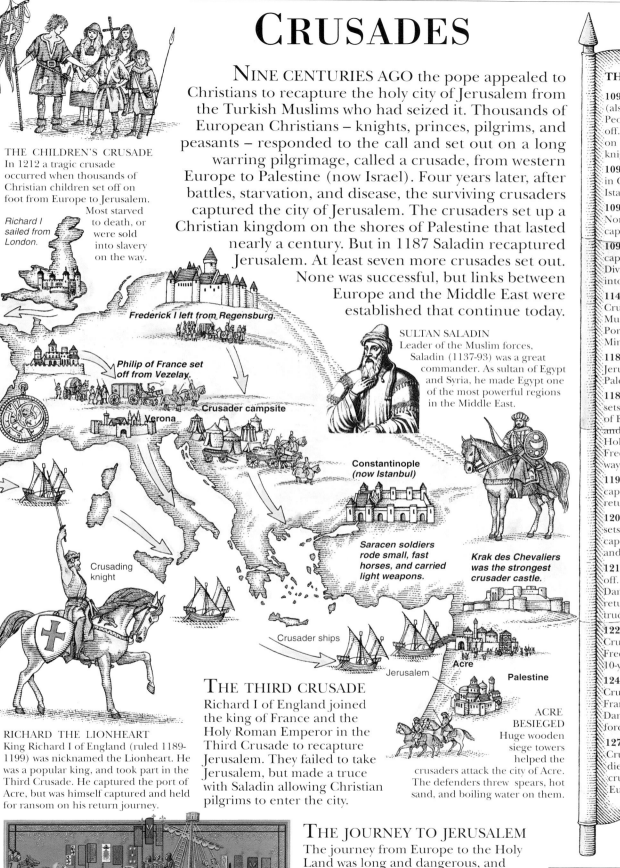

THE CHILDREN'S CRUSADE
In 1212 a tragic crusade occurred when thousands of Christian children set off on foot from Europe to Jerusalem. Most starved to death, or were sold into slavery on the way.

Richard I sailed from London.

Frederick I left from Regensburg.

Philip of France set off from Vezelay.

Verona

Crusader campsite

SULTAN SALADIN
Leader of the Muslim forces, Saladin (1137-93) was a great commander. As sultan of Egypt and Syria, he made Egypt one of the most powerful regions in the Middle East.

Constantinople (now Istanbul)

Saracen soldiers rode small, fast horses, and carried light weapons.

Krak des Chevaliers was the strongest crusader castle.

Crusading knight

Crusader ships

Jerusalem

Acre

Palestine

RICHARD THE LIONHEART
King Richard I of England (ruled 1189-1199) was nicknamed the Lionheart. He was a popular king, and took part in the Third Crusade. He captured the port of Acre, but was himself captured and held for ransom on his return journey.

THE THIRD CRUSADE
Richard I of England joined the king of France and the Holy Roman Emperor in the Third Crusade to recapture Jerusalem. They failed to take Jerusalem, but made a truce with Saladin allowing Christian pilgrims to enter the city.

ACRE BESIEGED
Huge wooden siege towers helped the crusaders attack the city of Acre. The defenders threw spears, hot sand, and boiling water on them.

THE JOURNEY TO JERUSALEM
The journey from Europe to the Holy Land was long and dangerous, and many of the crusaders died on the way. Those who went back to Europe from Palestine took silks and spices with them as well as Islamic learning such as mathematics and astronomy.

THE CRUSADES

1096 First Crusade (also known as the People's Crusade) sets off. Many peasants die on the way, though knights survive.

1097 Crusaders arrive in Constantinople (now Istanbul).

1098 French and Norman armies capture Antioch.

1099 Crusaders capture Jerusalem. Divide coastal land into four kingdoms.

1147-49 Second Crusade attacks Muslims in Spain, Portugal, and Asia Minor.

1187 Saladin conquers Jerusalem and most of Palestine.

1189 Third Crusade sets off led by the kings of England and France and Frederick I, the Holy Roman Emperor. Frederick dies on the way.

1191-92 Crusaders capture Acre but return to Europe.

1202-4 Fourth Crusade sets off. Crusaders capture Constantinople and steal treasure.

1217 Fifth Crusade sets off. Crusaders capture Damietta, Egypt, but return it and make a truce.

1228-29 Sixth Crusade. Emperor Frederick II makes a 10-year truce.

1248-50 Seventh Crusade. Louis IX of France captures Damietta but is forced to return it.

1270 Eighth Crusade. Louis IX dies. This final crusade returns to Europe.

Find out more

ARABS, HISTORY OF
CASTLES
WEAPONS

DAMS

EVERY DAY, FACTORIES and homes use up huge amounts of water. For example, an oil refinery uses 10 times as much water as the petrol it makes. Dams help to provide us with much of the water we need by trapping water from flowing rivers. Building a dam across a river creates a huge lake, called a reservoir, behind the dam. Reservoirs also provide water to irrigate large areas of farmland. A dam can store the water that falls in rainy seasons so that there is water during dry periods. By storing water in this way, dams also prevent floods. Flood barriers can stop the sea from surging up a river and bursting its banks. Dams may provide electricity as well as water. Many dams contain hydroelectric power stations powered by water from their reservoirs.

CONCRETE DAMS

There are two main types of concrete dam: arch dams and gravity dams. Arch dams are tall, curved shells of concrete as little as 3 m (10 ft) thick. Because their arched shape makes them very strong, they do not burst. Large gravity dams are also made of concrete. Their vast weight keeps them from giving way.

HOOVER DAM
The Hoover Dam in the United States, one of the world's highest concrete dams, is 221 m (726 ft) high. It is an arch dam that spans the River Colorado, supplying water for irrigation and electricity to California, Arizona, and Nevada. Lake Mead, the reservoir formed by the dam, is 185 km (115 miles) long.

Lake Mead

Lift shaft inside dam goes down to hydroelectric power station.

Water from the reservoir enters the intake towers.

Roadway along top of dam

Arched, concrete dam wall

Water flows down pipes to hydroelectric power station.

Pipes carry excess water to the Colorado River so that the dam does not break or overflow.

Dam shown with water removed from one side.

Water flows down to Colorado River.

Hydroelectric power station

Overflow water

Tunnel that was excavated to divert river while dam was built.

EMBANKMENT DAMS

The biggest dams are embankment dams, made by piling up a huge barrier of earth and rock. A core of clay or concrete in the centre keeps water from seeping through the dam. The side is covered with stones to protect it from the water. The world's highest dam is the Rogunsky Dam in Tajikistan, an embankment dam 325 m (1,066 ft) high.

Waterproof core

FLOOD BARRIERS

Movable dams, called flood barriers, are built on rivers to control flooding. A barrier across the River Thames in England protects London from flooding. Large, curved gates rise if the river gets too high.

THE EFFECTS OF DAMS

The reservoir that forms in the valley behind a dam floods the land, often damaging the environment. For example, the Aswan High Dam in Egypt was built to control the flooding of the River Nile, but changing the river's flow has destroyed the fertility of the surrounding land.

A dam prevents fish, such as salmon, from swimming up and down a river. Some dams have a fish ladder, a pipe, or pools through which fish can swim past the dam.

Find out more
ELECTRICITY
FARMING
LAKES
RIVERS
WATER

DANCE

THE CHAIN DANCE
In one of the most common folk-dancing patterns, the dancers weave in and out along a line or in a circle. In this 12th century "chain dance" they move from left to right, clasping alternate hands as they pass.

RITUAL DANCE
In religious rituals, dance is a way of thanking the gods or asking for their help. These North American Indians are performing a fertility dance. It is important that the steps are always danced in the same order.

WHEN PEOPLE HEAR music, they often tap their feet and clap their hands. Dancing is a natural activity, and there are many different styles of dance, ranging from the hectic breakdance to the graceful, elegant waltz. However, all forms of dance share the same rhythmic movements that people have enjoyed since time began. Prehistoric cave paintings show people moving in a lively way. They kept time by clapping and stamping. Later, dancers began to move in patterns with more formal steps, and dancing in couples or in groups at balls or dances became a part of social life. In many countries special costumes are part of the folk-dancing tradition.

MIME

Love – putting on a ring

Marriage – tying the love knot around the bride's neck

Mime mixes dance and acting to create a language without words which can be understood by people from many cultures. The dancer shown here is from India, but mime is also part of other Eastern dance styles.

SQUARE DANCING
Square dancing is very sociable. Sets of dancers move around in the shape of a square, changing partners in a sequence of moves. This traditional North American dance has many variations.

Books about the waltz and other dances sometimes have diagrams to show the dancers the steps.

WALTZ
This elegant, gliding dance originated in Austria in the 18th century. It became one of the most popular of all formal dances. Composers such as Johann Strauss (1825-99) of Vienna, Austria, wrote music especially for the waltz.

MODERN DANCE
Most traditional dances have a prearranged series of steps and movements, but modern dancers are free to move as they choose. Rock and roll dances of the 1950s were among the first modern dances; today dancing is influenced by the music of many different cultures.

Find out more
BALLET
FILMS
THEATRE

DEEP-SEA WILDLIFE

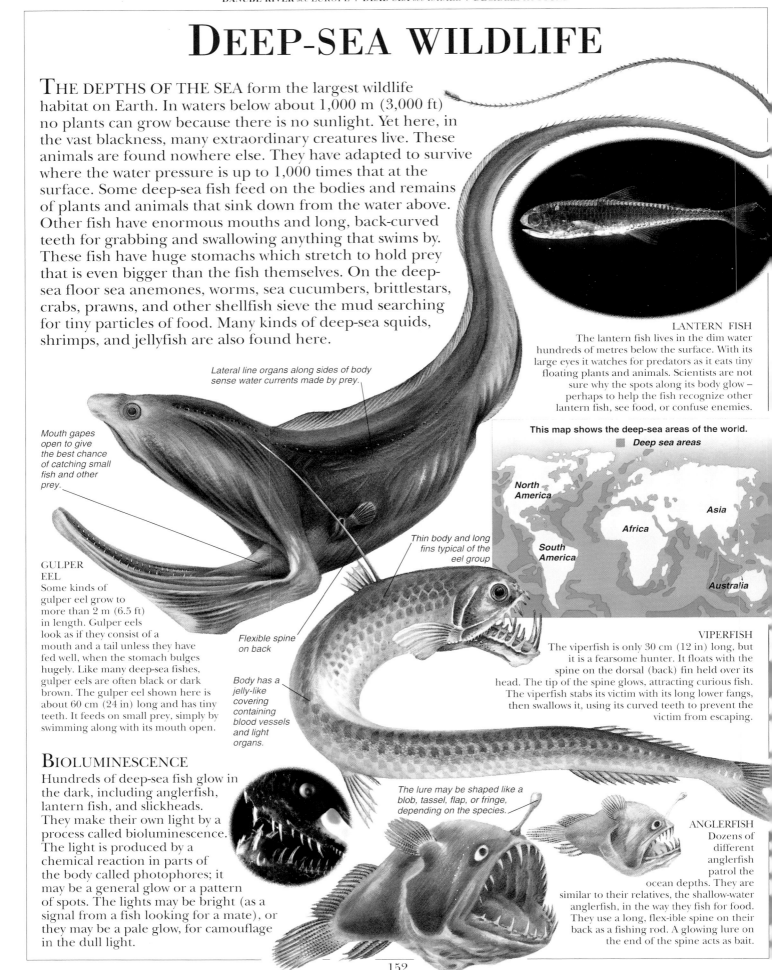

THE DEPTHS OF THE SEA form the largest wildlife habitat on Earth. In waters below about 1,000 m (3,000 ft) no plants can grow because there is no sunlight. Yet here, in the vast blackness, many extraordinary creatures live. These animals are found nowhere else. They have adapted to survive where the water pressure is up to 1,000 times that at the surface. Some deep-sea fish feed on the bodies and remains of plants and animals that sink down from the water above. Other fish have enormous mouths and long, back-curved teeth for grabbing and swallowing anything that swims by. These fish have huge stomachs which stretch to hold prey that is even bigger than the fish themselves. On the deep-sea floor sea anemones, worms, sea cucumbers, brittlestars, crabs, prawns, and other shellfish sieve the mud searching for tiny particles of food. Many kinds of deep-sea squids, shrimps, and jellyfish are also found here.

Lateral line organs along sides of body sense water currents made by prey.

Mouth gapes open to give the best chance of catching small fish and other prey.

LANTERN FISH
The lantern fish lives in the dim water hundreds of metres below the surface. With its large eyes it watches for predators as it eats tiny floating plants and animals. Scientists are not sure why the spots along its body glow – perhaps to help the fish recognize other lantern fish, see food, or confuse enemies.

This map shows the deep-sea areas of the world.

■ **Deep sea areas**

North America

South America

Africa

Asia

Australia

GULPER EEL
Some kinds of gulper eel grow to more than 2 m (6.5 ft) in length. Gulper eels look as if they consist of a mouth and a tail unless they have fed well, when the stomach bulges hugely. Like many deep-sea fishes, gulper eels are often black or dark brown. The gulper eel shown here is about 60 cm (24 in) long and has tiny teeth. It feeds on small prey, simply by swimming along with its mouth open.

Flexible spine on back

Thin body and long fins typical of the eel group

Body has a jelly-like covering containing blood vessels and light organs.

VIPERFISH
The viperfish is only 30 cm (12 in) long, but it is a fearsome hunter. It floats with the spine on the dorsal (back) fin held over its head. The tip of the spine glows, attracting curious fish. The viperfish stabs its victim with its long lower fangs, then swallows it, using its curved teeth to prevent the victim from escaping.

BIOLUMINESCENCE
Hundreds of deep-sea fish glow in the dark, including anglerfish, lantern fish, and slickheads. They make their own light by a process called bioluminescence. The light is produced by a chemical reaction in parts of the body called photophores; it may be a general glow or a pattern of spots. The lights may be bright (as a signal from a fish looking for a mate), or they may be a pale glow, for camouflage in the dull light.

The lure may be shaped like a blob, tassel, flap, or fringe, depending on the species.

ANGLERFISH
Dozens of different anglerfish patrol the ocean depths. They are similar to their relatives, the shallow-water anglerfish, in the way they fish for food. They use a long, flex-ible spine on their back as a fishing rod. A glowing lure on the end of the spine acts as bait.

CONSERVATION

Unlike other wildlife areas such as the rain forests, the deep sea is not in great danger from habitat loss or pollution. However, harmful polluting chemicals have been found at great depths. Fishing boats have also overfished many shallow seas and are now fishing in deeper waters. Deep-sea fish such as these orange roughie fish (right) may soon be in danger because of overfishing.

Fang tooth has a lure on head to attract small fish.

Needlelike teeth give the fang tooth fish its name.

Thin body shape and light organs along underside may reduce the risk of being seen from below by a predator.

Hatchetfish

Eyes have large yellow lenses to spy prey, especially small glowing fish and shellfish.

SULPHUR VENTS

At some places on the sea floor, hot water and gases bubble up through the rocks. These places are called sulphur vents. They emit (give out) energy-rich chemicals which are used by bacteria for growth. Other animals feed on the bacteria. Blind crabs and giant worms 3 m (10 ft) long live around the vents. They are the only creatures that do not depend on the sun for energy.

HATCHETFISH

The deep-sea hatchetfish has a tall, thin body, shaped like an axe-head. It looks like its relative, the freshwater hatchetfish. The deep-sea hatchetfish stays about 500 m (1,700 ft) below the surface by day and swims up at night to eat tiny shellfish and other floating food.

SEA LILY

This animal is an upside-down version of its relative, the starfish. It is fixed to the sea bed by a stalk. Its branched tentacles gather and trap food, then sweep it to the mouth in a stream of mucus (spit).

DEEP-SEA SQUID

Squid swim among the sea lilies, hunting for fish and other prey. The giant squid also swims near the sea bottom.

SEA CUCUMBER

The cylindrical-shaped sea cucumber is an animal, and a relative of the starfish. It has a frill of tentacles at one end, around the mouth. These tentacles sweep up bits of food from the muddy floor as the sea cucumber moves along on its many tubed feet.

Sea cucumber

LIFE ON THE SEA BED

Many kinds of animals filter, sieve, and sift the water and muddy sludge on the sea floor for tiny pieces of food. In places where ocean currents bring abundant food, these creatures cover the sea bed. Most of them are blind and slow-moving. When some deep-sea fish are brought to the surface, the decrease in water pressure makes them swell and burst. Scientists study them with special remote-control submersibles which can carry cameras as deep as 6,000 m (20,000 ft).

Sea lily

DEER, ANTELOPES, AND GAZELLES

The pronghorn antelope of North America is one of the fastest animals on land. It sprints at almost 90 km/h (55 mph) – as fast as a car.

Male red deer is called a stag or buck.

REINDEER
Reindeer, or caribou, live in Scandinavia, North America, and Siberia, in the Russian Federation. Both male and female caribou have antlers. Only the males of other kinds of deer have antlers.

MAJESTIC ANTLERS and graceful movements give deer an impressive appearance. Deer and their relatives, antelopes and gazelles, are well equipped to flee from danger. Their brown or grey colouring acts as camouflage, and their excellent hearing, sight, and smell help them to detect predators and leap away with great speed. There are 36 kinds of deer. They are mainly woodland creatures, but some, such as reindeer (caribou), live in the frozen Arctic. Antelopes and gazelles are found mostly in deserts and open grasslands. Other members of this group include the wildebeest, or gnu, and the dik-dik.

Male fallow deer's antlers are palmate (flattened).

A gazelle's horns grow in a spiral pattern.

Female deer is called a hind or doe.

Points (tips of topmost antler branches)

Soft layer of velvety fur covers growing antler.

Tines (tips of lower antler branches)

Layers of bone inside antler

Bony connection to skull

Soft fleshy layer of "velvet" covers growing antler

Reindeer stags rutting

Deer, antelopes, and gazelles graze on plants in the same way as cows and sheep.

HORNS AND ANTLERS
Antelopes, cattle, and gazelles have horns on their heads which grow throughout life. Horns are made of keratin, like fingernails, and some are twisted like corkscrews. Male deer have antlers on their heads, made of a hard, bony substance. The deer sheds and grows a new set of antlers each year.

Eland measures up to 2 m (6 ft) high at the shoulder and 3.4 m (11 ft) in length.

Royal antelope measures 25 cm (10 in) at the shoulder.

10-year-old child measures about 1.2 m (4 ft).

Young red deer is called a fawn.

HERDS
Most deer, antelopes, and gazelles live in groups called herds. During the autumn, male deer battle with each other to gain a territory and a harem – a group of females. Red deer males roar at each other, lock antlers, and try to push their opponent to the ground. This behaviour is called rutting. Usually the largest, strongest males win. These large males then defend their group and its territory against other herds.

FAWN
The red deer calf, or fawn is born in late spring and stays hidden in the undergrowth. Its spotted coat provides good camouflage in the dappled shade. The spots soon fade and the coat changes to rusty reddish brown.

ANTELOPES
There are about 100 different kinds of antelopes. These hoofed mammals are closely related to cattle and goats. The eland is the largest antelope. It is found in grassland areas of central and southern Africa. Elands do not need to drink often because they absorb enough water from the plants they eat. Elands live for about 15 years. The royal antelope, from western Africa, is the smallest antelope.

Find out more
AFRICAN WILDLIFE
FOREST WILDLIFE
NORTH AMERICAN WILDLIFE

DEMOCRACY

THE WORD *DEMOCRACY* COMES FROM the Ancient Greek words *demos,* which means "people", and *kratia,* which means "power". Democracy means "rule by the people". Within a democracy, all persons have the right to play a part in the government of their country. In the United Kingdom, for instance, everybody over the age of 18 can elect a member of parliament to represent them in the national government; and a councillor – their representative in local government. Occasionally they vote about an issue in a referendum. Twenty-five hundred years ago the people of Athens, Greece, practised a form of democracy. Men met in one place to decide on laws for their community. Today most democracy is representative. Because there are usually too many people in a country to be involved in making every decision, the people elect representatives to make decisions on their behalf.

BALLOT BOX
When people vote in an election, they mark their votes on a piece of paper which they then drop into a ballot box. Their vote is secret, because no one can tell who marked each piece of paper. Today, electronic voting booths are replacing ballot boxes.

REPRESENTATIVE DEMOCRACY
Representative democracy means that citizens vote for certain people to represent them. People form political parties and citizens vote for their favoured party in elections. The different parties compete with each other for votes in election campaigns. Getting the right to vote (suffrage) has been a dedicated struggle for both men and women. Today, adult men and women in most countries can vote.

Political parties campaign for votes in the United States, 1908.

MAJORITY RULE
Democracy means government by the people, but one group of people might want to do one thing and another group something completely different. In that case, the view of the majority (the larger group of people) rules. This could lead to the views of the minority being ignored, so many democratic countries and organizations have a constitution (a set of rules) that safeguards the rights of individuals and minorities. A few countries still do not have a democracy and are ruled by just one person, usually called a "dictator".

Minority vote

Majority vote

VOTING
India is the biggest representative democracy in the world: more than 500 million people are able to vote. In the general election of 1996, close to 400 million people went to the polling stations to vote for their representatives in the national parliament. So many people mean it can take several days for all the votes to be counted.

EASTERN EUROPE
From 1989, people in Communist Eastern Europe demanded democratic governments. They felt they did not have enough say in how their countries were run. In 1990, what was then Czechoslovakia became the first of many Eastern European Communist countries to declare themselves a real democracy.

Find out more
COMMUNISM
GOVERNMENTS
GREECE, ANCIENT
LAW

DENTISTS

CARING FOR YOUR TEETH is an everyday task, but there are some problems that even good diet and regular brushing cannot solve. Dentists are trained to find and treat problems in teeth and gums before they become too serious. With the aid of x-rays they can even identify unhealthy teeth that look normal from the outside. When teeth decay, dentists drill out the damaged area. Then they fill the cavity with amalgam – a combination of ground metals mixed with mercury – or with synthetic resin that hardens when light shines on the tooth. Dentists can also repair a broken tooth with an artificial crown, and only where there is no alternative will today's dentists extract (pull out) teeth, replacing them with dentures (artificial teeth). Our ancestors were less fortunate: 18th-century dentures were made from teeth stolen from graveyards, pulled from soldiers killed in battle, and even extracted by force from unwilling victims!

X-ray machine

Suction tube removes saliva and waste from mouth.

High-powered lamp on adjustable arm

Water supply to wash mouth

Adjustable seat

Equipment tray

Drills come in different shapes and sizes

Drills revolve 300,000 times a minute to remove decay in seconds.

THE DENTIST'S VIEW
To spot decay, the dentist uses an angled mirror. A bright lamp lights up every tooth, and a suction hose takes away saliva so the patient need not swallow.

FILLING TEETH

Drilling

Filling

Mobile trolley

Drilling removes the decayed part of the tooth. To seal the hole the dentist pushes amalgam or plastic resin into the tooth.

DENTAL SURGERY
Technology has made dental treatment safe, effective, and nearly painless. Dentists use some disposable equipment and sterilize other instruments. They also use pain-killing anaesthetics.

TOOTH X-RAY
An x-ray photograph reveals the root of a tooth inside the gum. Dentists can use the pictures to check developing teeth in young people and to correct crooked or uneven teeth at an early stage. This treatment is called orthodontics.

STREET DENTISTS
Modern hygienic dental treatment is expensive. Street dentists offer basic extractions and fillings in parts of the world where people cannot afford anaesthetics and germ-free conditions.

ORAL HYGIENE

Brushing teeth regularly reduces plaque, a deposit on teeth in which harmful bacteria live. The bacteria break down sugar in the food we eat to form the acids which destroy teeth.

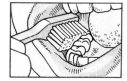

Teeth should be brushed individually with small strokes. Hard brushing can wear grooves in the enamel.

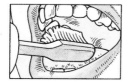

A rolling movement of the brush cleans the surface of the teeth from all directions. Work the bristles into gaps between teeth.

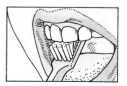

Even though it cannot be seen, the back of each tooth is as important as the front. Good brushing stimulates the gums.

Find out more
HEALTH
TEETH
X-RAYS

DEPRESSION
OF THE 1930s

1929	1930	1931	1932
1 billion	800 million	600 million	400 million

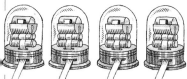

IN OCTOBER 1929, prices on the New York Stock Exchange crashed, and investors lost vast amounts of money. This was the beginning of an economic depression, or slump, which was to affect the whole world throughout the following decade. The crash caused untold panic, a loss of confidence, and the collapse of the American economy. Banks stopped lending money, factories closed, and trade declined. The result was mass unemployment: by 1932, 13.7 million U.S. workers were unemployed. The depression quickly spread across the world and hit almost every nation. Many countries had relied on loans from the United States to help them recover from World War I (1914-18). Now these loans stopped. Businesses collapsed, and millions of people were thrown out of work. Unemployment caused misery and poverty. Disillusioned and frightened people turned to extreme right-wing political parties, such as the National Socialist German Workers' (Nazi) Party in Germany. The build-up to World War II ended the depression, because increased production of arms created jobs.

DUST BOWL

During the 1930s, a terrible drought turned the soil in the American Midwest into dust. High winds blew clouds of dust over fields and farms, which hid the sunlight. The region became known as the Dust Bowl. Many ruined farmers were forced to trek across the country to find work in the orchards and farms of California, United States.

TENESSEE VALLEY AUTHORITY

When Franklin D. Roosevelt became U.S. President in 1932, he set up many programmes to improve the economy. The Tennessee Valley Authority was given money to employ people to build massive dams and hydroelectric power stations in the eastern United States.

Amount of sales on the New York Stock Exchange 1929-32.

WALL STREET CRASH

On 24 October, 1929, known as "Black Thursday", the boom years that had followed World War I came to an end. To get richer, people had been investing a lot of money in the New York Stock Exchange. When it crashed, people wildly tried to sell their shares. In two months, share values had declined by one third. Many people lost all their savings, and thousands of companies collapsed.

JARROW MARCH

In Britain, mass unemployment led to "hunger marches". In 1936, 200 out-of-work and hungry men marched 483 km (300 miles) from Jarrow, in the northeast of England, to the capital, London, in order to draw people's attention to their plight.

Find out more

GERMANY, HISTORY OF
ROOSEVELT, FRANKLIN DELANO
WORLD WAR I
WORLD WAR II

DESERT WILDLIFE

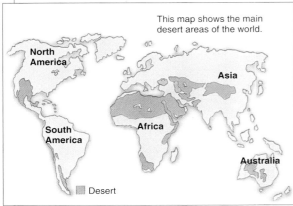

This map shows the main desert areas of the world.

North America

Asia

South America

Africa

Australia

Desert

THE VAST, DRY expanse of a desert may look uninhabited, but all kinds of plants and animals survive in these sandy regions – including insects, reptiles, mammals, and fish. Deserts are the driest places on Earth; some have less than 100 mm (4 in) of rainfall each year. Desert animals have adapted to the lack of water in various ways. Camels, for example, can survive for a long time without drinking. Other animals find enough water in the plants and insects they eat, so they never have to drink at all. Plants such as baobab trees have deep-growing roots to search for water underground.

Other problems for desert wildlife are the extremes of temperature and the lack of shelter. Some deserts are scorching hot; others are freezing cold. Desert mammals have thick fur to keep out heat as well as cold. Many find shelter from the sun and icy winds by digging burrows. In hot deserts animals stay in their burrows by day and hunt at night when the temperature is lower.

MONGOOSE

These adaptable mammals hunt by day for all kinds of small animals, including bees, spiders, scorpions, mice, and snakes. A mongoose has extremely quick reactions, so it can easily dodge an enemy such as a snake. The mongoose then leaps onto the snake and kills it with one bite.

TAWNY EAGLE

The tawny eagle survives well in desert conditions. Its incredible eyesight enables it to spot a rabbit or lizard thousands of metres away. When it sees prey, the tawny eagle dives at great speed and grabs the victim in its powerful talons.

COBRA

The hooded cobra kills small mammals, frogs, and lizards by biting them with its deadly fangs full of venom (poison). When this snake is in danger, it rears up its head and spreads out the ribs in the loose skin of its neck to form a hood. The hood makes the cobra look bigger and more threatening.

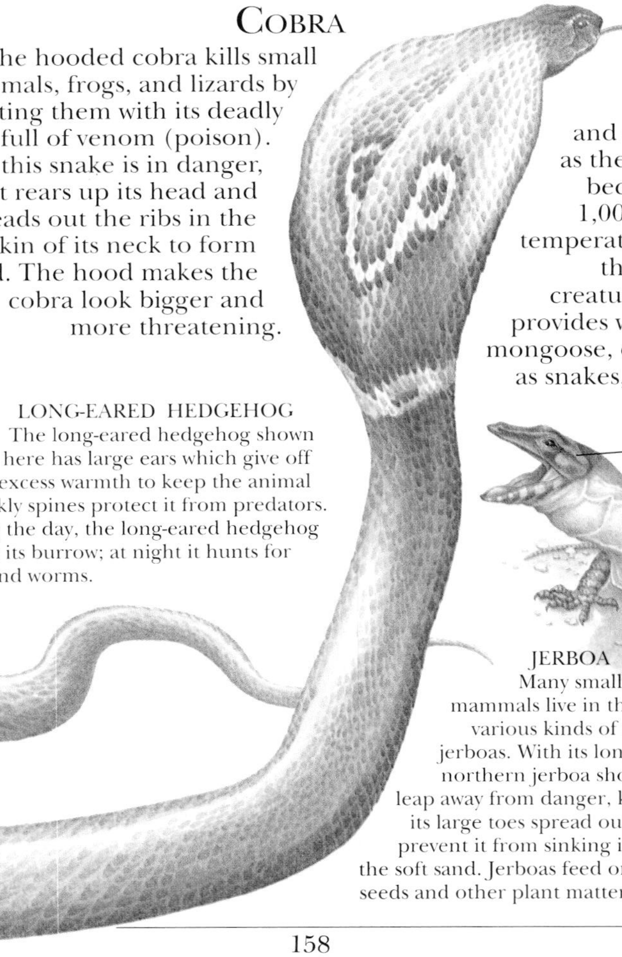

COLD DESERTS

It is often bitterly cold at night and during the winter in deserts such as the Gobi Desert in Asia. This is partly because the Gobi is very high – about 1,000 m (3,500 ft) above sea level. Day temperatures rise as high as 50° C (122° F), then fall to -40° C (-40° F). For some creatures, a burrow is the only place that provides warmth. Some animals, such as the mongoose, dig their own burrow; others, such as snakes, take over an empty burrow or kill and eat the occupier.

LONG-EARED HEDGEHOG

The long-eared hedgehog shown here has large ears which give off excess warmth to keep the animal cool. Prickly spines protect it from predators. During the day, the long-eared hedgehog stays in its burrow; at night it hunts for insects and worms.

Long-eared hedgehog

Many lizards prowl across the dry sand, flicking their tongues in and out to taste the air. This monitor lizard eats eggs belonging to birds and other reptiles.

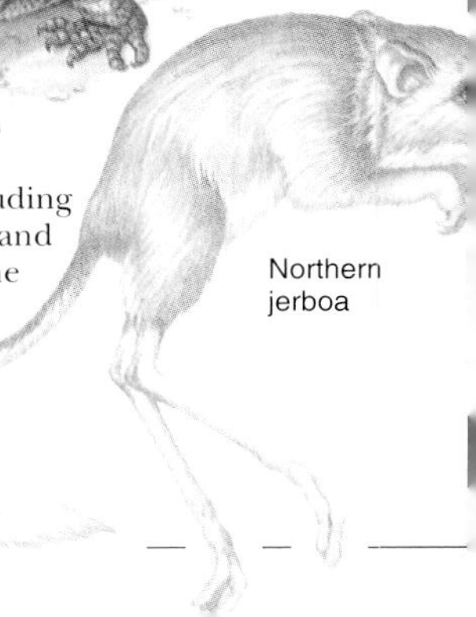

JERBOA

Many small mammals live in the desert, including various kinds of mice, gerbils, and jerboas. With its long back legs, the northern jerboa shown here can leap away from danger, keeping its large toes spread out to prevent it from sinking in the soft sand. Jerboas feed on seeds and other plant matter.

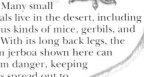

Northern jerboa

CONSERVATION

Most desert wildlife is not in urgent need of conservation measures because deserts are not seriously threatened by habitat destruction. However, some deserts are being turned into farmland for growing cereals, fruit, and other crops, and this destroys the unique desert plant life.

DORCAS GAZELLE

Dorcas gazelles are found across northern Africa, the Middle East, and India. They are an endangered species because they are being forced out of their natural habitat by farm animals and crops.

DATE PALM

The date palm tree has many different uses. The nourishing date fruits are food for people and animals, the stringy bark and wood are made into matting and ropes, and the leaves are fashioned into roofs and sunshades.

Dorcas gazelle

CACTUS

The cactus stores water in its swollen stem. Sharp prickles protect it from plant-eating animals. The cactus shown here is called the prickly pear cactus. The fruit is edible.

HOT DESERTS

The Sahara in Africa is the world's largest and hottest desert. At midday in the Sahara, the scorching sand is so hot that it can burn through skin in seconds. The temperature in the shade soars to more than 55°C (130°F). Few animals are active. Yet as the sun sets and the air and sand cool, many creatures emerge from under rocks and out of burrows. Dew forms at night, providing the plants and animals with much-needed moisture.

ADDAX

This large grazing antelope from the Sahara never drinks – it obtains enough water from its food. Like other sandy desert dwellers, the addax's feet splay out widely to spread the animal's weight and keep it from sinking in the sand. The addax's horns have spiral ridges. The horns are used for defence and in contests for control of the herd.

ROADRUNNER

The roadrunner can fly, but it usually races along the ground and runs into the undergrowth if it is disturbed. Roadrunners live in deserts and dry, open country in North America, feeding on all kinds of small animals, including grasshoppers, snakes, eggs, and certain fruits.

SIDEWINDER

A row of S-shaped marks in the sand at daybreak is a sign that a sidewinder snake passed during the night, probably on the trail of a mouse or a rat. This snake's wavelike way of moving means that only two small parts of its body touch the ground at any time, giving a better grip on the shifting sand.

NAKED MOLE RAT

This hairless rat is virtually blind and lives in underground tunnels in groups called colonies. The colonies are organized in a similar way to an ant's nest, with one queen who gives birth to all the young. Naked mole rats feed only on tubers which they find in the soil.

YUCCA MOTH AND YUCCA PLANT

The yucca is a desert lily. It has pale scented flowers which attract the tiny female yucca moth. The moth climbs into the flower and gathers pollen, then flies to another yucca. Here the yucca moth lays its egg in the flower's ovary (egg-bearing part), as well as transferring pollen. As the yucca's fruit ripens, the moth caterpillar feeds on it. The yucca moth and the yucca flower could not exist without each other.

PINK FAIRY ARMADILLO

Measuring only 15 cm (6 in) long, the pink fairy armadillo lives in the deserts of South America. It leaves its tunnel at nightfall to dig up ants, worms, and other food.

Find out more

BUTTERFLIES AND MOTHS
DEER, ANTELOPES,
and gazelles
DESERTS
NORTH AMERICAN WILDLIFE
REPTILES
SNAKES

DESERTS

A FIFTH OF THE EARTH'S LAND consists of dry, hostile regions called deserts, empty of all but a few plants, the hardiest of animals, and some wandering tribes. Life for desert dwellers, such as the Bedouin nomads who roam the Middle East, is a constant fight for survival, because food and water are scarce.

Little rain falls in deserts because the air is warm and no clouds can form. The clear skies make most deserts scorch with the sun's heat by day, but with no clouds to trap heat, the temperature may drop below freezing at night. Not all deserts are blazing hot and covered with vast stretches of sand; many are strewn with rocks, and deserts in some parts of Asia are often cold because they lie at high altitude. New deserts can form in regions where droughts often occur and where people cut down all the trees or allow their animals to eat all the plants, a process called overgrazing. During the 1970s, drought and overgrazing turned the Sahel region of central Africa into desert, and the problem still exists today.

MONUMENT VALLEY
Fantastic columns of rock adorn Monument Valley, a desert region in the United States. Sand carried by the wind wears away the rock to form pillars with extraordinary shapes.

SAND

Desert temperatures soar by day and plunge by night. Rock continually expands and contracts as it warms and cools, and its surface breaks up into fragments. These fragments are blown by the wind and grind down other rocks. Eventually millions of tiny pieces of rock cover the desert as sand. But the wind may also blow away the sand and leave bare rock or stony ground.

SAND DUNES
Many deserts contain huge mounds of sand called dunes. The wind heaps up sand to form the dunes, which slowly advance over the desert as the wind blows. The dunes are like waves of sand and can be 33 m (100 ft) high or more.

SAND STORMS
Strong winds blow sand and dust which sweep over the desert in swirling clouds. High winds can blow fine particles of dust across entire continents.

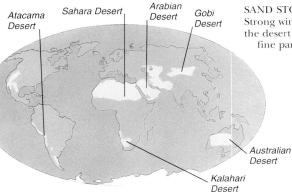

Atacama Desert · *Sahara Desert* · *Arabian Desert* · *Gobi Desert* · *Australian Desert* · *Kalahari Desert*

DESERTS OF THE WORLD
Two great belts of desert climate encircle the world on either side of the equator. Deserts also form in regions sheltered from rain by high mountains. The largest desert in the world is the Sahara in North Africa, covering an area of more than 9 million square km (3.5 million square miles). Some cold deserts lie in the hearts of continents where the winds are dry.

OASES
Desert travellers often seek an oasis, where water is abundant. The water comes from a great distance and flows under the desert, reaching the surface in springs. This oasis is in the Tamerza Desert, Tunisia.

IRRIGATION

Irrigation changes desert regions into green and fertile land. The water may come from dams across nearby rivers, or it may be pumped up from wells in the ground.

Find out more
CAMELS AND LLAMAS
CLIMATES
DESERT WILDLIFE

DESIGN

THE OBJECTS AROUND US have been carefully shaped to do their jobs as well as possible. Deciding the best shape is the work of a designer. Good design means that an object fits its purpose well. A chair that is stable and comfortable is well designed. If it is also attractive, inexpensive, and does not burn easily, its design is even better. A designer needs to understand the quality of the materials being used and to think about safety and convenience. Computers are increasingly useful for solving design problems in the aircraft and car industries. They can be used to make complex technical drawings and build up three-dimensional models very rapidly. Graphic designers use their skills to influence us through words and colour in advertising and on the printed page. In fact, designers influence every area of our lives.

Most 19th-century furniture was highly decorative.

Shaker chair, 19th century.

The Shakers thought simple designs were less wasteful.

Modern painted Memphis chair

FASHION DESIGN
Nothing changes faster than the design of clothes. Each year designers create new garments that will appeal to the fashion-conscious public. Designers use new fabrics that are easy to care for, and keep out wind, rain, and cold. Some clothes are specially designed to suit the needs of mountaineers, sailors, and other people who work or play outdoors. Some are designed for comfort and hard wear. Even nappies are designed for easy fitting and maximum absorption. But many clothes are made just to look colourful, appealing, or outrageous.

CHANGING CHAIRS
Design evolves to suit changing tastes and the availability of new materials. Much 19th-century furniture was ornamental, except for the simple furniture designed by the deeply religious Shaker sect. The 1850 Thonet chair used wood shaped in a new way which cut costs. The shape of Bauhaus chairs stressed their purpose of supporting the sitter's weight. Rethinking how people sit produced the kneeling chair. And today designers are introducing ornamentation once more, as on the Memphis chair (above left).

Thonet chair, 1850

COFFEEPOT

Container holds grounds, for easy cleaning

Secure, lipped lid

Insulated handle

High, drip-free spout

Wide, stable base

Vents keep base cool.

The perfect coffeepot not only holds coffee and looks good. It has also been designed to have a spout that does not drip, an insulated handle that does not burn your hand, a lid that does not fall off when the pot is tipped, and a heat-proof base that does not burn the table.

Kneeling chair, 1970s

Chair made at the 1920s German Bauhaus art school

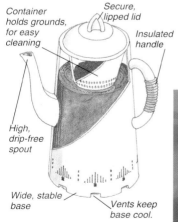

COMPUTERS IN DESIGN
By using a computer to simulate the shape of an aircraft or a car, a designer can "fly" or "drive" the vehicle before it is even built.

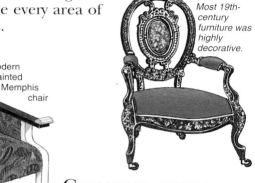

BEDROOM DESIGN
Designers have made sure that most things in this bedroom are comfortable, safe, and easy to use. There may be space-saving bunk beds, washable wallpaper, flameproof carpets, easy-care bedding, safety-tested light fixtures, adjustable shelves, and washable, nontoxic toys.

Find out more
ADVERTISING
ARCHITECTURE
CLOTHES
FURNITURE

DINOSAURS

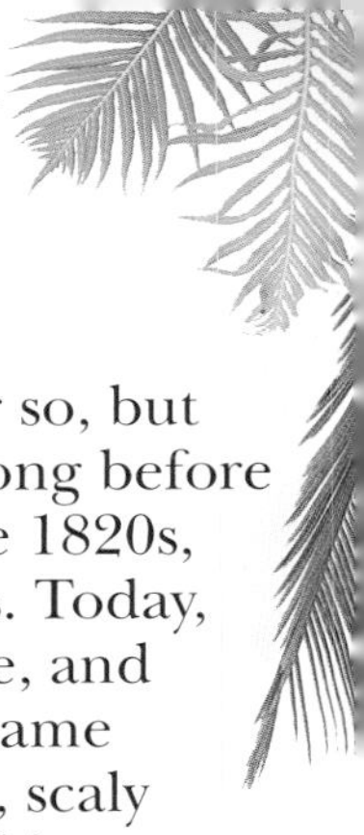

WE HAVE KNOWN ABOUT DINOSAURS for only 150 years or so, but these great creatures roamed the Earth for 160 million years – long before humans appeared. Scientists first learned about dinosaurs in the 1820s, when they discovered the fossilized bones of unknown creatures. Today, these fossils show us where dinosaurs lived, what they looked like, and what they ate. Dinosaurs were reptiles and lived on land. Their name means "terrible lizard", and like lizards, many of them had tough, scaly skin. There were hundreds of different kinds of dinosaurs, divided into two main groups. The Ornithischians (bird-hipped dinosaurs), such as *Protoceratops*, had hipbones similar to birds; the Saurischians (lizard-hipped dinosaurs), such as *Diplodocus*, had hipbones similar to lizards. Not all dinosaurs were giants – *Compsognathus* was the size of a chicken and *Heterodontosaurus* was the size of a large dog. Some dinosaurs, such as *Tyrannosaurus*, were carnivores (meat eaters); others, such as *Stegosaurus*, were herbivores (plant eaters). About 65 million years ago, dinosaurs and the swimming and flying reptiles that lived at the same time died out. The reason for this is still a mystery.

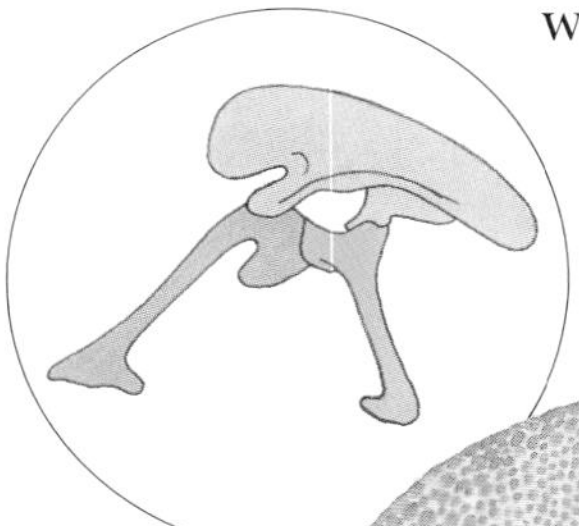

REPTILES

Dinosaurs were reptiles, like crocodiles, alligators, and the lizard shown above. Like other reptiles, dinosaurs had scaly skin, and laid eggs. Unlike lizards and other reptiles, dinosaurs had long legs, so they could move faster on land.

Tyrannosaurus rex *belonged to the group of lizard-hipped dinosaurs called Saurischians.*

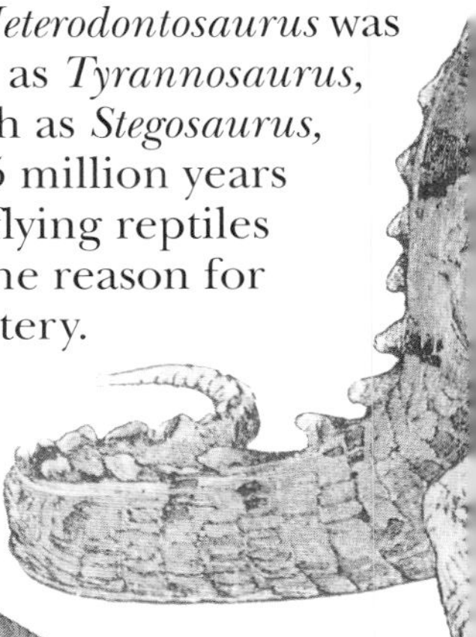

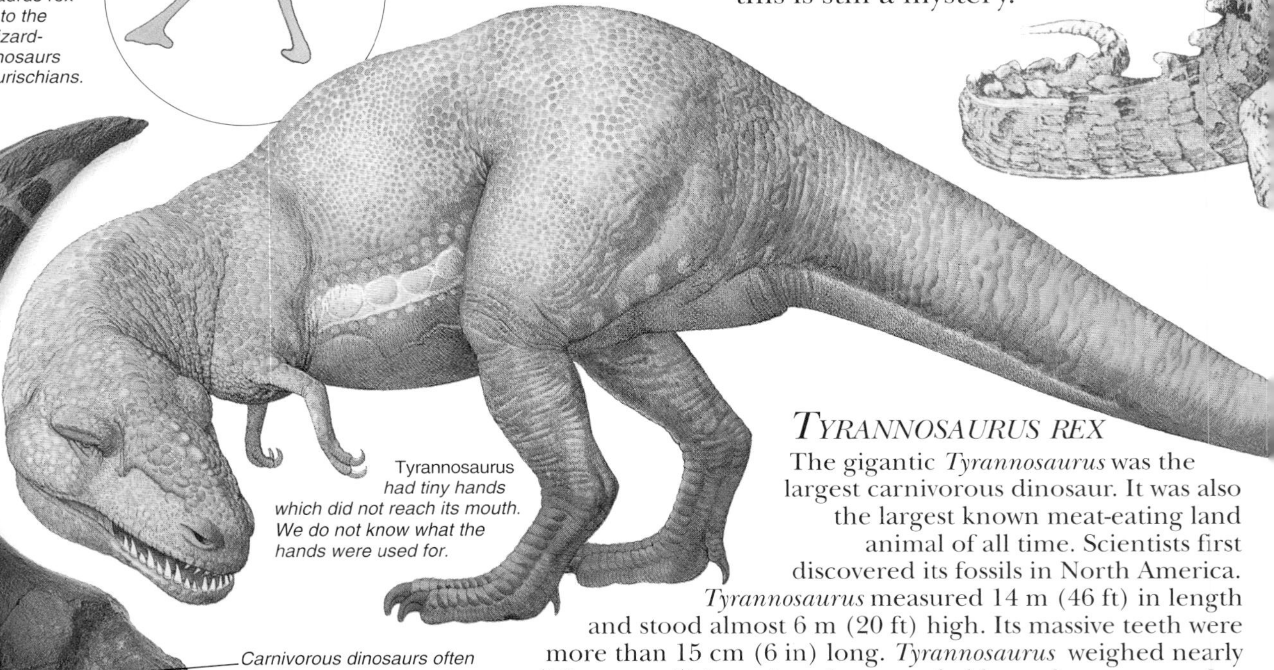

Tyrannosaurus *had tiny hands which did not reach its mouth. We do not know what the hands were used for.*

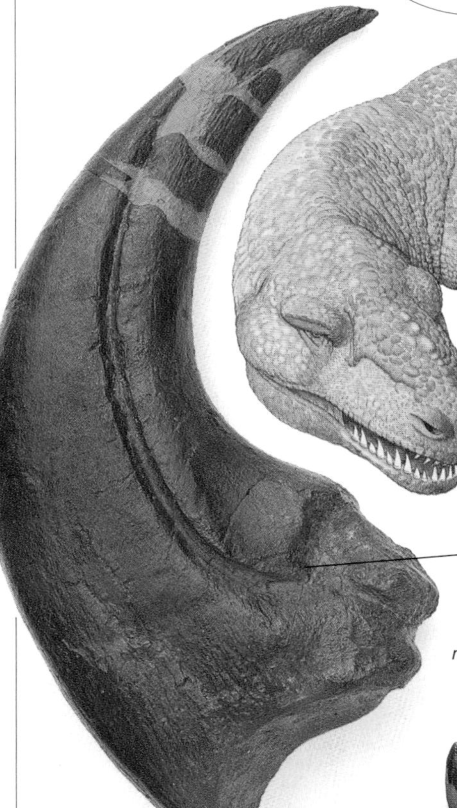

Carnivorous dinosaurs often *had large, strong claws for grabbing their prey. The claw shown here belonged to* Baryonyx, *which is nicknamed "Claws."*

TYRANNOSAURUS REX

The gigantic *Tyrannosaurus* was the largest carnivorous dinosaur. It was also the largest known meat-eating land animal of all time. Scientists first discovered its fossils in North America. *Tyrannosaurus* measured 14 m (46 ft) in length and stood almost 6 m (20 ft) high. Its massive teeth were more than 15 cm (6 in) long. *Tyrannosaurus* weighed nearly 7.3 tonnes (7.1 tons), so it was probably too heavy to run fast and hunt down other dinosaurs. *Tyrannosaurus* fed on small creatures, sick animals, and the bodies of dead dinosaurs.

Gorgosaurus jawbone

GORGOSAURUS

Carnivous dinosaurs such as the *Gorgosaurus* had huge teeth and powerful jaw muscles for a strong bite. Not all dinosaur teeth were this large, however; some were as small as human teeth.

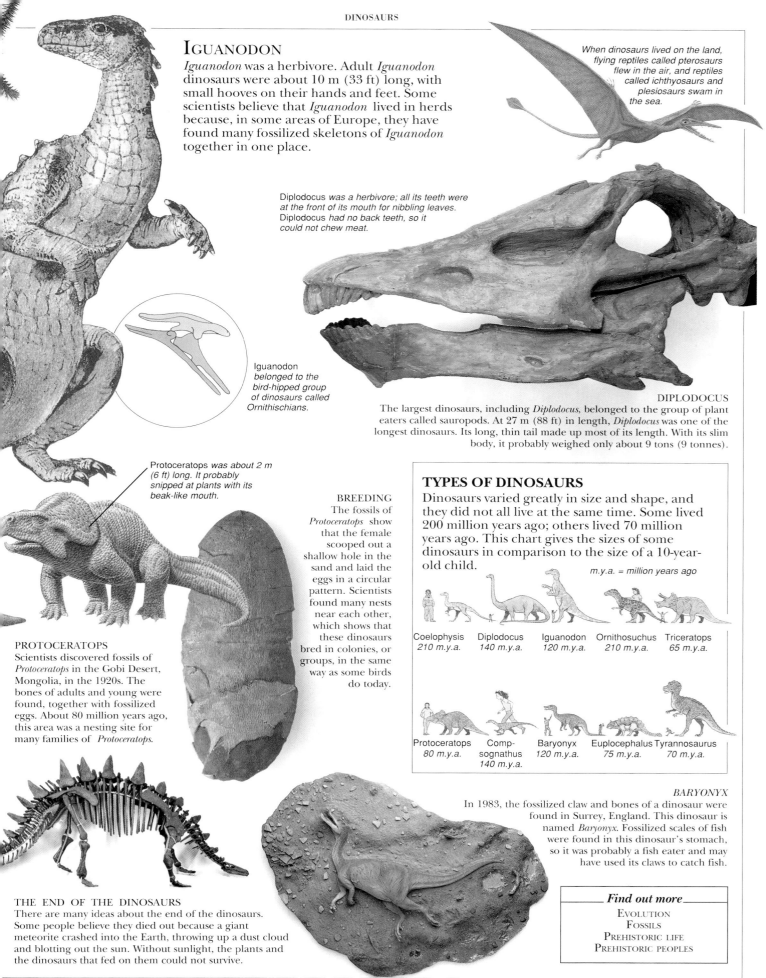

IGUANODON

Iguanodon was a herbivore. Adult *Iguanodon* dinosaurs were about 10 m (33 ft) long, with small hooves on their hands and feet. Some scientists believe that *Iguanodon* lived in herds because, in some areas of Europe, they have found many fossilized skeletons of *Iguanodon* together in one place.

When dinosaurs lived on the land, flying reptiles called pterosaurs flew in the air, and reptiles called ichthyosaurs and plesiosaurs swam in the sea.

Diplodocus *was a herbivore; all its teeth were at the front of its mouth for nibbling leaves.* Diplodocus *had no back teeth, so it could not chew meat.*

Iguanodon *belonged to the bird-hipped group of dinosaurs called Ornithischians.*

DIPLODOCUS

The largest dinosaurs, including *Diplodocus*, belonged to the group of plant eaters called sauropods. At 27 m (88 ft) in length, *Diplodocus* was one of the longest dinosaurs. Its long, thin tail made up most of its length. With its slim body, it probably weighed only about 9 tons (9 tonnes).

Protoceratops *was about 2 m (6 ft) long. It probably snipped at plants with its beak-like mouth.*

BREEDING

The fossils of *Protoceratops* show that the female scooped out a shallow hole in the sand and laid the eggs in a circular pattern. Scientists found many nests near each other, which shows that these dinosaurs bred in colonies, or groups, in the same way as some birds do today.

PROTOCERATOPS

Scientists discovered fossils of *Protoceratops* in the Gobi Desert, Mongolia, in the 1920s. The bones of adults and young were found, together with fossilized eggs. About 80 million years ago, this area was a nesting site for many families of *Protoceratops*.

TYPES OF DINOSAURS

Dinosaurs varied greatly in size and shape, and they did not all live at the same time. Some lived 200 million years ago; others lived 70 million years ago. This chart gives the sizes of some dinosaurs in comparison to the size of a 10-year-old child.

m.y.a. = million years ago

Coelophysis 210 m.y.a.	Diplodocus 140 m.y.a.	Iguanodon 120 m.y.a.	Ornithosuchus 210 m.y.a.	Triceratops 65 m.y.a.
Protoceratops 80 m.y.a.	Compsognathus 140 m.y.a.	Baryonyx 120 m.y.a.	Euplocephalus 75 m.y.a.	Tyrannosaurus 70 m.y.a.

BARYONYX

In 1983, the fossilized claw and bones of a dinosaur were found in Surrey, England. This dinosaur is named *Baryonyx*. Fossilized scales of fish were found in this dinosaur's stomach, so it was probably a fish eater and may have used its claws to catch fish.

THE END OF THE DINOSAURS

There are many ideas about the end of the dinosaurs. Some people believe they died out because a giant meteorite crashed into the Earth, throwing up a dust cloud and blotting out the sun. Without sunlight, the plants and the dinosaurs that fed on them could not survive.

Find out more

EVOLUTION
FOSSILS
PREHISTORIC LIFE
PREHISTORIC PEOPLES

DISEASE

AT SOME POINT in your life you may have a disease. It may be relatively harmless or it may be quite serious. Disease is a sickness of the body or mind. There are thousands of diseases that can strike almost every part of the body. They range from measles and the common cold to heart disease and emotional disorders such as depression. Some diseases are chronic (lasting for a long time); arthritis is a chronic disease that makes the joints swell painfully. Other diseases, which are called acute, occur in short, sharp attacks and include flu (influenza). There are many different causes of disease. Harmful micro-organisms (microscopic plants or animals) can invade the body and cause infectious disease. Poor living conditions can also cause disease. Some diseases occur at birth; others may be passed from parent to child. The reasons for some diseases such as cancer are unclear. Scientists are constantly working to understand the causes of diseases and find possible cures.

ENVIRONMENTAL DISEASE
Living conditions affect people's health. Nuclear radiation in the atmosphere can cause cancer; pollution of the air from chemicals such as lead can affect health, particularly that of children; and swimming in water that is polluted with sewage can cause serious infections such as hepatitis, typhoid, and cholera.

Viruses are tiny, smaller than a living cell. Viruses cause disease when they enter healthy cells in order to reproduce. The flu virus is spread from person to person by coughing and sneezing.

There are several different types of bacteria (below). Each consists of a single living cell. Some bacteria cause disease in humans and animals, but most are harmless.

Causes boils

Causes typhoid

Causes sore throat

BACTERIA AND VIRUSES
Infectious diseases are the only diseases that can spread from person to person. Most are caused by microscopic organisms called bacteria and viruses that invade the body. Typhoid and cholera are examples of diseases caused by bacteria; chicken pox and measles are caused by viruses.

Heart disease is often caused by blockage of blood vessels in the heart.

AIDS
Our bodies have natural defences which help us fight disease. One is the immune system, which attacks diseases that invade our bodies. In the 1980s, a new disease began to spread. Known as acquired immunodeficiency syndrome (AIDS), it stops the immune system from working correctly and can result in death.

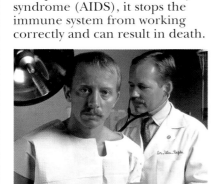
Doctor examining AIDS patient

HEREDITARY DISEASES
Parents can pass on certain diseases, called hereditary diseases, to their children. Sickle cell anaemia is a hereditary blood disease. Hereditary diseases do not usually affect all the children in a family, and may appear late in life. Diseases that appear at birth such as spina bifida, a defect of the spinal cord and nervous system, are called congenital diseases.

A hereditary disease may affect only one child in a family.

NUTRITIONAL DISEASES
In parts of the world, particularly Africa and Asia, many people do not have enough to eat. Lack of food can cause many disorders, including anaemia, rickets, and scurvy. In places such as Europe and North America, many people eat too much. Overeating can also cause disorders, including obesity (fatness), diabetes, and heart disease.

EPIDEMICS
When a disease affects many people at the same time, it is called an epidemic. Epidemics of AIDS and of malaria, a disease carried by mosquitoes, affect many parts of Africa. AIDS epidemics are also affecting industrialized countries. In Western countries, too, so many people suffer from heart disease and cancer that these diseases are sometimes described as epidemic.

Find out more
DOCTORS
DRUGS
HEALTH
HOSPITALS
MEDICINE
MEDICINE, HISTORY OF

DOCTORS

IF YOU ARE ILL, you may need to see a doctor. A doctor is someone who is trained to recognize what is wrong with sick people and know what will make them well. A general practitioner is usually the first doctor you see. These doctors, who are also called physicians, have a knowledge of many different types of illness. They also perform checkups and give vaccinations. Depending on your illness, the doctor may send you to a surgeon or some other specialist. Surgeons are doctors who carry out surgery or operations. They cut open the patient's body and take out or repair the sick organ. Other specialists include pediatricians, who specialize in treating children. To be licensed as a doctor takes five to six years of study at a medical school, and one year as a house officer in a hospital.

HIPPOCRATIC OATH
Doctors have existed since ancient times. Hippocrates was a famous Greek doctor who lived 2,500 years ago. He swore an oath to preserve life and to work for the benefit of everyone. Today doctors still swear the same oath when they complete their training.

The stethoscope enables the doctor to listen to the lungs, and to hear blood flowing.

The inflatable cuff of the sphygmomanometer temporarily stops the flow of blood, so that the doctor can measure its pressure.

DOCTOR'S TOOLS
Physicians use x-rays and a variety of special instruments to help them find out what is wrong with their patients.

X-ray photographs reveal broken bones and some diseases, such as lung cancer.

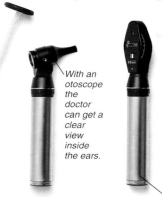

With an otoscope the doctor can get a clear view inside the ears.

A hammer tap below the knee tests the reflexes: a healthy patient's knee jerks.

An ophthalmoscope is used for examining the eyes.

DOCTOR'S OFFICE
A family doctor sometimes visits sick patients in their homes; patients who are well enough visit the doctor in his or her surgery. There the doctor asks questions and examines the patient, then makes a diagnosis (decides what is wrong). Before giving any treatment the doctor may also need to take x-rays or do blood tests.

MICROSURGERY
With the aid of microscopes, surgeons can see and operate on minute parts of the body. This technique, called microsurgery, makes it possible to repair or cut out damaged organs that are too small to work on without magnification. Microsurgeons can operate on delicate structures in the eye and the ear, and reconnect fingers or toes that have been cut off.

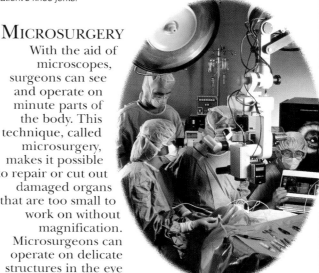

TRAVELLING DOCTORS
In remote parts of the world doctors travel from village to village to treat health problems. If there are not enough doctors health workers can learn to treat common health problems. In Australia and Canada "flying doctors" reach isolated areas by aeroplane.

Find out more
DISEASE
HEALTH
HOSPITALS

DOGS
WOLVES, AND FOXES

EARLY DOGS
Domestic dogs first existed in the Stone Age. We can see how they looked from early cave paintings.

WHEN A PET DOG BARKS at a stranger, or walks around in a circle before settling down to sleep, it is behaving in the same way that its wild wolf cousins did thousands of years ago. The dog family is made up of about 35 different species, one of which is the group of domestic dogs. There are many different breeds of domestic dogs, from large labradors to small terriers. Other members of the dog family are the Asian dhole, the African wild dog, many kinds of foxes, and four species of jackals. These muscular, fast running hunters are built for chasing prey in open country; their elongated skulls are thought to be adaptations for seizing prey on the run. Many wild dogs, such as wolves and dingos, are social and live in extended family groups called packs. Each pack has a leader, to whom all the other animals in the pack submit. A well-trained domestic dog sees its owner as a pack leader and is willing to obey that person's commands.

GREY WOLF
This wolf is believed to be the ancestor of our domestic dogs. It is the largest member of the dog family, measuring at least 2 m (6 ft) in length, including its tail. Where food is readily available, wolves may form a pack consisting of up to 20 wolves. When food is difficult to find, a large pack of wolves splits up into smaller groups of about seven animals.

Reasonable eyesight in daylight; night vision weak.

Extremely sensitive nose for tracking animals and people

Long, strong legs for fast, sustained running

GERMAN SHEPHERD
This dog has a long muzzle and large ears, and still resembles its wolf ancestors. It is a strong, agile, extremely intelligent breed of dog – popular both as a working dog and as a pet.

Tail is used to give social signals, such as wagging when happy.

Good hearing, with ears that turn to locate the source of a sound

Dogs have four claws on each paw. The tough toe pads help them grip well when they run.

Fur coat keeps animal warm and dry.

Meat-eating teeth, with large pointed canines for seizing and tearing at prey

DOMESTIC DOGS
Dogs have lived in harmony with humans for more than 10,000 years. It is quite possible that over thousands of years, humans have caught and tamed several members of the dog family, at first to help with hunting, herding, and guarding, and, much later, to keep as pets. Today more than 130 breeds of domestic dogs are recognized in Britain, and about 160 in the United States.

WORKING DOGS
Dogs are trained to do many jobs for humans. Some tasks, such as herding sheep or guarding property, involve the dog's natural instincts. Other jobs include guiding the blind, pulling sleds, and racing. Many dogs are trained by the police and the army to find people who are trapped or in hiding.

RED FOX

Few animals are as adaptable as the red fox, which lives in almost every country north of the equator. Red foxes eat almost anything, including insects and fish. The fox springs up and pounces on its prey like a cat. This creature's legendary cunning helps it survive in suburban gardens and city dumps. In towns and cities, it feeds on scraps from dustbins and rubbish heaps.

Mongrels are domestic dogs that are not pedigree – such as the three dogs shown here.

COYOTE

The North American coyote is closely related to wolves, jackals, and domestic dogs. Like most dogs, the female is pregnant for nine weeks before giving birth to about five puppies. The puppies feed on their mother's milk for up to seven weeks. After the first four weeks they also eat food regurgitated, or brought up, by their parents. Coyotes were thought to live alone, but we now know that some form small packs.

A female coyote usually has one litter of puppies each year.

PANTING

When a dog becomes hot, it cannot lose heat from its skin by sweating because its fur is so thick. Instead, the dog opens its mouth and pants, or breathes quickly, to give off heat from its mouth and tongue.

YORKSHIRE TERRIER
This small dog measures only 18 cm (7 in) in height. It is an agile runner, originally bred for chasing rabbits out of their holes.

MANED WOLF
The maned wolf is being bred in zoos and parks in an attempt to save it from extinction.

TOY DOGS

Dog breeders have created dogs of all sizes and shapes by mating dogs with unusual features, such as short legs or small ears. The smallest breeds, known as toy dogs, have become quite different from their distant ancestors, the wolves. A chihuahua, one of the smallest recognized breeds, can weigh less than 1 kg (2 lb).

CRAB-EATING FOX
The crab-eating fox, also called the common zorro, is from South America. It eats many kinds of food, including crabs, as it forages along the coast. Other crab-eating foxes live far inland in woods and grassland and never even see a crab.

PUPPIES
Young dogs such as the labrador puppy shown here spend much of their time in play, tumbling, jumping, and biting and shaking things. These games help the young dog develop hunting skills for adult life.

CONSERVATION

The long-legged maned wolf from South America is one of many members of the dog family that are officially listed as in danger of extinction. Many wolves and foxes, including the grey wolf, have been hunted not only for their beautiful fur, but also because they sometimes attack farm animals. One of the greatest threats to the dog family is the loss of the natural areas where they live, which are now used for farmland, houses, and factories.

Find out more
AFRICAN WILDLIFE
ANIMAL SENSES
ANIMALS
AUSTRALIAN WILDLIFE
CONSERVATION
and endangered species
MAMMALS
POLAR EXPLORATION

DRAWING

EARLY PEOPLE MAY HAVE BEGUN TO DRAW by scratching images in the dirt with sticks or their fingers, possibly outlines copied from shadows. They then learned to use natural earth pigments and charcoal to draw on other surfaces. They may have started to draw in order to communicate ideas. Points of soft lead, tin, copper, and other metals were used from ancient times to the 18th century. Today, people draw with chalk, charcoal, crayon, pastel, pencil, or pen and ink. Paper is the most practical medium for drawing. Creative drawings are often done as preparations for paintings or sculptures; a painter may sketch out an idea in a drawing before starting to paint a picture. But many drawings are seen as finished works of art. Drawing has practical as well as artistic uses. An architect has to draw up detailed, accurate plans in order for a building to be constructed properly. Courtroom artists draw pictures of scenes during a trial where photographers are not allowed. And before photography was invented, artists drew battles and other events for newspapers.

ALBRECHT DÜRER
The German artist Albrecht Dürer (1471-1528) made many drawings of people, landscapes, and animals. His brush drawing *Praying Hands* (above) was a study for part of an altarpiece for a German church. Dürer also produced a variety of paintings, engravings, and woodcuts.

Pencils range from 7H, which gives a hard, fine line, to 8B, which gives a soft, dark line.

Charcoal sticks were used by early peoples to sketch on the walls of caves.

Pastels are powdered pigments bound together with gum or resin.

Drawing ink is generally water resistant.

Conté crayons are made by mixing chalk and pigment with fatty materials such as wax.

Metal nib pen

Coloured pencils

PENS AND PENCILS
The "lead" pencil we use today is a mixture of graphite and clay fired at a high temperature and mixed with wax. This kind of pencil was not developed until the end of the 18th century. To get the best results, good-quality paper is necessary. Paper sometimes has a textured surface which adds to the character of the drawing.

TECHNICAL DRAWING
Architects, engineers, and designers make technical drawings of their designs with the aid of instruments such as T squares and compasses. Technical drawings show exactly how to construct things, from bridges to aeroplanes, so they must be very accurate. A technical artist needs to have a steady hand and pay great attention to detail. A mistake in the drawing could be disastrous.

SKETCH
Artists often make sketches – quick drawings – to record things that they see or to prepare for a finished work. The Italian artist Leonardo da Vinci (1452-1519) made thousands of sketches to record his observations. He filled notebooks with drawings of human anatomy, machines, plants, and plans of cities. Above is one of his sketches: a study for the *Head of Leda*.

Find out more

ARCHITECTURE
CARTOONS
PAINTING

DRUGS

IF YOU ARE ILL, the doctor might give you a drug. Drugs, or medicines, are substances used in the treatment of illnesses. They can relieve the symptoms (effects) of a disease, ease pain, and prevent or cure illnesses. Drugs are also used to treat a wide range of emotional disorders such as depression.

There are thousands of different kinds of drugs in use today. Each drug has a specific function and often acts on a single part of the body, such as the stomach. There are many sources of drugs. They may be natural or synthetic (artificial). Medicinal plants and herbs yield natural drugs which have been in use for thousands of years. Scientists search constantly for new drugs and often make them from chemicals. In many cases, the discovery of a drug has eased suffering and saved many lives. Antibiotics such as penicillin, for example, cure infections that would have been fatal 50 years ago.

Many drugs are taken orally (by mouth). The drug passes through the digestive system and into the bloodstream, which carries the drug to the relevant part of the body.

Drugs can be dangerous. Today, many containers are made with specially designed tops that are difficult to remove.

Some drugs, such as antihistamines for treating allergies (sensitivity to certain substances), work more quickly if they are injected directly into the bloodstream through a needle and syringe.

The body can absorb creams and ointments through the skin. Medicinal creams are often used to treat skin disorders.

Some drugs, particularly those for young people, are dissolved in a sweet-tasting syrup. Special spoons that hold a fixed amount of liquid ensure that the patient receives the correct dose.

Some powdered drugs dissolve in water, which makes them go into the bloodstream more rapidly than if they are taken as pills.

Tablets containing drugs are made with a smooth shape so that they are easy to swallow.

Tablets and capsules contain carefully measured amounts of drugs. When they are swallowed, the drugs slowly filter into the bloodstream via the digestive system. Some tablets have a coating which dissolves slowly, releasing the drug at a controlled rate.

TYPES OF DRUGS

Different drugs have different uses. They range from antibiotics (for treating infections) to painkillers, such as aspirin. Anaesthetics are used to put patients to sleep before surgery. There are different ways of taking drugs. They can be swallowed, injected, put on the skin, used in a spray, or inhaled.

DRUG ADDICTION

Many drugs, including some drugs recommended by doctors, are addictive. This means that the drug user depends on the drug. Drug addiction can lead to illness and death. The use of many dangerous drugs such as heroin, crack, and cocaine is illegal. However, other addictive drugs, such as alcohol and nicotine (from cigarettes), are not controlled by law.

SOURCES OF DRUGS

In the past, all drugs came from natural sources, particularly herbs and plants. Today, most drugs are made from chemicals, and some are made by genetic engineering, a method in which the cells in bacteria or yeasts are altered to produce drugs.

Some drugs such as insulin (for treating diabetes) can be obtained from pigs and cattle.

The heart drug digitalis comes from a flower called the foxglove.

The painkiller aspirin is made from chemicals.

The antibiotic penicillin first came from a mould called penicillium.

__Find out more__
DISEASE
DOCTORS
FLOWERS AND HERBS
HEALTH
MEDICINE
MEDICINE, HISTORY OF

DUCKS, GEESE, AND SWANS

A swan weighs about 13 kg (28 lb).

To reach takeoff speed, it has to run over the water.

The swan has to flap its wings very hard.

Large, powerful wings lift the swan into the air.

During flight, the feet tuck under the body.

For landing, the feet are used as brakes.

The feet serve as paddles for swimming.

WATERFOWL IS THE NAME GIVEN TO the ducks, geese, and swans that live on the lakes and rivers of the world. Many waterfowl have long, flexible necks that allow them to reach down into the water for food. They spend much of their time preening and spreading oils over their feathers with their beaks. The oils are made in special glands; they keep the plumage waterproof and help keep the bird warm. Most waterfowl live in flocks except in the breeding season; some, such as barnacle and brent geese, migrate long distances to their nesting grounds. Many waterfowl are kept by people for their eggs, meat, and feathers. Eiderdown, often used to stuff quilts, is the soft, downy under-feathers of the eider duck.

Canada

United States

SWAN
The female black-necked swan carries her fluffy cygnets (young swans) on her back when she is swimming, to keep them warm and safe from predators. Cygnets can fly about three months after hatching.

CANADA GEESE
Each spring, Canada geese fly from Mexico and the southern United States to breeding grounds in Canada. They fly in V-shaped formations and often change position so the leader of the flock does not get too tired. Canada geese nest in grass-lined hollows on islands and marshes. Like most geese and swans, Canada geese stay with their partners for many years. Both geese bring up the young goslings (baby geese), and the family stays together until the next breeding season.

Canada geese fly north in pairs to breed.

DIVING DUCKS AND DABBLING DUCKS
The two main groups of ducks are divers and dabblers. Dabblers, such as mallard ducks, pintail, widgeons, and teals, feed at the surface or stick their tails in the air and dabble just below the surface. They sweep their bills from side to side, sieving out seeds, flies, and other bits of food. Diving ducks, such as pochards and tufted ducks, swim down below the surface to peck at water plants, worms, shellfish, and other small water creatures.

Legs are at the back of body, for efficient swimming.

WEBBED FEET
Most waterfowl have short legs and webbed feet that work well as paddles but make it difficult to walk on land.

Webbed foot has claws on the toes for scratching in the earth.

TUFTED DUCK
Tufted ducks eat zebra mussels, a type of freshwater shellfish, as well as small fish, tadpoles, and water insects.

MALLARD
Most male dabbling ducks are more colourful than the females, with bright patches on both wings.

Find out more

BIRDS
FLIGHT IN ANIMALS
LAKE AND RIVER WILDLIFE
MIGRATION

EAGLES
AND OTHER BIRDS OF PREY

IN THE SAME WAY that sharks are hunters in the sea and lions are hunters on land, eagles are powerful hunters of the sky. Birds of prey, such as eagles, falcons, hawks, owls, and vultures, are also called raptors. There are about 280 different kinds, and they all have extremely sharp eyesight. They can spy their prey on the ground from a great height. Raptors have long, strong legs with sharp claws, called talons, for grasping their victims, and a sharp, hooked beak for tearing flesh. One of the largest, most majestic eagles is the Australian wedge-tailed eagle, with a wingspan of 2.5 m (8 ft). The Eurasian kestrel is a common bird of prey, often seen hovering alongside roads watching for prey in the grass. Many birds of prey are rare because the countryside where they live has been turned into farmland, and pesticides poison their food.

FISH EAGLE

The African fish eagle has long feathers on the tips of its wings to help it control its gliding. Its sharp eyes are always on the lookout for fish as it patrols the lakes, swamps, and rivers of Africa south of the Sahara Desert.

HAWK

The sparrow hawk is a nimble woodland hunter of smaller birds. It can swoop down on its prey with a surprise dive, or chase it with twists and turns among the trees.

Huge, powerful wings for soaring and diving

Excellent eyesight for spying fish

Large, strong beak for tearing flesh

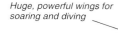

Long, sharp talons on toes for grasping prey

FALCONRY

For hundreds of years, falcons, hawks, and other birds of prey have been trained to hunt from a gloved hand. Birds such as this Eurasian kestrel are hooded before the hunt, to keep them calm. Falconry is especially popular in the Middle East.

BALD EAGLE

Because of their size and strength, eagles are popular symbols and emblems. The American bald eagle (left), a type of fish eagle, is the national emblem of the United States. It is not really bald but looks that way because the white feathers on its head contrast with the dark body.

CONDOR

Condors are among the largest flying birds. Their huge wings measure 3 m (10 ft) from tip to tip. The South American Andean condor can glide for hours and hours high above remote mountains.

SCAVENGERS

Vultures and condors feed mainly on dead and dying animals, known as carrion. They circle on high, watching for food. When one vulture sees a meal, it drops quickly, followed by other vultures nearby. Soon there may be 50 or more vultures pecking over the dead body.

KING VULTURE

Like all vultures, the colourful South American king vulture has a bald head and neck. This vulture lives in rain forests, and soars over the treetops, marshes, and grasslands in search of dead animals to scavenge. The king vulture also hunts small reptiles and mammals.

A brilliant orange head and a grey feather collar make the king vulture look dressed to kill.

Find out more
ANIMALS
BIRDS
FLIGHT IN ANIMALS
OWLS

EARS

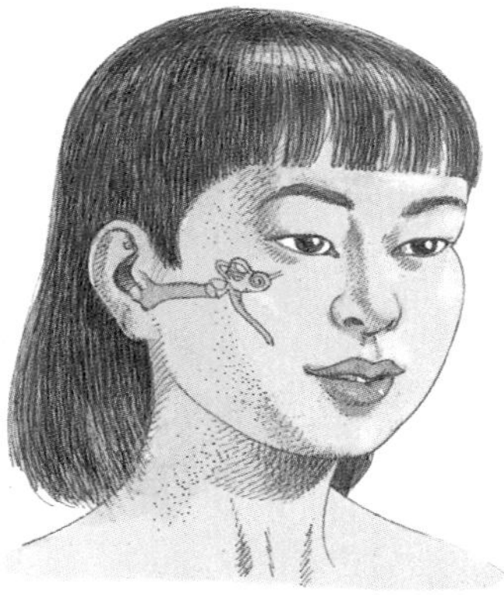

THE EARS ARE the organs of hearing and balance. They collect sound vibrations from the air and turn them into messages called nerve signals which are passed to the brain. Each ear has three main parts – the outer ear, the middle ear, and the inner ear. The outer ear is the part you can see. It consists of the ear flap, or auricle, and the ear canal. The middle ear consists of the eardrum and three tiny bones called the ossicles. The bones themselves are called the malleus (hammer), incus (anvil), and stapes (stirrup). These three bones send sounds from the eardrum to the inner ear. The main part of the inner ear is the snail-shaped cochlea, which is full of fluid. The cochlea changes vibrations into nerve signals. The inner ear also makes sure that the body keeps its balance. Although we can hear many different sounds, we cannot hear as wide a range as most animals. Also, unlike rabbits and horses, we cannot swivel our ears towards the direction of a sound – we have to turn our heads.

Ultrasonic sound is above the human range of hearing.

Human Dog Dolphin Bat

INSIDE THE EAR
The ear canal is slightly curved. It measures about 2.5 cm (1 in) in length. The delicate parts of the middle and inner ear lie well protected deep inside the skull bone, just behind and below the level of the eye.

INNER EAR
The stirrup bone presses on a thin, flexible part of the cochlea's wall, called the oval window, and passes its vibrations to the fluid inside the cochlea. The vibrations shake microscopic hairs on cells along a thin membrane in the cochlea. This movement creates nerve signals which are sent along the cochlear nerve to the brain.

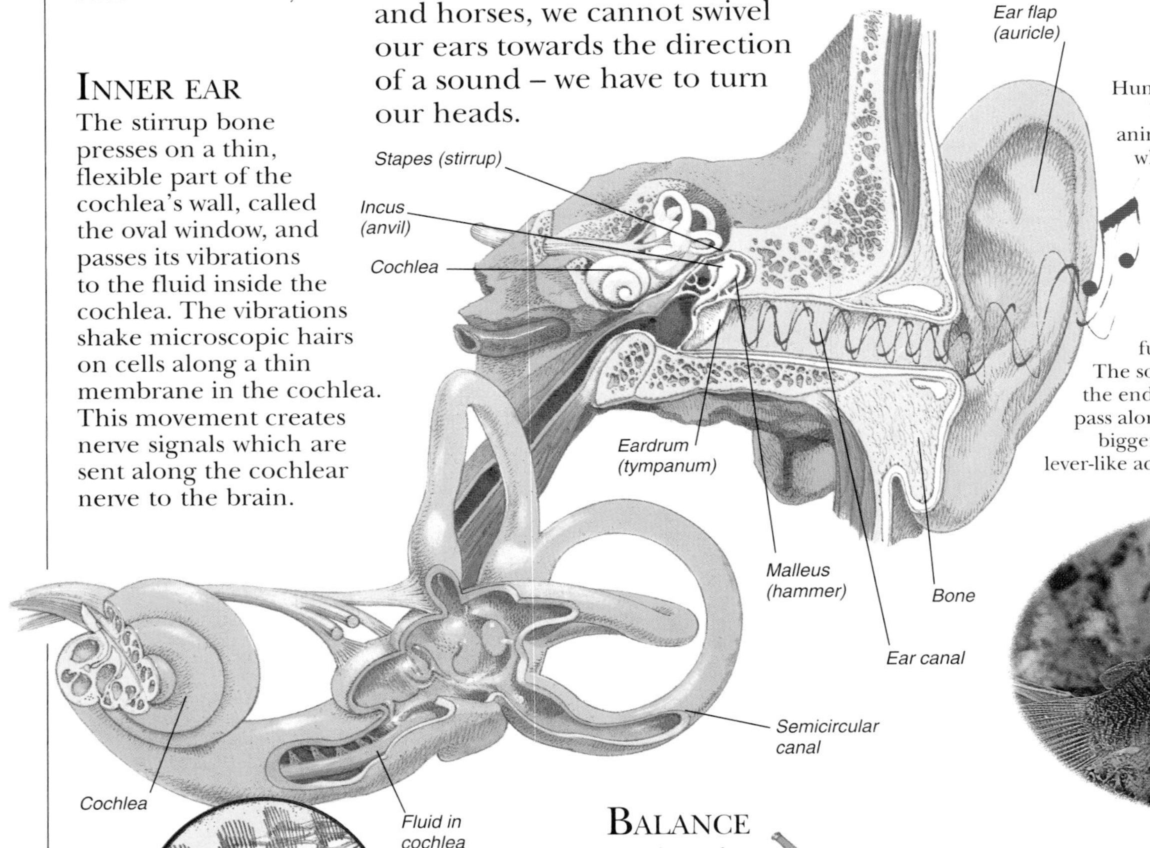

Ear flap (auricle)

Stapes (stirrup)

Incus (anvil)

Cochlea

Eardrum (tympanum)

Malleus (hammer)

Bone

Ear canal

Semicircular canal

Cochlea

Fluid in cochlea

Hair cell

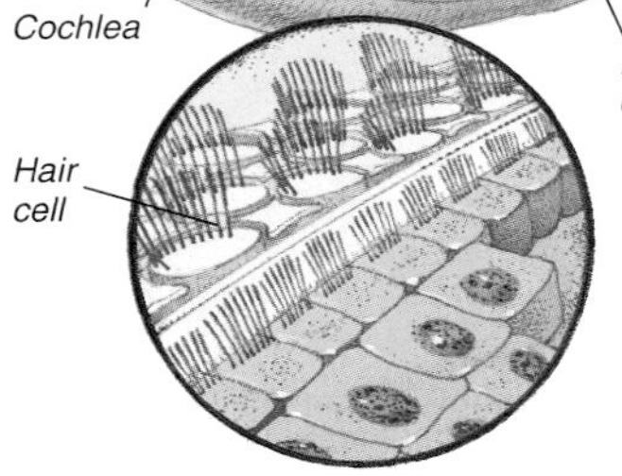

There are more than 20,000 microscopic hair cells inside the cochlea. Sound vibrations make cochlear fluid flow over the hairs; this is how the hair cells receive sound vibrations to convert into nerve signals which travel to the brain.

RANGE OF HEARING
Humans can hear sounds that vary from a low growl to a piercing scream. Many animals, including dogs, can hear sounds which are far too high-pitched for us to detect. A human's range of hearing is 30-20,000 hertz (vibrations per second); a bat's range of hearing is up to 100,000 hertz.

OUTER AND MIDDLE EAR
The ear flap on the side of the head funnels sound waves into the ear canal. The sound waves bounce off the eardrum at the end and make it vibrate. These vibrations pass along the ossicles, each of which is hardly bigger than a rice grain. The ossicles have a lever-like action that makes the vibrations louder.

BALANCE
The ears help us keep our balance. The three semicircular canals inside the ear contain fluid. As you move your head, the fluid flows around. Tiny hair cells sense this movement and produce nerve signals to tell the brain which way "up" you are.

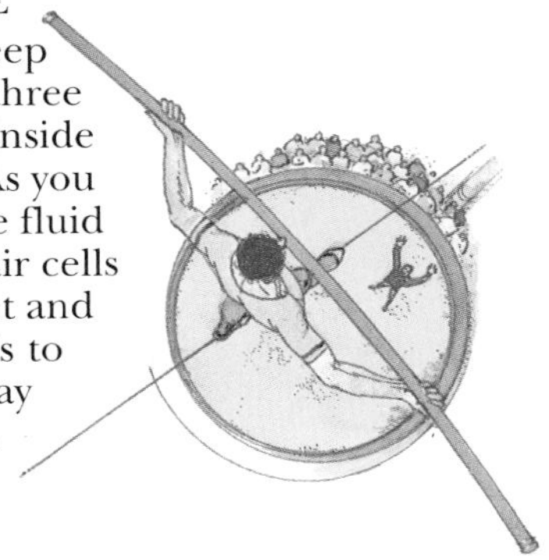

ANIMAL HEARING
Creatures such as fish and squid have sense organs to detect vibrations in the water. Fish have a lateral line – a narrow groove along each side of the body. Hair cells in the lateral line can sense the sound or movement of nearby animals. The catfish shown here also has whiskers called barbels which can sense vibrations.

Find out more
HUMAN BODY
SKELETONS
SOUND

EARTH

A LARGE BALL OF ROCK spinning through space is our home in the universe. This is the Earth, one of the nine planets that circle around the sun. The Earth is the only place we know of that can support life. It has oxygen in its atmosphere and water in its oceans, both of which are essential for life. And of all the planets in the solar system, the Earth is at just the right distance from the sun to be neither too hot nor too cold. Land makes up less than a third of the surface of the Earth; more than two thirds is the water in the oceans. The Earth's interior consists of layers of rock that surround a core made of iron and nickel.

The processes that support life on Earth are in a natural balance. However, many people are worried that pollution, human over-population, and misuse of resources may destroy this balance and make the Earth unsafe for plants and animals.

EARTH IN SPACE
When astronauts first saw the Earth from space, they were enthralled by the beauty of our blue planet. This picture shows the Earth rising over the moon's horizon.

ATMOSPHERE
A layer of air called the atmosphere surrounds the Earth. It is roughly 2,000 km (1,250 miles) deep and contains mainly the gases nitrogen and oxygen. The atmosphere shields the Earth from harmful ultraviolet rays coming from the sun and prevents the Earth from becoming too hot or too cold.

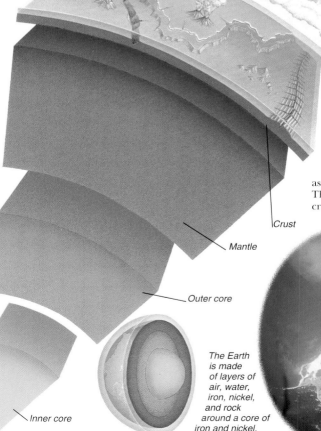

Clouds containing tiny drops of water float low in the atmosphere, carrying water from the seas and land which falls as rain.

Atmosphere

OCEANS
The oceans are large water-filled hollows in the Earth's crust. Their average depth is 3.5 km (2.2 miles).

MANTLE
Under the crust is the mantle, a layer of rock about 2,900 km (1,800 miles) thick. The temperature rises to 3,700°C (6,700°F) at the base of the mantle, but high pressure there keeps the rock solid.

OUTER CORE
The core of the Earth consists of two layers – the outer core and the inner core. The outer core is about 2,000km (1,240 miles) thick and is made of liquid iron. Its temperature is approximately 2,200°C (4,000°F).

INNER CORE
A ball of solid iron and nickel about 2,740 km (1,712 miles) across lies at the center of the Earth. The temperature at the centre is about 4,500°C (8,100°F).

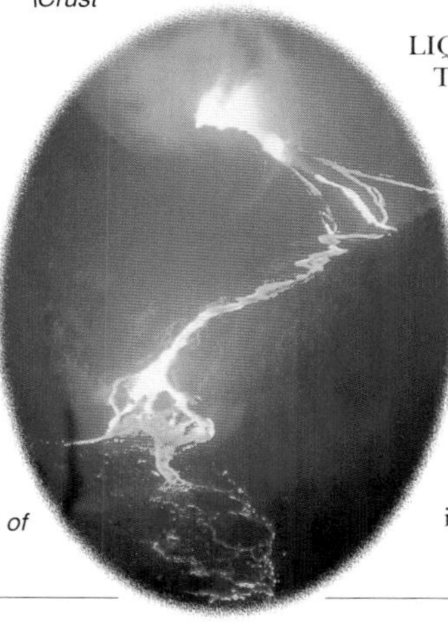

CRUST
The top layer of rock at the surface of the Earth is called the crust. It is up to 70 km (44 miles) deep beneath the continents, but as little as 6 km (4 miles) deep under the oceans. The temperature at the bottom of the crust is about 1,050°C (1,900°F).

Crust

Mantle

Outer core

Inner core

The Earth is made of layers of air, water, iron, nickel, and rock around a core of iron and nickel.

LIQUID ROCK
The interior of the Earth is very hot, heated by radioactive decay of the rocks inside the Earth. The temperature is so high that some rock inside the Earth may melt. This liquid rock rises to the surface at volcanoes, where it is called lava.

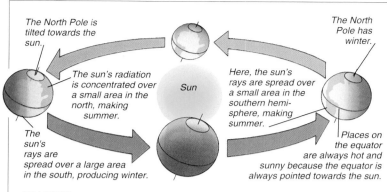

The North Pole is tilted towards the sun.

The North Pole has winter.

The sun's radiation is concentrated over a small area in the north, making summer.

Here, the sun's rays are spread over a small area in the southern hemisphere, making summer.

The sun's rays are spread over a large area in the south, producing winter.

Places on the equator are always hot and sunny because the equator is always pointed towards the sun.

Sun

SEASONS

Away from the equator, seasons change as the Earth moves around the sun. The Earth is tilted at an angle of 23.5° compared to its orbit, which makes the Poles point toward or away from the sun at different times of the year.

EARTH FACTS

Diameter at equator	12,756 km (7,926 miles)
Diameter at poles	12,714 km (7,900 miles)
Circumference at equator	40,075 km (24,901 miles)
Land area	29.2% of Earth's surface
Ocean area	70.8% of Earth's surface
Mass	6,000 billion billion tonnes (5,900 billion billion tons)
Time for one spin	23 hours 56 minutes 4 seconds
Time to orbit sun	365 days 6 hours 9 minutes 9 seconds
Distance from sun	150 million km (93 million miles)

The Earth spins around its axis, which passes through the North and South Poles. It also orbits the sun at the same time.

1 A cloud of gas and dust contracted (shrank) to form the sun about 4,600 million years ago. The rest of the cloud then contracted further and broke up into large clumps of particles of ice and rock. After a short time, the particles stuck to each other and began to form the planets.

2 The Earth may have taken about 100 million years to grow into a ball of rock. The new planet became hot as the rock particles crashed into one another. The surface was molten, and the young Earth glowed red-hot.

FORMATION OF THE EARTH

Scientists have calculated that the Earth is nearly 4,600 million years old. Some moon rocks and meteorites (pieces of rock that fall to Earth from space) are the same age, which suggests that the whole solar system formed at the same time. The sun, Earth, and the other planets were formed from a huge cloud of gas and dust in space.

3 Radioactivity in the rocks caused more heat, and the whole planet melted. Molten iron then sank to the centre of the Earth to form its core. Lighter rocks floated above the iron, and about 4,500 million years ago the surface cooled to form the crust. Volcanoes erupted and poured out gases, which formed the atmosphere, and water vapor, which condensed (changed into liquid) to fill the world's oceans.

GEOTHERMAL ENERGY

The heat from the interior of the Earth provides a source of safe, clean energy, called geothermal energy. Hot rocks lie close to the surface in Iceland, Italy, and other parts of the world. The rocks heat underground water and often make it boil into steam. Wells dug down to these rocks bring up the steam and hot water, which are used to generate electricity and heat buildings.

Water that filled the oceans may have also come from comets that collided with the young Earth.

THEORIES OF THE EARTH

People once believed that the Earth was flat. About 2,500 years ago, the Greeks found out that the Earth is round. Aristarchus, a Greek scientist, suggested in about 260 B.C. that the Earth moves around the sun. It was not until 1543 that Polish astronomer Nicolaus Copernicus (1473-1543; right) confirmed this idea. New theories are still evolving. For instance, one idea called the Gaia theory suggests that the whole planet behaves as a living organism.

4 Tiny living things began to grow at least 3,500 million years ago. Some produced oxygen, which began to build up in the atmosphere about 2,300 million years ago. The continents broke up and slowly moved into their present-day positions. They are still moving slowly today, a process called continental drift.

Find out more

ATMOSPHERE
CLIMATES
CONTINENTS
GEOLOGY
OCEANS AND SEAS
ROCKS AND MINERALS
UNIVERSE

EARTHQUAKES

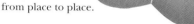

ONCE EVERY 30 SECONDS, somewhere in the world, the Earth shakes slightly. These earth tremors are strong enough to be felt, but cause no damage. However, every few months a major earthquake occurs. The land shakes so violently that roads break up, forming huge cracks, and buildings and bridges collapse, causing many deaths. Earthquakes are caused by the movements of huge plates of rock in the Earth's crust. They occur in places that lie on the boundaries where these plates meet, such as the San Andreas fault which runs 435 km (270 miles) through central California.

In some cases, scientists can tell in advance that an earthquake is liable to occur. In 1974, for example, scientists predicted an earthquake in China, saving thousands of lives. But earthquake prediction is not always accurate. In 1989, a major earthquake struck San Francisco, United States, without warning, killing 67 people.

INSTANT CHAOS
Destruction can be so swift and sudden that people have no time to escape. Falling masonry crushes cars and blocks roads.

CAUSES OF EARTHQUAKES

The Earth's crust consists of several vast plates of solid rock. These plates move very slowly and sometimes slide past each other. Most severe earthquakes occur where the plates meet. Sometimes the edges of the plates grip each other and cannot move, so pressure builds up. Suddenly the plates slip and lurch past each other, making the land shake violently.

The rocks suddenly slip along the fault: a movement of a few metres is enough to cause a severe earthquake.

FAULT
A deep crack, or fault, marks the boundary of two plates.

Rocks grip along the fault.

The place within the Earth where an earthquake occurs is the focus.

The earthquake is usually strongest at the epicentre, the point on the Earth's surface directly above the focus.

RICHTER SCALE
The severity of an earthquake is measured on the Richter scale, which runs from 0 to 9. An earthquake reaching 8 on the scale can flatten a city. The Richter scale measures the movement of the ground, rather than the damage an earthquake causes, which varies from place to place.

A rare photograph of a tsunami crashing through Hilo Harbor, Hawaii, in 1946. This person is in great danger.

SEISMOLOGY

Sensitive equipment can pick up vibrations far from an earthquake. This is because the sudden slip of rocks produces shock waves which move through the Earth. The study of earthquakes and the shock waves they cause is called seismology.

TSUNAMIS
Earthquakes occur on the ocean floor, often producing a wave called a tsunami which races towards the shore. The wave is not very high in mid-ocean. But it begins to rise as it nears the coast, sometimes growing to about 76 m (250 ft) high. The tsunami smashes onto the shore, destroying buildings and carrying boats far inland. Tsunamis, which are often wrongly called tidal waves, are also caused by volcanic eruptions.

EARTHQUAKE BELTS
Earthquakes occur only in certain parts of the world. This map shows the world's earthquake belts, which also extend through the oceans. Most severe earthquakes happen near boundaries between plates in the Earth's crust, so the belts follow the edges of the plates.

Find out more

CONTINENTS
EARTH
GEOLOGY
VOLCANOES

ECOLOGY AND FOOD WEBS

WE CAN LOOK AT NATURE in the same way that we look at a complicated machine, to see how all the parts fit together. Every living thing has its place in nature, and ecology is the study of how things live in relation to their surroundings. It is a relatively new science and is of great importance today. It helps us understand how plants and animals depend on each other and their surroundings in order to survive. Ecology also helps us work towards saving animals and plants from extinction and solving the problems caused by pollution. Plants and animals can be divided into different groups, depending on their ecological function. Plants capture the sun's light energy and use it to produce new growth, so they are called producers; animals consume (eat) plants and other animals, so they are called consumers. All the plants and animals that live in one area and feed off each other make up a community. The relationships between the plants and animals in a community is called a food web; energy passes through the community via these food webs.

ECOSYSTEM

A community and its surroundings, including the soil, air, climate, and the other communities around it, make up an ecosystem. The Earth can be seen as one giant ecosystem spinning through space. It recycles its raw materials such as leaves and other plant matter, and is powered by energy from the sun.

The European kingfisher has little to fear. Its brightly coloured plumage warns predators that it is foul-tasting. The kingfisher is well named – it is extremely skilful at fishing.

FOOD CHAINS AND FOOD WEBS

A plant uses the sun's energy to grow. A herbivore (plant eater) eats the plant. A carnivore (meat eater) or an omnivore (plant and meat eater) then eats the herbivore. This series of events is called a food chain.

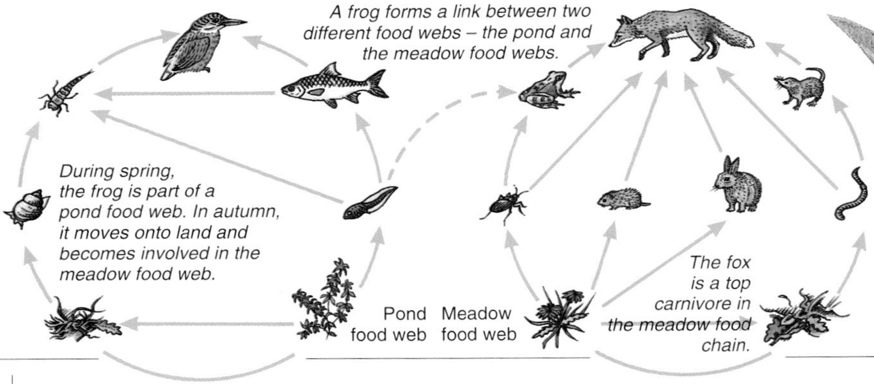

A frog forms a link between two different food webs – the pond and the meadow food webs.

During spring, the frog is part of a pond food web. In autumn, it moves onto land and becomes involved in the meadow food web.

Pond food web   Meadow food web

The fox is a top carnivore in the meadow food chain.

CARNIVORE
The adult frog is carnivorous; it catches flies and other small creatures.

OMNIVORE
Many small fish are omnivores, feeding on whatever they can find – from water weeds to tiny animals such as tadpoles.

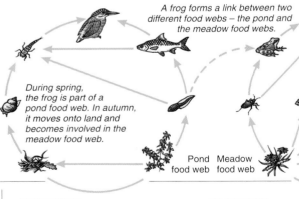

Plants form the beginning of the food chain in a pond, as they do on land.

DETRITIVORE
Leeches and water snails are called detritivores because they eat detritus, or rotting matter, at the bottom of a pond or river. They help recycle the materials and energy in dead and dying plants and animals.

HERBIVORE
As a young tadpole, the frog is a herbivore, eating water weeds.

KINGFISHER
Some carnivores are called top carnivores because they have almost no predators. Their usual fate is to die of sickness, injury, or starvation, at which time they become food for scavengers. The European kingfisher shown here eats a wide variety of food, including small fish such as minnows and sticklebacks, water snails and beetles, dragonfly larvae, tadpoles, and small frogs. The kingfisher is therefore at the top of a complex food web.

HABITAT

A habitat is a place where a certain animal or plant usually lives. There are several characteristic habitats, such as oak forests, mangrove swamps, and chalk cliffs. A habitat often has one or a few main plants, such as the pampas grass which grows in the grassland habitats of South America. Certain characteristic animals feed on these plants. Some animals live in only one or two habitats; the desman, for example, is a type of muskrat found only in fast-running mountain streams. Other animals, such as red foxes and brown rats, are able to survive in many different habitats. The coral reef shown here is one of the Earth's richest habitats. Its warm, shallow water is full of nutrients, and the sunlight encourages many different forms of life.

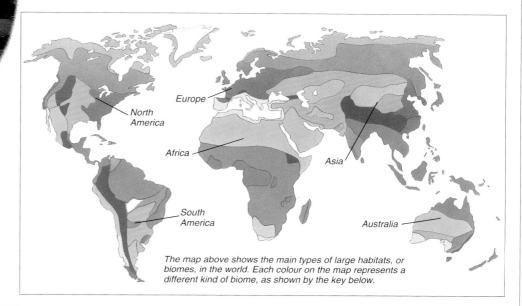

The map above shows the main types of large habitats, or biomes, in the world. Each colour on the map represents a different kind of biome, as shown by the key below.

BIOME

A biome is a huge habitat, such as a tropical rain forest or a desert. The deserts of Africa, central Asia, and North America each have distinct kinds of plants and animals, but their ecology is similar. Each of these large habitats, or biomes, has a big cat as a top predator – the caracal (a kind of lynx) in Africa, the bobcat in North America, and Pallas's cat in central Asia. The major types of plants that grow in a biome are determined by its climate. Areas near the equator with very high rainfall become tropical rain forests, and in cold regions near the Arctic and Antarctic only tundra plants can survive.

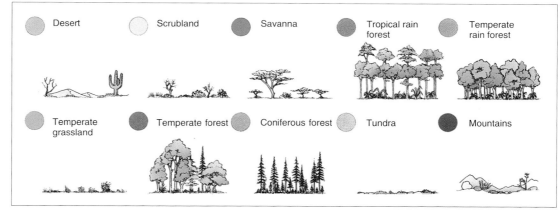

Desert   Scrubland   Savanna   Tropical rain forest   Temperate rain forest

Temperate grassland   Temperate forest   Coniferous forest   Tundra   Mountains

PESTICIDES

Farmers and gardeners use pesticides to kill insects that are pests on vegetable and cereal crops. In 1972, the insecticide called DDT was banned in the United States because it caused great damage to wildlife. When DDT is sprayed on crops, some of it is eaten by herbivores such as mice and squirrels. The insecticide builds up inside the animal's body. A bird of prey such as a hawk eats the animal, and the DDT becomes concentrated (builds up) in the bird's body. The DDT causes the bird to make very thin or deformed eggshells, which break and kill the developing chicks inside. Since DDT was banned, the number of falcons has slowly risen.

Today, falcons and other birds of prey are rare. Many have died as a result of the pesticides used by farmers to kill insects on farm crops.

Find out more

ANIMALS
CONSERVATION
and endangered species
EAGLES AND
other birds of prey
LAKE AND RIVER WILDLIFE
PLANTS
POLLUTION

EDUCATION

LEARNING DOES NOT ONLY take place at school. Education - the process of acquiring knowledge - begins when we are born and continues throughout life. Learning to speak, for instance, is a basic skill we acquire at an early age by imitating and repeating the sounds produced by our family and others around us. As we grow older, travelling, reading, and other pastimes also increase our knowledge. Formal education begins when we have learned certain basic skills, such as speech, and can benefit from going to school. Through nursery, primary and comprehensive school, we learn vital skills and valuable knowledge. At 16, some students go on to the sixth form or to tertiary college, where they widen their general knowledge and study one or more subjects in depth. School and college can also help us recognize and develop the individual talents and skills that each of us possesses, and show us how we can use this potential in a career and to benefit society as a whole. University, polytechnic, and different colleges provide education to match an individual's chosen career.

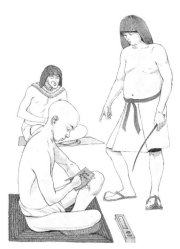

SCRIBE SCHOOLS
In Ancient Egypt only educated scribes could read and write. Boys who trained to be scribes laboriously wrote and copied each day. At first they wrote on useless objects such as broken pottery; when their work improved they were allowed to write on papyrus, a precious kind of paper. Girls were educated at home, learning domestic skills from their mothers.

UNIVERSITY
Many students continue their education at university, polytechnic, or college. Studies usually take three or four years. Students receive degrees – qualifications showing they have completed the course.

CHOICES IN EDUCATION
No two people are the same. For this reason education offers students a wide choice. From the arts, or humanities, students may choose subjects such as fine art (painting and sculpture), languages, and law. From science subjects there is the choice of pure science, such as physics; applied science, such as engineering; and medicine.

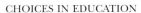

PHRENOLOGY
BY
L.N. FOWLER.

Scientists in the 19th century believed that portions of the human brain were reserved for specific kinds of knowledge.

EDUCATION FOR THE FEW
Free education for all has become available only during the last 100 years. Before then only the very wealthy could afford education. During the 13th century, Latin was the language of learning in Europe; it was essential for those who wanted to work in the church, the army, or in law.

GREEK EDUCATION
The Ancient Greek philosopher Aristotle held strong views about education. He believed that, from the age of seven, children should learn gymnastics, music, reading, writing, and drawing. Later studies would include physics, philosophy, and politics. Aristotle's ideal was an active and enquiring mind in a healthy body.

PRACTICAL LEARNING
Education is designed to meet society's needs. The children of tribes who live in tropical rain forests learn survival skills such as building boats and hunting. But in developing societies the educational system must produce the scientists and engineers the country needs in order to industrialize.

Find out more
MIDDLE AGES
MONASTERIES
SCHOOLS

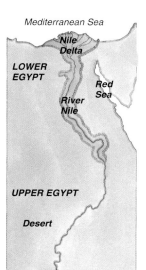

ANCIENT
EGYPT

THE RICH, FERTILE SOIL OF THE NILE VALLEY gave birth to Egypt, a civilization that began over 5,000 years ago and lasted more than 3,000 years. The River Nile made the black soil around it productive, and the civilization of Egypt grew wealthy. For much of its history Egypt was stable. Its pharaohs ruled with the help of officials called viziers who collected taxes and acted as judges. The Egyptians worshipped many gods and believed that when they died they went to the Next World. Pharaohs built elaborate tombs for themselves; the best known are the magnificent pyramids. The Egyptians also made great advances in medicine. Gradually, however, the civilization broke down, leaving it open to foreign invasion. In 30 B.C. the Romans finally conquered the empire.

PHARAOHS
The rulers of Ancient Egypt were called pharaohs, meaning "Great House". They were thought to be divine and had absolute power: all the land in Egypt belonged to them. People believed the pharaohs were the sons of Re, the sun god. Above is a famous pharaoh, Tutankhamun, who died when he was only 18.

PYRAMIDS
The Egyptians believed in an eternal life after death in a "perfect" version of Egypt. After their bodies had been preserved by embalming, pharaohs were buried in pyramid tombs. The earliest pyramids had steps. People believed the dead king's spirit climbed the steps to join the sun god at the top. Later, the pyramids were built with smooth slanted sides. However, people could rob the pyramid tombs easily, so later pharaohs were buried in unmarked tombs in the Valley of the Kings and guarded day and night.

Limestone casing

Chambers to relieve weight from above

Abandoned burial chamber

Escape shaft

Original burial chamber

Cutaway view of the Great Pyramid of Khufu (Cheops) at Giza, Egypt.

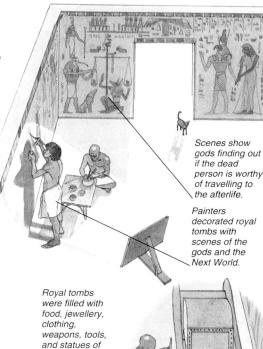

Scenes show gods finding out if the dead person is worthy of travelling to the afterlife.

Painters decorated royal tombs with scenes of the gods and the Next World.

Painting of the time shows cattle being transported across the River Nile in special wide boats.

Royal tombs were filled with food, jewellery, clothing, weapons, tools, and statues of servants.

TRANSPORT AND TRADE
The quickest way to travel in Egypt was by water. Barges carried goods along the Nile, and Egyptian traders travelled to ports around the eastern Mediterranean and the Red Sea in wooden reed ships. Using a system called bartering, they exchanged gold, grain, and papyrus sheets for silver, iron, horses, cedar wood, and ivory.

Mediterranean Sea

Nile Delta

LOWER EGYPT

Red Sea

River Nile

UPPER EGYPT

Desert

Inside a tomb

RIVER NILE
Each year, the River Nile burst its banks and spread water and fertile silt over the land. This "inundation" of the Nile Valley made the land fertile for about 10 km (6 miles) on either side of the river. The Egyptians planned their agricultural system around this, farming the land by storing the floodwaters. The desert on either side provided a natural defensive barrier and a rich source of minerals and stone.

FARMING AND FISHING

Most Egyptians were farmers who worked for priests, wealthy landowners, or the pharaoh. They were paid in crops. They watered the lands with floodwaters trapped in lagoons or with water-lifting machines called shadoofs. Crops grown included emmer for bread, barley for beer, beans, onions, dates, melons, and cucumbers. People also fished from the Nile.

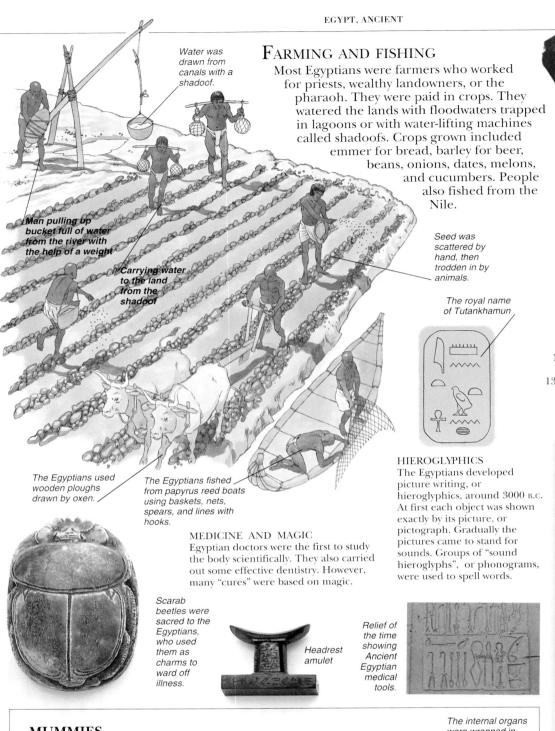

Water was drawn from canals with a shadoof.

Man pulling up bucket full of water from the river with the help of a weight

Carrying water to the land from the shadoof

Seed was scattered by hand, then trodden in by animals.

The Egyptians used wooden ploughs drawn by oxen.

The Egyptians fished from papyrus reed boats using baskets, nets, spears, and lines with hooks.

The royal name of Tutankhamun

MEDICINE AND MAGIC

Egyptian doctors were the first to study the body scientifically. They also carried out some effective dentistry. However, many "cures" were based on magic.

Scarab beetles were sacred to the Egyptians, who used them as charms to ward off illness.

Headrest amulet

Relief of the time showing Ancient Egyptian medical tools.

HIEROGLYPHICS

The Egyptians developed picture writing, or hieroglyphics, around 3000 B.C. At first each object was shown exactly by its picture, or pictograph. Gradually the pictures came to stand for sounds. Groups of "sound hieroglyphs", or phonograms, were used to spell words.

NEFERTITI

Nefertiti was the wife of the pharaoh Ikhnaton, who ruled from 1367 to 1355 B.C. She had great influence over her husband's policies. Usually, however, the only women who held important titles were priestesses.

ANCIENT EGYPT

c.10,000-5000 B.C. First villages on the banks of the Nile. Slow growth of the two kingdoms of Upper and Lower Egypt.

c. 2630 B.C. First step pyramid built at Saqqara.

c. 2575 B.C. During Old Kingdom period, bronze replaces copper. Pyramids built at Giza. Dead bodies are embalmed.

c. 2134 B.C. Old Kingdom ends with power struggles.

c. 2040 B.C. Middle Kingdom begins. Nobles from Thebes reunite the country. Nubia conquered.

c. 1640 B.C. Middle Kingdom ends.

1550 B.C. New Kingdom begins. Permanent army.

1400 B.C. Egypt reaches height of its power.

1070 B.C. Egyptian power begins to decline.

332 B.C. Alexander the Great conquers Egypt.

51 B.C. Cleopatra rules.

30 B.C. Egypt becomes a Roman province.

MUMMIES

The Egyptians thought that if they preserved their bodies after death, they would "live" forever. So they made "mummies" – corpses that did not decay.

Embalmers removed the liver, lungs, and brain from the dead body, leaving the heart inside. They then coated the body with saltlike natron crystals to preserve it, and finally wrapped the whole package in bandages.

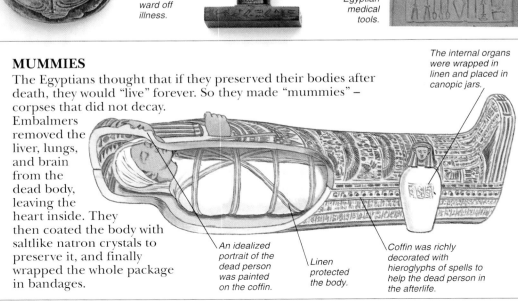

The internal organs were wrapped in linen and placed in canopic jars.

An idealized portrait of the dead person was painted on the coffin.

Linen protected the body.

Coffin was richly decorated with hieroglyphs of spells to help the dead person in the afterlife.

___

Find out more

AFRICA, HISTORY OF
ALPHABETS
ARCHAEOLOGY

ELECTRICITY

A FLASH OF LIGHTNING that leaps through the sky during a thunderstorm is one of the most visible signs of electricity. At almost all other times, electricity is invisible but hard at work for us. Electricity is a form of energy. It consists of electrons – tiny particles that come from atoms. Each electron carries a tiny electric charge which is an amount of electricity. When you switch on a light, about one million million million electrons move through the bulb every second.

Cables hidden in walls and ceilings carry electricity around houses and factories, providing energy at the flick of a switch. Electricity also provides portable power. Batteries produce electricity from chemicals, and solar cells provide electricity from the energy in sunlight. Lamps, motors, and dozens of other machines use electricity as their source of power. Electricity also provides signals which make telephones, radios, televisions, and computers work.

Electricity flows into homes through cables that run either underground or above street level on poles.

CURRENT ELECTRICITY
Electricity comes in two forms: electricity that flows, and static electricity, which does not move. Flowing electricity is called current electricity. Billions of electrons flow along a wire to give an electric current. The electricity moves from a source such as a battery or power station to a machine. It then returns to the source along another wire. The flow of electric current is measured in amperes (A).

Some power stations generate electricity by burning coal and oil. Other stations are powered by nuclear energy.

A transformer boosts the voltage (force) of the electricity to many thousands of volts.

Tall pylons support long cables that carry the electricity safely above the ground to all parts of an area.

Another transformer reduces the voltage of the electricity to a lower, safer level.

SUPERCONDUCTORS
Conductors resist the flow of electricity a little. However, this resistance disappears when certain materials are very cold. The conductor becomes a superconductor. Within a superconductor a strong current can flow without dying away.

A superconductor can produce a strong magnetic field which makes a small magnet hover above it.

Batteries produce direct current, which flows one way around a circuit.

Battery pushes electric current around the circuit.

Power stations produce alternating current, which flows first in one direction and then the other.

ELECTRIC CIRCUITS
Electric current needs a continuous loop of wire to flow around. This is called a circuit. If the circuit is broken, the electricity can no longer flow.

Wires connect battery and bulb to form a circuit.

Bulb in bulb holder

CONDUCTORS AND INSULATORS
Electricity flows only through materials called conductors. These include copper and many other metals. Conductors can carry electricity because their electrons are free to move. Other substances, called insulators, do not allow electricity to flow through them. This is because their electrons are held tightly inside their atoms.

Most plastics are insulators.

Electrons flow through copper conductor.

STATIC ELECTRICITY
There are two types of electric charge, positive (+) and negative (–). Objects usually contain equal numbers of both charges so they cancel each other out. Rubbing a balloon against a shirt makes the balloon pick up extra electrons, which carry a negative charge. This charge is called static electricity. It produces an electric force which makes the balloon stick to a wall and attract light objects such as hair.

GENERATOR

Generators produce electricity from the energy of movement. A coil of wire moves between the poles of a magnet. This produces an electric current in the coil. Small, simple generators that power bicycle lamps are called dynamos. Large generators in power stations produce huge amounts of electricity for homes and factories.

Basic generator

Coil of wire

Magnetic field produced by magnet

A simple generator (above) contains a coil of wire that spins between the poles of a magnet. A current flows in the coil where the coil moves through the magnetic field.

Instead of a simple magnet, there is a set of electromagnets – coils that use electricity to produce a strong magnetic field.

Electromagnets spin inside another set of coils. This produces electricity in the outer set of coils.

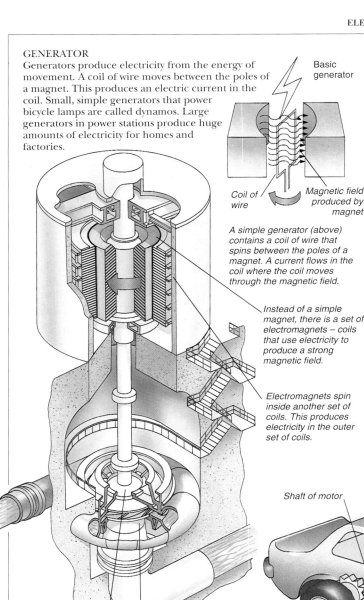

A shaft connected to the turbine (a set of vanes) drives the generator.

In a hydroelectric power station, water falling from a dam spins a turbine.

ELECTRICITY FROM CHEMICALS

Chemical energy from food changes into movement in your muscles. Chemical energy can also change into electrical energy. This is how a battery works. Chemicals react together inside a battery and produce an electric current. When there are no fresh chemicals left, the current stops. Fuel cells also produce electricity from chemicals in the form of gases.

ELECTRIC EEL

The rivers of South America are the home of the electric eel. This eel has special organs in its long body that work like batteries to produce electricity. With a powerful electric shock, the electric eel can stun its prey.

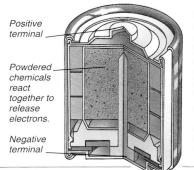

Positive terminal

Powdered chemicals react together to release electrons.

Negative terminal

BATTERY

Connecting a battery in a circuit makes the chemicals inside react to produce an electric current. The battery provides a force which pushes electrons around the circuit. The strength of this force is measured in units called volts.

Electrons flow around the circuit from the negative terminal and back to the positive terminal.

Shaft of motor

The magnetic force of the magnet pulls on the coil and makes it spin around.

Gears connect motor to wheels of car.

Coil of wire

Magnet produces magnetic field.

Electric current flows from battery into coil, producing a magnetic field.

ELECTRIC MOTOR

Many machines are powered by an electric motor, which contains a coil of wire placed between the poles of a magnet. The electric current fed to the motor flows through the coil, producing a magnetic field. The magnet attracts the coil and makes it spin around and drive the shaft of the motor.

ELECTRIC SHOCKS

Living things make use of electricity. Weak electric signals pass along the nerves to and from the brain. These signals operate the muscles, maintain the heartbeat, and control the way in which the body works. A strong electric current can give an electric shock that damages the human body and may even cause death. *Never* play with the main electricity supply because of the danger of electric shock.

--- *Find out more* ---

ATOMS AND MOLECULES
ELECTRONICS
ENERGY
FISH
HOUSEHOLD APPLIANCES
MAGNETISM

DISCOVERY

About 2,500 years ago, the Ancient Greeks found that rubbing amber (a yellow solid) produces a charge of static electricity. The Greek for amber is *elektron*, which is how electricity got its name. Around 1750, American scientist Benjamin Franklin (left) discovered that lightning is electricity and explained what electric charges are. At the end of the 18th century, Italian scientists Luigi Galvani and Alessandro Volta produced the first electric current.

Benjamin Franklin (1706-90) studied the electrical nature of lightning by flying a kite during a thunderstorm.

A bird sitting on an electric cable does not get an electric shock. The electricity does not pass into its body because the bird is touching only one wire and does not complete an electric circuit.

ELECTRONICS

The semiconductor silicon comes from sand, which is a compound of silicon and oxygen.

A diode is made from the junction between pieces of n- and p-type semiconductors.

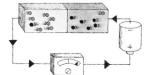

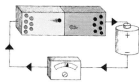

A diode allows current to flow through it in only one direction. The current is carried by the flow of holes and electrons.

If a battery is connected the other way around, holes and electrons meet and cancel out one another so that current cannot flow.

ELECTRICITY IS a source of power that drives machines and provides heat and light.
Electricity is also used to produce signals that carry information and control devices. Using electricity in this way is called electronics. We are surrounded by thousands of electronic machines including computers, cassette recorders, telephones, and televisions. All these machines contain circuits through which electric currents flow. Tiny electronic components in the circuits control the flow of the current to produce signals. For instance, a varying current may represent sound in a telephone line, or a number in a computer. The most important electronic component is the transistor. A small radio receiver may contain a dozen transistors; a computer contains thousands of miniaturized transistors inside microchips.

SEMICONDUCTORS
Most electronic components are made of materials such as silicon, which are called semiconductors. Semiconductors control the flow of current because they contain a variable number of charge carriers (particles that carry electricity). In n-type semiconductors, the charge carriers are negatively charged electrons; in p-type semiconductors, the charge carriers are positively charged "holes" – regions where electrons are absent.

CIRCUIT BOARD
An electronic device such as a telephone contains an electronic circuit consisting of several components joined together on a circuit board. Every circuit is designed for a particular task. The circuit in a radio, for instance, picks up and amplifies (boosts) radio waves so they can be converted into sound.

Capacitor stores electric charge. In a radio circuit, capacitors help tune the circuit so that it picks up different radio frequencies.

Resistor reduces the amount of current flowing in the circuit.

Diode allows current to pass in only one direction.

Transistor boosts the strength of electrical signals.

Variable resistor allows the flow of current to be varied.

Wires are used to connect some components.

Microchip in plastic casing

Metal tracks on the underside of the board connect components.

CONTROLLING CURRENT
Electronic circuits do several basic jobs. They may amplify current; they may produce an oscillating current – one that rapidly changes direction, essential for generating radio waves; or they may switch current on and off.

Oscillation: Some circuits convert a steady one-way current (direct current, or DC) into a varying alternating current (AC).

Amplification: An amplifier circuit generates a strong AC current that is an accurate copy of a weaker AC current.

Switching: In computers, electronic circuits rapidly switch current on and off in a code that represents data.

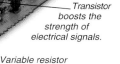

MICROCHIPS
Microchips, or silicon chips, contain circuits consisting of hundreds of thousands of microscopic components. These circuits are squeezed onto the surface of a semiconductor less than 25 mm (1 in) square.

TRANSISTOR
Transistors lie at the heart of most electronic machines. They boost current and voltage in amplifier circuits, store information in computers, and perform many other tasks. Physicists William Shockley, John Bardeen, and Walter Brattain invented the transistor in 1947.

Find out more

COMPUTERS
ELECTRICITY
RADIO
SOUND RECORDING
TECHNOLOGY

ELEPHANTS

WOOLLY MAMMOTH
The prehistoric mammoth became extinct about 10,000 years ago. Frozen remains of mammoths have been found in Alaska and Siberia.

GREAT TUSKS, huge ears, and a strong trunk make the elephant one of the most magnificent creatures on Earth. Elephants are the largest living land mammals and among the most ancient. They are extremely strong and highly intelligent, and have been trained to work for humans for thousands of years. There are two kinds of elephants – African and Asian (Indian). African elephants are slightly bigger than Asian elephants, with much larger ears. A large African male measures more than 3 m (10 ft) high at the shoulder and weighs more than 5.4 tonnes (5.3 tons). The elephant's trunk reaches to the ground and high into the trees to find food. The trunk is also used for drinking, smelling, greeting other members of the herd, and as a snorkel in deep water.

TRUNK
The trunk is formed from the nose and the long upper lip. It is extremely sensitive to touch and smell. The elephant uses its trunk to grasp leaves, fruits, and shoots, and place them in its mouth. In order to drink, the elephant must squirt water into its mouth because it cannot drink through its trunk.

Head and jaws are huge, with wide, ridged teeth for chewing plant matter.

Huge ears help to cool elephant by allowing heat to escape.

Ears are used to threaten other animals.

When bathing, the elephant sucks water into its trunk, then squirts it over the body.

Tusks are massive upper canine teeth, made of ivory. They can split bark from trees and gouge roots from the ground.

Wide, flat, soft-soled feet leave hardly any tracks.

Two nostrils at tip of the trunk

ASIAN ELEPHANT

There are probably fewer than 50,000 Asian elephants left in the wild, in remote forests of India, China, and Southeast Asia. Female or cow elephants are quite easy to tame between the ages of about 10 and 20 years. They are caught and kept in captivity, and used for clearing forests and towing logs. Asian elephants are also dressed and decorated for ceremonies and processions.

BREEDING
A newborn elephant calf weighs 100-120 kg (220-260 lb) at birth. It sucks milk from the teats between its mother's front legs until it is about four years old. A young elephant stays with its mother for the first 10 years of its life. By the age of six it weighs about one tonne, and at about 15 years of age it is ready to breed.

AFRICAN ELEPHANT

In the late 1970s there were about 1.3 million elephants in Africa. Today there are half that number. Poachers kill them for their ivory, and farms are built on the land where they live. In reserves, however, where elephants are protected, their numbers have increased. Here, they are culled (killed in a controlled way) to prevent them from damaging the countryside. Today elephants are on the official list of endangered species, and the trade in elephants and ivory is controlled by international agreement.

A six-year-old male African elephant

Find out more

AFRICAN WILDLIFE
ANIMALS
CONSERVATION
and endangered species
MAMMALS

ELIZABETH I

1533 Born, the daughter of Henry VIII and Anne Boleyn.

1536 Mother is executed for treason.

1554 Imprisoned in the Tower of London.

1558 Crowned queen.

1559 Establishes Protestant Church of England by the Act of Supremacy.

1587 Orders execution of Mary Queen of Scots.

1588 Faces the Armada.

1603 Dies.

MORE THAN FOUR HUNDRED YEARS AGO one woman brought 45 years of peace and prosperity to England through her determination and wisdom. Queen Elizabeth I began her life as a neglected princess, whose mother had been executed by her father. She was ignored and imprisoned as a girl, but upon the death of her half sister, Queen Mary, Elizabeth became a strong and popular queen. She tried to end years of religious conflict between Catholics and Protestants by insisting that the Church of England should be only moderately Protestant, so that it included as many people as possible. Elizabeth avoided expensive foreign wars for many years. Her most dangerous conflict was with Philip II, king of Spain, who sent the Armada (fleet of ships) against England. The queen's court was a centre for poets, musicians, and writers. Her reign is often called The Golden Age.

SIR WALTER RALEIGH

One of Elizabeth's favourite courtiers was Sir Walter Raleigh (1552-1618). In 1584 she knighted him, and later made Raleigh her Captain of the Guard. He made several voyages across the Atlantic, set up an English colony in Virginia, and brought tobacco and potatoes from the Americas to Europe.

ELIZABETHAN AGE

Elizabeth was the first monarch to give her name to an age. During her reign the arts of music, poetry, and drama flourished. Despite foreign threats and religious unrest at home, she won the loyalty and admiration of her subjects.

SPANISH ARMADA
In July 1588 Philip II, king of Spain, launched his Armada of nearly 150 ships to invade England and restore the Catholic religion. Sir Francis Drake (1540-1596) sailed in command of a large group of warships to oppose the Armada. Aided by stormy weather, the English defeated the great fleet.

MARY QUEEN OF SCOTS
Mary was Elizabeth's Catholic cousin and heir. Forced to abdicate her own throne in Scotland, she fled to England to seek Elizabeth's protection. Mary became involved in Catholic plots against Elizabeth, who reluctantly ordered her execution.

Find out more
SPAIN AND PORTUGAL, history of
THEATRE
UNITED KINGDOM, history of

ENERGY

THE MOVEMENT OF a car, the sound of a trumpet, the light from a candle – all these things occur because of energy. Energy is the ability to make things happen. For example, when you throw a stone you give it energy of movement which shows itself when the stone smashes glass. All life on Earth depends on energy, almost all of which comes from the sun. The sun's energy makes plants grow, which provides the food that animals eat; the energy from food is stored in an animal's muscles, ready to be converted into movement. Although energy is not an object that you can see or touch, you can think of it as something that either flows from place to place, or is stored. For instance, energy is stored by water high at the top of a waterfall. As soon as the water starts to fall, the stored energy changes into moving energy which flows to the bottom of the waterfall.

WORK, ENERGY, AND POWER
When a force moves an object, energy is transferred, or passed, to the object or its surroundings. This transfer of energy is called work. The amount of work done depends on the size of the force and how far it moves. For instance, this weightlifter does a lot of work lifting a heavy weight through a large distance. Power is the rate of doing work. The weightlifter produces more power the faster he lifts the weight.

POTENTIAL ENERGY
Energy can be stored as potential energy until it turns into another form such as movement. Examples include water in a raised reservoir waiting to flow through turbines, chemical energy in a battery waiting to drive an electric current, and a coiled spring waiting to be released.

KINETIC ENERGY
An object such as an aeroplane needs energy to make it move. Moving energy is called kinetic energy. When the plane stops, it gives up kinetic energy. This often appears as heat – for instance, in the plane's brakes.

TYPES OF ENERGY
Energy takes many forms, and it can change from one form into another. For example, power stations turn the chemical energy stored in coal or oil into heat energy which boils water. Turbines change the heat energy of the steam into electrical energy which flows to homes and factories.

ENERGY RESOURCES
The Earth's population uses a huge amount of energy. Most of this energy comes from coal, oil, gas, and the nuclear fuel uranium. However, these fuels are being used up and cannot be replaced. Today, scientists are experimenting with energy sources, called renewable resources, that will not run out. These include the sun, wind, waves, and tides.

Heat energy, such as the warmth of the sun, is carried by invisible waves called infrared or heat radiation.

Light is one form of energy that travels in waves. Others include X-rays and radio waves.

Sound waves are vibrations of the air, so they carry kinetic energy.

Some power stations produce electricity from nuclear energy, which comes from the nuclei (centres) of atoms.

Electrical devices turn the energy of electric currents into many other forms of energy, including heat, light, and movement.

Oil and coal contain stored chemical energy which changes into heat and light when these fuels are burned.

ENERGY CYCLE
Energy cannot be created or destroyed; it can only change from one form into another. The only exception might seem to be when matter changes into energy in a nuclear reactor. However, the rule still applies because matter and energy are really the same and one can be converted into the other.

A battery runs out when all its stored energy has been converted into heat in the wires and heat and light in the bulb.

Rows of solar panels for producing electricity

Find out more

ELECTRICITY
HEAT
LIGHT
NUCLEAR ENERGY
SOUND
SUN
WATER
WIND

ENGINES

Piston 2 rises and compresses (squeezes) fuel-air mixture.

Piston 4 rises and pushes waste gases out through exhaust valve.

Piston 3: mixture explodes, and expanding gases push piston down.

Piston 1 moves down and sucks fuel-air mixture in through inlet valve.

Valves open and close to admit and expel the fuel-air mixture.

Spark plug produces electrical spark that ignites fuel-air mixture.

The piston moves up and down inside the cylinder.

Engines have between four and eight cylinders. These work in sequence to produce continuous movement.

Crankshaft changes the up-and-down movement of the pistons into circular movement which drives the wheels.

WHEN PREHISTORIC PEOPLE discovered fire, they found a way of obtaining energy, because burning releases heat and light. About one million years later the steam engine was invented, and for the first time people could harness that energy and turn it into movement. Today there are many different kinds of engines which drive the world's transport and industry. All engines serve one function – to use the energy stored in a fuel such as oil or coal and change it into motion to drive machines. Before engines were invented, tasks such as building and lifting depended on the strength of people and their animals. Today, engines can produce enough power to lift the heaviest weights and drive the largest machines. The most powerful engine is the rocket engine; it can blast a spacecraft away from the pull of the Earth's gravity and out into space.

INTERNAL-COMBUSTION ENGINE

The engine that powers almost all the world's cars is the internal-combustion engine. It uses the power of gases created by exploding fuel to produce movement. A mixture of air and tiny droplets of petrol enters the engine's cylinders, each of which contains a piston. An electrical spark ignites (sets alight) the fuel mixture, producing gases which thrust each piston down.

ELECTRIC MOTORS

Petrol and diesel engines produce waste gases that pollute the air and contribute to the greenhouse effect (which causes the Earth's temperature to rise). Electric motors are clean, quiet, and produce no pollution. Several car manufacturers are developing cars powered by electric motors. Most electric cars are still experimental; one remaining problem is that sufficiently light, efficient batteries have not yet been developed.

DIESEL ENGINE

Many trains and lorries have powerful diesel engines, which are internal-combustion engines that burn diesel fuel instead of petrol. The engine works in the same way as a petrol-fueled engine, but does not have spark plugs. Instead, each cylinder has an injector that squirts diesel fuel into the cylinder. The piston compresses the air, making it very hot. The hot air makes the diesel fuel explode.

JET ENGINE

The jet, or gas turbine, engine now powers most high-speed aircraft. The engine blasts a jet of hot, fast-moving air backwards out of its exhaust; this pushes the engine forwards. Fans at the front of the engine spin and suck air into the engine and squeeze it at high pressure into several combustion chambers. There, flames of burning kerosene heat the air, which expands and rushes towards the exhaust. As the air streams out, it spins a turbine, which drives the fans at the front of the engine.

FRANK WHITTLE

In 1928, English pilot and engineer Frank Whittle (1907-) suggested the idea of the jet engine. Whittle's engine powered an experimental aircraft for the first time in 1941. However, the first jet-powered flight was made during the 1930s in Germany, where engineer Hans von Ohain had developed his own jet engine.

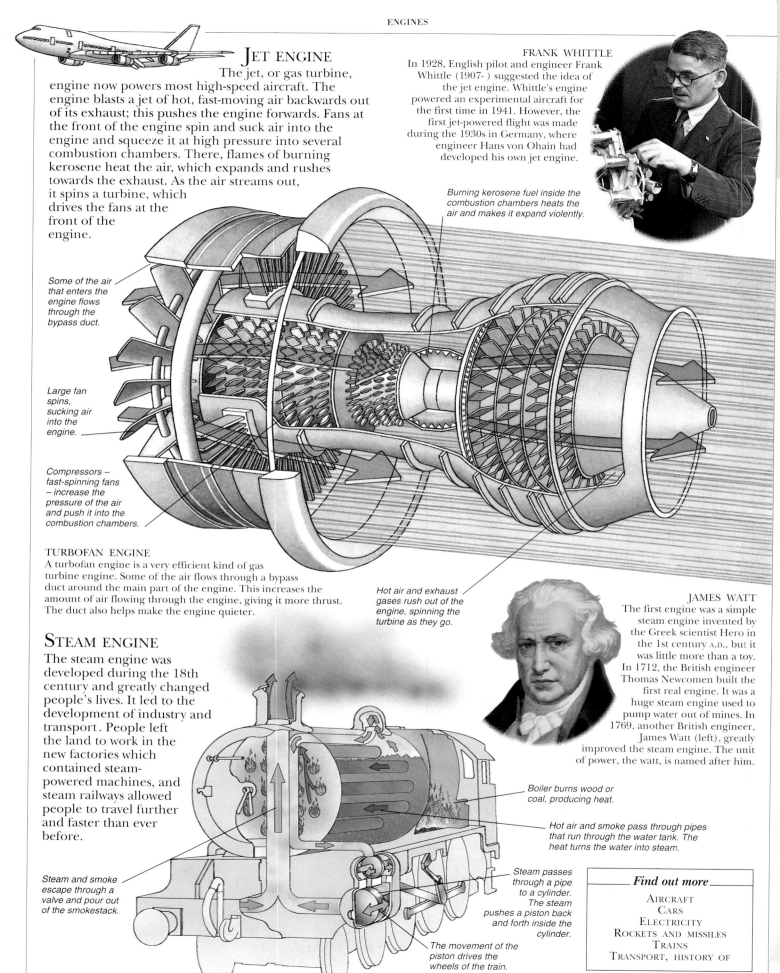

Burning kerosene fuel inside the combustion chambers heats the air and makes it expand violently.

Some of the air that enters the engine flows through the bypass duct.

Large fan spins, sucking air into the engine.

Compressors – fast-spinning fans – increase the pressure of the air and push it into the combustion chambers.

TURBOFAN ENGINE

A turbofan engine is a very efficient kind of gas turbine engine. Some of the air flows through a bypass duct around the main part of the engine. This increases the amount of air flowing through the engine, giving it more thrust. The duct also helps make the engine quieter.

Hot air and exhaust gases rush out of the engine, spinning the turbine as they go.

STEAM ENGINE

The steam engine was developed during the 18th century and greatly changed people's lives. It led to the development of industry and transport. People left the land to work in the new factories which contained steam-powered machines, and steam railways allowed people to travel further and faster than ever before.

JAMES WATT

The first engine was a simple steam engine invented by the Greek scientist Hero in the 1st century A.D., but it was little more than a toy. In 1712, the British engineer Thomas Newcomen built the first real engine. It was a huge steam engine used to pump water out of mines. In 1769, another British engineer, James Watt (left), greatly improved the steam engine. The unit of power, the watt, is named after him.

Boiler burns wood or coal, producing heat.

Hot air and smoke pass through pipes that run through the water tank. The heat turns the water into steam.

Steam and smoke escape through a valve and pour out of the smokestack.

Steam passes through a pipe to a cylinder. The steam pushes a piston back and forth inside the cylinder.

The movement of the piston drives the wheels of the train.

Find out more

AIRCRAFT
CARS
ELECTRICITY
ROCKETS AND MISSILES
TRAINS
TRANSPORT, HISTORY OF

ESCALATORS AND LIFTS

WORKING, SHOPPING, and travelling in a city would be difficult without escalators and lifts. People would have to walk up and down stairs in skyscrapers, big department stores, high blocks of flats, and deep underground stations.

A lift travels up and down between the floors of a building. People and goods ride inside the lift. An escalator is a staircase in which the steps move up or down. Some lifts and escalators travel up and down the outside of a building, giving a bird's-eye view of the surroundings.

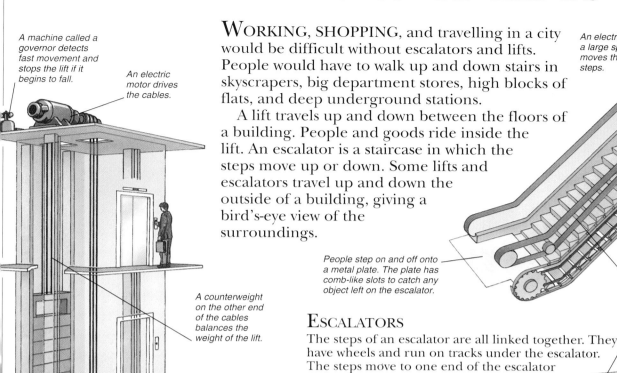

A machine called a governor detects fast movement and stops the lift if it begins to fall.

An electric motor drives the cables.

A counterweight on the other end of the cables balances the weight of the lift.

LIFT CAR
Push buttons operate automatic controls that send the lift to the right floor. A double-decker lift has two cars, one above the other, and stops at two floors at the same time.

There are separate doors in the lift car and at each floor. They open only when the car stops at a floor.

Lift car slides along guide rails.

Brakes grip the guide rails if the lift starts to fall.

An electric motor turns a large sprocket that moves the steps.

The motor also drives the handrail, which is an endless belt.

Handrail

People step on and off onto a metal plate. The plate has comb-like slots to catch any object left on the escalator.

ESCALATORS

The steps of an escalator are all linked together. They have wheels and run on tracks under the escalator. The steps move to one end of the escalator and return to the other end beneath the steps that are carrying people.

Steps flatten out at ends of escalator.

Steps form part of a continuous loop which runs beneath the escalator.

Each step has two pairs of wheels. The wheels run along pairs of tracks on each side of the escalator.

Returning steps

Sprocket

Steel tracks support the chain.

The tracks move apart at each end of the escalator so that the steps level out. People can then easily walk on and off the escalator.

CABLE CARS
A moving cable pulls cable cars and ski lifts up mountain slopes and steep hills. These cable cars are in Hong Kong.

LIFTS

Most lifts have strong steel cables that support the car, which travels along guide rails up and down a shaft. Some lifts are pushed up from below by a long steel tube. The world's fastest lifts rise about 610 m (2,000 ft) in a minute.

THE OTIS SAFETY LIFT
In 1854, the engineer Elisha Otis demonstrated his safety lift. While standing on the lift, he ordered the rope to be cut. A safety mechanism automatically gripped the guide rails and kept the lift from falling. Otis's invention made the building of skyscrapers possible. All lifts now have safety mechanisms of this kind.

Find out more
ARCHITECTURE
BUILDING
MACHINES

ESKIMOS (INUITS)

THE FROZEN ARCTIC was one of the last regions of the world to be inhabited by humans. The Eskimo (Inuit) people, who originally came from Asia, settled in the Arctic about 4,000 years ago. A Native American tribe named them *Eskimo*, which means "eaters of raw meat"; but the newcomers called themselves *Inuit*, which simply means "real men". Eskimos were nomadic. They moved about in family groups, hunting animals such as seals and caribou. Eskimo families survived the bitter cold of winter by digging shelters into the ground. They made roofs for the shelters from driftwood or whalebone, with a covering of turf. For clothes, they used double layers of caribou or polar bear fur. Today most Eskimos live in small settlements or towns, but they are proud of their culture. They preserve it in language, art, and song, and hunting is still an essential part of Eskimo life.

North Alaskan Eskimos
Polar Eskimos
West Greenlan Eskimos
Pacific Eskimos
Caribou Eskimos

Eskimos live in Siberia in the Russian Federation, in Alaska, Canada, and Greenland. There are many different groups, each named after the area in which they live. The Polar Eskimos of Greenland live the furthest north of all the world's peoples.

Today Eskimos hunt on snowmobiles instead of sledges.

A hunting trip takes many days, and supplies are carried by snowmobile.

Eskimo artists use their skills to decorate everyday tools, such as this arrow straightener.

HUNTING
Eskimos hunt for food to eat, and furs to sell. They do not hunt animals for sport. They respect foxes, caribou, seal, walrus, and other Arctic wildlife, and their hunting does not threaten the long-term survival of these animal species. Hunting takes patience and skill, and some Eskimos travel 5,000 km (3,000 miles) a year on hunting trips. When they are hunting away from home in winter, Eskimos build temporary shelters, called igloos, from blocks of snow.

To catch a seal, the Eskimo cuts a hole in the sea ice. When the seal comes up to the hole to breathe, the Eskimo shoots it.

Eskimos eat raw and cooked seal meat.

ESKIMO ART
During the long winter months there is little daylight in the Arctic, so the hours of hunting are limited. In the past, skilled Eskimo carvers used the time to work wood, bone, soapstone (soft rock), and walrus tusks. They created beautiful statues of animals, people, and especially favoured hunting scenes. Today museums and collectors eagerly seek good Eskimo carvings.

INUIT
The Eskimos of Greenland and North America are called Inuit. There are about 25,000 Inuit in North America. Most live in wooden houses equipped like a typical North American home. Some Inuit are still full-time hunters; most others work in many different businesses and industries.

A team of 10 to 15 husky dogs pull the traditional Eskimo sledge. With an expert driver at the reins, a dog team can travel 80 km (50 miles) in a day.

Find out more
ANTARCTICA AND THE ARCTIC
CANADA
POLAR EXPLORATION
POLAR WILDLIFE

EUROPE

COMPARED TO ITS mighty eastern neighbour, Asia, Europe is a tiny continent. But the culture of Europe has extended far beyond its boundaries. Europe has a long history of wealth, industry, trading, and empire building. Much of its prosperity comes from its green and fertile land, which is watered by numerous rivers and plenty of rain. Yet the climate varies considerably across the continent. The countries of southern Europe border the Mediterranean Sea. Holiday-makers visit the coast of this enclosed sea to enjoy its long, hot summers. The far north, by contrast, reaches up into the icy Arctic Circle. There are also a number of high mountain ranges within Europe, including the Alps and the Pyrenees. The 786 million people of Europe are as varied as the landscape. The Nordic people of the north have blond hair, fair skin, and blue eyes, while many southern Europeans have darker skin and dark, curly hair.

EUROPEAN UNION
The aim of the European Union (EU) – previously called the European Economic Community (EEC) then the European Community (EC) – is to promote political and economic union between the member states. The 12 stars in its flag represent the 12 original members. The Union now has 15 members.

LOCATION
Europe lies to the north of the Mediterranean Sea and overlooks the northern part of the Atlantic Ocean. It includes the surrounding islands, such as the British Isles and Iceland. The Ural Mountains in the Russian Federation mark the long eastern frontier with Asia.

Old European buildings may look picturesque, but the architecture is more than decorative. The mellow brick and stone provided essential protection against the cool, damp weather.

DANUBE RIVER
Europe's second-longest river is the Danube. The Danube flows from the Black Forest in Germany to the Black Sea and passes through nine European countries: Germany, Austria, Slovakia, Hungary, Croatia, Yugoslavia, Romania, Bulgaria, and Ukraine.

Austrian composer Johann Strauss Jr. (1825-1899) named his famous waltz tune The Blue Danube *after the river.*

TOWNS AND CITIES
A large proportion of Europeans are town dwellers. From early times, towns developed where people came to do business and to trade in the markets. As a result, Europe is dotted with towns and cities, such as Paris, whose origins are ancient. Beautiful old buildings grace many of these cities' centres. Some are historic monuments that have been restored and now house modern shops and businesses.

INDUSTRY
Large-scale industry began in Europe. Labor-saving inventions of the 18th and 19th centuries enabled workers in European factories to manufacture goods cheaply and in large numbers. The Industrial Revolution soon spread to other parts of the world, including the United States, India, and Japan. Manufacturing industries still play a vital role in most European countries.

To meet increasing competition from abroad, particularly from Japan, European companies have modernized their factories.

EUROPE

STATISTICS
Area: (10,498,000, sq km) 4,053,309 sq miles
Population: 749,000,000
Number of independent countries: 44
Religions: Christianity, Islam, Eastern Orthodox, Judaism
Highest point: Mount Elbrus (Russian Federation)5,642 m (18,510 ft)
Longest river: Volga (Russian Federation), 3,531 km (2,194 miles)
Main occupations: Agriculture, manufacturing, industry
Main exports: Machinery and transport equipment
Main imports: Oil and other raw materials

EUROPEAN COUNTRIES AND THEIR POPULATIONS
Countries that appear on a separate map are marked with a •

ALBANIA
3,300,000

ANDORRA •
58,000

AUSTRIA
7,800,000

BELGIUM •
10,000,000

BELORUSSIA •
10,300,000

BOSNIA AND HERZEGOVINA
4,500,000

BULGARIA
8,900,000

CROATIA
4,900,000

CZECH REPUBLIC
10,400,000

DENMARK •
5,200,000

ESTONIA •
1,600,000

FINLAND •
5,000,000

FRANCE •
57,400,000

GERMANY •
80,600,000

GREECE
10,200,000

HUNGARY
10,500,000

ICELAND •
300,000

IRELAND, REPUBLIC OF •
3,500,000

ITALY •
57,800,000

LATVIA •
2,700,000

LIECHTENSTEIN
29,386

LITHUANIA •
3,800,000

LUXEMBOURG •
400,000

MACEDONIA
1,900,000

MALTA •
400,000

MOLDAVIA •
4,400,000

MONACO •
28,000

NETHERLANDS •
15,300,000

NORWAY •
4,300,000

POLAND
38,500,000

PORTUGAL •
9,900,000

ROMANIA
23,400,000

RUSSIAN FEDERATION in Europe •
108,950,000

SAN MARINO •
23,000

SLOVAKIA •
5,300,000

SLOVENIA •
2,000,000

SPAIN •
39,200,000

SWEDEN •
8,700,000

SWITZERLAND •
6,900,000

TURKEY in Europe
5,400,000

UKRAINE •
52,200,000

UNITED KINGDOM •
57,800,000

VATICAN CITY •
1,000

YUGOSLAVIA
10,600,000

In 1992 U.N. peacekeeping forces entered war-torn Sarajevo, capital of Bosnia.

EASTERN EUROPE
This refers to countries such as Albania and Poland that came under Soviet control in 1945. It also refers to what was the western Soviet Union. From 1989, the Communist regimes in Eastern Europe collapsed and were replaced by more democratic governments. Some countries kept their boundaries, others changed. Croatia, Slovenia, and Bosnia and Herzegovina split away from what was Yugoslavia. In the early 1990s, bitter fighting broke out as Serbian, Croatian, and Muslim forces contested ethnic areas of Croatia and Bosnia and Herzegovina.

ATLANTIC OCEAN

R. Tagus

✳️ Lisbon

PORTUGAL

R. Guadalquivir

PYRENEES
The Pyrenees mountains lie on the border between France and Spain. The mountain range stretches from the Bay of Biscay to the Mediterranean Sea, a distance of 435 km (270 miles). The climate of the Pyrenees is mild and humid. The mountains offer fishing, sightseeing, and winter sports. There are also health spas with hot springs.

ICELAND

NORWEGIAN SEA

FAEROE
ISLANDS

SHETLAND
ISLANDS

ORKNEY
ISLANDS

HEBRIDES

SWEDEN

FINLAND

Lake Onega

NORWAY

Helsinki

RUSSIAN
FEDERATION

Oslo

Stockholm

BALTIC
SEA

Tallinn

ESTONIA

Lake
Ladoga

R. Volga

UNITED
KINGDOM

NORTH SEA

Lake
Vänern

Lake
Vättern

LATVIA

Riga

Shannon

DENMARK

LITHUANIA

Moscow

Dublin

Pennines

Copenhagen

RUSSIAN
FEDERATION

Vilnius

PUBLIC
RELAND

R. Severn

NETHERLANDS

Minsk

R. Thames

Amsterdam

GERMANY

R. Vistula

BELORUSSIA

London

Berlin

R. Elbe

Warsaw

Brussels

R. Rhine

Bonn

BELGIUM

LUXEMBOURG

POLAND

Kiev

R. Seine

Paris

Prague

UKRAINE

R. Loire

LIECHTENSTEIN

R. Danube

CZECH
REPUBLIC

SLOVAKIA

R. Dniester

R. Dnieper

FRANCE

Lake
Constance

Vienna

Bratislava

MOLDAVIA

BAY OF
BISCAY

Jura Mts.

Lake
Geneva

Berne

AUSTRIA

Budapest

Chisinau

SEA OF
AZOV

R. Garonne

SWITZERLAND

Alps

Ljubljana

Lake
Balaton

HUNGARY

Mont
Blanc

R. Po

SLOVENIA

Zagreb

ROMANIA

PAIN

Pyrenees

R. Rhône

SAN
MARINO

CROATIA

Belgrade

Bucharest

BLACK SEA

Madrid

MONACO

BOSNIA AND
HERZEGOVINA

Sarajevo

YUGOSLAVIA

BULGARIA

ANDORRA

CORSICA

ITALY

Sofia

Rome

Apennine Mts.

MACEDONIA

VATICAN
CITY

Tirana

Skopje

Ankara

SARDINIA

BALEARIC
ISLANDS

GIBRALTAR (UK)

ALBANIA

GREECE

TURKEY

MEDITERRANEAN SEA

SICILY

Athens

0   300 miles

MALTA

0   500 km

Valletta

CRETE

193

TRADE

Europeans have always been great traders. Between the 15th and 18th centuries, the countries of Europe were the most powerful in the world. They took their trade to all corners of the globe, and their settlers ruled parts of the Americas, Africa, India, Southeast Asia, and Australia. Almost all of these regions are now independent, but many still retain traces of European culture.

European trade and money formed the basis of the world's banking system.

SCANDINAVIA

A great hook-shaped peninsula encloses most of the Baltic Sea in northern Europe and extends into the Arctic Circle. Sweden and Norway occupy this peninsula. Together with Denmark to the south, they make up Scandinavia. Finland, to the east of the Baltic, and the large island of Iceland in the North Atlantic, are often also included in the group.

The people paint the houses white to reflect the heat of the sun.

In the warm climate of the Mediterranean region olives, oranges, lemons, sunflowers, melons, tomatoes, and aubergines grow well.

Goats and sheep are more common than cattle, which require richer pasture.

MEDITERRANEAN

Ten European countries border the Mediterranean Sea: Spain, France, Monaco, Italy, Slovenia, Croatia, Bosnia and Herzegovina, Yugoslavia, Albania, and Greece. A small part of Turkey is also in Europe. The Mediterranean people have traditionally lived by farming (above), but many of these countries now have thriving industries. Though the climate around the Mediterranean is much warmer than that of northern Europe, winters can still be quite chilly.

ART AND CULTURE

Europe has its own traditions of art and culture which are quite distinct from those of other parts of the world. Oil painting, classical music, and ballet had their origins in Europe. The traditions of European theatre, music, literature, painting, and sculpture all began in ancient times.

The port of Tallinn, Estonia

BALTIC STATES

Lithuania, Latvia, and Estonia, low-lying agricultural countries on the eastern coast of the Baltic Sea, are together called the Baltic States. They were formed in 1918 and remained independent until 1940 when they were occupied by the Soviet Union. In 1990, Lithuania became one of the first of the former Soviet republics to declare independence, followed, in 1991, by Estonia and Latvia.

Find out more
FRANCE
GERMANY
ITALY
RUSSIAN FEDERATION
SCANDINAVIA
SPAIN AND PORTUGAL
UNITED KINGDOM

EVOLUTION

LESS THAN 150 YEARS AGO, an English naturalist named Charles Darwin shocked the world when he wrote a book suggesting that humans were related to apes. Today Darwin's idea still forms the basis of what we call the theory of evolution. The word *evolution* means unfolding, and it is used to describe the way that all living things evolve, or change with time. There are three main parts to the theory. The first is called variation. All living things vary in size, shape, colour, and strength. No two animals or plants are exactly the same. The second part of the theory is that these variations affect whether or not a living thing can survive and breed. Certain features, such as colour, may mean that one animal or plant has a better chance of surviving than another. Some animals and plants have features that suit their surroundings. In other words, they are better adapted, and these useful features are called adaptations. The third part of the theory is inheritance. The adaptations that help a living thing to survive, such as its colour or shape, may be passed onto its offspring. If the offspring inherits the adaptations, they too will have a better chance of survival. Gradually, over many generations, the better-adapted plants and animals flourish, and those which are less well adapted die out. Many people believe that this process of evolution has led to the millions of different species that inhabit the Earth today.

NATURAL SELECTION
Charles Darwin wrote a book called *On the Origin of Species*, published in 1859, which explained his theory of evolution. Many people laughed at Darwin's idea that humans were related to animals. Above is a cartoon of the time, picturing Darwin as a monkey.

African elephant of today

Evolution of the elephant

Moenitherium lived about 38 million years ago.

Woolly mammoth lived about two million years ago.

Platybelodon lived from 12 to 7 million years ago.

Trilophodon lived from 26 to three million years ago.

EVIDENCE FROM THE PAST

Fossils, the remains of animals and plants preserved in rocks, provide evidence for evolution. They show how animals and plants have gradually changed through time. For example, each of the elephants shown above lived for a certain amount of time, as we know by the age of their fossilized bones. Scientists cannot be certain that the first type of elephant gradually evolved into the next, but it is unlikely that each elephant appeared, completely separate from the others. It is far more likely that these elephants were related. As we find more fossils, the relationships between various kinds of animals and plants become clearer.

EVIDENCE FROM THE PRESENT
Animals and plants alive today also provide evidence for evolution. In Hawaii there are several kinds of honeycreepers that look similar. It is unlikely that this is by chance. More likely, these different honeycreeper birds all evolved from one kind of honeycreeper. This first honeycreeper flew to the islands five million years ago. Since that time, natural selection has produced several similar, but separate, species.

There are 28 species of honeycreepers on the Hawaiian islands. Scientists believe they evolved from one species of bird.

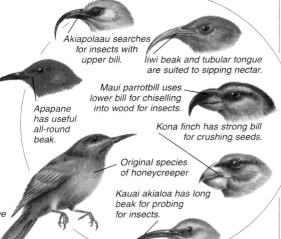

Akiapolaau searches for insects with upper bill.

Iiwi beak and tubular tongue are suited to sipping nectar.

Apapane has useful all-round beak.

Maui parrotbill uses lower bill for chiselling into wood for insects.

Kona finch has strong bill for crushing seeds.

Original species of honeycreeper

Kauai akialoa has long beak for probing for insects.

HOW EVOLUTION OCCURS

Imagine some green frogs, living and breeding in green surroundings. Most of the young inherit the green colouring of their parents. They are well camouflaged and predators do not notice them in the grass. Their green colour is an adaptation which helps them to survive. A few of the young have different colours, because of variation. Predators can see them in the grass and these frogs are soon eaten – this is natural selection at work. Then the environment slowly changes to yellow as the grass dies. Now the green frogs show up on the sand, and predators eat them. Gradually, the following generations of frogs change from mainly green to mainly yellow. A new species has evolved.

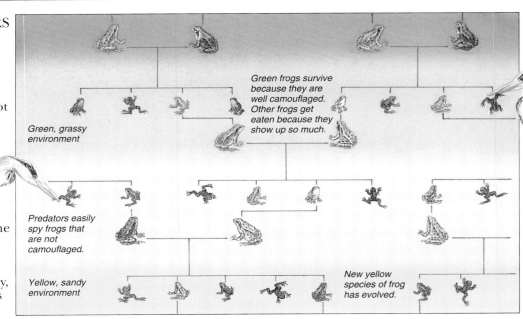

Green, grassy environment

Green frogs survive because they are well camouflaged. Other frogs get eaten because they show up so much.

Predators easily spy frogs that are not camouflaged.

Yellow, sandy environment

New yellow species of frog has evolved.

CHANGING ENVIRONMENTS

As the environment changes, living things evolve. About 200 years ago in Britain, peppered moths had mostly light-coloured wings that matched the light-coloured tree trunks where they rested, so birds of prey could not see them easily. During the Industrial Revolution, smoke from factory chimneys made the tree trunks darker in some areas. Light-coloured moths became easier to see. Gradually, more dark-coloured moths evolved, which were better camouflaged on the dark tree trunks.

The ichthyosaur is an extinct reptile. Its paddle-like front limb had many small bones.

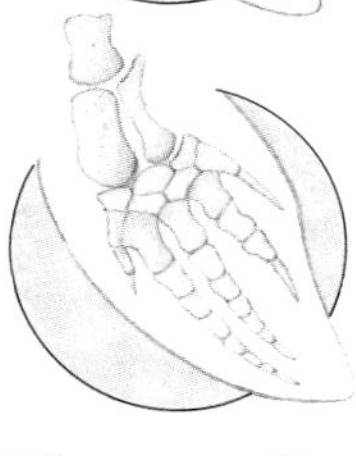

The dolphin is a mammal. Its paddle has the typical bones of the mammal arm and hand.

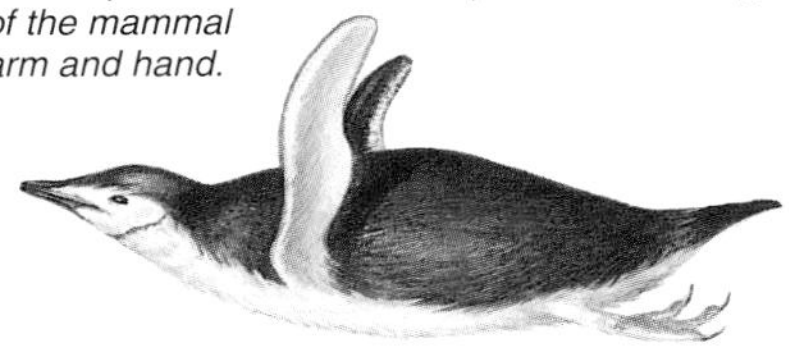

The penguin is a bird that cannot fly. It has the typical bird's wing bones in its paddle.

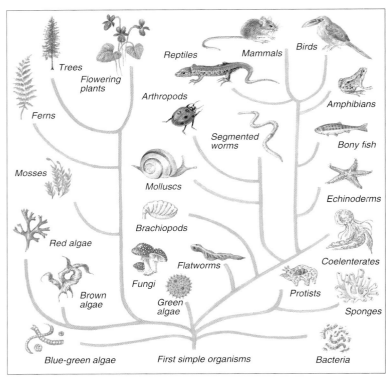

Trees

Flowering plants

Ferns

Reptiles

Mammals

Birds

Arthropods

Amphibians

Mosses

Segmented worms

Bony fish

Molluscs

Red algae

Brachiopods

Echinoderms

Flatworms

Coelenterates

Brown algae

Fungi

Green algae

Protists

Sponges

Blue-green algae

First simple organisms

Bacteria

EVOLUTIONARY TREE

Scientists believe that all living things are related and that they have evolved from the same ancestors over millions of years. This chart is called an evolutionary tree. It has lines between the main groups of animals and plants alive today, showing which ones are most closely related.

CONVERGENT EVOLUTION

Evolution sometimes makes different animals and plants look similar. This is called convergent evolution. It means that different animals or plants that live in the same environment, such as the sea, gradually take on the same adaptations, such as body shape. All the animals shown above have evolved, or developed, the same streamlined body form, because this is the best shape for moving speedily through water.

Find out more
ANIMALS
DINOSAURS
FOSSILS
GEOLOGY
PREHISTORIC LIFE
PREHISTORIC PEOPLES

EXPLORERS

TODAY PEOPLE ARE AWARE of the remotest corners of the world. But hundreds of years ago many did not know that countries apart from their own even existed. In the 6th century the Irish Saint Brendan is said to have sailed across the Atlantic in search of a land promised to saints. But it was not until the early 15th century that strong seaworthy ships were developed and Europeans such as Christopher Columbus were able to explore in earnest. Turkish Muslims had been controlling the overland trade route between Europe and the Indies (the Far East) since the 11th century. They charged such high prices for Eastern goods that European merchants became eager to find a direct sea route to the Far East which would bypass the Turks. The sailors who searched for these routes found the Americas and other lands previously unknown to Europeans. Of course, people already lived in most of these "newly discovered" lands, and the results of these explorations were not always happy. All too often the new arrivals exploited and enslaved the native peoples, destroying their cultures.

VIKINGS
The Vikings came from Norway, Sweden, and Denmark. Looking for new lands in which to settle, they sailed to Iceland, Greenland, and North America in their long ships, navigating by the sun and the stars.

PACIFIC ISLANDS
Europeans exploring the Pacific Ocean in the 1500s were amazed to find that prehistoric peoples had found the Pacific Islands before them. In about 30,000 B.C., the original Polynesians moved from southeast Asia to the islands in the Western Pacific, sailing in fragile canoes. By A.D. 1000, they had settled on hundreds of other islands.

Maori ancestors leaving for New Zealand

EARLY IDEAS
The first explorers had few maps. Early ideas about the shape of the world were hopelessly inaccurate. Many scholars thought the world was flat and that those who went too far might fall off the edge. Some believed that the world was supported by a tortoise (above).

PERILS OF THE SEA
Early sailors faced many natural dangers such as storms, reefs, icebergs, and fog. The sea was an alien territory, and rumours and legends spoke of huge sea monsters which swam in unknown seas. These stories were probably based on sightings of whales and other marine creatures. They were exaggerated by returning sailors telling tall tales of their adventures. Writers and artists added more gruesome details to these descriptions and so the myths grew.

DISCOVERIES
Explorers took gold, treasure, and exciting new vegetables from the Americas to Europe; they also carried silks, jewels, and spices from the East. People in Europe were eager to obtain these and wanted more. This led to a great increase in trade with both East and West.

Silk from the East

Potatoes from North America

Tomatoes and chillies from the Americas

Spices from the East

Chocolate was made from cacao beans from the Americas.

INQUISITIVE EUROPEANS

Once Europeans had an idea of the correct shape of the world, they set out to explore it more thoroughly. Some were driven by curiosity, some by greed, and some by a desire to convert the peoples who lived in faraway places to Christianity. All faced hardships and dangers.

SIR HENRY MORTON STANLEY (1841-1904)

Welshman Henry Stanley worked for a New York newspaper. He led an expedition into Africa to find the missing Scottish explorer David Livingstone. When he found him, Stanley uttered the famous words "Dr. Livingstone, I presume?" Stanley later explored much of central Africa around Lake Victoria.

MARY KINGSLEY (1862-1900)

A fearless and determined Englishwoman, Mary Kingsley travelled in West Africa, trading and making scientific studies. On her travels, she met and was entertained by cannibals. She was one of the first to demand fair treatment for the people of Africa by their colonial rulers.

AMERIGO VESPUCCI (1451-1512)

The first European to explore the Brazilian coast, Italian-born Amerigo Vespucci gave his name to America. He was in charge of a school of navigation in Seville, Spain. Vespucci believed in a southwestern route to the Indies around South America.

FERDINAND MAGELLAN (1480-1521)

Leader of the first European expedition to sail around the world, Portuguese explorer Magellan proved that there was a southwestern route to the Indies through the Pacific.

VASCO DA GAMA (1469-1524)

Despite bad weather and hardships on the voyage, Portuguese-born Vasco da Gama reached the East African coast and proved that there was a southeastern route to India. He was the first European to sail around the southern tip of Africa.

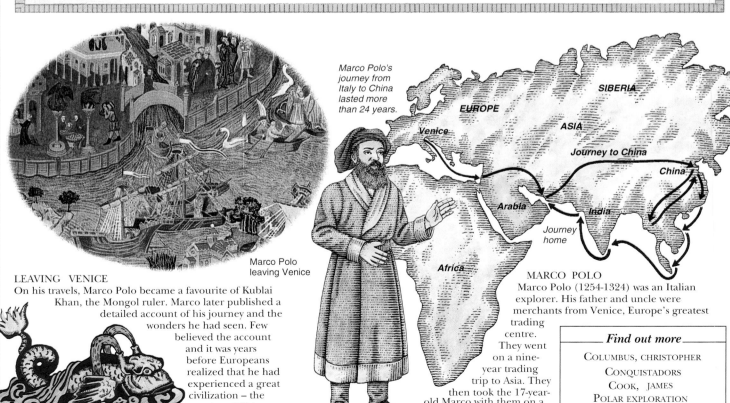

LEAVING VENICE

On his travels, Marco Polo became a favourite of Kublai Khan, the Mongol ruler. Marco later published a detailed account of his journey and the wonders he had seen. Few believed the account and it was years before Europeans realized that he had experienced a great civilization – the empire of China.

Marco Polo leaving Venice

Marco Polo's journey from Italy to China lasted more than 24 years.

SIBERIA

EUROPE

ASIA

Venice

Journey to China

China

Arabia

India

Journey home

Africa

MARCO POLO

Marco Polo (1254-1324) was an Italian explorer. His father and uncle were merchants from Venice, Europe's greatest trading centre. They went on a nine-year trading trip to Asia. They then took the 17-year-old Marco with them on a journey from Italy to China.

Find out more

COLUMBUS, CHRISTOPHER

CONQUISTADORS

COOK, JAMES

POLAR EXPLORATION

EYES

EAGLE SIGHT A golden eagle has the sharpest eyesight in the world. It can see rabbits and other prey from a distance of more than 1 km (half a mile).

AS YOU READ THIS PAGE, you are using the two organs of sight – the eyes. Our eyes enable us to learn a great deal about the world around us. Each eyeball measures about 25 mm (1 in) across and sits in the front of the skull in the eye socket, or orbit. The eyes can swivel around in their sockets so that you can see things above, below, and to the side. Each eye has an adjustable lens and sees a slightly different view of the same scene. The eyes work together, controlled by the brain. This is called binocular vision. The lens of each eye allows rays of light to enter from the outside and project a picture onto the retina – the inner lining of the eye. The retina converts the light into nerve signals which travel along optic nerves to the brain, where images are formed.

Tear (lacrimal) gland

Tear duct

Tear sac

EYE SOCKETS
The eyelid and eyelashes protect the front of the eye. When you blink, the eyelids sweep moisture over the eyeball, keeping it clean. The moisture is produced in the tear glands above the eyes. These glands also produce tears when you cry. Tiny holes called tear ducts drain the fluid into the tear sac, to the inside of the nose.

OUTER EYE
Light rays enter the curved front of the eye called the cornea, where they are partly focused. They pass through the pupil, which enlarges in dim conditions to let in more light and shrinks in bright conditions to protect the inside of the eye from too much light. The rays are then focused onto the retina by the lens.

Choroid, containing nourishing blood vessels

Muscles anchored at back of eye socket move the eye.

Cornea is like a transparent window in the front of the eyeball. The cornea partly focuses light rays.

Retina, bearing light-sensitive cells

Sclera – tough outer covering

Fat

Iris makes pupil larger or smaller.

Pupil is a hole within the iris.

EYEBALL
Three pairs of muscles turn the eyeball to look up, down, and from side to side. Pads of fat cushion the eye and the optic nerve, which is stretched and pulled by eye movements.

Conjunctiva – thin covering layer

Optic nerve to brain

Lens fine-focuses light rays.

Blind spot, containing no light-sensitive cells, where optic nerve leaves eye

INNER EYE
Inside the eye is the retina, which contains about 120 million rod cells, mainly around the sides, and seven million cone cells, mainly at the back. When an image lands on the retina it is upside down, but nerve signals reaching the brain turn the image right side up.

Vitreous fluid

RODS AND CONES
The retina contains millions of light-sensitive cells called rods and cones. The rods are sensitive to black and white, and the cones are sensitive to different colours. Rods and cones produce nerve signals when light falls on them.

LONGSIGHTEDNESS AND SHORTSIGHTEDNESS
Clear vision depends on the lens bending light rays to the correct angle so that the rays form a sharp picture on the retina. In longsighted people, either the lens is too weak or the eyeball is too small for its focusing power. In the shortsighted, the lens is too strong, or the eyeball is too big. Glasses and artificial lenses, such as contact lenses, help the eye's own lens to focus the rays correctly.

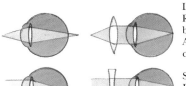

LONGSIGHTEDNESS
Rays are focused behind the retina. A convex lens corrects the focus.

SHORTSIGHTEDNESS
Rays are focused in front of retina. A concave lens corrects the focus.

Find out more
CAMERAS
COLOUR
EARS
HUMAN BODY
LIGHT

FARM ANIMALS

Female sheep are called ewes, males are rams, and the young are called lambs.

Merino sheep have the finest wool. The ancestor of today's Merino sheep is the Spanish Merino – a breed of sheep that is about 1,000 years old.

Meat from adult sheep is called mutton.

The Suffolk is an English breed that was first developed about 100 years ago.

Female chickens are called hens. Males, like the one shown here, are usually more colourful. They are called cocks, cockerels, or roosters.

HAMBURGERS, sausages, butter, and cheese are produced from animals that we keep on farms. Many other foods, including eggs, bacon, and yogurt, also come from farm animals. Farm animals include pigs, cows, sheep, rabbits, goats, and chickens. People keep these animals for their meat, milk, fur, and skins. We use the skins, or hides, of cows, pigs, and sheep to make shoes, and the wool of sheep, goats, and rabbits to make clothes. People have been keeping animals on farms for at least 9,000 years. Many are kept in small enclosed areas called pens, others in fields, and still others in cages. The first farm animals were wild creatures that people captured and domesticated, or tamed. Today's chickens are descended from tropical forest birds of Southeast Asia. Through the ages, farmers have bred (mated together) the healthiest, most docile animals with the best milk, meat, or wool production, to produce the breeds that we know today.

The female pig is called a gilt before she has any young, and a sow once she has young. Male pigs are called boars.

AMERICAN HAMPSHIRE PIG
The American Hampshire pig has little fat on its body, so the pork and bacon from this pig are lean (that is, they have little fat).

The Rhode Island Red is named after the state of Rhode Island in the United States. It is a good egg layer and is well known for its meat.

Chicks are sold for meat when they are about eight weeks old and weigh about 2 kg (4.5 lb).

POULTRY
Many people keep chickens as a source of meat and eggs. These chickens scratch around in farmyards and fields, eating seeds, worms, insects, and scraps. They lay their eggs in a small chicken coop or any other secluded place. This is called free-range rearing – the chickens are able to wander freely. In some parts of the world chickens are raised indoors, in huge buildings.

PLYMOUTH ROCK
There are about 7,000 million chickens around the world, and about 500 breeds. The Leghorn is the most common egg-laying hen. The Plymouth Rock shown here is a fast-growing chicken that produces tasty meat in a short time.

SHEEP
Wool comes from sheep, goats, rabbits, alpacas, and vicunas. Young sheep, or lambs, produce the softest, finest wool. The largest flocks of sheep are in Australia, where there are about 140 million sheep. The sheep we farm for wool are sheared for their fleeces (coats) once a year. An expert shearer with electric clippers can shear one sheep every 40 seconds. The wool is washed and combed, then stretched and twisted into yarn for woollen fabric. Here, a woman in Nepal, Asia, is spinning wool by hand to make into carpets and rugs.

INTENSIVE REARING

Some farm animals such as pigs and chickens are kept under controlled conditions in huge hangar-like buildings. Chickens are raised by the thousands in this way, for their meat or their eggs. These chickens sit in wire cages and cannot run around freely or scratch for their food. The food, temperature, and light in the building are controlled so that each chicken lays up to 300 eggs each year. Pigs are kept in pig units like the one shown here. They are fed an exact mixture of nutrients that makes them put on the most weight in the least time. Some kinds of pigs gain more than 0.7 kg (1.5 lb) in weight each day. A pig may be sold for pork when it is only three months old.

PIG

There are about 400 million pigs in Asia, and another 400 million scattered around the rest of the world. Some pigs are allowed to roam freely to feed on roots, worms, and household scraps; others are kept inside buildings (see above). There are more than 80 breeds of pigs, and some of the largest weigh more than 200 kg (440 lb). Almost every part of a pig can be eaten, including the trotters, or feet. Pork is the name for fresh pig meat; cured or preserved pig meat is called bacon or ham.

ZEBU

Cattle are the most numerous of farm animals, with 200 million in India and about 1,000 million in the rest of the world. They were first used to pull carts. Today some cattle are bred for their meat (beef breeds), others for their milk (dairy breeds), and some for both (dual-purpose breeds). There are about 200 breeds of cattle. The Zebu cattle shown here have a hump at the shoulders, and a long, narrow face. They were originally from India and are suited to hot climates. Zebu are also used to pull ploughs.

TURKEY

Today's most common breed of turkey is the White Holland, which was developed from the Bronze turkey, shown here. Turkeys came originally from North America. When Europeans first travelled to North America in the 16th century, they domesticated (tamed) turkeys and took some back to Europe.

Every year on 25 December, millions of turkeys are eaten at Christmas.

Male turkeys, or toms, are often twice the weight of the female hens. Young turkeys are called poults.

In many parts of the world, people keep goats for their milk, which is made into cheese and yogurt.

DUCKS AND GEESE

Waterfowl such as ducks and geese are kept mainly for their meat, especially in Southeast Asia. They also provide fluffy down (underfeathers) for stuffing mattresses, quilts, and clothing. Geese are good guards in the farmyard, as they hiss at strangers. The most common egg-laying waterfowl are Indian runner ducks, khaki campbell ducks, and Emden and Chinese geese.

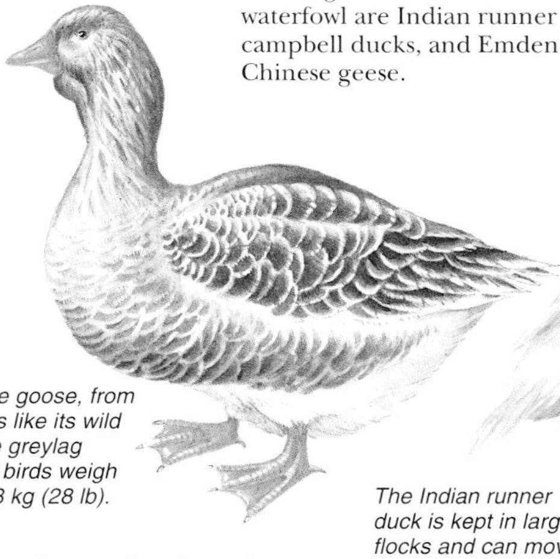

The Toulouse goose, from France, looks like its wild ancestor, the greylag goose. Adult birds weigh more than 13 kg (28 lb).

The Indian runner duck is kept in large flocks and can move swiftly on its long legs.

GOAT

The goat was one of the first animals to be domesticated. Goats feed on thorny bushes, spiky grasses, and woody stems, and they can leap up easily into the branches of small trees to eat the leaves. Almost 500 million goats are kept worldwide, often in dry and mountainous regions. They are used for their milk, meat, skins, and wool. The main dairy breed is the Anglo-Nubian, which produces up to 660 litres (1,200 pints) of milk each year.

Find out more

COWS, CATTLE, AND buffaloes
DUCKS, GEESE, AND SWANS
FARMING
FARMING, HISTORY OF
HORSES, ZEBRAS, AND ASSES
MOUNTAIN WILDLIFE

FARMING

To stock the food shelves of supermarkets in Europe and the United States farmers make nature and technology work in harmony. They use machinery to plough and reap great fields of wheat; they fertilize and irrigate greenhouses full of vegetables and orchards of fruit; and they rear animals indoors to fatten them quickly. Through this intensive agriculture, Western farmers feed up to ten people from land that once fed one.

However, not all the world's farmers can be so productive. Those who have plots on hilly land cannot use machines. Instead they graze a few animals or cultivate the land with inefficient hand tools. Farmers in dry climates must be content with lower yields or choose less productive crops that will tolerate dry soil. And farmers who cannot afford machines and fertilizers are forced to use wasteful farming methods that have not changed for centuries.

SUBSISTENCE FARMING

In some developing countries, most farming families grow only sufficient food for themselves. This is called subsistence farming. In a good year it provides enough food for all. But a drought or an increase in the population may lead to famine and starvation.

CROPS

Most crops grown today are the descendants of wild plants. However, special breeding has created varieties that give high harvests. Grain crops such as wheat have especially benefitted. Modern varieties have much larger grains than traditional species. However, this new "superwheat" is not as resistant to disease as other varieties and must be grown carefully.

Superwheat

Ordinary wheat

Ploughing

Planting seeds

Harvesting

Spraying

FARM MACHINERY

Modern grain farming requires special machinery at different times of the year. In spring a plough breaks the soil into furrows for planting. A seed drill puts a measured amount of seed into the prepared soil and covers the seed so that birds do not eat it. A sprayer covers crops with pesticides to kill harmful diseases and pests. Finally a combine harvester cuts the crop and prepares it for storage.

A baler rolls up the straw – the cut stalks of wheat left after the grain has been harvested – and ties it into tight round bundles called bales.

ORGANIC FARMING

Some farmers in Western countries prefer to grow crops and raise animals in a natural or organic way. They do not use artificial pesticides or fertilizers. Organic food is more expensive, but it may be healthier to eat.

Organic farmers use natural fertilizers such as seaweed or animal dung to make the soil more productive.

INTENSIVE FARMING

The purpose of intensive farming is to increase the production of crops and animals and cut food prices. Food animals such as chickens and pigs are kept indoors in tiny, overcrowded pens. Many people feel this is unnatural and cruel and prefer to eat only "free-range" animals – animals which have been allowed to move freely in the farmyard.

In intensive chicken houses conveyor belts carry food to the hens in the crowded cages, and take away the eggs.

Find out more

FARM ANIMALS
FARMING, HISTORY OF

HISTORY OF
FARMING

EARLY FARMING
The first farmers domesticated (tamed) wild animals and kept them in herds to provide meat, milk, hides, and wool. Some people became nomadic herders rather than farmers; they moved their animals continuously in search of new pasture. The picture shown here was painted in a cave in the Sahara Desert in Africa about 8,000 years ago, at a time when the desert was grassland.

GROWING CROPS AND breeding animals for food are among the most important steps ever taken by humankind. Before farming began, people fed themselves by gathering berries and other plant matter and hunting wild animals. People were nomadic – they had to move around to find food. About 12,000 years ago in the Middle East, people discovered they could grow cereal crops such as wheat. These people were the first farmers. With the start of farming, people began to settle permanently in one place. Villages grew into towns and cities. Farmers produced enough food to support the population, so some people were free to do other jobs such as weaving and making pottery and tools. Since everyone depended on farming for their food, however, many people died of starvation when the crops failed because of bad weather. Over the centuries people have tried many different ways of producing better crops. In the agricultural revolution of the 1700s, new scientific methods helped overcome the problem of crop failure. Today, farming is a huge international industry.

CROP GROWING
In about 10,000 B.C., farmers in the Middle East began to plant crops to provide food. Cereals, such as wheat, barley, millet, and corn, were the main crops. In the Far East, people first grew rice in about 5,000 B.C.

The huge Berkshire pig was first bred for meat in the 18th century.

IRRIGATION
Farmers need a good supply of water for their crops. In China and other Far Eastern countries, where rice is the main crop, water flows along channels on the terraced hillsides to make the paddies for growing rice.

MEDIEVAL FARMING
In the 11th century the hard horse collar was introduced to Europe from China. It allowed horses, rather than oxen, which are weaker, to pull ploughs. In the 12th and 13th centuries European farms consisted of vast open fields divided into strips so that each peasant farmer had a piece of land in each field. By the 14th century much of the land was enclosed with ditches or hedges.

Seed drill

AGRICULTURAL REVOLUTION
During the 18th century a revolution occurred in agriculture. New methods were developed – the use of fertilizer, the introduction of new crops such as turnips – and breeds of livestock were improved, such as the huge Berkshire pig (above). The invention of new machines, such as the seed drill shown above, allowed farmers to produce more crops.

Steam tractor

MECHANIZATION
The development of steam power during the 19th century, and the combustion engine in the 20th century, changed agriculture forever. Tractors replaced horses as the main source of power, and railroads and refrigerated ships meant that food could be transported all over the world.

Find out more
ENGINES
FARM ANIMALS
FARMING
U.S.S.R., HISTORY OF

FESTIVALS AND FEASTS

ALL OVER THE WORLD people set aside special times during the year for festivals and feasts. Most of these celebrations are linked to a society's religious or other beliefs. Festivals also celebrate the changing seasons and special events in a country's history. Rituals such as singing or exchanging gifts often form part of annual festivals, and in many societies certain actions, pictures, and objects take on a special meaning at festival time. For instance, at Chinese New Year golden fish become symbols of wealth. Very different cultures sometimes share the same symbols in their festivals: Christians light candles at Christmas, and Hindus do the same at their festival of Diwali. Dressing up in elaborate costumes and sharing meals are festive activities common to many parts of the world.

MAYPOLE
In Britain, young people once celebrated the coming of spring by dancing around a maypole. This was usually a hawthorn or may tree decorated with blossoms and ribbons for the May Day festival.

CHINESE NEW YEAR

New Year in the Chinese calendar falls in late January or early February. Chinese people living in other countries remember the customs of their homeland by holding processions led by huge dragons and exploding firecrackers.

The procession is lit by lanterns.

People carry crackling fireworks.

CARNIVALS
Carnivals began in Roman Catholic countries such as Mexico as a way of using up foods that were forbidden during the fast of Lent, which precedes Easter. At the famous Mardi Gras in New Orleans, Louisiana, United States, the streets are filled with music, dancing, and long processions of people wearing colourful costumes.

THANKSGIVING

In the autumn of 1621 a group of European settlers in North America celebrated their first harvest by inviting the native Indians to join them in a thanksgiving feast because the Indians had taught them how to grow the native crops. Today families gather together on Thanksgiving Day, a national holiday celebrated in November, to share the traditional dinner of turkey and pumpkin pie.

HALLOWEEN
Lighting candles inside frightening pumpkin faces scares away evil spirits at Halloween, 31 October.

Find out more
BUDDHISM
CHRISTIANITY
HINDUISM
ISLAM
JUDAISM
RELIGIONS

FILMS

IN A PARIS café in December 1895, people sat down to watch the world's first motion picture. It was shown by two French brothers, Louis and Auguste Lumière, and though it consisted only of a few short, simple scenes, films have been popular ever since. The first films were silent, with titles on the screen to explain the story. A pianist accompanied the film with the right type of music – for example, fast and furious music during a chase scene. The United States took the lead in making films. Soon the public began to select its favourite actors and actresses, and the first film stars were created, such as Rudolph Valentino. In 1927, the first full-length "talkie" – film with sound – was shown, and from then on the public would settle for nothing less. Technical improvements continued. In the United States, Metro-Goldwyn-Mayer and a few other powerful studios made 95 per cent of the films. During the 1950s, television captured people's attention and the film industry went into decline. In recent years films have become popular again. Russia, Germany, France, and Japan have produced films that have influenced filmmaking throughout the world, and there are many national film industries.

CHARLIE CHAPLIN
The British actor Charles Chaplin (1889-1977) created a movie character that touched the hearts of millions: a silent little tramp with a funny walk.

HOLLYWOOD
Southern California, United States, had the ideal climate and scenery for making films. Between 1907 and 1913 a Los Angeles district called Hollywood became the centre of the American film industry. Not all stars were human: King Kong (above) was an animated model.

The senior electrician on the film set is called the gaffer.

Teams of expert makeup artists and dressers prepare an actress or actor for a day's shoot.

The art director designs the sets and chooses suitable locations for filming away from the studio.

A continuity worker makes sure that scenes shot out of order match each other. He or she notes the details of each shot, to ensure that there are no mistakes when the scenes are put in order.

Sound technicians follow the actors with microphones suspended from long poles (booms).

Lighting experts operate huge lamps, to ensure that the light looks as natural as possible in a film. Lighting is needed on location as well as in the studio.

The producer chooses the script, finds financial backing, picks the director and the technical teams, oversees the filming, and organizes publicity.

The director guides the actors' performances, the action, and the camera angles, and gives the film its style and character.

The cinematographer leads a team which also includes the camera operator and camera assistants, who help with focusing, load magazines, and operate the clapper board. Workers called grips move the camera down tracks or rails for the camera to run along smoothly.

FILM SET

Set builders make film sets – from city streets to tropical jungles – inside huge buildings like aircraft hangars, or outdoors on studio grounds. Hundreds of people are involved in getting things ready for the first filming of the day. When all is satisfactory, a red warning light goes on, the studio is told to stand by for a take (an attempt at a scene), sound and cameras roll, and the director shouts "Action!"

Acting on the big screen is very different from the theatre. In close-ups, every movement can be seen, and actors have to play their part with subtle facial expressions. They must also be able to act the story out of sequence.

Stuntmen and stuntwomen take the place of actors in dangerous action. They risk their lives performing stunts such as falling from a great height, crashing a car, or leaping from a moving train.

SPECIAL EFFECTS

Special effects have created a vast new fantasy world in films. In a technique known as back projection, first used as early as 1913, the cinematographer projects a previously filmed background onto a screen from behind. Actors or models are filmed in front of the screen, giving the impression that they are actually at that location. The camera can also be set up to shoot through a glass screen on which parts of the set are painted, carefully matched to the background behind. Sometimes models are used near the camera to look much larger than the action beyond, and stop-frame animation is used to bring models to life. The camera can also shoot through glass screens painted with outdoor scenes. Lifelike models can produce gruesome horror effects, such as the model shark in *Jaws* (1975). The convincing spacecraft in films such as *Star Wars* (1977) were models filmed in a studio.

FILMING FLYING

To make Supergirl fly, the film crew shoots two sequences. One shows Supergirl in a flying pose; the other, shot from an aircraft, shows the landscape over which she seems to travel. Then, in a special optical laboratory, the two sequences are combined by printing (copying) them in a special way.

In the studio Supergirl is filmed lying on a hidden support against a plain background. A fan makes her cloak flap as it would if she were flying.

First the camera crew films Supergirl against a background which is a special shade of blue.

Printing the sequence onto special film makes a black "mask". This mask records the special blue background as black, and leaves a clear space shaped like Supergirl's outline.

Printing a copy of this mask creates a second mask with black and clear areas reversed – Supergirl in black, and the background clear.

Finally, the optical laboratory prints the first black mask, and the studio sequence of Supergirl, to fill the "hole" in the landscape with the flying figure.

Now the film crew shoots the landscape over which Supergirl seems to fly.

Printing the landscape together with the second mask leaves a "hole" in the scene for Supergirl to fly in.

SPIELBERG

Directors often become "stars" in their own right. Director Steven Spielberg was born in 1946. He shot his first film when he was 12 and won a contract with Universal Studios, Hollywood, after leaving college. He became the most successful American director of the 1970s, 1980s, and 1990s with blockbusters such as *Jaws* (1975), *Jurassic Park* (1993), and Oscar winners such as *Schindler's List* (1993).

EDITING

The film editor sees that all the pieces of film are joined together in the right order, and that the film lasts the right amount of time. But editing is more complex than that. A good editor can improve the film by cutting out sequences that slow down the action or inserting close-up shots to make a scene more dramatic. Editing is a highly skilled process. Director and film editor work together for hours to get the right combination of shots in each scene.

FILMS

1895 First public film show held in Paris.

1905 In the United States the first nickelodeon film theatre opens.

1907 Hollywood founded.

1927 *The Jazz Singer* (USA) is first full-length film with sound.

1929 First Academy Awards.

1928 American cartoonist Walt Disney (1901-66) launches his most popular cartoon character, Mickey Mouse, in the film *Steamboat Willie*.

1935 First full-spectrum Technicolor feature, *Becky Sharp*, released.

1947-54 House Un-American Activities Committee investigates communists in Hollywood.

1953 First CinemaScope (wide screen) movie, *The Robe*, released.

1995 *Toy Story*, first completely computer-animated feature film released.

DUBBING

The sound editor is responsible for assembling the soundtrack for the film. This consists of dozens of separate tracks including all the dialogue, music, sound effects, and background sound. After editing, these sounds have to be balanced against each other and blended onto a master tape in a process called dubbing. Technicians known as mixers watch the film and operate controls on a sound console to get perfect timing and balance of sounds.

Find out more
CAMERAS
CARTOONS
TELEVISION AND VIDEO
THEATRE

FIRE

A BOLT OF LIGHTNING hitting a tree, or the red-hot lava from a volcano, can start a fire in seconds. It was probably from natural events such as these that prehistoric people discovered fire about one million years ago. Later they learned how to make fire for themselves by rubbing sticks together or by striking certain stones, such as flint. Today, fire works for us in many ways. The heat from fire cooks food, warms homes, and provides energy in engines and power stations. Fire is the heat and light that are produced when something burns. Burning occurs when a substance rapidly combines with oxygen gas, which makes up about one fifth of the air around us. Each material has a certain temperature, called its ignition temperature, above which it will burst into flame. Once it is burning, it produces so much heat of its own that it continues to burn. When fire gets out of control, it can be very dangerous. Every year, fires kill and injure thousands of people and cause great damage to property.

MATCHES
Fire requires three things: fuel, heat, and oxygen. When striking a match, rubbing the match against the box produces heat. The heat makes chemicals in the head of the match burst into flame as they combine with oxygen from the air.

Fire engines carry ladders, oxygen tanks, lamps, crowbars, and many other items of equipment that the fire crew may need as they fight a fire.

FIRE ENGINE
There are several kinds of fire engines. All contain powerful pumps that force water through hoses at high pressure.

A cage raised on a long motorized boom carries firefighters high in the air to rescue people and spray water or foam over the flames.

When people are trapped by fire, firemen use tools such as hatchets to break open windows and doors. Firefighters wear strong waterproof clothing and breathe with the aid of oxygen tanks so they can work in smoke or fumes.

Fire produces smoke, ash, and dangerous gases which can make people collapse or die.

Water tank contains a limited supply of water for the hoses.

FIRE HYDRANT
Fire hydrants, like large taps on the street, provide unlimited water from the city supply for fighting fires.

Firefighters may give oxygen to people who have breathed in too much smoke.

HOW FIRES SPREAD
Fires are often the result of carelessness: a smouldering match or cigarette left on the ground has caused many huge forest fires. Once started, a fire can spread in three ways. Currents of hot air can carry burning fragments which start new fires. Heat radiation from the flames can set nearby objects alight. And metal objects can conduct the heat of a fire to another place, starting a new fire.

In 1988, huge forest fires occurred in Yellowstone National Park, United States.

FIRE BRIGADE
Firefighters are specially trained to put out fires quickly and safely. They race to the scene of a fire as soon as the alarm is raised. The firefighters first task is to rescue people who are trapped in a burning building. Then they pump water or foam over the flames to put out the fire.

Squeezing the handle punctures a cylinder of compressed carbon dioxide gas. The gas expands and forces the water out of the nozzle.

Water should never be used on electrical fires because water conducts electricity.

FIRE EXTINGUISHER
There are different kinds of fire extinguishers for tackling different kinds of fires. A water extinguisher puts out wood and paper fires because it removes heat from the flames. Other types, such as foam extinguishers, kill fire by smothering it and depriving it of oxygen.

Find out more

HEAT
OXYGEN
PREHISTORIC PEOPLES

FIRST AID

IN AN EMERGENCY, quick, calm help is vital. For example, someone who chokes on food cannot wait for a doctor. Instead, non medical people close by must remove the obstruction immediately so that the choking person can breathe. This sort of rapid treatment is called first aid, and it varies depending on the injury. For slight injuries such as cuts, a doctor may not be needed. Instead, first aid consists of cleaning the wound and applying a bandage. Some accidents result in broken bones. Then first aid involves keeping the injured person calm and still, and getting him or her to a hospital. And in a major emergency, such as a traffic accident or a heart attack, first aid may involve re-starting the injured person's heart while waiting for an ambulance. Unskilled first aid can do more harm than good, but training is easy. A course lasting half a day is enough to learn skills that could help you save lives.

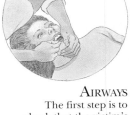

AIRWAYS
The first step is to check that the victim's airways, or breathing passages, are clear of obstructions.

BREATHING
Mouth-to-mouth resuscitation blows air into the victim's lungs.

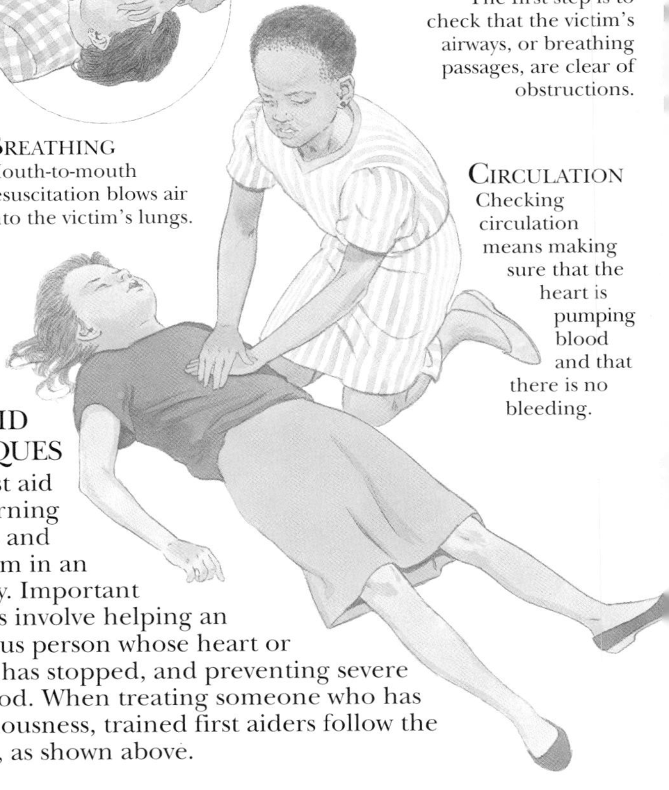

CIRCULATION
Checking circulation means making sure that the heart is pumping blood and that there is no bleeding.

FIRST-AID TECHNIQUES
Skilled first aid means learning basic skills and staying calm in an emergency. Important techniques involve helping an unconscious person whose heart or breathing has stopped, and preventing severe loss of blood. When treating someone who has lost consciousness, trained first aiders follow the ABC code, as shown above.

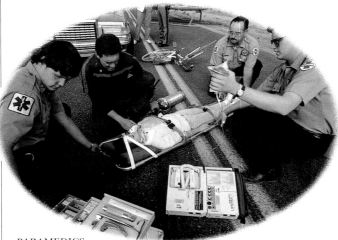

PARAMEDICS
At the scene of an accident, paramedics give emergency treatment to the injured. Paramedics are highly trained first-aid professionals. Their emergency ambulances contain life-saving equipment such as defibrillator machines, which are used to restart the hearts of heart attack victims. Paramedics save many lives because treatment starts before the patient reaches the hospital.

FIRST-AID KIT
Every home and car should have a first-aid kit containing items needed for emergency treatment. Keep the box clean and dry and clearly labelled. Replace items as soon as you use them or if the protective seal is accidentally broken.

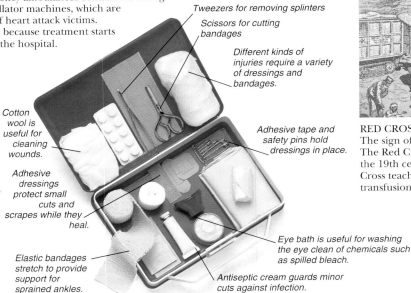

Tweezers for removing splinters

Scissors for cutting bandages

Different kinds of injuries require a variety of dressings and bandages.

Cotton wool is useful for cleaning wounds.

Adhesive dressings protect small cuts and scrapes while they heal.

Adhesive tape and safety pins hold dressings in place.

Elastic bandages stretch to provide support for sprained ankles.

Eye bath is useful for washing the eye clean of chemicals such as spilled bleach.

Antiseptic cream guards minor cuts against infection.

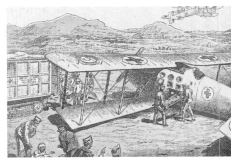

RED CROSS
The sign of a red cross is recognized everywhere. The Red Cross organization began in Europe in the 19th century. Today, members of the Red Cross teach first aid, collect blood for transfusions, and carry out welfare work.

Find out more
DISEASE
HEALTH
HOSPITALS
MEDICINE

FISH

FEATURES OF A FISH

The cod has all the features of a typical fish – a streamlined body for speed, a powerful tail, and fins for balance and steering. The lateral line along the body is a row of sense organs. These organs detect movements made by other creatures in the water.

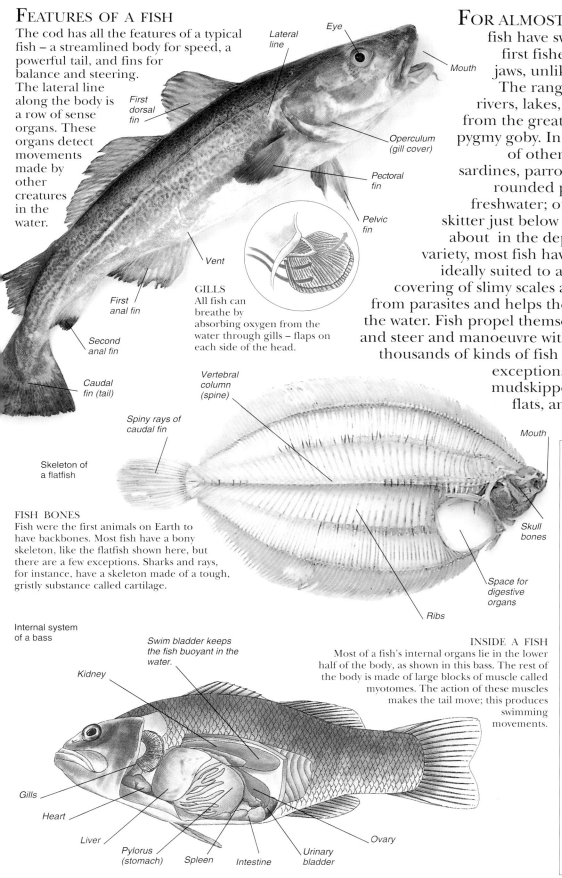

Lateral line

Eye

Mouth

First dorsal fin

Operculum (gill cover)

Pectoral fin

Pelvic fin

Vent

GILLS
All fish can breathe by absorbing oxygen from the water through gills – flaps on each side of the head.

First anal fin

Second anal fin

Caudal fin (tail)

Vertebral column (spine)

Spiny rays of caudal fin

Skeleton of a flatfish

FISH BONES
Fish were the first animals on Earth to have backbones. Most fish have a bony skeleton, like the flatfish shown here, but there are a few exceptions. Sharks and rays, for instance, have a skeleton made of a tough, gristly substance called cartilage.

Mouth

Skull bones

Space for digestive organs

Ribs

Internal system of a bass

Kidney

Swim bladder keeps the fish buoyant in the water.

Gills

Heart

Liver

Pylorus (stomach)

Spleen

Intestine

Urinary bladder

Ovary

INSIDE A FISH
Most of a fish's internal organs lie in the lower half of the body, as shown in this bass. The rest of the body is made of large blocks of muscle called myotomes. The action of these muscles makes the tail move; this produces swimming movements.

FOR ALMOST 500 MILLION YEARS, fish have swum in the oceans. The first fishes had no scales, fins, or jaws, unlike those we know today. The range of fish that live in our rivers, lakes, and seas is enormous – from the great whale shark to the tiny pygmy goby. In between are thousands of other fish, such as swordfish, sardines, parrotfish, and the comically rounded puffer fish. Some live in freshwater; others in saltwater. Some skitter just below the surface; others dart about in the depths. Despite their wide variety, most fish have a streamlined shape, ideally suited to a watery environment. A covering of slimy scales and mucus protects fish from parasites and helps them slip rapidly through the water. Fish propel themselves along by their tail, and steer and manoeuvre with their fins. Among the thousands of kinds of fish are some extraordinary exceptions. Hagfish have no jaws, mudskippers can skip across mud flats, and catfish can crawl and have no scales at all.

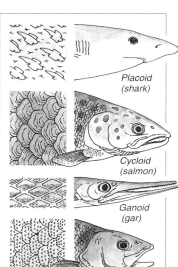

Placoid (shark)

Cycloid (salmon)

Ganoid (gar)

Ctenoid (perch)

SCALES
Bony discs called scales are embedded in the skin. They protect the body and overlap to allow movement. Although there are four main kinds, most fish have the cycloid or ctenoid kind.

STRANGELY SHAPED FISH

Each kind of fish is suited to its own way of life. The butterfly fish uses its long nose to pick food from crevices in rocks. Flying fish use their enlarged fins as "wings" for gliding as they leap out of the water. The bright colours on a lionfish warn other creatures of the deadly poison in its fin spines.

Lionfish

Flying fish

Long-nosed butterfly fish

SCHOOL OF FISH

Small fish often live in large groups called schools, or shoals, twisting and turning together as they search for food. A predator is sometimes so confused by their numbers and quick, darting movements that it cannot single out a fish to attack.

School of sea goldfish on a Red Sea coral reef

FEEDING

Fast predatory fish such as barracudas and pikes have long, slim, streamlined bodies and sharp teeth. Slower swimmers usually have more rounded bodies. Despite its shape, the parrotfish is an agile swimmer. It slips through cracks in the rock in search of food.

Parrotfish pulls weed from the rocks with its hard, beaklike mouth.

Sea horses

SEA HORSE

Sea horse eggs are injected by the female into the male's front pouch, where they develop for about four weeks. When the eggs hatch, the young sea horses emerge from the pouch.

Sea horses use their tails to cling to seaweed.

BREEDING

Most fish reproduce by depositing their eggs and sperm in the water, then leave the eggs to develop into fish. Some fish, such as sticklebacks and bowfins, look after the eggs and the young (called fry) once they have hatched. Other fish, such as some types of sharks, give birth to fully formed young fish after the eggs have developed in the mother's body.

MOUTHBREEDERS

The cichlid fish, found in African lakes, keeps its eggs safe inside its mouth. When the young hatch they swim out, then return to the parent's mouth for safety.

Cichlid fish and young

EUROPEAN EELS

Adult eels lay eggs in the Sargasso Sea. The eggs hatch into larvae which swim north during the next three years. When the larvae reach Europe they change into elvers and swim inland. There, they grow into yellow eels, then adults.

Yellow eels change into adult eels, then return to the Sargasso Sea to breed.

Larvae swim north and change into elvers.

Young elvers travel inland along rivers, where they change into yellow eels.

Eggs develop into larvae.

Royal gramma fish

TROPICAL OCEAN FISH

Fish, especially those from tropical waters, are among the brightest of all animals. Their dazzling colours and lively patterns have many different purposes. They help fish hide from predators among the coral, warn neighbouring fish to keep out of their territory, show other creatures that they are poisonous, or advertise for a mate.

Find out more

ANIMALS
DEEP-SEA WILDLIFE
MIGRATION
OCEAN WILDLIFE
SEASHORE WILDLIFE

FISHING INDUSTRY

THE WORLD'S RIVERS, seas, and oceans provide one of the most important of all foods. Fish are a rich source of protein and other vital nutrients. It is possible to catch a few fish using just a hook on the end of a piece of string. But to feed large numbers of people, a huge industry exists to catch millions of fish. Japanese fishing boats, for instance, catch more than 35,000 tons (31,000 tonnes) of fish each day. Fishing fleets use different methods to catch these vast numbers of fish, such as nets, traps, and hooks. Some nets are several miles long and can catch more than 100 million fish in one haul. Baskets, boxes, and other traps are left in the sea for shellfish, such as crabs, lobsters, and crayfish.

Hooks are arranged in a longline – a single line carrying hundreds of hooks – that is attached to a fishing boat and can trap huge numbers of fish at one time.

WHALING
For two centuries whaling has been a major industry and has made some species of whale almost extinct. As whales come to the surface to breathe, whale hunters shoot them with harpoons – huge explosive arrows fired from guns.

Drift nets are up to 60 miles (95 km) long. They catch fish very effectively, but may also harm other marine life.

FISHING GROUNDS
Fishing boats catch most fish near the coast in the seas above the continental shelf (shown in the dark blue on the map). This shelf is an extension of the continents covered by shallow sea water. Deep-water currents rich in nutrients rise onto the shelf and create good feeding grounds for fish.

At night lights attract fish into the dip nets.

The purse seiner tows its net in a huge circle to enclose the fish.

SEA FISHING

Seines are nets that float down from the surface. Drawing the net into a circle around a school, or group, of fish forms a huge bag which encloses the catch. Gill nets are long curtains of net which trap fish by the gills. Some gill nets float on the surface as drift nets; others are fixed to the sea bottom with anchors. A trawl is a large net bag towed behind a boat. Dip nets are hung over the side of the fishing boat on a frame. Lifting the frame catches the fish.

Weights keep the mouth of the trawl net open.

FREEZING FISH
Once a fish is dead, its flesh quickly rots. Freezing, canning, drying, smoking, and pickling all slow the decay and preserve the fish. Freezing is the best method. Large fishing boats have freezing plants on board to preserve the catch – the harvest of fish – before returning to port.

FISH FARMS
Not all fish are caught in the wild. Some fish, such as carp, salmon, trout, and shellfish, can be bred in controlled conditions on fish farms. In the United States, fish farmers raise catfish for food. Fish farmers build pens in lakes, ponds, or estuaries (river mouths). They hatch fish from eggs, then keep the fish until they are big enough to sell.

Find out more
FARMING
FISH
FOOD
OCEAN WILDLIFE

FLAGS

BRIGHTLY COLOURED flags, flying in the wind, have special meanings. They are used to send messages, greet the winner of a race, or encourage people to fight for their country. Every nation now has its own flag, which is a symbol of that country. Most organizations, such as the International Red Cross, also have their own flags. A flag is a piece of cloth with an easily recognized pattern. One edge is fixed to a pole, and the rest flaps freely.

Flags have always been important in battles. The leader of each warring army carried a flag. In the confusion of war, soldiers looked for their flag to see where their leader was. Capturing the enemy's flag often meant winning the battle. Before telephones or radio were invented, flags were a quick way to send messages. Today, signal flags are rarely used, but some flag codes have kept their meaning. Waving a white flag in war means that you want to surrender. And flying a flag halfway up the mast is a sign of respect for someone who has died.

The cap provides a neat, decorative top to the flagpole.

Flags can be any shape, but most national flags are rectangular.

The edge of the flag is the part most exposed to the wind, so it will be the first to show wear and tear.

The sleeve or heading is made of tough material into which the hoist rope is sewn.

The halyard is the long rope used to raise the flag.

NATIONAL FLAGS

The flags of many nations have symbols to represent the qualities or traditions of the country and its people. The Australian flag has a Union Jack – the British flag – to show the country's historic connection with Great Britain. The small stars on the flag are in the shape of the constellation *Crux Australis* (Southern Cross), which is visible only in the Southern Hemisphere.

CHECKERED FLAG

Waving a black and white checkered flag at the end of a motor race shows that the winner has crossed the finish line. Other flags are used as signals to drivers in car racing. A black flag indicates that the driver must make a pit stop. A yellow and red striped flag warns drivers that there is oil on the track. A red flag tells drivers to stop at once.

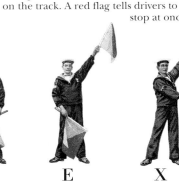

SEMAPHORE

With just two flags a signaler can spell out messages. Each flag position represents a different letter of the alphabet or a number. This system is called semaphore. Using large, plain, but colourful flags, messages can be sent over long distances, as far as the eye can see.

C E X

FLYING FLAGS

Flags make impressive decorations when they fly in a group in front of a building. Important buildings belonging to international organizations, such as the United Nations, may fly the flags of all their different members. Similar rows of flags brighten up hotels, supermarkets, and factories.

SIGNAL FLAGS

One of the earliest uses of flags was to send signals at sea. There was a flag for each letter of the alphabet and each number. Signalers spelled out words or used special combinations of flags to represent whole words. In the message above, for instance, "have" or "they have" is spelled with the flags for A, E, and L.

N
D
Q

Sharks

A
E
L

Have

F
L
G

Eaten

R
K
K

My

C
T
W

Captain

End of message flag

Find out more

KNIGHTS AND HERALDRY
NAVIES
SHIPS AND BOATS
UNITED STATES OF AMERICA

FLIES AND MOSQUITOES

Housefly can walk upside down.

SOME OF THE SMALLEST creatures in the world are the most dangerous to humans. Flies and mosquitoes carry some of the world's most serious diseases. With their habit of sucking blood and scavenging on rubbish, many of these insects spread cholera, malaria, and yellow fever. There are about 90,000 kinds of flies, including bluebottles, horseflies, fruit flies, tiny gnats, and almost invisible midges. We call many small, winged insects flies, but the only true flies are those with two wings; they belong to the insect group Diptera. All flies lay eggs. The eggs hatch into larvae called grubs or maggots. The maggots feed and grow into pupae or chrysalises, from which the adult flies finally emerge. Despite their unpopularity with humans, flies play a vital role in nature. They pollinate flowers and recycle nutrients as they scavenge, and they are a source of food for many larger animals.

Housefly has excellent eyesight and sponge-like mouthparts.

Eggs

Larva (maggot)

The bluebottle, or blowfly, lays thousands of eggs in dustbins and on meat. Within just a few weeks these eggs will produce thousands more flies.

Housefly feeding on rotting meat

Compound eye

Antenna

Tiny hairs and hooks on feet enable fly to walk on the ceiling.

Wing

MOSQUITO

The mosquito has needle-shaped mouthparts that pierce the skin to suck the blood of humans, horses, and other animals. If a female *Anopheles* mosquito bites a person with malaria, it takes in blood infected with the microscopic organisms that cause this disease. When the mosquito goes on to bite another victim, the organisms pass into that person's blood, and so the disease spreads. The map below shows those parts of the world where malaria is most severe.

North America

Asia

Africa

South America

Australia

Areas where malaria occurs

Malaria is one of the most serious and widespread diseases. It kills about one million people each year.

FLIES AND DISEASE

Houseflies, bluebottles, and similar flies feed and lay their eggs in rotting matter, including rubbish and excrement. Their mouthparts and feet become infected with bacteria, or germs, which rub off when they walk over our food, dishes, and kitchen equipment. The illnesses which spread in this way range from minor stomach upsets to deadly infections such as typhoid.

Hoverfly's wing tips make a figure of eight pattern with each wing beat.

HOVERFLY

The hoverfly is one of the most expert fliers. It can hover perfectly still, even in a wind, then dart straight up, down, sideways, or backwards. Tiny ball-and-stick structures behind the wings called halteres rotate rapidly and act as stabilizers during flight.

LIFE CYCLE OF A FLY

The drone fly is a kind of hoverfly. It resembles a bee in appearance and makes a low droning sound in flight. After mating, the female lays her eggs near a puddle, a polluted pond, or other stagnant (non-moving) water. The larvae, known as rat-tailed maggots, live in the water, breathing through the long tail which acts like a snorkel. The rat-tailed maggots wriggle to drier soil before changing into pupae. When the adults emerge from the pupal cases, they fly off to feed on pollen and nectar from flowers.

Female drone fly lays eggs near water in a drain.

Adult fly emerges 4-6 weeks after eggs are laid.

Rat-tailed maggots (larvae) feed on rotting and decaying plant and animal matter in the drain.

Maggots (larvae) crawl out of water and change into pupae (pupate).

Find out more
ANIMALS
DISEASE
FLIGHT IN ANIMALS
INSECTS

FLIGHT IN ANIMALS

BIRDS, BATS, AND INSECTS are the only animals that truly fly. Other animals, such as flying squirrels, flying fish, and flying lizards, swoop or glide but cannot climb upwards into the air under their own power. Life in the air has several advantages for flying animals – some birds, such as hawks, can hunt their prey in midair; other birds can quickly escape from predators. Birds are also able to migrate very long distances to find more suitable feeding areas in a cold season – the Arctic tern, for example, migrates about 18,000 km (11,000 miles) from the North Pole to the South Pole each year. Another bird, the swift, spends much of its life in the air, landing only to nest. A swift eats and drinks on the wing for nine months of the year. Birds, bats, and insects are also able to find food on land quickly and efficiently – a hummingbird hovers to gather nectar, a fruit bat flies into a tree to feed on fruit, and a dragonfly swoops over a pond to catch small flies. All flying animals from bees to buzzards need plenty of food to provide them with the energy to take to the air.

Animals first began to fly about 300 million years ago, when Earth's prehistoric coal swamps were becoming overcrowded with all kinds of creatures. Through evolution, special features began to develop, such as a flap of skin on the body for gliding. In order to fly, an animal needs a lightweight body and strong muscles with which to flap its wings. Birds have hollow bones to save weight when they are in flight, so that a huge bird such as the golden eagle weighs less than 4 kg (9 lb).

ARCHAEOPTERYX
The first bird known to have existed is called *Archaeopteryx*. Prehistoric remains date back 150 million years. *Archaeopteryx* could glide and fly through the air.

Elastic fibres allow the wings to shrink so the bat can fold them neatly.

WINGS

The wings of a flying animal are light so that they can be flapped easily. They are broad and flat, to push the air downwards and give lift. Wings must also be flexible for control in the air. An insect's wings are made of a thin membrane stiffened by tube-like veins. A bird's wings have bones and muscles at the front; feathers form the rest of the surface. A bat's wings consist of a thin layer of muscles and tough fibres sandwiched between two layers of skin that are supported by bones.

Flight feathers are light and stiff with strong shafts and large, smooth vanes.

Primary flight feathers help to reduce turbulence.

Feathers near the wing root shape the wing smoothly into the body.

Covert feathers are at the front of the wing. They are small and packed closely together, to give a smooth edge.

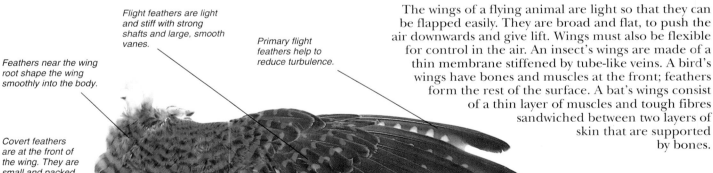

Wing of a kestrel

HOVERING

Only a few kinds of animals can hover. Staying still in midair requires great control and delicate balance as the animal adjusts its wingbeats to the slightest breeze. A few animals, such as some moths, hover as they gather food. Hummingbirds also hover expertly to feed. As they sip nectar from flowers, hummingbirds hover, go straight up and down, and fly backwards – just like helicopters. Hummingbirds beat their wings 20 to 50 times per second; this produces the humming sounds.

Hummingbird in flight

SOOTY TERN
The sooty tern lives on the wing for up to 10 years. It returns to the ground only to breed.

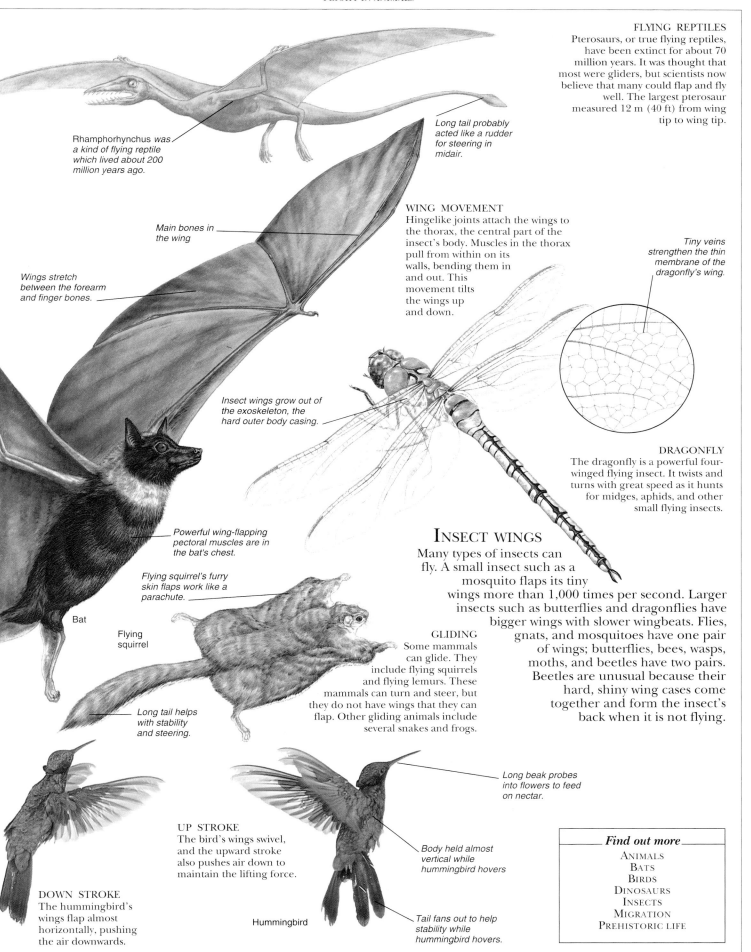

Pterosaurs, or true flying reptiles, have been extinct for about 70 million years. It was thought that most were gliders, but scientists now believe that many could flap and fly well. The largest pterosaur measured 12 m (40 ft) from wing tip to wing tip.

Rhamphorhynchus *was a kind of flying reptile which lived about 200 million years ago.*

Long tail probably acted like a rudder for steering in midair.

WING MOVEMENT
Hingelike joints attach the wings to the thorax, the central part of the insect's body. Muscles in the thorax pull from within on its walls, bending them in and out. This movement tilts the wings up and down.

Main bones in the wing

Wings stretch between the forearm and finger bones.

Tiny veins strengthen the thin membrane of the dragonfly's wing.

Insect wings grow out of the exoskeleton, the hard outer body casing.

DRAGONFLY
The dragonfly is a powerful four-winged flying insect. It twists and turns with great speed as it hunts for midges, aphids, and other small flying insects.

Powerful wing-flapping pectoral muscles are in the bat's chest.

INSECT WINGS
Many types of insects can fly. A small insect such as a mosquito flaps its tiny wings more than 1,000 times per second. Larger insects such as butterflies and dragonflies have bigger wings with slower wingbeats. Flies, gnats, and mosquitoes have one pair of wings; butterflies, bees, wasps, moths, and beetles have two pairs. Beetles are unusual because their hard, shiny wing cases come together and form the insect's back when it is not flying.

Flying squirrel's furry skin flaps work like a parachute.

Bat

Flying squirrel

GLIDING
Some mammals can glide. They include flying squirrels and flying lemurs. These mammals can turn and steer, but they do not have wings that they can flap. Other gliding animals include several snakes and frogs.

Long tail helps with stability and steering.

Long beak probes into flowers to feed on nectar.

UP STROKE
The bird's wings swivel, and the upward stroke also pushes air down to maintain the lifting force.

Body held almost vertical while hummingbird hovers

DOWN STROKE
The hummingbird's wings flap almost horizontally, pushing the air downwards.

Hummingbird

Tail fans out to help stability while hummingbird hovers.

Find out more
ANIMALS
BATS
BIRDS
DINOSAURS
INSECTS
MIGRATION
PREHISTORIC LIFE

FLOWERS AND HERBS

THE EXQUISITE BEAUTY, COLOUR, and perfume of flowers have inspired artists and poets for centuries. Flowers are among the most brightly coloured of all living things. They include sun-loving desert marigolds, hardy poppies in the snowy Arctic, tropical orchids, and cultivated garden roses, as well as some tiny inconspicuous flowers. Without the thousands of different flowers and herbs that exist, bees could not make honey, butterflies and hummingbirds would have no food, we would have no flowerbeds, and perfume would have no fragrance. For most of us, the word "flower" describes any flowering plant that is particularly colourful or pretty. To the botanist, however, who studies plants, a flower refers strictly to the reproductive part of a plant – its bloom or blossom. The word "herb" is an everyday name we give to smaller, less colourful flowering plants whose leaves and blossoms have a strong, pleasant scent and taste.

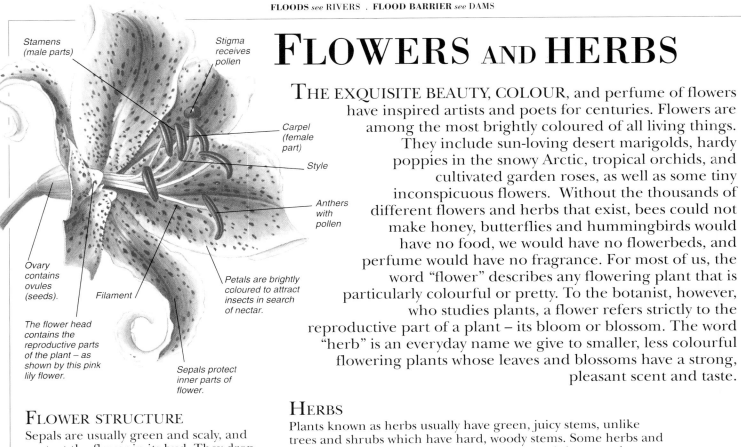

Stamens (male parts)

Stigma receives pollen

Carpel (female part)

Style

Anthers with pollen

Ovary contains ovules (seeds).

Filament

The flower head contains the reproductive parts of the plant – as shown by this pink lily flower.

Petals are brightly coloured to attract insects in search of nectar.

Sepals protect inner parts of flower.

FLOWER STRUCTURE

Sepals are usually green and scaly, and protect the flower in its bud. They drop off once the flower has blossomed. Petals may be large and colourful to attract bees and butterflies. The male cells lie in the pollen grains, contained in the anthers. The female cells are inside the ovary, below the style.

HERBS

Plants known as herbs usually have green, juicy stems, unlike trees and shrubs which have hard, woody stems. Some herbs and other flowering plants are described as annuals because they grow, flower, produce seeds, and die all in one year. Others are known as biennials because their life cycle takes two years; perennials live for an indefinite number of years.

HERB GARDEN
Tending the herb garden was once an important part of daily life because people relied on natural products which they grew themselves. Herbs are used to add flavour to food, scent the air, help us relax, and treat illnesses. Many of our modern medicines contain herbs; peppermint, for example, is used in many anti-indigestion pills. Herbal oils, known as essential oils, are extracted from herbs and used in the production of perfume and bath oils.

Thyme is a fragrant addition to meats, as a garnish, and for mouth, throat, and chest illnesses.

Basil is popular in Mediterranean cooking and is also used as an insect repellent.

Parsley is a garnish, an ingredient in sauces, and a treatment for urinary illness.

Sage flavours many dishes, from pork to poultry, and is used to treat sore throats and colds.

Rosemary is a companion to lamb dishes, and brewed in tea for headaches and upset stomachs.

Bay adds flavour to casseroles and stocks.

Oregano (wild marjoram) is used for meat, stuffing, and pizza, and to aid digestion.

Tarragon is often used in French cooking.

Mint is used to make tea and mint jelly; it also clears a stuffy nose and eases indigestion.

POLLINATION

To produce a seed, the male cell in a pollen grain must fertilize a female cell in the ovule. For this to happen the pollen must travel from its anther to the female stigma. In some flowers, the pollen is small and light, with wings, and is blown from one flower to another by the wind.

Wild dog rose

Cultivated tea rose

HORTICULTURE

From the beginnings of civilization, people have cultivated flowers for their scent and colour. Today's garden roses have been bred from wild ancestors so that they have larger, more numerous, and more colourful petals, sweeter scents, and a longer flowering time. The art of gardening is called horticulture.

BEES AND FLOWERS

Bees help pollination. As a bee feeds on nectar and pollen, more pollen inside the flower sticks to the bee's legs and body and is carried by the bee to the next flower, where it pollinates the female parts.

NECTAR

Butterflies, moths, bats, and birds feed on the sweet, energy-rich nectar inside each flower. Bees convert nectar into honey in the beehive.

BIRD-OF-PARADISE FLOWER

The bird-of-paradise plant comes originally from riverbanks in southern Africa and is now grown in many parks and gardens. Each plant has brilliant orange flowers which form a shape that looks like the head and beak of a bird of paradise. The bird-of-paradise flowers rise one after the other from a long, stiff, green-pink casing.

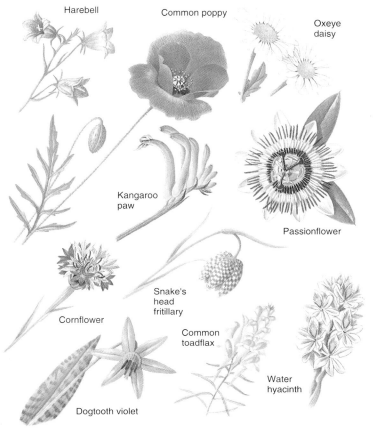

Harebell

Common poppy

Oxeye daisy

Kangaroo paw

Passionflower

Cornflower

Snake's head fritillary

Common toadflax

Water hyacinth

Dogtooth violet

PERFUME

A flower's smell attracts butterflies, bees, and people too. Lily of the valley and rose are used in the manufacture of perfumes and soaps.

Lily of the valley flowers have a sweet scent. Their leaves are scented too.

WILD FLOWERS AND CONSERVATION

Many wild flowers are in danger of extinction. Marshes are drained, and forests are felled for farmland and buildings, so the flowers that grow there are destroyed. Rare and beautiful blooms are at risk because they are dug up illegally by plant collectors. To save rare flowers, the places where they grow must be protected. As forests are cut down, thousands of flowers are disappearing even before they are known to science.

Find out more

BEES AND WASPS
CONSERVATION
and endangered species
FRUITS AND SEEDS
PLANTS

FOOD

ALL LIVING THINGS need food; it is the basic fuel of life. It keeps us warm, gives us energy, and helps us grow. Our daily pattern of eating and drinking is called our diet. Diets vary across the world according to the availability of food. Humans can digest a wide range of foods from both plant and animal sources, but some people, called vegetarians, choose not to eat meat for health, religious, or other reasons. Lack of the right kinds of food can lead to disease, inadequate growth, and eventually starvation. Eating too much of the wrong kinds of food can cause heart disease and other illnesses.

Fruit and vegetable market

FOOD PRESERVATION
Food goes bad because of bacteria (harmful organisms) which can grow in it. Bacteria cannot thrive in salted, smoked, frozen, high-acid, or high-sugar foods. Tinned food has all the air drawn out and is heat-treated to stop decay from within. Irradiating foods with gamma rays to kill bacteria is the most modern method of preservation, but some doubt its safety.

NUTRITION
A balanced diet is one that provides everything the body needs for health and growth. Energy-giving foods contain carbohydrates and fats, which are burned up slowly by the body. Energy in food is measured in calories. A 10-year-old needs about 2,000 calories a day. Body-building food is called protein and comes mainly from meat, fish, milk, eggs, nuts, and cereals. Vitamins are necessary to keep skin and eyes healthy and blood vessels strong. Water helps dissolve and digest food. Small quantities of minerals are needed for growth: calcium helps keep teeth strong, and iron is necessary for healthy blood. Fibre in food cannot be digested, but it enables our intestines to grip the food as it passes through.

FAMINE AND PLENTY
The world's farms produce enough to feed everyone, but food does not reach the hungry. Western nations have surplus food, yet elsewhere 40 million people starve each year.

Pasta and rice are basic or "staple" foods and provide bulk, energy, and protein. Grains, cereals, and legumes such as peas and beans are also staple foods. Their use varies from country to country.

Poultry and meat provide protein for body building and fat for energy.

REGIONAL FOOD
Food varies across the world according to climate, local customs, and religious beliefs. French cooks gather snails, and near coastlines the sea provides seaweed – a source of free green vegetables. The diet of some Aboriginal Australians and Africans includes insects and grubs.

Nuts are a good source of protein and fat.

Fungi provide small amounts of fibre and minerals.

Fruits and vegetables provide vitamins, fibre, and natural sugar. Some vegetables such as potatoes provide carbohydrates for energy.

Eggs and milk products provide a great deal of fat. They are also high in protein, vitamins, and minerals.

Fish and shellfish are rich in body-building protein, minerals, and vitamins.

Find out more

COOKING
FARMING
FISHING INDUSTRY
HEALTH
SHOPS AND SHOPPING

FOOD AND DIGESTION

HUMANS MUST EAT TO LIVE. The body needs food to work properly and to grow and repair itself. Food contains water and five vital nutrients – proteins, carbohydrates, fats, vitamins, and minerals. For food to be useful, the body has to break it down, or digest it, and combine it with oxygen. The digestive system consists of a long tube called the alimentary canal which runs from the mouth to the anus. Each part does a particular job. The stomach is like a bag where chewed food is mixed with acids and digestive juices. The small intestine pushes the food along by a squeezing action called peristalsis. The tiny particles of digested food pass easily through the walls of the small intestine and into the bloodstream, to be used by the body. The large intestine absorbs water from the food and turns the waste products into semi-solid lumps called faeces.

DIGESTION

Digestion begins in the mouth, as teeth crush the food. Watery saliva moistens the food and makes it easy to chew and swallow. The muscular walls of the stomach churn the food into a soup-like liquid and mix it with powerful digestive juices. The broken-down nutrients are small enough to seep through the lining of the small intestine and into the blood vessels in its wall.

Teeth chew, crunch, and grind food into a pulp.

Tongue tastes different flavours.

Salivary glands produce a watery liquid to mix with food and help with swallowing.

Oesophagus pushes swallowed food down through the chest, behind the windpipe and heart, into the stomach.

Stomach is where muscles crush food into a pulp and mix it with digestive juices.

Small intestine absorbs digested food into the body.

Large intestine absorbs water from undigested pieces of food.

Rectum is the last part of the large intestine.

Liver

EATING FOOD
When you swallow food, it enters your throat. A flap called the epiglottis folds over the entrance to the windpipe so that food goes into the oesophagus and not into the lungs, where it could cause choking.

LIVER
The liver is the body's "chemical factory". It receives digested nutrients from the intestines and converts them into more easily used forms, such as glucose (blood sugar) for muscle fuel.

SMALL INTESTINE
The small intestine is coiled into the lower part of the body. It is very long, measuring about 6 m (20 ft) in length. Its lining has many folds and ridges, so that it can absorb as many nutrients as possible.

Pancreas produces digestive juices.

LARGE INTESTINE
The large intestine is much shorter than the small intestine, but three times as wide, measuring up to 7 cm (2.5 in) in width.

Anus is where waste products leave the body as faeces.

STOMACH
This J-shaped bag is lined with a thick layer of slimy mucus. Tiny glands in the lining produce strong digestive juices, which contain substances such as enzymes and acids.

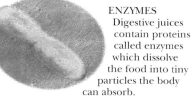

Bitter

Sour

Salty

Sweet

TONGUE
The tongue is a flexible muscle. On its surface are tiny nodules called taste buds which sense different flavours. The tip of the tongue can taste sweet flavours, the part behind the tip tastes salty flavours, the sides taste sour flavours, and the back tastes bitter flavours.

VILLI
Each fold of the lining of the small intestine has thousands of microscopic finger-shaped projections called villi. The villi allow the small intestine to absorb more nutrients.

ENZYMES
Digestive juices contain proteins called enzymes which dissolve the food into tiny particles the body can absorb.

Find out more
FOOD
HEALTH
HUMAN BODY
MUSCLES AND MOVEMENT

FOOTBALL

AT PACKED STADIUMS in almost every country, football fans cheer the teamwork and individual skills of their favourite players. Association football is the most popular spectator sport in the world, and more people actually play football themselves than any other team sport. More than 169 countries play association football, or soccer, at the international level. Other forms of football are equally popular, but less widespread. Soccer is played with a round ball, but in the United States football is played with an oval ball. It is now the top U.S. spectator sport, with professional and college-level games drawing huge crowds. Some European countries have also taken up the game, and the Canadians play a similar sport. Rugby football players, who also use an oval ball, compete mainly in Britain, France, Australia, Italy, New Zealand, and South Africa. Other varieties of football include Gaelic football, played in Ireland, and Australian Rules football, which is very popular in the city of Melbourne.

ANCIENT FOOTBALL
Mob football was the ancestor of modern football. It was a violent game played in England, with few rules, and was banned in the 14th century.

FOOTBALL

In American football, players aim to advance the ball across their opponents' goal line to score a touchdown, which counts six points. Each team has 11 players, selected from a squad of up to 45.

American football

SOCCER
In soccer, the most popular form of football, two teams of 11 aim to send the ball into the opposing goal with their feet and head. Only one team player, the goalkeeper, is allowed to touch the ball with his or her hands.

American football

FOOTBALL GROUNDS
The American football field is 100 yards (90 m) long and 160 ft (48 m) wide. The overall dimensions of the other types of football fields may vary, but the goal lines and internal markings are standard.

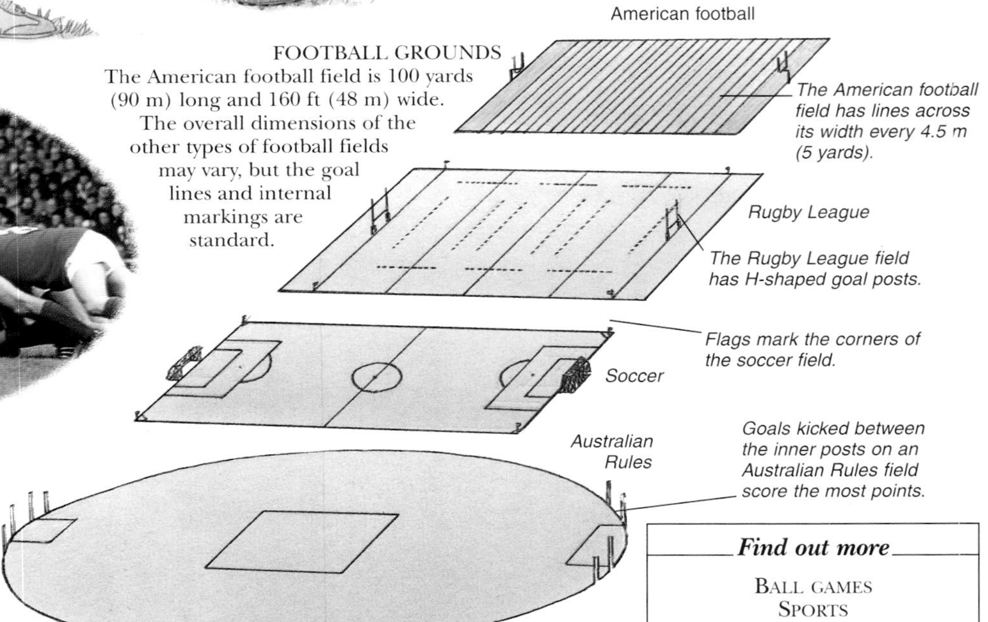

The American football field has lines across its width every 4.5 m (5 yards).

Rugby League

The Rugby League field has H-shaped goal posts.

Flags mark the corners of the soccer field.

Soccer

Australian Rules

Goals kicked between the inner posts on an Australian Rules field score the most points.

RUGBY SCRUM
In rugby, teams sometimes battle for possession of the ball in the "scrum." In the Rugby Union scrum, the eight forward players of each team bend forward and put their arms around their opponents. Then they use their feet to pass the ball to players outside the scrum.

Find out more

BALL GAMES
SPORTS

FORCE AND MOTION

WHAT IS IT THAT makes objects move? Why does a boat float? How does a magnet work? Left to itself, any object would remain still, but when it is pushed or pulled it begins to move. Something that pushes or pulls is called a force. Forces often produce motion, or movement. For example, an engine produces a force that pushes a car forward. There are several different kinds of forces. A magnet produces a magnetic force which pulls pieces of iron towards it, and a rubber band produces an elastic force when you stretch it. Liquids produce forces too. A boat floats because of the force of water pushing upwards on the hull. And a drop of water holds together because of a force called surface tension which makes all liquids seem as though they have an elastic skin around them. From the smallest particle inside an atom to the largest galaxy, the whole universe is held together by powerful forces. One of these forces is gravity, which holds us onto the surface of the Earth.

CENTRIFUGAL FORCE

Moving in a circle, as in a fairground ride, causes you to swing outwards away from the centre of the circle. It feels as though a force is pushing you. In fact, this force, called centrifugal force, is an illusion. You feel as though you are pushed outwards because your body is trying to move straight ahead rather than in a circle.

ACCELERATION

The action of a force produces motion, making an object accelerate (speed up). For example, the force produced by the engine makes a ship accelerate. The stronger the force, the greater the acceleration.

A small boat accelerates quickly and soon reaches constant speed. This is because water and air resist motion, producing a force called drag. Drag increases as speed increases. When drag force balances the driving force of the engines, speed stays constant.

ACTION AND REACTION

A rowing boat moves by action and reaction. The force of the oars pushing on the water is the action. The moving water exerts an equal and opposite reaction on the oars. This reaction force pushes the boat forward.

INERTIA

It takes a strong force to start a heavy object moving. In the same way, a strong force is needed to make it slow down and stop. This reluctance to start or stop moving is called inertia. The heavier the object, the greater its inertia.

NEWTON'S LAWS OF MOTION

In 1687, the English scientist Isaac Newton (1642-1727) published his three laws of motion. The first law explains that an object stays at rest or moves at a constant speed unless a force pushes or pulls it. The second law explains how force overcomes inertia and causes acceleration. The third law explains that when a force (or action) pushes one way, an equal force (or reaction) always pushes in the opposite direction.

In an arch bridge, the piers (ends of the bridge) support the weight of the arch.

FRICTION

When two surfaces rub against each other, they produce a force called friction that opposes motion. For example, brakes use friction to slow a wheel down. Friction produces heat and wastes energy. Putting a layer of oil between the moving parts of a machine reduces friction and improves efficiency.

STATIC FORCES

When two teams in a tug of war pull equally hard on the rope, neither team moves. This is because the forces produced by the teams balance exactly. Forces that balance and produce no movement are called static forces. A bridge stays up because of the balance of static forces. Its weight pushing down is balanced by parts of the structure pushing up.

Find out more

ATOMS AND MOLECULES
BRIDGES
GRAVITY
MAGNETISM
PHYSICS

FOREST WILDLIFE

This map shows the main forest areas of the world.

North America
Asia
Africa
South America
Australia

■ Tropical
■ Broad-leaved
■ Coniferous

TREES ARE THE most important inhabitants of a forest. They provide all kinds of animals, including monkeys, squirrels, and parrots, with food, homes, and escape routes from predators. The most common tree in any kind of forest often gives the forest its name, from the pine forests in the cold north, to the steamy teak forests in the tropical regions.

A forest consists of different layers of vegetation. The forest floor is covered with leaf litter. Here parts of trees and other plants rot into the soil, helped by the millipedes, worms, and other small creatures that feed on them. The next layer of the forest is called the herb layer. It consists of small flowers and ferns that grow wherever enough sunlight filters through the trees. Bushes, shrubs, and young trees make up the understory of the forest. Next is a layer of tall tree trunks, laced with trailing vines and creepers. The uppermost part of the forest is called the canopy. Leaves grow in the sunlight, insects, birds, and bats pollinate the flowers, and fruit ripens to feed a host of creatures.

LONG-EARED OWL
The long-eared owl swoops silently among the trees at twilight and during the night. These owls roost by day in a tree, and their mottled brown plumage provides good camouflage. The tufts on the feathers on this owl's head look like long ears – hence the name.

WOLVERINE
The wolverine of northern forests is an exceptionally strong animal for its size. It tackles animal prey much larger than itself and also eats carrion (dead animals), fruits, and berries. The wolverine is nicknamed the glutton because of its large appetite.

Woodchuck

WOODCHUCK
The North American woodchuck, also called the groundhog, belongs to the squirrel family and hibernates (rests and sleeps) during winter. Woodchucks search for seeds, roots, bulbs, and other plant matter on the forest floor, as well as insects, snails, and worms.

CONIFEROUS FORESTS
Pines and firs make up coniferous forests. These trees are evergreen – they keep their leaves all year, providing shelter for animals. The leaves are very tough, and only a few animals can eat and digest them. A few types of conifer, such as the larches, lose their leaves in autumn.

ROE DEER
The roe deer's reddish brown coat blends in well with the bracken where it lives. It lives alone for most of the year, feeding at twilight on the buds, shoots, and leaves of trees and shrubs.

Ferns such as bracken grow quickly and rapidly cover clearings. Bracken is common on every continent except Antarctica. It spreads by sending out branching underground stems.

BROAD-LEAVED FORESTS
The trees in a broad-leaved forest are called deciduous trees because their leaves drop off in the autumn, to be replaced by new leaves the next year. These trees blossom in the spring, which is the main animal breeding time. The new shoots provide food for animals. In the autumn, animals feed on the fruits, nuts, and berries of these trees, so they can survive the winter.

Bluebells are one of the spring woodland flowers. They grow from bulbs underground. Some bluebells have pink flowers; others have white ones.

Wood anemone

Several heavy-bodied, strong-legged birds live in the forest, including pheasants such as the blue peacock shown here. These birds can fly, but they often avoid danger by running into the dense forest undergrowth.

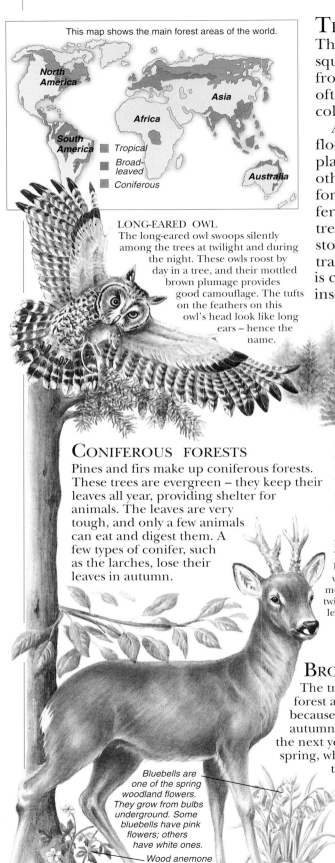

CONSERVATION

As the forests are cut down or burned, animals lose their homes. Tree-living creatures such as this American uakari monkey are most at risk. These monkeys depend on the flowers and fruits from the large old trees in rain forests. Worldwide conservation organizations are trying to stop the destruction of the rain forests in order to save monkeys and thousands of other creatures.

TANAGER

The paradise tanager is a noisy, active bird that lives high up in the rain forest canopy. Paradise tanagers keep their bright plumage all year and flutter from tree to tree in search of insects and ripe fruit.

TROPICAL FORESTS

In the tropics, there are wet and dry seasons, rather than summer and winter. Warm temperatures and heavy rainfall make tropical rain forests some of the richest places for wildlife. There are many more species of trees than in any other kind of forest, and thousands more kinds of animals.

SLOTH

Few animals move more slowly than the sloths of Central and South America. They hang from branches with their curved claws, eat leaves, and move so slowly that tiny green simple plants called algae grow on their coats. The algae help camouflage the sloths among the trees.

PARROT

The male and female eclectus parrots shown here are so differently coloured that for many years people believed they were two different species of birds. These parrots live in the forests of New Guinea and Australia. Like all parrots, they have huge bills for cracking seeds.

TOUCAN

With its large, light bill, the toucan is an excellent berry picker. Its bright colours help it advertise for a mate in the breeding season. There are 42 kinds of toucans, and they are all found in tropical South America. Toucans nest in tree holes and eat birds' eggs and nestlings, fruits, insects, frogs, and lizards.

Several kinds of frogs, lizards, snakes, and squirrels have evolved, or developed, ways of gliding through the air from a high branch to escape from predators or to reach food. The gliding snake flattens its ribs as it leaps, to make a streamlined ribbon shape.

Atlas moth resting on a bromeliad flower

ARROW-POISON FROG

It is so damp in rain forests that frogs spend their lives in the trees and do not need to find water elsewhere. Frogs lay their eggs, or spawn, in pools of rain which collect on leaves, fungi, and in flowers such as bromeliads, which grow on trees. Arrow-poison frogs live in the rain forests of South America. Their bright colours warn predators of the deadly poison in their skin.

ATLAS MOTH

The atlas moth is one of the largest moths in the world, with a wingspan of 30 cm (12 in). Today atlas moths are rare. In the past people killed thousands of them simply for their butterfly collections.

LEMUR

There are 22 different kinds of lemurs. These mammals are related to monkeys, and they live in trees in Madagascar, an island off the east coast of Africa. Mouse lemurs weigh only 60 gm (2 oz).

Ground ginger is a spice made from the root of the ginger plant, which came originally from the forests of Asia.

Leaf roller ants curl up leaves on the forest floor and join the edges into a tube to make a nesting site.

___ ***Find out more*** ___

BIRDS
BUTTERFLIES AND MOTHS
CONSERVATION
and endangered species
FROGS AND OTHER AMPHIBIANS
OWLS

FOSSILS

THE FIRST PLANTS, the earliest animals, the beginnings of human life – we know about prehistoric times because of fossils. Fossils are the remains of dead animals and plants that have been preserved for thousands or millions of years. A fossil might be the tooth of a dinosaur embedded in rock, or the outline of a leaf on a stone. By studying fossils, we can learn what ancient creatures and plants looked like and how they lived. Most fossils are of plants and animals that lived in water. When the living plant or animal died, its soft parts rotted away, leaving the hard pieces such as bones or leaf veins. Gradually layers of mud piled up and squeezed the remains of the plant or animal at great pressure. Slowly the mud, bones, and other remains fossilized, or turned to rock, in the place where they lay underground. Over many thousands of years, the movements of the Earth twisted and buckled the rocks, lifting the fossils closer to the surface of the soil. Sun, rain, and wind wore away the rocks and exposed the fossil.

AMMONITE
Some of the most common fossils are the shells of sea creatures called ammonites. Ammonites were related to squid and octopuses. They were very widespread about 250 million years ago. The smallest ammonites measured less than 2 cm (1 in) across; the largest measured about 2.5 m (8 ft) across. Ammonites died out with the dinosaurs about 65 million years ago.

Fossil collecting is a hobby that anyone can enjoy. You can find fossils in rocks, on beaches, and in quarries.

Fossil of a fish called Sparnodus – an ancestor of the sea bream

Fin on back for steering and stability

Backbone

Powerful two-lobed tail

Long jaws and short, sharp teeth

Large eye socket

Ribs

Front paddle for steering

Rear paddle

TYPES OF FOSSILS
When rock-forming minerals slowly replace the original parts of a dead creature or plant, they make a mineralized fossil. Sometimes the parts of a creature or plant rot away after being buried, leaving a hole in the rock; this is called a mould fossil. If the hole fills up with rock minerals, it becomes a cast fossil. The fossilized signs of animals, such as footprints, droppings, and tracks, are called trace fossils.

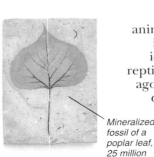

Mineralized fossil of a poplar leaf, 25 million years old

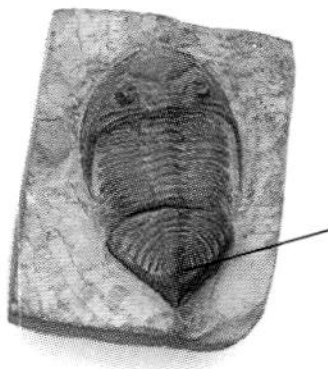

Cast fossil of a creature called a trilobite, which lived in the sea

ICHTHYOSAUR
Sometimes the outline of an animal's skin is preserved as well as its bones. This happened to the ichthyosaur shown above – a sea reptile from about 150 million years ago. The ichthyosaur looked like a dolphin, so it probably led a life similar to that of dolphins.
The outline of this fossil shows a fin on the back and a two-lobed tail. The dozens of sharp teeth in the long jaws tell us that this animal grabbed fish and other slippery prey.

The word *fossil* means "dug up". People who study fossils are called palaeontologists.

> ### Find out more
> DINOSAURS
> EVOLUTION
> PREHISTORIC LIFE
> ROCKS AND MINERALS

FRANCE

THE LARGEST COUNTRY in western Europe is France – a land of green, open spaces dotted with picturesque towns and small cities. Its many fine old country palaces, or chateaux, are reminders of France's long history. But it is a modern nation, too, with flourishing industries. France is also one of the leading countries in the European Union (EU), the organization that promotes political and economic union between the member states.

Northern France has cool, wet weather. The south, with its Mediterranean coast, is drier and warmer. Rolling hills rise from the coasts and valleys, providing good farmland. The rugged hills of the Massif Central occupy the middle of the country. The mountains of the Pyrenees and the Alps line the southwest and eastern borders. France also includes the Mediterranean island of Corsica, and some islands thousands of kilometres away in the Pacific Ocean and the Caribbean Sea. A democratically elected government and president rule France from Paris.

France shares its long eastern border with Italy, Switzerland, Germany, Luxembourg, and Belgium. Spain is to the south. The south of France lies on the Mediterranean Sea coast, and the Atlantic Ocean is to the west.

Workers on small, family-run estates may still pick grapes by hand. Many people spend their holidays grapepicking, but it is hard work.

Even the smaller winemakers now use some modern equipment, such as stainless-steel fermentation vats.

WINE MAKING

France produces about a fifth of the world's wine. Many famous wines are named after French regions, such as Champagne and Bordeaux. Most French wine comes from co-operatives – local groups of farms that share wine-producing and bottling facilities. Some wine, however, is still made on the small estates attached to the old chateaux. The grapes are picked in the early autumn. Pressing the grapes extracts the juice, which then ferments (reacts with yeast) in large vats to produce the alcohol and the delicious taste of the wine. Only when this process is complete can the wine be bottled.

The Louvre, in Paris, is one of the world's most famous art galleries. The glass pyramids were added in 1989.

MARSEILLES

France's biggest seaport is Marseilles, on the Mediterranean coast. The warm climate of southern France makes possible the lively, outdoor lifestyle of the city. There is a long history of trade with the rest of the Mediterranean. Marseilles has a large Arab population, mainly from North Africa.

PARIS

People have lived on the River Seine where Paris now stands since ancient times. Paris is the capital of France. France has a population of over 57 million; one fifth live in and around Paris. It is one of Europe's great cities, with wide, tree-lined streets called boulevards, and many famous monuments and museums. The city of today was largely replanned and rebuilt during the 19th century.

FRANCE

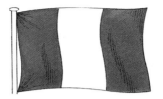

STATISTICS
Area: 551,500 sq km (212,936 sq miles)
Population: 57,400,000
Capital: Paris
Language: French
Religion: Roman Catholic
Currency: French franc
Main occupations: Manufacturing, farming
Main exports: Machinery, vehicles, farm products
Main imports: Machinery, petroleum, iron, steel

NORMANDY
The region of Normandy lies between Paris and the English Channel. Normandy is a farming area, known throughout France for its dairy products and its apples. By grazing their cattle in the orchards, many local farmers get double use from the land. They sell the apples as dessert fruit, or turn them into cider and a delicious apple brandy called calvados. Cream from the Normandy cattle makes some of France's most famous cheeses, including Brie and Camembert.

RIVER LOIRE
The valley of the River Loire is famous for its beautiful castles, called châteaux, such as this one at Gien. Kings, nobles, or wealthy landowners built the châteaux as their homes. They often chose a site on high ground and surrounded the château with a moat, which made it easy to defend the château from attackers. The Loire valley is also an important wine-producing area.

ENGLISH CHANNEL

CHANNEL ISLANDS (UK)

• Cherbourg
Le Havre •
• Caen
Normandy

• Brest
Brittany
• Saint-Malo
Saint-Brieuc

• Rennes
Laval •
Le Mans •

• Lorient
Carnac 𝖎𝖎𝖎

BELLE-ILE

• St-Nazaire
• Nantes
Rezé •
• Angers
R. Loire
Tou
R. Vier
• Cholet
La Roche-sur-Yon •
Poitou
Châtellerault •

N
W — E
S

Poitiers •
• Niort

ILE DE RÉ

• La Rochelle
ILE D'OLÉRON
• Rochefort

0 ————— 100 miles
0 ————— 150 km

• Saintes
Angoulê •

BAY OF BISCAY

Périgueu

Mérignac •
Bordeaux • B•
Pessac • Talence •

Landes
R. Garonne

•Mont-de-Marsan

Bayonne •
Biarritz •
• Pau

• Lourdes
Pyrenees

SPAIN

226

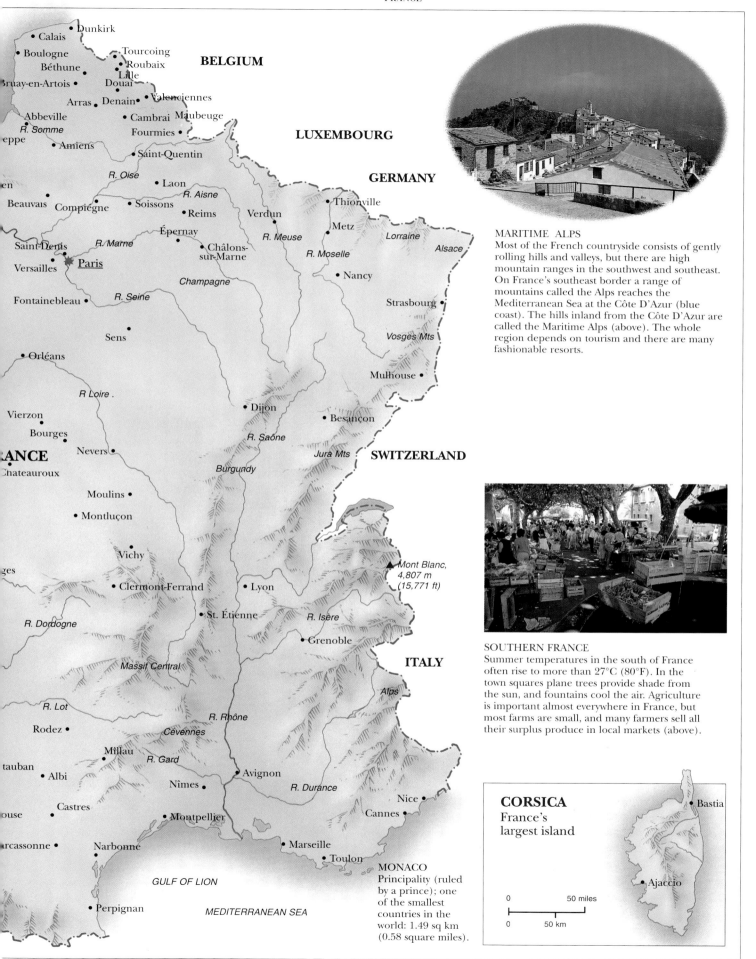

BELGIUM

LUXEMBOURG

GERMANY

Dunkirk
• Calais
• Boulogne
Béthune
Tourcoing
• Roubaix
Lille
Bruay-en-Artois •
Douai
Arras • Denain • Valenciennes
Abbeville • Cambrai Maubeuge
R. Somme
Fourmies •
eppe
• Amiens
Saint-Quentin •
R. Oise
• Laon
R. Aisne
en
• Soissons
• Reims
Verdun •
Beauvais Compiégne
• Thionville
• Metz
Lorraine
Épernay
R. Meuse
Saint-Denis R. Marne
Châlons-
sur-Marne
R. Moselle
Alsace
Versailles • Paris
• Nancy
Champagne
Fontainebleau •
R. Seine
Strasbourg •
Sens •
Vosges Mts
• Orléans
Mulhouse •
Vierzon •
R Loire .
• Dijon
Bourges •
• Besançon
ANCE
Nevers •
R. Saône
Jura Mts
SWITZERLAND
Chateauroux
Burgundy
Moulins •
• Montluçon
Vichy •
Mont Blanc,
4,807 m
(15,771 ft)
• Clermont-Ferrand
• Lyon
R. Dordogne
• St. Étienne
R. Isère
Massif Central
• Grenoble
ITALY
R. Lot
Alps
Rodez •
R. Rhône
Cévennes
tauban
Millau •
R. Gard
• Albi
Nîmes •
Avignon •
Nice •
Castres •
R. Durance
Cannes •
ouse
• Montpellier
arcassonne •
Narbonne •
• Marseille
• Toulon
GULF OF LION
• Perpignan
MEDITERRANEAN SEA

MARITIME ALPS
Most of the French countryside consists of gently
rolling hills and valleys, but there are high
mountain ranges in the southwest and southeast.
On France's southeast border a range of
mountains called the Alps reaches the
Mediterranean Sea at the Côte D'Azur (blue
coast). The hills inland from the Côte D'Azur are
called the Maritime Alps (above). The whole
region depends on tourism and there are many
fashionable resorts.

SOUTHERN FRANCE
Summer temperatures in the south of France
often rise to more than 27°C (80°F). In the
town squares plane trees provide shade from
the sun, and fountains cool the air. Agriculture
is important almost everywhere in France, but
most farms are small, and many farmers sell all
their surplus produce in local markets (above).

MONACO
Principality (ruled
by a prince); one
of the smallest
countries in the
world: 1.49 sq km
(0.58 square miles).

CORSICA
France's
largest island

• Bastia

0   50 miles

0   50 km

• Ajaccio

FOOD

French cooks are considered among the best in the world. There are numerous good restaurants, even in quite small towns, and the quality of ordinary daily food is very high. Food specialists who take great pride in their work produce outstanding cooked meats, pastries, and bread, including the famous stick-shaped baguette. French cheeses, such as Camembert, are eaten all over the world.

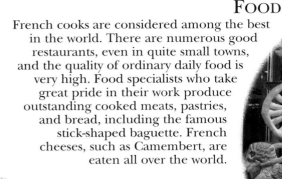

A patisserie specializes in sweet, delicious pastries, and produces a wide range for its customers every day.

TOUR DE FRANCE
Cycling is an enormously popular pastime in France. The world's most famous cycling race is the Tour de France (tour of France), which takes place every summer. The route follows ordinary – through closed roads, covering about 3,500 km (2,200 miles), primarily in France and Belgium, but briefly in four other countries. The race is done over 26 days, and the world's best cyclists take part.

In fine weather, café owners put tables and chairs out on the pavements so their customers can eat and drink in the open air.

The town square is the traditional spot for games such as boules or petanque, French versions of bowling.

The extract of scented flowers, such as lavender, is a major ingredient in perfume.

COUNTRY TOWNS

Much of France consists of open country where most working people earn a living from farming. One in every five French people lives and works in the countryside. The farming communities spread out around small market towns, which provide markets, banks, restaurants, and shops and supermarkets. Each town contains a *mairie*, the offices of the local government administration. The *mairie* often overlooks the central square, where people meet to talk and perhaps enjoy a game of *boules*.

PERFUME AND FASHION
Two of France's best-known industries are the manufacture of perfume and *haute couture,* or high fashion. Many of the most famous and most expensive brands of perfume are French. French designers have dominated fashion for most of this century. The Paris collections, shown in the spring of each year, are the most important of the international fashion shows and are attended by designers from all over the world. They set the trends which the rest of the world will follow.

CHARTRES
France is a mainly Roman Catholic country. There are churches in every village, and cathedrals in the cities. The cathedral of Chartres, in northern France, was completed in 1260. It is famous not only for its fine architecture but also for its magnificent stained-glass windows. There are 173 windows, covering a total area of 2,600 sq m (28,000 sq ft), the equivalent of 10 tennis courts.

Find out more

CHURCHES AND CATHEDRALS
EUROPE
FRANCE, HISTORY OF
FRENCH REVOLUTION
NORMANS

HISTORY OF
FRANCE

THE AREA OF EUROPE that we call France took its name from a tribe of warriors who conquered the region more than 1,000 years ago. The Franks ruled much of Europe for more than four centuries and were the first people to dominate all of France after the Roman Empire collapsed in A.D. 476. Frankish power was strongest under Charlemagne at the start of the ninth century, but ended in 895 when Vikings from Scandinavia settled in northern France. These Northmen, or Normans, as they became known, invaded England in 1066, establishing a link between these lands that was to last for 500 years. The English at one time dominated France, but by 1453 were driven out of everywhere except Calais. Over the next 300 years, the French kings gained immense power and set a pattern for other European royal families of the time. However, the monarchy became increasingly unpopular with the common people, and in 1789 King Louis XVI was overthrown in a revolution that shocked and inspired people all over the world. The French people abolished royal rule and instead chose to govern themselves. They set up the first of a series of republics that have made France one of the most powerful countries in the western Europe.

CARNAC

The ancient Stone Age inhabitants of France were highly developed. More than 7,500 years ago they built many long straight rows of standing stones at Carnac in Brittany. These stones were probably used in religious ceremonies.

ROMAN ENGINEERING

The Romans occupied Gaul from 58 B.C. to A.D. 486. They constructed many roads and towns, which they supplied with running water from canals. To carry the canals across valleys they built aqueducts, such as this one crossing the River Gard.

FRANKISH SOLDIERS

When the Roman Empire withdrew from Gaul (ancient France), different invading armies colonized parts of the region. Only when the fearsome Frankish warriors swept through Europe was France united again.

Landowners built huge fortresses with the great wealth they made from the feudal system. The château, or castle, was at the centre of the system.

FEUDAL FRANCE

For almost 1,000 years, during the Middle Ages, French peasants laboured under the feudal system. They had no land of their own and had to work for the local landowners. The system was finally abolished by the French Revolution.

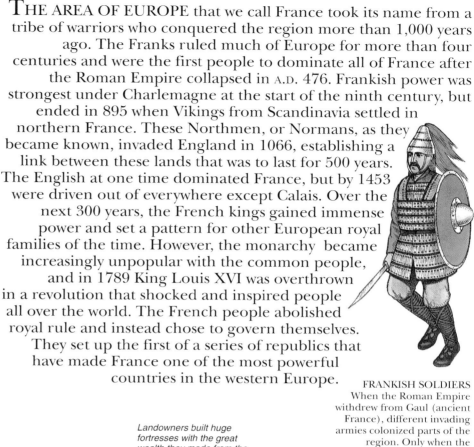

Peasants worked hard on the owner's land, and in return were allowed to grow their own food.

The peasants worked the land with ploughs drawn by oxen.

FIELD OF THE CLOTH OF GOLD

By the 16th century France was a major power in Europe. In 1520, the French king Francis I met Henry VIII of England at a lavish ceremony to sign a peace treaty between the two countries. The place where they met was later called the Field of the Cloth of Gold.

VERSAILLES
Under King Louis XIV and his successors in the 18th century, the arts and crafts in France were among the finest in Europe. Louis built a magnificent palace at Versailles, outside Paris. Ornate sculptures and fountains filled the grounds.

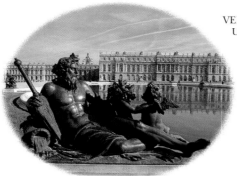

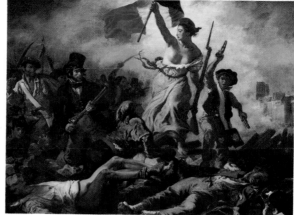

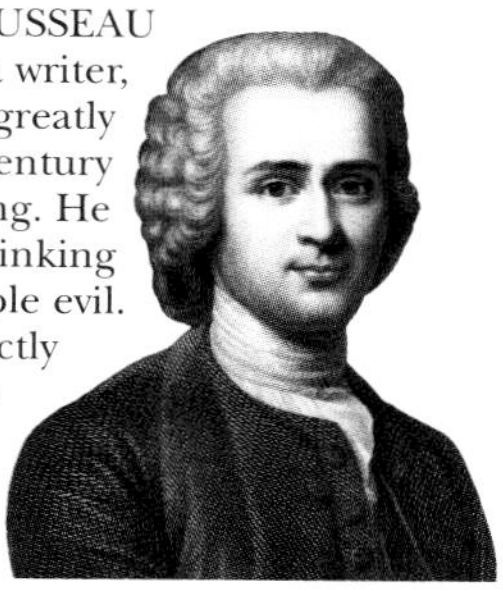

JEAN JACQUES ROUSSEAU
A philosopher and a writer, Rousseau (1712-78) greatly influenced 18th-century French thinking. He criticized society, thinking that it made people evil. His ideas directly influenced the development of the 1789 French Revolution.

REVOLUTIONS
France has a strong tradition of revolutions by the people against absolute domination by a king. In the July revolution of 1830, the people rose up against Charles X, who tried to rule with the total power of Louis XIV. This uprising is shown in a patriotic painting by Eugene Delacroix (above).

PARIS

The French capital has always been at the centre of the country's politics. In 1871 the city rebelled against the terms the government had accepted to end a war against Prussia. The Parisians barricaded the streets and set up a commune to run the city. The government savagely crushed the rebellion, killing 17,000 people. After the commune the architect Baron Haussmann (1809-91) made the streets of Paris wider to make the setting up of barricades impossible.

The engineer Alexandre Gustave Eiffel (1832-1923) built his famous Eiffel Tower to celebrate the 100th anniversary of the French Revolution.

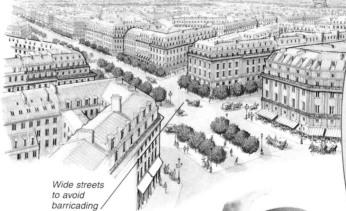

Wide streets to avoid barricading

FRANCE, HISTORY OF

5700 B.C. Carnac constructed.

58 B.C.-A.D. 486 Roman occupation.

500 Franks settle in country.

768-814 Charlemagne rules Frankish empire.

895 Vikings begin to raid France.

1337-1453 Hundred Years' War against England.

1431 Joan of Arc is burned to death by the English.

1515-47 Reign of Francis I.

1562-98 Wars of Religion between Catholics and Protestants.

1643-1715 Reign of Louis XIV.

1789 Outbreak of French Revolution.

1792 France becomes a republic.

1799 Napoleon seizes power.

1815 Defeat of Napoleon at Waterloo; king restored.

1830 July Revolution throws out king.

1848 Second Republic set up.

1852 Napoleon III sets up Second Empire.

1870-71 Prussia defeats France in Franco-Prussian War. Leads to Third Republic.

1914-18 World War I. France at war with Germany.

1940 Germany invades France.

1944 France liberated from Germany.

1954-62 War with Algeria.

1957 France and other western European nations set up the European Community.

1958-69 Charles De Gaulle is president.

1981 France elects its first socialist president, François Mitterand; he served until 1995.

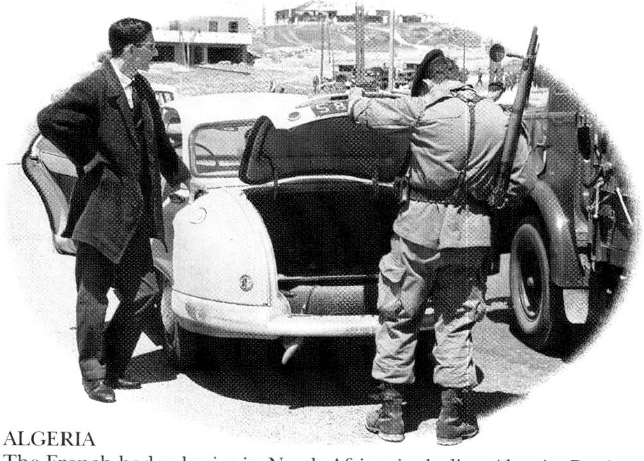

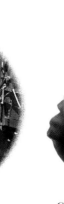

ALGERIA
The French had colonies in North Africa, including Algeria. During the 1950s many colonies gained independence, but France wanted to keep Algeria, home to almost a million French settlers. Discontent and bad living conditions led the Algerians to revolt, and a war followed. French troops occupied Algeria (above). In 1962, after much fighting, France finally granted Algeria independence.

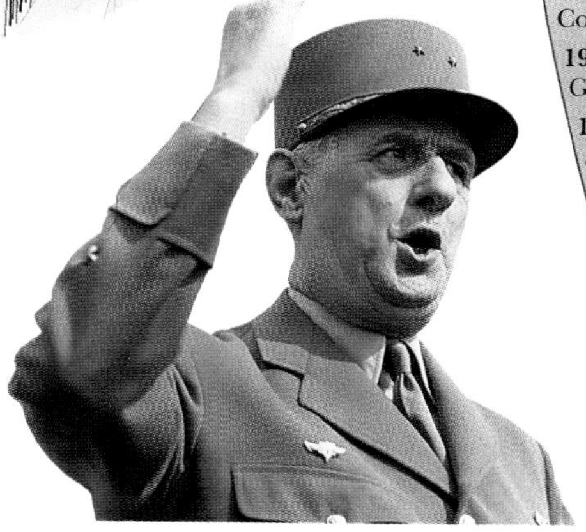

CHARLES DE GAULLE
During World War II, De Gaulle (1890-1970) was leader of the Free French. He became president of France in 1958. As president he led France through difficult times during which Algeria became independent. De Gaulle retired in 1969.

Find out more

FRANCE
FRENCH REVOLUTION
JOAN OF ARC
LOUIS XIV
NAPOLEON BONAPARTE

FRENCH REVOLUTION

THE EXECUTION OF LOUIS XVI
"Because the country must live, Louis must die". With those words, the king of France died on the guillotine on 21 January 1793.

"LIBERTY! EQUALITY! FRATERNITY!". This slogan echoed through France in 1789 as the hungry French people united to overthrow the rich noblemen who ruled the country. The Revolution put ordinary people in control of France and gave hope to oppressed people all over the world. The Revolution started when the bankrupt king Louis XVI summoned the French parliament for the first time since 1614. Instead of helping him raise taxes, they seized power. In Paris, a crowd stormed the Bastille prison, the symbol of royal authority. The king had to support the Revolution, but in 1792 France became a republic, and Louis was executed. Counterrevolution broke out in parts of France in 1793, which led to a Reign of Terror that undid many of the benefits of the Revolution. In 1799 a military takeover put Napoleon in power and ended the Revolution.

THE REVOLUTION

May 1789 Estates General (parliament) meets at Versailles.

July 1789 Paris crowd storms Bastille prison.

Aug 1789 Declaration of the Rights of Man

June 1790 Nobility is abolished.

June 1791 Louis XVI tries to flee from Paris.

Aug 1792 King Louis imprisoned.

Sept 1792 Monarchy abolished and France becomes a republic.

Mar 1793 Counter-revolution in Vendée region

Sept 1793 Start of Reign of Terror

July 1794 Terror ends when Robespierre is overthrown.

Nov 1795 A new republic, the Directory, takes power.

Nov 1799 Napoleon Bonaparte overthrows Directory and assumes power.

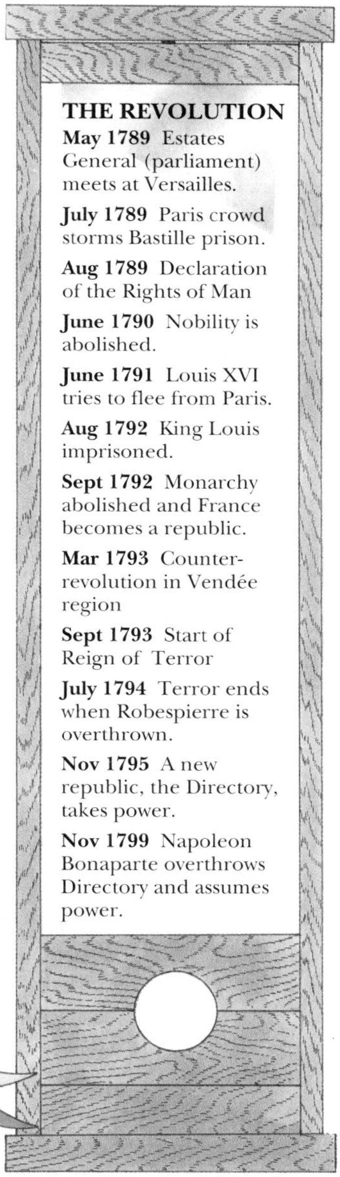

MAXIMILIEN ROBESPIERRE
When 35-year-old lawyer Robespierre came to power in 1793, he took severe measures to safeguard the Revolution. He presided over the Reign of Terror but was himself executed in 1794.

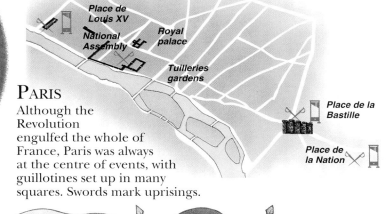

PARIS
Although the Revolution engulfed the whole of France, Paris was always at the centre of events, with guillotines set up in many squares. Swords mark uprisings.

Place de Louis XV
National Assembly
Royal palace
Tuilleries gardens
Place de la Bastille
Place de la Nation

MARIANNE
The new revolutionary calendar started from the day the king was overthrown. Marianne – a symbolic but imaginary revolutionary woman shown here on a stamp – illustrated the first month.

The red bonnet worn by the revolutionaries, and the republican tricolor flag

SANS-CULOTTES
The well-dressed aristocrats sneered at the revolutionaries and called them sans-culottes, or people without trousers. The revolutionaries adopted this name as their own. Their simple clothes came to symbolize the new way of life in revolutionary France.

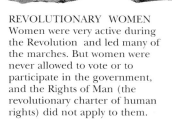

REVOLUTIONARY WOMEN
Women were very active during the Revolution and led many of the marches. But women were never allowed to vote or to participate in the government, and the Rights of Man (the revolutionary charter of human rights) did not apply to them.

Find out more

FRANCE, HISTORY OF
NAPOLEON BONAPARTE
NAPOLEONIC WARS

FROGS AND OTHER AMPHIBIANS

AMPHIBIANS ARE A GROUP OF creatures that are able to live both on land and in the water. The group includes frogs, toads, salamanders, newts, and caecilians. Amphibians have existed for millions of years and are found everywhere but Antarctica and Greenland. Frogs are the most widespread amphibians, surviving in deserts, rain forests, and mountainous regions. The limbless caecilian is found only in tropical areas. Caecilians burrow in the earth and swim by wriggling like eels. Frogs, by contrast, can swim, hop, and climb trees using their long back legs. Most amphibians breed in water, where they lay eggs that develop into larvae (tadpoles). During the larval stage, amphibians breathe through gills; as adults they develop lungs for breathing on land. Several kinds of frogs and salamanders are brightly coloured, and some have glands in the skin that produce toxins (poisons) to ward off predators.

Frogs rely on their eyes to watch for prey. They also use their eyes to judge distances when they are leaping.

Front legs act as shock absorbers when frog lands.

AMPHIBIANS
Many frogs and other amphibians lay spawn (eggs) in water; others lay eggs out of water, on leaves, or in holes underground. The frog spawn you see in a pond hatches into limbless tadpoles. As the tadpoles grow in the water, their limbs form. They gradually change into frogs and climb onto the land. This process is called metamorphosis.

After hatching from its egg, the tadpole starts to swim, breathing through gills.

About 16 weeks after hatching, the young frog leaves the water.

Tail becomes smaller and eventually disappears.

Limbs form, and internal lungs develop. Tadpole begins to gulp air from the surface of the water.

Frog's toes are sticky.

RED-EYED TREE FROG
Tree frogs often have longer, leaner bodies than frogs that live mainly in water. A frog's long back legs can kick powerfully for swimming and leaping away from predators. The red-eyed tree frog shown here has sticky discs on its toes that give a good grip on leaves and bark. Today red-eyed tree frogs are in danger of extinction.

SALAMANDER
After the tadpole stage, the fire salamander crawls up onto land and lives among leaves in moist woodland areas. The females return to the water to give birth to 10 to 15 live young. The fire salamander is so called because it hides in the logs that people use to make fires.

Fire salamander

Mandarin newt

NEWT
Salamanders and their relatives, the newts, resemble lizards in shape. In the breeding season newts often become brighter in colour, and may be red, yellow, or orange, such as the mandarin newt shown here. These colours warn predators that the glands in the skin produce horrible-tasting or poisonous fluids.

CANE TOAD
The cane or marine toad shown here originated in Central and South America. During the 1930s it was brought to Australia to eat the beetles that were pests in sugar cane plantations. Today the cane toad itself is regarded as a pest.

Cane toad grows up to 23 cm (9 in) in body length.

Asian leaf frog

Tomato frog

Find out more
ANIMALS
AUSTRALIAN WILDLIFE
CONSERVATION
and endangered species

FRUITS AND SEEDS

ALL FLOWERING PLANTS, from tiny duckweeds to mighty oaks, develop from seeds. Each seed contains an embryo (a young plant) plus a store of food for the embryo's growth. A fruit is the seed container; it protects the developing seeds until they are dispersed by animals or the wind to grow into new plants.

Fruits include lemons, melons, cherries, and tomatoes. The hard little stones or pips inside are the seeds. Many fruits, such as oranges and black-currants, are an important source of food. They contain large amounts of vitamin C, necessary for good health. People have cultivated fruits for centuries; today fruit growers produce millions of tonnes of fruit every year. Strangely enough, some foods that we call vegetables, such as cucumber, are in fact fruits, bursting with tiny seeds. So too are spices such as whole chillis and peppercorns. Yet rhubarb, which is often cooked as a fruit, is really the pink stem of a leaf.

Seeds (pips)

Core

There are more than 1,000 varieties of cultivated apples.

APPLE
The apple's flesh, which is what we eat, grows from the receptacle of the flower, so it is a false fruit. The apple core is formed from the ovary, and the pips inside are the seeds. Pears, quinces, and hawthorn berries are formed in the same way; they are also known as pomes.

TRUE AND FALSE FRUITS
Fruits have different names, depending on which part of the flower develops into the main part of the fruit. Fruits are usually described as either true or false fruits. A true fruit develops from the female parts of the flower. A false fruit is one that includes some other part of the flower, such as the receptacle, or flower base.

The bright red fruits of the mountain ash (rowan) develop from clusters of white flowers.

GRAPE
Berries are juicy, succulent, true fruits with pips inside. They include grapevine berries, which we call simply grapes. About 5,000 kinds of grapes are used to make wine or are dried into currants and raisins for cakes and biscuits. Other berries include gooseberries, tomatoes, and bananas. Citrus fruits, such as oranges, lemons, and grapefruits, are also berries.

PLUM DRUPE
Drupes are juicy, succulent true fruits like berries. Unlike berries, however, drupes do not have pips. Instead, they have a hard stone which contains the seed. Plums, cherries, and coconuts are all drupes. A blackberry is a collection of drupes.

Cherry

Plum

Runner bean pod

PEA LEGUME
Legumes are dry, non-juicy fruits. Their seeds are contained in a long outer casing called a pod. Pods are found on pea and bean plants, as well as sweet peas and laburnums. We eat the fruits of pea and bean plants.

Pea

Pea pod

POPPY CAPSULE
Capsules are hard, dry fruits found on poppies, violets, snapdragons, and the horse chestnut tree. The poppy capsule is like a saltshaker. The tiny seeds fall through holes at the top when the wind blows.

NUT

A nut is a dry, hard-cased fruit such as an acorn or hazelnut, with only one seed inside. Most hard, woody fruits or seeds are called nuts, but the fruit of the walnut is actually a drupe, and the Brazil nut is really a seed.

Walnut fruit (drupe)

Walnut "nut" is the seed.

Outer shell of Brazil nut

Hard casing

Brazil "nuts" are the seeds of a South American tree. The seeds grow in melon-sized fruit pods.

Brazil nut (seed)

Sunflower seeds are used in margarine, animal food, and as a snack.

Seed case

Seed head

Seed

SUNFLOWER
The sunflower grows about 2.5 m (8 ft) high. After fertilization, the large flower ripens to form a plate-sized seed head. Sunflower seeds contain large amounts of vitamins and edible oil.

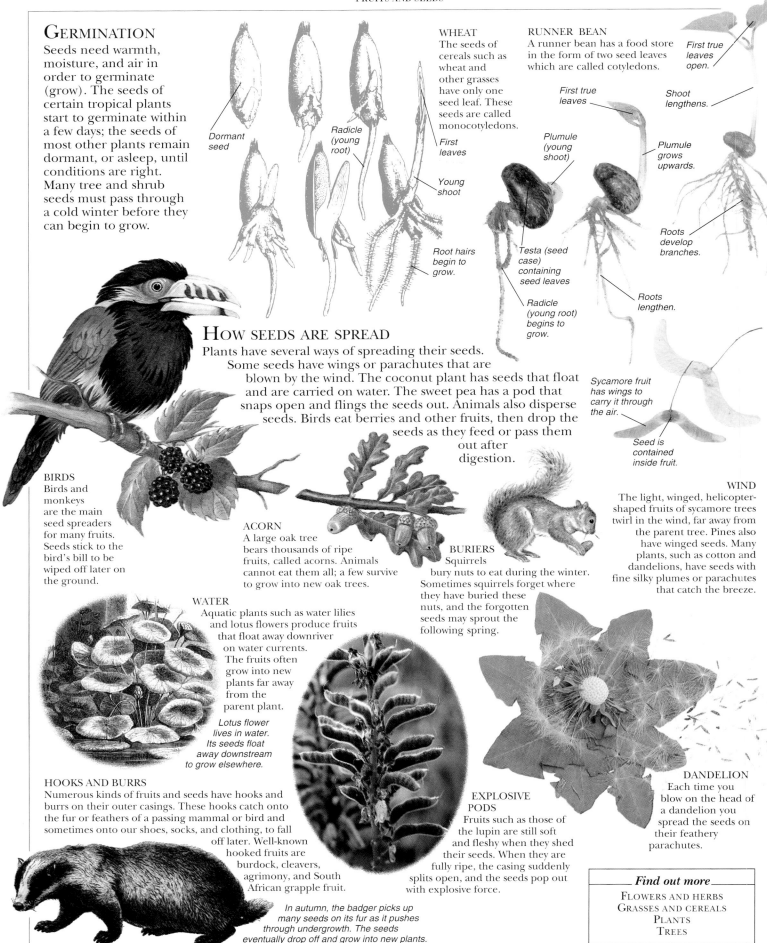

GERMINATION

Seeds need warmth, moisture, and air in order to germinate (grow). The seeds of certain tropical plants start to germinate within a few days; the seeds of most other plants remain dormant, or asleep, until conditions are right. Many tree and shrub seeds must pass through a cold winter before they can begin to grow.

Dormant seed

Radicle (young root)

Root hairs begin to grow.

WHEAT
The seeds of cereals such as wheat and other grasses have only one seed leaf. These seeds are called monocotyledons.

First leaves

Young shoot

RUNNER BEAN
A runner bean has a food store in the form of two seed leaves which are called cotyledons.

First true leaves open.

First true leaves

Plumule (young shoot)

Shoot lengthens.

Plumule grows upwards.

Testa (seed case) containing seed leaves

Radicle (young root) begins to grow.

Roots develop branches.

Roots lengthen.

Sycamore fruit has wings to carry it through the air.

Seed is contained inside fruit.

HOW SEEDS ARE SPREAD

Plants have several ways of spreading their seeds. Some seeds have wings or parachutes that are blown by the wind. The coconut plant has seeds that float and are carried on water. The sweet pea has a pod that snaps open and flings the seeds out. Animals also disperse seeds. Birds eat berries and other fruits, then drop the seeds as they feed or pass them out after digestion.

BIRDS
Birds and monkeys are the main seed spreaders for many fruits. Seeds stick to the bird's bill to be wiped off later on the ground.

ACORN
A large oak tree bears thousands of ripe fruits, called acorns. Animals cannot eat them all; a few survive to grow into new oak trees.

BURIERS
Squirrels bury nuts to eat during the winter. Sometimes squirrels forget where they have buried these nuts, and the forgotten seeds may sprout the following spring.

WIND
The light, winged, helicopter-shaped fruits of sycamore trees twirl in the wind, far away from the parent tree. Pines also have winged seeds. Many plants, such as cotton and dandelions, have seeds with fine silky plumes or parachutes that catch the breeze.

WATER
Aquatic plants such as water lilies and lotus flowers produce fruits that float away downriver on water currents. The fruits often grow into new plants far away from the parent plant.

Lotus flower lives in water. Its seeds float away downstream to grow elsewhere.

HOOKS AND BURRS
Numerous kinds of fruits and seeds have hooks and burrs on their outer casings. These hooks catch onto the fur or feathers of a passing mammal or bird and sometimes onto our shoes, socks, and clothing, to fall off later. Well-known hooked fruits are burdock, cleavers, agrimony, and South African grapple fruit.

In autumn, the badger picks up many seeds on its fur as it pushes through undergrowth. The seeds eventually drop off and grow into new plants.

EXPLOSIVE PODS
Fruits such as those of the lupin are still soft and fleshy when they shed their seeds. When they are fully ripe, the casing suddenly splits open, and the seeds pop out with explosive force.

DANDELION
Each time you blow on the head of a dandelion you spread the seeds on their feathery parachutes.

Find out more

FLOWERS AND HERBS
GRASSES AND CEREALS
PLANTS
TREES

FURNITURE

WHEN WE SIT DOWN to work or eat, when we lie down to sleep, furniture supports our bodies comfortably. When we carry out tasks in the office, school, or kitchen, furniture has surfaces at just the right height so that we don't bend or stretch. And furniture organizes all our belongings close at hand yet out of sight. We take for granted our chairs, beds, tables, and cabinets because we use them every day. But until the 19th century furniture was handmade, and few families could afford very much. Most homes had a table but only simple stools or benches to sit on. People stored their few clothes and possessions in a chest and slept on mattresses on the floor. Today most furniture is made in factories. Much of it is very practical, with easy-to-clean surfaces at convenient heights. But there are other styles, too, to fit in with any interior. Reproduction furniture, for example, imitates the styles of the past, with rich upholstery and carved wood.

A bed from the Ancient Roman town of Pompeii

EARLY FURNITURE
More than 2,000 years ago wealthy Roman citizens used bronze tables in the town of Pompeii, Italy. In Egypt the tomb of Tutankhamun contained exquisite furniture that was buried with the boy-king 3,500 years ago.

ANTIQUES
When carpenters such as Englishman Thomas Chippendale (1718-1779) were making furniture by hand, many of the objects they crafted were both beautiful and easy to use. Today these items of furniture are called antiques. Some are valuable and highly prized.

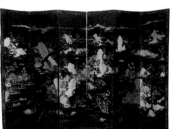

Antique screen from Japan

MOVABLE FURNITURE
European and North American families don't move into new homes often, so their furniture is made to stay in one place. But nomadic people carry their homes with them, so big chairs and tables are not practical. For example, the Bedouin of the Middle East furnish their desert tents with easy-to-pack rugs, cushions, and bedrolls.

South American Indians invented the hammock as a bed they could carry easily.

The woven rush back holds the sitter upright.

The covering material is attractive and hardwearing.

The chair frame of jointed wood supports the upholstery.

Padding is thick and even for comfort.

Horsehair was once the traditional material for padding; most furniture makers now use plastic foam.

The upholsterer stretches cotton webbing across the frame.

Coiled steel springs make the chair soft to sit on.

Sturdy material such as hessian covers the springs and distributes the sitter's weight.

UPHOLSTERY
The padding on chairs and sofas is called upholstery. It stops the hard frame of the furniture from digging into your body. Many different materials are needed to make a comfortable seat, because upholstery must be firm in some places to provide support and prevent backache, but soft and yielding elsewhere for comfort.

TYPES OF FURNITURE
Furniture designs have evolved to suit their role. For example, kitchen cabinets have solid doors to hide pots and pans, but the doors of china cabinets are glass to display attractive crockery.

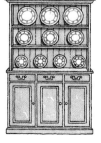

Drawers in the cupboard store cutlery and keep it clean. The upper part shows off the best china.

A well-designed desk is a miniature office. The locking drawers hide precious documents, and compartments keep stationery clean.

The cotton-filled futon is a sofa which folds out to make a bed. It originated in Japan as a way to save space in small homes.

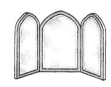

Glassmakers first made mirrors in the 16th century. The three hinged panels enable the user to see his or her face from the side.

Find out more
DESIGN
EGYPT, ANCIENT
HOUSES

GAMES

SKIPPING in the playground and playing world championship chess have one thing in common – they are both games. Some games are similar to organized sports and, like sports, games provide pleasure, relaxation, excitement, and a challenge. There are thousands of different games. Some, such as chess, have the same rules everywhere. But others vary from place to place; for example, there are many variations on the rules of the card game poker. Many games share the same playing equipment: dice are similar all over the world, but players use dice in a huge range of games. Not all games require special equipment: you can make the playing pieces for some games in a few minutes from string, toothpicks, sticks, or stones. Some games make you think, others call for physical skills, and some require both. You can play some games by yourself, some need two to play, while others are fun only when played in a group.

COMPUTER GAMES
To operate computer games, players use buttons, a keyboard, or levers called joy sticks. People play against the computer or against each other.

DICE
Throwing dice, usually in pairs, adds chance and luck to a game. In many board games, such as Monopoly, the number of spots facing up when the dice come to rest determines the number of squares or sections players may move along. Standard dice have from one to six spots. Variations include poker dice, which have faces similar to playing cards.

SKIPPING
Players usually chant traditional songs when skipping. With a long enough rope, several players can skip together.

TAG
In tag, the player chosen to be "it" tries to catch the other players.

HOPSCOTCH
Most hopscotch games have 9 to 12 numbered squares. Hopscotch calls for good balance when hopping between squares.

PIGGY IN THE MIDDLE
Two players throw a ball to each other. The "piggy" in the middle tries to catch it.

PLAYGROUND GAMES
Around any playground you will see a variety of games taking place. Some, such as skipping, occupy a small corner and people wait their turn. Others, such as tag, need more space.

SUITS
A pack of playing cards has four suits or groups, each with thirteen similar cards. The four suits are, from left to right, hearts, clubs, diamonds, and spades.

Some card games, such as the old English game of Happy Families, require a pack of special cards.

Cards in suits are numbered from one, or ace, to ten, and there are three "royal" cards: jack, queen, and king.

BOARD GAMES
People first marked out boards to play games 4,000 years ago. Board games such as chess and draughts originally represented the field of battle, in which the players captured enemy soldiers. In backgammon, players take their pieces through enemy territory. Many modern board games imitate peaceful aspects of life, such as buying and selling property, as in Monopoly.

CARD GAMES
A standard set of cards is called a pack or deck. With its 52 cards you can play countless games of skill or chance. The game of bridge requires good concentration and an excellent memory. But you can learn to play snap in a few seconds, and all you need are quick reflexes.

PARCHEESI

A variation of backgammon, parcheesi is the national game of India. Two or four players throw dice and try to get their counters to the inner centre of the board.

Find out more
COMPUTERS
SPORTS
TOYS

GAS

FORMATION OF NATURAL GAS

The natural gas we use today is millions of years old. It was formed from the remains of prehistoric plants that lived on land and in the sea. New gas deposits are still being created.

1 In the sea tiny plants sink, and a layer of dead plants builds up on the sea bed. The sea plants are buried in mud.

2 On land too, mud covers dead plants and trees. Slowly the mud hardens into rock. More layers of rock form above and press down on the plants, burying them deeper and heating them up.

3 The pressure and heat slowly change the sea plants into oil and then into gas. Land plants turn first to coal before becoming oil and gas. A layer of rock now traps the gas in a deep deposit. Earth movements may have raised the rocks containing the gas above sea level, so that the gas now lies under the land.

GAS DELIVERY

Natural gas is piped to homes for use in cookers and heaters. Gas stored in metal bottles supplies homes that are not connected to the pipeline.

6 Gas flows from terminals to large tanks, where it may be frozen and stored as a liquid. The gas can also be stored in huge underground caverns. Pumps push gas along pipes to the places where it is needed.

5 Raw gas has to be cleaned and dried before it can be used. The gas terminal removes impurities and water.

Gas storage tank

BURNING GAS to make heat is a quick and easy way to warm the home and to cook. Gas is also used in industry, both for heat and as a raw material. Most of the gas we use for fuel is natural gas. It is extracted from deposits buried deep underground or under the sea bed. Gas for burning can also be made by processing coal to produce coal gas. These fuel gases are not the only kinds of gas: there are many others with different uses. For instance, the air we breathe is made up of several gases mixed together.

Huge drills on a production platform sink wells to reach gas deposits, which lie as deep as 6 km (4 miles) below the sea bed.

4 Gas flows up the well to the production platform, and a pipeline takes it to a terminal on land. Gas from inland wells flows straight to the terminal.

GAS FOR INDUSTRY

Not all gas is used in the home. Many power stations burn gas to generate electricity. In dry places, such as deserts, the heat from burning gas is used to process sea water in order to produce salt-free drinking water. Gas is also used as a fuel in factories processing all kinds of things, from roasted peanuts to cars. Chemicals made from gas are vital ingredients in the manufacture of plastics, fertilizers, paints, synthetic fibres, and many other products.

Gas deposit

Oil deposit

A gas layer often forms above a layer of oil.

The pressure of the gas helps force the oil up wells to the production platform.

USEFUL GASES

Gas wells produce several different sorts of gas. Methane is the main component, but other fuel gases, called propane and butane, also come from gas deposits. The gas terminal stores these gases in metal cylinders for use in houses that the gas pipe does not reach. Gas deposits are also a source of helium. Helium is used to fill balloons because it is very light and does not burn. Air is another source of useful gases. Carbon dioxide, the gas that makes the bubbles in fizzy drinks, comes from air. Air also contains a little neon gas. Some advertising signs are glass tubes filled with neon. The gas glows when electricity passes through it.

Neon sign

Helium gas balloons

Find out more
AIR
COAL
HEAT
OIL
OXYGEN

GEMS AND JEWELLERY

A RING MOUNTED with beautiful gems, such as diamonds, seems to flash with fire as it catches the light. Yet the gems were once dull stones buried in rock. Their beauty is the work of gem cutters who shape the gems, and jewellers who mount them in settings of gold, silver, and other precious metals. Gems are stones used to make jewellery. They are either precious stones, such as sapphires and emeralds, or semiprecious stones, such as opal and jade.

Gems also have industrial uses: rubies are used in lasers, and diamond-tipped drills dig through rock in the search for oil. Most gems are hard; diamond, for instance, is the hardest material in the world.

CROWN JEWELS
Priceless gems line the British crown jewels. The Royal Sceptre (above) contains the world's largest cut diamond, the 106 g (3.7 oz) Star of Africa.

Polished blue sapphire

Jade is a hard gem made up of many tiny crystals.

This ruby crystal, called the Edwardes Ruby, is famous for its size and quality.

Cut ruby

PRECIOUS STONES

Gems such as diamonds come from transparent minerals found in rocks. In their pure form, these minerals are colourless. But metals and other impurities in the minerals produce colour. The metal chromium turns the colourless mineral beryl green, producing emerald, a precious stone. Gemstones are often found in riverbeds. They are long-lasting and remain in the bed after running water has worn away the surrounding rock.

The sheen and colours of titanium metal make it ideal for jewellery.

Setting made of gold

Tiger's-eye consisting mainly of quartz

Vein of opal embedded in sedimentary rock

Polished white opal

Imitation diamond brooch made from cut glass

Pearls form inside the shells of oysters.

Coral forms from the remains of tiny sea creatures.

Lapis lazuli jewellery has been known for more than 6,000 years.

SAPPHIRE AND RUBY
The crystals of coloured minerals make valuable gems. Sapphires and rubies are varieties of a mineral called corundum. The presence of iron and titanium turns corundum blue, to produce sapphires; chromium produces red rubies.

OPAL
Beautiful patterns of rainbow-like colours glisten inside opals. These gems consist mainly of silica, the same mineral found in sand. Opals do not need facets; instead tiny spheres of silica within opal reflect and scatter light, producing colours from milky white to black, the most highly prized opal.

JEWELLERY

Rings, brooches, bracelets, earrings, and necklaces are worn as jewellery by both men and women. Fine pieces are made from gold, diamonds, and other precious materials. But semiprecious stones and organic materials such as pearls and amber also make lovely jewellery. So too do inexpensive materials such as shells, coral, wood, and plastic. Some jewellery contains imitation gems made of cheap materials, such as glass, instead of precious stones.

CUTTING GEMS

A gem sparkles because it has many angled sides, or facets, that reflect light striking and entering the gem. Gem cutters split gemstones and then carve and polish the pieces to form the facets. There are several different kinds of cuts, some with complex patterns of facets.

Table cut   Cabochon   Rose cut

Step cut   Pear brilliant   Round brilliant

Find out more
CORALS, anemones, and jellyfish
METALS
ROCKS AND MINERALS
SHELLS AND SHELLFISH

GEOLOGY

OUR EARTH CHANGES all the time. Mountains rise and wear away. Continents move, causing oceans to widen and narrow. These changes are slow. It would take a million years to notice much difference. Other changes, such as when an earthquake shakes the land or a volcano erupts, are sudden. Geology is the study of how the Earth changes, how it was formed, and the rocks that it is made of.

Clues to the Earth's history are hidden in its rocks. Geologists survey (map out) the land and dig down to the rocks in the Earth's crust. The age and nature of the rocks and fossils (remains of prehistoric plants and animals) help geologists understand the workings of the Earth. Geologists also help discover valuable deposits of coal, oil, and other useful minerals. They study land before a large construction such as a dam is built, to make sure that the land can support the great weight. Geologists also warn people about possible disasters. Using special instruments, they detect the movement of rocks and try to predict volcanic eruptions and earthquakes.

GEOLOGISTS AT WORK
Rocks at the Earth's surface reveal their past to the expert eyes of geologists. For example, huge cracks in layers of rock show that powerful forces once squeezed the rocks.

SATELLITE MAPPING
Satellites circle the Earth and send back photographs of the surface from space. The pictures show features of the land in great detail and help geologists identify the rocks. Satellites also measure the size and shape of the Earth.

Studying the rocks in the ocean floor can reveal the slow movements of the Earth's crust.

AERIAL SURVEYS
Aeroplanes carry special cameras that produce three-dimensional views of the land below, and instruments that measure the strength of the Earth's magnetism and gravity.

SEISMIC TESTS
Special trucks strike the ground with huge hammers, producing shock waves, called seismic waves, which bounce off the layers of rock below. Computers use these waves to draw pictures of the layers of rock within the Earth.

DRILLING
Rigs bore shafts as deep as 3,000 m (10,000 ft) below the ground and bring up samples of the rock layers beneath.

RADIOACTIVE DATING
Rocks contain substances which decay over millions of years, giving off tiny amounts of nuclear radiation. By a process called radioactive dating, which measures this radioactivity, geologists can find out how old the rocks are.

SANDSTONE
The top and youngest layer of rock is sandstone. It sometimes forms from desert sands. The crisscross pattern shows how the wind blew sand to form the rock.

SHALE
A layer of shale rock shows that the land must have been beneath shallow water. Mud from a nearby river built up and compacted, forming shale.

BASALT
Lava from a volcano formed this layer of basalt. The land rose from the sea, and a volcano erupted nearby to cover the rock below with lava.

LIMESTONE
The lowest and oldest layer contains fossils of tiny creatures, showing that 100 million years ago, during the time of the dinosaurs, the region was under the sea.

ROCK SAMPLE
The layers of rock in this sample (above) come from deep underground.

THE HISTORY OF GEOLOGY

The Ancient Greeks and Hindus were the first peoples to study and date the rocks of the Earth. During the late 18th century, the Scottish scientist James Hutton became the first European geologist to realize that the Earth is millions of years old and that it changes constantly. But his ideas were not accepted until after his death. In 1912, Alfred Wegener, a German meteorologist, proposed that the continents move. But it was more than 50 years before his idea was found to be true.

In 1795, James Hutton founded the modern science of geology with his book *The Theory of the Earth.*

EXAMINING THE EARTH

The Earth's crust is made of layer upon layer of different kinds of rock which have been laid down over millions of years. The topmost layers usually formed most recently and the lowest layers are the oldest. By uncovering these layers of rock, geologists can go back through the history of the Earth.

Find out more

COAL
CONTINENTS
EARTH
EARTHQUAKES
FOSSILS
GAS
OIL
ROCKS AND MINERALS

GERMANY

THE LAND OF GERMANY occupies a central position in northern Europe. The 80.6 million German people also play a central role in the economy, way of life, and traditions of Europe. Germany is an old land, and its borders have changed often over the centuries. For much of the second half of the 20th century, Germany consisted of two separate nations: West Germany (the Federal Republic of Germany) and East Germany (the German Democratic Republic). In 1990 they became one nation. Germany is a rich and fertile land, and its farms are among the world's most productive. The landscape rises gently from the sandy coasts and islands on the North Sea and Baltic Sea. Flat plains dominate the northern part of the country, and in the south there are forests and the soaring Alps. The region's cool, rainy weather helps agriculture. Farms produce livestock and dairy products, cereals, potatoes, sugar beet, fruits, and vegetables. Most people, however, live in and around the towns where Germany's energetic industries are based.

LOCATION

Germany dominates the map of northern Europe. The Netherlands, Belgium, Luxembourg, and France are to the west; Switzerland and Austria are to the south; Poland and the Czech Republic are to the east; and the Baltic Sea, Denmark, and the North Sea are to the north.

Beer gardens attached to bars and pubs are popular in warm weather.

The Brandenburg Gate stands on the line that once divided East and West Berlin.

WURST AND BEER

Germany produces some excellent wine and is also famous for its beer. Germans often drink beer with the traditional snack of a sausage (or wurst) and a bread roll, accompanied by a large dollop of mild mustard. There are numerous kinds of wurst, and every region has its speciality. Frankfurters came originally from the German city of Frankfurt.

Sausage sellers specialize in the various kinds of wurst and often sell their wares from tiny stalls or vans.

Leitz camera factory

BERLIN

Reinstated as the capital of all Germany in 1990, Berlin grew up on the banks of the River Spree. Canals also link Berlin to the Elbe and Oder rivers. Berlin was devastated in World War II. In 1949 the city was split between the two states of East and West Germany. For many years a wall separated the people in the eastern and western sectors, and the two parts of the city still look very different. New buildings have made western Berlin look like any other modern European city. But eastern Berlin remains dull and uninviting.

INDUSTRY

There is a wide range of industries in Germany, producing electrical goods, computers, tools, textiles, and medicines. Coal mines in the central Ruhr region produce large quantities of brown coal, or lignite, to fuel the factories. Western Germany is famous for high-quality precision goods, such as BMW cars and Leitz cameras.

RIVER RHINE

The Rhine is the longest river in Germany. It begins in Switzerland and later forms the German border with France. Then it cuts through the western part of Germany towards the Netherlands and the sea. Large river barges can sail up the Rhine as far as Basle, Switzerland. Vineyards on the steep banks of the southern part of the river produce much of Germany's famous white wine.

Many parts of Bonn are modern.

BONN

Between 1949 and 1990, Bonn was the capital of West Germany. Bonn, an ancient city, stands on the River Rhine on the site of a Roman camp. It is an old university town with many beautiful buildings in traditional German style. Bonn was the birthplace of composer Ludwig van Beethoven (1770-1827).

SPORTING ACHIEVEMENT

Germany has produced some excellent athletes over the last few decades: at the 1988 Olympic Games in Seoul, athletes from East and West Germany together won more medals than competitors from any other country. The German government encourages sports, mainly because it promotes good health. Prizewinning athletes also bring great honour to their country.

The joining of East and West Germany brought together some of the world's finest athletes. When the two countries were rivals East German competitors were aided by excellent sports facilities, and special privileges gave them time to train. They won many more events than West German counterparts.

RUHR VALLEY

Much of Germany's heavy industry is concentrated in the valley of the River Ruhr. Huge coal seams provide the valley with a rich source of power, and factories in the region produce iron, steel, and chemicals.

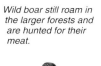

Wild boar still roam in the larger forests and are hunted for their meat.

FORESTS

Great forests cover many of the hills and mountains of the central and southern regions of Germany. These forests are prized for their beauty and for their valuable timber, which is used widely in industry. The most famous forests include the Thüringer Wald, the forests of the Harz Mountains in central Germany, and the Schwarzwald, or Black Forest, in southwest Germany.

OBERAMMERGAU

Once every 10 years an extraordinary event takes place in this small town in the Bavarian Alps in southern Germany. The inhabitants of Oberammergau get together to perform a passion play, which tells the story of Christ's crucifixion. The villagers first performed the play in 1634 in an effort to stop the plague. They have maintained the custom ever since. It is now a major tourist attraction, and thousands of visitors from Germany and abroad attend.

Find out more

EUROPE
GERMANY, HISTORY OF

GERMANY

DRESDEN
The city of Dresden in eastern Germany was once the capital of a historic German state called Saxony. Although there are still some beautiful buildings in Dresden, including the former royal palace (right), most of the city's fine architecture was destroyed by Allied bombing in World War II (1939-45). Dresden has now been completely rebuilt, and many of the buildings restored.

STATISTICS

Area: 356,945 sq km (137,816 sq miles)
Population: 80,600,000
Capital: Berlin
Language: German
Religions: Protestant, Roman Catholic
Currency: Deutsche mark
Highest point: Mount Zugspitze 2,963 m (9,721 ft)
Longest river: Rhine 1,320 km (820 miles)
Main occupations: Manufacturing and service industries
Main exports: cars, chemicals, iron, steel, machinery
Main imports: Food, fuels, industrial raw materials

GERMAN BORDERS

Germany is positioned in the very centre of Europe, and has land borders with no less than nine countries. It is not surprising, then, that it is Europe's biggest trading nation. All kinds of raw materials flow into Germany across its borders, for the nation has few natural resources. Manufactured goods cross Germany's borders in the opposite direction. Of all Germany's borders, that with France is the busiest: about one eighth of all German trade is with France.

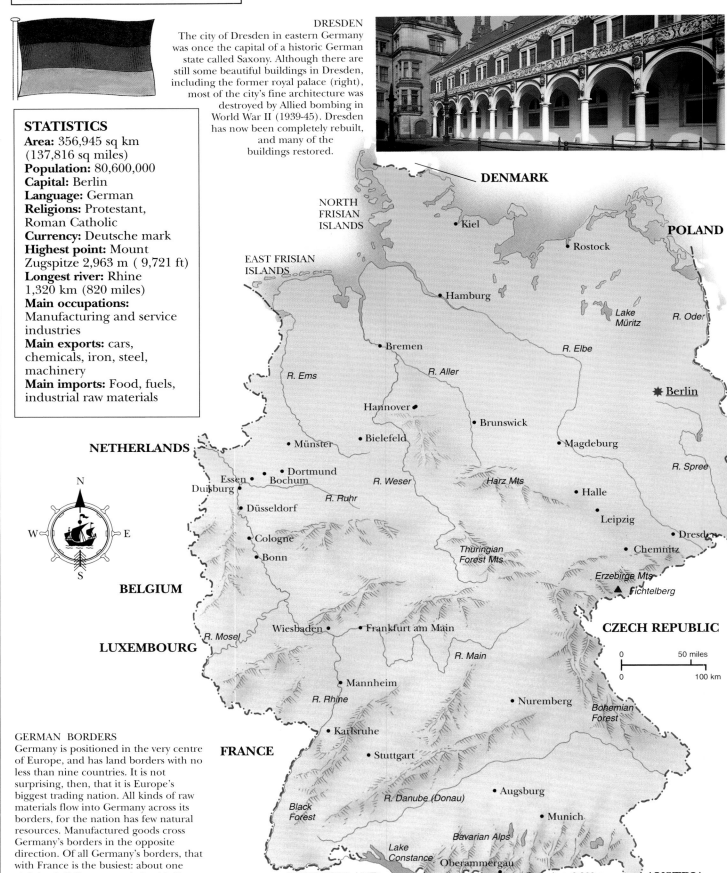

DENMARK

NORTH FRISIAN ISLANDS

EAST FRISIAN ISLANDS

POLAND

- Kiel
- Rostock
- Hamburg

Lake Müritz

R. Oder

R. Elbe

- Bremen

R. Ems

R. Aller

❋ Berlin

- Hannover
- Brunswick
- Münster
- Bielefeld
- Magdeburg

R. Spree

- Dortmund
- Essen Bochum
- Duisburg

R. Weser

Harz Mts

- Halle

R. Ruhr

- Düsseldorf
- Leipzig
- Dresden

- Cologne
- Bonn

Thuringian Forest Mts

- Chemnitz

Erzebirge Mts
▲ Fichtelberg

NETHERLANDS

BELGIUM

CZECH REPUBLIC

R. Mosel

- Wiesbaden
- Frankfurt am Main

LUXEMBOURG

R. Main

- Mannheim

R. Rhine

- Nuremberg

Bohemian Forest

- Karlsruhe

FRANCE

- Stuttgart

50 miles
100 km

R. Danube (Donau)

- Augsburg

Black Forest

- Munich

Bavarian Alps

Lake Constance

Oberammergau

Zugspitze, 2,963 m (9,721 ft)

SWITZERLAND

AUSTRIA

HISTORY OF
GERMANY

FOR MOST OF ITS HISTORY, the land of Germany has consisted of many small independent states, each with its own ruler and set of laws. Over the years there have been many attempts to unite these states into one country. In the 800s Charlemagne, emperor of the Franks, ruled most of Germany and what is now France. His successors tried to maintain this union by setting up the Holy Roman Empire. This empire consisted of Germany and surrounding areas, but Germany was united only in name, for the different states fiercely protected their independence. During the 1500s the Reformation, a movement to reform the Church, divided Germany into Protestant and Catholic states. Prussia emerged as the strongest state, challenging the dominance of the Austrian Hapsburg family. In 1871, the various states of Germany became one country under Prussian rule. But after Germany was defeated in World War II (1939-45), the country was divided again into two separate states – Communist East Germany (German Democratic Republic) and non-Communist West Germany (Federal Republic of Germany). In 1990, East and West Germany were once again united into one country.

FRANKISH KINGDOM
During the 3rd century the Franks, one of many warlike tribes in Germany, settled along the River Rhine. By the 800s the West Franks ruled what is now France, and the East Franks governed Germany. The Franks were skilled metalworkers, as shown by the bronze buckle and belt fitting above.

PEASANTS' WAR
In 1524, the German peasants rose against their lords. They demanded better social and economic conditions, including the right to elect their clergy and to hunt and fish. They were encouraged by the teachings of Martin Luther (1483-1546), who wanted to reform the Church. But Luther supported the lords, who crushed the revolt without mercy a year after it had begun.

Prussian territories 1740

Baltic Sea

North Sea

East Prussia

West Prussia

Brandenburg

Poland

Tecklenburg

Ravensburg

Cleves

Mark

PRUSSIA
Following the Thirty Years' religious war, which destroyed Germany, there was no central power, until Prussia began its rise to power. Prussia was originally a small state in what is now northern Poland. It slowly grew in size until, under the leadership of King Frederick the Great (reigned 1740-86), it became the most powerful state in Germany.

FRANKFURT PARLIAMENT
In 1815 a German Confederation was set up to protect the independence of the 39 separate states that existed in Germany at the time. But Germany was less advanced and prosperous than other European countries. Many people were dissatisfied and wanted unity. In 1848 a group of politicians set up a parliament (law-making group) to meet in Frankfurt to prepare for German unity. The plan failed in 1849 when the Prussian king, Frederick William IV, refused to be emperor. Soon the German Confederation was re-established.

OTTO VON BISMARCK
In 1871, statesman Otto von Bismarck (1815-98), chancellor of Prussia, united Germany under Prussian leadership. Bismarck built the new republic of Germany into a great power. He was famous for his political skill.

KRUPPS FACTORY
Arms manufacturers, such as Krupps (above), founded in 1811, helped create a powerful German army for the new united Germany.

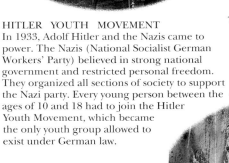

HITLER YOUTH MOVEMENT
In 1933, Adolf Hitler and the Nazis came to power. The Nazis (National Socialist German Workers' Party) believed in strong national government and restricted personal freedom. They organized all sections of society to support the Nazi party. Every young person between the ages of 10 and 18 had to join the Hitler Youth Movement, which became the only youth group allowed to exist under German law.

DEPRESSION
The German economy was hit badly by the peace settlements after World War I (1914-18). By 1931, the country, like the rest of the world, was in an economic slump. Thousands of people were out of work and had to line up for food. In desperation, many supported extreme political parties, such as the Nazis, to help them out of their poverty.

Berlin

German democratic republic

Federal republic of Germany

Czechoslovakia

France

Austria

UNITED GERMANY
In 1961 the Communists built a big wall of concrete and barbed wire in Berlin, the former German capital, dividing it into East and West Berlin. This was to block the escape route into West Germany where living and working conditions were much better. In 1989, the people of Berlin demolished the wall, and the following year, East and West Germany united.

DIVIDED GERMANY
After losing World War II, Germany was divided into two: the Federal Republic of Germany (non-Communist) in the west, and the German Democratic Republic (Communist) in the east.

GERMANY

200s Franks settle along the River Rhine.

c. 800 Charlemagne creates a huge Frankish kingdom in western Europe, uniting Germany for the first time.

843 East Franks form the first all-German kingdom.

962 King Otto I is crowned the first Holy Roman Emperor; the empire consists of a loose grouping of German states.

1300s Austrian Hapsburg family begins to dominate Germany.

1517 Martin Luther begins Reformation in Wittenberg.

1524-25 Peasants' War

1555 Religious conflict following the Reformation ends at the Peace of Augsburg.

1740-86 Prussia emerges as the most powerful German state.

1815 German Confederation established.

1848-49 Frankfurt Parliament attempts to unify Germany.

1862 Otto von Bismarck becomes chancellor of Prussia.

1914-18 Germany and Austria fight Russia, France, and Britain in World War I.

1919 Treaty of Versailles imposes harsh peace terms on Germany, which becomes a republic.

1933 Nazi party takes power.

1939-45 Germany invades rest of Europe during World War II.

1945 Russian, American, and British troops defeat Hitler and occupy Germany.

1949 Germany is divided into Communist East Germany and non-Communist West Germany.

1961 Berlin Wall divides city.

1989 People of Berlin demolish Berlin Wall.

1990 East and West Germany unite.

Find out more
CHARLEMAGNE
GERMANY
REFORMATION
WORLD WAR II

GLACIERS
AND ICECAPS

GLACIERS
Glaciers often join together, just as small rivers meet to form bigger rivers. The ice may be more than 1 km (0.5 mile) deep.

SNOW FALLING on the world's tallest mountain peaks never melts. The temperature rarely rises above freezing, and fresh falls of snow press down on those below, turning them to ice. A thick cover of ice, called an icecap or ice sheet, builds up, or snow collects in hollows. Ice flows down from the hollows in rivers of ice called glaciers. They move very slowly, usually less than 1 m (1 yd) a day, down towards the lower slopes. There it is usually warmer, and the glaciers melt. However, in the Arctic and the Antarctic, glaciers do not melt. Instead they flow down to the sea and break up into icebergs or form a floating ice shelf. A huge icecap covered much of North America and Europe a million years ago during the last Ice Age. When the weather became warmer, about 10,000 years ago, some ice melted, and the ice sheet shrank. Ice sheets now exist only in Greenland and Antarctica.

ICECAP
Icecaps cover vast areas. When the thickness of the ice reaches about 200 ft (60 m) its enormous weight sets it moving.

VALLEY GLACIER
The ice fills a valley, moving faster at the centre than at the sides of the glacier. Cracks called crevasses open in the surface.

MORAINE
The glacier acts like a huge conveyor belt, carrying broken rocks, called moraines, down from the mountaintop. The moving ice also plucks stones and boulders from the base and sides of the valley. This material is carried along within the glacier, and is called englacial moraine.

CIRQUES
The hollow where the ice collects to start the glacier is called a cirque or corrie.

A river flows down the centre of the valley.

Streams of water form as the glacier melts.

SHAPING THE LANDSCAPE
Glaciers slowly grind away even the hardest rock and reveal a changed landscape when they retreat. Deep valleys and lakes, together with rivers and waterfalls, now exist where there were none before.

Waterfall

Deep U-shaped valley carved out by the glacier

Lake formed behind moraines

FROZEN MAMMOTHS
In the Russian Federation, ice and frozen soil have preserved huge hairy elephants, called mammoths, just as if they were in a deep freeze. The last mammoths lived in North America, Europe, and Asia during the Ice Age.

Rocks in the melting ice build up a wall called a terminal moraine.

ICEBERGS
Huge pieces of floating ice are called icebergs. Nine tenths of the ice floats below the water, so icebergs are a danger to ships. In 1912 the ocean liner *Titanic* sank after colliding with an iceberg.

ICE AGE
A deep ice sheet covered about a third of the world's land during the last Ice Age. Ice extended as far south as St. Louis, Missouri, and London. There had been ice ages before the last one, and there could be more in the future.

FJORDS
The sea rose at the end of the Ice Age, drowning valleys formed by glaciers. These deep, steep-sided inlets are called fjords. The coast of Norway has many fjords.

Find out more
ANTARCTICA AND THE ARCTIC
MOUNTAINS
POLAR WILDLIFE
RAIN AND SNOW

GLASS AND CERAMICS

STICKY CLAY and dry sand are more familiar on the end of a spade than on the dinner table. Yet these are the basic ingredients in the manufacture of the pottery plates we eat from, and the jars and bottles in which we buy preserved food and drink. Glass and ceramic materials share some useful qualities: they resist the flow of heat and electricity, and they have a hard, non-reactive surface. But they are different in other ways: light passes through glass but not ceramics, and ceramics stay strong when they are heated. In their most basic forms glass and ceramic objects are brittle, but special additives and manufacturing methods make both materials much tougher.

Glass and ceramics are ancient materials. The Egyptians made decorative glass beads more than 5,000 years ago, and pottery is even older.

Spark plug for car engine

STAINED GLASS
Strips of lead hold together the many pieces of coloured glass in the stained glass windows that decorate homes, churches, and castles.

GLASS
Containers of clear glass protect their contents and display them to good advantage. Lenses are specially shaped pieces of glass that bend and concentrate light. But not all glass is functional; some glassware is simply decorative.

Glass bottle for holding medicines

Glass bottle for holding ink

Ornate glassware jug made in the 1930s.

CERAMICS
Damp clay is easy to mould into pottery and tiles; heat sets the shape permanently. Ceramics resist heat and electricity, so they are ideal for insulating objects that get hot, such as spark plugs.

Pottery mug

Ceramic tile

ENAMEL
Enamel is a glasslike layer on metal and other objects that protects them from damage and corrosion. Coloured enamel gives ornaments a beautiful appearance.

Magnifying glass which is a large convex lens.

MAKING GLASS

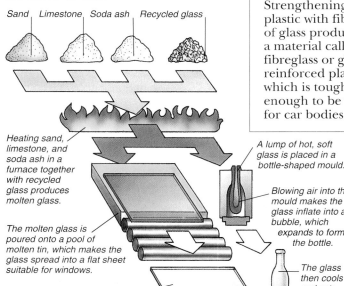

Sand Limestone Soda ash Recycled glass

Heating sand, limestone, and soda ash in a furnace together with recycled glass produces molten glass.

The molten glass is poured onto a pool of molten tin, which makes the glass spread into a flat sheet suitable for windows.

The glass sets and hardens on the cooler tin.

A lump of hot, soft glass is placed in a bottle-shaped mould.

Blowing air into the mould makes the glass inflate into a bubble, which expands to form the bottle.

The glass then cools and sets hard.

FIBREGLASS
Strengthening plastic with fibres of glass produces a material called fibreglass or glass-reinforced plastic, which is tough enough to be used for car bodies.

HEAT RESISTANCE
Ceramics can withstand very high temperatures. Ceramic tiles keep the astronauts cool even when the space shuttle glows red from the intense heat of re-entry.

GLASS BLOWING
The breath of the glass blower inflates soft glass on the end of a tube into a bubble. Skilful shaping makes the bubble into fine glassware as it cools.

Find out more

CHURCHES AND CATHEDRALS
LIGHT
PLASTICS
POTTERY

GOVERNMENTS

ORGANIZING EVEN THE SMALLEST enterprise involves a group of people making decisions that affect many others. In a restaurant, for example, the chef and the manager plan the menu; they do not consult every waiter. When the enterprise is as big as a whole nation, day-to-day decisions cannot involve the whole population. Instead, the government makes the decisions. Governments have many roles: they decide how the money raised through taxes will be divided among the different public services, such as health, education, welfare, and defence. Governments also maintain the police and armed forces to defend the country. There are two main types of government: democratic and autocratic. In a democracy, the people vote in an election to choose their government, selecting the people who will represent them from a list of candidates. Most Western countries are democracies. Autocratic governments are not elected, or there is no choice of candidates in the election. A dictatorship is where an autocracy is controlled by one ruler known as a dictator.

PLATO
More than 2,000 years ago the Greek philosopher Plato wrote the first book about governments and how they rule people – what we today call politics. His book, *The Republic*, set out ideas for democracy, a Greek word meaning "government by the people".

PRESIDENCY

In a republic such as the United States, three branches of government share power: the president leads the members of the executive branch in deciding the government's policy (its aims and objectives); members of the legislature make the laws; and the judges, who are appointed by the executive branch, interpret the laws (decide what they mean).

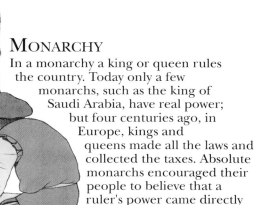

MONARCHY

In a monarchy a king or queen rules the country. Today only a few monarchs, such as the king of Saudi Arabia, have real power; but four centuries ago, in Europe, kings and queens made all the laws and collected the taxes. Absolute monarchs encouraged their people to believe that a ruler's power came directly from God.

ANARCHISM
Not everyone believes in governments. Anarchists prefer a society without central control. The 19th-century Russian anarchist Peter Kropotkin encouraged violent anti-government protests.

PARLIAMENT

The British government consists of the Queen, the House of Commons, and the House of Lords. Together they are called Parliament. The job of Parliament is to pass laws, raise taxes, and to carry out the work of governing the country. The House of Commons is the real governing body. It consists of 651 members of Parliament who are elected by the people. The House of Lords consists of dukes, earls, bishops, and other lords. Members are not elected. The British Parliament meets in the Houses of Parliament, London.

The Houses of Parliament, London, England

Find out more

COMMUNISM
DEMOCRACY
FRENCH REVOLUTION
LAW
RUSSIAN REVOLUTION

GRASSES AND CEREALS

THERE ARE MORE THAN 10,000 different kinds of grasses throughout the world. They include garden lawns, fields of barley, towering bamboos, and the African grasslands, where huge ostriches graze. Grasses are slender, flowering plants, with stiff stems and long narrow leaves called blades. Their many small roots are matted together. The flowers are feathery tufts without petals at the top of the stem. Grasses are pollinated by the wind, and seeds develop from the flowers in the same way as other flowering plants. Inside each seed is a grain, a rich food store for the plant, and also for us. Grasses are the major source of food for humans. We eat cereal grains in the form of bread, biscuits, and cakes, and also feed them to animals. Wheat and barley were two of the first plants cultivated (grown) by humans, about 10,000 years ago. Today wheat, rice, and corn are among the world's most important food crops.

Harvesting cereal grain by hand is slow, hard work. A modern combine harvester can do the work of up to 100 farm hands.

CEREALS

The ripe seeds of cereals such as oats, wheat, barley, rye, and corn are farmed to make breakfast cereals and other kinds of food. The stems are woven into baskets and turned into straw for animal bedding and thatching on houses. The leaves and stalks are put into a tower or a pit called a silo, where they are kept soft and damp. In time they turn into silage, or animal fodder.

BARLEY
Most barley is made into animal food. It is also brewed into alcoholic drinks.

MILLET
Millet seeds are made into flat breads and porridges. Millet is also common in birdseed and animal fodder.

Oats

Wheat

Barley

Millet

BAMBOO
Bamboo is a grass that grows up to 27 m (90 ft) tall. Its hollow, woody stems are used for making houses and furniture; it also makes very strong scaffolding.

SUGAR CANE
Sugar cane plants grow up to 4.5 m (15 ft) high. At harvest time, the cane is cut off close to the ground and stripped of its leaves, then brought to a sugar mill. In the sugar mill the canes are shredded and then squeezed, and the syrup is turned into sugar for cooking and making sweets.

Single rye grass flower

Stamen (male part)

Rye

WHEAT
There are more than 30 kinds of wheat. Durum wheat is used to make spaghetti, macaroni, and other pastas. Bread wheat is ground into flour to make bread and other baked foods.

RYE
Rye is used to make bread. It is also fed to farm animals and made into straw.

Rice

RICE
Rice belongs to the grass family. It is an important source of food in many parts of the world. Rice is also made into breakfast cereals.

THATCH
Dried grasses are used for thatching the roofs of houses.

Find out more
FRUITS AND SEEDS
GRASSLAND WILDLIFE
PLANTS
SOIL

GRASSHOPPERS AND CRICKETS

THE CHIRPING OF A GRASSHOPPER or a cricket is one of nature's most recognizable sounds. The sound is made by a male to attract a female or to warn off rival males. The insect produces the sound by rubbing together the ridged veins on the front wings, or by rubbing part of the back leg against the wing vein. Grasshoppers and crickets belong to the insect group called Orthoptera – a group that also includes katydids and locusts. There are more than 20,000 kinds of grasshoppers and crickets, living in all but the coldest regions. Grasshoppers are herbivores (plant eaters), feeding on leaves and stems, and crickets are omnivores (plant and meat eaters). A few of these creatures live underground and eat roots or digest nutrients in the soil. Most crickets and katydids have long antennae, sometimes longer than their bodies. Grasshoppers and locusts have much shorter antennae. All these insects have long back legs adapted for leaping. A large grasshopper can jump over a metre in one leap.

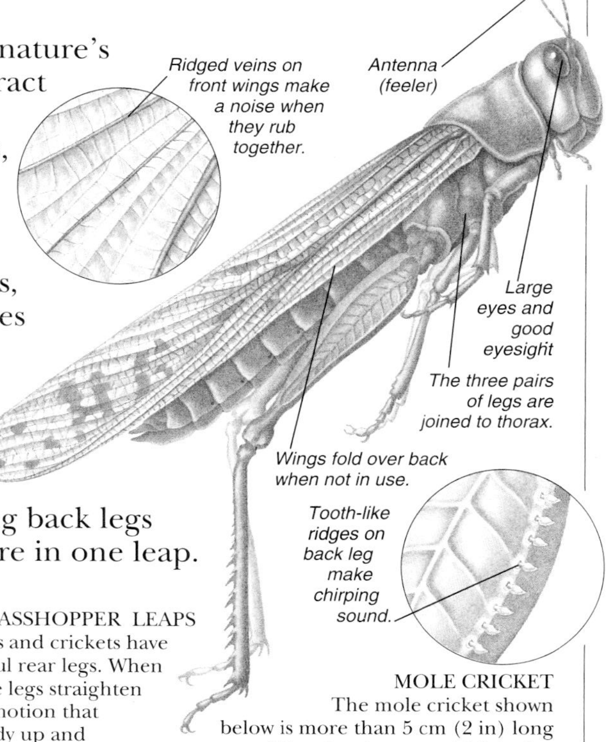

Ridged veins on front wings make a noise when they rub together.

Antenna (feeler)

Large eyes and good eyesight

The three pairs of legs are joined to thorax.

Wings fold over back when not in use.

Tooth-like ridges on back leg make chirping sound.

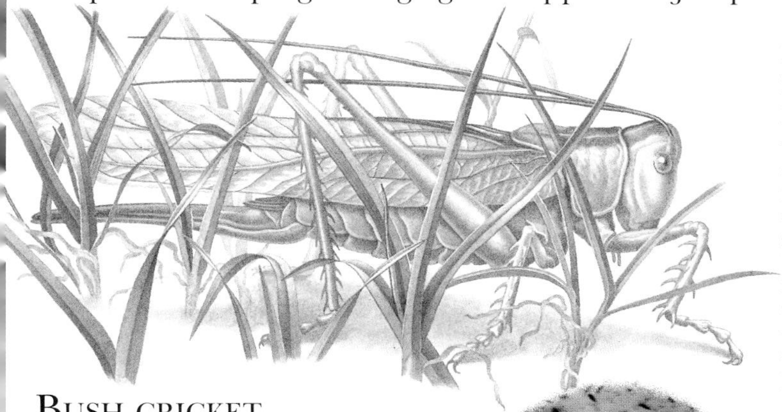

HOW A GRASSHOPPER LEAPS
Grasshoppers and crickets have long, powerful rear legs. When they leap, the legs straighten with a lever motion that flings the body up and forward, the feet giving a final kick. Many grasshoppers and crickets have spines on the legs and feet that they use for defence. These spines can cause wounds when the insect kicks out at a predator.

MOLE CRICKET
The mole cricket shown below is more than 5 cm (2 in) long and lives in a burrow which it digs with its shovel-shaped front legs. In the breeding season the male sits and sings at the burrow entrance, which is specially shaped so that the song carries more than 1.6 km (1 mile). Females lay eggs in underground nests and watch over them until they hatch.

BUSH CRICKET
The bush cricket's green colour provides good camouflage in hedges and bramble bushes. The wings of the male are longer than its body. The female has a long flattened egg-laying tube, called the ovipositor, at the rear end of the body. Bush crickets eat leaves and small insects.

LOCUST
Desert and migratory locusts breed quickly when weather and vegetation conditions are suitable. They form vast swarms of more than 50 billion locusts. These swarms devastate farm crops, causing famine and starvation.

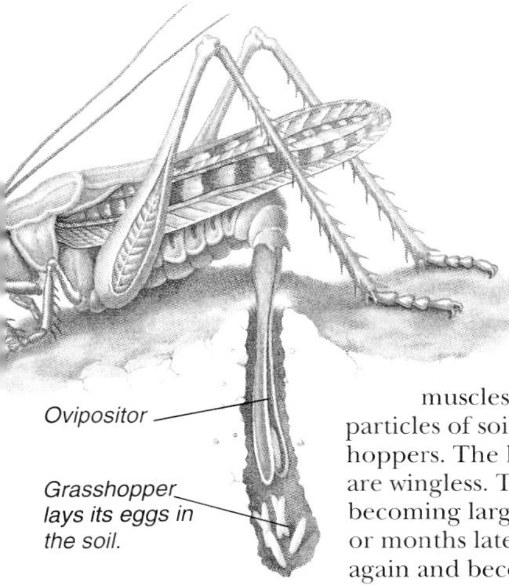

Many grasshoppers and crickets are active fliers. They have two pairs of wings. The front pair are leathery and protect the delicate fan-like wings at the back. As the insect leaps, the wings open.

Back legs kick out as grasshopper leaps forward.

Ovipositor

Grasshopper lays its eggs in the soil.

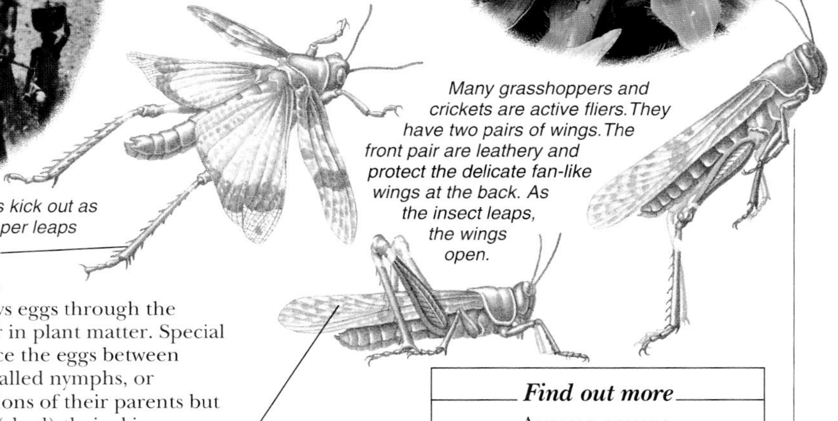

BREEDING
After mating, the female grasshopper or cricket lays eggs through the ovipositor, usually in soil or in plant matter. Special muscles stretch the abdomen and force the eggs between particles of soil. The eggs hatch into larvae called nymphs, or hoppers. The hoppers look like smaller versions of their parents but are wingless. They feed hungrily and moult (shed) their skin, becoming larger and more like the adults each time. Several weeks or months later, after about five moults, the hoppers shed their skin again and become full-sized winged adults.

Wings close as grasshopper lands.

Find out more
ANIMAL SENSES
ANIMALS
INSECTS

GRASSLAND WILDLIFE

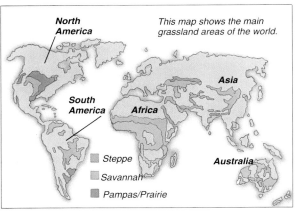

This map shows the main grassland areas of the world.

North America

Asia

South America

Africa

Australia

☐ Steppe
☐ Savannah
☐ Pampas/Prairie

GRASSLAND AREAS
The main grassland areas in the world are the Asian steppes, African savannas and grasslands, North American prairies, and South American pampas, which blend into tropical Amazonian grasses. There are also tropical grasslands in parts of India and northern Australia, and temperate grasslands in southern Australia.

VAST AREAS OF AFRICA, the Americas, Asia, and Australia consist of grasslands – areas too dry for trees but not too dry for grasses. Grasses themselves are flowering plants that can grow again quickly after animals eat them. Grasses also recover quickly if fire sweeps across the plains in the hot, dry season. The fire burns only the upper parts of the grass, so the roots and stems are not damaged. Grasslands provide a home for many different animals; each survives by feeding on a different part of the grass plants. Zebras, for example, eat the upper parts of grasses; wildebeest (gnu) graze on the middle layers; and Thomson's gazelles nibble close to the ground. Grasshoppers, ants, and termites shelter among the grass stems and roots; these insects, in turn, are food for larger animals such as anteaters and armadillos. The lack of trees in grassland areas means that small animals and certain birds have to dig burrows for shelter and for breeding. Each type of grassland has burrowing rodents; prairie dogs and pocket gophers live in North America, susliks in Asia, ground squirrels in Africa, and vizcachas and tuco-tucos in South America.

Thistles grow in grassy areas throughout the world. Their prickles protect them against grazing animals. The flowers are often purple, and form fluffy white seed heads.

SOUTH AMERICAN PAMPAS
The largest mammals on the South American pampas are the pampas deer, guanaco, and rodents such as the vizcacha, which burrows for shelter and safety. A fast-running bird called the rhea also lives on the South American pampas, feeding on grasses and other plants.

VIZCACHA
The vizcacha is related to the guinea pig. A male vizcacha weighs about 8 kg (17 lb), almost twice the size of the female. Vizcachas dig a system of burrows with their front feet and pile up sticks and stones near the various entrances. They eat mainly plant leaves and stems.

GIANT ANTEATER
With large claws on its second and third fingers, the giant anteater can easily rip a hole in an ants' nest or a termite mound as it searches for food. The giant anteater uses its long, sticky tongue to lick up the ants and termites. Its tongue measures about 60 cm (24 in) in length.

BURROWING OWL
The burrowing owl lives on the South American pampas. It often makes its nest in an empty burrow taken over from a vizcacha. Burrowing owls eat grasshoppers, insects, small mammals, birds, lizards, and snakes.

Tail protects anteater's body as it sleeps in a shallow hole, listening for predators such as pumas.

PAMPAS GRASS
The white, fluffy seed heads of pampas grass are a familiar sight in parks and gardens. Wild pampas grass covers huge areas of Argentina, in South America. Pampas leaves have tiny teeth, like miniature saws, that easily cut human skin.

JACKAL

Golden jackals eat whatever they can find on the African savanna, including fruits, small mammals, eggs, birds, and the carcasses (dead bodies) of larger animals such as zebras.

Jackals sometimes hunt in groups, pursuing small grazing animals such as these Thomson's gazelles.

The crested porcupine lives on the African savanna.

THOMSON'S GAZELLE

These swift-moving mammals live on the grassy plains of Africa in herds of up to 100 animals. They all have horns, but those of the male are larger than those of the female. Thomson's gazelles are often the prey of other grassland animals, such as the cheetah and the jackal.

SAVANNA

The huge grassland areas of eastern and southern Africa are called savannas. These areas are home to the world's largest herds of grazing animals, including zebra, wildebeest, and hartebeest. Many large grazers wander from one area to the next, following the rains to find fresh pasture. Acacia and baobab trees dot the landscape, providing shade for resting lions, ambush cover for leopards, and sleeping places for baboons.

CONSERVATION

Many grassland areas are now used for farmland, and the natural wildlife is being squeezed into smaller areas. As a result, these areas become overgrazed and barren. Grassland animals are also threatened by human hunters. In the past the Asian saiga antelope shown here was killed for its horns. Today it is protected by law, and its numbers have recovered.

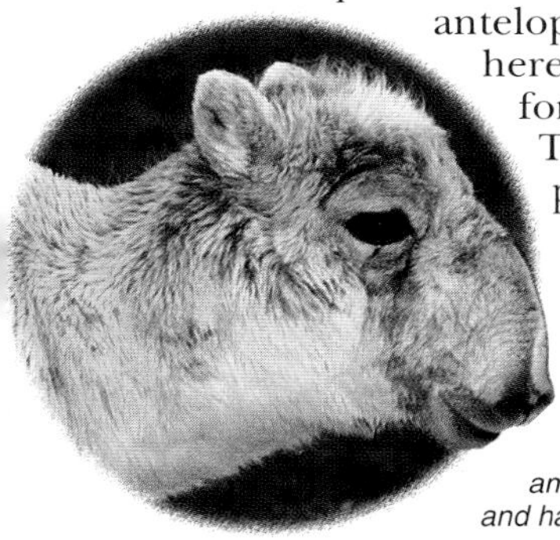

A newborn saiga antelope is fluffy and has no horns.

CRESTED PORCUPINE

The crested porcupine has sharp spines on its back for protection. It warns enemies to stay away by rattling the hollow quills on its tail. If an intruder ignores these warnings, the porcupine runs backwards into the enemy, and the quills come away and stick into the intruder's flesh.

Wild peonies are found in many grassy habitats around the world. Many garden peony plants came originally from the hardy wild peonies that grow in grassland areas.

STEPPE

The vast plains of Asia are called steppes. In the western part of Asia the rainfall is more than 25 cm (10 in) each year, and grasses and other plants grow well. Towards the eastern part of Asia there is less than 6 cm (2.5 in) of rainfall yearly, and the grasses fade away into the harsh Gobi Desert. Saiga antelopes, red deer, and roe deer graze on the rolling plains.

GRASS SNAKE

The grass snake lives on riverbanks and in marshes, mainly in Europe and Asia. Grass snakes are good swimmers.

PALLAS'S CAT

This long-furred cat lives in mountains, high steppes, and open country across central Asia. At night it hunts for hares, birds, and mice.

Head-body length of about 60cm (24 in)

Strong, agile, stout body with short legs

Soft, thick fur to keep out the cold winds

BROOK'S GECKO

Sharp claws and sticky toe pads enable the gecko to climb well over smooth rocks, along crevices, and in cracks. The Brook's gecko is active at night, catching insects, and hides by day under rocks or in an empty termite or ant nest.

PALLAS'S SANDGROUSE

The mottled plumage (feathers) of Pallas's sandgrouse gives it excellent camouflage among the brownish grasses and stones of the Asian steppe. It needs little water and can survive on very dry, tough seeds and other plant parts.

Find out more

AFRICAN WILDLIFE
HORSES, ZEBRAS, AND ASSES
LIONS, TIGERS,
and other big cats
LIZARDS

GRAVITY

FALLING

Earth's gravity makes falling objects accelerate (speed up). Their speed does not depend on how heavy they are: a light object falls as fast as a heavy object unless air slows it down. The Italian scientist Galileo Galilei (1564-1642) noticed this about 400 years ago.

A heavy rock weighs much more than an egg of the same size. However, both objects fall at the same rate and hit the ground at the same time.

THE EARTH MOVES around the sun, travelling about 50 times faster than a rifle bullet. A strong force holds the Earth in this orbit. This is the force of gravity; without it, the Earth would shoot off into space like a stone from a catapult. Everything possesses gravity; it is a force that attracts all objects to each other. However, the strength of the force depends on how much mass is in an object, so gravity is only strong in huge objects such as planets. Although you cannot feel it, the force of gravity is also pulling on you. The Earth's gravity holds you to the surface of the Earth, no matter where you are. This is because gravity always pulls towards the centre of the Earth. Sometimes you can see or feel the effects of gravity. For example, the effort you feel when you climb up a flight of stairs is because you are fighting against the force of gravity.

When you drop a ball, it falls because gravity is pulling it toward the centre of the Earth.

Gravity pulls all objects down towards the centre of the Earth.

MASS AND WEIGHT

An object's mass is the amount of material it contains. Mass stays the same wherever the object is in the universe. The weight of an object is the force of gravity pulling on it. Weight can change. Because the moon is smaller than the Earth, its gravity is weaker, about one sixth as strong as Earth's. Therefore, an astronaut on the moon weighs only one sixth of her weight on Earth, but her mass remains the same.

MOON AND EARTH

Gravity keeps the moon moving in its orbit around the Earth. The moon's gravity has effects on the Earth, too. When the moon is directly over the sea, its gravity pulls the sea water towards it, which produces a high tide; low tide follows when the Earth rotates away again.

Objects fall in the opposite direction on the other side of the Earth.

The force of gravity gets weaker as you go further from the centre of the Earth. On top of a high mountain, gravity is slightly weaker than at sea level, so objects weigh fractionally less.

EARTH'S GRAVITY

People on the opposite side of the Earth are upside down in relation to you. But they do not fall off into space. They are held on to the surface of the Earth just as you are. This is because the force of gravity pulls everything towards the centre of the Earth. Down is always the direction of the Earth's centre.

ISAAC NEWTON

The great British scientist Isaac Newton (1642-1727) was the first person to understand the force of gravity. In 1666, after watching an apple fall to the ground, he wondered whether the force of gravity that makes things fall also holds the moon in its orbit. This was a daring idea, and it took Newton many years to prove it to be true. He declared his law of gravity to be a universal law – a law that is true throughout the universe.

CENTRE OF GRAVITY

It is best to carry a large, unwieldy object such as a ladder by holding it above its centre. The weight of the ladder balances at the centre, which is called its centre of gravity or centre of mass. An object with a large or heavy base has a low centre of gravity. This stops it from falling over easily.

Objects such as a loaded tray balance if supported directly beneath their centre of gravity.

Find out more

ASTRONAUTS
PHYSICS
PLANETS
SCIENTISTS AND INVENTORS
UNIVERSE
WEIGHTS AND MEASURES

ANCIENT GREECE

MANY OF OUR words, monuments, ideas, and sources of entertainment have their roots in the world of Ancient Greece. About 2,500 years ago, the Greeks set up a society that became the most influential in the world. Greek architects designed a style of building that is copied to this day. Greek thinkers asked searching questions about life that are still discussed. Modern theatre is founded on the Ancient Greek plays that were performed under the skies thousands of years ago. And the Greeks set up the world's first democracy (government by the people) in Athens. However, only free men born in Athens were actually allowed to have a say in government. Ancient Greek society went through many phases, with a "golden age" between around 600 and 300 B.C. Arts and culture flourished at that time. The Macedonians, under Philip of Macedon, finally conquered the civilization, but it continued under Philip's son Alexander, who spread Greek culture and thinking throughout the Middle East and North Africa.

TEMPLE OF HERA
The Greeks built temples to worship their many gods. This temple at Paestum, Italy, was built to honour the goddess Hera, who was the protector of women and marriage.

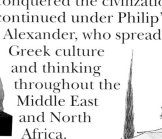

PERICLES
As leader of Athens, Pericles (c.490-429 B.C.) carried out a programme to beautify the city. This included the building of the Parthenon, a temple to the goddess Athena.

There were many busy markets in Athens, where people came to buy and sell their goods.

ATHENS
During the golden age, the Greek world consisted of independent, self-governing cities, known as city-states. With its own superb port at Piraeus, Athens was the most important city-state. It became the centre of Greek civilization and culture, attracting many famous playwrights and thinkers, such as Socrates. Athens practised the system of *demokratia* (democracy). People gathered together in the Agora (marketplace) to shop and talk. The Acropolis (high city) towered above Athens.

SPARTA
The second major city-state of Greece, Sparta, revolved around warfare. Spartans led tough, disciplined lives. Each male Spartan began military training at the age of seven and remained a soldier until 60. Women kept very fit by running and wrestling. The fierce Spartan hoplites (foot soldiers) were feared throughout the Greek world.

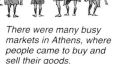

Athens and dependent states, c. 450 B.C.

GREEK WORLD
The Greek world consisted of many city-states and their colonies, spread throughout the Mediterranean region.

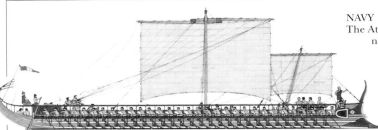

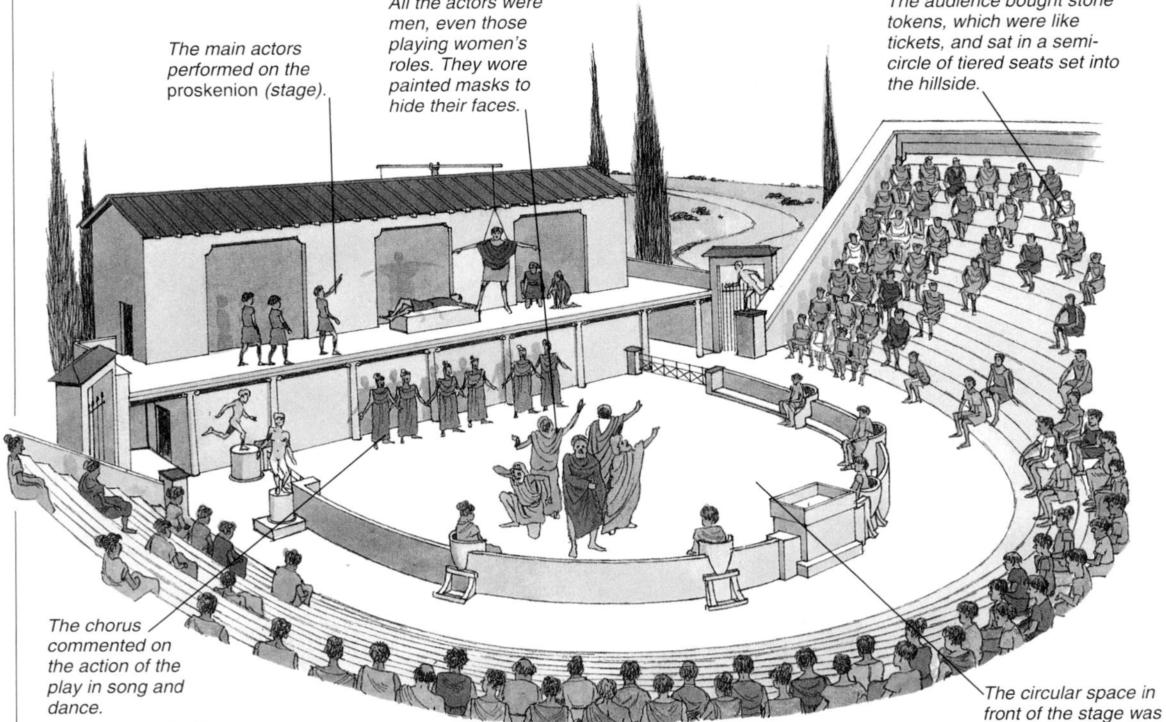

Modern reconstruction of a Greek trireme

NAVY
The Athenians possessed a powerful navy, consisting of a fleet of more than 200 triremes – warships powered by a square sail and rowed by 170 men seated in three ranks. The battle tactic involved rowing furiously and ramming the enemy's ship. In 480 B.C., during wars against the Persians, the Athenian navy crushed the Persian fleet at the sea battle of Salamis.

The main actors performed on the proskenion (stage).
All the actors were men, even those playing women's roles. They wore painted masks to hide their faces.
The audience bought stone tokens, which were like tickets, and sat in a semi-circle of tiered seats set into the hillside.
The chorus commented on the action of the play in song and dance.
The circular space in front of the stage was called the orchestra.

GREEK THEATRE

Drama was born in Athens. It began as singing and acting as part of a religious festival to honour the god Dionysus. The audience watched a series of plays; at the end of the festival, prizes were given for the best play and best actor. From these beginnings, playwrights such as Sophocles and Aristophanes started to write tragedies and comedies. Tragedies involved dreadful suffering; comedies featured slapstick humour and rude jokes.

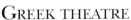

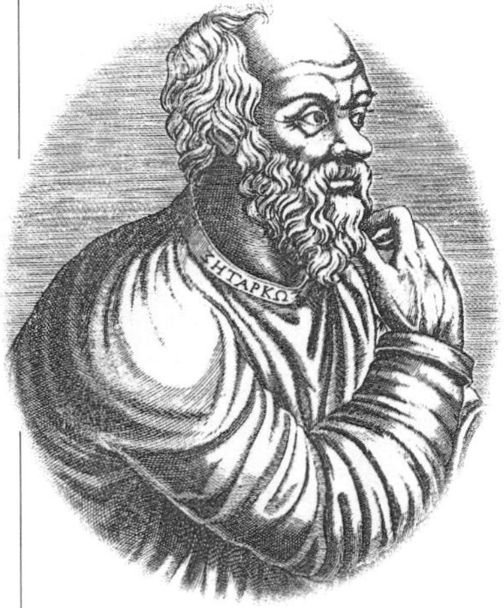

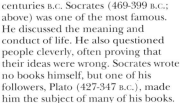

THINKERS
Great thinkers from Athens dominated Greek learning and culture during the 5th and 4th centuries B.C. Socrates (469-399 B.C.; above) was one of the most famous. He discussed the meaning and conduct of life. He also questioned people cleverly, often proving that their ideas were wrong. Socrates wrote no books himself, but one of his followers, Plato (427-347 B.C.), made him the subject of many of his books.

Amphora (vase) from Attica shows Zeus, king of the gods, at the birth of Athena, his daughter.

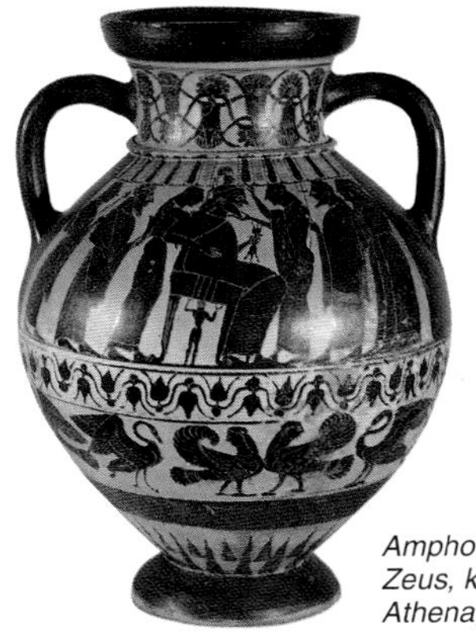

VASE PAINTING

Painted scenes on Greek pottery give us clear clues about daily life in Ancient Greece. The paintings often show a touching scene, such as a warrior saying good-bye to the family as he goes off to war. They also show the many gods that the Greeks worshipped.

ANCIENT GREECE

1500 B.C. Minoan civilization (on island of Crete) at its height.

c. 1400 Mycenaean civilization, centred in great palaces on the Greek mainland, dominates Greece.

c. 1250 Probable date of the Trojan Wars between Mycenaeans and the city of Troy.

c. 1000 Greek-speaking peoples arrive in Greece and establish the first city-states.

776 First Olympic Games held at Olympia, Greece.

750s First Greek colonies founded.

c. 505 Democracy is established in Athens.

400s Golden age of Greek theatre.

490-479 Persian Wars; Greek states unite to defeat Persians.

490 Greeks defeat Persians at Marathon.

480 Greeks destroy the Persian fleet at the Battle of Salamis.

479 Final defeat of Persians at Plataea.

461-429 Pericles rules in Athens; Parthenon built.

431-404 Peloponnesian War between Athens and Sparta leads to Spartan domination of Greece.

359 Philip becomes king of Macedonia.

338 Philip of Macedonia conquers Greece.

336-323 Alexander the Great, son of Philip, sets up Greek empire in Middle East.

Find out more

ALEXANDER THE GREAT
ARCHITECTURE
DEMOCRACY
MINOANS
SCULPTURE
THEATRE

GUNS

THE FIRST GUNS, called cannons, appeared during the early 14th century. They consisted of a thick metal tube which was closed at one end and was packed with gunpowder. Lighting the fuse caused the gunpowder to explode, blasting a steel ball out of the end of the tube. In the 16th century, pistols were invented to be used as concealed weapons and for personal protection. However, they were useless at a range of more than 9 m (10 yd), and once fired had to be laboriously reloaded. Modern guns range from large, powerful artillery weapons to small, light pistols. Sophisticated engineering has given guns great accuracy and power, and many guns can be fired several times without reloading. However, even the most modern guns work on the same basic principle as the early cannon.

Eighteenth-century highwaymen, armed with early pistols, attacking a stagecoach.

Hammer drives firing pin into the back of the cartridge, making the charge explode.

Rear sight

To aim the pistol, the front and rear sights are lined up.

When the gun is fired, bullet shoots along barrel.

Pulling the trigger releases the spring-loaded hammer to fire the gun.

Magazine is loaded with cartridges which are pushed towards the firing chamber by a spring. To reload the gun, a new magazine is slid into place.

AUTOMATIC PISTOL
The pistol is loaded with cartridges, each of which contains a lead bullet and a small charge of explosive. When the hammer of the gun strikes the charge it explodes, producing gases that expand violently. The force of the expanding gases pushes the bullet along the barrel. The gun recoils, or jerks backwards, when it is fired. In automatic or self-loading weapons such as machine guns, this jerk forces another cartridge into place, ready for firing.

Pulling trigger makes firing pin strike the cartridge, detonating its explosive charge.

Recoil pushes back slide which ejects spent cartridge case; the next cartridge springs into firing chamber.

The slide snaps back into place, pushing new cartridge into place, ready for firing.

BULLETS
When a bullet is fired, its casing remains behind. The force of the explosion ejects the spent cartridge case through a slot in the barrel.

ARTILLERY
Heavy guns, or artillery, are used to bombard enemy positions. They fire shells – hollow bullet-shaped cylinders packed with high explosive – over distances of more than 32 km (20 miles). The latest artillery weapons are guided by computers and laser rangefinders, and their shells are equipped with special homing devices so that they can hit their targets with great accuracy.

Pakistani soldiers aiming a light artillery weapon high up in the Himalayas.

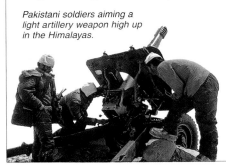

KINDS OF GUN
There are four main types of hand-held gun: pistols for personal protection, rifles for accurate firing over long distances, submachine guns which produce a spray of bullets, and shotguns which fire a mass of lead fragments for sport shooting.

SUBMACHINE GUN
With one squeeze of the trigger, a submachine gun can fire several bullets in quick succession. It is small and light so that a soldier can carry it easily into battle.

REVOLVER
Revolvers have a rotating drum with six chambers, allowing six shots to be fired without reloading.

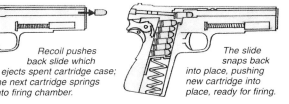

RIFLE
A rifle is a long-barrelled gun that is fired from the shoulder. Inside the barrel is a spiral of grooves which make the bullet spin as it is fired. The flight of a spinning bullet is very stable, which makes the rifle a very accurate weapon. A rifle bullet can travel at about 3,540 km/h (2,200 mph).

MACHINE GUN
A machine gun is often mounted onto a jeep or armoured vehicle because it is too heavy to hold. It is fed with bullets fixed on a long belt and can fire about 600 rounds per minute.

Find out more

ARMIES
TANKS
WEAPONS

HAPSBURGS

DURING THE 900s a family named Hapsburg owned some land in France and Switzerland. From this they rose to dominate European history for more than 1,000 years. The name Hapsburg comes from one of the family's first castles, the Habichtsburg, in Switzerland. Through a series of wars, inheritances, and careful marriages, the family gained land. By the 1500s it owned most of southern and central Europe and much land in the Americas. The Hapsburg possessions became so big that in 1556 the Hapsburg emperor, Charles V, split the land between members of his family. Philip II governed one half from Madrid, Spain, while Ferdinand of Austria governed the other half from Vienna, Austria. The Spanish Hapsburgs died out in 1700, but the Austrian Hapsburgs continued to increase their lands. In the 19th century, however, Hapsburg power began to weaken because the empire contained so many different peoples. When it collapsed after World War I (1914-18), four new nations emerged: Austria, Czechoslovakia, Hungary, and Yugoslavia.

FAMILY CREST
The crest of the Hapsburg family was the black double-headed eagle. It appeared on all their flags and banners.

CHARLES V
Under Charles V, who reigned as Holy Roman Emperor from 1519 to 1556, the Hapsburgs reached the height of their power. Charles V ruled a vast empire, as shown by this map.

Joseph II and family

JOSEPH II
From the time of Rudolf I onwards, the Hapsburg family extended its power throughout Europe. Joseph II, son of Maria Theresa, was appalled by the living conditions of his poorer subjects. He began reforms that included freeing serfs and abolishing privileges.

HAPSBURGS

1273 Rudolf I becomes the Holy Roman Emperor.

1282 Albert I becomes first Hapsburg ruler of Austria.

1438 Albert II becomes Holy Roman Emperor.

1519 Charles V becomes Holy Roman Emperor.

1526 Ferdinand, brother of Charles, acquires Bohemia.

1556 Charles V splits Hapsburg lands in half.

1700 Charles II, last Spanish Hapsburg monarch, dies.

1740-1780 Maria Theresa increases Hapsburg power in Europe.

1781 Joseph II, son of Maria Theresa, introduces major reforms and frees serfs.

1867 Austrian empire split between two monarchs: Austrian and Hungarian.

1918 Charles I, last Hapsburg emperor, gives up throne.

MARIA THERESA
In 1740, Maria Theresa came to the Austrian throne. She was only 23 and her empire was bankrupt. Over the next 40 years, she pulled Austria back from poverty and restored Hapsburg power in Europe.

AUSTRIA
Under Maria Theresa, Austria became the leading artistic centre of Europe. Austria was home to the composers Franz Joseph Haydn and Wolfgang Amadeus Mozart. Artists and architects came from all over Europe to work on great palaces such as the Schönbrunn in Vienna (above).

Find out more
CHARLEMAGNE
GERMANY, HISTORY OF
SPAIN AND PORTUGAL, history of

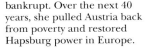

HEALTH

ARE YOU HEALTHY? Before answering, think about what you understand by "health". It doesn't just mean freedom from disease. Health is a measure of how sound and vigorous both your body and mind are. A truly healthy person has a sense of physical and mental well-being. Our health is precious and easily damaged. But there is much we can do to maintain it. Eating well, exercising, and getting enough sleep all help keep us healthy. Standards of health and health hazards are different from place to place. In some parts of the world many people have serious health problems because they are poor, hungry, and without clean drinking water. In other places stress at work, lack of exercise, and too much food bring their own health problems, such as heart disease. People also damage their health through the use of alcohol, tobacco, and dangerous drugs.

Regular, vigorous exercise helps prevent heart disease.

Better hygiene and a more balanced diet could eliminate much ill health in developed nations.

KEEPING HEALTHY

Food plays a large part in health. A healthy diet includes fresh fruit and vegetables, meat, fish, bread, eggs, and milk, but not too many fatty, salty, or sugary foods. Exercise keeps the heart strong and prevents us from gaining weight.

A doctor or nurse usually gives immunizations by injection.

IMMUNIZATION

Good health includes preventing disease. Immunization, sometimes called inoculation or vaccination, involves injecting the body with a vaccine. This is a tiny dose of the infecting agent of the disease, which has been specially treated to render it safe. The vaccination provides immunity, or protection, against the disease. It is now possible to immunize against diphtheria, polio, tetanus, measles, mumps, rubella, and tuberculosis. Immunization has completely eliminated one disease, smallpox.

PUBLIC HEALTH

Dirt and lack of hygiene damage health. During the 1840s, pioneers of public health in Europe worked to introduce clean water supplies and good sewage systems.

MENTAL HEALTH

A healthy mind is just as important as a healthy body. Stress, drug abuse, physical disease, and family problems such as divorce can all damage mental health. Specialist doctors who treat mental health problems are called psychiatrists. Other sources of help include drug therapy, counselling, and self-help groups.

To reveal cancer cells on a microscope slide, technicians stain the tissue sample with coloured dyes.

HEALTH CHECKUPS

Through routine medical checkups, doctors can detect health problems such as cancer at the early stages, when treatment is most effective. Checkups can also reveal hereditary health problems – diseases that pass from parents to children at birth.

Find out more

DENTISTS
DISEASE
DOCTORS
FIRST AID
FOOD
FOOD AND DIGESTION
MEDICINE

HEART AND BLOOD

OUR BODIES CONTAIN about 4.5 litres (8 pints) of blood. Throughout life the organ inside the chest, the heart, pumps blood to every part of the body, keeping us alive. The heart is such a powerful pump that it takes only about a minute for each blood cell to travel all the way around the body and back to the heart. Travelling along tubes called blood vessels, blood carries oxygen and nourishment from digested food to every part of the body. Blood also carries away harmful waste products such as carbon dioxide. Blood consists of red and white blood cells, platelets, and a watery liquid called plasma. A drop of blood the size of a pinhead contains about five million cells. About once every second the muscular walls of the heart contract, squeezing blood out of the left side of the heart and into blood vessels called arteries. The arteries divide many times until they form a network of tiny blood vessels called capillaries. The capillaries gradually join up again to form veins, which carry the blood back to the heart, where it is sent to the lungs for fresh oxygen.

INSIDE THE HEART

The heart has four chambers, two on each side. The upper chamber is called the atrium. Blood from the veins flows into the atrium, and then into the lower chamber, called the ventricle. The thick, muscular walls of the ventricle force the blood out into the arteries. The heart consists of two pumps, working side by side. The left pump sends blood full of oxygen (oxygenated) around the body. As the blood passes its oxygen to various parts of the body, it becomes stale (deoxygenated) and returns to the heart through the right pump. The right pump sends it to the lungs for fresh oxygen, then back through the left pump again to be sent around the body once more.

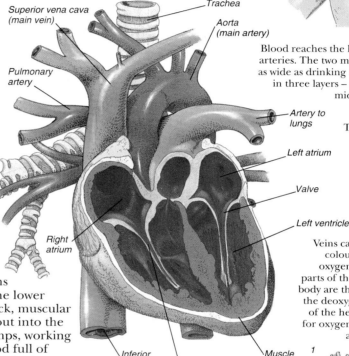

Superior vena cava (main vein)

Pulmonary artery

Right atrium

Inferior vena cava

Right ventricle

Trachea

Aorta (main artery)

Artery to lungs

Left atrium

Valve

Left ventricle

Muscle

HUMAN HEART
The heart is protected by the rib cage. An adult's heart is the size of a clenched fist and weighs about 300 g (9 oz).

ARTERIES
Blood reaches the heart muscle through coronary arteries. The two main coronary arteries are about as wide as drinking straws. Arteries have thick walls in three layers – a tough outer layer, a muscular middle layer, and a smooth lining.

CAPILLARIES
The tiny blood vessels that carry blood between the smallest arteries (arterioles) and the smallest veins (venules) are called capillaries. Capillaries allow oxygen and nutrients to pass through their walls to all the body cells.

VEINS
Veins carry deoxygenated blood (blue-coloured blood which contains little oxygen) back to the heart from other parts of the body. The largest veins in the body are the two venae cavae, which carry the deoxygenated blood to the right side of the heart, to be pumped to the lungs for oxygen. Veins are thinner, less elastic, and less muscular than arteries.

1

Blood enters atria (upper chambers).

2

Blood flows through to ventricles (lower chambers).

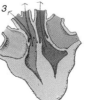

3

Ventricles contract to pump blood into arteries.

4

Atria refill with blood.

HEART BEAT
On average, an adult's heart beats 60 to 70 times each minute, and this rises to more than 150 beats after strenuous activity. Each heartbeat has two main phases. The phase when the heart muscle is fully contracted, squeezing out blood, is called systole. The phase when the heart relaxes and refills with blood is called diastole.

BLOOD CELLS
There are three types of blood cells. Red blood cells carry oxygen from the lungs to the rest of the body. White blood cells protect the body against illness and fight infection. Platelets, which are the smallest type of blood cell, help to make the blood clot. All blood cells are produced in the bone marrow, inside the bones.

White cell

Red cell

Platelet

HOW BLOOD CLOTS
When you cut yourself and blood flows out of the wound, platelets in the blood stick together and a fine meshwork of fibres forms. This meshwork traps more blood cells and forms a clot to seal the wound.

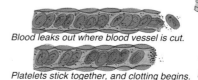

Blood leaks out where blood vessel is cut.

Platelets stick together, and clotting begins.

Tiny meshwork of platelets begins to form.

Blood clot forms, sealing the cut.

Find out more
BRAIN AND NERVES
HUMAN BODY
LUNGS AND BREATHING
MUSCLES AND MOVEMENT

White-hot steel

HEAT

STAND IN THE SUNSHINE: you feel warm. Go for a fast run: you will get hot. The warmth of sunshine comes from heat generated in the centre of the sun. Your body also produces heat all the time, and this heat keeps you alive. Heat is important to us in many ways. The sun's heat causes the weather, making winds blow and rain fall. The Earth's interior contains great heat, which causes volcanoes to erupt and earthquakes to shake the ground. Engines in cars, aircraft, and other forms of transport use the heat from burning fuel to produce movement. Power stations change heat into electricity which comes to our homes. Heat is a form of energy. Everything, even the coldest object, contains heat – a cold object simply has less heat than a hot object. All things are made of tiny particles called molecules. Heat energy comes from the vibrating movement of molecules. Hot objects have fast-moving molecules; molecules in colder objects move more slowly.

A solid, such as ice, has rows of molecules that vibrate back and forth. The molecules are locked together, so solids are often hard and cannot be squashed.

SOLIDS, LIQUIDS, AND GASES
A substance can be a solid, a liquid, or a gas, depending on how hot it is. Changing the temperature changes the substance from one state to another. For instance, liquid water becomes a solid – ice – when it is cold and a gas – steam – when it is hot.

A gas, such as steam, has molecules that move about freely so that the gas spreads out to fill its container.

BOILING POINT
At a temperature called the boiling point, a liquid changes to a gas. Below the boiling point the gas changes back to a liquid again. The boiling point of water is 100°C (212°F).

MELTING POINT
Heating a solid makes it melt into liquid. This happens only at a certain temperature, which is called the melting point. Below this temperature, the liquid freezes to a solid again. The melting point of water is 0°C (32°F).

Warm rising air

A process called convection spreads heat through gases and liquids. For example, hot air above a heater rises. Cold air flows in to take its place, becomes hot, and rises. In this way, a circular current of air moves around a room, carrying heat with it.

Convection heater

A liquid, such as water, has molecules that are close together. The molecules can move around more easily than in a solid, so a liquid can flow.

A liquid slowly changes into a gas at a temperature lower than its boiling point. This is called evaporation. A puddle dries up because the water evaporates and turns into water vapor.

All objects give out heat rays that travel through air and space. The heating element of an oven cooks food with heat rays. The transmission (movement) of heat by heat rays is called radiation. It is not the same as nuclear radiation.

Heat travels through solid objects by a process called conduction. Metal conducts heat well. For instance, a metal spoon in a cup of coffee gets hot quickly. Other substances, such as wood and plastic, do not conduct heat well. They are called insulators and are used to make saucepan handles.

Cool incoming air

HEAT ENERGY
Heat is just one of many forms of energy. Sources of heat change one type of energy into heat energy. A burning fire, for example, changes chemical energy in its fuel into heat energy. Electric heaters change electrical energy into heat.

The digestive system of an animal or person changes chemical energy from the food into heat inside the body.

INFRARED RAYS
Heat rays are also called infrared rays. They are invisible rays very similar to red light rays, which is why the rays are called infrared. All objects give out these rays, and hot objects produce stronger infrared rays than cold objects. Some electric heaters have curved reflectors that send heat rays forward just as a mirror reflects light rays.

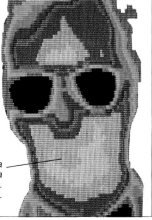

This is a thermogram (heat picture) of a person's face. It was taken by a special camera that uses infrared rays instead of light rays. The hottest parts are yellow in the picture.

TEMPERATURE

Temperature is a measure of how hot an object is. A hot object has a higher temperature than a cold object. When objects are extremely cold, they have negative temperatures: a minus sign indicates how many degrees the temperature is below zero on the temperature scale.

Centre of the sun, about 15 million°C (27 million°F)

Centre of the Earth, about 4,500°C (8,100°F)

Aluminium melts, 660°C (1,220°F)

Water boils, 100°C (212°F)

Normal body temperature, 37°C (98°F)

Water freezes, 0°C (32°F)

Oxygen becomes liquid, -218°C (-360°F)

Absolute zero, -273°C (-460°F)

FAHRENHEIT
Temperatures marked with an *F* are recorded using the Fahrenheit scale of temperature. In the Fahrenheit scale, water freezes at 32°F and boils at 212°F. A few countries, including the United States, use the Fahrenheit scale.

Digital display accurately records temperature within one tenth of a degree.

Column of coloured alcohol

Level of column indicates temperature against scale

ABSOLUTE ZERO
The lowest temperature of all is called absolute zero. At absolute zero, -273°C (-460°F), molecules stop moving. Scientists have cooled substances almost to absolute zero, but the exact temperature can never be reached.

CELSIUS
Temperatures marked with a *C* are recorded in the Celsius (also called Centigrade) scale of temperature. In this scale, water freezes at 0°C and boils at 100°C. Scientists and most countries of the world use the Celsius scale.

EXPANSION AND CONTRACTION

All things expand (get slightly larger) when they get hot. They contract (shrink) again when they cool. This happens because the molecules inside an object make larger, more rapid vibrations as the object heats up. The molecules therefore take up more space, causing the object to expand. The supersonic airliner *Concorde* expands by about 25 cm (10 in) while in flight. The aircraft heats up because of the friction of the air rushing over it at more than 2,400 km/h (1,500 mph)).

THERMOMETER

A thermometer is an instrument that measures temperature. A digital thermometer has a display that shows the temperature in numbers. Glass thermometers contain a thin column of mercury (a liquid metal) or coloured alcohol that expands and rises in the thermometer as the temperature increases.

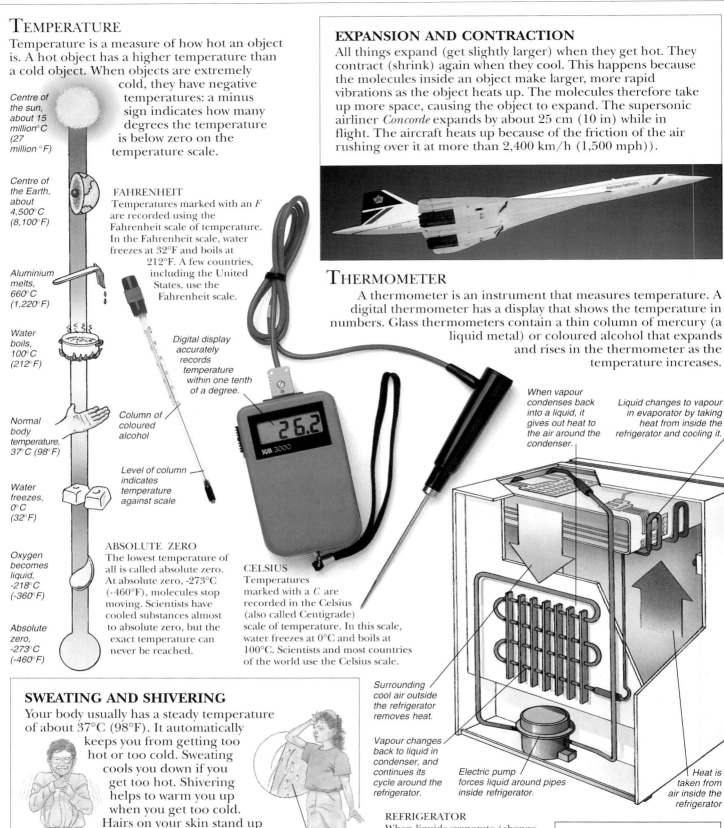

When vapour condenses back into a liquid, it gives out heat to the air around the condenser.

Liquid changes to vapour in evaporator by taking heat from inside the refrigerator and cooling it.

Surrounding cool air outside the refrigerator removes heat.

Vapour changes back to liquid in condenser, and continues its cycle around the refrigerator.

Electric pump forces liquid around pipes inside refrigerator.

Heat is taken from air inside the refrigerator

26.2

SWEATING AND SHIVERING

Your body usually has a steady temperature of about 37°C (98°F). It automatically keeps you from getting too hot or too cold. Sweating cools you down if you get too hot. Shivering helps to warm you up when you get too cold. Hairs on your skin stand up when your body gets cold and help to trap a layer of air around the skin, which stops heat loss.

Shivering makes muscles move and produce heat.

Drops of sweat evaporate, which cools the skin.

REFRIGERATOR
When liquids evaporate (change into a gas), they take heat from their surroundings. In a refrigerator, a liquid circulates, going through a cycle of evaporation and condensation (changing back into a liquid again). As the liquid evaporates, it takes heat from the food in the refrigerator.

Find out more
ATOMS AND MOLECULES
EARTH
ENGINES
FIRE
STARS
SUN
VOLCANOES

HEDGEHOGS
MOLES, AND SHREWS

NIGHT-TIME IS WHEN hedgehogs, moles, and shrews are most active. These small mammals are well adapted to living in the dark. Their eyesight and hearing are poor, but their sense of smell is keen, and their sensitive whiskers enable them to feel their way in the dark. Hedgehogs measure about 23 cm (9 in) in length, with short ears, a short tail, a long snout, and stiff needle-like spines covering the top of the body. Most hedgehogs rest in burrows during the day and emerge at night to hunt for insects and earthworms. The common European mole spends most of its life underground. Its soft, velvety fur lies flat and smooth in any direction, which enables the mole to move around easily in the earth. The mole uses its curved front feet and long claws for digging tunnels in search of insects. Shrews are also suited to dark conditions. They look like mice but are smaller, with a longer nose and tiny eyes. Most shrews live on land; the water shrew has adapted to life in rivers and streams where it hunts for fish and tadpoles. Hedgehogs, moles, and shrews all belong to a large animal group called insectivores (insect eaters).

A hedgehog can shuffle along surprisingly fast.

When alarmed, the hedgehog rolls itself into a ball. The legs and face are gradually hidden.

The hedgehog usually peeps out to check that the danger has passed, before rolling over onto its front.

HIBERNATION
During winter, hedgehogs roll up into a ball and hibernate, or sleep until spring arrives.

EUROPEAN HEDGEHOG
When it senses danger, the European hedgehog rolls itself into a ball. It tucks its head and feet into the centre of the ball, and a ring of muscles around the lower part of its body tightens like a drawstring on a purse. Hedgehogs have about 5,000 spines; when danger threatens, the spines stick straight out.

MOLEHILL
A molehill is made from the excess soil that the mole pushes out of the way as it digs. The large burrow shown here is where the mole rests and raises its young.

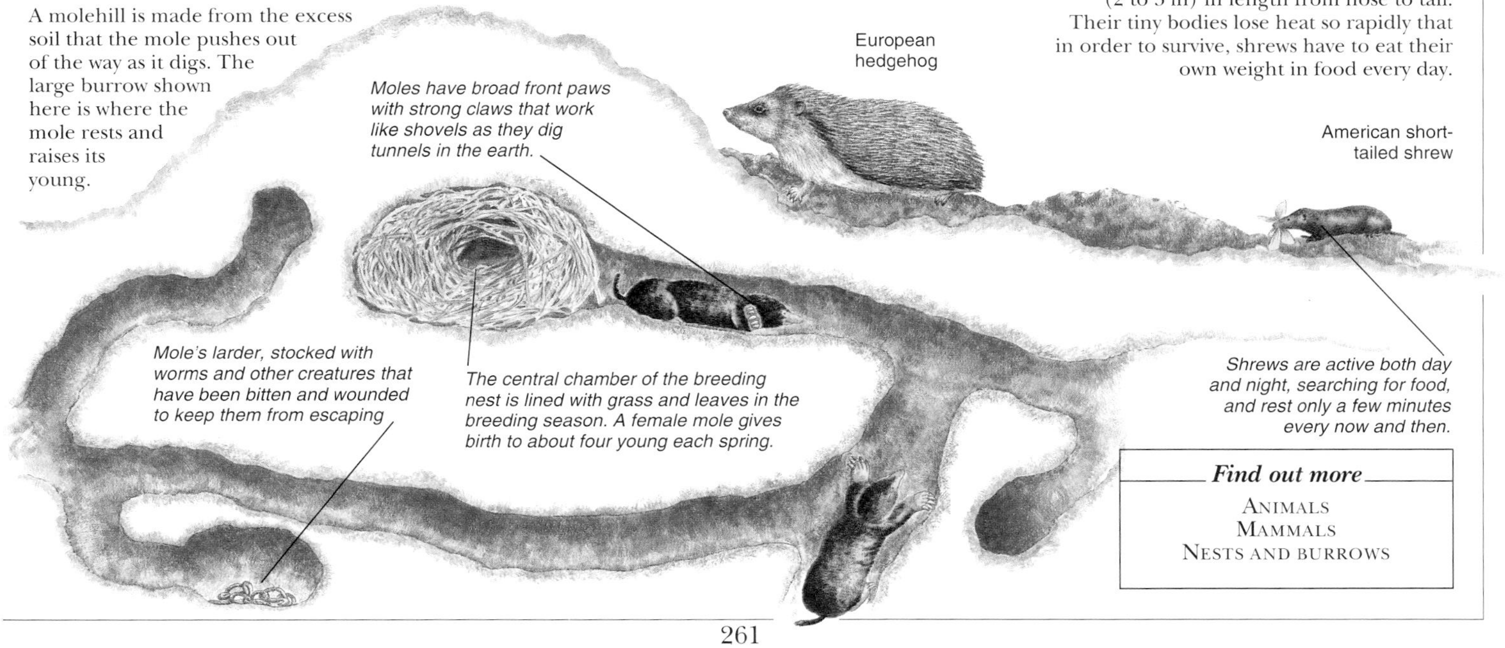

STAR-NOSED MOLE
The star-nosed mole shown here has an unusual nose which is very sensitive to touch and vibrations. The mole's nose helps it find worms and beetles in the darkness.

MOLE
There are about 20 different kinds of moles, found throughout the world. Like other moles, the European mole shown here lives mainly underground, digging new tunnels daily, each about 5 cm (2 in) wide. The mole patrols the tunnels regularly in search of worms and insects that have fallen through the walls.

SHREW
The smallest shrews measure just 5 to 8 cm (2 to 3 in) in length from nose to tail. Their tiny bodies lose heat so rapidly that in order to survive, shrews have to eat their own weight in food every day.

European hedgehog

American short-tailed shrew

Moles have broad front paws with strong claws that work like shovels as they dig tunnels in the earth.

Mole's larder, stocked with worms and other creatures that have been bitten and wounded to keep them from escaping

The central chamber of the breeding nest is lined with grass and leaves in the breeding season. A female mole gives birth to about four young each spring.

Shrews are active both day and night, searching for food, and rest only a few minutes every now and then.

Find out more
ANIMALS
MAMMALS
NESTS AND BURROWS

HELICOPTERS

OF ALL FLYING machines, the helicopter is the most versatile. It can fly forwards, backwards, or sideways. It can go straight up and down, and even hover in the air without moving. Because helicopters can take off vertically, they do not need to use airport runways and can fly almost anywhere. They can rescue people from mountains, fly to oil rigs out at sea, and even land on the roofs of skyscrapers. Helicopters come in many shapes and sizes. Some are designed to carry only one person; others are powerful enough to lift a truck. All helicopters have one or two large rotors. The rotor blades are shaped like long, thin wings. When they spin around, they lift the helicopter up and drive it through the air.

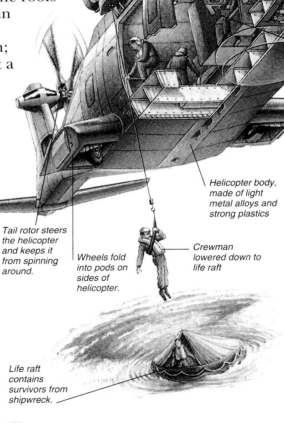

Gas turbine engine (one of three)

Rotor blades, made of ultra-strong plastics

Cockpit with automatic flight control system

ALL-PURPOSE HELICOPTER
The EH101 can transport 30 passengers or troops, carry 16 stretcher patients as an air ambulance, or lift a load of over 6 tonnes (5.9 tons). It flies at 280 km/h (170 mph).

Radar dome contains radar antenna.

Mission control console, equipped with radar screens and computers

Tail plane and fins keep the helicopter stable as it flies.

Tail rotor steers the helicopter and keeps it from spinning around.

Wheels fold into pods on sides of helicopter.

Helicopter body, made of light metal alloys and strong plastics

Crewman lowered down to life raft

Life raft contains survivors from shipwreck.

TAKING OFF
The rotor blades produce a lifting force which supports the helicopter.

The "collective pitch" stick adjusts the rotors so the helicopter can go up, hover, or go down.

Another control, the cyclic pitch stick, makes the main rotor tilt so that it can pull the helicopter in any direction – backwards, forwards, or sideways.

The tail rotor keeps the helicopter from spinning around. Pedals control the tail rotor so the helicopter can be turned to face any direction.

DEVELOPMENT
The Italian artist and scientist Leonardo da Vinci sketched a simple helicopter about 500 years ago, but it was never built. It was not until 1907 that a helicopter carried a person. It was built by a French mechanic named Paul Cornu.

Igor Sikorsky, a Russian-American, built the VS-300 in 1939. It was the first single-rotor helicopter, and it set the style for machines to come.

TWIN-ROTOR HELICOPTER
Large helicopters, such as this Boeing Chinook, may be twin-rotor machines. They have two main rotors that spin in opposite directions, and no tail rotor. The largest helicopter in the world is the Russian Mil Mi 12. It has twin rotors and is powered by four gas turbine engines.

Main rotor

Main rotor

Find out more

AIRCRAFT
ARMIES
MILITARY AIRCRAFT
PLASTICS

HIBERNATION

MANY WARM-BLOODED ANIMALS need extra energy in order to stay warm in the cold winter months, but the source of that energy – food – is scarce in winter. Some animals survive winter by migrating to a warmer place; others, such as bats and hedgehogs, hibernate, or sleep, in a safe and unexposed place such as a nest, burrow, or cave. In true hibernation, the body processes slow down almost to a standstill – the heartbeat occurs only every now and then, and the lungs breathe very slowly. The body temperature falls to only a few degrees above the outside temperature – as low as 0°C (32°F) in a hamster. If the outside temperature drops below zero, chemical reactions in the animal's body switch on to keep it from freezing to death. A hibernating animal feasts on extra food in the autumn so it can build up reserves of fat in its body and survive the winter months without food.

Senses such as hearing and sight are inactive during hibernation.

Dormouse curls up into a ball shape to reduce heat loss from its body.

Dormouse builds nest on or near ground, using stems, moss, and leaves.

Furry tail wraps around face for protection and insulation.

Up to half of body weight is lost during hibernation.

DORMOUSE

One of the best-known hibernators is the dormouse. In autumn it feeds eagerly to build up stores of body fat, then settles into a winter nest among tree roots or in dense undergrowth. Its heart slows to only one beat every few minutes, and its breathing slows down. Its body temperature also drops to a few degrees above the surroundings.

BLACK BEAR

The winter sleep of bears, skunks, and chipmunks is not as deep as the true hibernation of bats and mice. The American black bear's body temperature drops, but the heartbeat hardly slows at all. This means that the bear can rouse itself from its winter sleep quite rapidly during a spell of slightly warmer weather. Although it wakes up, the bear does not eat and continues to live off its body fat until the spring. Some female bears give birth during the winter months.

TORPOR

To save energy, some small, warm-blooded animals such as bats and hummingbirds allow their bodies to cool and their heartbeat and breathing to slow down for part of the day or night. This is called torpor. Large animals such as bears do not become torpid because they would need too much energy to warm up again afterwards. Bats often huddle together as they hang upside down to prevent too much heat loss. When the cold season comes, bats fly to a special cave or tree called a hibernaculum, where they begin true hibernation.

ESTIVATION

Many desert animals sleep during the hot, dry season to survive the intense heat. This is called estivation – the opposite of hibernation. Many desert creatures estivate, including lizards, frogs, insects, and snails. Before estivation begins, snails seal their shell openings with a film of mucus that hardens in the heat.

Snails cluster on grass stems to estivate, away from predators on the ground.

Find out more
BATS
BEARS AND PANDAS
MICE, RATS, AND SQUIRRELS
MIGRATION
SNAILS AND SLUGS

HINDUISM

MORE THAN 5,000 YEARS ago Hinduism, one of the world's oldest religions, began in India. Hinduism has no single founder but grew gradually from early beliefs. Today there are many different Hindu groups or sects. They may worship the same Hindu gods, but they do not all share the same religious beliefs. Nevertheless, most Hindus believe that people have a soul which does not die with them. Instead the soul moves from body to body. People who live good lives are reincarnated, or born again in a higher state. Bad deeds lead to rebirth as an animal or an insect. It is possible to escape from the need to be born again by improving with each life. This is called reaching the state of Moksha. Hindus are born into castes, or groups, which give them their rank in society. Rules restrict how people of different castes may mix and marry. Today there are about 660 million Hindus in the world. They live mainly in India and East Africa.

HINDU FESTIVALS

Holi Two-day festival in spring.

Janmashtami August/September; festival in honour of Krishna.

Dussehra 10 days in September/October.

Diwali Festival of lights.

New Year

Temple festivals are held once a year.

GODS

Stories of the gods and their battles against evil are told in ancient Indian poems such as the Mahabharata. Many Hindu gods are related to each other. Although most Hindus have a favourite god who is special to them, there are three gods – Vishnu, Brahma, and Shiva – who are more important than the rest. Vishnu, the preserver, appears in ten different forms. Two of the most popular are Rama and Krishna.

More gentle than the fierce Shiva, Vishnu comes to restore order and peace to the world.

The four heads of Brahma, the creator, show that he has knowledge of all things.

Shiva, the destroyer, rules over the death and life of everything in the world. It is thought that when Shiva dances, he creates life.

MARRIAGE

Family life and marriage are very important to Hindus. Parents are often involved in their children's choice of partner. Women are required to be dutiful and obedient to their fathers and husbands. A wedding ceremony is accompanied by music and feasting. The bride and groom wear colourful garlands of flowers and make solemn promises to each other before a holy man.

TEMPLES

In southern and central India there are large temples which contain ornate carvings and statues of the many Hindu gods. Priests look after the temples. Visitors come to pray and bring offerings of flowers and food. After the food has been blessed, it is shared by the worshippers or given to the poor.

Find out more

FESTIVALS AND FEASTS
INDIA
RELIGIONS

HORSES
ZEBRAS, AND ASSES

FOR THREE THOUSAND years before trains and cars were invented, horses were a fast, efficient method of transport. These swift, graceful creatures are among the most intelligent of all animals, and easy for humans to train. Today there are more than 75 million domestic (tame) horses, and they are divided into more than 100 different breeds.

Horses, asses, and zebras belong to the equid family, a group that includes donkeys and mules. Equids are long-legged mammals with hoofed feet, flowing tails, and a mane on the upper part of the neck. They can run or gallop with great speed. A keen sense of smell, good eyesight, and sharp hearing mean that they are always alert and ready to flee from danger. Horses, asses, and zebras are grazing animals that feed almost entirely on grasses, which they crop with their sharp front teeth.

TEETH
Experts can tell the age of a horse by the number and size of its teeth, and the way the teeth have worn down with use. Most adult horses have between 40 and 42 teeth.

UNICORN
The unicorn is an imaginary horselike creature. It often appears in legends and folktales as a symbol of purity.

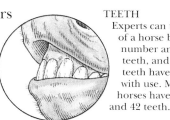

Poll

Forelock

Large ears can swivel to detect which direction a sound comes from.

Mane covers upper neck.

Eyes are on upper parts of head for good all-round vision.

Withers

Back

Flank

Croup

Dock

Muzzle

Long jaws and strong cheek muscles for chewing grass

Neck

Chest

HOOVES
Horses walk on the tips of their toes. On each foot is a strong, hard hoof made of bone. There is a pad on the sole of the hoof called the frog. The frog acts like a shock absorber when the horse runs. People also put metal horseshoes on a horse's hooves to protect them on hard roads and rough ground.

Heel

Knee

Frog

Sole

Horseshoe

Cannon

Bones

Elbow

Horse uses long, coarse hairs of tail as a fly-whisk and as a social signal.

Fetlock

Pastern

Hoof

Today's domestic horse

Eohippus

THE FIRST HORSES
Eohippus, one of the first horses, lived in woodland areas more than 50 million years ago. It was only 60 cm (2 ft) high. Through evolution, horses gradually became larger and began to live in more open grassland areas.

An adult male horse is called a stallion; an adult female is a mare. Young males are called colts; young females are fillies.

HORSES AND HUMANS
Domestic horses are trained to do many jobs, from pulling carts to carrying soldiers into battle. Many sports and leisure activities involve horses, such as show jumping, polo, rodeo, flat racing, and steeplechasing. Champion horses are worth millions of pounds, and the first prize at a famous horse race may be thousands of pounds.

In some countries horses and mules are still used instead of cars. They are also used on farms to till fields, fertilize the crops, and pull produce to market.

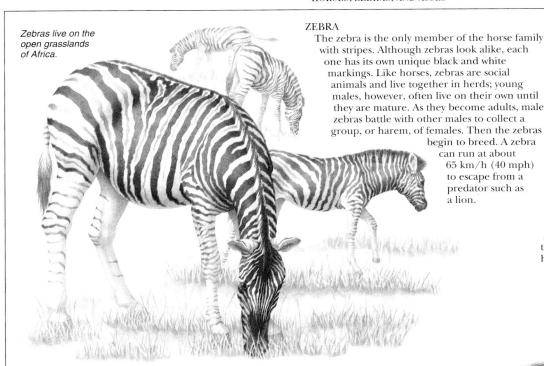

Zebras live on the open grasslands of Africa.

ZEBRA

The zebra is the only member of the horse family with stripes. Although zebras look alike, each one has its own unique black and white markings. Like horses, zebras are social animals and live together in herds; young males, however, often live on their own until they are mature. As they become adults, male zebras battle with other males to collect a group, or harem, of females. Then the zebras begin to breed. A zebra can run at about 65 km/h (40 mph) to escape from a predator such as a lion.

DONKEY

A donkey is a domesticated ass. Donkeys, together with horses and asses, have been hauling loads for people for thousands of years. They are often called beasts of burden. Another beast of burden, the mule, is the offspring of a female horse and a male donkey.

ASS

There are two kinds of wild ass – the African ass and the Asian ass. The African ass lives in dry, rocky areas of North Africa; the Asian ass is found in Asia. Asses need very little water and survive in the wild by eating tough, spiky grasses. Like other members of the horse family, the female ass has one young at a time, called a foal. The foal can walk a few minutes after birth.

A wild African ass and a smaller domesticated ass, or donkey

PRZEWALSKI'S HORSE

Also called the Asian horse or "wild horse", Przewalski's horse is closely related to the domestic horse. Herds of these horses once lived on the high plains of Mongolia, in northern Asia. Today there are only a few hundred left in zoos and wildlife parks around the world.

GALLOPING

Horses move at a walk, trot, canter, or gallop, in increasing order of speed. When a horse gallops, all its hooves are off the ground for a split second during each stride. The fastest race horses can gallop at more than 65 km/h (40 mph) over a short distance.

TYPES OF HORSES

There are three main kinds of horses – draught horses such as Shires; light horses such as Arabian horses; and ponies such as Shetland ponies. Draught horses pull ploughs, and light horses take part in races.

HOW WE MEASURE HORSES

Horses are measured in hands from the ground to the withers (the highest point of the shoulder). One hand equals 10 cm (4 in). Shire horses are the largest and Shetland ponies are the smallest horses.

Shetland pony is 120 cm (12 hands, 4 ft) high.

Appaloosa is about 150 cm (15 hands, 5 ft) high.

Shire horse may be more than 183 cm (18 hands, 6 ft) at the shoulders and weigh more than 1,135 kg (2,500 lb).

Find out more

ANIMALS
MAMMALS
TRANSPORT, HISTORY OF
WILD WEST

HOSPITALS

A MACHINE THAT CAN make sick people well sounds like an inventor's dream, but it already exists – it is a hospital. Like a machine, a hospital is a well-run unit that contains all the equipment and facilities needed to treat every kind of illness. But unlike a machine, a hospital is a human place staffed by doctors, nurses, and operating staff, all of them trained to make patients well. Hospitals are needed because there are some disorders that physicians cannot treat in the home or the doctor's office. Someone needing surgery, for instance, usually has to spend a day or more in the hospital. Other people may visit the hospital for a short time during the day, perhaps to see a skin specialist, or for medical tests such as x-rays. In this way hospitals provide both long- and short-stay help. They also provide facilities for diagnosing illness, and care for people who are not ill at all, such as women giving birth.

EARLY HOSPITALS
Until the 19th century, hospitals were unhealthy, crowded places where the poor were treated. People with dangerous infectious diseases were also taken to hospitals to prevent them from infecting others.

GENERAL HOSPITALS
Some hospitals treat only certain patients, such as those with mental illnesses, but general hospitals treat patients suffering from all kinds of problems. Most towns and cities have a general hospital. General hospitals contain medical wards, surgical wards for people having operations, maternity wards for women having babies, and children's wards. They also have intensive care units, casualty departments, and operating rooms.

ACCIDENTS AND EMERGENCIES
People who are injured or suddenly taken very ill may be rushed by ambulance to the casualty department.

A powerful lamp lights the area where the surgeon operates.

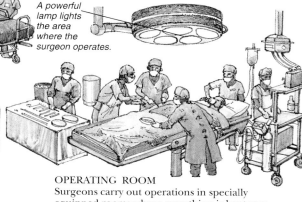

OPERATING ROOM
Surgeons carry out operations in specially equipped rooms where everything is kept very clean to prevent infection.

In the intensive care unit the staff uses electronic monitoring devices to keep constant track of the condition of seriously ill patients.

Nurses carefully monitor the medication that each patient receives.

WARDS
Some patients stay in a ward – a room with several beds. Hospital departments, such as surgery, are also called wards.

NURSING
A nurse is a man or a woman who is trained to care for the ill and injured. Nurses check the condition of their patients, give them medication, and keep them as comfortable as possible.

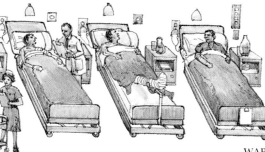

CHILDREN'S HOSPITALS
Some cities have special hospitals that are only for children. Nurses and doctors who work in children's hospitals are specially trained to care for babies and children. Parents can usually stay with their children throughout the day and, if necessary, can sleep in the hospital at night.

Find out more
DOCTORS
MEDICINE
MEDICINE, HISTORY OF
X-RAYS

HOUSEHOLD APPLIANCES

UNTIL THIS CENTURY, most people had to do their household tasks by hand. Laundry and house cleaning took up hours every day, leaving little time for leisure. Today, there are household appliances that answer almost every need. Cooking and cleaning have become simple tasks with the aid of efficient cookers, microwave ovens, vacuum cleaners, and dishwashers. In addition to machines that ease household chores, there is a whole range of appliances that make homes safer and more comfortable. Many houses are protected by complex burglar alarms that not only produce a loud warning siren but also automatically send a telephone message to the police station. Heating systems warm houses in cold climates, and air conditioning units keep rooms cool and fresh in hot weather. With the development of electronics, many homes today use increasing amounts of technology.

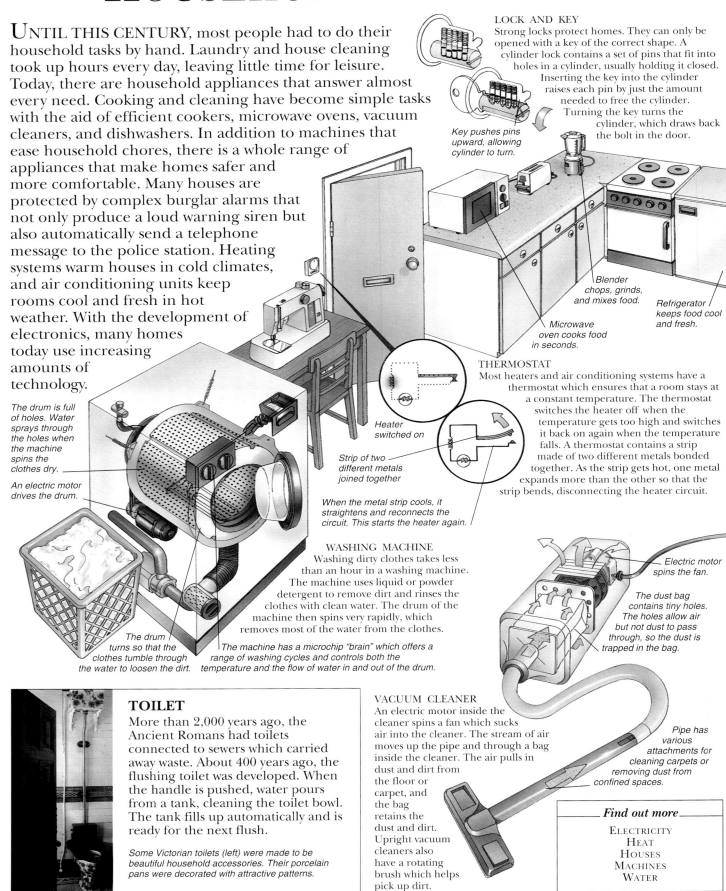

LOCK AND KEY
Strong locks protect homes. They can only be opened with a key of the correct shape. A cylinder lock contains a set of pins that fit into holes in a cylinder, usually holding it closed. Inserting the key into the cylinder raises each pin by just the amount needed to free the cylinder. Turning the key turns the cylinder, which draws back the bolt in the door.

Key pushes pins upward, allowing cylinder to turn.

Blender chops, grinds, and mixes food.

Refrigerator keeps food cool and fresh.

Microwave oven cooks food in seconds.

The drum is full of holes. Water sprays through the holes when the machine spins the clothes dry.

An electric motor drives the drum.

Heater switched on

Strip of two different metals joined together

When the metal strip cools, it straightens and reconnects the circuit. This starts the heater again.

THERMOSTAT
Most heaters and air conditioning systems have a thermostat which ensures that a room stays at a constant temperature. The thermostat switches the heater off when the temperature gets too high and switches it back on again when the temperature falls. A thermostat contains a strip made of two different metals bonded together. As the strip gets hot, one metal expands more than the other so that the strip bends, disconnecting the heater circuit.

WASHING MACHINE
Washing dirty clothes takes less than an hour in a washing machine. The machine uses liquid or powder detergent to remove dirt and rinses the clothes with clean water. The drum of the machine then spins very rapidly, which removes most of the water from the clothes.

The drum turns so that the clothes tumble through the water to loosen the dirt.

The machine has a microchip "brain" which offers a range of washing cycles and controls both the temperature and the flow of water in and out of the drum.

Electric motor spins the fan.

The dust bag contains tiny holes. The holes allow air but not dust to pass through, so the dust is trapped in the bag.

Pipe has various attachments for cleaning carpets or removing dust from confined spaces.

TOILET
More than 2,000 years ago, the Ancient Romans had toilets connected to sewers which carried away waste. About 400 years ago, the flushing toilet was developed. When the handle is pushed, water pours from a tank, cleaning the toilet bowl. The tank fills up automatically and is ready for the next flush.

Some Victorian toilets (left) were made to be beautiful household accessories. Their porcelain pans were decorated with attractive patterns.

VACUUM CLEANER
An electric motor inside the cleaner spins a fan which sucks air into the cleaner. The stream of air moves up the pipe and through a bag inside the cleaner. The air pulls in dust and dirt from the floor or carpet, and the bag retains the dust and dirt. Upright vacuum cleaners also have a rotating brush which helps pick up dirt.

Find out more
ELECTRICITY
HEAT
HOUSES
MACHINES
WATER

HOUSES

LEARNING THE ART of building enabled our ancestors to escape from the dark caves in which they sheltered from the weather and from hungry beasts. Building houses as they went, these first settlers moved to parts of the world where there was no natural shelter. Even in the icy wastes of the Arctic the Eskimo people learned to use ice to build domed igloos. Most houses, though, consist of walls and a roof, built in a huge variety of styles. Local materials dictate the kind of house that rises in a particular place, but climate is important too. For instance, houses in the mountains of the Alps have steep roofs to shed the heavy layers of snow that fall in the winter.

Modern houses are often complex structures, hiding in their walls networks of pipes and cables that supply water and energy and carry away waste. But in central Turkey, some people live in caves like those that provided the first shelter in prehistoric times.

MOBILE HOMES
The horse-drawn caravan which took fairground workers from place to place was the forerunner of today's mobile home.

MUD HOUSES
The people of New Mexico traditionally use dried mud to build houses. Because there is little rain, the mud stays hard, and building and repairs are quick and easy. Thick walls and small windows keep out the sun's fierce heat and retain warmth at night.

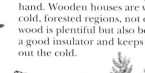

Mud was one of the first materials to be used for building houses.

HOUSEBOATS
A floating house solves the problem of finding a place to live in an overcrowded city where there is no more room to build. The houseboats are usually permanently moored.

This kind of houseboat is found in Hong Kong.

WOODEN HOUSES
American Pioneers built their houses with wood, the best building material at hand. Wooden houses are well suited to cold, forested regions, not only because wood is plentiful but also because it is a good insulator and keeps out the cold.

The earliest wooden houses were crude log cabins. The walls and roof of this house are made of sawed timber.

FLATS
City and town flats house hundreds of families on small plots of land, where there is room for just a few low-rise homes. The tallest buildings are made of strong materials such as steel and concrete.

HOUSE OF THE FUTURE
The newest building techniques aim to conserve energy. In the future people may live in better-insulated homes that need little fuel. The wind will generate electricity, the sun's rays will heat water, and computers will control the windows and heating system.

SHANTYTOWN
Many cities are ringed with shantytowns because people crowd in to seek work but can find nowhere to live. Some build their own homes with any materials they can find. Others remain homeless, sleeping on the streets.

Find out more
ARCHITECTURE
BUILDING
ESKIMOS
FURNITURE

HUMAN BODY

FROM THE MOMENT we are born to the moment we die, our bodies do not stop working for a second. The human body is a complex collection of more than 50,000 million living units called cells. There are about 200 different types of cells, including nerve cells, called neurons, and specialized cells called gland cells. Glands produce substances such as hormones and enzymes, which they release into the body for different purposes. Each type of cell in the body does a particular job. Cells that do similar jobs are grouped together to form tissues, such as muscle tissue and nerve tissue. Tissues, in turn, are grouped together to form organs, which are the main separate parts of the body. The lungs, heart, liver, and kidneys are some of the main organs. The organs work together as systems, and each system carries out one major function. For example, the heart, blood vessels, and blood form the circulatory system, which carries oxygen and nutrients around the body and carries away waste products. All the different systems work together, controlled by the brain. The entire body is a living marvel of design.

THE BODY'S ABILITIES
The human body is capable of amazing feats of balance and coordination. Many animals can run faster or jump higher, but our bodies are very adaptable. An extremely complex brain controls the body and gives us the intelligence to use our physical abilities to the best advantage.

CELL

Every second, millions of cells die and millions more replace them. An average cell measures about 0.025 mm (one thousandth of an inch) across, but there are many different kinds of cells in the body, each shaped for a certain job. Nerve cells are long and thin. Like wires, the nerves conduct (carry) electrical nerve signals. Red blood cells are doughnut-shaped and contain chemicals that carry oxygen around the body. Epithelial cells on body surfaces, such as the lining of the mouth, are broad and flat and fit together like paving stones.

Fat cell

Muscle cell   *Nerve cell*

SKIN
The body is covered by skin. Skin is flexible and helps protect the body. It keeps water and harmful bacteria out, and keeps body fluids in. Skin is also wear-resistant because it continually renews itself. The base of the upper layer, or epidermis, divides constantly to make new cells. The new cells move upwards as if on a conveyor belt, to replace cells that are worn out.

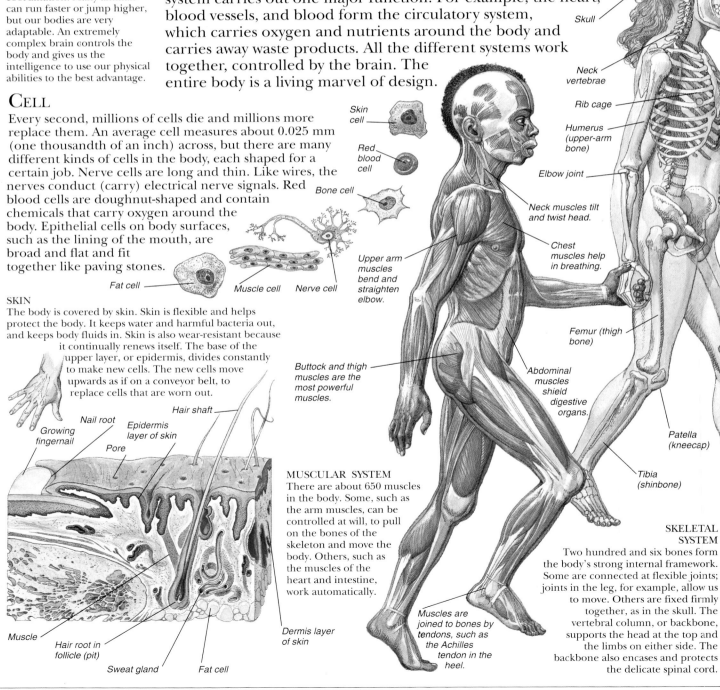

Skin cell

Red blood cell

Bone cell

Skull

Neck vertebrae

Rib cage

Humerus (upper-arm bone)

Elbow joint

Neck muscles tilt and twist head.

Chest muscles help in breathing.

Upper arm muscles bend and straighten elbow.

Femur (thigh bone)

Abdominal muscles shield digestive organs.

Buttock and thigh muscles are the most powerful muscles.

Patella (kneecap)

Tibia (shinbone)

Hair shaft

Nail root

Epidermis layer of skin

Growing fingernail

Pore

MUSCULAR SYSTEM
There are about 650 muscles in the body. Some, such as the arm muscles, can be controlled at will, to pull on the bones of the skeleton and move the body. Others, such as the muscles of the heart and intestine, work automatically.

Muscle

Hair root in follicle (pit)

Sweat gland   *Fat cell*

Dermis layer of skin

Muscles are joined to bones by tendons, such as the Achilles tendon in the heel.

SKELETAL SYSTEM
Two hundred and six bones form the body's strong internal framework. Some are connected at flexible joints; joints in the leg, for example, allow us to move. Others are fixed firmly together, as in the skull. The vertebral column, or backbone, supports the head at the top and the limbs on either side. The backbone also encases and protects the delicate spinal cord.

GROWTH AND DEVELOPMENT

As the human body grows, it develops many skills. Babies learn to smile, sit up, crawl, walk, and talk. Learning continues at school. On average, the peak of physical abilities is reached at about 18 to 25 years of age. Later, more changes occur with age. The skin becomes wrinkled and less elastic, the joints are less flexible, bones become more brittle, muscles are less powerful, and there is some loss of height and greying of hair.

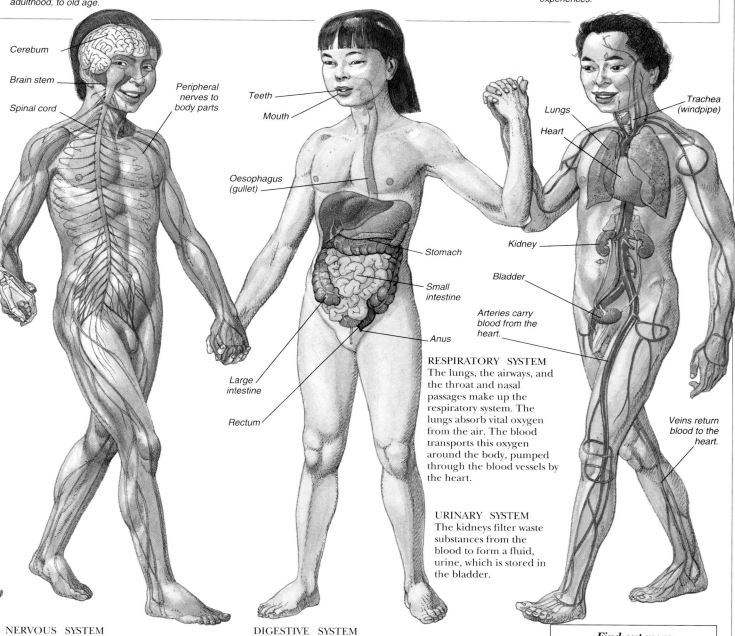

There are several stages of development in everyone's lifetime – from birth through childhood, adolescence, and adulthood, to old age.

In many older people, decrease in physical strength is offset by the wisdom and knowledge gained from a lifetime of experiences.

Cerebum

Brain stem

Spinal cord

Peripheral nerves to body parts

Teeth

Mouth

Oesophagus (gullet)

Stomach

Small intestine

Anus

Large intestine

Rectum

Lungs

Heart

Trachea (windpipe)

Kidney

Bladder

Arteries carry blood from the heart.

Veins return blood to the heart.

RESPIRATORY SYSTEM

The lungs, the airways, and the throat and nasal passages make up the respiratory system. The lungs absorb vital oxygen from the air. The blood transports this oxygen around the body, pumped through the blood vessels by the heart.

URINARY SYSTEM

The kidneys filter waste substances from the blood to form a fluid, urine, which is stored in the bladder.

NERVOUS SYSTEM

The brain and the nerves make up the nervous system. Nerves spread from the brain to all body parts, carrying signals in the form of tiny electrical impulses. The signals bring information from the sense organs to the brain and take instructions from the brain to the muscles. The brain controls many processes automatically, such as breathing, heartbeat, and digestion, without our having to think about them.

DIGESTIVE SYSTEM

The mouth, oesophagus, stomach, and intestines are part of the digestive system. These organs work together to break down food into particles that are small enough to pass through the lining of the intestine and into the blood. The mouth and teeth chop and chew food, and the stomach churns it with powerful digestive chemicals. The liver is the main organ for converting absorbed nutrients into forms more suitable for use by the various organs. The large intestine deals with wastes and leftover food.

Find out more
BRAIN AND NERVES
EARS
EYES
HEART AND BLOOD
LUNGS AND BREATHING
REPRODUCTION
SKELETONS
TEETH

INCAS

IN THE 12TH CENTURY a tribe of Native Americans moved down from the Andes mountains in South America to settle in the fertile Cuzco valley. By the end of the 15th century they had conquered a huge territory of 1,140,000 sq km (440,000 square miles) containing more than 10 million people. The Incas won this land with their powerful army and then controlled it with a remarkable system of communications. Inca engineers built a network of paved roads that crisscrossed the empire. Relays of imperial messengers ran along these roads (there were no horses or wheeled vehicles), travelling 240 km (150 miles) a day as they took messages to and from the capital city of Cuzco. At the head of the empire was the chief Inca, who was worshipped as a god and held absolute power over all his subjects. But in 1525 the chief Inca, Huayna Capac, died, and civil war broke out between two rivals for his throne. In 1532 a small force of Spanish soldiers arrived in the country and found it in disarray. They quickly overwhelmed the Incan army, and by 1533 the Inca empire was completely under Spanish rule.

South America

Inca empire

INCA EMPIRE
In 1525, at its height, the Inca empire stretched for more than 3,200 km (2,000 miles) along the Pacific coast of South America, ruling over much of present-day Ecuador, Peru, Bolivia, and Chile.

MACHU PICCHU
Covering an area of 13 sq km (5 square miles), the fortress city of Machu Picchu was built on a series of terraces carved into the side of a mountain more than 2,280 m (7,480 ft) above sea level.

Llamas have been used as pack animals for 4,000 years.

QUIPU
The Incas could not read or write. Instead, they used quipus – lengths of knotted string – to record every aspect of their daily life. Historic events, laws, gold reserves, population statistics, and other items of information were all stored accurately in this way.

Colour, number of knots, and length of string indicated what was recorded on the quipu.

The Incas were expert goldsmiths and often placed gold figurines (below) in their graves. Much of the Incan gold was melted down by the Spanish invaders.

WEAVING
The Incas wove lengths of beautiful, colourful cloth with elaborate patterns. The wool they used came from the mountain animals – llamas, alpacas, and vicunas, which the Incas kept on their farms. Many of their designs depicted jaguars and pumas.

TERRACE FARMING
The Incas were expert at farming every available piece of fertile land in their mountainous empire. They built terraces along the steep hillsides and watered them with mountain streams so that crops could be grown and animals kept to feed all the people who lived in the cities.

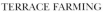

Find out more
CAMELS AND LLAMAS
CONQUISTADORS
SOUTH AMERICA,
  history of

INDIA
AND SUBCONTINENT

Traditional wooden printing blocks are still used in the production of colourful Indian textiles.

A TRAVELLER IN INDIA would need to speak more than 1,000 languages to understand conversations in every part of the country. Hindi and English are the two official languages, and 14 other languages are spoken nationwide. Many people, however, speak a local language of their own. The majority of Indians are Hindu in religion, but there are many Muslims, Sikhs, Christians, and Buddhists. Geographically, the country is very varied too. The north is mountainous, and in the centre the River Ganges waters a rich plain of productive farmland. In the south a hot and fertile coastal region surrounds a dry inland plateau. With a population of more than 896 million, India is the second most heavily populated country in the world (China is the first). About 70 per cent of the people live in small, often very poor villages, and work on the land. The rest live in big cities where some work in modern factories and offices. Recent advances in farming have made the land more productive, and after many years of famine, India can now feed itself.

India, Pakistan, Nepal, Bhutan, Bangladesh, and Sri Lanka occupy the Indian subcontinent. China is to the north, and to the east lie the jungles of Southeast Asia. The Indian Ocean washes the southern shores; the mountains and deserts of Iran and Afghanistan enclose the subcontinent on the west.

TEA
Most of the world's tea comes from the Indian subcontinent. The low tea bushes grow well on the sheltered, well-drained foothills of the Himalayas. Only the leaves near the tip of the plant are picked; they are then dried, rolled, and heated to produce the final product. Tea also grows in southern India and Sri Lanka.

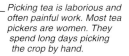

Picking tea is laborious and often painful work. Most tea pickers are women. They spend long days picking the crop by hand.

TEXTILES
The production of textiles, carpets, and clothing is one of the major industries in India. Millions of people work at spinning, weaving, and finishing a wide range of cotton and other goods, often printed with designs that have been in use for centuries. Many of these products are exported. There are large factories, but some people also work in their own homes.

KARAKORAM MOUNTAINS
A high mountain range separates the Indian subcontinent from China to the north. Most of the range is part of the Himalayas. At its western end, the Himalayas continue as the Karakoram range, which forms Pakistan's northern border. Few people have their homes in these mountainous regions. Nevertheless, the mountains have a great influence on people living thousands of kilometres away. Most of the rivers that irrigate the fertile plains of the Indian subcontinent begin in the Himalayas.

MODERN INDIA
India is one of the most industrial countries in Asia, with a wide range of engineering, electronic, and manufacturing industries. Its railway system is one of the world's biggest. However, traditional costumes and ways of life coexist with modern industries.

Ancient monument | Volcano | Highest mountain | Capital city | City/town

INDIA STATISTICS
Area: 3,166,829 sq km (1,222,714 sq miles)
Population: 896,600,000
Capital: New Delhi
Languages: Hindi, English, many local languages
Religions: Hinduism, Islam, Christianity, Sikhism, Buddhism
Currency: Rupee
Main occupation: Agriculture
Main exports: Gems, tea, clothing and textiles
Main imports: Petroleum, iron, steel, machinery

INDIAN PEOPLE
India has one of the most diverse populations in the world. Throughout history, one race after another has settled in India, each bringing its own culture, customs, and languages. The races often intermarried, but not all aspects of society became mixed and diluted: many groups clung to their traditions. For instance, there is no one Indian language, and people in different parts of the country often have their own unique local language.

AFGHANISTAN

PAKISTAN

IRAN

Mohenjo-Daro

Central Makran Range

R. Indus

Hyderabad

Karachi

Tropic of Cancer

0   200 miles
0   400 km

BANGLADESH
Area: 143,998 sq km (55,598 sq miles)
Population: 122,200,000
Capital: Dhaka
Language: Bengali
Religion: Islam
Currency: Taka
Main occupation: Agriculture

PAKISTAN
Area: 796,095 sq km (307,372 sq miles)
Population: 128,100,000
Capital: Islamabad
Language: Urdu
Religion: Islam
Currency: Pakistani rupee
Main occupation: Agriculture

BHUTAN
Area: 46,500 sq km (17,954 sq miles)
Population: 1,700,000
Capital: Thimphu
Language: Dzongkha, English and Nepali
Religion: Buddhism
Currency: Ngultrum

SRI LANKA
Area: 65,610 sq km (25,332 sq miles)
Population: 17,900,000
Capital: Colombo
Languages: Sinhalese, Tamil
Religion: Buddhism
Currency: Sri Lanka rupee
Main occupations: Agriculture
Main exports: Tea, textiles and clothing, gemstones
Main imports: Oil, machinery, food and drinks

NEPAL
Area: 147,181 sq km (56,827 sq miles)
Population: 21,100,000
Capital: Kathmandu
Language: Nepali
Religion: Hinduism
Currency: Nepalese rupee
Main occupation: Agriculture
Main exports: Food grains, jute, timber, oilseeds
Main imports: Textiles, oil, iron, steel, machinery

KERALA
The state of Kerala in southwest India borders the Arabian Sea. The eastern part of the state is hilly, but much of the land area is a flat plain. Kerala is one of the most densely populated states in India. Fishing is important for the local economy. Near the coast, the people of Kerala grow crops of cashew nuts, coconuts, and rice, and there are tea, rubber, coffee, and pepper plantations to the east. Although the government has encouraged modern farming techniques, traditional methods of agriculture and transport are common, such as the canoe in the picture above. Forestry is also important in Kerala. In the mountains there are forests of teak, ebony, and rosewood and a wide variety of wildlife.

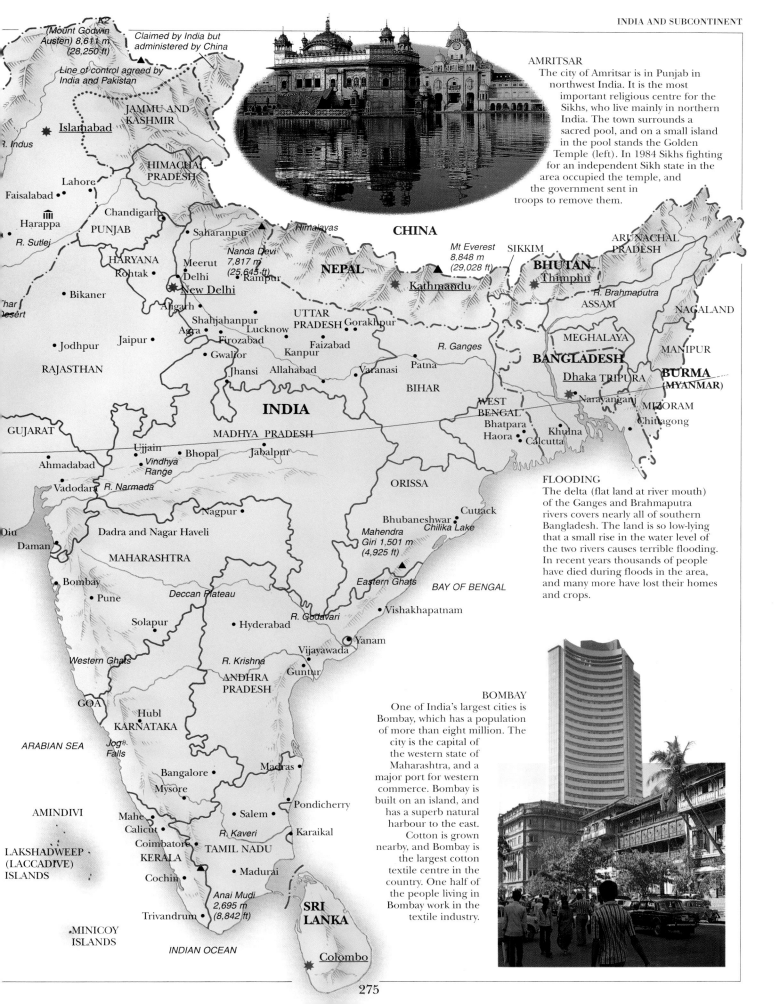

K2
(Mount Godwin
Austen) 8,611 m
(28,250 ft)

Claimed by India but
administered by China

Line of control agreed by
India and Pakistan

JAMMU AND
KASHMIR

R. Indus

Islamabad

HIMACHAL
PRADESH

Lahore

Faisalabad

Chandigarh

Harappa

R. Sutlej

PUNJAB

Saharanpur

Himalayas

CHINA

ARUNACHAL
PRADESH

HARYANA

Rohtak

Meerut

Delhi

Nanda Devi
7,817 m
(25,645 ft)

Rampur

Mt Everest
8,848 m
(29,028 ft)

SIKKIM

BHUTAN

Thimphu

NAGALAND

Bikaner

New Delhi

Aligarh

Shahjahanpur

NEPAL

Kathmandu

R. Brahmaputra

ASSAM

MEGHALAYA

MANIPUR

Jodhpur

Jaipur

Agra

Lucknow

UTTAR
PRADESH

Gorakhpur

BANGLADESH

Firozabad

Faizabad

Dhaka TRIPURA

BURMA
(MYANMAR)

Thar
Desert

RAJASTHAN

Gwalior

Jhansi

Kanpur

Allahabad

R. Ganges

Patna

Narayanganj

MIZORAM

Varanasi

BIHAR

Chittagong

INDIA

MADHYA PRADESH

WEST
BENGAL

Bhatpara

GUJARAT

Ujjain

Bhopal

Jabalpur

Haora

Khulna

Calcutta

Ahmadabad

Vindhya
Range

Vadodara

R. Narmada

Diu

Daman

Dadra and Nagar Haveli

Nagpur

ORISSA

Cuttack

Bhubaneshwar

Chilika Lake

Mahendra
Giri 1,501 m
(4,925 ft)

MAHARASHTRA

Deccan Plateau

Eastern Ghats

BAY OF BENGAL

Bombay

Pune

Solapur

Hyderabad

R. Godavari

Vishakhapatnam

Western Ghats

R. Krishna

Vijayawada

Yanam

ANDHRA
PRADESH

Guntur

GOA

Hubl

KARNATAKA

ARABIAN SEA

Jog
Falls

Bangalore

Madras

Mysore

AMINDIVI

Mahe

Salem

Pondicherry

LAKSHADWEEP
(LACCADIVE)
ISLANDS

Calicut

Coimbatore

TAMIL NADU

Karaikal

R. Kaveri

KERALA

Madurai

Cochin

Anai Mudi
2,695 m
(8,842 ft)

SRI
LANKA

Trivandrum

MINICOY
ISLANDS

INDIAN OCEAN

Colombo

AMRITSAR

The city of Amritsar is in Punjab in
northwest India. It is the most
important religious centre for the
Sikhs, who live mainly in northern
India. The town surrounds a
sacred pool, and on a small island
in the pool stands the Golden
Temple (left). In 1984 Sikhs fighting
for an independent Sikh state in the
area occupied the temple, and
the government sent in
troops to remove them.

FLOODING

The delta (flat land at river mouth)
of the Ganges and Brahmaputra
rivers covers nearly all of southern
Bangladesh. The land is so low-lying
that a small rise in the water level of
the two rivers causes terrible flooding.
In recent years thousands of people
have died during floods in the area,
and many more have lost their homes
and crops.

BOMBAY

One of India's largest cities is
Bombay, which has a population
of more than eight million. The
city is the capital of
the western state of
Maharashtra, and a
major port for western
commerce. Bombay is
built on an island, and
has a superb natural
harbour to the east.
Cotton is grown
nearby, and Bombay is
the largest cotton
textile centre in the
country. One half of
the people living in
Bombay work in the
textile industry.

Indian musicians play a drum called the tabla, and the tambura and sitar, which are both stringed instruments.

FILMS
Bombay and Madras are the centres of the Indian film industry, which produces even more films than Hollywood, United States. The films of the late Satyajit Ray, a leading Indian film director, are shown and admired worldwide.

MUSIC AND DANCING
Traditional Indian music is very complex, with a wide range of rhythms. Melodies are based on ragas – a fixed series of notes the performer must play as a basis for improvising or making up the tune. In recent years, bhangra, a new music combining traditional Indian music from the province of Punjab with western rock music, has become popular among young people.

Many of the traditional steps and postures in Indian dance have special meanings. Here the dancer depicts the God of Love about to shoot an arrow.

Dance is an important part of music making in India.

The holy city of Varanasi (or Benares) on the banks of the River Ganges

RIVER GANGES
From its source in the Himalayas, the River Ganges flows eastward across India, then turns south. The river's 2,510 km (1,560-mile) course takes it through Bangladesh to reach the sea in the Bay of Bengal. Hindus consider the river to be sacred.

Cows are sacred to Hindus in India and must not be harmed.

DELHI
The ancient city of Delhi lies on the hot plains of northern India. In 1638 it became the capital city of the Indian Mogul empire. When the British took control of India in the 1800s, they moved the capital to Calcutta, in the east of the country. In 1912, the British began to build a new city in the outskirts of Delhi from where they could govern their vast Indian empire. Since 1931 New Delhi has been the capital city of India.

TAJ MAHAL
This huge mausoleum, or memorial building, is a monument to Mumtaz Mahal. She was the wife of Shah Jahan, the Mogul emperor of India. When she died in 1631, her husband ordered the Taj Mahal to be built in her memory. The building is covered in white marble and inlaid with semi-precious stones.

Find out more
ASIA
BUDDHISM
FILMS
HINDUISM
INDIA, HISTORY OF
SOUTHEAST ASIA, HISTORY OF

HISTORY OF
INDIA

NEARLY 5,000 YEARS AGO, a civilization grew up around the Indus River in southern Asia. The peoples of this region built the world's first cities. Since that time India has been the birthplace of two great religions, Hinduism and Buddhism. Over the centuries, India has had many rulers and has been invaded many times. The first invaders were the Aryans, from the northwest. At the time, India consisted of several city-states, often in conflict. The Maurya dynasty, or ruling family, finally emerged, and under the Maurya emperor Asoka, India entered a period of peace. The Gupta dynasty came next, followed by the Moguls, who created a splendid civilization. But differences between various religious groups of Muslims, Sikhs, and Hindus weakened India. Between the 17th and 18th centuries, the British East India Company took control of much of the country; a century later the British government took over India. Many Indian people wanted independence. In 1947 India gained freedom from Britain, but was plunged into conflict between Muslims and Hindus. British and Indian leaders divided the country into two nations: India and Pakistan.

INDUS VALLEY CIVILIZATION
The peoples of the Indus Valley used the water from the River Indus to enrich their soil. They built Mohenjo-Daro and Harappa, the world's first cities. Craftsworkers created elegant and beautiful figures of people, animals, and gods, such as this seal in the form of a bull.

GUPTA EMPIRE
A family of wealthy landowners, the Guptas, founded their empire in A.D. 320, under Chandra Gupta I. Within a century the empire covered much of northern and eastern India. A golden age of cultural life began. The Guptas devised the decimal system of counting and writing numbers that we still use today. The empire collapsed in the seventh century after tribes invaded from central Asia.

EAST INDIA COMPANY
In 1600, the British founded the East India Company to trade with India. By 1765, the company was governing parts of India itself, but in 1858 the British government took over. The company ceased to exist in 1873. The drawing on the right shows an Englishman travelling by Indian elephant.

MOGUL EMPIRE
In 1526, Babur, the Mogul ruler, united India with the Mogul empire. The Moguls were Muslims, and they built some of the most magnificent mosques (Muslim places of worship) and palaces in the world. In 1858, the British abolished the empire.

BRITISH RAJ

From the early 16th century, Portugal, France, Britain, and the Netherlands all tried to take control of India. The British were the most successful. By the mid-1800s, they ruled the entire Indian subcontinent. In 1876 the British queen, Victoria, became empress of India. The government of India was called the British Raj (from an Indian word meaning "rule"). The Raj employed a civil service to administer the country from the capital city of New Delhi, which was completed in 1931.

MOHANDAS GANDHI

The leader of the movement for Indian independence from British rule was Mohandas Gandhi (1869-1948). Called the Mahatma, meaning "great soul", Gandhi attempted to unite all of India's different religions and peoples. He stressed the importance of *satyagraha*, or non-violent resistance to British rule.

NEHRU FAMILY

The first prime minister of India was Jawaharlal Nehru (1889-1964; above). Two years after his death, his daughter, Indira Gandhi (right), became prime minister. She remained India's leader almost continuously until she was assassinated in 1984, when her son Rajiv succeeded her. In 1989, he resigned; in 1991 he too was assassinated.

PAKISTAN AND BANGLADESH

When the British ruled the country most Indians were Hindus, but there were Muslims also. There was much conflict between Hindus and Muslims. In 1947 when India achieved independence, the British partitioned (divided) India.

A train bound for Pakistan carries terrified Muslim refugees.

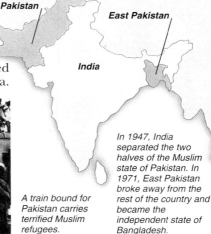

West Pakistan

East Pakistan

India

In 1947, India separated the two halves of the Muslim state of Pakistan. In 1971, East Pakistan broke away from the rest of the country and became the independent state of Bangladesh.

INDIA

c.2500 B.C. Indus Valley civilization sets up cities.

c.1500 B.C. Aryan invaders destroy Indus Valley civilization and introduce Hinduism.

c.A.D. 320-c.550 Gupta dynasty rules country.

500s Huns from central Asia overthrow Guptas.

700s Arab traders arrive in India; Turks introduce Muslim religion of Islam.

900s Muslim invasion.

1206-1526 The Delhi Sultanate (first Muslim kingdom) rules most of the country.

1526 Babur unites India with Mogul Empire.

1877 Queen Victoria is empress of India.

1885 Indian National Congress formed to campaign for Indian independence.

1906 Muslim League formed to campaign for a separate Muslim state in India.

1947 British India divided into India and Pakistan. More than 500,000 people killed during partition.

1948 Hindu fanatic assassinates Mohandas Gandhi.

1956, 1961 India takes over remaining French and Portuguese colonies in India.

1962 Border dispute with China leads to war.

1964 Death of Prime Minister Nehru.

1965 War between India and Pakistan over province of Kashmir.

1966 Indira Gandhi becomes prime minister.

1971 Bangladesh achieves independence.

1984 Indira Gandhi assassinated.

1991 Rajiv Gandhi assassinated.

Find out more

BUDDHISM
HINDUISM
INDIA
SOUTHEAST ASIA, HISTORY OF
TM

NATIVE AMERICAN
INDIANS

THE FIRST PEOPLE to live in North America arrived from Asia more than 20,000 years ago. They wandered over the Bering Strait, which was a land bridge at the time and now separates Asia and North America, following animals they were hunting. Gradually these early people settled into different tribes. Over the centuries the tribes developed organized societies. During the 1500s Europeans arrived in North America for the first time. They thought they were in the "Indies", or Asia, so they called the native Americans "Indians", a misleading name. The Europeans wanted land and threatened the existence of native North Americans. The Indians fought many wars with the new settlers. During the 1800s, the tribes resisted when the United States government tried to make them leave their homelands. After a bitter struggle the native Americans were moved onto reservations – areas of land set aside for them – where many still live today.

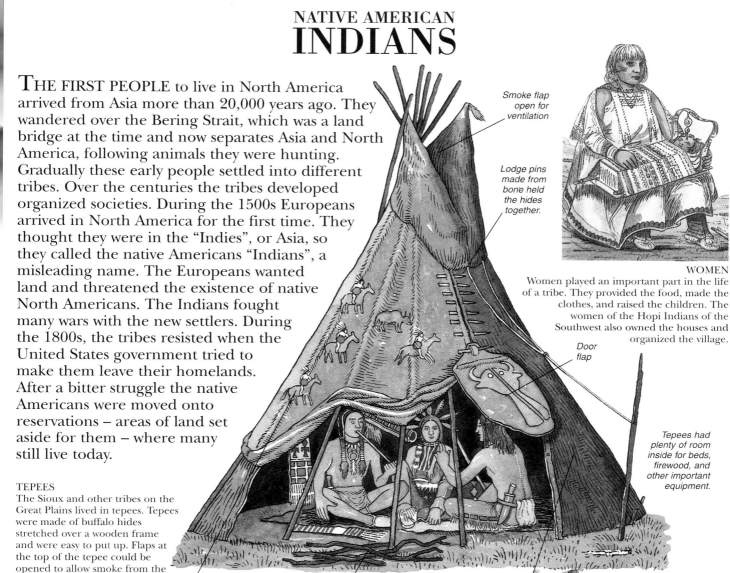

Smoke flap open for ventilation

Lodge pins made from bone held the hides together.

Door flap

Tepees had plenty of room inside for beds, firewood, and other important equipment.

WOMEN
Women played an important part in the life of a tribe. They provided the food, made the clothes, and raised the children. The women of the Hopi Indians of the Southwest also owned the houses and organized the village.

TEPEES
The Sioux and other tribes on the Great Plains lived in tepees. Tepees were made of buffalo hides stretched over a wooden frame and were easy to put up. Flaps at the top of the tepee could be opened to allow smoke from the fire to escape

Paintings that told a story decorated the hides.

A fire was lit in the entrance for cooking and warmth.

Buffalo hide was used to make the tepee cover.

SIGN LANGUAGE
Each Indian tribe spoke its own language. But Indians from different tribes were able to communicate with each other using a special sign language they all understood.

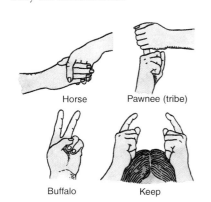

Horse

Pawnee (tribe)

Buffalo

Keep

GERONIMO
One of the most successful Indian chiefs in leading resistance to the "white man" was Geronimo (1829-1909), of the Chiricahua Apache Indians. Geronimo led raids across the southwestern states and into Mexico. In 1886, he was captured and exiled to Florida. Later he was released and became a national celebrity.

TRIBES
The native peoples of North America belonged to numerous tribes. Most of them hunted, fished, and farmed. Among the best known tribes are the Cheyenne, Comanche, and Sioux, who lived on the Great Plains; the Apache, Navajo, and Pueblo, who lived in the Southwest; and the Iroquois, Huron, and Cherokee, who lived in the East.

SIOUX

The Sioux lived on the Great Plains. They hunted buffalo on horseback, using the skins for clothing and tepees, the meat for food, and the bones and horns for tools. The Sioux were noted for their bravery and fighting skills and fought a long series of battles with European settlers and gold miners who took over their territory in the 1880s. In 1876, the Sioux defeated the U.S. cavalry at the now famous Battle of the Little Bighorn in Montana. But eventually the Sioux were driven onto reservations.

PUEBLOS

The Pueblos were peaceful tribes that lived in the Southwest. They farmed vegetables for food and were skilled craftsworkers, weaving brightly coloured cloth from homespun cotton and making pots. Their multi-storeyed houses were built of stone or adobe (sun-dried clay bricks) and were occupied by several families. Today many Pueblos live on reservations in Arizona and New Mexico.

TRIBAL LANDS

Quinault
Colville
Blackfeet
NORTHWEST COAST
Leech Lake
Menominee
Isabella
Crow
Standing Rock
CALIFORNIA-INTERMOUNTAIN
Uintah and Ouray
PLAINS
EASTERN WOODLANDS
Navajo
SOUTHWEST
Osage
Cherokee
Apache
Papago
Big Cypress

Last lands given up by the Indians 1890
Present-day reservations

TRIBAL LANDS

Before the Europeans arrived, the Indians occupied most of what later became the United States. The tribes were roughly grouped into six geographical regions. European settlement gradually forced the Indians to the west and southwest, so that by 1890 they were living on a few scattered reservations.

INDIAN WEAPONS

Indians used bows and arrows, knives, and clubs as weapons. Many also carried tomahawks. During the 16th century they got rifles from European traders.

Bow, made of wood

Quiver, used for holding arrows

Bow case holds the bow when not in use.

Tomahawks were axes with stone or iron heads. It was the Europeans who first made a combined axe blade and tobacco pipe.

CRAFTSWORK

Many Indians were skilled craftsworkers. They produced beautifully decorated clothes and headdresses. This pair of men's moccasins, from the Blackfeet tribe of western Canada, are made of stitched leather decorated with leather thongs and embroidered with coloured beads.

MODERN RESERVATIONS

The 1.5 million Indians in the United States live on reservations which they govern themselves. The Navajo reservation, for example, covers over 6 million hectares in Arizona, New Mexico, and Utah. Recently several tribes, such as the Pacific Northwest Coast Indians, have protested successfully and regained lost land.

Find out more

AZTECS
CANADA, HISTORY OF
COWBOYS
INCAS
UNITED STATES OF AMERICA, history of
WILD WEST

INDUSTRIAL REVOLUTION

THE WORLD WE LIVE IN TODAY, with its factories and huge cities, began less than three hundred years ago in Britain, then spread to Europe and the United States. Beginning in about 1760, great changes took place that altered people's lives and methods of work forever, changes that are known today as the Industrial Revolution. Machines powered by water and, later, steam were invented to produce cloth and other goods more quickly. It took many workers to run these big machines, so poor people moved from the country into the new industrial towns to be near the factories. There were more jobs and higher wages in the cities, but life was often miserable. Although the Factory Act in 1833 banned young children in Britain from factories, there were no laws to control how long people worked each day, or to make sure the machines were safe.

FACTORY OWNERS
Robert Owen (1771-1858) was a generous British factory owner who tried to improve working conditions. Many other owners grew rich by demanding long hours of work for low wages.

NEW TOWNS
Factory towns were built as fast and as cheaply as possible. Large families were crowded into tiny houses, and the water supply was often polluted. Diseases spread rapidly, and many people died young.

Factory workers lived in overcrowded houses, which often became slums.

Barges on new canals carried factory goods from one town to another.

Chimneys from the new factories created a lot of smoke. This made the towns dirty and polluted.

NEW TECHNOLOGY
Stronger metals were needed to make machines, so cast iron and, later, steel were developed. Steam to drive the new engines was made by burning coal to boil water. Coal mines were driven deep into the ground. Cotton cloth was the first product to be made completely by machine. The new goods were produced in large numbers so they were cheap to buy.

Cotton replaced wool as the main material for making clothes.

DAVY LAMP
In 1815 British inventor Sir Humphry Davy developed a miner's safety lamp.

Cast iron, which could be moulded into any shape, became common.

BEDSTEAD
Iron was even used for making beds.

INDUSTRIAL REVOLUTION

1708 Englishman Abraham Darby invents coke smelting of iron.

1733 John Kay, England, develops "flying shuttle" which mechanizes weaving.

1760 Start of Industrial Revolution, Britain.

1765 James Hargreaves invents "spinning jenny", England. It increases output of spun cotton. Scotsman James Watt develops steam engine which is used to drive machinery in cotton industry.

1769 Richard Arkwright's water frame used to spin strong thread. Speeds up production, early beginning of Factory Age, England.

1779 English weaver Samuel Crompton develops spinning "mule" which spins many threads at once.

1784 Henry Cort develops puddling furnace and rolling mill, England. Produces high quality iron.

1789 First steam-powered spinning loom, England. Speeds up textile production.

1793 Eli Whitney's cotton gin mechanizes cotton production, United States.

1804 Englishman Richard Trevithick builds first railway locomotive, England.

1825 First public railway from Stockton to Darlington, England.

1828 Development of hot-blast smelting furnace, England.

1842 Mines Act, Britain, bans women and children from working underground.

1851 Great Exhibition, London, displays new industrial products and techniques.

1856 Bessemer converter developed in England. Changes pig iron into steel.

1870 Industrialization established in Britain, Germany, United States.

MILLS

The first factories were water-driven cotton mills which produced cloth. They were noisy, dangerous places to work. Mill owners employed many women and children because they could pay them lower wages than men.

STEAM HAMMER

Unlike humans, steam-powered machines could work tirelessly, turning out vast quantities of goods. This steam hammer, invented in 1839, could hammer iron forgings with tremendous power and great accuracy.

The Clifton suspension bridge, Avon

BRUNEL

Isambard Kingdom Brunel (1806-1859) was probably the greatest engineer of the Industrial Revolution. His most famous bridge was the Clifton suspension bridge across the Avon Gorge. He also designed and built the Great Western Railway and the *Great Britain*, which was the first large steamship with an iron hull and a screw propeller.

CO-OPS AND UNIONS

Working people fought to improve their conditions. Some set up labour unions to fight for shorter hours and better pay. Others created co-op stores to provide wholesome food at reasonable prices. These stores later grew into a co-operative movement.

Find out more
FARMING
SCIENTISTS AND INVENTORS
TEXTILES
TRADE AND INDUSTRY
VICTORIAN AGE

INSECTS

THE EARTH IS CRAWLING with insects; in fact, they make up the largest group of animals. There are at least one million different species, including beetles, butterflies, ants, and bees. Insects first appeared on Earth more than 500 million years ago and are found in almost every kind of habitat, from cold mountains to tropical rain forests. Although all insects have six legs and a body covered by a hard exoskeleton (outer skeleton), they vary enormously in size and shape. The goliath beetle weighs more than 100 gm (3.5 oz); the tiny fairyfly is almost invisible to the human eye.

Some insects cause problems for humans. Flies spread disease, and weevils and locusts eat farm crops. Parasites such as ticks and lice live and feed on farm animals and sometimes on humans, too. But insects are a vital part of nature. They pollinate flowers and are an important source of food for many birds, bats, and reptiles. Certain insects are also very useful to humans – without bees, for example, there would be no honey.

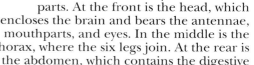

COCKROACH

A typical insect such as the common cockroach above has a body in three main parts. At the front is the head, which encloses the brain and bears the antennae, mouthparts, and eyes. In the middle is the thorax, where the six legs join. At the rear is the abdomen, which contains the digestive and reproductive organs. The hard, outer skeleton is made mainly of a substance called chitin.

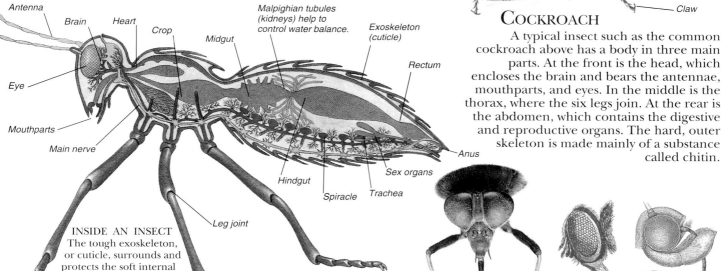

INSIDE AN INSECT
The tough exoskeleton, or cuticle, surrounds and protects the soft internal organs. An insect breathes through tiny air tubes called tracheae, which form a network inside its body. The tubes open at holes called spiracles in the cuticle. Water-dwelling insects such as the grubs of pond beetles breathe through gills, which are formed from delicate folds of cuticle.

Bugs such as aphids have needlelike piercing mouthparts.

Housefly sucks up liquid food through its padded, spongelike mouthparts.

Butterfly's tubular mouthparts are coiled like a watch spring.

FEEDING

Insects feed on almost anything – wood, blood, nectar, paper, shoe polish, seaweed, and other insects. The mouthparts of most insects, however, are specialized for a particular kind of food. Some mouthparts are adapted to bite, others to pierce, suck, sponge, scrape, and probe. The mouthparts have four main structures. The mandibles are hard jaws that bite and chew; the maxillae are secondary jaws; the labrum and labium are the upper and lower lips.

COMPOUND EYE
An insect's eye is made up of many rod-shaped units called ommatidia. A housefly eye has about 4,000 ommatidia. Each single ommatidium detects the amount and colour of light entering the eye, but it cannot form an image by itself. Together, all the thousands of ommatidia in the eye produce a mosaic-like view of the outside world made up of light and dark patches.

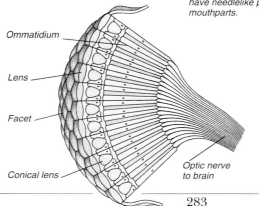

COURTSHIP

Some insects, such as the praying mantises shown here, have complicated courtship behaviour. After mating, the female mantis often grasps and eats the male mantis; the nutrients in the body of the male help the eggs to develop.

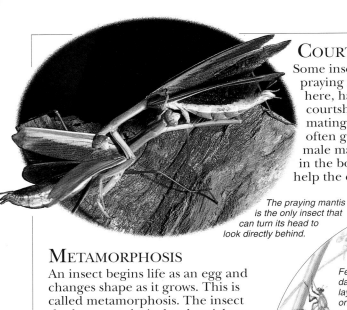

The praying mantis is the only insect that can turn its head to look directly behind.

Indian beetle has antler-like antennae.

Weevil has elbow-jointed antennae.

ANTENNAE
Sense organs called antennae detect smells and vibrations in the air and in solid objects. Often the male has larger, more branched antennae than the female. These help detect the scent that she releases into the air at mating time.

METAMORPHOSIS

An insect begins life as an egg and changes shape as it grows. This is called metamorphosis. The insect sheds, or moults its hard cuticle so that the new one beneath can expand and harden. In insects such as butterflies, the egg hatches into a larva or caterpillar, then a pupa or chrysalis, and finally an imago or mature adult. These great changes in form are known as complete metamorphosis. In other insects, such as grasshoppers, the young insect resembles the parent when it hatches. Each time the young insect moults its skin it looks more like an adult. This is called incomplete metamorphosis.

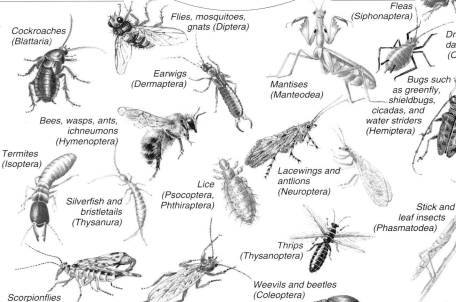

Female damselfly lays eggs on stem of reed.

Emerging nymph climbs up reed stem.

Adult emerges from nymph skin.

Young nymph (larva)

Older nymph (larva) develops wings.

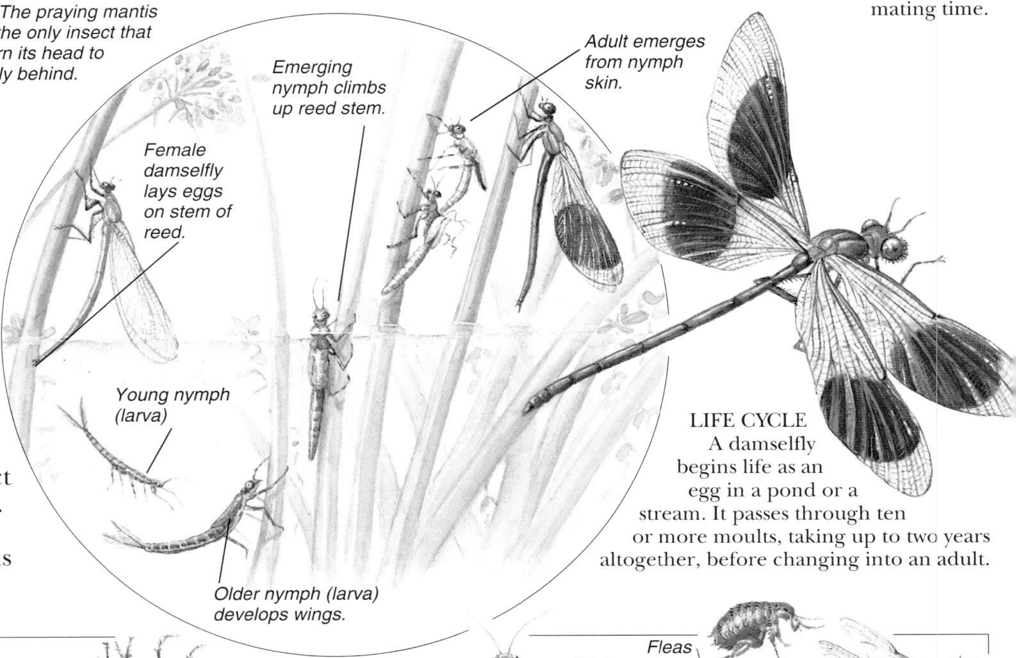

LIFE CYCLE
A damselfly begins life as an egg in a pond or a stream. It passes through ten or more moults, taking up to two years altogether, before changing into an adult.

TYPES OF INSECTS

There are about 20 main groups of insects. Beetles and weevils form the largest single group of insects, which contains more than 300,000 species known to entomologists (scientists who study insects). Most insects have wings at some stage during their life cycle; bristletails, silverfish, and firebrats do not. Fleas are also wingless; their wings have disappeared during the course of evolution.

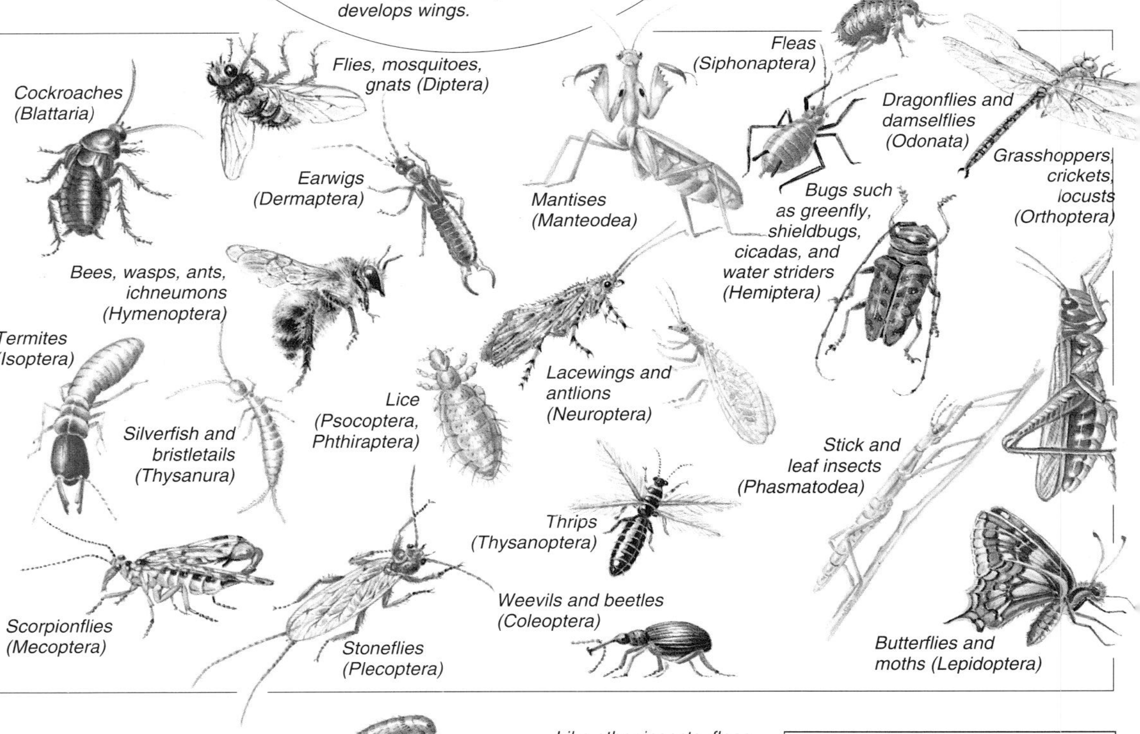

Cockroaches (Blattaria)

Flies, mosquitoes, gnats (Diptera)

Earwigs (Dermaptera)

Fleas (Siphonaptera)

Dragonflies and damselflies (Odonata)

Grasshoppers, crickets, locusts (Orthoptera)

Mantises (Manteodea)

Bugs such as greenfly, shieldbugs, cicadas, and water striders (Hemiptera)

Bees, wasps, ants, ichneumons (Hymenoptera)

Termites (Isoptera)

Silverfish and bristletails (Thysanura)

Lice (Psocoptera, Phthiraptera)

Lacewings and antlions (Neuroptera)

Stick and leaf insects (Phasmatodea)

Thrips (Thysanoptera)

Scorpionflies (Mecoptera)

Stoneflies (Plecoptera)

Weevils and beetles (Coleoptera)

Butterflies and moths (Lepidoptera)

FLEA

A flea can leap more than 30 cm (12 in) up into the air – the same as a person jumping 245 m (800 ft), which is higher than a 70-story building, or St. Paul's Cathedral in London, England.

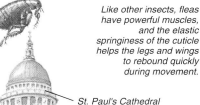

Legs kick down for extra acceleration.

Like other insects, fleas have powerful muscles, and the elastic springiness of the cuticle helps the legs and wings to rebound quickly during movement.

St. Paul's Cathedral

Find out more

ANTS AND TERMITES
BEETLES
BUTTERFLIES AND MOTHS
FLIES AND MOSQUITOES
GRASSHOPPERS
and crickets

IRELAND

Ireland is the smaller of the two main British Isles. The other – Britain – is to the east, and the Atlantic Ocean is to the west. Ireland is divided into the Republic of Ireland, which is independent, and the province of Northern Ireland, which is part of the United Kingdom.

OFF THE NORTHWEST COAST of Europe lies one of the most beautiful islands in the world. For centuries, writers and singers have praised the lush countryside and wild mountains of Ireland. Despite its beauty, Ireland is not a rich country and has few natural resources. It has no coal, no iron ore or vast reserves of oil. Nevertheless, Ireland's influence has been far-reaching, for the country is rich in its people and their distinctive Gaelic culture. Few corners of the world lack an Irish community whose members keep alive the memory and customs of their homeland. In 1973, the Republic of Ireland (Eire) joined the European Economic Community (now the European Union). Until then, its powerful neighbour and former ruler, the United Kingdom, had always dominated the country's economy. As a member of the Union, Eire is slowly becoming more prosperous and independent of the United Kingdom. New high-tech industries are replacing traditional agriculture and textiles as the main sources of employment.

Blocks of peat – carbon-rich soil consisting of decomposed plant life – are dug up from the marshy countryside and left to dry before being used as fuel.

DUBLIN

The capital city of the Republic of Ireland is Dublin. It lies on the River Liffey not far from the Irish Sea. The Vikings founded Dublin in the 9th century, and the city has many historic buildings and beautiful town squares.

COUNTRYSIDE

Wet west winds blow across Ireland from the Atlantic Ocean, soaking parts of the country with more than 200 cm (80 in) of rain each year. This makes the farmland very productive; about 16 per cent of the people work in farming and food processing industries.

GEOGRAPHY

Mountains to the south, west, and north surround Ireland's large, central plain. The plain is marshy in places, and there are many lakes, called loughs. Lough Neagh (right) in Northern Ireland, the biggest lake in the British Isles, is famous for its wildfowl and salmon.

Pipes, fiddles, and banjos are all used in traditional Irish music.

CULTURE

Many famous writers, including W.B. Yeats (1865-1939) and James Joyce (1882-1941), have been born in Ireland. There is also a strong musical tradition: Irish artists are well known internationally in both classical and rock music.

INDUSTRY

Once renowned for its traditional industries of glass, lace, and linen, Ireland now also produces medicine, electronics, and other modern goods. Many people work in the tourism industry.

Find out more
CELTS
EUROPE
IRELAND, HISTORY OF
UNITED KINGDOM
UNITED KINGDOM, HISTORY OF
VIKINGS

IRELAND

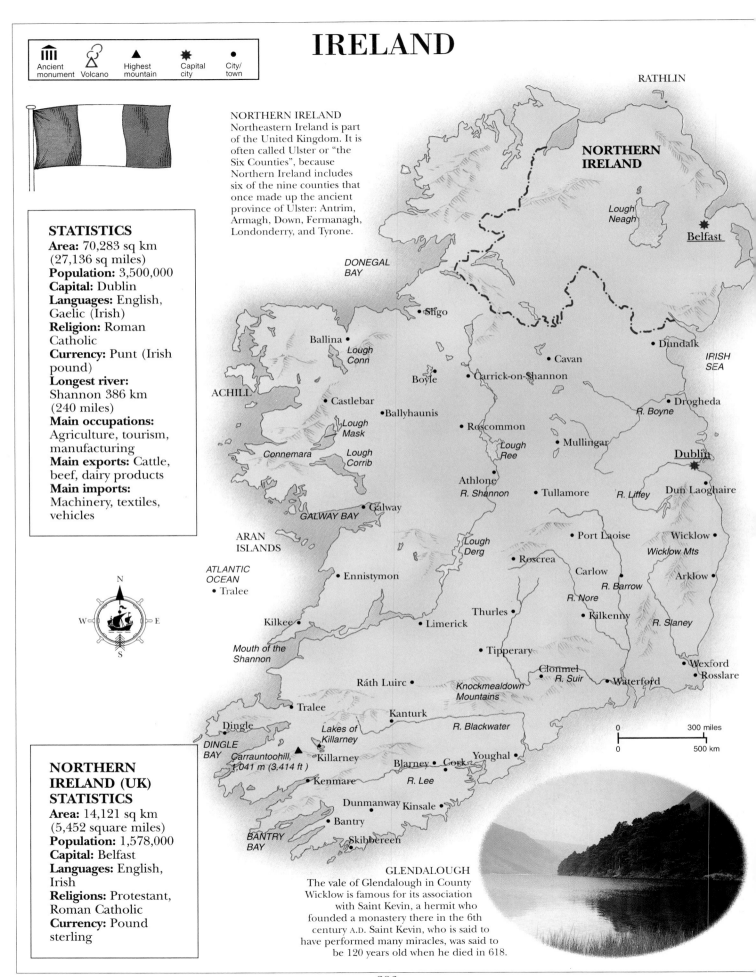

Legend:
- Ancient monument
- Volcano
- Highest mountain
- Capital city
- City/town

NORTHERN IRELAND
Northeastern Ireland is part of the United Kingdom. It is often called Ulster or "the Six Counties", because Northern Ireland includes six of the nine counties that once made up the ancient province of Ulster: Antrim, Armagh, Down, Fermanagh, Londonderry, and Tyrone.

STATISTICS
Area: 70,283 sq km (27,136 sq miles)
Population: 3,500,000
Capital: Dublin
Languages: English, Gaelic (Irish)
Religion: Roman Catholic
Currency: Punt (Irish pound)
Longest river: Shannon 386 km (240 miles)
Main occupations: Agriculture, tourism, manufacturing
Main exports: Cattle, beef, dairy products
Main imports: Machinery, textiles, vehicles

NORTHERN IRELAND (UK) STATISTICS
Area: 14,121 sq km (5,452 square miles)
Population: 1,578,000
Capital: Belfast
Languages: English, Irish
Religions: Protestant, Roman Catholic
Currency: Pound sterling

Map labels:

RATHLIN · NORTHERN IRELAND · Lough Neagh · Belfast · DONEGAL BAY · Sligo · Ballina · Lough Conn · ACHILL · Castlebar · Ballyhaunis · Boyle · Carrick-on-Shannon · Cavan · Dundalk · IRISH SEA · Drogheda · R. Boyne · Lough Mask · Roscommon · Mullingar · Connemara · Lough Corrib · Lough Ree · Dublin · Athlone · R. Shannon · Tullamore · R. Liffey · Dun Laoghaire · Galway · GALWAY BAY · ARAN ISLANDS · Lough Derg · Port Laoise · Wicklow · Wicklow Mts · ATLANTIC OCEAN · Ennistymon · Roscrea · Carlow · Arklow · Tralee · R. Barrow · R. Nore · R. Slaney · Kilkee · Thurles · Kilkenny · Limerick · Mouth of the Shannon · Tipperary · Clonmel · R. Suir · Wexford · Rosslare · Ráth Luirc · Knockmealdown Mountains · Waterford · Tralee · Kanturk · R. Blackwater · Dingle · Lakes of Killarney · DINGLE BAY · Carrauntoohill, 1,041 m (3,414 ft) · Killarney · Blarney · Cork · Youghal · Kenmare · R. Lee · Dunmanway · Kinsale · Bantry · BANTRY BAY · Skibbereen

Compass: N, E, S, W

Scale: 0 — 300 miles · 0 — 500 km

GLENDALOUGH
The vale of Glendalough in County Wicklow is famous for its association with Saint Kevin, a hermit who founded a monastery there in the 6th century A.D. Saint Kevin, who is said to have performed many miracles, was said to be 120 years old when he died in 618.

HISTORY OF
IRELAND

ARDAGH CHALICE
During the golden age Irish craftworkers made many magnificent treasures. The silver Ardagh chalice, one of the most famous, is decorated with bronze and gold.

THE FIRST STONE AGE hunters arrived in Ireland from Europe. The Celts followed and divided Ireland into small kingdoms. The Celtic age produced fantastic legends and wonderful stories of gods, battles, and heroes. In 432, St. Patrick brought Christianity to the land, and became Ireland's patron saint. A golden age followed during which Irish Christians studied, painted, and wrote literature. Ireland became the cultural centre of Europe. In 795, Viking raiders shattered this peace. They built settlements, including Dublin, the capital. During the 12th century the Normans gained control of most of Ireland. Monarchs Henry VIII, Elizabeth I, and James VI all used the planting of Protestant English and Scottish people on lands seized from the Irish as a way of increasing subjects loyal to the British crown. This worked especially well in areas of Ulster, which accounts for much of today's conflicts in Northern Ireland.

BATTLE OF THE BOYNE
In 1690 the Protestant William III of England defeated the exiled Catholic King James II of England at the Battle of the Boyne, and James gave up his efforts to regain his throne. William III's victory began a long period of harsh English rule over the Irish Catholics. This was called the Penal Law.

POTATO FAMINE
In the 1800s, most Irish people lived on small holdings and were very poor. They ate mainly potatoes. The crop failed many times, but 1845 and 1848 were the worst years. More than 750,000 people starved and thousands emigated.

EASTER REBELLION
On Easter Monday in 1916, Irish Republicans impatient with the delay in implementing Home Rule rose up in armed revolt. The British army crushed the rebellion and executed 15 of the rebels. The dead rebels became heroes, and support for the Republican cause grew.

THE TROUBLES
In 1922 the Irish Free State (South) was created. In Northern Ireland the Protestant majority ran the government. In 1968 Catholic marches for Civil Rights were suppressed, and years of mistrust sparked off new violence. The British army was called in to keep peace but conflict developed with them. People from all sides of the community still seek a peaceful solution.

IRELAND
C. 600 B.C. Celts invade Ireland
A.D. 795 Vikings raid Ireland.
1014 King Brian Boru defeats the Vikings at Clontarf.
1170 Normans land in Ireland.
1641 Rebellion by the Irish against English government.
1690 Battle of the Boyne followed by Protestant domination.
1798 United Irishmen rebellion for a Republic is defeated.
1845-49 Potato famine. Population falls by three million.
1916 Easter Rebellion.
1919-23 War of Independence. Six counties of Ulster remain with the UK. Anglo-Irish treaty causes Civil War in the south.
1973 Ireland joins the E.C.
1997 Belfast-born Mary McAleese succeeds Mary Robinson as Ireland's president.

Find out more

CIVIL WAR, ENGLISH
IRELAND
UNITED KINGDOM, HISTORY OF

IRON AGE

This razor is around 2,500 years old and would have been as sharp as a modern razor.

IN SEVERAL EARLY LANGUAGES the word for iron meant "metal from the sky". This was probably because the first iron used to make tools and weapons came from meteorites which fell to Earth from space. Ironworking probably began in the Middle East some 6,000 years ago. At first people hammered iron while it was cold. Later people learned how to smelt iron – heat the iron ore so they could extract the iron and work with it properly. Unlike bronze, which early people also used, iron did not melt. Instead it was reduced to a spongy mass which people hammered and reheated until it was the right shape. Special furnaces were needed to reach the right temperature. The Hittites, who lived in what is now Turkey, were the first people we know of who traded in iron. But it was not until around 1000 B.C. that knowledge of smelting spread and the Iron Age truly began. In western Europe, the Celts were one of the first peoples to make and use iron.

IRON AGE

4000 B.C. First iron objects, made from meteoric iron, appear in the Middle East.

c. 1500 B.C. People in the Middle East find out how to extract (smelt) iron from iron ore and how to work it by heating and hammering (wrought iron). The Hittites dominate the trade.

1000 B.C. Iron Age begins in the Middle East and Greece. Iron-working also develops in India.

c. 800 B.C. Use of iron spreads across Europe. Celts become expert workers in iron.

c. 400 B.C. Chinese discover how to make cast-iron objects by melting iron ore and pouring it into moulds.

1760 A.D. Industrial revolution leads to a renewed use of iron. Also leads to great advances in ironworking techniques.

HILL FORT
The Celts fortified hill tops with ditches and ramparts. These forts were places of refuge in wartime; they were also administrative and trading centres, and enclosures for livestock.

Iron horseshoe

Heating iron ore in a furnace

IRONWORKING
Early furnaces were shallow stone hearths which people filled with iron ore and charcoal. Bellows helped raise the temperature to about 1,200°C (2,192° F), hot enough to make the iron workable. The Celts used deeper furnaces in which the iron collected at the bottom and impurities, called slag, gathered at the top.

Hammering the iron into shape

Spring

Iron pin

Brooch made of glass discs

TOOLS
People made useful tools from iron such as a saw with a serrated edge (far left) and tongs (left); the tongs were used to hold metal while beating it into shape.

WEAPONS
Iron weapons were greatly superior to bronze ones. They had sharper edges and were more effective. This dagger has a handle shaped like a human figure.

CLOTHING
The Celts loved decoration. Celtic clothes were woollen, often with checked patterns. Richer men and women wore heavy twisted neckbands called torcs in gold or bronze, and cloaks fastened with ornate brooches.

Find out more

BRONZE AGE
CELTS
INDUSTRIAL REVOLUTION
IRON AND STEEL

IRON AND STEEL

HUGE STRUCTURES such as oil tankers and bridges, and tiny objects such as nuts and bolts are made from steel. The world produces about 680 million tonnes (670 million tons) of steel each year; it is the most widely used of all metals. Steel is made from iron, one of the most common metals in the Earth's crust, and carbon, which comes from coal. Iron has many uses which include making car engine parts and magnets. Our bodies need iron to work properly. A healthy diet must include foods such as green vegetables, which contain iron. Pieces of iron fall to Earth in meteorites from space. But most iron comes from iron ore in rock. Heating the ore with coke (from coal) produces iron. The Hittites of Turkey perfected iron smelting about 1500 B.C. This was the beginning of the Iron Age, during which iron gained widespread use for making weapons and tools.

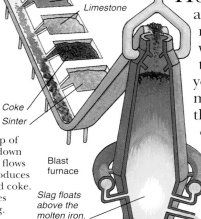

Iron and steel were once used to make weapons and armour, such as this 16th-century helmet.

MAKING STEEL

RAW MATERIALS
Iron making starts with iron ore, coke (a form of carbon from coal), and limestone. They are mixed and treated to make lumps called sinter.

Iron ore
Limestone
Coke
Sinter

BLAST FURNACE
The ingredients enter the top of the blast furnace and move down inside. A blast of very hot air flows up the furnace. The heat produces molten iron from the ore and coke. Limestone removes impurities which form a layer called slag.

Blast furnace

Slag floats above the molten iron.

Molten iron is drained from the furnace into large ladles.

Oxygen is blown through pipe onto surface of pig iron.

STEEL CONVERTER
Molten iron from the blast furnace is poured into a steel converter where hot air or oxygen is blown over it. The heat burns up most of the carbon from the iron, leaving molten steel. Steel from old cars and other waste can be recycled by adding it to the converter.

After blowing with oxygen, the converter tilts to discharge molten steel.

The molten steel may be cast into large blocks called ingots.

Molten steel from converter

Continuous casting

MAKING IRON AND STEEL
Making metals by heating their ores is called smelting. Huge factories smelt iron ore by heating it with coke to produce iron, which is rich in carbon. Removing most of the carbon produces steel. Steels of different quality are made by adding metals, such as nickel.

CONTINUOUS CASTING
Molten steel from the converter sets as it cools and is held in shape by rollers. The long slab is then cut up into lengths and rolled into steel products.

USES OF STEEL

Different kinds of steel are made by varying the amount of carbon and other metals in it. Low-carbon steel goes into car bodies; stronger medium-carbon steel is used for making ships and steel beams that support structures. High-carbon steel is very strong but difficult to shape, and is used for springs and rails that get much wear. Steel containing tungsten metal resists heat and is used in jet engines.

RUST
Iron and steel objects get rusty when they are left outside in damp conditions. Moist air causes rust. It changes iron into iron oxide, a red-brown compound of iron and oxygen. Rusting weakens the metal so that it crumbles away.

STAINLESS STEEL

Adding the metals chromium and nickel produces stainless steel, which does not rust. Cutlery and saucepans are often made of stainless steel. This metal is also used to make equipment which must be kept very clean in places such as hospitals and dairies.

Casting uses molten steel from the converter.

Forging

Rolling

SHAPING STEEL
Passing a hot slab between rollers presses the soft steel into plates or sheets. A forge presses the steel into more complex shapes. Casting uses a mould, in which molten steel cools and sets into shape.

ISLAM

IN THE 7TH CENTURY the prophet Muhammad founded a religion in Arabia which was to become a powerful force in the world. The religion is Islam and its followers are called Muslims (or Moslems). Muslims believe that many prophets or teachers have been sent by God, including Moses and Jesus Christ, but that Muhammad was the greatest of them all. Like Christians and Jews, Muslims believe in one God, Allah. Islam means "submission to the will of God", and Muslims commit themselves to absolute obedience to Allah. Islamic life is based on a set of rules called the five pillars of Islam. Muslims believe that by following these rules, they will reach heaven. There is also a strict code of social behaviour. Some Muslim women wear clothes that cover their bodies completely, and alcohol and gambling are forbidden. Today there are more than 900 million Muslims living mainly in the Middle East, Asia, and Africa, and Islam is still growing rapidly. Its popularity has been increased by Islamic fundamentalists – extremely religious people who call for a return to strict, traditional Islamic values.

KORAN
The sacred book of Islam is the Koran. Muslims believe the Koran is the direct word of God as revealed to his messenger, Muhammad.

ISLAMIC FESTIVALS
Day of Hijrah First day of Islamic year.

Ramadan Month-long fast.

Eid ul-Fitr Feast to mark the end of Ramadan.

Lailat ul-Qadr Revelation of Koran to Muhammad.

Meelad ul-Nabi Muhammad's birthday.

Lailut ul-Isra Death of Muhammad.

MOSQUES
The Muslim place of worship is the mosque. Before entering, Muslims remove their shoes and wash. The faithful kneel to pray with their heads touching the floor. At prayer time Muslims face the mihrab, an empty recess which shows the direction of Mecca. Although they must attend the mosque on Fridays, at other times Muslims pray wherever they are.

MINARETS
Five times a day muezzins, or criers, stand at the top of tall towers called minarets to call fellow Muslims to prayer.

BLUE MOSQUE
The first mosques were very simple, but some later buildings such as the Blue Mosque at Istanbul, Turkey (right), are magnificent examples of Islamic art. Islam forbids realistic images of humans or other living things, so the tiled walls are decorated with intricate designs and beautifully written texts.

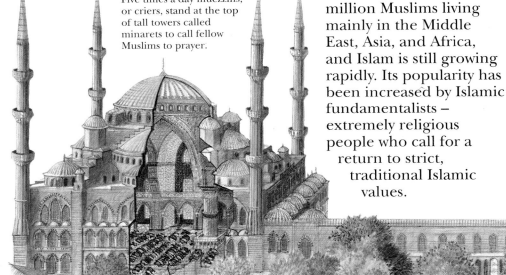

Before kneeling in prayer in the mosque, Muslims wash their faces, hands, and feet.

MUHAMMAD
The shahada is the Islamic declaration of faith. "None is to be worshipped save Allah: Muhammad is his prophet."

MECCA
The birthplace of Muhammad is Mecca, Saudi Arabia, and every Muslim tries to visit the holy city at least once in a lifetime. The Kaaba, the sacred shrine, is the central point of this pilgrimage. Inside the Kaaba is a black stone which dates from ancient times.

Muslim pilgrims must walk seven times around the Kaaba.

Find out more
ARABS
ARABS, HISTORY OF
CRUSADES
FESTIVALS AND FEASTS
RELIGIONS

ISRAEL

THE MODERN STATE OF ISRAEL has existed only since 1948. It was created on the sites where there had been Jewish settlements in earlier times. Jews from all over the world flocked to the new state, especially the survivors of Nazi anti-semitism. They revived the ancient language of Hebrew as the national language of Israel. But there have been many problems. The region had previously been the land of Palestine, and many Arab Palestinians had to leave when the country became Israel. However, others have remained, and today they make up about 15 per cent of Israel's 5.4 million population. Israel has also fought wars with neighbouring Arab countries to secure its borders. It still occupies some territory gained in these wars, causing continual Palestinian unrest. Israel is now a wealthy country. The Israelis have converted large areas of desert into farmland and developed a wide range of modern industries.

Israel lies at the eastern end of the Mediterranean Sea. Lebanon lies to the north, Syria and Jordan to the east, and Egypt to the southwest.

OCCUPIED TERRITORIES
Israel occupied the Gaza Strip, the West Bank, and the Golan Heights in wars with its neighbours. These Arab nations want the land back before they begin peace talks with Israel. The Jewish families who have settled in these occupied territories live under constant threat of attack.

KIBBUTZ
Careful organization is needed to grow crops in the hot, dry countryside. Israel has introduced a particular type of farming called a kibbutz, or gathering. A kibbutz is a farm where families live, work, and share everything together as a community. Nearly half of Israel's food is produced on such farms.

WAILING WALL
Israel occupies much of the "Holy Land" described in the Bible. The land is sacred not only to Jews but also to Christians and Muslims. The Wailing Wall in Jerusalem is the most sacred Jewish monument. It is all that remains of a temple built by King Herod 2,000 years ago. Visitors gave the wall its name when they heard the sad sound of devout Jews mourning the destruction of the temple.

Tel Aviv's centre symbolizes the modern, prosperous face of Israel.

TEL AVIV-JAFFA
The main commercial and industrial centre of Israel is Tel Aviv-Jaffa, the country's second largest city. It was once two separate towns, but Tel Aviv grew rapidly and absorbed its neighbour, the ancient port of Jaffa.

DEAD SEA
The world's saltiest sea, the Dead Sea, is also the lowest area of water on Earth, 400 m (1,312 ft) below the level of the Mediterranean Sea. The River Jordan flows into this hot, barren place. The water evaporates in the heat of the sun, but the salt in the water is left behind. Over the centuries the salt has become very concentrated.

Visitors to Dead Sea resorts bathe in mud because they believe it is good for their skin.

Find out more
ARABS
CRUSADES
JEWS, HISTORY OF THE
JUDAISM
MIDDLE EAST

ITALY

SHAPED LIKE A BOOT, complete with heel and toe, Italy juts out far into the Mediterranean Sea from southern Europe. Between the country's east and west coasts rise the Apennine mountains, which divide Italy into two along its length. Northern Italy is green and fertile, stretching from the snow-capped Alps to the middle of the country. It includes farmlands in the great flat valley of the Po river, and big industrial towns, such as Turin and Milan. Factories in the north produce cars, textiles, clothes, and electrical goods. These products have helped make Italy one of the most prosperous countries in Europe. Southern Italy, by contrast, is dry and rocky. There is less farming and less industry, and people are poorer. Sicily and Sardinia, the two largest islands of the Mediterranean, are also part of Italy. Rome, the capital, lies at the centre of the nation. It is the home of Italy's democratic government and also the Vatican, the headquarters of the Roman Catholic Church.

Many Italian farmhouses are old and picturesque; the machinery is usually modern.

Italy is in southern Europe and forms part of the northern coast of the Mediterranean Sea. It has borders with France, Switzerland, Austria, and Slovenia.

AGRICULTURE
Italian farmers grow almost enough to feed Italy's population of 58 million. They also export fresh and processed food. Italy is famous for its olives and olive oil, tomatoes, wine, pasta, cheese, fruit, and meat products such as salami and ham. Italy also grows large quantities of grain, particularly wheat, as well as rice, potatoes, and sunflowers, which are used to make cooking oil. Almost one third of Italians live in rural areas.

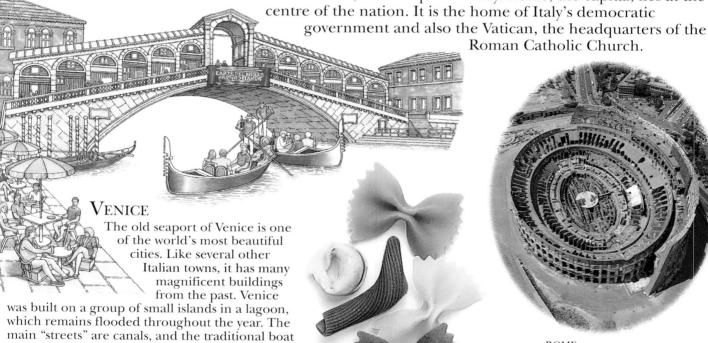

VENICE
The old seaport of Venice is one of the world's most beautiful cities. Like several other Italian towns, it has many magnificent buildings from the past. Venice was built on a group of small islands in a lagoon, which remains flooded throughout the year. The main "streets" are canals, and the traditional boat called a gondola is still a common form of transport.

ROME
A walk through Rome is like a walk through history. Since the city was first built, more than 2,500 years ago, each new generation has added something. Today, modern city life goes on around Ancient Roman arenas, 15th-century churches, and 17th-century palaces. Like many of Italy's historic towns, Rome attracts thousands of tourists every year.

Ferrari makes one of the leading Grand Prix racing cars.

CARS
The Italian motor industry produces some of Europe's finest cars. Italian manufacturers, such as Alfa Romeo, Ferrari, Lamborghini, and Lancia, have always had a reputation for speed and stylish design. Fiat, which is based in Turin, is the largest company. Fiat produces family cars, trucks, tractors, and buses.

PASTA
There are at least 200 shapes of pasta, including ravioli, spaghetti, and macaroni. Pasta is a kind of dough made from wheat flour. Served with a tasty sauce, it is Italy's favourite dish.

Find out more

EUROPE
ITALY, HISTORY OF
RENAISSANCE
ROMAN EMPIRE

ITALY

SWITZERLAND

AUSTRIA

Alps Dolomites

Mont Blanc 4,807 m (15,771 ft)

R. Piave

SLOVENIA

Lake Como Lake Garda

Como

Trieste

Lake Maggiore

Brescia

Novara

Milan

Verona

Venice

Turin

R. Adige Padua Padova

Piacenza

R. Po

Alessandria

Ferrara

Modena

Genoa

Bologna

Ravenna

La Spezia

Pisa R. Arno Florence

SAN MARINO

Livorno

Siena

ADRIATIC SEA

STATISTICS
Area: 301,268 sq km (116,320 sq miles)
Population: 57,800,000
Capital: Rome
Language: Italian
Religion: Roman Catholic
Currency: Lira
Highest point: Mont Blanc 4,807 m (15,771 ft)
Main occupations: Manufacturing, agriculture
Main exports: Machinery, vehicles, textiles, clothing
Main import: Machinery

SAN MARINO
One of the world's smallest countries, with an area of just 61 sq km (23 sq miles), San Marino is also the world's oldest republic.

ST. PETER'S CHURCH
St. Peter's Church, Vatican City, Rome, is the world's largest Christian church. Shaped like a cross, it is nearly 210 m (700 ft) long and about 137 m (450 ft) at its widest point.

FRANCE

In 1814 French emperor Napoleon Bonaparte (1769-1821) was banished to the small island of Elba.

N
W   E
S

ELBA

CORSICA (FRANCE)

Perugia

Lake Bolsena

Apennines ITALY

R. Tiber

VATICAN CITY
Vatican City, in Rome, is ruled by the pope. It is the smallest independent state in the world, with an area of 0.44 sq km (0.17 sq miles).

Rome

Foggia

Bari

Sassari

Naples Vesuvius

Salerno

R. Bradano

Taranto

R. Tirso

CAPRI

GULF OF TARANTO

SARDINIA

TYRRHENIAN SEA

Cagliari

STROMBOLI

LIPARI ISLANDS

Messina

MILAN
Milan is the second largest city in Italy. It is situated in the north, near the Alps, and has been an important trading centre for hundreds of years. Today this lively city is Italy's leading financial and manufacturing centre.

Palermo

Reggio di Calabria

Mt Etna

SICILY

Catania

MEDITERRANEAN SEA

0   100 miles

0   150 km

HISTORY OF
ITALY

FOR 500 YEARS Italy was at the centre of the powerful Roman Empire. In 476 the empire fell. Various tribes conquered Italy and divided it between them. The Italian popes became prominent in both religion and politics and managed to drive out the strongest tribe, the Lombards. During the 1300s, independent "city-states" developed from cities that had grown rich through industry, trade, and banking. These city-states became very powerful, and their wealthy rulers supported Renaissance artists during the 15th century. For a time, Italian ideas and styles dominated the whole of Europe. But the city-states, weakened by constant squabbling and wars among themselves, were taken over by the Hapsburg family of Austria and Spain. In 1796 Napoleon invaded Italy and a movement for unification of the various city-states grew. This unification was achieved in 1861. But Italy never regained her former power in Europe. Dictator Benito Mussolini (1883-1945) involved Italy disastrously in World War II. Since then, Italy has become a leading European country.

ETRUSCANS
The Etruscans lived in an area of western Italy called Etruria in about 800 B.C. They were great traders, farmers, artists, and engineers and built a civilization of small city-states. The Romans eventually conquered the Etruscans but adopted many of their customs, including gladiatorial fights and chariot racing. Above is an Etruscan chariot running over a fallen man.

Wealthy citizens owned land outside the city walls.

Merchant ships travelled in search of trade.

CITY-STATES
During the Renaissance (a flourishing of arts and learning), Italian city-states such as Venice and Florence were important centres of learning. Many city-states were ruled by princes elected by rich citizens who owned huge estates outside the city walls. The estates produced food for the craftworkers and scholars who lived in the city. Most city-states were near the sea, making it easy for Italian merchants to travel to distant countries in search of trade.

DOGE'S BARGE
Venice, the most powerful Italian city-state, was built on a lagoon and crisscrossed by canals. Its huge fleet of ships enabled it to set up a rich empire in the eastern Mediterranean. Each year the ruler of Venice, called the doge, went to sea in his magnificent barge and gave thanks for this wealth by "marrying" the sea with a golden ring. The doge lived in the doge's palace, shown right.

Italian city-states 1494

- Savoy
- Milan
- Venice
- Florence
- Siena
- Papal states
- Corsica
- Rome
- Naples
- Kingdom of the two Sicilies

PRE-UNIFICATION ITALY
At the end of the Renaissance, rivalry and constant fighting weakened the city-states. Italy became easy prey and an attractive prize for invaders from Spain, Austria, and France, who had claims to the land.

GARIBALDI

In 1860, Giuseppe Garibaldi (1807-82) became an Italian hero. He led a small army of 1,000 volunteer soldiers, called red shirts, to free Sicily from the rule of the king of Naples, so that the island of Sicily could become part of a new united Italy.

CAVOUR

Camillo di Cavour (1810-61), prime minister of Piedmont city-state, was a brilliant statesman who dreamed of a united Italy. He led the movement to unite all the Italian states into one country.

MUSSOLINI

In 1922 Benito Mussolini (below) became premier of Italy. Two years later he was dictator, leading a new movement called fascism, under which the government controlled everything in the country. Mussolini's vast building projects created jobs, but his secret police silenced his opponents. Mussolini, who was also called Il Duce (the leader), wanted to make Italy great, but he became unpopular when his armies were defeated in World War II.

Benito Mussolini making a speech

NAPOLEON

Napoleon Bonaparte (above, on horseback) invaded Italy and defeated the Austrian Hapsburgs, who ruled it at the time. He destroyed the old system of many different governments and introduced a single system with the same laws. For the first time since the days of Ancient Rome, Italians from different regions were ruled in the same way. Many began to dream of a united Italy, free from foreign rulers.

PALIO

Each summer a colourful festival takes place in the ancient Etruscan city of Siena, northern Italy. This pageant, called the Palio, celebrates the power of the city-state, and comes to a climax with a horse race staged in the main square of the city. The race is fast and dangerous. Each *contrada* (city district) is represented by a colourful flag and symbol, and competes fiercely for the honour of winning.

ITALY

509 B.C. Romans drive out Etruscans and establish the Roman republic.

A.D. 476 German barbarians depose last Roman emperor, Romulus Augustulus. Invading German tribes break up empire.

c. 1300 Renaissance begins in Italy.

1796 Napoleon Bonaparte invades and seizes Italy.

1815 Napoleon defeated at Waterloo. Representatives from Austria, Great Britain, Prussia, and Russia (the victorious nations) meet at the Congress of Vienna. Most of Italy is returned to its old rulers.

1858 Cavour, prime minister of the kingdom of Piedmont, makes a treaty with Napoleon III of France to defend the kingdom from the Austrians.

1859 Combined French and Piedmontese army defeats Austrians.

1861 All of Italy, except Venice, San Marino, and the city of Rome, join to become the kingdom of Italy. Victor Emmanuel II, king of Piedmont, becomes king of Italy.

1871 Rome becomes capital of Italy, but the Pope's territory of Vatican City remains an independent state.

1915 Italy joins World War I, fighting with the Allies (Britain, France, Russia, and the United States).

1922 Benito Mussolini becomes premier of Italy.

1940 Italy joins World War II, fighting for the Germans.

1943 Italy surrenders to Allies.

1945 Italian resistance fighters kill Mussolini.

1946 Italy becomes a republic.

1949 Italy joins North Atlantic Treaty Organization (NATO) with 11 other Western countries, to protect against Soviet expansion.

1957 Italy joins the E.E.C.

Find out more

ITALY
NAPOLEON BONAPARTE
NAPOLEONIC WARS
RENAISSANCE
ROMAN EMPIRE

JAPAN

THE TOPS OF A SUBMERGED mountain chain form the islands of Japan. About three quarters of the country is too steep to farm or build on. Japan has a population of 125 million, most of whom live in valleys and on the narrow coastal plain. Japan is a leading industrial nation, but its success is fairly recent: until 1853 the country was closed to foreigners and the government refused to import modern machines. More recently, Japanese companies have been very successful in exporting their own goods, so Japan sells more than it buys and has become very wealthy. Western influence is strong, but the Japanese are very proud of their traditional culture and religion. They continue to practise old customs while developing more modern technology. Most people follow both the Buddhist and Shinto religions. The head of state is an emperor, but the government is democratic. In the past the country was ruled by noblemen and samurai, professional soldiers who had a strict code of honour. Although the samurai have long been disbanded, their code still influences everyday life.

BONSAI
Japanese bonsai trees are pruned so that they do not grow more than a few centimetres high.

Japan is located in the Pacific Ocean, off the east coast of Asia. North and South Korea are to the west, and the Russian Federation to the north. There are four main islands, covering almost 370,000 sq km (144 square miles).

TOKYO

The largest city in Japan is the capital, Tokyo. More than 18 million people live in the city and suburbs, and the whole area is extremely overcrowded. Fumes from cars and industry are a major problem, but effective measures are being taken to reduce pollution.

INDUSTRY
Although Japan has few raw materials such as metal ores or coal, Japanese industry is the most successful in the world. The country's main resource is a human one – that of its workers. Japanese workers are very loyal to their companies, and workers take their holidays together, exercise together, and sing the company song daily. Managers are equally devoted to the company and pride themselves on their cooperation with the workers. New technology and techniques are introduced quickly and help boost prosperity.

BULLET TRAIN
Japan has more than 25,000 km (16,000 miles) of railways. The most famous train is the Shinkansen, or bullet train, which runs from Tokyo to Fukuoka. The train covers the 1,176 km (731 miles) in less than six hours at an average speed of 195 km/h (122 mph) per hour.

SUSHI
Traditional Japanese food consists mainly of fish and rice. Often the fish is eaten raw or lightly cooked in dishes called sushi.

Mount Fuji, a 3,776 m (12,389 ft) tall volcano is sacred to the Japanese.

SUMO
The national sport of Japan is sumo wrestling. It attracts large crowds and is shown on television. The two contestants try to push each other out of a small ring. Success depends on strength and weight, so sumo wrestlers go to schools where they train and follow a special diet. Successful wrestlers may become extremely rich and famous. The sport is traditional and follows an elaborate pattern controlled by officials in decorative costume.

Japanese people travel more by train than do travellers in any other country.

Find out more

ASIA
DEMOCRACY
JAPAN, HISTORY OF
WEAPONS

JAPAN

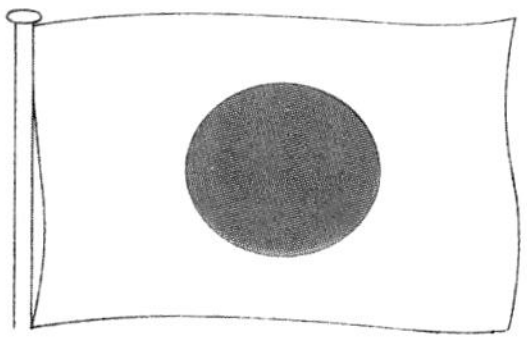

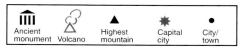

Ancient monument | **Volcano** | **Highest mountain** | **Capital city** | **City/town**

STATISTICS
Area: 377,801 sq km (145,835 sq miles)
Population: 125,000,000
Capital: Tokyo
Language: Japanese
Religions: Shintoism, Buddhism, Confucianism
Currency: Yen
Highest point: Mount Fuji 3,776 m (12,388 ft)
Main occupation: Manufacturing
Main exports: Cars, steel, electronic equipment, iron, textiles, ships, vehicles
Main imports: Oil, machinery, coal, iron ore, timber, wheat, food

OSAKA
Japan's third largest city is Osaka, on the south coast of the island of Honshu. Osaka is a major industrial centre, with steel, chemical, and electrical industries. It is also one of the oldest cities in Japan:and has many Buddhist and Shinto temples. Osaka is the site of an impressive castle built in the 16th century by the shogun (warlord) Toyomoti Hideyoshi, who once ruled Japan. In 1970 Osaka was the host city for the World's Fair.

KYUSHU
The southernmost island of Japan, Kyushu, is mountainous; the highest point is a volcano, Mount Aso. Kyushu is the most densely populated of the Japanese islands, and is linked to Honshu island by a railway tunnel under the Shimonoseki Strait.

Colourful plant life flourishes in Kyushu's subtropical climate

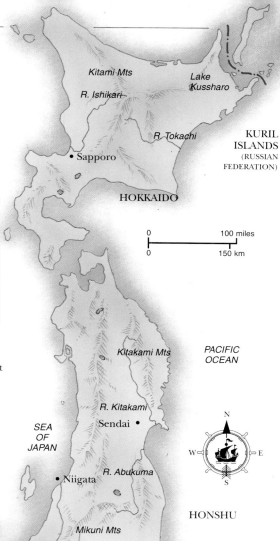

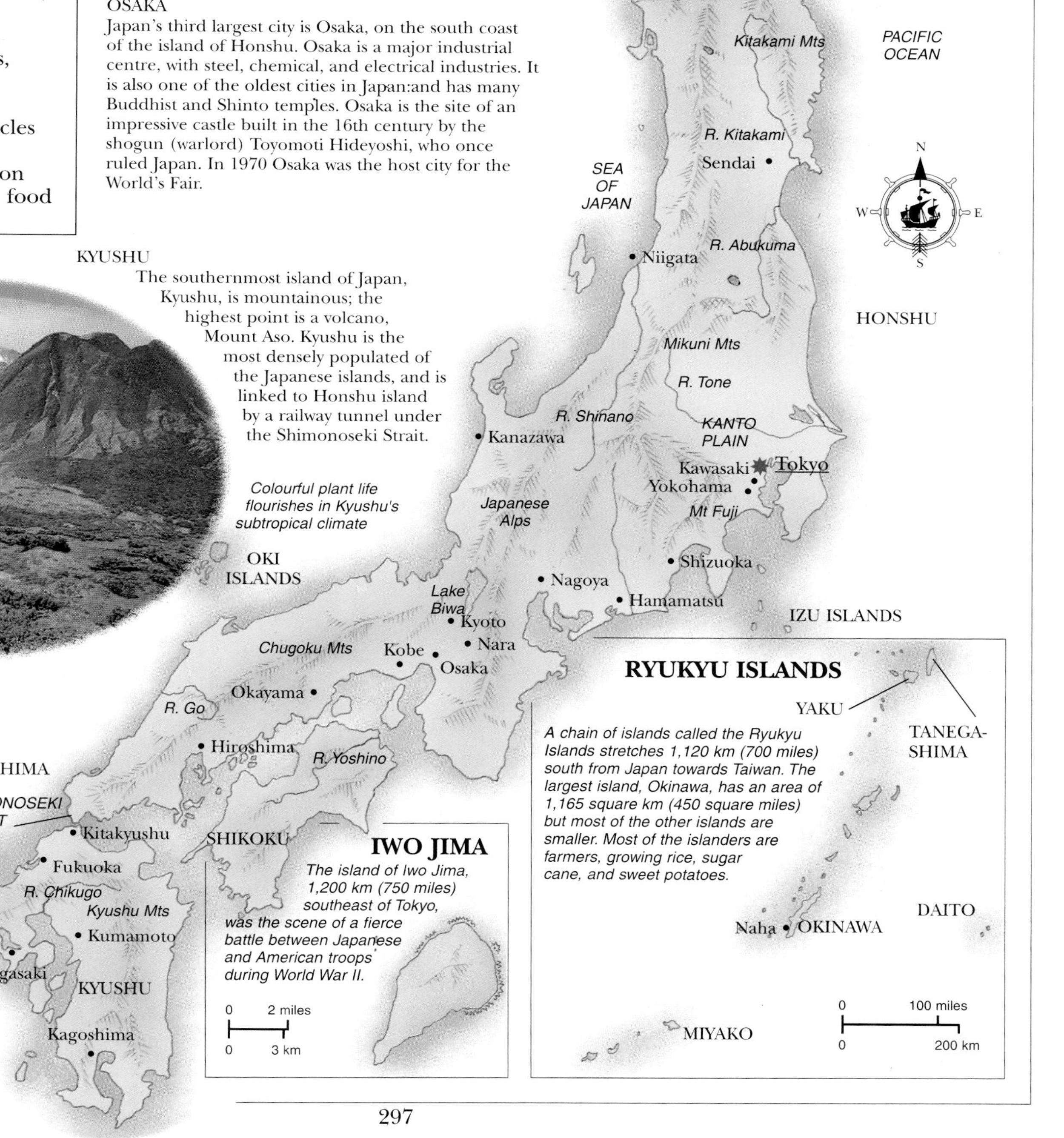

KURIL ISLANDS (RUSSIAN FEDERATION)

HOKKAIDO

Kitami Mts
R. Ishikari
Lake Kussharo
R. Tokachi
Sapporo

0 — 100 miles
0 — 150 km

Kitakami Mts

PACIFIC OCEAN

R. Kitakami
Sendai

SEA OF JAPAN

R. Abukuma
Niigata

HONSHU

Mikuni Mts
R. Tone

KANTO PLAIN
R. Shinano
Kanazawa
Kawasaki ★ Tokyo
Yokohama
Mt Fuji
Japanese Alps
Shizuoka
Nagoya
Hamamatsu
IZU ISLANDS

OKI ISLANDS
Lake Biwa
Kyoto
Chugoku Mts
Kobe · Nara
Okayama · Osaka
R. Go
Hiroshima
R. Yoshino

KOREA STRAIT

TSUSHIMA
SHIMONOSEKI STRAIT
Kitakyushu
Fukuoka
R. Chikugo
Kyushu Mts
Kumamoto
Nagasaki
KYUSHU
GOTO ISLANDS
Kagoshima

SHIKOKU

IWO JIMA
The island of Iwo Jima, 1,200 km (750 miles) southeast of Tokyo, was the scene of a fierce battle between Japanese and American troops during World War II.

0 — 2 miles
0 — 3 km

RYUKYU ISLANDS
YAKU
TANEGA-SHIMA

A chain of islands called the Ryukyu Islands stretches 1,120 km (700 miles) south from Japan towards Taiwan. The largest island, Okinawa, has an area of 1,165 square km (450 square miles) but most of the other islands are smaller. Most of the islanders are farmers, growing rice, sugar cane, and sweet potatoes.

DAITO
Naha · OKINAWA

MIYAKO

0 — 100 miles
0 — 200 km

HISTORY OF
JAPAN

THE GROUP OF ISLANDS THAT IS JAPAN remained isolated from the rest of the world until quite recently. During the 6th century A.D., Japan absorbed ideas from its neighbour, China. It also adopted China's Buddhist religion and the Chinese system of imperial rule. But 200 years later, Chinese influence declined, and the imperial system broke down. Until the 1860s powerful families, and then shoguns (military generals), ruled Japan in the name of the emperor. People rarely invaded Japan successfully. The Mongols tried and failed in the 13th century. During the 16th century European traders were also unsuccessful. But in 1868, Japan began to look towards the West. Within 50 years it had built up a strong, modern economy and a large empire. All this was destroyed in World War II (1939-45). However, Japan recovered and is once more a rich power.

NARA
Nara, the first capital city of Japan, was the political and religious centre of the country. It was the site of the Buddhist Horyuji Temple (above).

SHOGUNATE
The shogunate was a hereditary military dictatorship. During shogun rule, an aristocratic class of knights called the Samurai gained considerable power. These warriors protected the lands of the daimyo (local lords) and followed a code of honour known as the Bushido – "the way of the warrior". Samurai warriors committed *hara kiri* (suicide) if they lost their honour.

Curved Samurai sword

Special suit of armour which a Samurai could get into quickly from the side or from below

THE TALE OF GENJI
In the early eleventh century a Japanese woman named Murasaki Shikibu wrote one of the world's first novels. More than 600,000 words long, *The Tale of Genji* describes the adventures of a young prince and his travels in search of love and education. The novel was written in Japanese at a time when the official language of the country was Chinese: only commoners and women were allowed to speak Japanese.

TEA CEREMONY
After the 14th century, the ritual ceremony of drinking tea became very popular in Japan. The ceremony was based on the Zen Buddhist principles of self-discipline and meditation and was very popular among the warlike shoguns and Samurai.

A.D. 400s Yamato clan unites Japan.

794 Capital city of Kyoto founded.

1192 Minamoto Yoritomo becomes first shogun.

1281 "Divine wind" saves Japan from Mongols.

1338-1573 Civil wars.

1542 Portuguese sailors visit Japan.

1549 St. Francis Xavier introduces Christianity to Japan.

1592, 1597 Japan invades Korea.

1639 Almost all Europeans leave.

1853 U.S. Navy forces Japan to trade with the West.

1868 Meiji restoration returns power to emperor.

1868 Tokyo becomes national capital.

1889 Constitutional government.

1904-5 Russo-Japanese War.

1910 Japan takes control of Korea.

1914-18 Japan fights Germany in World War I.

1937-45 Japan invades China, Southeast Asia; bombs Pearl Harbour in 1941, bringing United States into World War II.

1945 U.S. drops first atomic bombs on Hiroshima and Nagasaki; Japanese surrender.

1989 Hirohito dies.

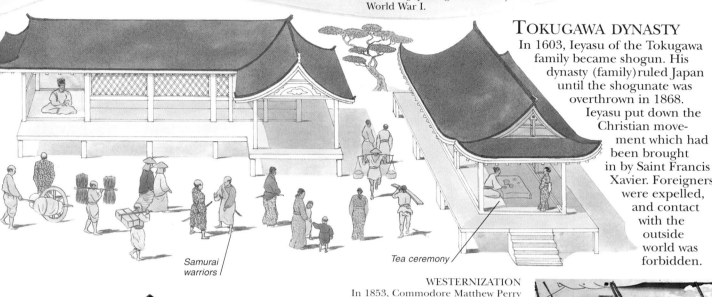

Samurai warriors

Tea ceremony

TOKUGAWA DYNASTY

In 1603, Ieyasu of the Tokugawa family became shogun. His dynasty (family) ruled Japan until the shogunate was overthrown in 1868. Ieyasu put down the Christian movement which had been brought in by Saint Francis Xavier. Foreigners were expelled, and contact with the outside world was forbidden.

WESTERNIZATION

In 1853, Commodore Matthew Perry of the U.S. Navy sailed into Tokyo Bay and demanded that Japan end its isolation and begin trading with the outside world. Dramatic changes followed. The shogunate ended, and the young emperor Meiji took power. Within 50 years, Japan became one of the world's leading industrial and economic powers. Factories and railways were built, a national education system was set up, and students were sent abroad to learn about Western life.

SINO-JAPANESE WAR

Japan went to war with China in 1894-5 over the control of Korea, and then with Russia in 1904-5 in order to gain colonies in Taiwan, Korea, and China. Both wars revealed the new Westernized Japan to be a powerful force in world affairs.

KAMIKAZE

In the 13th century, a storm destroyed the Mongol fleet and saved the Japanese. They called the storm kamikaze, meaning "divine wind". During World War II, the Japanese used kamikaze pilots, who crashed their bomb-laden planes on to American warships. These "suicide pilots" believed that they, like the storm, were saving Japan, and were blessed by the emperor, whom they believed to be divine.

HIROHITO

According to tradition, the first emperor of Japan was descended from the sun goddess and took power around 660 B.C. An unbroken line of descent then stretched to Hirohito, who in 1926 became the 124th emperor. In 1946, after the Japanese defeat in World War II, Hirohito publicly rejected the divinity of the emperor. He died in 1989. His son Akihito became emperor in 1990.

Find out more
CHINA, HISTORY OF
JAPAN
NUCLEAR AGE
WORLD WAR I
WORLD WAR II

JESUS CHRIST

ONE OF THE WORLD'S major religions – Christianity – was inspired by a man named Jesus Christ. We know about Jesus from the New Testament gospels, which were written by Matthew, Mark, Luke, and John, men who knew him. The gospels declare that Jesus was a Jew born in Bethlehem, in the Roman province of Judea, and was believed to be the Son of God. At the age of 30 he began to travel around Palestine (then under Roman rule) preaching a new message. He told stories called parables to explain his ideas. The gospels also describe miracles – amazing things he did such as raising the dead. However, some people thought his ideas might cause rebellion against Roman rule. He was arrested, tried, and sentenced to death. When Jesus appeared to his disciples (closest followers) after his death, they were convinced that God had raised him from the dead. The Christian church was founded on the belief, and soon his ideas swept across the Roman Empire.

NATIVITY
The birth of Jesus, which took place in a stable in Bethlehem, is called the Nativity. Every year, on 25 December, Christians celebrate Jesus' birthday.

WHERE JESUS LIVED
Jesus spent his childhood in Nazareth. He preached mainly in Judea and Galilee.

Jesus' travels around the Holy Land

Sidon
Tyre
Galilee
Nazareth
Tiberias
Caesarea
Samaria
Jericho
Judea
Jerusalem
Bethlehem
Gaza
Dead Sea

SERMON ON THE MOUNT
Jesus taught that God was a kind, loving father, and that people should not fight back when attacked but should "turn the other cheek". He stressed the importance of love. His Sermon on the Mount contained new ideas describing how ordinary people who were humble, gentle, and poor would go to heaven. He also taught his followers a special prayer – the Lord's Prayer.

LAST SUPPER
Near the end of his life Jesus shared a last supper with his 12 disciples. Using bread and wine as symbols of his body and blood, Jesus told them to remember him by this feast. To this day, the last supper is re-enacted during communion, when Christians take wine and wafers of bread as part of church services.

CRUCIFIXION
Jesus was accused of treason against Rome and tried by the Roman governor, Pontius Pilate. He was sentenced to be crucified – nailed to a cross on a hill called Calvary, outside Jerusalem. After his death his body was sealed in a tomb.

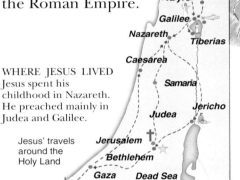

RESURRECTION
On Sunday morning, three days after Jesus' death, the tomb in which his body had been placed was found empty. The gospels tell how he appeared to his disciples and, after 40 days of teaching them, rose to heaven.

Find out more

CHRISTIANITY
JEWS, HISTORY OF
RELIGIONS

HISTORY OF THE
JEWS

ACCORDING TO THE OLD TESTAMENT, about four thousand years ago, in Canaan (modern Israel), a man named Abraham became the ancestor of a people called Hebrews. These were the ancestors of today's Jews. Later they moved south to Egypt to escape famine. They lived there for about 500 years until their leader, Moses, led them away from the wicked Egyptian pharaoh (king) and into Canaan, the land promised to them by their god. There they prospered under three great kings, Saul, David, and Solomon. The kingdom split into two after Solomon's death – Israel in the north and Judah in the south. The word *Jew* comes from *Judah*. Major invasions ended Jewish independence, and for a time the Jews lived in Babylon. In 63 B.C., the Romans conquered Palestine (formerly Canaan) and expelled the Jews. The Jews scattered around the world, from India to Spain. In 1948, the Jewish state of Israel was created for the Jews to live in. But they face threats from Arab neighbours.

EXODUS
In about 1290 B.C., the Jews fled from slavery in Egypt and, led by Moses, migrated to Canaan. The arduous journey through the Sinai Desert took them about 40 years. The leaving of Egypt is known as the Exodus (from the Greek word for "marching out").

Religious ceremonies took place in a central building.

Giant basin of water for priests to use in ceremonies

Yellow star that Jews were forced to wear

TEMPLE OF SOLOMON
King Solomon (reigned 961-922 B.C.) built the first Jewish temple in Jerusalem, which became the capital of Israel. The limestone temple was 50 m (164 ft) long and 30 m (98 ft) wide and housed the Ark of the Covenant, a sacred wooden chest containing the Ten Commandments – laws by which to live given to Moses by God. In 587 B.C., the Babylonians burned down the temple when they captured Jerusalem.

ZIONISM
Most Jews longed for a homeland where they could be free from anti-Semitism. In 1897, an Austrian journalist named Theodor Herzl organized a conference in Basel, Switzerland, "to secure for the Jewish people a home in Palestine". This movement, known as Zionism, gained international support following the Nazi massacre of the Jews during World War II (1939-45).

HOLOCAUST
For centuries, some people have hated and persecuted the Jews. This is called anti-Semitism. Anti-Semitism reached a horrific peak between 1933 and 1945. In what became known as the Holocaust, the Nazi Party of Germany rounded up, and systematically murdered more than six million European Jews in concentration camps set up for that purpose. Thousands more lost their homes and property and were driven into exile.

JEWS

- **c. 2000 B.C.** Jews settle in Palestine under Abraham.
- **c. 1800 B.C.** Jews settle in Egypt.
- **c. 1290 B.C.** Moses leads Jews out of Egypt back to Palestine.
- **c. 1020 B.C.** Saul becomes the first Jewish king.
- **c. 1000-961 B.C.** Reign of David.
- **961-922 B.C.** Reign of Solomon.
- **922 B.C.** Jewish kingdom splits into Israel and Judah. Keeps Jerusalem as its capital.
- **722 B.C.** Assyrians capture Israel.
- **587 B.C.** Babylonians invade Jerusalem. Diaspora (dispersal) of Jews begins all around the world.
- **A.D. 70** Romans destroy Jerusalem.
- **1492** Jews expelled from Spain.
- **1897** Zionist movement begins.
- **1948** Israel founded.
- **1967** Six-day Arab-Israeli War.

Find out more
CRUSADES
ISRAEL
JUDAISM
MIDDLE EAST
RELIGIONS

JOAN OF ARC

IN THE EARLY 15TH CENTURY the French finally defeated the English, who ruled much of their country. The warrior who led them into battle was a woman who has since become one of the best-loved heroines of French history. Joan of Arc was born into a poor family in 1412. She never learned to read or write, but she was inspired and stubborn and could argue with educated people. When Joan was a young girl, she heard "voices" of saints and angels. The voices told her that she must restore the rightful king to the throne of France. Joan managed to convince the heir to the throne, later to be Charles VII, to support her, and in 1429, when she was only 17, she led the French army to victory at Orléans. Joan led her country's troops in other successful battles, but in 1430 she was caught by the Burgundians, a powerful group of the French people. They sold her to the English, who imprisoned her and then put her on trial as a heretic – a person who does not believe in the teachings of the Church. Joan was found guilty, and on May 30 1431, she was executed in Rouen by being burned alive. After her death the English were driven out of France, and Joan's reputation as a heroine grew. Legends grew up about Joan and in 1920 she was made a saint.

The standard flown by Joan in battle

THE MAID OF ORLEANS
Joan of Arc was a brave fighter who wore a suit of armour and had her hair cut short like a man's. She was deeply religious, and prayed for guidance before going into battle.

JOAN'S HELMET
Joan may have worn this helmet in battle against the English. There is a hole in the side made by an arrow or a crossbow bolt.

THE DEATH OF JOAN
A crowd of people watched Joan being burned to death. As the flames rose she begged for a cross, and a priest held up the crucifix from the altar of a nearby church.

THE HUNDRED YEARS' WAR
In 1337, the English king Edward III claimed the French throne and invaded France. When Joan was born, the English controlled more than half of France, including the capital city of Paris. The French and Burgundians ruled the rest. War between England and France continued until 1453, although between the battles there were many periods of peace. The war, now called the Hundred Years' War, caused much suffering in France: many people were killed, and the English troops looted the conquered towns. Joan's successful battles weakened the English, and within a few years of her death, they held only the northern seaport of Calais.

Joan leading the French troops into battle against the English at Orléans

CROSS OF LORRAINE
During World War II (1939-45) France was occupied by Germany. French Resistance fighters adopted the cross of Lorraine, originally Joan's symbol, because they shared her aim – to rid their country of foreign rule.

____ *Find out more* ____

FRANCE, HISTORY OF

JUDAISM

JEWISH FESTIVALS

Rosh Hashanah (New Year) Early autumn.

Yom Kippur (Day of Atonement) Tenth day of New Year; holiest of festivals, with 24 hours of fasting.

Passover (Pesach) Eight-day spring festival.

Shavuot (Feast of Weeks) Harvest festival in early summer.

Sukkoth (Feast of Tabernacles) Nine-day autumn festival.

Hanukkah (Festival of Lights) Eight-day winter festival.

Purim (Feast of Lots) Early spring festival.

THE HISTORY OF THE Jewish people and their religion, Judaism, are closely linked. All Jews believe in one God who, more than 4,000 years ago, made a special agreement with their ancestor, Abraham. They were to become God's chosen people. In return they promised to obey his laws and to spread his message to others. Jews believe that a Messiah, God's messenger, will one day come to transform the world into a better place and to restore the ancient Jewish kingdom that was destroyed in the 6th century B.C. Judaism aims for a just and peaceful life for all people on earth. Jewish scriptures explain that to achieve this aim, correct behaviour is very important. Orthodox Jews – those who interpret the scriptures very strictly – obey many rules about their day-to-day activities, including how to dress and what to eat. For example, they do not eat pork or shellfish. Many Jews, however, are not orthodox and apply the rules less strictly. For all Jews, Hebrew is the language of worship. It is also the national language of Israel, the Jewish homeland. However, Jews live and work all over the world, speaking many different languages. Their strong family life and the laws which guide them unite them wherever they live.

Jews light candles in a menorah, or branched candlestick, during Hanukkah.

Jewish men wear a skull cap called a yarmulke or kipa.

TORAH

The first five books of the Hebrew Bible – the Torah – contain the laws of Judaism and the early history of the Jewish people. Other sections of the Hebrew Bible contain the psalms, the words of the prophets, and other holy writings. For Jews the Torah is the most important of books.

During prayers Jewish men wear a tallith, or prayer shawl, over their shoulders.

The Jewish scriptures are written in Hebrew and Aramaic.

TALMUD

Jewish religious leaders are called rabbis. They are responsible for teaching and explaining the laws of Judaism. They study two holy books: the Talmud, and the Torah which is kept as a scroll. The Talmud contains instructions for following a Jewish way of life and understanding Jewish laws.

SYNAGOGUE

Jews worship in the synagogue. Prayer, study, and special family occasions such as weddings and bar and bat mitzvahs (the celebrations of children becoming adult Jews) take place here.

Find out more

FESTIVALS AND FEASTS
ISRAEL
JEWS, HISTORY OF
RELIGIONS

MARTIN LUTHER
KING

IN 1963 A BAPTIST MINISTER from Alabama, United States, led 250,000 people in a march on Washington, D.C., and delivered a moving and powerful speech. He was Martin Luther King, Jr., and his mission in life was to achieve equality and freedom for black Americans through peaceful means. Under his leadership the civil rights movement won many victories against segregation laws; laws that prevented blacks from voting, separated blacks from whites in schools and other places, and gave white people better opportunities and more freedom. Martin Luther King encouraged people to practice non-violent protest: demonstrations, "sit-ins", and peaceful disobedience of the segregation laws. King went to jail several times and faced constant threats of violence and death, but he continued to work for civil rights. Some white people hated him because he was black, and some black people disliked him because he refused to use more extreme and violent methods. King was assassinated in 1968, but his dream of a country without racial discrimination lives on today. In 1986, the US began to observe a national holiday in his name.

1929	Born, Atlanta, U.S.A.
1954	Baptist minister.
1955	Philosophy Doctorate.
1955-56	Leads Montgomery bus boycott.
1957	Southern Christian Leadership Conference.
1961	Freedom Rides to support desegregation.
1963	March on Washington.
1964	Nobel Peace Prize.
1965	Selma–Montgomery march.
1968	Assassinated.
1986	Holiday established.

PUBLIC SPEAKER

Martin Luther King's words inspired millions of Americans, black and white. At the August 1963 march on Washington, King made a speech that has since become famous. He said: "I have a dream that one day this nation will rise up and live out the true meaning of its creed: We hold these truths to be self-evident; that all men are created equal."

CIVIL RIGHTS MOVEMENT

Black Americans remained second-class citizens throughout the southern states until very recently. They were not allowed to vote, and restrictions were placed on where they could sit in buses and restaurants. During the late 1950s a movement arose demanding equal rights for all Americans. Martin Luther King and others organized non-violent protests designed to force changes in the law. In 1964-65 racial discrimination was finally outlawed throughout the United States.

BUS BOYCOTT

In December 1955, Rosa Parks, a black seamstress who worked in an Alabama department store, was arrested for refusing to give up a bus seat reserved for white people. For one year, Martin Luther King and his friends persuaded people to boycott (refuse to use) every bus in Montgomery, Alabama, until the segregation of the bus seats was declared illegal.

Find out more

CIVIL WAR, AMERICAN
SLAVERY
UNITED STATES OF AMERICA,
history of

KITES AND GLIDERS

CHINESE KITES
Flowing, painted tails in the shape of dragons, birds, and butterflies are typical of traditional Chinese kites. This centipede-like kite is made from 15 round paper and bamboo kites strung together.

Without a line to hold it at the correct angle to the wind, a kite would not be able to fly.

NO FLYING
machine is as old as the kite. People in China were flying silk kites more than 3,000 years ago, and legends tell how in 202 B.C. General Huan Theng terrified his enemies with kites whose taut strings wailed eerily in the breeze. Fifteen hundred years later, Marco Polo, the great Italian traveller, came back from China with tales of vast kites that hoisted prisoners into the air to test the wind. In Europe children have played with toy kites for more than 1,000 years. Gliders owe their origins to kites, and they too are old. In about 1800, the English inventor George Cayley found that a kite with arched wings and a tail could glide through the air without a breeze to lift it or a string to guide it. Later, Cayley built a glider large enough to carry a person. This rough prototype (test model) was the forerunner not only of the streamlined gliders of today but of all winged aircraft.

FLAT KITES
The oldest and simplest kites are diamond-shaped and have flat frames. They can also be strung together to make spectacular writhing serpents.

DELTA KITES
Triangular "delta" kites are simple to build and fly well in light winds. Hang gliders are based on the delta kite.

BOX KITE
Elaborate box kites have a frame that may be a combination of squares, triangles, and rectangles. Box kites are the most stable fliers of all.

HANG GLIDERS
The hang glider is the cheapest and simplest form of aircraft, and hang gliding is becoming an increasingly popular sport. When a hang glider takes to the air, the fabric of the wings arches up to give an aerofoil shape, like an ordinary aircraft wing. Without this, the craft would plummet, not glide, through the air.

The wing is made from lightweight Dacron fabric stretched over a long aluminium tube. On some hang gliders, curved spars help give the wing its aerofoil shape.

The pilot hangs under the wing and steers by shifting body weight to one side or the other.

Straps hold the pilot safely in position.

Gliders have long, thin wings which give a lot of lift (upward force) but keep air resistance to a minimum.

Eventually the glider loses height and lands.

The pilot looks for isolated clouds, which often indicate a thermal.

GLIDERS
Because a glider has no engine, it ultimately can fly only downwards. Modern gliders are streamlined and made of light fibreglass so that they lose height very slowly. However, a glider needs help to fly far. To take off, an aeroplane or a truck tows the glider into the air. Then the pilot looks for pockets of rising warm air, called thermals, to keep the glider flying high in the sky.

As the truck moves off, the glider rises into the air.

Once the glider is high enough, the pilot releases the winch line, and the glider flies free.

Warm air rising over a city or a sun-warmed field carries the glider upward in a spiral.

Find out more
AIRCRAFT
CHINA, HISTORY OF
PLASTICS

KNIGHTS AND HERALDRY

Argent a mullet
azure

Vert a lily or

Ermine a cross
crosslet gules

Azure a dolphin
argent

Sable a bee or

Gules a lion
rampant or

Or a chief
indented purpure

Argent a talbot
statant sable

Azure a fess
erminois

A THOUSAND YEARS AGO men who fought in battle on horseback were called knights. At first they were just powerful warriors who terrified the foot soldiers. But by the 13th century the knights of western Europe had an important role in society. They fought in the armies of the king or queen, in return for land. Knights also protected the peasants who lived and worked on the land, and in exchange the peasants gave the knight their service and produce.

Heraldry developed as a way of identifying knights in battle. Armour completely covered the knights' faces and bodies, and they all looked alike. So each knight chose "arms" – a unique coloured pattern or picture which everyone could recognize. He displayed his arms on a linen tunic worn over his armour. This was his "coat of arms". The chosen pattern remained in the knight's family and was passed on from father to son.

KNIGHTS HOSPITALLERS
Knights from northwest Europe fought in the Crusades, religious wars that took place in the Middle East between the 12th and 13th centuries. They formed alliances which soon became powerful groups. One of these was the Knights Hospitallers. This group looked after the hospitals along the Crusaders' routes to war.

Stirrups and a high saddle enabled the knight to stay on his horse at the moment of impact.

TOURNAMENTS AND JOUSTING

Tournaments began in France in the middle of the 11th century as peacetime training exercises for knights. They soon developed into major events with elaborate rules. Big groups of knights fought fierce mock battles over large areas of land, and the losing side paid a ransom or lost possessions. In the 13th century, tournaments became more organized and took place in a single field. Here just two knights jousted, or fought with blunt weapons. Later, tilting replaced jousting. The knights used lances to knock their rivals to the ground.

Gules a
lymphad argent

Azure an owl
argent

Vert a garb or

Vair a chevron
sable

Argent a rose
gules

Sable a boar's
head erased or

Or a bend
gules

Azure a
harpy or

Gules
Aescu

CAMELOT

King Arthur and his knights sat around a legendary round table in the ancient capital of Camelot. If it really did exist, Camelot was probably built in the west of Great Britain about 12 centuries ago. According to legend, Arthur led his Celtic knights in battle against Anglo-Saxon invaders. The knights of Camelot became heroes and had many adventures.

Caerleon Castle, Wales, possible site of Camelot.

Even though lances used in tilting had blunt tips, a fall from horseback (which meant defeat) often injured the knight.

The knight's coat of arms was painted or sewn onto all his equipment.

SHIELD

A knight displayed his arms on a shield. The shield had two parts: the field, or surface, which may have been a plain colour or a pattern; and the charge, which was a symbol, or a picture, such as an animal or a bird. Sometimes, a coat of arms also included above the shield a picture of a helmet with a crest, a silk wreath, and mantling – a cloth for protection from the sun. Below the shield there may have been a motto, or slogan. Together, these things were called a heraldic achievement (heralds were experts in arms).

Wooden barriers, called lists, kept the tilting knights apart, and protected spectators.

NAMING SHIELDS
The blazon, or description, below each shield names the field and charge and gives their colours in old French.

The field on this shield is or (gold).

The charge is a dragon vert (green). He is sitting "sejant" – that is, sitting forepaws on the ground

KNIGHTHOOD
The training to become a knight started at seven years of age. A boy (girls were not allowed to become knights) began as a page in the household of his father's lord. Pages learned the rules of knight service and how to use weapons. At the age of 15 or 16, a page became a squire. The squire was the personal servant to his master and learned the skills needed for fighting on horseback. After five years the squire could become a knight. At first this was an honour that any knight could bestow on a squire. Today, only English kings and queens can give knighthoods, but the title is a formal one and has lost most of its meaning.

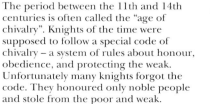

Dubbing a squire, or touching him on the shoulders with a sword, made him into a knight.

In English legend, Saint George was a chivalrous knight who killed a dangerous dragon.

CHIVALRY
The period between the 11th and 14th centuries is often called the "age of chivalry". Knights of the time were supposed to follow a special code of chivalry – a system of rules about honour, obedience, and protecting the weak. Unfortunately many knights forgot the code. They honoured only noble people and stole from the poor and weak.

Vert a castle argent

Or a lion passant gules

Sable a bobbin palewise argent

Chequy or and azure a canton vert

Ermine a millrind sable

Azure a fleur de lys or

Argent a martlet gules

Vert a unicorn rampant argent

Gules a barrel palewise or

Purpure fretty or

Sable a cross engrailed or

Argent an eagle displayed sable

Gyronny argent and gules

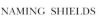

Or a dragon sejant vert

Argent a thistle proper

Find out more
ARMOUR
CASTLES
CRUSADES
MIDDLE AGES
WEAPONS

LAKE AND RIVER WILDLIFE

THE WATER IN LAKES and rivers is teeming with all kinds of plants and animals. Grasses, reeds, and other plants grow along the water's edge, providing food and shelter for insects, nesting birds, and mammals such as water voles and muskrats. In rivers, the fast-flowing water sweeps away plants, but in lakes, tiny floating plants are food for small creatures such as water fleas and shrimps, which are in turn eaten by bigger fish. Larger floating waterweeds provide shade for basking fish. Fallen leaves, animal droppings, and rotting plant matter form a rich mud at the bottom of rivers and lakes, where worms, snails, and other small animals live. Today, many lakes and rivers are suffering from serious pollution. Industrial chemicals, farm fertilizers, untreated sewage, and a host of other damaging substances discharged into lakes and rivers have upset or destroyed the natural wildlife balance.

FRESH WATER
The water in lakes and rivers is called fresh water. Although it makes up only about one three-thousandth of all the water on Earth, fresh water is home to thousands of different plants and animals.

Pickerell weed grows at the water's edge of lakes and rivers.

MUSKRAT
The muskrat is a rodent that usually eats water plants but also feeds on small animals such as fish, frogs, and freshwater shellfish.

Muskrat swims powerfully with its webbed back feet and uses its long, hairless tail as a rudder for steering.

RUDDY DUCK
The ruddy duck is found in open waters in many parts of Europe. It has a stiff, upward-pointing tail and dives in search of plants, small water insects, larvae, and worms.

GIANT OTTER
The largest member of the otter family lives in South America. The giant otter grows to more than 1.5 m (5 ft) long including its tail. It hunts catfish, piranhas, and other fish. Unlike other otters, the giant otter prefers to stay in streams and pools and is not often seen on land. Today, this otter is very rare and is on the official list of endangered species.

PIKE
The northern pike is a large, fearsome predator with a huge mouth and sharp teeth for seizing many kinds of fish, as well as frogs, water birds, and small mammals. Pike live in lakes and slow-moving rivers; the biggest pike grow to more than 1 m (3 ft) long.

FALSE MAP TURTLE
One of the many water creatures that suffer from pollution of rivers and lakes is the false map turtle from North America, shown here. The harmful chemical waste that we pour into the water has also reduced this turtle's food of snails and shellfish.

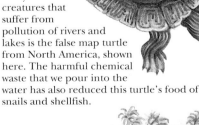

RIVER PLANTS
The speed of the water in a river has a great effect on the wildlife. In a fast river the water sweeps the riverbed clean of sand and mud, leaving only pebbles. Nothing can grow in the middle of a river, and the river bank consists mainly of plants such as willows that hang over the water. In a slow river, sand and mud can settle, and plants such as irises take root more easily.

Pond weed is food for many different lake and river fish.

CRAYFISH
The crayfish, found in rivers, is a freshwater relative of sea-living lobsters. It is active mainly at night and walks along the river bed on its four pairs of legs, eating a wide range of food, from plant matter to worms, shellfish, and small fish.

Cattail grows to 2.5 m (8 ft) high.

LAKE WILDLIFE

Trees such as willows and alders line the edge of many lakes; rushes, tussock sedges, reeds, and other marshy plants grow closer to the water. Plants such as water lilies and water horsetails grow in the shallow water and stick up above the surface. Each type of plant is food for a different assortment of animals.

HERON
Many kinds of herons visit lakes and rivers around the world. Herons wade slowly in shallow water, sometimes standing perfectly still for several minutes, then suddenly striking at a frog or a fish with their long, spear-shaped bills.

WILLOW
The willow tree thrives in the damp soil of river banks and the shores of lakes. Its long, penetrating roots help strengthen the bank.

MOORHEN
During the breeding season the male and female moorhen build a nest among the vegetation at the water's edge, and the female lays up to 11 eggs. The moorhen's long, splayed toes enable it to walk on floating leaves on rivers, lakes, and marshes. These birds eat pond weeds, fruits, and sometimes insects.

Dragonflies are a familiar sight around lakes and rivers during the summer months.

WATER LILIES
There are about 200 kinds of water lilies. Their leaves and flowers float on the surface of the water, and their long stems stretch down about 2 m (6 ft) to the roots embedded in the mud below.

WATER BOATMAN
This aquatic insect uses its paddle-like legs to row across the surface of the water. The back swimmer, a similar creature, swims upside down, often near the surface.

WATER SNAKE
Many snakes can swim; the water snake is an expert swimmer. It glides across the lake with hardly a ripple. Water snakes prey on small mammals, frogs, fish, and small water birds and their eggs and nestlings.

Diving beetles breathe by trapping air under the hard wing cases that cover the body.

MIRROR CARP
Carp are fish that live in slow-flowing rivers and weed-filled lakes. Mirror carp are so-named because their bodies are covered with large, shiny, mirror-like scales. Mirror carp search the river bottom for small plants, shellfish, and worms.

Insect larvae, fish fry (young), and other small creatures shelter among the plants along the water's edge.

DIVING BEETLE
The diving beetle is a fierce predator. It hunts tadpoles, small fish, water worms, and insects.

CONSERVATION
The axolotl shown here is a kind of Mexican salamander. It cannot survive on land and is found only in lakes such as Lake Xochimilco, Mexico. Like many other lake and river creatures, the axolotl is threatened by pollution. Thousands of lakes in the world are now lifeless, because of the damaging substances that flow into them. Today many lakes and rivers are being turned into nature reserves in order to protect the birds, fish, mammals, and other wildlife they contain.

Axolotl means "water beast".

Find out more

ANIMAL SENSES
DUCKS, GEESE, AND SWANS
FISH
FROGS AND OTHER AMPHIBIANS
SNAKES

LAKES

WATER FROM RIVERS, mountain springs, and rain fills hollows in the ground and forms lakes, which are areas of water surrounded by land. Lakes also form in depressions dug out of the ground by glaciers, or in holes in limestone rocks. Some lakes are artificial: reservoirs are lakes made by building dams across rivers. Several landlocked seas such as the Caspian Sea and the Dead Sea are really lakes. The Caspian Sea, which lies between Europe and Asia, is the world's biggest lake. Its surface covers an area almost as large as Japan.

Lakes sustain a wealth of plant and animal life and are often surrounded by fertile land. Freshwater lakes provide water for towns and cities, and recreation areas for swimming, sailing, and water-skiing. Large lakes, such as the Great Lakes, are used to transport goods in ships. However, lakes do not last forever. Silt and plants can fill up a lake over a period of years and turn it into a swamp.

SALTY LAKES
Salt collects in lakes that have no outlet, such as the Dead Sea between Israel and Jordan. The water is so salty that people can float in it without swimming.

VOLCANIC LAKES
Rainwater fills the volcanic crater at the summit of Mount Mazama, Oregon, United States, to form Crater Lake. It is 589 m (1,932 ft) deep, making it the deepest lake in the United States.

KINDS OF LAKES

Lakes form in hollows dug by glaciers during the Ice Age, and in places where glaciers have left barriers of rock across valleys. Water dissolves huge holes in limestone regions which often fill with rainwater to create lakes. Lakes can also form in volcanic craters.

FRESHWATER LAKES
The water in freshwater lakes is not salty like the sea, because the lakes are constantly fed and drained by rivers. The largest group of freshwater lakes are the Great Lakes in the United States and Canada. Lake Superior (left) is the largest of the Great Lakes.

Plants grow on the damp, fertile soil.

SWAMPS AND MARSHES

The Everglades is a large region of swamps in the United States. Swamps, or marshes, can form at the edge of a lake where the ground is soaked with water or covered with shallow water. They also form on land where water cannot drain away.

THE LIFE OF A LAKE

Lakes are not permanent features of the landscape. Some may come and go as their water supply rises and falls. Lakes can slowly fill with soil and stones washed down from the land above the lake. The outlet river may deepen and drain the lake.

River flows into lake.

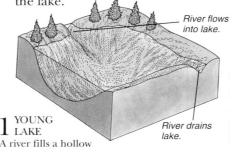

1 YOUNG LAKE
A river fills a hollow in the ground to create the lake. The water flows through the lake, running out into another river.

River drains lake.

2 SHRINKING LAKE
The river carries soil, which falls to the bottom as it enters the lake. A layer of soil builds up along the edge of the lake.

3 DYING LAKE
The soil layers extend into the lake. Plants grow and the layers become land. This continues until the lake vanishes.

Soil and mud build up at sides and bottom of lake.

LANGUAGES

OUR ABILITY TO TALK is one of the skills that makes humans different from the rest of the animal world. Some mammals and birds have simple "languages" of just a few noises, but human speech is much more highly developed. In English, for example, most people use a vocabulary (a list of words) of about 5,000 words in talking, and 10,000 in writing. A language is a way of organizing spoken sounds to express ideas. Human language developed over thousands of years, and people in different countries use different languages. Some languages share words with the languages of nearby countries. For instance, *book* is *libro* in both Italian and Spanish, and *livre* in French; in English we get the word *library* from the same source. There are now some 5,000 different languages and many dialects – local versions of major languages.

TOWER OF BABEL
At the beginning of this Bible story everyone spoke the same language. But when people tried to build a tower to reach heaven, God became angry. He made many languages so people could not understand and help one another.

LATIN
For many centuries, educated people of many nationalities spoke Latin as well as their native, or first, language. Throughout Europe, scholars, governments, and the Christian Church used Latin.

English is spoken by 330 million people as a first language, and by about 600 million as a second or third language.

About two thirds of China's population, 803 million people, speak Mandarin Chinese.

France once ruled many countries in West Africa, and people there still speak French as well as their local languages.

There are at least 845 languages in India. Hindi and English are the official languages.

Some people have no difficulty in learning foreign languages and can speak several fluently; the record is about 28.

There are about 700 languages in Papua New Guinea.

COMMON LANGUAGES
A map of national languages shows how European nations have explored the world: for example, English settlers took their language to the United States, Canada, Australia and New Zealand. Spain conquered much of South America, and Spanish is still spoken there. But many people using these languages also have their own local language.

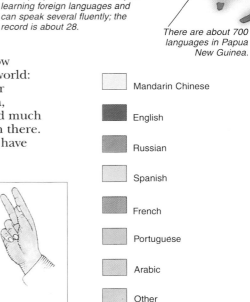

Mandarin Chinese

English

Russian

Spanish

French

Portuguese

Arabic

Other

SIGN LANGUAGE
Human speech and hearing make language possible. People who have difficulty speaking or hearing cannot use a spoken language. Instead they communicate using hand signals. There are signs and gestures for all the common words, and signs for individual letters.

S P E A K

Find out more
ALPHABETS
EDUCATION

LASERS

IF SOMEONE ASKED you what is the brightest, most intense light of all, you might say sunlight. You would be wrong. The light from lasers is even brighter; in fact, it is the brightest light known. A laser produces a pencil-thin beam of coloured light which can be so intense that it will burn a hole through steel, or so straight and narrow that it can be aimed precisely at a tiny mirror on the moon, 384,401 km (238,855 miles) away.

A scientist named Theodore Maiman built the first laser in 1960. Maiman created the beam by flashing ordinary light into a special rod of synthetic ruby. Today's lasers work with many other materials, as well as ruby. Gas lasers, for instance, use gases such as argon which gives a low-power beam ideal for delicate surgery. By contrast, powerful solid-state lasers produce a beam with solid rods of crystals such as emerald.

LASER SHOW
Multicoloured lasers produce spectacular light shows for rock concerts and public celebrations.

In ordinary light, such as that from a flashlight, light waves are jumbled up together and spill out in all directions.

Laser light bounces back and forth between the mirrors at either end of the tube. Some light gets through the half-silvered mirror at the front.

Gas atoms in laser tube produce laser light.

Tube contains mixture of gases, such as helium and neon.

Electric discharge excites the gas atoms into firing off photons.

LASER
An electric spark gives energy to atoms in the laser tube. This extra energy makes some atoms fire off photons – tiny bursts of light. These photons hit other atoms, making them fire off photons too. Mirrors reflect the photons back and forth along the tube, making them bump into more atoms as they go. Some of the photons surge through a "partial" mirror at the front of the laser to form the beam.

Lasers produce a straight, narrow beam, and laser light itself is "coherent", which means that all the light waves travel in step.

Gas laser

An atom has electrons moving around its nucleus.

Electrical energy from power supply boosts an electron into a different energy state.

When the electron returns to its original state, it gives out a photon of laser light.

This laser sends out a continuous beam of light. "Pulsed" lasers emit the beam in regular rapid bursts.

Laser light hits other atoms, which in turn produce laser light.

HOLOGRAMS
A hologram is a photograph made with laser light. When you look at a hologram, you see a three-dimensional view of the object, just as with the real thing. Holograms are made by splitting a laser beam into two. One beam, the reference beam, goes straight to the photographic film; the other hits the object of the hologram first, breaking up its neat pattern of light waves. The film records the way the disturbed "object" beam upsets the undisturbed reference beam, producing a three-dimensional image.

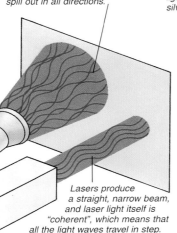

USES OF LASERS
Lasers are used in industry to drill steel and engrave microchips with speed and precision; by engineers to line up bridges and skyscrapers with pinpoint accuracy; in phone networks to carry calls swiftly and clearly through optical fibres; and by doctors to treat cancer and perform delicate eye operations.

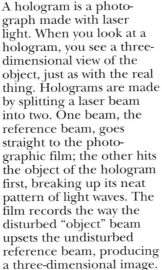

Laser beams are bounced off satellites in space to help scientists track the movement of the Earth's continents.

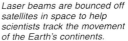

Find out more
GAS
GEMS AND JEWELLERY
LIGHT
SHOPS AND SHOPPING
SOUND RECORDING

LAW

EVERY SOCIETY HAS its own set of laws to safeguard the rights of its citizens and to balance individual freedom against the needs of the broad mass of people. On the simplest level, there are laws to protect citizens from attack or robbery as they walk along the street. These and other similar rules are called criminal laws. However, the law does much more than provide simple protection. It also settles arguments between individuals. For example, if you believe that you have bought damaged goods, and the person who sold them disagrees, the law must decide who is right. The branch of law that deals with arguments such as these is called civil law. The law is very complex because it must meet the different needs and expectations of society's millions of members. It includes not only civil and criminal branches but also other smaller divisions, such as family law which settles arguments when people divorce. Understanding the law takes a long time; lawyers, who apply and interpret the law, study for many years. Most lawyers specialize in just one area of the law.

JUDGES
The judge helps the jury understand the laws relating to the trial, and passes sentence (decides the punishment) if there is a guilty verdict.

Prisoner on trial

Jury of 12 people

Defence lawyer addressing the jury

Prosecution tries to prove guilt.

FAIR AND JUST LAW
Statues representing justice wear a blindfold to show that the law does not favour any one person. However, not all law is good law, for governments can make laws that remove freedoms as well as safeguard them. The scales show that justice weighs opposing evidence like a balance weighs goods. The sword represents punishment.

Defence tries to convince the jury that the prisoner is not guilty.

DEATH PENALTY

Until the 18th century, death was the punishment for many crimes. Some countries still execute people for murder and other serious crimes.

JURY TRIAL

Anyone accused of a serious crime has the right to a trial by a jury, a group of men and women (usually 12) chosen by chance. A prosecuting lawyer tries to convince the jury that the defendant – the accused person – is guilty. A defence lawyer sets out to prove the defendant's innocence. Witnesses tell the court what they know about the crime. The jury listens to the facts, or evidence, and decides whether the prosecution has proved guilt.

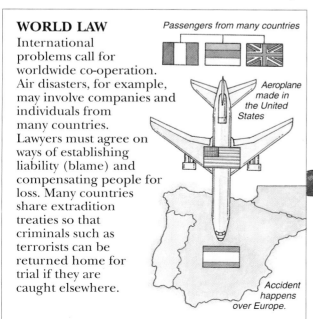

WORLD LAW

International problems call for worldwide co-operation. Air disasters, for example, may involve companies and individuals from many countries. Lawyers must agree on ways of establishing liability (blame) and compensating people for loss. Many countries share extradition treaties so that criminals such as terrorists can be returned home for trial if they are caught elsewhere.

Passengers from many countries

Aeroplane made in the United States

Accident happens over Europe.

ALTERNATIVES TO PRISON
Electronic tags locked to the legs of criminals keep them at home and out of trouble. A box next to the offender's telephone monitors the range of the tag. If the wearer of the tag moves too far away, the box dials up a central computer and sounds the alarm.

Heavy labour is sometimes part of the prison sentence for serious offenders.

PRISON AND PUNISHMENT
People found guilty of serious crimes usually go to prison. This is partly to punish them and partly to protect others from danger. Prisons also aim to reform offenders and discourage them from further crime.

Find out more

GOVERNMENTS
POLICE
WOMEN'S RIGHTS

LIGHT

WITHOUT LIGHT, LIFE on Earth would be impossible. Sunlight provides the energy to make plants grow and keep all living things alive. Light itself is a form of energy which travels in tiny, invisible waves. Light waves carry tiny packets of energy called photons. When photons enter our eyes they stimulate special light-sensitive cells so that we can see. Other forms of energy which travel in waves include radio waves, x-rays, and microwaves in microwave ovens. These are all types of electromagnetic waves. Just as there is a spectrum of colours in light, so too is there an electromagnetic spectrum. In fact, light waves are also a type of electromagnetic wave, and the colours in light form a small part of the electromagnetic spectrum. Light waves and all other electromagnetic waves travel at more than 300,000 km per second (186,000 miles per second), which is so fast that they could circle the world almost eight times in a second. Nothing in the universe can travel faster than the speed of light.

LIGHT BULB

In the middle of every electric light bulb is a tiny spiral of tungsten wire called the filament. When an electric current is sent through the filament, it warms up so much that it glows white hot. It is the brightly glowing filament that produces light.

Filament made of tungsten metal

Bulb is filled with an inert gas such as argon to keep the filament from catching fire and burning out, as it would do in air.

Filament and electric terminals are sealed into an airtight glass bulb.

Electrical contact is made when the bulb terminal is screwed into the socket.

The explosion of gunpowder inside a firework produces a burst of coloured light.

BRIGHTNESS OF LIGHT

The further you are from a light, the less bright it will seem. This is because light spreads out in all directions from its source. So when you are far away, the light is spread over a wide area. Many stars, for instance, are much brighter than our sun, but their light is spread out over so vast an area that by the time it reaches us, the stars seem no brighter than a candle.

Nuclear reactions inside the centre of the sun produce intense heat and light. Stars in other galaxies also produce light from nuclear reactions.

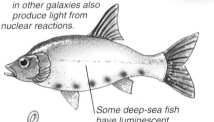

Some deep-sea fish have luminescent stripes and spots along their bodies that give out light.

Searchlights give out very intense light, often produced by a spark which bursts between two pieces of carbon.

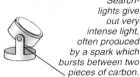

SOURCES OF LIGHT

Many different objects give off light. The sun, electric light bulbs, and fireworks are incandescent, which means they glow because they are hot. But not all lights are hot. Chemicals, not heat, produce the glowing spots on the bodies of some deep-sea fish. All cool lights, including fluorescent lights, are called luminescent.

Shine a torch on a wall and watch the pool of light grow larger and dimmer as you move the flashlight further away.

A candle is a wide source of light, so it produces a fuzzy shadow.

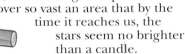

Candles and lanterns give out light.

When things burn they give out light as well as heat.

LIGHT AND SHADOW

Light travels in straight lines, so, in most cases, it cannot go around obstacles in its path. When light rays hit a solid object, some bounce back and some are absorbed by the object, warming it up a little. The area behind receives no light rays and is left in shadow.

FLUORESCENT LIGHT

A lot of energy in an electric light bulb is wasted as heat. Fluorescent tubes are cooler and more economical. When an electric current is passed through the gas in the tube, gas atoms emit invisible, ultraviolet light. The ultraviolet light strikes phosphors – chemicals in the tube's lining – and makes them glow with a brilliant white light.

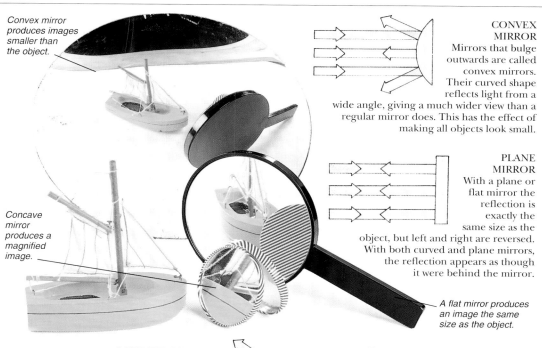

Convex mirror produces images smaller than the object.

Concave mirror produces a magnified image.

CONVEX MIRROR

Mirrors that bulge outwards are called convex mirrors. Their curved shape reflects light from a wide angle, giving a much wider view than a regular mirror does. This has the effect of making all objects look small.

PLANE MIRROR

With a plane or flat mirror the reflection is exactly the same size as the object, but left and right are reversed. With both curved and plane mirrors, the reflection appears as though it were behind the mirror.

A flat mirror produces an image the same size as the object.

MIRRORS

Light passes easily through transparent substances such as glass and water, but not through opaque objects such as paper. Most opaque objects have a rough surface which scatters light in all directions. However, a mirror has a smooth surface, so it reflects light in a regular way. When you look at your face in a mirror, the light bounces straight back, producing a sharp image. Most mirrors are made of glass; your face is reflected from a shiny metal coating at the back of the mirror, not from the glass.

CONCAVE MIRROR

A concave mirror, which is curved inwards, forms two kinds of image. If the object is close to the mirror, the reflection is larger than the real thing. If the object is far away, the image formed is small and upside down.

MIRAGE

In the hot desert, weary travellers are often fooled by the sight of an oasis (a fertile area where water rises to the surface). The oasis appears on the horizon, only to vanish as the travellers hurry towards it. What they have seen is an illusion called a mirage. The oasis may exist but it lies beyond the horizon. Light from the oasis is refracted (bent) by a layer of hot air near the ground, making the oasis look closer than it really is.

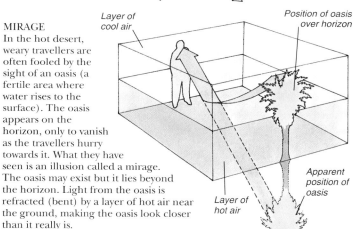

Layer of cool air

Position of oasis over horizon

Apparent position of oasis

Layer of hot air

LENSES AND REFRACTION

Glasses, cameras, telescopes, and microscopes use lenses to create particular kinds of images. The lenses in a telescope, for example, produce a magnified view of a distant object. All lenses work on the principle that although light always travels in straight lines, it travels slower through glass than through air. If a light ray strikes glass at an angle, one side of the ray will hit the glass just before the other and will slow down earlier. The effect is to bend the light ray slightly, just as a car pulls to one side if it has a puncture. This bending of light is called refraction.

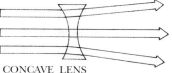

CONCAVE LENS

A concave lens is thicker at the edges than in the centre, so it spreads light rays out. If you look through a concave lens, everything appears smaller.

Focus

CONVEX LENS

Convex lenses bring light rays together. At the focus, where light rays from a distant object meet, they form an image of the object which can be seen on a screen.

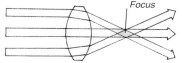

Magnifying glasses are convex lenses.

FIBRE OPTICS

Fibre optic cables are channels that carry light. They are flexible so they can carry light around corners. The fibres are long, thin filaments of glass; the light bounces back and forth along the inner surface of the glass. Fibre optics are valuable for seeing into awkward places. Doctors can use fibre optic endoscopes to see inside a patient's body without opening the body up.

Light refracts when it passes through water, because the water slows it down. This makes objects look as though they are bent.

Find out more

CAMERAS
COLOUR
EYES
LASERS
PHOTOGRAPHY
PLANTS
SUN
TELEPHONES

ABRAHAM
LINCOLN

ONE OF THE MOST FAMOUS PRESIDENTS in history is Abraham Lincoln. But when he was elected in 1860, less than half the country supported him, and he remained very unpopular with many people for the entire five years of his presidency. Lincoln did not approve of slavery, and many landowners in the southern United States still kept slaves. As a result of his election, 11 southern states left the Union and declared themselves an independent Confederacy, or alliance. Civil war then broke out between the Union and the Confederacy. Lincoln was a capable war leader. He struggled to keep the remaining states united behind his leadership. Many people in his own government opposed him. But in 1865 he led the Union states to victory. Afterwards, Lincoln tried to repair the damage done by the war and bring together the two opposing sides.

LINCOLN'S BIRTHPLACE
This log cabin in Kentucky, United States, is a replica of the birthplace of Abraham Lincoln. The poverty of Lincoln's childhood influenced his political ideas.

1809 Born in Kentucky.

1831 Moves to New Salem, Illinois, where he worked as a storekeeper, surveyor, and postmaster while studying law.

1834 Elected to state legislature.

1836 Qualifies as a lawyer.

1847-49 Elected to Congress.

1855, 1858 Runs unsuccessfully for Senate.

1860 Elected president.

1863 Issues Emancipation Proclamation.

1864 Re-elected president.

1865 Assassinated.

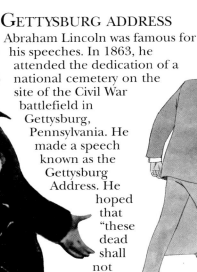

GETTYSBURG ADDRESS
Abraham Lincoln was famous for his speeches. In 1863, he attended the dedication of a national cemetery on the site of the Civil War battlefield in Gettysburg, Pennsylvania. He made a speech known as the Gettysburg Address. He hoped that "these dead shall not have died in vain".

THE DEATH OF LINCOLN
On 14 April, 1865, Abraham Lincoln was watching a play at Ford's Theatre in Washington, D.C. John Wilkes Booth, an actor who supported the southern states in the Civil War, crept quietly into the president's box and shot him. The president died of his wounds the next day.

ABOLITION
The move to abolish slavery in the United States grew under Lincoln. Led by white middle-class Northerners, many freed slaves joined the abolition movement. Some, such as Andrew Scott (right), fought in the Union army during the Civil War. Slaves fled from South to North (and freedom) via the Underground Railroad – a secret escape route. Harriet Tubman, a famous pioneer of the railroad, helped 300 slaves to escape in this way.

MOUNT RUSHMORE
The faces of four American presidents – Abraham Lincoln, George Washington, Thomas Jefferson, and Theodore Roosevelt – are carved out of rock on the side of Mount Rushmore in the Black Hills of South Dakota, United States.

___*Find out more*___
CIVIL WAR, AMERICAN
SLAVERY
UNITED STATES OF AMERICA, history of

LIONS
TIGERS, AND OTHER BIG CATS

FEW CREATURES ARE held in such awe as lions, tigers, cheetahs, and leopards, which we often call the big cats. These agile predators have strong, razor-sharp teeth and claws, muscular bodies, and excellent senses. Their beautiful striped and dappled fur camouflages them among the trees, allowing them to leap from the shadows to ambush unwary zebras, giraffes, and other prey. There are seven kinds of big cats. The tiger is the largest. A fully grown tiger may measure more than 3 m (10 ft) from nose to tail; a fully grown lion is almost as big.

The first large cats lived 45 million years ago. Many, including the lion, cheetah, and leopard, still inhabit parts of Africa. Snow leopards dwell in the mountains and forests of Asia. Jaguars are the largest of the big cats in North and South America. They are equally at home swimming in lakes or climbing in trees.

CUBS
Like all young big cats, tiger cubs have pale markings when they are born. After a few months, the pale stripes change to black and orange.

HUNTING PREY
Lions live mainly on savannas (grassy plains) and scrubland, and the females do most of the hunting. This picture shows two adult lionesses charging at a young gazelle, separating it from the rest of the herd.

LION PRIDE
Lions are the only big cats that live in groups, called prides, which may be up to 30 strong. The pride roams over an area of 100 sq km (40 square miles) or more, depending on the abundance of prey in the area. The large male lion protects the pride's territory against other prides. The lion also defends the females against other males.

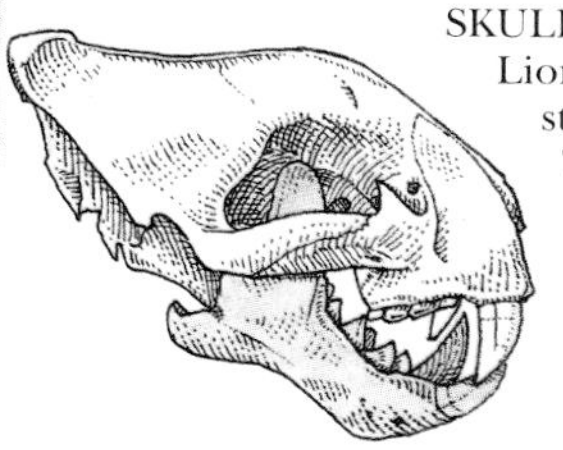

SKULL AND TEETH
Lions and other big cats have short, strong skulls with powerful jaws. Their spearlike canine teeth pierce and rip their victim's flesh. The large molar teeth tear flesh and gristle as the jaw opens and closes.

Lion has a thick, shaggy mane.

Large, strong canine teeth for tearing prey

Large feet and sharp claws

The chief lion is the strongest member of the pride. It can measure 2.4 m (8 ft) in length, and 1 m (3 ft) high at the shoulder.

CARNIVORES
Lions, tigers, and other big cats are true carnivores (flesh eaters). Lions usually eat large prey such as antelopes and zebras. One giraffe is often enough to feed a whole pride of lions.

CLAWS OUT
When a cat pounces on a victim or climbs up into a tree, it unsheathes its sharp claws. Muscles in the feet pull the claws out and draw back the sheaths.

CLAWS IN
Most of the time, a cat's claws are protected in muscular sheaths. This keeps the claws sharp and less likely to break. The claws are extended when the cat cleans its feet.

LEOPARD
The leopard weighs about 60 kg (130 lb), and its body measures about 1.5 m (5 ft). Leopards are adaptable creatures. They can survive in hot tropical forests or on cold mountainsides. They may also live close to towns and villages.

CLIMBING
Leopards are excellent climbers. They sleep, rest, and watch for prey from the branches of trees. They also drag their uneaten food up into a tree to store it and to keep it away from scavengers.

PANTHER
The black panther (right) is a type of leopard. In daylight, its spots show black in its dark grey-brown fur.

JAGUAR
The jaguar (below) stalks its prey in the same way as the tiger. Jaguars eat a variety of other creatures, including tapirs, fish, frogs, rodents, sloths, and small caimans (South American crocodiles).

ROARING
Only the big cats can roar, and they do so loudly, although the jaguar and snow leopard roar only rarely. The roar is a way of expressing anger, and warns other creatures to keep away.

TIGER
Unlike most cats, the tiger does not mind water. A tiger sometimes pulls its dead prey near the water's edge, because it needs to take frequent drinks during a meal. Tigers stalk their prey through dense undergrowth, then bound over the last 16 m (50 ft) or so, taking their victim by surprise. On average, a tiger consumes about 18 kg (40 lb) of meat a day.

CHEETAH
No animal can outrun a cheetah over a short distance. Cheetahs can speed along at about 100 km/h (60 mph) – as fast as a car. Unlike other cats, the cheetah cannot withdraw its claws into sheaths, so the claws are always extended. This gives the cheetah extra grip as it starts its run. If a stalking cheetah is detected before it gets within about 183 m (200 yards) of its prey, it does not make the final dash. Only about half of a cheetah's hunting chases are successful.

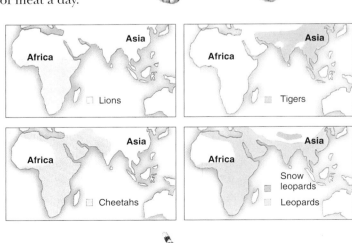

Africa | Asia | □ Lions
Africa | Asia | ▪ Tigers
Africa | Asia | □ Cheetahs
Africa | Asia | ▪ Snow leopards / ▫ Leopards

CONSERVATION
Leopards and other big cats have been overhunted for their fur and because they attack livestock and, very rarely, people. The trade in big cats and fur products is now banned by an international agreement. The maps show the main areas of the world where these big cats still live.

Find out more
AFRICAN WILDLIFE
ANIMALS
CAMOUFLAGE
CATS
CONSERVATION
and endangered species
MAMMALS
ZOOS

LITERATURE

THROUGH LITERATURE – which includes plays, poems, and novels – people write about their thoughts, ideas, and hopes. But not everything that is written down is literature. Writing becomes literature only if it is well written and covers subjects of lasting interest to people of all societies. For example, the English playwright William Shakespeare (1564-1616) often based his plays on old or well-known stories that nobody would call literature. But Shakespeare was a very skilled writer and had a great understanding of human nature. So hundreds of years after he wrote his plays, they still excite audiences of all nationalites.

Authors, or writers, have often used literature to protest injustice in the world and influence the opinions of peoples or governments. For instance, in *The Grapes of Wrath*, American John Steinbeck (1902-68) drew public attention to the suffering of homeless farmers fleeing from Oklahoma to California in the Great Depression of the 1930s.

GULLIVER'S TRAVELS

English author Jonathan Swift (1667-1745) wrote *Gulliver's Travels* in 1726. Although he did not write the book for children, the first two parts have long been popular with young people.

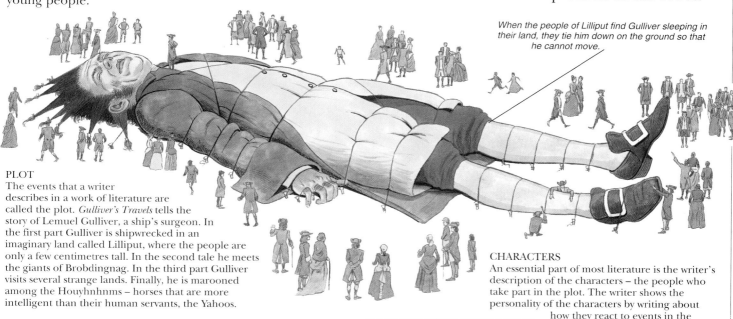

When the people of Lilliput find Gulliver sleeping in their land, they tie him down on the ground so that he cannot move.

PLOT

The events that a writer describes in a work of literature are called the plot. *Gulliver's Travels* tells the story of Lemuel Gulliver, a ship's surgeon. In the first part Gulliver is shipwrecked in an imaginary land called Lilliput, where the people are only a few centimetres tall. In the second tale he meets the giants of Brobdingnag. In the third part Gulliver visits several strange lands. Finally, he is marooned among the Houyhnhnms – horses that are more intelligent than their human servants, the Yahoos.

CHARACTERS

An essential part of most literature is the writer's description of the characters – the people who take part in the plot. The writer shows the personality of the characters by writing about how they react to events in the story. For example, Swift shows that Gulliver was a kindhearted man by describing how he entertained the tiny Lilliputian people: "I would sometimes lie down, and let five or six of them dance on my Hand. And at last the Boys and Girls would venture to come and play at Hide and Seek in my Hair."

ORAL LITERATURE

People created stories long before writing was invented. Oral literature is a spoken story passed on from one storyteller to another. A storyteller, Scheherazade, is the main character in a traditional Arabic story called *The Thousand and One Nights*. Her cruel husband vows to kill her in the morning, but she charms him with a story and delays her death. Next night, she tells another story and lives one more day. After many stories her husband changes his mind, and Scheherazade's life is spared.

THEME

The plots and characters in literature can be entertaining, but writers use them to give the reader a much more general message. The theme of a work of literature is this message. It is often about a social or political subject. *Gulliver's Travels* seems to be an adventure story but Swift's theme was the character of 18th-century England. The Lilliputians represent different types of English people, and their good and bad qualities.

EPICS AND SAGAS

Epics and sagas tell the story of legendary heroes and their deeds. An epic tells the story as a long poem; a saga is in prose – it does not rhyme as the verses of a poem do. The English epic *Beowulf* is more than 3,000 lines long. The story was probably first told in the 6th century, but the version we know today comes from a 10th- century manuscript written in Old English. It tells the story of Beowulf, a Swedish hero. He destroys the flesh-eating monster Grendel and his mother, who attacked the court of the Danish king Hrothgar.

BIOGRAPHY

A book which tells the true story of someone's life is called a biography. In an autobiography the writer tells the story of his or her own life. Justin Kaplan's biography *Mr. Clemens and Mark Twain* takes its title from the famous American author's real name, Samuel Langhorne Clemens.

POETRY

Poetry is different from other forms of literature because it usually has rhythm and rhyme. In a poem with rhythm the accents or beats in each line follow a pattern that is repeated in each verse, like the verses of a song. In poems that rhyme, lines end with words that sound similar. Poets enjoy the rhyme and rhythm of words, and Englishman Edward Lear (1812-88) used both in his nonsense verses for children (above).

A Hans Christian Andersen story tells how a pea beneath a pile of mattresses keeps a princess awake.

STORIES

Most stories describe a single incident or cover a short period of time. There are children's stories about every subject from adventures to ghosts. One of the best-known story writers was Danish author Hans Christian Andersen (1805-75), who wrote *The Emperor's New Clothes* and *The Ugly Duckling*.

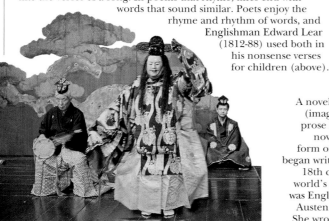

DRAMA

Literature that is written to be performed by actors is called drama. Different countries have their own forms of drama. In Noh drama (above), which began in Japan in the 14th century, there is very little scenery. The actors use dance, mime, and masks to perform the plays, which can last several hours. The religious beliefs of Buddhism and Shintoism have influenced Noh drama.

NOVELS

A novel is a long story about fictitious (imaginary) characters, written in prose rather than poetry. Today, novels are the most popular form of literature, but people began writing them only in the 18th century. One of the world's greatest novelists was Englishwoman Jane Austen (1775-1817). She wrote *Pride and Prejudice* and other books about English life, customs, and morals.

The first page of an unfinished novel by Jane Austen.

Jane Austen

Find out more

BOOKS
PRINTING
THEATRE
WRITERS AND POETS

LIZARDS

THE LARGEST GROUP of reptiles is the lizard family, with about 3,700 kinds. Lizards live in almost every habitat except the open sea and the far north. The huge Komodo dragon is the largest, and tiny geckos are the smallest – some are less than 2 cm (1 in) long. A typical lizard such as the iguana has a slim body, a long tail, legs that splay out sideways, and five-toed feet. There are many variations, however; skinks are often extremely long, with short legs. They seem to move effortlessly through loose soil with a wriggling motion. Snake-lizards are even more snake-like, with no front legs and small, paddle-shaped back legs. Several kinds of lizards, including the slow-worm, have lost their limbs during the course of evolution. Like other reptiles, most female lizards lay eggs, which they bury in the soil or hide under rocks until the young hatch.

Lizards can hear through their ear openings.

Green iguana

Long tail for balance

CRESTED WATER DRAGON

This lizard is found in Asia and lives mainly in trees that grow close to water. Like most lizards, the water dragon is able to swim. Unlike most other lizards, however, which move on all four legs, the crested water dragon runs on two legs if it is threatened, which gives it more speed on land.

Typical scaly skin like other reptiles, such as snakes and crocodiles

Outstretched claws give extra balance.

LIZARD TAILS

In the same way that a starfish regrows its arms, a lizard can regrow its tail. When a predator such as a bird or cat grabs a lizard by its tail, the lizard sheds the tail in order to escape. The vertebrae (backbones) along the tail have cracks in them, so the tail breaks off easily. The broken-off part of the tail often twitches for a few minutes, confusing the enemy while the lizard runs away. The tail grows back to its original length in about eight months.

Loose skin around neck looks like a huge collar.

The more the frilled lizard opens its mouth, the more the frill expands.

Tail waves around to frighten enemy.

Tree skink has lost the end of its tail.

Tail has regrown fully within a few months.

Tokay gecko

FRILLED LIZARD

The Australian frilled lizard has a flap of loose skin around its neck which folds flat along the body. The lizard raises the frill to make itself look bigger in order to scare away a predator. It also waves its tail and head around to alarm its enemy, then scuttles away.

TOKAY GECKO

The pads on the feet of the tokay gecko are covered with about one million microscopic hair-like structures which help the gecko grip on to surfaces. The rubber soles of plimsolls and walking boots look like the soles of the gecko's feet.

Five claws
on feet

Forked
tongue

TEGU LIZARD

The young tegu lizard shown left is found in tropical areas of South America. It feeds mostly on young birds and mammals, and also eats other lizards. Like most lizards, the tegu has a tough, scaly skin, a forked tongue, five claws on its feet, and movable eyelids.

Male anole lizard inflates its red throat sac.

ANOLE LIZARD

Anole lizards belong to the iguana family of lizards. There are many different kinds, found in tropical areas of Central and South America. Anole lizards are territorial (they guard their territory). The males inflate their red-coloured throat sacs, which they display to each other as a sign of aggression. Anole lizards are sometimes called American chameleons.

KOMODO DRAGON

The komodo dragon is the largest lizard – up to 3 m (10 ft) long. It scavenges on dead animals and also catches deer, pigs, and wild boars. Komodo dragons live on the island of Komodo and other islands east of Java.

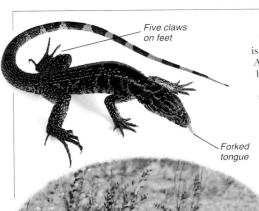

Komodo dragon lizards feasting on the carcass (dead body) of a deer

GILA MONSTER

Only two lizards have a poisonous bite – the Gila monster and the Mexican beaded lizard, both from southern North America. The Gila monster, shown here, is found in dry, scrubby areas. It hides in a burrow by day and emerges at night to eat small animals such as mice and the eggs of birds and other reptiles.

Gila monster feeding on newborn mice

THORNY DEVIL

The extraordinary looking thorny devil is also called the moloch. Spines protect its body from nose to tail. Thorny lizards live in dry parts of Australia, where they forage for ants. When the young molochs hatch from their eggs, they look like tiny, spiny versions of their parents.

GREEN GECKO

Many lizards are coloured to blend in with their surroundings. Tree-climbing lizards such as this green gecko are often bright green to match the leaves; desert-dwelling lizards are sand-coloured or brown. Many kinds of chameleons can change their colour according to their surroundings.

IGUANA

Like all lizards, iguanas depend on heat from the environment to keep their bodies warm and active. They spend much of the day basking in the sun, absorbing its warmth to prepare for activity. At night they become slow and sluggish as their body temperature falls. The Galapagos marine iguanas shown here dive to more than 11 m (35 ft) deep into the sea in search of seaweed.

After each dive, Galapagos marine iguanas sunbathe on the rocks to warm up again.

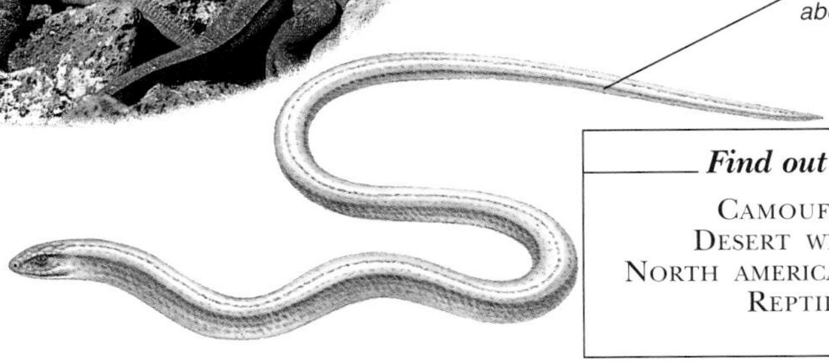

Slowworms grow to about 50 cm (20 in) in length.

SLOW-WORM

The slow-worm is not really a worm, but a lizard. It is not slow either; when disturbed, slowworms can wriggle away rapidly to safety. Slow-worms are found in fields and scrubland in Europe, northern Africa, and southwest Asia. They feed on slugs, spiders, and insects. Unlike most lizards, slowworms give birth to fully formed young.

Find out more

CAMOUFLAGE
DESERT WILDLIFE
NORTH AMERICAN WILDLIFE
REPTILES

LOUIS XIV

IN 1643 LOUIS XIV became king of France. He ruled for 72 years and made his country the most powerful in Europe at that time. While Louis was still young, his mother and his chief minister, Cardinal Mazarin, ruled on his behalf. During this time the nobility rose up against the throne and tax policies in a rebellion called the Fronde. However, when Louis was 23 he took complete charge of France and ruled as an absolute monarch, making all decisions himself. He moved his court to Versailles, just outside Paris, and appointed Jean Colbert, a French statesman, as his finance minister. Under Colbert's control trade and industry flourished. Louis XIV fought a series of wars and increased the territory of France. But the many wars cost France a lot of money, and the country was nearly bankrupt. Taxes were raised to pay off debts, causing much hardship among the poor.

VERSAILLES PALACE

The palace at Versailles was magnificent. Its many rooms included a hall of mirrors that was 73 m (240 ft) in length and lavishly decorated. Formal gardens with fountains and sculpted hedges surrounded the palace. Louis spent one tenth of all France's wealth on its upkeep. Even so, many parts of the palace were overcrowded, dark, and cold. Today Versailles palace is open to the public.

Detailed embroidery on chair typical of Louis XIV style furniture

The hall of mirrors at the palace of Versailles was a place for nobles to congregate.

FURNITURE
Louis XIV employed groups of expert craft workers to make furniture for his palace at Versailles. The style of the furniture, such as this walnut chair, was elaborate and ornate. It became known as the Louis XIV style.

SUN KING
Louis XIV surrounded himself with splendour. His court was a centre for the great writers, artists, and musicians of the time. He said of himself *"L'état c'est moi"* or "I am the state". Louis was given the nickname the Sun King after the Greek god Apollo, who was also a patron of the arts.

Find out more

FRANCE, HISTORY OF
FRENCH REVOLUTION

LUNGS AND BREATHING

WE NEED OXYGEN TO LIVE, and we get oxygen by breathing air. When we breathe in, air is sucked through the nose or mouth, down the windpipe, and into the lungs, two powerful organs in the chest. The lungs absorb as much oxygen from the air as possible. The oxygen travels in the blood from the lungs to every part of the body. Our bodies use oxygen to burn up the food we eat and convert it into energy. Then the harmful carbon dioxide is breathed out of the body by the lungs. The whole process is called respiration. The lungs, together with the airways, throat, and nasal passages, form the respiratory system. Each lung is surrounded by a thin covering or membrane called the pleura. The lungs themselves contain air tubes, blood vessels, and millions of tiny air sacs called alveoli. If you spread these air sacs out flat, they would cover the area of a tennis court.

HOW WE MAKE SOUNDS
We use the air flowing in and out of our lungs to make sounds. We speak, shout, laugh, and cry by making air flow over two small leathery flaps called the vocal cords. These are in the larynx (voice box), in the lower part of the throat.

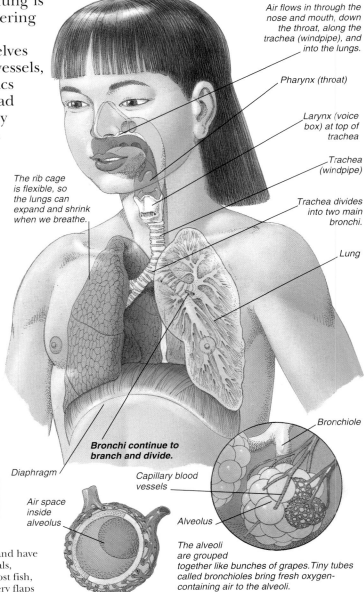

Air flows in through the nose and mouth, down the throat, along the trachea (windpipe), and into the lungs.

Pharynx (throat)

Larynx (voice box) at top of trachea

Trachea (windpipe)

Trachea divides into two main bronchi.

Lung

The rib cage is flexible, so the lungs can expand and shrink when we breathe.

Bronchiole

Bronchi continue to branch and divide.

Diaphragm

Capillary blood vessels

Alveolus

The alveoli are grouped together like bunches of grapes. Tiny tubes called bronchioles bring fresh oxygen-containing air to the alveoli.

BREATHING

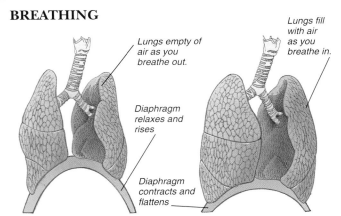

Lungs empty of air as you breathe out.

Lungs fill with air as you breathe in.

Diaphragm relaxes and rises

Diaphragm contracts and flattens

BREATHING OUT
When you breathe out, the diaphragm and chest muscles relax. The lungs are spongy and elastic, so they spring back to their smaller size after they have been stretched. This blows air back out of the lungs.

BREATHING IN
When you breathe in, the diaphragm contracts (becomes flatter) and pulls down the base of the lungs. Muscles between the ribs contract to swing the ribs up and out. These actions stretch and enlarge the lungs, so that air is sucked in.

LUNGFISH
Most animals that live on land have lungs. Many water animals, however, including most fish, breathe using feathery flaps called gills. Oxygen in the water passes through the thin gill coverings to the blood inside the fish's body. The lungfish shown here is an unusual animal because it has lungs and gills, so it can breathe in both ways and can survive out of water for a long time.

Air space inside alveolus

ALVEOLUS
Each alveolus is surrounded by a network of very fine blood vessels called capillaries. Oxygen passes from the air space inside the alveolus, through the lining, and into the blood. Carbon dioxide passes in the opposite way.

Find out more

BRAIN AND NERVES
HEART AND BLOOD
HUMAN BODY
MUSCLES AND MOVEMENT
OXYGEN
SKELETONS

MACHINES

INCLINED PLANE

Simple machines reduce the effort needed to move or lift an object, but the object has to travel a greater distance. The simplest machine is the ramp, or inclined plane. You need less force to push an object with a downwards load up an inclined plane than you need to lift it straight up. This is because the object moves a greater distance along the plane. The gentler the slope, the further you have to push, but the easier it is.

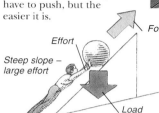

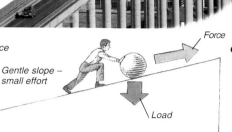

Effort

Force

Steep slope – large effort

Load

Gentle slope – small effort

Force

Load

WHAT DO A SAW and a computer have in common? Both are machines. One is simple and the other is very complex, but both are tools that do work for us. Machines perform tasks that we would find difficult or even impossible to do. You cannot cut through wood with your bare hands, for example, but it is easy with a saw. Likewise, a computer can do calculations rapidly that would take you an enormous amount of time. All machines need a source of energy. Mechanical machines, such as a corkscrew, use the energy of movement. A motor or a person's muscles drive the machine with a certain amount of force called the effort. The machine then applies this movement but produces a larger force called the load. For example, your fingers operate a can opener, but the blade of the can opener moves with much more force than that produced by your fingers. Many hand-powered machines help us perform tasks for which we do not have enough strength. They use devices known as simple machines. These include levers, gears, pulleys, and screws.

SCREW

A screw moves forward a shorter distance than it turns. It therefore moves forward with a much greater force than the effort needed to turn it. The screw bites into the wood with great force and is held strongly.

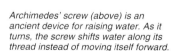

The screw makes use of the principle of the inclined plane.

Archimedes' screw (above) is an ancient device for raising water. As it turns, the screw shifts water along its thread instead of moving itself forward.

The thread of the screw is like a slope wrapped around a cylinder.

PLOUGH
The plough has a cutting blade that bites into the soil and a V-shaped blade that turns the soil over.

PERPETUAL MOTION

Many inventors have tried to build a machine that, once started, would never stop. It would run on its own without any source of energy. However, such a perpetual motion machine is impossible. This is because all machines lose some energy as they work. Without a constant source of energy, a machine always slows down and stops.

In this machine, the motion of the balls was supposed to keep the wheel turning.

WEDGE
The wedge is a form of inclined plane. Instead of moving a load along a slope, the wedge is a slope that pushes a load aside or upward as it moves forward. The wedge pushes with greater force than the effort needed to move the wedge. Sharp blades are thin wedges that make cutting an easy task.

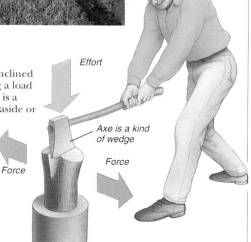

Effort

Axe is a kind of wedge

Force

Force

PULLEYS

Lifting a heavy load is easy with a pulley system. It contains a set of wheels fixed to a support. A rope goes around grooves in the wheels. Pulling the rope raises the lower wheel and the load. A pulley system allows you to lift a heavy load with little effort, but you must pull the rope a large distance to raise the load by a small amount.

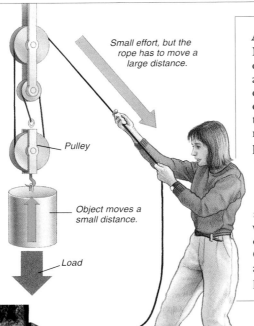

Small effort, but the rope has to move a large distance.

Pulley

Object moves a small distance.

Load

AUTOMATIC MACHINES

Many machines do not need to be operated by people. These are automatic machines. They contain mechanisms or computers to control themselves. These machines may simply perform a set task whenever it is required; automatic doors, for example, open as people arrive. Other machines are able to check their own work and change the way they operate to follow instructions. One example is an aircraft autopilot, which guides the plane through the skies.

Traffic lights are machines that control traffic automatically.

Fulcrum

GEARS

Gears are intermeshing toothed wheels. They can increase force or speed depending on the relative size of the wheels and their number of teeth. A gearwheel driven by a smaller wheel turns less quickly than the smaller wheel but with greater force. A wheel driven by a larger wheel turns faster but with less force.

Mechanical clocks and watches contain gears that turn the hands at different speeds.

LEVER

A long stick propped up on a small object (a fulcrum) helps you move a heavy load. The stick is a simple machine called a lever. Pushing down on the end furthest from the fulcrum raises the other end with greater force, helping you move the load. Other kinds of levers can increase either the force applied to, or the distance moved by, a load.

Effort

A pair of scissors consists of two levers hinged together.

Load

Fulcrum

Fulcrum

A wheelbarrow is a second-class lever. The load lies between the fulcrum and the effort.

Load

Effort

There are three types of lever. A crowbar is called a first-class lever. The fulcrum is between the load and the effort, which is the force that you apply.

WHEEL AND AXLE

Several machines use the principle of the wheel and axle. One example is the winch, in which a handle (the wheel) turns a shaft (the axle) that raises a load. The handle moves a greater distance than the load rises. The winch therefore lifts the load with a greater force than the effort needed to turn the handle.

Effort

Force

Load

STEERING WHEEL

The steering wheel on a car is an example of the wheel and axle. The shaft turns with greater force than the effort needed to turn the steering wheel.

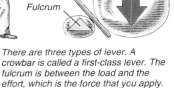

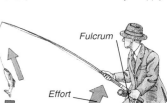

Fulcrum

Effort

Load

A fishing rod is a third-class lever. The load moves a greater distance than the effort, but with less force. The effort pushes between the load and the fulcrum.

Find out more

ENGINES
HOUSEHOLD APPLIANCES
INDUSTRIAL REVOLUTION
ROBOTS
TECHNOLOGY

MAGAZINES

WHATEVER YOUR INTEREST, you'll find a magazine that tells you more about it. Like newspapers, new issues of a magazine go on sale regularly – usually weekly or monthly. But magazines last longer than newspapers. Often two or three people read the magazine before discarding it. And some magazines, such as scientific journals, are more like reference books. Their buyers keep them to refer to months or even years later. The simplest magazines, such as neighbourhood newsletters, are sheets that have been roughly photocopied and stapled together. Other magazines cover topics with a wide appeal. They are printed in colour on glossy paper and have many pictures. The editor in chief decides what goes into the magazine. Other editors and journalists write the features and articles. The art director is responsible for the style and look of the magazine. Designers choose pictures and lay out the pages.

LIFE MAGAZINE
The first magazines began in Europe in the 17th century. But modern magazines started only when it was possible to print photographs on their pages. One of the greatest of picture magazines is *Life*, which first appeared in 1936. *Life* tells stories with a series of pictures and few words.

COMICS
Children and adults read comics. The word *comic* is short for *comic strip*, because the first comics were collections of comic strips from newspapers. They were originally called funnies. A new type of comic, containing adventure stories, first appeared in the 1930s and led to the many different comics of today.

© 1982 DC Comics Inc. Used with permission

Superman, one of the world's best-known comic-strip heroes, first appeared in Action Comics in 1938.

Pictures in geography magazines show remote corners of the world.

Popular science magazines explain new discoveries in simple terms.

Food magazines contain recipes and restaurant reviews.

Publishers may produce different editions of a fashion magazine for readers in each country.

Fan clubs produce magazines about their pop heroes.

MAGAZINES FOR EVERYONE
There are magazines for every reader's interest. There are fashion, beauty, and family magazines as well as magazines on every activity from sailing and fishing to computers and the arts. Magazines such as *Time* and *Newsweek* give the background to current events in more depth than newspapers or television news. Specialist magazines cover subjects such as science or hobbies. Fanzines are magazines about pop stars. Trade magazines are for businesses such as publishing, mining, or engineering.

NEWSSTANDS
At a newsstand you can choose from a huge range of national and foreign magazines.

JOURNALIST
Magazines are sometimes called journals, so the editors and writers who create them are called journalists. An editor decides what will appear in the magazine and chooses the writer. The writer carries out research or interviews and writes the article. Then the editor corrects errors and makes sure the article fits into the space on the page.

Find out more

ADVERTISING
CARTOONS
NEWSPAPERS

MAGIC

TWO HUNDRED YEARS AGO, a television set might have seemed like magic, because nobody would have been able to explain how it worked. Today we find a little magic in everything we cannot explain through science or logic. Magic means more than this, however. Magic also refers to special powers that very few people are supposed to possess. The tribal priest is an important figure in places where belief in magic is still quite strong, such as Haiti. People consult this "shaman", who possesses magic powers, when they want help with events in their lives. They believe that the shaman is in touch with the world of spirits and can explain signs or look into the future. Magic powers can be used for either good or evil purposes, and people sometimes wear charms or perform ritual actions in order to protect themselves against bad magic.

FAIRY FOLK
In European folklore, fairies were tiny people with magic powers. They visited homes of new babies to tell what the future held for them. Fairies could disappear when they chose, so they could live among people unseen.

SPEAKING WITH SPIRITS
Some cultures believed that animal horns had magic powers. This antelope horn from central Africa was used for communicating with a spirit.

LOOKING INTO THE FUTURE
Some people believe that the shapes reflected in mirrors, glass, or water can reveal the future. Crystal balls are part of a fortune teller's equipment.

SALEM WITCH TRIALS
In the 16th and 17th centuries innocent women often took the blame for bad crops and human misfortunes. People called the women witches and believed the devil had given them special powers. In 1692 fear became hysteria in Salem, Massachusetts, United States, when groups of women stood trial as witches and several were executed.

There are 78 tarot cards. They are used for fortune telling.

CONJURERS
Tricks and illusions are also called magic, and conjurers throughout history have fascinated people by doing what seems to be impossible. Some of the most bewildering tricks, such as sawing someone in half, are clever illusions. In this picture, the illusionist suspends his assistant in mid-air. He shows that there are no invisible wires by passing a hoop along her body.

WATER DIVINING
To find underground sources of water or minerals, dowsers or diviners use Y-shaped twigs of hazel or willow. The diviner holds one end in each hand and walks around until the rod twitches or points towards the ground, showing where to dig. No one has successfully explained what gives dowsers this magical power.

Find out more

MYTHS AND LEGENDS
RELIGIONS

MAGNETISM

ORIGIN OF MAGNETISM
Iron contains millions of tiny magnets called magnetic dipoles. Normally all the dipoles point in different directions so their magnetism cancels out. In a magnet, the dipoles point the same way so that their magnetism combines.

MAGNETIC FIELD
The area around a magnet in which its magnetic force works is called its magnetic field. For instance, a paper clip is pulled towards the magnet (right) when it is placed within the magnetic field of the magnet.

All magnets attract iron and steel objects but not plastic or wooden ones.

THE FORCE OF magnetism is invisible, yet you can see its power when a magnet drags a piece of metal towards it. A material that attracts certain metals such as iron is called a magnet. Materials that are attracted by a magnet are called magnetic. Every magnet has two poles – places at which magnetic objects cluster. The Earth itself is a huge magnet; its magnetic poles are close to the geographical North and South Poles. One pole of a magnet is attracted to the Earth's northern magnetic pole and is called the magnet's north pole; the other is attracted to the south and is called the magnet's south pole. Materials that retain their magnetism all the time are called permanent magnets. An electric current flowing in a coil of wire produces a magnet called an electromagnet that can be switched on and off. Electromagnets are used in electric motors, loudspeakers, and many other devices.

MAGNETIC POLES

The north pole of one magnet and the south pole of another magnet attract each other.

A magnetic pole, such as a south pole, repels (pushes away) another pole of the same kind.

LODESTONE
Magnetite is an iron ore that often possesses magnetism. It was once commonly called lodestone, which means "guiding stone", because early navigators used it as a compass.

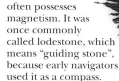

The magnetic north and south poles lie a small distance away from geographical north and south.

GEOMAGNETISM
The Earth produces a magnetic field which makes it seem as though it has a huge "bar" magnet inside it. Electric currents flowing within the Earth's liquid iron core cause the Earth's magnetism, which is called geomagnetism.

The geographical North and South Poles lie on the Earth's axis, which is the line around which the Earth spins.

The pattern of lines shows the Earth's magnetic field. The field is strongest where the lines are closest together.

ELECTROMAGNETS
An electromagnet is a coil of wire. An electric current within the coil creates a magnetic field. The field can be made stronger by winding the wire around a piece of iron. Turning off the current switches off the magnetic field. Some cranes use an electromagnet instead of a hook.

COMPASS
The needle inside a magnetic compass is a thin, light magnet, balanced so that it swings freely. The needle's north pole points towards the Earth's magnetic north pole, which is very close to geographical north. People use magnetic compasses to navigate at sea and on land.

Find out more
EARTH
ELECTRICITY
MAPS
NAVIGATION

MAMMALS

THE ANIMAL GROUP CALLED MAMMALS includes the heaviest, tallest, and fastest animals on land – the elephant, the giraffe, and the cheetah. Mice, whales, rhinoceroses, bats, and humans are also mammals. Like birds, mammals are warm-blooded, but three features set them apart from all other creatures. All mammals are covered in fur or hair, all feed their young on milk, and all have a unique type of jawbone joint. The jawbone joint helps us to identify the fossilized bones of prehistoric mammals that lived on Earth millions of years ago. Mammals are also members of the group known as vertebrates because they all have vertebrae (backbones). Today there are about 4,000 kinds of mammals, including carnivores (flesh eaters) such as tigers; herbivores (plant eaters) such as rabbits; and omnivores (flesh and plant eaters) such as bears. Cattle, sheep, goats, and most other farm animals are mammals, and many pets are mammals too, including cats, dogs, and guinea pigs. Mammals live nearly everywhere. They are found on land, in the sea, and in the sky, from the coldest Arctic to the most searing heat of the desert.

A mammal's body is covered in fur

MARSUPIAL YOUNG
Marsupials are very tiny when they are born. At birth, a kangaroo is less than 2.5 cm (1 in) long. It crawls through its mother's fur into a pocket-like pouch on the abdomen, where it attaches itself to her teat and suckles milk.

A kangaroo's large tail is so strong that it can act as a prop for the kangaroo to lean on.

Young male joey

PLACENTAL MAMMALS
Most mammals, including monkeys, cats, and dogs, are called placental mammals because the young develop inside the mother's womb, or uterus, and are fed by means of the placenta. The placenta is a specialized organ embedded in the wall of the womb. It carries nutrients and other essential materials from the mother's blood to the baby's blood. These nutrients help the young grow and develop. After the young are born, the placenta comes out of the uterus as afterbirth.

MARSUPIAL MAMMALS
Kangaroos, opossums, wallabies, koalas, wombats, and bandicoots are all known as marsupials, or pouched mammals. These animals carry their young in their pouches until the young are able to fend for themselves. Once it has left the pouch, the joey (young kangaroo) returns to the pouch to suckle milk. Marsupials are found in Australia and New Guinea, South America, and North America. A few marsupials, such as the shrew opossum of South America, do not have pouches.

MONOTREME MAMMALS
Three kinds of mammals lay eggs. They are called monotreme mammals, and include the platypus and the two types of echidna (spiny anteater). All are found in Australasia. After about 10 days, the young hatch out of the eggs, then feed on their mother's milk.

PRIMATES
Monkeys, apes, and humans belong to a group called primates. Primates are able to grasp with their hands. Most primates have thumbs and big toes, with flat fingernails rather than claws. Members of the primate group range in size from the mouse lemur, which weighs only 60 g (2 oz), to the gorilla, which weighs up to 275 kg (610 lb).

SPINY ANTEATER
The short-beaked spiny anteater, or echidna, lays a single egg in a temporary pouch on its abdomen. The young echidna hatches, then sucks milk from mammary glands on its mother's abdomen.

MAMMAL GROUPS

There are about 18 main groups of placental mammals. Rodents make up almost half of all mammals; bats account for a quarter. There are only two kinds of elephants, and the aardvark is in a group of its own.

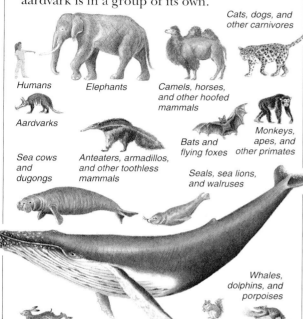

Humans

Elephants

Camels, horses, and other hoofed mammals

Cats, dogs, and other carnivores

Aardvarks

Bats and flying foxes

Monkeys, apes, and other primates

Sea cows and dugongs

Anteaters, armadillos, and other toothless mammals

Seals, sea lions, and walruses

Whales, dolphins, and porpoises

Hares, rabbits, and pikas

Hedgehogs, moles, and other insectivores

Squirrels, rats, mice, and other rodents

Tree shrews

Most puppies feed on their mother's milk for two or three months. A mother shrew suckles her young for four weeks; a mother whale feeds her youngster for six months or more.

MAMMAL MILK

Mammals are the only creatures that feed their young with milk. When the female is about to give birth, she starts to produce milk in mammary glands on the chest or abdomen. When the young are born, they suck the milk from the mother's teats. Mother's milk is an ideal food for the young – warm and nourishing, and full of special substances which protect the young from disease. As the babies grow larger and stronger, they take less milk and begin to eat solid foods. This process is called weaning.

GESTATION

Rhinoceros

The time between mating and birth, when the young develop in the mother's womb, is called the gestation or pregnancy period. In general, large mammals have longer pregnancies and fewer young than small mammals.

The gestation usually lasts for 15 months; one young is born.

Rabbit

Gestation usually lasts for 30 days; as many as eight young are born in a litter.

Dirty fur harbours pests and also lets heat escape, so many mammals spend time cleaning or grooming their fur.

HAIR AND FUR

Fur or hair protects the mammal's skin from injury and the sun's rays. It also keeps heat in and moisture out. The colours and patterns of the fur provide camouflage. Water-dwelling mammals such as beavers have special oily, waterproof fur. The porcupine's spines and the rhinoceros's horn are also made from strong hairs tightly packed together.

ARMADILLO

Some mammals, such as armadillos and pangolins, have reptile-like scales instead of fur. These scales, or scutes, are made of a type of horn and bone that grows from the skin. Hairs grow between the scutes and also cover the animal's soft-skinned underbelly.

BODY TEMPERATURE

Mammals and birds are called warm-blooded animals because they can maintain a high body temperature even in cold conditions. Mammals do, however, need plenty of food to provide the energy for warmth. The heat to warm a mammal is produced by chemical reactions in the body, particularly in the muscles.

Huskies are able to stay warm in deep snow because of their thick fur.

Find out more

ANIMAL SENSES
ANIMALS
AUSTRALIAN WILDLIFE
FARM ANIMALS
FLIGHT IN ANIMALS
HIBERNATION
PREHISTORIC LIFE

MAO ZEDONG

ONE MAN TRANSFORMED CHINA from a backward peasant society into one of the most powerful nations in the world. That man was Mao Zedong. Mao was born to a peasant family, and as a young man he travelled widely, observing the conditions of the poor. He became interested in communism as a way to improve people's lives and, in 1921, helped set up the Chinese Communist Party. There followed a long period of struggle between the Communists, led by Mao, and the Nationalist Party (who believed in strong national government), led by Chiang Kai-shek. The struggle ended in a civil war. In October 1949, the Communist Party was victorious and took power in China. Mao proclaimed China a People's Republic. Under his leadership, the Communists put everything in China under state control. Mao's face became a familiar sight. Young people in particular supported Mao, and many tried to introduce his ideas into their own countries.

1893 Born in Shaoshan, Hunan province.

1921 Founding member of Chinese Communist Party.

1928 Establishes Chinese Soviet (Communist) Republic in Kiangsi province.

1934-35 Leads Long March.

1945-49 Leads Communists in fight to overthrow Nationalist government.

1958 Great Leap Forward

1966-69 Cultural Revolution

1976 Dies.

The Long March

LONG MARCH

In October 1934, Mao led his Communist supporters from their stronghold in Kiangsi province to Shensi province in northwest China. Kiangsi was under attack from Chiang Kai-shek. More than 100,000 men and their families marched for more than a year, covering 9,700 km (6,000 miles). Only 30,000 marchers survived the ordeal.

Route of the Long March

Yenan

Kunming

Juichin

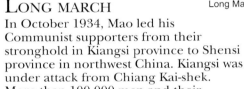

CULTURAL REVOLUTION

After the failure of the Great Leap Forward, Mao lost influence inside the Communist Party. In 1966, he launched the Cultural Revolution, a campaign to regain power and get rid of foreign influences. For three years China was in turmoil as every aspect of society was criticized by the Red Guards, followers of Mao. They armed themselves with the *Little Red Book*, which contained Mao's thoughts.

GREAT LEAP FORWARD

In 1958 Mao launched a plan to improve the Chinese economy. The Great Leap Forward, as it was called, set up huge agricultural communes and encouraged the growth of small, labour-intensive industries. However, a series of bad harvests and poor economic planning caused the policy to fail.

PERSONALITY CULT

Mao Zedong encouraged a cult of his personality to unite the country. His round face with the familiar mole on the chin adorned every public building in China. He was praised as the father and leader of his nation, and huge rallies were held at which he addressed his followers.

Find out more

CHINA, HISTORY OF
COMMUNISM

MAPS

EARLY TRAVELLERS FOUND their way by asking directions from strangers they met. Their guides created the first maps by scratching rough drawings of the route on the ground. Maps still show the positions of different places, but travellers today need many different maps. For local journeys, they use large-scale maps which cover a small area but show lots of detail. For longer journeys travellers may use a small-scale map that shows a larger area in less detail, or they may use an atlas (a book of maps) of whole countries. There are also special-purpose maps; political maps, for example, show legal boundaries. Utility companies need large-scale maps to show them where to dig for power lines and water pipes. Sailors use a special kind of map, called a chart, which shows coastlines and water depths.

MAPPA MUNDI
An English priest created the Mappa Mundi, or map of the world, between 1280 and 1300. It shows how Christians of that time viewed their world but was of little use to travellers. For religious reasons, Jerusalem is at the centre, and east is at the top of the map.

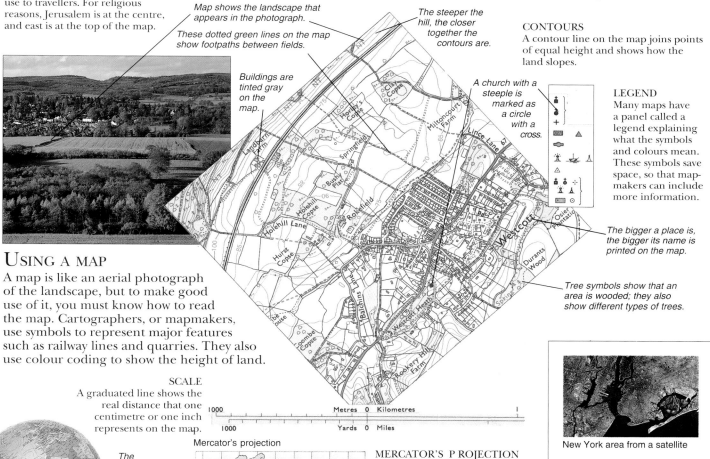

Map shows the landscape that appears in the photograph.

These dotted green lines on the map show footpaths between fields.

Buildings are tinted gray on the map.

The steeper the hill, the closer together the contours are.

A church with a steeple is marked as a circle with a cross.

CONTOURS
A contour line on the map joins points of equal height and shows how the land slopes.

LEGEND
Many maps have a panel called a legend explaining what the symbols and colours mean. These symbols save space, so that map-makers can include more information.

The bigger a place is, the bigger its name is printed on the map.

Tree symbols show that an area is wooded; they also show different types of trees.

USING A MAP
A map is like an aerial photograph of the landscape, but to make good use of it, you must know how to read the map. Cartographers, or mapmakers, use symbols to represent major features such as railway lines and quarries. They also use colour coding to show the height of land.

SCALE
A graduated line shows the real distance that one centimetre or one inch represents on the map.

1000		Metres 0 Kilometres	
1000		Yards 0 Miles	

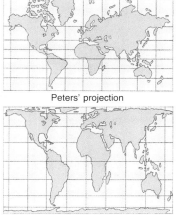

The equator is 0° latitude.

LONGITUDE AND LATITUDE
Lines of longitude, or meridians, run between the North and South Poles on a world map showing you how far east or west you are. Longitude is measured in degrees from the meridian that runs through Greenwich, England. Lines of latitude are parallel to the equator and show how many degrees north or south you are.

Mercator's projection

Peters' projection

MERCATOR'S PROJECTION
To represent the round Earth on a flat sheet of paper, mapmakers use a projection. Imagine a glass globe with a light at its centre. The light projects shadows of the continents onto a flat screen. All projections distort the world's shape, areas or distances. The most familiar world map is Gerhard Mercator's projection made in 1569. This shows the correct shapes of the continents but distorts their areas. Arno Peters' projection, published in 1973, distorts the shapes of countries but shows their true areas. It counteracts the focus on Europe encouraged by Mercator, whose map makes Europe look bigger than it really is.

New York area from a satellite

SATELLITE MAP
Satellites can now map every part of the world. Their sensors send video photographs of the Earth's surface to ground stations, which turn them into maps.

Find out more
EXPLORERS
MAGNETISM
NAVIGATION
SATELLITES

MARSH AND SWAMP WILDLIFE

THE FRESHWATER HABITATS of swamps and marshland are called wetlands. Marsh and swamp wildlife includes crocodiles, frogs, birds, fish, and countless plants. At different times of the year the water level of marshes and swamps rises and falls. In summer the land dries up, and in winter it floods. Wetlands are generally unsuitable for large mammals – except the African swamps where hippopotamuses live. Smaller mammals such as muskrats live in North American swamps, and the European marshes are home to many birds. The main plant life consists of reeds, rushes, saw grass, and cattail. Large trees are found only in the tropical mangroves, where the trees form dense thickets. Willows and other waterside trees grow in the higher, drier ground around the marsh.

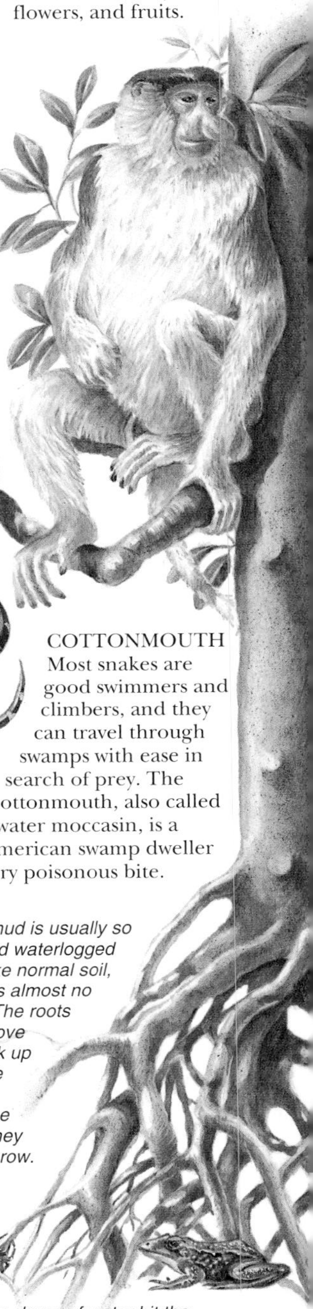

PROBOSCIS MONKEY
This large-nosed monkey lives among the mangrove trees of river and coastal swamps. The proboscis monkey is a good swimmer. Proboscis monkeys eat leaves, flowers, and fruits.

CONSERVATION
Farming and industry threaten many swamplands, but some animals, such as the marsh harriers shown here, are protected. They live in the Coto Doñana National Park in Spain – one of Europe's most important wetlands.

PELICAN
These fish-eating birds build their nests in remote marshland areas. Some species breed on the ground, some in trees. Others, such as spot-billed and Dalmatian pelicans, are very rare, because of destruction of their nesting sites.

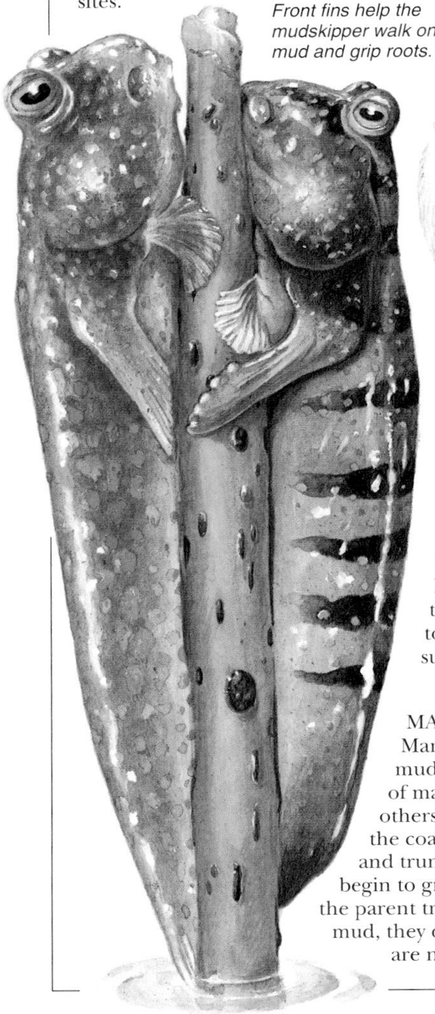

Front fins help the mudskipper walk on mud and grip roots.

COTTONMOUTH
Most snakes are good swimmers and climbers, and they can travel through swamps with ease in search of prey. The cottonmouth, also called the water moccasin, is a North American swamp dweller with a very poisonous bite.

Swamp mud is usually so dense and waterlogged that, unlike normal soil, it contains almost no oxygen. The roots of mangrove trees stick up above the mud, to absorb the oxygen they need to grow.

SWAMP RABBIT
This large rabbit from North America can swim well and dives to escape from predators, kicking with outspread toes. Swamp rabbits eat water plants, grasses, and other vegetation.

MUDSKIPPER
This unusual fish has a store of water in its large gill chambers which allows it to live out of water for long periods. From time to time it skitters over the mud to a pool to take in a new supply of water.

MARSHLAND
Marshes are nursery areas for many insects whose larvae live in water, such as dragonflies, damselflies, and mosquitoes. Insect larvae and worms form the main diet of many fish and water birds. Frogs and toads also breed in marshland, and their tadpoles are food for numerous larger creatures.

The drops of water hit the insect like tiny bullets.

MANGROVE SWAMPS
Mangroves are trees that grow in muddy tropical swamps. Some kinds of mangrove trees grow in fresh water; others tolerate salty water and grow on the coast or in river estuaries. Their roots and trunks trap mud, and their seeds begin to grow while they are still attached to the parent tree. When the seeds drop into the mud, they quickly establish roots so they are not washed away.

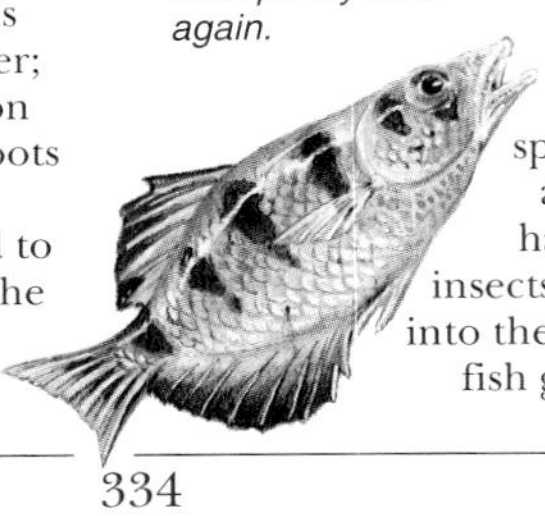

Archer fish adjusts its aim if it misses, and quickly fires again.

ARCHER FISH
The archer fish spits drops of water at insects on over-hanging twigs. The insects fall off the twigs, into the water, where the fish gulps them down.

> ### Find out more
> BIRDS
> FISH
> MONKEYS AND APES
> RABBITS AND HARES
> SEASHORE WILDLIFE
> SNAKES

MATHEMATICS

PROBABILITY THEORY
Probability theory is the analysis of chance. For instance, if you repeatedly roll two dice, you can use probability theory to work out how often you can expect a certain number to come up.

SENDING A SPACECRAFT to a distant planet is like trying to throw a stone at an invisible moving target. Space scientists do not use trial and error; instead they use the science of mathematics to direct the spacecraft precisely to its target. Mathematics is the study of number, shape, and quantity. There are several different branches of mathematics, and they are valuable both in science and in everyday life. For instance, arithmetic consists of addition, subtraction, multiplication, and division of numbers; it helps you work out change when you buy something. Geometry is the study of shape and angle; it is useful in carpentry, architecture, and many other fields. Algebra is a kind of mathematical language in which problems can be solved using symbols in place of varying or unknown numbers. Branches of mathematics that relate to practical problems are called applied mathematics. However, some mathematicians study pure mathematics – numerical problems which have no known practical use.

INFINITY
Pure mathematicians study the fundamental ideas of numbers and shapes. One such idea is the concept of infinity, which means "never-ending" .This pattern is called a fractal. It is produced by a computer according to a strict formula (rule). You can enlarge any part of the pattern again and again, but you will still get a pattern that is just as intricate. The pattern is infinitely complex.

NUMBERS
The number system that most people use today was probably invented by the Hindus about 1,400 years ago. During the 10th century, the Arabs brought the Hindu system to Europe; this is why modern numbers are often called Arabic numbers.

The Babylonians invented a number system based on 10 about 3,500 years ago.

I II III IV V VI VII VIII IX X

The Ancient Roman number system goes back to about 500 B.C. It is still sometimes used today.

About 200 B.C., the Hindus used a number system based on 10. About 1,400 years ago they modified it to include zero.

By the 15th century, Hindu-Arabic numbers had replaced Roman numerals as the most popular number system.

0 1 2 3 4 5 6 7 8 9 10

Today, most countries in the world use a modern version of the Hindu-Arabic number system.

ABACUS
The abacus, or counting frame, is an ancient calculating device which comes from China. It consists of rows of beads that represent units, tens, hundreds, and thousands. People in Asian countries still use the abacus as a rapid tool for adding, subtracting, multiplying, and dividing.

PROBLEM SOLVING
These cards have 50 choices of hairstyles, eyes, noses, and mouths. It would take many hours to find out the number of possible faces by moving the cards. However, with mathematics, the problem is easy to solve.

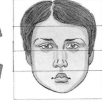

For each choice of hairstyle there are 50 choices of eyes, making 50 x 50 combinations. For each of these there are 50 different noses, and for each of those combinations there are 50 different mouths, making a total of 50 x 50 x 50 x 50 = 6,250,000 faces.

Arranging cards for hair, eyes, noses, and mouths produces different faces.

Find out more

ARABS, HISTORY OF
COMPUTERS
ROMAN EMPIRE
WEIGHTS AND MEASURES

MEDICINE

TWO HUNDRED AND FIFTY years ago, most people lived no longer than 35 years. Today, in the industrialized parts of the world, the average lifespan has increased to more than 70 years. Better food and hygiene have helped, but one of the main reasons for this change is the advances made in medicine. Medicine is the branch of science concerned with the prevention, diagnosis (identification), and treatment of disease and damage to the human body. Medical scientists are constantly searching for new ways of treating diseases. Treatments include drugs, radiation therapy, and surgery. Preventive measures, such as vaccinations against infections, are becoming an increasingly important part of modern medicine.

DIAGNOSIS
A doctor's first step with a sick patient is to diagnose the illness. This can be done in various ways – by asking the patient about his or her symptoms (physical feelings), by carrying out medical tests, and by making a physical examination of the ill person.

BRANCHES OF MEDICINE
Medicine is a huge subject and nobody can hope to know it all. Thus doctors, nurses, and other medical workers often become expert in a single area of medicine, a process which can take years and years of study.

Neurology is concerned with disorders of the brain and nerves.

Ophthalmology is the treatment of disorders of the eyes.

Orthopaedics is the care of the spine, bones, joints, and muscles.

Psychiatry is the treatment of mental illness.

Cutting into the body to cure illness is called surgery.

Dermatology is concerned with the skin and skin diseases.

Paediatrics is the medical care of children.

SURGERY
Medical treatments may include drugs or surgery. Surgery is the branch of medicine that involves operating, or cutting into the body, to treat the cause of an illness. Today surgery is so advanced that surgeons can repair or replace organs such as the kidneys and the heart.

RECOVERY
Recovery from an illness or an operation may take only a few hours or as long as several weeks. Much depends on the severity of the illness and the impact the treatment has on the body.

MEDICAL TECHNOLOGY
Modern medicine makes use of a wide range of technology. Latest developments include body scanners which use x-rays or ultrasound (very high-frequency sound waves) to produce an image of the interior of the human body. Such equipment has revolutionized medicine.

Doctors use brain scanners to check patients for tumours or damage to the brain.

Rue is an ancient cure for headaches.

Catmint is a cold cure that was first used by prehistoric people.

Mint is used for settling a stomach upset.

HOLISTIC MEDICINE
The word *holistic* means "of the whole". The principle of holistic medicine is to treat the whole person – body and mind – rather than just the affected part. Holistic therapies (treatments) include acupuncture (stimulating the nerves by inserting needles into the skin) and aromatherapy (treatment using oils containing fragrant plant extracts).

Find out more
DISEASE
DOCTORS
DRUGS
FIRST AID
HEALTH
HOSPITALS
MEDICINE, HISTORY OF

HISTORY OF
MEDICINE

SINCE THE EARLIEST TIMES, people have looked for ways of curing their illnesses. Early people believed that disease was a punishment from the gods. They also believed that priests and magicians could heal them. In Ancient Greece, people visited temples when they were ill and sacrificed animals to Asclepius, the Greek god of healing. They also drank and bathed in medicinal waters and followed strict diets in the hope of being cured. During the fifth century B.C. the Greek doctor Hippocrates declared that it was nature, not magic, that caused and cured disease. Hippocrates was famed as "the father of medicine", and he and his followers wrote many medical books. The spirit of enquiry, which was part of the Renaissance (a cultural movement in 14th-century Europe), encouraged experiments that put European medicine on a firm scientific basis. Many people began to question the traditional ideas about medicine. Scientists such as Vesalius (1514-1564) began to study the bodies of dead people to learn more about disease and how to treat it. Since then, there have been many more discoveries in medicine, and the battle against disease continues.

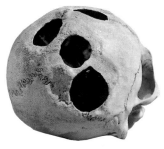

TREPANNING
Ten thousand years ago, the first doctors tried to cure an ill person by cutting a hole in his or her skull. They believed that the hole in the head released evil spirits that caused pain. This was known as trepanning.

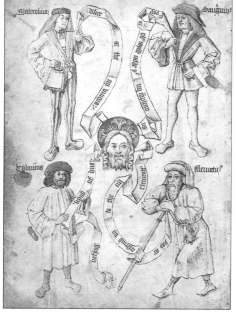

HUMOURS
The Greek physician Galen (A.D. c. 130 - 200) introduced the idea that the body contained four fluids called humours – blood, phlegm, yellow bile, and black bile. He believed that a person's mood depended on which of these four fluids ruled the body, and that if the fluids were not balanced, illness would result.

WILLIAM HARVEY
In 1628, an English doctor named William Harvey (1578-1657) discovered that blood constantly circulates around the body. He described how blood is pumped by the heart into the arteries and returns to the heart in the veins. He showed that valves in the veins stop the blood from flowing backwards. At first, Harvey was scorned for contradicting old ideas, but later he became physician to Charles I, king of England.

HERBALISM
For thousands of years, people have used herbs and plants in healing. Herbalists wrote lists of herbs and their uses. Monks were also famed for their knowledge of herbs. The first pharmacists, called apothecaries, used herbs to make potions, or medicines. But in Europe during the Renaissance many herbalists were accused of being witches. Many people are now turning to herbs as a natural way of treating illnesses.

Harvey drew detailed diagrams to explain his theory of circulation.

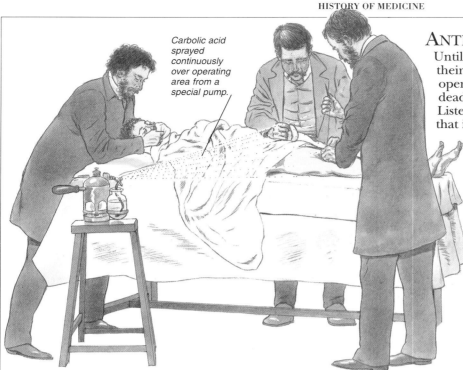

Carbolic acid sprayed continuously over operating area from a special pump.

ANTISEPTICS

Until the late 19th century, surgeons did not wash their hands or their medical instruments before operating on a patient. Many patients died from deadly infections following an operation. Joseph Lister (1827-1912), an English surgeon, guessed that infection with bacteria might be the cause of these deaths. In 1865, Lister developed an antiseptic spray called carbolic acid. This spray could destroy bacteria in the operating room, so there was a dramatic drop in the number of deaths following operations.

BLOOD-LETTING
Doctors once believed that too much blood in the body was the cause of disease. They removed the excess blood by blood-letting. Doctors either cut open a vein to let the blood out, or they applied bloodsucking creatures called leeches to the body. The exact spot for blood-letting depended on what was wrong with the patient.

FLORENCE NIGHTINGALE

Before the 19th century most nurses apart from midwives were untrained. Sick people were usually looked after at home by female relatives. Florence Nightingale (1820-1910) started a training school in London to improve the standards of nursing. She was already famous for her tireless work in nursing wounded soldiers during the Crimean War (1854). She walked 6 km (4 miles) past soldiers' beds every night and was known as "the lady with the lamp" because of the lamp that she carried.

HISTORY OF MEDICINE

c. 8000 B.C. Early healers practise trepanning.

400s B.C. Hippocrates, a Greek, begins scientific medicine.

1543 Vesalius publishes first scientific study of human body.

1615 Santorio, an Italian doctor, designs mouth thermometer.

1683 Anton van Leeuwenhoek, a Dutch scientist, discovers bacteria.

1796 Edward Jenner gives first smallpox vaccination.

1816 Rene Laennec, a French doctor, invents stethoscope.

1842 American surgeon, Horace Long, operates using general anaesthetic.

1895 Wilhelm Roentgen, a German physicist, discovers x-rays, which enable doctors to see inside the human body.

1900s Polish-born Marie Curie and her husband, Pierre Curie of France, discover the chemical element radium to treat cancer.

1900s Scottish bacteriologist, Alexander Fleming, discovers penicillin.

MEDICAL PIONEERS

Through the centuries many people have shaped modern medicine. The Flemish doctor Vesalius produced accurate drawings of the human body; Dutchman Anton van Leeuwenhoek (1632-1723) first discovered microbes, now called bacteria; and the English doctor Edward Jenner (1749-1823) discovered vaccinations – a way of preventing certain diseases by injection.

LOUIS PASTEUR
Frenchman Louis Pasteur (1822-1895) showed that bacteria caused disease. He invented pasteurization – the heating of milk and beer to destroy harmful bacteria.

SIGMUND FREUD
The Austrian doctor Sigmund Freud (1856-1939; below) was interested in finding out how the mind works. He treated patients with mental disorders by listening to them talk about their dreams and thoughts. This treatment was called psychoanalysis.

___ ***Find out more*** ___

DRUGS
EGYPT, ANCIENT
GREECE, ANCIENT
MEDICINE

METALS

IMAGINE A WORLD without metals. There would be no cars or aeroplanes, and skyscrapers would fall down without the metal frames that support them. Metals have countless uses because they possess a unique combination of qualities. They are very strong and easy to shape, so they can be used to make all kinds of objects from ships to bottle tops. Almost all metals conduct electricity. Some are ideal for wires and electrical equipment. Metals also carry heat, so they make good cooking pots. These qualities can be improved by mixing metals with others to make alloys. Most metal objects are made of alloys rather than pure metals.

There are more than 80 kinds of pure metals, though some are very rare. Aluminium and iron are the most common metals. A few metals, such as gold, occur in the ground as pure metals; the rest are found as ores in rock. Metals can also be obtained by recycling old cars and tins. This reduces waste and costs less than processing metal ores.

Gold watch

Mercury thermometer

Copper wire

Silver-plated frame

PURE METALS

The rarity and lustre of gold and silver have been prized for centuries. Other pure metals have special uses. Electrical wires are made of copper, which conducts electricity well. Mercury, a liquefied metal, is used in thermometers.

Aeroplane fuselage made of aluminium alloys

ALUMINIUM

The most common metal in the Earth's crust is aluminium. The metal comes from an ore called bauxite, which contains alumina, a compound of aluminium and oxygen. Aluminium is light, conducts electricity and heat, and resists corrosion. These qualities mean the metal and its alloys can be used in many things, including aircraft and bicycles, window frames, paints, saucepans, and electricity supply cables.

A lump of bauxite

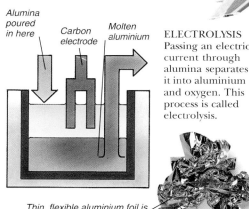

Alumina poured in here

Carbon electrode

Molten aluminium

ELECTROLYSIS Passing an electric current through alumina separates it into aluminium and oxygen. This process is called electrolysis.

Thin, flexible aluminium foil is useful for cooking and storing food because it is nonreactive and can stand high temperatures.

ALLOYS

Most metal objects are made of steel or other alloys. This is because alloys are often stronger or easier to process than pure metals. Copper and tin are weak and pliable, but when mixed together they make a strong alloy called bronze. Brass is a tough alloy of copper and zinc that resists corrosion. Alloys of aluminium are light and strong and are used to make aircraft.

METAL FATIGUE
Metals sometimes fail even though they may be very tough and strong. Corrosion weakens some metals, as in the case of rusty steel. Repeated bending can cause metal parts to break, an effect called metal fatigue.

Keys may break after considerable use.

METALWORKING

There are many ways of shaping metal. Casting is one method of making objects such as metal statues. Hot, molten metal is poured into a mould where it sets and hardens into the required shape. Metal can also be pressed, hammered, or cut into shape.

WELDING
Metal parts can be joined by welding. Welders apply heat, from a gas flame or an electric spark, to the edges of two pieces of metal. The heat causes the edges to melt so that they can be joined together.

Find out more
BRONZE AGE
IRON AGE
IRON AND STEEL
ROCKS AND MINERALS
SCULPTURE

MEXICO

THE WEALTH OF MEXICO has traditionally come from the land. Precious metals lie buried in the mountains and rich crops grow in the valleys. Oil flows from wells on the coast. The Mexican people began to exploit these advantages centuries ago. Farming supported most of the people, and from the country's mines came silver to make beautiful jewellery. The mineral wealth of the country attracted invading European soldiers in the 16th century, and Spain ruled Mexico for three centuries. A revolt against Spanish rule gave the Mexican people independence in 1821. The discovery of oil early this century brought new wealth to Mexico. The government invested this in new factories, and in social services to relieve hunger and improve health and education. In 1994, the North American Free Trade Agreement (NAFTA) reduced trade barriers between Mexico, Canada, and the United States, promising long-term economic benefits. However, the border between Mexico and the U.S. has been strengthened as a result of U.S. concern over the estimated 850,000 illegal crossings each year.

Mexico is part of the continent of North America and lies between the United States to its north and Central America to its south.

José Guadalupe Posada (1852-1913) drew humorous illustrations, many of which supported the Mexican revolution.

POLITICS AND REVOLUTION
Mexico was a Spanish colony from 1521 to 1821, when it became an independent republic. After a long period of political unrest, there was a revolution in 1910, in which half a million people died. Since 1929, the Institutional Revolutionary party has governed Mexico. Under its strong rule, the country has benefitted from radical social reforms and political stability.

MEXICO CITY
More than 13 million people live in and around Mexico City, the capital of Mexico, making it the most populated city in the world. The city lies 1.6 km (1 mile) above sea level in a natural basin surrounded by mountains. These mountains trap the pollution from the city's industries. As a result, Mexico City is one of the world's most unhealthy cities, with an inadequate water supply, a lack of housing, and the constant threat of earthquakes adding to its many problems.

FARM PRODUCE

Sweet potatoes

Cinnamon sticks

Mangoes

Chillies

Corn

Bananas

Beans

More than half the population of Mexico lives and works on the land, growing staple or food crops. Increasingly, however, farmers are growing coffee, cotton, sugar, and tomatoes for export. These cash crops take vital land away from the crops that the Mexican people themselves need for food. Most of the farmers are members of co-operatives, pooling their limited resources to help one another.

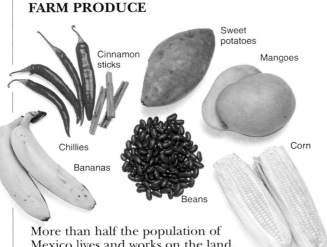

Mexican artisans are skilled at making fine jewellery from the many gemstones found in their country.

MINERAL WEALTH
Copper, silver, zinc, mercury, and other valuable metals are among the many minerals found in Mexico. Oil is the most important resource. In 1974 vast new reserves were discovered in the south of the country.

Find out more

CENTRAL AMERICA
CONQUISTADORS

MEXICO

STATISTICS
Area: 1,972,544 sq km (761,600 sq miles)
Population: 90,000,000
Capital: Mexico City
Languages: Spanish, Indian languages
Religion: Roman Catholic
Currency: Mexican peso
Main exports: Oil, cotton, machinery, coffee
Main imports: Machinery, vehicles, chemicals

MEXICAN FABRICS
Mexican people have been expert weavers since ancient times. They are skilled at producing brightly coloured fabrics, with bold, geometric designs, like the striped skirt worn by the girl on the right. Today most Mexican fabrics are mass-produced in large factories, but a few craftworkers still produce textiles in the traditional way, using hand looms.

Lower California is also called Baja California. The peninsula is in Mexico, and is not part of the US state with which it shares a name.

The tallest peak of Ixtacihuatl rises to 5,340 m (17,520 ft)

SIERRA MADRE
The main mountain system of Mexico, the Sierra Madre, runs 2,400 km (1,500 miles) southeast from the border with the United States. There are three ranges, in the east, south, and west, and they enclose Mexico's central plateau. Mexico's third highest mountain, Ixtacihuatl (above), is in the Sierra Madre del Sur, the southern range. The mountain has three separate summits, and its name means "White Woman" in the Aztec language, because the peaks resemble a woman wearing a hood.

GUANAJUATO
Spanish prospectors searching for gold founded Guanajuato (left) in 1554. The town is the capital of Guanajuato state in the mountains of central Mexico and rises more than 2,050 m (6,726 ft) above sea level. It is built in a ravine and has steep, winding streets.

MICE
RATS, AND SQUIRRELS

THE LITTLE HOUSE MOUSE is the second most numerous mammal on Earth after humans. It has beady black eyes, a long thin tail, and large front teeth, and belongs to the mammal group called rodents. This group includes rats and squirrels. All rodents have chisel-like incisor teeth for nibbling nuts and berries. The teeth wear down as the animal gnaws, but continue to grow throughout life. There are more than 1,000 kinds of rats and mice, found in every kind of habitat. Mice have small bodies, almost hairless tails, pointed noses, and sensitive whiskers; rats resemble mice but are larger. The most common rats are brown and black rats, which live in large groups. Rats are well known as carriers of the bubonic plague (Black Death). They also damage buildings and electrical wires with their gnawing and tunnelling. Most squirrels are similar to rats and mice in shape, but have bushy tails. Tree squirrels such as red, grey, and flying squirrels live in woodland areas, often high up in trees. Ground squirrels such as chipmunks have shorter tails and never climb trees.

Strong chewing muscles and cheek pouches for carrying food

Big ears and good hearing

Keen sense of smell

House mice and brown rats are often a nuisance to humans, eating stored grain and spoiling crops.

Rodent skull

Molars (cheek teeth) for chewing

Chisel-like front incisors for gnawing

HARVEST MOUSE

A typical mouse has round black eyes, large ears, and sharp claws. The harvest mouse is one of the smallest mice. Its body is only 6.5 cm (2.5 in) long and weighs 10 g (one third of an ounce). The harvest mouse feeds on corn and wheat stalks. Using grass stems, it weaves a breeding nest the size of a tennis ball among the corn. Harvest mice also live and nest in the long grass of bushes, shrubs, and woodland clearings.

Large eyes stick out of head for all-round vision.

BROWN RAT

The brown rat, also called the common rat or Norway rat, is fast and agile. It swims well, eats almost anything, and can gnaw its way through wood, stonework, and metal plates in order to get at food. It has spread to all parts of the globe, even surviving in sewers. A brown rat grows up to 50 cm (20 in) long from the tip of its nose to the tip of its tail.

LEMMING
These small rodents are related to mice but have a blunt snout, squat body, short tail, and very thick fur. Lemmings live in the most northern parts of the world. They can survive the coldest winters by burrowing under the snow and eating mosses, roots, stems, and bulbs. Contrary to popular belief, lemmings do not deliberately hurl themselves off cliffs to drown in the sea. When they migrate in great numbers to find more food, however, some die of starvation or are drowned as they try to cross deep rivers.

Tail is used as a counterbalance.

SQUIRREL

With its sharp claws for clinging to the bark and its long, fluffy tail to help with balance, the squirrel is well adapted for life in the trees. Squirrels are great acrobats, able to leap through the treetops with ease. The American grey squirrel was introduced to Europe two centuries ago and is now widespread in forests and parks. The European red squirrel, however, has become rarer in some areas, particularly in Britain. Squirrels rest and sleep in a drey – a ball-shaped nest of twigs and leaves. In the breeding season the female makes an extra-strong drey where she raises two or three young.

Red squirrel

Squirrel sleeps in the drey during the coldest weather but may come out on warmer days to look for food.

BREEDING

Mice and other small rodents have to breed at a fast rate in order to replace those killed by predators and bad weather. In good conditions, when few die, their numbers soar. One female house mouse can give birth to more than 50 young in one year. After about two weeks the young are covered in fur, they can see and hear, and they begin to explore away from the nest. Within three weeks the young have finished feeding on their mother's milk and are ready to leave the nest. After only six weeks her first litter of mice also starts to breed.

Newborn mice are bald, blind, and deaf; they stay warm and hidden in the nest.

GERBIL

Many rodents line their nests with shredded plant material such as stalks, stems, and bark. The Mongolian gerbil shown here is from the dry areas of central Asia. Gerbils are popular pets.

CHIPMUNK

The chipmunk belongs to the squirrel family and is sometimes known as the ground squirrel. Chipmunks hold pieces of food in their front paws and nibble skilfully, using their incisors as levers to crack a nut or seed at its weakest point. Chipmunks are bold and curious, and they are often seen looking for titbits in parks and picnic areas of North America. Whatever a chipmunk cannot eat, it carries back to its nest in its bulging cheek pouches.

Like all rodents, voles groom their fur and spread special body oils through it to keep it untangled, free of pests, and water-repellent. If the fur became soggy, the animal would soon die of cold.

VOLE

The vole is a close relative of the lemming and has a similar blunt-nosed, stocky shape. There are almost 100 different kinds of voles living in all sorts of habitats from the snowy Arctic to subtropical forests. The muskrat of North America is one of the largest voles. Another, the water vole, is often mistaken for a brown rat when it is swimming.

Find out more

ANIMALS
BLACK DEATH
MAMMALS
NESTS AND BURROWS

MICROSCOPES

WITHIN ALL OBJECTS THERE is a hidden world, much too tiny for us to see. With the invention of the microscope in the 16th century, scientists were able to peer into this world and unravel some of the great mysteries of science. They discovered that animals and plants are made of millions of tiny cells, and later were able to identify the minute organisms called bacteria that cause disease. Early microscopes consisted of a single magnifying lens; today's microscopes have several lenses and can be used to see very tiny objects. Electron microscopes are even more powerful. Instead of light they use a beam of electrons – tiny particles which are normally part of atoms – to magnify objects many millions of times. Scientists use electron microscopes to study the smallest of living cells and to delve into the structure of materials such as plastics and metals.

Observer looks through eyepiece.

Objective lenses of different power can be swung into position when needed.

The objective lens produces an image which the eyepiece magnifies (makes larger).

The object being studied rests on a glass slide.

Condenser lenses focus a beam of light onto the object.

A strong beam of light strikes a mirror under the microscope. The beam shines onto the object from below.

OPTICAL MICROSCOPE

The optical, or light, microscope has two main lenses: the objective and the eyepiece. High-quality microscopes contain several additional lenses which help to give a clear, bright image. Different objectives can be fitted which give a range of magnification from about 10 times to 1,500 times normal size.

USING OPTICAL MICROSCOPES
Optical microscopes can reveal living cells such as these cells which come from a human cheek. They are magnified more than 200 times.

ELECTRON MICROSCOPES
Objects must be cut into thin slices in order to see them with a microscope. However, a scanning electron microscope can magnify a whole object such as this ant, which is about 15 times normal size.

With a scanning electron microscope the image appears on a monitor screen.

INVENTING THE MICROSCOPE

EN LAN 2000

Although the Romans used magnifying lenses about 2,000 years ago, the first true microscope appeared around 1590, built by Dutch spectacles makers Hans and Zacharias Janssen. In 1663, English scientist Robert Hooke studied insects and plants with a microscope. He found that cork was made up of tiny cells, a discovery of great scientific importance. Microscopes aroused great interest in microscopic life, as this old etching shows.

IMAGING ATOMS
Special electron microscopes can show individual atoms, which are so small that a line of 0.5 million atoms would only span the width of a human hair. This piece of silicon is magnified 45 million times, revealing its atoms.

Find out more
ATOMS AND MOLECULES
LIGHT
MICROSCOPIC LIFE

MICROSCOPIC LIFE

Dust mite

ALL AROUND US THERE are living things that we cannot see because they are too small. They float in the air. They swim in puddles and oceans, and they coat rocks, soil, plants, and animals. Microscopic life includes bacteria and viruses; single-celled animals, called protozoa; and single-celled plants, called algae. It also includes the microscopic stages in the lives of larger plants and animals, such as the tiny pollen grains of flowers and the spores of mushrooms. All, from bacteria to algae, are so small that we can see them only through a microscope. Viruses, which are the smallest and simplest of all living things, must be magnified one million times before we can see them. Microscopic life has a crucial role to play. Plankton consists of millions of algae and protozoa and is an important food for water creatures. Bacteria in soil help to recycle nutrients. Some microscopic life, such as viruses, can cause disease.

DUST MITE
This microscopic animal can be found in everyone's home. It lives among dust, fluff, cat fur, and bits of dirt. Dust mites eat the dead skin you shed every day.

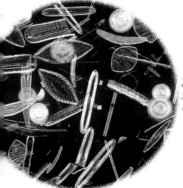

DIATOM
Microscopic plants called diatoms live in lakes, rivers, and oceans. There are thousands of different kinds of diatoms, providing food for many insects and water creatures. Diatoms live and grow by using sunlight and the nutrients in the water. Around their bodies are strong shell-like walls made of silica – the same material found in sand grains.

POLLEN
Microscopic grains of pollen grow on the male part of a plant, called the stamen. Each kind of plant has a different type of pollen grain with its own pattern and shape.

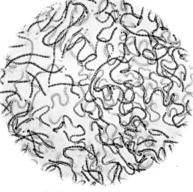

ALGAE
The slimy scum that you see on the surface of a stagnant pond is blue-green algae. These algae are not true plants. They are more closely related to bacteria. Blue-green algae were among the first forms of life to appear on Earth more than 2,000 million years ago.

AMOEBA
The amoeba is a single-celled animal called a protozoan. It lives in ponds and puddles. We need to magnify an amoeba at least one thousand times before we can see it. The amoeba moves by stretching out a part of its body known as a pseudopod, or "false foot". The rest of the body then flows into the pseudopod. Amoebas feed by engulfing prey such as bacteria with their pseudopods; then the whole body flows over the prey.

Amoeba divides in half, forming two daughter cells.

Food is stored in a small bag called the food vacuole.

Pseudopod (false foot)

Nucleus – control centre of amoeba

Cell membrane, the skin around the cell

HOW AN AMOEBA REPRODUCES
To reproduce, the amoeba divides into two. This is called fission. First the nucleus splits in two, then the rest of the body divides in half to form two separate amoebas. These are called daughter cells.

Passionflower pollen grain

Hollyhock pollen grain

Find out more

DISEASE
HUMAN BODY
MICROSCOPES
OCEAN WILDLIFE

MIDDLE AGES

LORDS AND LADIES feasting in castle banquet halls, peasants working on the land, knights in armour – all these are associated with a period in history known as the Middle Ages, or the medieval period. The Middle Ages was a time of change in western Europe between the fifth and 15th centuries. During the fifth century the Roman Empire fell, to be replaced by invading German tribes. Western Europe then broke up into many kingdoms. Trade collapsed, and people had to make their living from the land. Gradually powerful landowners or lords emerged and the feudal system developed. The early Middle Ages are sometimes called the Dark Ages because the learning of Ancient Greece and Rome almost disappeared. But the Christian Church gave leadership to the people. Trade gradually improved. By about the 13th century the Middle Ages had reached their height. Feudalism governed society, and monasteries (where monks lived) were the centres of learning. The Middle Ages ended in the 15th century when the Renaissance swept through Europe.

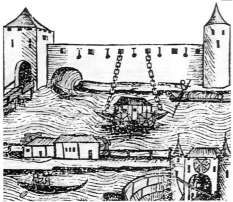

FAIRS
Great fairs were held every year in towns such as Winchester, England, which were on important trade routes. Merchants travelled from all over Europe to sell their goods at these fairs.

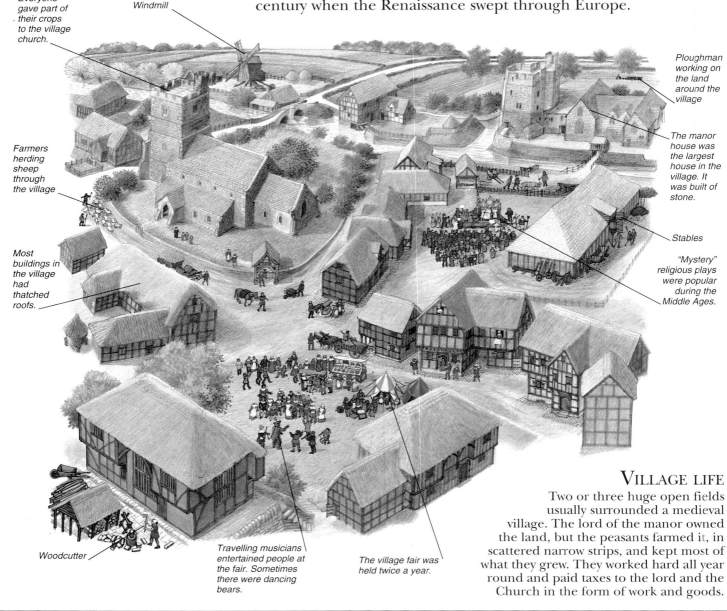

Everyone gave part of their crops to the village church.

Windmill

Ploughman working on the land around the village

Farmers herding sheep through the village

The manor house was the largest house in the village. It was built of stone.

Most buildings in the village had thatched roofs.

Stables

"Mystery" religious plays were popular during the Middle Ages.

Woodcutter

Travelling musicians entertained people at the fair. Sometimes there were dancing bears.

The village fair was held twice a year.

VILLAGE LIFE

Two or three huge open fields usually surrounded a medieval village. The lord of the manor owned the land, but the peasants farmed it, in scattered narrow strips, and kept most of what they grew. They worked hard all year round and paid taxes to the lord and the Church in the form of work and goods.

Shoemakers

People bought fabric to make their own clothing.

The poultry trader sold geese.

TOWN SCENE

Trade increased in the later Middle Ages making merchants wealthy and powerful. Towns became important trading centres with a new class of craftspeople. The craftspeople created organizations called guilds to control the prices and quality of their goods.

FEUDALISM

Kings gave their vassals – powerful nobles – tracts of land called fiefs. In return for this land the vassals fought for the king when required. The vassals divided their land into manors (estates), which they gave to lesser nobles and knights. In return, the knights and lesser nobles worked for the lord of the manor, and had to fight for him when called on.

14th-century manuscript shows feudal structure, with the king at the top.

Hunting (above) was a popular sport for upper-class medieval women.

A French medieval woman, Christine de Pisan (left), earned her living as a writer.

WOMEN

Peasant women worked very hard all their lives. They brought up their children, spun wool and wove clothing, and helped with all the farmwork. Upper class women also led busy lives. They often ran the family estates while their husbands were away travelling around their lands, fighting against neighbouring lords, or on a Crusade to the Holy Land. Women also nursed the sick and provided education for children in their charge.

MIDDLE AGES

A.D. 400 Roman empire begins to decline.

450 German tribes – Angles, Jutes, and Saxons – settle in Britain.

480s Franks set up kingdom in Gaul (now France).

800 Charlemagne, king of the Franks, unites western Europe.

900-1000s Europe is divided into feudal estates; there is widespread poverty and disease in the region.

1066 Normans conquer England.

1000s-1200s High Middle Ages: trade improves, population grows, towns develop, and learning flourishes.

c. 1100 First universities are founded.

1215 Magna Carta: English barons win power and rights from King John.

1300-1500 Late Middle Ages.

c. 1320 Renaissance, a rebirth of arts and learning, begins in Italy.

1337 Hundred Years' War begins between England and France.

1348 Black Death, a killing plague, reaches Europe. Eventually it wipes out one third of the population of Europe.

1378-1417 Great Schism: Catholic Europe is divided in support of two different popes, Urban VI and Clement VII.

1454 Johannes Gutenberg, a German, develops movable type. Printing begins in Europe.

Find out more
BLACK DEATH
CHURCHES AND CATHEDRALS
KNIGHTS AND HERALDRY
MONASTERIES
RENAISSANCE
ROMAN EMPIRE

MIDDLE EAST

LESS THAN 100 YEARS AGO, many of the inhabitants of the Middle East were Bedouins – desert-dwelling nomads who lived in tents and led their animals in search of food. The rest of the population lived in small towns and villages and made a living as farmers or craftsworkers. Almost everyone was poor and uneducated. Today, the lives of their children and grandchildren have been transformed by the discovery of oil. Many people have grown rich from the new industries and services related to oil production and refining. In some countries, notably Kuwait and Bahrain, there is free schooling and medical care for everyone.

Oil transformed the international importance of the Middle East as well. The region had little influence in world affairs. Now it controls one quarter of the world's oil production, and decisions made in the Middle East affect the economies of Europe, North America, and the Far East. But despite this massive change, traditional customs have not been completely abandoned, and the religion of Islam continues to dominate daily life throughout the Middle East, as it has done for more than 1,300 years.

The Middle East consists of 15 independent countries. They sit at the crossroads of three great continents – to the northwest lies Europe, to the southwest Africa, to the north and east are the Caucasus and Central Asian republics, all part of Asia.

MODERNIZATION
The discovery of oil brought great wealth to the Middle East very quickly. But governments in the region recognize that the oil will eventually run out. So they have spent some of the money they earned from selling oil in encouraging and modernizing local industry and business. Many Middle East countries have also invested in property and businesses in other nations throughout the world.

The areas of desert bordering the great waterways of the Middle East are swamps and marshlands. In these regions, small boats replace the camel as the most common means of transport.

At a banking school in the Middle East, students learn the skills that will help them modernize business in their country.

LANDSCAPE AND CLIMATE
Most of the Middle East consists of hot, dry, rocky deserts. A crescent of fertile land stretches west from the Tigris and Euphrates rivers through northern Iraq and Syria and then south into Lebanon and Israel. Turkey and Iran are mountainous, as are the southern parts of the Arabian peninsula. In the southeast of Saudi Arabia lies the Rub' al Khali, a vast, uninhabited sandy desert known as the Empty Quarter.

Camels are well adapted to the harsh conditions of the Middle East, and are still a popular form of transport.

OIL

Deposits of oil and natural gas were first discovered in the Gulf in the early years of this century. Today, more than half the world's oil reserves are located in the gulf. The oil industry has made several of the countries very rich, particularly Saudi Arabia, the United Arab Emirates, Bahrain, and Kuwait.

Desert oil rigs flare (burn off) natural gas that is pumped out of the ground with the oil.

UNITED ARAB EMIRATES

Like many Middle East nations, the United Arab Emirates has no democratic government. Instead, the country is ruled by a group of wealthy emirs (kings) who have absolute power over their people. Each emir controls his individual emirate, or kingdom, but they meet in the Federal Supreme Council of Rulers to make decisions that affect the whole country. Today, oil provides most of the country's wealth, but shipping has traditionally been important, and there are major ports at Abu Dhabi, Dubai, and Sharjah.

The port at Sharjah is built to accommodate the most modern container ships.

MIDDLE EAST WARS

Muslim guerrillas fight in the streets of Lebanon.

Bitter wars have caused much suffering and death in the Middle East. Israel and her Arab neighbours have fought four wars over the last 50 years. Throughout the 1980s Iran and Iraq were constantly at war, and Lebanon was devasted by a civil war that threatened to pull the country apart. In 1990 Iraq invaded Kuwait, drawing foreign troops to the area. In January 1991, hostilities broke out.

The Kurdish people of northern Iraq and eastern Turkey have been fighting for independence since 1918. Many have been made homeless by the battles.

Palm trees grow right up through the canopies that shade Bahrain streets.

SUEZ CANAL

More than 160 km (100 miles) in length, the Suez Canal links the Mediterranean Sea and the Red Sea. The canal took ten years to build, and when completed in 1869, it cut more than 11,000 km (7,000 miles) from the distance that sailing ships travelled to reach the Far East. Today, nearly 50 ships pass through the canal each day. The Suez Canal is an important trade route and has often been at the centre of conflict in the Middle East. The waterway has been closed by war and political disagreements several times, most recently by the Arab-Israeli Six Day War of 1967.

BAHRAIN

The island of Bahrain is little more than 50 km (30 m) long. Oil wells and refineries on the tiny island provide employment for many people, but tourism is important, too; in 1986 a causeway was opened, linking Bahrain to Saudi Arabia. Since then, many Saudis have visited Bahrain to enjoy themselves, because the island is much more free-and-easy than Saudi Arabia, which has strict Islamic laws.

Find out more
ARABS
ARABS, HISTORY OF
ISLAM
ISRAEL
JEWS, HISTORY OF THE

MIDDLE EAST

STATISTICS
Area: 6,192,321 sq km (2,390,867 sq miles)
Population: 205,600,000
Number of independent countries: 15
Languages: Arabic, Greek, Turkish, Hebrew, French, English
Main occupations: Agriculture, service industries
Main exports: Oil, farm produce
Main imports: Raw materials, machinery

ABU DHABI
The rulers of many Middle East states invested income from sales of oil to improve the living conditions of their people and develop the economies of their nations. In the 1960s the city of Abu Dhabi was just a fishing village on the Gulf. Today it is the capital city of the Abu Dhabi sheikdom in the United Arab Emirates, complete with an international airport and high-rise downtown area.

Istanbul • R. Sakarya
Bursa •
Eskisehir • **Ankara**
• Izmir **TURKEY**
Konya • Kayseri •
Taurus Mts
Gaziant
Adana • Aleppo
MEDITERRANEAN SEA R. Orontes
CYPRUS Nicosia Homs •
Ceasefire line dividing Greek and Turkish areas. **LEBANON**
Beirut
Damascus
ISRAEL Mt Hermon
Israeli-occupied areas Irbid •
Jerusalem **Amman**
Suez Canal *Negev Desert* *Dead Sea*
Israeli-occupied areas **JORDAN**
Sinai Peninsula
EGYPT Medina •
Jiddah • Mecca
RED SEA
SUDAN
ETHIOPIA

 ## BAHRAIN
Area: 678 sq km (262 sq miles)
Population: 500,000
Capital: Manama
Religion: Islam
Currency: Bahrain dinar

 ## CYPRUS
Area: 9,251 sq km (3,571 sq miles)
Population: 700,000
Capital: Nicosia
Religions: Orthodox Church of Cyprus, Islam
Currency: Cyprus pound

 ## IRAN
Area: 1,648,000 sq km (636,297 sq miles)
Population: 63,200,000
Capital: Tehran
Religion: Shia Islam
Currency: Rial

 ## IRAQ
Area: 438,317 sq km (169,235 sq miles)
Population: 19,900,000
Capital: Baghdad
Religion: Shia Islam
Currency: Iraqi dinar

 ## ISRAEL
Area: 20,770 sq km (8,017 sq miles)
Population: 5,400,000
Capital: Jerusalem
Religion: Judaism
Currency: Shekel

 ## JORDAN
Area: 97,740 sq km (37,737 sq miles)
Population: 4,400,000
Capital: Amman
Religion: Sunni Islam
Currency: Jordanian dinar

 ## KUWAIT
Area: 17,818 sq km (6,879 sq miles)
Population: 1,800,000
Capital: Kuwait
Religion: Islam
Currency: Kuwaiti dinar

 ## LEBANON
Area: 10,400 sq km (4,015 sq miles)
Population: 2,900,000
Capital: Beirut
Religions: Islam, Christian, Druze
Currency: Lebanese pound

 ## OMAN
Area: 212,457 sq km (82,030 sq miles)
Population: 1,700,000
Capital: Muscat
Religion: Ibadite sect of Islam
Currency: Omani rial

 ## QATAR
Area: 11,000 sq km (4,247 sq miles)
Population: 500,000
Capital: Doha
Religion: Islam
Currency: Qatar riyal

 ## SAUDI ARABIA
Area: 2,175,589 sq km (839,996 sq miles)
Population: 16,500,000
Capital: Riyadh
Religion: Sunni Islam
Currency: Saudi riyal

 ## SYRIA
Area: 185,180 sq km (71,500 sq miles)
Population: 13,800,000
Capital: Damascus
Religion: Sunni Islam
Currency: Syrian pound

 ## TURKEY
Area: 779,452 sq km (300,948 sq miles)
Population: 59,600,000
Capital: Ankara
Religion: Islam
Currency: Turkish lira

 ## UNITED ARAB EMIRATES
Area: 83,600 sq km (32,278 sq miles)
Population: 1,700,000
Capital: Abu Dhabi
Religion: Islam
Currency: Dirham

 ## YEMEN
Area: 527,968 sq km (203,850 sq miles)
Population: 13,000,000
Capital: Sana
Religion: Islam
Currency: Yemeni rial, dinar

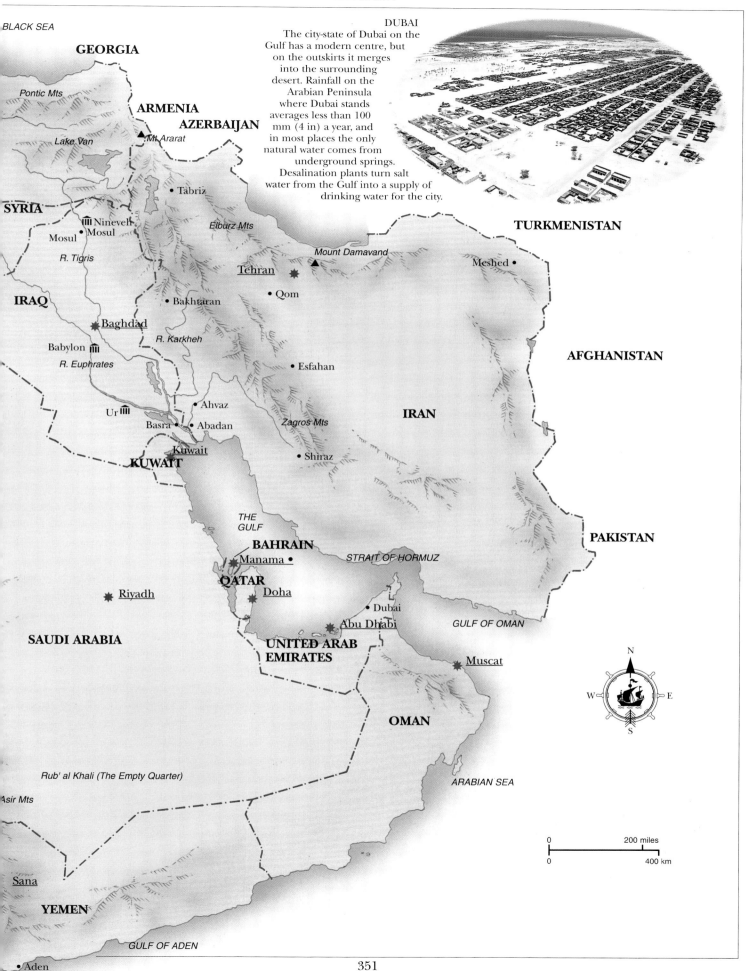

BLACK SEA

GEORGIA

Pontic Mts

ARMENIA

AZERBAIJAN

Lake Van

▲ Mt Ararat

• Tabriz

Elburz Mts

DUBAI
The city-state of Dubai on the
Gulf has a modern centre, but
on the outskirts it merges
into the surrounding
desert. Rainfall on the
Arabian Peninsula
where Dubai stands
averages less than 100
mm (4 in) a year, and
in most places the only
natural water comes from
underground springs.
Desalination plants turn salt
water from the Gulf into a supply of
drinking water for the city.

TURKMENISTAN

SYRIA

🏛 Nineveh
• Mosul
Mosul

R. Tigris

Mount Damavand ▲

Tehran ✴

Meshed •

• Qom

IRAQ

• Bakhtaran

✴ Baghdad

R. Karkheh

Babylon 🏛

AFGHANISTAN

R. Euphrates

• Esfahan

Ur 🏛

• Ahvaz

IRAN

Basra • • Abadan

Zagros Mts

Kuwait ✴

• Shiraz

KUWAIT

PAKISTAN

THE
GULF

BAHRAIN

✴ Manama •

STRAIT OF HORMUZ

QATAR

✴ Riyadh

✴ Doha

GULF OF OMAN

• Dubai

✴ Abu Dhabi

SAUDI ARABIA

**UNITED ARAB
EMIRATES**

✴ Muscat

OMAN

N

W ⚓ E

S

Rub' al Khali (The Empty Quarter)

ARABIAN SEA

Asir Mts

0   200 miles

0   400 km

Sana

YEMEN

GULF OF ADEN

• Aden

351

MIGRATION

MANY ANIMALS LIVE in the same areas all their lives, rarely going far. But others undertake migrations – long journeys in search of food, warmth, or a suitable place to breed and raise young. Some animals migrate seasonally. During the dry season, for example, buffaloes may set off in search of water holes or fresh pasture. Some creatures migrate to avoid the harsh winter cold; others to avoid the scorching summer sun. Migration can cover thousands of kilometres and often involves a return journey. Birds such as cuckoos and swallows, for instance, spend the summer in Europe and winter in Africa. Some animals, such as lemmings and locusts, migrate only when they become so numerous that the area can no longer feed them.

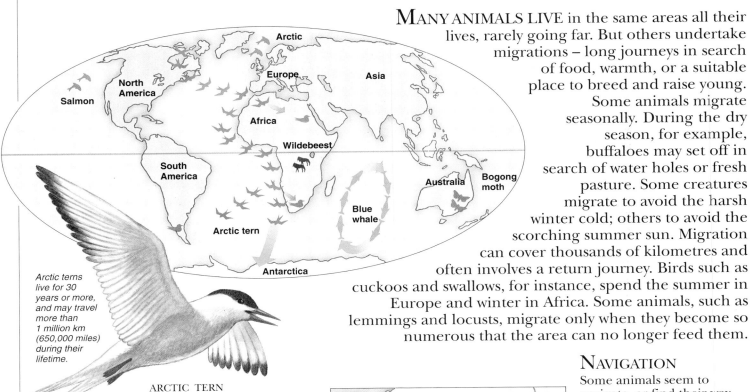

Arctic terns live for 30 years or more, and may travel more than 1 million km (650,000 miles) during their lifetime.

ARCTIC TERN
The longest migration in the world is made by the Arctic tern. This champion migrator travels from the top of the globe to the bottom each year and back again. Arctic terns spend the summer in the Arctic, where they rear their young and feed on insects, fish, and shellfish. After the short summer they fly south, and some reach the Antarctic. The direct journey is 15,000 km (9,000 miles), yet many terns go even farther, flying east across the North Atlantic, then west across the South Atlantic. After another summer near the South Pole, they migrate north again.

Wildebeest wander north to find fresh pasture.

Serengeti National Park in Africa

Adult male wildebeest patrol the migrating herds to keep the females together and to protect against predators.

SALMON
Salmon hatch from eggs in rivers and streams, then swim to the ocean, where they spend most of their lives. As adults they migrate thousands of kilometres back to the river where they were born, to breed. They are so sensitive to the chemicals in the stream where they hatch that they can find their way back to the same spot even after a few years. Salmon are powerful swimmers, and leap out of the water as they fight their way upstream.

NAVIGATION
Some animals seem to navigate, or find their way, by following the position of the sun, moon, or stars. Others may have a built-in compass that senses the Earth's magnetic field or the electric field of ocean currents. Scientists cannot be sure how animals know where to migrate, especially young animals that have never made the journey before.

WILDEBEEST
During the dry season in Africa, huge herds of gnus (also called wildebeest) set out in search of fresh grassland and water. Sometimes they travel more than 1,500 km (900 miles) before they reach a suitable place.

Spring
Adult bogong moths migrate to mountain regions above 1,200 m (4,000 ft).

Summer
Adults gather in mountain caves and among rocks to rest during the hot, dry season.

BOGONG MOTH
Some animals migrate in summer rather than winter. During the hot, dry summer in southeast Australia, bogong moths sleep in cool caves and rock crevices high in the mountains. This type of hibernation is called estivation. In autumn the moths fly down over the lowlands. Some keep flying when they reach the coast, and perish at sea.

Autumn
Adult moths wake and fly down to the lowlands to lay eggs.

Find out more
ANIMALS
BIRDS
BUTTERFLIES AND MOTHS
FISH
HIBERNATION

MILITARY AIRCRAFT

JUST A FEW YEARS after the Wright brothers' historic first powered flight of 1903, aeroplanes took to the air as weapons of war. These early aircraft were fragile machines made only of wood and fabric held together with steel wire, and were armed with one or two machine guns. By the end of World War I in 1918, military aircraft had developed into large, long-range bombers for attacking distant cities or military installations, and small, manoeuvrable fighters for destroying enemy aircraft. However, these machines seem primitive by comparison with military aircraft of today. The latest aeroplanes are built of the lightest, strongest materials, powered by jet engines which drive them through the air as fast as a rifle bullet, and armed with a fearsome array of weaponry. They are also very adaptable; with only minor modifications a single aircraft may be used as a fighter, as a bomber, or for aerial reconnaissance (scouting) operations.

FIGHTER AIRCRAFT

Generally considered to be the world's most advanced fighter aircraft, the *F-15E Eagle* is equipped with sophisticated electronic instruments for detecting and attacking other aircraft and ground targets. The aeroplane has a top speed of more than 2,980 km/h (1,850 mph) and can fly to a height of 18,290 m (60,000 ft), which is twice that of Mount Everest.

Fuselage made of composite plastic materials and light metal alloys

Cockpit carries a crew of two: the pilot and the weapons systems operator.

Ejector seats allow crew to escape from the aircraft if it is in danger of crashing.

Infrared heat-sensitive camera enables crew to fly in the dark.

Two powerful turbofan (jet) engines

Radar antennas for detecting other aircraft

Aircraft needs only a short runway (the length of ten Olympic swimming pools) to take off and land.

Rotary cannon, which can fire more than 6,000 rounds of ammunition per minute

One of four air-to-air missiles for attacking other aircraft

Large, transparent canopy allows crew to look out for enemy aircraft.

Terrain-following radar enables plane to fly at high speed only a couple of hundred metres above the ground.

Missiles may be guided by laser beams, or by sensors which detect the heat of their target's engines.

STEALTH BOMBER

Built at great cost, the U.S. Air Force B-2 *Stealth* bomber is designed to approach targets without being noticed. It is made of composite plastic materials and has a special shape which makes it difficult to detect by radar. It first flew on 17 July 1989.

HELICOPTER
Armies, navies, and air forces use helicopters for a wide variety of operations. Helicopter gunships are designed to attack troops and tanks on the ground.

AERIAL RECONNAISSANCE
The *SR-71A Blackbird* flies at more than 3,200 km/h (2,000 mph) and at very high altitudes, so it can photograph enemy territory secretly.

TRANSPORT PLANE
Armed forces need huge transport aeroplanes to carry tanks and other equipment into battle. Aircraft of this type can carry loads weighing over 150 tonnes (about 150 tons).

VERTICAL TAKE-OFF
The *Harrier* jump jet is one of few aircraft that can take off and land vertically and change direction very rapidly while in flight. As a result, Harriers can operate from confined spaces such as ships or jungle clearings.

Find out more

AIRCRAFT
AIR FORCES
GUNS
HELICOPTERS
ROCKETS AND MISSILES
WORLD WAR I
WORLD WAR II

MINOANS

FOR NEARLY A THOUSAND YEARS a glittering civilization dominated the Mediterranean. Its people were known as the Minoans, after their legendary king Minos. In about 6000 B.C. settlers had travelled from mainland Greece to the island of Crete. Blessed with rich soil and a fruitful sea, these people became prosperous and developed a rich culture that reached its height between 2200 B.C. and 1500 B.C. They built huge palaces, such as the palace at Knossos, their main city. The Minoans were great seafarers. They traded throughout the Mediterranean region and with Egypt, carrying passengers, wine, oil, cloth, and bronze in their ships. They grew wheat, vines, and olives and herded sheep on the mountain slopes. Quite suddenly a huge volcanic eruption devastated the Minoan civilization. It was not until early this century that an archaeologist uncovered the palace at Knossos and amazed the world.

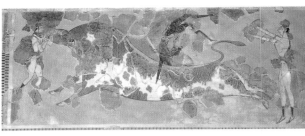

BULL DANCE
Young Minoan men and women performed life-threatening acrobatic feats, probably for religious reasons. They took turns leaping through the horns of a charging bull. After the dance they sacrificed the bull and spread its blood on the land. Few would have survived this type of sport.

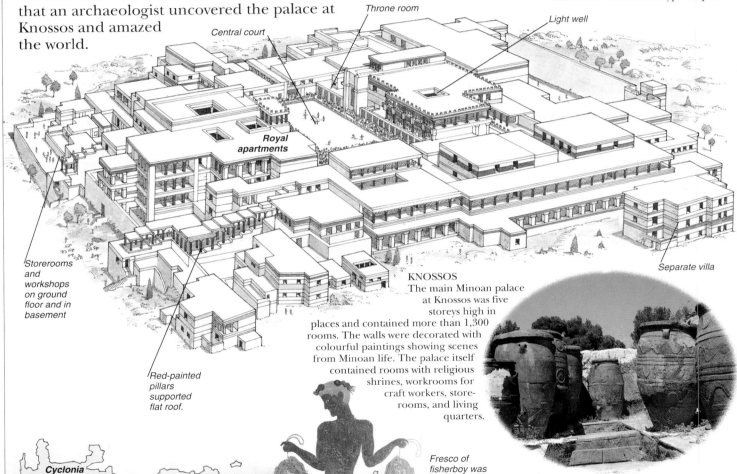

Throne room

Light well

Central court

Royal apartments

Storerooms and workshops on ground floor and in basement

Red-painted pillars supported flat roof.

Separate villa

KNOSSOS
The main Minoan palace at Knossos was five storeys high in places and contained more than 1,300 rooms. The walls were decorated with colourful paintings showing scenes from Minoan life. The palace itself contained rooms with religious shrines, workrooms for craft workers, storerooms, and living quarters.

Fresco of fisherboy was discovered in a house on the island of Thera. (Fresco is the ancient art of painting on plaster.)

Cyclonia

CRETE

Knossos

Phaestos

MINOAN POTTERY
The Minoans produced outstanding pottery. They used potter's wheels to make eggshell-thin, finely decorated pots and huge storage jars called pithoi (above). Oil, wine, and grain were kept in the pithoi.

MINOAN EMPIRE
The Minoans built a network of towns on the island of Crete and set up many trading posts around the shores of the eastern Mediterranean. After the volcanic eruption on the nearby island of Thera in about 1550 B.C., peoples from mainland Greece overran Crete. They were called Mycenaeans. The Minoan civilization then went into decline.

FISHING
Minoan sailors fished the stormy waters around Crete and traded all over the eastern Mediterranean. Fishing was the basis of the Minoan economy.

Find out more

EGYPT, ANCIENT
GREECE, ANCIENT

354

MONASTERIES

DURING THE MIDDLE AGES men who wanted to devote their lives to the Christian religion often became monks and entered a monastery. They promised to give up all their possessions and never to marry. They followed a hard routine of worship and work. Monks attended up to eight services each day in the abbey church. Regular hours were set aside for working, praying, studying, and recreation. Most monks never left their monastery. They grew their own food, raised their own animals, and made most of the things they needed. Monasteries helped the sick and gave food to the poor. They were also important centres of learning.

LEARNING
Many monasteries had schools and large libraries where trained monks copied and decorated books by hand.

MONASTERIES
The abbey church was the centre of monastery life and the largest building. Monks ate in the refectory.

Cloisters (covered walkways)

Dormitory where monks slept

11th-century monastery

Herb garden for medicine and food

Bees kept for honey and wax

Orchard for growing fruit

Refectory where monks ate

Sick people were cared for in the infirmary, or hospital.

Monasteries had rooms where travellers could stay.

CLOTHING
Monks wore sandals on their feet and coarse robes called habits. The tops of their heads were shaved in a hairstyle called a tonsure; this represented Christ's crown of thorns.

ORDERS OF MONKS
Different types, or orders, of monks organized their lives in different ways. Some orders devoted most of their time to prayer and meditation; others spent more time at physical work.

NUNS AND NUNNERIES
Religious houses for women were called nunneries. Some nuns entered nunneries for religious reasons; others went to escape from brutal husbands. Nuns taught, prayed, and studied, and followed the same hard routine as monks. Some orders were very strict; others were more relaxed.

Find out more

CHRISTIANITY
HOSPITALS
MIDDLE AGES
RELIGIONS

MONEY

THE NEXT TIME YOU ARE about to buy something, look at your money. Coins and notes are just discs of metal and sheets of paper, yet the shop accepts them as payment for useful, valuable goods. Money is a token which people trade for goods of an agreed value, and strange objects have been used for money throughout the world. Tibetans once used blocks of dried tea! It does not really matter what you use as money, provided everyone can reach agreement about what it is worth.

Many early coins were made from precious metals, such as gold and silver, but in 11th-century China, paper bank notes, or bills, first appeared. Unlike gold, bank notes had no real value. However, the bank that issued them promised to exchange them for gold. English bank notes still have the same promise printed on them. The United States government stopped exchanging bills for gold in 1971.

MINT
A government-controlled factory called a mint produces coins and paper money. Each coin is stamped with a special design, including its value, and often the year of manufacture. This stamping process is known as "minting".

Some North American Indians used wampum belts made of clamshell beads for money.

A strip of plastic or metal thread is embedded in the paper.

The first Chinese coins were made of bronze in the shape of tools, such as the head of a hoe.

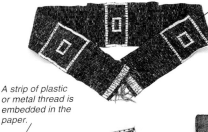

The weight of a coin made of precious metal indicates its value.

Specially made paper includes a watermark, which is visible only when the note is held up to the light.

The loops and whirls are machine-engraved and extremely difficult to copy.

1422 WILLIAM CAXTON 1491

THOMAS DE LA RUE AND COMPANY LIMITED

PROOF NO. 398 D/5

COINS
People from ancient Lydia (now Turkey) were the first to make coins, about 2,700 years ago. Their coins were made from electrum, a mixture of gold and silver. Today coins are used only for small denominations (sums of money). Paper money is used for larger sums, because notes are more difficult to forge than coins.

The metal of a modern coin is almost worthless, so the value of the coin is stamped on it.

BANK NOTES
Governments issue bank notes and guarantee their value. It is a crime for anyone else to copy and print bank notes. The crime is called forgery or counterfeiting, and bank notes have complicated designs to make copying difficult. Thomas De La Rue & Company is one of the world's most successful bank note printers. Their specimen note includes various security features which make their notes very difficult to copy.

All credit cards have to be signed by the user and can be used only by that person.

Many credit cards incorporate holograms which are difficult to copy.

Bank of Montreal Banque de Montréal

BB Multi-Branch Banking Inter-Service

Access

SPECIMEN

NATIONAL bank VISA

5224 999 00035 65

1265 VALID FROM 00/00 UNTIL END 00/00
MR A SPECIMEN

BANKS
Most people deposit, or store, their money in a bank. Banks keep this money safe in a vault or lend it to their other customers. The bank has an account, or record, of how much each of its customers has deposited. Banks pay out notes and coins when their customers need money to make purchases. People with bank accounts can also buy things by writing cheques – notes which the bank promises to exchange for cash.

The raised letters imprint your name and card number on the receipt.

CREDIT CARDS
A credit card is a piece of plastic that can be used in place of money. When you use it to buy something, you sign a receipt. The credit card company pays for the goods, and you pay the credit card company a month or so later. Credit cards are carefully made to reduce the risk of forgery or misuse.

Find out more

GOVERNMENTS
ROCKS AND MINERALS
SHOPS AND SHOPPING
TRADE AND INDUSTRY

MONGOL EMPIRE

IN THE LATE 1100s a masterful chieftain united a group of wandering tribes into a powerful army. He was called Genghis Khan; the tribes were the Mongols. All were toughened by a harsh life spent herding on the treeless plains of northeastern Asia. Determined to train the best army of his time, Genghis built up a formidable cavalry force. Using new weapons such as smoke bombs and gunpowder, they were invincible. In 1211, the Mongols invaded China, then swept through Asia. They moved at incredible speed, concentrating their forces at critical moments. All their military operations were planned to the smallest detail. Looting and burning as they came, they struck terror into the hearts of their enemies. In 1227, Genghis Khan died, leaving a huge empire to his four sons, who extended it through Asia Minor into Europe. However, the empire broke apart as rival khans (Mongol kings) battled for control.

GENGHIS KHAN
Temüjin (1162-1227) was the son of a tribal chief. His father was murdered when Temüjin was still a child, and when he grew up he defeated his enemies, united all other tribes under his control, and took the title Genghis Khan, "prince of all that lies between the oceans". He aimed to conquer the world.

Cavalry controlled horses with their feet to leave their hands free for fighting.

Armour-piercing arrow

Khanate of the Golden Horde

Khanate of Jagatai

Empire of Kublai Khan

Khanate of Hulagu

MONGOL KHANATES
After Genghis's death, the Mongol Empire was divided into four khanates, or states, with different rulers. Kublai, grandson of Genghis, ruled the eastern khanate. The smaller western empires, although briefly united in the 1300s by Tamerlane the Great, gradually disintegrated.

MONGOL EMPIRE

1206 Temüjin conquers Mongolia.

1219 Mongols invade Persia.

1223 Mongols invade Russia.

1237 Batu, grandson of Genghis Khan, invades north Russia.

1240 Batu invades Poland and Hungary.

1260 Mamelukes, Egyptian warriors, defeat Mongols.

1279 Kublai Khan defeats China.

1370 Tamerlane the Great conquers three western khanates.

Strung bow

Horses in battle gear

Unstrung bow

YURTS
Tribes wandered the Mongolian steppes following their herds of sheep, goats, cattle, and horses. They lived in circular tents called yurts, which they took with them when they moved. The women drove wagons which held the yurts; the men hunted, looked after the herds, and traded for grain and metal. Mongols of today still live in yurts.

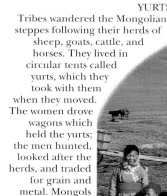

COMPOSITE BOW
Mongols made their deadly bows out of wood, horn, and sinew, which gave the bows incredible power. The Mongols were superb archers, able to string, aim, and fire at full gallop. They developed armour-piercing arrows, whistling arrows for signalling, and even arrows tipped with grenades.

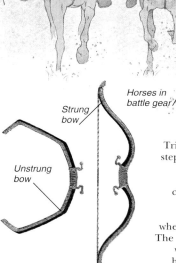

Find out more

CHINA, HISTORY OF
EXPLORERS
RUSSIA, HISTORY OF

MONKEYS AND APES

AMONG THE MOST intelligent creatures on Earth are the apes – chimpanzees, gorillas, gibbons, and orang-utans. They have large brains, long arms, fingers, and toes, and their bodies are covered in hair. In body shape and intelligence these creatures resemble humans, which also belong to the ape family. Closely related to apes are monkeys, a larger group of animals that includes baboons, macaques, colubuses, and marmosets. Monkeys and apes have a similar body plan, although monkeys tend to be smaller. A pygmy marmoset weighs only 150 g (5 oz), whereas a huge male "silverback" gorilla weighs as much as 180 kg (400 lb). Both monkeys and apes have a rounded face with a flat snout, small ears, and large eyes which face forward. They use their front limbs like arms, and their hands can grasp strongly and manipulate delicately. Most monkeys have tails, which they use as a counterbalance as they swing through trees. In some monkeys the tail is strong and prehensile (grasping); apes, however, have no tails. Apes and monkeys feed on a variety of foods, including fruit, leaves, insects, and birds' eggs.

ORANG-UTAN

The richly coloured orang-utan is found in the forests of Borneo and Sumatra in South-east Asia. Orang-utans spend most of their time high up in the trees searching for fruit, shoots, leaves, and insects. They live alone, except during the breeding season.

Prehensile hand can grasp.

Arms are very long in relation to the body.

Shaggy coat of reddish-brown hair

Today, orang-utans are in danger of extinction because their forest homes are being cleared for timber and farmland.

GORILLA

Measuring up to 2 m (6 ft) in height, gorillas are the largest apes. Gorillas are slow, gentle creatures – unless disturbed – and they spend their time resting and eating leaves, stems, and shoots. Gorillas live in small groups that travel slowly through the forest, eating some but not all of the food in one area before moving on to another feeding area.

BREEDING
A gorilla group contains between five and 10 animals. There is one large male, several females, and their young of various ages. The young are born singly; a female gives birth about every four years.

PRIMATES
All monkeys and apes belong to the mammal group called primates. Other primates include bush babies, pottos, tarsiers, and humans. Today many primates, including gibbons and the other apes, are on the official list of endangered species.

MACAQUE MONKEY
Monkeys and apes show behaviour that we describe as "intelligent". These creatures communicate well, have good memories, and are able to solve problems. A famous example is the Japanese macaque monkey which discovered that by washing its food in water it could get rid of the dirt and sand on it. Other members of the troop saw what the monkey was doing and copied it.

GIBBON

A gibbon's muscular arms and hands are so long that the knuckles touch the ground even when the gibbon stands upright. Gibbons live in family groups of a male, a female, and two to four young. There are nine kinds of gibbons; the largest is the siamang, which weighs about 10 kg (22 lb). The siamang is so heavy that it cannot swing out to the tips of thin branches as other gibbons can.

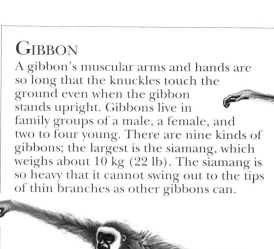

The acrobatic gibbon swings through the trees of Southeast Asia and rarely comes down to the ground.

Gibbons feed mainly on fruit and young leaves.

Young chimpanzees spend much of their time playing with objects and chasing each other. This helps prepare the chimp to find food and fight off enemies in adult life.

Most monkeys and apes depend on trees for shelter and food, particularly in the rain forests.

COMMUNICATION

Many monkeys communicate by sounds. The howler monkey of South America produces extremely loud howling noises using its specialized larynx (voice box). These sounds warn other howler troops to stay out of the group's territory. The leading male howler is usually the main shouter and can be heard nearly 3 km (2 miles) away.

CONSERVATION

The forests where monkeys and apes live are being cut down at a great speed. Newly planted trees are soon removed for timber, so they do not provide homes for the local wildlife. Dozens of different kinds of monkeys are at risk. Among them is the woolly spider monkey of Brazil.

CHIMPANZEE

Chimpanzees are the animals which remind us most of ourselves – because of their facial expressions and the way they play games, make tools, and solve puzzles. Chimpanzees live in groups which sometimes fight with neighbouring groups. Their main foods are fruits and leaves, seeds, flowers, insects, and sometimes larger creatures such as monkeys and deer. Chimpanzees live deep in the forests and open grassland of Africa. Pygmy chimps or bonobos are found only in the thick forests of Zaire (central Africa).

BABOON

The African baboon can climb but usually walks or gallops on all fours. Baboons are easy to study because they live in open country, and scientists have learned much about their social life. Baboons live in troops. Each troop is based around senior females and their offspring. Growing males tend to live alone while they are maturing. When a male becomes an adult he joins a troop, but has to battle with other males to establish his rank. The troop protects itself against predators such as lions and against other baboon troops that stray into its territory.

Find out more

AFRICAN WILDLIFE
ANIMALS
CONSERVATION
and endangered species
FOREST WILDLIFE
MAMMALS

MOON

Lava once flowed from the moon's interior following huge meteorite impacts more than 4,000 million years ago. The lava solidified into smooth-floored plains called seas or maria.

OUR NEAREST NEIGHBOUR in space is the moon. It orbits, or circles, the Earth keeping the same face pointed towards us. The moon is a hostile place. It has no atmosphere to keep the temperature constant, as Earth does. Instead, temperatures range from a scorching 115°C (240°F) during the moon's day to an icy -160°C (-260°F) at night. There is no water, so no plants or animals can live there. Great plains stretch over the moon's surface, dotted with huge mountains and scarred by numerous craters. The moon does not produce light of its own. We see the moon because it acts like a huge mirror, reflecting light from the sun. The moon is a natural satellite – something that orbits around a planet or a star. There are many moons circling the other planets in the solar system.

Craters were formed by meteorite impacts. A few are a result of volcanic activity within the moon.

BIRTH OF THE MOON
There have been many theories to explain the formation of the moon. Scientists have suggested that the moon may be a piece of the Earth that broke away millions of years ago. Today, however, most astronomers believe that the moon and Earth formed together from the same cloud of gas and dust about 4.5 billion years ago.

The gravitational attraction of the moon causes tides to rise and fall in the Earth's oceans.

1 New moon (moon invisible)   3 Half moon (first quarter)   5 Full moon   7 Half moon (last quarter)

2 Crescent moon   4 Gibbous moon (waxing)   6 Gibbous moon (waning)   8 Old moon

Moon seen from here

PHASES OF THE MOON
As the moon orbits the Earth, different shapes, or phases, appear, depending on the amount of the sunlit side of the moon that is visible from Earth.

LUNA 3
Until 1959, the far side of the moon had never been seen. In October of that year, the Russian space probe *Luna 3* (right) sent back the first photographs of this part of the moon.

OTHER MOONS
Our solar system contains more than 60 known moons. Nearly all circle the giant outer planets and are made of ice mixed with rock. The largest planet, Jupiter, has at least 16 moons, three of them larger than our own moon. One, Io (seen alongside Jupiter, left), is alive with active volcanoes. Another, Ganymede, is the largest satellite in the solar system. Some of Saturn's moons are very small and orbit in the outer sections of the planet's rings.

Armstrong's crew member, Edwin Aldrin, stands by the lunar module.

LUNAR LANDINGS
In 1966, the Russian *Luna 9* spacecraft made the first controlled landing on the moon. It was only three years later, in July 1969, that American astronaut Neil Armstrong climbed down from the *Apollo 11* lunar module to become the first person on the moon..

MOON FACTS

Distance from Earth	384,401 km 238,855 miles
Diameter at equator	2,160.5 miles (3,477.8 km)
Time for each orbit	27 days, 7 hours, 43 minutes
Time between full moons	29 days, 12 hours, 43 minutes
Gravity at surface	1/6 of Earth's surface gravity
Brightness	1/425,000 brightness of sun

Find out more

ASTRONOMY
EARTH
OCEANS AND SEAS
PLANETS
SPACE FLIGHT

MOSSES, LIVERWORTS
AND FERNS

MISTY TROPICAL RAIN FORESTS and moist, shady woodlands shelter some of the simplest land plants. These are mosses and liverworts, also seen on logs, stone walls, and garden lawns. Together they make up a plant group of their own, quite separate from other plants. They have no true root systems, flowers, or seeds. Instead, mosses and liverworts have tiny rootlets that absorb only a small amount of water from the soil, and short-stemmed leaves that take in moisture from the air.

Ferns are also flowerless. They are an ancient group of plants that have grown on Earth for more than 300 million years. Unlike mosses and liverworts, ferns do have true roots, with tubes inside their stems that carry water to the leaves. The giant tree ferns are the largest of all ferns. They grow up to 20 m (65 ft) high and look like palm trees. The smallest ferns in tropical rain forests are tiny, with leaflike fronds less than 1 cm (0.5 in) long. Ferns grow in most kinds of soil, but not in hot desert sand.

Horsetails are fernlike plants with no flowers. About 300 million years ago, forests of giant horsetails grew up to 46 m (150 ft) high. Their remains have turned into coal.

Carpet of moss covers wet bark on log.

HOW MOSS REPRODUCES
The leafy moss plant has male and female organs. The fertilized eggs grow in the brown spore-containing capsules, which are held above the leaves on long stalks.

FERN
A new fern frond gradually unfurls. When it is mature, brown dots called sori appear on the frond. These sori contain spores. The spores grow into tiny heart-shaped plants, which bear male and female organs.

Tip of frond uncurls.

Polypody fern fronds stay green all winter.

Curled-up frond of polypody fern

Sori are on the underside of fern frond.

Fern

MOISTURE-LOVING PLANTS
Mosses and liverworts grow beside streams and rivers because they need the moisture from the water. Many do not have roots to absorb water from the soil and pass it to their leaves. Instead, their leaves take in moisture from the air.

Liverwort

BRACKEN
Bracken is found on every continent except Antarctica. It has far-reaching roots and creeping stems, and spreads quickly across grassland and woodland. Bracken is a nuisance to many farmers and gardeners because it is very difficult to remove once it has become established.

LIVERWORT
The liverwort grows close to the ground, from which it soaks up moisture. Some liverworts, mosses, and ferns grow on trees and other plants, which they cling to for support.

Liverworts take their name from their shape, which looks like the human liver.

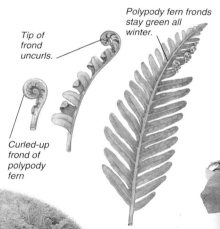

Bracken spreads into a pasture, reducing the grazing area.

BOG MOSS
Sphagnum moss is one of the few plants found in wet, marshy areas. It grows very well in swamps, forming wet, spongy hummocks. As the sphagnum dies, it rots slowly, and over many centuries turns into mossy peat below the surface.

MOUNTAIN WILDLIFE

LAMMERGEIER
The lammergeier is one of the biggest vultures. It has a wingspan of about 3 m (10 ft) and soars over the high mountain peaks of Africa, Asia, and Europe. This bird of prey feeds mostly on carrion (bodies of dead animals).

THE MOUNTAIN RANGES of the world are home to all kinds of wildlife – from tiny beetles to huge bears. The lower slopes are often covered with lush vegetation and are rich in animal life. Higher up the mountain the temperature is lower, and there is less wildlife. Mammals living here have thick fur to survive the cold. In places too steep for most creatures to climb, sure-footed goats and chamois leap with ease over the rocks. Near the top of the mountain the wind is so strong that only powerful birds such as condors can fly. In some windy areas the insects have lost their wings during the course of evolution; wings would be useless to them. Spiders and wingless insects live higher up the mountain than any other creature. As you climb higher the temperature drops by 6.5°C (3.6°F) for every 300 m (1,000 ft) of height. Above about 2,400 m (8,000 ft) small shrubs grow, bent and twisted by the icy winds. Higher up still, only mosses and lichens grow, and at the very top – where nothing lives – there is permanent snow and ice.

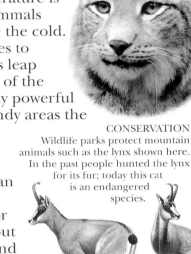

CONSERVATION
Wildlife parks protect mountain animals such as the lynx shown here. In the past people hunted the lynx for its fur; today this cat is an endangered species.

This map shows the main mountain ranges of the world.

North America

Europe
Alps

Africa

Asia

South America

Australia

■ Mountains

The mountain goat is a North American relative of the European chamois. Its body is more thickset and sturdy, and it is three times the weight of a chamois. The mountain goat moves slowly and deliberately through deep snow.

CHAMOIS
A rubbery hoof pad allows the chamois to grip stony surfaces with ease as it leaps nimbly among rocks in search of grasses, herbs, and flowers. Chamois live in groups of up to 30 females and young. The males live alone except in the breeding season.

SPECTACLED BEAR
The only bear in South America is the spectacled bear, so-named because of the markings around its eyes. It lives in the Andes Mountains and is found in warm, moist forests and mountains at heights of 3,500 m (11,500 ft). Spectacled bears eat a wide range of foods, including leaves, fruits, insects, eggs, small deer, and other mammals.

MOUNTAIN PLANTS
High up where trees do not grow, alpine flowers bloom in the short summer. The word *alpine* means above the tree line. The leaves of most alpine flowers grow low and flat so they are protected from the bitter winds. These flowers are pollinated mainly by flies, butterflies, and other insects that have survived the winter as eggs or as adults under the snow.

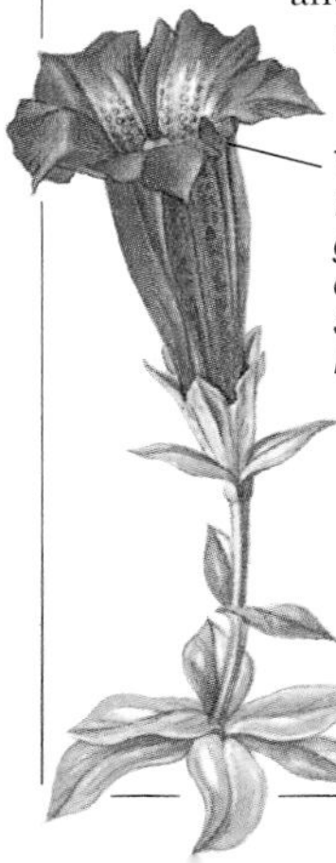

The trumpet gentian is named from its deep trumpet of petals. It grows in stony places and in damp, short turf at heights of 3,000m (10,000 ft), in the Alps, Pyrenees and Apennines of Europe.

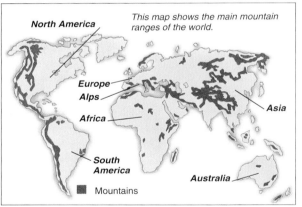

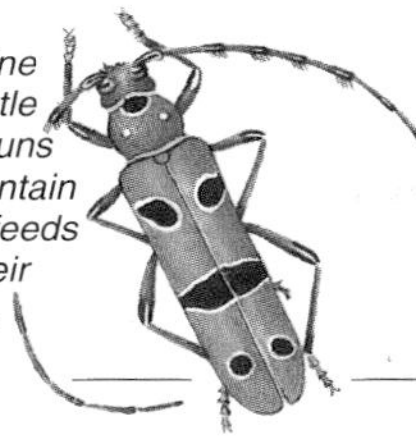

Today the edelweiss is a protected plant in many areas.

The alpine longhorn beetle shown here suns itself on mountain flowers and feeds on their pollen.

Hyraxes eat mainly grasses.

ROCK HYRAX
The small, furry, stoutly built hyrax of Africa is the closest living relative of the elephant – the largest animal on land. Rock hyraxes live at heights of up to 4,000 m (13,300 ft) in rocky places such as Mount Kenya.

Find out more
BEARS AND PANDAS
CONSERVATION AND endangered species
EAGLES and other birds of prey
LIONS, TIGERS, and other big cats
MOUNTAINS

MOUNTAINS

CONTINENTS COLLIDE and grind against one another, while hot, molten rock bubbles beneath the Earth's surface. These powerful forces thrust up mountains reaching as high as 8 km (5 miles). Many mountains are still growing, and those that formed long ago are slowly wearing away. Some mountains are volcanoes, made of layers of solidified lava which build up as the volcano erupts. There are mountains under the oceans and on other planets. The highest known mountain is on Mars; it is three times as high as Mount Everest.

The Earth has two vast mountain ranges. The Rocky Mountains and Andes run through North and South America; the mighty Himalayas, Alps, and Atlas Mountains stretch across Asia, Europe, and North Africa. These mountains are "young": they formed during the last 50 million years. Other ranges, such as the Urals in the Russian Federation, are much older and lower. The forces of erosion have worn them down since they were first formed more than 200 million years ago.

High on the mountaintop it is so cold that plants cannot grow. There is only snow and bare rock.

Higher still, only plants that are adapted to the cold are able to grow.

Forests of pine trees grow higher up the mountain where it is colder.

MOUNT EVEREST
The world's highest mountain is Mount Everest, on the border of China and Nepal. It rises 8,848 m (29,028 ft). Above are Edmund Hillary of New Zealand (left) and Tenzing Norgay of Nepal who first climbed Everest in 1953.

MOUNTAIN CLIMBING
Mountain climbing requires special equipment, such as ropes to prevent falls and crampons – steel spikes fixed to mountaineers' boots which grip ice.

AVALANCHE
Snow and ice can suddenly crash down a steep mountainside. This is called an avalanche, and it often occurs in spring as the snow melts.

MOUNTAIN ZONES
A high mountain has several zones, or regions, containing different kinds of plants. Forests cover the mountain's lower reaches. Further up is a zone of small, low-lying plants. Snow covers the summit, which is bare of plant life. Zones occur because the air becomes colder higher up the mountain.

Forests of broad-leaved trees and a wide range of other vegetation grow at the base of the mountain.

FAULTING AND FOLDING
As the continents move, they squeeze layers of rock. These movements produce huge cracks, or faults, and push up blocks of rock which form block mountains. The movements also make the Earth's surface buckle, forming fold mountains. Dome mountains appear when molten granite pushes the rock above it into a huge hump.

Formation of block mountains

Squeezing action pushes up blocks of rock.

Block wears away over many years to produce a mountain.

Formation of fold mountains

As layers of rock are squeezed, they form zigzag folds.

The rocks then crack and wear away at the top of the curve, forming jagged mountains.

EROSION
Ice, wind, and running water break up rock, slowly wearing it away over millions of years. This process of erosion carves out deep valleys and creates high peaks. Continuing erosion wears away the peaks, so that the mountains become lower and more rounded.

Find out more
CONTINENTS
GLACIERS AND ICECAPS
MOUNTAIN WILDLIFE
OCEANS AND SEAS
VOLCANOES

MUSCLES AND MOVEMENT

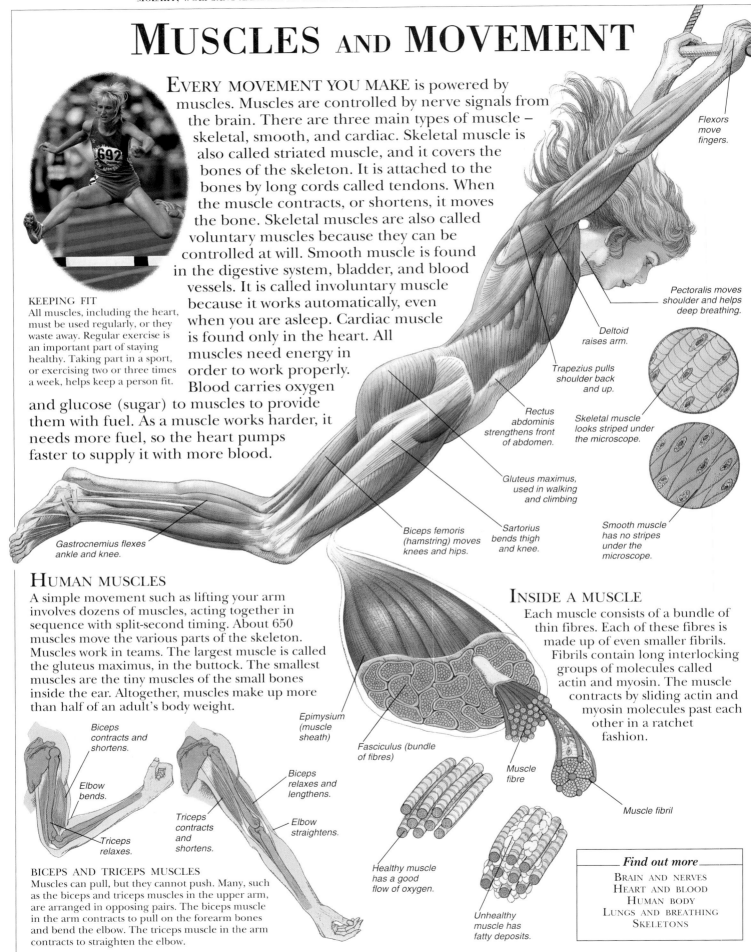

EVERY MOVEMENT YOU MAKE is powered by muscles. Muscles are controlled by nerve signals from the brain. There are three main types of muscle – skeletal, smooth, and cardiac. Skeletal muscle is also called striated muscle, and it covers the bones of the skeleton. It is attached to the bones by long cords called tendons. When the muscle contracts, or shortens, it moves the bone. Skeletal muscles are also called voluntary muscles because they can be controlled at will. Smooth muscle is found in the digestive system, bladder, and blood vessels. It is called involuntary muscle because it works automatically, even when you are asleep. Cardiac muscle is found only in the heart. All muscles need energy in order to work properly. Blood carries oxygen and glucose (sugar) to muscles to provide them with fuel. As a muscle works harder, it needs more fuel, so the heart pumps faster to supply it with more blood.

KEEPING FIT
All muscles, including the heart, must be used regularly, or they waste away. Regular exercise is an important part of staying healthy. Taking part in a sport, or exercising two or three times a week, helps keep a person fit.

Flexors move fingers.

Pectoralis moves shoulder and helps deep breathing.

Deltoid raises arm.

Trapezius pulls shoulder back and up.

Rectus abdominis strengthens front of abdomen.

Skeletal muscle looks striped under the microscope.

Gluteus maximus, used in walking and climbing

Smooth muscle has no stripes under the microscope.

Biceps femoris (hamstring) moves knees and hips.

Sartorius bends thigh and knee.

Gastrocnemius flexes ankle and knee.

HUMAN MUSCLES
A simple movement such as lifting your arm involves dozens of muscles, acting together in sequence with split-second timing. About 650 muscles move the various parts of the skeleton. Muscles work in teams. The largest muscle is called the gluteus maximus, in the buttock. The smallest muscles are the tiny muscles of the small bones inside the ear. Altogether, muscles make up more than half of an adult's body weight.

Biceps contracts and shortens.

Elbow bends.

Triceps relaxes.

Triceps contracts and shortens.

Biceps relaxes and lengthens.

Elbow straightens.

BICEPS AND TRICEPS MUSCLES
Muscles can pull, but they cannot push. Many, such as the biceps and triceps muscles in the upper arm, are arranged in opposing pairs. The biceps muscle in the arm contracts to pull on the forearm bones and bend the elbow. The triceps muscle in the arm contracts to straighten the elbow.

Epimysium (muscle sheath)

Fasciculus (bundle of fibres)

Muscle fibre

INSIDE A MUSCLE
Each muscle consists of a bundle of thin fibres. Each of these fibres is made up of even smaller fibrils. Fibrils contain long interlocking groups of molecules called actin and myosin. The muscle contracts by sliding actin and myosin molecules past each other in a ratchet fashion.

Muscle fibril

Healthy muscle has a good flow of oxygen.

Unhealthy muscle has fatty deposits.

Find out more
BRAIN AND NERVES
HEART AND BLOOD
HUMAN BODY
LUNGS AND BREATHING
SKELETONS

MUSHROOMS
TOADSTOOLS, AND OTHER FUNGI

BRIGHTLY COLOURED toadstools, delicate mushrooms, and the furry green mould on a rotting piece of bread all belong to a unique group of organisms called fungi. Fungi are neither plants nor animals. They are the great decomposers of the natural world. Fungi feed by releasing chemicals called enzymes which rot away whatever they are feeding on. The dissolved nutrients and minerals are absorbed and recycled by the fungi. Many kinds of fungi grow in damp woodlands and lush, grassy meadows, especially during autumn. There is no scientific difference between mushrooms and toadstools, but toadstools are often more colourful, and some are extremely poisonous. The part of a mushroom that we eat is called the cap. It contains spores – minute cells which grow into new mushrooms when they are released from the cap. Some harmful fungi cause diseases on plants and ringworm in humans. Yeast is a fungus used to make bread and doughnuts rise. Another fungus is used to make the antibiotic drug penicillin.

Champignon mushrooms grow in a ring in meadows and in gardens. Many people used to believe these were magic fairy rings.

MOULD
The decaying parts of plants and animals are rotted away by pinmould, which grows on damp bread, and the blue mould growing on this peach.

EDIBLE FUNGI

Many mushrooms and other fungi are edible; some are not only delicious but also are a good source of minerals and fiber. Cultivated mushrooms are farmed in dark, damp sheds on beds of peat. Collecting wild fungi to eat can be very dangerous. Some deadly poisonous fungi look just like edible mushrooms.

Ring where rim of cap was attached to stalk

Cap

Gills inside cap

Stalk

Young cap

Spores are released from between the gills of mature cap.

BEEFSTEAK FUNGUS
This fungus grows on trees. It is called the beefsteak bracket because it looks like a piece of undercooked steak.

OYSTER MUSHROOM
The oyster mushroom is common on beech trees; its cap looks like the shell of an oyster. Oyster mushrooms are tasty and keep well when they are dried.

FIELD MUSHROOM
During the autumn, field mushrooms spring up overnight in damp pastures and meadows.

MOREL
Prized for its flavour, the morel's cap is crisscrossed with patterned ridgework.

CHANTERELLE
The funnel-shaped cap of the chanterelle mushroom is yellow and smells like an apricot. It is found in oak, beech, and birch woods. It grows slowly, preserves well, and is much prized by chefs.

GIANT PUFFBALL
When the giant puffball ripens, its top breaks open, and clouds of tiny spores puff out with the slightest breeze or the smallest splattering of rain.

DUTCH ELM DISEASE
Dead and dying elm trees are a familiar sight in Europe and North America. A deadly fungus carried on the bodies of elm bark beetles, which live on elm trees, has killed millions of trees. The fungus grows through the bark, blocking the water-carrying tubes inside the trunk.

POISONOUS FUNGI

People die every year from eating poisonous fungi. Some of these are brightly coloured toadstools which are easily recognized. Others, such as the destroying angel, look harmless, but cause death rapidly if they are eaten.

Death cup

The bright red fly agaric toadstool is poisonous. Small amounts can cause unconsciousness.

The harmless-looking death cup is one of the most poisonous fungi. Less than 28 g (1 oz) can kill a person in only a few hours.

Fly agaric

Find out more
DRUGS
FOOD
FOREST WILDLIFE
PLANTS
SOIL

MUSIC

MUSICIANS MAKE MUSIC by carefully organizing sounds into a regular, pleasing pattern that anyone can appreciate. Notes are the starting point for all music. A note is a regular vibration of the air which musicians create with musical instruments or with their voices. The more rapid the vibration, the higher the pitch of the note – the higher it sounds to a listener. Certain notes sound better together than others. Most music uses these notes, organized into a scale. A scale is a series of notes that increase gradually and regularly in pitch. Musicians usually play or sing notes at fixed time intervals. We call this regular pattern of notes the rhythm or meter of the music. A melody or tune is a combination of the rhythm, the notes the musician plays, and their order. The melody is the overall pattern that we hear and remember – and whistle or hum days or perhaps weeks later.

Ancient musicians from Ur in Sumer (now Iraq) played lutes, flutes, pipes, and percussion instruments.

THE FIRST MUSIC
The chanting of prehistoric people was probably the earliest music. The oldest surviving musical instruments are mammoth bones from Northern Eurasia; musicians may have banged them together or blown them to make notes about 35,000 years ago.

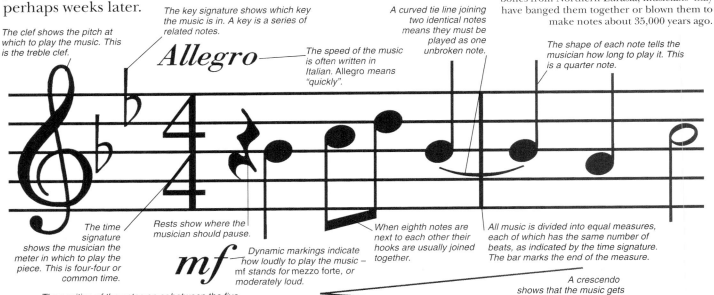

The clef shows the pitch at which to play the music. This is the treble clef.

The key signature shows which key the music is in. A key is a series of related notes.

The speed of the music is often written in Italian. Allegro means "quickly".

A curved tie line joining two identical notes means they must be played as one unbroken note.

The shape of each note tells the musician how long to play it. This is a quarter note.

The time signature shows the musician the meter in which to play the piece. This is four-four or common time.

Rests show where the musician should pause.

Dynamic markings indicate how loudly to play the music – mf stands for mezzo forte, or moderately loud.

When eighth notes are next to each other their hooks are usually joined together.

All music is divided into equal measures, each of which has the same number of beats, as indicated by the time signature. The bar marks the end of the measure.

A crescendo shows that the music gets gradually louder.

The position of the notes on or between the five horizontal staff lines indicates their pitch. Musicians use letters of the alphabet as names for each of the eight notes in an octave.

c d e f g a b c

NOTATION
Composers need a way of writing down the music they create. Musical notation is a code of symbols and signs that records every aspect of the music. Monks were the first to use musical notation in the 9th century, to help them remember the tunes of holy songs. The system in use today had developed fully by about A.D. 1200.

JAZZ
The essential ingredient of jazz is improvisation – the musicians make up some or all of the music as they play it. Black musicians created the very first jazz music at the beginning of the 20th century in New Orleans.

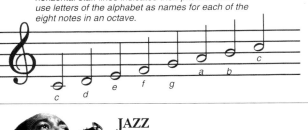
Charlie "Bird" Parker (1920-55) popularized a new form of jazz, called bebop, in the 1940s.

CHAMBER MUSIC
Classical – rather than pop – music for small groups of instruments is called chamber music. Chamber music was so called because it began as music for enjoyment in chambers, or rooms, in the home. Composers wrote different types of music for theatres or churches. Today performances of chamber music often take place in concert halls.

Many South American salsa songs share similar melodies but have very different lyrics, or words.

TRADITIONAL MUSIC

In much traditional music the composer is unknown, and the music itself may not be written down. Performers learn the tunes "by ear" – by listening to each other play – so they do not need a written score. Musicians sometimes make small changes as they play, so there are often many slightly different versions of the same traditional melody.

MILITARY AND MARCHING MUSIC

Music with a strong, steady beat helps soldiers march in step. Today military bands are not the only ones to play marching music. American high schools and football teams often have their own marching bands, which entertain the crowds at halftime and on special occasions.

Cheerleaders keep time with marching music and encourage spectators to join in songs and chants.

Buddhist monks blow large horns as part of their religious ceremonies.

Swedish folk musicians in modern and traditional costume.

RELIGIOUS MUSIC

Music has always played an important part in religion. In religious ceremonies, music inspires people to think about their God or gods. It accompanies religious songs and sacred dances. Composers also choose religious themes for music that is not part of worship: *Messiah* by the German composer George Frideric Handel (1685-1759) sets part of the Bible to music.

FOLK MUSIC

Peoples of the world make their own particular kinds of music; different regions within each country create different styles of music too. This folk music is full of character and often accompanies traditional dances. Some composers, such as Hungarian Béla Bartók (1881-1945), studied the folk tunes of their country and included them in their music.

ROCK MUSIC

During the 1950s a new form of popular music was heard for the first time. Rock and roll songs had a powerful beat and words that young people could relate to. This form of music began in the United States, where it grew from traditional rhythm and blues played by black musicians. Over the years it has influenced many other musical forms.

American-born singer Elvis Presley (1935-77) sold millions of rock and roll records and starred in 33 movies.

Find out more

COMPOSERS
MUSICAL INSTRUMENTS
OPERA AND SINGING
ORCHESTRAS
POPULAR MUSIC

MUSICAL INSTRUMENTS

THE POUNDING BEAT of an electric guitar might seem far removed from the delicate trill of a classical violin, yet these two instruments make their different sounds in a similar way. Both use a stretched string to create the vibrations we hear as music. The guitar and the violin have similar beginnings, but they actually belong to different families of musical instruments. String instruments such as the violin make their notes when the musician plucks the strings or draws a stretched bow – a bundle of horsehair – across them. Electric instruments, such as the electric guitar, produce weak vibrations that must be amplified for the audience to hear the music. There are five other groups: woodwind, percussion, brass, keyboard, and electronic. This short list includes a huge variety: some instruments, such as the hollow wooden flute, are very simple; others, such as the synthesizer, are highly complex.

CONCH HORNS
Conch sea shells made fine trumpets in ancient times – as they still do in modern Peru.

STRING INSTRUMENTS

Vibrating strings stretched across these instruments make the musical note: the finer the string and the shorter its length, the higher the note. The size of the instrument also affects its sound. The small violin, for example, produces higher sounds than the large double bass. Musicians pluck the strings of guitars, harps, and lutes, and usually use a bow to play the violin, viola, cello, and double bass.

Playing the violin

CELLO
The four cello strings make a rich, mellow sound.

VIOLIN
To play the violin the musician holds it under the chin.

WOODWIND INSTRUMENTS

Blowing into a woodwind instrument makes the air inside vibrate; this produces the musical notes. Covering the holes in the tube with fingers or keys changes the length of the vibrating air, producing different notes. The instruments with the shortest tubes, such as the piccolo, make the highest notes. Other woodwind instruments are the bassoon, English horn, saxophone, clarinet, oboe, and flute.

FLUTE
To play a side-blown flute such as this one, you blow across the tube.

Keys

Body joint

Head joint

Lip plate

Blowhole

Bell joint

Reed

Upper joint

Keys

OBOE
The mouthpiece of an oboe is a double reed (a piece of thin wood). The instrument makes a clear, sad sound.

Reed

Tip

OBOE REED
Most professional oboe players make their own reeds by binding two pieces of split cane to a tube called a staple.

A flautist playing a side-blown concert flute

Playing the oboe

Staple

A wood frame pulls horse-hair tight across the bow. Sliding the bow across the strings makes them vibrate.

BRASS

Some of the most exciting sounds in music come from brass instruments. This group includes the French horn, trumpet, bugle, cornet, trombone, and tuba. The instruments are long tubes of brass or other metal curved around for easier handling. Sounds produced by the musician's lips on the mouthpiece vibrate down the tube. Pressing the valves opens more of the tube, making the pitch of the note lower. The trumpet has a long history. When the Egyptians buried King Tutankhamun more than 3,000 years ago, they placed a trumpet in his tomb.

Playing the horn

THE CORNET

Musicians in military and brass bands often play the cornet, which is descended from the horns that were blown to announce the arrival of a mailcoach. The cornet is one of the smallest brass instruments, with a tube about 1.5 m (4.5 ft) long.

Cornet player

FRENCH HORN

Uncurled, this horn is 5 m (17 ft) long. It developed from an 18th-century hunting horn and makes a rich, warm sound. The Austrian composer Wolfgang Amadeus Mozart created four pieces of music for the French horn.

PERCUSSION

Bells, gongs, and drums are percussion instruments and there are many more, because all over the world people find different objects, such as beads and seeds, that make a noise when beaten or shaken. Some percussion instruments, such as the xylophone and timpani, are tuned to play definite notes.

Bass strings

Tuning pins

Strings

SNARE DRUM

The wire spring on the bottom skin of the snare drum vibrates when the player strikes the top skin.

Sounding board

KEYBOARDS

Hammers strike strings in the piano when the pianist presses a key. Pedals keep the note sounding when the key is released.

Iron frame

Pedals

Keyboard

Dampers

Hammers

TRADITIONAL INSTRUMENTS

Musicians in symphony orchestras play only a few of the world's vast range of musical instruments. Many more are used in the traditional or folk music of individual countries. Some of these instruments developed unique shapes in different parts of the world, as musicians explored the music-making potential of local materials. However, some are remarkably similar: the bagpipes are played in Europe, Asia, and Africa.

A flute player from Thailand

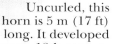

ELECTRONIC INSTRUMENTS

These instruments can produce an exciting array of sounds, by either simulating existing instruments or synthesizing completely new sounds. The musician can feed sounds into the memory of the instrument and then play them back together to simulate a whole orchestra.

Find out more

COMPOSERS
MUSIC
ORCHESTRAS
POPULAR MUSIC

MYTHS AND LEGENDS

BEFORE THERE WERE any books, storytelling was an important way of passing on knowledge and beliefs from one generation to the next. Often the stories took the form of myths which explained mysteries of nature, such as the origins of thunder. Ancient peoples told stories about gods and goddesses, and about human heroes with special powers. These myths became part of art and literature. Legends, though, were often based on real people and real-life events. To make a better tale, parents exaggerated the details as they repeated the legends to their children. Every country has its own legends. Paul Bunyan, the hero of stories told by North American lumberjacks, supposedly carved out the Grand Canyon by dragging his pick behind him. Sometimes legendary monsters were created, such as the werewolf which appears in stories from many cultures.

THE TROJAN HORSE LEGEND
Greek soldiers conquered the besieged city of Troy by hiding in a huge wooden horse. When the Trojans took the horse inside the city walls, the Greeks emerged and conquered Troy.

The Greek sun god, Apollo

SUN GODS
The same myths can be found in widely different cultures thousands of kilometres apart. This is because natural things such as the rain, the sea, and the moon are common to everyone. Many peoples worshipped sun gods: Surya in India and Apollo in Ancient Greece were both believed to ride across the sky in chariots of flame.

The Indian sun god, Surya

WILLIAM TELL
A famous Swiss legend describes how William Tell insulted his country's hated Austrian rulers. His punishment was to shoot an apple balanced on his son's head. He succeeded and later led a revolt against Austrian rule.

The Egyptian sun god, Ra

CREATION MYTHS
Most peoples used myths to explain how the world may have begun. This North American Indian myth was told by members of the Kwakiutl tribe.

A raven, flying over water, could find nowhere to land. He decided to create the world by dropping small pebbles to make islands.

Then he created trees and grass. Beasts lived in the forest, birds flew in the air above, and the sea was filled with fish.

After many failed attempts, the raven succeeded in making the first man and woman out of clay and wood. At last his world was complete.

GODS AND GODDESSES
The ancient Greeks worshipped many gods and goddesses. The goddess Athena took part in battles and loved bravery. Athens, the capital of Greece, is named after her.

Quetzalcoatl appears in Mexican mythology as one of the greatest Aztec gods. As god of air, Quetzalcoatl created the winds that blew away the rain.

Find out more
GREECE, ANCIENT
LITERATURE
MAGIC
RELIGIONS

NAPOLEON BONAPARTE

15 August 1769 Born on the island of Corsica.

1779-84 Military school

1799 Becomes ruler of France.

1804 Crowned Emperor.

1812 Defeated in Russia.

1814 Exiled to island of Elba in the Mediterranean.

1815 Returns to France; defeated at Waterloo.

5 May 1821 Dies in exile on the island of St. Helena.

IN A LAVISH CEREMONY IN 1804, Napoleon Bonaparte crowned himself Emperor of the French. He was an unlikely figure to lead his country, and spoke French with a thick Corsican accent. Yet he was one of the most brilliant military leaders in history. Napoleon first caught the public eye in 1793, when he commanded an attack against the British fleet occupying the French port of Toulon. In 1795 he crushed a revolt in Paris and soon led the French armies to victory in Italy. By 1799 Napoleon was strong enough to take power with help from the army. He made himself First Consul and restored the power of the French government after the chaos left by the French Revolution. He introduced many social reforms, laying the foundations of the French legal, educational, and financial systems. Napoleon was a military genius who went on to control Europe from the English Channel to the Russian border. But he suffered a humiliating defeat in Russia, and when the British and Prussians beat him at the Battle of Waterloo in 1815, Napoleon was sent out of France into exile on a British island in the South Atlantic. He died six years later.

THE NAPOLEONIC EMPIRE

At the height of his power in 1812, Napoleon ruled Europe from the Baltic to the south of Rome, and his relations ruled Spain, Italy, and parts of Germany. The rest of Germany, Switzerland, and Poland were also under French control, and Denmark, Austria, and Prussia were allies. Only Portugal, Britain, Sweden, and Russia were independent.

Battle of Waterloo

Military school near Paris

Napoleon's home in exile on the island of Elba

Birthplace in Corsica

EMPEROR
On 2 December 1804, Napoleon crowned himself Emperor of the French in a ceremony at Notre Dame Cathedral in Paris. He had already changed his Italian-sounding name, Buonaparte, to the French name of Bonaparte. Now he was to be known as Napoleon I.

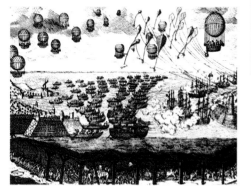

1812 AND THE RETREAT FROM MOSCOW
Napoleon invaded Russia in June 1812 with a force of more than 500,000 men. The Russians retreated, drawing the French army deeper into the country. Napoleon captured the capital, Moscow, but was forced to retreat because he could not supply his army. The harsh Russian winter killed many troops as they returned to France.

THE INVASION OF ENGLAND
In 1805 Napoleon assembled an army of 140,000 soldiers by the English Channel and drew up plans to invade England. These included crossing the Channel by ship and balloon, and digging a tunnel under the sea. The invasion was cancelled when the British admiral Nelson defeated the French fleet at the Battle of Trafalgar.

Find out more

FRANCE, HISTORY OF
FRENCH REVOLUTION
NAPOLEONIC WARS

NAPOLEONIC WARS

Two centuries ago a series of bloody wars engulfed Europe, causing hardship to millions of people and disrupting trade. Sparked off by the French Revolution, the Napoleonic Wars began in 1792 and continued for nearly a quarter of a century. On one side was revolutionary France, and on the other the old kingdoms of Britain, Austria, Russia, and Prussia. At first the countries encircling France fought the new republic because they wanted to put down the Revolution. But after Napoleon became ruler in 1799, the French conquered most of Europe, until only Britain remained free. The French army was the most powerful in Europe, but paying the troops required high taxes. Too few people volunteered to join the army, so the government had to force people to fight. These measures were unpopular in the countries that France occupied, and led to revolts in Spain and elsewhere.

SPANISH CAMPAIGN
Napoleon invaded Spain in 1808 and put his brother on the Spanish throne. The Spanish fought back with what they called a guerrilla or little war. Many were executed or died in the fighting.

NAPOLEONIC WARS
1792 France declares war on Austria.

1793 France declares war on Britain, Holland, and Spain.

1799 Napoleon takes power.

1803 Britain declares war on France.

1805 Napoleon defeats Russians and Austrians.

1806 Defeats Prussians.

1807 Napoleon defeats Russians at Friedland.

1808 France occupies Spain and Portugal.

1812 Napoleon's invasion of Russia ends in disaster.

1813 Austrians, Prussians, and Russians defeat Napoleon at Leipzig.

1814 Napoleon exiled to island of Elba, off Italy.

1815 Napoleon escapes, marches on Paris. Final defeat at Waterloo.

French field gun unit

WAR ON LAND
Napoleon organized his army brilliantly. His genius lay in making the right decisions at the right time and in using his forces in the most effective way. With superior tactics he often beat far larger forces.

BATTLE OF TRAFALGAR
Horatio Nelson was an admiral in the British navy. At the battle of Trafalgar in 1805, Nelson destroyed the French fleet by attacking in a fan formation, rather than by sailing side by side, as the French had expected. He died in the battle.

Traditional sea battle

How Nelson attacked the French fleet

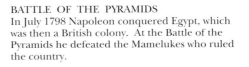

BATTLE OF THE PYRAMIDS
In July 1798 Napoleon conquered Egypt, which was then a British colony. At the Battle of the Pyramids he defeated the Mamelukes who ruled the country.

DUKE OF WELLINGTON
"A Wellington Boot, or the Head of the Army". Cartoons made fun of everyone in the wars, including Wellington, the British army commander and victor of Waterloo.

Find out more
FRANCE, HISTORY OF
NAPOLEON BONAPARTE

NAVIES

IN THE DAYS BEFORE cars and aircraft, sea travel was the fastest way to get around the world. However, it was also dangerous: pirates robbed cargo ships, and in wartime opposing countries raided each other's vessels. The Ancient Greeks, Persians, and Romans were among the first to build ships for war at sea. In the 16th century European nations organized navies as a way of protecting civilian shipping from attack. They used the ships to defend cargo and passenger vessels visiting their new colonies overseas. In wartime modern navies do their traditional job. They guard merchant ships and sail out in groups, or fleets, to attack the enemy until the sea is secure for trade again. Naval ships also transport soldiers to the war zone and supply invasion forces with food and ammunition. In peacetime the oceans are safe for shipping, so navies train for war and are useful in other ways. Sailors help with rescue work after an earthquake or hurricane. Navies also pay goodwill visits to promote friendship between countries.

PRESSGANG
An 18th-century sailors life was harsh, and few volunteered. The pressgang forced or "impressed" men to join the navy. The sailors in the pressgang kidnapped those who refused to join.

BATTLE OF TRAFALGAR
The first navies relied on wind power, and sea battles were tests of both fighting and sailing skills. At the Battle of Trafalgar in 1805 the British navy defeated a combined French and Spanish fleet, sinking or capturing more than half the enemy ships.

AIRCRAFT CARRIERS

Fighter planes based on aircraft carriers defend the fleet from enemy air attack. The runway deck is short, so a catapult gives aeroplanes added power on takeoff. Carriers are huge and have few guns, and other warships must protect them in battles.

To increase launch speed and give aircraft added lift, the carrier steams into the wind while aircraft take off.

USS *FORRESTAL*
A typical aircraft carrier, such as the USS *Forrestal* of the United States navy, carries about 90 aircraft. Most are fighters, but one fifth are used as supply planes or for scouting. Most of the interior of the ship is taken up by hangars, repair areas, and ammunition stores.

Parking area

Aircraft on the hangar deck are raised on giant lifts for takeoff.

Aircraft wings fold to save storage space.

Crew's living quarters

NAVAL SHIPS
A navy needs many different ships. Aircraft carriers act as floating airfields. Fast-moving destroyers and frigates attack enemy ships. Nuclear submarines defend the fleet and carry missiles to hit targets on land. Patrol craft are very fast and are used to defend ports and other land sites.

Aircraft carrier

Destroyer

Frigate

Submarine

Patrol craft

Takeoff area is short, so steam catapults give aircraft extra speed.

UNIFORMS

Each nation has its own naval uniform, carrying information about the person wearing it. There are many different tasks on board a ship; jobs also vary from ship to ship. Uniforms therefore vary too. For example, a gunner on a destroyer wears a helmet, and a deck hand on an aircraft carrier wears goggles and earphones.

United States   United Kingdom   China   Russia

Find out more

NAVIGATION
SHIPS AND BOATS
WARSHIPS
WORLD WAR I
WORLD WAR II

NAVIGATION

EVEN IN A CITY with signs and street names to help you, it is easy to get lost. But imagine you were out in the open country or sailing in a boat without a map. How would you find your way? The earliest sailors faced this problem as they made their voyages of discovery. The answer was to watch the sun by day and the stars by night. Because the sun always rises in the east and sets in the west, sailors could work out which direction they were travelling in. The position of stars in the sky also gave them their direction: Polaris, the North Star, for instance, is almost in line with the Earth's North Pole.

Navigation is the process of working out where you are and in what direction you are travelling. This can be on land, at sea, or in the air. Today, navigators have many aids to help them find their way. There are detailed maps of almost every part of the world, and electronic systems which use radar and satellites can fix the position of an aircraft or ship to within a few hundred metres. Such advances in navigation make even the longest journey easy and safe.

MAP AND COMPASS
Marks on a map show paths, hills, and other features. A magnetic compass shows which way to point a map so that it represents the landscape. The Chinese first used magnetic compasses about 1,000 years ago; about 2300 B.C. the first map was drawn in Babylon.

NAVIGATION SYSTEMS

Today, ships and aircraft routinely travel around the world without danger of becoming lost. Navigators use a gyrocompass, which gives the direction in which they are travelling even more precisely than a magnetic compass. In addition, ships and aeroplanes are packed with electronic navigation systems which guide them automatically.

Radar warns a navigator of nearby objects such as other boats or aircraft. A radar scanner sends out a beam of radio waves as it rotates, and receives the echoes bouncing back from any object within range.

For safety, a boat or aircraft travelling at night carries a red light on the port side (left) and a green light on the starboard side (right). This tells others the direction it is travelling in.

Navigation satellites beam radio signals to Earth. A computer on board a boat or aeroplane uses these signals to guide the vessel anywhere in the world with great precision.

A radio receiver on board a boat compares the times that signals arrive from land-based radio beacons and uses this information to calculate the boat's position. This system is called radio direction finding.

SEXTANT
For more than 250 years, navigators have used a device called a sextant. A sextant gives a measurement of the angle between two objects in the sky, such as two stars. From this angle, it is possible to calculate the position of a ship or an aircraft.

Buoy with radar reflector

A sonic depth finder measures depth of water, which is important for navigating around coasts. It beams high-pitched sound waves towards the sea bed. The time taken for the echo to return gives the depth.

LIGHTHOUSE
Coastal waters can be dangerous because of rocks or tides. Lighthouses send out a bright beam of light to warn ships. The interval at which the light flashes identifies the lighthouse and so helps navigators find their position.

BUOYS
Floating markers called buoys mark dangers such as hidden rocks. Buoys either mark a safe channel or indicate the dangerous areas themselves. The shape and colour of the buoys show on which side a boat should pass.

AUTOPILOT
The autopilot will keep a boat or a plane on a chosen course by adjusting the steering gear automatically. The autopilot of an airliner controls the plane for most of its flight. Some computerized autopilot systems can even guide a plane through take-off and landing.

Find out more
AIRCRAFT
MAGNETISM
MAPS
RADAR
SATELLITES
SHIPS AND BOATS

NESTS AND BURROWS

MOST ANIMALS need shelter and a place to bring up their young. A nest in a tree or a burrow underground protects an animal against predators and extremes in temperature. Many creatures, including birds and squirrels, build nests. Some creatures weave complicated nests. The harvest mouse makes a ball-shaped nest among corn stalks, where it rests and sleeps. Other animals, including birds, build a nest only during the breeding season, in which they lay eggs or give birth to live young. They line the nest with moss, grass, fur, or feathers to keep it warm and dry. Rabbits and foxes dig burrows, or tunnels, in the ground; a desert tortoise digs a burrow in which to hide from the midday sun. Some burrows are shallow; others, such as rabbit warrens, are deep, with escape routes, dead ends, and a separate burrow for the breeding nest.

Nesting boxes and dovecotes encourage many birds to breed in the same place each year.

Natural building materials from the surrounding area, such as lichens, help camouflage the nest.

Nest has a soft, thick lining of moss, hair, and feathers to keep eggs warm.

Wagtail weaves twigs and stems together to strengthen the nest.

Flamingo nests are cone-shaped and made of mud.

FLAMINGO

Many animals such as these African flamingos nest in large groups called colonies. Predators can see the flamingos easily, but there are so many parents making such a noise that few predators dare to enter the colony. In a flamingo colony there is safety in numbers.

NESTS

Many birds spend weeks making a nest in a sheltered place. Each kind of bird has its favourite materials, such as twigs, grass, or fur. Each also chooses a particular place to make the nest, such as a tree or a spot on the ground. A pied wagtail, for example, often builds its nest around farm buildings and uses twigs, straw, leaves, and moss, with a lining of hair and feathers. A grey wagtail builds its nest beside fast-flowing water and uses grasses and moss, with a lining of hair.

TRAP-DOOR SPIDER

The trap-door spider digs a small burrow in loose soil and hides in it. Using silk that it produces from its body, the spider glues particles of soil together to make a neatly fitting, well-disguised door. As an insect or other prey passes by, the spider flips open the door and grabs the victim.

Young platypuses stay in the breeding nest in a burrow underground and suckle milk from their mother for up to four months.

PLATYPUS BURROW

The Australian platypus digs a complex breeding burrow up to 30 m (90 ft) long in the riverbank. Here the female lays eggs and raises the young when they hatch. Each time the platypus enters or leaves the burrow to feed, it digs its way out and rebuilds the series of doors made of mud along the tunnel to protect its young from intruders.

Trap door is fixed by a silken hinge.

Door fits into specially shaped top of hole.

Tunnel is up to 38 cm (15 in) deep and lined with silk.

Find out more

ANTS AND TERMITES
BEES AND WASPS
BIRDS
MICE, RATS, AND SQUIRRELS
RABBITS AND HARES

NETHERLANDS

WE OFTEN REFER to the Netherlands as Holland, but Holland is really the name of just two of its 12 provinces. The Dutch, the people of the Netherlands, call their country Nederland, which means "low country", because nearly one third of the Netherlands is below sea level. Over the last four centuries, Dutch engineers have reclaimed more land by pushing back the North Sea with a network of barriers, or dykes. Even so, land is still scarce, and the 15.3 million Dutch people are crowded together in their small country. The Dutch countryside is rich, fertile, and green, with a cool, rainy climate. Farming is important. Canals and roads link towns together. The major industries produce iron and steel, natural gas, clothing and textiles, and electrical equipment. The Netherlands is a member of the European Union (EU), the trade alliance that unites 15 European nations. The country has a democratic government based in The Hague, although Amsterdam is the capital. There is a Dutch royal family, but the government makes all important political decisions.

The Netherlands lies in northern Europe, with Germany to the east and Belgium to the south. It overlooks the North Sea and has a jagged coastline.

LAND RECLAMATION

To reclaim land from the sea, engineers build dykes which enclose areas of the shallow water. Pumps then drain out the water. The reclaimed areas of land are called polders. Most of the polders are used as farmland.

The flat landscape of the Netherlands makes bicycling a popular way to get around.

BULB FIELDS

The Dutch have been famous for their flower bulbs since these plants first arrived in Europe from the Middle East in the 16th century. In springtime the dazzling colours of daffodils and tulips fill the bulb fields.

Windmills once powered the pumps which kept the polders drained of water.

ROTTERDAM

The largest city in the Netherlands is Rotterdam. It is also the world's largest and busiest port. A deep river connects Rotterdam to the sea 28 km (17 miles) away. Europoort, Rotterdam's huge modern port, can handle 300 cargo ships at a time.

Adding herbs to Edam and Gouda cheeses gives them extra flavour.

CHEESE

Much of the cheese produced in the Netherlands is made from the milk of cows which graze on the polders. The most famous cheeses are Gouda, and Edam, with its rind of red wax.

THE TOUR OF 11 TOWNS

If the canals freeze over in winter, a famous skating race may take place. It is called the Elfstedentocht, or Tour of 11 Towns. The skaters race along the canals that connect the towns, covering a distance of some 200 km (125 miles). Some 16,000 people take part in the Elfstedentocht, including the nation's top skaters. The winners complete the course in about six hours.

Find out more

EUROPE
NETHERLANDS, HISTORY OF
PORTS AND WATERWAYS

HISTORY OF THE
NETHERLANDS

IN THE GOLDEN AGE of the Netherlands, riches flowed into the country from its extensive empire, making it a centre during the 17th century for banking, industry, and the arts. This rise to prominence followed a long period of rule by other nations. Between the 9th and 15th centuries control of the Netherlands passed from the Frankish empire to the dukes of Burgundy and finally to Spain. The Protestant Dutch eventually rebelled against the Catholic Spanish king and achieved their independence in 1648 after 80 years of war. The flowering of Dutch trade and culture that followed was short-lived. Wars with England and France weakened the country, and by the 18th century the Netherlands was in decline. In this century, World War II meant a brief return to foreign invasion – this time by Germany. The country was a founder member of the European Economic Community in 1957 and is today involved in other moves towards a united Europe.

A LAND BELOW THE SEA
Throughout their history, the Dutch have had to battle with the North Sea to keep it from washing over their low-lying land. Flood protection measures such as windmills and dykes are a common motif in the arts and crafts of the country.

Dutch East Indiaman, or ocean-going cargo ship

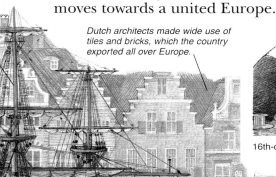

Dutch architects made wide use of tiles and bricks, which the country exported all over Europe.

16th-century Amsterdam merchant

Oriental spice imports stacked on the quayside

THE NETHERLANDS

1477 Netherlands under the control of Spain.

1568 Dutch revolt begins.

1602 Dutch East India Company formed to trade with East Indies.

1619 First colony founded in East Indies.

1648 Dutch win independence from Spain.

1652-54 First war against England.

1652 Dutch found colony in South Africa.

1672-78 War against France.

1688-1702 William III reigns as King of England.

1815 Belgium united with Netherlands.

1830 Belgium declares its independence.

1940-45 Occupied by Germany in World War II.

1957 Founding of European Economic Community.

A TRADING NATION
The Dutch have made their living and their wealth from the sea. In the 17th century they built up a maritime empire and traded gold, spices, and other goods around the world.

Dutch trade routes

THE DUTCH REVOLT
When the Dutch won their independence from Spain in 1648 they set up a government to rule the country (the States-General), which met in The Hague beneath captured Spanish army banners. A tradition of religious and political tolerance was established and continues today.

THE GOLDEN AGE
During the 17th century, rich Dutch merchants built fine houses. Many had pictures painted of their homes and families. The artist Jan Vermeer (1632-1675) became especially skilled at painting these Dutch interiors.

BELGIUM
Belgium was a Spanish and then an Austrian province until 1815, when it was transferred to the Netherlands. The Belgians did not like their new masters and rebelled in 1830, declaring their independence.

___*Find out more*___

EUROPE, HISTORY OF
NETHERLANDS
TRADE AND INDUSTRY

NETHERLANDS
BELGIUM AND LUXEMBOURG

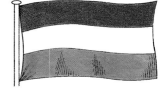

NETHERLANDS STATISTICS
Area: 41,864 sq km (16,164 sq miles)
Population: 15,300,000
Capital: Amsterdam
Seat of Government: The Hague
Language: Dutch
Religions: Roman Catholic, Dutch Reformed Church
Currency: Dutch guilder
Main occupations: Manufacturing, farming

BELGIUM STATISTICS
Area: 30,514 sq km (11,781 sq miles)
Population: 10,000,000
Capital: Brussels
Languages: French, Dutch, German
Religion: Roman Catholic
Currency: Belgian franc
Main occupation: Industry

LUXEMBOURG STATISTICS
Area: 2,586 sq km (998 sq miles)
Population: 400,000
Capital: Luxembourg
Languages: Letzeburgesch, French, German
Religion: Roman Catholic
Currency: Luxembourg franc
Main occupations: Industry, commerce, service industries, tourism

Motor cruisers provide visitors to Amsterdam with an excellent view of the city's fine buildings.

AMSTERDAM

More than 80 km (50 miles) of waterways crisscross Amsterdam, and for visitors a boat trip is a leisurely and pleasant way to view the city. The canals link Amsterdam with the River Rhine and the rest of the Netherlands. Amsterdam is the capital and largest city of the Netherlands, situated in the north of the country. It is an international centre for the diamond cutting and polishing industry. The Rijksmuseum has an outstanding collection of Dutch paintings.

Zeebru
Ostend • Bru

RIVER MOSELLE

Small towns and villages line the west bank of the River Moselle in Luxembourg. The river forms the southeast border of the tiny country, dividing it from its giant neighbour, Germany. Farmers in the Moselle valley grow grapes and other crops on the slopes above the river. However, agriculture provides little of the country's income; its biggest exports are iron and steel, produced by huge mills in the south which employ one third of all Luxembourg workers.

FRANCE

LANGUAGES
The French-speaking part of Belgium lies in the south of the country, close to the border with France. North of Brussels, most people are Flemings, who speak Dutch. In all, 42 per cent of the Belgian population are French-speakers.

Much of northern Netherlands lies below sea level. Drainage of the land began in the 11th century, and today a total of 7,700 sq km (3,000 sq miles) has been reclaimed from the sea.

WEST FRISIAN ISLANDS

WADDENZEE

• Leeuwarden   • Groningen

Barrier Dam

NETHERLANDS

Den Helder •

NORTH SEA

IJsselmeer

Northeast Polder

Alkmaar •

Markerwaard Polder

• Zwolle

Beverwijk •

Flevoland Polder

The 11th-century town of Delft is famous for its hand-made pottery and tiles, called delftware.

• Zaandam

Almelo •

Haarlem •   ✳ Amsterdam

Bussum •

• Deventer   • Hengelo
                   Enschede •

• Leiden   Hilversum •   • Apeldoorn

☙ The Hague

• Utrecht

Delft •   R. Lek   Arnhem •   • Rheden
  Schiedam •
Vlaardingen • • Rotterdam   R. Waal   Nijmegen •
  Dordrecht •   R. Rhine

R. Maas   • 's Hertogenbosch

GERMANY

Breda •   • Tilburg

• Roosendaal   Helmond •
Bergen op Zoom •   Eindhoven •   Venlo

R. Westerschelde

Turnhout •

Merksem •
  • Antwerp
Sint Niklaas • Hoboken •   Genk •   Geleen •
  • Lokeren   • Lier   • Heerlen
• Ghent   Mechelen •   Hasselt • Maastricht
  R. Schelde   •
Jette •   • Louvain
Anderlecht ☙ Brussels
  Forest

• Ronse

BELGIUM   • Liège

nai

• Mons Jumet •   Namur •   R. Meuse   Verviers •
       • Charleroi   ▲ Botrange Mt

R. Sambre

▲ Buurgplaatz (Bourgplatz)

Ardennes Mts

FRANCE

LUXEMBOURG

Luxembourg ✳   R. Moselle

• Esch-sur-Alzette

LUXEMBOURG

The city of Luxembourg (below) is the capital of the country with which it shares a name. The official name of the country is the Grand Duchy of Luxembourg, and it is ruled by a grand duke or duchess. Luxembourg city is a financial, banking, and transportation centre. It began in the middle of the 10th century as a castle. Because of its important site overlooking the River Alzette, Luxembourg grew into one of the strongest walled cities in Europe. Most of the Luxembourg people speak French and German but they may use a local language, called Letzeburgesch, in their homes.

Markets in Luxembourg city sell antiques and curios from open-air stalls.

BRUSSELS

Belgium is one of the world's top trading nations, and its capital, Brussels, is the site of the Belgian World Trade Centre (below). Approximately 4 per cent of all world imports and exports pass through Belgium, even though it is a relatively tiny country with a small population. As a member of the European Union, Belgium has been leading the way to remove the extra costs and artificial barriers that arise between nations who want to buy and sell each other's goods.

WTC

NEW ZEALAND

THE ISLAND NATION of New Zealand is a fascinating mixture of cultures and peoples. Maori people were the original inhabitants of the country, which they call Aotearoa, and they still live there, together with the descendants of the early British settlers and immigrants from other European and Asian countries. Only 3.5 million people live in New Zealand, and there are few large towns. The people are young – more than half of them are less than 30 years old – and the number of births per 1,000 of population is higher than in other developed nations. Since 1907, New Zealand has been an independent dominion of Britain. It is a leading Pacific nation and has strong links with many of the small island countries in the region, such as Niue. The landscape of New Zealand is varied. There are towering mountains containing glaciers, and volcanoes which spurt lava and heat lakes until the water steams.

New Zealand lies in the Pacific Ocean, east of Australia. There are two large islands – North Island and South Island – and many smaller ones, making a total area of 268,000 sq km (103,700 square miles).

KIWI
New Zealand lies far from other land masses, and as a result its wildlife has developed in an unusual way. The kiwi, which cannot fly, is the most famous of all New Zealand creatures. There are several other species of flightless birds.

WELLINGTON
The capital of New Zealand is Wellington, which stands at the southern tip of North Island. The city lies around a large natural harbour and is a busy port. Older wooden buildings stand close to recent structures built in a more modern style.

MAORI CULTURE
The Maoris, a Polynesian people, arrived in New Zealand around A.D. 950 from islands further north. Today their descendants keep alive the rich culture of wood carving, weaving, and music which they brought with them.

Sheep shearers work very quickly: some can clip a lamb in under a minute.

FARMING
New Zealand has a warm, moist climate which is ideal for many types of farming. Sheep and cattle ranching are the biggest businesses. There are three cattle and 20 sheep for every human in New Zealand. The country exports more dairy produce and lamb than any other nation and is the second largest exporter of wool. Over the past 15 years production of other crops, such as kiwi fruits, oranges, and lemons, has increased. Newly built fishing boats have helped New Zealand's fleet increase its catch, and today the country is a major seafood exporter.

SOUTH ISLAND
Although South Island is the largest New Zealand island, it has fewer inhabitants than North Island. The western side of the island is covered by the Southern Alps, a region of mountains and glaciers, parts of which have not been fully explored. The rest of the island consists of farmland, grazing land for sheep and cattle, and a few ports and coastal cities.

Find out more
NEW ZEALAND, HISTORY OF
OSTRICHES AND EMUS
PACIFIC ISLANDS

NEW ZEALAND

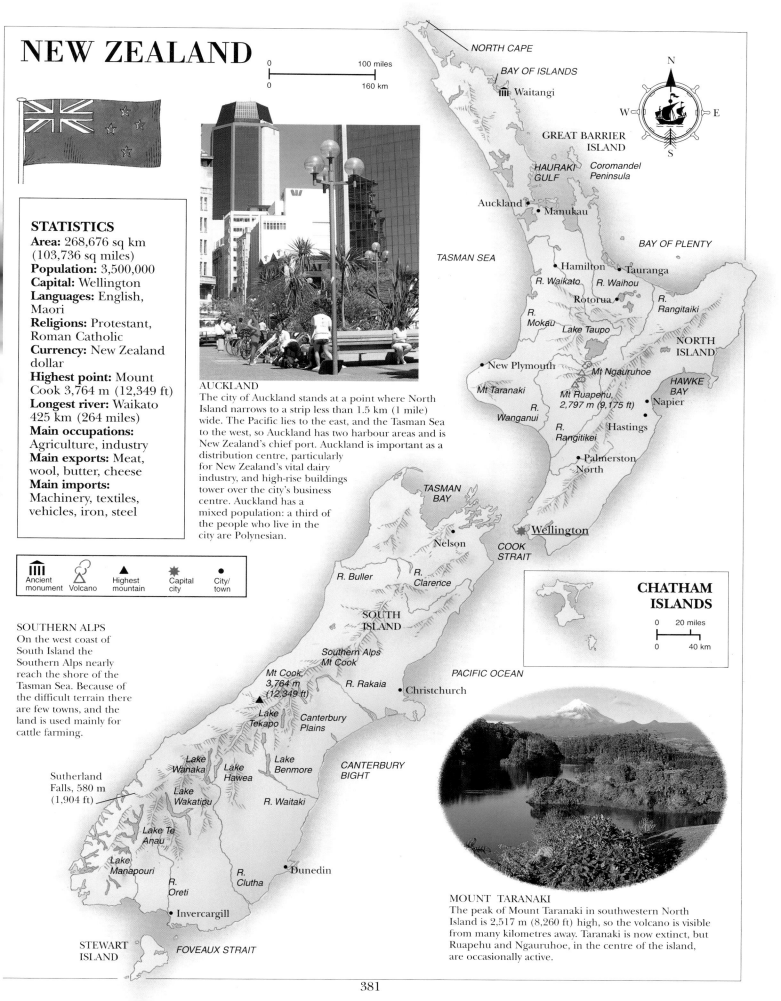

Scale:
0 ——— 100 miles
0 ——— 160 km

STATISTICS

Area: 268,676 sq km
(103,736 sq miles)
Population: 3,500,000
Capital: Wellington
Languages: English,
Maori
Religions: Protestant,
Roman Catholic
Currency: New Zealand
dollar
Highest point: Mount
Cook 3,764 m (12,349 ft)
Longest river: Waikato
425 km (264 miles)
Main occupations:
Agriculture, industry
Main exports: Meat,
wool, butter, cheese
Main imports:
Machinery, textiles,
vehicles, iron, steel

AUCKLAND

The city of Auckland stands at a point where North
Island narrows to a strip less than 1.5 km (1 mile)
wide. The Pacific lies to the east, and the Tasman Sea
to the west, so Auckland has two harbour areas and is
New Zealand's chief port. Auckland is important as a
distribution centre, particularly
for New Zealand's vital dairy
industry, and high-rise buildings
tower over the city's business
centre. Auckland has a
mixed population: a third of
the people who live in the
city are Polynesian.

Map legend

| ▥ Ancient monument | ☁△ Volcano | ▲ Highest mountain | ✳ Capital city | ● City/ town |

SOUTHERN ALPS

On the west coast of
South Island the
Southern Alps nearly
reach the shore of the
Tasman Sea. Because of
the difficult terrain there
are few towns, and the
land is used mainly for
cattle farming.

MOUNT TARANAKI

The peak of Mount Taranaki in southwestern North
Island is 2,517 m (8,260 ft) high, so the volcano is visible
from many kilometres away. Taranaki is now extinct, but
Ruapehu and Ngauruhoe, in the centre of the island,
are occasionally active.

Map labels

NORTH CAPE
BAY OF ISLANDS
▥ Waitangi
GREAT BARRIER ISLAND
HAURAKI GULF
Coromandel Peninsula
Auckland ●
● Manukau
BAY OF PLENTY
TASMAN SEA
● Hamilton   ● Tauranga
R. Waikato   R. Waihou
Rotorua ●
R. Mokau   R. Rangitaiki
Lake Taupo
NORTH ISLAND
● New Plymouth   △ Mt Ngauruhoe
Mt Taranaki   Mt Ruapehu, 2,797 m (9,175 ft)
R. Wanganui   ● Napier
HAWKE BAY
R. Rangitikei   ● Hastings
● Palmerston North
TASMAN BAY
★ Wellington
● Nelson
COOK STRAIT
R. Buller   R. Clarence
SOUTH ISLAND
Southern Alps Mt Cook
▲ Mt Cook, 3,764 m (12,349 ft)
R. Rakaia
PACIFIC OCEAN
● Christchurch
Lake Tekapo   Canterbury Plains
Sutherland Falls, 580 m (1,904 ft)
Lake Wanaka   Lake Hawea   Lake Benmore
CANTERBURY BIGHT
Lake Wakatipu   R. Waitaki
Lake Te Anau
Lake Manapouri
R. Oreti   R. Clutha   ● Dunedin
● Invercargill
STEWART ISLAND   FOVEAUX STRAIT

Compass rose

N
W — E
S

CHATHAM ISLANDS

0 ——— 20 miles
0 ——— 40 km

HISTORY OF
NEW ZEALAND

ABOUT 1,000 YEARS AGO, a group of people ventured ashore on a string of islands in the South Pacific. These people were the Maoris, and they had travelled in canoes across the Pacific Ocean from the distant islands of Polynesia to a land they called Aotearoa. For about 700 years, the Maoris lived on the islands undisturbed. In 1642, the Dutch explorer Abel Tasman visited the islands, and named them New Zealand, after a province in the Netherlands. Soon American, Australian, and European sealers and whalers were exploiting the rich coastal waters, and in 1840 the British founded the first European settlement. The Maoris fought protest wars until 1870, when they lost control of their lands. As a British colony, New Zealand grew wealthy by exporting its agricultural produce. In 1907, New Zealand became independent. More recently, New Zealand has formed several alliances with its neighbours in the South Pacific.

Traditional Maori cloak made out of feathers

MAORIS
Long before the Europeans arrived in New Zealand, the Maoris had established a thriving agricultural community. They grew sweet potatoes and caught fish and fowl. They wore colourful clothes woven from flax. They lived in houses made of rushes and wood.

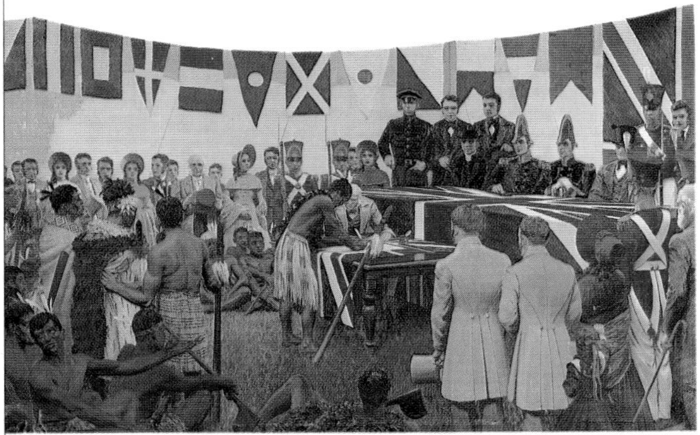

TREATY OF WAITANGI
In 1840, the Maoris granted sovereignty or ownership of their country to Britain. In return Britain promised protection of their rights and property. New Zealand then became a colony of the British Empire.

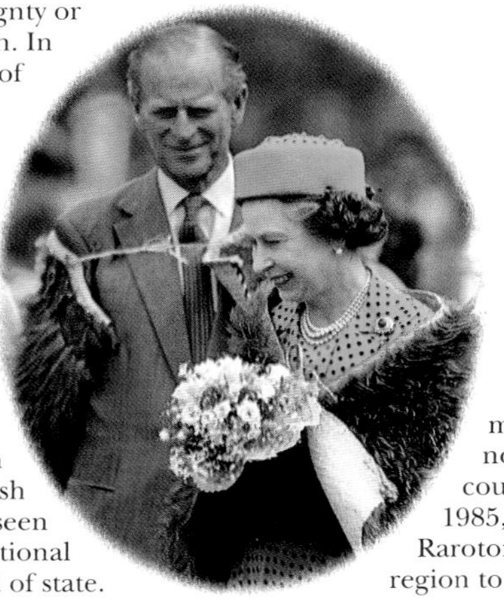

INDEPENDENCE
In 1852, Britain granted New Zealand self-government. The country gave pensions to workers and was the first in the world to give the vote to women. In 1907, New Zealand gained full independence, but ties with Britain remained strong. The British monarch, Queen Elizabeth II, seen here with Prince Philip in a traditional Maori cloak, is the nation's head of state.

NUCLEAR-FREE ZONE
In 1983, anti-nuclear protestors blockaded the U.S.S. *Phoenix* nuclear submarine in Auckland harbour. The following year New Zealand prime minister David Lange declared that no nuclear weapons were to enter the country in visiting foreign warships. In 1985, New Zealand signed the Treaty of Rarotonga, which declared the South Pacific region to be a nuclear-free zone.

Find out more

COOK, JAMES
NEW ZEALAND

NEWSPAPERS

THE PAGES OF A NEWSPAPER keep everyone in touch with local, national, and world events for a few pence a day. Newspapers provide more detail about events than television news programmes have time for, and stories in the paper cover a wide range of topics. In addition to news, there is information about politics, the arts, sports, fashion, business, technology, science, and the environment. Newspapers also contain opinions or points of view; some newspapers support a political party, and others try to remain independent. Local newspapers concentrate on events in one city or neighbourhood; national newspapers sell countrywide and cover events at home and abroad. A big newspaper has a large staff of editors, reporters, feature writers, cartoonists, photographers, typesetters, printers, and many others who work through the night to deliver the latest news each morning.

THE BROADSIDE
Before the first newspaper was published in 17th-century Germany, people read the news in "broadsides". These were single sheets of printed paper.

ON THE NEWSSTAND
Every country has its own newspapers. Some are published daily, others weekly. Some sell millions of copies a day, others just a few thousand a week. Each newspaper has a unique format – a special type style and general layout that sets it apart from others on the newsstand.

International edition of the American Herald Tribune

France

Spain

International Arabic paper

NEWS ROOM
The heart of a newspaper is the news or editorial room. Here national news and reports from all over the world come pouring in via the telephone, fax machine, and Internet. Here too reporters write their stories, assistant editors check them, and editors make decisions about how important each story is and what to include in the newspaper.

PRINTING PRESS
The thunder of the press as it prints newspapers each night shakes the floor. Huge reels of paper up to 8 km (5 miles) long roar through the press. Some machines can print, fold, cut, and stack more than 1,000 newspapers a minute. Lorries and trains rush the papers to newstands so people can buy them first thing in the morning.

FRONT PAGE
Big headlines and photographs of important, newsworthy events feature on the front page. In an eventful day the editor may need to change the leading story several times before the last copies of the paper are printed. Front pages carry the news that makes history – the outbreak of war, for example, or the sinking of an ocean liner, such as the *Titanic*.

Short pieces of text called captions explain what is happening in the pictures.

Find out more
ADVERTISING
CARTOONS
MAGAZINES
PRINTING

NORMANS

BAYEUX TAPESTRY
Dating to the 11th century, the Bayeux tapestry was produced to record the Norman Conquest of England. It shows scenes of battle, and can be seen today at Bayeux, in France.

Today SOLID STONE CASTLES in England, Sicily, and France stand as reminders of the Normans, warriors from northern France who transformed Europe during the 11th and 12th centuries. The Normans were descendants of the Norsemen, or Vikings, and were formidable fighters. They settled in northern France during the early 900s in an area now known as Normandy. The Normans were not only warriors but also skilled administrators. Their dukes created a complex and efficient society, dividing their kingdom into areas called fiefs. A knight controlled each fief. The Normans reached their height of power under William, Duke of Normandy who led the conquest of England in 1066. They quickly transformed England into a Norman kingdom, building castles to defend their conquests, as well as churches, monasteries, and cathedrals. The Normans continued to rule England until 1154. After this, the Saxons and Normans began to merge into one nation. In 1204 the king of France conquered Normandy and took it over.

WILLIAM THE CONQUEROR
William, Duke of Normandy (c. 1028-87) was a brilliant but ruthless general and administrator. He led the Norman invasion of England and, after defeating the Saxon king, Harold II, was crowned king of England.

Sovereign states

Conquered territory

Unconquered territory

Scotland

Ireland

Wales

England

Paris

Brittany

Aquitaine

DOMESDAY BOOK
In 1085 King William I ordered a complete survey of England. Known as the Domesday Book, it contained thorough details of people, goods, animals, and lands for every single village in the country.

EMPIRE
At their height of power under Henry II (reigned 1154-89) the Normans had conquered northern France, England, southern Italy, and Sicily. They did not survive as a separate group, but merged with the peoples they had conquered.

ARCHITECTURE
The Normans were skilled architects. They built strong castles to guard their conquests, such as the Tower of London, which stands to this day. They also built churches, cathedrals, and monasteries. Norman churches have intricately carved arches over the doors and windows and massive walls and pillars.

___ *Find out more* ___
CASTLES
FRANCE, HISTORY OF
UNITED KINGDOM,
history of
VIKINGS

NORTH AMERICAN WILDLIFE

THE CONTINENT OF NORTH AMERICA has a stunning array of wildlife, including golden eagles, bobcats, coyotes, cacti, and giant redwood trees. There are ice-covered Arctic islands across the far north, bordered by cold, treeless tundra where the ground is frozen for many months each year. Reindeer scratch in the tundra snow searching for mosses and lichens. South of the tundra is a vast belt of coniferous forests, with pines, spruces, larches, and firs. Today large areas of these forests are logged (cut down), but wolves, bears, and lynx still live in the wilderness areas. In the midwest are great grassland prairies; in the east are maple and hickory forests that were once huge; and in the west are mountains and redwood forests. Harsh, dry deserts such as Death Valley are found in the southwest, with swamps in the far southeast, and desert merging into the tropical forests of Central America.

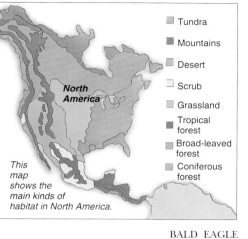

Tundra
Mountains
Desert
Scrub
Grassland
Tropical forest
Broad-leaved forest
Coniferous forest

This map shows the main kinds of habitat in North America.

BALD EAGLE
The bald eagle is the national emblem of the United States; it has a wingspan of about 2 m (6 ft). Bald eagles feed mainly on fish.

CACTUS
The giant saguaro cactus is found mainly in Arizona. It is a slow-growing cactus, but it may reach a height of 14 m (45 ft). Its white flowers attract many insects, including swallowtail butterflies.

DESERTS
The cactus is one of many plants that survive in the North American southwest, despite the dry climate. Cacti have plump stems which store water, and spines to prevent animals from eating them. In Mexico there are hundreds of different kinds of cacti.

WETLANDS
The lakes, swamps, and marshes of the southeast are called the wetlands. They are home to many plants, fish, and reptiles, including the water hyacinth plant and the American alligator, which can measure about 6 m (18 ft) long. Many other water creatures also live here, including frogs, toads, and red-eared turtles.

COTTONTAIL RABBIT
Like many dryland plant eaters, the desert cottontail rabbit stays near rocks or undergrowth and dashes to safety if it spies an approaching predator. The cottontail is so-named because its white bobtail resembles a boll (seed head) of cotton.

GRASSLANDS
Most of the natural prairie that once covered the North American midwest is now farmland. However, many animals are able to survive, particularly small burrowing rodents such as prairie dogs. Their tunnelling helps break up the soil, improve drainage, and recycle nutrients.

ALFALFA
This plant is a member of the pea family, originally from South America. Today farmers grow it for animal feed; humans also eat alfalfa.

PRAIRIE DOG
These animals are so-named because they make a sharp yipping sound like the barking of a small dog. Prairie dogs live in small groups called coteries, consisting of a male, a few females, and their young. The coteries are grouped into wards, and the wards are grouped into towns. Some prairie dog towns cover more than 40 hectares (100 acres) and form a massive maze of interlinked tunnels.

COLLARED LIZARD
This lizard eats other lizards and insects. Collared lizards measure up to 50 cm (20 in) long.

Ring of soil around burrow entrance keeps out rainwater.

PUMA

The American puma is a member of the cat family. It is also called the cougar or mountain lion. The puma can survive in thick forest or open semi-desert. A large male puma may measure nearly 1.8 m (6 ft) long and weigh almost 100 kg (220 lb). Pumas prowl mainly at night, hunting prey that ranges from rats and rabbits to adult deer. In the past, people hunted and killed pumas because they sometimes attack farm animals.

NORTH AMERICAN FORESTS

In the vast conifer forests to the north, summer is short and winter is long and bitterly cold. In autumn, bears begin to sleep in their dens, spruce grouse turn to their tough winter diet of pine needles and twigs, and migratory birds such as warblers fly south. Moose and reindeer shelter among the trees, scratching for mosses and lichens in the snow, and watching out for wolves. In the spring the migratory birds return, insects begin to buzz among the branches, and deer feed on the new growths of leaves and water plants.

REDHEADED WOODPECKER

Woodpeckers probe under bark and in wood for grubs, beetles, and similar animals. They use their stiff tail as a prop against the trunk as they hammer with their sharp bill.

SNOWY OWL

In the far north of the continent, the snowy owl swoops by day on voles, mice, lemmings, rabbits, Arctic hares, ducks, and other birds. Male snowy owls are usually white or slightly flecked; females are larger and more striped.

Snowy owl

MOOSE

The moose is the largest deer in the world. A large male moose has huge flattened antlers and measures up to 2.1 m (7 ft) at the shoulder. Female moose are smaller and do not have antlers. In summer, moose wade into the thawed marshes, lakes, and rivers to chew on water plants. In winter, they survive on buds, twigs, and other woody plant matter. Unlike many deer, moose live alone except in the breeding season.

Moose live in the forest areas of North America and also in Europe, where they are called elks.

MOUNTAINS

The Rocky Mountains provide many different habitats for wildlife. Above about 1,370 m (4,500 ft) the surrounding grassland changes to sagebrush and juniper trees, then to firs and pines at 2,000 m (6,600 ft). Above 3,200 m (10,500 ft), only mountain grasses and small flowers grow during the short summer. These rugged mountains are a refuge for spectacular animals such as bears, wolverines, and bighorn sheep and Rocky Mountain goats which are preyed on by the lynx.

The porcupine is a good tree climber.

Virginia creeper plant

AMERICAN WOODCOCK

This bird lives in forest areas in North America. Woodcocks probe in soft soil with their long bills searching for worms and grubs. They detect their prey partly by smell, and by using the sensitive tip of the bill.

PORCUPINE

The North American porcupine feeds on conifer needles and tree bark. In summer it spends more time on the ground, where it feeds on stems, flowers, seeds, and fruit. Porcupines have long spines on their backs for defence. Although they look like hedgehogs, the two animals are not related.

Find out more

DEER, ANTELOPES, and gazelles
EAGLES and other birds of prey
LIONS, TIGERS, and other big cats
LIZARDS
OWLS
RABBITS AND HARES

NUCLEAR AGE

IN 1945, THE FIRST atomic bombs were dropped on the Japanese cities of Hiroshima and Nagasaki. The years since 1945 have sometimes been called the nuclear age because the knowledge that nuclear bombs can destroy civilization has affected political decisions and attitudes towards war. The term nuclear age also describes the growth of nuclear energy. In 1953, U.S. President Eisenhower launched the Atoms for Peace campaign to develop nuclear power for peaceful uses, such as generating electricity. At first nuclear energy was welcomed; today many people believe that it is dangerous. The nuclear arms "race" between the United States and the then Soviet Union, which began in 1945, caused political tension for years. By the 1980s, the United States and the Soviet Union owned enough nuclear weapons to destroy every living thing on Earth. Many people wanted to rid the world of nuclear weapons, and in the late 1980s both superpowers began to disarm.

NUCLEAR FISSION
In 1939, the German scientists Fritz Strassman (left) and Otto Hahn discovered that energy could be created by splitting uranium atoms into two. This process, called nuclear fission, was later developed to produce the energy to create electricity and the explosion to make a nuclear bomb.

HIROSHIMA
On 6 August, 1945, an American warplane dropped an atomic bomb on the city of Hiroshima to force Japan to surrender in World War II. The city was destroyed, and about 130,000 people were killed. The people of Hiroshima commemorate the event every year in "Peace City", a place where the ruins have been left untouched in memory of those killed.

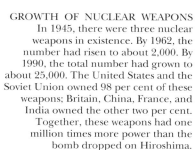

GROWTH OF NUCLEAR WEAPONS
In 1945, there were three nuclear weapons in existence. By 1962, the number had risen to about 2,000. By 1990, the total number had grown to about 25,000. The United States and the Soviet Union owned 98 per cent of these weapons; Britain, China, France, and India owned the other two per cent. Together, these weapons had one million times more power than the bomb dropped on Hiroshima.

1945: only three nuclear weapons exist.

1962: the number of nuclear weapons is in the thousands.

1990: the number of nuclear weapons is over 25,000.

NUCLEAR ENERGY
In 1954, the world's first nuclear power station opened in the Soviet Union. Today there are nearly 400 nuclear power stations producing 15 per cent of the world's energy. Above is a 1950s cooking demonstration: a woman cooks hamburgers by atomic power.

ANTI-NUCLEAR MOVEMENTS
Opposition to nuclear weapons began in the 1950s as people realized that nobody would survive a nuclear war. Throughout the world people adopted the peace symbol (left) as they demonstrated against nuclear weapons.

NUCLEAR DISARMAMENT
During the late 1980s, the United States and the former Soviet Union discussed nuclear disarmament. In 1987, U.S. President Reagan and Soviet Premier Gorbachev agreed to dismantle some intermediate-range nuclear weapons (left). In 1993, U.S. President Bush and Russian President Yeltsin signed a treaty agreeing to reduce their nuclear arsenals by two-thirds within ten years.

Find out more

NUCLEAR ENERGY
UNITED STATES OF AMERICA, history of
U.S.S.R., HISTORY OF
WORLD WAR II

NUCLEAR ENERGY

THE ATOMS THAT make up everything in the universe are the source of a huge amount of energy called nuclear energy. Nuclear energy produces the searing heat and light of the sun, the deadly explosions of nuclear weapons, and vast amounts of electricity in nuclear power stations. Nuclear energy is based on the fact that matter and energy are different forms of the same thing, and one can be converted into the other. In a nuclear reaction, a tiny amount of matter changes into an enormous amount of energy. The nuclear reaction occurs in the nuclei (centres) of atoms. This can happen in two ways: when the nucleus of a heavy atom splits, in a process called fission, and when two lightweight nuclei join together, in a process called fusion. In nuclear weapons, fission or fusion occurs in a split second. By contrast, nuclear power stations produce electricity from fission reactions that work at a controlled rate.

Experimental nuclear fusion reactor near Oxford, England

Hydrogen nucleus
Neutron
Hydrogen nucleus with extra neutrons
Helium nucleus

NUCLEAR FUSION
Scientists are trying to build reactors that use nuclear fusion, a process which produces less dangerous waste than nuclear fission (below). Nuclear fusion occurs when hydrogen atoms smash together and join to form heavier atoms of helium. However, nuclear fusion is extremely difficult to achieve. Hydrogen atoms must be squeezed by a magnetic field and held at a temperature higher than that in the sun's centre for fusion to occur.

Neutron hits nucleus of uranium atom.

Fission occurs, releasing energy and neutrons.

NUCLEAR FISSION
Nuclear power stations produce energy from the fission of atoms of uranium metal. The impact of a particle called a neutron makes an atom of uranium split. This releases heat energy and two or three neutrons. The neutrons strike other uranium atoms and make them divide. Soon many atoms begin to split, producing a huge amount of energy.

Reactor core contains pellets of uranium oxide fuel held in fuel rods. Two thimble-sized pellets would produce enough electricity for a person for one year.

Pump for high-pressure water system

Protective clothing worn when handling nuclear waste

If neutrons travel too rapidly, they bounce off uranium atoms without producing fission. The fuel is surrounded by water, which slows the neutrons down so they produce fission. A material that slows neutrons in a reactor is called a moderator.

Metal control rods absorb neutrons and slow down the nuclear reaction. In an emergency, the control rods drop into the reactor core and shut off the nuclear reaction.

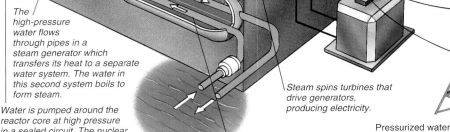

The high-pressure water flows through pipes in a steam generator which transfers its heat to a separate water system. The water in this second system boils to form steam.

Water is pumped around the reactor core at high pressure in a sealed circuit. The nuclear reactions heat the water to more than 300°C (570°F), but the high pressure keeps it from turning into steam.

Steam spins turbines that drive generators, producing electricity.

A third water circuit acts as a coolant, changing the steam back into water which returns to the steam generator once again.

Pressurized water reactor (PWR)

NUCLEAR RADIATION
Some waste from nuclear power stations is radioactive – it produces deadly nuclear radiation consisting of tiny particles or invisible waves that can damage living cells. Some radioactive waste may last for thousands of years, so it is buried underground in sealed containers. Many people are concerned about the dangers of nuclear waste and are demanding an end to nuclear energy production.

NUCLEAR POWER STATION
A fission reaction becomes continuous only if there is a certain amount of fuel present, called the critical mass. In a nuclear reactor, rods contain uranium fuel. The fuel rods are placed close together to provide the critical mass that starts the reaction.

Find out more

ATOMS AND MOLECULES
ENERGY
NUCLEAR AGE
PHYSICS
U.S.S.R., HISTORY OF
WEAPONS

OCEAN WILDLIFE

LIFE BEGAN IN THE OCEANS millions of years ago. Today, oceans cover 71 per cent of the planet's surface and provide homes for countless fish, octopuses, seals, sharks, and jellyfish. Ocean wildlife is at its richest in the warm shallow waters of coral reefs, where dazzlingly colourful angelfish and butterfly fish live. In deeper waters, whales, dolphins, and porpoises are found. Most plants and animals live close to the water's surface. Sunlight filters through the surface, allowing microscopic plants such as diatoms to flourish. An intricate web of small animals feeds on these microscopic organisms; larger sea creatures eat the smaller ones, and so on, up the food chain to the large predators such as sharks. Today, many marine plants and animals are threatened; we dump chemical wastes in the oceans, fertilizers flow into the oceans from rivers, and we catch so many fish that fish-eating sea mammals such as seals and dolphins have to compete with us for their food.

COELACANTH

The coelacanth is a survivor from prehistoric times, although scientists first discovered it in 1938. The coelacanth lives around the Comoro Islands, off southeast Africa, in water 70 to 400 m (230 to 1,300 ft) deep. Adult coelacanths measure about 1.7 m (5.5 ft) in length. Today this fish is threatened because of fish collectors and souvenir hunters.

Common squid

Finback whale

PLANKTON

Billions of tiny plants and animals float in sea water. Together they are called plankton, from the Greek word *planktos*, meaning "wanderer". Plankton are food for many fish and other sea creatures.

FINBACK WHALE

The finback whale is the second largest living animal (the blue whale is the largest) and is found from the Poles to the tropics. Finbacks grow to about 25 m (85 ft) in length and weigh 73 tonnes (71 tons). They feed by straining shrimplike creatures called krill from the water, using fringes of baleen hanging from the upper jaws.

SAND TIGER

Sharks are the most aggressive hunters in the ocean. The ferocious sand tiger shark hunts even before it is born, when it is still in its mother's womb. There are 10 to 15 embryo sharks in the womb, and as they develop, they eat each other until there are only two left. The two survivors are born fully formed, then swim away to begin their fish-eating lives, growing to 3.5 m (12 ft) in length.

OPEN OCEAN

Many animals in the open sea are streamlined (sleek in shape) so that they can swim away quickly from predators and chase after prey. There are fish of all shapes and sizes in the open ocean, as well as enormous schools of jellyfish, and mammals such as seals. Sea birds such as albatrosses, petrels, and shearwaters feed at the surface.

HERRING

There were once vast shoals of herring in the oceans; they were an easy catch for fishing boats, and people valued them for their tasty flesh. Today herring is much less common because people have overfished the oceans. Herring feed on plankton.

SARDINE

Pacific sardines are related to herrings. Other members of the herring family are the sprat and the shad. All of them are hunted by bigger ocean dwellers such as seals.

SWORDFISH

This spear-nosed hunter is one of the fastest fish in the sea; it can swim in bursts at speeds of 95 km/h (60 mph). The swordfish resembles the marlin and sailfish, and weighs up to 675 kg (1,500 lb). Swordfish injure their prey with side-to-side slashes of the sword, and then devour them.

Swordfish

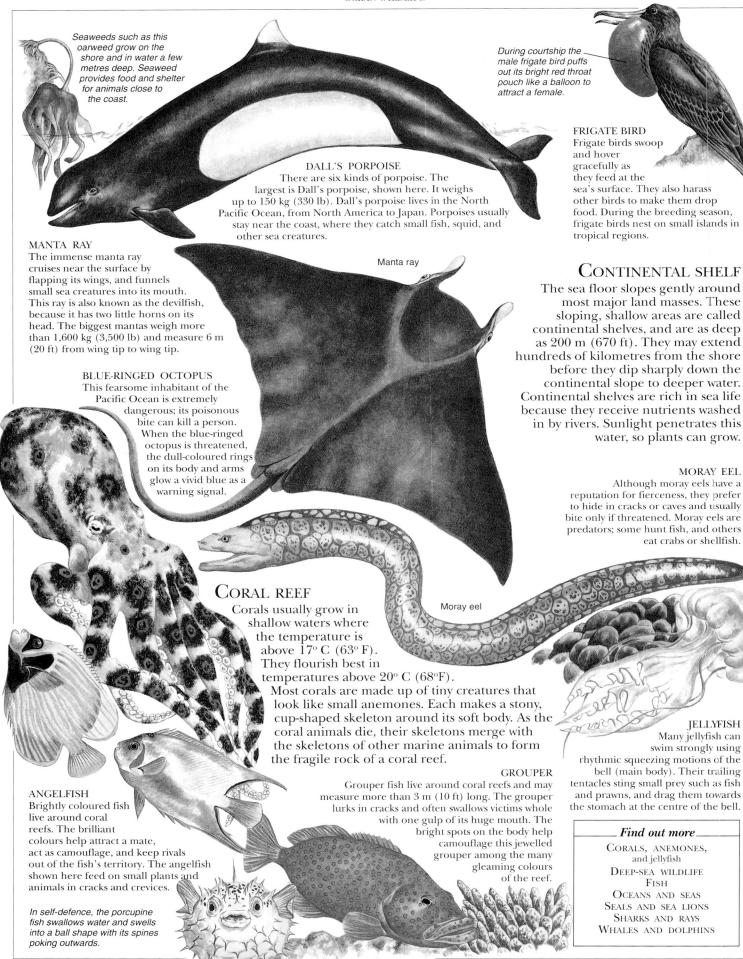

Seaweeds such as this oarweed grow on the shore and in water a few metres deep. Seaweed provides food and shelter for animals close to the coast.

During courtship the male frigate bird puffs out its bright red throat pouch like a balloon to attract a female.

FRIGATE BIRD
Frigate birds swoop and hover gracefully as they feed at the sea's surface. They also harass other birds to make them drop food. During the breeding season, frigate birds nest on small islands in tropical regions.

DALL'S PORPOISE
There are six kinds of porpoise. The largest is Dall's porpoise, shown here. It weighs up to 150 kg (330 lb). Dall's porpoise lives in the North Pacific Ocean, from North America to Japan. Porpoises usually stay near the coast, where they catch small fish, squid, and other sea creatures.

Manta ray

MANTA RAY
The immense manta ray cruises near the surface by flapping its wings, and funnels small sea creatures into its mouth. This ray is also known as the devilfish, because it has two little horns on its head. The biggest mantas weigh more than 1,600 kg (3,500 lb) and measure 6 m (20 ft) from wing tip to wing tip.

CONTINENTAL SHELF
The sea floor slopes gently around most major land masses. These sloping, shallow areas are called continental shelves, and are as deep as 200 m (670 ft). They may extend hundreds of kilometres from the shore before they dip sharply down the continental slope to deeper water. Continental shelves are rich in sea life because they receive nutrients washed in by rivers. Sunlight penetrates this water, so plants can grow.

BLUE-RINGED OCTOPUS
This fearsome inhabitant of the Pacific Ocean is extremely dangerous; its poisonous bite can kill a person. When the blue-ringed octopus is threatened, the dull-coloured rings on its body and arms glow a vivid blue as a warning signal.

MORAY EEL
Although moray eels have a reputation for fierceness, they prefer to hide in cracks or caves and usually bite only if threatened. Moray eels are predators; some hunt fish, and others eat crabs or shellfish.

CORAL REEF
Corals usually grow in shallow waters where the temperature is above 17° C (63° F). They flourish best in temperatures above 20° C (68°F).

Most corals are made up of tiny creatures that look like small anemones. Each makes a stony, cup-shaped skeleton around its soft body. As the coral animals die, their skeletons merge with the skeletons of other marine animals to form the fragile rock of a coral reef.

Moray eel

JELLYFISH
Many jellyfish can swim strongly using rhythmic squeezing motions of the bell (main body). Their trailing tentacles sting small prey such as fish and prawns, and drag them towards the stomach at the centre of the bell.

GROUPER
Grouper fish live around coral reefs and may measure more than 3 m (10 ft) long. The grouper lurks in cracks and often swallows victims whole with one gulp of its huge mouth. The bright spots on the body help camouflage this jewelled grouper among the many gleaming colours of the reef.

ANGELFISH
Brightly coloured fish live around coral reefs. The brilliant colours help attract a mate, act as camouflage, and keep rivals out of the fish's territory. The angelfish shown here feed on small plants and animals in cracks and crevices.

In self-defence, the porcupine fish swallows water and swells into a ball shape with its spines poking outwards.

Find out more

CORALS, ANEMONES, and jellyfish
DEEP-SEA WILDLIFE
FISH
OCEANS AND SEAS
SEALS AND SEA LIONS
SHARKS AND RAYS
WHALES AND DOLPHINS

OCEANS AND SEAS

YOUR FEET MAY BE RESTING firmly on the ground. But more than two thirds of our planet is covered with water. Oceans and seas make up 71 per cent of the Earth's surface. They influence the climate, supply us with food, power, and valuable minerals, and provide a home for a fascinating range of plant and animal life.

The oceans and seas began millions of years ago when the Earth cooled from its original molten state. Water vapour escaped from inside the Earth in volcanic eruptions, cooled, and fell as rain. It filled vast hollows and basins surrounding rocky land masses. These gradually moved around to form the continents and oceans as they exist today. As rivers formed on the land and flowed into the seas, they dissolved minerals from the rocks, making the oceans and seas salty.

OCEAN HUNTERS
Fishing boats sail the oceans and seas to bring us the fish and other sea creatures that we eat. The best fishing grounds are in shallow seas, where the water teems with fish. But catches must be controlled; otherwise the numbers of fish will fall as the fish fail to breed.

TIDES

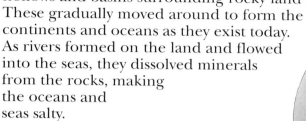

Sun · Moon · Earth · Rise in water level

SPRING TIDES
High, spring tides occur when the Earth, sun, and moon are in line.

Twice a day the level of the seas rises and falls. These changes in level are called tides. They are caused mainly by the pull of the moon's gravity on the Earth. When the moon lies directly over the ocean, its gravity pulls the water towards it. Water also rises on the opposite side of the Earth, because the Earth itself is pulled towards the moon.

THE WORLD'S OCEANS AND SEAS
Oceans are vast bodies of water, usually separating the continents. The Pacific Ocean, which is the largest and deepest, lies between America and Asia and covers more than a third of the globe. The others, in order of size, are the Atlantic, Indian, and Arctic oceans. The Arctic Ocean lies between the land masses around the North Pole and is largely covered by ice. Seas, bays, and gulfs are smaller bodies of water that lie between arms of land, or between islands and land masses. Some, such as the Caspian and Dead seas, are entirely surrounded by land and are really not seas but large lakes.

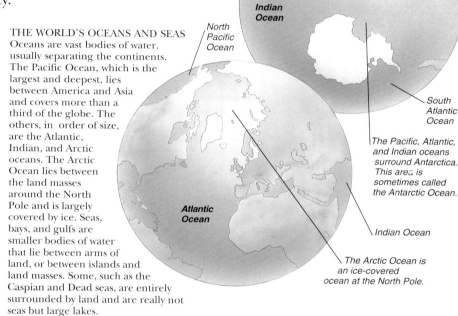

Pacific Ocean

Indian Ocean

North Pacific Ocean

South Atlantic Ocean

The Pacific, Atlantic, and Indian oceans surround Antarctica. This area is sometimes called the Antarctic Ocean.

Indian Ocean

Atlantic Ocean

The Arctic Ocean is an ice-covered ocean at the North Pole.

OCEAN CURRENTS

The water in the oceans is constantly moving in great circular streams, or currents, which can flow about as fast as you walk. Winds blow the surface layer of the oceans to form these currents, which carry warm or cold water along the shores of continents, greatly affecting the weather there. Sometimes currents flow deep below the surface, moving in the opposite direction to surface currents. For example, surface currents carry warm water away from the equator, while currents deep beneath the sea bring cold water back to the equator. Most seas have strong currents. But the waters of the Sargasso Sea, which lies in the North Atlantic Ocean, are almost still, causing the sea to become choked with seaweed.

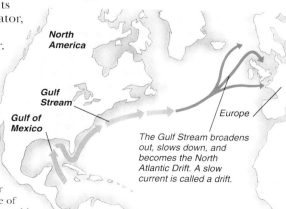

North America

Gulf Stream

Gulf of Mexico

Europe

The Gulf Stream broadens out, slows down, and becomes the North Atlantic Drift. A slow current is called a drift.

THE KON TIKI EXPEDITION
Early peoples may have used the currents to travel across oceans. In 1947 the Kon Tiki expedition, led by Norwegian explorer Thor Heyerdahl, tested this theory by sailing a light wooden raft from Peru to the Polynesian Islands.

GULF STREAM
Water heated by the sun flows out from the Gulf of Mexico. This warm current crosses the Atlantic Ocean and flows around the shores of western Europe. There the winter weather is mild, while places on the other side of the ocean away from the current are freezing cold.

Long, wide ocean ridges run through most oceans.

Undersea mountains rise from the sea bed.

Long, deep trenches lie near the edges of some oceans.

UNDER THE OCEANS

A strange landscape lies hidden beneath the oceans. There are huge cliffs, great ranges of mountains, and deep chasms, all far larger than any on land. Much of the ocean floor is a vast flat plain which lies up to 6 km (4 miles) below the surface. Trenches descend as deep as 11 km (7 miles), more than the height of the highest mountain on land. Undersea mountains and volcanoes rise from the plain, many poking their summits above the waves to form islands. The seas around the shores of most continents are not very deep. Most offshore islands are high land rising from the shallow sea bed. Coral reefs and atolls grow up from the sea bed in warm seas.

Some volcanoes rise up from the deep ocean floor to form islands.

Many continents extend out into the ocean and have a wide undersea continental shelf which is about 130 m (400 ft) deep.

Large offshore islands rise from the ocean floor or continental shelf.

The continental shelf ends in a cliff called the continental slope.

OCEANOGRAPHY

Our knowledge of the oceans comes from oceanographers, who study the oceans. They sail in special ships with instruments that take samples of the water and mud on the sea bed, chart ocean currents, and map the ridges and trenches in the ocean floor. The scientists also dive in submersibles and use underwater robots to see the strange creatures that live in the depths. Satellites look down from space and send back information about the oceans.

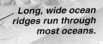

WAVES

The surface of the sea is restless, even on the calmest day. Waves ceaselessly rise and fall, eventually reaching the land to lap or crash on the shore. Waves are caused by winds blowing over the ocean. The energy from waves can be used to power generators and produce electricity. However, tsunamis (wrongly called tidal waves) are very destructive. They are caused by earthquakes and volcanic eruptions and are very powerful.

SHORES AND COASTS

High land at the shore ends in cliffs, and low land slopes gently to form beaches. The waves hurl stones at the base of cliffs, causing rocks to fall and forming coasts with bays and headlands. Strange rock formations and caves may result. The waves batter the rocks and break them up into pebbles and then into sand. Beaches form at the base of cliffs, and the sea also sweeps pebbles and sand along the shore to form beaches elsewhere.

Water reaches base of circle in trough of wave.

Water reaches top of circle in crest of wave.

Crest topples over to break on shore.

HOW WAVES MOVE

The water in a wave does not move forwards. It moves in a circle, so the water only goes up and down as a wave passes. The approaching shore holds back the base of the wave, making the top of the wave move faster to break on the shore.

Find out more

CONTINENTS
DEEP-SEA WILDLIFE
EARTHQUAKES
FISHING INDUSTRY
OCEAN WILDLIFE
SEASHORE WILDLIFE

OCTOPUSES AND SQUID

SEA CREATURES SUCH AS THE OCTOPUS and squid have always held a strange fascination for humans. With their powerful tentacles and strange shape, they were once thought of as sea monsters. Octopuses and squid are clever, active creatures, the biggest and most intelligent of all the invertebrates (animals without backbones). They have sharp eyesight, a large brain, fast reactions, and the ability to remember. Octopuses, squid, and their relatives the cuttlefish are molluscs, related to shelled animals with soft bodies such as snails and clams. Unlike snails and clams, octopuses, squid, and cuttlefish have no outer shells, though squid have a very thin shell called a pen inside the body. The white oval cuttlebones of cuttlefish are often seen washed up on beaches. An octopus has eight "arms" covered with suckers which it uses for moving around. Squid and cuttlefish have eight short "arms" and two long tentacles which curl and uncurl. They use their arms as rudders for swimming and their tentacles for catching prey.

Some large octopuses measure 9 m (30 ft) across with their "arms" spread out. However, stories of giant octopuses that swallow divers whole are untrue.

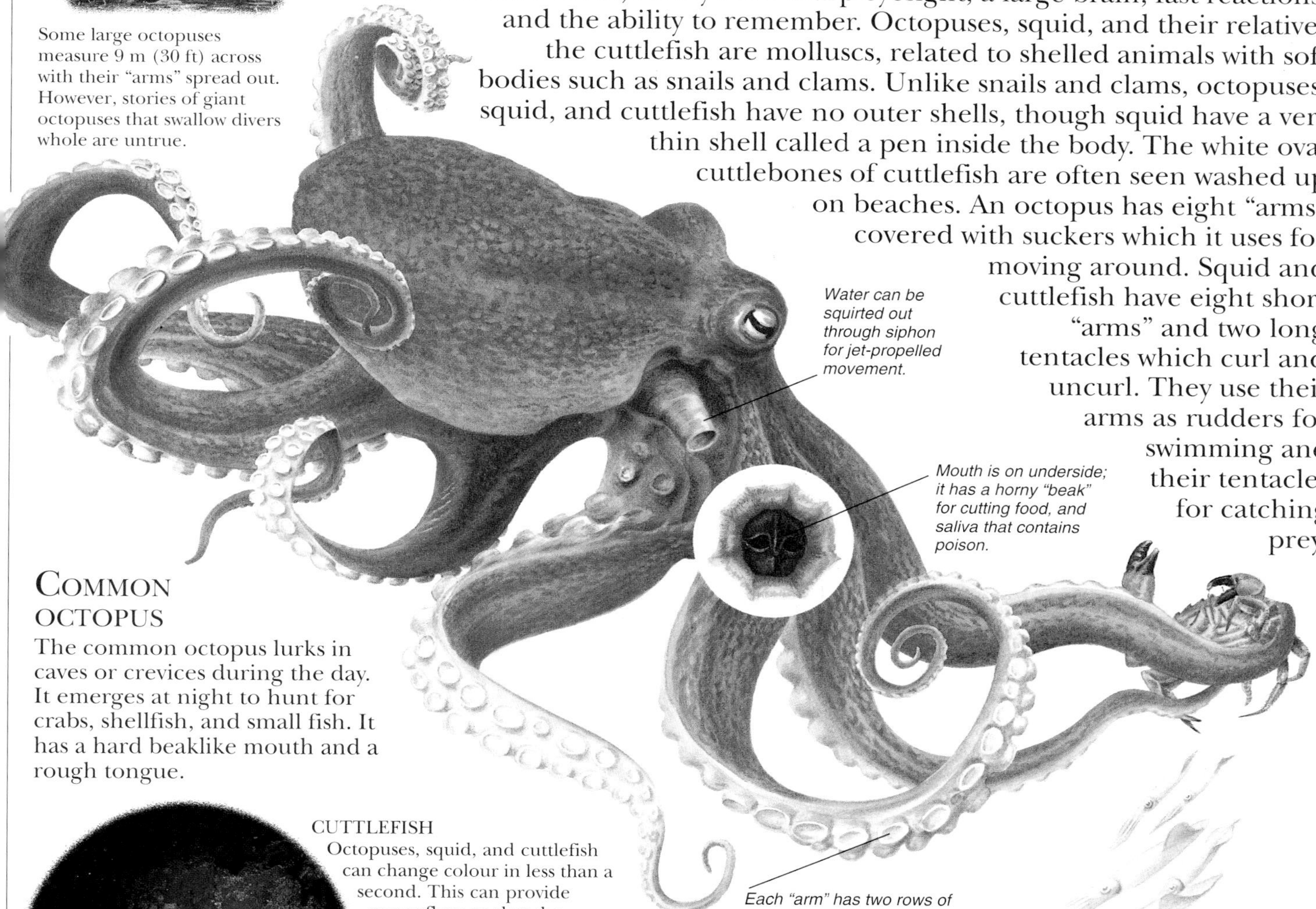

Water can be squirted out through siphon for jet-propelled movement.

Mouth is on underside; it has a horny "beak" for cutting food, and saliva that contains poison.

COMMON OCTOPUS

The common octopus lurks in caves or crevices during the day. It emerges at night to hunt for crabs, shellfish, and small fish. It has a hard beaklike mouth and a rough tongue.

CUTTLEFISH

Octopuses, squid, and cuttlefish can change colour in less than a second. This can provide camouflage so that the creature blends in with the surroundings. It may also indicate a change of mood – a male cuttlefish turns black with rage when it is angry. The dappled red colouring of the cuttlefish shown here is a good disguise among the coral.

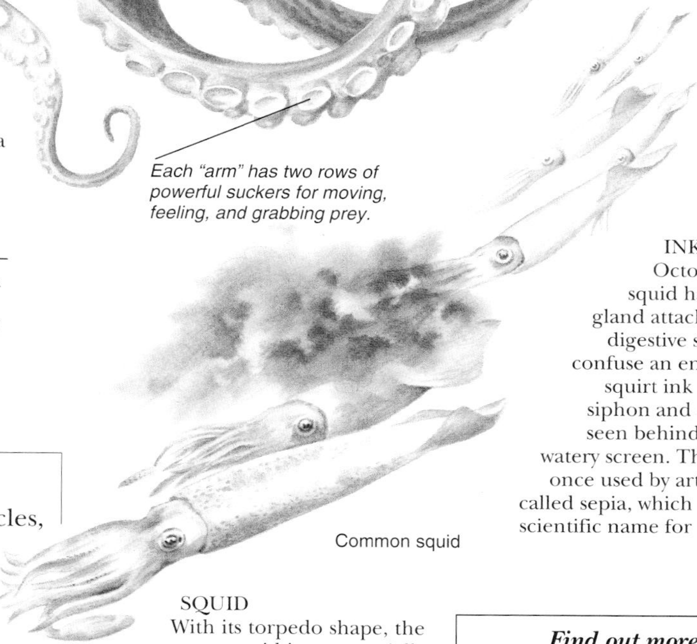

Each "arm" has two rows of powerful suckers for moving, feeling, and grabbing prey.

INK CLOUD

Octopuses and squid have an ink gland attached to the digestive system. To confuse an enemy, they squirt ink out of the siphon and cannot be seen behind the dark, watery screen. This ink was once used by artists and is called sepia, which is also the scientific name for cuttlefish.

Common squid

GIANT SQUID

Measuring 20 m (60 ft) in length including its tentacles, the giant squid is the world's largest invertebrate. It is an important source of food for sperm whales.

SQUID

With its torpedo shape, the common squid is an especially fast swimmer. Powerful muscles inside the body squirt water rapidly through the siphon, pushing the creature along through the water.

Find out more

ANIMALS
DEEP-SEA WILDLIFE
OCEAN WILDLIFE

OIL

WITHOUT OIL, modern life would grind to a halt. Oil is needed to make the fuels that drive cars, lorries, diesel trains, ships, and aircraft. Power stations burn oil to produce much of the world's electricity, and many homes use oil-burning boilers for heating. Oil is also very important because it is needed to make plastics, textiles, and other useful products. Oil is a dark, thick liquid which lies deep underground and beneath the sea bed. Oil wells are bored to obtain oil, which is also called crude oil or petroleum. Crude oil contains a mixture of chemicals and many different types of oil. Lubricating oil is made from crude oil. It helps machine parts slide easily so that the machine works well.

OIL REFINERY
The crude oil that comes from a deposit is a mixture of chemicals and many kinds of oil. Crude oil is taken to an oil refinery, where it is heated. This makes the oil break down, or separate, into petrol and other fuels, lubricating oils, chemicals, and bitumen for making roads.

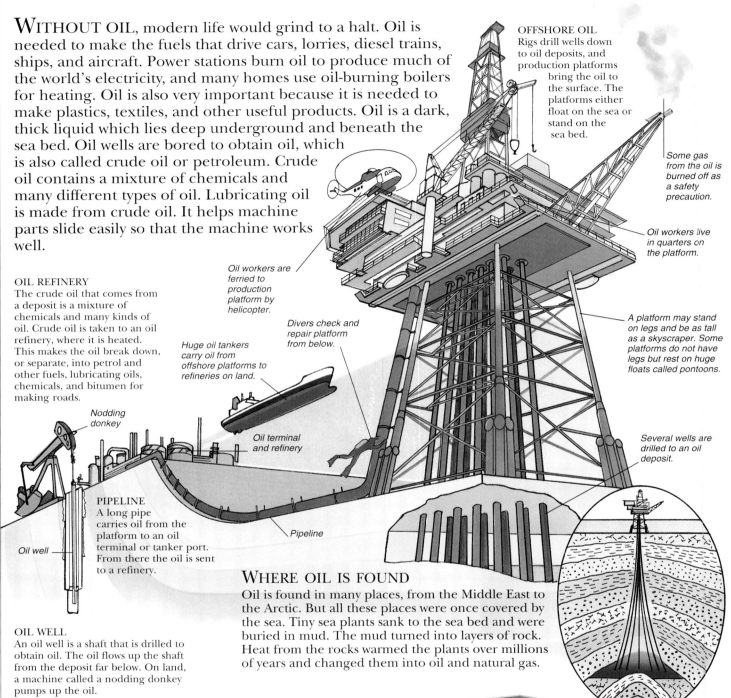

OFFSHORE OIL
Rigs drill wells down to oil deposits, and production platforms bring the oil to the surface. The platforms either float on the sea or stand on the sea bed.

Some gas from the oil is burned off as a safety precaution.

Oil workers live in quarters on the platform.

A platform may stand on legs and be as tall as a skyscraper. Some platforms do not have legs but rest on huge floats called pontoons.

Oil workers are ferried to production platform by helicopter.

Divers check and repair platform from below.

Huge oil tankers carry oil from offshore platforms to refineries on land.

Oil terminal and refinery

Several wells are drilled to an oil deposit.

Nodding donkey

PIPELINE
A long pipe carries oil from the platform to an oil terminal or tanker port. From there the oil is sent to a refinery.

Oil well

Pipeline

OIL WELL
An oil well is a shaft that is drilled to obtain oil. The oil flows up the shaft from the deposit far below. On land, a machine called a nodding donkey pumps up the oil.

WHERE OIL IS FOUND
Oil is found in many places, from the Middle East to the Arctic. But all these places were once covered by the sea. Tiny sea plants sank to the sea bed and were buried in mud. The mud turned into layers of rock. Heat from the rocks warmed the plants over millions of years and changed them into oil and natural gas.

VEGETABLE OILS
Plants and vegetables, such as olives, peanuts, sunflowers, and corn, provide valuable oils. Olive oil is made by crushing ripe olives; sunflower oil comes from sunflower seeds. These oils are used in cooking, and sunflower oil is used to make margarine. Factories treat plant and vegetable oils to make other products, such as soap and paints.

Olive oil

Olives

CHEMICALS FROM OIL
An oil refinery produces many chemicals from crude oil, which are called petro-chemicals. Factories use these chemicals to make plastics, textiles, and other products. Polythene, for example, is made from a gas that comes from oil. Chemicals from oil are also used to make drugs, fertilizers, detergents, and dyes and paints in all colours.

PETROL
Petrol is one of the most important of all oil products. Diesel fuel is another kind of motor fuel made from oil.

Find out more
GAS
GEOLOGY
PLASTICS
ROCKS AND MINERALS
TEXTILES

OLYMPIC GAMES

EVERY TWO YEARS, the world's best athletes compete in the Summer or Winter Olympics. About 10,000 athletes from nearly 200 nations take part in the Summer Olympics, in more than 25 sports. The Winter Games are smaller, with 1,800 athletes from nearly 70 countries competing in seven sports.

Five interlocking rings make up the Olympic symbol.

The inspiration for today's Olympics came from Ancient Greek games of more than 2,000 years ago. The modern Olympics began in Athens, Greece, in 1896. Individual excellence and team achievement are the theme of the Olympic Games, not competition between nations. So the International Olympic Committee (IOC) chooses a city, not a country, to host the games. No one country "wins" the games, and there is no prize money. Instead, individuals and teams compete for gold medals (first place), silver (second), and bronze (third) – and for the glory of taking part.

ANCIENT GAMES
The ancient Olympics began as a religious festival. At first they consisted of just one race, but at their height the games lasted five days and included sports such as wrestling and chariot racing. Only men could compete in or watch the ancient Olympics. Women held their own games in honour of the goddess Hera.

The opening ceremony for the Olympics is a spectacular occasion.

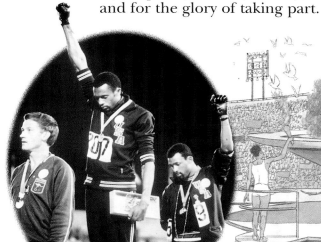
The black power salute

The Olympic Flame burns high above the stadium.

POLITICS AND THE GAMES
The huge international audience for the Olympics ensures that political protests and terrorist acts there gain maximum publicity. In 1968, winning athletes raised clenched fists to show that they supported a campaign to give black people more power. Four years later Palestinian terrorists caused the deaths of 11 Israeli athletes at Munich, Germany.

OLYMPIC TORCH
The Olympic Games open with a spectacular ceremony. The most important part is the lighting of the Olympic Flame from a burning torch. Teams of runners carry the torch from Olympia, in Greece, site of the ancient games, to the stadium where the games are to be held. This ceremony dates back to 1928, when Baron Pierre de Coubertin, founder of the modern Olympics, urged the athletes to "keep alive the flame of the revived Olympic spirit".

Ski jumping, shown here, is one of the most exciting events in the Winter Olympics.

WINTER OLYMPICS
A separate Winter Games takes place every four years, midway between the Oympics. It includes ice and snow sports such as skating and skiing.

The Games include a variety of team and individual sports. New ones are added, and old ones are sometimes dropped.

Javelin Field Hockey Running Canoeing Archery

Find out more
BALL GAMES
GREECE, ANCIENT
SPORTS
TRACK AND FIELD SPORTS

OPERA AND SINGING

THE HUMAN VOICE is a versatile musical instrument that has inspired many composers to write beautiful solo songs and works for groups of singers, or choirs, as well. Every voice is unique. Some women have a high soprano voice; others a deep, rich contralto. The male voice can range from a very high countertenor to a low bass. There are also variations in between. In the Middle Ages monks sang as part of their religious life, and wandering troubadours sang poetic songs of bravery and love. In the 17th century a new form of sung drama called opera began in Italy. New musical forms required trained voices, and by the 18th century great professional singers were delighting audiences everywhere. Today, singers perform all kinds of historical music, but constantly explore new ways of using their voices.

SYDNEY OPERA HOUSE
This striking opera house overlooking Sydney Harbour in Australia caused much debate when it opened in 1973. It was designed to match the shape of ships in the harbour. Hanging ceilings beneath the roofs create the right acoustics.

FAMOUS SINGERS

The greatest opera singers are those who can touch the emotions of their audience. Some, like Nellie Melba, moved people with the beauty of their voices. Maria Callas brought characters such as Aida and Tosca to life through superb acting as well as singing. Singers such as Kiri Te Kanawa and Placido Domingo sing popular songs as well as opera.

Maria Callas

GRAND OPERA

In grand opera every word is sung. Most of the main characters have an opportunity to show off their voices by singing arias, or solos. Some arias, such as "One fine day" from Puccini's *Madame Butterfly*, are very well known. Operas composed by Puccini, Verdi, Wagner, and Mozart also include fine music for the chorus, a group of opera singers who are not featured in solos.

MUSICALS

Musical comedies first became popular in the United States at the beginning of this century. Like opera, they have solos and a chorus, but the stories are mostly spoken. Spectacular dance routines are an important ingredient in musicals such as composer and conductor Leonard Bernstein's *West Side Story*. Many successful musicals are later made into films.

WORK SONGS

In the days before steam was used to power ships, special songs called sea chanties or shanties were a popular accompaniment to heavy work. Singing them helped the sailors keep a steady, repetitive rhythm as they hauled on ropes to lift a sail or raise the anchor.

FIDDLER ON THE ROOF
Popular musicals can turn performers into stars. Topol (above) found fame in *Fiddler on the Roof*, directed by choreographer Jerome Robbins.

Find out more
COMPOSERS
MUSIC
ORCHESTRAS
THEATRE

ORCHESTRAS

THE THRILLING SOUND made by an orchestra is no accident. An orchestra is not just a random collection of instruments brought along by the musicians; it is a carefully planned group of different families or types of instruments. Each family has its own part to play in the performance of a piece of music. The symphony orchestra is the largest group of musicians who perform together. They play four main sections of instruments: strings, woodwinds, brass, and percussion. Orchestra in the past were not so well organized, and for a long time musicians simply played whatever instruments they owned. But in the 18th century composers wanted to make sure that their music would sound the same whenever it was played. So they wrote on the piece of music which instruments of the orchestra should play each part of the tune. By the early 20th century the form of the symphony orchestra was established, and many large cities in Russia, the United States, and Europe had their own symphony orchestras.

GAMELAN
Indonesian orchestras are called gamelans. Most of the instruments belong to the percussion family: gongs, metallophones, xylophones, and gong-chimes. Flutes, two-stringfiddles, and zithers complete the gamelan, which has about 30 players.

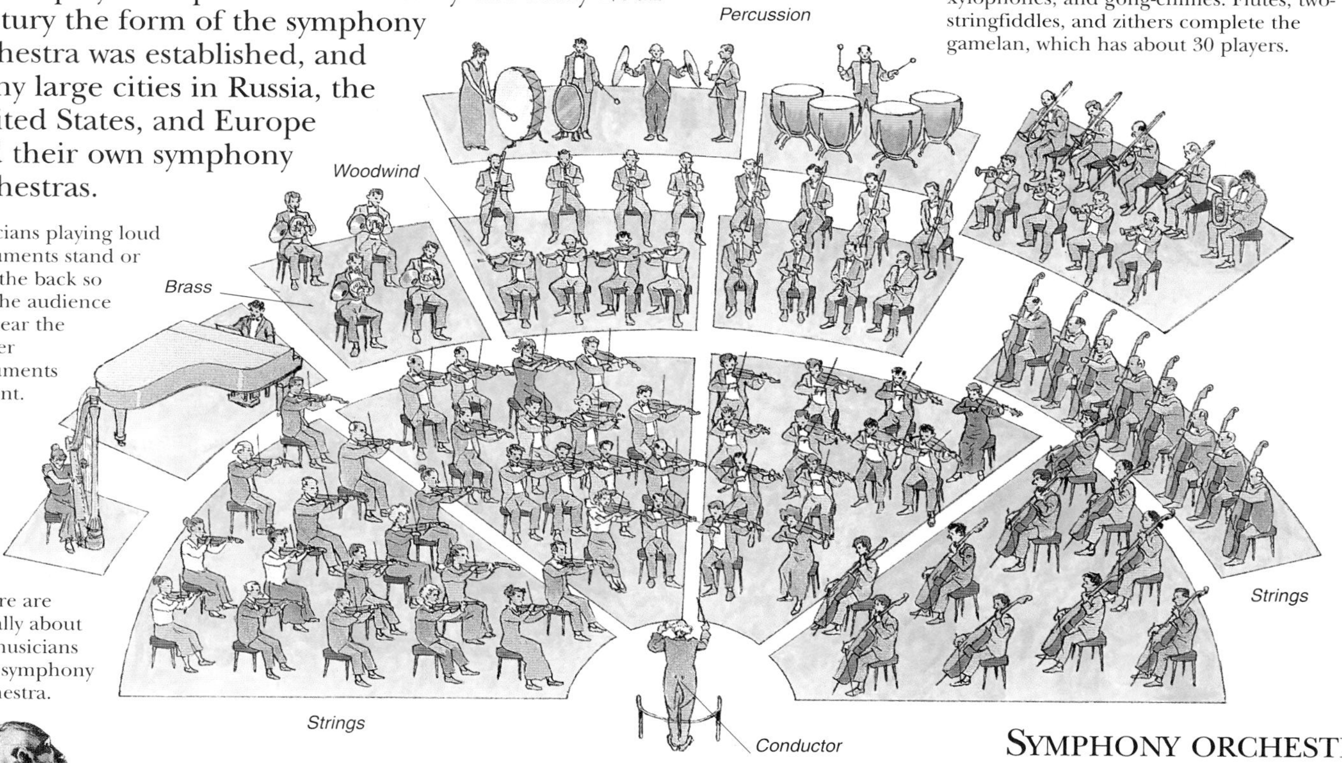

Musicians playing loud instruments stand or sit at the back so that the audience can hear the quieter instruments in front.

Percussion

Woodwind

Brass

Strings

There are usually about 90 musicians in a symphony orchestra.

Strings

Conductor

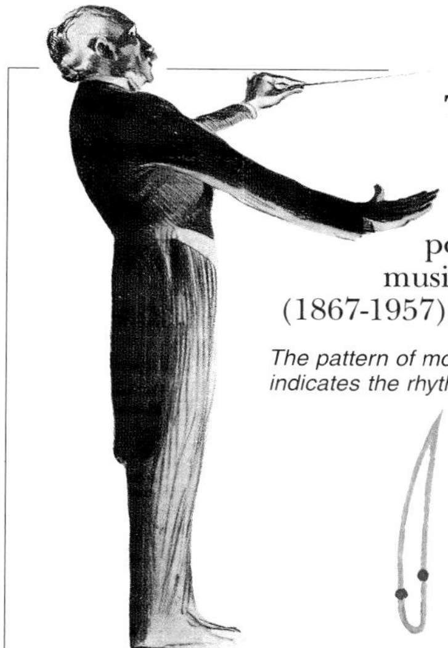

THE CONDUCTOR
The conductor uses hand motions or a baton – a small stick – to give the orchestra the tempo, or speed, of the music. Conductors don't just direct the orchestra like a police officer directing traffic; they interpret the composer's music, so that each performance is special. Arturo Toscanini (1867-1957), shown here, was an exciting conductor.

The pattern of movement of the conductor's baton indicates the rhythm of the music to the orchestra.

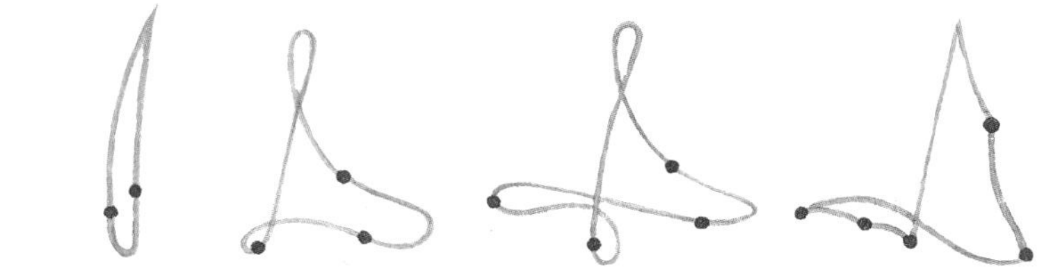

2 beats in a bar   3 beats in a bar   4 beats in a bar   5 beats in a bar

SYMPHONY ORCHESTRA
Great composers such as Wolfgang Amadeus Mozart (Austria) and Ludwig van Beethoven (Germany) wrote major pieces of orchestral music called symphonies. Symphony orchestras take their name from this sort of music, but they also play other kinds of classical music and music for films, television, and pop songs.

> ### *Find out more*
> COMPOSERS
> MUSIC
> MUSICAL INSTRUMENTS
> OPERA AND SINGING

OSTRICHES AND EMUS

THERE ARE MANY kinds of birds that cannot fly, including ostriches and emus, and most of these birds are large. Ostriches are the biggest of all living birds, at more than 2.5 m (8 ft) high. They live in the dry grassland areas of Africa, and their feathers are soft and fluffy because they are not needed for flying. Ostrich eggs are the biggest of any living bird. The egg shells are only 3 mm (⅛ in) thick but very hard. Ostriches and emus are speedy runners on land, and emus also swim well. The emu is a well-known pest to farmers in Australia, where it tramples on wheat fields. Other flightless birds include the secretive cassowary, which lives in the dense forests of Australasia, and the kiwi, which is found only in New Zealand. Kiwis are about 30 cm (1 ft) high, with tiny, useless wings. The rhea, a fast- running flightless bird, lives in the grassland areas of Brazil and Argentina, in South America. Rheas gather in large flocks in winter.

BIGGEST EGG
An ostrich egg is 20 cm (8 in) long and 30 times heavier than a hen's egg. This makes ostrich eggs the largest bird's eggs in the world.

Male ostrich spreads out wings to defend chick against predator.

Female ostrich guards chicks.

YOUNG
Both ostriches guard the chicks, but the male usually looks after the eggs until they hatch. Within a month of hatching, the young ostrich chicks can run fast and feed themselves. Adult ostriches have strong, powerful legs and large, flexible feet for running quickly.

Newly hatched ostrich young have speckled necks at first.

FASTEST BIRD ON LAND
The ostrich runs faster than any other bird and faster than most animals. It can run at 50 km/h (30 mph) for several minutes and may reach 70 km/h (45 mph) in short bursts.

EMU
The Australian emu grows to 2 m (6 ft) tall, which makes it the second-largest living bird. Emus eat a varied diet of seeds, leaves, fruit, shoots, and insects. The female lays up to 15 green eggs in a shallow nest on the ground. The newly hatched young are striped and stay with their parents for the first 18 months.

RHEA
The male rhea makes a shallow nest called a scrape which can contain up to 60 eggs. This Darwin's rhea is about 1 m (3 ft) tall.

CASSOWARY
Three different kinds of cassowary live in Australasia, wandering the dense, dark forests in search of fruits and seeds. The female common cassowary usually lays about five bright green eggs in a shallow nest lined with leaves. The male cassowary sits on the eggs to keep them warm and stays with the chicks after they hatch for up to one year.

Find out more

AUSTRALIAN WILDLIFE
BIRDS
GRASSLAND WILDLIFE

OTTOMAN EMPIRE

DURING THE LATE 13th century, a group of nomadic Turkish tribes settled in Anatolia, in modern Turkey. They were led by Osman, their first sultan, or ruler. He gave his name to the Ottoman Empire – one of the greatest empires in the world. By 1566, the empire had spread along the Mediterranean Sea across the Middle East to the Persian Gulf. The Ottomans owed their success to their military skill. Their armies included many Christian recruits organized into groups of highly trained foot soldiers called Janissaries. The empire grew wealthy on the trade it controlled throughout the Middle East. Art and architecture flourished within its borders. Discontent with Ottoman rule eventually weakened the empire, and it declined during the 19th century before it finally collapsed in 1918. The country of Turkey emerged out of its ruins.

Ottoman Empire at its greatest extent

SULEIMAN THE MAGNIFICENT
The greatest of all Ottoman sultans was Suleiman I (1495-1566), known as Suleiman the Magnificent. During his reign the Ottoman Empire reached the height of its power. A patron of the arts, Suleiman reformed the educational and legal systems.

Public letter writers wrote letters for people.

Janissaries could be recognized by their elaborate headdresses

THE OTTOMANS
Although the Ottomans were Muslims, they allowed Christians and Jews to practise their own religions and tolerated the many different peoples who lived within their empire. The sultans lived in great luxury and wealth and encouraged the arts and learning. Ottoman women had to live in a separate section of the household called a harem.

OTTOMAN EMPIRE

1281-1324 Osman founds Ottoman Empire.

1333 Ottomans capture Gallipoli, Turkey, giving them a foothold in Europe.

1453 Ottomans capture city of Constantinople (now Istanbul), the capital of the Byzantine Empire; the city becomes the capital of the new empire.

1566 Ottoman Empire reaches its greatest extent.

1571 Christian navy destroys Turkish fleet at Lepanto.

1697-1878 Russia slowly expels the Turks from the lands around the Black Sea.

1878-1913 Turks expelled from most of their European possessions.

1914-18 Ottoman Empire fights with Germany and Austria in World War I.

1918 Troops of several allied nations including Britain and Greece occupy the Ottoman Empire.

1922 Last sultan is overthrown. Turkey is declared a republic.

BATTLE OF LEPANTO
To stop the growth of Ottoman power, Pope Pius V formed a Christian league that included Spain, Venice, Genoa, and Naples. In 1571 the Christian forces defeated the Turks at the Battle of Lepanto, off the coast of Greece. The defeat was the first major setback to the Ottoman Empire and ended Turkish naval power in the Mediterranean Sea.

SICK MAN OF EUROPE
During the 19th century, the Ottoman Empire lost its grip on its European possessions and was in danger of falling apart. The empire became known as the "Sick Man of Europe".

A CONSULTATION ABOUT THE STATE OF TURKEY.

Find out more
BYZANTINE EMPIRE
ISLAM

OUTLAWS AND BANDITS

PEOPLE WHO LIVE outside the law are called outlaws or bandits. They do not just break one or two laws: their whole way of life is illegal, or against the law. Some outlaws and bandits are criminals who hope to get rich by stealing. Many of the famous bandits of the Wild West lived like this. It was easy for them to avoid getting caught, because there were so few people to enforce the law.

But other outlaws are "social bandits". They are outlaws because they try to change and improve society. Many countries have laws that benefit rich and powerful people and punish the poor and weak. These are the laws that social bandits break. Social bandits often escape capture for many years because lots of ordinary people support them. From their supporters the bandits can get food and shelter. There have been social bandits in most countries of the world at one time in their history. Some have become legendary figures, and people still tell stories of their daring deeds.

REWARD
($5,000.00)
Reward for the capture, dead or alive, of one Wm. Wright, better known as
"BILLY THE KID"
Age, 18. Height, 5 feet, 3 inches. Weight, 125 lbs. Light hair, blue eyes and even features. He is the leader of the worst band of desperadoes the Territory has ever had to deal with. The above reward will be paid for his capture or positive proof of his death.
JIM DALTON, Sheriff.
DEAD OR ALIVE!
"BILLY THE KID"

REWARDS
Rewards encouraged people to tell lawmen or police where outlaws were hiding. If there was a reward for the capture of an outlaw, he was said to have "a price on his head". Rewards were printed on posters such as the one above.

NED KELLY
Australian outlaw Ned Kelly (1855-1880) was the son of a convict who had been sent to Tasmania as punishment for crimes in Ireland. He took up crime, and soon the British-led police were on his trail. Kelly and his gang became outlaws after they shot three policemen in 1878. Local people hid them, but the police trapped the gang in a hotel in 1880. Protected by homemade armour, Ned (left) tried to shoot his way out. The police caught him, and he was executed.

ROBIN HOOD

One of the most famous outlaws was Robin Hood. People believe he lived in England around 1300. He and his band of followers, or "merry men", hid in Sherwood Forest, close to Nottingham. They defended the peasants from the unjust rule of the landowners. Robin Hood robbed rich people so that he could give their money and possessions to the poor.

BELLE STARR
One of the handful of female outlaws was Belle Starr. She was the partner of several male outlaws and shared their lives of crime. In 1880, she and a Cherokee Indian named Sam Starr had a large ranch in Oklahoma. It became a hideout for outlaws. An unknown killer shot Belle Starr in 1889.

HIGHWAYMEN

In 18th-century England, bandits were called highwaymen. They stopped stagecoaches on lonely roads and robbed the wealthy travellers inside. The most famous of the highwaymen was Dick Turpin (1705-39). He robbed coaches on the busy roads to the northeast of London. He had a reputation for generosity and for giving away the valuables that he stole.

Find out more
AUSTRALIA, HISTORY OF
MYTHS AND LEGENDS
PIRATES
WILD WEST

OWLS

MOST OWLS HUNT BY NIGHT and are not often seen during the day. There are 133 different kinds, and more than 20 of these kinds are on the official list of threatened species. Many owls that live in tropical forests are rare and in danger of extinction because their homes are being destroyed. An owl is easily recognized by its big face and huge eyes. It has powerful feet and claws called talons for seizing prey, and a hooked bill for tearing flesh. An owl has a small body, big wings, and soft wing feathers so it can swoop down silently on its prey. The snowy owl, from the Arctic and other northern regions, is about 60 cm (2 ft) long and hunts during the day. The elf owl of North America, which makes its nest hole in a cactus, is no bigger than a sparrow. Eagle owls, the largest owls, weigh about 4 kg (9 lb).

Fringed edges on wing feathers help produce silent flight.

WISE OLD OWL
Most people think of owls as wise birds because they have big eyes and an intelligent appearance.

TAWNY OWL
The tawny owl lives in northern Asia and Europe and hunts all sorts of small mammals and birds. Its prey also includes worms, snails, and even fish.

BARN OWL
Throughout the world the barn owl is known as the farmer's friend because it catches rats and mice that live in barns and eat grain.

This pellet has soft fur, hair, and feathers wrapped around the sharp bones and teeth inside.

Tawny owl pellets also contain the remains of other birds, such as the starling skull and lower bill shown here.

Contents of owl pellet

Starling skull

Lower bill

Remains of three field mice

Skulls

Leg bones

Hipbones

OWL PELLETS
Owls swallow their prey whole, but do not digest the bones, fur, feet, or beaks. Instead, the owl regurgitates, or coughs up, these remains in the form of pellets which fall to the ground under the owl's roost, where it perches. Take a pellet apart, and you can tell what the owl has eaten recently.

SIGHT AND SOUND
Owls have good eyesight and hearing. Their eyes are at the front of the head, so they can see ahead with both eyes, unlike most birds, whose eyes are on each side of the head. Owl eyes cannot swivel in their sockets, but the bird has a very flexible neck, and can turn its head right around to see behind – as shown by this eagle owl.

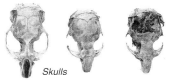

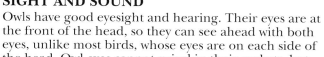

Find out more
BIRDS
EAGLES
and other birds of prey
FLIGHT IN ANIMALS
NORTH AMERICAN WILDLIFE

OXYGEN

WE CANNOT SEE, SMELL, or taste oxygen, yet without oxygen, none of us could survive longer than a few minutes. It is fortunate, then, that oxygen is the most common substance on Earth. Oxygen is a gas. Mixed with other gases, it makes up about one fifth of the air we breathe. Most of the oxygen in the world, though, does not float free as a gas. Instead, the oxygen is bound up in combination with other substances – in a solid or liquid form. This is because oxygen is chemically reactive: it readily combines with other substances, often giving off energy in the process. Burning is an example of oxygen at work. When a piece of timber burns, oxygen is combining with the wood and giving off heat. Oxygen is also found in water, combined with atoms of another gas, hydrogen. Oxygen can be extracted from water by passing an electric current through it. The electricity breaks the water into its parts (the gases oxygen and hydrogen), and oxygen bubbles off.

RESPIRATION

Our bodies need oxygen to make the energy consumed when we use our muscles. The oxygen we breathe in is used to "burn" the food we eat, producing energy. This process is called respiration. Blood carries the oxygen from the lungs, which extract it from the air, to the muscles where it is needed to make energy.

BURNING

Nothing can burn without oxygen. In outer space there is no air or oxygen, so it would be impossible to light a fire. The rocket motors used to launch spacecraft need oxygen to burn the rocket fuel and propel the craft upwards. Spacecraft therefore carry their own supply of pure oxygen which mixes with the fuel in the rocket motor. When anything burns in pure oxygen, it produces a very hot flame. In welding machines a fuel gas is burned with pure oxygen, producing a flame hot enough to melt metal.

OXYGEN CYCLE

Breathing air or burning fuel removes oxygen from the atmosphere and gives off carbon dioxide. Plants do the reverse. During the day, they produce energy for growth by the process of photosynthesis. The green parts of the plant take in sunlight, water, and carbon dioxide to make new cells, and give off oxygen. So oxygen continually passes into and out of the air. This is called the oxygen cycle.

People and animals breathe in oxygen

Green plants absorb carbon dioxide breathed out by living creatures

Mountain climbers, astronauts, and undersea divers carry a supply of oxygen to breathe. A special valve releases the oxygen at the correct pressure for breathing.

OXYGEN IN WATER

Sea water contains dissolved oxygen. Fish use this oxygen to breathe. Water flows over their gills, which extract the oxygen. Unlike other fish, sharks can breathe only when moving in the water. To avoid suffocating, they must swim constantly, even when asleep.

Find out more

AIR
CHEMISTRY
FIRE
HUMAN BODY
PLANTS
ROCKETS AND MISSILES

PACIFIC ISLANDS

ON A MAP OF THE PACIFIC Ocean, the sunny, tropical Pacific islands look like tiny grains of sand scattered on the sea. The first adventurous settlers of these islands sailed from Southeast Asia. They spread gradually across the region, travelling over the vast expanses of ocean in their light wooden sailing boats. Today the islands are divided into three main groups: Micronesia to the north, Melanesia to the south, and Polynesia to the east. There are twelve independent countries in the Pacific, including Fiji, Tonga, and Nauru, one of the world's smallest nations. Europeans first arrived in the Pacific in the sixteenth century, and a number of islands maintain strong links with Europe. New Caledonia, for instance, is French. Many Pacific islanders lead lives that have barely changed for centuries, but there are a number of important modern industries, including large-scale fishing and mining, as well as tourism.

There are some 25,000 Pacific islands, but only a few thousand are inhabited. They stretch across the central part of the Pacific Ocean, straddling the equator and occupying an area larger than the whole of Asia. To the west and southwest lie Southeast Asia, Australia, and New Zealand; North and South America are to the east.

Wooden sailing boats called outriggers have a main hull and floats on either side, like a catamaran.

Those taking part in the spectacular traditional dances of Papua New Guinea wear costumes decorated with feathers and beads.

United States military bases cover virtually all of some Pacific Islands, mainly in Micronesia.

ISLAND LIFE
Many Pacific islands are very small. They are the tops of submerged mountains. Coral reefs protect them from the Pacific waves. On the remoter islands, people live much as their ancestors did. Their simple houses have thatched roofs made of palm fronds. Families keep pigs and chickens and grow fruit and vegetables. They use traditional boats for fishing and for trade between the islands.

EASTER ISLAND
Tiny, remote Easter Island is one of the furthest east of the Pacific islands. A Dutch admiral gave the island its name when he landed there on Easter Day in 1722. More than 1,000 years ago the islanders' Polynesian ancestors carved mysterious stone statues, which still dot the dry, barren landscape.

WAKE ISLAND
The United States controls a number of Pacific islands, including Wake Island (above) and Midway, which was the scene of a major battle in World War II. The islands of Hawaii form one of the 50 states.

There are more than 600 of these huge heads on Easter Island, some over 20 m (65 ft) tall.

PAPUA NEW GUINEA
New Guinea, one of the world's largest islands, is part of Melanesia. Half of it belongs to Indonesia and is called Irian Jaya. The other half is a mountainous independent country called Papua New Guinea. Its thick tropical forests are the home of many remote tribes who have little contact with the outside world.

Find out more
OCEANS AND SEAS
WORLD WAR II

PACADIFIC ISLANDS

STATISTICS
Area: 522,271 sq km (201,649 sq miles)
Population: 5,877,386
Number of independent countries: 12
Languages: English, local languages and dialects
Religions: Protestant, Roman Catholic, Hindu
Highest point: Mount Wilhelm (Papua New Guinea) 4,509 m (14,793 ft)
Main occupations: Agriculture, fishing

 ### FIJI
Area: 18,274 sq km (7,055 sq miles)
Population: 700,000
Capital: Suva
Currency: Fiji dollar

 ### KIRIBATI
Area: 728 sq km (281 sq miles)
Population: 75,000
Capital: Tarawa
Currency: Australian dollar

 ### MARSHALL ISLANDS
Area: 181 sq km (70 sq miles)
Population: 48,000
Capital: Majuro
Currency: U.S. dollar

 ### MICRONESIA
Area: 702 sq km (271 sq miles)
Population: 101,000
Capital: Kolonia
Currency: U.S. dollar

 ### NAURU
Area: 21 sq km (8 sq miles)
Population: 10,000
Government Centre: Yaren
Currency: Australian dollar

PAPUA NEW GUINEA
Area: 461,691 sq km (178,260 sq miles)
Population: 4,100,000
Capital: Port Moresby
Currency: Kina

 ### PALAU
Area: 302 sq km (188 sq miles)
Population: 16,386
Capital: Koror
Currency: U.S. dollar

 ### SOLOMON ISLANDS
Area: 28,446 sq km (10,983 sq miles)
Population: 400,000
Capital: Honiara
Currency: Solomon Islands dollar

 ### TONGA
Area: 748 sq km (289 sq miles)
Population: 101,000
Capital: Nuku'alofa
Currency: Tongan pa'anga

TUVALU
Area: 25 sq km (10 sq miles)
Population: 9,000
Capital: Funafuti
Currency: Australian dollar

NEW CALEDONIA
The Isle of Pines (above) is one of the smallest inhabited islands in the New Caledonia group. Like many of the Pacific Islands, New Caledonia is governed by a larger, more powerful country. France rules New Caledonia, and French aid provides one third of the country's income. Most of the rest comes from the export of nickel – the islands have 40 per cent of the world's reserves of the metal.

 ### VANUATU
Area: 12,190 sq km (4,706 sq miles)
Population: 155,000
Capital: Vila
Currency: Vatu

WESTERN SAMOA
Area: 2,934 sq km (1,133 sq miles)
Population: 162,000
Capital: Apia
Currency: Tala

DEPENDENCIES
Besides the twelve independent nations listed at the top of the page, there are many other island groups in the Pacific. Most of these islands states depend on aid from a larger country, and some have very low populations. Pitcairn, for example, is a British colony and is the home of less than 100 people.

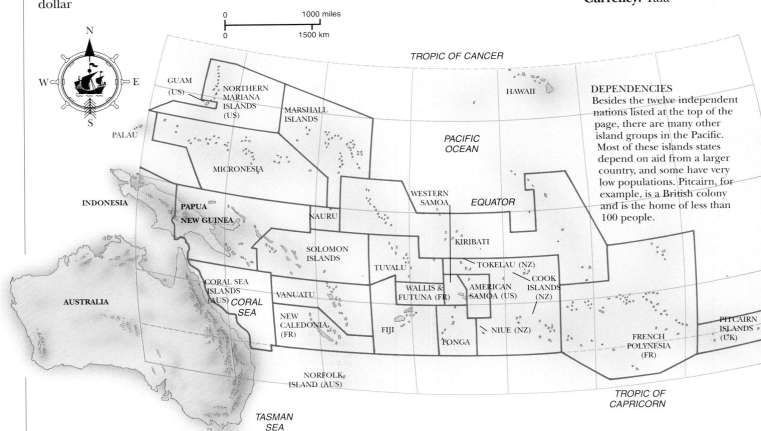

PAINTERS

ARTISTS USE PAINT in the same way that writers use words to convey ideas on paper. Painters capture the likeness of a face or a flower, but they can do much more than just paint a realistic image. Painters work skilfully with colour, texture, and shape to create all kinds of eye-catching images of the world as they see it. Every culture throughout history has produced its own great painters, from Giotto in the 14th century to Picasso in the 20th century. There have been many different groups, or movements, in painting, such as classicism, cubism, and pop art. Painters change the way we see the world. Rembrandt's portrait paintings, for example, are powerful studies from real life, whereas Salvador Dali's strange surrealist (dreamlike) landscapes are drawn from his imagination. Painters use all kinds of paint to create a picture – thick blobs of oil colour daubed onto a canvas with a palette knife; delicate brushstrokes of watercolour on a sheet of paper. Some painters dab paint on with sponges, rags, even their fingers; others flick paint onto a surface. Whatever the medium (materials) used, each great painter has his or her own distinctive style.

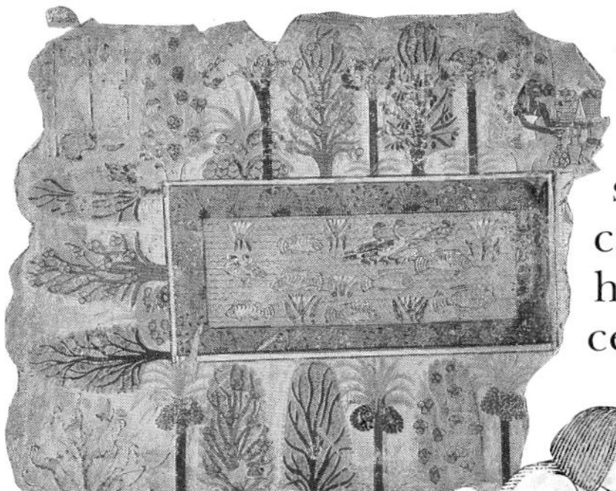

EARLY PAINTERS
The artists of Ancient Egypt decorated the walls of tombs with scenes of gods and goddesses and of hunting and feasting. The Minoan people of early Greece painted their houses and palaces with pictures of dancers, birds, and flowers. Roman artists painted gods and goddesses and scenes from classical mythology.

MEDIEVAL PAINTERS
Up until the 14th century, Western artists painted mostly Christian subjects – the life of Christ and the saints. Painters used rich colours and thin layers of gold to make these religious paintings. These early artists used different methods of painting people than did later Western painters, but although the paintings may look flat to us, they are no less powerful. Artists worked on wood panels for altarpieces and painted directly on church walls.

People in medieval paintings sometimes look stiff and expressionless, like the figures in this 11th-century picture of an emperor, a saint, and an angel (left).

The Sistine Chapel ceiling, painted by Michelangelo.

RENAISSANCE
One of the greatest periods in European painting was the Renaissance, which reached its height in Italy in the early part of the 16th century. During the Renaissance, painters developed more realistic styles of painting. They studied perspective and the human body, painted more realistic landscapes, and developed portrait painting.

MICHELANGELO
Michelangelo Buonarroti (1475-1564) is one of the best-known Italian Renaissance painters. Much of his work was for Pope Julius II, who commissioned him to paint the ceiling of the Sistine Chapel in the Vatican, in Rome, between 1508 and 1512.

Michelangelo had difficulty in reaching certain parts of the ceiling in the Sistine Chapel, so he built a scaffold and sometimes lay on his back to paint.

GIOTTO
The Italian artist Giotto (c.1266-1337) painted at the beginning of the Renaissance. He brought a new sense of naturalness to paintings. The painting shown above is called *The Flight into Egypt*. It shows Mary and Jesus on a donkey being led by Joseph.

REMBRANDT

Most people know the Dutch artist Rembrandt H. van Rijn (1606-69) only by his first name. He is well known for his portraits, which are full of expression. The painting shown here is one of many self-portraits.

ROMANTIC MOVEMENT

During the late 18th and early 19th centuries, painters such as the French artist Eugène Delacroix (1798-1863) began a new style of painting, which became known as the Romantic Movement. The romantics used bright colour and a free handling of paint to create their dramatic pictures. The English painter J.M.W. Turner (1775-1851) painted landscapes and seascapes flooded with light and colour.

EASTERN PAINTERS

While European art was developing, Eastern artists were evolving their own styles of painting. The Chinese observed nature accurately and painted exquisite pictures with simple brushstrokes in ink on silk and paper. Some Japanese artists, such as Hokusai (1760-1849), made beautiful prints.

This painting is by the modern Japanese painter Kaii Higashiyama (1918-); it is called Flowery Glow.

This is a detail from the painting by the French artist Fragonard (1732-1806) called The Swing.

The Poppy Field, *by Claude Monet*

PICASSO

Many people believe that the Spanish painter Pablo Picasso (1881-1973) was the most creative and influential artist of the 20th century. From a very young age, Picasso was extremely skilful at drawing and painting. His restless personality led him to paint in many different styles. One style was his "blue period" of painting, when he concentrated on blue as the main colour for his pictures. In 1907, Picasso painted a picture called *Les Demoiselles D'Avignon*, which shocked many people — it was a painting of human figures represented by angular and distorted shapes. This led to a style of painting called cubism.

This photograph shows Picasso with a painting of his children, Claude and Paloma. He is on his way to show this painting at an exhibition of his work.

MONET

Claude Monet (1840-1926) was the leader of the impressionists. He painted many pictures of the flowers in his garden at Giverny and in the French countryside, including the picture above right, called *The Poppy Field*. Seen close up, the picture consists of many brushstrokes of different colours, but from a distance the dabs of colour come together to form a field of red flowers.

IMPRESSIONISM

At an exhibition in Paris in 1874 a painting by the French artist Claude Monet caused an uproar. Art critics and the public were used to seeing realistic objects in pictures, but the impressionists, as Monet and his fellow artists were called, painted in dabs of colour to create the effect of light and shade. Other great artists of the impressionist movement were Camille Pissarro, Pierre Auguste Renoir, and Alfred Sisley.

HOCKNEY

David Hockney (born 1937) is a well-known British painter. He is famous for his pictures of California, especially paintings of swimming pools such as this one, called *A Bigger Splash*. Hockney works with many different materials, including photographs and colour photocopies.

MODERN PAINTERS

Since the beginning of the 20th century, painters have experimented with different ways of creating pictures. Picasso and Georges Braque stuck fabric, sand, and newsprint on to canvases to make collages. Piet Mondrian painted in straight lines and right angles. Action painting was developed by the American artist Jackson Pollock, who splashed paint on to huge canvases on his studio floor.

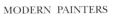

___Find out more___
DRAWING
PAINTING
RENAISSANCE
SCULPTURE

PAINTING

SINCE PREHISTORIC PEOPLE first applied natural pigments to cave walls, artists have painted to express themselves. Paintings can be important historical documents, providing clues as to how people dressed at the time of the painting and what their customs and interests were. Training is not necessary in order to paint, but it can be a help in learning basic techniques. A painting can be done with oil paints, watercolours, or as a fresco – that is, painting onto wet plaster. The type of paint depends on what the powdered pigment or colour is mixed with to allow it to be brushed onto the painting. Oil paints use a vegetable oil such as linseed or poppy oil. Before oil paints were developed in the 15th century, artists made tempera paintings in which the pigments were mixed with an emulsion such as egg yolk. Artists may paint onto almost any surface: from rock and wood to fabric, paper, metal, plastics – even skin. They may also choose any subject, such as a still life or something abstract like random shapes.

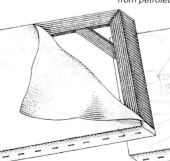

CAVE PAINTING
Eighteen thousand years ago people used burned bones and wood, and different-coloured earth mixed with water or animal fat, to paint scenes on cave walls. South African bushmen produced this cave painting. It shows men hunting an eland, a type of deer.

OIL PAINTING

Oil paint has the advantage of drying slowly. This gives the artist time to change things on the painting while the paint is still wet, and makes it easier to blend colours and tones or even scrape off the paint where it is not working success-fully. Oil paint can be applied thickly or thinly. It is flexible enough to be built up in layers to produce a particular effect. The paint is applied to a canvas (a piece of fabric stretched onto a frame) with brushes, a painting knife, or the fingers.

Thumb hole allows artist to hold palette with one hand while painting with the other.

Linseed oil is a popular binder for oil paint.

Turpentine for thinning paint

Palette

The best brushes for oil painting are made from hog's hair or sable. Some brushes are made of synthetic fibres.

Pigments for making oil paints may come from natural sources such as berries, bark, roots, and earth, or from petroleum and metals.

The artist staples the canvas to a wooden frame. This makes the canvas taut.

A coat of primer prevents the canvas from absorbing the paint; then an outline is done.

The artist applies oil paint in layers. When dry, the painting will be coated with varnish to protect it against dirt.

PREPARING FOR OIL PAINTING
Linen or cotton canvas is a popular surface or "support" for oil painting. Before beginning, the canvas must be specially prepared (left). Once it is ready, the painter can begin to apply layers of paint. Some artists draw outlines in charcoal or pencil on the canvas first; others put the paint straight on. Oil paint can be thinned down with turpentine to produce an effect rather like a watercolour.

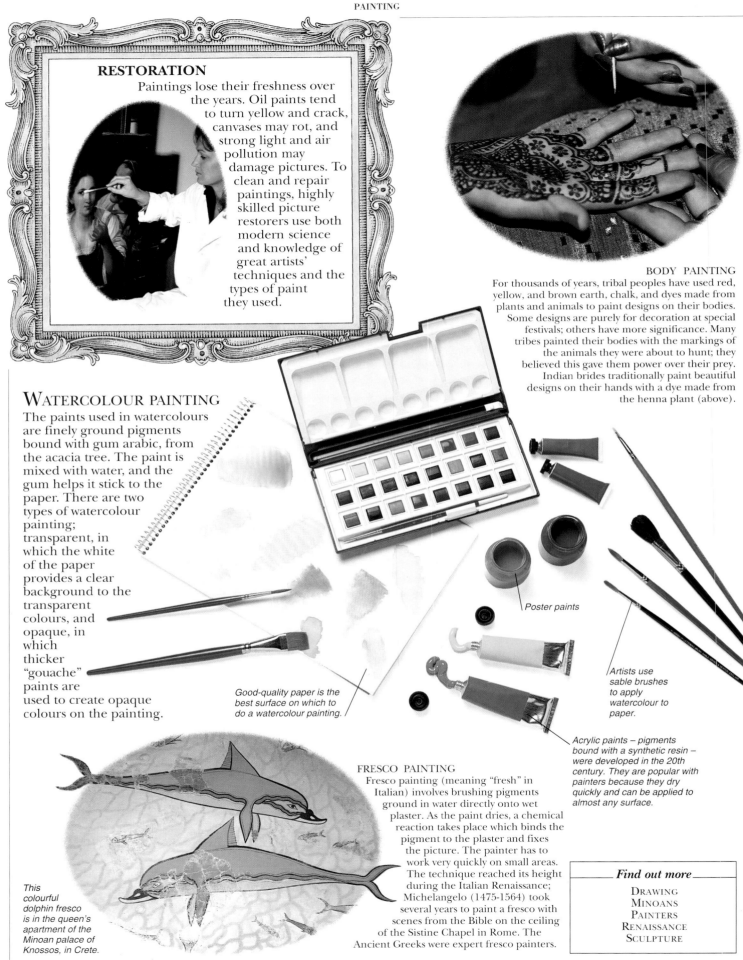

RESTORATION

Paintings lose their freshness over the years. Oil paints tend to turn yellow and crack, canvases may rot, and strong light and air pollution may damage pictures. To clean and repair paintings, highly skilled picture restorers use both modern science and knowledge of great artists' techniques and the types of paint they used.

BODY PAINTING

For thousands of years, tribal peoples have used red, yellow, and brown earth, chalk, and dyes made from plants and animals to paint designs on their bodies. Some designs are purely for decoration at special festivals; others have more significance. Many tribes painted their bodies with the markings of the animals they were about to hunt; they believed this gave them power over their prey. Indian brides traditionally paint beautiful designs on their hands with a dye made from the henna plant (above).

WATERCOLOUR PAINTING

The paints used in watercolours are finely ground pigments bound with gum arabic, from the acacia tree. The paint is mixed with water, and the gum helps it stick to the paper. There are two types of watercolour painting; transparent, in which the white of the paper provides a clear background to the transparent colours, and opaque, in which thicker "gouache" paints are used to create opaque colours on the painting.

Poster paints

Good-quality paper is the best surface on which to do a watercolour painting.

Artists use sable brushes to apply watercolour to paper.

Acrylic paints – pigments bound with a synthetic resin – were developed in the 20th century. They are popular with painters because they dry quickly and can be applied to almost any surface.

FRESCO PAINTING

Fresco painting (meaning "fresh" in Italian) involves brushing pigments ground in water directly onto wet plaster. As the paint dries, a chemical reaction takes place which binds the pigment to the plaster and fixes the picture. The painter has to work very quickly on small areas. The technique reached its height during the Italian Renaissance; Michelangelo (1475-1564) took several years to paint a fresco with scenes from the Bible on the ceiling of the Sistine Chapel in Rome. The Ancient Greeks were expert fresco painters.

This colourful dolphin fresco is in the queen's apartment of the Minoan palace of Knossos, in Crete.

Find out more

DRAWING
MINOANS
PAINTERS
RENAISSANCE
SCULPTURE

PAPER

TEAR A PIECE of paper, and you will see tiny fibres along the tear. These are plant fibres, and a piece of paper contains millions of them stuck together. Paper may also contain other materials, such as a filler to make it stiff, resin to keep ink from soaking into the fibres, and dye to colour the paper. Using different materials produces different kinds of paper, from stiff, heavy cardboard to light, fluffy tissues. The plant fibres in paper come mainly from trees. Millions of trees are cut down every year to provide us with paper, and new trees are planted in their place. Rags are also used to make some paper, and wastepaper can be reused to make new paper. Recycled paper is paper made completely or partly from wastepaper. Making paper in this way saves forests, uses much less energy, and reduces air and water pollution.

Paper is named after papyrus, a reedlike plant which the Ancient Egyptians used as a writing material more than 5,000 years ago. The Chinese invented the paper that we use about 2,000 years ago. But wasps have been making paper for much longer. They chew up wood and plant fibres to make paper nests.

ORIGAMI
Folding a sheet of paper into a decorative shape is called origami. The art of origami is at least 300 years old and began in Japan.

Wallpaper

Party decorations

DECORATION
Wallpaper gives a special look to a room. The pattern is printed on the surface of heavy paper or pressed paper. People hang paper decorations at parties and other festive occasions.

Paper napkin

Cardboard packaging

Newspaper

Tissues

Cheque

Tea bag

Photograph

PAPER IN THE HOME
Paper is good for tasks such as cleaning because it can be thrown away after use. Light paper soaks up liquid and is used to make tissues and paper towels.

INFORMATION
A huge amount of information is recorded on paper, either as printed words and pictures or as photographs. People also use paper for money, in the form of banknotes and cheques.

Writing paper

Note-paper

Wrapping paper

Handmade paper

PAPER MAKING
A paper mill is a large factory that turns trees into big rolls of paper. The trees are ground up and mixed with water to make wood pulp. A machine then presses and rolls a layer of pulp into paper.

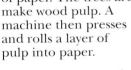

Wastepaper added to pulping machine to make recycled paper

Pulping machine

Fillers and dyes are added to pulp.

Trees are cut down and sawn into logs. The logs are then sent to paper mills.

The bark is removed and the logs are cut into tiny chips.

PAPER TYPES
There are many different types of paper. They range from the most delicate handmade papers to the toughest cardboard, and they have many uses. The colour, strength, and texture of the paper can be changed by printing and dyeing, and by mixing it with materials such as wax or plastic.

TREES FOR PAPER
A big tree has to fall to provide each person with a year's supply of paper. A new tree is planted in its place, usually at a special tree farm. It takes between 15 and 50 years for a freshly planted tree to grow large enough to be used for paper making.

PAPER-MAKING MACHINE
Wet wood pulp flows onto a belt with a mesh of tiny holes. Water is sucked out, and the wet paper passes through rollers and heated cylinders that press and dry it. The finished paper is wound onto a large roll.

Find out more
BOOKS
NEWSPAPERS
POLLUTION
PRINTING
TREES

ANCIENT
PERSIANS

MORE THAN 3,000 years ago, the present-day country of Iran was home to various tribes, including the Medes and the Persians. For many years, the Medes ruled the area, but in 549 B.C. Cyrus, the Persian king of a small state called Ashan, conquered the Medes and set out to create a vast kingdom. Within 30 years Persia had become the most powerful nation in the world, and the Persian Empire covered all of Mesopotamia, Anatolia (Turkey), the eastern Mediterranean, and what are now Pakistan and Afghanistan.

For more than 200 years the Persian Empire was the greatest the world had ever seen. The Persians were skilled warriors, horse riders, and craft workers. They were also highly organized. Under Darius I, also called Darius the Great, the empire was divided into provinces called satrapies. A network of roads linked the provinces and enabled people to trade easily. Darius introduced a postal system and a single currency to unify the empire. The empire flourished until the Greek leader Alexander the Great conquered Persia in 331 B.C.

CYRUS THE GREAT
Cyrus (ruled 549-529 B.C.) founded the Persian Empire. During his reign many different peoples, including Babylonians, Egyptians, Greeks, and Syrians, lived in the Persian Empire.

People bringing gifts to the royal palace

Reliefs show people arriving for a festival on New Year's Day.

PERSEPOLIS
In about 520 B.C. Darius I began to build the city of Persepolis. Building continued in the reign of Xerxes I (486-465 B.C.). Persepolis was the site of many beautiful buildings, including the royal palace. The city was used only once a year at New Year, when the peoples of the empire brought tributes (gifts) to the king.

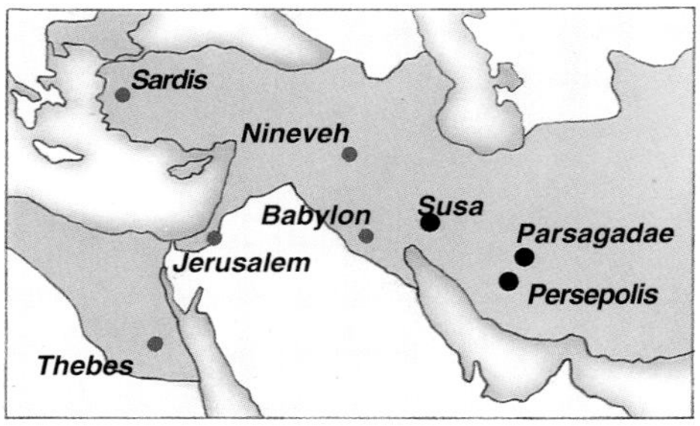

Remains of Persepolis include statues such as the carved head of this horse in the Central Palace.

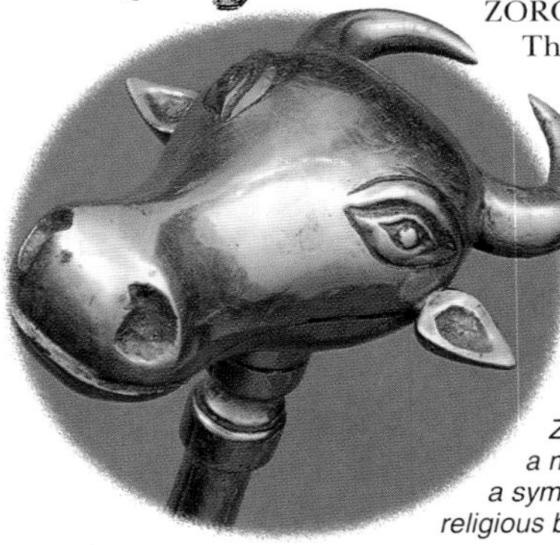

ZOROASTRIANISM
The Persian people followed the teachings of a prophet named Zoroaster, who lived from about 628 to 551 B.C. Zoroastrianism was the main religion in Persia until the country became Muslim in the 7th century A.D.

Zoroastrian priests carried a mace with a bull's head as a symbol of the priests' religious battle against evil.

PERSIAN EMPIRE
At its height, the Persian Empire stretched from the borders of India to the River Nile in Egypt. The city of Susa was the administrative capital of the empire, Persepolis was the royal capital, and Parsagadae was the city where kings were crowned.

Map labels: Sardis, Nineveh, Babylon, Susa, Parsagadae, Persepolis, Jerusalem, Thebes

PERSEPOLIS TODAY
When Alexander the Great invaded the Persian Empire, he burned Persepolis to the ground. But the ruins of the city, including the royal palace, can still be seen today in southern Iran.

ANCIENT PERSIANS

549 B.C. Cyrus the Great defeats the Medes peoples and forms the Persian Empire.

538 B.C. Cyrus conquers the Babylonian Empire.

529 B.C. Cyrus dies.

525 B.C. Persians conquer Egypt.

521-486 B.C. Reign of Darius the Great.

510 B.C. Persians invade southeast Europe and central Asia.

500-449 B.C. Persian Wars between Persian Empire and Greek states, because Persian kings felt threatened by the democracy of Greece.

490 B.C. Greeks defeat Persians at the Battle of Marathon.

480 B.C. Greek navy defeats Persians at the Battle of Salamis.

334 B.C. Alexander the Great invades Persia.

331 B.C. Alexander defeats Persians at the Battle of Gaugamela. Persian Empire collapses.

Find out more
ALEXANDER THE GREAT
ASSYRIANS
BABYLONIANS
GREECE, ANCIENT
MIDDLE EAST

PETS

LIKE TRUSTED FRIENDS, pets give us comfort and affection. In return, pets need people to provide food and shelter and care for their health. Pets are tame animals kept for companionship or because they are attractive to look at. Humans first tamed animals for their milk or meat 11,000 years ago, but people have kept pets only since about 2000 B.C. At that time the Ancient Egyptians tamed hyenas, cats, and even lions for company. Choosing the right pet is an important decision. Some pets, such as large dogs, need space to run around, so it is cruel to keep them in a city home. Cats thrive almost anywhere, but enjoy exploring outdoors. And many pets need very little attention or space – there's room in even the smallest home for a fish tank or a birdcage.

CATS
Mammals make rewarding pets because they are affectionate and often become fond of their owners. Cats and dogs are the most common pets; there are more than 50 million pet cats in the United States alone.

KEEPING PETS
In their natural habitat, animals look after themselves. But few pets can hunt or exercise in a natural way. It is therefore important to understand a pet's requirements and give it what it needs to stay healthy. Exercise and a suitable diet are most important, but all pets also need a clean living area and the care of a vet when they get sick.

Canaries

Seeds and fruit provide the basic diet for most kinds of pet birds.

Budgerigar

BIRDS
Because of their cheerful songs, canaries make charming pets. Some cage birds, especially parrots and mynah birds, can be trained to imitate human speech. The world's most talkative bird was an African grey parrot that knew more than 800 words.

Hamsters exercise by running inside a wheel.

The hamster drinks from a drip feeder.

Hamsters keep their teeth sharp by gnawing, so their cages have to be made with sturdy metal bars.

Hamsters eat dried food such as seeds and nuts, as well as fresh vegetables.

GUINEA PIGS
In warm weather guinea pigs can live in outdoor cages and feed on fresh grass. Some special breeds have long, glossy coats, which have to be kept well brushed. Guinea pigs are not actually pigs at all, but small rodents which came originally from South America.

Gerbils like to play in cardboard tubes, but they also tend to gnaw them.

Terrapins like to swim, so they have to be kept in tanks containing pools of water.

BREEDING PETS
All pets may produce young if adult males and females are put together. In a large aviary, (above) birds will pair off and make nests, just as they do in the wild. For especially valuable pets, breeding pairs are carefully selected, since the best males and females usually produce the best young.

TRAINING
Any pet that lives outside a cage has to be trained so that it does not soil the home. Without training, dogs can be especially destructive and even dangerous.

At dog shows, prizes are awarded to the most well-trained dogs.

UNUSUAL PETS
Almost any animal could be a pet, but unusual pets require special care and some knowledge about how these animals live and behave in the wild.

Pythons kill their prey by strangling them. If handled correctly, they make good pets.

Find out more
CATS
DOGS, WOLVES, AND FOXES
FARM ANIMALS
HORSES, ZEBRAS, AND ASSES
VETERINARIANS

PHOENICIANS

Purple dye is made from the liquid produced by crushing murex seashells.

A TINY GROUP of cities perched along the coast of the Mediterranean produced the most famous sailors and traders of the ancient world. These seafaring people were called the Phoenicians. The cities of Phoenicia were linked by the sea, and they traded in many goods, including purple dyes, glass, and ivory. From 1200 to 350 B.C. the Phoenicians controlled trade throughout the Mediterranean. They spread their trading links to many points around the coast. Their most famous trading post was Carthage on the north coast of Africa. During its history, Phoenicia was conquered by several foreign empires, including the Assyrians, Babylonians, and Persians. These foreign rulers usually allowed the Phoenicians to continue trading. But in 332 B.C. Alexander the Great conquered Phoenicia, and Greek people came to live there. The Greeks brought their own culture with them, and the Phoenician culture died out.

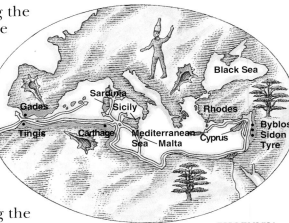

PHOENICIA
Phoenicia lay on the coast of the eastern Mediterranean roughly where Lebanon is today. The Phoenicians spread throughout the Mediterranean, to Carthage, Rhodes, Cyprus, Sicily, Malta, Sardinia, Gades (Cadiz), and Tingis (Tangier).

When arriving at a new place to trade, the Phoenicians would lay their goods out on the beach and let the local people come and look at what they had brought.

Sculptures show that Phoenician men wore distinctive conical hats.

Phoenician glassware, such as this glass jar, was a luxury in the ancient world.

Phoenicians traded in a vast array of goods from the Mediterranean, including metals, farm animals, wheat, cloth, jewellery, and gemstones.

DYEING
The Phoenicians were the only people who knew how to produce a vivid purple dye from murex shells. The dye was considered to be exceptionally beautiful but it was also very expensive. Only high government officials, for example, could wear purple dyed cloth in the Roman Empire.

PHOENICIAN SHIPS
The Phoenicians' ships were famous all over the Mediterranean, and were the main reason for the Phoenicians' success as traders. The ships had oarsmen, sails, and heavy keels, which enabled them to sail in any direction.

PHOENICIAN GLASSWARE
Ancient Egyptians made glass many years before the Phoenicians did, but Egyptian glass was cloudy, whereas Phoenician glass was clear. The Phoenicians were able to make clear glass because their sand contained large amounts of quartz.

BYBLOS
The Phoenician port of Byblos was famous for its trade in papyrus – a kind of paper made in Egypt by pressing together strands of papyrus reeds. The Greeks called papyrus "biblos" after the port of Byblos. A number of our words concerned with books, such as Bible and bibliography (a list of books), come from *biblos*.

The papyrus reed grows in the warm, damp conditions of the River Nile in Egypt.

Find out more
ALPHABETS
ASSYRIANS
BABYLONIANS
GREECE, ANCIENT
PERSIANS, ANCIENT

PHOTOGRAPHY

MORE THAN TWO MILLION times each day, a camera shutter clicks somewhere in the world to take a photograph. There are family snapshots capturing happy memories, dramatic news pictures, advertising and fashion shots, identity photographs, pictures of the planet beamed back from satellites in space, and much more. The uses of photography are already numerous, and new applications are being found all the time.

The first photographs were made by coating sheets of polished metal with light-sensitive chemicals, but the image appeared in shades of dull, silvery grey and could only be seen from certain angles. Now the chemicals are spread onto a film of cellulose (a kind of plastic), and the photograph can be either black and white or full colour. Alternatively, photographs can be made electronically on computer disks, using a still-video camera. These video photos can be viewed immediately on a television set and can be transmitted across the world instantly by satellite. Someday, all photographs may be made electronically.

Cameras have become smaller and simpler to use; animals and young babies, however, are still difficult to photograph.

HIGH-SPEED PHOTOGRAPHY
With the use of special cameras and lights, high-speed photography can reveal movement too fast for the eye to see. A brief burst of light from an electronic flash, lasting less than one millionth of a second, freezes objects moving at hundreds of kilometres per hour.

ACTION PHOTOS
Atheletes can improve their technique by studying action sequences, which are made by firing a series of electronic flashes in quick succession using a special lamp called a stroboscope. All the flashes are recorded on a single photograph.

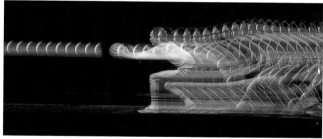

WIDE-ANGLE VIEW
Photography can create strange and dramatic views of familiar objects. Photographs taken with a wide-angle lens can distort objects to emphasize their size and power.

HISTORY OF PHOTOGRAPHY
A Frenchman named Joseph Niépce took the first photograph in 1826. The exposure took eight hours to make, and the picture was fuzzy and dark. In 1837, another Frenchman, Louis Daguerre, discovered how to make sharp photographs in a few minutes. Just two years later an English scientist, William Fox Talbot, invented the photographic process which is used for films today.

People in early portraits often look uncomfortable and stiff because they had to keep still for several minutes.

CLOSE-UP PHOTOGRAPHY
Macro or close-up photography magnifies tiny details barely visible to the naked eye, such as the beautiful gold-coloured eye of a leaf frog (right).

THE PHOTOGRAPHIC PROCESS

In a black-and-white photograph, the picture is made up of millions of tiny grains of black silver which are visible under a microscope but too small to be seen by the naked eye. Where there are many grains, the picture appears dark. Where there are fewer grains, the picture appears light. Film contains chemicals called silver salts which are affected by light. When film is made, the transparent backing is coated with grains of these salts, held in place by a thin layer of gelatin, the same substance as in jelly. Because this coating, or emulsion, is sensitive to light, it must be kept in darkness, so both the film canister and the camera must be completely lightproof.

1 EXPOSURE
When a picture is taken, light coming through the lens briefly strikes the film. Each grain of silver struck by light is subtly changed, and the photograph is recorded in an invisible pattern of changed grains. The film must be processed before the picture can be seen.

Chemicals

Timer

2 DEVELOPER AND FIXER
The film is immersed in a bath of chemicals called developer. This makes the silver salt grains that were struck by light change into silver metal. After a quick rinse with water, the film is placed in a bath of fixer – a chemical solution which dissolves away the unexposed silver salt grains. After fixing, the black silver image is left permanently on the film.

3 NEGATIVE
Once the film is fixed, it is washed thoroughly in running water to remove all traces of chemicals, then hung up to dry. If you look at the drying film against the light, you can see each picture clearly. But the pictures are negative, which means the light and dark areas are reversed.

GEORGE EASTMAN
In the early days, photography was for enthusiasts only. Cameras were bulky, and for each picture, photographers had to carry a separate glass plate and process it in messy chemicals. Then, in 1888, American George Eastman invented a camera called the Kodak. The Kodak was small and light and came already loaded with a roll of film rather than plates. Taking a picture became so easy that soon millions of people were taking up photography.

4 ENLARGER
To see the picture properly, the negative is printed. This means it is re-photographed on white paper in a lightproof darkroom using an enlarger. Like a camera, an enlarger has a lens to keep the image sharp. The enlarger lens also magnifies the negative by projecting a big version of the picture onto the print paper. Like film, print paper is coated with light-sensitive emulsion. When the enlarger is switched on, silver salts in the emulsion record the magnified picture in the same way as film.

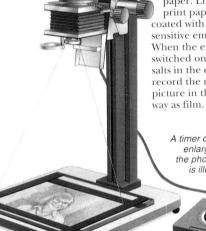

A timer connected to the enlarger ensures that the photographic paper is illuminated for the correct time.

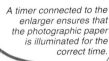

5 DEVELOPING
After exposure to the enlarger light, the print paper is developed and fixed in chemicals in the same way as film.

6 PRINT
After it has been developed, the print is washed and laid flat to dry.

COLOUR FILM

The dyes in colour print film are yellow, magenta, and cyan. When the picture is printed, they produce red, green, and blue on the print.

Colour photography depends on the fact that every colour we see can be made by mixing three primary colours – red, blue, and green. Colour film has three layers of light-sensitive emulsion, each of which reacts to one of these colours. The layers record how much of each colour there is in each part of the scene. After processing, coloured dyes are produced in each layer, and together they form the colour image.

Find out more
CAMERAS
COLOUR
FILMS
LIGHT
TELEVISION AND VIDEO

PHYSICS

THE SCIENCE OF PHYSICS used to be called natural philosophy, which means thinking about and investigating the natural world. Physicists seek to understand and explain the universe from the largest, most distant galaxy to the tiniest invisible particle. Great physicists have wrestled with fundamental questions such as what is it that holds us to the Earth, what is time, and what is inside an atom.

Physicists work with a mixture of theory and experiment. They conduct experiments and then think of a theory, or idea, that explains the results. Then they try new experiments to test their theory. Some theories have become so good at explaining nature that many people refer to them as the laws of physics. For example, one such law states that nothing can travel faster than the speed of light. The German physicist Albert Einstein (1879-1955) proposed this in 1905 as part of his revolutionary theory of relativity.

ASTROPHYSICS
Astronomers use physics to find out about the origins and interiors of the sun and stars. This branch of physics is called astrophysics.

BRANCHES OF PHYSICS
Physics is the science of energy and matter (the materials of which everything is made). There are several branches of physics. They cover a range of subjects from atoms to space.

OPTICS AND THERMAL PHYSICS
Heat and light are important forms of energy: the sun sends out light and heat that make life possible on Earth. The physics of light is called optics; the branch of physics concerned with heat is called thermal physics.

STATICS
Statics is the branch of physics concerned with calculating and understanding forces that support buildings and bridges.

MECHANICS
The study of force and movement is a branch of physics known as mechanics.

ELECTRICITY
One of the most useful forms of energy is electricity. Physicists study the nature of electricity and find ways of using it in electrical applicances, microchips, and computers.

MAGNETISM
Physicists study magnets and the forces that magnets produce. This includes the Earth's magnetism, which comes from the movements of the molten metal core at the centre of the Earth.

QUANTUM MECHANICS
Physicists have discovered that energy can only exist in tiny packets called quanta. This idea is very important in the study of atoms, and it has given rise to a branch of physics called quantum mechanics.

NUCLEAR PHYSICS
Physicists are constantly searching for a greater understanding of the particles that make up the nucleus (centre) of an atom. This branch of physics is called nuclear physics.

ELECTROMAGNETISM
Physicists have discovered a group of mostly invisible rays called electro-magnetic waves. They include light, heat, x-rays, and radio waves. The physics of these waves is called electromagnetism.

MOLECULAR PHYSICS
Physicists use the idea of molecules to explain the way solids, liquids, and gases behave. This branch of physics is called molecular physics.

ACOUSTICS
Physicists study the nature of sound and how it travels. They also use sound to study the interior of the Earth and the oceans. The science of sound is called acoustics.

GEOPHYSICS
The interior of the Earth is hidden from us, but physicists have developed ways of studying its structure. They have discovered that there is great heat and pressure at the Earth's centre. Geophysics is the branch of physics concerned with the Earth.

English physicist Stephen Hawking (1942–) developed new theories about the nature of matter, black holes in space, and the origin of the universe that have opened doors to new possibilities in physics.

Find out more
ELECTRICITY
FORCE AND MOTION
GRAVITY
HEAT
LIGHT
MAGNETISM
SCIENTISTS AND INVENTORS
SOUND

PILGRIM FATHERS

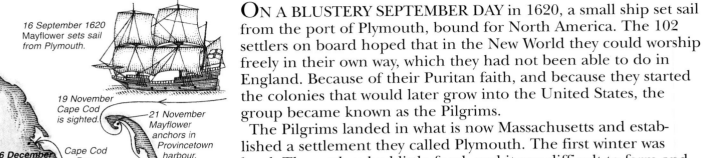

16 September 1620
Mayflower *sets sail
from Plymouth.*

19 November
Cape Cod
is sighted.

21 November
Mayflower
anchors in
Provincetown
harbour.

Cape Cod
Bay

**26 December
Plymouth
colony founded,
Massachusetts**

MAYFLOWER
The Pilgrim Fathers sailed
to North America in a two-
masted ship, the *Mayflower*.
The ship was about 30 m
(90 ft) long and was
built to carry wine
and other cargo.

ON A BLUSTERY SEPTEMBER DAY in 1620, a small ship set sail
from the port of Plymouth, bound for North America. The 102
settlers on board hoped that in the New World they could worship
freely in their own way, which they had not been able to do in
England. Because of their Puritan faith, and because they started
the colonies that would later grow into the United States, the
group became known as the Pilgrims.

The Pilgrims landed in what is now Massachusetts and established a settlement they called Plymouth. The first winter was
hard. The settlers had little food, and it was difficult to farm and
fish. But with help from the local Native Americans, the settlement
eventually prospered. The Pilgrims replaced their wooden homes
with more secure dwellings and started trading furs with the
Native Americans. More groups of Puritans came to join the
original settlers; together they created one of the first successful
European settlements in North America.

EARLY SETTLEMENT

The first settlements in
Plymouth were built of
wood from the local
forests. The chimneys
were made of sticks
held together with clay,
and the roofs were
waterproofed with bark.

*Every member of
the family had to
work hard to build
a house and plant
crops for food.*

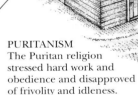
*Splitting logs to
make planks*

PURITANISM
The Puritan religion
stressed hard work and
obedience and disapproved
of frivolity and idleness.

*The Pilgrims held prayer meetings
outside until they built churches.*

GOVERNMENT
The early Plymouth settlers
elected their own government
which met annually to make laws
and levy taxes.

PURITANS

The people known as the
Puritans wished to purify the
English church of its pomp and
ritual. They dressed in simple
clothes and lived their lives
according to the Bible.

THANKSGIVING
In the autumn of 1621, the
Pilgrims celebrated their first
successful harvest. They invited
the local Native Americans to
join them in a feast of
thanksgiving. Thanksgiving,
which became a national
holiday in 1863, is celebrated
in the United States on the
fourth Thursday in November.

Find out more

FESTIVALS AND FEASTS
UNITED STATES OF AMERICA,
history of

PIRATES

IN TALES ABOUT pirates, shady figures row through the moonlight to bury treasure on tropical islands. The reality of a pirate's life, though, was very different from the storybook version. Most pirates were simply criminals who robbed ships at sea and often murdered the crews. Pirates first appeared when trading ships began to cross the Mediterranean about 4,000 years ago. They have flourished ever since in every ocean of the world, but were particularly active from 1500 to 1800. Some pirates, such as Blackbeard, cruised the Caribbean Sea, which was also called the Spanish Main. Others, such as Captain Kidd, attacked ships in the Indian Ocean. Sometimes countries at war encouraged piracy, but only against enemy shipping. They called the pirate ships privateers and gave them letters of marque – official licenses to plunder enemy ships. Today there are still pirates in the South China Sea. They rob families fleeing by boat from Vietnam.

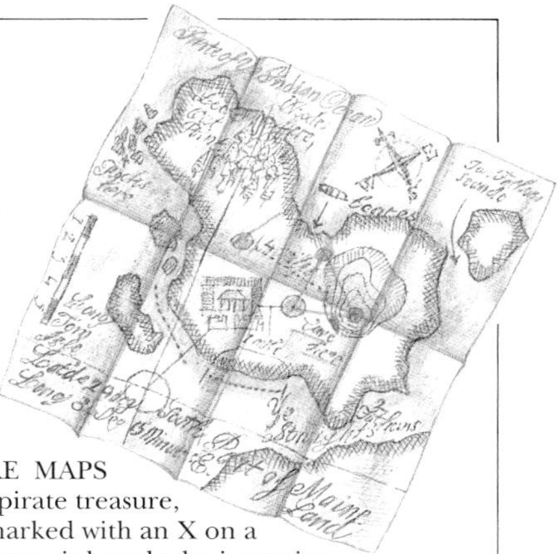

TREASURE MAPS
Buried pirate treasure, marked with an X on a map, is largely the invention of adventure writers. Most of the time pirates attacked lightly armed merchant ships, stealing food and weapons.

PIRATE SHIPS

Traditional pirate vessels were generally small, fast, and manoeuvrable. They floated high in the water so they could escape into shallow creeks and inlets if pursued. They were armed with as many cannons as possible. Some cannons were heavy guns which fired large metal balls; others were lighter swivel guns which fired lead shot.

ANNE BONNY
Anne Bonny was born in Ireland. She fell in love with the pirate "Calico Jack" Rackham and sailed with him. On a captured ship she met another woman pirate, Mary Read. The women pirates were arrested in 1720 but escaped the gallows, as they were both expecting babies.

BLACKBEARD
One of the most terrible pirates was Edward Teach. His nickname was Blackbeard, and his favourite drink was rum and gunpowder. In battle he carried six pistols and wore burning matches twisted into his hair. He died on a British warship in 1718.

DOUBLOONS
The pirate's currency was a Spanish gold dollar called the doubloon. Doubloons were also called *doblón de a ocho*, meaning pieces of eight, because each was worth eight Spanish gold escudos.

Find out more
ELIZABETH I
OUTLAWS AND BANDITS

PLANETS

THE EARTH IS one of nine huge, roughly spherical objects that move around our sun. These objects are planets – vast balls of rock, metal, and mixtures of gases that orbit a star. Some, such as Earth and Venus, are surrounded by a layer of gases called an atmosphere. The largest planets, such as Jupiter and Saturn, also have rings of dust around them. The planets vary greatly in temperature: Mercury, the planet closest to the sun, is hotter than an oven during the planet's day; Pluto, at the edge of the solar system, is 10 times colder than a deep freeze at night. All the planets move around the sun in elliptical (oval-shaped) orbits. They travel in the same direction and spin as they move. Through a telescope, the planets appear to be discs of light that move across the night sky. However, they do not produce light themselves, but reflect light from the sun. As far as we know, Earth is the only planet in our solar system that supports life. However, there are millions of other stars like our sun in the universe, many believed to have their own planets. It is possible that, like the Earth, some of these planets have life forms too.

In this picture the planets are drawn to scale.

JUPITER
Jupiter is the largest planet in the solar system. It has 16 moons. Belts of swirling gas clouds cover its surface, which is made of a mixture of liquids and gases. It is a cold planet, surrounded by a ring-shaped band of dust.

THE SUN
The sun is a star – a vast ball of hot gas, far larger than any of the planets.

EARTH
The Earth has an atmosphere of air. It also has oceans filled with water. The Earth's average temperature is 22°C (72°F). Air and liquid water are essential for life on the planet. If Earth were any hotter, the water would evaporate; if it were any colder, the water would freeze.

The moon

MARS
Mars is a small, dry planet with a red, rocky surface. It is cold – about -23°C (-9°F) – and has two polar caps of ice and frozen gas. It has two tiny moons named Phobos and Deimos.

ASTEROIDS
Thousands of tiny planets called asteroids orbit the sun, mainly between Mars and Jupiter. Most of them are lumps of rock and metal just a few kilometres in diameter.

MERCURY
Mercury (below) is so close to the sun that it has no atmosphere or oceans. It has a rocky surface that rises to a temperature of about 350°C (662°F).

VENUS
Thick clouds cover the whole surface of Venus. They trap the sun's heat, making Venus the hottest planet in the solar system. The surface temperature of Venus is about 480°C (896°F).

PLANET PICTURES
Space technology has enabled us to discover what the other planets in the solar system look like and what they are made of, and to establish it is very unlikely that they can support life. By 1993, no close-up pictures of Pluto had been taken.

The heavily cratered surface of Mercury is revealed in this composite photograph taken by the space probe Mariner 10.

Photograph taken by the Pioneer-Venus probe shows thick yellowish clouds covering the surface of Venus.

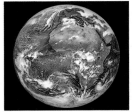

Picture of the Earth taken by the Meteosat weather satellite. Colours have been enhanced using a computer.

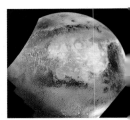

Picture of Mars constructed from 100 images taken by the Viking 1 space probe.

SATURN'S RINGS

Jupiter, Saturn, Uranus, and Neptune are all surrounded by rings. Saturn's rings, which consist of millions of fragments of ice-coated rock floating in space, are the most spectacular. Scientists are not sure how the rings formed. They may have formed at the same time as the planet, or they may be the remains of a large, icy moon that broke apart.

NEPTUNE

Neptune (right) has a striking blue atmosphere of hydrogen with clouds of methane gas. It has a rocky core about as large as the Earth. Neptune has three rings and eight moons.

PLUTO

Pluto is the outermost and smallest planet, with a diameter only one fifth the Earth's. It is the coldest planet in the solar system, with a temperature of about -230°C (-382°F). Pluto has one moon which is almost half its size.

URANUS

Uranus (left) has a solid core of metal surrounded by ice and gases. Its blue-green atmosphere is made of gases, including methane, hydrogen, and helium. Uranus is extremely cold – about -214°C (-353°F).

SATURN

Saturn is huge, almost as big as Jupiter. Bands of storm clouds circle the planet, giving it a ringed appearance. It has a solid core surrounded by ice and hydrogen gas. Saturn has more moons than any other planet; astronomers believe that it has more than 20 moons.

VOYAGER SPACE PROBE

We have incredible pictures of the planets and their moons because space probes have flown to all of the planets except Pluto. *Voyager 2* was one of the most successful interplanetary spacecraft. It travelled for more than a decade photographing the planets, and in 1990, it made its way out of the solar system. *Voyager 2* made use of the gravity of the planets to give it an extra push on its long journey – a similar effect to stepping off a merry-go-round while it is moving.

SOLAR SYSTEM

The solar system consists of the sun, planets, moons, asteroids, and comets. It formed about 4,500 million years ago from a huge cloud of gas and dust. The sun's force of gravity holds all the planets in their orbits. The planets are grouped in two bands. The inner band consists of Mercury, Venus, Earth, and Mars; in the outer band are Jupiter, Saturn, Uranus, Neptune, and Pluto.

Neptune
Jupiter
Uranus
Saturn
Venus
Mercury
Mars
Earth
Pluto

Close-up picture of Miranda, one of the moons of Uranus, taken by Voyager 2

...ger 1 picture of Jupiter ...ing the Great Red ... which is thought to be ...ge storm.

Image of Saturn and its beautifully coloured rings taken by the Voyager 1 probe.

Voyager 2 image of Uranus. Its atmosphere looks blue because clouds of methane gas cut out red light.

Voyager 2 photograph of Neptune. The two dark blurs are enormous storms in Neptune's atmosphere.

Find out more

ASTRONOMY
GRAVITY
MOON
SUN
UNIVERSE

PLANTS

LIFE ON EARTH could not exist without plants. Humans and animals need plants for food and oxygen. The cereal you eat for breakfast, the orange juice you drink, even the jeans you wear, are all derived from plants. Trees provide us with wood for fuel, furniture, and tools. In almost every country, flowers and vegetables are grown by the millions for food and pleasure. Scientists use plants to make drugs such as digitalis (from foxglove), and morphine (from poppies). Plants range from microscopic green plankton in the sea to gigantic coniferous trees so tall you cannot see their tops. What they all have in common is their unique ability to capture and use the sun's light as an energy source. This process is called photosynthesis, and it powers all plant life and growth. About 400,000 plants are already known to us, from rare exotic flowers to common garden vegetables. Even more plants await discovery, especially in tropical regions. Today, however, more than 25,000 different trees, flowers, and other plants are in danger of extinction due to the destruction of their natural habitats.

STEM
The sturdy stem supports the leaves and flowers and carries water and food materials to the leaves and fruits.

FLOWERS
The flowers of a plant contain the reproductive parts, the pollen and egg cells. These ripen to form the fruits.

LEAVES
Green leaves capture light energy from the sun by the process known as photosynthesis.

Palisade cell containing chloroplasts

Upper epidermis

Mesophyll cell

Inside a leaf

Leaf vein

Air space

Seed is inside fruit (bean pod).

Stoma

Guard cell

FRUIT
The fruits contain seeds which eventually grow into new plants. The large fruits on this plant are called beans.

STRUCTURE OF A PLANT
During its lifetime, a typical flowering plant such as this runner bean grows a stem, roots, shoots, leaves, flowers, and fruits. Trees, which are huge plants, have a trunk – a stiff, woody stem full of fibres.

Carbon dioxide is taken in from air through tiny holes called stoma.

Light energy from sun

Oxygen is given off into the air through stoma.

Water is taken in from soil through roots.

PHOTOSYNTHESIS
In order to grow, plants use energy from sunlight. This process is called photosynthesis. A green substance called chlorophyll is contained in the cells of a plant's leaves. Chlorophyll captures energy in the light waves from the sun, then carries out chemical reactions in which carbon dioxide gas from the air is combined with water from the soil. This process creates sugars and other substances which the plant uses for energy and growth.

ROOTS
From the soil, the roots take in water and minerals which pass to the leaves and fruits through tiny tubes in the stem. Roots also anchor the plant firmly in the ground.

Xylem (water-carrying tube)

Phloem (sap-carrying tube)

Cortex

Root hair

Inside a root

Root cap

REPRODUCTION
Most plants reproduce sexually. Pollen fertilizes the ovules in the ovaries, which ripen into fruits that contain seeds. Other plants, such as the potato, reproduce asexually. They grow by tubers which develop into new plants that look like the parent plant.

Parent strawberry plant

Flower

HOW A STRAWBERRY PLANT REPRODUCES
The parent strawberry plant sends out runners along the ground. Buds and roots develop on these runners and grow into new strawberry plants. This is a form of asexual reproduction, also called vegetative propagation.

Runner

Runner

New strawberry plant

MAIN GROUPS OF PLANTS

The plant kingdom is made up of many different groups. These groups are divided into flowering and non-flowering plants, as shown here.

Non-flowering plants

Microscopic plants are so small that we can see them only through a microscope.

Lichen is a combination of algae and fungi. It has no true leaves, stems or roots.

Ferns grow in all parts of the world. Some are as large as trees; others are tiny and look like moss.

Club mosses are among the first plants with true stems.

Flowering plants

Vegetables are edible flowering plants that are rich in vitamins and minerals. They include carrots, potatoes, spinach, tomatoes, and beans.

Herbs have scented leaves. They include basil and oregano.

Weeds are flowering plants that include dandelions, nettles, and buttercups.

Grasses include lawn grass and cereals such as wheat, rice, barley, and corn.

Seaweed is an alga that grows in sea water and attaches itself to rocks.

Liverworts are small non-flowering plants related to mosses.

Fruit trees provide many kinds of fruits, including apples, lemons, and bananas. All are rich in vitamins.

True flowering plants include roses, tulips, and other garden plants.

Deciduous trees are also called broadleaved trees. They lose their leaves each autumn.

Moss grows on logs and walls and in moist, shady woodland areas.

Horsetails were among the earliest plants on Earth.

Coniferous trees include fir trees and pine trees. They are also called evergreen trees.

Bushes are woody plants which are smaller than trees. They usually have one main stem.

Shrubs are woody plants with more than one main branch growing from the ground.

WEEDS

A weed is simply a plant growing where it is troublesome to humans. Most weeds grow fast, come into flower quickly, then spread their seeds. Some weeds, such as the convolvulus shown here, have pale, delicate flowers; others are colourful, such as the dandelions and buttercups that grow on lawns.

CHOCOLATE

Inside every large fruit, or pod, of the tropical cacao tree are about 40 cacao beans. These beans are roasted, shelled, then ground into a paste. The cacao paste is mixed with sugar at a high temperature in a strong air current. The result is chocolate.

FOOD FROM PLANTS

We grow plants for food on farms and in gardens, too. Food plants include cereals such as rice, fruits such as oranges, and vegetables such as carrots. Spices such as cinnamon are parts of plants and are used for flavouring. Some plant parts cannot be eaten because they are bitter, sour, or poisonous. Potatoes are an important food crop, but we eat only the tuber that grows underground. The fruits and leaves of the potato plant which grow above ground are poisonous.

THE BIGGEST FLOWER

The giant rafflesia is a parasitic plant. It has no leaves and obtains its food by living on a liana creeper. It has the world's largest flower, at 1 m (3 ft) across. Because of its smell, it is also called the stinking giant.

FLESH-EATING PLANTS

Some plants obtain extra food from animals. One plant, commonly called the Venus's-flytrap, usually grows in swamps, where the soil is poor. Flesh-eating or carnivorous plants trap and digest insects and other small creatures.

Venus's-flytrap flower

The flytrap shuts in one fiftieth of a second, when trigger hairs at the base of each leaf are moved.

MISTLETOE

This plant "steals" its food and energy by growing and feeding on trees. It grows high up in the branches, and its roots grow into the bark and absorb the tree's nutrients.

When a small creature touches sensitive hairs on the leaves of the Venus's-flytrap, the leaves snap shut with one of the fastest movements in the plant world.

Find out more

FLOWERS AND HERBS
FRUITS AND SEEDS
GRASSES AND CEREALS
MOSSES,
liverworts, and ferns
SOIL
TREES

PLASTICS

MANY MATERIALS that we use are natural materials, such as cotton, wool, leather, wood, and metal. They come from plants or animals, or they are dug from the ground. Plastics can be used in place of natural materials, and they are used to make clothes, parts for cars, and many other products. Plastics are synthetic materials, which means that they are made from chemicals in factories. The chemicals come mainly from oil, but also from natural gas and coal. An important quality of plastics is that they are easy to shape. They can be used to make objects of all kinds as well as fibres for textiles. Extra-strong glues, long-lasting paints, and lightweight materials that are stronger than metal – all of these products are made of plastics with special qualities. None can be made with natural materials.

Bakelite was invented in 1909 by the American chemist Leo Baekeland. It was the first plastic to be made from synthetic chemicals.

PVC
Electrical wires have a coating of flexible PVC (polyvinyl chloride), which is also used to make inflatable toys.

POLYTHENE
Plastic bags are often made of polythene, a plastic that can be made into a tough, flexible film. When produced in thicker layers, polythene is also used to make bottles, bowls, and other household containers.

KINDS OF PLASTICS
There are thousands of different plastics. Some of the most common types are shown below.

NYLON
Fibres of nylon, a strong but flexible plastic, are used to make ropes and hard-wearing fabrics. Solid nylon is used to make gearwheels and other hardware.

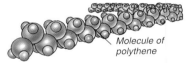

POLYMERS

Molecule of polythene

Plastics are polymers, which are substances with molecules composed of long chains of atoms. This is why the names of plastics often begin with *poly*, which means "many". Long molecules give plastics their special qualities, such as flexibility and strength.

POLYSTYRENE
Packaging made from polystyrene is light and rigid. Tough plastics often contain polystyrene.

POLYCARBONATE
Goggles need to be clear and strong, two qualities of polycarbonate plastic. Other uses include car lights and crash helmets.

BEECH STARSHIP 1
In aircraft, composites can be used to replace many metal parts. This aircraft is made almost entirely of composites which are highly resistant to corrosion and cracking,

COMPOSITES
Strong fibres are put into tough plastics to create materials called composites, which are very strong yet light and easily shaped. Thin fibres of glass, carbon, or Kevlar (a strong plastic) are used.

Carbon-fibre sheet
Layer of epoxy (plastic adhesive)
Honeycomb of tough plastic
Epoxy layer
Carbon-fibre sheet

POLAR EXPLORATION

THE COLDEST PLACES on Earth were also the very last to be explored. At the North and South Poles fierce, icy winds lash the surrounding masses of snow. The first European explorers to reach the Poles risked their lives in the attempt, and some of them never returned. They used primitive equipment and simple transport. Explorers travelled part of the way by ship, then used skis for the remaining distance, carrying their equipment on sledges pulled by husky dogs or ponies. They faced terrible hazards. The low temperatures made frostbite common, and they had to carry with them everything they needed, including enough food for the long journey to the Pole and back. These early explorers used the position of the sun to tell them when they had reached their goal, because there were no landmarks in the polar landscapes. Later explorers had the advantage of more modern vehicles, but it was not until the middle of the 20th century that both polar regions had been fully explored.

ROBERT PEARY
Commander Robert Peary (1856-1920) was the first to reach the North Pole on 6 April, 1909, together with one other American and four Eskimos.

Scott's ship Discovery

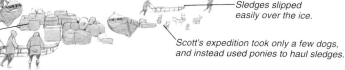

Food and other supplies were stored in dumps, ready for recovery by the party returning from the Pole.

Sledges slipped easily over the ice.

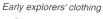

Scott's expedition took only a few dogs, and instead used ponies to haul sledges.

AMUNDSEN AND SCOTT

In 1912 the specially built wooden ship *Discovery* took an expedition led by British Captain Robert Scott (1868-1912) to within 1,450 km (900 miles) of the South Pole. When Scott's party reached the Pole, they discovered that they were not the first. A Norwegian team led by Roald Amundsen (1872-1928) had arrived at the South Pole on 14 December 1911, well ahead of their British rivals. Scott's group died before they could complete their return journey.

Early explorers' clothing

A heavy hood slowed heat loss from the head.

Fur mittens

MODERN RESEARCH
Today explorers have been replaced by scientists who carry out research at the Poles using more advanced equipment, but in the same harsh and unfriendly environment.

NORTH POLE
982 Viking Eric the Red discovers Greenland.

1607 Hudson tries to sail around northern Canada.

1827 Sir William Parry tries to reach the Pole using dog sledges.

1893-96 Norwegian ship freezes in pack ice and drifts close to the Pole.

1909 Peary reaches Pole.

1926 First flight to Pole.

1959 U.S. submarine *Skate* surfaces at Pole.

SOUTH POLE
1820 First sighting of Antarctic continent.

1821 A Russian sails around Antarctica, and an American sets foot on it.

1911 Five expeditions race to the Pole; Roald Amundsen wins.

1928 First aeroplanes used in Antarctica.

Goggles prevented sunlight from dazzling the explorers.

___*Find out more*___

ANTARCTICA AND THE ARCTIC
EXPLORERS
GLACIERS AND ICECAPS

POLAR WILDLIFE

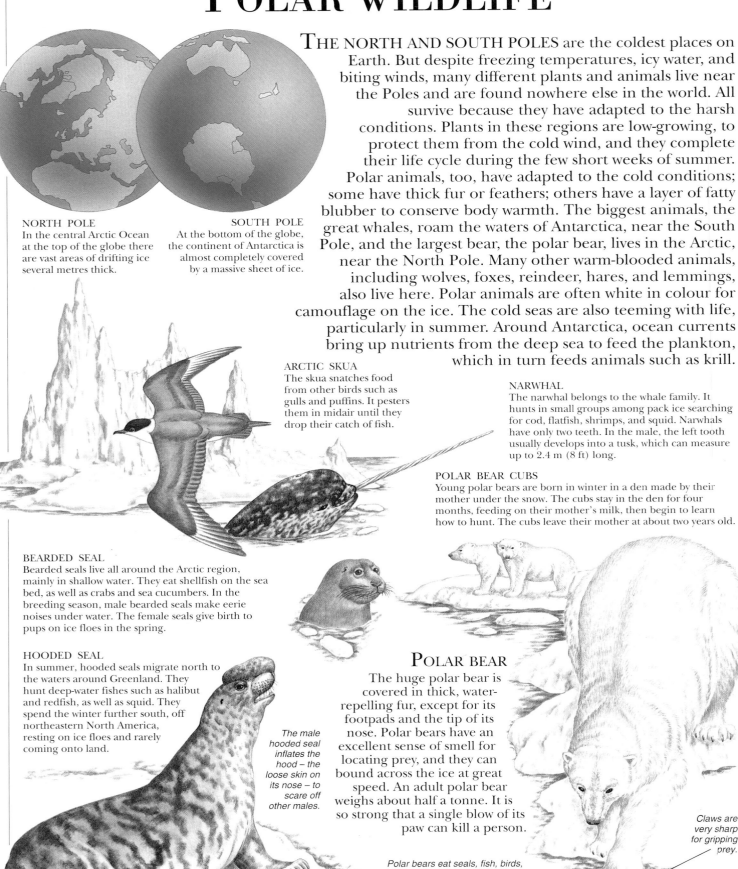

THE NORTH AND SOUTH POLES are the coldest places on Earth. But despite freezing temperatures, icy water, and biting winds, many different plants and animals live near the Poles and are found nowhere else in the world. All survive because they have adapted to the harsh conditions. Plants in these regions are low-growing, to protect them from the cold wind, and they complete their life cycle during the few short weeks of summer. Polar animals, too, have adapted to the cold conditions; some have thick fur or feathers; others have a layer of fatty blubber to conserve body warmth. The biggest animals, the great whales, roam the waters of Antarctica, near the South Pole, and the largest bear, the polar bear, lives in the Arctic, near the North Pole. Many other warm-blooded animals, including wolves, foxes, reindeer, hares, and lemmings, also live here. Polar animals are often white in colour for camouflage on the ice. The cold seas are also teeming with life, particularly in summer. Around Antarctica, ocean currents bring up nutrients from the deep sea to feed the plankton, which in turn feeds animals such as krill.

NORTH POLE
In the central Arctic Ocean at the top of the globe there are vast areas of drifting ice several metres thick.

SOUTH POLE
At the bottom of the globe, the continent of Antarctica is almost completely covered by a massive sheet of ice.

ARCTIC SKUA
The skua snatches food from other birds such as gulls and puffins. It pesters them in midair until they drop their catch of fish.

NARWHAL
The narwhal belongs to the whale family. It hunts in small groups among pack ice searching for cod, flatfish, shrimps, and squid. Narwhals have only two teeth. In the male, the left tooth usually develops into a tusk, which can measure up to 2.4 m (8 ft) long.

POLAR BEAR CUBS
Young polar bears are born in winter in a den made by their mother under the snow. The cubs stay in the den for four months, feeding on their mother's milk, then begin to learn how to hunt. The cubs leave their mother at about two years old.

BEARDED SEAL
Bearded seals live all around the Arctic region, mainly in shallow water. They eat shellfish on the sea bed, as well as crabs and sea cucumbers. In the breeding season, male bearded seals make eerie noises under water. The female seals give birth to pups on ice floes in the spring.

HOODED SEAL
In summer, hooded seals migrate north to the waters around Greenland. They hunt deep-water fishes such as halibut and redfish, as well as squid. They spend the winter further south, off northeastern North America, resting on ice floes and rarely coming onto land.

The male hooded seal inflates the hood – the loose skin on its nose – to scare off other males.

POLAR BEAR
The huge polar bear is covered in thick, water-repelling fur, except for its footpads and the tip of its nose. Polar bears have an excellent sense of smell for locating prey, and they can bound across the ice at great speed. An adult polar bear weighs about half a tonne. It is so strong that a single blow of its paw can kill a person.

Claws are very sharp for gripping prey.

Polar bears eat seals, fish, birds, and small mammals. They also scavenge on the carcasses (dead bodies) of whales.

CONSERVATION

Today polar bears and whales are protected from hunting by law. But many polar animals are still threatened by oil spills from ships and by over-fishing. Fishing boats catch huge quantities of fish, which affects the numbers of animals that depend on fish for food.

KRILL

The shrimplike creatures shown left are called krill. They are the main food for baleen (whalebone) whales, such as the blue whale, which scoop up thousands of krill from the ocean every day.

PENGUINS

There are 16 different kinds of penguins; all live in the southern hemisphere. Penguins cannot fly, but they are expert swimmers and divers. They can speed along in the water after fish and squid using their flipper-shaped wings.

EMPEROR PENGUIN

The emperor penguin breeds in the coldest place on Earth – on Antarctic ice where the average temperature is – 20° C (– 4° F). After the female has laid an egg, the male penguin keeps it warm between his feet and belly for about 60 days. The newborn chicks stay warm by standing on their parents' feet.

ICE FISH

The blood of most fish freezes solid at about – 35° C (– 32° F), and the waters in the polar regions sometimes drop even lower. The icefish, also called the crocodile fish, has special chemicals in its blood to stop it from freezing.

TUNDRA

The lands on the edge of the Arctic Ocean are bleak and treeless. This region is called the tundra. The brief summer in the Arctic allows small plants such as sedges, cushion-shaped saxifrages, heathers, mosses, and lichens to grow. These plants provide food for many insects and the grazing caribou. Birds such as snow geese breed along the shores and migrate south in autumn.

LEOPARD SEAL

The four main kinds of seals around Antarctica are the leopard, crabeater, Ross, and Weddell seals. The leopard seal measures up to 3 m (10 ft) in length. It patrols the pack ice and island coasts hunting for penguins and other seals, especially crabeater seals.

There is little life on the continent of Antarctica itself, apart from a few mosses, lichens, and tiny creatures such as mites.

MUSK OX

The musk ox is related to goats and sheep. It is the only large mammal that can survive winter on the tundra. The musk ox's thickset body has dense underfur and a thick, shaggy outer coat of tough hairs. Musk oxen stand together in a herd for warmth and as protection against predators such as wolves.

SNOW GOOSE

About 100 kinds of birds migrate to the tundra to breed in spring. Snow geese arrive two weeks before there are any plants to eat, but they have a store of body fat which allows them to make a nest and lay eggs before they eat. Later they feed the chicks on the newly growing grasses.

Dwarf willows are among the world's smallest shrubs. They grow low and spread sideways to stay out of the icy winds.

ARCTIC SAXIFRAGE

The cushion shapes of tundra flowers such as saxifrage and crowberry help prevent the plants from freezing. These plants also provide shelter for the tiny creatures living inside them.

___*Find out more*___

ANTARCTICA AND THE ARCTIC
BEARS AND PANDAS
FISH
SEA BIRDS
SEALS AND SEA LIONS
WHALES AND DOLPHINS

POLICE

ALL SOCIETIES HAVE rules or laws to protect the rights of their citizens. In a few remote communities the people themselves enforce the laws and identify and catch anyone who breaks them. But in most societies law enforcement is the job of the police. Police officers have many different duties. They chase dangerous criminals, stop motorists who drive too fast, and patrol neighbourhood streets. Some work in offices, carefully studying information for clues in order to solve a crime. The police arrest people suspected of committing a crime, then charge the suspects (accuse them of the crime) and hand them over to the courts for trial. The police must be careful to enforce only existing laws and not to arrest people for imagined crimes. In some countries, such as the United States, the police are civilians who are employed by the government. In other countries the police are similar to soldiers. And in many nations the government uses police to hold on to power and stop political opposition.

PEELERS

British police officers first appeared in the early 19th century. Politician Sir Robert Peel (1788-1850) argued for their introduction to try and make London a more law-abiding city. People nicknamed these first policemen "peelers" or "bobbies" after the founder of the force.

The pattern on the skin of every person's hands is unique. Detectives look for the fingerprints of the suspect at the scene of the crime.

Detectives produce a composite picture of the suspects they are seeking from descriptions provided by witnesses.

Detectives carefully label evidence to show where it was found.

Police keep fingerprint records of every known criminal.

DETECTIVES

Police officers with special training in investigating crime are called detectives. When a crime has been committed, one detective takes charge of the investigation. Detectives interview witnesses – people who saw the crime happen – and search for evidence. First they look for evidence that will help track down the person who committed the crime. When they have arrested a suspect, detectives look for evidence that will prove the suspect's guilt.

Plastic bags keep small pieces of evidence safe.

Brushing special powder onto shiny surfaces reveals fingerprints.

Some riot police are specially trained personnel; others are regular officers with special riot equipment such as helmets, shields, and heavy truncheons.

RIOT POLICE

Sometimes large demonstrations or marches become violent. The demonstrators may loot stores or attack members of the public. Riot police move in to control such disturbances. They try to stop the violence by arresting the troublemakers and dispersing the crowd so that peace returns.

UNIFORMED POLICE

Detectives often wear ordinary clothes, but most police officers wear a uniform. The uniform enables members of the public to recognize the police officers. In some countries traffic police wear a completely different uniform from the criminal investigation police. A uniform must be practical, with pockets for a two-way radio, notebooks, handcuffs, a truncheon, and other equipment. In some countries, such as the United States, the police are armed. In other countries, such as Britain, police do not usually carry guns.

Japan   Zimbabwe   United Kingdom   Thailand

Find out more

GOVERNMENTS
LAW
SPIES AND ESPIONAGE

POLLUTION

OIL ON BEACHES, vehicle exhaust fumes, litter, and many other waste products are called pollutants, because they pollute (dirty) our environment. Pollutants can affect our health and harm animals and plants. We pollute our surroundings with all kinds of chemical waste from factories and power stations. These substances are the unwanted results of modern living. Pollution itself is not new – a hundred years ago factories sent out great clouds of poisonous smoke. Today, there are many more factories and many more pollutants. Pollution has spread to the land, air, and water of every corner on Earth, even to Antarctica and Mount Everest. Scientists still have much to learn about pollution, but we do know more about how to control it. We can also reduce pollution by recycling waste and using biodegradable materials which eventually break down in the soil and disappear.

ACCIDENTAL POLLUTION
As well as everyday pollution, there is also accidental pollution – for example, when a ship leaks oil and creates a huge oil slick in the ocean. This kind of pollution causes damage to the environment and kills millions of fish and sea birds, like the oil-covered birds shown above.

ATMOSPHERIC POLLUTION
Ozone is a kind of oxygen present in the atmosphere high above the Earth's surface. It forms a protective layer that blocks out the sun's ultraviolet radiation, which can cause skin cancer in humans. Chemicals called CFCs (chloro-fluorocarbons), which are used in refrigerators, spray cans, and packaging, destroy the ozone. Scientists have discovered holes in the ozone layer above Antarctica and the Arctic.

Many factories release chemicals as a by-product. These chemicals can build up and pollute the air, rivers, and oceans.

Farmers spray crops with fertilizers to help them grow, and pesticides to control pests and weeds, but these chemicals harm the other kinds of wildlife that live and feed on the crops.

ACID RAIN
Vehicle exhausts produce fumes that contain nitrogen oxides. The coal we burn in power stations produces sulphur dioxide. When these two substances mix with water in the air, they turn into acids, then fall as acid rain. Acid rain damages trees, eats into buildings, and kills wildlife in rivers. Today, it is possible to reduce the amount of sulphur dioxide given off by power stations, but the process is expensive.

RECYCLING
If we save the glass, metal, plastics, and paper that we use every day, they can be recycled and used again. This helps preserve the Earth's natural resources. Recycling cuts down litter, reduces air and water pollution, and can save energy. Many towns have "bottle banks" to collect glass for recycling.

Ships leak oil into the sea, which is harmful to sea creatures.

Every day we drop litter on the ground – sweet wrappers, paper bags, empty tin cans, bottles, and cigarette packets. Litter is ugly, unhygienic, and a fire risk, and it can kill animals that eat it.

TRAFFIC POLLUTION
Lorry, car, and bus exhausts belch out lead (which can damage the nervous system), carbon monoxide, carbon dioxide, and nitrogen oxides which cause acid rain and the smog called photochemical smog. Some of these harmful substances are reduced by special catalytic converters attached to vehicle exhausts.

WASTE DUMPING
In many parts of the world people bury toxic (poisonous) chemicals and other dangerous waste products. These substances leak into the soil and water, killing wildlife. We treat the seas as waste dumps, and the North Sea is now seriously polluted. In order for the wildlife in the oceans and seas to survive, we must produce less harmful waste products.

Find out more
ATMOSPHERE
CLIMATES
CONSERVATION
and endangered species
NUCLEAR ENERGY
OIL
RAIN AND SNOW

POPULAR MUSIC

THE ELECTRIFYING APPEAL of popular music crosses all barriers of culture and language. It creates the same excitement in a TV audience of millions as it does in an audience of one on a personal stereo. Pop music is entertaining, memorable, and easy to listen to, and it comes in a wide range of styles, such as jazz, country-western, and blues. Much of this music originates in the traditional music of individual countries or peoples. For example, jazz, blues, and rap all have their roots in black American music. Each era produces its own styles of popular music. Some of this music, such as swing, vividly captures the atmosphere of the age in which it was written. Truly great pop songs have lasting appeal. Some even became serious music in later generations. For instance, waltzes were the pop songs of the 19th century!

ELECTRIC GUITAR
Electrical detectors called pick-ups on the body of an electric guitar turn the quiet vibrations of the strings into electric currents; the amplifier and loudspeakers change the current into musical notes.

Narrow neck makes playing chords easier.

Fret markers give position of notes.

Six metal strings

Body is made of solid wood.

Pick-ups are usually in two or three sets.

Tremolo arm bends the pitch of notes.

Controls to alter volume and tone

Cable from output leads to amplifier.

DANCE BAND
By modern standards, the dance bands that were so popular in the 1930s and 1940s were more like orchestras. But then, as now, dance music was rhythmical, light, and easy to listen to.

The performers wear earphones so that they can hear the other musicians and their instruments.

A soundproof window separates the studio from the control room.

The engineers can listen to the recording on monitor speakers in the control room.

Knobs on the mixing desk control the tone and volume of each track individually.

RECORDING STUDIO
Popular music reaches its enormous audience because it can be recorded and then distributed on tape and discs. Cables route the signals from the microphones and instruments in the studio to a special tape recorder, which records each instrument or voice on a separate track. The producer and engineers later mix the 24 or more tracks together to create a two-track stereo recording.

Pink Floyd in concert

LIVE MUSIC
Watching a performance at a live concert is far more thrilling than listening to a recording. Behind the scenes at any large concert are many people who help to make the show run smoothly. Engineers produce exciting sound and lighting effects. Stage crews, road managers, costume designers, makeup artists, and management complete the team.

THE BEATLES
Paul McCartney, Ringo Starr, John Lennon, and George Harrison from Liverpool, England, were a phenomenal success as the Beatles in the early 1960s. Lennon and McCartney composed many songs, such as *Yesterday*, that have since become pop classics. The Beatles separated in 1970.

Find out more

COMPOSERS
DANCE
MUSIC
MUSICAL INSTRUMENTS

PORTS AND WATERWAYS

SHIPS LOAD AND UNLOAD their cargoes at ports, or harbours – sheltered places on coasts or rivers with cranes and warehouses to handle ships, passengers, and goods. Road and rail connections link the ports with inland areas. The earliest ports were simply landing places at river mouths. Here ships were safe from storms, and workers on board could unload cargo into smaller boats for transport upriver. Building walls against the riverbanks created wharfs to make loading easier. In the 18th and 19th centuries, port authorities added docks – deep, artificial pools – leading off the rivers. Ships and boats use waterways to sail to inland towns or as shortcuts from one sea to another. Waterways can be natural rivers, or artificial rivers called canals. One of the world's largest waterway systems, based on the Mississippi River links the Great Lakes with the Gulf of Mexico. It includes 24,000 km (15,000 miles) of waterways.

Navigation lights guide ships safely into the port.

Ships and boats unload at wharfs.

Huge tanks at the terminal store the oil until it is needed.

Because oil burns easily, oil tankers use special terminals to unload their cargo.

DOCKS

Huge gates at the entrance to the docks maintain the water level inside. The warehouses and cranes of the old-style docks are disappearing today as more ships carry goods in containers – large steel boxes of standard size that are easy to stack and move.

LOADING AND UNLOADING
Ships carry nearly two thirds of all goods in containers, but many items do not fit neatly inside them. Cranes lift these individual large pieces of cargo on and off the ships. Loose cargo such as grain is sucked up by huge pumps and carried ashore through pipes. Vehicles drive onto special ships known as "ro-ros": roll-on, roll-off ferries.

CONTAINERS
A special wheeled crane handles containers. It lifts them off the ship and can either stack them nearby or lower them onto the back of a truck. Cranes, ships, and trucks around the world have the same size fittings so that they can move containers easily between different countries.

SINGAPORE
At the centre of the sea routes of southern Asia lies Singapore, one of the busiest ports in the world. Its large, modern docks handle goods from all over the world. Many large ships from Europe and the Americas unload their cargoes here into smaller vessels for distribution to nearby countries.

HOW A LOCK WORKS

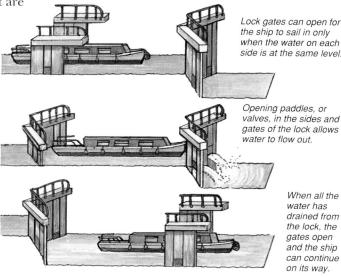

Lock gates can open for the ship to sail in only when the water on each side is at the same level.

Opening paddles, or valves, in the sides and gates of the lock allows water to flow out.

When all the water has drained from the lock, the gates open and the ship can continue on its way.

LOCKS
To raise or lower ships from one water level to another, canals and harbours have locks. If a ship is going to a lower water level, the lock fills with water and the ship sails in. Closing the upper gates and letting out the water gradually lowers the ship to the level of the water outside the lower gates.

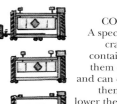

PANAMA CANAL
Ships travelling around the South American coast from the Caribbean Sea to the Pacific Ocean must sail nearly 10,000 km (6,000 miles). So the United States built a huge canal through Panama in Central America where the Pacific and the Caribbean are just 82 km (51 miles) apart. The canal opened in 1914.

__Find out more__
NAVIGATION
SHIPS AND BOATS
TRADE AND INDUSTRY

POSTAL SERVICES

MILLIONS OF LETTERS pass through the postal system each day. But even those posted to you from the other side of the world reach your home within only a few days. To accomplish this miracle, the postal system relies on a network of sorting offices. Every letter passes through several sorting processes at different offices. If you post a letter to a friend far away, workers from the post office first collect your letter from the postbox. Then they take it back to the sorting office and put it into a sack along with others destined for the same county or urban area. Vans, trains, or aeroplanes rush the sack to the correct destination, where more postal workers empty out the sack and sort the letters once more – this time by town, or by city district. Again, the post travels onwards to the local sorting office, then on to a neighbourhood office. There, postal workers sort the letters by street and by house before delivering them on foot or by van.

HILLTOP BEACONS
Fires carried messages long before there was a regular postal service. During the 16th century a chain of hilltop fires warned the British of the danger of a Spanish invasion. Watchers on each hilltop lit their beacon when they saw a flame on the horizon. The signal travelled from beacon to beacon faster than a messenger could ride on horseback.

Cancellation with a postmark means a stamp cannot be re-used.

The name and address must be easy for the postal worker to read.

The street or district address is shown in the form of a post-code too.

Stamps are always placed in the top right-hand corner.

Phosphor dots reveal the post-code to the sorting machine.

STAMPS
The first postage stamps appeared in Britain in 1840. They were prepaid; postage cost one penny regardless of how far the letter had to travel. In 1847 the United States started producing stamps, and other countries soon followed. Today, every country produces stamps in a range of prices, often changing the illustrations to commemorate national events and famous citizens.

Parcels and packages still need to be sorted by hand.

SORTING SYSTEM
The use of machines has made the task of sorting mail much quicker and easier. Machines read and postmark the stamps so they cannot be used again. A keyboard operator translates the postal codes into a series of phosphor dots that can be sorted automatically. A modern sorting system can deal with 350,000 letters per hour.

PONY EXPRESS
In 1860 in the United States, the pony express company introduced a fast postal service between Missouri and California. Stagecoach post took six weeks, but the relays of riders employed by the pony express cut this to eight days, with each rider covering up to 120 km (75 miles) a day. There were 80 riders. One of them was 14-year-old William Cody, later famous as Buffalo Bill. The service was short-lived and was soon replaced by the telegraph.

Find out more

TRADE AND INDUSTRY
TRANSPORT,
history of
WILD WEST

POTTERY

HEATING CLAY DUG from the ground transforms it from oozing wet mud to the strong, hard, waterproof material that we call pottery. Pottery has many uses because its properties are so different from those of clay. The potter (pot maker) can easily mould the soft clay into a wide variety of shapes, from flat plates for eating, to deep jars for storage. Firing, or baking the pot, sets its shape forever.

The potter's art is very old. The first potters worked in the Middle East 9,000 years ago. They made simple pressed pots and coiled pots as shown below left. And 3,500 years ago potters started to use small turntables, now called potter's wheels, to make their pots perfectly round. We know this because pottery does not decay in the ground as wood does. Archaeologists use pottery fragments to learn about the people who made the pots centuries ago.

PRESSED POTS
A potter can make many identical pots by pressing clay into a plaster mould.

COILED POTS
Pots can be made without a wheel by coiling long, thin rolls of clay.

SLIP CASTING
Pouring liquid clay (slip) into the plaster mould of a pot coats the inside. When dry, the clay forms a perfect replica of the mould.

PORCELAIN
By adding sand to clay, potters create a special kind of pottery called porcelain. The sand turns to glass in firing, making the porcelain almost transparent. The Chinese invented porcelain more than 1,200 years ago, but their art remained a secret until the 18th century.

FIRING
Pots must dry out after shaping. Then the potter stacks them carefully in the kiln – a big oven. Gas or electricity heats the kiln to more than 600°C (1,100°F) to turn the dry, brittle clay into rigid pottery. To make pots, the potter must control the temperature of the firing and how long it lasts.

The potter measures the firing temperature with a special thermometer or by placing small ceramic cones in the kiln. The cone melts when the temperature is high enough to fire the pots.

GLAZING
After the first firing, pottery is porous – water can still seep through it. Glazing the pottery completely seals its surface with a very hard, glasslike coating. Glaze is a mixture of metal oxides and minerals in water. The potter dips the pot into the glaze or pours the glaze on. The glaze dries, then the pot goes back into the kiln for a second firing. This melts the glaze and makes it stick to the pot.

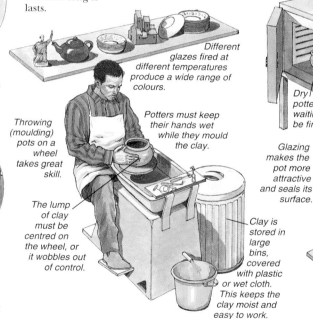

Different glazes fired at different temperatures produce a wide range of colours.

Throwing (moulding) pots on a wheel takes great skill.

Potters must keep their hands wet while they mould the clay.

The lump of clay must be centred on the wheel, or it wobbles out of control.

Dry pottery waiting to be fired.

Glazing makes the pot more attractive and seals its surface.

Clay is stored in large bins, covered with plastic or wet cloth. This keeps the clay moist and easy to work.

Before glazing their pots, potters decorate them with slip, underglaze colours, or enamel.

TRADITIONAL POTTERY

Potters in every culture have shaped and decorated their pots in unique ways. Many made useful pots such as bowls and cooking vessels. But craft potters as far apart as South America and Korea also made objects for decoration and enjoyment, including beads and musical instruments.

MAKING POTS

There are three main stages in making pots: shaping the clay, firing, and glazing. Potters use many different methods of shaping clay. To make perfectly circular objects, they "throw" the pot from a lump of clay on a revolving wheel. As the wheel spins, the potter uses both hands to draw the lump of clay upward and form the sides of the vessel.

___ *Find out more* ___
CHINA, HISTORY OF
GLASS AND CERAMICS
ROCKS AND MINERALS

PREHISTORIC LIFE

WHEN PLANET EARTH FORMED more than 4,600 million years ago, there was no life. Torrential storms raged, lightning bolts flashed, volcanoes poured out poisonous gases, and there was no atmosphere to protect the Earth from the sun's radiation. Slowly, warm shallow seas formed. In these seas the first forms of life appeared, protected by the water. We call these early beginnings "prehistory" because they happened before written history. Fossils – the preserved remains of plants and animals – provide the only records of prehistoric life. We know from fossils more than 2,000 million years old that some of the earliest forms of life were bacteria. Gradually plants called blue-green algae evolved, or developed. These produced oxygen – the gas that plants and animals need for life. Oxygen was released into the air from the sea and formed a protective blanket of ozone in the atmosphere. The ozone screened out the sun's radiation, and living things began to invade the land and take to the air. Millions of kinds of animals and plants have existed since the first signs of life – some, such as insects, have thrived; others, such as the dinosaurs, have died out as the Earth's environment has changed.

2,000 MILLION YEARS AGO
The earliest forms of life were bacteria and blue-green algae. The algae grew in rings or short columns called stromatolites, which are fossilized in rocks. Today stromatolites still form in shallow tropical seas.

Some of the earliest forms of life on Earth are fossils called stromatolites.

600 MILLION YEARS AGO
Rare fossils of soft-bodied creatures show us that many different animals had evolved by this time. They included the first kinds of jellyfish, corals, sea pens, and worms.

Sea pens existed 600 million years ago.

450 MILLION YEARS AGO
Fossils from this time are much more common, because animals had developed hard shells that preserved well. They include trilobites, nautiloids, sea urchins, and giant eurypterids, or sea scorpions, more than 2.5 m (8 ft) long.

Trilobites were common 450 million years ago. They are ancient relatives of crabs.

One of the first fishes, about 390 million years old

390 MILLION YEARS AGO
Fish were the first creatures with backbones. They evolved quickly into many different kinds. Gradually they developed jaws and fins. The first small land plants, such as mosses, appeared on the swampy shores.

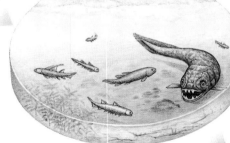

Cooksonia was one of the first land plants to appear on Earth.

HOW WE KNOW THE AGE OF FOSSILS

Stages		Million years ago (mya)
	Quaternary period	2 to today
	Tertiary period	65 to 2 mya
	Jurassic and Cretaceous periods	195 to 65
	Triassic period	230 to 195
	Carboniferous and Permian periods	345 to 230
	Devonian period	395 to 345
	Ordovician and Silurian periods	500 to 395
	Cambrian period	570 to 500
	Pre-cambrian period	4,000 to 570

Scientists called palaeontologists find out how old a fossil is from the age of the rocks around it. This is called relative dating. They also measure the amounts of radioactive chemicals in the rocks and fossils to find out when they formed. This is called absolute dating.

Prehistoric time is divided into different stages, called eras, which are further divided into periods. Each of these stages lasted for many millions of years. If you dig deep down into the Earth's surface, you can find fossils of animals and plants that lived during the different periods.

350 MILLION YEARS AGO
As plants became established on land, they were soon followed by the first land animals, such as millipedes and insects. Woody trees that looked like conifers stood more than 30 m (100 ft) high. Sharks and many other fish swam in the seas.

EXTINCTION

We are concerned because many animals and plants are in danger of dying out, or becoming extinct. But ever since life began, animals and plants have died out, to be replaced by others. This process is part of nature. As the conditions on Earth change, some living things cannot adapt; they eventually become extinct. Scientists believe that 99 per cent of all the different plants and animals that ever lived have died out naturally. In prehistoric times there were mass extinctions when hundreds of different things died out together. These extinctions were often due to dramatic changes in climate. About 225 million years ago, 90 per cent of all the living things in the sea died out. Today, animals and plants are dying out more quickly because humans damage and destroy the areas where they live.

STEGOSAURUS
This dinosaur lived about 150 million years ago in North America. It became extinct about 140 million years ago.

NEANDERTHAL PEOPLE
These people lived from about 120,000 to 35,000 years ago. They were the same species as ourselves, but smaller. As modern humans (*Homo sapiens*) evolved (developed), these people died out.

150 MILLION YEARS AGO
Dinosaurs ruled the land. Reptiles such as plesiosaurs ruled the seas, and other reptiles, the pterosaurs, flew in the air. There were also birds and mammals at this time. Ammonites were common in the seas.

Insects such as the dragonfly evolved about 350 million years ago.

Mosasaur was one of the first sea reptiles. Its sharp teeth show that it was a meat eater, and it probably hunted fish.

The first bats existed about 50 million years ago.

300 MILLION YEARS AGO
The first amphibians had crawled from the water about 50 million years earlier. Gradually they developed stronger limbs and thicker skins, so they could live on land. They still had to return to the water to lay their eggs. Giant ferns and horsetails grew in the warm swamps.

Sabre-toothed cats existed 19 – 2 million years ago. Their huge teeth enabled them to attack and kill large prey.

65 MILLION YEARS AGO
Trees with blossoms, such as the magnolia, began to appear on Earth more than 100 million years ago. Later, about 65 million years ago, dinosaurs and many other living things became extinct (died out). During the next few million years different kinds of mammals and birds became more common.

GREAT ICE AGE
About 2 million years ago, several ice ages gripped the Earth, with warmer stretches between. Humans evolved – probably in Africa – and soon spread around the world. In the north, they hunted woolly mammoths, woolly rhinos, and sabre-toothed cats. About 18,000 years ago, ice sheets covered much of northern Europe, northern Britain, and North America.

Find out more
COAL
DINOSAURS
EVOLUTION
FOSSILS
PREHISTORIC PEOPLES

PREHISTORIC PEOPLES

COMPARED WITH the rest of life on Earth, human beings arrived quite recently, after the dinosaur age and the age of mammals. The whole story of human evolution is incomplete, because many parts of the fossil record have never been found. Human-like mammals first emerged from the ape family about five million years ago in central Africa. They came down from the trees and began to walk on two legs. Hominids, or early humans, were more apelike than human and lived in the open. Over millions of years they learned to walk upright and developed bigger brains. These large brains helped them to develop language and the ability to work together. Hominids lived in groups and shared work and food, wandering through the countryside gathering fruits, roots, nuts, berries, and seeds, and hunting animals. Standing upright left their hands free to make tools and weapons, shelters and fire. They lived in caves and in shelters made from branches and stones. These early humans spread slowly over the rest of the world and soon rose to dominate life on Earth.

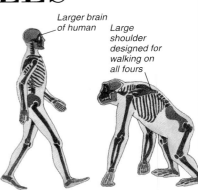

Larger brain of human

Large shoulder designed for walking on all fours

HUMAN OR APE?
Humans have smaller jaws and larger brains than apes. The human hand has a longer thumb; apes have longer fingers. The human pelvis and thigh have developed to allow upright motion, giving the spine an S-shaped curve. People have longer legs than arms; apes have the reverse. Unlike apes, humans cannot use their big toes as extra thumbs; the foot has adapted to walking and can no longer grasp.

WISDOM TOOTH
Early people needed wisdom teeth in order to eat roots and berries. Today we no longer need wisdom teeth, and many people do not even develop them.

Lucy's remains were found at Hadar.

Lucy gathered fruit to eat.

Fossil remains of the earliest hominids have all been found in East Africa.

Homo habilis

Simple stone tool

Homo erectus

Homo erectus *made more advanced tools, such as this spear.*

Simple clothing

Neanderthal man

Sophisticated carving

Sewn leather clothing

Rough woven cloth

Modern people wore shoes.

LUCY
In 1974 archaeologists discovered a complete fossil hominid skeleton in Ethiopia, northeastern Africa. She was nicknamed Lucy, after the song "Lucy in the Sky with Diamonds". Lucy was 3 million years old. Although nearly human, she was probably not one of our direct ancestors.

When alive, Lucy was about the same height as a ten-year-old girl, and weighed 30 kg (66 lb)

FROM HOMINIDS TO HUMANS
About 2,500,000 years ago hominids called *Homo habilis* (meaning "handy man") shaped crude stone tools and built rough shelters. Other, more advanced hominids, called *Homo erectus*, moved out of Africa into Europe and Asia. They lived in camps, made use of fire, and probably had a language. After the Ice Age, Neanderthals lived in Europe. Neanderthals looked much like people today, wore clothes, made flint tools and fire, and buried their dead. They vanished about 30,000 years ago and were replaced by "modern people," who invented farming about 9,000 years ago and began to settle down in communities. Shortly after, the first civilizations began.

MODERN PEOPLE
When humans learned to domesticate animals and grow crops, they stopped wandering and settled down on farms. Thus towns began to develop.

Find out more
ARCHAEOLOGY
BRONZE AGE
EVOLUTION
PREHISTORIC LIFE
STONE AGE

PRINTING

HAVE YOU EVER thought about how many times you look at print each day? Printed words and pictures have found their way into almost every part of our lives: on advertisements, road signs, food labels, records, clothes, newspapers, and, of course, in books such as this. Today we take this information for granted, but before the invention of printing, all information had to be laboriously written by hand, and only a few people had access to education.

The introduction of printing caused a revolution. Printing means that numerous identical copies of words and pictures can be made quickly and cheaply. Printing presses use a mirror image of the original to apply ink to paper, cardboard, and other materials. In the old days, printers used to set type (form words) in "hot" metal. They put pages together from metal blocks, each one of which printed either a single letter or a single line of text. Nowadays, the mirror image of an entire page can be made almost instantly on sheets of transparent film, and many printers use computers to speed up the process.

1 TYPESETTING
To set the type for a book, the words are typed into a computer. The computer sends signals to a machine containing a laser that prints the words onto a plastic, light-sensitive film, called the type film.

2 COLOUR SEPARATION
All the colours and illustrations in this book are reproduced with just four coloured inks; each is printed with a plate made from a separate film. To make the separate films (called colour separations), all the pictures are laid on a spinning drum. A laser scans over the pictures four times – once for each separation.

Yellow colour separation

Cyan colour separation

Magenta colour separation

Black colour separation

Original picture containing all colours

3 PRINTING PRESS
The printing plates are made photographically, by shining light through the type and colour films so that the details are recorded by the plate's light-sensitive coating. Each of the plates is treated with chemicals to bring out the print image, then fitted onto rollers in the printing press. There are four plates altogether, one for each of the coloured inks. As the paper runs through the press, it passes over each of the four inked plates in turn. These plates add the four colours one by one. Separate rollers run over the plates and keep them wet with fresh ink. The paper emerges at the far end as printed pages in full colour.

Adding yellow ink

Adding cyan ink

Adding magenta ink

Adding black ink

Page printed with yellow ink only.

Final printed page built up from yellow, cyan, magenta, and black inks.

After the paper is printed on one side, it is fed back through the press for printing on the other side.

THE HISTORY OF PRINTING
In A.D. 868, the Chinese were printing books using carved wooden blocks. In about 1440, Johannes Gutenberg of Germany developed movable type, in which separate pieces of type print each letter on a handpress (right). This process remained in use for 350 years until the invention of power-driven presses which allowed books to be printed more easily.

Gutenberg and his press

FOUR-COLOUR PRINTING
All the colours you see on this page are made up of dots printed with just four different coloured inks: yellow, magenta (blue-red), cyan (green-blue), and black. More colours are sometimes used for high-quality prints, but this costs more, since most printing presses are set up to print in four colours only.

Find out more

BOOKS
COLOUR
NEWSPAPERS
PAPER

PUPPETS

THE PUPPET SHOW is one of the oldest forms of theatre, and each age has produced new traditions. In Africa, China, and India puppets were used in early times to dramatize legends and religious stories. In the 18th century the Bunraku puppets of Japan acted out dramatic stories to the words of a narrator with the puppeteers in full view. Punch and Judy in England and Petrushka in Russia are puppets that grew out of the characters of Italian comedy of the 16th to 18th centuries. There are many different ways to work a puppet. It takes just one hand to work simple finger puppets, but some complicated Japanese puppets require three operators. Puppets sometimes comment on what is going on in the real world and can be quite mischievous. Modern puppeteers such as the late Jim Henson, the creator of the Muppets, have replaced the strings and rods of traditional puppets with electronic mechanisms.

MARIONETTES

String puppets, or marionettes, require two hands and great skill. The operator controls the puppet by moving a wooden bar to which the strings are attached. Some strings are linked to synchronize movements; for example, raising one leg lowers the other.

FINGER PUPPETS

Making a finger puppet is simple – and operating one is just as easy. With a little practise, you can stage a whole puppet play using just the fingers of both hands.

Several operators are needed to control the body puppet.

The puppet's eyes can open and close.

So that the mouth can move, it is attached to the frame by hinges.

The person inside the puppet can hear directions from the operator.

A television set shows the operator what the viewer sees.

The puppet is moved by a cable link to the operator.

BODY PUPPETS

Life-size puppets are a real team effort. The person inside the suit manoeuvers the limbs while other operators control the face. The puppet is made from foam rubber over a rigid frame, so it is very light and easy to move.

The television camera films only the puppet; Jim Henson (center) and the other operators below remain hidden.

SHADOW PUPPETS

In this ancient form of puppetry the operator holds the puppet close to a screen. The light behind casts a shadow which the audience can see from the other side of the screen. Javanese puppets such as this one can be more than 1 m (3 ft) tall. The arms are moved by rods held from below. These puppets are traditionally made from buffalo hide and are brightly coloured in golds, reds, and blues.

HAND PUPPETS

Glove puppets are very simple to operate. A hand inside makes the puppet move, with the index finger supporting and turning the head. The arms of these Muppets are moved by a combination of glove and rod techniques.

Find out more

THEATRE

RABBITS AND HARES

ONE FEMALE wild rabbit produces more than 20 young each year, making the common rabbit one of the most numerous mammals. Originally from Europe, rabbits are now found in every region except Antarctica. In many places they are serious pests to farmers because they eat crops, but in recent years a disease called myxomatosis has reduced their numbers. The common rabbit belongs to a large group of animals called lagomorphs. They include hares, cottontails, and a small, furry creature called the pika. Rabbits and hares are fast, agile runners. They can walk but usually hop at great speeds. Rabbits and hares have sensitive whiskers and sharp senses. They also have long rodent-like front teeth to gnaw grass, roots, and leaves. Rabbits and hares have an unusual method of double digestion. They eat food, digest some of it, expel soft droppings, and then eat these to obtain more nutrients. Finally they leave small, hard pellets on the ground. Rabbits build burrows; hares live in open country. Young hares are born covered in fur with their eyes open; newborn rabbits are bald at first, and their eyes are closed.

Small white tail is used as a danger signal to other rabbits.

Large ears swivel to find direction of a sound.

Whiskers help rabbit find its way in tunnels and at night.

Body is about 40 cm (16 in) long.

Eyes stick out for all-round vision.

COMMON RABBIT

Most common rabbits usually stay within 140 m (150 yards) of their warren. Although rabbits usually feed at twilight and at night, they sometimes come above ground by day. Rabbits nibble grasses and other plants, cropping them close to the ground. Each rabbit spends much time grooming its coat with its claws, tongue, and teeth to remove dirt and the fleas that may carry the disease called myxomatosis.

PIKA

The pika, found in Asia and North America, is much smaller than its relative, the rabbit. In summer it breaks off stems of grass, leaves them to dry in the sun, then piles the dried grass into tiny haystacks. The pika uses the dried grass as a food store during the winter months.

Long ears and excellent hearing

Large, round eyes give hare keen eyesight.

WARREN
The warren is a system of tunnels dug among tree roots or in a bank or sand dune. It is home to about 10 adult rabbits and their young. Other smaller burrows in the rabbits' territory are used in emergencies. A doe (female rabbit) often raises her kits (young) in a separate tunnel called a stop.

HARE

Hares are larger and longer than rabbits, with longer hind legs and ears. Male hares are called jacks, and females are called jills. The jill gives birth to two or three young, called leverets. While the mother is away feeding, the young crouch in a shallow scoop in the grass called a form. The young are well camouflaged – as long as they keep perfectly still.

European hare

White tail

Body measures more than 50 cm (20 in) in length.

Long, powerful back legs

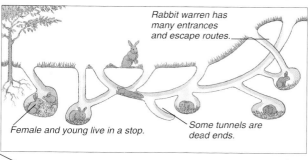

Rabbit warren has many entrances and escape routes.

Female and young live in a stop.

Some tunnels are dead ends.

Hare has long, slim front legs.

JACK RABBIT
Despite its name, the North American jack rabbit is actually a hare. Jack rabbits are speedy animals; some can run at more than 80 km/h (50 mph), outpacing many other creatures. In hot deserts jack rabbits lose excess heat through their huge ears. The black-tailed jack rabbit causes much damage by eating crops in the western part of North America.

___ **Find out more** ___

ANIMALS
CAMOUFLAGE
MAMMALS
NESTS AND BURROWS
WEASELS,
stoats, and martens

RADAR

FROM HUNDREDS OF kilometres away, a radar operator can track the movements of ships and aircraft even in dark or cloudy conditions. Radar finds objects by bouncing high-frequency radio waves off them and detecting the reflected waves. Radar is an extremely valuable tool. It helps aircraft find their way safely through crowded skies, warns weather forecasters of approaching storms, and reduces the risk of collisions at sea. Astronomers use radar to study the planets, and armies, air forces, and navies use radar for aiming missiles and locating opposing forces.

In the 1930s, a group of British scientists headed by Sir Robert Watson-Watt (1892-1973) developed an early radar system. During World War II (1939-1945), this system gave early warning of bombing attacks, which allowed defending aircraft time to take to the air.

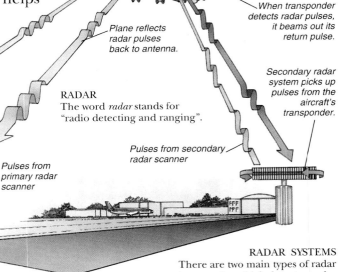

Radar in aircraft's nose detects bad weather.

Plane reflects radar pulses back to antenna.

When transponder detects radar pulses, it beams out its return pulse.

Secondary radar system picks up pulses from the aircraft's transponder.

RADAR
The word *radar* stands for "radio detecting and ranging".

Pulses from secondary radar scanner

Pulses from primary radar scanner

Radar antenna spins slowly to scan for aircraft in all directions.

HOW RADAR WORKS

A radar antenna sends out short bursts, or pulses, of radio waves. Between pulses the antenna listens for a return signal which has bounced off the target plane or ship. The direction in which the antenna is pointing gives the direction of the target. The delay between the transmitted pulse and the return pulses shows the distance of the target.

RADAR SCREEN

A radar screen inside a ship or aircraft displays a computer-generated map of the nearby land and sea. A central dot indicates the position of the ship or plane; other craft are represented by symbols on the screen.

Ship's radar

Radar image of coastline

Yellow line indicates direction of ship's travel.

RADAR SYSTEMS

There are two main types of radar systems: primary radar, which detects a radar "echo", and secondary radar, which detects a pulse transmitted by the target. Secondary radar is important for air traffic control. Airliners carry a transponder, a device which sends out a signal whenever a pulse from an air traffic control radar system strikes the plane. The transponder signal carries information such as the aircraft's identity, height, and speed.

MILITARY RADAR

Long-range ground-based radar scans the skies for intercontinental missiles; radar on high-altitude planes searches for low-flying aircraft approaching beneath the long-range beams. High-speed fighter aircraft have some of the most advanced radar systems. The radar scans the ground ahead so that the plane can fly rapidly just above the treetops and attack an enemy without warning.

Radio waves from speed trap

Radio waves bounce back off speeding car.

Radar scanner

SPEED TRAP

Police officers use radar to measure the speed of passing cars. A radar scanner sends out a beam of radio waves which bounce off an approaching car. The car's forward movement squeezes up the waves, so the reflected signal has a fractionally shorter wavelength than the original signal. The radar set measures the change in wavelength and calculates the car's speed.

The change in the wavelength of a signal caused by the movement of its source is called the Doppler effect.

Find out more
AIRCRAFT
AIRPORTS
MILITARY AIRCRAFT
NAVIGATION
RADIO

RADIO

EARLY RADIO WAS often called "wireless" because radio uses invisible waves instead of wires to carry messages from one place to another. Today, radio waves carry many kinds of information. Television signals carry picture and sound information; radio-control signals carry pulses that operate model planes and cars. Radio waves also occur naturally in space. Astronomers use them to learn about galaxies, supernovas (exploding stars), and other objects far from Earth.

Within the circuits of a radio transmitter, rapidly varying electric currents generate radio waves that travel to your radio receiver. Radio waves are a type of electromagnetic (EM) wave, like light and x-rays. Like these waves, radio waves travel at the speed of light, 299,792 km (186,280 miles) per second, nearly one million times the speed of sound waves.

MORSE CODE
Early radio signals consisted of beeps, made by tapping a key. Operators tapped out a message using a series of short and long beeps called Morse code, invented by Samuel Morse (1791-1872) in 1837.

RADIO STUDIO
A microphone converts sound waves from the announcer's voice into electrical signals, which are then transmitted as radio waves.

RADIO FREQUENCIES
Radio waves consist of rapidly oscillating (varying) electric and magnetic fields. The rate of oscillation is called the frequency of the wave, measured in hertz (Hz). One Hz equals one oscillation per second; one kilohertz (kHz) equals 1,000 hertz. Bands of certain frequencies are used to transmit different kinds of information.

A transmitter receives radio programmes by cable from the studio. The transmitter antenna beams radio waves that spread out like ripples in water.

Radio stations usually have a range of antennas to transmit radio waves of different frequencies.

Communications satellites pick up and rebroadcast radio programmes using super-high-frequency waves with frequencies of more than 3 billion Hz.

UHF (ultra-high-frequency) radio waves (300,000-3,000,000 kHz) carry television programmes.

Long waves (30-300 kHz) can travel almost 1,000 km (about 600 miles). They are used for national broadcasts and to send weather information to ships.

Programmes on medium-frequency (300-3,000 kHz) channels, called medium wave, travel for a few hundred kilometres. Many radio stations use the medium-wave band.

VHF (very-high-frequency) radio waves (30,000-300,000 kHz) move in straight lines so they cannot travel over the horizon. Police, fire brigade, and citizens band radios use VHF waves for short-range communications.

Short waves (3,000-30,000 kHz) can travel great distances. They bounce around the world, reflected off the ionosphere (a layer in the atmosphere) and the Earth's surface. International radio stations and amateur radio enthusiasts use short-wave radio signals.

MARCONI
In 1864, Scottish physicist James Clerk Maxwell developed the theory of electromagnetic waves, which are the basis of radio. In 1888, Heinrich Hertz, a German physicist, discovered radio waves. Italian Guglielmo Marconi (1874-1937, right) made the first radio system in 1895, and in 1901 he sent radio signals across the Atlantic.

RADIO RECEIVER
When radio waves hit the metal antenna of a radio set, they produce tiny varying electric currents within the antenna. As the tuner knob is turned, an electronic circuit selects a single frequency from these currents corresponding to a particular radio channel. This signal is amplified (boosted) to drive the loudspeaker, which converts the signal into sound waves.

Find out more
ASTRONOMY
NAVIGATION
RADAR
TELEPHONES
TELEVISION AND VIDEO

RAIN AND SNOW

THE WATER THAT FALLS from the sky as rain or snow is taking part in a continuous cycle. It begins when the water on the Earth's surface evaporates, or dries out, and enters the air as invisible water vapour. Rising air carries the vapour into the sky. The air cools as it rises, and the water vapour turns into tiny water droplets. These droplets are so small that they float in the air, and a cloud forms. A rain cloud contains millions of water droplets which merge together to form larger drops. When these drops become too large and heavy to float, they fall to the ground as rain and the cycle starts all over again. If the air is very cold, the water in the cloud freezes and forms snowflakes or hailstones. However, rainfall and snowfall are not equal all over the world. Deserts have hardly any rain at all; tropical regions can have so much rain that there are severe floods, while in the polar regions snow falls instead of rain.

LIFE-GIVING RAIN
Rain is vital to life on Earth. Plants need water to grow, providing food for us and other animals. Rain also fills the rivers and lakes which provide our water supply.

WATER CYCLE
Water enters the air from lakes, rivers, seas, and oceans through the process of evaporation. In addition, plants, animals, and people give out water vapour into the atmosphere. The vapour stays in the air for an average time of 10 days and then falls as rain or snow. It joins the sea, rivers, and underground watercourses, and the cycle begins once more.

Trees and other plants release water vapour into the air from their leaves.

Cloud begins to form from water vapour in the atmosphere.

Water joins rivers and streams and flows down to the sea.

Water droplets fall from a cloud especially over high ground where the air is cooler. The general name for rain, snow, sleet, hail, mist, and dew is precipitation.

Wind and the sun's heat cause water to evaporate from the oceans and other large areas of water.

Water seeps underground through a layer of porous rock and flows down to the sea.

RAINBOW
If the sun shines on a shower of rain, you may see a rainbow if you are looking towards the rain and the sun is behind you. The raindrops in the shower reflect the sun's light back to you. As the sunlight passes through the raindrops, it splits up into a circular band of colours. You see the top part of this circle as a rainbow.

SNOW AND HAIL
In cold weather, the water in a cloud freezes and forms ice crystals. These crystals stick together and fall as snowflakes. The snow may melt slightly as it falls, producing sleet. In some clouds, strong air currents can toss frozen raindrops up and down. Each time they rise and fall, the frozen drops collect more ice crystals and water, and frozen layers build up like the skin around an onion. Eventually they become so heavy that they fall to the ground as hailstones.

ICE CRYSTAL
A microscope reveals that snowflakes are made of tiny six-sided ice crystals. No two crystals are exactly the same.

Find out more
COLOUR
RIVERS
STORMS
WATER
WEATHER
WIND

REFORMATION

ON 31 OCTOBER, 1517, German monk Martin Luther pinned a list of 95 theses, or complaints, on a church door in Wittenberg, Saxony. This sparked off a movement known as the Reformation because its followers demanded the reform of the Catholic Church. The Catholic Church was the most powerful force in Europe. But many people, including Luther, believed it was corrupt, and attacked the wealth of the Church and the sale of indulgences (pardons for sins). In 1521, Luther was expelled from the Church. He set up his own church which became known as Protestant because its followers were protesting against Rome. Protestantism spread through Europe. Then, in a movement called the Counter-reformation, the Catholic Church began to reform itself. The Counter-reformation led to religious persecution and bitter civil wars in Europe.

MARTIN LUTHER
Martin Luther (1483-1546) inspired the Reformation. He attacked the sale of indulgences, and said that no amount of money paid to the clergy could pardon him for his sins. Only through faith could people be saved.

Catholic *Protestant* *Catholic and Protestant*

PROTESTANTISM
By 1560, Europe had two main religions – Roman Catholic and Protestant. Protestantism began in Germany. Many German rulers adopted the new religion so that they could break away from the control of the pope and the Holy Roman Emperor (the "political" Catholic ruler).

People were thrown out of windows during the war.

Battle scene during Thirty Years' War

THIRTY YEARS' WAR
The Thirty Years' War lasted from 1618 to 1648. It began as a religious struggle between Catholics and Protestants in Germany. Then it expanded into a war between the Hapsburg rulers of the Holy Roman Empire and the kings of France for possession of land. In 1648, by the Peace of Westphalia, the Protestants won the struggle.

COUNCIL OF TRENT
The Counter-reformation began when Catholic leaders met at the Council of Trent in 1545. The council established the main principles of Catholicism and set up places for training priests and missionaries. During this time the Jesuits, an important teaching order founded in 1534, became popular.

INQUISITION
In 1231, the pope set up the Inquisition – a special organization that searched out and punished heretics (those who did not conform to the Catholic faith). Inquisitors arrested, tortured, and executed heretics and witches (above). During the Reformation, 300 years later, the Inquisition tried to crush the new Protestant religion, but failed.

Find out more
EUROPE
FRANCE, HISTORY OF
GERMANY, HISTORY OF
HAPSBURGS
UNITED KINGDOM, HISTORY OF

RELIGIONS

THERE ARE MANY EVENTS in life which are impossible to control. Nobody can stop the seasons from changing or guess where lightning will strike. People have always searched for explanations of these events, and religions may be the result. A religion is a set of beliefs that tries to explain those aspects of life we do not fully understand. Most religious people believe in one God or several gods. Gods are supreme beings who created the world or who control what happens in it. Animism was the very first religion. Animists believe that there is a spirit or a god in every object, from animals to rocks. The belief that there might be only one God was first held by followers of Judaism around 4,000 years ago. Christians and Muslims also believe in a single, all-powerful God. Some religions are highly organized. People are told how to behave and live their lives.

They worship in special buildings and have priests to guide them. Other religions have less formal rules. Many people follow their beliefs in their own more individual way.

MOTHER GODDESSES
Pregnant female figures have been found at many ancient and holy places. Early peoples may have worshipped mother goddesses because they associated women with the production of new life.

ISLAM
The world's second largest religion, Islam, was founded by the prophet Muhammad 1,400 years ago. Followers of Islam are called Muslims, and most of them live in the Middle East. They believe in one God.

Early Christian symbol

CHRISTIANITY
The Christian religion has one God. Christians believe that God's son, Jesus Christ, lived on Earth about 2,000 years ago. Christianity has more followers than any other religion.

HINDUISM
The Indian religion of Hinduism began more than 5,000 years ago. Hindus worship many different gods, and most Hindus share a belief in reincarnation, or rebirth.

The main symbol of Hinduism is the word Om *– the name of God.*

A shaman or holy man from Taiwan in a trance

The Jewish Star of David symbol

The Buddhist wheel of life represents the cycle of birth and rebirth.

BUDDHISM
The teachings of an Indian prince, Siddharta Gautama, form the basic beliefs of Buddhism. Buddhists believe that people are reborn after death and are rewarded in their next life for good deeds in their present life.

JUDAISM
The religion of Jewish people is called Judaism. Jews were the first people to worship one God. Judaism began in the Middle East around 4,000 years ago.

DEATH AND HEAVEN
Religious people of many faiths believe that the human body is just a temporary container for the soul, or personality. After death the soul is reborn in another body or goes to heaven to join the gods. In some faiths, such as Christianity, heaven is a reward for good deeds or suffering on earth. Most religions have special rituals or funerals to honour and remember the dead.

JERUSALEM
For three religions Jerusalem is a holy place. Jews pray at the Wailing Wall, the ruins of a temple destroyed in A.D. 70. The Dome of the Rock mosque is sacred to Muslims. It is the site of Abraham's attempt to sacrifice his son. The Church of the Holy Sepulchre is one of many places associated with Jesus Christ.

RELIGIOUS EXPERIENCE
Many religious people feel the need to be closer to their God. Meditation, prayer, and chanting are all used to heighten this sense of closeness, and can produce a dreamlike state called a trance. In a trance people feel that holy spirits enter and control their bodies.

___*Find out more*___

BUDDHISM
CHRISTIANITY
FESTIVALS AND FEASTS
HINDUISM
ISLAM
JUDAISM

RENAISSANCE

ITALY IN THE 15TH CENTURY was an exciting place. It was here that educated people began to develop new ideas about the world around them and rediscover the arts and learning of Ancient Greece and Rome. For a period of about 200 years that became known as the Renaissance, meaning rebirth, people made great advances in learning and thinking. Helped by the invention of printing, the Renaissance gradually spread from Italy to the rest of Europe. Although the Renaissance affected only the wealthy, it had an enormous impact on the way that everybody lived and thought about the world around them. The Renaissance produced great artists such as Michelangelo and Raphael. It also produced a new way of thinking called humanism, as scholars and thinkers such as Erasmus began to challenge the authority of the Church. Humanism gave human beings more importance. It meant that artists such as Leonardo da Vinci began to produce more realistic images rather than symbolic scenes. Scientists, too, began to challenge old ideas about the nature of the universe and to conduct experiments.

COPERNICUS
By observing the movement of planets and stars, astronomers such as Nicolaus Copernicus (1473-1543) began to challenge ideas about the solar system which had been accepted since the time of the Ancient Greeks.

TECHNOLOGY
Renaissance scientists invented or developed new scientific instruments to help them in their work. The armillary sphere, a skeleton sphere with the Earth in the centre, was used to measure the position of the stars. Galileo invented the proportional compass, which could be set at any angle.

Armillary sphere

Proportional compass

Galileo at work

GALILEO
Galileo (1564-1642) was an Italian astronomer and physicist. He disproved many of the Ancient Greek thinker Aristotle's theories, including the theory that heavy bodies fall faster than light ones. He perfected a refracting telescope and observed that the Earth and all the planets of the solar system revolve around the sun.

LEONARDO DA VINCI
People sometimes describe Italian-born da Vinci (1452-1519) as a "universal man". This was a Renaissance ideal describing somebody who was skilled in many different areas. Da Vinci was not only a painter and a sculptor, he was also immensely knowledgeable about anatomy, architecture, astronomy, botany, and science.

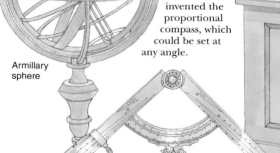

Leonardo was well ahead of his time, he designed several extraordinary machines including a tank, a parachute, and a type of airplane (above).

ERASMUS
Desiderius Erasmus (1466-1536) was a Dutch priest who wanted to reform the Catholic Church. He wrote many books criticizing the superstitions of the clergy. He also published studies of the Old and New Testaments to give people a better understanding of the Bible. A leading Renaissance humanist, he put humans before the Church, a shocking idea at the time.

BOTTICELLI

The paintings of Sandro Botticelli (1444-1510) show many of the features typical of Renaissance art: clear lines, even composition, and an emphasis on human activity. Renaissance artists painted realistic, mythological, and biblical subjects. Most tried to make their paintings as realistic as possible by using perspective to give scenes an appearance of depth. Above is the Botticelli painting *Venus and Mars*.

MEDICIS

The Medicis were a great banking family who ruled Florence for more than 300 years. They became very powerful. Many of them, particularly Lorenzo "the Magnificent" (1449-1492), encouraged artists such as Michelangelo, and helped them financially.

MICHELANGELO

Michelangelo (1475-1564) was a very skilled Italian artist and sculptor. His marble statue of David (left) is one of the finest examples of Renaissance sculpture. People admired the statue's youthful strength and beauty, which demonstrated the new realistic style of art.

Dome rises more than 120 m (400 ft) from the floor of the church.

ST. PETER'S

Situated in Vatican City, Rome, Italy, St. Peter's Church has a rich history. Ten different architects worked on its construction. Michelangelo designed the dome. The Italian architect Bernini (1598-1680) designed the inside of the church and the majestic piazza outside the church. St. Peter's houses many fabulous works of art, and marble and detailed mosaics decorate the walls.

SCULPTURE

Renaissance sculptors made great use of marble, copying the style of Ancient Roman statues. A new understanding of anatomy inspired sculptors to carve nude figures, with accurate depictions of muscles and joints. Some sculptors even dissected corpses to discover how the human body works.

ARCHITECTURE

Renaissance architecture was modelled on classical Roman building styles. Architects featured high domed roofs, vaulted ceilings, decorative columns, and rounded arches in their buildings. One of the most influential architects was Andrea Palladio (1508-1580). The classical designs used by Palladio for his many villas and palaces were widely copied by later architects.

RENAISSANCE

1420-36 Architect Filippo Brunelleschi develops the system of perspective.

1430-5 Donatello sculpture of David is the first large nude statue since the Roman Empire.

1480-5 Sandro Botticelli paints *The Birth of Venus*.

1497 Leonardo da Vinci paints *The Last Supper*.

1501 Petrucci publishes first printed music in Venice.

1501-4 Michelangelo sculpts David.

1502 Leonardo paints the *Mona Lisa*.

1505 Architect Donato Bramante begins the new St Peter's in Rome. Completed in 1655.

1508 Artist Raphael begins to decorate the pope's apartments in the Vatican.

1508-12 Michelangelo decorates the Sistine chapel.

1509 Erasmus writes *In Praise of Folly*, criticizing the Church.

c.1510 Renaissance art in Venice reaches its peak with artists such as Titian, Veronese, and Tintoretto.

1532 Niccolo Machiavelli's book *The Prince* is published, suggesting how a ruler should govern a state.

1543 Astronomer Copernicus claims that the Earth and the other planets move around the sun.

1552 Architect Palladio begins to build the Villa Rotunda in Venice.

1593 Galileo develops the thermometer.

1608 Galileo develops the telescope.

REPRODUCTION

FOR LIFE TO CONTINUE on Earth, humans and other animals must produce young. The process of creating new life is called reproduction. Human beings reproduce in much the same way as other mammals. From birth, a woman has many tiny pinhead-sized ova (egg cells) in two glands inside the abdomen called ovaries. From puberty onwards, one of these egg cells is released each month as part of the menstrual cycle. Throughout life, a man produces small tadpole-shaped cells called sperm in sex organs called the testes. During sexual intercourse, sperm cells leave the man's body and enter the woman's body, swimming towards her ovaries. If a sperm meets a ripe egg cell, the two join together. This is called fertilization. The egg cell can only be fertilized for about three days after ovulation. Fertilization makes the egg cell begin to develop in the woman's uterus. During the following nine months the tiny egg develops into a fully formed baby, ready to be born.

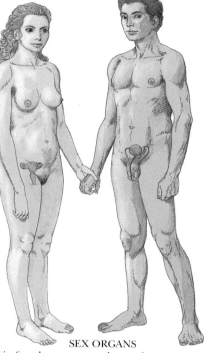

SEX ORGANS
The main female sex organs, the ovaries, are inside the abdomen. The main male organs, the testes and penis, hang outside the abdomen. Other differences between males and females, such as the woman's breasts, are called secondary sexual characteristics.

FOETUS
A developing baby lives in a watery world inside the uterus, cushioned from bumps, bright lights, and noises from outside by the amniotic fluid. However, the baby can hear the regular thump of the mother's heartbeat and the gurgling of food in her intestines.

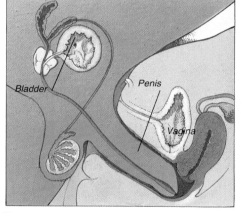

Bladder

Penis

Vagina

SEXUAL INTERCOURSE
During sexual intercourse, the man's penis becomes stiff enough to insert into the woman's vagina, which also enlarges. After a while muscular contractions squeeze sperm cells from the man's testes out of the penis and into the vagina, in a fluid called semen. This process is called ejaculation. The sperm cells swim through the uterus, propelled by their tails, and travel along the Fallopian tube. Sometimes, one of these sperm cells reaches the egg cell and fertilizes it, resulting in pregnancy.

FERTILIZATION
An egg cell begins to divide and develop into a baby only when it is joined by a sperm cell. After intercourse, hundreds of sperm cells reach the egg. But only one breaks through the outer layer. Once this occurs, genetic material in the sperm – the instructions needed to make a new human – joins the genetic material inside the egg. The coming together of sperm and egg and their genes is called fertilization, or conception.

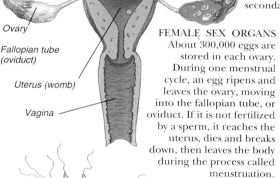

Ovary

Fallopian tube
(oviduct)

Uterus (womb)

Vagina

FEMALE SEX ORGANS
About 300,000 eggs are stored in each ovary. During one menstrual cycle, an egg ripens and leaves the ovary, moving into the fallopian tube, or oviduct. If it is not fertilized by a sperm, it reaches the uterus, dies and breaks down, then leaves the body during the process called menstruation.

Sperm cells cluster around egg cell in Fallopian tube. Only one sperm penetrates egg to fertilize it.

Fertilized egg divides into two cells within 36 hours, then into four within 48 hours, then into eight, and so on. Barrier around dividing cells keeps out other sperm cells.

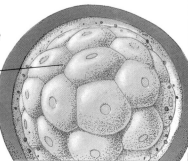

Embryo enters uterus about three days after fertilization in the form of a solid ball of 16-32 cells.

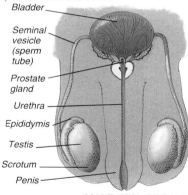

Bladder

Seminal vesicle (sperm tube)

Prostate gland

Urethra

Epididymis

Testis

Scrotum

Penis

MALE SEX ORGANS
Each testis makes more than 250 million sperm cells every day. The cells are stored in the testis itself and in a long, winding tube called the epididymis. If they are not released, they break down and are reabsorbed into the bloodstream.

PREGNANCY

About one week after fertilization, the ball of cells embeds itself in the blood-rich lining of the uterus and feeds off the nutrients there. The cells continue to divide and become different, forming the first body tissues such as blood vessels and nerves. Gradually the ball of cells folds and twists, to give the basic body shape. Meanwhile, other cells form the placenta, a saucer-shaped organ in the lining of the uterus. Inside the placenta, the baby's blood flows very close to the mother's blood. Vital oxygen and nutrients pass from mother to baby, while wastes go in the opposite direction.

5 WEEKS

The developing baby is now about 10 mm (1/2 in) long. It has a recognizable head, back, and heart, and the beginnings of a mouth and eyes. The limbs are forming as stubby buds. At this stage, the developing baby is called an embryo.

8 WEEKS

The baby is about 25 mm (1 in) long, and all the major parts of the body have formed – even the fingers and toes. The developing baby is now called a foetus.

12 WEEKS

Cells are still active in the baby, dividing and growing and putting the finishing touches on the body, such as eyelids, fingernails, and toenails. The baby is about 13 cm (5 in) long. There are still 28 weeks to go before it is born.

GENETICS

Certain characteristics, such as eye or hair colour, are handed down to children from their parents. This is called heredity. Genetics is the study of heredity. All of us inherit characteristics called genes from our parents. The genes are parcelled into structures called chromosomes. Each cell in the body (except egg and sperm cells) contains 46 chromosomes, consisting of 23 pairs. Egg and sperm cells have half the regular amount of chromosomes. When the egg and sperm cells join together at fertilization, the new cell has the correct number, 46 chromosomes.

Father XY   Mother XX

At fertilization, the 23 chromosomes in the female egg combine with 23 in the male sperm to form the full set of 46.

Daughter XX   Son XY

In a female all the sex chromosomes are the same, called X. In a male the sex chromosomes are either X or Y. At fertilization, one chromosome pairing determines whether a baby is a girl (XX) or a boy (XY).

PUBERTY

Babies and children have sex organs, but they are not able to release egg or sperm cells. At puberty these organs mature (become fully developed). Other changes occur at this time too, particularly a spurt in growth. Chemicals called sex hormones control these changes. The sex hormones are released into the bloodstream from hormonal glands. In a girl, the ovaries produce progesterone and oestrogen, which cause the breasts to develop and cause fatty tissue to form and give the body a more rounded shape.

In a boy, the testes produce the sex hormone called testosterone. Testosterone makes hair begin to grow on the face and body during puberty. It also makes the voice deeper, encourages muscle development, and begins sperm production.

MENSTRUAL CYCLE

Beginning at puberty (10 to 15 years), a woman's body undergoes a monthly process called the menstrual cycle. Changing levels of hormones thicken the uterus lining and enrich it with blood, to nourish a fertilized egg if it arrives.

1st week | 2nd week | 3rd week | 4th week

Lining of uterus breaks down and passes out of the vagina as menstrual blood flow, called menstruation.

Lining starts to thicken again in preparation for next egg. Next egg begins to ripen in ovary.

Ripe egg is released from ovary. Egg can be fertilized for up to 36 hours in Fallopian tube.

Egg reaches uterus and implants if fertilized, breaks down if not fertilized.

CHROMOSOMES

Chromosomes are in the nucleus of cells. They carry genetic information and give a unique mixture of genetic material to each person. Deoxyribonucleic acid (DNA) is found inside chromosomes. DNA is the main carrier of genetic information in almost all living things.

Chromosomes are thread-like structures visible only under a microscope.

Find out more

ANIMALS
HUMAN BODY

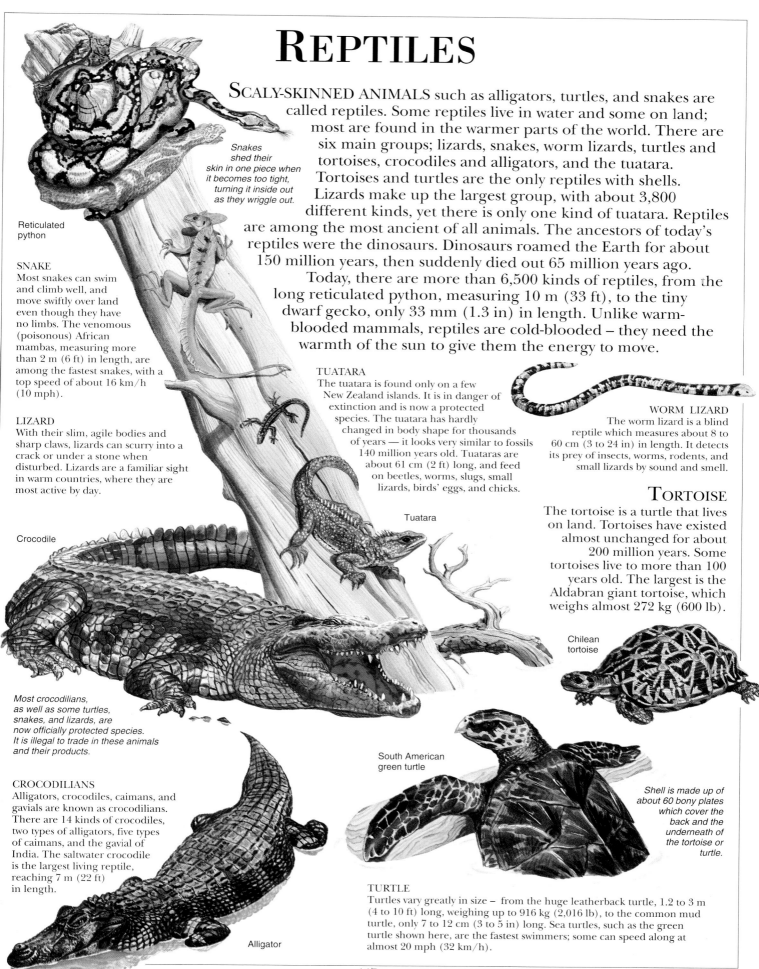

REPTILES

SCALY-SKINNED ANIMALS such as alligators, turtles, and snakes are called reptiles. Some reptiles live in water and some on land; most are found in the warmer parts of the world. There are six main groups; lizards, snakes, worm lizards, turtles and tortoises, crocodiles and alligators, and the tuatara. Tortoises and turtles are the only reptiles with shells. Lizards make up the largest group, with about 3,800 different kinds, yet there is only one kind of tuatara. Reptiles are among the most ancient of all animals. The ancestors of today's reptiles were the dinosaurs. Dinosaurs roamed the Earth for about 150 million years, then suddenly died out 65 million years ago. Today, there are more than 6,500 kinds of reptiles, from the long reticulated python, measuring 10 m (33 ft), to the tiny dwarf gecko, only 33 mm (1.3 in) in length. Unlike warm-blooded mammals, reptiles are cold-blooded – they need the warmth of the sun to give them the energy to move.

Snakes shed their skin in one piece when it becomes too tight, turning it inside out as they wriggle out.

Reticulated python

SNAKE
Most snakes can swim and climb well, and move swiftly over land even though they have no limbs. The venomous (poisonous) African mambas, measuring more than 2 m (6 ft) in length, are among the fastest snakes, with a top speed of about 16 km/h (10 mph).

LIZARD
With their slim, agile bodies and sharp claws, lizards can scurry into a crack or under a stone when disturbed. Lizards are a familiar sight in warm countries, where they are most active by day.

TUATARA
The tuatara is found only on a few New Zealand islands. It is in danger of extinction and is now a protected species. The tuatara has hardly changed in body shape for thousands of years — it looks very similar to fossils 140 million years old. Tuataras are about 61 cm (2 ft) long, and feed on beetles, worms, slugs, small lizards, birds' eggs, and chicks.

Tuatara

WORM LIZARD
The worm lizard is a blind reptile which measures about 8 to 60 cm (3 to 24 in) in length. It detects its prey of insects, worms, rodents, and small lizards by sound and smell.

TORTOISE
The tortoise is a turtle that lives on land. Tortoises have existed almost unchanged for about 200 million years. Some tortoises live to more than 100 years old. The largest is the Aldabran giant tortoise, which weighs almost 272 kg (600 lb).

Chilean tortoise

Crocodile

Most crocodilians, as well as some turtles, snakes, and lizards, are now officially protected species. It is illegal to trade in these animals and their products.

South American green turtle

Shell is made up of about 60 bony plates which cover the back and the underneath of the tortoise or turtle.

CROCODILIANS
Alligators, crocodiles, caimans, and gavials are known as crocodilians. There are 14 kinds of crocodiles, two types of alligators, five types of caimans, and the gavial of India. The saltwater crocodile is the largest living reptile, reaching 7 m (22 ft) in length.

Alligator

TURTLE
Turtles vary greatly in size – from the huge leatherback turtle, 1.2 to 3 m (4 to 10 ft) long, weighing up to 916 kg (2,016 lb), to the common mud turtle, only 7 to 12 cm (3 to 5 in) long. Sea turtles, such as the green turtle shown here, are the fastest swimmers; some can speed along at almost 20 mph (32 km/h).

BREEDING

Most reptiles lay eggs, from which the young hatch. Snake and lizard eggs usually have a leathery, flexible shell; the eggs of crocodiles and tortoises are hard and rigid, like birds' eggs. The loggerhead turtle shown here digs a deep hole in the beach sand and lays its eggs under cover of darkness. The eggs take several weeks to hatch and are at risk from foxes and monitor lizards, which dig them up and eat them. After hatching, the young turtles have to avoid sea birds and crabs as they scuttle down to the sea.

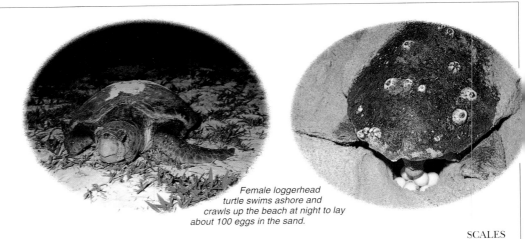

Female loggerhead turtle swims ashore and crawls up the beach at night to lay about 100 eggs in the sand.

BLUE-TONGUED SKINK

The reptile tongue has several uses. Lizards and snakes use it to detect their surroundings. The tongue flicks out to pick up chemicals in the air and carries them back to Jacobson's organs, special sensory organs in the roof of the mouth. When in danger, the Australian blue-tongued skink opens its mouth wide, thrusts out its bright blue tongue, hisses, and puffs up its body to frighten away a predator.

SCALES

A reptile's scaly skin provides good protection against predators and stops the animal from drying out. The arrangement of the scales helps scientists identify species. Some reptiles, such as chameleons, have special cells in the skin. These cells make the coloured pigments inside the skin expand or contract. This is how the chameleon changes its colour, for camouflage.

WALL GECKO

Wall geckos have tiny sticky pads on their toes which enable them to run up smooth glass windows and upside-down across the ceiling.

Wall gecko

During the hot midday sun the lizard stays in the shade to avoid overheating.

TEMPERATURE REGULATION

We often describe reptiles as cold-blooded, but this is not strictly true. Reptiles cannot generate body heat internally, in the way that mammals do, but they can control their body temperature by their behaviour. Reptiles bask in the sun to absorb warmth, then hide in the shade when they become too hot.

At dawn the lizard sunbathes with the side of its body facing the sun to absorb maximum heat.

At dusk the lizard basks with its head facing the sun to keep up its body temperature.

LARGEST AND SMALLEST REPTILES

The saltwater crocodile is the largest reptile, although some snakes, such as the reticulated python, are longer, growing to 10 m (33 ft) in length. The largest lizard is the Komodo dragon, a type of monitor lizard. The smallest of all reptiles are some kinds of geckos, only about a centimetre long when fully grown.

COELOPHYSIS

The first reptiles appeared on Earth more than 300 million years ago and gradually took over from amphibians as the largest animals on land. Dinosaurs such as *Coelophysis* shown here were early reptiles that evolved about 200 to 220 million years ago. *Coelophysis* was about the size of an adult human.

Coelophysis probably hunted lizard-like reptiles and other small animals of the time.

Find out more
ANIMALS
CROCODILES AND ALLIGATORS
DINOSAURS
LIZARDS
SNAKES

AMERICAN
REVOLUTIONARY WAR

EVERY YEAR ON 4 JULY, Americans celebrate the birth of their nation. Independence Day is a reminder of the moment when the 13 American colonies declared that they would no longer be ruled by Britain. The colonists did this because they had to pay British taxes, yet could not elect representatives to the British Parliament. The colonists had tried to make peace with Britain. At the First Continental Congress in 1774 representatives of each colony met to try and arrange fairer taxation. They failed, and fighting broke out between British soldiers and colonists at Lexington, Massachusetts, the following year. The colonists formed an army, led by George Washington. A second Congress again failed to make peace, and on 4 July 1776, the Americans declared their independence. France sent aid to the colonies which helped defeat the British. In 1781, the war ended. Britain recognized the independence of the United States two years later.

PAUL REVERE'S RIDE
On the night of 18 April 1775, silversmith Paul Revere took his now-famous ride from Charlestown, Massachusetts, to warn the people that the British army was coming.

THE BATTLE OF LEXINGTON

British soldiers set out from Boston, Massachusetts, on 19 April 1775, to capture the military stores at Concord. On their way, the British met a group of armed Americans at Lexington. The fighting that followed was the first battle of the war.

BOSTON TEA PARTY

In 1773, the British government cut the tax on tea in Britain but kept the rate the same in America. The colonists had no legal way of objecting because they did not have a Member of Parliament in Britain. On the night of 16 December a group of colonists dressed as Indians boarded three tea ships in Boston harbour and threw all the tea into the water as a protest.

AMERICAN REVOLUTIONARY WAR

1767 Britain imposes high taxes on American colonies.

1773 Boston Tea Party protests unfair taxation.

1774-1775 Continental Congress against Britain.

A NEW FLAG
The first flag of the new country of the United States consisted of 13 stripes and 13 stars, one for each of the original states.

1775 Battle of Lexington marks start of War.

1775 Battle of Bunker Hill won by British but strengthens American resistance.

1776 Declaration of Independence.

1777 Americans win Saratoga campaign.

1778 France supports American cause.

1781 General Cornwallis surrenders at Yorktown to Americans and French.

1783 Britain recognizes American independence in the Peace of Paris.

Find out more

UNITED STATES OF AMERICA, history of
WASHINGTON, GEORGE

RHINOCEROSES
AND TAPIRS

THE FIRST RHINOCEROSES existed about 30 million years ago and some evolved into the largest land mammals that ever lived. Today, few creatures are in such a desperate plight as the rhinoceros. Thousands have been killed for their horns, and all are on the official list of endangered species. Rhinoceroses are herbivores, or plant eaters. There are five different kinds – the white and black rhinoceroses of Africa, and the Indian, Javan, and Sumatran rhinoceroses of Asia. Rhinos are solitary creatures, usually living on their own. They are near-sighted animals, but have good hearing and an excellent sense of smell. Tapirs are closely related to rhinoceroses. They are stout, piglike mammals that live mainly in forests. Tapirs are most active at night, when they feed on plants. They are good swimmers and spend much of their time in water. Tapirs are rare in many areas today, because of overhunting by humans.

WHITE RHINOCEROS
With a weight of more than 2 tonnes, this is the second-largest animal on land (the elephant is largest). It is very nearsighted and sometimes charges at objects it does not recognize. It snips off grasses and other ground plants with its broad, blunt lips. White rhinoceroses are poached for their horns, which some people believe have medicinal properties.

BLACK RHINOCEROS
The black rhinoceros shown here is slightly smaller than the white rhinoceros. Black rhinos are found in central and southern Africa. They cannot focus clearly on things further than about 30 m (100 ft) away and sometimes charge at suspicious objects. Black rhinoceroses feed mainly at night on trees and bushes. They grasp the leaves and shoots with their long, hooked lips.

American tapir

Black rhinoceros

White square-lipped rhinoceros

FACES
American tapirs and black rhinoceroses have long, hooked upper lips. The white rhinoceros has a square-shaped mouth.

RHINOCEROS HORN
Horn is made of hairlike fibres pressed together into a hard mass; there is no bone inside. The Indian rhinoceros (right) and the Java rhinoceros have only one horn; the other kinds of rhinoceros have two horns.

Tough, leathery hide

Movable ears and good hearing

Poor eyesight

Horn on nose

Very keen sense of smell

Hooked lip for grasping plant food

Mud baths keep rhinoceroses cool and coat their skin for protection against biting insects.

RHINOCEROS HIDE
Rhinoceros skin, or hide, is extremely thick and tough. It hangs in flat sheets, with folds and creases around the legs and neck. It looks like a suit of armour on the Indian rhinoceros shown here. Only the Sumatran rhinoceros has hair on its body; all other rhinoceroses are bald.

MALAYAN TAPIR
Tapirs give birth to one young after a gestation (pregnancy) of 400 days. A newborn Malayan tapir has a spotted coat which gives good camouflage in the dappled forest undergrowth. At about six months, the spots and stripes fade and the tapir begins to look like its parents. An adult tapir has a large white patch on its black body, which helps to break up the animal's shape in dim light.

Find out more

AFRICAN WILDLIFE
ANIMALS
CONSERVATION AND
endangered species
MAMMALS

RIVERS

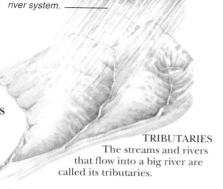

Rain feeds the river system.

WATER RUNS DOWN from high ground, cutting out a channel in the rock as it moves. This flowing water forms a river, which can be fed by a melting glacier, an overflowing lake, or a mountain spring. Rivers shape the landscape as they flow: the water sweeps away soil and eventually creates deep valleys in the land. One of the world's deepest valleys, cut by the River Kali Gandak through the Himalayas, is 5.5 km (3.4 miles) deep. Rivers also flow deep underground, slowly wearing away limestone rocks to form caves.

Rivers are important for transport and as a source of water, which is why most big cities lie on rivers. The longest rivers are the River Nile in Africa, which is 6,670 km (4,145 miles) long, and the River Amazon in South America, which is 6,448 km (4,007 miles) long.

TRIBUTARIES
The streams and rivers that flow into a big river are called its tributaries.

WATERFALL
The river plunges over a shelf of hard rock to form a waterfall.

RIVER SYSTEM

Small rivers and streams feed a large river with water. A river system consists of the whole group of rivers and streams. A watershed, or high ridge, separates one river system from another. Streams flow in opposite directions on either side of a watershed.

GORGE
The waterfall slowly wears away the rock, cutting a deep gorge.

RAPIDS
Fast, swirling currents form where water flows down a steep slope. These parts of the river are called rapids.

NIAGARA FALLS
The Niagara River plunges almost 55 m (180 ft) at Niagara Falls, which is situated on the border of the United States and Canada.

RIVER VALLEY
The river carries along stones and mud, which grind against the riverbed and sides, deepening and widening the V-shaped valley.

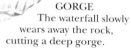

Weathering on the valley sides breaks up soft rock and soil. This material falls into the river and is carried away by the current.

OXBOW LAKE
The river cuts through the neck of a loop by wearing away the bank. Material is deposited at the ends of the loop eventually forming a lake.

FLOODS
Rivers can overflow when rain is heavy, or when water surges up from the sea. Flooding is severe in low-lying places, such as parts of Brazil in South America, which is often hit by tropical storms. Destruction of surrounding forests may be increasing the flow of water, making floods worse.

FLOOD PLAIN
Further down the river, the valley flattens out. This area, called the flood plain, is sometimes submerged during floods. The river runs through the plain in loops called meanders.

USES OF RIVERS

Great rivers that flow across whole countries carry boats that take goods from place to place. Some rivers have dams which build up huge stores of water in reservoirs. This water is used to supply towns and cities, irrigate crops, and generate electricity in hydroelectric power stations. Rivers are also a source of fish, but many rivers are now polluted by farms and factories.

DELTA
The river sometimes fans out into separate streams as it reaches the sea. The streams dump mud which forms an area of flat land called a delta.

Some rivers do not form deltas, but flow into the sea through a single wide channel called an estuary.

RIVER RHINE
The River Rhine is an important trade route. Barges carry goods between towns in northern Europe.

Find out more
DAMS
GLACIERS AND ICECAPS
LAKE AND RIVER WILDLIFE
LAKES
RAIN AND SNOW
WATER

ROADS AND MOTORWAYS

THE UNITED STATES has more roads than any other country. They stretch more than 6 million km (nearly 4 million miles). You would have to drive nonstop at 80 km/h (50 mph) for almost nine years to travel all of them. Great networks of roads and motorways cover most countries. Major motorways link cities, and minor roads crisscross cities and towns to reach neighbourhoods and homes. Cars, coaches and buses speed along roads and motorways carrying people from place to place. Trucks and lorries bring the goods that we buy in shops.

In most countries, motorists drive on the right-hand side of the road. In some countries, including Britain, India, Japan, and Australia, motorists drive on the left. Most large cities contain systems of one-way streets which help traffic to flow smoothly.

ANCIENT ROADS

The Ancient Romans were great road builders. They constructed a system of roads throughout their European empire about 2,000 years ago. These and many other old roads still exist, now surfaced for motor vehicles. Ancient roads were also trade routes. From as early as the 3rd century B.C., the Silk Road was used to bring silk from China across Asia to Europe.

Narrow roads twist through the countryside and over hills, often following old tracks and paths.

Bypass carries traffic around the edge of the city, avoiding the city centre.

Roundabouts allow vehicles to change roads without crossing other lines of traffic.

Feeder road links two roads.

The pavement is for pedestrians.

Traffic meets at crossroads, and the vehicles on one road yield to those on the other road.

Vehicles stop at crossings for pedestrians.

ROAD BUILDING
To build a major road that carries heavy traffic, bulldozers first clear and level the ground and build embankments or dig trenches if necessary. Drains are laid to carry rainwater away, and the road is then built in several layers. One or more layers of crushed stone are placed on the soil. The top layer can be made of concrete, or a "blacktop" of tar and stone chips. Steamrollers squash down each layer to make it firm.

Tarmac or concrete

Layers of crushed stone

Compressed soil

MOTORWAYS
Motorways carry traffic nonstop between cities and around city centres. They are very wide, usually with three lanes in each direction, so they can carry large amounts of traffic. A central barrier separates the two sides of the road.

TRAFFIC CONTROL
Road signs, such as speed limits and warnings of hazards ahead, help make the traffic move more safely. Road markings keep traffic in lanes, and traffic signals keep vehicles from colliding at crossroads. Police officers monitor busy roads using video cameras, and computers control city traffic, operating groups of signals to speed traffic flow and prevent jams.

TRAFFIC JAM

Almost 300 million vehicles fill the world's roads. This makes roads congested and causes serious pollution.

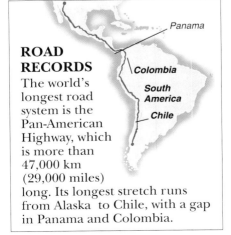

Panama

Colombia

South America

Chile

ROAD RECORDS
The world's longest road system is the Pan-American Highway, which is more than 47,000 km (29,000 miles) long. Its longest stretch runs from Alaska to Chile, with a gap in Panama and Colombia.

Find out more
BRIDGES
BUILDING
CITIES
ROMAN EMPIRE
TUNNELS

ROBOTS

WHEN PEOPLE THINK of robots, they often imagine the metal monsters of science fiction movies. However, most robots at work today look nothing like this. A robot is a computer-controlled machine that carries out mechanical tasks. The Czech playwright Karel Capek invented the word *robot*, which comes from a Czech word meaning "forced labour". Indeed, robots do jobs that would be dangerous or boring for people to do. Many factories have robots that consist of a single arm that is fixed in one spot. The robot simply repeats a task that it has been instructed to perform, such as spray-painting car parts. Today, engineers are developing much more sophisticated robots. These robots can move around, and their electronic detectors enable them to sense their surroundings. They also have "intelligence", which means that they can understand what they see and hear and make decisions for themselves. Intelligent robots are designed to act as guards and firemen, and may travel into space to study distant worlds.

SCIENCE FICTION ROBOTS
The robots of science fiction, such as *C3-P0* from the film *Star Wars*, are often anthropoid (human-like). In reality, anthropoid robots are rare. However, Japanese engineers have built experimental robots with two legs.

ROBOT ARM
Sophisticated robots work in factories, assembling, spraying, and welding components (parts). A skilled welder or painter will have programmed the robot by leading it (or a similar robot) through the task. Some robots can understand simple spoken instructions too. Robots often have sensors such as laser vision systems which help the robots to find and work on complex parts.

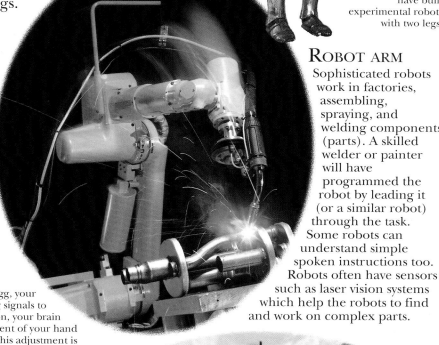

Held too tightly – loosen grip.

Brain sends nerve signals to muscles in the hand, adjusting the strength of the grip so the egg is neither dropped nor squashed.

Held too loosely – tighten grip.

Touch sensors in your hand detect how hard you are pressing on the egg.

FEEDBACK
When you pick up an egg, your senses begin sending signals to your brain. From this information, your brain automatically adjusts the movement of your hand and the pressure of your fingers. This adjustment is called feedback. Advanced robots control their actions by feedback from electronic detectors such as lasers, television cameras, and touch sensors.

SPACE ROBOT
In 1976, two unmanned *Viking* landers made automatic touchdowns on Mars. These robot spacecraft studied the planet and searched for signs of life. Robot space probes such as these are designed to obey instructions from controllers on Earth, but decide for themselves how to carry out the orders.

Space probes need to be able to work independently because radio instructions could take minutes or even hours to travel from Earth.

REMOTE CONTROL
Mobile robots do dangerous jobs such as repairing and dismantling nuclear reactors and detonating concealed bombs. These robots are remotely controlled – a human operator controls the general actions of the robot from a safe distance, and onboard computers control detailed movements.

This bomb disposal robot runs on tracks so that it can climb into awkward places. It carries cameras to send back pictures to the operator, and a gun for detonating the bomb.

Find out more
COMPUTERS
TECHNOLOGY
TRADE AND INDUSTRY

ROCKETS and MISSILES

THE INVENTION OF the rocket engine was a landmark in history. Not only did it give humankind a tool with which to explore space, but it also produced the missile, a weapon of terrible destructive power. A rocket engine is the most powerful of all engines. It has the power to push a spacecraft along at more than 40,000 km/h (25,000 mph), the speed necessary for it to break free from Earth's gravity. In a rocket engine, fuel burns to produce gases that rush out of the nozzle at the back, thrusting the rocket forward. However, unlike other engines, rockets do not need to use oxygen from the air to burn their fuel. Instead they carry their own supply of oxygen, usually in the form of a liquid, so that they can operate in space where there is no air. There is one major difference between a missile and a space rocket: missiles carry an explosive warhead instead of a satellite or human cargo.

After a few seconds booster fuel is expended.

Third stage fires for about 12 minutes, carrying its satellite payload into orbit about 320 km (200 miles) above the Earth's surface.

First stage propels rocket for about three minutes, by which time rocket is more than 50 km (30 miles) above the Earth.

Once first stage has run out of fuel, it falls away and second stage takes over, burning for about two minutes.

SPACE ROCKET

Most space rockets are made up of several stages, or segments, each with its own rocket engines and propellant, or fuel. By detaching the stages as they are used, the rocket can reach higher speeds because its weight is kept to a minimum. There are two main types of rocket propellant: solid and liquid. Solid fuel burns rapidly and cannot be controlled once ignited. But rockets powered by liquid propellant can be controlled by opening and closing valves which adjust the flow of fuel into the engine.

NUCLEAR MISSILES

Deadly nuclear warheads and precise navigational systems make nuclear missiles the most dangerous weapons in the history of warfare. A single warhead has the power to destroy a large city and cause thousands of deaths. Nuclear missiles can be launched from submarines, aircraft, trucks, and hidden underground launch sites.

ARIANE ROCKET

Vehicle equipment bay contains satellite which is being carried into orbit.

Guidance systems keep rocket on the correct course.

Third stage with one liquid-propellant rocket

Tank containing oxidizer, a liquid which contains oxygen

Tank containing highly inflammable liquid fuel

Pumps push fuel and oxidizer to the nozzle, where they burn and produce a violent rush of hot gases which pushes the rocket upwards.

Second stage with one liquid-propellant rocket

Two solid-propellant and two liquid-propellant strap-on booster rockets give space rocket an extra push in the first part of its flight.

First stage with four liquid-propellant rocket engines

TYPES OF MISSILES

Huge intercontinental ballistic missiles (ICBMs) blast up into space and come down on their targets thousands of kilometres away. However, not all rocket-powered missiles travel into space; many have replaced guns for short-range attacks on tanks, ships, and aircraft. Many of these missiles home in on their targets automatically.

ICBM armed with nuclear warhead

Anti-aircraft missile, usually launched from a ship

Size of rockets compared to a child 1.2 m (4 ft) tall

Radar-guided anti-ship missile. It can be launched from the air, from land, or from a warship.

Anti-tank missile, guided to target by remote control

DEVELOPMENT OF ROCKETS

In the 13th century, the Chinese used a simple type of rocket powered by gunpowder to scare enemy horses. Six hundred years later, Englishman Sir William Congreve developed a gunpowder rocket that the English forces used during the Napoleonic Wars. During World War II (1939-45), German scientist Wernher von Braun invented the first successful long-range rocket, the V-2, the forerunner of the ICBM.

Early Chinese rockets

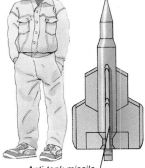

Find out more

MILITARY AIRCRAFT
NAPOLEONIC WARS
NUCLEAR AGE
NUCLEAR ENERGY
SPACE FLIGHT
SUBMARINES
WEAPONS
WORLD WAR II

ROCKS AND MINERALS

WE LIVE ON THE SURFACE of a huge ball of rock, the Earth. The landscape everywhere is made up of rocks. Most are covered by soil, trees, or grass. Others, such as Ayer's Rock in Australia, a massive lump of sandstone 335 m (1,100 ft) high, rise from the ground and are visible. The oldest rocks on Earth are about 3,800 million years old. Other rocks are much more recent, and new rocks are forming all the time. All rocks contain substances called minerals. Marble consists mainly of calcite, for example, and granite contains the minerals mica, quartz, and feldspar.

Rocks form in different ways: from molten rock within the Earth, from the fossils of animals and plants, and by the action of heat and pressure on ancient rocks inside the Earth. But no rocks, however hard, last forever on the Earth's surface. They are slowly eroded, or worn away, by the action of wind, rain, and other weather conditions.

HOW ROCKS FORM

All rocks started out as clouds of dust in space. The dust particles came together and formed the rocks that make up the planets, moons, and meteorites. There are now three main kinds of rocks at the Earth's surface: igneous, sedimentary, and metamorphic rocks. Each kind of rock forms in a different way.

GIANT'S CAUSEWAY
The steps of this unusual rock formation in Northern Ireland are made of columns of basalt, rock which developed when lava from a volcano cooled and set. The rock cracked into columns as it cooled.

Bubbles of gas trapped in the lava created holes in this piece of rock.

When lava from a volcano cools on the Earth's surface, it forms basalt.

IGNEOUS ROCKS
Deep underground the heat is so intense that some rock is molten (melted). When it cools, this molten rock, or magma, sets hard to produce an igneous rock. This may happen underground, or the magma may rise to the surface as lava and solidify.

Mud and pebbles are buried and squashed together, producing a hard sedimentary rock called conglomerate.

SEDIMENTARY ROCKS
Ice, wind, and running water wear away rocks into pebbles and small particles called sediment. Layers of sediment containing sand, clay, and animal skeletons are buried and squeezed so that they slowly change into hard rocks called sedimentary rocks.

Sedimentary rocks, such as conglomerate, form on the beach at the mouth of a river.

River carries sediment from the land to the sea.

Lava flows from a volcano and solidifies, forming basalt, an igneous rock.

Red-hot magma heats surrounding limestone, turning it into marble.

Hot magma solidifies, forming granite, an igneous rock.

Shale forms from clay at the river bed.

When magma slowly cools deep underground it often forms granite, a hard rock which is used as a building material.

Limestone contains the remains of shellfish. Chalk, another kind of limestone, is made of the skeletons of sea animals.

Clay forms shale, a sedimentary rock that crumbles easily. This rock is slate, the metamorphic rock which forms from shale.

METAMORPHIC ROCKS
Heat and pressure deep underground bake and squeeze sedimentary and igneous rocks. The minerals within the rocks change, often becoming harder. In this way they form new rocks called metamorphic rocks. After millions of years, the top rocks are worn away and metamorphic rocks appear on the surface.

Heating and compressing limestone turns it into marble, a hard metamorphic rock.

MINERALS

An impressive rock collection will feature rocks that contain beautiful mineral crystals. Minerals are the different substances of which rocks are made. For example, limestone and marble contain the white mineral calcite. Minerals include precious stones such as diamonds, and ores – minerals that contain metals such as iron and aluminium. Almost all metals are produced by mining and quarrying ores, and then treating the ores to extract their metals.

DESERT ROSE
The mineral gypsum forms petal-shaped crystals in deserts and dry regions. This happens as water dries up, leaving mineral deposits behind. The crystals often look like flowers, so they are called desert roses or gypsum flowers.

TURQUOISE
Jewellers cut beautiful gemstones and ornaments from turquoise, a blue-green mineral that often runs in a thin vein through other rocks.

HALITE
Table salt comes from the mineral halite. Halite forms where sea water dries at the shore. Underground deposits of halite are the remains of ancient salt lakes. Pure salt has no colour, but impurities in halite give it a pink colour.

SULPHUR
Yellow crystals form when molten sulphur cools. Large underground deposits in places such as the United States provide sulphur for making rubber and chemicals.

GALENA
Glistening grey crystals of galena stick out from a piece of white limestone. Galena forms cubic crystals. It is the main ore in which lead is found, and it often appears as a vein in limestone. Lead is combined with sulphur in galena. Smelting the ore by heating it in a furnace removes the sulphur and leaves lead metal.

CRYSTALS

Minerals often form crystals – solids which grow in regular shapes with flat sides. Light sparkles from crystals because they are often transparent and have smooth, shiny surfaces. Each mineral forms crystals with particular shapes, such as columns and cubes. Crystals grow from molten minerals or minerals that are dissolved in liquids, such as water.

Hexagonal crystals form in six-sided columns.

Cubic crystals form in four-sided columns.

Some minerals, such as solecite, form needle-shaped crystals.

Crystals form in columns, such as in this piece of the mineral beryl.

QUARTZ
Quartz is one of the most common minerals. Electronic clocks and watches contain small cut pieces of quartz that control time-keeping with great accuracy.

USES OF ROCK

Rocks in one form or another surround us in towns, cities, and the countryside. Hard rocks such as granite, sandstone, and limestone provide good building materials for houses and walls, and roads contain fragments of crushed rock. Soft rocks have uses too. Heating clay or shale with crushed limestone produces cement for making concrete and laying bricks. Bricks themselves are made by baking clay in moulds.

The first tools were made of stone. Early people broke pieces of rocks and stone to make sharp cutting implements such as axes.

Sculptors work rocks, stones, and pure minerals to make statues and ornaments.

Find out more

ATOMS AND MOLECULES
CLOCKS AND WATCHES
COMETS AND METEORS
FOSSILS
GEMS AND JEWELLERY
GEOLOGY
VOLCANOES

ROMAN EMPIRE

TWO THOUSAND YEARS AGO a single government and way of life united most of western Europe, the Middle East, and the north coast of Africa. The Roman Empire was based on good organization and centralized control. Towns in different countries were planned in exactly the same way. A network of stone-paved roads (parts of which remain today) connected every area to Rome. The reign of the first emperor, Augustus, began a long period of stability known as the Pax Romana, or Roman Peace, which lasted for about 200 years. Strong border defences manned by the Roman army protected the empire, while a skilled civil service governed it. Trade flourished and the people were united. The empire reached the height of its power in about A.D. 200 and then began to decline slowly. It was divided into two parts in 284. In 476 barbarian tribes conquered the Western Empire (based in Rome). The Eastern Empire (based in Constantinople, now called Istanbul, Turkey) continued until 1453.

ROMAN GRAFFITI
The Romans were fond of making fun of each other. This caricature was found on a wall in Pompeii. It is a mockery of a leading local citizen – probably a noble, judging from his laurel wreath.

Temple where people worshipped Roman gods.

Traders sold their wares at market stalls.

Public baths.

ROMAN CITY LIFE

Roman cities were carefully planned with straight streets, running water, and sewers. The forum, or central market-place, was surrounded by shops, law courts, and the town hall. The rich, always Roman citizens, lived in fine villas; the poor lived in apartment-style buildings. There were many temples. Most of the hard work was done by slaves, who had none of the rights granted to citizens, such as access to the baths.

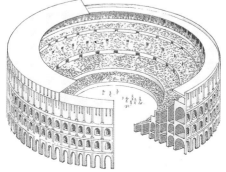

COLOSSEUM
Emperors paid for expensive public games, such as chariot racing, in order to be popular with the crowds. In Rome a massive theatre called the Colosseum held 45,000 people, who watched gladiators and wild animals fight to the death.

ROMAN BATHS

The Romans loved bathing. They scraped off the dirt, rubbed oil into their skin, relaxed in steam rooms, swam in warm pools, and plunged into icy water.

HYPOCAUST
The hypocaust system circulated hot air under the floors and through the walls to heat houses and baths.

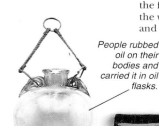

People rubbed oil on their bodies and carried it in oil flasks.

Bathers scraped the sweat and dirt off their bodies with strigils.

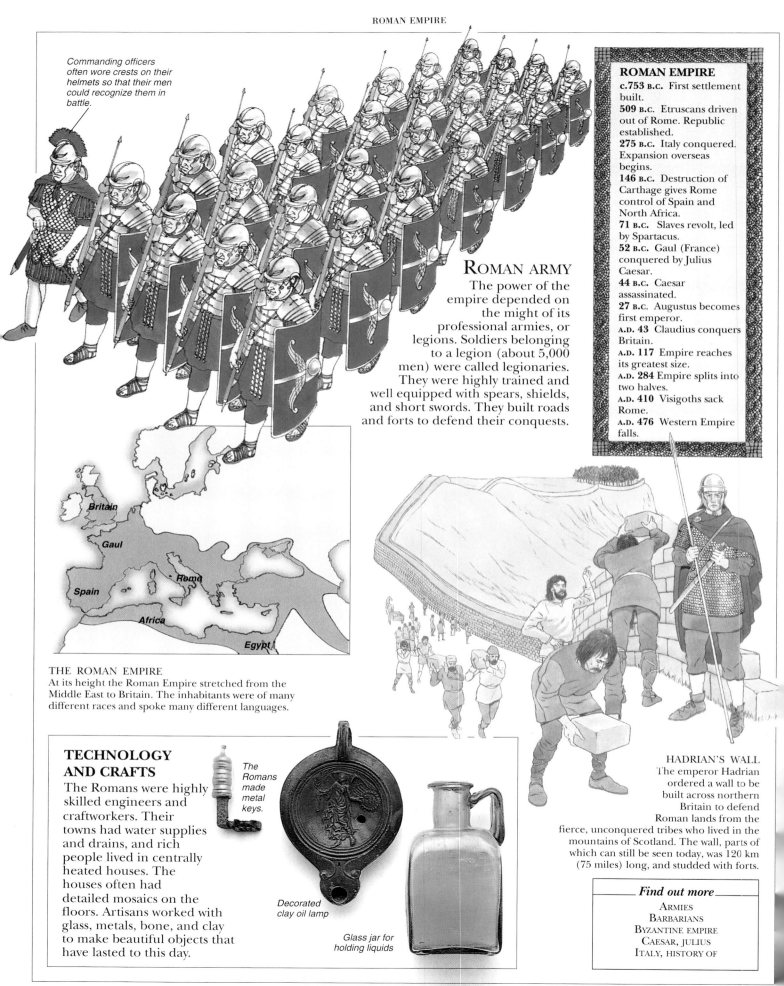

Commanding officers often wore crests on their helmets so that their men could recognize them in battle.

ROMAN ARMY

The power of the empire depended on the might of its professional armies, or legions. Soldiers belonging to a legion (about 5,000 men) were called legionaries. They were highly trained and well equipped with spears, shields, and short swords. They built roads and forts to defend their conquests.

ROMAN EMPIRE

c.753 B.C. First settlement built.

509 B.C. Etruscans driven out of Rome. Republic established.

275 B.C. Italy conquered. Expansion overseas begins.

146 B.C. Destruction of Carthage gives Rome control of Spain and North Africa.

71 B.C. Slaves revolt, led by Spartacus.

52 B.C. Gaul (France) conquered by Julius Caesar.

44 B.C. Caesar assassinated.

27 B.C. Augustus becomes first emperor.

A.D. 43 Claudius conquers Britain.

A.D. 117 Empire reaches its greatest size.

A.D. 284 Empire splits into two halves.

A.D. 410 Visigoths sack Rome.

A.D. 476 Western Empire falls.

Britain

Gaul

Rome

Spain

Africa

Egypt

THE ROMAN EMPIRE

At its height the Roman Empire stretched from the Middle East to Britain. The inhabitants were of many different races and spoke many different languages.

TECHNOLOGY AND CRAFTS

The Romans were highly skilled engineers and craftworkers. Their towns had water supplies and drains, and rich people lived in centrally heated houses. The houses often had detailed mosaics on the floors. Artisans worked with glass, metals, bone, and clay to make beautiful objects that have lasted to this day.

The Romans made metal keys.

Decorated clay oil lamp

Glass jar for holding liquids

HADRIAN'S WALL

The emperor Hadrian ordered a wall to be built across northern Britain to defend Roman lands from the fierce, unconquered tribes who lived in the mountains of Scotland. The wall, parts of which can still be seen today, was 120 km (75 miles) long, and studded with forts.

Find out more

ARMIES
BARBARIANS
BYZANTINE EMPIRE
CAESAR, JULIUS
ITALY, HISTORY OF

FRANKLIN DELANO
ROOSEVELT

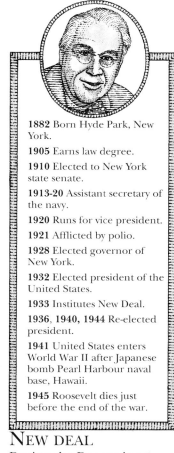

IN 1932 THE UNITED STATES was at one of its lowest points in history. Thirteen million people – nearly one third of the country's work force – were unemployed. Then a new president was elected with a mission to make Americans prosperous again. When Franklin Delano Roosevelt was disabled by polio in the summer of 1921, it appeared to be the end of a promising political career. But Roosevelt was a fighter and, helped by his wife, Eleanor, he regained the partial use of his legs. In 1928 he was elected governor of New York, then ran for president in 1932. He won a landslide victory, and for 13 years – the longest time any United States president has ever served – Roosevelt worked to overcome the effects of unemployment and poverty, telling Americans that "the only thing we have to fear is fear itself". He launched the New Deal – a series of social reforms and work programmes. During World War II, Roosevelt proved to be an able war leader, and with his Soviet and British allies he did much to shape the postwar world.

NEW DEAL
During the Depression of the 1930s, Roosevelt promised a New Deal. The government provided jobs for the unemployed and tried to return the country to prosperity. New laws were passed that provided better conditions for workers and pensions for retired workers.

The New Deal as seen by a cartoonist of the time.

FIRESIDE CHATS
President Roosevelt was an expert communicator who used the then-new medium of the radio to explain his controversial policies to the nation. These informal "fireside chats" established firm links between the President and the American people.

ELEANOR ROOSEVELT
Throughout her life President Roosevelt's wife, Eleanor (1884-1962), was a tireless campaigner for human rights. After 1945 she represented her country in the United Nations.

YALTA CONFERENCE
In February 1945, President Roosevelt, Winston Churchill, the British prime minister (far left), and Joseph Stalin, Soviet premier (far right), met in the Soviet resort of Yalta to discuss the postwar world. Together they decided to set up the United Nations.

Find out more
DEPRESSION
of the 1930s
UNITED NATIONS
UNITED STATES OF AMERICA,
history of
WORLD WAR II

HISTORY OF
RUSSIA

BEFORE THE NINTH CENTURY A.D., Russia consisted of scattered tribes from eastern Europe who farmed a barren landscape of marshes, forests, and steppes. In 882, the first Russian state was established at Kiev, an important trading centre. But in the 1200s, huge Mongol armies destroyed much of Russia. The Russian princes survived the attack only by brutally taxing their own people on behalf of the Mongols. Their methods began a long-lasting system of cruel government in Russia. In the 15th century, after the Mongols had withdrawn, Moscow became the capital of Russia. Over the next 300 years, the czars (emperors) conquered new lands so that Russia became the largest country in the world. However, it seemed unable to modernize, so its industry and people remained backward. After 1900, Russia slowly began to emerge into modern life, but its newfound strength was wasted in wars. There was a huge contrast between the czar's wealth and the poverty of the people. In 1917, the Russian Revolution overthrew czarist rule. The Communists took power, and from 1917 to 1991, Russia was the largest republic in the Soviet Union. With the collapse of the Soviet Union in 1991, Russia became independent once more.

KIEV

In 882 a Viking named Oleg captured Kiev and made it the capital of Russia. After this, Russian princes, who recognized Kiev's importance as a trade route between the Baltic Sea and the Black Sea, ruled the city. In 988, Prince Vladimir I of Kiev became a Christian and made Christianity the state religion. It was called Russian Orthodox religion. In 1240, Kiev fell to the Mongols.

MOSCOW

It was under Mongol control that Moscow (then called Muscovy) rose to power. The Mongols let Prince Ivan I (nicknamed "Moneybags") collect taxes for them. He kept some of the money and began to expand Russia's territory. He also made Moscow the religious centre of Russia. Ivan III (the Great) enlarged Moscow's territory. He also drove out the Mongols, leaving Moscow the most powerful city in Russia.

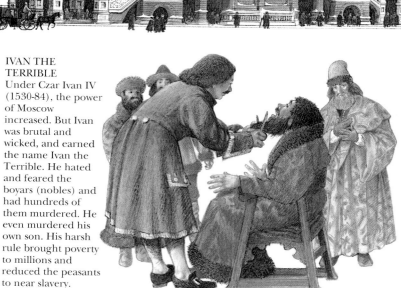

ST. BASIL'S CHURCH

In 1552, Ivan the Terrible built St. Basil's Church, Moscow. It was very ornate to show the great wealth and prosperity of Moscow. Legend has it that Ivan had the architects blinded to prevent them from designing anything as beautiful again.

The colourful decorations and onion-shaped domes on the outside of St. Basil's are typical of Russian Orthodox churches.

IVAN THE TERRIBLE

Under Czar Ivan IV (1530-84), the power of Moscow increased. But Ivan was brutal and wicked, and earned the name Ivan the Terrible. He hated and feared the boyars (nobles) and had hundreds of them murdered. He even murdered his own son. His harsh rule brought poverty to millions and reduced the peasants to near slavery.

PETER THE GREAT

In 1682 Peter the Great became czar. During his reign he modernized the army, defeated Sweden, and gained control of the Baltic coast, giving Russia an outlet to the West. He built a new capital at St. Petersburg and improved industry and education. He travelled through Europe in disguise to learn about Western life and tried to modernize Russia by using Western methods. He cut off the beards of the Orthodox Russians as a symbol of all he intended to change.

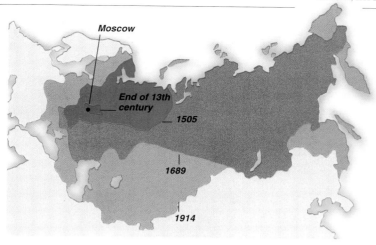

Moscow

End of 13th century

1505

1689

1914

RUSSIAN EXPANSION

From the 14th century, Russia grew in size as a result of conquest. Part of the reason for this expansion was the search for a port which was ice-free all year round. The pioneers who settled in the new areas, such as Poland, lived mostly on tiny farms, scratching out a miserable existence. Power lay in the hands of the czar and a few very rich nobles. Communications across such vast distances were difficult, so the czars had no idea of the problems and poverty of their people.

882 Vikings establish first Russian state at Kiev.

988 Prince Vladimir I forces all Russians to accept the Russian Orthodox faith.

1237 Mongols invade Russia.

1480 Ivan III breaks Mongol control of Russia; brings other cities under Moscow's control.

1547 Ivan IV introduces serfdom, which forces the peasants to stay in one place and work for a landowner.

1604-13 "Time of Troubles". Russia suffers civil wars as rival groups struggle for power.

1613 Michael Romanov becomes czar. Romanovs rule Russia until 1917.

1703 Czar Peter the Great begins to build his new capital at St. Petersburg. Brings in experts to modernize industry.

1774 Peasants' revolt.

1812 French emperor Napoleon invades Russia. Most of his army dies in the freezing Russian winter.

1825 "Decembrist Uprising". Army officers demand an elected government.

1905 Japan defeats Russia in Russo-Japanese War. A workers' revolution forces Nicholas II to establish a parliament, called the Duma.

1914-17 Russia fights against Germany in World War I. Discontent pushes the people into revolution.

1917-91 Communists control Russia.

1991 Soviet Union collapses; Russia independent.

CATHERINE THE GREAT

During Catherine's reign (1762-96) Russia's territory expanded. Catherine created a glittering court which was much admired outside Russia. She increased the power of the nobles but did nothing for the peasants. They were used as slave labour in distant areas and suffered untold misery.

Russian peasants working on the land

Catherine the Great

FABERGÉ EGG

In 1884, Peter Fabergé became jeweller to the czars. He created magnificent pieces covered in gold, jewels, and coloured enamel for the rich nobles of the Russian court. His most famous creations were the Easter eggs he made for czars Alexander III and Nicholas II.

ALEXANDER II

Czar Alexander II (1818-81) realized that Russia had to keep up with the West in order to succeed. He freed the peasants and helped them buy land. But they were disappointed with the quality of their land and the high taxes they had to pay. In 1881, a revolutionary group assassinated Alexander.

Find out more

COMMUNISM
NAPOLEONIC WARS
RUSSIAN FEDERATION
RUSSIAN REVOLUTION
U.S.S.R., HISTORY OF

RUSSIAN FEDERATION

Moscow's GUM department store

The Russian Federation stretches from eastern Europe in the west across the entire width of Asia to the Pacific Ocean in the east, and from the Arctic Circle in the north to Central Asia in the south.

THE LARGEST NATION in the world is the Russian Federation. Also called Russia, it consists of 20 autonomous (self-governing) republics, and more than 50 other regions. It covers one tenth of the earth's land area – one third of Asia, and two fifths of Europe. Russia has a very varied climate and a landscape that ranges from mountains in the south and east to vast lowlands, and rivers in the north and west. The population is varied too, although most of the 149 million people are of Russian origin and speak the Russian language. The Russian Federation came into being in 1991 after the break up of the Soviet Union, or U.S.S.R. After 1991, the Russian people experienced greater political freedom but also economic hardship as their country changed from a state-planned to a free-market economy. The Russian Federation has vast agricultural resources. It is also rich in minerals, and has considerable industry. In the early 1990s, the Russian government sought international investment to help overcome its economic problems.

MODERN RUSSIA
Large Russian cities look similar to cities elsewhere in the world, but the bright lights hide economic problems. Both luxury and essential goods are often in short supply. Lining up for food is a daily occupation, and clothes and consumer goods are scarce and often of poor quality. Most homes are rented from the government, but housing is in limited supply, which means that overcrowding is common.

MOSCOW
The capital city of the Russian Federation is Moscow. It was founded during the 12th century. At the city's heart on the banks of the River Moscow lies the Kremlin, a walled fortress housing all the government buildings. Nearby St. Basil's Cathedral was built in the 16th century to celebrate a military victory; it is now a museum.

A typical Russian Orthodox Church

Nevsky Prospect is St. Petersburg's busiest shopping street.

RUSSIAN ORTHODOX CHURCH
The chief religion in Russia is the Russian Orthodox Church. Under Communism, all religions were persecuted. In the late 1980s, freedom of worship returned to Russia, and today millions of people worship without fear. The Russian Federation also contains many Muslims, Jews, and Buddhists.

ST. PETERSBURG
The second largest city in the Russian Federation, St. Petersburg has a population of 4.5 million. Before 1917 St .Petersburg (called Leningrad from 1924 to 1991) was the capital of Russia. It still contains many beautiful, historical buildings, such as the Hermitage Art Gallery, once the summer palace of the czars.

462

AGRICULTURE

Most agriculture in the Russian Federation takes place on the fertile Russian plain that stretches from the western border into Central Asia. Here, farmers produce wheat and other cereals, meat, dairy products, wool, and cotton. The Russian Federation is one of the world's biggest cereal producers, but often fails to grow enough food to feed its own population and has to import grain.

RUBLES AND KOPECKS

The unit of Russian money is the ruble, which is divided into 100 kopecks. Visitors to the Russian Federation can buy rubles at government banks. However, the official exchange rate is unfavourable, and unofficial money changers offer higher rates to those willing to break the law.

The Bolshoi Theatre, home of the Bolshoi Ballet

PEOPLE

Most people in the Russian Federation are Russian in origin. But there are at least 100 minority groups, including Tatars, Ukrainians, Bashkirs, and Chukchis. Some, such as the Yakut hunters shown here in traditional clothing, are Turkish in origin; other groups are Asiatic. The population is not spread evenly through this vast nation. About 75 per cent live west of the Ural Mountains; less than 25 per cent live in Siberia and the far east of the country.

BOLSHOI BALLET

The world-famous Bolshoi Ballet dance company was founded in Moscow in 1773. It became famous touring the world with performances of Russian folk dances and classic ballets such as *Swan Lake*. Other Russian art forms have not enjoyed the same freedom of expression until recently. Artists opposed to the Communist government worked in secret. For example, the novels of Aleksandr Solzhenitsyn (born 1918) were banned for many years. His most famous works, such as *The Gulag Archipelago*, were smuggled in from Europe or retyped by readers and circulated secretly.

TECHNOLOGICAL ACHIEVEMENTS

As part of the Soviet Union, Russian science developed very unevenly. Today, the Russian Federation leads the world in some medical techniques, particularly eye surgery (right), but lags far behind Western Europe and the United States in areas such as computers. In the field of space also, the Soviet Union led the world, launching the first satellite in 1957 and putting the first man in space in 1961. More recently, the Russians have launched orbiting space stations in which astronauts live for months at a time.

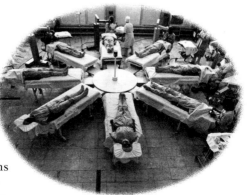

Ленингра́д

CYRILLIC WRITING

In the Russian Federation over 112 languages are spoken. Russian is the official language and is taught in every school. Russian writers use the Cyrillic alphabet, shown here.

Find out more

COLD WAR
COMMUNISM
RUSSIA, HISTORY OF
RUSSIAN REVOLUTION
U.S.S.R., HISTORY OF

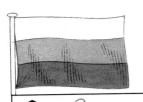

RUSSIAN FEDERATION

STATISTICS
Area: 17,075,400 sq km
(6,592,812 sq miles)
Population: 149,000,000
Capital: Moscow
Languages: Russian, many regional languages
Religions: Russian Orthodox
Currency: Ruble
Highest point: Klyuchevskaya Sopka 4,749 m (15,580 ft)

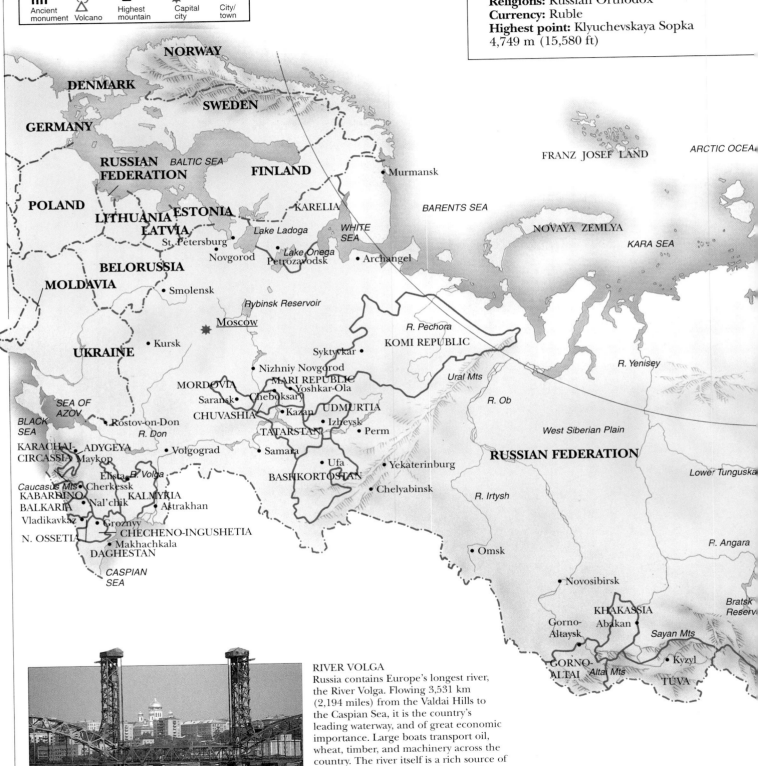

Ancient monument
Volcano
Highest mountain
Capital city
City/town

NORWAY
DENMARK
SWEDEN
GERMANY
RUSSIAN FEDERATION
BALTIC SEA
FINLAND
POLAND
LITHUANIA
ESTONIA
LATVIA
KARELIA
• Murmansk
BARENTS SEA
FRANZ JOSEF LAND
ARCTIC OCEA
NOVAYA ZEMLYA
KARA SEA
Lake Ladoga
WHITE SEA
St. Petersburg
Novgorod
Lake Onega
Petrozavodsk
• Archangel
BELORUSSIA
MOLDAVIA
• Smolensk
Rybinsk Reservoir
R. Pechora
KOMI REPUBLIC
R. Yenisey
Moscow
• Kursk
Syktyvkar •
UKRAINE
• Nizhniy Novgorod
Ural Mts
MORDOVIA
MARI REPUBLIC
Yoshkar-Ola
R. Ob
Saransk •
Cheboksary
West Siberian Plain
SEA OF AZOV
CHUVASHIA
• Kazan
UDMURTIA
BLACK SEA
• Rostov-on-Don
TATARSTAN
• Izhevsk
R. Don
• Perm
KARACHAI-CIRCASSIA
ADYGEYA
• Volgograd
• Samara
RUSSIAN FEDERATION
Maykop
• Ufa
• Yekaterinburg
Lower Tunguska
Elista
R. Volga
BASHKORTOSTAN
Caucasus Mts
Cherkessk
• Chelyabinsk
R. Irtysh
KABARDINO-BALKARIA
• Nal'chik
KALMYKIA
Vladikavkaz
• Astrakhan
R. Angara
• Groznyy
CHECHENO-INGUSHETIA
N. OSSETIA
• Makhachkala
DAGHESTAN
• Omsk
CASPIAN SEA
• Novosibirsk
Bratsk Reserv
KHAKASSIA
Gorno-Altaysk
Abakan •
Sayan Mts
GORNO-ALTAI
Altai Mts
• Kyzyl
TUVA

RIVER VOLGA
Russia contains Europe's longest river, the River Volga. Flowing 3,531 km (2,194 miles) from the Valdai Hills to the Caspian Sea, it is the country's leading waterway, and of great economic importance. Large boats transport oil, wheat, timber, and machinery across the country. The river itself is a rich source of fish, particularly sturgeon. Sturgeon's roe is pickled to make the delicacy caviar.

Largest lake: Lake Baikal
31,500 sq km (12,162 sq
miles)
Longest river: Lena 4,400
km (2,734 miles)
Main occupation: Service
industries, manufacturing
Main exports: Oil
Main imports: Machines
and equipment

SIBERIA

The vast region of Siberia is in the
northeast of the Russian
Federation, and stretches from the
Ural Mountains in the west to the
tip of Alaska in the east. Although
Siberia occupies nearly 80 per cent
of the land area of the Russian
Federation, it is thinly populated.
Most Siberian people live close to
the route of the Trans-Siberian
Railway, which runs for 9,438 km
(5,864 miles) between Moscow and
Vladivostok. Much of northern
Siberia lies inside the Arctic circle,
and during the summer months
the sun never sets, but simply dips
close to the horizon at night (left).

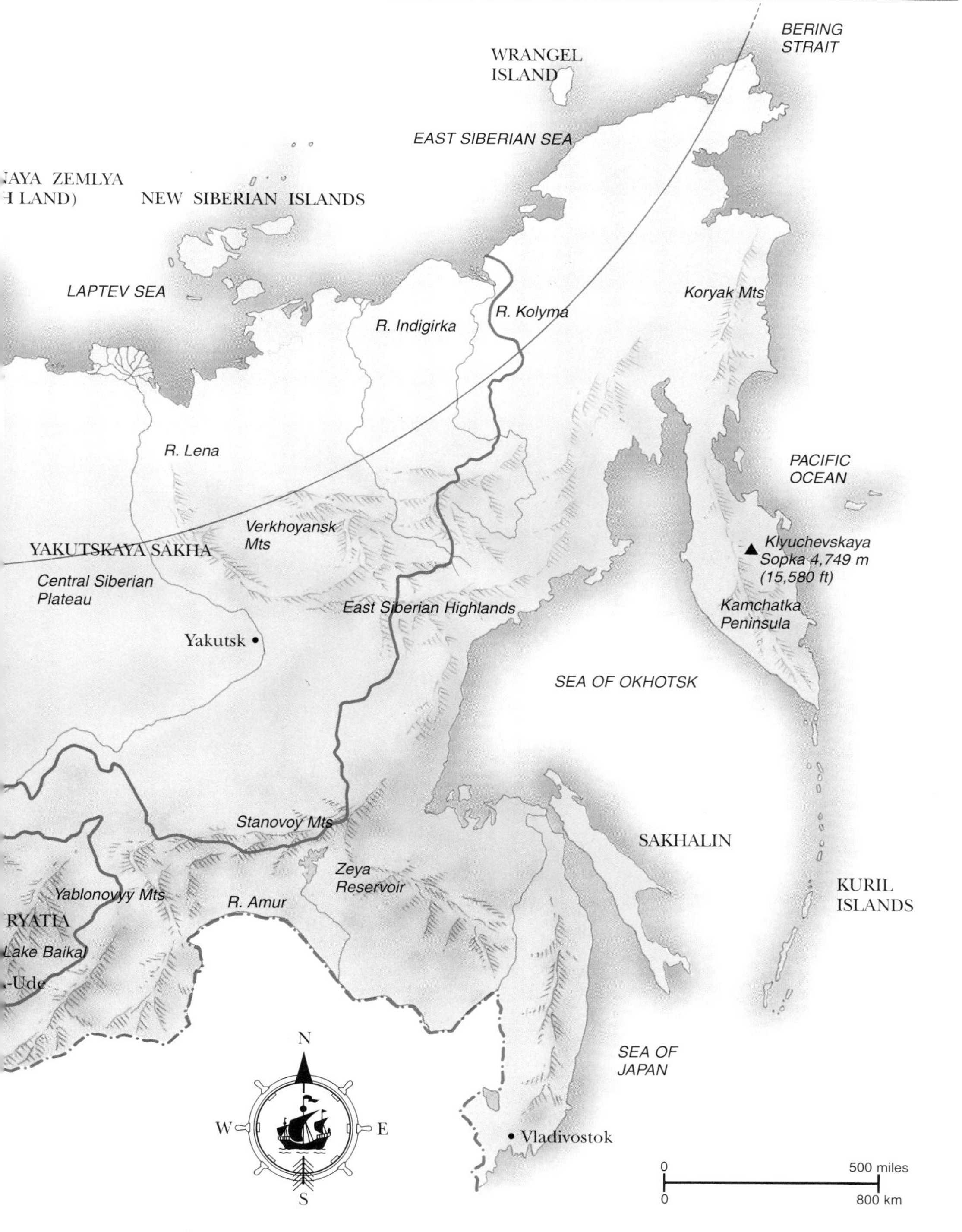

AUTONOMOUS REPUBLICS OF THE RUSSIAN FEDERATION:

ADYGEYA
Capital: Maykop

BASHKORTOSTAN
Capital: Ufa

BURYATIA
Capital: Ulan-Ude

CHECHENO-INGUSHETIA
Capital: Groznyy

CHUVASHIA
Capital: Cheboksary

DAGHESTAN
Capital: Makhachkala

GORNO-ALTAI
Capital: Gorno-Altaysk

KABARDINO-BALKARIA
Capital: Nal'chik

KALMYKIA
Capital: Elista

KARACHAI-CIRCASSIA
Capital: Cherkessk

KARELIA
Capital: Petrozavodsk

KHAKASSIA
Capital: Abakan

KOMI REPUBLIC
Capital: Syktyvkar

MARI REPUBLIC
Capital: Yoshkar-Ola

MORDOVIA
Capital: Saransk

NORTH OSSETIA
Capital: Vladikavkaz

TATARSTAN
Capital: Kazan

TUVA
Capital: Kyzyl

UDMURTIA
Capital: Izhevsk

YAKUTSKAYA SAKHA
Capital: Yakutsk

BERING
STRAIT

WRANGEL
ISLAND

EAST SIBERIAN SEA

...AYA ZEMLYA
...H LAND) NEW SIBERIAN ISLANDS

LAPTEV SEA

R. Indigirka R. Kolyma

Koryak Mts

R. Lena

PACIFIC
OCEAN

Verkhoyansk
Mts

YAKUTSKAYA SAKHA

▲ Klyuchevskaya
Sopka 4,749 m
(15,580 ft)

Central Siberian
Plateau

East Siberian Highlands

Kamchatka
Peninsula

Yakutsk •

SEA OF OKHOTSK

Stanovoy Mts

SAKHALIN

Zeya
Reservoir

KURIL
ISLANDS

Yablonovyy Mts

...RYATIA

R. Amur

...Lake Baikal

...-Ude

SEA OF
JAPAN

• Vladivostok

N
W   E
S

0   500 miles
0   800 km

RUSSIAN REVOLUTION

IN 1917, THE PEOPLE OF RUSSIA staged a revolution that was to change the course of modern history. The Russian people were desperate for change. Russia was suffering serious losses against Germany in World War I. Food and fuel were scarce. Many people were starving. Czar Nicholas II, ruler of Russia, was blamed for much of this. In March 1917 (February in the old Russian calendar) a general strike broke out in Petrograd (today St. Petersburg). The strike was in protest against the chaos caused by the war. Nicholas was forced to give up his throne, and a group of revolutionaries, called the Mensheviks, formed a provisional government. This government soon fell, because it failed to end the war. In November, the Bolsheviks, a more extreme revolutionary group, seized power. They ended the war with Germany and, led by Vladimir Lenin, set up the world's first Communist state. They declared the country a Soviet republic. This revolution was the first Communist takeover of a government. It inspired more to follow.

1905 REVOLUTION
In 1905 unarmed workers marched on Nicholas II's Winter Palace in St. Petersburg. The czar's troops fired on the crowd. Nicholas set up an elected parliament, or Duma. But the Duma had no real power, so distrust of the czar grew.

OCTOBER REVOLUTION
What is known as the October Revolution broke out on 7 November, 1917 (25 October in the old Russian calendar used before the revolution). The cruiser *Aurora* fired blanks across the River Neva at the headquarters of the Menshevik government in the Winter Palace. The Bolsheviks also attacked other important buildings in Petrograd.

LENIN
Vladimir Lenin (1870-1924), founder of the Bolshevik party, believed in the ideas of the German writer Karl Marx. He lived mostly in exile from Russia, until the October Revolution. He was a powerful speaker whose simple slogan of "Peace, land, and bread" persuaded many Russians to support the Bolsheviks. He ruled Russia as dictator.

NICHOLAS II
Russia's last czar, Nicholas (1868-1918), was out of touch with his subjects. They blamed him for the Russian defeats in World War I (1914-18), where he fought at the front. His sinister adviser, a monk named Rasputin, was widely hated and feared. After Nicholas gave up the throne, he and his family were arrested. The Bolsheviks shot them all the following year.

RUSSIAN REVOLUTION
1914 Russia joins World War I against Germany and Austria.

1916 One million Russian soldiers die after German offensive. Prices in Russia rise.

1917 March International Women's Day march in Petrograd turns into bread riot. The Mensheviks set up a provisional government. The Bolsheviks organize another government made up of committees called soviets.

July Lenin flees Russia.

October Lenin returns to Petrograd.

7 November Armed workers seize buildings in Petrograd.

15 November Bolsheviks control Petrograd.

Find out more
COMMUNISM
RUSSIA, HISTORY OF
U.S.S.R., HISTORY OF
WORLD WAR I

SAILING AND BOATING

ONCE A VITAL MEANS of transport, sailing is now a pastime and a sport. The smallest sailing boats are one-person crafts, but ocean-going racing yachts have a crew of 20 or more. Anyone can learn to sail a simple sailing boat. There is a rudder to point it in the right direction, and a keel or centreboard to stop it from slipping sideways. The skill of sailing lies in the positioning of the sail according to the direction of the wind. Rowing and canoeing do not rely on the wind. Rowing with two oars is called sculling. Canoeing is a popular way of touring rivers and lakes at a leisurely pace. "White-water" canoeing is far from leisurely. Canoeists have to paddle through fast-flowing rivers while avoiding hidden rocks.

AMERICA'S CUP

One of the world's most famous ocean sailing races is the America's Cup. Two yachts, which represent two different nations, race over a triangular course, and the nation that wins receives the cup as a prize. The trophy is named for the U.S. yacht *America,* which won the cup in 1851. The New York Yacht Club kept the cup for 132 years by beating all challengers.

RACING SAILBOAT

Most races are for matched boats of the same class, or type. In this way, sailing skill and tactics determine the winner, rather than the boat's design. Even the simplest training sailboat can compete in races. Some racing sailboats require a crew of more than one.

Pieces of coloured wool show the crew how the wind is blowing across the sail.

Aluminium mast is lighter and stronger than traditional timber.

Sails are made of artificial fibre such as Dacron.

The spinnaker pole supports the billowing spinnaker sail that the crew raises when the wind is behind the boat.

The centreboard drops into a slot to keep the boat on course, but lifts out so the boat can sail in shallow water.

Windows enable the crew to see through the sail.

Ropes on sailing vessels are called sheets or lines.

The mainsheet adjusts the position of the mainsail.

Rudder steers the boat through the water.

Hull is made of glass-reinforced plastic, which is lightweight but very strong.

Tiller extension bar lets the helm turn the rudder while leaning out to balance the boat.

The crew member who controls the boat's direction is called the helm.

CANOEING

The kayak, an enclosed canoe, is used for touring or racing. It is propelled with a double-bladed paddle. Canoeists use a single-bladed paddle in open canoes. In Canada canoe racers use a similar paddle and race in a high kneeling position.

Kayak

Open touring canoe

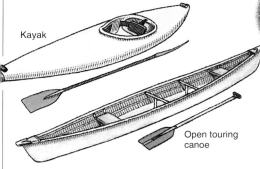

THE UNIVERSITY BOAT RACE

Every year since 1829 crews from Oxford and Cambridge universities in England have held a now-famous rowing match. The two rowing boats race over a winding 6.4 km (4 mile) course on the River Thames in London.

SAFETY

Sailors must always take safety precautions, such as wearing a life jacket. A sailing boat should have a bucket for bailing out water and a paddle in case the wind drops.

Find out more

NAVIGATION
PORTS AND WATERWAYS
SHIPS AND BOATS

SATELLITES

Polar orbit, used by Earth observation satellites

SATELLITE ORBITS

A communications satellite takes exactly 24 hours to orbit the Earth, so it appears to remain fixed over one spot. This kind of orbit is called geostationary. A polar orbit allows a satellite to see the whole Earth in a series of strips. In an elliptical orbit, a satellite can pass low over a selected part of the Earth.

Geostationary orbit, used by communications satellites

Elliptical orbit, used by spy satellites

Solar panels generate electricity from sunlight to power the satellite.

Radar altimeter provides data on wind speed, ocean currents, and tides.

Infrared scanner measures water vapour in the atmosphere and the temperatures of seas and cloud tops.

Earth observation satellite ERS-1

Antenna for transmitting data back to Earth.

WHEN AIRCRAFT AND balloons first took to the skies, the people in them were amazed at their new view of the world. From hundreds of metres up they could see the layout of a large city, the shape of a coastline, or the patchwork of fields on a farm. Today, we have an even wider view. Satellites circle the Earth, not hundreds of metres, but hundreds of kilometres above the ground. From this great height, satellites provide a unique image of our planet. Some have cameras that take photographs of land and sea, giving information about the changing environment on Earth. Others plot weather patterns or peer out into space and send back data (information) about planets and stars. All of these are artificial satellites that have been launched into space from Earth. However, the word *satellite* actually means any object that moves around a planet while being held in orbit by the planet's gravity. There are countless natural satellites in the universe: the Earth has one, which is the moon.

ARTIFICIAL SATELLITES

There are many types of artificial satellites. Weather satellites observe rain, storms, and clouds, and measure land and sea temperatures. Communications satellites send radio and television signals from one part of the Earth to another. Spy satellites observe military targets from low altitudes and send back detailed pictures to ground stations. Earth observation satellites monitor vegetation, air and water pollution, population changes, and geological factors such as mineral deposits.

MAPPING THE EARTH

Resources satellites take pictures of the Earth's surface. The cameras have various filters so they can pick up infrared (heat) radiation and different colours of light. Vegetation, for instance, reflects infrared light strongly, showing up forests and woodlands. Computer-generated colours are used to pick out areas with different kinds of vegetation and minerals.

SPUTNIK 1

On 4 October 1957, the Soviet Union launched the world's first artificial satellite, *Sputnik 1*. The satellite carried a radio transmitter which sent signals back to Earth until *Sputnik* burned up in the atmosphere 92 days later.

Satellite map image of San Francisco Bay, California. Clearly visible are two bridges: the Golden Gate Bridge on the left and the Bay Bridge on the right.

NATURAL SATELLITES

There are more than 60 known natural satellites, or moons, in the solar system. Most orbit (move around) the four giant outer planets: Jupiter, Saturn, Uranus, and Neptune. The largest moons are larger than Pluto, the smallest planet; the smallest moons are only a few kilometres across and have irregular, potato-like shapes.

The planet Jupiter with two of its moons, Io (left) and Europa (right)

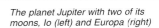

Find out more

ASTRONOMY
GEOLOGY
NAVIGATION
SPACE FLIGHT
TELEPHONES
TELEVISION AND VIDEO

SCANDINAVIA

AT THE FAR NORTH of Europe are the countries of Scandinavia, which have much in common yet in some ways could not be more different. Their economies are closely linked, but each uses its own currency. They are all independent nations; but in times past, several of them have been bound together in a single union. Each country has its own language, yet strong cultural ties exist between the nations.

Cross-country skiing is a popular sport in many parts of Scandinavia.

Landscapes are different, however. Denmark is flat – the biggest hill is only 179 m (590 ft) high – and most of the country is very fertile; but both Norway and Iceland are mountainous with little farmland. Sweden and Finland are dotted with lakes – more than 60,000 in Finland alone. Greenland is almost entirely covered in ice and snow. Politically, the different countries co-operate through the Nordic Council, which aims to strengthen ties between the nations. Denmark, Finland, and Sweden are members of the European Union, a trade alliance of European nations. Most Scandinavians enjoy a high standard of living and an active cultural life. Norway and Sweden award the annual Nobel Prizes for sciences, literature, and peace.

Geographically Scandinavia consists of the Norway and Sweden peninsula. But it is also used widely to include Denmark and Finland. The Faeroe Islands, Iceland and Greenland are often associated with Scandinavia.

The frozen north of Scandinavia, called Lapland, is the home of 40,000 Lapplanders. Many of them live by herding reindeer for their hide and meat.

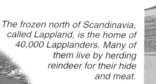

FINLAND

Although Finland is part of Scandinavia, it is closely tied to the Russian Federation, and the two countries share a long frontier. Until 1917, Finland was a province of the old Russian empire. Today Finnish trade is still conducted with the Russian Federation. Forests cover two thirds of Finland, and the paper industry dominates the economy. Shipbuilding and tourism are also important. One third of the country lies within the Arctic Circle, and throughout the winter months only the southern coastline is free of ice.

The Swedish capital of Stockholm is built on numerous islands.

SWEDEN

The biggest of the Scandinavian countries, Sweden is also the wealthiest. Over the years, the Swedes have developed a taxation and social welfare system that has created a good standard of living for everybody. As a result few people in Sweden are either very rich or very poor. The population numbers about 8.7 million, most of whom live in the south and east of the country; the mountainous north lies within the Arctic Circle and is almost uninhabited.

NORWAY

Shipping, forestry, and fishing were the traditional Norwegian industries. But in 1970, oil was discovered in the Norwegian sector of the North Sea, and the country's fortunes were transformed. Today, the four million Norwegians enjoy a high standard of living, low taxes, and almost no unemployment. But Norway has almost no natural resources apart from oil and timber. The wooded country is mountainous and indented with numerous inlets, or fjords, from the North Atlantic Ocean. These fjords make communications difficult between the cities in the south and the more sparsely populated regions in the north.

Deep-sea fishing is a major occupation throughout Scandinavia.

Find out more

ANTARCTICA AND THE ARCTIC
EUROPE
SCANDINAVIA, HISTORY OF

SCANDINAVIA

🏛	Ancient monument
🌋	Volcano
▲	Highest mountain
✶	Capital city
•	City/ town

DENMARK
Area: 43,077 sq km (16,632 sq miles)
Population: 5,200,000
Capital: Copenhagen
Language: Danish
Religion: Evangelical Lutheran
Currency: Danish krone

SWEDEN
Area: 449,964 sq km (173,731 sq miles)
Population: 8,700,000
Capital: Stockholm
Language: Swedish
Religion: Evangelical Lutheran
Currency: Swedish krona

FINLAND
Area: 338,127 sq km (130,551 sq miles)
Population: 5,000,000
Capital: Helsinki
Languages: Finnish, Swedish
Religion: Lutheran
Currency: Markka

NORWAY
Area: 323,895 sq km (125,056 sq miles)
Population: 4,300,000
Capital: Oslo
Language: Norwegian
Religion: Evangelical Lutheran
Currency: Norwegian krone

Scandinavia is the geographical name for Norwa and Sweden. But it also includes other places w Nordic people live, including Denmark, Finlan and Iceland. Greenland, the world's largest isla is a self-governing part of Denmark, but geographically it is part of North America. It ha nearly double the land area of all the other Scandinavian countries combined. Most of Greenland lies inside the Arctic Circle. The Fae Islands are also ruled by Denmark, though the islands themselves control local affairs. Iceland an independent republic.

DENMARK
Copenhagen (above) is the capital of Denmark, and about one quarter of all Danish people live in and around the city. Copenhagen is on the east coast of Zealand, the largest of 482 islands that make up about 30 per cent of Denmark. The low-lying Jutland peninsula to the west makes up the rest of the land area.

SWEDEN
The fertile soil in the Swedish lowlands makes this area the richest farmland in Sweden. The area around Nordingrå (right), close to the Gulf of Bothnia, is best known for its dairy produce. Many Swedish farmers belong to agricultural cooperatives which process and distribute their crops.

GREENLAND
Area: 2,175,600 sq km (839,780 sq miles)
Population: 56,000

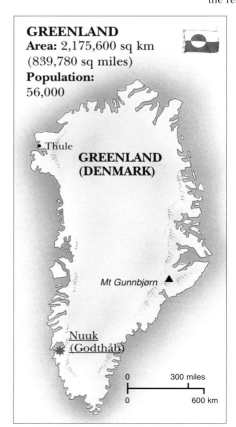

- Thule

GREENLAND (DENMARK)

Mt Gunnbjørn ▲

Nuuk (Godthåb)

| 0 | 300 miles |
| 0 | 600 km |

ICELAND
Area: 103,000 sq km (39,768 sq miles)
Population: 300,000

Akureyri
Seydhisfjördhur
ICELAND
Vatnajökull Glacier
R. Thjórsa
Hvannadalshnúkur ▲
Reykjavik
Mt Hekla △
SURTSEY

| 0 | 60 miles |
| 0 | 100 km |

FAEROE ISLANDS (DENMARK)
Area: 1,399 sq km (540 sq miles)
Population: 47,000

✶ Tórshavn
FAEROE ISLANDS

NORWEGIAN SEA

Sogne Fjord

Bergen •

Hardanger Fjörd

NORTH SEA

• Thorshavn
SKAGERRA K

Ålborg
DENMAI
• Holstebro
Jutland   R
•Esbjerg   Århu
•Kolding
Odense •

| 0 | 40 miles |
| 0 | 60 km |

GERMANY

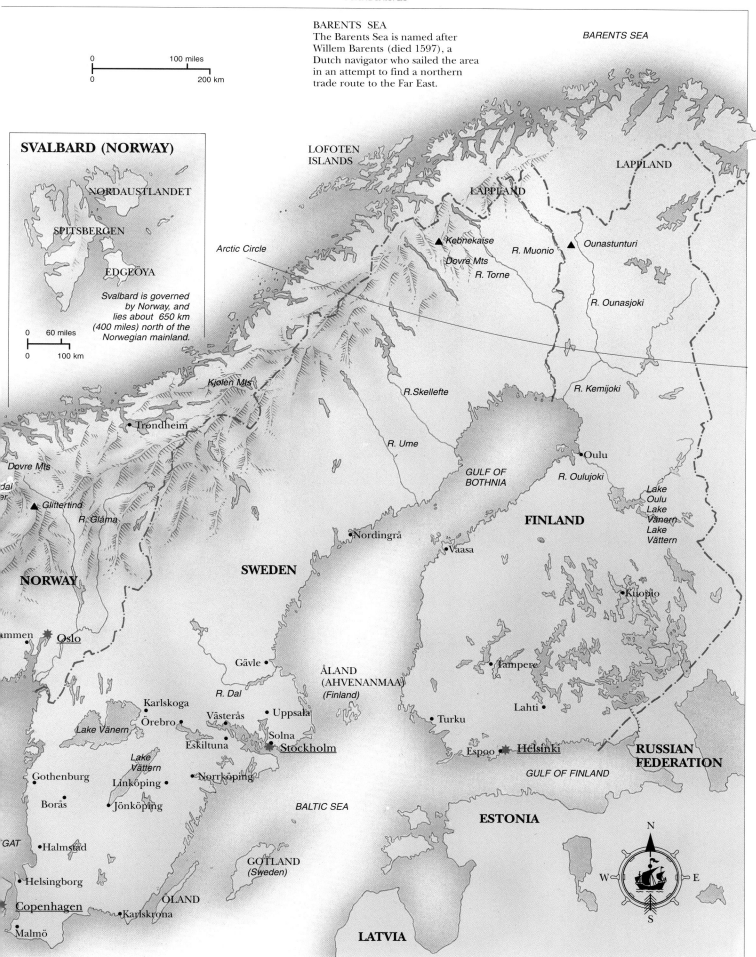

BARENTS SEA

BARENTS SEA
The Barents Sea is named after
Willem Barents (died 1597), a
Dutch navigator who sailed the area
in an attempt to find a northern
trade route to the Far East.

SVALBARD (NORWAY)

NORDAUSTLANDET

SPITSBERGEN

EDGEÖYA

*Svalbard is governed
by Norway, and
lies about 650 km
(400 miles) north of the
Norwegian mainland.*

0   60 miles

0   100 km

LOFOTEN
ISLANDS

LAPPLAND

LAPPLAND

▲ Kebnekaise

Dovre Mts

R. Torne

R. Muonio

▲ Ounastunturi

R. Ounasjoki

Arctic Circle

Kjölen Mts

R.Skellefte

R. Kemijoki

Trondheim

R. Ume

•Oulu

R. Oulujoki

Dovre Mts

GULF OF
BOTHNIA

Lake
Oulu
Lake
Vänern
Lake
Vättern

▲ Glittertind

R. Gläma

FINLAND

•Nordingrå

•Vaasa

SWEDEN

•Kuopio

NORWAY

ammen

Oslo

Gävle •

ÅLAND
(AHVENANMAA)
(Finland)

•Tampere

R. Dal

Lahti •

Karlskoga

Västerås

• Uppsala

• Turku

Örebro

Eskiltuna

Solna

Stockholm

Espoo•

Helsinki

RUSSIAN
FEDERATION

Lake Vänern

GULF OF FINLAND

Gothenburg

Lake
Vättern

•Norrköping

Linköping •

Borås

Jönköping

BALTIC SEA

ESTONIA

GAT

•Halmstad

GOTLAND
(Sweden)

N

•Helsingborg

OLAND

W   E

Copenhagen

•Karlskrona

•Malmö

LATVIA

S

HISTORY OF
SCANDINAVIA

KING CANUTE
In 1014, Canute (c.995-1035) became king of Denmark. He invaded England in 1015 and conquered Norway in 1028. Canute ruled his huge empire with justice and fairness until his death.

HISTORICALLY the region called Scandinavia, in northern Europe, consisted of Norway, Sweden, and Denmark. Today Finland and Iceland are also considered part of Scandinavia. All are independent countries, but their history has been intertwined since ancient times. Seafaring Vikings were among the earliest people to live in the region of Scandinavia, more than 1,000 years ago. During the 900s the three separate nations of Denmark, Norway, and Sweden emerged for the first time. Over the next few centuries, the three countries were often united. During the 16th century, Sweden broke away to build its own empire and became a huge European power. This left Norway and Denmark closely linked. In 1814, Norway came under Swedish rule. But in 1905, Norway became an independent nation. Today, the Scandinavian nations are world leaders in environmental and health issues.

MARGARET I
Margaret I (1353-1412) became queen of Denmark, Norway and Sweden. In 1397 she united the three countries in the Kalmar Union.

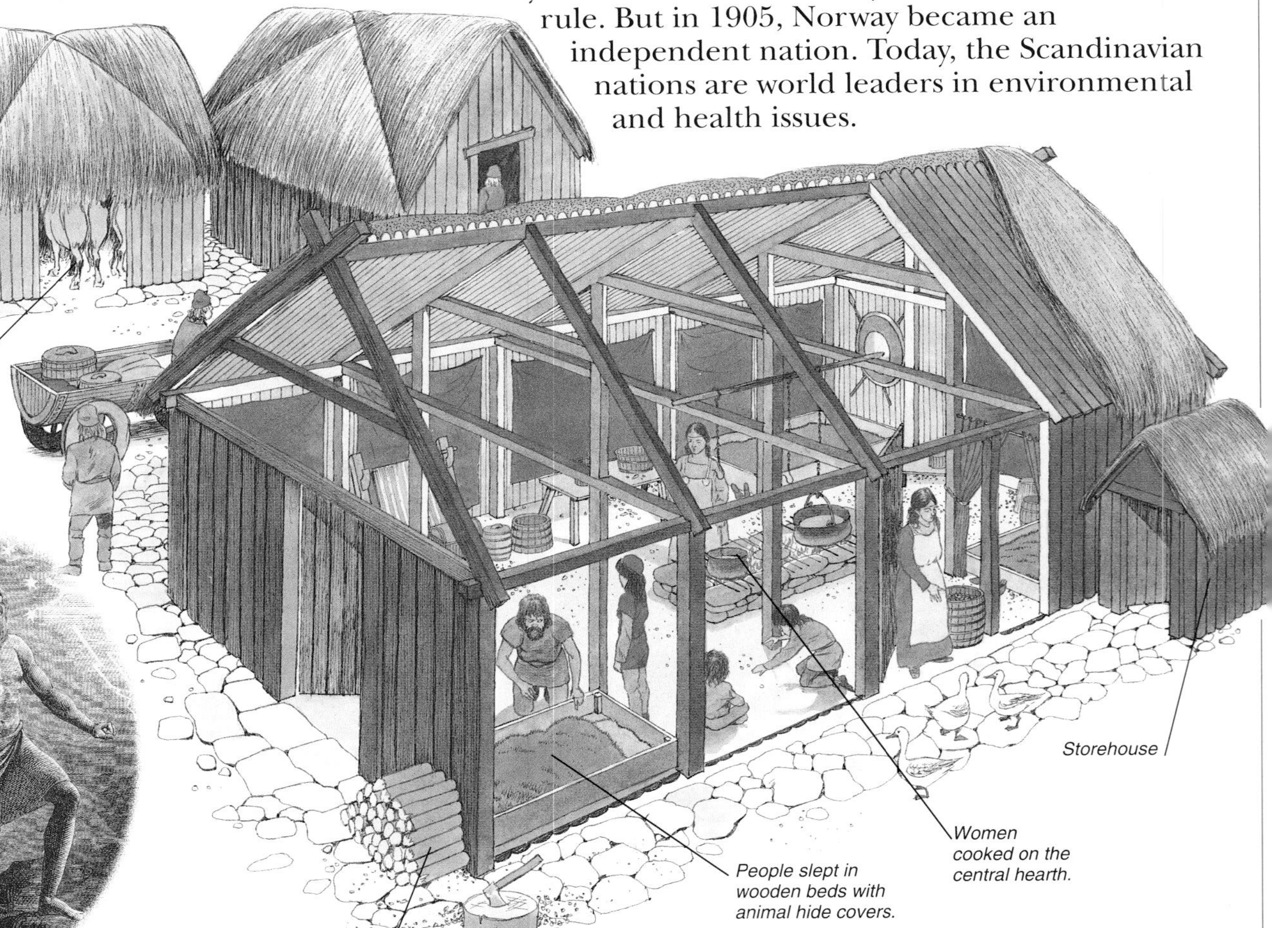

Thatched roof

Cowshed

Storehouse

Women cooked on the central hearth.

People slept in wooden beds with animal hide covers.

Chopped firewood

THOR
The Vikings worshipped many different gods. Thor was one of the most powerful. As ruler of the sky, he controlled the weather and was the god of thunder, lightning, rain, and storms. Vikings prayed to him for good harvests and good luck. He gave his name to Thor's day, or Thursday.

VIKING HOUSE
The Vikings built sturdy one-storey houses with sloping roofs. The houses had timber frames, wooden or stone walls, and thatched roofs. The hearth was the central feature in the house. It provided heat, light, and a place to cook. Viking houses had no windows, so the one room was usually very smoky.

SWEDEN

In 1523, Sweden left the Kalmar Union and declared independence under King Gustavus I (1496-1560). Gustavus introduced many reforms to strengthen Sweden. He made Protestantism the state religion, built up an efficient army, and improved the country's economy. During the reign of Gustavus II, which lasted from 1611 to 1632, Sweden became a major European power. Gustavus increased Swedish territory, gaining most of Finland from Russia. He built a strong navy, but the flagship *Vasa* (right), capsized in Stockholm harbour on its maiden voyage in 1628.

SCANDINAVIA

A.D. 800s-1000s Vikings raid Europe for land and trade.

1014-35 King Canute of Denmark rules vast empire.

1319 Norway and Sweden united.

1375-1412 Margaret I rules Denmark.

1397-1523 Kalmar Union unites Denmark, Norway, and Sweden as Scandinavia.

1523 Sweden becomes independent under Gustavus I; Norway remains part of Denmark until 1814.

1500s-1700s Sweden and Russia fight for control of Finland.

1612-32 Reign of Gustavus II of Sweden; Sweden becomes major European power.

1658 Swedish power at its height.

1700-21 Great Northern War ends Swedish power in the Baltic.

1814-1905 Norway ruled by Sweden.

1901 First Nobel Prizes awarded.

1905 Norway independent.

1917 Finland declares independence from Russia following Russian Revolution.

1914-18 Scandinavian nations are neutral during World War I.

1940-45 Germany occupies Norway and Denmark during World War II.

1986 Olof Palme, Prime Minister of Sweden, assassinated.

EDVARD GRIEG

During the 19th century, Sweden ruled Norway. The Norwegian composer Edvard Grieg (1843-1907) supported independence. He became known as the Voice of Norway, because he wrote patriotic music based on old Norwegian folk songs. His most famous work is music for the playwright Ibsen's *Peer Gynt*.

GREAT NORTHERN WAR

Between 1563 and 1658, the Swedes fought wars with their neighbours that resulted in Swedish domination of the Baltic Sea, an important waterway. For the next 40 years there was an uneasy peace in the region. Then, in 1700, Russia, Denmark, and Poland declared war to end Swedish power. The Great Northern War, as it was called, lasted for 21 years. The Swedes lost lands in the east to Russia.

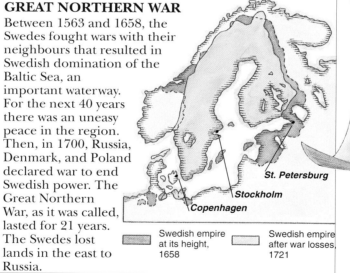

St. Petersburg

Stockholm

Copenhagen

Swedish empire at its height, 1658

Swedish empire after war losses, 1721

CHRISTIAN X

Germany invaded Norway and Denmark during World War II (1939-45). The Norwegian king, Haakon VII, went into exile in Britain, and Vidkun Quisling, a German supporter, took over. The word *quisling* is still used today to describe a traitor. In Denmark, King Christian X (left) led passive resistance to German rule. The Germans demanded that all Jews wear a yellow star, so Christian stated that he too would wear a star. The Danes then helped most Jews escape to neutral Sweden.

GRO BRUNDTLAND

In 1987, Norwegian Prime Minister Gro Brundtland published *Our Common Future: The Brundtland Report*, a major work that described environment problems and their effects on the poor of the world. It also suggested solutions.

NOBEL PRIZE

Swedish chemist Alfred Nobel (1833-96) invented dynamite. He disliked its military uses, and left money in his will to fund prizes to promote peace and learning. Prizes – for physics, chemistry, medicine, literature, and peace – have been awarded since 1901.

Find out more

SCANDINAVIA
VIKINGS

SCHOOLS

MOST PEOPLE REMEMBER starting school. Schools vary depending on culture, but most of us experienced the same mixture of confusion and excitement on our first day at school. Many of us share other early school experiences, too. Schools everywhere aim to teach the basic skills that we need to live in society. For this reason most schoolchildren take classes in reading, writing, and arithmetic. In most Western countries, these early school years are called primary or elementary school, because they are a preparation for later years of education. Reading skills, for example, are vital for everyone throughout their lives. In some other countries, though, for many children school ends at the age of 10, sometimes earlier. Schooling is expensive, and only the wealthier countries can afford to operate free schools for all beyond the first four or five years. Even in countries where primary education is free and compulsory, many families need the money that younger children can earn; so millions of children work as well as – or instead of – attending school.

MEDIEVAL TEACHING
Discipline was strict and the school day was long for the 13th-century student. There was little reading and writing, and students learned mainly by listening to the teacher and asking questions. However, by the end of the 15th century, books of Latin grammar were a popular teaching aid.

SCHOOLS IN THE 19TH CENTURY
In the last century free schooling for all became common in many European countries and the United States. The school schedule was similar to that of today, but learning was not nearly as exciting as it now is. For example, 19th-century teachers expected children to remember long lists of facts which they recited out loud in the classroom.

THE SOCIAL SIDE
School life includes learning to share, communicate, and get along with others. Members of a class must learn to work together and listen to other people's opinions and ideas. The school is also a place where young people learn how to make friends and cope with differences.

OPEN-AIR CLASSROOMS
In parts of Africa and India where money is too scarce to provide enough school buildings, many classes take place out of doors. In countries where the population is scattered, schools are far apart and children may walk several kilometres to learn. And when the nearest school is very distant, as in Australia, a two-way radio brings the school to the pupil.

BRAILLE
Children with a mental or physical disability may find learning difficult. Special equipment helps them study. Braille books with raised letters enable the sight-impaired to read. Children with a hearing loss learn sign language or lip reading.

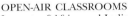

Learning about other peoples and places helps us understand the world around us.

Physical education teaches health, fitness, and teamwork.

Playing a musical instrument demands co-ordination and precise timing; playing with other musicians means learning the skill of co-operation.

Most people find it easier to learn a second language at school than when they are older.

The ability to calculate and measure is essential in everyday life, as well as in many careers.

Computer skills improve logic and aid problem solving in other scientific subjects.

Both boys and girls study food technology and domestic crafts to prepare them for an independent adult life.

Most schoolchildren enjoy painting and sculpture; experience at school can lead to an appreciation of the great artists.

Find out more

EDUCATION
WOMEN'S RIGHTS

SCIENTISTS AND INVENTORS

ANCIENT TIMES

Early people first invented things such as tools about 2 million years ago. About 10,000 years ago, people began to settle in communities and started farming and building. The first civilizations grew up in the Middle East, Africa, India, and China. There people studied the sun and stars, built simple clocks, developed mathematics, and discovered how to make metals and pottery.

This stone blade was used about 200,000 years ago in Egypt.

The wheel was invented in about 3500 B.C.

The plough was invented in about 4000 B.C.

The pump was invented in the second century B.C.

Hero of Greece built the first simple steam engine in the first century A.D.

Archimedes' screw was a device for raising water.

A balloon first carried people in 1783.

In 1608, Dutch optician Hans Lippershey invented the telescope.

GREEKS AND ROMANS

From about 600 B.C., the Greeks began to study their world. Great philosophers (thinkers) such as Pythagoras developed the "scientific method" – the principle of observation and experiment that is still the basis of science today. The Greeks studied mathematics and astronomy and invented simple machines. At around the same time, the Romans used Greek scientific ideas to help them build great structures.

ARCHIMEDES
Greek scientist Archimedes (287 - 212 B.C.) explained how levers and pulleys work and discovered how things float. This idea is said to have come to him while he was in his bath.

SPACE TRAVEL, computers, and reliable medical care are just a few of the things that owe their existence to scientists and inventors. Scientists study the natural world, from distant galaxies to tiny atoms, and try to explain what they see. The work of a scientist is based on a cycle of experiment, observation, and theory. For instance, in the 17th century, English scientist Isaac Newton experimented with sunlight passing through a prism. From the spectrum (bands of colours) that he observed, he suggested the theory that white light is a mixture of colours.

Inventors are people who think of a new idea that can be put into practice. Sometimes an invention is the result of a scientific discovery, such as the laser, which Theodore Maiman (born 1927) built because of his knowledge of light and atoms. However, this is not always the case. Early people invented the lever before they knew how it worked. Whatever their chosen fields, scientists and inventors have one thing in common: they are men and women of rare insight who make discoveries new to the world.

A.D. 1000-1600

During this period, Arabic civilizations made several discoveries, particularly about the nature of light. After about A.D. 1000, people in Europe began to use the scientific method of the Ancient Greeks. Polish astronomer Nicolaus Copernicus (1473-1543) suggested that the Earth orbits the sun, and Flemish doctor Andreas Vesalius (1514-64) made discoveries about human anatomy.

LEONARDO DA VINCI
The great Italian artist and inventor Leonardo da Vinci (1452-1519) designed many machines, including a parachute and a helicopter. However, these machines were never built.

In 1438, Johannes Gutenberg of Germany (c.1398-1468) invented the modern printing process.

1600-1800

Italian scientist Galileo Galilei (1564-1642) made discoveries about force, gravity, and motion. Modern astronomy began in 1609 when German astronomer Johannes Kepler (1571-1630) discovered the laws of planetary motion and Galileo built a telescope to observe the heavens. During the 1700s, the first engines were built by inventors such as James Watt (1736-1819) of Scotland. Chemistry advanced as scientists discovered how everything is composed of chemical elements such as oxygen and hydrogen.

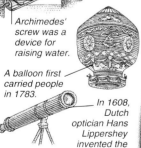

ISAAC NEWTON
In 1666, Isaac Newton (1642-1727) proposed the daring idea that gravity is a universal force, keeping planets and moons in their orbits as well as causing things to fall to the ground. Newton also put forward the famous laws of motion, and found that white light is composed of the colours in the rainbow.

1800-1900

The invention of the battery by Italian Alessandro Volta (1745-1827) led to discoveries about electricity and magnetism by scientists such as Englishman Michael Faraday (1791-1867) and many electrical inventions such as electric light. Englishman John Dalton (1766-1844) and other scientists found out that everything is made of tiny atoms. Frenchman Louis Pasteur (1822-1895) showed that bacteria cause disease, which led to better health care. Transport advanced with the invention of locomotives, powered ships, and cars.

In 1801 Englishman Richard Trevithick invented the steam locomotive.

The telephone was invented by a Scottish-American, Alexander Graham Bell, in 1876.

In 1895, Italian scientist Guglielmo Marconi invented radio transmission.

THOMAS EDISON
Thomas Edison (1847-1931) was one of the world's most successful inventors. He made more than 1,000 inventions, including the record player (patented 1878) and a system for making motion pictures. Edison was also one of the inventors of the electric light bulb.

1900 TO THE PRESENT

Scientists delved into the atom, finding electrons and the nucleus, and then studied the nucleus itself. This led to the invention of nuclear power and to the science of electronics, which brought us television and the computer. Scientists also explored living cells and found new ways of fighting disease. Astronomers studied stars, planets, and distant galaxies. The invention of aircraft and space flight allowed people to travel into the air and out into space.

Several scientists developed television during the 1920s. The first public television service started in the 1930s.

Theodore Maiman and Charles Townes invented the first working laser in 1960.

Artificial satellites were first launched in 1957.

WRIGHT BROTHERS
In 1903, the world watched in wonder as Orville Wright (1871-1948) and his brother Wilbur (1867-1912) made the first powered aeroplane flight.

WILLIAM SHOCKLEY
Computers, televisions, and other electronic devices depend on the transistor, invented in 1948 by a team of scientists headed by William Shockley (born 1910). Now millions of transistors can be packed into a tiny microchip.

In 1946, a team of American scientists built the first fully electronic computer.

ALBERT EINSTEIN
In 1905 and 1915, the German scientist Albert Einstein (1879-1955) proposed his theories of relativity. They showed that light is the fastest thing in the universe, and that time would slow down, length would shorten, and mass would increase if you could travel at almost the speed of light. The sun's source of energy and nuclear power, and how black holes can exist in space are explained by his discoveries.

MAX PLANCK
In about 1900, German scientist Max Planck (1858-1947) published his quantum theory, which explained the nature of energy and led to many new ideas. For example, although we usually think of light as waves, quantum theory explains how light sometimes seems to behave as tiny particles called photons.

Find out more
BIOLOGY
CHEMISTRY
MEDICINE, HISTORY OF
PHYSICS
RENAISSANCE
TECHNOLOGY

HISTORY OF
SCOTLAND

THE NAME SCOTLAND comes from "Scots": peoples from Ireland who raided the country in the sixth century. Tribal communities of Picts already lived there, and in 843, Kenneth MacAlpin united the Picts and the Scots to become the first king of the whole of Scotland. From then until 1603, Scotland had its own king and government and was entirely independent of England. There was fierce rivalry with the southern neighbour, England, over the frontier. Raids were common and full-scale wars were frequent. In 1603, the Scottish king, James VI, inherited the English throne from his cousin Elizabeth I and ruled both countries separately. A century later a full union was achieved between the two countries when their parliaments were merged in the Act of Union of 1707. However, Scotland kept its own legal and educational systems and has remained quite different from England in many other ways.

IONA CHURCH
In 563, the Irish missionary Saint Columba set up a monastery on the island of Iona, off the west coast of Scotland. From there monks travelled throughout the country converting the people to Christianity.

In the Battle of Culloden in 1746, the English finally defeated the Scots.

ROBERT BRUCE
In 1306, Robert Bruce (1274-1329) was crowned king of Scotland against English wishes. In secret, he trained an army which relied on guerrilla tactics – surprise raids and attacks on castles. In 1314, the Scottish defeated the English at the Battle of Bannockburn. Fighting between the two countries continued until the English recognized the independence of Scotland in 1328.

BATTLE OF CULLODEN
In 1714, the Stuart family was kept off the British throne because they were Catholic and most British people were Protestant. In 1745, Charles Edward Stuart (1720-88), known as Bonnie Prince Charlie, was supported by the Highland Scots in his attempt to regain the throne.

CLEARING THE HIGHLANDS
In the late 1700s and early 1800s, landowners cleared people out of the Highlands of Scotland and set the land aside for sheep and cattle grazing in order to make more money. Many Scots were forced to emigrate to Australia or Canada to find work.

INDEPENDENCE
Although Scotland has been united with England since 1707, many Scots want to be independent again. In 1928, the Scottish National Party (SNP) was founded to promote Scottish nationalism. The discovery of oil in the North Sea during the 1970s increased support for the party. The oil has created enough wealth to allow Scotland to become economically independent of England.

SCOTLAND

843 Kenneth MacAlpin becomes the first king of a united Scotland.

1296 English invade and occupy Scotland.

1314 Robert Bruce defeats English at Battle of Bannockburn.

1603 James VI unites the crowns of England and Scotland.

1707 Act of Union formally unites the two countries under one parliament.

1745 Stuart family tries to regain throne.

1746 The English defeat Charles Stuart at Culloden.

1800s Highlands are cleared of people.

1928 Scottish National Party (SNP) founded.

1970s Oil is discovered off east coast of Scotland.

1997 Yes vote for Scottish parliament.

Find out more
ELIZABETH I
UNITED KINGDOM
UNITED KINGDOM, HISTORY OF

SCULPTURE

BY CARVING SOLID MARBLE or pouring liquid metal, a sculptor can create art in three dimensions. Like paintings and drawings, the resulting sculpture is a vivid image from the artist's imagination. But unlike paintings, which are flat, sculpture is solid, so that you can often walk around it. Sometimes you can touch the sculpture and feel its texture. But it is the depth of sculpture that makes it so interesting. Looking at a sculpture from a different angle changes its appearance completely. For this reason, city planners often use sculpture to brighten up public parks and other outdoor places. Sculptures of people and animals are called statues. But modern sculptors also create abstract sculptures – works which do not represent any real thing but make the space they occupy more interesting, exciting, or restful.

BAS-RELIEF

Not all sculptures are freestanding. Some, called bas-reliefs, are like raised pictures made of wood, metal, or stone. The sculpted figures project a bit from the background, giving a more lifelike quality. Ancient civilizations often recorded great events in their history in bas-relief panels.

Woodcarvers hit their sharp chisels with a wooden mallet to remove large pieces of wood.

For finer work, they shave wood away by pushing the chisel with their hands.

Modelling clay is so soft that even lightweight tools can shape it.

Metal scrapers are useful for shaving the surface of set plaster.

SCULPTOR'S TOOLS

Because sculptors create their art from many different materials, they use a great variety of tools. Hard materials such as stone require powerful cuts from heavy chisels. But to make a sculpture that will be cast in bronze, scrapers and other small tools are all that is needed.

Heavy hammer helps chip stone into shape.

WOOD SCULPTURE

African carvers are experts in wood sculpture. They cut, shave, and polish the wood to make gleaming statues of people and forest or grassland animals. In Europe, woodcarvers decorated the insides of many churches and cathedrals. English sculptor Grinling Gibbons (1648-1720) carved fruits and flowers from wood and decorated St. Paul's Cathedral, London.

STONE SCULPTURE

Sculptors work with many kinds of stone, but marble is popular because it does not fracture unpredictably when the sculptor strikes it. Before starting work, the sculptor generally makes a plaster maquette, or small model, of the sculpture. Chipping away with chisels and hammer, the sculptor shapes the stone roughly before making the final cuts. A final polish gives the stone a beautiful finish.

BRONZE CASTING

Most cast sculptures are made of bronze – an alloy, or mixture, of copper and tin. The sculptor creates the original work in a soft material such as clay or plaster. From this master, the sculptor can make an identical copy in wax. Covering the model in plaster and heating it melts away the wax and leaves a perfect mould. Filling the mould with the molten (liquid) metal creates the sculpture. Finally, the sculptor cuts off unwanted metal and sometimes polishes the finished work.

MODERN SCULPTURE

Artists sometimes use sculpture to express ideas about society. American artist Javacheff Christo (born 1935) wraps landscapes and buildings to make people think about the packaging that covers everything they buy.

By wrapping the Pont Neuf, Paris, *Christo transformed this French landmark into a work of art.*

Find out more
METALS
PAINTERS
PAINTING
RENAISSANCE

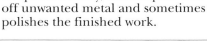

SEA BIRDS

Albatrosses and petrels, such as this storm petrel, are called tubenoses because they have tube-shaped nostrils on the bill.

ALL KINDS OF BIRDS live near the sea, gliding over the waves and feeding along the shore or diving for fish. Sea birds are not one single bird group. They are several different groups of birds, all of which live near the sea. Most have webbed feet for swimming, waterproof feathers, and sharp bills for gripping slippery fish. Sea birds include razorbills and guillemots, whose small wings act like flippers for swimming. Other sea birds, such as albatrosses and petrels, have long, slim wings for soaring high in the sky. Gulls and skuas are scavengers and take almost any food, from dead flesh to other sea birds' eggs and chicks. The great skua attacks birds in midflight, making them drop their food, which it then catches. Gannets and boobies dive for fish from 30 m (100 ft). Penguins cannot fly, but they swim expertly with their wings, chasing fish in the oceans south of the equator.

WANDERING ALBATROSS

There are 14 kinds of albatross, and most live south of the equator. Their wings are the longest of any bird, more than 3 m (10 ft) from tip to tip. They glide over the oceans for hours without flapping, picking fish from the water.

HERRING GULL

Noisy and aggressive, herring gulls live in Europe, North America, North Africa, and Asia. They trail after fishing boats for leftovers, visit rubbish dumps, and follow the farmer's plough to feed on worms, insects, and small mammals.

GANNET
A gannet collects grasses for its nest, then returns to the gannetry, its cliff-top breeding colony. Sometimes more than 50,000 gannets nest in the same place.

Spear-shaped bill for piercing fish

Long, narrow albatross wings are a perfect shape for gliding on the wind.

Atlantic puffin

BREEDING COLONIES

Most sea birds raise their young on cliffs and small islands. Their food is nearby, and the chicks are safe from predators on the steep ledges. The noise of a sea bird colony is deafening. Kittiwakes, cormorants, and guillemots are nesting together here, but each nest is well out of the way of all the other birds' stabbing bills.

Cormorants, kittiwakes, and guillemots share the same cliff-top nesting place.

Guillemot egg has pointed tip.

PUFFIN
The Atlantic puffin can hold a dozen sand eels or small fish in its big, bright bill. When its bill is full, the puffin carries the food to its chick in the burrow.

A kittiwake's nest is made of pieces of seaweed and plant stuck together with droppings.

EGGS
Guillemots do not make nests. Their eggs are pointed at one end, so they spin in a circle if they roll, and do not fall off the cliff edge.

Find out more
BIRDS
FLIGHT IN ANIMALS
MIGRATION
SEASHORE WILDLIFE

SEALS AND SEA LIONS

WITH THEIR STREAMLINED BODIES, seals and sea lions are well equipped for life in the ocean. Despite their large size, they are speedy, energetic swimmers. Their oily, glossy fur keeps them warm in cold waters, helped by a thick layer of blubber under the skin. Seals swim gracefully with alternate strokes of their back flippers. On land, however, they are clumsy without water to support their bodies, so they clamber over the shore by wriggling along on their bellies. Unlike seals, sea lions waddle along quickly on land. Sea lions also sit up on rocks, supported by their front flippers, and tuck their back flippers under the body. They use their front flippers like oars as they speed after fish in the sea. There are more than 30 kinds of seals and sea lions.

HARP SEAL
Newborn harp seals have white fur to camouflage them on the ice. After a few weeks the coat changes to grey.

CALIFORNIA SEA LION
The best-known performing seals are California sea lions. Thousands of them live off the coast of California, in the United States. They feed on squid, fish, and other small sea creatures.

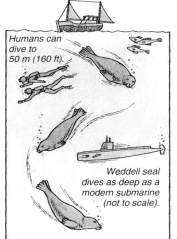

Humans can dive to 50 m (160 ft).

Weddell seal dives as deep as a modern submarine (not to scale).

WEDDELL SEAL
This seal can dive to nearly 600 m (2,000 ft), holding its breath for almost an hour. Only a submarine can dive to the same depth.

COMMON SEAL
This seal is also known as the harbour seal, as it is often seen around harbours, ports, and even a short way up rivers. Fish is its main food, and it lives around the northern shores of the Atlantic and Pacific oceans.

BREEDING COLONIES
Seal colonies are very crowded places during the breeding season – in spring and early summer. All kinds of seals and sea lions come ashore to breed, and live together in their hundreds. The males, or bulls, battle for a territory, as these two huge elephant seal bulls are doing. Once the bulls have established their territory, the pregnant females arrive. Each female gives birth to one pup and feeds it with her milk for several weeks. At 3 tonnes (3 tons) in weight, the elephant seal is the heaviest member of the seal family.

WALRUS
The icy Arctic Ocean is the home of the walrus, a close relative of the seal. Males can grow to more than 3 m (10 ft) in length; females are slightly smaller. These sea mammals paddle with their back flippers and steer with the front ones. Their tough skin is 2.5 cm (1 in) thick, covered with short, coarse hairs. Females give birth to one walrus calf every other year, and it may stay with its mother for the first two years. Walruses can live for up to 40 years.

WALRUS TEETH
Walruses have huge canine teeth, or tusks, that grow more than 50 cm (20 in) long. Tusks are a status symbol, and the male with the largest tusks usually becomes the leader of the herd. Walruses use their strong tusks for chopping holes in the ice and for hauling themselves out of the water and on to ice floes to rest.

Find out more
ANIMALS
MAMMALS
OCEAN WILDLIFE
POLAR WILDLIFE

480

SEASHORE WILDLIFE

SEASIDE DANGERS

Most of these baby turtles, hatching from eggs buried by their mother in the sand, will die. They are food for gulls, crabs, lizards and other hunters. Humans also steal the eggs. Conservation efforts are now being made to protect the turtles.

A SEASHORE is formed wherever the land meets the sea, and can be a polar ice cliff or a tropical beach. The endless motion of the waves, and the tide going in and out, means the shore changes constantly with time. Each seashore has its own selection of plant and animal life that is specially adapted to an environment governed by the rhythm of the tides. Inhabitants of the seashore must survive pounding waves, salty sea water, fresh rainwater, drying winds, and hot sunshine. Plants thrive along rocky coasts and in some muddy areas, providing food and shelter for creatures, but they cannot grow on shifting sand or pebbles. Here the inhabitants depend on the tide to bring new supplies of food, in the form of particles floating in the water. Successful seashore animal groups include molluscs and crustaceans, both of which are protected by hard casings.

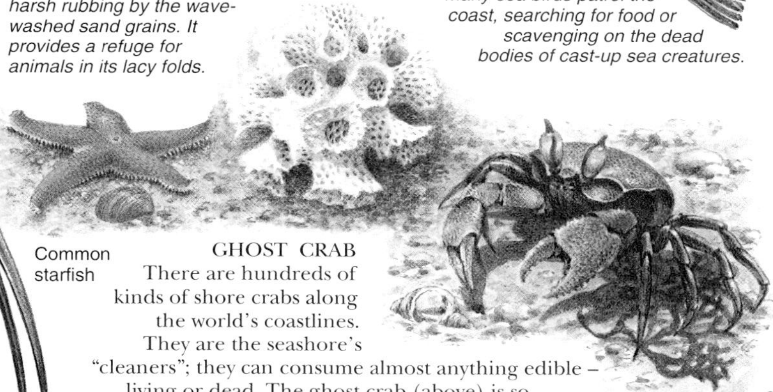

Lace coral can survive harsh rubbing by the wave-washed sand grains. It provides a refuge for animals in its lacy folds.

Many sea birds patrol the coast, searching for food or scavenging on the dead bodies of cast-up sea creatures.

SANDY BEACHES

Waves roll and tumble the tiny grains of sand on the beach. Plants cannot get a firm hold on this type of shore, so they usually grow higher up. Although the sandy beach often looks deserted, dozens of creatures are just below the surface. Sand makes an ideal hiding place for burrowing creatures. Many filter food from the sea water when the tide is in or digest tiny edible particles in the sand.

WADING BIRDS

Waders probe into sand or mud with their long, narrow bills to find shellfish and worms. Large species with the longest bills, such as the curlew (above), reach down several centimetres for deeply buried items. Smaller waders, such as the black-bellied dunlin, take food from just below the surface.

Common starfish

GHOST CRAB

There are hundreds of kinds of shore crabs along the world's coastlines. They are the seashore's "cleaners"; they can consume almost anything edible – living or dead. The ghost crab (above) is so called because of its ghostly pale colour.

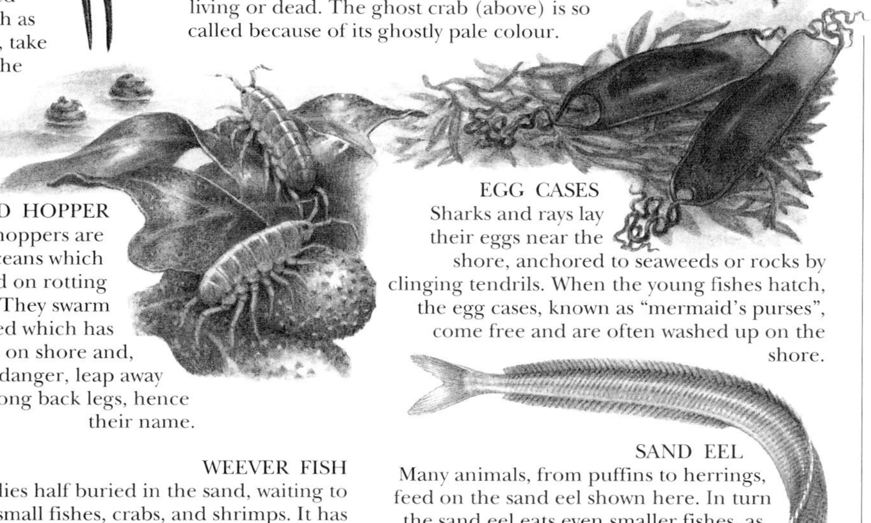

EGG CASES

Sharks and rays lay their eggs near the shore, anchored to seaweeds or rocks by clinging tendrils. When the young fishes hatch, the egg cases, known as "mermaid's purses", come free and are often washed up on the shore.

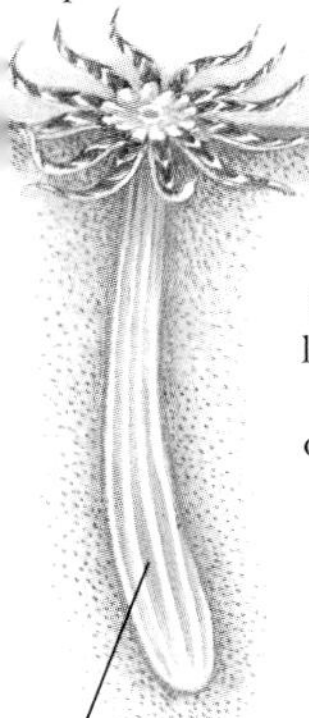

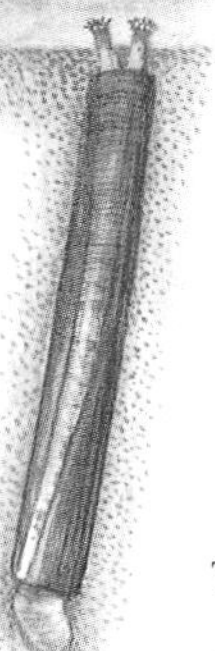

RAZOR CLAM

So-called because it looks like an old-fashioned cut-throat razor, the razor clam has two shells. The mollusc inside digs quickly by pushing its strong, fleshy foot into the sand and then pulling the shell down.

SAND HOPPER

Sand hoppers are crustaceans which feed on rotting vegetation. They swarm over seaweed which has washed up on shore and, when in danger, leap away on their strong back legs, hence their name.

The burrowing sea anemone's arms spread out to sting and catch small prey. Its stalk, up to 30 cm (12 in) long, is used to hold on to the sand.

WEEVER FISH

The weever lies half buried in the sand, waiting to gobble up small fishes, crabs, and shrimps. It has poisonous spines on its fins, which give a nasty sting if the fish is stepped on.

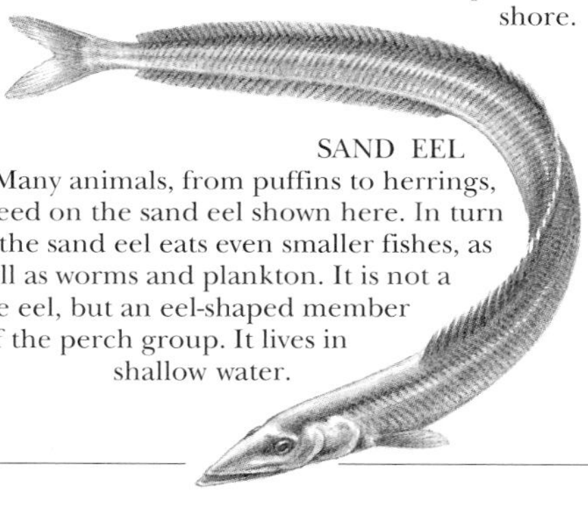

SAND EEL

Many animals, from puffins to herrings, feed on the sand eel shown here. In turn the sand eel eats even smaller fishes, as well as worms and plankton. It is not a true eel, but an eel-shaped member of the perch group. It lives in shallow water.

SALT MARSHES

Salt marshes form at the back of the shore, where the tide floods flat areas of land near a river's mouth. Plants such as cordgrass, glasswort, eelgrass, sea club rush, and sea starwort are able to survive in the salt that builds up in the soil. Birds such as geese, gulls, and terns can feed on salt marshes all year round, especially in winter, when inland areas are frozen hard. Some birds use salt marshes as summer breeding grounds, some as stop-overs while migrating.

Some large seaweeds are called kelps, such as sugar kelp and oarweed.

CLIFFS

Only a few very agile land animals, such as snakes, can reach precarious cliff ledges. So the ledges are safe nesting sites for a variety of birds, from gannets to gulls, razorbills, and cormorants. A few plants, like thrift ("sea pink"), also gain a foothold, provided they can withstand strong winds and salty spray.

Periwinkles seal themselves to the rock with mucus as the tide retreats, to keep them from losing water and drying out.

SEAWEED

There are three main kinds of rocky-shore seaweeds, also known as algae: brown, red, and green. They do not have roots, stems, or leaves, like other plants. Instead most anchor themselves to the rocks by structures called holdfasts. The larger brown and red weeds have stem-like stipes, ending in leaflike blades known as laminae or fronds.

ROCKY SHORES

Rocks provide a firm surface for plant roots, and many creatures shelter among the vegetation. But the plants still face problems. Waves smash them against the hard stony surface, and they are regularly submerged by salt water, then left high and dry at low tide. Shellfish cling to the rocks, and a variety of fishes and crabs adapt themselves to the ever-changing conditions, hiding from predators in holes and crevices.

WHELKS

These rocky-shore scavengers hunt for dead or dying animals. They are relatives of land snails and find prey by "smelling" the water, which they draw in through a periscope-like siphon.

ANEMONES

These jellyfish relatives use their tentacles to sting small fishes, shrimps, and other creatures and draw them into the mouth in the stalk. When the tide goes out, the tentacles fold inwards for protection.

Barnacle

CHITON

Chitons are also called "coat of mail" shells because they look like chainmail armour. Each chiton has an eight-part shell set into its broad, fleshy body. It can grip a rock very firmly. These molluscs feed on small algae from the rock surface.

MANTIS SHRIMP

The mantis shrimp, a crustacean, hides in a hole waiting for prey. When a fish or other victim approaches, the shrimp stuns it by a lightning blow from its club-shaped second "leg".

Branching holdfast provides shelter for small animals

Red seaweed

SEA STAR

The biscuit sea star feeds on shellfish, sea squirts, corals, sponges, and other animals. It glides along on dozens of tiny, sucker-tipped hydraulic tube feet located on its underside.

Find out more

CORALS, ANEMONES, and jellyfish
CRABS AND OTHER CRUSTACEANS
FISH
OCEAN WILDLIFE
SEA BIRDS
SHELLS AND SHELLFISH
STARFISH AND SEA URCHINS

SHARKS AND RAYS

A PERFECT SHAPE FOR SPEED, an incredible sense of smell, and a mouth brimming with razor-sharp teeth make sharks the most fearsome fish in the sea. Sharks have existed for 350 million years, and their shape has hardly changed at all during this time. They have no predators and fear nothing in the ocean. The great white shark is the largest predatory fish, at more than 9 m (27 ft) in length and 2.7 tonnes (2.7 tons) in weight. Dozens of huge teeth line its jaws. The great white shark prowls the ocean, eating any kind of meat, alive or dead, and often swallows its prey in one gulp. Sharks have to keep moving or they sink, and the great white travels more than 483 km (300 miles) in a day.

Although most fish have bony skeletons, sharks and their relatives, the rays, have rubbery skeletons made of a substance called cartilage. Rays are flat-bodied, with a wide mouth on the underside and blunt teeth for crushing clams and other shellfish. Rays live close to the sea bed and move gracefully by flapping their huge wings.

Good sense of smell for hunting

Long tail used for rounding up fish in the water

The thresher shark lashes the water with its tail to sweep fish into a group. Then, with its mouth open, the shark charges through, gobbling them up.

Excellent eyesight for spying prey

THRESHER SHARK
This shark measures 6 m (20 ft) in length. It lives mainly in the warm coastal waters of the Atlantic and Pacific oceans but sometimes strays north in summer.

FIN
A shark's dorsal (back) fin cuts the sea's surface as the shark circles before attacking. The dolphin's fin is more crescent-shaped.

Stingrays have a poison spine on the tail.

STINGRAY
There are about 100 kinds of stingrays – the biggest measures 4 m (12 ft) across.

TEETH
Sharks have many rows of teeth. As they grow, the teeth move from inside the mouth to the outside edge, where they are used for tearing flesh. Eventually the teeth wear away or break off, only to be replaced by the teeth behind.

Shark tooth

Huge wings

Sharks' teeth have a serrated edge so they can saw through flesh.

Dorsal fin

Dorsal fin

SKIN
Shark skin is covered with toothlike scales, and rips whatever it touches.

WHALE SHARK
The harmless whale shark cruises slowly through the tropical oceans, feeding by filtering tiny floating animals (plankton) from the water. It is a peaceful creature and is the biggest fish of any kind, at 15 m (45 ft) long.

Upper lobe of caudal fin (tail)

Pectoral fin

Nostrils are excellent at detecting the smell of blood in the water.

SWIMMING MACHINE
The shark's swimming power comes from its tail. The larger upper lobe drives it down with each stroke and helps keep the body level; otherwise the creature's weight would tilt its head down. A shark cannot swivel its fins to stop quickly. It must veer to one side instead.

A human can swim safely with the gentle whale shark, the biggest fish in the sea.

HAMMERHEAD
The eyes and nostrils of the hammerhead shark are on the two "lobes" of its head. Hammerheads prey on stingrays, unharmed by the poison in their spines.

Find out more
ANIMAL SENSES
ANIMALS
FISH
OCEAN WILDLIFE

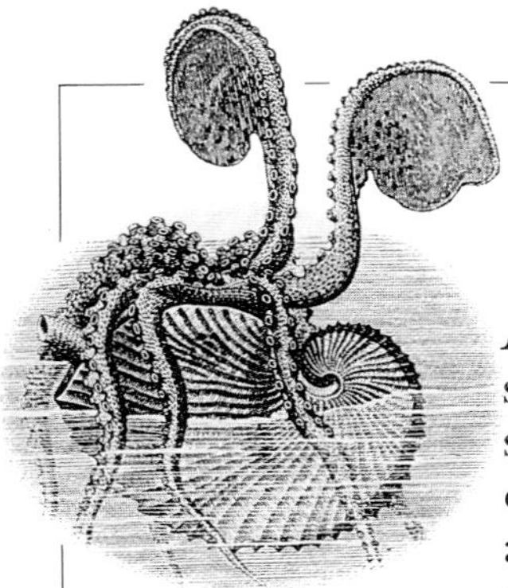

SHELLS AND SHELLFISH

ALL THE WONDERFUL shells you find on the seashore were once the homes of soft-bodied sea creatures. These creatures are commonly known as shellfish, although they are not fish at all, but molluscs, like slugs and snails. There are thousands of different kinds of shellfish living in the sea, including mussels, oysters, and clams. Many, such as the winkle, have small, delicate shells; others, such as the queen conch, have big, heavy shells. The shell itself is like a house, built by the shellfish. As it feeds, the shellfish extracts calcium carbonate from the water. This mineral is used by the shellfish to build up layers of shell, little by little. As the creature grows bigger, its shell grows bigger too. Some shellfish live in a single, coiled shell; others, known as bivalves, have a hinged shell with two sides that open and close for feeding.

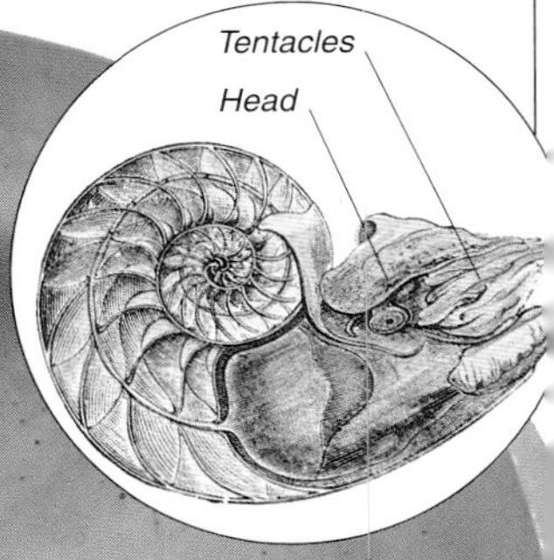

ARGONAUT
The paper nautilus is a type of octopus which makes a thin shell to keep its eggs in. It is also known as the argonaut, after the sailors of Greek legend, because people believed it used its papery shell as a boat.

Tentacles
Head

INSIDE A SHELL
The pearly nautilus has a shell with many chambers. As it grows, the animal shuts off more chambers by building a "wall" and lives only in the last chamber.

NAUTILUS
This predator and scavenger hunts at night. It lives in the Indian and Pacific oceans, and has more than 30 tentacles for catching prey.

HOW SHELLS GROW
Shellfish begin life as eggs, then develop shells. Creatures with single coiled shells, such as this triton, grow by adding layers of shell-building material (calcium carbonate) to the open end. Hinged-shell creatures, such as cockles, add calcium carbonate to the rounded edges, in the form of coils called growth rings.

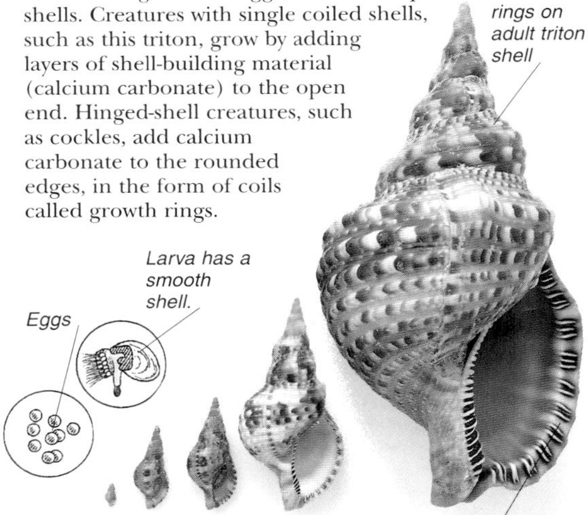

Growth rings on adult triton shell

Larva has a smooth shell.

Eggs

Young shells are tiny and have few coils.

Growth rings are slowly added to the open end.

HINGED SHELLS
The two sides of a hinged shell (bivalve) are joined together by a tough ligament. Powerful muscles keep the valves closed for protection. The valves open slightly to allow the creature to breathe and feed.

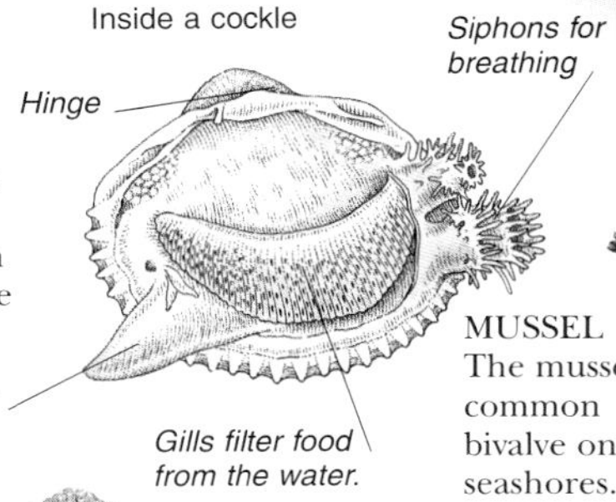

Inside a cockle

Hinge

Foot

Siphons for breathing

Gills filter food from the water.

MUSSEL
The mussel is a common bivalve on many seashores.

COCKLE SHELL
The spiny cockle buries itself in sand and feeds when the tide comes in.

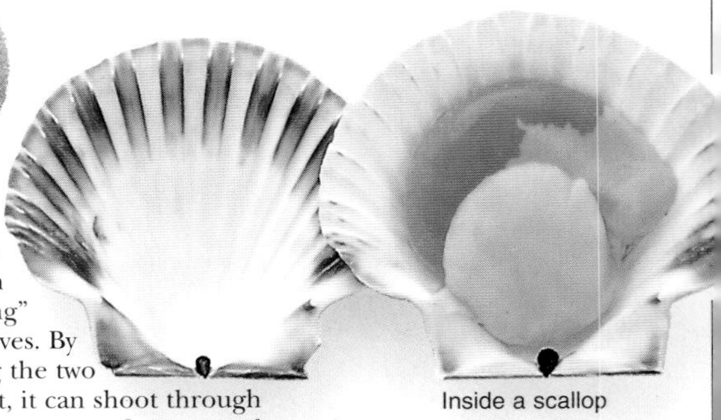

SCALLOP
The scallop is able to swim by "flapping" its two valves. By snapping the two sides shut, it can shoot through the water to escape from a predator.

Inside a scallop

HOW A PEARL IS MADE
If a piece of grit gets lodged in an oyster's shell, the oyster covers it with mother-of-pearl (nacre), a substance lining its shell.

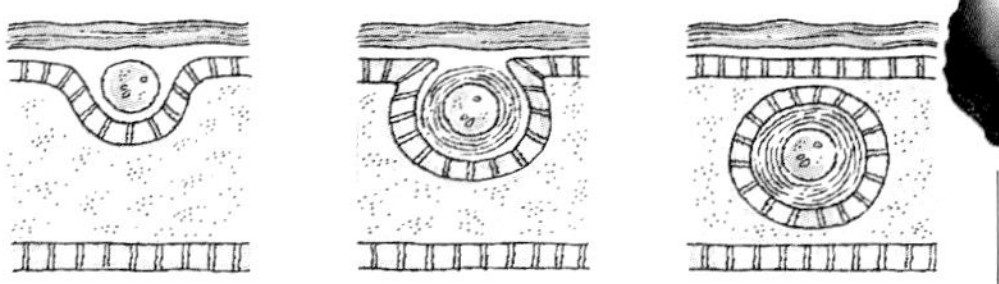

Tiny piece of grit irritates oyster.

Mother-of-pearl (nacre) forms over grit.

Pearl comes free, removing the irritation.

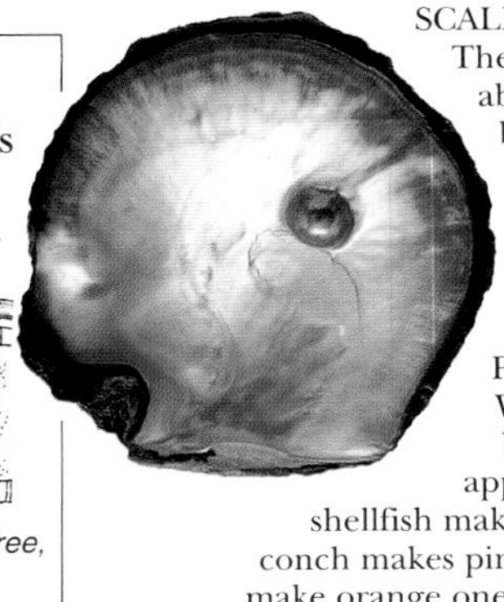

PEARL
We value oyster pearls highly because of their white, shiny appearance, but other kinds of shellfish make pearls too. The Caribbean conch makes pink pearls, and some shellfish make orange ones. The pearl shown here is a "blister pearl" on a black-lipped oyster shell.

Find out more
ANIMAL SENSES
ANIMALS
FOOD
SEASHORE WILDLIFE
OCEAN WILDLIFE

SHIPS AND BOATS

Traditional craft such as this Chinese junk are still used in some parts of the world.

EVER SINCE OUR EARLIEST ancestors discovered that wood floats on water, ships and boats have played a major part in human history. The first boats helped people cross streams and rivers and carried hunters into shallow waters so they could go fishing. Better ways of building ships and boats began to develop when people left their homes to explore new territories. Since more than two thirds of the Earth is covered by water, these early explorers had to put to sea to discover new lands, and they needed vessels that could make long voyages. Ships and boats changed and improved over thousands of years as distant nations began to trade and opposing navies fought battles at sea. Today there are thousands of different types of ships and boats. Ships are seagoing vessels; boats are generally smaller and travel on coastal or inland waters.

SHIPBUILDING
Modern ships are built of steel plates welded together. Shipbuilders build all the parts separately and finally assemble the ship in the shipyard. After months of sea trials to check its safety, the ship is ready for service.

A crane (called a derrick), driven by steam or electricity, is used to load and unload cargo.

A powerful diesel engine drives one or more propellers at the stern (back) of the ship.

Weight of ship pushing downwards

Upthrust from water pushing upwards

HOW SHIPS FLOAT
Although metal is very heavy, a ship contains large spaces filled with air. The hull (main body) of a ship pushes water out of the way, and the water pushes back on the ship with a force called upthrust. The upthrust balances the weight of the ship and keeps it afloat.

Rudder

Propeller

RUDDER AND PROPELLER
A rotating propeller forces the ship through the water, and the rudder steers the ship. When the rudder twists, the weight of water thrusting against it turns the ship.

The captain commands the ship from the bridge, which houses the steering wheel and navigation instruments such as compasses, radar equipment, and charts.

Cabins for crew to sleep in when not on duty.

Main body of the ship is called the hull.

The front end of a ship is called the bow.

CARGO SHIP
Every year, cargo ships carry millions of tonnes of goods across the world's oceans. Some cargo ships, called container ships, carry huge loads piled up in large, steel boxes that stack together like building blocks. The largest ships of this kind carry more than 4,000 such containers.

KINDS OF SHIPS
There are many kinds of ships. They range from passenger vessels to cargo ships that carry goods of all types to and from the world's ports.

Cargo is stored in a large compartment below deck, called a hold. Large modern cargo vessels may have 12 or more holds. Ships that carry fresh food have refrigerated holds.

FERRY
Ferries take people and goods across a stretch of water. Large ferries carry cars, trucks, and trains as well as people.

OIL TANKER
Oil is transported at sea in huge tankers. The engines and bridge are at the stern to give more storage space.

CRUISE LINER
Liners are large ships that carry passengers on scheduled routes. Most liners are like floating hotels and take tourists on lengthy cruises.

TRAWLER
Trawlers are engine-powered fishing boats that drag a net (the trawl) along the sea bed in order to catch fish that swim near the bottom of the sea.

HISTORY OF SHIPS AND BOATS

The development of ships began more than 6,000 years ago with rafts and reed boats, and continues today with the introduction of nuclear-powered ships and boats made of light, strong plastics.

HIDE BOAT

About 6,000 years ago the Ancient Egyptians used boats made of a wicker framework covered with animal skins. In about 3200 B.C., the Egyptians invented sails.

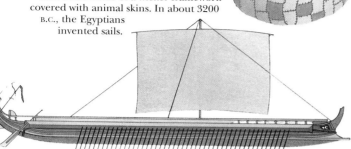

TRIREME

The Greeks invented the trireme (above) in about 650 B.C. It had sails and lines of rowers to carry it along at speed. The Romans built similar ships for trade and war.

Groups of rowers were positioned on two levels.

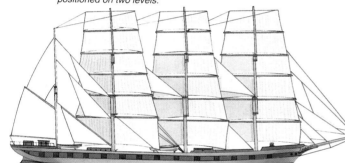

CLIPPER

Fast sailing ships called clippers (above) appeared during the 19th century, the height of the age of sailing. They carried many sails and had sleek lines to increase speed. Clippers were used mainly for trade.

STEAMSHIPS

Oceangoing steamships (below) took to the seas early in the 19th century. The earliest vessels had paddles connected to the engine and sails to gain extra speed in high winds. Ships with propellers entered service during the 1840s.

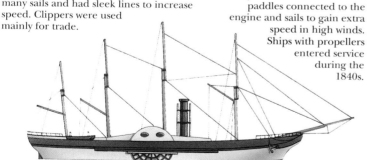

KINDS OF BOATS

Different boats have different uses. Many boats, such as yachts, are pleasure craft; tugs and fishing boats, however, are the workhorses of coastal waters.

POWERBOAT

Powerboats are small, fast boats driven by powerful petrol or diesel engines. They are used either for pleasure or for racing.

TUGBOAT

Tugs tow larger vessels, guiding them through difficult or shallow waters at sea or on inland waterways such as canals.

HYDROFOIL

A boat's engine has to work hard to overcome the resistance of the water. Light, fast boats called hydrofoils avoid this problem because they rise up on skis at high speeds. With the hydrofoil travelling so rapidly, water behaves as if it were a solid, so the hydrofoil skims over the water surface just like an aeroplane wing in air.

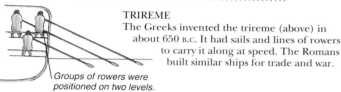

Any force can be divided into two parts at right angles to each other. The part along the length of the boat drives the boat forwards.

Air rushing past the sail produces a force that tends to move the boat at right angles to the wind.

Wind rushing past sail

Wind pushing on sail

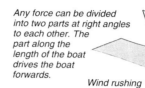

HOW A BOAT SAILS

Modern sailing boats do not need the wind behind them to move – they can travel in almost any direction. In the same way that air rushing over the wings of an aeroplane produces an upward force called lift, wind moving past a sail produces a force at right angles to the sail. Adjusting the sail makes the boat move in different directions.

Centreboard prevents boat from drifting with the wind and stops the boat from capsizing.

With the wind behind the boat, the sail is stretched out across the boat.

Direction of wind

Direction of movement

A sailing boat cannot travel directly into the wind. Instead, it must follow a zigzag path. This is called tacking.

The boat heads into the wind with the sail drawn in as tightly as possible.

With the wind to the side of the boat, the sail is drawn in more tightly. The boat travels fastest with the wind in this position.

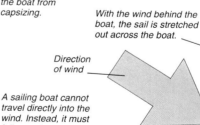

Direction of movement

YACHT

Yachts are pleasure boats. They have engines or sails. Racing yachts are built purely for speed and are made of strong, light materials.

Find out more

NAVIES
NAVIGATION
PORTS AND WATERWAYS
SAILING AND BOATING
SUBMARINES
WARSHIPS

SHOPS AND SHOPPING

IF YOU NEED TO BUY FOOD, or perhaps a book for school, there is probably a shop or a department store close to your home that sells just what you want. But shopping has not always been so easy. Shops started only with the introduction of money in Ancient China. In earlier times people used barter: in exchange for the goods they needed, they traded crops or objects they had made. The first shops sold just a few specialized products; the butcher sold meat, and the baker sold bread.

In 1850 the first department store, a shop which sells many different items under one roof, opened in Paris. Self-service stores developed in the United States in the 1930s. They replaced the old methods of serving customers individually by selling prepackaged goods straight from the shelves. Modern supermarkets have car parks and provide customers with trolleys so they can shop weekly instead of daily. Nowadays you do not even have to leave home to go shopping. You can shop by post, by telephone, or through a computer terminal straight to the warehouse.

COWRIE SHELLS
People in the Pacific Islands and parts of Africa once used cowrie shells as money.

MEDIEVAL SHOPPING
In the middle ages shoppers liked to test the goods and argue over the price. Traveling pedlars carried their goods from place to place, selling and trading.

MAIL ORDER
Shopping by post has been possible for a hundred years. It was introduced for people who lived in remote areas a long way from any shops.

FRONTIER STORE
The frontier store supplied early American settlers with everything from food to tools. There was no packaging and little choice of goods. Supplies often ran out, and sometimes customers could not pay until they had sold their crops.

SHOPPING MALL
The modern shopping mall is an enclosed collection of shops. It is usually air-conditioned and has benches and restaurants to make shopping a pleasant social experience.

MARKETS
Markets are found in all parts of the world. They were the earliest kind of shops where people could bring their surplus goods to exchange or sell. They grew up at important trading places where roads crossed.

BAR CODES
The packages of most modern products identify the contents both in words and with a code of black-and-white stripes. A laser scanner at the till reads the price and other information from this bar code. The till records the price, adds up the bill, and tells a central computer when to reorder the item.

CASH REGISTERS
Cash registers, or tills, were invented in Ohio in 1879. They recorded each sale and kept the money safe. Modern electronic tills add up the bill and print a receipt.

___ *Find out more* ___

ADVERTISING
FOOD
MONEY
TRADE AND INDUSTRY

SKELETONS

INSIDE THE BODY, hundreds of bones link together like scaffolding to form the skeleton. Without a skeleton, the body would collapse. The skeleton holds the body rigid and gives shape to all the softer parts. It also protects the organs – the skull surrounds the brain, and the ribs act like a protective cage around the lungs and heart. The skeleton is also an anchor for the muscles, which move the different parts of the body. Bone is made of living cells surrounded by a framework of minerals, particularly calcium and phosphate, and a stringy, elastic substance called collagen. In a newborn baby, many of the bones are made of a soft, rubbery substance called cartilage. As a baby grows, the cartilage gradually turns into hard bone. Our wrists and ankles are among the last to become bone. In later life, bones gradually become more fragile and brittle, and therefore break more easily.

INTERNAL SKELETONS

Humans and other mammals, fish, birds, and reptiles all have an inner skeleton, or endoskeleton, made of many separate bones. The central part of the skeleton is the spine (vertebral column or backbone). The spinal joints can move only a little, but the spine as a whole is very flexible. Some creatures, such as worms, have no bones. Instead the pressure of fluid inside their bodies helps them keep their shape. They are said to have a hydrostatic skeleton.

Lizard has an internal skeleton, like other vertebrates.

HUMAN SKELETON

There are 206 bones in the human skeleton, including 29 in the skull, 26 in the spine, 32 in each arm, 31 in each leg, and 25 in the chest. The largest bone is in the thigh, and the smallest ones are the ossicles, which are three tiny bones inside each ear.

Skull
Maxilla (upper jaw)
Mandible (lower jaw)
Cervical (neck) vertebrae
Clavicle (collarbone)
Scapula (shoulder blade)
Thorax
12 pairs of ribs
Humerus (upper-arm bone)
Lumbar (lower back) vertebrae
Radius and ulna (forearm bones)
Carpals (wrist bones)
Metacarpals (palm bones)
Phalanges (finger bones)
Pelvis (hipbone)
Ball-and-socket joint
Femur (thighbone)
Patella (kneecap)
Tibia and fibula (shin bones)
Tarsals (ankle bones)
Metatarsals (foot bones)
Phalanges (toe bones)

BONE

Living bone is tough and slightly flexible – only dead bone is white and brittle. Blood vessels pass through small holes in the bone's surface, and carry a steady supply of blood to the bone. Some bones contain a jelly-like substance called bone marrow, which makes blood cells.

Soft, spongy bone inside
Bone marrow
Hard, compact bone outside
Thin, tough outer layer called the periosteum

JOINTS

Bones are linked together at joints. There are several types of joints, including fixed, hinge, and ball-and-socket joints. Fixed joints, such as those between the separate bones in the skull, cannot move; hinge joints, such as those in the elbow, allow movement in one direction, like a hinge. Ball-and-socket joints, such as the hip, allow the bones to swing in two directions and also to twist.

Upper-arm bone
Shoulder blade
Hinge-type elbow joint moves mainly back and forth.
Forearm bone

Cup-shaped socket in hipbone
Ball-and-socket-type hip joint allows leg to swivel and twist.
Ball-shaped end of thighbone

EXTERNAL SKELETONS

Insects, spiders, and crabs have a hard casing or shell, called an exoskeleton. This kind of skeleton cannot grow larger. As the animal grows, it has to shed its old skeleton, and a new, bigger skeleton hardens beneath.

Find out more

BRAIN AND NERVES
HEART AND BLOOD
HUMAN BODY
LUNGS AND BREATHING
MUSCLES AND MOVEMENT

SLAVERY

FIVE THOUSAND YEARS AGO the Sumerians put their prisoners to work on farms as slaves. The workers had no rights and no pay, and their masters regarded them as property. In ancient Greece and Rome, slaves produced most of the goods and also worked as household servants. During the 16th century European nations began to colonize the Americas, and imported thousands of Africans to work as slaves on their plantations and silver mines. Between 1500 and 1800, European ships took about 12 million slaves from their homes to the new colonies. By the 19th century, those against slavery set up movements in the United States and Britain to end it. Slavery was formally abolished, or ended, in the British Empire and the United States in the mid-1800s. Sadly, it continues today in many parts of the world, most often affecting children and immigrants.

ROMAN SLAVES
Most wealthy Roman citizens owned slaves. Some slaves lived as part of the family; others were treated very badly. Some earned manumission (a formal release from slavery) through loyalty to a master.

TRIANGLE OF TRADE

The British trade in slaves was known as the triangular trade. Ships sailed from British ports laden with goods such as guns and cloth. Traders exchanged these goods with African chiefs for slaves on the west coast of Africa. The slave ships then carried their cargo across the Atlantic to the Americas and the Caribbean. Here, slaves were in demand for plantation work, so the traders exchanged them for sugar, tobacco, rum, and molasses. The ships then returned to Britain carrying this cargo, which was sold at huge profits.

Ships sailed back to Europe with goods.

Ships departed from Britain carrying guns and cloth.

Ships carried slaves across the Atlantic.

BRITAIN

NORTH AMERICA

Tobacco

Rum, sugar, and molasses

SOUTH AMERICA

AFRICA

Slave coast

SLAVE SHIPS
Slavers (slave traders) packed their ships with Africans to sail on what was known as the middle passage across the Atlantic. The slaves were chained and kept below deck for most of the voyage. Unclothed and underfed, thousands of Africans died on the Atlantic crossing.

SLAVE MARKET
Once the slaves had reached the West Indies or the southern states of America, they were auctioned at a slave market. Here, they were treated like animals. Families were sometimes separated, and people were sold singly to plantation owners. Slaves were put to work on cotton, sugar, and tobacco plantations. Many received cruel treatment. Severe whipping was a common punishment for slaves who tried to escape.

SLAVE REBELLIONS
Many Africans fought against slavery. In 1791, one of the most famous rebellions began in the French colony of Haiti. A slave named Toussaint L'Ouverture led an army of slaves against the French soldiers in a rebellion that lasted 13 years. L'Ouverture was captured and died in prison in 1803. In 1804, Haiti gained independence and became the world's first black republic.

Find out more

AFRICA, HISTORY OF
CARIBBEAN
CIVIL WAR, AMERICAN
LINCOLN, ABRAHAM

SNAILS AND SLUGS

SLIMY, SLOW-MOVING SNAILS and slugs belong to a group of creatures called gastropods, meaning "stomach foot". These animals seem to slide along on their stomachs; in fact, the underside is itself a special organ which produces movement. There are about 70,000 kinds of slugs and snails, all belonging to the larger group of animals called molluscs, a group that also includes clams and octopuses. In addition to the familiar land snails and slugs, there are seashore gastropods such as sea slugs, winkles, and limpets, and freshwater species such as pond snails and ramshorn snails. Slugs and snails are similar in shape. Snails have shells to protect their bodies; slugs have no shells. Both have tentacles on their heads, with eyes on the ends of the tentacles. Snails and slugs are hermaphrodites. This means that they have both male and female reproductive organs. Most slugs and snails hide away and hibernate during the cold or dry season. During hibernation, snails seal the mouth of their shell with a film of dried mucus.

Diameter of shell increases as snail grows.

Eyes on tips of rear pair of tentacles

Front pair of tentacles

Lip or mouth of shell

Mantle, the fold of flesh that envelops the body

Lower surface or foot

Mouth and rasping tongue

Dark-lipped banded snail has dark band around shell mouth.

GARDEN SNAIL
The snail's shell protects the animal from predators and prevents the soft, moist body from drying out. The shell is made of calcium carbonate and other minerals. As the snail grows, it adds more material to the mouth of the shell, making it larger. The snail's tongue is called a radula. It is small and filelike, with as many as 150,000 tiny teeth for rasping at plant food.

YOUNG
After mating, the snail or slug lays eggs, either singly or in batches in mucus. The young snails and slugs hatch from their eggs after about two to four weeks.

SLIME
Snails and slugs make several types of slime. As the slug crawls along, it lays down one kind of slime in patches. Another kind of slime is given off when the creature is attacked by a predator. A slug crawls by waves of muscle contractions passing along its foot.

SLUG
Slugs are unpopular with gardeners because they do serious damage to vegetables. Most slugs have no shells; some have a very small shell embedded in the back. Slugs avoid drying out by living in damp places and emerging only at night or after rain.

SEA SLUG
There are many beautifully coloured sea slugs in the shallow coastal waters of the world, particularly around coral reefs. Many have feathery or tufted gills for absorbing oxygen from the water. Sea slugs are predators, feeding mainly on sponges, barnacles, sea mats, and sea anemones.

TOPSHELL
The purple top-shell snail lives close to the high-tide mark.

Find out more
OCEAN WILDLIFE
SEASHORE WILDLIFE
SHELLS AND SHELLFISH

490

SNAKES

LONG, LEGLESS, SCALY, and slithering, snakes are a very successful group of reptiles. They are found everywhere except the coldest regions, highest mountain peaks, and a few islands. Most snakes can swim and climb well. All snakes are hunters. Some, such as pythons and boa constrictors, squeeze and suffocate their prey to death; others, such as cobras, paralyse their victims with a poisonous bite. Fast-moving snakes such as sand snakes hunt down insects, small birds, and mammals. Blind snakes are burrowers that eat ants and termites. More than 400 kinds of snakes are venomous (poisonous), but only some can give a fatal bite to humans. Deadly poisonous snakes include cobras, boomslangs, and mambas.

FANGS
The pair of hollow teeth at the front of the upper jaw are called fangs. The fangs lie flat along the jaw and swing forward when the snake strikes. Muscles pump venom from glands down the fangs into the victim.

RATTLE
Rattlesnakes are so named because they shake the tip of the tail (the rattle), to scare off predators. The rattle consists of a row of hollow tail segments which make a noise when the snake shakes them.

Rattle at tip of tail

SNAKE CHARMING
This is an ancient entertainment in Africa and Asia. Snake charmers fascinate snakes with movements that make the snakes sway to the music.

RATTLESNAKE
At more than 2 m (7 ft) long, the eastern diamondback is the largest rattlesnake, and the most poisonous snake in North America. The rattlesnake feeds mainly on rats, rabbits, and birds. Unlike many other snakes, which lay eggs, the rattlesnake gives birth to about 10 live young in late summer.

Emerald tree boa constricts or squeezes its prey.

Snake's long belly has large scales called ventral scutes which overlap like tiles on a roof.

MILK SNAKE
The non-venomous milk snake shown left is found all over North America, down to the north of South America. It looks similar to the poisonous coral snake, but the milk snake has yellow bands bordered by black, whereas the poisonous coral snake has black bands bordered by yellow. The milk snake hunts small mammals, birds, and other reptiles, including rattlesnakes. It coils around its prey and chokes it to death.

YOUNG SNAKES
Some snakes are described as viviparous, because they give birth to fully formed young. Others lay eggs in a burrow or under a log, leaving the young to hatch and fend for themselves. Certain kinds of pythons coil around the eggs and protect them until they hatch.

The sea snake's body follows S-shaped curves, pushing sideways and backwards.

Young grass snake hatches from its egg head first and flicks its tongue to sense its surroundings.

CONSTRICTOR
Boas and pythons are called constrictors because they constrict or coil around their prey and suffocate it. There are 66 kinds of boas and pythons; they include some of the largest snakes on Earth. Anacondas are boas of the Amazon region in South America. These massive snakes reach more than 8 m (25 ft) in length and weigh 227 kg (500 lbs).

SEA SNAKE
There are 50 kinds of sea snakes – the yellow-bellied sea snake shown left is the most common. It measures up to 80 cm (32 in) in length, preys on fish, and gives birth to about five young at sea. Sea snakes spend their lives swimming in the warm waters of the Indian Ocean, around Southeast Asia and Australia, and in the western Pacific.

Find out more
ANIMALS
AUSTRALIAN WILDLIFE
DESERT WILDLIFE
FOREST WILDLIFE
REPTILES

SOIL

FERTILIZER
Farmers add fertilizers to poor soil. The fertilizer is rich in minerals that help the crops to grow.

IF YOU REACH DOWN and pick up a handful of soil, you will be holding one of the Earth's most basic and valuable resources. Soil teems with life. A plot of earth the size of a small garden may contain millions of insects and micro-organisms, plus organic matter from dead or dying plants and animals. Soil provides the foundation for roots, a source of food for plants, and a home not only for burrowing animals, such as moles, but also for millions of spiders and centipedes.

There are many different types of soil, from thick silt and loose sand to waterlogged mud and dry desert. Soil is formed from the wearing down of rocks and takes many years to develop. Each 6.5 sq cm (1 sq in) of soil, for instance, may take 100 to 2,000 years to form. The quality of soil varies from region to region. In hot countries such as Africa and Australia, where there is little rain, the soil is very dry. In temperate regions such as Europe and North America much of the soil is rich and fertile. But soil can be destroyed in just a fraction of the time it takes to form. Overfarming the land, for example, has led to soil erosion in many parts of the world.

TYPES OF SOIL
Soil may be black, brown, red, yellow, orange, or cream in colour, depending on the minerals it contains. Rich, dark, peaty soil is ideal for garden plants.

Peaty soil

Clay soil

Chalky soil

Sandy soil

SOIL EROSION
In overfarmed areas, or where natural vegetation is removed, soil is no longer protected from rain or held in place by roots. Winds blow away the loose particles as dust, and rains wash them away as mud. The land becomes infertile and cannot support life. Today soil erosion affects more than 513,000 sq km (198,000 square miles) in the United States alone.

SOIL LAYERS

Soil is formed from several different layers that merge into one another. On top is a layer of humus, consisting of dead and rotting leaves. Underneath this layer is the topsoil where decayed plant and animal matter is broken down and recycled by insects, fungi, and bacteria. The subsoil layer, which contains less organic matter, lies below the topsoil and above a loose layer of partly weathered rock. A hard layer of solid bedrock lies below all the other layers.

HUMUS
Humus is the layer of decaying leaves and other plant material in the soil.

TOPSOIL
Topsoil is full of burrowing bugs, worms, and other creatures. It also gives anchorage to plants with shallow root systems.

Moles tunnel in the upper metre of rich soil, where there are many worms to eat.

Slug

Beetle

Snail

Caterpillar

Earthworm

Beetle

Centipede

POTATO
All plants, including the potato, use the energy in sunlight, mineral nutrients in the soil, water, and carbon dioxide from the air to grow. The potato plant stores its food reserves in the potatoes that we eat.

Potato tuber

COMPOST
Fungi, bacteria, worms, and insects thrive in a compost heap, helping the contents to decay and be recycled.

RECYCLING
All living things eventually rot away, back into the soil. The compost heap is a valuable recycler. In time, it turns domestic organic rubbish such as apple peelings, banana skins, eggshells, and grass cuttings into humus, a food supply for the soil. In this way, valuable resources are recycled.

SUBSOIL
The subsoil layer is reached only by deep-rooted plants such as trees.

PARTLY WEATHERED ROCK ZONE
This is a layer of crumbled rocks.

Tree roots reach into subsoil layer.

Find out more
FLOWERS AND HERBS
MUSHROOMS
toadstools, and other fungi
PLANTS
TREES

SONGBIRDS

MOST BIRDS MAKE SOME KIND OF SOUND. Some birds make loud, complicated warbles and whistles which are so pleasing to our ears that we call these birds songbirds. There are about 4,000 kinds of songbirds, also called perching birds because they perch in trees to sing. Many songbirds are small and dull-coloured, and stay hidden in trees. In dark, shady woodlands, a loud, clear singing voice is more useful for communicating with others than brightly coloured feathers. The male is usually the chief singer. He sings to show other birds where his territory is and to attract a female. Each kind of songbird has its own way of singing. Birdsongs vary from place to place, in the same way that humans pronounce words in different ways. Among the most outstanding singers are the robin chats of Africa, the warblers of Europe and Asia, and the babblers and bellbirds of Australasia.

DAWN CHORUS
As soon as the sun rises, birds finish their nightly rest and begin the day's activities. Many birds sing loudly at this time, and sing again at dusk. Each bird's song tells neighbours that it has survived the night and is still occupying its territory.

SONG THRUSH
This bird has a loud, cheerful, musical song. Its favourite singing perches include television aerials and high tree branches. Song thrushes eat snails, often breaking the shell open on a stone to extract the flesh.

ROBIN REDBREAST
During the spring, when robins have paired off to build a nest and raise young, the male robin's sweet, sad song tells intruders to stay out of his territory. The robin's warning call, a sharp *tic-tic-tic*, warns other birds of a nearby cat or hawk.

NIGHTINGALE
Many people describe the nightingale's song as the most beautiful of all. It has inspired poets and musicians through the ages. The nightingale (right) sings both day and night, but its song is noticed most at night.

BIRDSONG
There are several ways of describing a bird's song with words and symbols. Tape recordings help people learn how to identify birds by their particular songs.

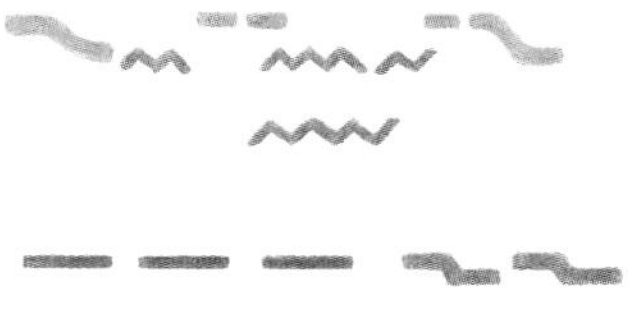

SARDINIAN WARBLER
Loud, fast warbles

NIGHTINGALE
Smooth, liquid sounds

YELLOW WARBLER
In North and Central America, the yellow warbler is well known in parks and orchards. Its song often starts with three or four sweet *wheet* sounds and ends with a quick burst of high and low notes. Yellow warblers feed on caterpillars, moths, beetles, and spiders.

Find out more
ANIMALS
BIRDS
FLIGHT IN ANIMALS
MIGRATION

SOUND

WE LIVE IN A NOISY world. The roar of city traffic, the music from a piano, the bark of a dog – all come to our ears as sound waves travelling through the air. Sound is generated when a disturbance sets air moving – for example, when someone plucks a guitar string. We hear sounds when sound waves – tiny vibrations in the air – strike our eardrums. Sound waves need a substance to travel through. This substance may be a liquid, such as water; a solid, such as brick and stone; or a gas, such as air.

Sounds such as musical notes have a certain pitch. A high-pitched sound makes the air vibrate backward and forward more times each second than a low-pitched sound. The number of vibrations per second is called the frequency of the sound and is measured in hertz (cycles per second). Humans cannot hear sounds with frequencies above about 20,000 hertz or below about 30 hertz.

LOUDNESS AND DECIBELS
The sound of a train is louder than the sound of a whisper because the train produces larger vibrations in the air. The loudness of sound also depends on how close you are to its source. Loudness is measured in decibels (dB). A jet airliner taking off is rated at about 120 dB; the rustling of leaves is about 33 dB.

ECHOES
If you shout in a large hall or near mountains, you can hear your voice echo back to you. An echo occurs when a sound bounces off a surface such as a cliff face and reaches you shortly after the direct sound. The clarity of speech and music in a room or concert hall depends on the way sounds echo inside it.

The distance from one region of highest pressure to the next is called the wavelength of the sound. The higher the pitch, or frequency, of the sound, the shorter the wavelength.

Region of high-pressure air

Region of low-pressure air

The noise of the boat's engine sends sound waves through the water.

SPEED OF SOUND
Sound travels in air at a speed of about 1,224 km/h (about 760 mph). It travels more slowly when the temperature and pressure of the air is lower. In the thin, cold air 11 km (7 miles) up, the speed of sound is about 1,000 km/h (620 mph) In water sound travels at 5,400 km/h (about 3,350 mph), much faster than in air.

SOUND WAVES
A sound wave consists of air molecules vibrating backward and forward. At each moment the molecules are crowded together in some places, producing regions of high pressure, and spaced out in others, producing regions of low pressure. Waves of alternately high pressure and low pressure move through the air, spreading out from the source of the sound. These sound waves carry the sound to your ears.

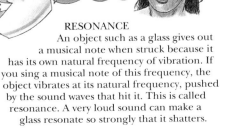

RESONANCE
An object such as a glass gives out a musical note when struck because it has its own natural frequency of vibration. If you sing a musical note of this frequency, the object vibrates at its natural frequency, pushed by the sound waves that hit it. This is called resonance. A very loud sound can make a glass resonate so strongly that it shatters.

HARMONICS
In a musical note, secondary frequencies, called harmonics, are mixed with the main frequency. Harmonics are characteristic of different instruments, which is why a note played on a piano sounds different from the same note played on a violin. Harmonics bring life to the sound of musical instruments: an electronically produced sound of a single pure frequency sounds artificial and dull.

Find out more
EARS
MUSIC
RADIO
SOUND RECORDING

SOUND RECORDING

TODAY WE CAN STORE sound and reproduce it at will. We can hear music whenever we wish, produce "talking books" for the blind, make quick notes into miniature recorders, and much more. All recording systems store sounds by making an image, or copy, of the sound waves. This image may be in the form of magnetism on a tape, the spiral groove in a record, or the pits in a compact disc. In a recording studio, sound is recorded with 24 or more microphones, each producing a recording on one track (a thin strip) of wide magnetic tape. The sound engineer can modify the music on each track separately to perfect the tonal quality and loudness of any instrument or singer. Some studios record sound directly into the memory of a computer. The studio recording is the master version of the music, which factories then use to make thousands of copies on compact discs, records, and cassette tapes.

Early gramophone featured in the famous trademark of the record company His Master's Voice (HMV)

RECORD PLAYER
The earliest recordings consisted of grooves cut into wax-coated cylinders. In 1887, German-American Emile Berliner first demonstrated the flat gramophone disc, or record, which was to be the most popular way of recording music for almost a century.

Protective grill prevents diaphragm from being damaged.

Fragile diaphragm made of plastic or thin metal foil

Coil of wire fixed to the diaphragm

MICROPHONE
Every recording begins with a microphone, which converts sound waves into electrical signals. A moving-coil microphone (right) contains a wire coil attached to a diaphragm (a thin, flexible disc). Sound waves make the diaphragm, and therefore the coil, vibrate. The coil moves within the magnetic field of a small magnet; this movement generates an electric current in the coil. The current fluctuates in strength in the same way as the sound wave.

Whenever a coil moves within a magnetic field, a current is produced in the coil.

Permanent magnet produces magnetic field.

TAPE RECORDING
A cassette contains a spool of thin plastic tape coated with tiny metal grains. The grains are magnetic, and when sound is recorded onto the tape, the magnetism of the grains changes. The new magnetic pattern represents the sound.

Capstan and pinch roller keep the tape moving at the correct speed past the tape head.

Tape head, containing a coil that both records and plays back sound on the tape

During recording, the tape head arranges the magnetic pattern of the grains to record an image of the sound onto the tape.

When a new recording is made, the tape passes the erase head, which disorders the magnetic particles on the tape so that a fresh recording can be made.

Before a recording is made, the magnetic grains in the tape point in all directions.

Compact discs reproduce sounds with very high quality.

Metal coating on the disc reflects the laser beam into the light detector.

At a place on the CD where there is no pit, the laser beam (above) bounces back to a photocell detector that converts the light into electric current. Where there is a pit, the beam is reflected away from the detector.

Miniature laser scans the underside of the disc.

Photocell detector

COMPACT DISC
A compact disc (CD) stores sounds as a sequence of millions of tiny pits which represent a series of coded numbers. As the disc spins, the CD player's laser beam reads the sequence of pits and adjusts a signal produced by the CD. This varying signal, once amplified, drives a loudspeaker which reproduces the sound.

LOUDSPEAKER
A loudspeaker changes electrical signals into sound waves. Inside a loudspeaker, a varying electric current from a source such as a CD player powers an electromagnet, producing a varying magnetic field. This field makes a cone-shaped diaphragm vibrate, producing sound.

Varying field in electromagnet moves cone to and from permanent magnet.

An amplifier boosts the signal from a CD player, a tape recorder, or a record player before it reaches the speaker.

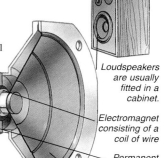

Loudspeakers are usually fitted in a cabinet.

Electromagnet consisting of a coil of wire

Permanent magnet

Cone vibrates, producing sound waves.

Find out more
LASERS
MUSIC
POPULAR MUSIC
SOUND

SOUTH AMERICA

THREE VERY DIFFERENT TYPES of landscape dominate the triangular continent of South America. Along the western coast the towering Andes Mountains reach to more than 6,700 m (22,000 ft) in height. Dense rain forest covers the hot and humid northeastern area. Further south are great open plains of grass and scrub. There are huge mineral deposits and rich farming lands. Despite this, some of the 12 nations which make up the continent are among the poorest in the world.

Until about 170 years ago Spain or Portugal ruled almost all of South America. Most people still speak Spanish or Portuguese. The population is made up of three groups: those descended from European settlers; native Amerindians; and people of mixed ancestry. Many people are desperately poor and can barely afford to buy food. Large sections of the population are uneducated and cannot read or write. Many South American governments are insecure or unstable. Most have borrowed large sums of money from wealthier nations. The cost of repaying these debts makes it hard for the South American countries to develop industries which would take advantage of the natural resources.

South America lies south of the isthmus of Panama, between the Atlantic and Pacific oceans. It covers 17.8 million square km (6.8 million square miles).

Care of the Argentine cattle is the job of cowboys called gauchos.

ARGENTINA

Argentina covers more than 2.75 million square km (1 million square miles) and includes much of the southeastern part of the continent. The pampas, a vast, open grassy plain, makes up most of central Argentina. Large herds of cattle roam on the pampas. Wheat, corn, and beans are grown in other areas, and the cities produce steel, textiles, and chemicals.

ANDES MOUNTAINS
Stretching the entire length of the continent, the Andes mountain chain is 47,250 km (4,500 miles) long. As well as mineral deposits, the Andes have rich farming land in mountain valleys and on the Altiplano, a large plateau in Peru and Bolivia.

Roads crossing the Andes follow routes through the few low passes.

PERU

With a population of nearly 23 million, Peru is one of the larger South American countries. It includes a long stretch of the Andes and part of the rain forest. Many people live on mountain farms and are very poor. Others work on plantations growing coffee, sugar, and cotton for export. Oil has recently been discovered and is bringing some wealth to Peru.

Coffee is still picked by hand in parts of South America.

INDUSTRY

South American industry is generally undeveloped. It is largely confined to the cities and mainly consists of the processing of farm products. Textile workers spin and weave cloth from the wool of sheep and llamas. Other factory workers process and tin meat, or prepare and freeze the meat for export. Many people are also employed in mining, forestry, and fishing.

BOLIVIA

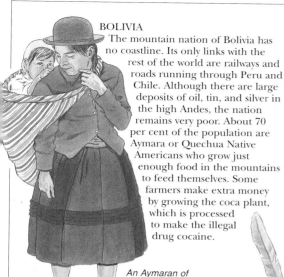

The mountain nation of Bolivia has no coastline. Its only links with the rest of the world are railways and roads running through Peru and Chile. Although there are large deposits of oil, tin, and silver in the high Andes, the nation remains very poor. About 70 per cent of the population are Aymara or Quechua Native Americans who grow just enough food in the mountains to feed themselves. Some farmers make extra money by growing the coca plant, which is processed to make the illegal drug cocaine.

An Aymaran of the Altiplano in traditional dress.

RIO DE JANEIRO

The great Brazilian city of Rio de Janeiro stands on one of the world's most beautiful bays, where tall mountains sweep down to the sea. A huge statue of Christ towers over the city. More than 12 million people live in Rio de Janeiro; it is South America's busiest port. Other major cities include Caracas, Bogotá, and Brasilia.

The statue of Christ, 40 m (131 ft) tall, stands on the summit of Mount Corcovado overlooking Rio.

The Native Americans of South American forests live in large huts shared by many families. They sleep in hammocks hung between the posts of the huts.

NATIVE AMERICANS

The first peoples of South America were Indians. In the lowlands the Indians lived in small villages and gathered food from the forest, but in the Andes they built great civilizations. The arrival of European explorers destroyed these great cultures, and today only a few remote tribes still live in the forest as their ancestors did. However, the destruction of the rain forest for farming and mining threatens to eliminate even these last traces of Native American society.

FALKLANDS

Since 1833, Britain has ruled the Falkland Islands, and the inhabitants, called kelpers, speak English. They live by fishing and raising sheep. However, Argentina claims the islands, which lie about 640 km (400 miles) off its coast, and calls them the Malvinas. In 1982 Argentine troops invaded the islands but were defeated by the British.

Penguins are common on the Falkland Islands.

AMAZON

The longest river in South America is the Amazon, which rises in the Andes and flows 6,400 km (4,000 miles) to the Atlantic. For most of its length the river flows through a vast rain forest which covers 6.5 million square km (2.5 million square miles). In recent years much of the rain forest has been cut down to provide farmland. Although the destruction continues, it is now slowing down.

___*Find out more*___

CONQUISTADORS
INCAS
SOUTH AMERICA, HISTORY OF

497

SOUTH AMERICA

STATISTICS
Area: 17,800,000 sq km (6,880,000 sq miles)
Population: 309,418,000
Number of independent countries: 12
Languages: Spanish, Portugese, French, Dutch, and Native American languages
Religions: Roman Catholic, Hinduism, Islam, Protestant
Main occupations: Farming, fishing
Main exports: Coffee, timber, bananas
Main imports: Machinery, petroleum

 ARGENTINA
Area: 2,766,889 sq km (1,068,304 sq miles)
Population: 33,500,000
Capital: Buenos Aires

BOLIVIA
Area: 1,098,581 sq km (424,195 sq miles)
Population: 7,700,000
Capitals: La Paz, Sucre

BRAZIL
Area: 8,511,965 sq km (3,286,726 sq miles)
Population: 156,600,000
Capital: Brasília

CHILE
Area: 736,905 sq km (284,519 sq miles)
Population: 13,800,000
Capital: Santiago

COLOMBIA
Area: 1,138,914 sq km (439,770 sq miles)
Population: 34,000,000
Capital: Bogotá

ECUADOR
Area: 270,670 sq km (104,506 sq miles)
Population: 11,300,000
Capital: Quito

FRENCH GUIANA (French dependency)
Area: 83,533 sq km (32,252 sq miles)
Population: 118,000
Capital: Cayenne

GUYANA
Area: 214,969 sq km (82,980 sq miles)
Population: 800,000
Capital: Georgetown

PARAGUAY
Area: 406,752 sq km (157,048 sq miles)
Population: 4,600,000
Capital: Asunción

PERU
Area: 1,285,216 sq km (496,260 sq miles)
Population: 22,900,000
Capital: Lima

SURINAM
Area: 163,265 sq km (63,041 sq miles)
Population: 400,000
Capital: Paramaribo

URUGUAY
Area: 177,414 sq km (68,500 sq miles)
Population: 3,100,000
Capital: Montevideo

VENEZUELA
Area: 912,050 sq km (352,170 sq miles)
Population: 20,600,000
Capital: Caracas

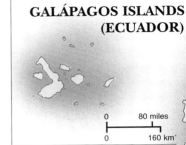

GALÁPAGOS ISLANDS (ECUADOR)

0   80 miles
0   160 km

Magdalen
Medellín
Manizales •
Ibagué •
• Cali
COLOMI
Quito ✳
Cotopaxi
ECUADOR
• Guayaquil   Iqu
R. Marañón
Andes Mts
PERU
R. Uc
PACIFIC OCEAN

LAKE TITICACA
In the Andes mountains on the border between Peru and Bolivia, Lake Titicaca is the highest large lake in the world. Its surface is 3,812 m (12,507 ft) above sea level. Some parts are 180 m (600 ft) deep. Although large ships operate on the lake, the local people still use reed to build their traditional fishing boats.

CHILE
Sandwiched between the Andes mountains and the sea, Ch is a narrow country. At its narrowest point, less than 25 (15 miles) of land separate Chile's southern fjords (k bordered by steep cliffs) from the border with Argentina. Chile is long as well as narrow; more than 4,100 (2,600 miles) separate the parched deserts of the north fr frozen glaciers in the sou

COFFEE
Farmers in many South American countries make a living by growing coffe for export all over the world. Coffee berries are picked by hand, then pulped to remove the fleshy outer parts. After washing and fermenting, the soft, blue-green beans lie in the sun to dry (left). The skins of the beans are removed and the coffee is then bagged for export. Coffee beans are usually roasted shortly before they are needed.

TIERRA DEL FUEGO
Tierra del Fuego means "land of fire". The Portuguese explorer Ferdinand Magellan (1480-1521 gave the islands this name in 15 because he saw signal fires burn on the mountains at night.

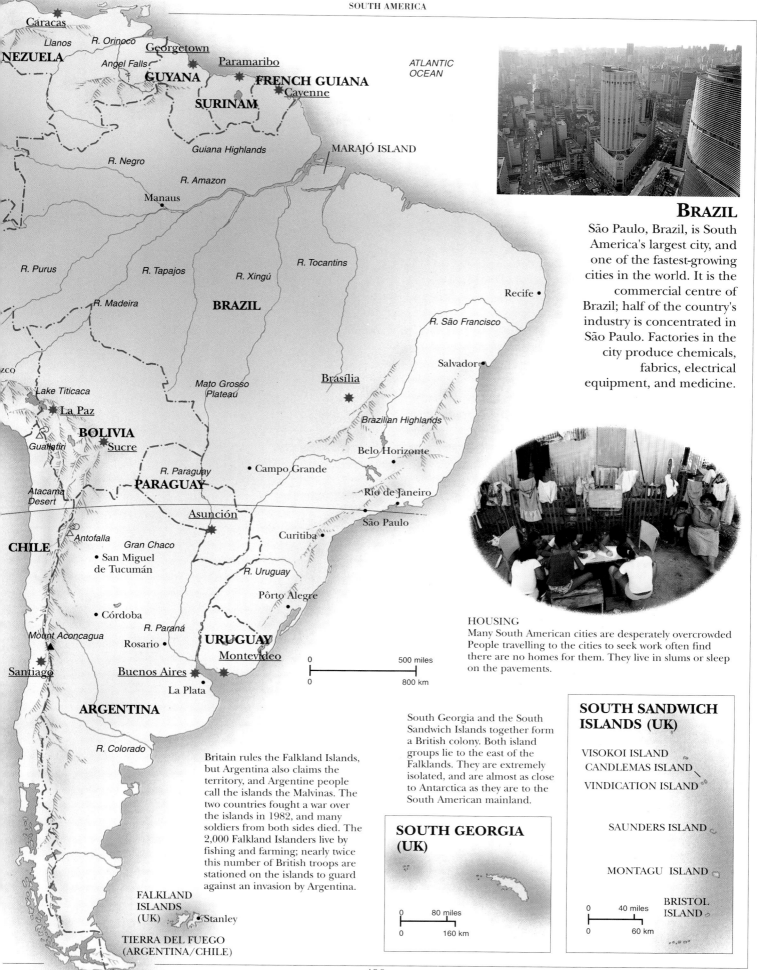

Caracas
Llanos   R. Orinoco Georgetown
NEZUELA   Angel Falls   Paramaribo
          GUYANA   FRENCH GUIANA
                    SURINAM   Cayenne

ATLANTIC
OCEAN

MARAJÓ ISLAND

Guiana Highlands

R. Negro

R. Amazon

Manaus

R. Purus   R. Tapajos   R. Xingú   R. Tocantins

R. Madeira   BRAZIL   R. São Francisco

zco   Brasília

Lake Titicaca   Mato Grosso Plateau

La Paz

BOLIVIA   Brazilian Highlands

Guallatiri   Sucre

R. Paraguay   Campo Grande   Belo Horizonte

Atacama   PARAGUAY   Rio de Janeiro
Desert   São Paulo
          Asunción

Antofalla Gran Chaco   Curitiba

San Miguel
de Tucumán   R. Uruguay

CHILE   Pôrto Alegre

Córdoba
Mount Aconcagua   R. Paraná   URUGUAY
Rosario   Montevideo

Santiago   Buenos Aires
              La Plata

ARGENTINA

R. Colorado

BRAZIL

São Paulo, Brazil, is South America's largest city, and one of the fastest-growing cities in the world. It is the commercial centre of Brazil; half of the country's industry is concentrated in São Paulo. Factories in the city produce chemicals, fabrics, electrical equipment, and medicine.

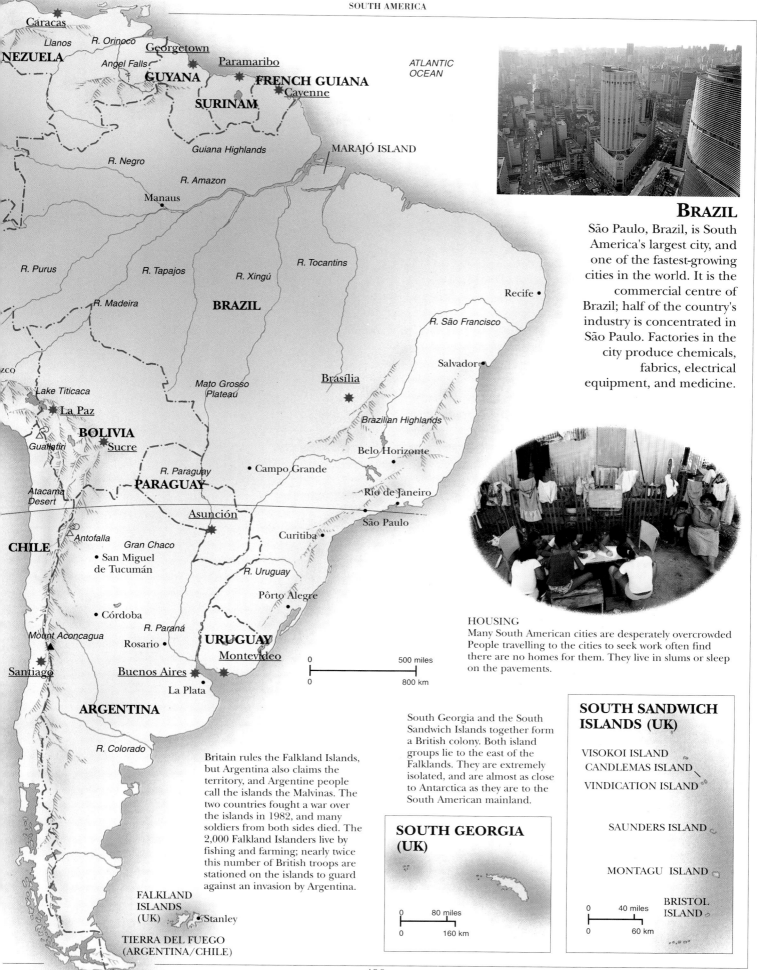

HOUSING
Many South American cities are desperately overcrowded People travelling to the cities to seek work often find there are no homes for them. They live in slums or sleep on the pavements.

Recife

Salvador

0   500 miles
0   800 km

Britain rules the Falkland Islands, but Argentina also claims the territory, and Argentine people call the islands the Malvinas. The two countries fought a war over the islands in 1982, and many soldiers from both sides died. The 2,000 Falkland Islanders live by fishing and farming; nearly twice this number of British troops are stationed on the islands to guard against an invasion by Argentina.

FALKLAND
ISLANDS
(UK)   Stanley

TIERRA DEL FUEGO
(ARGENTINA/CHILE)

South Georgia and the South Sandwich Islands together form a British colony. Both island groups lie to the east of the Falklands. They are extremely isolated, and are almost as close to Antarctica as they are to the South American mainland.

SOUTH SANDWICH ISLANDS (UK)

VISOKOI ISLAND
CANDLEMAS ISLAND
VINDICATION ISLAND

SAUNDERS ISLAND

MONTAGU ISLAND

BRISTOL
ISLAND

0   40 miles
0   60 km

SOUTH GEORGIA (UK)

0   80 miles
0   160 km

CHIMU EMPIRE

The Chimu empire centred on the vast capital city of Chan Chan, in what is now northern Peru. The empire covered much of the Pacific coast of South America and reached the height of its power in the 15th century. In 1460, the Incas conquered the Chimu empire, and Chan Chan fell into ruin.

HISTORY OF
SOUTH AMERICA

Gold mask

Dead Chimu king is prepared for burial in a sitting position.

Chimu burial ceremony

Attendants, uniformly dressed, carry the dead king on a bier.

FOR THOUSANDS OF YEARS, the continent of South America developed independently from the rest of the world. Great cultures rose and fell, among them the Nazcas, Chimus, and Incas, all of which developed highly advanced civilizations of great wealth and achievement. In 1532 the Spaniards invaded the Inca empire and within a few years ruled over most of the continent. The Portuguese established control over Brazil. Soon Spanish and Portuguese became the main languages of South America, and for the next 300 years the affairs of South America were decided in Europe. The native peoples were almost wiped out by disease and ill treatment. When Spain and Portugal became involved in the Napoleonic wars in Europe, the South Americans seized the chance to win their independence. Afterwards, the new countries were ruled by European families who had settled in South America. Many more Europeans arrived during the 19th and early 20th centuries. The nations of South America have only recently begun to control their destinies.

SOUTH AMERICA

200 B.C – A.D. 600 Nazca empire in Peru.

600 City-states of Tiahuanaco and Huari in Peru.

1000-1470 Chimu empire in Peru.

1200 Inca empire in Bolivia, Chile, Ecuador, and Peru.

1494 Treaty of Tordesillas divides New World between Spain and Portugal.

1499-1510 Amerigo Vespucci explores coast of South America; the continent is named for him.

1530 Portuguese colonize Brazil.

1532-33 Spanish led by Francisco Pizarro conquer Inca empire.

1545 Silver discovered in Peru.

1808-25 Liberation wars: Spanish and Portuguese colonies

1822-89 Empire of Brazil

1879-84 Border wars between Peru, Chile, and Bolivia

1932-35 War between Paraguay and Bolivia over disputed territory

1946 Juan Perón becomes president of Argentina.

1967 Che Guevara killed in Bolivia.

Line of demarcation 1494

Portuguese territories

Spanish territories

TREATY OF TORDESILLAS
In the 1494 Treaty of Tordesillas Spain and Portugal divided the non-European world between them. They drew a rough line down the Atlantic Ocean, giving Spain the lands to the west and Portugal the lands to the east.

NATIVE AMERICANS
The Native Americans were put to work as slaves in the silver mines and in the big plantations of sugar and other crops that were exported to Europe. Most Indians died of overwork, poor conditions, and European diseases they had no immunity against.

SPANISH DOMINATION
From 1532 to 1810 Spain controlled the whole of South America apart from Portuguese-owned Brazil. The vast Spanish empire was divided into three vice royalties – New Granada in the north, Peru in the centre, and Rio de la Plata in the south. On the right is Santiago, the patron saint of Spanish soldiers.

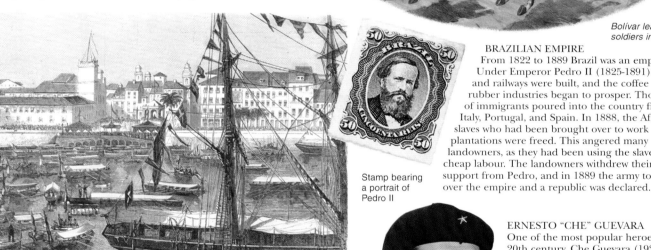

SIMÓN BOLÍVAR

In 1808 Spain was involved in a war with French emperor Napoleon Bonaparte; the South American colonies took this opportunity to declare their independence. Led by Simón Bolívar (1783-1830) and José de San Martín (1778-1850), the colonies fought against Spanish control; all gained their freedom by 1825. Bolívar hoped to unite all of South America, but many disliked his dictatorial approach. In 1822, Brazil declared its independence from Portugal, leaving only Guiana in the north under European control.

ROMAN CATHOLIC CHURCH

When the Spanish arrived in South America, they brought the Roman Catholic religion with them. Catholic priests tried to stamp out local religions and convert the Native Americans to their faith. In the end the priests were forced to include parts of the old Native American religions in their services. In some places, the priests tried to protect the Native Americans against Spanish rulers who were cruel to them, but most priests upheld the Spanish colonial government. During the 20th century the Catholic Church began to take a more active role in supporting the poor against powerful landlords and corrupt governments.

Bolívar leads soldiers into battle

BRAZILIAN EMPIRE

From 1822 to 1889 Brazil was an empire. Under Emperor Pedro II (1825-1891) roads and railways were built, and the coffee and rubber industries began to prosper. Thousands of immigrants poured into the country from Italy, Portugal, and Spain. In 1888, the African slaves who had been brought over to work the plantations were freed. This angered many landowners, as they had been using the slaves for cheap labour. The landowners withdrew their support from Pedro, and in 1889 the army took over the empire and a republic was declared.

Stamp bearing a portrait of Pedro II

Pedro arrives in Recife (formerly Pernambuco), a prosperous town in the empire.

ERNESTO "CHE" GUEVARA

One of the most popular heroes of the 20th century, Che Guevara (1928-1967) was born into a rich Argentinian family. Guevara was a doctor before choosing to spend his life supporting revolutions against oppressive South American governments. In 1959, he helped Fidel Castro overthrow the Cuban government. Guevara served under Castro until 1965, when he went to Bolivia to start a revolution there among the poor tin workers. In 1967 he was killed by the Bolivian army. His death made him a hero for revolutionaries everywhere. In 1997 he was reburied in Cuba.

JUAN PERÓN

From 1946 to 1955, Argentina was ruled by president Juan Perón (1895-1974). Poor people living in the cities supported Perón and his wife, Eva. He introduced many reforms but did not allow anyone to oppose him. After Eva died in 1952, Perón was much less popular. In 1955, the army overthrew him. In 1973, Perón again held power but died the following year. His third wife, Isabel Martínez de Perón, succeeded him as president.

Find out more

CENTRAL AMERICA
CONQUISTADORS
INCAS
SOUTH AMERICA

SOUTHEAST ASIA

AT ITS SOUTHEAST CORNER, the continent of Asia extends far out into the sea, in two great peninsulas and a vast chain of islands. In this region, which is called Southeast Asia, over 469 million people live in ten independent countries. The area has a rich and varied culture, and music and dancing are particularly important. Their performance is often governed by strict rituals and rules, some of them religious. There are several different religions in the area: most people on the mainland are Buddhist; Indonesia is chiefly Muslim; and Christianity is the religion of the Philippines.

For much of this century the lives of many Southeast Asian people have been disrupted and destroyed by wars. The fighting made normal trade, agriculture, and industry impossible and turned Laos and Cambodia into the two poorest nations on Earth. In Cambodia guerrilla warfare continues to claim the lives of soldiers and civilians. Other Southeast Asian countries, particularly the island nations, have escaped the worst fighting. These countries are now more prosperous and peaceful.

Southeast Asia is the part of Asia to the south of China, and east of India. The mainland portion has an area of 1.6 million sq km (640,000 square miles). The region continues to the south as a chain of islands which separate the Pacific and Indian oceans. The island of Sumatra is 1,720 km (1,070 miles) long; other islands are tiny.

THAILAND
There are 56.9 million people in Thailand, and the country is among the wealthiest in the region. Most people in the cities work in mining and industry; in the countryside most are farmers, growing rice, sugar, and rubber trees. The country's rich heritage includes ritual temple dances and beautiful architecture.

Singapore City began as a small British trading station; today giant skyscrapers dominate the skyline.

Plantation workers drain the sticky sap from the trees in the morning when the flow of sap is fastest.

RUBBER
One of the most important products of Southeast Asia is rubber. The industry began about a century ago when British traders brought rubber trees to the region from Brazil. The sap of the trees is collected, then mixed with acid to form solid sheets of latex, which are hung out to dry.

SINGAPORE
The tiny island state of Singapore occupies just 620 sq km (240 square miles) off the coast of Malaysia. The nation is highly industrialized and very rich. Most of Singapore's 2.8 million people earn their living from industries such as oil refining, textiles, and electronics.

JAVA
The country of Indonesia is made up of 13,677 islands. Java is the most populated island, with 107 million people. Many are farmers producing large quantities of rice. The capital city, Jakarta, is a centre for the textile industry. The island has much unique wildlife, including species of tiger and rhinoceros found nowhere else.

The 8th-century Borobudur Temple, Java

Find out more

SOUTHEAST ASIA, HISTORY OF
VIETNAM WAR

HISTORY OF
SOUTHEAST ASIA

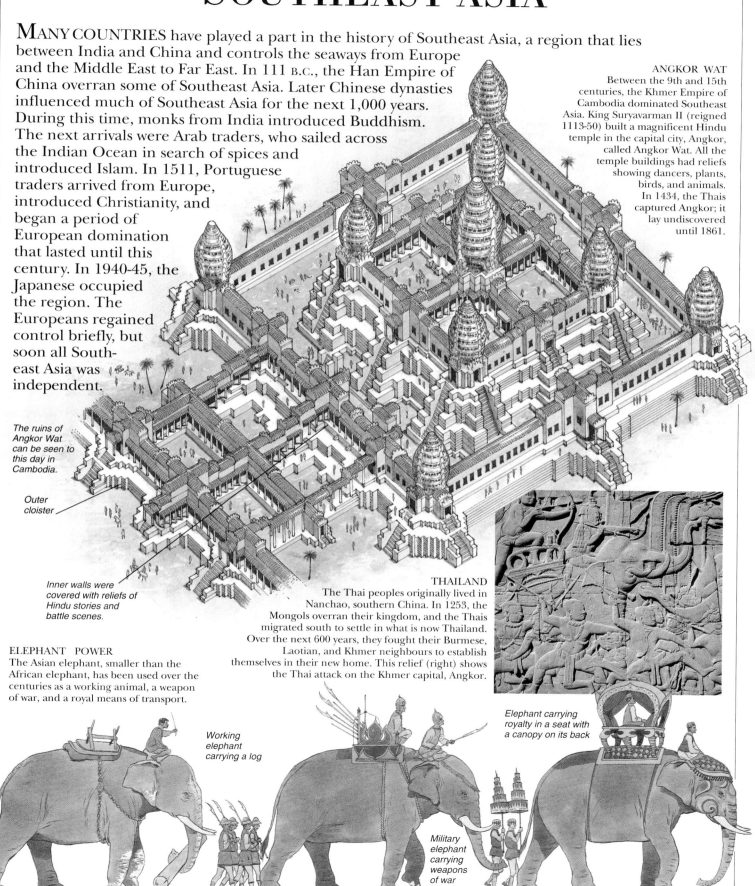

MANY COUNTRIES have played a part in the history of Southeast Asia, a region that lies between India and China and controls the seaways from Europe and the Middle East to Far East. In 111 B.C., the Han Empire of China overran some of Southeast Asia. Later Chinese dynasties influenced much of Southeast Asia for the next 1,000 years. During this time, monks from India introduced Buddhism. The next arrivals were Arab traders, who sailed across the Indian Ocean in search of spices and introduced Islam. In 1511, Portuguese traders arrived from Europe, introduced Christianity, and began a period of European domination that lasted until this century. In 1940-45, the Japanese occupied the region. The Europeans regained control briefly, but soon all Southeast Asia was independent.

ANGKOR WAT
Between the 9th and 15th centuries, the Khmer Empire of Cambodia dominated Southeast Asia. King Suryavarman II (reigned 1113-50) built a magnificent Hindu temple in the capital city, Angkor, called Angkor Wat. All the temple buildings had reliefs showing dancers, plants, birds, and animals. In 1434, the Thais captured Angkor; it lay undiscovered until 1861.

The ruins of Angkor Wat can be seen to this day in Cambodia.

Outer cloister

Inner walls were covered with reliefs of Hindu stories and battle scenes.

THAILAND
The Thai peoples originally lived in Nanchao, southern China. In 1253, the Mongols overran their kingdom, and the Thais migrated south to settle in what is now Thailand. Over the next 600 years, they fought their Burmese, Laotian, and Khmer neighbours to establish themselves in their new home. This relief (right) shows the Thai attack on the Khmer capital, Angkor.

ELEPHANT POWER
The Asian elephant, smaller than the African elephant, has been used over the centuries as a working animal, a weapon of war, and a royal means of transport.

Working elephant carrying a log

Elephant carrying royalty in a seat with a canopy on its back

Military elephant carrying weapons of war

SOUTHEAST ASIA

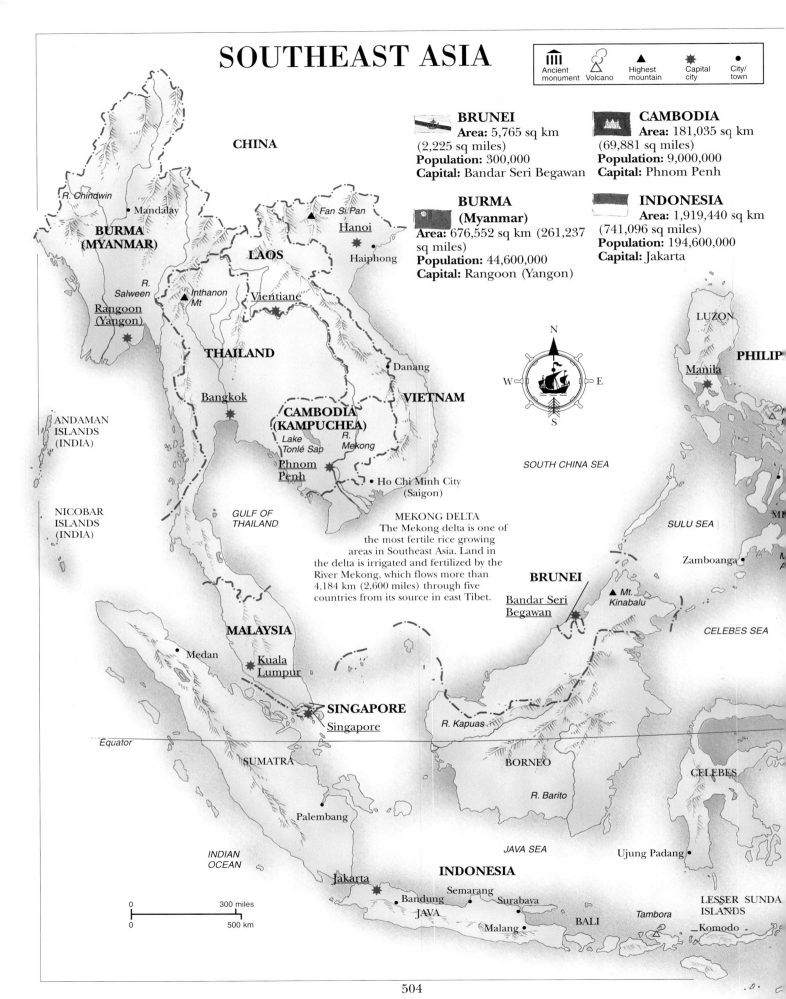

| Ancient monument | Volcano | Highest mountain | Capital city | City/town |

CHINA

R. Chindwin

• Mandalay

BURMA (MYANMAR)

R. Salween

Rangoon (Yangon)

ANDAMAN ISLANDS (INDIA)

NICOBAR ISLANDS (INDIA)

▲ *Fan Si Pan*

Hanoi

Haiphong

LAOS

▲ *Inthanon Mt*

Vientiane

THAILAND

Bangkok

CAMBODIA (KAMPUCHEA)

Lake Tonlé Sap

R. Mekong

Phnom Penh

• Danang

VIETNAM

• Ho Chi Minh City (Saigon)

GULF OF THAILAND

BRUNEI
Area: 5,765 sq km (2,225 sq miles)
Population: 300,000
Capital: Bandar Seri Begawan

BURMA (Myanmar)
Area: 676,552 sq km (261,237 sq miles)
Population: 44,600,000
Capital: Rangoon (Yangon)

CAMBODIA
Area: 181,035 sq km (69,881 sq miles)
Population: 9,000,000
Capital: Phnom Penh

INDONESIA
Area: 1,919,440 sq km (741,096 sq miles)
Population: 194,600,000
Capital: Jakarta

LUZON

PHILIP

Manila

SOUTH CHINA SEA

MEKONG DELTA
The Mekong delta is one of the most fertile rice growing areas in Southeast Asia. Land in the delta is irrigated and fertilized by the River Mekong, which flows more than 4,184 km (2,600 miles) through five countries from its source in east Tibet.

SULU SEA

Zamboanga •

CELEBES SEA

BRUNEI
Bandar Seri Begawan

▲ *Mt. Kinabalu*

MALAYSIA

• Medan

Kuala Lumpur

SINGAPORE
Singapore

R. Kapuas

Equator

SUMATRA

BORNEO

R. Barito

CELEBES

Palembang •

INDIAN OCEAN

JAVA SEA

Ujung Padang •

Jakarta

INDONESIA

• Bandung

Semarang

Surabaya

LESSER SUNDA ISLANDS

Tambora

0 — 300 miles
0 — 500 km

JAVA

• Malang

BALI

Komodo

LAOS
Area: 236,800 sq km (91,435 sq miles)
Population: 4,600,000
Capital: Vientiane

 MALAYSIA
Area: 329,749 sq km (127,326 sq miles)
Population: 19,200,000
Capital: Kuala Lumpur

 PHILIPPINES
Area: 300,000 sq km (115,839 sq miles)
Population: 66,500,000
Capital: Manila

 SINGAPORE
Area: 618 sq km (239 sq miles)
Population: 2,800,000
Capital: Singapore

 THAILAND
Area: 513,115 sq km (198,129 sq miles)
Population: 56,900,000
Capital: Bangkok

 VIETNAM
Area: 329,558 sq km (127,252 sq miles)
Population: 70,900,000
Capital: Hanoi

PACIFIC OCEAN

INDONESIA
Although more than 17,500 islands make up the Republic of Indonesia, only about 6,000 are inhabited. Most Indonesian people live in the countryside and work on farms. But many people live in towns and cities. The city of Yogyakarta (above), on the southern coast of the heavily populated island of Java, is typical. It has a population of about 400,000.

STATISTICS
Area: 4,477,761 sq km (1,728,975 sq miles)
Population: 433,303,000
No. of independent countries: 10
Religions: Buddhism, Islam, Taoism, Christianity, Hinduism
Largest city: Jakarta (Indonesia) 7,829,000
Highest point: Puncak Jaya (Indonesia) 5,030 m (16,503 ft)
Longest river: Mekong 4,184 km (2,600 miles)
Main occupation: Farming
Main exports: Sugar, fruit, timber, rice, rubber, tobacco, tin
Main imports: Machinery, iron and steel products, textiles, chemicals, fuels

PHILIPPINES
Most of the islands in the Philippines are mountainous and forested. The Filipino people live in towns and villages on the narrow coastal plains, or on plateaus between the mountain ranges. The volcanic cone of Mount Mayon, 320 km (200 miles) southeast of Manila, is one of the most beautiful in the world. However, its beauty hides its dangerous character. The volcano is still active, and past eruptions have destroyed parts of the nearby city of Albay.

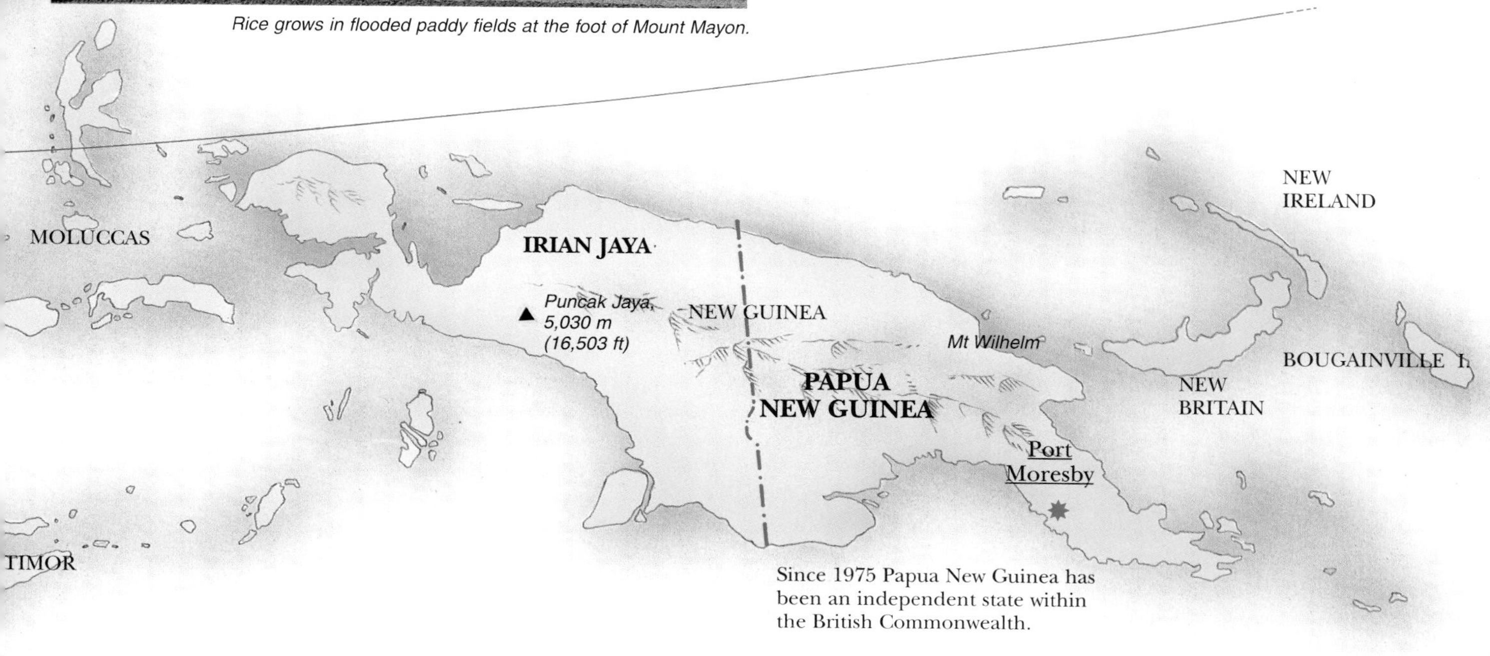

Rice grows in flooded paddy fields at the foot of Mount Mayon.

Davao

MOLUCCAS

IRIAN JAYA

▲ Puncak Jaya 5,030 m (16,503 ft)

NEW GUINEA

Mt Wilhelm

PAPUA NEW GUINEA

Port Moresby

NEW IRELAND

BOUGAINVILLE I.

NEW BRITAIN

TIMOR

Since 1975 Papua New Guinea has been an independent state within the British Commonwealth.

SPICE TRADE

During the 15th century, European explorers who arrived in the islands of Southeast Asia were delighted to find a wide variety of spices, such as nutmeg, pepper, and cloves, which were in great demand for cooking but were very expensive in Europe. As a result first the Portuguese and the Spanish, then the Dutch and the British, fought for control of the profitable spice trade.

Rich Dutch merchants landed on Asian shores to trade with the local people.

SINGAPORE

In 1824, Britain took control of the island of Singapore because it had an important harbour. But in 1942, during World War II (1939-45) Japanese troops took over the island, forcing the British to surrender (left). Several years later Britain reoccupied the country. In 1965, Singapore became an independent nation.

SOUTHEAST ASIA

111 B.C. Chinese invade Vietnam; dominate northern area until A.D. 939

A.D. 0-500 Buddhism spreads throughout Southeast Asia.

802 Khmers establish empire in Cambodia and Laos.

1113-1150 Construction of Angkor Wat temple.

1300s Arab traders introduce Islam to Indonesia.

1434 Thais capture Angkor Wat and overrun Khmer Empire.

1564 Spanish conquer Philippines.

1700 British East India Company establishes a trading base in Borneo.

1766-69 China invade Burma.

1786 British East India Company establishes a base in Malaya.

1799 Dutch take over all Indonesia.

1819 Singapore founded by British merchant Sir Stamford Raffles. Becomes richest port in region.

1824-1886 British take control of Burma.

1859-1893 French take control of Vietnam, Cambodia, and Laos.

1800s Thailand is only country in region independent of Europe.

1896 Britain establishes control over Malaya.

1940-1945 Japanese occupy Southeast Asia during World War II.

1946-54 French fight to maintain control of their empire in Southeast Asia.

1948 Burma independent.

1949 Dutch grant independence to Indonesia.

1953 Cambodia and Laos win independence from France.

1956 Civil war begins in Vietnam.

1957 Malaya independent.

1967 Formation of ASEAN.

1965-73 US fully involved in Vietnam War.

1975 Vietnam War ends, north Vietnamese take control.

CORAZON AQUINO

From 1986 to 1992, Corazon Aquino became president of the Philippines. She entered politics when her husband, Benigno, a popular political leader, was assassinated by the dictator, Ferdinand Marcos, who ruled the Philippines for 20 years. Marcos attempted to prevent Corazon from winning the country's general election. But the people rose up against him, and he was forced to flee the country.

INDONESIA

On 11 August, 1945, Sukarno (1901-70) declared Indonesia's independence from Dutch rule and became president of the Republic of Indonesia. The Dutch transferred sovereignty four years later. By the end of the 1950s, Malaysia, Laos, Vietnam, Cambodia, and Burma had all become independent.

Find out more

JAPAN, HISTORY OF
SOUTHEAST ASIA
VIETNAM WAR

SPACE FLIGHT

SPACE SHUTTLE

A space shuttle is an aircraft that can make repeated flights into space. Both the United States and Russia have built space shuttles. The American space shuttle has powerful engines and huge booster rockets to blast it into space; the Russian shuttle rides into space on the back of the enormous *Energia* rocket.

A large fuel tank feeds the main engines. It breaks away at a height of 110 km (70 miles), just eight minutes after launch.

Smaller engines guide the shuttle into orbit.

The booster rockets break away at a height of about 47 km (29 miles). They are recovered from the ocean and used again.

A spacecraft must reach a speed of about 28,000 km/h (17,500 mph) in order to get into orbit. If it attains a speed of 40,000 km/h (about 25,000 mph), it can break free from the Earth's gravity and travel out into space. This speed is called the Earth's escape velocity.

ONLY A FEW decades ago, stories about space flight were found only in science fiction books. Today spacecraft blast off regularly from the Earth, placing artificial satellites in orbit around the planet and carrying space probes and astronauts into space. Space flight became a reality because of two inventions: the rocket engine, which is the only engine that can work in the vacuum of space; and the computer, which is needed to guide a spacecraft on its mission. Spacecraft do many jobs in space. Much of their work consists of launching satellites which have a range of functions such as mapping the Earth or providing communication links between countries. However, the most exciting part of space flight is the exploration of space itself. Spacecraft have carried astronauts to the moon. Although this dramatic journey took three days it covered only a tiny speck of the universe. The real space explorers are *Voyager, Pioneer,* and other unmanned probes which travel many years through the solar system and beyond, photographing planets, moons, and other objects on their way.

SPACE ROCKET
Most spacecraft make only one flight into space. The launch rocket consists of several parts called stages, each with its own rocket engine. Each stage breaks away as it uses up its fuel, eventually leaving only the spacecraft to fly in space. Spacecraft that return to Earth use a small rocket engine to slow them down until they fall out of orbit. They then land by parachute.

At the launch pad, a tall gantry enables astronauts to enter the shuttle. The shuttle's rocket engines fire, and the spacecraft lifts off to begin its journey into space.

Curved doors open to release satellites and space probes.

The main engines burn liquid hydrogen and liquid oxygen from the shuttle's fuel tank. Smaller engines burn chemicals. They are used to manoeuvre the shuttle into position.

A robot arm handles and moves the cargo. The astronauts control the arm from inside the shuttle.

The flight cabin houses the controls for two pilots to fly the shuttle.

The astronauts work, eat, and sleep in the crew quarters. At the rear is an air lock through which they can go outside into space to work.

The payload bay holds the shuttle's cargo, which consists of satellites, space probes, and equipment for carrying out experiments in space.

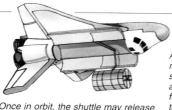

Once in orbit, the shuttle may release satellites and space probes, or retrieve damaged satellites for repair.

At the end of its mission, the shuttle turns around and fires its engines to slow it down.

FIRSTS IN SPACE

1957 The first artificial satellite, *Sputnik 1* (U.S.S.R.), goes into orbit around the Earth.

1959 *Luna 3* (U.S.S.R.), the first successful space probe, flies past the moon and sends back the first picture of the moon's far side.

1961 Russian Yuri Gagarin becomes the first person to fly in space, making one orbit of the Earth.

1962 *Mariner 2* (U.S.), the first successful planetary space probe, flies past Venus.

1969 Neil Armstrong becomes the first person to walk on the moon.

1971 The first space station, *Salyut 1* (U.S.S.R.), goes into orbit.

1977 *Voyager 2* (U.S.) leaves Earth and flies past Jupiter (1979), Saturn (1981), Uranus (1986), and Neptune (1989).

1981 U.S. space shuttle *Columbia* makes its first test flight into space.

1986 European space probe *Giotto* sends back close-up pictures of the nucleus (centre) of Halley's Comet.

1997 *Pathfinder* (U.S.) sends back images and data from Mars.

Once the shuttle is travelling slowly enough, it leaves its orbit and begins to descend towards Earth.

When the shuttle enters the Earth's atmosphere, friction of the air makes the heat-proof underside of the shuttle glow red-hot.

The shuttle lands on the runway and rolls to a halt. After months of intensive checking, it is ready to fly again.

The shuttle glides down towards a runway, just like an ordinary aircraft.

SPACE PROBES
Space probes leave the Earth and travel out into space. They are equipped with cameras and all kinds of sensors that collect information about space and the planets, which is beamed back to Earth by radio.

Radio antenna to communicate with Earth

Instruments for studying Jupiter's surface

Atmospheric entry probe

GALILEO
In 1989, the *Galileo* probe (left) was launched on a six-year journey to Jupiter. It dropped an "entry" probe into Jupiter's atmosphere on its arrival, and should continue orbiting the planet until 1999.

A parachute lowered the entry probe into Jupiter's atmosphere.

Instruments in the probe measured conditions in Jupiter's atmosphere. They worked for only 75 minutes because Jupiter's gravity crushed the probe like an egg when it got close to the planet's surface.

Heat shield

Module for experimenting with materials manufacture

Russian space station *Mir*

Soyuz *spacecraft brings crew members to station and returns them to Earth.*

Docking section connects spacecraft to space station.

Solar panels generate electricity from sunlight to power the space station.

INSIDE *MIR*
While on board *Mir*, Russian cosmonauts conduct experiments and repair equipment under weightless conditions. In 1997 the space station ran into trouble after colliding with a space module.

SPACE STATION
People can make the longest space flights on board space stations – large spacecraft that spend several years in orbit around the Earth. Smaller spacecraft carry teams of astronauts to the space station, where they will live and work for weeks or months at a time. Supplies and relief crews come aboard in spacecraft that dock, or link up, with the space station.

Scientific module where cosmonauts conduct experiments under weightless conditions.

Progress M *cargo spacecraft brings supplies to space station.*

Mir base block containing living quarters for cosmonauts.

Find out more

ASTRONAUTS
COMETS AND METEORS
GRAVITY
MOON
PLANETS
ROCKETS AND MISSILES
SATELLITES

SPAIN AND PORTUGAL

In many parts of Spain and Portugal, the donkey cart is still a common form of transport.

ALTHOUGH THEY ARE NEIGHBOURS, Spain and Portugal are very different countries. Spain is the fourth largest country in Europe, and both its landscape and its people are varied. The centre of Spain is a hot, dry plateau with snowcapped mountain ranges to the north and south. The southern province of Almeria contains Europe's only desert. The people of Spain differ widely in temperament from one region to another, and a quarter of them speak a language other than Spanish.

Portugal is much smaller than Spain. The Tagus River divides the country in two. To the north the land is hilly; to the south it is low-lying. Trees cover much of Portugal, and winds coming off the Atlantic Ocean cool the country. Unlike the Spanish, the Portuguese all speak the same language. For much of their recent history Spain and Portugal were ruled by dictators. However, in the mid-1970s both countries formed democratic governments. This change allowed them to join the European Community in 1986 and to benefit from the higher standard of living in the rest of Europe.

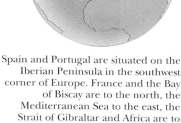

Spain and Portugal are situated on the Iberian Peninsula in the southwest corner of Europe. France and the Bay of Biscay are to the north, the Mediterranean Sea to the east, the Strait of Gibraltar and Africa are to the south, and the vast Atlantic Ocean washes the west coast.

Flamenco is the traditional dance of Gypsies from Andalucia in the south of Spain.

FLAMENCO DANCING

The exciting and colourful flamenco dance is very popular in Spain. Dancers are usually accompanied by guitars and their own hand-held percussion instrument called castanets.

TOURISM

More than 60 million tourists from all over Europe and the United States visit Spain and Portugal each year. They come to enjoy the sun, because the climate is mild in the winter and hot in the summer. Both countries have fine beaches, and their old towns and cities are full of interesting buildings and fine works of art.

During the Christian Holy Week that leads up to Easter, processions commemorating the holiday take place in many towns and villages.

BULLFIGHTING

Men fight with bulls to entertain crowds in both Spain and Portugal. In Spain, the matador, or bullfighter, stands in the bullring and teases the bull into a rage before he kills it with a sword. In Portugal, the bullfighter is on horseback but does not kill the bull. Bullfighting is very popular, but many people consider it to be a cruel sport.

The bullfighter wears an elaborate costume. He carries a red cape and waves it to make the bull charge.

RELIGION

The Roman Catholic Church plays an important part in the lives of most Spanish and Portuguese people. Nearly everybody is a member of the church and attends mass on Sundays. The priest is an influential member of the community, and the church is a centre of local activities.

SPAIN AND PORTUGAL

Ancient monument | Volcano | Highest mountain | Capital city | City/town

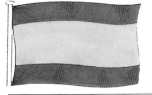

SPAIN STATISTICS
Area: 504,782 sq km (194,898 sq miles)
Population: 39,200,000
Capital: Madrid
Languages: Spanish, Catalan, Basque, Galician
Religion: Roman Catholic
Currency: Peseta
Main occupations: Manufacturing, agriculture, service industry, tourism

PORTUGAL STATISTICS
Area: 92,389 sq km (35,671 sq miles)
Population: 9,900,000
Capital: Lisbon
Language: Portuguese
Religion: Roman Catholic
Currency: Escudo
Main occupations: Agriculture, fishing, industry, service industry

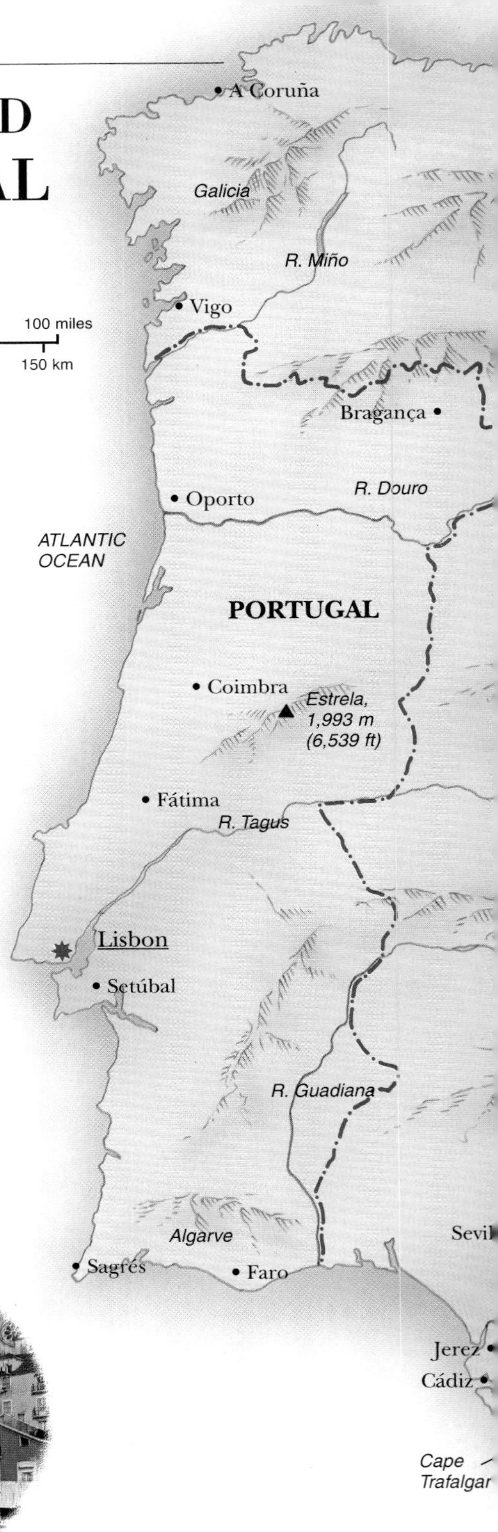

0 — 100 miles
0 — 150 km

N
W · E
S

ATLANTIC OCEAN

· A Coruña

Galicia

R. Miño

· Vigo

Bragança ·

· Oporto

R. Douro

PORTUGAL

· Coimbra

▲ Estrela, 1,993 m (6,539 ft)

· Fátima

R. Tagus

✳ **Lisbon**
· Setúbal

R. Guadiana

Algarve   Sevi

· Sagres   · Faro

Jerez ·
Cádiz ·

Cape Trafalgar

MADRID
Spain's largest city, Madrid, lies at the centre of the country, surrounded by a broad plain. Madrid has been Spain's capital city since the 16th century. Recently it has become an important centre for commerce and industry. Madrid's main roads radiate out from the Plaza del Sol (left), which is positioned at the heart of the old city. The newer parts of the city lie to the east.

LISBON
The port of Lisbon is Portugal's capital city and the home of about one fifth of all Portuguese people. The city has one of the finest harbours in southern Europe, where ships load ceramics, cork, sardines, tomato paste, and wine for export all over the world. Lisbon's cathedral (right) overlooks the commercial district.
Lisbon is an ancient city, but many of the buildings that stand today date from the 18th century. They were constructed after an earthquake destroyed two thirds of the city in 1755.

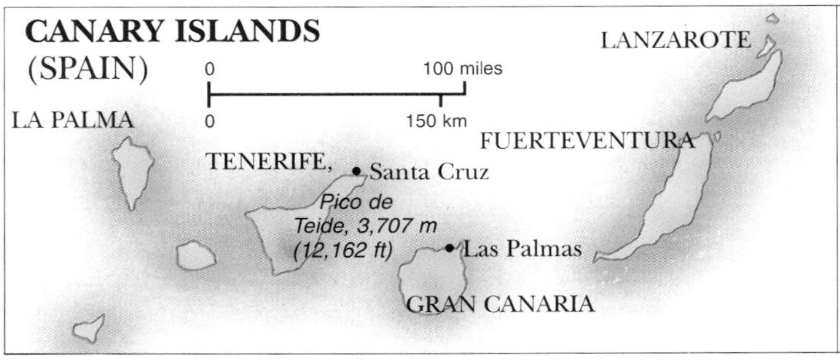

CANARY ISLANDS (SPAIN)
0 — 100 miles
0 — 150 km

LANZAROTE

LA PALMA

FUERTEVENTURA

TENERIFE,
· Santa Cruz
Pico de Teide, 3,707 m (12,162 ft)
· Las Palmas

GRAN CANARIA

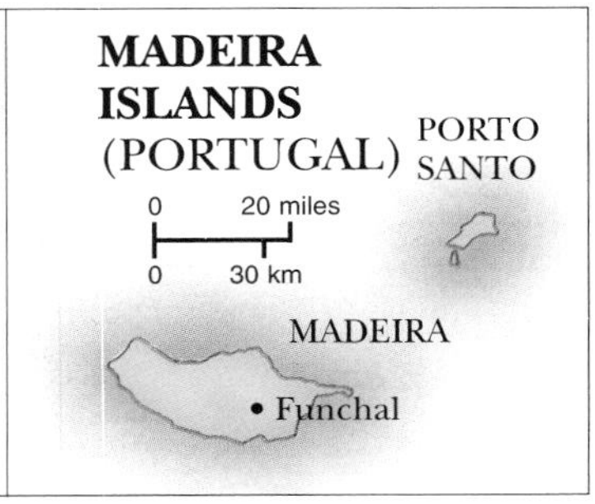

MADEIRA ISLANDS (PORTUGAL)
PORTO SANTO

0 — 20 miles
0 — 30 km

MADEIRA

· Funchal

CANARY ISLANDS
It was not a bird but a dog that gave its name to the Canary Islands. In ancient times the islands were the home of many dogs: *Canary* comes from the same word in the Latin language as *canine*. The islands lie about 100 km (60 miles) off the northwest coast of Africa, and in winter they are a popular resort for tourists from Europe.

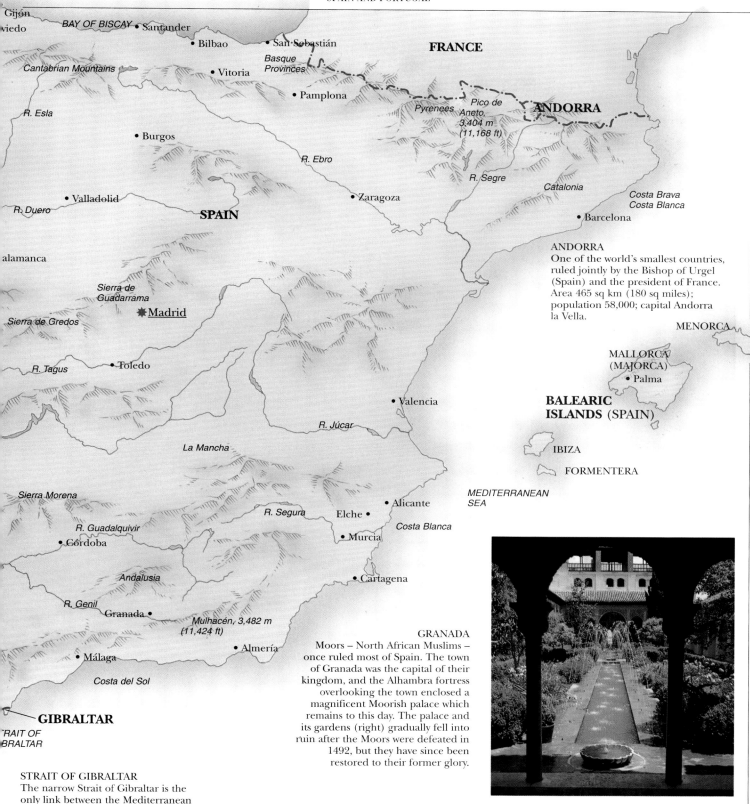

Gijón
Oviedo
BAY OF BISCAY • Santander
• Bilbao
• San Sebastián
FRANCE
Cantabrian Mountains
• Vitoria
Basque
Provinces
R. Esla
• Pamplona
Pyrenees
Pico de
Aneto,
3,404 m
(11,168 ft)
ANDORRA
• Burgos
R. Ebro
R. Segre
• Zaragoza
Catalonia
Costa Brava
Costa Blanca
• Valladolid
SPAIN
• Barcelona
R. Duero
Salamanca
Sierra de
Guadarrama
Sierra de Gredos
✳ Madrid
MENORCA
R. Tagus
• Toledo
**MALLORCA
(MAJORCA)**
• Palma
• Valencia
**BALEARIC
ISLANDS (SPAIN)**
R. Júcar
IBIZA
La Mancha
FORMENTERA
Sierra Morena
• Alicante
*MEDITERRANEAN
SEA*
R. Segura
Elche •
R. Guadalquivir
Costa Blanca
• Córdoba
• Murcia
Andalusia
R. Genil
• Cartagena
Granada •
*Mulhacén, 3,482 m
(11,424 ft)*
• Málaga
• Almería
Costa del Sol
GIBRALTAR
STRAIT OF
GIBRALTAR

ANDORRA

One of the world's smallest countries, ruled jointly by the Bishop of Urgel (Spain) and the president of France. Area 465 sq km (180 sq miles); population 58,000; capital Andorra la Vella.

GRANADA

Moors – North African Muslims – once ruled most of Spain. The town of Granada was the capital of their kingdom, and the Alhambra fortress overlooking the town enclosed a magnificent Moorish palace which remains to this day. The palace and its gardens (right) gradually fell into ruin after the Moors were defeated in 1492, but they have since been restored to their former glory.

STRAIT OF GIBRALTAR

The narrow Strait of Gibraltar is the only link between the Mediterranean Sea and the Atlantic Ocean beyond. At the narrowest point, only 13 km (8 miles) separate Spain from Africa. The sun evaporates the waters of the Mediterranean, making them saltier than those of the Atlantic, and this causes currents to flow through the Strait of Gibraltar. Water from the Atlantic flows through the strait at the surface, while the saltier Mediterranean water flows in the other direction at a greater depth.

AZORES

The Azores are a region of Portugal, though the islands are about 1,200 km (800 miles) west of the mainland across the Atlantic Ocean. The islands are volcanic, and there have been several eruptions and earthquakes. More than a quarter of a million people live on the Azores, and many more visit to holiday in the semi-tropical climate.

**AZORES
(PORTUGAL)**
TERCEIRA
PICO
SAO MIGUEL
• Ponta
Delgada
0   100 miles
0   150 km

PAINTING

Many great artists lived and worked in Spain and Portugal. Diego Velasquez (1599-1660) was famous for his pictures of the Spanish royal family. Several modern painters, including Pablo Picasso (1881-1973) and Salvador Dali (1904-1989), were born in Spain.

Velasquez included himself as the painter in his picture The Maids of Honour.

INDUSTRY

Agriculture and fishing are major industries in both Spain and Portugal. Citrus and other fruits, wheat, and olives are grown in Spain. Portugal exports olive oil, nuts, tuna, sardines, and cork. Both countries are major producers of wine. Iron, coal, and other minerals are mined in the Cantabrian Mountains in the north of Spain, and the country is rapidly becoming a major producer of cars. Although Portugal is less industrialized, it has a large textile and clothing industry. Both countries make a wide range of electrical and household goods.

In the coastal towns of Spain and Portugal, many people work in fishing or in the related industries of boatbuilding and netmaking.

BARCELONA

The city of Barcelona lies on the Mediterranean coast of eastern Spain. It is the second largest city in the country (Madrid is the largest) and is a bustling port of almost two million people. Barcelona is the capital of the province of Catalonia. Its people speak Catalan, a language that sounds similar to Spanish but has many differences. The city is renowned for its beautiful architecture and many historic buildings.

The cathedral of Sagrada Familia in Barcelona was designed by Antonio Gaudi and begun in 1882. It is still not finished today.

GIBRALTAR

Spain claims that Gibraltar, at its southern tip, is Spanish. However, since 1713 this rocky outcrop has been a British colony. Gibraltar is just 6.5 sq km (2.5 square miles) in area. Most of the 32,000 inhabitants work in tourism.

The Rock of Gibraltar towers over the entrance to the Mediterranean Sea

Portugal is famous for its colourful pottery and its port and madeira wines. These are produced by mixing brandy with table wine. Sherry is a similar product from Spain.

Find out more

ARABS,
history of
EUROPE
SPAIN AND PORTUGAL,
history of

HISTORY OF
SPAIN AND PORTUGAL

By 1550, SPAIN AND PORTUGAL had become the two greatest powers in Europe. Both had explored other lands and set up huge empires with colonies in Africa, the Americas, the Caribbean, and Asia. Because Spain and Portugal are neighbours (the land they share is called the Iberian Peninsula), much of their history is intertwined. Their early story is one of visiting conquerors. From about 1000 B.C., the Phoenicians, then the Carthaginians and Greeks, built trading colonies on the peninsula. The Romans, and then the Visigoths, a Germanic tribe, occupied the whole land. In A.D. 711 Muslim Moors from North Africa invaded. By the end of the 15th century Spain and Portugal had driven out the Moors, and rivalry between the two countries grew as they competed in building up their empires. Beginning in 1580, Spain occupied Portugal for 60 years. After this, the Portuguese became determined to remain independent of Spanish rule. The two countries even fought against each other during the Napoleonic Wars with the French. More recently, both countries were ruled by dictators until the mid-1970s. Now they have democratic governments.

HISPANIA
In 201 B.C. the Romans conquered Spain and Portugal. The Romans named the region Hispania and introduced Latin as the official language. They also built huge aqueducts (such as the one in Segovia, Spain, above) which carried water to cities. Several of Rome's greatest emperors, including Hadrian and Trajan, were born in Hispania.

ALHAMBRA
Begun in 1248, the Alhambra palace in Granada was the last stronghold of the Moors in Spain. The outer wall is made of red bricks, which gave the palace its name (*alhambra* is the Arabic word for red). It also has thirteen towers. The Alhambra contains the finest examples of Moorish art in Europe.

HENRY THE NAVIGATOR
During the European age of discovery in the late 1400s, Spain and Portugal, on the edge of the Atlantic, were in an ideal spot to send out explorers. Prince Henry the Navigator (1394-1460) built a school of navigation at Sagrés in Portugal to train sailors.

EL CID
During the Moorish occupation, the people of Castile in northern Spain emerged as champions of Christianity. Rodrigo Díaz de Vivar (1040-1099) was a nobleman and soldier who heroically fought the Christian cause under King Sancho II of Castile. But when Sancho's brother Alfonso became king, he banished Rodrigo. Rodrigo quickly gathered a small army and fought the Moors. In 1094, he captured the city of Valencia from the Moors. He was given the title El Cid (from the Arabic word *sidi*, meaning "lord") and is one of Spain's national heroes. He died immensely wealthy, ruler of his own kingdom.

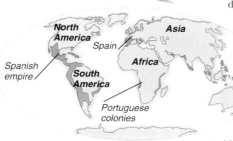

North America
Spain
Asia
Spanish empire
Africa
South America
Portuguese colonies

The Spanish empire, 1588

SPANISH EMPIRE
In the Treaty of Tordesillas the Pope divided the non-European world between Spain and Portugal, to avoid wars between them. In 1588, when Spain and Portugal were united, the Spanish Empire was at the height of its power.

PHILIP II

King Philip II (1527-98) ruled Spain at the height of its power. Under him, Spanish art, writing, and fashions led Europe. He united Spain with Portugal and conquered the Philippine islands. He was involved in many wars; during a war against the English, the Spanish Armada (fleet) was destroyed. Poverty spread throughout Spain because of these wars, and after Philip died, Spanish power began to fail.

Battle scene during the Portuguese revolt

PORTUGUESE REVOLT

During the Thirty Years War (1618-48) Spain lost much money fighting the Catholic cause against the Reformation (a movement to reform the Catholic church which led to Protestantism). This weakened the country, and the Portuguese, led by John, Duke of Braganza, revolted and drove out their Spanish rulers. John then became King John IV of Portugal.

SPANISH CIVIL WAR

In February 1936 a left-wing (radical) Republican government was elected in Spain. Most of the Spanish army (right-wing and conservative) rebelled and tried to overthrow the government. Led by General Franco, the army fought bitterly with the Republicans for nearly three years. Mussolini sent Italian troops, and Hitler sent German troops to help the right-wing cause. Thousands of Spaniards died in this bloody civil war. In 1939, the Republican armies collapsed, and Franco emerged as dictator of Spain.

FRANCO

General Francisco Franco (1892-1975) had a successful army career before he became dictator of Spain. He kept Spain out of World War II (1939-45). After the war there was rapid economic growth, and the standard of living improved. But many people were unhappy with Franco's restrictions on personal freedom. Many Spaniards were arrested and executed by Franco's police for protesting and demanding more freedom.

BASQUES

The Basque people have lived in the Pyrenees (mountains between France and Spain) for thousands of years. They have their own language, called Euskera. In the 1960s the Spanish Basques demanded a separate, independent Basque state. Some Basques formed terrorist groups to fight against the Spanish government. The Basques now have their own parliament and some control over their government.

SPAIN & PORTUGAL

800-200 B.C. Phoenicians, Carthaginians, and Greeks set up trading colonies along the coast of Spain.

201 B.C Roman control begins.

711 A.D. Visigoths invade. Muslim Moors from North Africa conquer Spain and Portugal.

1094 El Cid captures Valencia.

1385 Spaniards attempt invasion of Portugal but are defeated.

1386 Portugal and England become allies.

1494 Treaty of Tordesillas. Spain and Portugal begin to carve out their empires.

1580 Philip II of Spain invades Portugal and unites the two countries.

1588 English navy defeats the Spanish Armada.

1640 Portugal rebels against Spanish rule; regains independence. John, Duke of Braganza, becomes King John IV.

1898 Spanish war with United States over Cuba leads to the end of the Spanish Empire.

1910 Portugal becomes a republic.

1928 Dr. Antonio Salazar becomes dictator of Portugal.

1931 King Alfonso XIII of Spain flees the country. Spain becomes a republic.

1936-39 Spanish Civil War.

1939 General Franco becomes dictator of Spain.

1975 Franco dies. Spain becomes a democracy.

1986 Spain and Portugal join the European Community (EC).

─── *Find out more* ───

COLUMBUS, CHRISTOPHER
HAPSBURGS
SOUTH AMERICA, HISTORY OF
SPAIN AND PORTUGAL

SPIDERS AND SCORPIONS

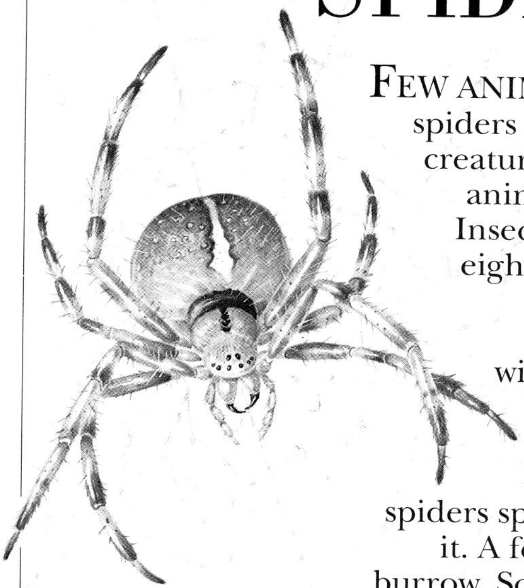

FEW ANIMALS ARE MORE feared but less understood than spiders and scorpions. We often call these scurrying little creatures insects, but they really belong to the group of animals called arachnids, along with ticks and mites. Insects have six legs; spiders and other arachnids have eight legs. There are about 35,000 kinds of spiders and 1,200 kinds of scorpions. All are carnivores (meat eaters). Scorpions hunt down their prey and kill it with their pincers. If the prey is big, or struggles, the scorpion uses the sting in its tail. Many spiders capture insects by spinning a silken web. The silk of some webs is stronger than steel wire of the same thickness. Not all spiders spin webs, however; some catch their prey by dropping a net of silk onto it. A few spiders, such as the trap-door spider, rush out at their victim from a burrow. Some scorpions and several spiders are dangerous to humans, including the Australian funnel web spider and the Durango scorpion of Mexico.

WEB
Spiders make webs with a special silken thread from glands at the rear end of the body. Tubes called spinnerets squeeze out the thread like toothpaste. The silk hardens as the spider's legs pull it out.

GARDEN SPIDER
Thousands of spiders live in our houses and gardens, feeding on flies, gnats, and moths. The common garden spider spins a beautiful, complicated web called an orb web, often between the stems of plants. Some spiders lie in wait for their prey in the centre of the web; others hide nearby. Many orb-web spiders spin a new web almost every day.

The female black widow has a deadly bite.

SPIDERLINGS
Young spiders are called spiderlings. They hatch from eggs inside a silken cocoon and feed on stores of yolk in their bodies. After a few days, weeks, or months, depending on the weather, they cut their way out of the cocoon and begin to hunt for food.

BLACK WIDOW
The female black widow spider is so named because it sometimes kills its mate. This spider is also one of the few spiders that can kill humans. The female black widow shown here is standing near its eggs, which are wrapped in a silken egg sac or cocoon.

TARANTULA
True tarantulas are shy spiders which live mainly in burrows. False tarantulas, such as the big spider shown here, include various large, hairy hunting spiders from North and South America. They are also called bird or monkey spiders. Their bite is painful to humans, but it is less poisonous than the bite of smaller spiders such as the black widow.

FOOD
Spiders eat animal prey. Their most common victims are insects, worms, sow bugs, and other spiders. The spider's venom subdues or paralyses the prey while the spider wraps it up in a silk bag to eat later.

YOUNG
Scorpions are born fully formed. At first the female scorpion carries the young on its back, where they are well protected from predators. After the young have moulted (shed their skin) for the first time, they leave their mother to fend for themselves.

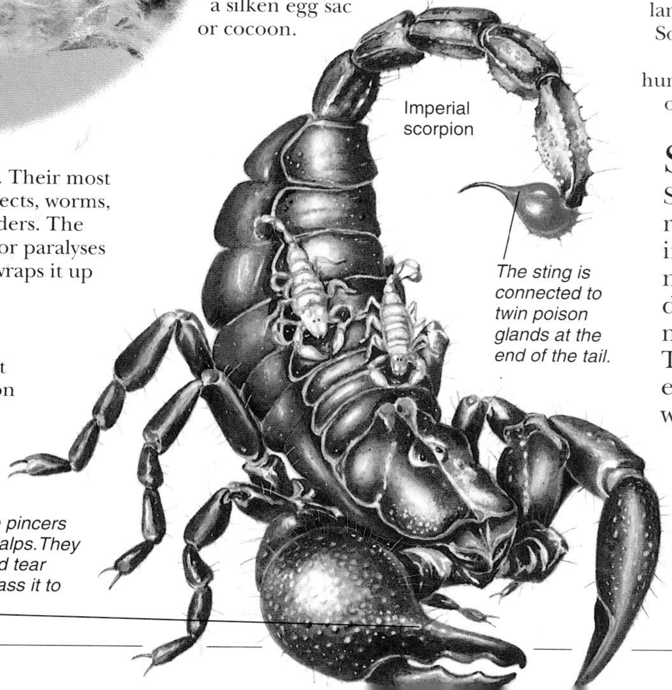

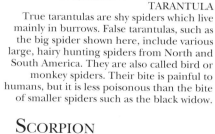

Imperial scorpion

The sting is connected to twin poison glands at the end of the tail.

Scorpion's large pincers are called pedipalps. They seize, crush, and tear the prey, then pass it to the jaws.

SCORPION
Scorpions live mainly in warm regions, lurking beneath rocks or in cracks or burrows. Most feed at night, ambushing or hunting down their prey. They feed mainly on insects and spiders. The scorpion uses the sting at the end of the tail in self-defence, as well as to subdue its prey.

Find out more

ANIMALS
AUSTRALIAN WILDLIFE
DESERT WILDLIFE

SPIES AND ESPIONAGE

MATA HARI
The most notorious spy of World War I was a dancer who worked in Paris using the stage name Mata Hari. She was born in the Netherlands as Gertrude Margarete Zelle in 1876. Mata Hari was probably a double agent: she spied on the Germans for their enemies the French, but she also gave French secrets to the Germans. She was arrested by the French and executed in 1917.

Charmed by Mata Hari's beauty, military men gave her secret information.

NATIONS AT WAR try hard to discover what their enemy will do next, so that they can mount a more secure defence or an effective attack. Secretly trying to discover the plans of an enemy or competitor is called spying, or espionage. The people who do it are called spies, and they have a difficult job. They often pretend to be working for one side while collecting information for the other. Their work is also dangerous: spies caught in wartime are executed.

Spying is an ancient trade, but it reached a peak during World War II (1939-45) and in the years that followed. Though the United States and the former Soviet Union were not at war, each feared attack from the other. So both sides used espionage to estimate the strength of the opponent's forces. Today, much spying is not military but industrial. By copying a competitor's plans, a manufacturer can make a similar product without the cost of research.

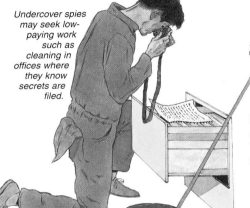

Undercover spies may seek low-paying work such as cleaning in offices where they know secrets are filed.

SECRET AGENTS

Spies may use false identities to hide their activities. They seem to lead regular lives but are secretly collecting information. These spies are called agents or secret agents. They may bribe people to steal secrets. Or they use blackmail: they find out damaging facts about someone who has access to secrets, then threaten to reveal these facts unless the victim becomes a spy.

Tiny bugs transmit signals that a spy can pick up a city block away.

Night-vision binoculars help spies see long distances in darkness.

Phone capsule transmitters broadcast telephone calls and are difficult to detect.

Even a cigarette pack is big enough to hide a tiny tape recorder.

Cameras hidden in watches enable spies to take photographs secretly.

Bug detectors disguised as pens give a warning that a spy has hidden a bug in the room.

SPY EQUIPMENT
Spies need special equipment so that they can watch and listen to people and send messages secretly. To hear private conversations, spies hide "bugs" – tiny microphones and radio transmitters – in their subjects' homes or offices. The spy tunes in a radio receiver to hear the signals transmitted by the bug. A spy can use a camera with a powerful magnifying lens to take embarrassing photographs with which to blackmail. Hacking into a computer to discover top-secret files of government and big business is a growing trend.

CODES

When spies send messages, they encode them – write them in code – to hide the meaning. The spy changes each letter for a different one, so that only someone else who knows the code can read the words. On this code disc, the letters of the message are marked in blue, and their coded form is in green. For example, C becomes X. HELP I AM TRAPPED would be SVOK R ZN GIZKKVW in code. This code is easy to break, or understand. But computer-generated codes are almost impossible to break.

SPY SATELLITES
In 1961, the United States launched the first spy satellite. It had cameras pointed at the ground to photograph troop movements. Today there are many spy satellites, and they are much more sophisticated. They can monitor radio signals and distinguish individual vehicles on the ground. Spying from space has greatly reduced the need for conventional spies.

Find out more

LAW
NUCLEAR AGE
POLICE
WORLD WAR II

SPORTS

EVERYONE WHO TAKES PART in a sport does so for his or her own individual reasons. Early-morning joggers feel good by keeping fit and trying to beat a personal best time. Backpackers enjoy the fresh air and like to learn outdoor survival skills. And in a sports competition, no experience can match the sensation of winning. Sports are games and activities that involve physical ability or skill. Competitive sports have fixed rules and are organized so that everyone has an equal opportunity to succeed.

Many of today's sports developed from activities that were necessary for survival, such as archery, running, and wrestling. Some sports, such as basketball and volleyball, are modern inventions. And as the equipment improves, the rules change to ensure that no competitor has an advantage. Sponsorship and television are now major influences on sports. Leading players become millionaires, and most popular events have huge international audiences.

Many ancient sports are still played today but some, such as foot-wrestling, have long been forgotten.

Officials make sure each game lasts the same time.

EQUIPMENT AND UNIFORMS

Uniforms are important in team sports. They help players and spectators quickly recognize fellow team members and tell them apart from the opposing side. Underneath the basic shirt and shorts or jersey and trousers, players wear protective gear, especially in games such as football and hockey. Shoes are designed to suit the playing surface – rubber-soled for a basketball court, for example, and cleated (spiked) for grass. Other equipment includes a standard ball and, for some sports, bats or rackets.

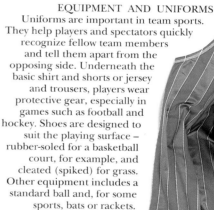

FIELD

The rules of every team sport include standard sizes for the field or court, its markings, and other features such as goal posts. There may be more than one standard if the game is played by both adults and young people. For example, the dimensions of the free-throw lane and the backboard are different for high school, college, and professional basketball. The rules of some sports, such as baseball and soccer, give the largest and smallest sizes allowed for the playing area.

TEAM SPORTS

In a team sport such as basketball, everybody must co-operate, or work together, in order to win. The stars in a team sport are usually the attacking players who score points or kick for a goal. However, if every player tried to be a star, there would be no one to play a defensive role and prevent the opposing team from scoring. So every player on the team has a special job, and each plays an equal part in a successful game.

Basketball hand signals

Personal foul

One free throw

Time out

RULES

Each team sport has its own rules so that everyone taking part knows how to play the game. Referees, umpires, or other judges stand at the edge of the playing area and make sure that the players obey the rules. In some sports, they use a loud whistle to stop and start play. They also signal with their hands or with flags to let the players know their decisions.

The ring of the basket stands 3 m (10 ft) above the floor.

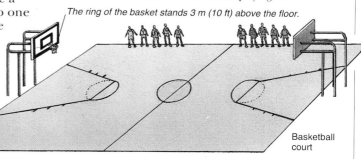

Basketball court

COMPETITION

In individual competition, contestants compete alone. Some try to beat a record; some measure their performance against other contestants. Players compete "one-on-one" in sports such as fencing, judo, and tennis. Several contestants compete together in racing sports such as horse racing or the 100-meter dash. In some sports, such as alpine skiing and archery, contestants compete separately to record the best times or scores. In other sports, such as diving or gymnastics, judges decide the scores.

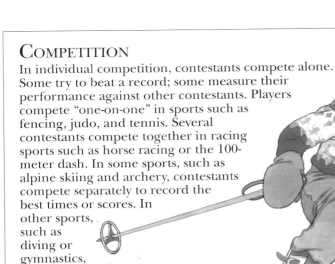

GYMNASTICS

In classic gymnastics, contestants perform exercises on the floor and on pieces of apparatus. This apparatus includes a padded stand called a horse, wooden rings hanging from straps, and arrangements of bars. Men and women do different exercises, and each is excluded from certain events. For instance, only men compete on rings, and only women use the balance beam.

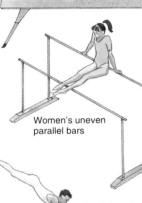

Men's rings

Men's pommel horse

Women's balance beam

Women's uneven parallel bars

Men's horse vault

Men's parallel bars

Women's floor exercises

TARGET SPORTS

Firing at targets began with archery, or bow and arrow practice, about 500 years ago. In modern archery, competitors shoot a series of arrows at a target from a range of distances. They score ten points for arrows that hit the center, or bull, and get lower scores the closer the arrow is to the edge of the target. Another target sport is shooting, in which competitors fire rifles or pistols at targets.

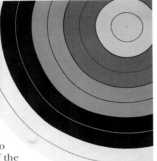

Archery target

COMBAT SPORTS

Modern combat sports originated in the fighting sports of ancient Greece, although people wrestled for sport 15,000 years earlier. Various styles of unarmed combat evolved – boxing and wrestling in the West and jujitsu in the East. The martial arts, such as judo, karate, aikido, and taekwondo, come from jujitsu.

WHEEL SPORTS

Competitions on wheels include everything from roller-skating to Grand Prix automobile racing. Physical skill and fitness are most important in unpowered wheel sports such as skateboarding, cycling, and bicycle motocross.

AIR SPORTS

Flying, gliding, and skydiving provide some of the greatest thrills in sport. Pilots race airplanes and, in aerobatics, perform maneuvers. Glider, balloon, and hang glider pilots use warm air currents to move around without power. Skydiving parachutists "free fall" for thousands of feet, linking hands in formation before opening their parachutes to land safely.

ANIMAL SPORTS

Greyhounds, pigeons, camels, and sled dogs compete in races, but horse racing is the best-known animal sport. Horse racing takes place over jumps as well as on flat ground. In harness racing, the horse pulls its driver around a track in a two-wheeled "sulky," like the chariot of ancient times. Other horse sports include show jumping, eventing, dressage, and polo.

In parasailing, a tow vehicle lifts the participant into the air with the aid of a special parachute.

Find out more

BALL GAMES
FOOTBALL
GAMES
OLYMPIC GAMES
TRACK AND FIELD SPORTS

STARFISH AND SEA URCHINS

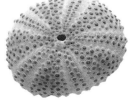

A sea urchin's shell is also known as a test. This one has lost all its spines.

THE SEA BED provides homes for many spiny-skinned creatures including starfish, sea urchins, and brittle stars. Starfish range in size from 8 cm (3 in) to 1 m (3 ft) across, and have a central body from which five arms radiate outwards. The sea urchin looks like a starfish whose arms have curled upwards and joined at the top to make a ball shape. Sea urchins have a hard outer skeleton covered with long spines. Starfish usually have short spines, like little bumps on the skin. Sea urchins graze on tiny animals and plants from rocks and the sea bed, and starfish feed on corals and shellfish. Both animals move using tubes inside the body which pump water in and out of hundreds of "tube feet". These tube feet lengthen and bend under the pressure of the water, propelling the creature along. Each tube foot has a sucker on the end. Using these suckers, a sea urchin can move up a vertical rock, and a starfish can wrench open a shellfish and eat the flesh inside.

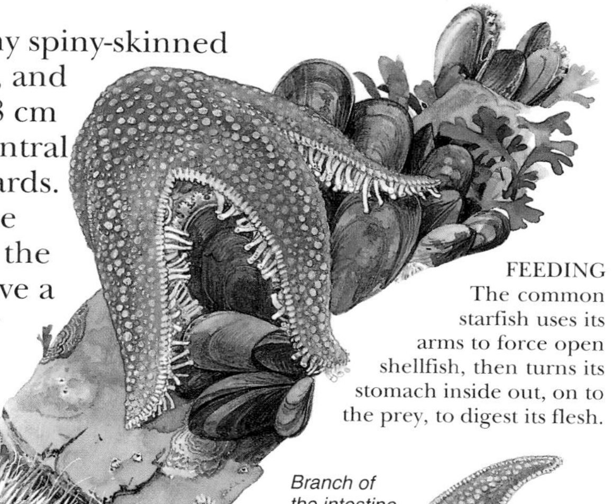

FEEDING
The common starfish uses its arms to force open shellfish, then turns its stomach inside out, on to the prey, to digest its flesh.

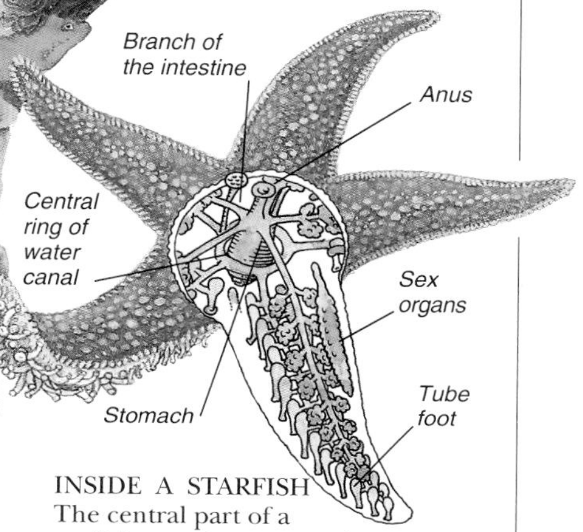

INSIDE A STARFISH
The central part of a starfish contains a stomach, with the mouth below and the anus above. Branches of the nerves, stomach, and water canals go into each arm.

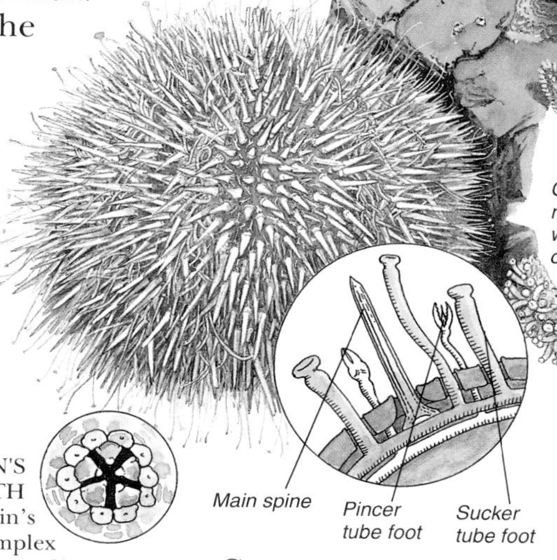

Branch of the intestine

Anus

Central ring of water canal

Sex organs

Stomach

Tube foot

SEA POTATO
Sea urchins such as sea potatoes burrow in sand with their flattened spines. Their tube feet are shaped at the tips for passing food to the mouth. An extra long tube foot reaches the surface of the sand like a periscope, so that the sea urchin can breathe. There is another tube foot for passing out waste products.

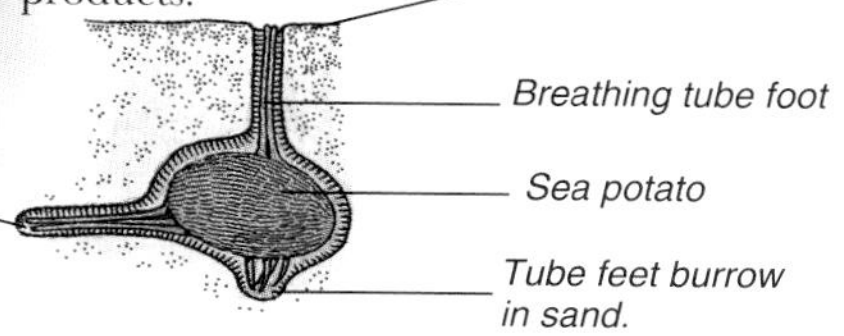

SEA URCHIN'S MOUTH
An urchin's mouth is a complex five-sided set of jaws.

Main spine

Pincer tube foot

Sucker tube foot

Waste-matter tube foot

Sand surface

Breathing tube foot

Sea potato

Tube feet burrow in sand.

SEA URCHIN
A sea urchin has long spines for defence. Around the spines are poison sacs, and between them wave the tube feet with suckers on the end. Some tube feet bear tiny pincers for clinging on to prey and others contain venom sacs that are full of poison.

GROWING NEW ARMS
Most starfish can grow new body parts, particularly arms, if the old ones are broken or bitten off. This means they can leave an arm behind to escape from a predator. A new arm grows within a few weeks.

Flexible arm

New arm will grow here.

Central disc

BRITTLE STAR
The brittle star shown here feeds by trapping food on its slimy mucus-covered arms. It pushes the food towards the mouth with its tube feet. This starfish moves by "rowing" with its arms, and is called a brittle star because its long, slim arms break off easily.

CROWN-OF-THORNS STARFISH
These large, prickly starfish eat living coral, and they have severely damaged many coral reefs, including Australia's Great Barrier Reef. Covered with razor-sharp poisonous spines, crown-of-thorns starfish attack coral reefs from Kenya to Tahiti.

The crown-of-thorns has more than a dozen arms covered with poisonous spines.

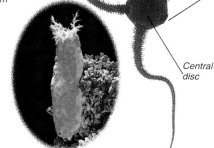

SEA CUCUMBER
This curious sea creature lies on its side looking like a cucumber. Feathery tentacles around the mouth gather tiny food particles from the water.

Find out more

ANIMALS
DEEP-SEA WILDLIFE
SEASHORE WILDLIFE

STARS

IF YOU LOOK up at the sky on a clear night, it is possible to see about 3,000 of the billions of stars in our galaxy. Although they appear to be tiny dots, they are really like our closest star, the sun – huge, hot balls of burning gas, deep in space. Some stars are gigantic – if placed in the centre of the solar system, they would stretch beyond the Earth's orbit. Others are much smaller, about the size of our planet, and give off a faint light. Stars are unimaginably distant; so distant, in fact, that light from our nearest star (apart from the sun) takes more than four years to reach us.

Ancient sky watchers noticed that stars form patterns in the sky. They imagined that the shapes represented pictures called constellations. These constellations, such as the Great Bear, are still useful for learning the positions of the stars. Astronomers identify individual stars according to their constellation and with Greek letters such as alpha, beta, and gamma (which stand for A, B, and C). For instance, the second brightest star in the constellation of Centaurus (the Centaur) is called Beta Centauri.

STARLIGHT
Inside a star, nuclear reactions produce light and heat. A star appears to twinkle because its light passes through the Earth's atmosphere, which is a moving blanket of gases. Seen from a spacecraft, stars shine steadily.

A group of growing stars called an open cluster

As the gas and dust in a mini-globule pack closer together, it moves faster and gets hotter. The mini-globule has become a protostar (a young star).

Death of a massive star

Death of a star about the size of the sun

NEBULA
Stars are born from great clouds of dust particles and hydrogen gas, called nebulae. The word *nebula* (plural nebulae) comes from the Latin for "mist".

BIRTH OF A STAR
Gravity pulls parts of a nebula into blobs called globules. These globules get smaller and spin faster, finally breaking up into a group of a few hundred smaller "mini-globules". Each of these will eventually become a star.

STAR STARTS TO SHINE
When the centre of the protostar reaches about 10 million°C (18 million°F), nuclear reactions begin which slowly change hydrogen into helium. The protostar begins to shine – it has become a true star.

RED GIANT
As the hydrogen fuel of a sunlike star runs low, it swells up into a cooler, larger star called a red giant. This will happen to our sun in about 5,000 million years.

LIFE AND DEATH OF A STAR
Throughout the universe, new stars form and old stars die. The birthplaces of stars are clouds of gas and dust scattered through space. Stars the size of the sun shine for about 10 billion years. The most massive stars (which contain 100 times as much matter as the sun) shine very brightly, but live for a shorter time – only about 10 million years.

SIZE, COLOUR, AND BRIGHTNESS
The colour of a star's light corresponds to the temperature of the star: red stars are the coolest, blue stars are the hottest. A star's brightness (the amount of energy it gives out) is linked to its mass (the amount of material it contains): heavier stars are brighter than lighter stars. Astronomers measure the colour and brightness of a star to give an indication of its size and distance from Earth.

VARIABLE STARS
Many stars, called variable stars, appear to vary in brightness. For example, some stars constantly swell and shrink, becoming alternately fainter and brighter. Other variables are really two stars that circle each other and block off each other's light from time to time.

Double stars circle around each other. When one star is in front of the other, the brightness falls. When both stars can be seen, the brightness rises.

Some variable stars are produced by exploding stars. The explosion makes the star appear much brighter than usual for a period that can last from a few days to a few years.

White dwarfs are small stars; some are smaller than the Earth.

Giants have diameters between 100 and 1,000 times larger than the sun's.

Yellow dwarfs, or medium-size stars, are about the same size as the sun.

Neutron stars (pulsars) are the smallest stars. They have about the same mass as the sun, but are only about 16 km (10 miles) in diameter.

Supergiants are the largest stars, with diameters up to 1,000 times that of the sun.

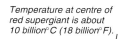

Temperature at centre of red supergiant is about 10 billion° C (18 billion° F).

PULSAR

A supernova may leave behind a pulsar – a spinning ball of matter with a mass greater than the sun's, yet only about 16 km (10 miles) across. As a pulsar spins it sends out beams of radio, light, and other waves, which sweep around the sky.

BLACK HOLE

The remains of a very massive star may collapse into a tiny space, forming a black hole. The gravitational pull of a black hole is so strong that matter and radiation (such as light) cannot escape from it.

RED SUPERGIANT

Some dying stars grow into huge, cool stars called red supergiants. Red supergiants can be up to 1,000 times the diameter of the sun. A red supergiant contains many different substances formed by nuclear reactions. Eventually the iron is formed, and the steady burning ends.

SUPERNOVA

When a massive star dies, it collapses in less than one second. A colossal explosion called a supernova follows. The explosion produces still more substances which are scattered through space in an expanding gas cloud.

PARALLAX

Astronomers use a technique called parallax to measure the distance of stars. As the Earth moves around the sun, the nearest stars seem to move very slightly compared with stars further away. Astronomers measure the position of a star once, and then again six months later. From their measurements, they can find the distance of a star.

CONSTELLATIONS

Today, astronomers group stars into 88 constellations. Each has a Latin name, such as Ursa Major (the Great Bear) or Corona Australis (the Southern Crown). The sun signs of astrology are the same as the 12 constellations of the zodiac – the band of sky along which the sun and planets appear to pass during a year.

Depending on the season, the constellation of Orion (above) can be seen from anywhere on Earth.

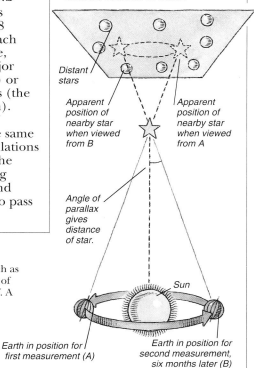

Distant stars

Apparent position of nearby star when viewed from B

Apparent position of nearby star when viewed from A

Angle of parallax gives distance of star.

Sun

Earth in position for first measurement (A)

Earth in position for second measurement, six months later (B)

PLANETARY NEBULA

Near the end of its life, the core of a sunlike star may collapse (cave in). The sunlike star flares up and throws off a "shell" of gas called a planetary nebula (above). A planetary nebula takes its name from its appearance through a telescope – it looks like a planet.

WHITE DWARF

At the end of its life, a solitary star such as the sun shrinks to about the size of the Earth, forming a white dwarf. A white dwarf is intensely hot, but because it is so small, it is very faint.

BLACK DWARF

After perhaps thousands of millions of years, a white dwarf will cool to become a dark, cold, black dwarf. However, none has been observed because there may not have been enough time since the beginning of our galaxy for any black dwarfs to appear.

Find out more

ASTRONOMY
GRAVITY
NAVIGATION
PLANETS
SUN
TELESCOPES
UNIVERSE

STATUE OF LIBERTY

ON A BRONZE PLAQUE inside the base of the Statue of Liberty are the words of a poem written by Emma Lazarus in 1883. Part of it reads: "Give me your tired, your poor,/ Your huddled masses yearning to breathe free,/ The wretched refuse of your teeming shore./ Send these, the homeless, tempest-tost to me./ I lift my lamp beside the golden door!" The "masses" were the people fleeing poverty and oppression in Europe; the "golden door", the opportunity to start a new life in the United States. The French historian Edouard de Laboulaye planned the statue in 1865 to symbolize liberty and to commemorate the friendship of France with the United States. It was designed by Frédéric Auguste Bartholdi and built by Alexandre Gustave Eiffel, whose famous Eiffel Tower dominates the skyline of Paris.

Mercury lamps light the torch of Liberty.

A 10-year-old child would look this size in the crown.

Observation platform in crown

Seven points signify liberty radiating out to the seven continents and across the seven seas.

Tablet bears date of American Declaration of Independence.

A staircase leads up the arm.

A double spiral staircase winds up 171 steps.

ELLIS ISLAND
The first thing millions of immigrants from Europe saw after a long voyage across the North Atlantic Ocean was the Statue of Liberty. They disembarked nearby on tiny Ellis Island, which, between 1892 and 1943, was the chief immigration station for the United States.

STATUE OF LIBERTY
Supported by four steel columns with a framework of iron, the copper-covered Statue of Liberty represents a woman dressed in a long classical robe, standing 46 m (151 ft) high. The head measures 3 m by 5 m (10 ft by 17 ft) the right arm holding the torch is 13 m (42 ft) long. The torch at the top of the statue is 93 m (305 ft) above the water.

MAKING THE STATUE
Alexandre Gustave Eiffel built the Statue of Liberty in a suburb of Paris, France. Then it was shipped to the United States in 214 cases aboard the French ship *Isére*. The parts were re-assembled in New York.

THE BASE
The statue stands on a pedestal of concrete faced with granite. Its base is surrounded by walls in the shape of an 11-pointed star, part of Fort Wood, a disused fort. The entire base and pedestal are 47 m (154 ft) high, almost the same height as the statue itself.

Visitors enter here and take a lift to the base of the statue.

IMMIGRATION 1870-1916

S. and E. Europe
12,412,144

N. and W. Europe
10,562,280

N. and S. America
1,940,051

Asia, Africa, and Oceania
740,242

Most immigrants into the United States between 1870 and 1916 came from southern and eastern Europe.

Find out more

UNITED STATES OF AMERICA, history of

STONE AGE

TWO AND A HALF MILLION YEARS AGO, stone was the most valuable raw material known to people. They made stone tools and weapons, usually from flint. These early people were called hominids, and were more apelike than us. They gradually learned to make specialized implements, such as knife blades. Stone Age people moved constantly, looking for hunting areas and setting up camps in small groups. A few groups lived in caves during the coldest seasons. They gathered fruits, berries, and roots, and hunted wild animals. By the start of the Mesolithic Age (Middle Stone Age; 10,000 years ago) many types of larger animals had died out. Mesolithic people, who were "modern people" (*Homo sapiens sapiens*) like us, used new stone-edged tools to fish and hunt deer and wild pigs. About 5,000 years ago some Neolithic (New Stone) Age people learned how to domesticate animals and grow crops. They settled on farms.

c. 2,500,000 B.C. Palaeolithic Age begins.

c. 2,000,000 B.C. Hominids make the first stone tools.

c. 1,500,000 B.C. First hand ax.

c. 125,000 B.C. Ice Age retreats; people return to Europe, hunt large animals.

c. 75,000 B.C. People use fire and bury their dead.

c. 20,000 B.C. Spear thrower invented. Also harpoon, bow and arrows, sewing, and cave painting.

c. 8300 B.C. Mesolithic Age.

c. 6500 B.C. Neolithic Age.

c. 3000 B.C. Metal tools and weapons replace stone.

MAMMOTH HUNT

From about 50,000 years ago, "modern people" hunted wild animals. By co-operating in groups and using their superior brainpower, they could kill creatures much larger than themselves. They sometimes slaughtered large numbers of deer and similar creatures by driving whole herds over cliffs. Elephant-like woolly mammoths were popular game; they are now extinct.

Mammoth has been lured into a pit trap covered in branches.

Hunters killed prey with sharp stone weapons.

Dwelling places made from animal hides and mammoth bones kept out the cold wind.

Woman cooks a hare on a spit over the fire.

Stretching hide to make clothing.

Man is using a bone hammer to chip away at a flint core.

MAKING FLINT TOOLS AND WEAPONS

1 The first flint implements were crude. People used the sharp edge of a broken rock as a cutting tool.

2 Later tools were much better. The toolmaker prepared a flint core by skillful chipping.

3 Hitting the core with a bone hammer made flakes, each one a special tool.

HAND AXE

The hand ax was the first deliberately shaped tool made by humans. It was gripped at the rounded end and used to cut meat or dig roots. Popular for over a million years, it was used longer than any other tool.

This flint hand axe was found in a desert area near Thebes, Egypt.

Find out more
ARCHAEOLOGY
EVOLUTION
PREHISTORIC PEOPLES

STORMS

TORNADOES

The most violent storms are tornadoes, or whirlwinds. A twisting column of rising air forms beneath a thunder cloud, sometimes producing winds of 400 km/h (250 mph). The air pressure at the centre is very low, which can cause buildings to explode. A waterspout is a tornado over water, formed when water is sucked up into the funnel of air. Dust devils are tornadoes which have sucked up sand over the desert.

Severe storms build up as moist air, heated by warm land or sea, rises. Storm clouds develop as the rising air cools and rain forms. Air rushes in to replace the rising air, and strong winds begin to blow.

The base of the tornado is fairly narrow – about 1.6 km (1 mile) across.

The rising air spirals up the column, sucking up dirt and objects as heavy as trucks from the ground.

ABOUT 2,000

thunderstorms are raging throughout the world at this very moment, and lightning has struck about 500 times since you started reading this page. Storms have enormous power: the energy in a hurricane could illuminate more light bulbs than there are in the United States. A storm is basically a very strong wind. Severe storms such as thunderstorms, hurricanes, and tornadoes all contain their own strong wind system as well as blowing along as a whole. Certain areas, such as the region around the Gulf of Mexico, are hit regularly by severe storms because of the local conditions. Storms can cause great damage because of the force of the wind and the devastating power of the rain, snow, sand, or dust which they carry along. One of the most destructive forces of a hurricane is a storm surge. The level of the sea rises because of a rapid drop in air pressure at the centre of the storm. This rise combines with the effect of the wind on the sea to create a huge wall of water which causes terrible damage if it hits the coast.

DESTRUCTION AND DEVASTATION

Winds of 320 km/h (200 mph) leave a trail of destruction (below) when the hurricane strikes the shore. The strongest winds are in a belt around the calm eye.

THUNDER AND LIGHTNING

Thunder clouds often form on hot, humid days. Strong air currents in the cloud cause raindrops and hailstones to collide, producing electric charges. Lightning flashes in giant sparks between the charges, and often leaps to the ground. A burst of heat from the flash makes the air nearby expand violently and produces a clap of thunder.

Negative charges in the bottom of the cloud attract positive charges in the ground. Eventually, a huge spark of lightning leaps from the cloud to the highest point on the ground.

Buildings are protected by lightning rods – strips of metal on the roof which attract the lightning and lead the electricity safely to the ground.

HURRICANES

When warm, moist air spirals upward above tropical oceans, it forms a hurricane – a violent storm which is also called a typhoon or a cyclone. The spin of the Earth causes the storm winds to circle around a calm centre called the eye. The eye usually moves along at about 24 km/h (15 mph). It can measure as much as 500 miles (800 km) across.

Find out more
CLIMATES
RAIN AND SNOW
WEATHER
WIND

SUBMARINES

THE GREAT POWER of a submarine lies in its ability to remain hidden. It can travel unseen beneath the waves, carrying its deadly cargo of missiles and torpedoes, and remain underwater for months at a time. However, the submarine had humble beginnings; legend states that during the siege of Tyre (Lebanon) in 332 B.C., Alexander the Great attacked the inhabitants from a submerged glass barrel. Aided by the invention of the electric motor for underwater propulsion and the torpedo for attacking ships, modern submarines developed into powerful weapons during the two world wars of this century. Today's submarines are powered either by a combination of diesel and electric motors or by nuclear-powered engines. There are two main types: patrol submarines, which aim to seek and destroy ships and other submarines, and missile-carrying submarines. Small submarines called submersibles are used mainly for non-military purposes, such as marine research.

NUCLEAR SUBMARINE
The most powerful of all weapons is the nuclear missile-carrying submarine. Its nuclear-powered engines allow it to hide underwater almost indefinitely without coming up for air, and it carries sufficient nuclear missiles to destroy several large cities.

Propeller drives the submarine through the water.

Diesel-electric engines are specially designed to make as little noise as possible.

Periscope and communication antennas

The Conning tower stands clear of the water when the submarine is on the surface.

Torpedoes ready for firing

Small movable wings called hydroplanes control the submarine's direction.

Tubes for launching torpedoes

HUNTER-KILLER SUBMARINE
A diesel engine powers this hunter-killer submarine when it travels on the surface, and an electric motor when it is underwater. Buoyancy tanks fill with water to submerge the submarine; to surface again, compressed air pushes the water out of the tanks.

Crew's living quarters are usually cramped. Some submarines carry a crew of more than 150.

Control room, from which the captain commands the submarine

TORPEDOES
Torpedoes are packed with explosives and have their own motors to propel them to their targets. They are launched by compressed air from tubes in the nose and rear of the submarine.

PERISCOPE
With a periscope, the captain can see what is on the surface while the submarine is submerged. A periscope is a hollow tube which extends from the conning tower. It contains an angled mirror at either end and a system of lenses which form an image of the object on the surface.

Anti-submarine helicopter trails active sonar system in the water.

SONAR
Helicopters, ships, and hunter-killer submarines are equipped with sonar (sound navigation and ranging) for detecting submarines. Passive sonar consists of microphones which pick up the sound of the submarine's engines. Active sonar sends out ultrasonic sound pulses which are too high-pitched to hear but bounce off a hidden submarine and produce a distinctive echo.

The missile-carrying submarine will dive to escape its attackers.

Hunter-killer submarine uses active sonar to detect enemy submarine.

Submarine captain sees helicopter through periscope.

Find out more
NAVIES
ROCKETS AND MISSILES
SHIPS AND BOATS
UNDERWATER EXPLORATION
WARSHIPS

SUN

THE NIGHT SKY is full of stars, so distant that they are mere points of light. The sun is one of these stars, but we are closer to it than to any other star. Along with the other planets of the solar system, the Earth moves around the sun, trapped in orbit by the force of gravity. The sun provides light and heat which sustains nearly all life on Earth, yet sunlight is produced by the same process that powers nuclear weapons. The sun is a ball of glowing gases, roughly three-quarters hydrogen and one-quarter helium, along with traces of other elements. Within its hot, dense core, gravity crushes hydrogen atoms together. This produces nuclear reactions that form helium, releasing energy as intense heat and light. The energy produced in these reactions is released from the surface as radiation. Energy sources that humans use to provide power originate from the sun. For example, coal is the remains of ancient plants, which trapped the sun's energy.

STORY OF THE SUN
The sun was born just under 5,000 million years ago from a cloud of hydrogen and helium mixed with dust which contracted (shrank) under its own gravity. The contraction heated the cloud until nuclear reactions began, converting the hydrogen into helium. At this point the sun began to shine steadily. Scientists believe that the sun will continue to shine for another 5,000 million years before it runs out of hydrogen fuel and begins to die.

SOLAR FLARES
Huge explosions on the sun's surface, called solar flares, fire streams of electrically charged particles into space. Some flares produce auroras – coloured lights in the sky above the Earth's poles. They also create magnetic storms, which cause power failures and interfere with radio reception.

Energy travels outwards in the form of electromagnetic waves such as heat, light, and radio waves.

Relatively cool, dark areas, called sunspots, form on the surface of the sun. Sunspots are caused by large changes in the sun's magnetic field.

Great streamers of glowing hydrogen gas, called prominences, frequently soar up from the sun. Prominences are often about 60,000 km (more than 37,000 miles) long.

Light from the sun takes about eight minutes to reach the Earth.

Core extends to about 175,000 km (about 110,800 miles) from the sun's centre.

The glowing, white-hot surface of the sun is called the photosphere (sphere of light). It is about 400 km (250 miles) deep.

A glowing red layer of hydrogen gas called the chromosphere (sphere of colour) lies above the photosphere. The chromosphere is a few thousand kilometres deep.

CORONA AND SOLAR WIND
A thin pearl-white atmosphere of gases called the corona extends for millions of kilometres around the sun. A stream of electrically charged particles, called the solar wind, shoots out from the corona at a rate of millions of tonnes each second. The Earth is protected from these particles by its magnetic field, but they can damage spacecraft and satellites.

The sun's diameter is 109 times the Earth's. More than 1,300,000 globes the size of the Earth could fit into the sun.

Warning: Never look at the sun, either directly or through dark glasses. The intense light could seriously damage your eyesight.

SOLAR ENERGY
Electronic devices called solar cells convert sunlight into electricity. Solar cells power satellites and produce electricity in experimental houses and cars. In 1987, the solar-powered *Sunraycer* car (below) drove across Australia at an average speed of 66.9 km/h (41.6 mph).

Umbra is the centreof the moon's shadow, where the sun is completely hidden.

Penumbra is the outer part of the moon's shadow, where part of the sun can be seen.

SUN FACTS
Earth–sun distance	149.6 million km (92.9 million miles)
Diameter at equator	1,392,000 km (864,950 miles)
Time to rotate once	25.4 days
Temperature at surface	5,500°C (9,932°F)
Temperature at center	15,000,000°C (27,000,000°F)

SOLAR ECLIPSES
When the moon passes between the Earth and the sun, the sun is hidden. This is called a solar eclipse. A total solar eclipse occurs at places on the Earth where the sun appears to be completely hidden (although prominences, chromosphere, and corona can be seen). Elsewhere the eclipse is partial, and parts of the sun can be seen.

Find out more

ASTRONOMY
ENERGY
STARS

TANKS

MILLIONS OF YEARS AGO, nature equipped animals such as turtles with armour in the form of a shell to protect them from enemies. As recently as this century, armies adopted the same idea in battle. The result was the tank – a steel monster that lumbered over the battle-fields of World War I (1914-18), destroying enemy defences and machine gun posts. Tanks have now developed into sophisticated weapons that combine fire power, protection, and mobility. Each tank is fitted with a powerful gun that is guided by computers and a laser rangefinder to ensure pinpoint accuracy. Hardened-steel armour, which may be up to 11 cm (4.3 in) thick, protects the crew. Tanks can manoeuvre their way over terrain that would defeat any other vehicle, and some light tanks can travel at speeds of more than 80 km/h (50 mph).

DA VINCI'S TANK
In 1482, Italian artist and scientist Leonardo da Vinci drew this design for a kind of tank, armed with a multitude of cannons. However, it is doubtful whether the tank was ever built.

MAIN BATTLE TANK
The *Leopard 2* main battle tank is one of the most powerful tanks in the world. It can travel at 72 km/h (45 mph) despite its weight of 55 tonnes (54 tons), which is equivalent to more than 30 small family saloon cars. It is armed with a main gun and two machine guns and carries a crew of four.

Smoke dischargers produce huge cloud of smoke to hide the tank if it is under attack.

Commander's cupola with periscopes which give all-round vision

Turret allows main gun to be aimed in any direction.

Machine gun, used to defend tank against aircraft

Main gun, guided by laser sight and computers

SELF-PROPELLED GUN
Because mobile artillery weapons are mounted on a tanklike vehicle, they can move rapidly into new positions.

Gun loader operates main gun and radio communications.

Periscope allows driver to see out from inside the hull of the tank.

Ammunition store with shells for main gun

Many tanks can plough through water more than 2 m (6.5 ft) deep so they can cross streams and rivers.

CATERPILLAR TRACKS
Tanks run on caterpillar tracks, which are endless belts running over several wheels. To turn the tank, the driver makes the tracks on either side of the tank run at different speeds.

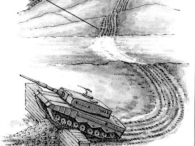

ARMOURED CAR
Armoured cars are perfect for reconnaissance (scouting) missions and patrols because they are small and fast.

DEVELOPMENT OF THE TANK
In 1916, the British Mark I became the first tank to be used in battle. Its strange shape allowed it to cross the wide trenches, mud, and barbed wire of the battlefield. Over the next 30 years, tanks evolved into advanced fighting machines. Recent developments are concerned with improving weaponry, speed, and armour of tanks.

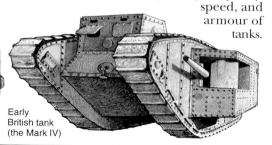

PERSONNEL CARRIER
Soldiers travel into battle in an armoured personnel carrier. It transports them on water and on land, propelled by its caterpillar tracks which work like paddles.

Early British tank (the Mark IV)

Find out more

ARMIES
GUNS
WEAPONS
WORLD WAR I
WORLD WAR II

TECHNOLOGY

THE INVENTION OF stone tools more than 2 million years ago marked the beginning of technology. For the first time in history, people found that jobs such as cutting or chopping were easier to do with tools than with their bare hands. Technology is the way in which people use the ideas of science to build machines and make tasks easier. Although technology began in prehistoric times, it advanced rapidly only after the Industrial Revolution which began in the 18th century. Since that time technology has dramatically changed our world. It has given us fast, safe transport, materials such as plastics, worldwide communications such as telephones and television, and many other useful appliances. Perhaps the greatest benefits of technology are from modern medicine, which has improved our health and lengthened our lives. However, technology has a negative side too – it produces weapons with the power to cause death and destruction.

Nuclear missiles fired from submarines are almost impossible to stop. Complex navigation systems guide them to their targets with great precision.

A calculator does arithmetic and other calculations correctly and almost instantly.

COMPUTERS

The development of computers has been one of the most important recent advances in technology. Computers can perform many different tasks and are used in banking, architecture, manufacturing, and many other businesses. Computers also aid new technology, because they can help design and invent new machines.

Microchips lie at the heart of every computer. These tiny devices store and process huge amounts of information at high speed.

Computers can be linked into worldwide networks. They exchange information via satellites or along telephone lines.

Rockets launch shuttles, satellites, and other spacecraft into space.

Computers and radar at an airport enable controllers to guide aircraft safely through the air.

Trains are the fastest kind of land transport.

MEDICAL TECHNOLOGY

Inventions such as x-ray machines and brain scanners help doctors detect and treat illness. Doctors can transplant organs, implant tiny electronic pacemakers to keep a heart beating, and repair damaged tissue with plastic surgery.

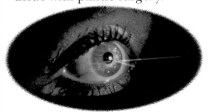

Laser surgery can correct many eye defects without the need for cutting into the eye.

Efficient road networks allow cars and trucks to carry people and goods quickly and safely.

Electronic aids such as sonar help trawlers find and catch fish.

Oil tankers are the largest ships. They carry oil from under-sea wells to oil terminals on land.

TRANSPORT

Technology enables us to transport goods throughout the world and travel almost anywhere – even into space. Inventors have developed powerful engines to drive cars, trains, ships, aircraft, and other vehicles. Engineers have built structures that make transport possible, including bridges, tunnels, roads, railway lines, harbours, and airports.

Oil rigs bore deep shafts to tap oil in deposits beneath the land and sea.

Tunnels carry trains and cars beneath rivers and sea channels.

Military aircraft use some of the most advanced technology for their navigation and weapons systems.

A space shuttle can make many flights into space. It is launched into orbit around the Earth and then returns to land on a runway.

Astronauts wearing spacesuits can leave a spacecraft to repair satellites that may have become damaged in space.

A communications satellite receives and sends signals to link different parts of the globe.

SMALL-SCALE TECHNOLOGY

People in the poorer countries of the world cannot afford to buy the latest technology that is common in North America, Japan, and Europe. Instead, they use smaller, simpler machines, such as windmills that drive pumps for irrigation.

Threshing machines help people separate the heads from the stalks of rice plants. Previously, this job had to be done by hand.

Television programmes are broadcast via satellites, television masts, or underground cables.

MILITARY TECHNOLOGY
Many machines were originally built for military uses, but now benefit civilians as well. The jet engine and radar, for example, were developed for war but are vital to modern airliners.

Sonar was invented to find submarines. Now it is also used to locate fish.

Undersea cables carry telephone signals between continents.

COMMUNICATIONS

Technology enables people on opposite sides of the globe to talk to each other, receive information, and watch television programmes. Electronics turns speech, pictures, and words into electric signals. Telephone, radio, and television systems transmit these signals along wires or by way of radio waves, often via communications satellites in space.

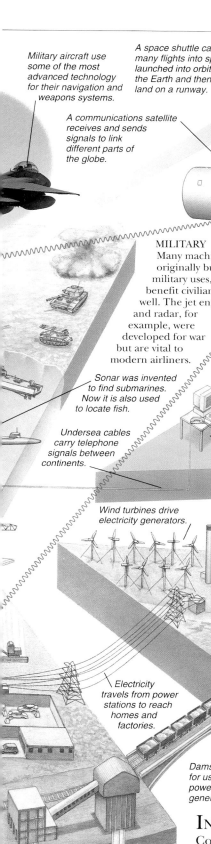

Wind turbines drive electricity generators.

Huge power stations produce electricity to keep the world's industry functioning.

There are millions of telephones all over the world linked by a system of wires, fibre-optic cables, and satellites.

Solar power stations convert the light and heat of the sun's rays into electricity.

ENERGY

The multitude of machines developed by modern technology requires an immense amount of energy to drive them. This energy comes mostly from fuels such as coal and oil, which are burned directly in engines or used to generate electricity in power stations. Burning fuels causes pollution, but engineers are developing safer ways of producing energy using wind, water, and sunlight.

Electricity travels from power stations to reach homes and factories.

Dams store water for use in hydroelectric power stations that generate electricity.

Electrical energy is very useful because it can be changed into many different kinds of energy.

INDUSTRY

Construction, manufacturing, and agriculture are large industries that depend on technology. Engineers design and construct high buildings, bridges, tunnels, and dams. Factories contain machines that make goods of all kinds – many of these machines are robots controlled by computers. Farms use tractors, pumps that milk cows, and many other machines.

Layers of minerals such as coal lie underground. Cutting machines extract these minerals from deep mines.

Find out more
COMPUTERS
ELECTRONICS
FARMING
HOUSEHOLD APPLIANCES
INDUSTRIAL REVOLUTION
MACHINES
MEDICINE
TRANSPORT, HISTORY OF

TEETH

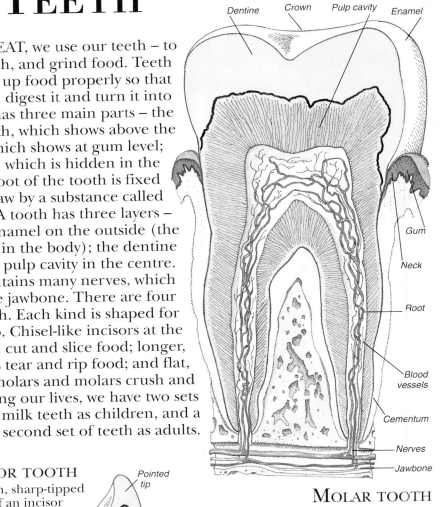

Dentine — Crown — Pulp cavity — Enamel

Gum

Neck

Root

Blood vessels

Cementum

Nerves

Jawbone

EVERY TIME WE EAT, we use our teeth – to bite, chew, crunch, and grind food. Teeth enable us to break up food properly so that our bodies can digest it and turn it into energy. A tooth has three main parts – the crown of the tooth, which shows above the gum; the neck, which shows at gum level; and the root, which is hidden in the jawbone. The root of the tooth is fixed securely in the jaw by a substance called cementum. A tooth has three layers – creamy white enamel on the outside (the hardest substance in the body); the dentine beneath; and the pulp cavity in the centre. The pulp contains many nerves, which connect to the jawbone. There are four main kinds of teeth. Each kind is shaped for a different job. Chisel-like incisors at the front of the mouth cut and slice food; longer, pointed canines tear and rip food; and flat, broad premolars and molars crush and grind it. During our lives, we have two sets of teeth – milk teeth as children, and a second set of teeth as adults.

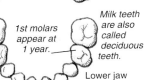

HEALTHY TEETH
It is important to take care of your teeth to keep them healthy. Teeth should be cleaned with a toothbrush, toothpaste, and dental floss after every meal. Sugary foods are damaging to the teeth and cause tooth decay.

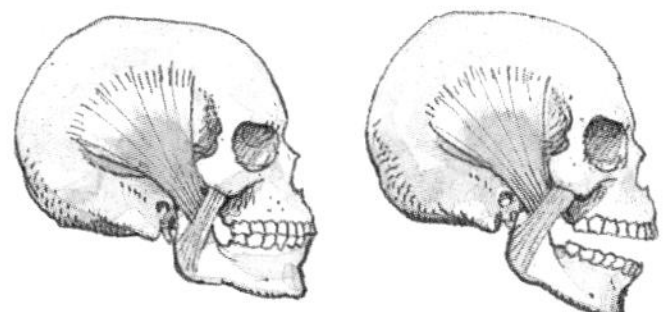

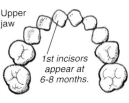

JAWS
The upper jaw is fixed to the skull and does not move. Powerful muscles in the cheeks and the side of the head pull the lower jaw up towards the upper jaw, so that the teeth come together with great pressure for biting. Other muscles pull the lower jaw sideways, so that we can chew with both up-and-down and side-to-side movements.

WISDOM TEETH
The four molar teeth at the very back of the jaw are called the wisdom teeth. They usually appear after about 20 years of age. In some people, wisdom teeth never emerge at all, but stay hidden in the jaw.

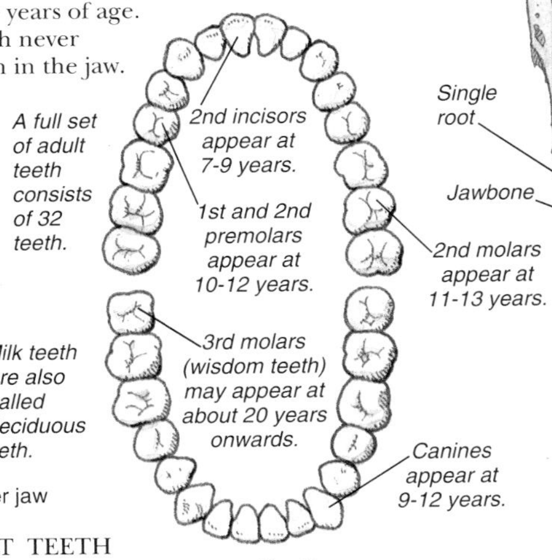

INCISOR TOOTH
The thin, sharp-tipped shape of an incisor tooth is ideal for snipping and cutting up food. The incisor has only one root, deeply embedded in the jawbone.

Pointed tip

Single root

Jawbone

MOLAR TOOTH
Molars have one, two, three, or occasionally four roots, which anchor them securely in the jawbone and withstand the great pressure of chewing hard food. The nerves and blood vessels pass out through tiny holes in the base of each root. The crown is broad and flat, for crushing and grinding.

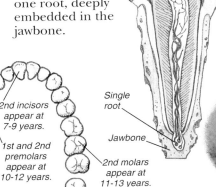

Upper jaw

1st incisors appear at 6-8 months.

A full set of adult teeth consists of 32 teeth.

Milk teeth are also called deciduous teeth.

1st molars appear at 1 year.

Lower jaw

2nd incisors appear at 7-9 years.

1st and 2nd premolars appear at 10-12 years.

3rd molars (wisdom teeth) may appear at about 20 years onwards.

2nd molars appear at 11-13 years.

Canines appear at 9-12 years.

MILK TEETH AND ADULT TEETH
Children have a first set of 20 milk teeth, which usually all appear by about two years of age. There are eight incisors, four canines, and eight molars. During childhood these teeth gradually fall out and are replaced by a second set of permanent, or adult, teeth.

TUSKS
Animals use their teeth for more than just eating food. Large teeth help in defence against enemies, or when battling with rivals during the mating season. The warthog's tusks shown here are huge canine teeth – like the tusks of an elephant. Tusks are used to frighten off predators and, sometimes, to dig up food.

Find out more

DENTISTS
FOOD AND DIGESTION
HUMAN BODY
SKELETONS

TELEPHONES

WITH THE PUSH of a few buttons on the telephone, it is possible to talk to someone nearly anywhere else in the world. By making instant communication possible, the telephone has done more to "shrink" the world than almost any other invention. A telephone signal can take several forms on its journey. Beneath the city streets it travels in the form of electric currents in cables, or as light waves in thin glass fibres. Telephone signals also travel as radio waves when they beam down to other countries via satellites, or when they carry messages to and from mobile phones. Many electronic devices "talk" to each other by sending signals via telephone links. Computers exchange information and computer programs with one another, and fax machines use telephone lines to send copies of pictures and text to other fax machines across the world within seconds.

Electronic circuits generate signals corresponding to each button as it is pressed. They also amplify (boost) incoming electric signals and send them to the receiver.

A loudspeaker, called the receiver, contains a thin metal disc that vibrates, converting electric signals into sound waves.

TELEPHONE HANDSET
A small direct (one-way) electric current flows in the wires connected to a telephone handset. Signals representing sounds such as callers' voices, computer data, and fax messages consist of rapid variations in the strength of this current.

Sound waves of the user's voice strike a microphone called the transmitter, creating an electrical signal that is sent down the telephone cable.

TELEPHONE NETWORK
Computer-controlled telephone exchanges make the connections needed to link two telephones. When a person dials a telephone number, automatic switches at the local exchange link the telephone lines directly. International calls travel along undersea cables or, in the form of radio waves, by way of satellites.

Fibre-optic cables use light waves to carry thousands of phone calls at one time.

Communication satellites orbit the Earth at such a height and speed that they remain stationary over the same part of the globe all the time. They receive telephone signals from one country on Earth, boost the signals, then beam them back down to another country.

Words and pictures printed by a fax machine have jagged edges because they are made up of thousands of dots.

FAX
A facsimile, or fax, machine scans a picture or a written page, measuring its brightness at thousands of individual points. The machine then sends a stream of signals along the telephone wire, each signal representing the brightness at one point. A printer inside the receiving fax machine prints a dot wherever the original picture is dark, building up a copy of the picture.

ALEXANDER GRAHAM BELL
The inventor of the telephone was a Scottish-American teacher named Alexander Graham Bell (1847-1922). In 1875, Bell was experimenting with early telegraph systems. For this he used vibrating steel strips called reeds. He found that when a reed at one end of the line vibrated, a reed at the other end gave out a sound. In 1876, Bell patented the first practical telephone.

PORTABLE PHONES
A cordless telephone has a built-in radio transmitter and receiver. One type, for use in the home, communicates with a unit that is connected to the regular telephone line. Other types of portable phones send messages over long distances with the aid of powerful relay stations.

Find out more

RADIO
SATELLITES

TELESCOPES

FROM FAR AWAY, a person looks like a tiny dot. But with a telescope, you can see a clear, bright image that reveals all the details of that person's face. Large modern telescopes make it possible to see incredibly distant objects. The Hale telescope on Mount Palomar, California, United States, can detect objects in space called quasars, which are about 30,000 million million million km (20,000 million million million miles) from the Earth. Less powerful telescopes are important too: they are valuable tools for mapmakers, sailors, and bird watchers. Telescopes have helped scientists make some of the greatest discoveries about the universe. In 1609, the Italian scientist Galileo first turned a telescope to the skies. His observations led him to suggest that the Earth moved around the sun and was not the centre of the universe, as people believed at that time. Since then astronomers have used telescopes to probe into the farthest reaches of our solar system and beyond, discovering new stars and planets.

OPERA GLASSES
Opera glasses are the simplest kind of binoculars. They consist of two small telescopes placed side by side.

Eyepiece lenses are adjustable to match the strength of each eye.

Prisms "fold up" the light inside the binoculars, which magnifies objects as much as a long telescope.

BINOCULARS
Binoculars are more complex than opera glasses. They contain a system of lenses and prisms that makes them powerful yet small in size.

A prism is a triangular-shaped piece of glass.

Light enters the front of the telescope.

Doors of observatory slide open to give telescope a view of the stars.

When the Hale telescope was first built, the observer sat inside the telescope itself to view the stars. Today there is an electronic detector placed there instead.

REFLECTING TELESCOPE
Most astronomers use reflecting telescopes, which are the best telescopes for picking up the faint light from distant stars. A large curved mirror catches the light and concentrates it to form an image. A smaller mirror then carries the image to a lens called the eyepiece. A camera or electronic light detector is often fitted to the eyepiece of astronomical telescopes.

Concave mirror is curved inward to focus the light. This mirror is called the objective mirror because it forms an image of a distant object.

The mountings allow the telescope to turn in order to follow the stars as the Earth moves.

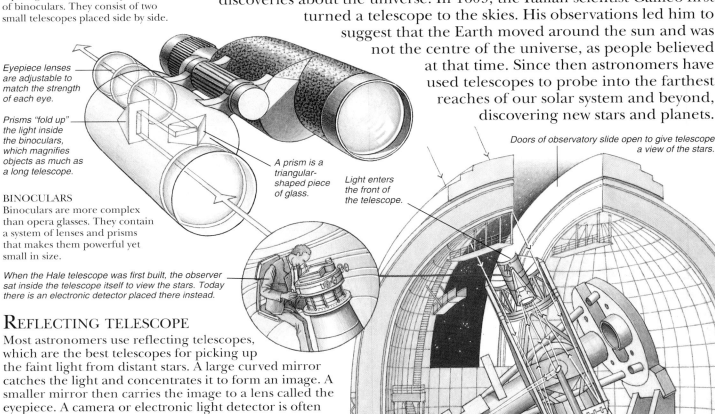

RADIO TELESCOPES
Stars and other objects in space give out invisible radio waves as well as light. Astronomers study the universe with radio telescopes, which are large dish-shaped antennas that pick up radio waves from space. Radio astronomy has led to the discovery of dying stars and distant galaxies that would not have been seen from their light alone.

The eyepiece lens focuses the image into the observer's eye.

The middle lens turns the image the right way up.

The objective lens is a convex lens which concentrates the light to form an image.

REFRACTING TELESCOPE
A large lens at the front of a refracting telescope refracts, or bends, the light to form an image of a distant object. The eyepiece lens is at the back. Some refractors have a third lens in the middle. Without this lens, the telescope would produce an upside-down image.

The mirror is made as large as possible to collect the maximum amount of light and distinguish fine details. The objective mirror on the Hale telescope (above) is 508 cm (200 in) wide and weighs 20 tonnes (20 tons).

Find out more

ASTRONOMY
LIGHT
MICROSCOPES
SCIENTISTS AND INVENTORS

TELEVISION AND VIDEO

The announcer reads the script from a TelePrompter. The words are printed on a monitor screen and reflected in a two-way mirror in front of the camera lens. An operator on the studio floor controls the speed at which the words move.

A television screen concealed in the desk shows the announcer the picture that is being broadcast.

Through a hidden earpiece, the control room sends information and instructions to the announcer, such as countdowns to a commercial or last-minute changes in the running order of the program.

Bright, hot lights illuminate the studio. A technician in the control room operates the lights.

Each camera continually sends pictures to the control room, but pictures from only one camera are broadcast at a given time. A red light on the front of each camera lights up when its signal is being broadcast.

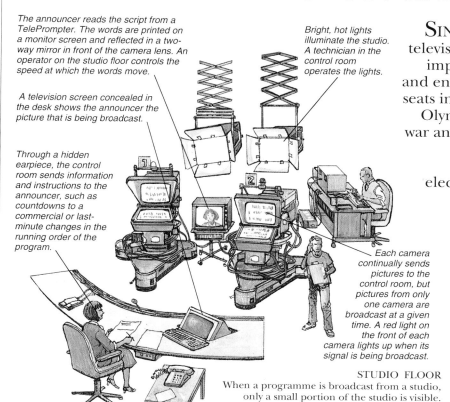

STUDIO FLOOR
When a programme is broadcast from a studio, only a small portion of the studio is visible. Hidden from view are the dozens of people and wide range of complex equipment needed to make the programme.

SINCE ITS INVENTION early this century, television has become one of the world's most important sources of information, opinion, and entertainment. Television gives us the best seats in the theatre, at a rock concert, or at the Olympic Games. It also beams us pictures of war and disaster, the conquering of space, and other world events as they happen. Television programmes are actually electronic signals sent out as radio waves by way of satellites and underground cables. A television set converts the signals into sound and pictures. Pictures also come to a television set from a videocassette recorder (VCR). With a VCR, people can watch films recorded on videotape, record programmes and watch them at a convenient time, and make their own films with a lightweight video camera. Closed-circuit (nonbroadcast) television cameras are used to guard shops and offices, monitor traffic conditions, and survey crowds at sports events.

TELEVISION STUDIO
Within the space of a few hours, the same studio might be used for a game show, a play, a variety show, and a panel discussion, so studio sets have to be changed very rapidly. Announcers and people working behind the cameras receive instructions from the control room via headphones. Most programmes are videotaped, sometimes months before they are broadcast.

Camera operator zooms and focuses remote control cameras from within the control room. In many studios, the camera operator controls the camera directly.

A production assistant tells everyone in the studio how much time is left on each film clip or news story.

The vision mixer operates the controls that select and combine pictures.

Engineers control the quality of lighting and pictures.

OUTSIDE BROADCAST

Away from the studio, outside broadcast teams use light, portable cameras when mobility is important, as in a news report, and large, fixed cameras for events such as football games. The pictures are recorded on videotape or beamed back to the studio via a mobile dish antenna.

CONTROL ROOM
The director selects what is to be broadcast from a bank of screens showing pictures from several sources: from cameras in the studio and at outside broadcast locations, from videotape machines, and from satellites. Other screens show still photographs, captions, and titles.

Microphones in the studio are mounted on stands or worn by performers and announcers. In a separate control room, sound operators select and mix the sounds with music and special effects.

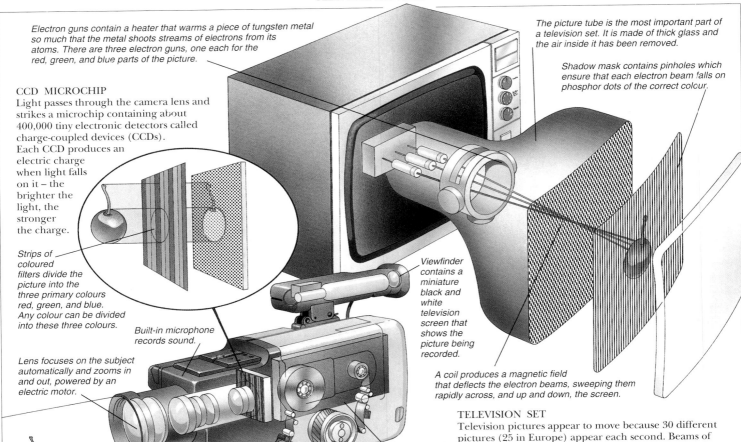

Electron guns contain a heater that warms a piece of tungsten metal so much that the metal shoots streams of electrons from its atoms. There are three electron guns, one each for the red, green, and blue parts of the picture.

The picture tube is the most important part of a television set. It is made of thick glass and the air inside it has been removed.

Shadow mask contains pinholes which ensure that each electron beam falls on phosphor dots of the correct colour.

CCD MICROCHIP
Light passes through the camera lens and strikes a microchip containing about 400,000 tiny electronic detectors called charge-coupled devices (CCDs). Each CCD produces an electric charge when light falls on it – the brighter the light, the stronger the charge.

Strips of coloured filters divide the picture into the three primary colours red, green, and blue. Any colour can be divided into these three colours.

Built-in microphone records sound.

Lens focuses on the subject automatically and zooms in and out, powered by an electric motor.

Viewfinder contains a miniature black and white television screen that shows the picture being recorded.

A coil produces a magnetic field that deflects the electron beams, sweeping them rapidly across, and up and down, the screen.

TELEVISION SET
Television pictures appear to move because 30 different pictures (25 in Europe) appear each second. Beams of electrons (tiny charged particles from atoms) sweep across the inside surface of the screen, hitting dots of chemicals called phosphors. The electrons cause the dots to glow red, green, or blue, depending on the kind of phosphor in the dot. These primary colours combine to reproduce every colour in the picture.

Video head spins at high speed, arranging the magnetic particles on the tape to record the pictures and sound.

CAMCORDER
A tiny videocassette recorder combined with a video camera is called a camcorder. Like all television and video cameras, camcorders turn a picture into an electrical signal that represents colour and brightness. The signal can then be recorded as a pattern of magnetic particles on videotape.

VIDEO
Videocassette recorders store television pictures on magnetic tape that is similar to audiotape but wider and longer. A pattern of magnetic particles in the tape records the picture in a series of diagonal tracks. This allows the vast amounts of information contained in television pictures to be packed into a small space on the tape.

INVENTION
In 1926, Scottish engineer John Logie Baird (1888-1946) gave the first public demonstration of television. At about the same time, the Russian-American engineer Vladimir Zworykin (1889-1982) invented the electronic camera tube, which was more sophisticated than Baird's system and is the basis of today's television sets. In 1956 the American Ampex company first produced video-tape; videocassette recorders appeared in 1969, produced by Sony of Japan.

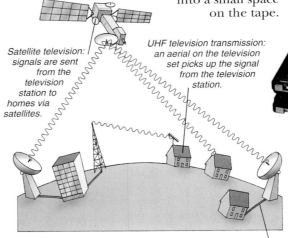

Satellite television: signals are sent from the television station to homes via satellites.

UHF television transmission: an aerial on the television set picks up the signal from the television station.

LCD TELEVISION
Instead of using a television tube which is very bulky, miniature televisions produce colour pictures using liquid crystal displays (LCDs), similar to that in a digital watch.

Cable television: a ground station picks up signals and sends them to homes via cables.

TELEVISION TRANSMISSION
Television signals can reach a viewer by several routes. Usually, transmitters broadcast television signals directly to homes as ultrahigh frequency (UHF) radio waves. Alternatively the signals go up to a satellite, which boosts them and rebroadcasts them to an area as large as a country. Dish antennas on individual homes receive the signals. In other cases, a ground station picks up the signals and sends them out along cables.

Find out more
CAMERAS
ELECTRONICS
RADIO
SOUND RECORDING

TEXTILES

SPINNING, WEAVING, AND KNITTING turn a mass of short fibres into something much more useful: a textile. We are surrounded by decorative textiles; most clothing is made from them. Textiles keep us warm because they trap air within their mesh of threads. The air acts as an insulator, preventing body heat from escaping. But textiles do much more than keep out the cold. Tightly woven artificial fibres are flexible but tough, so they are ideal for making knapsacks, sails, and parachutes. The loose-weave loops of natural fibres in a towel have a great thirst for water, drying us quickly after a bath. Some special textiles are as strong as armour; Kevlar fabric, for instance, can stop a bullet.

Textiles date back to the taming and breeding of animals about 12,000 years ago. The people of Mesopotamia (now Iraq) rolled sheep wool into a loose yarn for weaving clothes. Plant fibres such as cotton came later, and synthetic fibres have been available only since the invention of nylon in 1938.

SPINNING WHEEL
Spinning thread by twisting fibres between the fingers is hard work. The pedal-powered spinning wheel made the process quicker and easier.

Wool thread

Fibres of wool

SOURCES OF TEXTILES
Natural fibres for textiles come from cotton bolls, flax (for linen), fleece (for wool), and silk cocoons. Synthetic fibres, such as nylon, are made of chemicals that are mostly produced from crude oil.

Cotton boll

SPINNING
Natural fibres in a boll or fleece are tangled together. Spinning machines separate the fibres. They then twist natural or synthetic fibres together so the fibres firmly grip each other and form a strong thread.

Crude oil

Fleece

SYNTHETIC FIBRES
Squeezing a liquid called a polymer through tiny holes makes synthetic fibres. The polymer sets as it emerges.

WEAVING AND KNITTING
Looms are machines that crisscross long threads to make woven textiles. Knitting by hand requires just a pair of needles, but a machine does the job more quickly. Pressing unspun fibres together produces a thick textile called felt that is often used for hats.

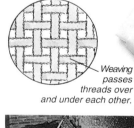
Weaving passes threads over and under each other.

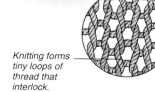

FINISHING TEXTILES
Many textiles are printed with beautiful patterns. Batik (above) uses wax or other materials to make a pattern by restricting where the dye penetrates the fabric. Special treatments make textiles fluffy or waterproof, or stop them from shrinking or wrinkling.

Knitting forms tiny loops of thread that interlock.

CARPET MAKING
A carpet loom weaves strong threads of wool, cotton, or synthetic fibres onto a mesh backing to make a carpet. The threads may also be knotted together or formed into loops. Cutting the loops turns the tufts of fibres into a carpet pile.

Find out more

BUTTERFLIES AND MOTHS
CLOTHES
INDUSTRIAL REVOLUTION
PLASTICS

THEATRE

AT THE HEART of all theatre lies the excitement of watching a live performance. Bringing a play to life involves many people. The words of the dramatist, or playwright, the ideas of the director, and the actors' skill combine to make an audience believe that what is happening on the stage – the drama – is real. Early theatre grew out of religious festivals held in Greece in honour of the god Dionysus, and included singing and dancing as well as acting. The different forms of theatre that emerged in India, China, and Japan also had religious origins. In the Middle Ages, European people watched "miracle plays", which were based on Bible stories. Later, dramatists began to write about all aspects of life, and companies of actors performed their plays in permanent theatres. Theatre changes to suit the demands of each new age for fantasy, spectacle, or serious drama.

OPEN-AIR THEATRE
Ancient Greek theatre made use of landscapes like this one at Delphi. Actors wore exaggerated masks so that characters could be recognized from afar.

HISTORY OF THE THEATRE

GREEK THEATRE
The audience sat in a semicircle of steplike seats. There was a circular orchestra – a space for dancing and singing – and a low stage for actors.

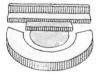

ROMAN THEATRE
Built on the level, the theatre was enclosed on three sides and a permanent wooden roof sheltered the raised stage.

THE OPEN STAGE
Some modern theatres have an open stage without a curtain. The actors can address the audience more directly, as if holding a conversation.

THEATRE-IN-THE-ROUND
Here the audience surrounds the cast on all four sides, bringing everyone close together. The actors enter through aisles between the seats.

THE GLOBE PLAYHOUSE
Shakespeare was an actor and a writer at this famous theatre on the south bank of the River Thames in London. There was room for more than 2,000 people in the round wooden building. The audience stood in the open yard or sat in the enclosed gallery to watch a performance. In 1995, the Globe was rebuilt at a nearby site in London.

INSIDE THE THEATRE

Fly ropes raise and lower the lights as they are needed.

Lowering the curtain, or tabs, hides the stage while stagehands change scenery.

Scenery and props wait in the wings for rapid scene changes.

By raising or angling the stage slightly the designer can change the audience's view.

Musicians may sit in an orchestra pit below the front of the stage.

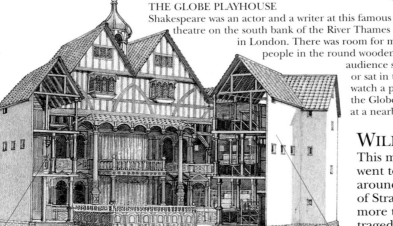

People could pay more to sit in galleries which protected them from the rain.

There was little scenery, and actors entered through doors at the back.

The walls were about 9 m (30 ft) high with tiny windows.

WILLIAM SHAKESPEARE

This most famous of all playwrights went to London as a young man around 1590 from his birthplace of Stratford-upon-Avon. He wrote more than 37 plays, including tragedies (*Hamlet*), comedies (*As You Like It*), and history plays (*Henry V*). He died in 1616 at the age of 52.

THE PICTURE FRAME
Clever use of scenery and a sloping stage helps to change the audience's view through the proscenium arch and makes the stage look deeper.

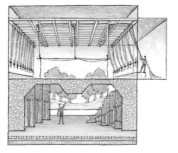

UP IN THE FLIES
High above the stage there is "fly" space in which scenery and equipment hang. A system of pulleys makes it possible to lower scenery.

DRAMA AND DRAMATISTS
Playwrights adapt drama to suit what they want to say. Watching the downfall of characters in a tragedy helps us to understand more about life. Comedy makes us laugh, but some dramatists, such as George Bernard Shaw, used it to say serious things about society. Modern dramatists such as Samuel Beckett and Bertolt Brecht have experimented with words and characters to push the boundaries of drama even further.

LAURENCE OLIVIER
Twentieth-century acting was dominated by Laurence Olivier. He took well-known roles such as Macbeth (left) and Henry V and found new ways to interpret them. Archie Rice in *The Entertainer* was one of his greatest roles. Olivier also directed plays and films, and part of the Royal National Theatre in London is named after him.

The flameproof safety curtain seals off the stage from the auditorium if fire breaks out.

Some of the actors share a dressing room where they put on makeup and change into costume.

Loudspeaker announcements warn the actors to get ready to make their entrance.

Actors who play the lead roles may have a dressing room to themselves.

The wardrobe department makes the costumes and stores them until needed.

PROFILE-SPOT
Stagehands control this light from the rear of the upper circle. They use the strong beam to pick out and follow an actor in a pool of brilliant light.

Actors enter and leave the theatre by the stage door.

The busy carpentry department builds the sets. Props, such as furniture, are stored here when not in use.

The elevator can lift an actor or prop onto the stage in a split second.

Most traditional theatres have a "picture frame" stage – the play takes place under a proscenium arch.

From the lighting control board or console, the operator can dim or brighten any light in the theatre. A lighting change can alter the mood of a play in seconds.

SOUND EFFECTS
Sound effects must happen at exactly the right moment. If an actor falls down before the sound of a gunshot, the whole scene is ruined. The sound operator listens and watches carefully for each cue.

Find out more

BALLET
LITERATURE
MUSIC
OPERA AND SINGING

TIME

HOURGLASS
Sand draining through an hourglass shows the passing of time. It takes one hour for the sand to run from the top to the bottom bulb.

HOUR FOLLOWS HOUR as time passes. Time always flows steadily in the same direction. Behind us in time lies the past, which we know. Ahead lies the future, which we cannot know. We cannot change time, but we can measure it. People first measured time in days and nights, which they could easily see and count. They also measured time in months, by watching the phases of the moon, and in years, by watching the cycle of the seasons. Today we have clocks and watches that can measure time in fractions of a second.

In 1905, a German physicist named Albert Einstein proposed the scientific theory of relativity. This says that time is not constant, but that it would pass more slowly if you could travel very fast (near the speed of light), or in strong fields of gravity. Scientists believe that time may even come to a stop in black holes deep in space.

In reality, the Earth is 400 times further away from the sun than it is from the moon.

Earth   Moon   Sun

YEARS AND MONTHS
A year is based on the time the Earth takes to go once around the sun, which is 365.26 days. Months vary from 28 to 31 days. They were originally based on the time the moon takes to go around the Earth, which is 27.3 days.

The International Date Line is at 180 degrees longitude.

3 p.m. in Moscow, Russian Federation

INTERNATIONAL DATE LINE
The western side of the International Date Line is one day ahead of the eastern side. When you cross the line, the date changes.

12 noon in London, Britain

TIME ZONES
The world is divided into 24 regions, called time zones, each with a different time of day. This was done to avoid having several time differences within one area, and to ensure that all countries have noon during the middle of the day.

2 p.m. in Cairo, Egypt

UNIVERSAL TIME
The time at the prime meridian is used as a standard time known as Universal Time (UT) or Greenwich Mean Time (GMT).

7 a.m. in New York City, U.S.A.

The Earth spins counterclockwise.

The prime meridian is at 0 degrees longitude.

UNITS OF TIME
One full day and night is the time in which the Earth spins once. This is divided into 24 hours: each hour contains 60 minutes, and each minute contains 60 seconds. The Babylonians fixed these units about 5,000 years ago, using 24 and 60 because they divide easily by 2, 3, and 4.

DAYS AND NIGHTS
The sun lights up one half of the Earth, where it is day. The other half, away from the sun, is dark, and there it is night. Days and nights come and go because the Earth spins once every 24 hours. But the day and night may last different lengths of time because the Earth is tilted at an angle to the sun.

9 a.m. in Rio de Janeiro, Brazil

The Hindu calendar is based on lunar months. Diwali, the Festival of Light, marks the start of the new year, which falls in October.

CALENDARS
The date is fixed by the calendar, which contains 12 months with a total of 365 days. Every fourth year is a leap year which has one extra day, February 29. Leap years are years that divide by four, such as 1996 and 2000. The calendar contains leap years because the Earth takes slightly longer than 365 days to go once around the sun. Prehistoric peoples may have used monuments such as Stonehenge, in southern England (below), to measure the sun's position and find the exact length of the year.

Twice a year the sun is directly overhead at 12 noon

Find out more
CLOCKS AND WATCHES
EARTH
PHYSICS
SCIENTISTS AND INVENTORS
STARS
UNIVERSE

TOYS

ALTHOUGH THE MAIN purpose of a toy is fun or amusement, toys have other functions too. Some toys prepare children for the activities of adult life. For example, hobby-horses helped children learn about horseriding long before they were old enough to sit in the saddle. Similarly, today's toy cars can teach driving skills. In the Middle Ages toys such as tops and rattles were popular, but in later centuries only rich families could afford the elaborate toys that became fashionable. In strict families the only toys allowed on Sunday were those associated with the Bible, such as a model of Noah's Ark. Today there are more toys than ever before. Children have a vast choice of mass-produced playthings, but there is still a demand for simple homemade toys just like those which amused Ancient Egyptian children.

HOOPS
With a little imagination everyday objects can become toys. A stick becomes a hobby-horse, an old box a doll's bed. For centuries children of many lands have used wooden wheels or rings from barrels as hoops. They can be rolled along, thrown in the air, or whirled around the body.

ANCIENT TOYS
Baked clay horses found in Egypt are almost 2,500 years old. Archaeologists in Rhodes, Greece, discovered small animals and riders which were even older. These ancient toys give us an idea of how children played long ago.

DOLLS
Dolls were among the first toys. They have been made from rags, wax, wood, and paper. During the last century dolls were beautifully dressed and had fragile china heads. Modern dolls are much sturdier and some are able to walk, talk, and eat.

The ball is a universal toy and is found in every society.

Blocks can be used for games of counting, balancing, and building.

ELECTRONIC TOYS
Battery-powered games test a player's mental agility and speed of reflexes. The computer brains inside are tiny, so even complex games are small enough to fit in a pocket.

TOY CARS
Both children and adults enjoy and collect model cars. Some toy cars move in any direction by remote control.

TEDDY BEARS
On a hunting trip in 1902, United States President Theodore "Teddy" Roosevelt refused to kill a bear cub. Soon after this was reported in the newspapers, a shopkeeper began to sell cuddly toys called "teddy bears". In Europe, a German company called Steiff made similar bears with movable arms and legs. This favourite toy now comes in all colours and sizes, but the basic shape remains the same.

CONSTRUCTION TOYS
Construction toys such as Lego really challenge building skills and imagination. Sections of various sizes fit together to create model forts, castles, and spacecraft.

Find out more
GAMES
PUPPETS

TRACK AND FIELD SPORTS

MOST SPORTS FANS like track and field sports, which have produced some of the greatest achievements in sports over the years. Track sports include sprinting, middle-distance running, walking, and hurdles, which involves leaping over low gates while running. They may take place on a track, a road, or a cross-country route. Field events are held in special arenas and include the high jump, the long jump, and several throwing events. All track and field events require stamina, speed, power, and determination. In the shortest sprinting events, competitors may reach speeds of 36 km/h (22 mph). Many people do not compete but pursue track and field sports purely for their fitness and health benefits.

MARATHON
Men and women of very mixed abilities take part in marathon races, run over a distance of 42.2 km (26 miles, 385 yards). Marathons usually follow a route around the closed streets of a city, such as New York.

RUNNING EVENTS
Races take place around the track in a counterclockwise direction. Runners in races up to 400 m (437 yds) must stay in lanes.

JUMPING EVENTS
These include triple jumps and the pole vault, for men only, and the broad and high jumps, for both men and women. Competitors in the broad and triple jumps land in sandpits; in the high jump and pole vault, they land on soft foam beds.

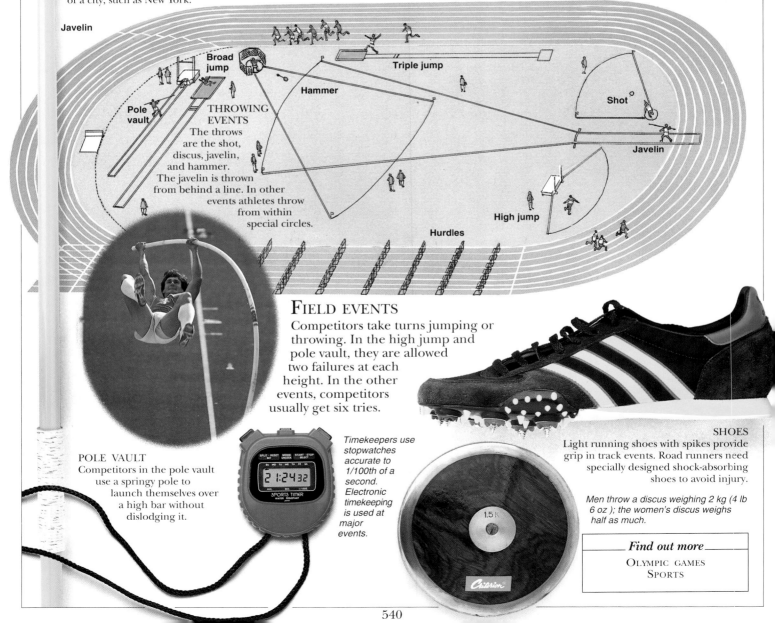

Javelin

Broad jump

Triple jump

Hammer

Pole vault

THROWING EVENTS
The throws are the shot, discus, javelin, and hammer. The javelin is thrown from behind a line. In other events athletes throw from within special circles.

Shot

Javelin

High jump

Hurdles

FIELD EVENTS
Competitors take turns jumping or throwing. In the high jump and pole vault, they are allowed two failures at each height. In the other events, competitors usually get six tries.

POLE VAULT
Competitors in the pole vault use a springy pole to launch themselves over a high bar without dislodging it.

Timekeepers use stopwatches accurate to 1/100th of a second. Electronic timekeeping is used at major events.

SHOES
Light running shoes with spikes provide grip in track events. Road runners need specially designed shock-absorbing shoes to avoid injury.

Men throw a discus weighing 2 kg (4 lb 6 oz); the women's discus weighs half as much.

Find out more
OLYMPIC GAMES
SPORTS

TRADE AND INDUSTRY

WITHOUT TRADE AND INDUSTRY, people would have to create everything they needed to live. If you wanted a loaf of bread you would have to grow wheat, grind the wheat to make flour, mix the dough, and bake it in an oven. You would also need to build the mill and make the oven! Industry organizes the production of bread, so that just a few farmers, millers, and bakers can make bread for everyone. Similarly, industry supplies us with most other essential and luxury goods, from fresh water to cars. Trade is the process of buying and selling. Trade gets the products from the people who make them to the people who need them. And through trade, manufacturers can buy the raw materials they need to supply their factories and keep production going. Together, the trade and industry of a nation are sometimes called the economy.

SILK ROAD
Trade between different regions and peoples goes back to ancient times. The Silk Road was one of the earliest and most famous trade routes. Traders led horses and camels along this route between 300 B.C. and A.D. 1600, carrying silk from China to Europe.

INTERNATIONAL TRADE
Goods move around the world by sea, land, and air. This international trade takes materials such as oil from the countries that have a surplus to those that have no oil deposits. International trade is also necessary because goods do not always fetch a high price in the country where they are made. For example, many clothes are made by hand in countries where wages are low. But the clothes are sold in another country where people are richer and can pay a high price.

India exports cotton textiles to Europe.

India exports tea to the Russian Federation.

India imports cars from Japan.

India imports oil from the Middle East.

India exports rice to Australia.

Imports

Exports

IMPORTS AND EXPORTS
Goods that are traded internationally are called imports and exports. Goods that one country sells to another are called exports; imports are goods that a country buys from another. In most nations, private businesses control imports and exports. But in others, the government imposes strict controls on what can be bought and sold.

TRADE AGREEMENTS
Some countries sign trade agreements in order to control trade between them. The agreement may simply fix the price at which the two countries buy and sell certain goods, such as wheat. The European Union (EU) has a complicated network of trade agreements which allow free exchange of goods between EU countries. The EU also restricts trade with countries that are not members of the community. This helps encourage industry in member countries.

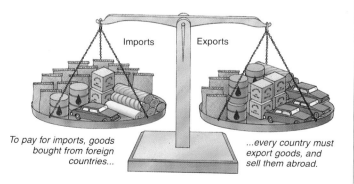

Imports

Exports

To pay for imports, goods bought from foreign countries...

...every country must export goods, and sell them abroad.

BALANCE OF PAYMENTS
Each country pays for imports with the money it earns by selling goods in other countries. This balance between imports and exports is called the balance of trade, or the balance of payments. Countries that do not export enough must borrow money abroad to pay for imports.

FACTORIES

Some industry takes place in people's homes, but workers in factories make most of the products that we buy. In a factory each person has a small task in the manufacturing process. He or she may operate a large machine or assemble something by hand. No one person makes an entire product. This process of mass production makes manufacturing cheaper and quicker. Most factories are owned by governments or large companies; a few factories are owned by the people who work in them.

SUPPLY AND DEMAND

In Communist countries the government decides what the factories will make and at what price it will be sold. In other countries, factories make and supply goods only if there is a demand for them. When fewer people buy the goods that the factory makes, demand falls, and the workers in the factory may lose their jobs.

A factory starts by making a small number of umbrellas.

Shops put a few umbrellas on sale at a high price.

Many people need umbrellas and buy them, increasing demand.

The factory employs more people to make more umbrellas.

When everyone has an umbrella, demand for umbrellas falls.

Prices drop, and the factory needs fewer umbrella workers.

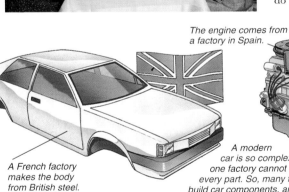

The restaurant industry provides the service of cooking and serving food and washing the dishes.

SERVICE INDUSTRIES

Not all industries make objects for sale. Some industries provide a service in return for money. A garage, for instance, might charge a fee to adjust a car so that it runs more efficiently. People pay for this service rather than do the work themselves.

The engine comes from a factory in Spain.

A French factory makes the body from British steel.

A modern car is so complex that one factory cannot make every part. So, many factories build car components, and an assembly plant builds the vehicle.

The transmission is made in Germany.

Final assembly of the car may take place in Spain.

MANUFACTURING

The basic form of industry is manufacturing. This means working on materials to manufacture, or make, a finished product. Almost everything we use is the product of manufacturing, and most manufacturing takes place in large factories. However, craftworkers manufacture goods alone or in small groups. Some goods go through many stages of manufacturing. For example, workers making cars assemble manufactured components or parts which in turn have been made in many other factories, often in other countries.

TRADE UNIONS

During the 19th century, workers began to form trade unions. The job of a trade union is to obtain better pay and conditions for its members. If the union is not successful, its members may go on strike – stop work – until their demands are met.

The successful strike of British women workers in a London match factory in 1888 encouraged other unskilled workers to join unions.

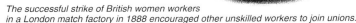

Find out more

ADVERTISING
DEPRESSION OF THE 1930s
INDUSTRIAL REVOLUTION
MONEY
SHOPS AND SHOPPING

TRAINS

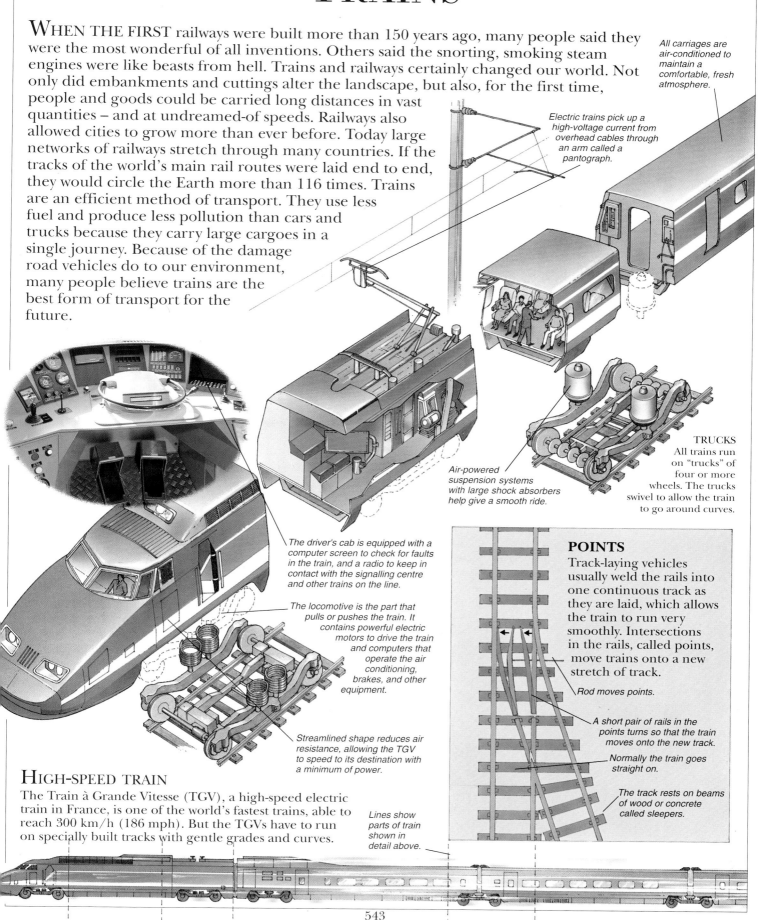

WHEN THE FIRST railways were built more than 150 years ago, many people said they were the most wonderful of all inventions. Others said the snorting, smoking steam engines were like beasts from hell. Trains and railways certainly changed our world. Not only did embankments and cuttings alter the landscape, but also, for the first time, people and goods could be carried long distances in vast quantities – and at undreamed-of speeds. Railways also allowed cities to grow more than ever before. Today large networks of railways stretch through many countries. If the tracks of the world's main rail routes were laid end to end, they would circle the Earth more than 116 times. Trains are an efficient method of transport. They use less fuel and produce less pollution than cars and trucks because they carry large cargoes in a single journey. Because of the damage road vehicles do to our environment, many people believe trains are the best form of transport for the future.

All carriages are air-conditioned to maintain a comfortable, fresh atmosphere.

Electric trains pick up a high-voltage current from overhead cables through an arm called a pantograph.

Air-powered suspension systems with large shock absorbers help give a smooth ride.

TRUCKS
All trains run on "trucks" of four or more wheels. The trucks swivel to allow the train to go around curves.

The driver's cab is equipped with a computer screen to check for faults in the train, and a radio to keep in contact with the signalling centre and other trains on the line.

The locomotive is the part that pulls or pushes the train. It contains powerful electric motors to drive the train and computers that operate the air conditioning, brakes, and other equipment.

Streamlined shape reduces air resistance, allowing the TGV to speed to its destination with a minimum of power.

HIGH-SPEED TRAIN

The Train à Grande Vitesse (TGV), a high-speed electric train in France, is one of the world's fastest trains, able to reach 300 km/h (186 mph). But the TGVs have to run on specially built tracks with gentle grades and curves.

Lines show parts of train shown in detail above.

POINTS
Track-laying vehicles usually weld the rails into one continuous track as they are laid, which allows the train to run very smoothly. Intersections in the rails, called points, move trains onto a new stretch of track.

Rod moves points.

A short pair of rails in the points turns so that the train moves onto the new track.

Normally the train goes straight on.

The track rests on beams of wood or concrete called sleepers.

RICHARD TREVITHICK

In 1801, a steam locomotive (right) built by Englishman Richard Trevithick ran on rails for the first time. Trevithick thought that steam power had a future, and bet that his steam engine could haul 9 tonnes (9 tons) of iron 15 km (9.5 miles) along a mine railway in Wales. Trevithick won his bet; the engine carried not only the iron but also 70 cheering coal miners who climbed aboard.

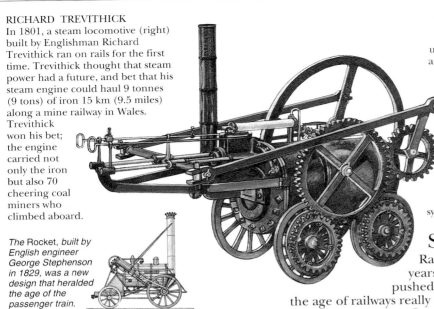

UNDERGROUND TRAINS

In crowded cities, underground trains are the quickest way to travel. The first underground system was opened in London in 1863. Now many cities have their own network. The Metro in Paris is one of the most efficient underground systems in the world.

The Rocket, *built by English engineer George Stephenson in 1829, was a new design that heralded the age of the passenger train.*

A front truck was introduced on early American locomotives to give a smoother ride around curves.

During the mid-1800s, England's railway system developed into a large network.

Engines could reach 200 km/h (126 mph) by the 1930s – the peak of the steam age.

Steam locomotives of the 1930s were very sophisticated compared to the first engines.

STEAM RAILWAYS

Railways date back 4,000 years to the Babylonians, who pushed carts along grooves. But the age of railways really began in the early 1800s when steam engines first ran on rails. In 1825, the first passenger line opened in England; 30 years later, vast railway systems stretched across Europe and North America. By the 1890s, steam engines could reach speeds of more than 160 km/h (100 mph).

SIGNALS AND SAFETY

Trackside signals tell the driver how fast to go and when to stop. In the past, signals were mechanical arms worked by levers in the signal box. Nowadays they are usually sets of coloured lights controlled by computers that monitor the position of every train.

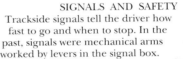

MAGLEVS AND MONORAILS

One day we may be whisked along silently at speeds of 480 km/h (300 mph) on trains that glide a small distance above special tracks, held up by magnetic force – which is why they are called Maglevs (for magnetic levitation). Some countries, such as Japan, already have Maglev lines. Other new designs include monorail trains, which are electric trains that run on, or are suspended from, a single rail.

ORIENT EXPRESS

Some trains have become famous for their speed, some for their luxury, and others for the length of their route. From 1883, the Orient Express, for example, provided a first-class service from Paris to Constantinople (Istanbul), Turkey. It still travels part of this route today. The world's longest train route is the Trans-Siberian Express, which runs 9,438 km (5,864 miles) across Siberia.

Find out more
BUSES
ENGINES
TRANSPORTATION, HISTORY OF

HISTORY OF
TRANSPORT

WE LIVE IN AN AGE when people can fly across the Atlantic Ocean in less than three hours. Straight roads link city to city across the world. Yet 7,000 years ago the only way that people could get from one place to another was by walking. In around 5,000 B.C. people began to use donkeys and oxen as pack animals, instead of carrying their goods on their backs or heads. Then, 1,500 years later, the first wheeled vehicles developed in Mesopotamia. From around A.D. 1500, deep-sea sailing ships developed rapidly as Europeans began to make great ocean voyages to explore the rest of the world. During the 1700s, steam power marked another milestone in transport. Steam engines were soon moving ships and trains faster than anyone had imagined. During the next century the first cars took to the road and the first flying machines took to the air.

STAGECOACH
So called because they stopped at stages on a route to change horses, stagecoaches were the most popular type of public land transport during the 17th and 18th centuries.

Railways began to appear in the United States in the 1820s. Trains could carry more goods and people than any other kind of transport.

LAND TRAVEL

Land travel is the most common kind of transport. It all began with walking. Two thousand years ago the Romans built a network of superb roads over which people travelled by foot or by horse-drawn cart. It was only in the 1800s that steam power took the place of horse power. Steam locomotives provided cheap long-distance travel for ordinary people. In the early years of this century, engine-powered cars, trucks, and buses were developed.

CARS
Cars are now the most popular form of private transport. Yet they were invented only a hundred years ago.

JUNK
One of the world's strongest sailing ships, the junk has been used in Asia for thousands of years. Mainly a trading vessel, it has large, highly efficient sails made of linen or matting.

BARGE
A barge is a sturdy boat which transports cargo, such as coal, from place to place along canals and rivers.

Ocean liners (below) are used as floating hotels. They take passengers on cruises and call at different resorts along the way.

SEA TRAVEL

Floating logs led to the first watercraft, the simple raft. In around 3500 B.C. the Sumerians and the Egyptians made fishing boats out of reeds from the riverbank. They also built watertight wooden ships with oars and a sail, for seagoing voyages. In the 19th century, steel replaced wood, and steam engines gradually took over from sails. Today's engine-powered ships can carry huge loads of cargo at speeds never reached under sail.

AIR TRAVEL

In 1783 the Frenchmen Pilâtre de Rozier and the marquis d'Arlandes made the first human flight in a hot air balloon. Then, in 1903, to everyone's amazement, brothers Orville and Wilbur Wright built and flew the first powered plane near Kitty Hawk, North Carolina. Aircraft developed rapidly in the two world wars that followed. In 1918, the U.S. Post Office began the first airmail service. Today it is hard to imagine a world without aircraft.

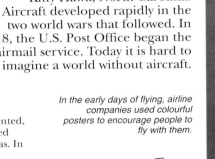

In the early days of flying, airline companies used colourful posters to encourage people to fly with them.

BALLOONS

Long before aeroplanes were invented, people flew in balloons – bags filled with hot air or a lighter-than-air gas. In 1783, the Montgolfier brothers of France built the first balloon to lift humans into the air. Balloons were used by the French emperor Napoleon as flying lookout posts, and later during the Civil War and World War I. Today, ballooning is a popular sport.

AEROPLANES

Today millions of people depend on aeroplanes for both business and pleasure. But the golden age of aeroplane development occurred only 80 years ago, when daring pilots took great risks in testing aeroplanes and flying long distances. Jet-powered passenger aeroplanes appeared in the 1950s. The first supersonic airliner, *Concorde*, entered service in 1976. At 2,494 km/h (1,550 mph), it travels faster than sound.

SPACE TRAVEL

Not content with the sky, humans wanted to explore space and distant planets as well. In 1957, the Soviets fired the first satellite, *Sputnik*, into orbit (a path around the Earth). In 1968, the United States sent the first manned craft around the moon. Then in 1969 astronaut Neil Armstrong became the first person to walk on the moon.

The Apollo II spacecraft

POLLUTION-FREE TRANSPORT

Many of today's forms of powered transport pollute the environment because their engines send out dangerous gases. Cars, in particular, upset the natural balance of the atmosphere. Lead-free petrol helps reduce the amount of poison which cars release into the air. The transport systems that cause the least pollution are those using natural power, such as wind. On land, people can help preserve our planet by walking, bicycling, or using animals to pull wheeled vehicles. At sea, large loads can be moved in sailing ships powered only by the wind.

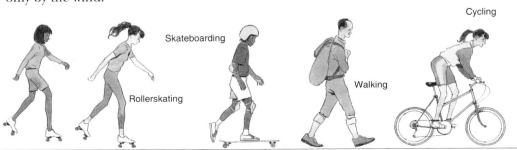

Skateboarding

Rollerskating

Walking

Cycling

Find out more
AIRCRAFT
BALLOONS AND AIRSHIPS
CARS
SAILING AND BOATING
TRAINS

TREES

WITHOUT PLANTS such as trees there could be no life on Earth. Trees take in carbon dioxide from the air and give off oxygen by the process of photosynthesis, so maintaining the balance of the atmosphere. Tree roots stabilize the soil so it is not washed away by the rain, and their leaves give off vast amounts of water vapour, which affects the balance of the world's weather. Forests cover about 39 million sq km (15 million square miles) of the planet's surface. Trees vary greatly in size, from huge redwoods to dwarf snow willows, only a few centimetres high. They supply food for millions of creatures, and produce wood to make buildings, furniture – even the pages of this book.

Giant sequoia trees are the largest living things – more than 90 m (270 ft) high, and 2,000 tonnes (1,970 tons) in weight; an elephant weighs about 5 tonnes (5 tons).

English oak tree in spring and autumn.

Leaves

Buds

Oak bark

Acorns are the fruits of the oak tree; they develop from the female flowers during autumn.

CONIFEROUS TREES

Pines, firs, cedars, and redwoods are called coniferous trees, or conifers, because they grow their seeds in hard, woody cones. The long, narrow leaves, called needles, stay on the tree all winter. These trees are also called evergreens, because they stay green all year.

CONES
Each tree has its own type of cone, which develops from the fertilized female flowers.

Larch cones

Scots pine needles grow in pairs.

Pine cones

Arolla pine needles

Conifer roots usually spread out sideways.

BROAD-LEAVED TREES

Oaks, beeches, willows, and many other trees are called broad-leaved because their leaves are broad and flat, unlike the sharp needles on coniferous trees. Some broad-leaved trees are also called deciduous, because their leaves die and drop off in autumn.

The roots of a deciduous tree may reach out sideways to the same distance as the tree's height.

Sitka spruce cone turns brown as it ripens.

NEEDLES
Every conifer has distinctively shaped needles that grow in a certain pattern. Sitka spruce needles are long and sharp.

Sitka spruce is an evergreen coniferous tree often seen in forest plantations.

LEAVES
Broad-leaved trees can be recognized by the shape of their leaves and the pattern in which the leaves grow on the twigs. In winter, you can identify a bare tree by its bark, buds, and overall shape.

Japanese maple leaves have deep notches.

Leaves of the holly tree are spiky.

The gingko tree has fan-shaped leaves.

Rowan or mountain ash trees have feathery leaves.

Sweet chestnut leaves have a jagged edge.

GROWTH

All trees grow from small seeds inside their fruits. Each seed contains a food store and a tiny embryo tree. The seed begins to grow when the temperature and moisture of the soil are suitable. A young tree is called a sapling.

Beech seed (or beechnut) is contained in hard seed case.

Root begins to emerge.

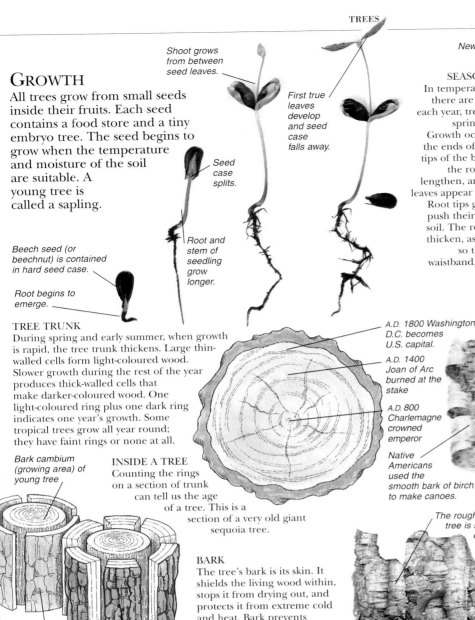

Shoot grows from between seed leaves.

First true leaves develop and seed case falls away.

Seed case splits.

Root and stem of seedling grow longer.

SEASONAL GROWTH

In temperate regions, where there are definite seasons each year, trees grow during spring and summer. Growth occurs mainly at the ends of the tree, the tips of the branches, and the roots. The twigs lengthen, and flowers and leaves appear from the buds. Root tips grow longer and push their way through the soil. The roots and branches thicken, as does the tree trunk, so that the tree's girth, or waistband, also increases in size.

New leaves develop each spring.

Twig tips grow.

Trunk and branches thicken.

Roots become fatter.

Root tips lengthen.

TREE TRUNK

During spring and early summer, when growth is rapid, the tree trunk thickens. Large thin-walled cells form light-coloured wood. Slower growth during the rest of the year produces thick-walled cells that make darker-coloured wood. One light-coloured ring plus one dark ring indicates one year's growth. Some tropical trees grow all year round; they have faint rings or none at all.

A.D. 1800 Washington, D.C. becomes U.S. capital.

A.D. 1400 Joan of Arc burned at the stake

A.D. 800 Charlemagne crowned emperor

Native Americans used the smooth bark of birch trees to make canoes.

INSIDE A TREE

Counting the rings on a section of trunk can tell us the age of a tree. This is a section of a very old giant sequoia tree.

Bark cambium (growing area) of young tree

Young bark is smooth.

Bark grows from the inside and pushes the older bark outwards.

Old bark cracks and flakes.

Coconut palm tree

BARK

The tree's bark is its skin. It shields the living wood within, stops it from drying out, and protects it from extreme cold and heat. Bark prevents damage from moulds, but some animals, such as deer and beavers, eat the bark, and a few wood-boring beetles can tunnel through. A tree with no leaves can be identified by the colour and texture of its bark.

The rough bark of the cork tree is stripped off every eight to ten years; it is used to make bottle stoppers and floor tiles.

PALM TREES

The 2,700 kinds of palm trees are found in warm Mediterranean and tropical regions. These tall, straight trees provide many products including palm oils, dates, and coconuts from the coconut palm.

The outer husk of the coconut is used to make coconut matting. Coconuts are a valuable source of milk, edible fats, and animal food.

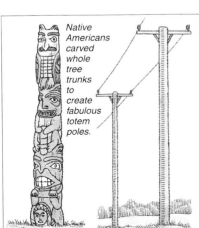

Native Americans carved whole tree trunks to create fabulous totem poles.

WOOD

Every year we use thousands of tonnes of wood for furniture, tools, building, fuel, cooking, and paper. As the world's population increases, vast areas of forests are cut down in ever-increasing numbers, particularly in South America, where much of the tropical rain forest has been destroyed.

People use whole tree trunks to make telephone poles.

In the past, loggers had to float logs downstream to the sawmill.

___*Find out more*___

FOREST WILDLIFE
FRUITS AND SEEDS
PLANTS
SOIL

TRUCKS AND LORRIES

FROM THE SMALLEST van to the largest juggernaut that towers over all other traffic, trucks and lorries play a vital role in all our lives. They are powerful, rugged vehicles designed to carry goods of all kinds. They transport food to shops, raw materials to factories, fuel to power stations, and much more. In many countries, trucks and lorries now carry all but the very bulkiest goods. Trains can carry larger loads, but they are not nearly as adaptable. A lorry or truck can pick up and deliver goods from door to door. It can be specially built to carry nearly any kind of load – big or small, heavy or light, liquid or solid. And a truck can reach remote places far from the nearest railway. For the icy settlements of Finland, the desert towns of the Middle East, and many starving people in countries such as Ethiopia, trucks are an essential lifeline.

ROUGH-ROAD LORRIES

Trucks and lorries are often the only way to get goods in and out of rugged mountain regions. But to survive the rough tracks, the trucks have to be tough and reliable. They also need big wheels to give plenty of ground clearance.

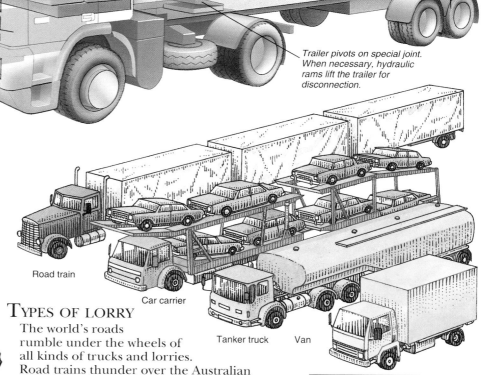

The air deflector, a specially shaped metal flap, helps air flow smoothly over the tractor and trailer and cuts down on fuel consumption.

Long-distance lorry drivers spend many hours on the road, so the cab is made as comfortable as possible. Many cabs contain a bed for overnight stops.

The turbocharged diesel engine is very powerful, because it must pull heavy loads. Some lorries have up to 20 forward and 10 reverse gears, allowing them to cope with all kinds of road conditions.

Double wheels to spread the load over a bigger road area

Cab tips forward to make the engine easier to work on.

Trailer pivots on special joint. When necessary, hydraulic rams lift the trailer for disconnection.

ARTICULATED LORRIES

Most large, modern lorries are articulated, or jointed. The load is pulled along on a separate trailer behind a tractor unit containing the engine and the driver's cab. Because an articulated lorry bends, it is much more maneuverable than a rigid one. Articulated lorries have different kinds of trailers that are built to carry a wide range of loads, such as food, wood, oil, and animals.

SPECIAL VEHICLES

There are several kinds of lorries and trucks that are designed for special purposes. Many carry particularly large or heavy loads, such as this coal truck (below), or the huge trailer that carries the space shuttle to its launch pad.

Road train

Car carrier

Tanker truck   Van

TYPES OF LORRY

The world's roads rumble under the wheels of all kinds of trucks and lorries. Road trains thunder over the Australian plains hauling two, or even three, trailers to keep costs low. Car carriers have trailers too, to take up to 18 cars. Tanker trucks carry petrol, wine, milk, and even flour. Most common are vans, which are able to carry many small loads.

Find out more
BUSES
CARS
TRANSPORTATION, HISTORY OF

TUNNELS

A CITY HIDES MANY of its most important structures from view; some we never see at all. Among these are tunnels, and a city may be honeycombed with them. Beneath the streets run tunnels carrying trains, pedestrians, motor vehicles, sewage, water supplies from reservoirs, and even small rivers. These kinds of tunnels serve cities and towns. Other tunnels allow trains and motor vehicles to pass through hills and mountains and under rivers and seas. Canals, which must be level, sometimes have tunnels to take boats under hills. Mine systems have the deepest tunnels of all. People dug tunnels in ancient times, hacking out the rock with picks. On the island of Samos in Greece, a tunnel dug in about 525 B.C. can still be seen. It is 1 km (3,400 ft) long. The tunnel was started from both ends, and the teams of diggers met in the middle of the mountain.

RECORD TUNNELS
The St. Gotthard Road Tunnel in Switzerland (above) is the world's longest road tunnel. It is 16 km (10 miles) long. The longest rail tunnel is the Seikan Rail Tunnel in Japan. It has a length of 54 km (33.5 miles). At 169 km (105 miles), a water supply tunnel in New York State, USA, is the longest of all.

KINDS OF TUNNELS
Many city tunnels are "cut-and-cover" tunnels. Machines excavate a deep trench; a cover is then placed over it. Other tunnels are bored through rock or soil, and may go much deeper. Still others, designed for use under rivers, are made in sections on land and joined together on the riverbed.

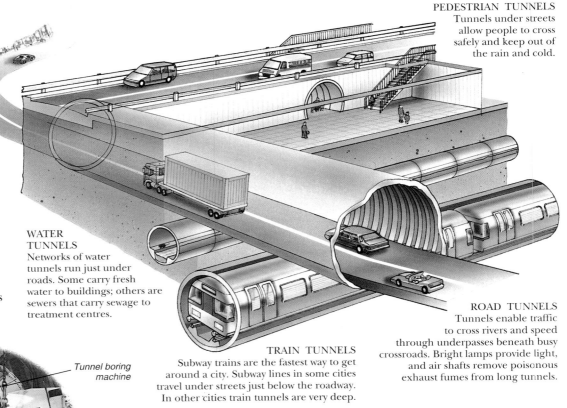

PEDESTRIAN TUNNELS
Tunnels under streets allow people to cross safely and keep out of the rain and cold.

WATER TUNNELS
Networks of water tunnels run just under roads. Some carry fresh water to buildings; others are sewers that carry sewage to treatment centres.

Tunnel boring machine

TRAIN TUNNELS
Subway trains are the fastest way to get around a city. Subway lines in some cities travel under streets just below the roadway. In other cities train tunnels are very deep.

ROAD TUNNELS
Tunnels enable traffic to cross rivers and speed through underpasses beneath busy crossroads. Bright lamps provide light, and air shafts remove poisonous exhaust fumes from long tunnels.

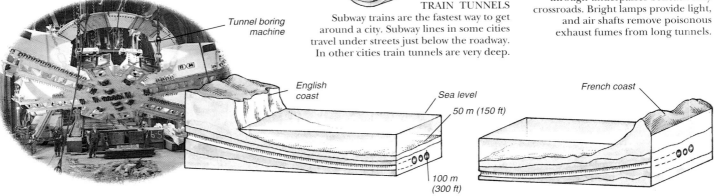

English coast

Sea level

50 m (150 ft)

French coast

100 m (300 ft)

BORING A TUNNEL
Huge tunnelling machines, often guided by lasers and computers, bore tunnels through rock and soil. At the front of the machine is a round cutting head that digs out the rock or soil. Sections of tunnel lining are fitted behind the cutting head. The lining supports the roof, floor, and sides of the tunnel.

CHANNEL TUNNEL
In 1987, work started on a 50- km (31-mile) rail tunnel under the English Channel, which links Britain and France. Special trains have been designed to carry cars through the tunnel. The Channel Tunnel opened for business in 1994.

Find out more

CITIES
COAL
TRAINS
WATER

UNDERWATER EXPLORATION

BENEATH THE WAVES lies another world waiting to be discovered. Divers go down to explore the edges of the underwater world. Only a few metres below the surface they can find fascinating sea creatures, beautifully coloured coral reefs, and strange rock formations. On the sea bed lie wrecks of ships which may have sunk hundreds of years ago. They contain pots, coins, and other objects which show how people lived in ancient times. Divers also work in the sea. They service underwater structures, such as oil rigs, and study life on the sea bed. But diving can be dangerous, and divers must follow strict safety rules.

The dark depths of the ocean lie beyond divers. Only submersibles, which are small submarines, can reach the ocean floor. There they have discovered previously unknown creatures and have studied undersea mountains and trenches that reveal the structure of the Earth.

DIVING BELL
Early underwater explorers used diving bells – air-filled chambers that were lowered to the sea bed.

SNORKELLING
By wearing a face mask and breathing through a tube called a snorkel, a swimmer can look down into the water and make short dives.

SCUBA DIVING
Self-contained underwater breathing apparatus (scuba for short) enables divers to swim underwater for an hour or so. The safe maximum depth for scuba diving is 50 m (160 ft).

REACHING THE DEPTHS

People can dive simply by holding their breath and swimming down into the water. But such dives are short-lived and shallow. In order to dive deeper, divers carry air cylinders or receive air pumped through tubes from the surface. Divers using special equipment can reach a maximum depth of approximately 500 m (1,600 ft). Underwater vessels take people on the deepest dives.

SUBMERSIBLES
Teams of people dive to the ocean floor in submersibles, which sometimes go as deep as 6,000 m (20,000 ft). The submersible dives from, and returns to, a mother ship on the surface.

Float contains petrol which keeps bathyscaphe weightless in the water.

UNDER-WATER ROBOTS
Robot submersibles are small and manoeuvrable. They collect samples and send television pictures to the surface.

Mechanical arms take samples and grip tools.

The steel cabin holds two crew members. Its spherical shape helps it withstand the enormous water pressure.

BATHYSCAPHES
Special deep-diving vessels called bathyscaphes can dive to the deepest sea bed. In 1960 the bathyscaphe *Trieste* dived almost 11 km (7 miles) to reach the very deepest part of the ocean, the Marianas Trench in the Pacific Ocean. The descent took nearly five hours.

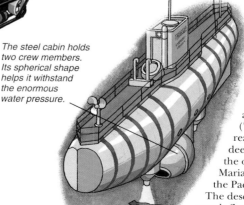

EXPLORING THE *TITANIC*
In 1986, the U.S. submersible *Alvin* explored the wreck of the great ocean liner *Titanic*. The crew used a robot submersible, called *Jason Junior* (left), to inspect the hull and look inside the ship. The *Titanic*, which was thought to be unsinkable, struck an iceberg on its maiden voyage in 1912. It sank more than 3.2 km (2 miles) to the floor of the North Atlantic Ocean.

SCUBA EQUIPMENT

A diver needs several pieces of equipment to survive underwater. An aqualung provides air, and a wet suit keeps the diver warm. A buoyancy jacket may also be necessary, since divers tend to sink in the water as they dive deeper. The diver maintains a constant depth by blowing air into or expelling air from the jacket.

A computer indicates the amount of air in the cylinder, the depth of the water, the duration of the dive, and the safe speed at which the diver should return to the surface.

Face mask made of rubber and toughened glass

Snorkel for use in emergencies

Weights on the belt cancel out the buoyancy of the diving suit and help the diver sink. The belt can be released in an emergency.

A film of water trapped between the rubber wet suit and the diver's body prevents heat from escaping and keeps the diver warm in cold water.

Knife

Scuba divers wear large fins, or flippers, to propel themselves through the water.

Mouthpiece for inflating buoyancy jacket in emergency

Mouthpiece and demand valve

Air from the aqualung inflates the buoyancy jacket. The emergency cylinder can be used if the main one fails, or the diver can blow into the mouthpiece.

Emergency air cylinder

Main air cylinder

Compass for navigating underwater

Lever opens and closes air inlet valve.

Diaphragm moves in and out as diver inhales and exhales.

Tube from air cylinder

Air outlet valve opens when diver breathes out.

Air inlet valve

AQUALUNG

The diver breathes from an aqualung, which consists of an air cylinder, a pressure-reducing valve, and a tube that leads air to the mouthpiece. The cylinder contains air at high pressure. The diver can only breathe in air at the same pressure as the surrounding water. The demand valve on the mouthpiece automatically controls the air pressure so the diver can breathe in and out easily.

Two Frenchmen, Jacques Cousteau (above) and Émile Gagnan, invented the aqualung in 1943. Later Cousteau became a famous underwater explorer.

ATMOSPHERIC DIVING SUIT

Divers can reach greater depths, make longer dives, and avoid the dangers of the bends by using an atmospheric diving suit. This suit encloses the diver's body, and has its own air supply so the diver can breathe normally.

Buoyancy tank

Hand-operated manipulators

Thrusters propel suit.

The spherical cabin can be released from Alvin to carry the crew back to the surface in an emergency.

DANGERS OF DIVING

Air contains nitrogen gas. Increasing pressure forces nitrogen into a scuba diver's blood as he or she dives deeper. Too much nitrogen is harmful, so the diver must not dive too deep or stay too long. The diver must return slowly from a deep dive, or the nitrogen forms bubbles in the blood. This condition, called the bends, is very painful and can cause permanent injury.

Spherical cabin resists the pressure of the surrounding water.

Thrusters for manoeuvring in the water

Ballast tanks to adjust buoyancy of submersible

Thrusters for propulsion

Batteries power motors

Television camera

Twin-lens stereo camera

Manipulator arm

Porthole

Equipment tray

UNDERWATER ARCHAEOLOGY

Ancient vessels often carried pottery containers called amphorae.

Divers are able to uncover the wrecks of old ships just as archaeologists on land dig up the remains of old buildings. They carefully recover objects from the shipwrecks, some of which contain treasure. A few ships have been raised to the surface and preserved.

THE *ALVIN* SUBMERSIBLE

Since it began service in 1964, *Alvin* has made more than 2,000 dives deep into the world's oceans. The submersible mainly undertakes scientific research. Three people – one pilot and two scientists – make dives of six to ten hours to a maximum depth of 4,000 m (13,120 ft).

Find out more

DEEP-SEA WILDLIFE
OCEANS AND SEAS
SUBMARINES

UNITED KINGDOM

BRITAIN, AS THE UNITED KINGDOM of Great Britain and Northern Ireland is usually known, is not one country but four. It is made up of England, Wales, and Scotland, which together form the island of Great Britain, and the province of Northern Ireland. Each of the four parts is quite different. The English countryside is famed for its gently sloping hills and rich farmland. Wales and Scotland are mostly wild and mountainous. Much of Northern Ireland is low-lying and marshy. Although English is the national language it is spoken with a strong accent in the different regions of the country. In Wales and parts of Scotland, many of the people speak a language of their own. Britain is a multicultural country, for the English, Scots, Welsh, and Irish are all separate peoples. And in the last 100 years refugees and immigrants from Europe, Africa, India, and the Caribbean have settled in Britain, bringing with them their own languages and religions. Britain is a rich country and once controlled a vast empire that stretched around the world. In recent years its economy has declined, but the discovery of oil in the North Sea has helped to make the country self-sufficient in energy.

The United Kingdom lies off the northwest coast of Europe. The North Sea lies to its east and the Atlantic Ocean to its north and west. The English Channel separates the country from the mainland.

Distinctive black taxis and double-decker buses ferry Londoners around their city.

LONDON
When the Roman armies invaded Britain almost 2,000 years ago, they built a fortified town called Londinium to safeguard the crossing over the River Thames. By 1100, the city of London had grown in size to become the capital of the entire country. Today, London is a huge city of nearly 7 million people and is the political, financial, and cultural centre of Britain. Tourists come from all over the world to admire the historic buildings, particularly the Tower of London (left), an 11th-century fortress.

Cricket began in Britain, and is the country's national sport. Many villages have their own teams.

CITY OF LONDON
The ancient heart of London is called the City. London is one of the world's leading financial centres, and most of the nation's banks and businesses have their headquarters here. The modern building shown on the left is the Lloyd's Building, where the world's shipping is registered and insured.

ENGLAND
The biggest and most populated part of the United Kingdom is England. Many people live in large towns and cities, such as London, Birmingham, and Manchester. Parts of the southeast and the north are very crowded. The English countryside is varied, with rolling farmland in the south and east and hilly moors in the north and west. England is dotted with picturesque villages where old houses and shops are often grouped around a village green.

The rose is the national flower of England.

UNITED KINGDOM

STATISTICS

Area: 244,017 sq km (94,215 sq miles)
Population: 57,065,000
Capital: London
Language: English
Religions: Protestant, Roman Catholic
Currency: Pound sterling
Highest point: Ben Nevis (Scotland) 1,343 m (4,406 ft)
Longest river: Severn (England, Wales) 354 km (220 miles)
Main occupations: Service industry, manufacturing, financial services
Main exports: Manufactured goods, machinery, vehicles, textiles, chemicals, electrical goods, metal products, aircraft
Main imports: Machinery, fruit, vegetables, metals, minerals, raw materials

ENGLAND
Area: 130,360 sq km (50,332 sq miles)
Population: 47,536,000
Capital: London

SCOTLAND
Area: 78,769 sq km (30,412 sq miles)
Population: 5,094,000
Capital: Edinburgh

WALES
Area: 20,767 sq km (8,018 sq miles)
Population: 2,857,000
Capital: Cardiff

NORTHERN IRELAND
Area: 14,121 sq km (5,452 sq miles)
Population: 1,578,000
Capital: Belfast

NORTHERN ENGLAND
The north of England has traditionally been the most heavily industrialized part of the United Kingdom. In the Industrial Revolution of the 19th century, factories and mills made goods for export to a British empire that covered half the world. Today the industrial cities of the north remain, but many of the factories stand empty because manufacturing is more profitable in other parts of the world. Northern England is also famous for its natural beauty; in the northwest is a rugged, mountainous region called the Lake District. Here deep lakes separate steep hills which rise to a height of more than 975 m (3,200 ft). The Lake District is beautiful and attracts many visitors and tourists.

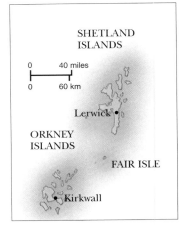

SHETLAND ISLANDS

| 0 | 40 miles |
| 0 | 60 km |

Lerwick

ORKNEY ISLANDS

FAIR ISLE

Kirkwall

SHETLAND AND ORKNEY
To the northeast of Scotland, two groups of islands form Britain's most northerly outposts. Orkney and Shetland comprise about 170 islands in all, but only the larger islands are inhabited. The landscape is bleak and there are few trees. The land is too poor to make farming profitable, and the traditional local industry is fishing. The islands are also famous for their hand-knitted wool clothes: Fair Isle has given its name to a distinctive knitting pattern.

PEOPLE
Britain is a large and crowded island. The most densely populated area is the southeast of England, and 12 per cent of Britain's population lives in the London metropolitan area alone. The southeast is also the most prosperous. Other parts of Britain are less crowded; although three quarters of Britain's land is farmed, few people have their homes in the countryside; most live in one of the large cities.

JERSEY AND GUERNSEY
The Channel Islands of Jersey and Guernsey are closer to France than they are to Britain. The French coast is just 24 km (15 miles) away from Jersey, the largest island. Close to Jersey and Guernsey are some smaller islands that are also part of the Channel Islands group. All of the islands have a mild climate, so one of the principal occupations is the growing of vegetables. The warm weather and ample sunshine also attract holidaymakers, who in the summer months swell the islands' usual population of 145,000.

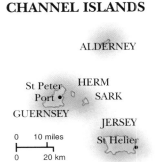

CHANNEL ISLANDS

ALDERNEY

St Peter Port

HERM

SARK

GUERNSEY

JERSEY

St Helier

| 0 | 10 miles |
| 0 | 20 km |

OUTER
HEBRIDES

THE
MINCH

John
o'Groats

SKYE

MORAY FIRTH

ATLANTIC
OCEAN

Loch
Ness

Aberdeen

SCOTLAND

▲ Ben Nevis,
1,343 m
(4,406 ft)

R. Tay

MULL

Grampian
Mountains

Dundee

JURA

Loch
Lomond

FIRTH OF FORTH

★ Edinburgh

IRELAND

ISLAY

Glasgow

ARRAN

R. Clyde

R. Tweed

Southern Uplands

Cheviot Hills

Giant's
Causeway

Hadrian's Wall

Newcastle upon Tyne

R. Tyne

Sunderland

R. Bann

SOLWAY FIRTH

Londonderry

NORTHERN
IRELAND

★ Belfast

Lake District

R. Eden

R. Tees

0   50 miles

0   40 km

R. Blackwater

Mourne
Mts.

Windermere

ISLE OF MAN

REPUBLIC OF
IRELAND

Pennine Chain

York

Blackpool

Bradford

R. Ouse

Kingston upon Hull

IRISH SEA

Leeds

R. Humber

NORTH SEA

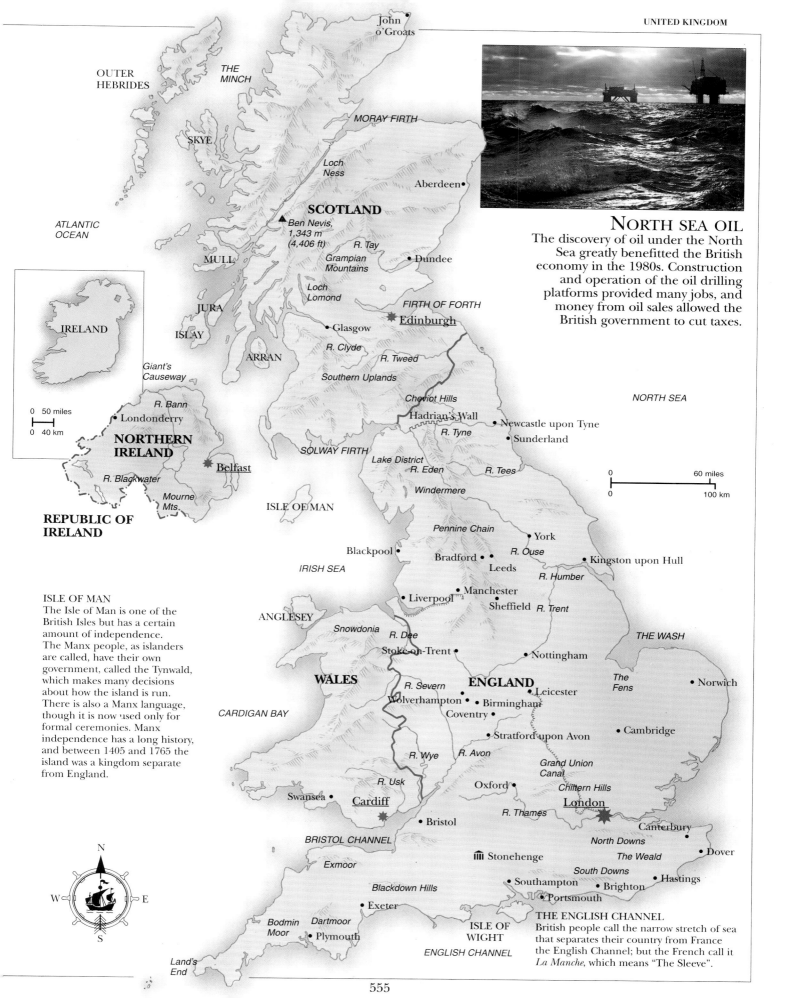

NORTH SEA OIL
The discovery of oil under the North Sea greatly benefitted the British economy in the 1980s. Construction and operation of the oil drilling platforms provided many jobs, and money from oil sales allowed the British government to cut taxes.

0   60 miles

0   100 km

ISLE OF MAN
The Isle of Man is one of the British Isles but has a certain amount of independence. The Manx people, as islanders are called, have their own government, called the Tynwald, which makes many decisions about how the island is run. There is also a Manx language, though it is now used only for formal ceremonies. Manx independence has a long history, and between 1405 and 1765 the island was a kingdom separate from England.

Manchester

Liverpool

Sheffield

R. Trent

ANGLESEY

Snowdonia

R. Dee

Stoke-on-Trent

THE WASH

Nottingham

WALES

ENGLAND

The
Fens

Norwich

R. Severn

Leicester

CARDIGAN BAY

Wolverhampton

Birmingham

Coventry

Cambridge

Stratford upon Avon

R. Wye

R. Avon

Grand Union
Canal

R. Usk

Oxford

Chiltern Hills

Swansea

Cardiff

London

Canterbury

Bristol

R. Thames

Dover

BRISTOL CHANNEL

North Downs

🏛 Stonehenge

The Weald

Exmoor

South Downs

Hastings

Blackdown Hills

Southampton

Brighton

Portsmouth

Exeter

ISLE OF
WIGHT

THE ENGLISH CHANNEL
British people call the narrow stretch of sea that separates their country from France the English Channel; but the French call it *La Manche*, which means "The Sleeve".

Bodmin
Moor

Dartmoor

Plymouth

ENGLISH CHANNEL

Land's
End

N
W   E
S

A Welsh village has the longest placename in the United Kingdom.

LLANFAIRPWLLGWYNGYLLGOGERYCHWYRN-DROBWLLLLANTYSILIOGOGOGOCH

PUBLIC HOUSES

Public houses, more usually called pubs, developed from inns which offered travellers food, drink, and shelter. The pub played a part in British culture, too. In the *Canterbury Tales* by Geoffrey Chaucer (1340-1400), pilgrims on their way to Canterbury in southeast England rest at pubs and tell each other tales. Many of the plays of William Shakespeare (1564-1616) were performed in the yards of London pubs. Today the pub is a social centre where adults meet to discuss the events of the day. Pubs often entertain their customers with music or poetry, and many British rock bands began their careers playing in a pub.

WALES

In 1282 the English conquered the principality, or prince's province, of Wales and have ruled it ever since. But Wales has preserved its own identity, and many people in northern Wales still speak the Welsh language. Most people live in the industrialized valleys of the south. The south was once a coal-mining region, but almost all the mines have closed down and most people now work in the car industry or the new computer and electronics industries. In the north and west of the country, most people work in farming or the tourist industry.

The leek is the Welsh National flower.

By custom, the first son of the British king or queen becomes Prince of Wales, and wears a gold crown.

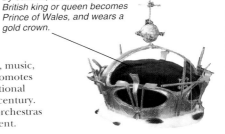

EISTEDDFOD

Every year a festival of poetry, music, and drama celebrates and promotes the Welsh language. This National Eisteddfod began in the 7th century. Today colourful choirs and orchestras compete for awards at the event.

SCOTLAND

Until 1603, Scotland was an independent nation. In that year, the king of Scotland also became king of England. The two countries were not formally united until 1707, and Scotland still maintains a distinct identity from England and has its own legal and educational system. Most of Scotland consists of high mountains and remote glens or valleys. The majority of Scots live in and around the two southern cities of Edinburgh and Glasgow. Every year Edinburgh hosts an international arts festival.

The Scottish emblem is the thistle.

The Irish shamrock emblem

NORTHERN IRELAND

In 1921, the British rulers of Ireland divided the country into two parts. The 26 southern counties became an independent nation, and the six counties in the north remained part of the United Kingdom. Northern Ireland is a centre for textiles and shipbuilding. Although light industry and farming are important sources of income, many people in the province are unemployed.

Find out more

EUROPE
IRELAND
SCOTLAND, HISTORY OF
UNITED KINGDOM, HISTORY OF

HISTORY OF THE
UNITED KINGDOM

In 1801, THE UNITED KINGDOM came into being with the Act of Union. Before that there had been four separate areas: England, Wales, Scotland, and Ireland. However, England had begun taking over the government of Wales in the 1000s, Ireland in the 1100s, and had shared a joint monarchy with Scotland since 1603. The United Kingdom is a small country, but by 1850 it had become the richest and most powerful nation in the world, controlling the largest empire in history. Even today, the British Commonwealth of Nations includes more than 40 independent countries that were once British colonies. The United Kingdom has often been forced to fight long and bitter wars, but has survived and prospered because of its island position and its strong navy. The British system of laws and government by Parliament has become a model which many other nations have copied.

PALAEOLITHIC SETTLERS
A quarter of a million years ago, during mild conditions between two Ice Ages, people began to settle in Britain. They walked across the bridge of land which then joined Britain to Europe.

BATTLE OF HASTINGS
In 1066, a battle changed the course of English history. A Norman army led by William the Conqueror defeated an English king, Harold of Wessex, at Hastings, southern England. William built castles in his new kingdom and gave land to powerful barons who agreed to fight for him. This system was called feudalism. William's descendants have ruled the country ever since.

HENRY VIII
A truly multitalented king, Henry VIII was an expert at many things, from jousting and archery to lute-playing and languages. His impact on England was tremendous. In 1541, he forced the Irish Parliament to recognize him as king of Ireland. He also broke from the Catholic Church, in order to divorce his wife, and became head of a new Church of England. He was an absolute ruler who executed anyone who displeased him, including two of his six wives.

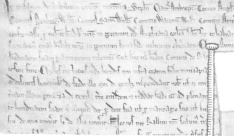

MAGNA CARTA
The Magna Carta (Great Charter) of 1215 was an agreement between the king and the nobles of England. It promised that the king would not abuse his power to tax them. It became important because it was the start of the belief that even kings must obey certain laws.

UNION FLAG
The flag of the United Kingdom is made up from the red crosses of St. George of England and St. Patrick of Ireland, plus the white St. Andrew's cross of Scotland, on a blue background. Wales has its own flag.

UNITED KINGDOM

43 A.D. Ancient Romans, under Claudius, invade Britain and make it part of their empire.

400 Romans leave Britain.

c. 500 Christian missionaries arrive in Britain and preach Christianity to the people.

c. 870 Viking conquest of Britain begins.

1066 Normans invade Britain.

1215 Magna Carta agreement between the king and the nobles of England.

1282 Edward I, king of England, conquers Wales.

1485 Battle of Bosworth. Henry VII becomes the first Tudor king.

1534 Parliament declares Henry VIII head of the Church of England.

1588 English navy defeats the Spanish Armada (fleet) sent by Philip II, king of Spain.

CHARLES II

The Parliamentary army defeated and executed King Charles I during the English Civil War (1642-49). For nine years Oliver Cromwell (1599-1658), a member of Parliament, and his army ruled the country as a republic. But in 1660, Charles' son returned from travels abroad (above) and claimed the throne as King Charles II. The nation, weary of the republic, welcomed him.

ADMIRAL NELSON

The most famous and daring commander of the British Royal Navy was Admiral Horatio Nelson (1758-1805). He defeated the Spanish and French at the Battle of Trafalgar. Before the battle he said "England expects every man to do his duty". His men fought hard but Nelson died of serious wounds.

CHARTISTS

During the 19th century, British people fought for the right to vote. Groups such as the Chartists (1836-48) organized demonstrations demanding a fairer system with representation for all, a secret voting system, and regular elections. Above is a Chartist riot being crushed by the police.

IMMIGRATION

Since the 1960s, the United Kingdom has become increasingly multiracial and multicultural. Immigrants have arrived from the Commonwealth countries in the Caribbean, and many nations in Asia. On the right recent arrivals from Jamaica line up for their meals at a hostel set up for them.

WELFARE STATE

In 1945, after World War II, the Labour government came into power and introduced a welfare state. This put some private businesses under public control. It also provided welfare for people "from the cradle to the grave", including free medical treatment under the National Health Service.

SOVEREIGNTY

In 1953, Elizabeth II (right) was crowned queen of the United Kingdom. Today the duties of the monarch are mainly ceremonial. The real power lies in the hands of the prime minister and the Cabinet (group of government advisers). In 1979, Margaret Thatcher (left) became the first British woman prime minister. Her term of office lasted for 11 years, until November 1990.

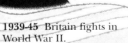

1642-49 Civil War between the king and Parliament.

1660 Charles II becomes king of England.

1707 Act of Union unites England, Wales, and Scotland.

1801 Ireland united with Great Britain.

1900 Britain is the strongest, richest country in the world.

1914-18 Britain fights in World War I.

1931 Commonwealth of Nations is established.

1939-45 Britain fights in World War II.

1945 Welfare state introduced.

1973 Britain becomes a member of the European Community (EC).

1997 Scotland votes in favour of its own parliament.

Find out more

CIVIL WAR, ENGLISH
ELIZABETH I
INDUSTRIAL REVOLUTION
IRELAND, HISTORY OF
NORMANS
UNITED KINGDOM
VICTORIAN AGE

UNITED NATIONS

IN 1945, AT THE END of World War II, the nations that opposed Germany, Italy, and Japan decided that such a war must never be repeated. They set up the United Nations, with the aim of preventing future conflicts, and drew up the United Nations Charter. The United Nations (UN) met for the first time in San Francisco in 1945. Today more than 170 nations belong to the UN. The UN consists of six main organs: the General Assembly, the Security Council, the Secretariat, the Economic and Social Council, the Trusteeship Council, and the International Court of Justice. Each is concerned with world peace and social justice. The UN also has agencies which deal with global issues such as health. Each member nation of the UN has a seat in the General Assembly; 15 nations sit on the Security Council. The UN is not without problems. Its members often disagree, and it suffers financial difficulties.

LEAGUE OF NATIONS
In 1919 the victors of World War I, including Great Britain, founded the League of Nations to keep peace. But in 1935 the League failed to prevent Italy from invading Ethiopia. In 1946, the League's functions were transferred to the UN. Haile Selassie, emperor of Ethiopia, is seen addressing the League, above.

UNITED NATIONS
The headquarters of the UN in New York City, United States, is where the General Assembly and Security Council meet, as well as many of the specialist agencies of the organization. Politicians from every member nation come to New York to address the UN, and many international disputes and conflicts are settled here.

SECURITY COUNCIL

The aim of the Security Council is to maintain peace in the world. It investigates any event which might lead to fighting. The council has five permanent members – Britain, the United States, the Russian Federation, France, and China – and ten members elected for two years each.

UN SYMBOL
The symbol of the United Nations (above) consists of a map of the world surrounded by a wreath of olive branches, symbolizing peace.

UNICEF

The United Nations Children's Fund (UNICEF) is one of the most successful agencies of the UN. UNICEF was originally founded to help child victims of World War II. The fund now provides education, health care, and medical help for children across the world, particularly in areas devastated by war or famine. Much of its work takes place in the poor countries of Africa and Asia.

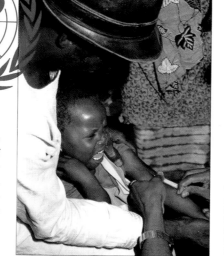

Children in underdeveloped countries are immunized against disease, thanks to UNICEF (left).

PEACEKEEPING
The UN is sometimes called on to send a peacekeeping force to a country in order to prevent war. In 1989, a UN force was sent to Namibia, southern Africa, to supervise the elections that led to Namibia's independence. More recently UN forces were sent to guard food supplies in war-torn Bosnia and Croatia.

> **Find out more**
> ARMIES
> GOVERNMENTS
> WORLD WAR I
> WORLD WAR II

UNITED STATES OF AMERICA

The United States covers much of the continent of North America. It reaches from the Atlantic to the Pacific oceans and from the Mexican border to Canada. The nation covers a total of 9.3 million sq km (3.6 million square miles).

ON THE FLAG OF the United States, 50 identical stars represent the country's 50 states. But the states themselves could not be more different. If the stars showed their areas, the largest, for Alaska, would be nearly 500 times bigger than the star for the smallest state, Rhode Island. If the stars showed population, Alaska's star would be the smallest, and the star for California, which has the most people, would be 60 times larger. The states vary in other ways, too. The Rocky Mountains in the western states reach more than 4,300 m (14,000 ft) in height, but flat plains extend for hundreds of kilometres across the country's centre. At Barrow, Alaska, the most northerly town, the average temperature is just -13°C (9°F), yet in Arizona temperatures have reached 57°C (134°F). The nation as a whole is the most powerful in the Western world. American finance, culture, and politics have spread outward from the United States. Products made in the United States are available in every country. People of all nations dance to American music. And decisions made by American politicians affect the lives of many people throughout the world.

The seemingly endless wheat fields of the Midwest.

MIDWEST

The United States is the world's largest exporter of wheat and produces nearly half of the corn on Earth. This enormous quantity of food is grown on the open plains which cover the Midwest between the Mississippi River and the Rockies. Grain farming is highly mechanized, with giant machines operating in fields hundreds of hectares in size. The United States also produces one quarter of the world's oranges, one seventh of the world's nuts, and half of the world's soya beans.

NEW YORK CITY

At the mouth of the Hudson River on the east coast of the United States is New York City, the country's biggest city. It is also one of the oldest. New York was founded in 1624 and is now an urban area with 8 million people. The city is the financial heart of the nation and houses the offices of many large companies and dozens of theatres, museums, and parks. Skyscrapers more than 300 m (1,000 ft) tall dominate the city centre, Manhattan.

Manhattan, the centre of New York, is built on a rocky island between the Hudson and East rivers.

STATE AND FEDERAL GOVERNMENT

The United States is a democracy and has a written constitution which sets out how government works. State governments, which meet in the state capital, have the authority to make laws affecting their own residents. The states were once nearly self-governing, but today the federal, or national, government has more power. It makes decisions on foreign policy and can pass laws which affect the entire country.

HAWAII AND ALASKA

Hawaii, a group of tropical islands in the Pacific Ocean, became the fiftieth state in 1959. The islands produce pineapples, sugar, and coffee. Polynesians first settled Hawaii in the 700s, and many native Polynesians still live here. Alaska lies outside the main United States, too, separated from the other states by Canada.

The Sugar Train on the Hawaiian island of Maui

CALIFORNIA

In 1848 gold was discovered in California, and many people rushed to the region to prospect for it. California is still the state with the most inhabitants. More than 29 million people live there. Most of the state has a mild, sunny climate and produces vast amounts of fruit.

Many towns in California have become resorts. Modern industries have started up in California; the so-called Silicon Valley, for example, is a centre for the computer business.

Cable cars still carry passengers up some of the 43 hills on which the city of San Francisco, California, is built.

AMERICAN PEOPLE

Native Americans, the original Americans, now make up only a small part of the total population of 257.8 million. Most people are the descendants of settlers from overseas and speak English. They live in the same neighbourhoods and mingle in everyday life. Their cultures have also mingled, producing a new form of English different from that spoken in England. Some groups, such as the Chinese and the Italians, also keep their own traditions and language alive in small, urban communities.

Baseball, the national sport, was first played between two organized teams in 1846.

The Grand Canyon is a favourite tourist attraction, and many people ride to the bottom on mules.

NASA

The United States is a world leader in technology, particularly in space research. The National Aeronautics and Space Administration (NASA) spends millions of dollars every year on satellites and spacecraft. In 1969, it was NASA's Apollo programme that placed humans on the moon. One of the organization's recent successes is the space shuttle, a reusable spacecraft.

GRAND CANYON

There are many natural wonders in the United States; one of the most impressive is the Grand Canyon in Arizona. The Colorado River took thousands of years to cut the canyon by natural erosion through solid rock. It is 29 km (18 miles) wide in places and more than 1,800 m (6,000 ft) deep.

Famous blues singer B.B. King (born 1925) has played his guitar, named Lucille, in concerts all over the world.

BLUES

During the 17th, 18th, and 19th centuries thousands of Africans were brought to America as slaves. Slavery was outlawed in 1865, and since then black writers, artists, and musicians have made their mark on American culture. The popular music known as blues originated among slaves in the southern states of America.

Find out more

GOVERNMENTS
INDIANS, NORTH AMERICAN
KING, MARTIN LUTHER
MUSIC
ROOSEVELT, FRANKLIN DELANO
UNITED STATES OF AMERICA,
history of
WILD WEST

UNITED STATES OF AMERICA

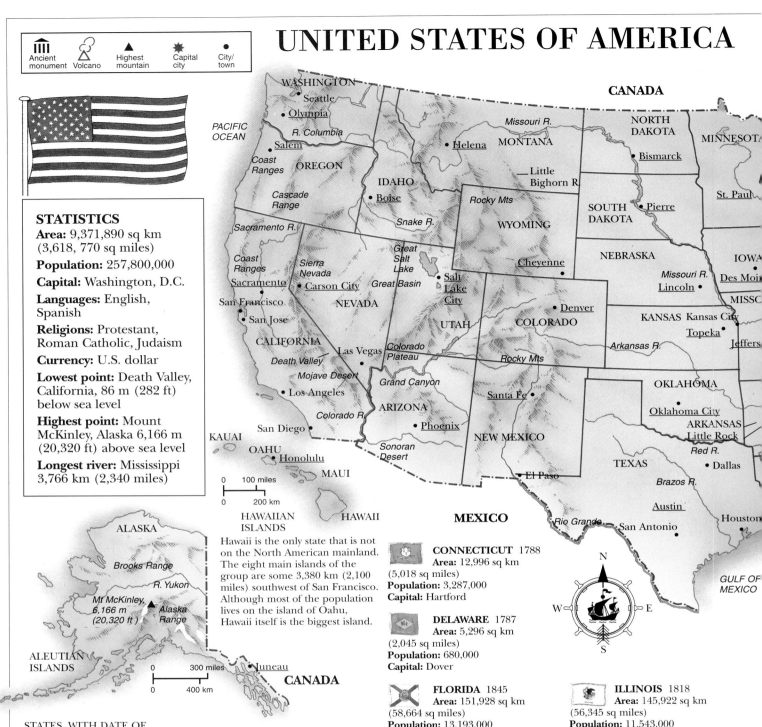

STATISTICS

Area: 9,371,890 sq km (3,618, 770 sq miles)

Population: 257,800,000

Capital: Washington, D.C.

Languages: English, Spanish

Religions: Protestant, Roman Catholic, Judaism

Currency: U.S. dollar

Lowest point: Death Valley, California, 86 m (282 ft) below sea level

Highest point: Mount McKinley, Alaska 6,166 m (20,320 ft) above sea level

Longest river: Mississippi 3,766 km (2,340 miles)

Hawaii is the only state that is not on the North American mainland. The eight main islands of the group are some 3,380 km (2,100 miles) southwest of San Francisco. Although most of the population lives on the island of Oahu, Hawaii itself is the biggest island.

CONNECTICUT 1788
Area: 12,996 sq km (5,018 sq miles)
Population: 3,287,000
Capital: Hartford

DELAWARE 1787
Area: 5,296 sq km (2,045 sq miles)
Population: 680,000
Capital: Dover

FLORIDA 1845
Area: 151,928 sq km (58,664 sq miles)
Population: 13,193,000
Capital: Tallahassee

GEORGIA 1788
Area: 152,565 sq km (58,910 sq miles)
Population: 6,623,000
Capital: Atlanta

HAWAII 1959
Area: 16,759 sq km (6,471 sq miles)
Population: 1,135,000
Capital: Honolulu

IDAHO 1890
Area: 216,414 sq km (83,564 sq miles)
Population: 1,039,000
Capital: Boise

ILLINOIS 1818
Area: 145,922 sq km (56,345 sq miles)
Population: 11,543,000
Capital: Springfield

INDIANA 1816
Area: 93,712 sq km (36,185 sq miles)
Population: 5,610,000
Capital: Indianapolis

IOWA 1846
Area: 145,740 sq km (56,275 sq miles)
Population: 2,795,000
Capital: Des Moines

KANSAS 1861
Area: 213,081 sq km (82,277 sq miles)
Population: 2,495,000
Capital: Topeka

STATES, WITH DATE OF ADMISSION TO UNION

ALABAMA 1819
Area: 133,906 sq km (51,705 sq miles)
Population: 4,040,000
Capital: Montgomery

ALASKA 1959
Area: 1,530,572 sq km (591,000 sq miles)
Population: 550,000
Capital: Juneau

ARIZONA 1912
Area: 295,237 sq km (114,000 sq miles)
Population: 3,665,000
Capital: Phoenix

ARKANSAS 1836
Area: 137,744 sq km (53,187 sq miles)
Population: 2,351,000
Capital: Little Rock

CALIFORNIA 1850
Area: 411,017 sq km (158,706 sq miles)
Population: 29,760,000
Capital: Sacramento

COLORADO 1876
Area: 269,575 sq km (104,091 sq miles)
Population: 3,295,000
Capital: Denver

The border between Canada and the United States is the longest land border between any two countries in the world.

ATLANTIC OCEAN

0 ————————— 300 miles

0 ————————— 500 km

MONTANA 1889

Area: 380,820 sq km
(147,046 sq miles)
Population: 808,000
Capital: Helena

NEBRASKA 1867

Area: 200,334 sq km
(77,355 sq miles)
Population: 1,593,000
Capital: Lincoln

NEVADA 1864

Area: 286,331 sq km
(110,561 sq miles)
Population: 1,284,000
Capital: Carson City

NEW HAMPSHIRE 1788

Area: 24,031 sq km
(9,279 sq miles)
Population: 1,105,000
Capital: Concord

NEW JERSEY 1787

Area: 20,167 sq km
(7,787 sq miles)
Population: 7,760,000
Capital: Trenton

NEW MEXICO 1912

Area: 314,902 sq km
(121,593 sq miles)
Population: 1,548,000
Capital: Santa Fe

NEW YORK 1788

Area: 127,180 sq km
(49,108 sq miles)
Population: 18,058,000
Capital: Albany

NORTH CAROLINA 1789

Area: 136,402 sq km
(52,669 sq miles)
Population: 6,737,000
Capital: Raleigh

NORTH DAKOTA 1889

Area: 183,104 sq km
(70,702 sq miles)
Population: 635,000
Capital: Bismarck

OHIO 1803

Area: 107,036 sq km
(41,330 sq miles)
Population: 10,939,000
Capital: Columbus

OKLAHOMA 1907

Area: 181,076 sq km
(69,919 sq miles)
Population: 3,175,000
Capital: Oklahoma City

OREGON 1859

Area: 251,400 sq km
(97,073 sq miles)
Population: 2,922,000
Capital: Salem

PENNSYLVANIA 1787

Area: 117,339 sq km
(45,308 sq miles)
Population: 11,961,000
Capital: Harrisburg

RHODE ISLAND 1790

Area: 3,139 sq km
(1,212 sq miles)
Population: 1,004,000
Capital: Providence

SOUTH CAROLINA 1788

Area: 80,576 sq km
(31,113 sq miles)
Population: 3,560,000
Capital: Columbia

SOUTH DAKOTA 1889

Area: 199,715 sq km
(77,116 sq miles)
Population: 703,000
Capital: Pierre

TENNESSEE 1796

Area: 109,145 sq km
(42,144 sq miles)
Population: 4,953,000
Capital: Nashville

TEXAS 1845

Area: 690,977 sq km
(266,807 sq miles)
Population: 17,349,000
Capital: Austin

UTAH 1896

Area: 219,871 sq km
(84,899 sq miles)
Population: 1,770,000
Capital: Salt Lake City

VERMONT 1791

Area: 24,898 sq km
(9,614 sq miles)
Population: 567,000
Capital: Montpelier

VIRGINIA 1788

Area: 105,578 sq km
(40,767 sq miles)
Population: 6,286,000
Capital: Richmond

WASHINGTON 1889

Area: 176,466 sq km
(68,139 sq miles)
Population: 5,018,000
Capital: Olympia

WEST VIRGINIA 1863

Area: 62,756 sq km
(24,232 sq miles)
Population: 1,801,000
Capital: Charleston

WISCONSIN 1848
Area: 145,425 sq km
(56,153 sq miles)
Population: 4,968,000
Capital: Madison

WYOMING 1890

Area: 253,306 sq km
(97,809 sq miles)
Population: 460,000
Capital: Cheyenne

DISTRICT OF COLUMBIA
When members of Congress passed laws in 1790 and 1791 to create the capital of the U.S.A., they wanted to avoid rivalry between states. So when George Washington chose the site for the capital city that bears his name, the region was created as a special district, called the District of Columbia (D.C.). However, D.C. is not a state, and although the people who live there take part in Congressional elections their delegate in the House of Representatives cannot vote.

KENTUCKY 1792

Area: 104,654 sq km
(40,410 sq miles)
Population: 3,713,000
Capital: Frankfort

LOUISIANA 1812

Area: 123,678 sq km
(47,752 sq miles)
Population: 4,252,000
Capital: Baton Rouge

MAINE 1820
Area: 86,150 sq km
(33,265 sq miles)
Population: 1,235,000
Capital: Augusta

MARYLAND 1788
Area: 27,089 sq km
(10,460 sq miles)
Population: 4,860,000
Capital: Annapolis

MASSACHUSETTS 1788
Area: 21,454 sq km
(8,284 sq miles)
Population: 5,996,000
Capital: Boston

MICHIGAN 1837
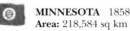
Area: 151,573 sq km
(58,527 sq miles)
Population: 9,368,000
Capital: Lansing

MINNESOTA 1858
Area: 218,584 sq km
(84,402 sq miles)
Population: 4,432,000
Capital: St. Paul

MISSISSIPPI 1817
Area: 123,505 sq km
(47,689 sq miles)
Population: 2,529,000
Capital: Jackson

MISSOURI 1821

Area: 180,501 sq km
(69,697 sq miles)
Population: 5,159,000
Capital: Jefferson City

HISTORY OF THE
UNITED STATES

TODAY THE UNITED STATES of America is the most powerful nation on Earth. Yet just 230 years ago the United States was a new and vulnerable nation. It occupied a narrow strip of land on the Atlantic coast of North America and had a population of only about four million people. Beyond its borders lay vast areas of unclaimed land. Throughout the 19th century, American settlers pushed the frontier westwards across that land, fighting the native Indians for control. At the same time, millions of immigrants from Europe were arriving on the East Coast. By 1900 the nation's farms and factories were producing more than any other country. That wealth and power led to more United States involvement in international affairs and drew the country into two wars in Europe. But the country continued to prosper. Since 1945 the system of individual enterprise that inspired the founders of the United States has made its people among the world's richest. American business, influence, and culture have spread to every other nation in the world.

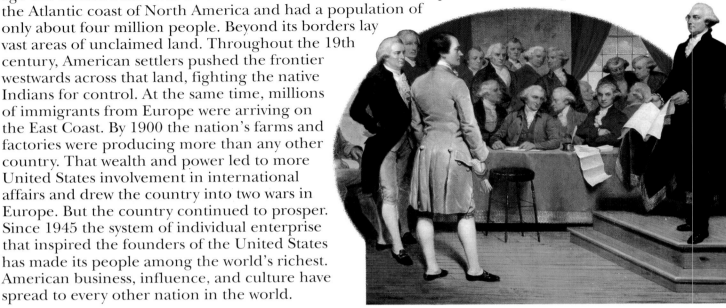

FOUNDING FATHERS
The United States originally consisted of 13 states, each with its own customs and history. In 1787 George Washington and others, sometimes called the Founding Fathers, drew up the Constitution, a document that established a strong central government. The Constitution, which also safeguards the liberties of the states and those of their people, has been in force since 1789.

STARS AND STRIPES
The first official flag was made in 1777 and had one stripe and one star for each of the original 13 states of the Union. After 1818, a new star was added to the flag each time a state joined the Union. Today there are 50 stars.

Map labels:
CANADA
Red River Basin 1818
13 original states 1763
Oregon county 1846
Louisiana Purchase from France 1803
Acquired by 1800
Granted by Mexico 1848
Gadsden Purchase 1853
MEXICO
Louisiana 1812
Texas 1845
Bought from Spain 1819

GROWTH OF THE UNITED STATES
The 13 original colonies on the East Coast gained their independence from Britain in 1783, and acquired all the land as far west as the Mississippi River. In 1803 the vast area of Louisiana was bought from France, and by 1848 the United States had reached the Pacific Ocean.

SPREAD OF THE RAILWAY
In 1860 there were more than 48,000 km (30,000 miles) of railways in the eastern United States, but almost none had been built west of the Mississippi River. On 10 May, 1869, the first continental railway was completed, and the two coasts of America were joined for the first time. A ceremony was held at Promontory Point in Utah to mark the occasion. The growth of the national railway network helped unify the country.

FALL OF THE SOUTH
The Civil War ended in 1865, leaving the South in ruinous poverty. The hatred and bitterness caused by the war lasted for many years as the central government took full control of the southern states.

IMMIGRATION

During the 19th century many Europeans crossed the Atlantic in search of new freedoms and opportunities. The United States welcomed Irish people escaping famine, eastern European Jews fleeing persecution, and countless others. By 1890, half a million immigrants were arriving each year in the United States. As a result, the country became a mixture of many different cultures and religions.

INDUSTRY

The United States offered an endless supply of raw materials to 19th-century industrialists, who soon took advantage of these resources. Manufacturers such as Ransom Olds pioneered mass production of cars and many other goods. In the Olds Motor Works, cars moved along a production line, with workers at intervals each performing a single task. This technique made assembly faster, and Henry Ford and other manufacturers quickly adopted it.

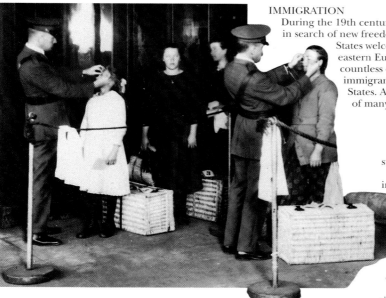

Immigrants arriving in the United States were examined at a reception centre on Ellis Island, New York.

UNITED STATES

1783 The 13 colonies win their independence from Britain.

1787 Constitution is drafted.

1789 George Washington becomes the first president.

1790 A new capital named Washington is built on the Potomac River.

1803 Louisiana Purchase doubles size of the country.

1845 Texas joins the Union.

1848 U.S. defeats Mexico and acquires California.

1861-65 Civil War divides country into north and south.

1869 First transcontinental railway is completed.

1917-1918 United States fights in World War I.

1929 Stock market crash starts economic depression.

1941 United States enters World War II.

1963 President Kennedy assassinated.

1969 Neil Armstrong walks on the moon.

1987 President Ronald Reagan signs treaty with Soviet Union to remove many nuclear weapons from Europe.

JOHN F. KENNEDY

In 1960 John F. Kennedy (1917-63) became the youngest man ever elected president. In 1961, Kennedy approved the invasion of Communist Cuba by U.S.-backed Cuban exiles. The invasion, at the Bay of Pigs, was a disaster, and Kennedy was severely criticized. In 1962 the Soviets stationed nuclear missiles on the island. For one week, nuclear war seemed unavoidable, but Kennedy persuaded the Soviet Union to remove the missiles. Kennedy's presidency ended tragically on 22 November, 1963, when he was assassinated during a visit to Dallas, Texas, United States.

THE UNITED STATES AT WAR

Until the United States entered World War I in 1917, its armed forces had never fought overseas. After the war ended the United States tried once again to stay out of conflicts overseas. But in 1941 the Japanese attacked Pearl Harbor naval base in Hawaii, bringing the U.S. into World War II. Since 1945, the U.S. has fought in several overseas wars, notably in Korea (1950-53) and Vietnam (1961–73).

The Iwo Jima monument in Arlington National Cemetery is a memorial to Americans who died in World War II. It shows Marines raising the flag on Iwo Jima Island in the Pacific. Many U.S. soldiers died in the battle for the island.

EQUAL OPPORTUNITIES

Since 1789, the U.S. Constitution has guaranteed every citizen equal rights. In reality, many minority groups are only now starting to achieve equality. The photograph above shows David Dinkins, New York City's first black mayor.

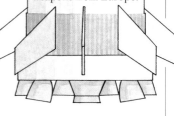

Find out more

CIVIL WAR, AMERICAN
NUCLEAR AGE
PILGRIM FATHERS
REVOLUTIONARY WAR, American
UNITED STATES OF AMERICA
WASHINGTON, GEORGE
WILD WEST

UNIVERSE

THE VAST EXPANSE of space that we call the universe contains everything there is. It includes the sun, the planets, the Milky Way galaxy, and all other galaxies too. The universe is continually growing, and each part is gradually moving further away from every other part. We know about the universe by using powerful telescopes to study light, radio waves, x-rays, and other radiations that reach Earth from space. Light from a star travels nearly 9.5 billion km (6 billion miles) in a year. We call this distance a light-year. The light from a distant star that you can see through a telescope may have travelled thousands of years to reach us. The universe consists of billions of galaxies. Most scientists believe that galaxies form out of the gas that was ejected by a massive explosion that happened in the universe billions of years ago. This idea is called the big bang theory.

Milky Way has a halo of stars and gas.

MILKY WAY
The sun is just one of 100 billion stars in the large spiral galaxy we call the Milky Way. Like most other spiral galaxies, the Milky Way has curved arms of stars radiating from a globe-shaped centre. The Milky Way is 100,000 light-years across, and the sun is 30,000 light-years from its centre.

GALAXIES
Galaxies, which contain gas, dust, and thousands of millions of stars, belong to one of three main groups – elliptical, irregular, or spiral. Most galaxies are elliptical, ranging from sphere shapes to egg shapes. A few galaxies are irregular. Others, such as the Milky Way, are spirals. Most galaxies belong to groups called clusters, which often contain thousands of galaxies of all three kinds.

Pieces of paper represent clusters of galaxies.

ELLIPTICAL GALAXY
Elliptical galaxies such as the one shown here consist mostly of older, red-coloured stars. These galaxies contain only small amounts of the gas and dust from which new stars are formed.

Balloon expands in the same way that the universe is expanding.

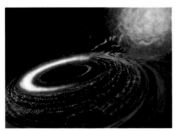

BLACK HOLES
Scientists believe that the gravitational pull of some stars is so strong that no light can escape. This creates what we call a black hole (above). A black hole is like an exit from our universe – anything that falls in is never seen again, because light and matter cannot escape from it. Although we cannot see the black hole itself, it can create a quasar – the brightest thing we know.

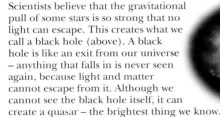

IRREGULAR GALAXY
The Large Magellanic Cloud is an irregular galaxy. It is a companion of the Milky Way – 160,000 light-years away and 30,000 light-years across.

THE EXPANDING UNIVERSE
You can get an idea of how the universe is expanding by imagining several small pieces of paper glued onto a balloon. Each piece represents a cluster of galaxies. As you blow up the balloon, all the paper pieces move further away from one another. In the same way, galaxy clusters are moving further away from one another. The further a cluster is, the faster it travels away from us.

LOOKING BACK IN TIME
If you look through a telescope you can see galaxies millions of light-years away. You are not seeing them as they are now but as they were long ago, when their light first set out on its journey – so in a sense, you are looking into the past.

Galaxy is 100 million light-years away. Light left this galaxy when the dinosaurs lived on Earth.

Dinosaurs lived on Earth 65-215 million years ago.

Find out more
COMETS AND METEORS
EARTH
LIGHT
MOON
PLANETS
STARS
SUN
TELESCOPES

HISTORY OF THE
U.S.S.R.

IN 1922, A NEW NATION came into being. The Union of Soviet Socialist Republics (U.S.S.R.) was the new name for Communist Russia, led by Vladimir Lenin (1870-1924). The years following the 1917 Revolution were difficult. Civil war between Communists and anti-Communists had torn Russia apart. More than 20 million people had died. When Lenin died, Joseph Stalin took over as dictator. In a reign of terror, he eliminated all opposition to his rule. He started to transform the Soviet Union into a modern industrial state. The huge industrial effort made the Soviet Union strong. It survived German invasion in 1941, although World War II (1939-1945) cost the nation many lives. After 1945 the Soviet Union became a superpower. But it still had difficulty providing enough goods for its people. In 1985, Mikhail Gorbachev came to power. He introduced reforms and began a policy of openess with the West. In 1991, the Communist Party was declared illegal, and the Soviet Union broke up.

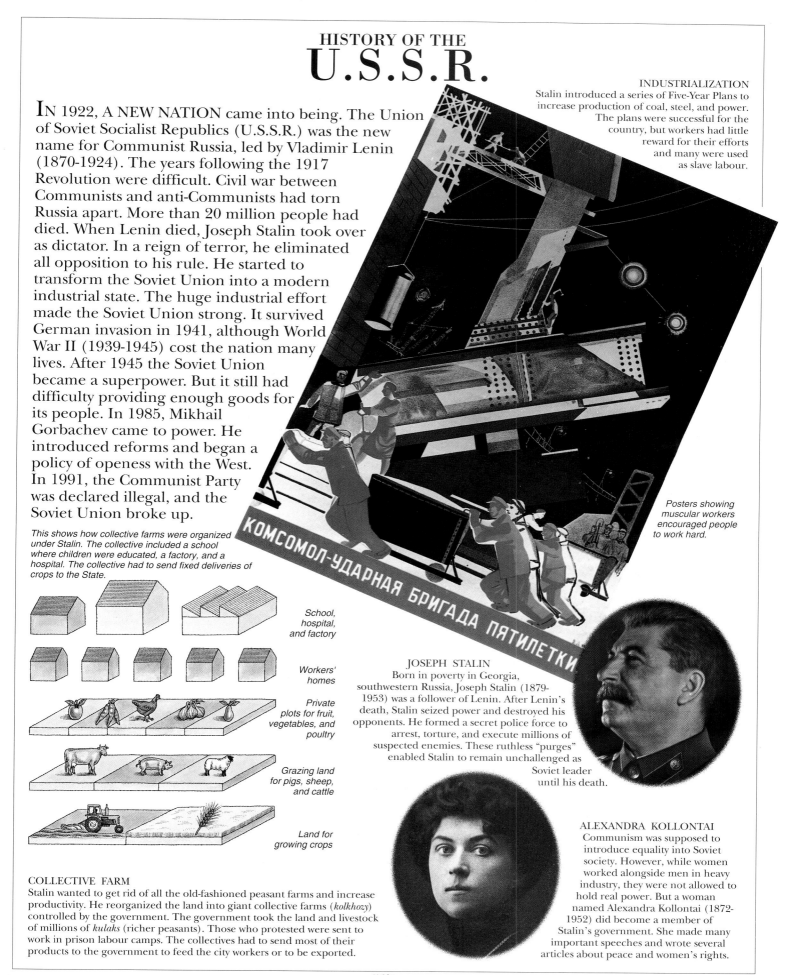

INDUSTRIALIZATION
Stalin introduced a series of Five-Year Plans to increase production of coal, steel, and power. The plans were successful for the country, but workers had little reward for their efforts and many were used as slave labour.

Posters showing muscular workers encouraged people to work hard.

This shows how collective farms were organized under Stalin. The collective included a school where children were educated, a factory, and a hospital. The collective had to send fixed deliveries of crops to the State.

School, hospital, and factory

Workers' homes

Private plots for fruit, vegetables, and poultry

Grazing land for pigs, sheep, and cattle

Land for growing crops

JOSEPH STALIN
Born in poverty in Georgia, southwestern Russia, Joseph Stalin (1879-1953) was a follower of Lenin. After Lenin's death, Stalin seized power and destroyed his opponents. He formed a secret police force to arrest, torture, and execute millions of suspected enemies. These ruthless "purges" enabled Stalin to remain unchallenged as Soviet leader until his death.

COLLECTIVE FARM
Stalin wanted to get rid of all the old-fashioned peasant farms and increase productivity. He reorganized the land into giant collective farms (*kolkhozy*) controlled by the government. The government took the land and livestock of millions of *kulaks* (richer peasants). Those who protested were sent to work in prison labour camps. The collectives had to send most of their products to the government to feed the city workers or to be exported.

ALEXANDRA KOLLONTAI
Communism was supposed to introduce equality into Soviet society. However, while women worked alongside men in heavy industry, they were not allowed to hold real power. But a woman named Alexandra Kollontai (1872-1952) did become a member of Stalin's government. She made many important speeches and wrote several articles about peace and women's rights.

WORLD WAR II

In 1941, German armies invaded the Soviet Union and reached the gates of Moscow, the capital. The Soviets resisted heroically. Stalingrad and Leningrad survived long and bitter sieges. New factories in the east began to produce advanced weapons, such as the T-34 tank, in large numbers. In 1943, Soviet armoured forces, led by Marshal Zhukov, fought and won the largest tank battle ever. But the Soviets paid a high price for victory. They suffered more military casualties than any other country in the war. More than 20 million people died.

U.S.S.R.

1922 U.S.S.R formed.

1924 Lenin dies and is replaced by Stalin.

1941-45 More than 20 million Soviets die in World War II.

1955 Warsaw Pact, an alliance of Communist states, created.

1962 U.S.S.R. builds missile bases on Cuba. U.S. Navy blockades island. U.S.S.R. removes missiles.

1980 Soviet invasion of Afghanistan.

1988 Soviet troops withdraw from Afghanistan.

1991 U.S.S.R breaks up as Lithuania, Latvia, and other republics declare their independence.

CHERNOBYL

In 1986 there was a major disaster at Chernobyl, near Kiev. A nuclear power plant exploded, killing at least 30 people and injuring hundreds more. Radioactive dust and smoke blew all over Europe and exposed thousands of people to contamination. Instead of keeping this disaster secret, the Soviets followed their new policy of *glasnost*, or openness, and warned the rest of the world of the danger.

SPACE RACE

On 4 October 1957, the whole world listened in amazement to a strange beeping sound that came from space. The Soviet Union had launched the first satellite, called *Sputnik 1,* into orbit around Earth. It was followed four years later by Yuri Gagarin, the first human in space.

GORBACHEV AND YELTSIN

Throughout the late 1980's, Soviet people suffered from terrible economic hardship. Many thought that the changes brought about by Gorbachev's policy of *perestroika* were too slow. Gorbachev (right) resigned in 1991. Boris Yeltsin (left) became the leader of the new Russian Federation. The Soviet Union broke up as the republics formed their own governments.

COLLAPSE OF COMMUNISM

After his appointment in 1985, Soviet premier Mikhail Gorbachev introduced policies of *glasnost* (openness) and *perestroika* (economic reform) to improve the poor state of the Soviet economy. People under Soviet control began to demand more freedom. The Communist Party ceased to be the only political party, and in 1989, Nicolae Ceausescu, the Communist dictator of Romania, was overthrown and executed. In the Soviet Union, anti-Communist demonstrations took place. People destroyed statues of Lenin and other Communist leaders. In Moscow, the statue of Felix Dzerzhinsky, head of the hated KGB, or security police, was toppled

Find out more
COLD WAR
COMMUNISM
RUSSIA, HISTORY OF
RUSSIAN REVOLUTION
WORLD WAR II

VETERINARIANS

UNLIKE HUMANS, ANIMALS cannot explain where the pain is when they are ill. This makes healing sick animals particularly difficult. It is the job of the veterinarian. Veterinarians are doctors who study the care and healing of animals. Originally, they treated horses and farm animals. Today veterinarians look after household pets, too. They carry out regular health checks on farm animals and help with delivering lambs and calves. Some veterinarians treat zoo animals, and some are animal dentists. If an animal is very sick or in great pain, a veterinarian may have to put it down (kill it painlessly) to relieve its suffering. The first veterinary schools opened in Europe in the 18th century. Today veterinarians study for five years or more to learn the skills they need.

FARRIERS

Before there were vets, farriers (blacksmiths) treated horses and other farm animals such as cattle, using traditional folk remedies.

VETERINARIAN'S SURGERY

Many different animals go to the veterinarian's surgery for treatment. To avoid fights and prevent the spread of infection, dogs must be kept on a lead and cats should stay in baskets. The veterinarian examines the animal and asks the owner what the signs of the illness are. The veterinarian may need to give medicine or injections, take x-rays, or operate.

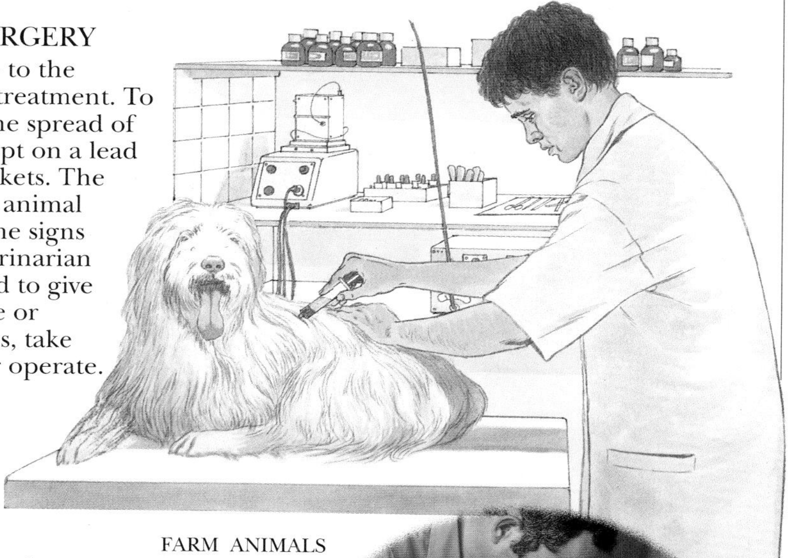

People wait with their pets in the waiting room.

FARM ANIMALS

Veterinarians are essential for intensive farming. Modern farm animals are bred to produce meat or eggs as efficiently as possible, but they need special care because their breeding may reduce resistance to disease. Veterinarians help the farmer keep livestock healthy.

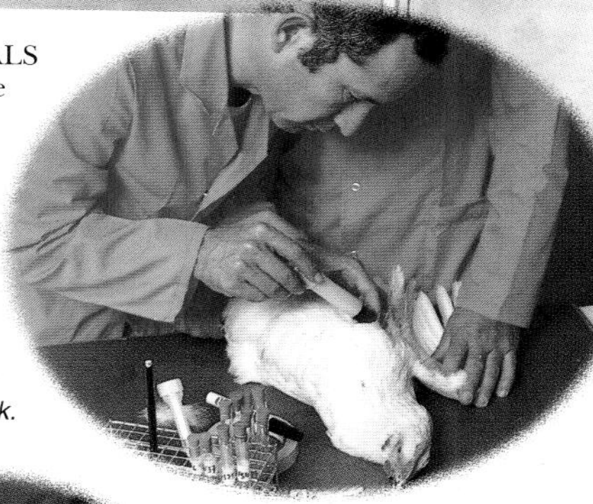

Inoculating chickens prevents one diseased bird from infecting the whole flock.

Vets sometimes have to use helicopters to locate and treat animals that range over wide areas.

CONSERVATION

Some veterinarians are involved in wildlife conservation and treating wild animals. Large or ferocious animals, such as lions and giraffes, may have to be given a calming drug before the veterinarian can handle them. The drug eventually wears off, and does not harm the animal.

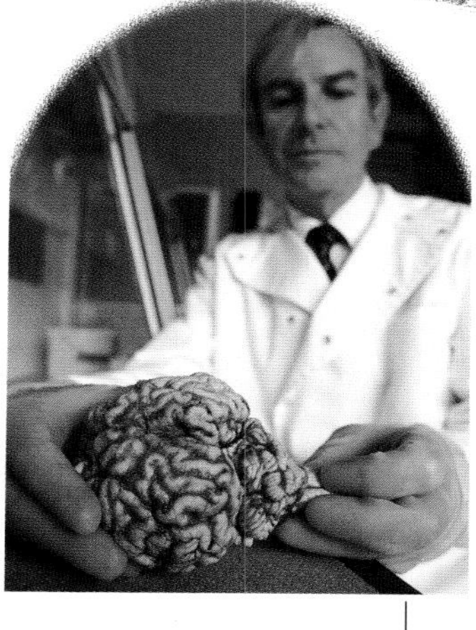

VETERINARY RESEARCH

Constant research is necessary to learn more about animal health. Research veterinarians look for cures to the diseases that make animals sick. They also try to control animal diseases that humans can catch, such as rabies.

Find out more

CONSERVATION
and endangered species
FARMING
PETS

VICTORIAN AGE

IN 1837, A YOUNG WOMAN named Victoria became queen of Great Britain. She was only 18 and was to rule for 64 years. She gave her name to an age in history, and when she died her empire was the largest the world has ever seen. Enormous changes took place during Victoria's reign. There were prosperous people everywhere, so shops got bigger and more servants were employed. But many other people were poor and lived in slums. Police forces, clean water supplies, sewage treatment, and public transport were introduced to make life easier in the new towns that sprang up. Many middle-class people believed in high moral standards, as Victoria did, and set up programmes to "improve" poor people. The Victorians thought they were more advanced than anyone else in the world.

QUEEN VICTORIA
A small figure, Victoria (1819-1901) is best remembered dressed all in black, in mourning for Albert, her husband, who died in 1861. She had great dignity and was highly respected by her subjects.

CRYSTAL PALACE
In 1851, a new building was built in Hyde Park, London, to house the Great Exhibition. It was made entirely of glass and cast iron. Joseph Paxton designed it so it could be moved later and rebuilt in south London.

VICTORIAN STYLE

Victorians loved elaborate decoration. Almost all Victorian objects, from lampposts to teaspoons, were covered in carvings, patterns, and other decorations. Large houses and public buildings, such as St. Pancras Station, London (right), looked like castles, cathedrals, and palaces.

THE GREAT EXHIBITION
In 1851, Prince Albert organized the first international exhibition in Britain. More than 6 million people visited Crystal Palace (above) to view the celebration of the wonders of the new industrial age. The 14,000 exhibits included a 24-ton lump of coal, a railway engine, the Koh-i-noor diamond (from India), and a stuffed elephant.

ALBERT
In 1840, Victoria married Albert (1819-61), a German prince. A sensitive and well-educated man, he had more influence on Victoria than anyone else in her life. Together they had nine children. Prince Albert believed in a simple and strict family life that would be an example to the nation. They are seen above on a family excursion. When Albert died, Victoria was heartbroken.

MUSIC HALLS

Working people went to music halls for cheap and popular entertainment. Audiences could eat and drink while enjoying melodramas, acrobats, comedians, and singers. Sentimental songs were especially popular.

Acrobats performed exciting feats on stage in music halls.

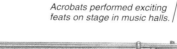

The Martini-Henry rifle appeared around 1871. It had a range of 275 m (300 yards).

EMPIRE BUILDING

During Victoria's reign, there were dozens of small wars as European nations carved out empires in Africa and Asia. The people who lived in these places stood little chance against trained troops equipped with rifles and automatic guns.

The Gatling gun fired bullets at a rate of 1,000 rounds per minute.

END OF AN ERA

Britain reached the height of her powers during Victoria's 64-year reign. When she died in 1901, the whole country went into mourning and people wept in the streets. It was the start of a new century and the end of a great era.

IRONCLAD BATTLESHIPS

Britain kept a huge navy to protect and control an empire which spanned the world. Fast gunboats and powerful battleships sailed to areas where there was trouble, protecting British interests wherever they were threatened.

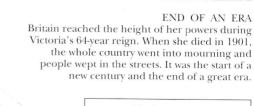

HMS *Warrior*

Find out more

INDUSTRIAL REVOLUTION
TRANSPORT,
history of
UNITED KINGDOM,
history of

VIETNAM WAR

BETWEEN 1965 AND 1975 Vietnam fought one of the most destructive wars in modern history. In 1954, Vietnam defeated French occupying forces and was divided into two countries – a Communist North and a non-Communist South Vietnam. The Viet Cong (Vietnamese Communists) rebelled against the South Vietnamese government and, helped by North Vietnam under Ho Chi Minh, fought to reunite the country. This brought in the United States, which believed that if Vietnam fell to the Communists, nearby countries would fall, too. During the 1960s the United States poured troops and money into Vietnam, but found itself in an undeclared war it could not win. Despite intensive bombing and the latest military technology, the Viet Cong were better equipped and trained for jungle warfare. Casualties in Vietnam were appalling, and strong opposition to the war developed in the United States. A cease-fire was negotiated, and in 1973 all American troops were withdrawn. Two years later North Vietnam captured Saigon, capital of South Vietnam, and Vietnam was united as a Communist country.

VIETNAM WAR

1859 France begins to colonize Vietnam.

1954 Vietnamese defeat French.

1956 Viet Cong lead rebellion against South Vietnamese government.

1961 United States sends advisers to train South Vietnamese army.

1964 Gulf of Tongking clash between North Vietnamese and U.S. naval craft leads to war.

1965 United States begins bombing of North; first U.S. combat troops arrive in South.

1968 Tet (Vietnamese New Year) offensive by Viet Cong

1968 American troops massacre My Lai villagers.

1968 Antiwar protests in U.S.

1973 Cease-fire signed in Paris; American troops leave Vietnam.

1975 Vietnam reunited under northern control.

VIETNAM
Vietnam is in Southeast Asia. The war was fought in the jungles of South Vietnam and in the skies above North Vietnam. Viet Cong fighters received supplies from the North along the Ho Chi Minh trail. At the end of the war, the country was reunited with its capital at Hanoi. Saigon, the southern capital, was renamed Ho Chi Minh City.

TROOPS
The first American military personnel arrived in Vietnam during 1961 to advise the South Vietnamese government. By 1969 there were about 550,000 American troops in Vietnam.

DESTRUCTION
The lengthy fighting had a terrible effect on the people of Vietnam. Their fields were destroyed, their forests stripped of leaves, and their houses blown up, leaving them refugees. Thousands were killed, injured, or maimed.

COSTS
It is unlikely that the exact cost of the Vietnam War will ever be known, but in terms of lives lost, money spent, and bombs dropped, it was enormous. Both sides suffered huge casualties and emerged with seriously tattered economies.

The United States spent $150 billion on the war; there are no figures for what North Vietnam spent.

Four times as many bombs were dropped by the American Air Force on Vietnam than were dropped by British and American bombers on Germany during the whole of World War II.

More than one million South Vietnamese and between 500,000 and one million North Vietnamese died in the war; over 58,000 American soldiers and nurses lost their lives.

The U.S. Air Force bombed the jungle with chemicals to strip the leaves off the trees. Much of Vietnam is still deforested today.

Find out more

SOUTHEAST ASIA, history of

UNITED STATES OF AMERICA, history of

VIKINGS

BETWEEN THE 8TH AND 12TH CENTURIES A.D., fierce warriors called Vikings terrorized the people of Europe. They came from Norway, Sweden, and Denmark, where the weather was cold and the soil was poor, to look for loot. At first they made lightning raids on coastal villages and lonely farms. They stole horses and food, captured prisoners for slaves, and robbed churches of their gold and silver. Later they conquered and settled in parts of England, France, Germany, Italy, and Russia. The Vikings were the finest shipbuilders of the time, and their swift, light boats could travel far from their homelands. They settled in Iceland and Greenland and were the first Europeans to reach North America. Although they are chiefly remembered for their conquests, most Nordic people lived peacefully in small settlements and worked as farmers, merchants, and craftworkers.

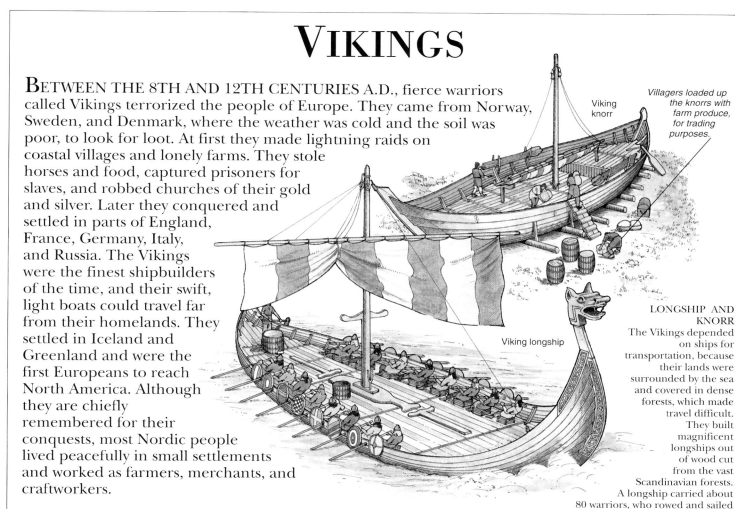

Viking knorr

Villagers loaded up the knorrs with farm produce, for trading purposes.

Viking longship

LONGSHIP AND KNORR
The Vikings depended on ships for transportation, because their lands were surrounded by the sea and covered in dense forests, which made travel difficult. They built magnificent longships out of wood cut from the vast Scandinavian forests. A longship carried about 80 warriors, who rowed and sailed the ship and then fought at the end of the journey. The Vikings also built smaller ships called knorrs, which they used for trading and transporting goods.

WARRIORS
Viking warriors usually fought with swords and battle axes, although some used spears, and bows and arrows. They carried wooden shields, and some wore armour made of layers of thick animal hides. Viking chieftains often wore metal helmets and chain-mail armour.

Swedish helmet (7th century)

A warrior used both hands to swing the long-handled battle axe at an enemy.

The sword was a Viking's most important weapon.

BURIAL GROUNDS
Important Vikings were buried with their ships. Relatives placed the body in a wooden cabin on the deck. Sometimes dogs, horses, cattle, and slaves were buried with their owners. The body of a great warrior might be burned on a pile of wood or placed on the deck of a longship which was then set alight.

Relatives have surrounded the body with the dead person's most treasured possessions, including his horse.

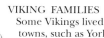

VIKING FAMILIES
Some Vikings lived in bustling trading towns, such as York, England. But most lived in isolated farming settlements. Everything the family needed had to be made or grown on the farm. Viking women had more rights than many other European women of the time. For instance, they were allowed to get divorced if they wished.

Find out more
NORMANS
SCANDINAVIA, HISTORY OF

VOLCANOES

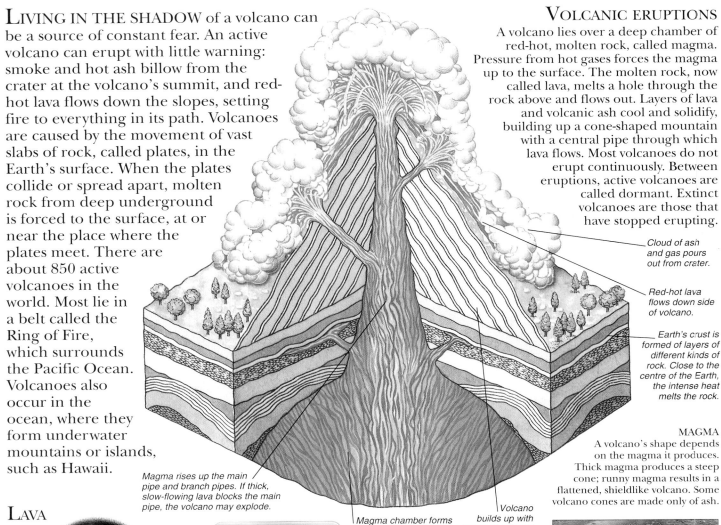

LIVING IN THE SHADOW of a volcano can be a source of constant fear. An active volcano can erupt with little warning: smoke and hot ash billow from the crater at the volcano's summit, and red-hot lava flows down the slopes, setting fire to everything in its path. Volcanoes are caused by the movement of vast slabs of rock, called plates, in the Earth's surface. When the plates collide or spread apart, molten rock from deep underground is forced to the surface, at or near the place where the plates meet. There are about 850 active volcanoes in the world. Most lie in a belt called the Ring of Fire, which surrounds the Pacific Ocean. Volcanoes also occur in the ocean, where they form underwater mountains or islands, such as Hawaii.

VOLCANIC ERUPTIONS

A volcano lies over a deep chamber of red-hot, molten rock, called magma. Pressure from hot gases forces the magma up to the surface. The molten rock, now called lava, melts a hole through the rock above and flows out. Layers of lava and volcanic ash cool and solidify, building up a cone-shaped mountain with a central pipe through which lava flows. Most volcanoes do not erupt continuously. Between eruptions, active volcanoes are called dormant. Extinct volcanoes are those that have stopped erupting.

Cloud of ash and gas pours out from crater.

Red-hot lava flows down side of volcano.

Earth's crust is formed of layers of different kinds of rock. Close to the centre of the Earth, the intense heat melts the rock.

Magma rises up the main pipe and branch pipes. If thick, slow-flowing lava blocks the main pipe, the volcano may explode.

Magma chamber forms deep underground.

Volcano builds up with layers of ash and solidified lava.

MAGMA
A volcano's shape depends on the magma it produces. Thick magma produces a steep cone; runny magma results in a flattened, shieldlike volcano. Some volcano cones are made only of ash.

LAVA

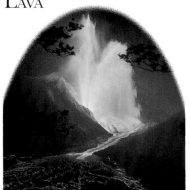

Molten rock which has escaped to the Earth's surface is called lava. A bubbling lake of molten rock fills the crater of the volcano, and fountains of fiery lava leap high into the air. Glowing streams of lava pour out of the crater and flow down the sides of the volcano like rivers of fire. The lava has a temperature of about 1,100°C (2,000°F), which is hot enough to melt steel.

PUMICE
Lava containing bubbles of gas hardens to form a rock called pumice, which is peppered with tiny holes. The holes make pumice very light; it is the only rock that can float in water.

POMPEII
In A.D. 79, Mount Vesuvius in Italy erupted, burying the Roman city of Pompeii and its inhabitants in a deep layer of hot ash. Archaeologists have now uncovered Pompeii, much of which is well preserved. The bodies of victims left hollows in the ash; the plaster cast below is made from such a hollow and shows the last moments of one victim. Vesuvius last erupted in 1944. It could erupt again at any time. One of the greatest of all volcanic disasters occurred when the island of Krakatoa, Indonesia, exploded in 1883.

GEYSERS
A jet of boiling water which suddenly shoots up from the ground is called a geyser. Hot rock deep below the surface heats water in an underground chamber so that it boils. Steam forces the water out in a jet. When the chamber refills and heats up, the geyser blows again.

Find out more
CONTINENTS
EARTHQUAKES
GEOLOGY
MOUNTAINS
ROCKS AND MINERALS

WARSHIPS

IN A MODERN NAVY, there are several different types of warship, each designed to carry out a special function. The largest warship is the aircraft carrier, which is like a floating runway about 300 m (more than 1,000 ft) long that acts as a base for up to 100 aircraft. Battleships are heavily armoured warships equipped with powerful guns that can fire shells over distances of about 32 km (20 miles). Other warships include destroyers for protecting fleets of ships; frigates, which are usually armed with missiles; minesweepers for clearing mines; and small coastal protection vessels.

The role of the warship has changed with the invention of nuclear arms. One of its most important functions is the ability to locate and attack missile-carrying submarines. Thus warships increasingly rely on advanced electronic equipment to detect their targets, and are armed with an array of guided missiles and guns.

FRIGATE
A frigate is a light, fast, medium-sized warship which is particularly useful for escorting other ships. Frigates carry equipment for seeking submarines, anti-ship missiles for defence against other warships, and an array of anti-aircraft weapons.

British-built Type 22 frigate

Anti-aircraft missiles

Radar for detecting enemy aircraft

Main living quarters for crew of about 250

Captain commands the ship from the bridge.

Ship's helicopter, used for reconnaissance (scouting), transport, rescue work, and anti-submarine warfare

Anti-aircraft missiles with a range of about 5 km (3 miles)

Control room, from where all weapons are fired and guided

Twin gas-turbine engines capable of producing a top speed of 55 km/h (35 mph) with a range of about 8,300 km (5,200 miles)

Hull made of aluminium, which is lighter than steel and makes the frigate faster and more manoeuvrable

Anti-ship missiles, for use against enemy warships up to 32 km (20 miles) away

The first modern battleship was the British Navy Dreadnought, which was introduced in 1906. The Dreadnought was armed with heavy guns and protected by thick steel armour.

The heavily armed galleon was developed by the Spanish in the early 15th century and used in their voyages of conquest in the Americas and Asia.

MODERN WARSHIPS
Many warships now carry missiles as well as guns. Warships have various types of missile. Some are used as a defence against aircraft. Other types of missile can attack enemy warships, which may be so distant that they are visible only on a radar screen.

HISTORY OF WARSHIPS
The first true warships were the galleys of Ancient Greece and Rome which used oars and sails for propulsion. Major leaps forward came with the invention of the cannon, steam power, and the use of steel in shipbuilding. During World War I (1914-18) and World War II (1939-45) warships developed into huge, heavily armed battleships, the forerunners of today's warship.

During the 9th century, Viking warriors used longships to travel from their homeland in Scandinavia to conquer countries of northern Europe.

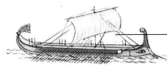

The trireme, or Roman galley, of 200 B.C. had three banks of oars. The pointed beak at the prow (front) of the ship allowed it to ram enemy vessels.

Find out more
NAVIES
ROCKETS AND MISSILES
SUBMARINES
WEAPONS
WORLD WAR I
WORLD WAR II

GEORGE
WASHINGTON

1732 Born in Westmoreland, Virginia.

1759-74 Member of the Virginia parliament

1775-81 Leads Continental forces in the Revolutionary War.

1787 Helps draft Constitution.

1789 Chosen as first president of the United States.

1793 Elected to second term as president.

1797 Retires as president.

1799 Dies at Mount Vernon.

"THE FATHER OF HIS COUNTRY" was a nickname that George Washington earned many times over. First, he led the American forces to victory against the British in the Revolutionary War, then he served the American people again as the first president of the United States. As a military leader, he was capable and strong-willed. Even when the British seemed set to win the war, Washington did not give up hope and continued to encourage the American troops. As president, he was an energetic leader who used his prestige to unite the new nation. Yet despite his many personal strengths, Washington was an unlikely figure to lead a revolution. He was born into a wealthy family and trained as a surveyor before serving in the local militia. He could have had a brilliant military career, but at the age of 27 he returned to farming in Virginia. He did the same at the end of the Revolutionary War, and only went back to national politics in 1787 because he felt the country needed his help once more.

VICTORY AT TRENTON

On Christmas night, 1776, George Washington led his troops across the icy Delaware River and attacked the British in Trenton, New Jersey, before they had time to prepare themselves for battle. The surprise attack did much to increase American morale at the start of the Revolutionary War.

Troops had to break the ice in order to make their way across the river.

CONTINENTAL CONGRESS

In 1774, the 13 British colonies in North America set up a Continental Congress to protest unfair British rule. George Washington was one of the delegates from Virginia. Although the Congress favoured reaching an agreement with Britain, fighting broke out between the two sides in 1775. The Congress raised an army under Washington and on 4 July 1776, issued the Declaration of Independence. Peace was declared in 1781 and the Congress became the national government of the newly formed United States of America. In 1789 it was abolished and a new government structure was established.

MOUNT VERNON
Built in 1743, Mount Vernon was the home of George Washington for more than 50 years. The wooden house overlooks the Potomac River near Alexandria, Virginia, and is now a museum dedicated to Washington.

____ *Find out more* ____

REVOLUTIONARY WAR,
American
UNITED STATES OF AMERICA,
history of

WATER

WE ARE SURROUNDED by water. More than 70 per cent of the Earth's surface is covered by vast oceans and seas. In addition, 10 per cent of the land – an area the size of South America – is covered by water in the form of ice. However, little new water is ever made on Earth. The rain that falls from the sky has fallen billions of times before, and will fall billions of times again. It runs down the land to the sea, evaporates (changes into vapour) into the clouds, and falls again as rain in an endless cycle. Water has a huge effect on our planet and its inhabitants. All plants and animals need water; life itself began in the Earth's prehistoric seas. Seas and rivers shape the land over thousands of years, cutting cliffs and canyons; icy glaciers dig out huge valleys. Water is also essential to people in homes and factories and on farms.

The force of surface tension holds water molecules together so that they form small, roughly spherical drops.

SURFACE TENSION
The surface of water seems to be like an elastic skin. You can see this if you watch tiny insects such as water striders walking on water – their feet make hollows in the surface of the water, but the insects do not sink. This "skin" effect is called surface tension. It is caused by the attraction of water molecules to each other. Surface tension has another important effect: it causes water to form drops.

Molecule at surface

Forces hold water molecules together.

In the body of the liquid, each water molecule is surrounded by others, so the forces on them balance out.

Molecules at the surface have other molecules pulling on them only from below. This means there is a force pulling on this top layer of molecules, keeping them under tension like a stretched elastic band.

WATER FOR LIFE
All plants and creatures, including humans, are made largely of water and depend on water for life. For instance, more than two thirds of the human body is water. To replace water lost by urinating, sweating, and breathing, we must drink water every day to stay healthy. No one can survive more than four days without water.

ICE
Water freezes when the temperature drops below 0°C (32°F). Water expands, or takes up more space, as it freezes. Water pipes sometimes burst in very cold winters as the water inside freezes and expands.

STATES OF WATER
Pure water is a compound of two common elements, hydrogen and oxygen. In each water molecule there are two hydrogen atoms and one oxygen atom; scientists represent this by writing H_2O. Water is usually in a liquid state, but it can also be a solid or a gas. If left standing, water slowly evaporates and turns into water vapour, an invisible gas. When water is cooled down enough, it freezes solid and turns to ice.

WATER
Salty water boils at a higher temperature and freezes at a lower temperature than fresh water, which is why salt is put on roads in winter to keep ice from forming.

WATER VAPOUR
Water boils at 100°C (212°F). At this temperature it evaporates so rapidly that water vapour forms bubbles in the liquid. Water vapour is invisible; visible clouds of steam are not water vapour but are tiny droplets of water formed when the hot vapour hits cold air.

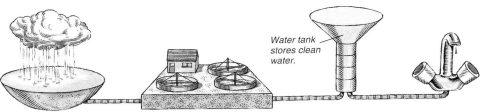

Water falls as rain and is collected in lakes and artificial reservoirs.

Water is cleaned in a treatment plant.

Once the water is treated, it is pumped up into a high tank, ready to be used.

With the water high above the ground, the tap can be opened and the water runs out.

Water tank stores clean water.

WATER TREATMENT
Water in a reservoir is usually not fit to drink. It must pass through a treatment centre which removes germs and other harmful substances. Chlorine gas is often dissolved into the water to kill bacteria and viruses. In addition, the water is stored in huge basins so that pieces of dirt sink to the bottom; filters made of stones and sand remove any remaining particles.

SOLUTIONS
Pure water is rarely found in nature because water dissolves other substances to form mixtures called solutions. For example, sea water is salty because there are many minerals dissolved in it. Water solutions are vital to life; blood plasma, for instance, is a water solution.

Sugar dissolves in water, making a sweet-tasting sugar solution.

The sugar disappears when it is completely dissolved.

HYDROELECTRIC POWER
People have used water as a source of power for more than 2,000 years. Today, water is used to produce electricity in hydroelectric (water-driven) power stations. Hydroelectric power stations are often built inside dams. Water from a huge lake behind the dam flows down pipes. The moving water spins turbines which drive generators and produce electricity. Hydroelectric power produces electricity without causing pollution or using scarce resources.

If three identical holes are drilled in the side of a water-filled container, water spurts out much further from the lowest hole because of the weight of the water above.

WATER PRESSURE
Water rushes out of a tap because it is under pressure; that is, it is pushed from behind. Pressure is produced by pumps that force water along using pistons or blades like those on a ship's propeller. Water pressure is also created by the sheer weight of water above. The deeper the water, the greater the pressure. If you dive into a pool, you can feel the water pressure pushing on your eardrums.

POLLUTION AND DROUGHT
In many places, such as East Africa, there is insufficient rain and constant drought. Plants cannot grow, and people and animals must fight a constant battle for survival. Fresh, clean water can also be difficult to obtain even in places with lots of rain. This is because waste from cities and factories pollute the water, making it unsafe to drink.

Fire fighters connect their hoses to fire engines which contain powerful pumps. The pumps increase the pressure so that the water can reach flames high up in buildings.

Deep underground water stores exist below the surface of the Earth. After a drought, these stores dry out; it may take years for them to be refilled.

Find out more

ELECTRICITY
HEAT
LAKES
OCEANS AND SEAS
RAIN AND SNOW
RIVERS

WATER SPORTS

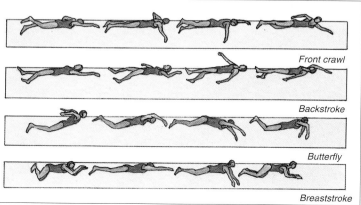

SPLASHING AROUND IN WATER – whether swimming, diving, surfing, or just floating on your back – is one of the most enjoyable ways of relaxing and keeping fit. Water sports are fun for people of all ages: even babies can learn to swim. And for the elderly or the physically handicapped, swimming provides a gentle yet vigorous way to exercise. Swimming became popular for fitness and recreation with ancient peoples in Egypt, Greece, and then Rome. Swimming races began in the 19th century and were included in the first Olympics, in 1896. Like swimming, surfing and water-skiing take place on the surface of the water. Scuba divers, however, dive deep below the waves. They can stay under water for an hour or more by breathing air from cylinders on their backs. Snorkelers swim to a depth of about 9 m (30 ft) with just a face mask, flippers, and a snorkel, or breathing tube.

WATER POLO
In water polo, seven players on each side try to throw the ball into their opponents' goal. The playing area measures 30 m by 20 m (98 ft by 66 ft). Only the goalkeeper may hold the ball with both hands.

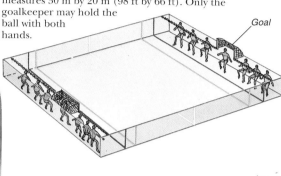

Goal

There are three types of competitive water-skiing: slalom, jumping, and trick skiing.

WATER-SKIING
A fast powerboat tows water-skiers along at the end of a rope. Skiers can cross from side to side behind the boat, and can jump through the air by skiing up a ramp in the water.

DIVING
In diving competitions, judges award points for technique as each competitor performs a series of dives. More difficult dives win higher points. Divers leap from a platform at 10 m (33 ft) above the water, and from a springboard at 3 m (10 ft).

WINDSURFING
Windsurfing, or sailboarding, began as a leisure activity in the 1960s and became a competitive Olympic event in 1984. The windsurfer balances the craft by holding on to a boom fixed around the sail. A daggerboard, or fin, on the underside of the board keeps the board upright in the water.

SWIMMING STROKES
The arm and leg actions of swimmers are called strokes. In the front crawl the swimmer uses left and right arms alternately. In the backstroke the swimmer is face up. In the butterfly and breaststroke, swimmers move both arms and legs together to pull themselves through the water.

Front crawl

Backstroke

Butterfly

Breaststroke

___ **Find out more** ___
SAILING AND BOATING
SPORTS
UNDERWATER EXPLORATION

WEAPONS

Spears could be thrown or used for stabbing.

Boomerangs return to the thrower if they miss their target.

Even simple bows can hurl arrows great distances.

PREHISTORIC HUNTERS LEARNED that they could kill their prey more quickly and safely with a stone knife than with their bare hands. This crude weapon later became refined into the dagger and the sword. Both are members of a group of weapons we now call side arms. However, an even less dangerous way to hunt was to use missile weapons. By throwing rocks or spears, early hunters could disable wild beasts and human enemies alike from a distance of 10 paces or more. Simple changes to a missile weapon made it much more effective: with slingshots or bows and arrows hunters could hit smaller, more distant targets. Since these early times, better technology has greatly increased the range and accuracy of weapons. Seven centuries ago the invention of gunpowder made possible much more powerful weapons. Gunpowder launched bullets and cannonballs much faster than an arrow could fly. Muskets and cannons were thus more deadly than bows, and quickly came to dominate the battlefield. Modern developments have increased both power and range still farther. Today nuclear weapons can destroy in seconds a whole city on the other side of the world.

Some fighting axes were made to be thrown.

The weighted ropes of the bolas wrap around an animal's legs and trip it up.

Powerful crossbows were even more deadly and accurate than simple bows.

Medieval dagger made about 1400

SWORDS

Armed with swords, warriors could inflict injuries at a greater distance than with daggers or knives. The earliest swords were made in about 1500 B.C., when bronze working first developed. Later swords were made of iron and steel. Many different types evolved. Some were for thrusting, others for cutting. Today pistols have replaced swords in close combat, but the sword still has a role to play. It is used as a symbol of power in military ceremonies, in courts of law, and in governments.

SAMURAI DAGGER
Very high-quality steel was used for Samurai weapons such as this dagger. It took craft workers many hours to produce them.

SAMURAI WARRIORS

Swordfighting and archery were the two most important skills of the Samurai warriors of Japan. These warriors first appeared in the 12th century as private armies of landowners. They became very powerful, and the shogun, head of all the Samurai war lords, controlled Japan for the next seven centuries.

The best Samurai swords were thought to have supernatural powers. They were given names and passed down from father to son.

RAPIER
Around 1580 a new type of sword, called the rapier, was invented. It was long and thin and was used for thrusting.

BRONZE AGE SWORD
Shaping the sword so that it was wider near the end of the blade made it more effective as a slashing weapon. The handle of this Bronze Age sword would have been wrapped in leather for comfort.

ARROWS

A well-made arrow must be perfectly straight and have the right weight and flexibility. The tip shape depends on the arrow's use.

Broad arrowhead for hunting

Narrow arrowhead for piercing armour

BOWS AND ARROWS

Before the invention of gunpowder the most powerful missile weapon was the bow and arrow. The springy wood of the bow stored the archer's energy as he gradually drew the string; letting go of the string released the energy and propelled the arrow further and more accurately than it could be thrown by hand. Cave paintings created more than 10,000 years ago show hunters using simple bows.

CROSSBOW

The crossbow was a short, very powerful bow mounted on a wooden "stock". Some crossbows were so strong that the archer needed a winch to draw the string. A catch held the string back while the archer loaded a short arrow called a bolt and took aim. Pulling a trigger fired the weapon.

Amerindian arrows from about 1800

How archers grip string and arrow

SHORT AND LONG BOWS

Early bows were very short. Native Americans used bows that were about 1m (3.5 ft) long. The powerful English longbow of the 14th to 16th centuries was as long as the archer was tall.

CANNONS

Lighting the charge of gunpowder at the closed end of a cannon caused a mighty explosion. The strong tube of the cannon directed the explosion forwards, hurling the stone or iron ball 1.6 km (1 mile) or more. Later, explosive shells replaced the simple ball.

Wadding holds ball and charge in place.

Fuse for lighting charge

MODERN WEAPONS

The grenade is a small explosive bomb which is set on a time fuse and thrown at the enemy. Modern soldiers are also armed with machine guns, which fire many bullets in rapid succession without the need for reloading. More sophisticated and powerful weapons used today include nuclear missiles, rockets, and explosive mines.

Cannonballs ready for loading

Damp rags put out sparks.

Cannonball

Explosive charge

Rammer forces charge into barrel.

Screw removes unburned powder.

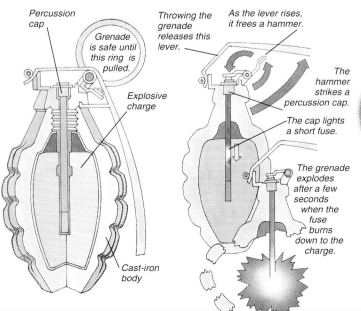

Percussion cap

Grenade is safe until this ring is pulled.

Explosive charge

Throwing the grenade releases this lever.

As the lever rises, it frees a hammer.

The hammer strikes a percussion cap.

The cap lights a short fuse.

The grenade explodes after a few seconds when the fuse burns down to the charge.

Cast-iron body

THE NUCLEAR DETERRENT

A single nuclear weapon can kill the population of an entire city, and a nuclear war might destroy all life on Earth. Some politicians call these weapons the nuclear deterrent. They believe that the terrible results of nuclear war discourage or deter a nation from launching a nuclear attack.

Nuclear weapons create an extremely powerful blast, searing heat, and lethal nuclear radiation.

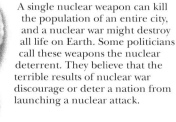

Find out more

ARMIES
ARMOUR
GUNS
NUCLEAR AGE
ROCKETS AND MISSILES

WEASELS
STOATS, AND MARTENS

WITH THEIR SHARP teeth and agile bodies, weasels, stoats, and martens are excellent hunters. These fierce, lean predators are speedy and muscular, ideally suited to chasing prey into tight spaces. Their eyesight and hearing are good, and they have a keen sense of smell to pick up the scent of their victim. Their teeth are pointed for gripping their prey. Weasels, stoats, and martens can leap and twist their bodies with great ease as they chase after mice, rabbits, and birds. Of the three animals, the weasel is the smallest – the least weasel, measuring only 20 cm (8 in) in length, can kill rabbits, which are much larger than itself. The stoat, also called the ermine, resembles the weasel in shape. Martens also look like weasels; they have thick brown fur with a yellowish patch on the chest. Weasels, stoats, and martens all belong to the family of animals called mustelids. This family includes polecats (or ferrets), mink, skunks, badgers, otters, and wolverines. Most of them raise their young in burrows. After a few weeks, the young leave the burrow to pounce and tumble in mock play, practising for their lives as hunters.

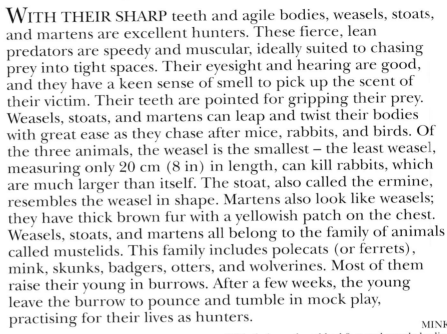

MARTEN
Although it hunts mainly on the ground, the pine marten is a skillful climber. It is so nimble in the treetops that it can easily catch a squirrel. Pine martens hunt beetles, mice, birds' eggs and chicks, and also eat berries.

STOAT
During the spring and summer months stoats are brown like weasels. In winter, however, their coats change colour to white, and this coat is known as ermine. In the coldest parts of northern Europe, North America, and Asia the stoat's white fur provides good camouflage as the animal hunts rabbits, lemmings, and mice in the snow. Like other members of the weasel family, stoats steal birds' eggs and raid chicken coops in search of eggs.

MINK
With their partly webbed feet and supple bodies measuring 40 to 50 cm (16 to 20 in) in length, mink are expert swimmers and divers. They live on the banks of rivers and lakes, where they feed on water birds, water voles, and fish. Many mink have been killed for their beautiful fur, and in some areas they are bred for this purpose.

Mink

POLECAT
The polecat is also called the ferret. There are three kinds – the European polecat, the steppe polecat, and the black-footed ferret from North America. Black-footed ferrets are on the official list of endangered species. They are threatened because their main source of food – the prairie dog – has been greatly reduced in numbers.

Markings on face enable ferrets to recognize one another.

Black-footed ferret

Lithe, muscular body

COMMON WEASEL
With its long, thin body and short legs, the European common weasel can dart into a rabbit burrow or rat tunnel to grab its prey. Weasels are so long and slender and flexible that they can easily perform a U-turn in a rabbit burrow. Weasels are fierce hunters, ripping a mouse or vole apart within seconds in a flurry of teeth and claws.

Sharp claws for digging and for catching prey

The weasel sniffs around a tunnel entrance in search of prey such as young rabbits.

Common weasel

When it finds a victim such as a rabbit, the weasel gives it a fatal bite to the back of the neck.

Find out more
ANIMALS
BADGERS AND SKUNKS
MAMMALS
RABBITS AND HARES

WEATHER

FROM ONE MOMENT to the next the weather can change. A warm, sunny day can be overtaken by a violent storm. Dark clouds form, high winds blow, and rain lashes the ground, yet it may be only a few minutes before the sunny weather returns. However, in some parts of the world, such as the tropics, the weather barely changes for months at a time. There it is always hot, and heavy rains fall. Weather describes conditions, such as rain, wind, and sunshine, that occur during a short period of time in a particular place; climate is the overall pattern of weather in a region. Meteorologists are scientists who measure and forecast the weather. They do this by studying clouds, winds, and the temperature and pressure of the Earth's atmosphere. But despite the use of satellites, computers, and other technology in weather forecasting, weather remains a force of nature that is hard to predict.

The air over the Sahara Desert is so stable and dry that rain almost never falls.

Cloud hangs over the hot and rainy tropics of central Africa.

Swirls of cloud mark patterns of winds.

Snow and ice cover the cold Antarctic continent.

WORLD WEATHER
The sun is the driving force for the world's weather. The heat of the sun's rays produces wind and evaporates water from the seas, which later forms clouds and rain. The direct heat above the equator makes the weather hot, while the poles, which get less of the sun's heat, are cold and cloudy.

MEASURING THE WEATHER
Several thousand weather stations on land, ships, and aircraft measure weather conditions around the world. The stations contain instruments that record temperature, rainfall, the speed and direction of wind, air pressure, and humidity (the amount of water vapour in the air). Balloons called radiosondes carry instruments to take measurements high in the air. Weather satellites in space send back pictures of the clouds.

A scale of hours on the cardboard shows at what times the sun was shining.

SUNSHINE RECORDER
The more direct sunshine a region receives, the warmer it becomes. An instrument called a sunshine recorder measures daily hours of sunshine. The glass ball works like a powerful lens, focusing the sun's rays, which leave a line of burn marks on a piece of cardboard.

The wind spins the cups, and the wind speed is shown on a dial.

Rain pours through a funnel into a container. Each day the collected water is poured into a measuring cylinder which gives a reading of the day's total rainfall.

Barograph gives a permanent record of air pressure on a chart.

RAIN GAUGE
Droplets of water and tiny ice crystals group together to form clouds, and water falls from the skies as rain and snow. Meteorologists measure rainfall, which is the depth of water that would occur if the rain did not drain away.

ANEMOMETER
The sun's heat produces winds – moving currents of air that flow over the Earth's surface. Meteorologists use anemometers to measure wind speed, which shows the rate of approaching weather.

BAROGRAPH
A barograph measures air pressure. This is important in weather forecasting because high pressure often brings settled weather; low pressure brings wind and rain.

CLOUDS

Low-lying clouds at the top of a hill cause the air to become cold, foggy, and damp. This is because the clouds contain many tiny droplets of water. Clouds form in air that is rising. The air contains invisible water vapour. As the air ascends, it becomes cooler. Colder air cannot hold so much vapour, and some vapour turns to tiny droplets or freezes to ice crystals, forming a cloud. Slow-rising air produces sheets of cloud. Air that is ascending quickly gives clumps of cloud.

CLOUD FORMATION

There are three main kinds of clouds which form at different heights in the air. Feathery cirrus clouds float highest of all. Midway to low are fluffy cumulus clouds. Sheets of stratus clouds often lie low in the sky; gray stratus bears rain. Cumulonimbus cloud, a type of cumulus cloud, towers in the sky and often brings thunderstorms.

Cirrus clouds

Anvil of cumulonimbus clouds

Cirrocumulus

Cumulonimbus

Altostratus

Altocumulus

Cumulus

Stratocumulus

Stratus

16 km (10 miles)

13 km (8 miles)

9.7 km (6 miles)

6.4 km (4 miles)

3.2 km (2 miles)

Ground level

CIRRUS CLOUDS

Cirrus clouds form high in the sky so they contain only ice crystals. Cirrocumulus (above) and cirro-stratus also form at high altitudes.

CUMULUS CLOUDS

Separate masses of cloud are called cumulus clouds. Altocumulus is medium-high patchy cloud, and low stratocumulus contains low, dense clumps of cloud.

AIR MASSES AND FRONTS

Huge bodies of air, called air masses, form over land and sea. Air masses containing warm, cold, moist, or dry air bring different kinds of weather as they are carried by the wind. A front is where two air masses meet. The weather changes when a front arrives.

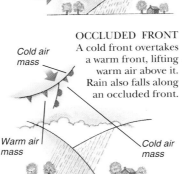

WARM FRONT

Long spells of rain occur as warm air rises above cold air before the front arrives on the ground.

Warm, moist air mass

Cold, moist air mass

COLD FRONT

Cold air moves in under warm air, bringing heavy rain followed by showers.

Cold air mass

Warm air mass

OCCLUDED FRONT

A cold front overtakes a warm front, lifting warm air above it. Rain also falls along an occluded front.

Cold air mass

Warm air mass

Cold air mass

WEATHER FORECASTING

The weather centres in different countries receive measurements of weather conditions from satellites and observers around the world. They use this data to forecast the weather that lies ahead. Supercomputers do the many difficult calculations involved and draw charts of the weather to come. Forecasters use the charts to predict the weather for the next few days, producing weather reports for television, newspapers, shipping, and aircraft.

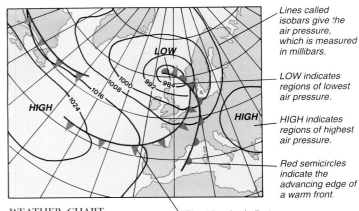

LOW

HIGH

HIGH

1024 1016 1008 1000 992 984

Lines called isobars give the air pressure, which is measured in millibars.

LOW indicates regions of lowest air pressure.

HIGH indicates regions of highest air pressure.

Red semicircles indicate the advancing edge of a warm front.

Blue triangles indicate the advancing edge of a cold front.

WEATHER CHART

A weather forecaster predicts the day's weather using a chart showing air pressure and fronts over a large region. Lines called isobars connect regions with the same atmospheric pressure. Tight loops of isobars of decreasing pressure show a low, where it is windy and possibly rainy. Isobars of rising pressure indicate a high, which gives settled weather.

HIGHS AND LOWS

The pressure of the air varies. Regions of low pressure are called cyclones or lows. The air rises and cools, bringing clouds and rain. An anticyclone, or high, is a region of high pressure. The air descends and warms, bringing clear, dry weather. Winds circle around highs and lows, as can be seen in this satellite picture of a cyclonic storm.

Find out more

ATMOSPHERE
CLIMATES
EARTH
RAIN AND SNOW
STORMS
WIND

WEIGHTS AND MEASURES

HOW FAR AWAY is the moon? How deep are the oceans? How tall are you? How hot is it on Mars? It is possible to measure all these things and many more. Every day we need to make measurements. In cooking, for example, a recipe requires the correct weight of each ingredient, and once mixed the ingredients have to be cooked at a certain temperature. We make measurements using measuring instruments. For example, a thermometer measures temperature, a ruler measures distance, and a clock measures time. All measurements are based on a system of units. Time, for example, is measured in units of minutes and seconds; length is measured in metres or feet. Precise measurements are very important in science and medicine. Scientists have extremely accurate measuring instruments to determine everything from the tiny distance between atoms in a piece of metal, to the temperature of a distant planet, such as Neptune.

Scale pan carries fixed weights in units of grams or ounces.

WEIGHT
Weighing scales measure how heavy things are. They compare the weight of an object in one pan to a known weight which sits in the other pan.

VOLUME
Volume measures the amount of space that an object or liquid takes up. A measuring jug measures the volume of a liquid. By reading the level of the liquid against a scale of units, you can find the volume of the liquid in the jug.

Thermometers measure temperature.

LENGTH AND AREA
Tape measures and rulers indicate length. They can also be used to calculate area, which indicates, for example, the amount of land a football pitch takes up or the amount of material needed to make a coat.

We can also measure things that we cannot see. This digital meter measures the strength of an electric current in amperes (A).

UNITS OF MEASUREMENT
When you measure something, such as height, you compare the quantity you are measuring to a fixed unit such as a metre or a foot. Scientists have set these units with great precision, so that if you measure your height with two different rulers, you will get the same answer. The metre, for example, is defined (set) by the distance travelled by light in a specific time. This gives a very precise measure of length.

TIME
Time is measured in hours, minutes, and seconds. A digital stopwatch can measure the time of a race to the nearest hundredth of a second.

METRIC SYSTEM
A system of measurement defines fixed units for all quantities such as weight and time. Most countries use the metric system, which began in France about 200 years ago. Then the metre was fixed as the distance between the North Pole and the equator divided by 10 million. The metre is now fixed using light.

The cubit and the hand were Ancient Egyptian units.

One cubit

The hand was divided into four fingers.

The foot originated in Ancient Rome.

BODY MEASUREMENTS
The earliest systems of units were based on parts of the human body, such as the hands or feet. Both the Ancient Egyptians (about 3000 B.C.) and the Romans (from about 800 B.C.) used units of this kind. However, body measurements present a problem. They always give different answers because they depend on the size of the person making the measurement.

Many imperial units were first used in Ancient Rome. The mile was 1,000 paces, each pace being two steps. The word mile *comes from the word for 1,000 in Latin.*

IMPERIAL SYSTEM
Units of the imperial system include inches and feet for length, pints and gallons for volume, and pounds and tons for weight. The imperial system is used mainly in the United States.

___*Find out more*___
CLOCKS AND WATCHES
EGYPT, ANCIENT
MATHEMATICS
ROMAN EMPIRE

WHALES AND DOLPHINS

TEN MILLION YEARS before humans first lived on Earth, whales were swimming in the oceans. Whales are among the most intelligent of all creatures. They are also the largest living animals, and among the gentlest and most graceful. Whales, dolphins, and porpoises make up a fascinating group of mammals. They are warm-blooded, but unlike seals, they have no fur; a thick layer of fatty blubber under the skin keeps them warm. The whale group is divided into those with teeth (toothed whales) and those without teeth (baleen whales). There are dozens of different toothed whales, including the friendly bottle-nosed dolphin and the ferocious killer whale, which eats almost anything in the sea. Toothless or baleen whales include the humpback and blue whales, which feed by sieving small sea creatures such as krill into their mouths. Since all whales and dolphins breathe air, they must swim to the surface of the water regularly. Whales and dolphins swim by moving their tails up and down; fish move their tails from side to side. Whales have suffered greatly from hunting by humans, and 21 kinds are on the official lists of endangered species. Today whaling is not allowed, in the hope that the population of whales will increase.

One of the most playful creatures in the world is the dolphin. This sociable animal lives in "schools" of up to 1,000. They race through the waves, and sometimes can be seen scooting along in front of boats.

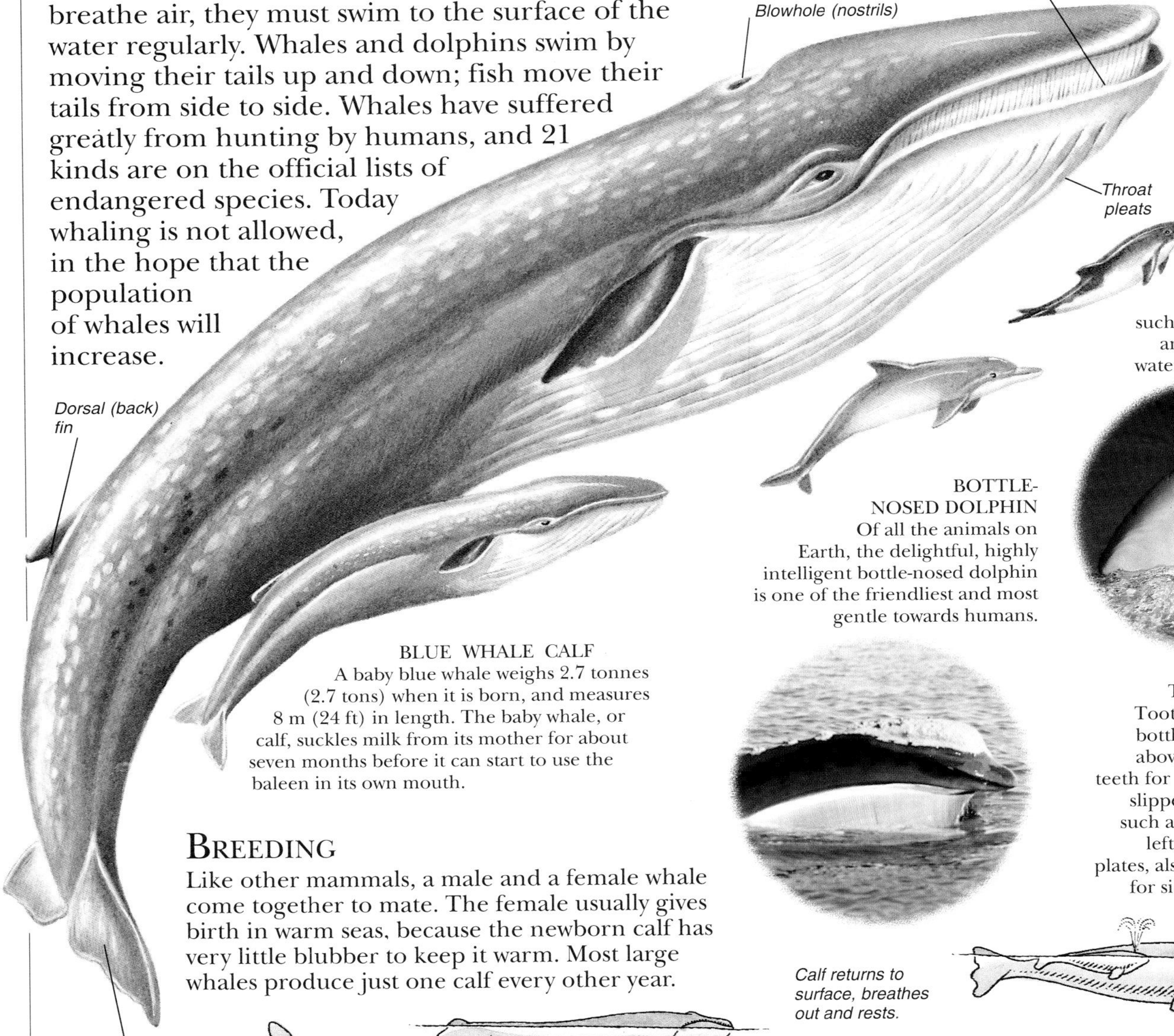

BLUE WHALE
The blue whale is the largest animal that has ever lived, and it roams all oceans. Blue whales can live to 80 years of age. The skin on the blue whale's throat has many grooves, and expands hugely as the whale feeds.

Baleen plates for feeding

Blowhole (nostrils)

Throat pleats

PORPOISE
There are six different kinds of porpoises. Common, or harbour, porpoises such as the one shown here are often seen in shallow water close to harbours and beaches

Dorsal (back) fin

BOTTLE-NOSED DOLPHIN
Of all the animals on Earth, the delightful, highly intelligent bottle-nosed dolphin is one of the friendliest and most gentle towards humans.

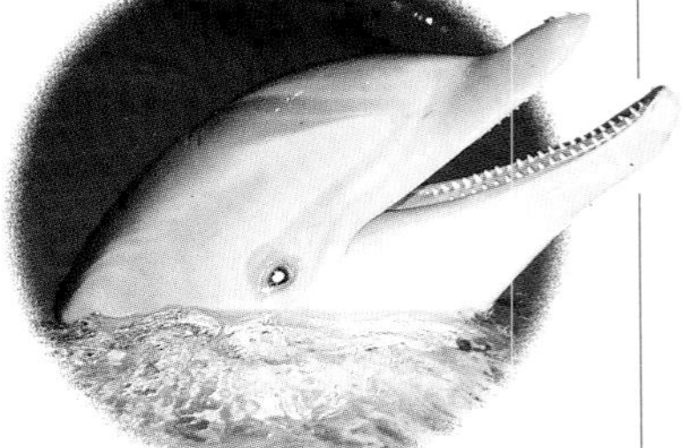

BLUE WHALE CALF
A baby blue whale weighs 2.7 tonnes (2.7 tons) when it is born, and measures 8 m (24 ft) in length. The baby whale, or calf, suckles milk from its mother for about seven months before it can start to use the baleen in its own mouth.

TEETH AND BALEEN
Toothed whales, such as the bottle-nosed dolphin shown above, have dozens of sharp teeth for gripping fish and other slippery prey. Baleen whales, such as the right whale shown left, have comb-like baleen plates, also known as whalebone, for sieving krill from the sea.

BREEDING
Like other mammals, a male and a female whale come together to mate. The female usually gives birth in warm seas, because the newborn calf has very little blubber to keep it warm. Most large whales produce just one calf every other year.

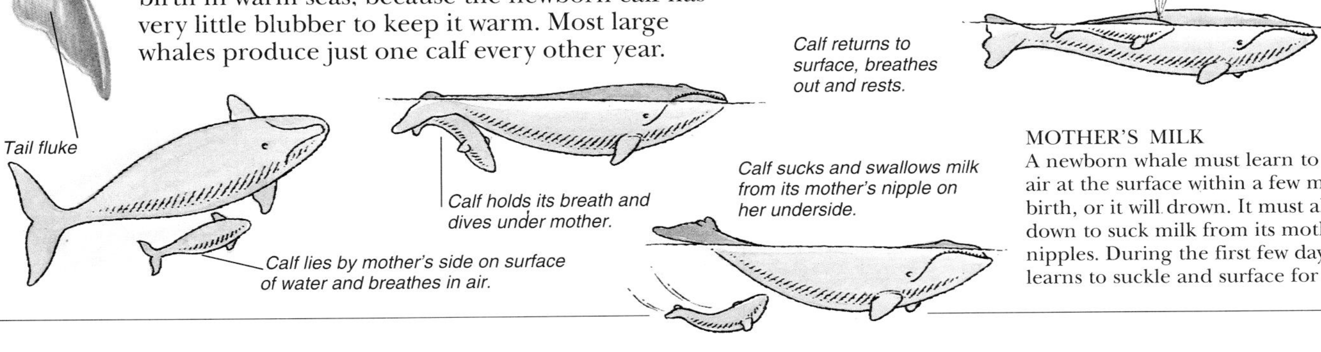

Calf returns to surface, breathes out and rests.

Tail fluke

Calf holds its breath and dives under mother.

Calf sucks and swallows milk from its mother's nipple on her underside.

Calf lies by mother's side on surface of water and breathes in air.

MOTHER'S MILK
A newborn whale must learn to breathe air at the surface within a few minutes of birth, or it will drown. It must also dive down to suck milk from its mother's nipples. During the first few days the calf learns to suckle and surface for air.

SPERM WHALE

The impressive sperm whale is the deepest diving sea mammal known to us. It swims down to at least 1 km (3,300 ft), holding its breath for more than an hour. Measuring more than 15 m (45 ft) in length, it is the largest of the toothed whales and has enormous teeth – up to 25 cm (10 in) long. The sperm whale feeds on squid and fish deep down near the sea bed. In the past, so many sperm whales were killed to make products from their fatty blubber, flesh, and the oil in their foreheads (spermaceti) that very few of these great creatures now exist.

The sperm whale's enormous forehead is filled with a waxy, oily substance called spermaceti, which helps keep the whale upright in the water.

THE LARGEST BRAIN
The brain of the sperm whale is the biggest of any animal, weighing more than 9 kg (20 lb).

Up to 50 teeth in lower jaw

BLOWHOLES
After a dive, whales rise to the surface to blow out warm, moist air from their lungs. As this air mixes with the cold ocean air, the moisture condenses (like your breath on a cold winter morning). This is what makes the watery-looking spout.

Blue whale

Right whale

Humpback whale

Sperm whale

WHALE SOUNDS
Whales make a variety of sounds, including squeals, groans, yips, and wails, which carry many kilometres through the water. Each male humpback whale has its own song, lasting for up to 35 minutes, which it sings over and over again. Dolphins in a group "talk" constantly to each other as they play and feed.

Melon organ in forehead

Shark is detected by dolphin.

Outgoing clicking sound and returning echoes

ECHOLOCATION
In addition to using their sight and hearing, dolphins are able to sense other creatures nearby by means of a special organ in their forehead called the "melon". By making a loud clicking sound which bounces off objects and makes echoes, the dolphin can tell the size and distance of another creature in the water. It can then warn other dolphins of any danger.

MIGRATION
Many whales spend the winter in warm seas and summer in colder waters, travelling great distances from ocean to ocean. Grey whales travel south to give birth to one calf in winter near California. Then the mother and baby begin a long journey up the coast towards the Bering Sea and the Arctic Ocean.

Bering Sea

Canada

United States

California

WHALES OF THE WORLD
All whales and most dolphins live in the sea; five kinds of dolphins live in rivers. Some whales, such as humpback and killer whales, inhabit all oceans; others, such as the narwhal and the beluga whale, live only in the Arctic region.

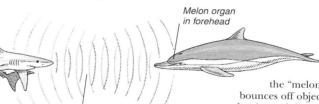

Humpback whale 16 m (50 ft) 26 tonnes (26 tons)

Killer whale (orca) 8 m (27 ft), 3.6 tonnes (3.5 tons)

Beluga, 1.4 tonnes (1.4 tons)

STRANDINGS
Whales sometimes swim too close to the land and are stranded. Without water to support their bodies, they cannot breathe, and soon die.

BIGGEST ANIMAL EVER
Blue whales are larger than the dinosaurs were – up to 30 m (100 ft) in length. They are the heaviest animals ever, weighing 136 tonnes (134 tons) – about as heavy as 2,000 people.

Human diver, 2 m (6 ft) in length. Blue whale 30 m (100 ft) in length.

Ganges river dolphin, 90 kg (200 lb)

Pacific white-sided dolphin, 90 kg (200 lb)

Narwhal, 1.4 tonnes (1.4 tons)

Find out more
ANIMAL SENSES
ANIMALS
MAMMALS
MIGRATION
OCEAN WILDLIFE

WHEELS

SOMETIMES THE SIMPLEST inventions are the most important. Although no one is sure exactly who invented the first wheel, the earliest records go back to about 5,500 years ago. The wheel has made possible a whole range of machines, from photocopiers to jet engines, that we take for granted today. Wheels have a unique characteristic – they are circular, without corners, enabling them to roll or spin evenly. This allows almost all forms of land transportation – bicycles, cars, trains, and trams – to roll smoothly along roads, rails, and rough ground. In addition, the circular motion of a wheel means that it can transmit power continuously from an engine. Other inventions are also based on wheels. The crane, for example, relies on pulleys (grooved wheels around which a rope is passed) which reduce the effort needed to lift heavy weights; gears multiply or reduce the speed and force of a wheel and are essential in countless machines including engines and aircraft.

AXLE AND BEARINGS
A wheel spins on a shaft called an axle. Wheels often have ball bearings – several small steel balls that run between the axle and the wheel, allowing it to turn smoothly. Without bearings, the great weight of a Ferris wheel (above) would squeeze the wheel against the axle and prevent it from turning.

Before wheels were invented, people had to push or drag heavy loads over the ground. Perhaps watching a smooth rock roll down a hill gave people the idea of using wheels for transport.

About 4,500 years ago, the Ancient Egyptians built great triangular pyramids as tombs and temples. Gangs of workers dragged huge blocks of stone with the aid of logrollers.

The first vehicle wheels were solid wooden wheels used for carts. They were made of two or three planks of wood fixed together and cut into a circle. They first appeared in about 3200 B.C.

INVENTING THE WHEEL
The first recorded use of a wheel dates back to around 3500 B.C. This was the potter's wheel, a simple turntable used in southwest Asia by Mesopotamian pottery workers to make smooth, round clay pots. About 300 years later, the Mesopotamians fitted wheels to a cart, and the age of wheeled transport had begun.

GYROSCOPES
A gyroscope is a rotating wheel mounted on a frame. When the wheel spins, its momentum makes it balance like a spinning top. Once a gyroscope is spinning, it always tries to point in the same direction. Aircraft, ships, and missiles use gyroscopes to navigate, or direct themselves, to their destinations.

Bibendum, the famous symbol of the French tyre company Michelin

Wheels with spokes developed in about 2000 B.C. Spoked wheels are lighter and faster than solid wheels and were fitted to war chariots.

Wheels held together by wire spokes appeared in about 1800. They are very light and strong, and were first used for cars, bicycles, and early aeroplanes. In the 1950s, metal wheels replaced wire wheels on cars.

Gears can change the direction of motion of a wheel – from horizontal to vertical, for example.

TYRES
Car and bicycle wheels have rubber tyres filled with air. They give a comfortable ride and have a tread (a pattern of ridges) to help them grip the road. Scottish engineer Robert W. Thomson invented the first air-filled tyre in 1845.

GEARS
Sets of interlocking toothed wheels are called gears. Gears transfer movement in machines and change the speed and force of wheels. For example, a large gear wheel makes a small gear wheel rotate faster, but the faster-moving wheel produces less force.

Find out more

BICYCLES AND MOTORCYCLES
CARS
TRANSPORT, HISTORY OF

WILD WEST

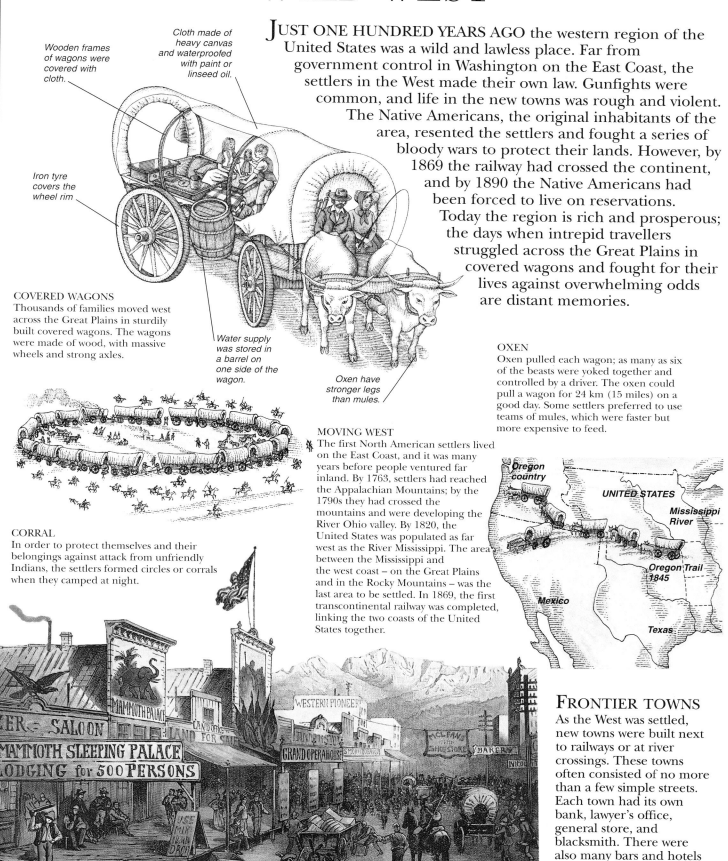

JUST ONE HUNDRED YEARS AGO the western region of the United States was a wild and lawless place. Far from government control in Washington on the East Coast, the settlers in the West made their own law. Gunfights were common, and life in the new towns was rough and violent. The Native Americans, the original inhabitants of the area, resented the settlers and fought a series of bloody wars to protect their lands. However, by 1869 the railway had crossed the continent, and by 1890 the Native Americans had been forced to live on reservations. Today the region is rich and prosperous; the days when intrepid travellers struggled across the Great Plains in covered wagons and fought for their lives against overwhelming odds are distant memories.

Wooden frames of wagons were covered with cloth.

Cloth made of heavy canvas and waterproofed with paint or linseed oil.

Iron tyre covers the wheel rim

Water supply was stored in a barrel on one side of the wagon.

Oxen have stronger legs than mules.

COVERED WAGONS
Thousands of families moved west across the Great Plains in sturdily built covered wagons. The wagons were made of wood, with massive wheels and strong axles.

CORRAL
In order to protect themselves and their belongings against attack from unfriendly Indians, the settlers formed circles or corrals when they camped at night.

OXEN
Oxen pulled each wagon; as many as six of the beasts were yoked together and controlled by a driver. The oxen could pull a wagon for 24 km (15 miles) on a good day. Some settlers preferred to use teams of mules, which were faster but more expensive to feed.

MOVING WEST
The first North American settlers lived on the East Coast, and it was many years before people ventured far inland. By 1763, settlers had reached the Appalachian Mountains; by the 1790s they had crossed the mountains and were developing the River Ohio valley. By 1820, the United States was populated as far west as the River Mississippi. The area between the Mississippi and the west coast – on the Great Plains and in the Rocky Mountains – was the last area to be settled. In 1869, the first transcontinental railway was completed, linking the two coasts of the United States together.

Oregon country

UNITED STATES

Mississippi River

Oregon Trail 1845

Mexico

Texas

FRONTIER TOWNS
As the West was settled, new towns were built next to railways or at river crossings. These towns often consisted of no more than a few simple streets. Each town had its own bank, lawyer's office, general store, and blacksmith. There were also many bars and hotels where the local people could enjoy themselves.

SALOON
MAMMOTH SLEEPING PALACE
LODGING for 500 PERSONS
MAMMOTH PALACE
LAND FOR SALE
WESTERN PIONEER
GRAND OPERAHOUSE
SMOKE TOBACCO
SHOE STORE
BAKERY

A SETTLER'S HOUSE

There were no trees or rocks to use as building materials on the grassy Great Plains of the American Midwest. So the first settlers built their houses from turf or sod, which they shaped into bricks. The simple but effective dwellings could last 10 years, but they were damp and often leaked when it rained.

FRONTIER LIFE
Life in the American Midwest was harsh and lonely for the settlers, many of whom lived far from any town. The whole family had to work long hours on the land to produce enough food to eat. There was little time for pleasure or company.

INDIAN WARS

As the settlers moved west, they claimed the land they found as their own. However, they first had to drive away the Native American population, which had farmed the valleys and hunted the plains for centuries. From 1861 the Native Americans fought a series of wars to keep their land, but by 1890 many Native Americans had been killed, and the settlers controlled most of the West.

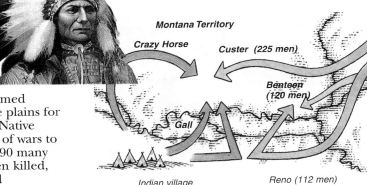

Montana Territory

Crazy Horse

Custer (225 men)

Benteen (120 men)

Gall

Indian village

Reno (112 men)

CUSTER'S LAST STAND
On 25 June 1876, about 3,000 Sioux and Cheyenne warriors gathered at Little Bighorn River, Montana, to fight for their lands. About 500 men of the 7th Cavalry attempted to attack the warriors. Lieutenant Colonel George Custer, who led one of the regiments, was a famous Native American fighter and a hero of the Civil War. Although Custer split his force into three, they were outnumbered and defeated by the Native Americans. Led by Gall and Crazy Horse, the Native Americans killed every man in Custer's group. The map shows the main groupings.

THE GOLD RUSH

In January 1848, the first gold fields were discovered in California. At first, only local people prospected (searched) for gold, but in 1849 a rush of prospectors came west to make their fortunes and invaded the state. In 1849 alone, the population of California rose from 20,000 to more than 100,000 people.

Pan for separating gold from rubble; gold dust stuck to the greasy bottom of the pan.

FRONTIER LAW
Many early settlers used guns to protect themselves and their property. The law was rough and ready, and sheriffs kept the peace as best they could. However, they were often powerless to prevent gunfights and other acts of violence.

THE WILD WEST

1836 Siege of the Alamo leads Texas to break away from Mexico and join the United States in 1845.

1842 Thousands of settlers begin to travel west along the Oregon Trail to live in the new territories.

1845-48 United States gains California, Nevada, and part of Utah, New Mexico, and Arizona in war with Mexico.

1847 Mormon settlers establish Salt Lake City, Utah.

1848 Gold discovered in California.

1849 Gold rush brings many prospectors to California.

1858 First regular stagecoach service between East and West coasts.

1861-65 Civil War splits nation over issue of slavery.

1861-90 Frequent wars between the Indians and settlers in the Midwest.

1862 Homestead Act offers settlers 65 hectares (160 acres) of virtually free land on the Great Plains; it leads to the population and cultivation of the Midwest.

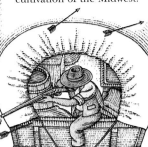

Find out more

COWBOYS
INDIANS,
Native American
UNITED STATES OF AMERICA,
history of

WIND

AS A GENTLE BREEZE OR A POWERFUL hurricane, wind blows constantly around the world. Winds are belts of moving air that flow from one area to another, driven by the sun's heat. Warm air is lighter than cold air, so warm air rises as it is heated by the sun and cold air flows in to take its place. This sets up a circular current of air which produces winds. Light, warm air exerts less pressure on the Earth than cold air, creating an area of low pressure towards which cold air flows. Similarly, cold air sinks and produces an area of high pressure from which air flows outwards. The greater the difference in pressure between two areas, the stronger the winds. Weather forecasters use the Beaufort scale to measure the speed of wind. It runs from 0 to 12: for example, force 2 is a light breeze; force 12 is a hurricane. The size and shape of areas of land and water affect local winds, which are often given special names such as the chinook in North America and the sirocco in Italy.

WIND DIRECTION
A wind is often named according to the direction from which it is coming. For example, a wind which comes from the west is called a westerly. Windsocks and vanes are used to show the wind direction.

At the equator, the sun's heat warms the air. In this area, the air rises, causing a belt of calm air called the doldrums.

When the air has risen very high, it cools and sinks back to the Earth in the horse latitudes.

Polar easterlies

Westerlies

Horse latitudes

NE trade winds

Doldrums

SE trade winds

Horse latitudes

Westerlies

The westerlies are warm winds which blow away from the horse latitudes in the direction of the poles.

The trade winds flow from the horse latitudes towards the equator.

In between the westerlies and the trade winds is an area of calm called the horse latitudes. The name may refer to the many horses that died on ships that were becalmed in this region.

The polar easterlies are cold winds which blow away from the poles.

WORLD WINDS
As well as local and seasonal winds, there are certain winds that always blow. These are called prevailing winds. There are three main belts of prevailing winds on each side of the equator. They are called the trade winds, the westerlies, and the polar easterlies. The direction they blow in is affected by the spin of the Earth. They are angled towards the left in the southern hemisphere and towards the right in the northern hemisphere.

MONSOONS

Winds that change direction with the seasons are called monsoons. For example, during the summer in southern Asia, the wind blows from the Indian Ocean towards the land, bringing heavy rains. In winter, the wind blows in the opposite direction, from the Himalayas towards the ocean.

WIND TURBINES
The earliest ships used wind power to carry them across the sea. Wind also powers machines: windmills were used in Iran as long ago as the 7th century for raising water from rivers, and later for grinding corn. Today huge windmills, or wind turbines, can produce electricity; a large wind turbine can supply enough electricity for a small town. Wind turbines cause no pollution but they are large and noisy and take up huge areas of land.

An experimental wind farm in the United States uses 300 wind turbines to produce electricity.

Find out more
CLIMATES
ENERGY
STORMS
WEATHER

WOMEN'S RIGHTS

TWO HUNDRED YEARS AGO women had few rights. They were not allowed to vote, and were considered the property of their fathers or husbands. By the middle of the 19th century, women were demanding equality with men. They wanted suffrage – the right to vote in elections – and an equal chance to work and be educated. They demanded the right to have their own possessions, to divorce their husbands, and to keep their children after divorce. The fight for women's rights was also called feminism, and involved many dedicated women. The first organized demand for the vote occurred in the United States in 1848. By the 1920s women had won some battles, particularly for the vote and education. In the 1960s women renewed their fight for equal rights. The new wave of protest was called the women's liberation movement. It led to the passage of laws in many countries to stop discrimination against women.

WORKING WOMEN
In the United States about 43 per cent of workers are women. But few hold important positions, and most earn less than men doing the same jobs.

1792 Mary Wollstonecraft publishes *A Vindication of the Rights of Woman.*

1848 First women's rights conference, U S A calls for voting rights for women.

1893 New Zealand is first country to grant voting rights to women.

1903 Emmeline Pankhurst launches Women's Social Political Union to fight for the vote in Britain.

1918 British women over 30 gain the vote.

1920 19th amendment to U.S. Constitution grants vote to women over 30.

1960 World's first woman prime minister in Sri Lanka.

1963 Federal Equal Pay Act outlaws paying women less than men for the same job.

1970 First Women's Liberation Conference, Oxford, England.

1970 Equal Pay Act, Britain.

1979 United Nations approves Convention on the Elimination of All Forms of Discrimination Against Women.

EMILY DAVISON
In 1913 British suffragette Emily Davison leaped under the king's horse at a race and died. Her protest drew attention to the Votes for Women campaign.

SUSAN B. ANTHONY
One of the leaders of the suffrage movement in the United States, Susan B. Anthony (1820-1906), helped launch *Revolution*, the first feminist newspaper.

Suffragettes publicised their campaign by chaining themselves to the railings of famous buildings.

SUFFRAGETTES

In 1905, a British newspaper used the word *suffragette* to insult women who were fighting for the vote. However, the suffragettes themselves were delighted. People have used the name ever since. Many suffragettes broke the law and went to prison for their beliefs. Women who used peaceful means to obtain the vote were called suffragists.

FORCE FEEDING
In 1909 suffragettes in prison refused to eat. Warders fed them by pouring food down tubes which they forced through the women's noses into their stomachs. It was painful and seriously injured some women. Force feeding ended in 1913.

WOMEN AT WAR
During World War I (1914-18), women in Britain worked to keep factories going while the men fought. They proved that women were just as capable as men. In 1918 British women over 30 gained the vote. Two years later American women also gained the vote.

WOMEN'S LIBERATION MOVEMENT
During the late 1960s and 1970s, the women's liberation movement fought for further improvements in women's rights. Women everywhere demonstrated for equal pay, better health care, and an end to pornography and violence against women.

Find out more
DEMOCRACY
LAW
SCHOOLS

WONDERS
OF THE ANCIENT WORLD

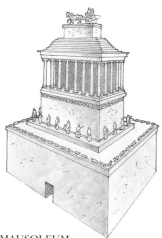

PYRAMIDS
Three pyramids were built at Giza, Egypt, in about 2600 B.C. as tombs for three Egyptian kings. The largest, made from more than two million huge limestone blocks, stands 147 m (482 ft) high.

TWO THOUSAND YEARS AGO Ancient Greek and Roman tourists visited the world's great landmarks just as we do today. Ancient "travel agents" compiled lists of amazing things that travellers should see. These "wonders" were outstanding examples of human artistic or engineering achievement. The seven most commonly listed monuments to human endeavour are called the Seven Wonders of the Ancient World. They all had qualities which made them stand out from the rest. Some were the most beautiful statues, others the largest structures of the day. Of the seven wonders, only one, the Great Pyramids, can still be seen today. The Hanging Gardens, the Temple of Artemis, the Statue of Zeus, the Mausoleum, the Colossus, and the Lighthouse at Pharos have all vanished or are in ruins.

HANGING GARDENS
In 605 B.C. Nebuchadnezzar II, king of Babylon, built the Hanging Gardens in his kingdom. He planted many exotic plants on a brick terrace 23 m (75 ft) above the ground. Machines worked by slaves watered the plants.

MAUSOLEUM
The Mausoleum at Halicarnassus (in modern Turkey) was a huge marble tomb built for Mausolus, a rich governor. It stood 41 m (135 ft) high, with a base supporting 36 columns, under a stepped pyramid. An earthquake destroyed most of the mausoleum.

LIGHTHOUSE
The Greek architect Sostratos designed the world's first lighthouse. It was built around 304 B.C. on the island of Pharos, Alexandria, Egypt. It stood about 134 m (440 ft) high. A fire burned at the top to mark the harbour entrance.

TEMPLE OF ARTEMIS
This, the largest temple of its day, was dedicated to Artemis, goddess of the moon and hunting. Built almost entirely of marble by the Greeks at Ephesus (in modern Turkey), it burned down in 356 B.C., leaving only a few broken statues.

COLOSSUS
The bronze statue of the sun god Helios towered 37 m (120 ft) over the harbour entrance on the island of Rhodes in the Aegean Sea. Built in 292 B.C., it was about the same size as the Statue of Liberty in New York.

ZEUS
The great Statue of Zeus, king of the Greek gods, stood 12 m (40 ft) high at Olympia, Greece. Phidias, a famous Greek sculptor, created the statue in about 435 B.C. The god's robes and ornaments were made of gold, and the skin was of ivory.

Olympia

Ephesus
Halicarnassus

Rhodes

Alexandria
Giza

Babylon •

LOCATION OF THE WONDERS
The map shows the location of the Seven Wonders of the Ancient World. Travellers visited many of them by ship. Most of the wonders were destroyed by earthquakes or fire, but some remains can still be seen in the British Museum in London, England.

Find out more

ALEXANDER THE GREAT
BABYLONIANS
EGYPT, ANCIENT

WORLD WAR I

BETWEEN 1914 AND 1918, a terrible war engulfed Europe. The war was called the First World War, or the Great War, because it affected almost every country in the world. It began because of the rivalry between several powerful European countries. Fighting started when the empire of Austria and Hungary declared war on Serbia. Soon other countries joined the war. They formed two main groups: the Allies, composed of Britain, France, Italy, Russia, and the United States, versus the Central Powers – Germany, Austria-Hungary, and Turkey. In the beginning everyone thought the war would be short and glorious. Young men rushed to join the armies and navies. But it soon became clear that none of the opposing armies was strong enough to win a clear victory. Thousands of troops died, fighting to gain just a few hundred metres of the battlefield. In the end, the war, which some called the "war to end all wars", had achieved nothing. Within a few years a worse war broke out in Europe.

ARCHDUKE FERDINAND
On 28 June, 1914, a Serbian terrorist shot Francis Ferdinand, heir to the throne of Austria and Hungary. Germany encouraged Austria to retaliate, or fight back, by declaring war on Serbia. A month after the assassination World War I had begun.

COUNTRIES AT WAR
The war involved nearly thirty countries – more countries than any previous war. There was fighting in the Middle East, Africa, and the Pacific. However, most of the war was fought in Europe. The western front in northern France was a line of trenches which stretched from Switzerland to the English Channel. Soldiers on the eastern front fought in what is now Poland. Fighting took place on land, at sea, and in the air.

Allied countries are green, Central powers are pink, and neutral countries are shown in beige

Norway

Denmark

Sweden

Great Britain

Netherlands

Germany

Poland

Russia

Belgium

English Channel

France

Austria-Hungary

Spain

Romania

Serbia

Bulgaria

Montenegro

RED BARON
World War I was the first war in which aeroplanes were used for fighting. Germany's Manfred von Richthofen (the Red Baron) became one of the first air aces.

YPRES
The Belgian city of Ypres was a battleground several times during World War I. It was here that the Germans first used poison gas on the western front. By 1918 the town was devastated (left).

TRENCH WARFARE
The armies advanced as far they could, then dug trenches for shelter. Life in the trenches was miserable. Soldiers were often up to their knees in mud. Lice and rats added to their discomfort. When soldiers left the trenches to advance further, the enemy killed them by the millions with machine guns. Each side also had artillery – guns that fired huge shells – which killed many more and churned up the battlefield into a sea of mud.

U-BOATS
German submarines called underwater boats or U-boats sank many cargo ships in the Atlantic, causing food shortages in Britain.

LUSITANIA
On 7 May, 1915, a German U-boat torpedoed the British passenger liner *Lusitania*. More than 100 American passengers drowned, some of whom were very rich and famous. This angered many Americans and turned them against Germany. The sinking helped to bring the United States into the war on the Allied side.

WORLD WAR I
June 1914 Assassination of Archduke Ferdinand

July 1914 Austria-Hungary declares war on Serbia.

August 1914 Germany declares war on Russia and France and invades Belgium. Britain declares war on Germany and Austria-Hungary.

May 1915 Italy joins Allies.

July 1916 Allies use tanks for the first time in France.

April 1917 United States enters the war.

March 1918 Russia signs treaty with Germany. Germany's final huge attack at Marne fails.

September 1918 Allies begin their final attack.

November 1918 Germany signs armistice, ending war.

WOMEN WORKERS
As thousands of men went off to war, women took over their jobs in the factories. Most women worked long hours, and many had dangerous jobs, such as making ammunition. Their efforts disproved the old idea that women were inferior to men, and eventually led to women gaining the right to vote. But when the troops returned after the war, there was massive unemployment, and women lost their jobs.

PROPAGANDA
Wartime posters and newspapers aimed to persuade people that the enemy was evil and that war must go on. The message of this propaganda, or government-controlled news, was that everyone should help by fighting, working, raising money, and making sacrifices. The poster (left) shows a frightening image of Germany with its hands on Europe.

COMMUNICATION
People at home had little idea of the real conditions of war. Officers read mail from soldiers and censored, or cut out, information that told the true story.
Troops returning home were often too sickened by life in the trenches to explain what it was really like or to tell how many soldiers had been killed or wounded.

GERMANS
Until 1918, it looked as if Germany and her allies might win. But they were outnumbered, and when the British navy blocked the ports and cut off supplies of food and vital war materials, the German people rioted. They demanded food and peace, and the kaiser – the German emperor – gave up his throne. Germany then made a peace treaty with the Allied forces. The Germans lost much land and took the blame for starting the war.

DEATH TOLL
Germany and Russia lost nearly two million soldiers each in the war. Britain lost nearly one million. In all, ten million died.

Find out more

DEPRESSION OF THE 1930S
WOMEN'S RIGHTS
WORLD WAR II

WORLD WAR II

IN 1939 GERMAN TANKS and bombers attacked Poland, and the bloodiest war in history began. Like World War I, World War II was a global war and was fought on the ground, in the air, and at sea. The war was a result of the rise to power of the German National Socialist or Nazi party, led by Adolf Hitler. The Nazis wanted to wipe out the memory of defeat in World War I. Within a year German armies, with help from Italy, had occupied much of Europe. Only Britain opposed them. In 1941, Hitler invaded the Soviet Union. But the Soviet people fought hard and millions died. In the Pacific the Japanese formed an alliance, called the Axis, with Germany and Italy. Japanese warplanes bombed the American naval base at Pearl Harbour, in Hawaii. This brought the United States into the war, and they joined the Soviet Union and Britain to form the Allies. By June 1945, Allied forces had defeated the Nazis in Europe; Japan surrendered in August. When the war ended, 45 million people had died and much of Europe was in ruins. Two new "super powers" – the Soviet Union and the United States – began to dominate world politics.

HITLER
In 1933, Adolf Hitler came to power in Germany as leader of the Nazi party. The Nazis were fascists: they were against communism and believed in strong national government. The Nazis ruthlessly crushed anyone who opposed them. They enslaved and murdered Jews, gypsies, and other minorities, whom they blamed for all Germany's problems, from defeat in World War I to unemployment and inflation.

The growth of Nazi Germany

British spitfire

German Messerschmitt

Norway

Sweden

Dunkirk

Poland

Britain

USSR

France

Nazi Germany

Czechoslovakia

Austria

Hungary

INVASION
In 1938 Hitler took control of Austria and parts of Czechoslovakia. Britain and France did not oppose him, and he went on to invade Poland. Britain and France then declared war on Germany. German troops smashed into France in 1940, sweeping aside the armies of Britain and France. Fleets of fishing boats and pleasure steamers from the south coast of England helped the Royal Navy to rescue the retreating Allied soldiers from the beaches at Dunkirk, on the coast of France.

BLITZ
Between August and October 1940 the British Royal Air Force fought the Luftwaffe – the German air force – in the Battle of Britain, and finally won. Without control of the skies Hitler could not invade Britain. His bombers began to bomb British cities during the night. This "blitzkrieg" or blitz, killed 40,000 people, mostly civilians.

EVACUATIONS
During the bombing of major cities, such as London, thousands of British children were evacuated to country towns and villages where they were much safer.

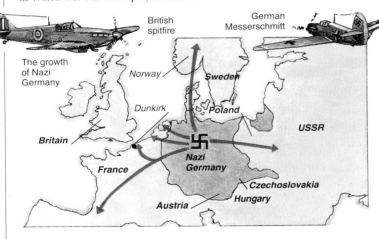

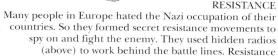

MIDWAY

Japan conquered many Pacific islands and invaded mainland Asia. But the United States fleet defeated the Japanese on 3 – 6 June, 1942, at the Battle of Midway. The battle turned the Pacific war in favour of the Allies.

RESISTANCE

Many people in Europe hated the Nazi occupation of their countries. So they formed secret resistance movements to spy on and fight the enemy. They used hidden radios (above) to work behind the battle lines. Resistance workers risked torture and death if they were discovered.

The defeat of Hitler's Germany, 1944-45

Britain

The Soviet advance

Held by Germany at end of war

Liberated by Allied forces

France

Neutral

Spain

Advance of Allies

PEACE IN EUROPE

By the spring of 1945, the Allies had recaptured most of occupied Europe and began to cross the River Rhine into Germany. In the east the Soviet army swept towards Berlin, Germany's capital. Crushed between these two powerful forces, the German armies surrendered. Hitler committed suicide, and the biggest and most expensive war in human history ended.

D-DAY

In June 1944, Allied troops invaded occupied Europe in the greatest seaborne landing ever mounted. Invasion day was code-named D-day. The D stood for deliverance. After a bitter struggle, and aided by resistance fighters, the Allied forces broke through, and the German soldiers retreated or were taken as prisoners.

CONCENTRATION CAMP

After Germany surrendered, Allied troops discovered horrifying concentration (prison) camps throughout Europe, where the Nazis had imprisoned up to 26 million people they considered "undesirable", including millions of Jews. The prisoners were starved and tortured, and many were eventually gassed to death.

VE DAY

On 8 May 1945, the Allies celebrated VE (Victory in Europe) Day. However, there were still another three months of bitter fighting in the Pacific. In August 1945 U.S. planes dropped two atom bombs on Japan, destroying the cities of Hiroshima and Nagasaki. This was done to force Japan to surrender quickly and so save Allied lives that would be lost if the Allies invaded Japan. Within a few weeks the Japanese surrendered and the war ended.

WORLD WAR II

1 September, 1939 Germany invades Poland. Britain and France declare war on Germany two days later.

April 1940 Germany invades Denmark and Norway.

May 1940 Germany invades Belgium, the Netherlands, and France.

June 1940 Germans enter Paris, and France signs an armistice (peace agreement) with Germany.

April 1941 Germany invades Greece and Yugoslavia.

June 1941 Germany invades the Soviet Union.

September 1941 Siege of Leningrad (U.S.S.R.) begins; lasts over two and a half years.

7 December, 1941 Japanese planes attack Pearl Harbour. The United States, Britain, and Canada declare war on Japan.

February 1942 Japanese capture many Pacific islands.

August 1942 German attack on Stalingrad (U.S.S.R.) begins.

November 1942 Allied troops land in North Africa to fight Germany and Italy. Under General Montgomery the British defeat Germany, led by Rommel, at El Alamein, Egypt.

February 1943 German armies besieging Stalingrad surrender.

May 1943 German armies in North Africa, under Rommel, surrender to the Allies.

July 1943 Allies invade Sicily.

September 1943 Italy surrenders.

September 1943 Allied forces land in Italy.

June 1944 Allied forces land in Normandy, north-west France, in the D-day invasion.

May 1945 German forces surrender; war in Europe ends.

August 1945 Allies drop atomic bombs on Japan.

2 September, 1945 Japan signs an unconditional surrender, ending World War II.

Find out more

CHURCHILL, SIR WINSTON
COLD WAR
NUCLEAR AGE
ROOSEVELT, FRANKLIN DELANO
WORLD WAR I

WORMS

WE DESCRIBE MANY long, slender, soft, legless creatures as worms. There are thousands of different kinds, ranging from the tiny hookworm to the much larger bootlace worm. The word *worm* is a fairly general term, and there are a number of distinct groups. Annelids, or segmented worms, include leeches, earthworms, and ragworms. Nematodes, or roundworms, have long tube-like bodies without segments. There are at least 12,000 kinds of roundworms. Some, including hookworms, cause serious diseases in humans such as river blindness and elephantiasis. Flatworms, or playhelminths, make up a third group. There are more than 30,000 kinds, and they include the parasitic flukes and tapeworms that infest sheep, pigs, and other animals.

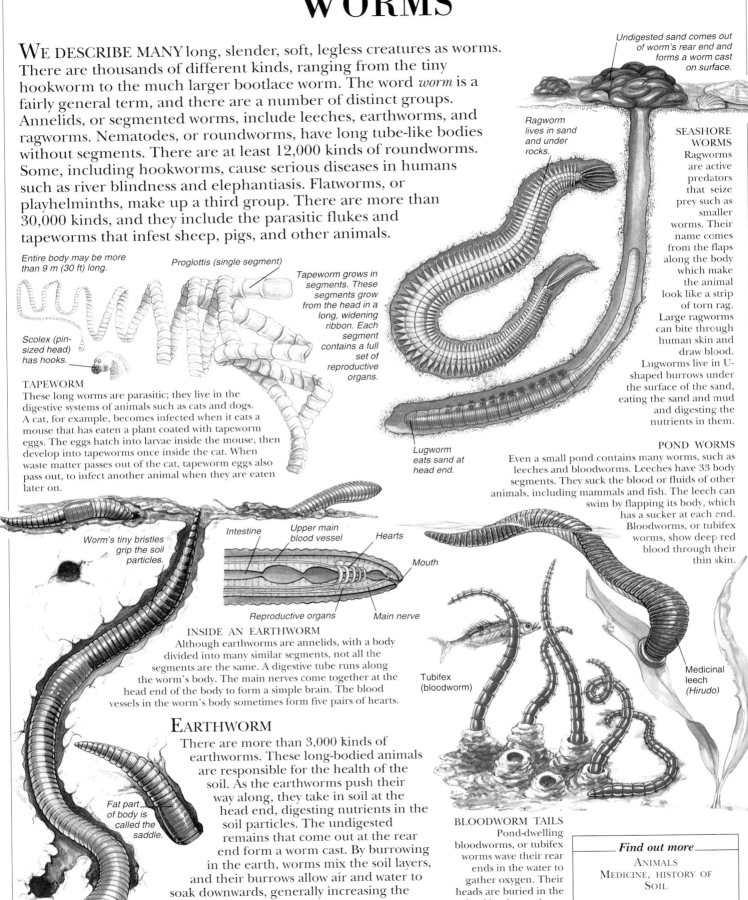

Undigested sand comes out of worm's rear end and forms a worm cast on surface.

Ragworm lives in sand and under rocks.

Entire body may be more than 9 m (30 ft) long.

Proglottis (single segment)

Tapeworm grows in segments. These segments grow from the head in a long, widening ribbon. Each segment contains a full set of reproductive organs.

Scolex (pin-sized head) has hooks.

TAPEWORM
These long worms are parasitic; they live in the digestive systems of animals such as cats and dogs. A cat, for example, becomes infected when it eats a mouse that has eaten a plant coated with tapeworm eggs. The eggs hatch into larvae inside the mouse, then develop into tapeworms once inside the cat. When waste matter passes out of the cat, tapeworm eggs also pass out, to infect another animal when they are eaten later on.

Lugworm eats sand at head end.

SEASHORE WORMS
Ragworms are active predators that seize prey such as smaller worms. Their name comes from the flaps along the body which make the animal look like a strip of torn rag. Large ragworms can bite through human skin and draw blood. Lugworms live in U-shaped burrows under the surface of the sand, eating the sand and mud and digesting the nutrients in them.

POND WORMS
Even a small pond contains many worms, such as leeches and bloodworms. Leeches have 33 body segments. They suck the blood or fluids of other animals, including mammals and fish. The leech can swim by flapping its body, which has a sucker at each end. Bloodworms, or tubifex worms, show deep red blood through their thin skin.

Worm's tiny bristles grip the soil particles.

Intestine

Upper main blood vessel

Hearts

Mouth

Reproductive organs

Main nerve

INSIDE AN EARTHWORM
Although earthworms are annelids, with a body divided into many similar segments, not all the segments are the same. A digestive tube runs along the worm's body. The main nerves come together at the head end of the body to form a simple brain. The blood vessels in the worm's body sometimes form five pairs of hearts.

Tubifex (bloodworm)

Medicinal leech (Hirudo)

EARTHWORM
There are more than 3,000 kinds of earthworms. These long-bodied animals are responsible for the health of the soil. As the earthworms push their way along, they take in soil at the head end, digesting nutrients in the soil particles. The undigested remains that come out at the rear end form a worm cast. By burrowing in the earth, worms mix the soil layers, and their burrows allow air and water to soak downwards, generally increasing the fertility of the soil.

Fat part of body is called the saddle.

BLOODWORM TAILS
Pond-dwelling bloodworms, or tubifex worms wave their rear ends in the water to gather oxygen. Their heads are buried in the mud, taking in nutrients.

Find out more
ANIMALS
MEDICINE, HISTORY OF
SOIL

WRITERS AND POETS

A READER'S IMAGINATION can be excited by the way in which writers and poets use words. Writers create fantasy worlds for readers to explore. Historical novelists and science fiction writers transport us back to the past or into the distant future. Others writers, such as journalists, write in a way that creates a lifelike picture of real events they have experienced. And poets arrange words into patterns or rhymes that bring pleasure just by their sound or their shape on the page. A writer is anyone who expresses facts, ideas, thoughts, or opinions in words. Most writers hope or expect that their work will be published – printed in books or magazines and read by thousands of people. But some writers, including diarists such as the Englishman Samuel Pepys (1633-1703), write for their own pleasure. They do not always expect their work to be published. Poets are people who write in verse, or poetry. Poets make sure the lines of their poems form a regular pattern, so that, unlike prose, or ordinary writing, the poem has a rhythmic sound.

HOMER
One of the world's first writers was the Ancient Greek poet Homer, who lived about 2,700 years ago. He wrote long epic verses called *The Iliad* and *The Odyssey*. In *The Odyssey* the beautiful singing of the bird-like sirens lured sailors to the island where the sirens lived.

WRITING
Even a short novel has more than 50,000 words, so writing can be hard work. To make it easier, most writers organize their work carefully. Writing methods are very individual. Although many authors use word processors, pen and paper are still popular writer's tools. American Raymond Chandler (1888-1959), who wrote detective novels, had a favourite way of writing throughout his working life.

Like any author, Chandler would have used maps to check his hero's movements around Los Angeles, the setting for many of his novels.

Chandler typed the first draft, or version, of his books on yellow paper. He used half-size sheets because he made changes by retyping, not by changing words with a pen. Retyping a whole sheet would have taken longer.

Books such as J. S. Hatcher's Textbook of Pistols *gave Chandler the accurate information he needed to make his stories seem lifelike and real.*

Chandler's secretary typed a clean version of the finished draft on white paper.

Chandler smoked a pipe and drank coffee as he worked. At times he also drank a lot of alcohol.

© 1990, Copyright by COSMOPRESS, Geneva & Anne FRANK-Fonds

ANNE FRANK
During World War II, the German Nazi government persecuted millions of European Jews. To escape, Anne Frank (born 1929) and her Jewish family hid in a secret attic in a Netherlands office. The diary that Anne wrote while in hiding was later published. It is a deeply moving and tragic account of her ordeal. Anne died in a prison camp in 1945.

MANUSCRIPT
A writer's original typed or handwritten version of a work is called a manuscript. The publisher writes instructions to the printer on the manuscript, and may also make changes and revisions to improve the writing. For example, F. Scott Fitzgerald (1896-1940) was bad at spelling, and his publisher corrected these errors.

The manuscript for this page, with the publisher's corrections

CHAUCER

Geoffrey Chaucer (c.1340-1400) was an English government official. He wrote poems in English at a time when most English writers were writing in French and Latin. Chaucer began his most famous work, the *Canterbury Tales*, in about 1386. It is a collection of stories told by pilgrims travelling from London to Canterbury. The stories tell us much about 14th-century life and are often very amusing.

HARRIET BEECHER STOWE

Uncle Tom's Cabin is a powerful anti-slavery novel written by Harriet Beecher Stowe (1811-96) in 1852. It became extremely popular all over the world, even in the southern states of America, where owning a copy was illegal at the time.

DICKENS

Some of the greatest novels in the English language are the work of Charles Dickens (1812-70). He wrote colourful and exciting novels, such as *Oliver Twist*, *Nicholas Nickleby*, and *David Copperfield*, which also drew attention to the poverty and social injustices of 19th-century England.

LONGFELLOW

During his lifetime, Henry Wadsworth Longfellow (1807-82) was the most popular poet in the United States. His *Song of Hiawatha*, which was published in 1855, sold more than a million copies while Longfellow was still alive. The poem tells the story of an Indian tribe before America was colonized by Europeans. Longfellow wrote on many subjects and in many styles, but he is best remembered for his romantic "picture poems" about American life.

NEIL SIMON

Playwright Neil Simon was born in New York City on 4 July 1927. He has written more than 25 plays and musicals, many of which have been made into films. Most of his plays deal with aspects of ordinary American life. However, the writer's insight and sense of humour ensure that his plays appeal to people of all nationalities.

The Goodbye Girl, one of Neil Simon's best-loved films, is set in New York.

c.2300 B.C. Ancient Egyptian writers create the world's first literature, the Book of the Dead.

c.600 B.C. Greek poet Sappho writes early lyric poetry (poetry accompanied by music).

c.500 B.C. Greek poet Aeschylus (525-456 B.C.) writes the earliest dramas.

c.A.D.100 Greek writer Plutarch (A.D. 46-120) writes *The Parallel Lives*, the first biography.

1420 Zeami Motokiyo (1363-1443), the greatest writer of Japanese Noh dramas, writes *Shikadosho* (Book of the Way of the Highest Flower).

1740-42 Englishman Samuel Richardson (1689-1761) writes one of the first English novels, *Pamela, or, Virtue Rewarded*.

1765 Horace Walpole (1717-97), an Englishman, writes the first ghost story, *The Castle of Otranto*.

1819-20 American Washington Irving (1783-1859) publishes one of the first books of short stories, which includes *The Legend of Sleepy Hollow* and *Rip Van Winkle*.

1841 American writer Edgar Allan Poe (1809-49) publishes *The Murders in the Rue Morgue*, the first detective story.

1847 English novelist Charlotte Brontë writes *Jane Eyre* under false name Currer Bell, because it is still unacceptable for "respectable" women to write fiction.

1864 Jules Verne (1828-1905), a Frenchman, writes the first science fiction story, *Journey to the Centre of the Earth*.

1956 The performance of *Waiting for Godot* by Irish-French dramatist Samuel Beckett (1906-89) opens the way for modern drama.

1993 American novelist Toni Morrison (born 1931), author of *Song of Solomon* and *Beloved*, becomes the first black American to win the Nobel Prize for Literature.

Find out more

BOOKS
LITERATURE
SLAVERY

X-RAYS

To THE EARLY pioneers of medicine, the thought of looking through the body of a living person would probably have seemed like magic. But today it is routine for doctors and dentists to take pictures of their patients' bones and teeth with an x-ray camera. X-rays are invisible waves, like light or radio waves. They can travel through soft materials just as light passes through glass. For example, x-rays can travel through flesh and skin. But hard materials such as bone and metal stop x-rays, so bone and metal show up as a shadow on an x-ray picture. X-rays have many uses: scientists use them to probe into the molecular structure of materials such as plastics, and engineers make x-ray scans of aircraft to find cracks that could cause mechanical failure. In addition, the sun, stars, and other objects in space produce x-rays naturally.

Scanner is lined with lead to prevent x-rays from escaping.

Array of photodiodes – electronic detectors which produce electrical signals when x-rays hit them

A metal object such as a pistol does not allow x-rays to pass through it, so the pistol shows up on screen.

Conveyor belt carries suitcases into the scanner.

X-ray tube produces x-rays.

Computer receives electrical signals from the photodiodes and converts them into an image of the case.

X-RAY TUBE
An x-ray tube is like a light bulb that produces x-rays instead of light.

A strong electric current heats a wire. The energy from the electric current knocks some electrons out of the atoms in the wire.

As the electrons crash into the target, atoms of the metal produce the x-ray beam.

A powerful electric field pulls electrons at high speed towards the metal target.

Monitor screen displays contents of case to security guards.

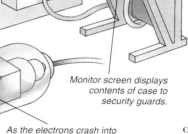

WILHELM ROENTGEN
The German scientist Wilhelm Roentgen (1845-1923) discovered x-rays in 1895. Roentgen did not understand what these rays were, so he named them x-rays.

BAGGAGE SCANNER
Airports have x-ray scanners (left) to check baggage for weapons and other dangerous objects. An x-ray tube produces a beam of x-rays, and a conveyor belt carries each suitcase into the path of the beam. Electronic detectors pick up the x-rays once they have passed through the case. A computer uses signals from the detectors to build up a picture of the contents of the case.

X-RAYS IN SPACE
Satellites containing x-ray telescopes orbit the Earth. The telescopes detect x-rays coming from the sun and stars, and from objects such as black holes. The satellites send x-ray pictures back to Earth. Astronomers use these pictures to discover and understand more of the universe.

MEDICAL X-RAYS
Doctors and dentists use x-ray machines to look inside their patients' bodies without using surgery. The machine makes an x-ray picture on a piece of photographic film. The photograph is a negative, and bones show up in white. Large doses of x-rays are harmful, so x-ray examinations must be carefully controlled.

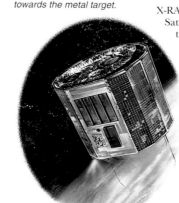

Find out more
AIRPORTS
ATOMS AND MOLECULES
DENTISTS
MEDICINE, HISTORY OF
STARS

ZOOS

PEOPLE BEGAN TO keep animals in zoological gardens, or zoos, more than 3,000 years ago, when rulers in China established a huge zoo called the Gardens of Intelligence. Today most cities have a zoo, wildlife park, or aquarium, which provides a chance to observe and study hundreds of different animals. However, many people do not agree on the value of zoos. Zoo supporters say that zoos give people the opportunity to be close to animals, which they would never otherwise experience; zoos help us appreciate the wonder of the natural world; and zoo staff carry out scientific research and important conservation work, such as breeding rare species. Zoo critics believe that it is wrong to keep animals in captivity; the creatures behave unnaturally, and in poorly run zoos they suffer because of stress, unsuitable food, dirty conditions, and disease.

EARLY ZOOS
In early zoos, animals such as elephants were taught to perform for the visitors, as shown in this picture. Animals are no longer trained to perform for the public. The purpose of a zoo is to enable people to see how wild animals behave in their natural surroundings. The ideal solution is to save wild areas, with their animals and plants, and allow people to visit these, but this is not always possible.

This huge bird cage is called an aviary.

Tonnes of animal food are delivered to the zoo each week from all over the world, including eucalyptus leaves from Australia for the koalas.

Storehouse, where food is stored. Zoo trucks take food from here to the animals.

Display boards and guide books full of information provide education.

Gardeners take care of the zoo grounds and look after all the plants.

Signposts around the zoo direct visitors to different areas.

Thousands of school-children visit zoos each year with their teachers.

Zoo vans collect dirty straw from each of the animal houses.

Zookeeper delivering straw to animals

Zoos have restaurants and cafés, where visitors can eat, drink, and relax.

Visitors can buy souvenirs in the zoo shop.

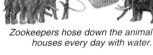

Zookeepers hose down the animal houses every day with water.

HOW ZOOS ARE RUN
A zoo employs zookeepers to look after the animals, zoologists (scientists who study animals), vets, accountants, architects, cooks, gardeners, builders, and many other people. The zoo manager must keep all these people organized because there are many jobs to do, such as ordering the correct food for each animal and running the souvenir shop and the restaurants. Visitors have to pay an entrance fee towards the upkeep of the zoo, but most zoos also need government funds.

MODERN ZOOS
In some zoos, such as the San Diego Zoo, United States, (left), animals range free in large enclosures with trees and other natural features. People view the animals through glass panels rather than iron bars. You can even see the animals from an open-topped bus. In most countries, inspectors can arrive unannounced to check the welfare of the creatures. A few zoos still treat their captives badly, and organizations such as Zoo Check work towards better conditions in zoos.

Find out more
ANIMALS
CONSERVATION
and endangered species

FACT FINDER

B.C.	7000	6000	5000	4000	3000	2000
AFRICA			Farming in Egypt begins: it is the dawn of the Egyptian empire.			Egyptian empire at gre extent
AMERICAS					Pottery produced, Ecuador, Colombia, South America	Metalworking, Peru
ASIA					Bronze casting in the Middle East	Rise of Sumer In Babylonian Empire
EUROPE	Copper working in Anatolia (now Turkey)				Minoan civilization, Crete	Bronze Age
OCEANIA	Oceania remains in Stone Age until A.D. 1770.					

AFRICA

1,500,000 B.C. – 2500 B.C. EARLIEST PEOPLES

1,500,000 B.C.
Our direct ancestors, *Homo erectus*, inhabit Africa and move outwards to Middle East and the rest of the world.

c.7000 B.C.
People begin to herd cattle in the Sahara.

c.3000 B.C.
Egyptians develop hieroglyphic writing.

c.2600 B.C.
Construction of the Great Pyramid at Giza, Egypt.

2500 B.C. – A.D. 1400 GREAT CIVILIZATIONS

c.1503 B.C.
Hatshepshut, woman pharaoh (ruler) of Egypt, begins her reign.

900 B.C.
Kingdom of Meroë established. Towns, temples, and pyramids are built, all showing influence of Egypt.

814 B.C.
Phoenicians found the city of Carthage in North Africa. Phoenician industries include dyeing, metal-working, glass-working, pottery, and carving.

c.671 B.C.
Assyrians conquer Egypt. They are great builders, and decorate their palaces with big stone reliefs.

500 B.C.
Nok culture begins in Nigeria. People produce terracotta sculptures.

332 B.C.
Alexander the Great conquers Egypt.

c.290 B.C.
World's greatest library founded in Alexandria, Egypt.

1400 – 1900 EUROPEAN IMPACT AND THE SLAVE TRADE

100 B.C.
Camel arrives in the Sahara from Arabia.

A.D. 100
Civilization of Aksum begins in Ethiopia. It trades at sea and exports ivory.

A.D. 641
Islamic Arabs occupy Egypt; they begin a conquest of North Africa.

A.D. 971
The world's first university is founded in Cairo, Egypt.

c.1300
West African kingdom of Benin excels in casting realistic figures in bronze.

1430
Great Zimbabwe is built and trades gold to Muslims on the East African coast.

1488
The Portuguese navigator Bartholomeu Diaz rounds the Cape of Good Hope.

1510
The first African slaves are shipped to the Caribbean.

1652
Boers - Dutch settlers - set up a colony in Cape of Good Hope.

1787
The British establish a colony in Sierra Leone, West Africa.

1795
British acquire the Cape of Good Hope from Dutch.

1822
United States sets up Liberia, West Africa, as a home for freed slaves.

1835-37
Boers trek north from the Cape to escape British rule.

1899-1902
Boer War is fought between the Boers and the British. War ends with treaty which makes Boer republics British colonies.

1900 – 1998 INDEPENDENCE AND THE MODERN WORLD

1910
Union of South Africa is created.

1935
Italy conquers Ethiopia; leads to end of League of Nations.

1914-1918
World War I: German colonies in Africa conquered by British and French.

1949
Apartheid (apart-ness of races) begins in South Africa.

1954
Gamal Abdel Nasser becomes premier of Egypt.

1957
Ghana becomes independent; it is the first African state to gain independence.

1962
Algeria wins independence from France.

1963
Organization of African Unity (OAU) is founded to promote unity among all the African states.

1965
Rhodesia declares independence from Britain.

1967-70
Civil war fought in Nigeria.

1975
Moroccans begin occupation of the Spanish Sahara.

1980
Rhodesia becomes independent and is renamed Zimbabwe.

1984
Ten-year drought leads to appalling famine in Ethiopia, Sudan, and Chad.

1989
Namibia, the last colony in Africa, becomes independent from South Africa.

1993
Eritrea becomes independent.

1994
Nelson Mandela, released in 1990, becomes president of South Africa.

1000	500	A.D. 100	400	500	600	800

Ironworking in Africa

Rise of kingdom of Ghana, West Africa

Rise of Olmec civilization, Mexico

Bronze Age begins, South and Central America

Rise of Mayan civilization, Mexico

...civilization

Shang rule first Chinese civilization

Start of Persian Empire

Gupta empire flourishes, India.

...yrian Empire

Greek city-states Athens and Sparta at height

Roman empire at greatest extent

Roman Empire ends; Barbarian tribes overrun western Europe.

Byzantine Empire at height

Feudalism, a system of rights between lords and their vassals, develops in western Europe.

Alexander the Great creates empire in Middle East.

AMERICAS

40,000 B.C. – 2000 B.C. EARLIEST PEOPLES

c.40,000 B.C.
The first peoples arrive in the Americas from Siberia across the Bering Strait.

c.15,000 B.C.
Cave art produced in what is now Brazil.

c.6500 B.C.
Farming begins in the Peruvian Andes, South America.

c.3200 B.C.
Pottery begins to be made in Ecuador, and Colombia, South America.

2000 B.C. – A.D. 1450 EMPIRES AND CIVILIZATIONS

2000 B.C.
The Mayan culture begins in Central America. Farmers begin to settle in villages.

c. 1150 B.C.
Olmec people in Mexico, North America, develop a picture-writing and number system that spreads through continent.

c.300 B.C.
Mayan culture develops. Large political and religious centres are built, such as Teotihuacán.

c. A.D. 300
Hopewell Indians build burial mounds and trade in North America.

c. A.D. 700
People weave tapestries in Peru, South America. Cotton and wool tapestry, above, shows jaguars.

c. A.D. 900
Toltecs conquer the Mayans and create an empire in Central America.

c. A.D. 1000
Vikings from Europe arrive in North America.

1450 – 1750 EUROPEAN CONQUEST AND TRADE

1492
Genoese explorer Christopher Columbus reaches the Caribbean and claims islands for Spain; other Europeans follow with horses and guns, seeking treasure.

1494
Treaty of Tordesillas divides the Americas between Spain & Portugal.

1499
Amerigo Vespucci explores the Amazon, South America; gives his name to the American continent.

c.1510
First African slaves are taken to the Caribbean.

1519
Hernando Cortés, a Spanish Conquistador, conquers Mexico; the Aztec empire, under emperor Montezuma, ends.

1620
Mayflower ship arrives in New England, North America, carrying Puritan refugees from Britain (the Pilgrim fathers).

1636
The first North American university, Harvard College, is founded.

1750 – 1900 THE NEW NATIONS

1783
Birth of Simón Bolívar, the liberator of South America.

1787
Dollar currency is introduced, United States.

1791
Slave revolt, led by Toussaint L'Ouverture, in Haiti, against the French.

1803
Louisiana Purchase: France sells a vast area of land back to the United States, doubling the size of the country.

1849
Gold rush begins in California.

1852
Elisha Otis invents the elevator.

1861-65
Civil War fought in United States. Slaves are freed.

1867
Canada becomes independent.

1869
Railway crosses United States from coast to coast.

1876
Battle of the Little Bighorn between Indians and white settlers.

1877
Thomas Edison invents the phonograph.

1895
King C. Gillette invents the safety razor, with a convenient disposable blade.

1900 – 1998 THE MODERN WORLD

1903
Wright brothers make the first flight.

1912
Henry Ford produces Model T Ford car.

1913
Hollywood becomes centre of film industry.

1917
United States enters World War I, following sinking of passenger ship *Lusitania*.

1920
Boom years:jazz age follows World War I (1914-18).

1929
The Wall Street crash: the U.S. Stock Exchange collapses; start of Depression of the 1930s.

1941
United States enters World War II.

1945
United Nations begins, San Francisco, United States.

1958
Silicon chip developed by Texas Instruments.

1959
Ernesto "Che" Guevara helps Fidel Castro overthrow Cuban government.

1961
Cuban exiles invade Cuba at the Bay of Pigs. Fidel Castro crushes the invasion.

1969
Apollo 11 takes U.S. astronauts to moon. Neil Armstrong is the first man to walk on moon.

1987
Intermediate-Range Nuclear Forces (INF) Treaty signed with Soviet Union.

A.D.	900	950	1000	1050	1100	1150

AFRICA — Great civilizations flourish in West Africa: Zimbabwe, Kingdom of Mali, Benin empire

AMERICAS

ASIA — Angkor kingdom, Cambodia, at greatest strength

EUROPE — Frankish ruler Charlemagne creates vast empire, western Europe (814). — Normans invade England; age of castle building begins.

OCEANIA — Maoris and aborigines live undisturbed on the Pacific islands.

ASIA

800,000 B.C. – 1500 B.C. — EARLIEST CIVILIZATIONS

800,000 B.C.
First humans arrive in Asia from Africa.

c.9000 B.C.
Palestinian sheep are the world's first domesticated animals identified so far.

c.8350 B.C.
Jericho, the world's first known walled city, is founded. It consists of mud brick houses behind a strong wall.

c.3500 B.C.
The Sumerians invent the wheel.

c.3250 B.C.
The Sumerians develop picture writing and build the world's first cities. They also grow barley, bake bread, and make beer.

Sumerian picture writing was called cuneiform, and was scratched onto clay tablets.

c.2698 B.C.
Legendary Chinese emperor Shen Nung writes Chinese "Canon of Herbs" with over 252 plant descriptions.

c. 2500 B.C.
Indus Valley civilization, based on agriculture, in India.

c.1750 B.C.
Hammurabi establishes the Babylonian Empire.

1500 B.C. – A.D. 1500 — EMPIRES AND RELIGIONS

c.1500 B.C.
Hindu religion begins to be established in India.

---

c.1200 B.C.
Beginning of Judaism, Palestine.

650s B.C.
World's first coins are produced in the Near East.

c.600 B.C.
Chinese philosopher Lao-tze philosophy of Taoism

c.563 B.C.
Birth of Siddhartha Gautama, the Buddha, founder of Buddhism, India

551 B.C.
Birth of Confucius, founder of a philosophical system in China

200s B.C.
Great Wall of China is built to keep out invaders.

C. A.D. 30
Jesus Christ is executed; Christianity is born in Judea.

C. A.D. 100
Paper is invented in China.

A.D. 606
First examinations for entry to public offices in China.

A.D. 632
Death of Muhammad, the Prophet. Spread of Islamic religion, led by caliphs (successors).

A.D. 868
World's first printed book, *Diamond Sutra*, in China

C. A.D. 1000
The Chinese perfect their invention of gunpowder.

A.D. 1206
Mongols begin conquest of Asia.

1259
Kublai Khan becomes Mongol ruler of China; sets up Yuan dynasty, which lasts 1279-1368.

1290
Ottomans (Turkish Muslims) rise to power.

1333
China suffers drought, famine, floods, and plague. Five million people die.

1421
Peking (now Beijing) becomes capital of China.

1453
Ottomans capture Constantinople, ending the Byzantine Empire.

1498
Portuguese navigator Vasco da Gama reaches India, via Africa.

1500 – 1900 — TRADE AND CONQUEST

1556
Akbar the Great, the greatest of the Mogul rulers, comes to power, India.

1600
English East India trading company is founded.

1639
Japan closed to foreigners.

1648
Taj Mahal is built in India by emperor Shah Jahan as a tomb for his favourite wife, Mumtaz Mahal.

1649
Russians conquer Siberia and reach the Pacific Ocean.

1857
Outbreak of Indian Mutiny against British rule. Put down by British a year later.

1900 – 1998 — THE MODERN WORLD

1911
China becomes a republic.

1918
Ottoman Empire collapses.

1920
Mahatma Gandhi begins campaign for Indian independence.

1921
Mao Zedong and Li Ta-chao found the Chinese Communist Party in Beijing.

1926
Hirohito becomes the emperor of Japan.

1934
Communists in China, led by Mao Zedong, begin Long March through the mountains of China to Yenan, where they set up government.

1941
Japanese attack U.S. fleet at Pearl Harbour.

1945
World's first atomic bombs are dropped on Japan.

1947
India and Pakistan independent.

1947
Partition of Palestine into Arab and Jewish states approved by United Nations, but opposed by Arabs. Leads to fighting between Arabs and Jews in Palestine.

1948
Jewish state of Israel founded.

1966
Mao Zedong starts Cultural Revolution in China.

1967
Six-Day War between Arabs and Israelis.

1980–1989
War between Iran and Iraq.

1989
Pro-democracy movement in Beijing is crushed by military force.

1990–1991
Gulf War. Iraq annexes Kuwait. U.N. intervenes.

1200	1250	1300	1350	1400	1450	1500

Portuguese establish first trading post in North Africa.

Songhai empire reaches its greatest height.

Portuguese set up trading posts, East Africa.

Rise of Aztec empire

Inca empire flourishes in South America.

Conquistadors destroy Aztec and Inca empires (1519).

Life of Tamerlane, who, based in Samarkand, conquered Mongol empire.

Portuguese set up trading posts, Indian Ocean – Christianity spreads throughout Asia.

Ghengis Khan dies, leaving huge Mongol empire to his sons (1227)

100 Years' War between England and France

Renaissance of art and learning

EUROPE

EARLY PEOPLES AND THE ANCIENT WORLD — 1,000,000 B.C. – A.D. 450

1,000,000 B.C.
First humans arrive in Europe.

6500 B.C.
First farming in Greece and the Balkans.

c.1900 B.C.
Civilization of Mycenae develops in Greece. The Mycenaeans build rich palaces.

c.1500 B.C.
Linear B script, used to write an early version of the Greek language, develops in Crete.

c.1250 B.C.
Trojan War between Mycenaean Greeks and the Trojans. After a ten-year siege, the Greeks enter Troy concealed in a huge wooden horse and destroy the whole city.

c.753 B.C.
Rome founded by the legendary brothers Romulus and Remus.

776 B.C.
First Olympic Games held in Greece.

750 B.C.
Homer composes the *Iliad*, an epic poem describing the Trojan War.

c.500 B.C
Celts occupy much of Europe.

146 B.C.
Romans conquer Greece.

RELIGION AND THE MIDDLE AGES — A.D. 450 – 1450

44 B.C.
Julius Caesar is assassinated.

A.D. 391
Christianity becomes the official religion of the Roman Empire.

A.D. 500
Barbarian tribes overrun much of western Europe.

793
Vikings raid northern Europe.

1096
First Crusade leaves England for Palestine.

c.1150
One of the first European universities is founded in Paris.

1290
Reading glasses are invented in Italy.

1348
A bubonic plague, called the Black Death, kills one third of the population of Europe.

1454
The German Johann Gutenberg publishes the Gutenberg Bible, the first printed book in Europe. It was printed with movable copper type.

EXPLORATION AND SCIENCE — 1450 – 1780

1453
Ottoman Turks capture Constantinople; end of Byzantine Empire.

1516
Hapsburg Empire expands under Charles V of Spain.

1517
German Martin Luther pins a list of complaints against the Catholic Church on a church door in Wittenberg; Reformation begins.

1519-1521
Portuguese Ferdinand Magellan leads the first voyage around the world.

1531
Polish astronomer Copernicus suggests that Earth revolves around the sun.

1555
Tobacco taken to Europe from the Americas.

1603
Union of Scotland and England.

1628
William Harvey, English doctor, discovers circulation of blood.

1665
English scientist Isaac Newton discovers principles of gravity.

1682
Peter the Great becomes czar of Russia.

1683
Ottoman Turks fail in their siege of Vienna.

1690
William III of England defeats the exiled Catholic James II and his Irish supporters at the Battle of the Boyne, Ireland.

1710
Russia conquers Swedish provinces in the Baltic.

REVOLUTION AND THE MODERN WORLD — 1760 – 1998

1789
French Revolution breaks out.

1805
British Admiral Nelson defeats French in the sea battle of Trafalgar.

1825
First passenger railway, Britain

1840
First postage stamp, the Penny Black, is issued in Britain.

1846
Potato crop failure in Ireland causes famine.

1848
Karl Marx writes *Communist Manifesto*.

1859
Charles Darwin publishes theory of evolution.

1876
Scottish teacher Alexander Graham Bell invents telephone.

1895
Italian Guglielmo Marconi invents the radio.

1902
Polish scientist Marie Curie and her French husband, Pierre, discover radium, a chemical element to treat cancer.

1914
World War I begins.

1917
Russian Revolution breaks out.

1922
The Irish Free State is formed.

1930s
Economic depression in Europe.

1939
German scientists Otto Hahn and Fritz Strassman discover that energy can be released by splitting uranium atoms into two.

1939
World War II begins when Germany and the Soviet Union attack Poland.

1949
North Atlantic Treaty Organization (NATO) formed.

1957
European Community formed.

1957
Soviets launch first space satellite.

1961
Berlin Wall built by East and West Germany.

1990
East and West Germany unite.

1991
Soviet Union collapses.

A.D.	1550	1600	1650	1700	1725	1750

AFRICA All major European powers begin to establish trading posts around African coast. Dutch set up colony, South Africa. Increasing European control over Africa

AMERICAS American Revolution. independence, create America

ASIA Dutch control spice trade, Southeast Asia. Japan closed to foreigners (until 1853).

EUROPE Elizabethan Age, England Thirty Years' War, Germany Industrial Revolution begins, Britain.

OCEANIA

OCEANIA

50,000 B.C. – A.D. 1600 FIRST SETTLERS

c. 40,000 B.C. Aboriginal people arrive in Australia from Southeast Asia.

c.2000 B.C. People arrive in New Guinea.

c.1300 B.C. People reach Fiji, Tonga.

c. A.D. 300 People reach Polynesia.

c. A.D. 950 Polynesians, later known as Maori people, settle in New Zealand and the Pacific islands.

1600 – 1850 CONQUEST AND COLONIZATION

1606 Dutch navigator Willem Jansz visits Australia.

1642 Dutch navigator Abel Tasman sails around Australia to New Zealand.

1770 English navigator Captain Cook claims Australia for Britain. He discovers species of animals and plants not yet heard of in Europe.

1788 First British convicts are transported from British prisons to Botany Bay, site of the first European settlement, Australia.

1826 English settlers and Aboriginals fight in the "Black War" in Tasmania.

1840 In the Treaty of Waitangi, Maori chiefs in New Zealand give sovereignty over New Zealand to Britain. New Zealand becomes British colony.

1851 Gold rush, Victoria, Australia. Settlers arrive from Europe.

1850 – 1998 THE MODERN WORLD

1860 Burke and Wills are the first people to cross Australia from coast to coast. Both die of starvation on the journey back from north to south, 1861.

1893 New Zealand women gain the vote.

1901 Australia gains independence from Britain.

1907 New Zealand gains independence from Britian.

1927 Canberra becomes the capital city of Australia.

1941-42 Japan invades the Pacific islands.

1945 Assisted passages to Australia for Europeans. Two million people emigrate.

1950s Nuclear testing carried out in the Pacific islands.

1951 ANZUS defence treaty between Australia, New Zealand, and the United States.

1985 South Pacific Forum treaty - Pacific declares itself a nuclear-free zone.

PRESIDENTS OF THE UNITED STATES

GEORGE WASHINGTON (1732-1799) Term of office: 1789-1797

JOHN ADAMS (1735-1826) Term of office: 1797-1801

THOMAS JEFFERSON (1743-1826) Term of office: 1801-1809

JAMES MADISON (1751-1836) Term of office: 1809-1817

JAMES MONROE (1758-1831) Term of office: 1817-1825

JOHN Q. ADAMS (1767-1848) Term of office: 1825-1829

ANDREW JACKSON (1767-1845) Term of office: 1829-1837

MARTIN VAN BUREN (1782-1862) Term of office: 1837-1841

W.H. HARRISON (1773-1841) Term of office: Mar.-Apr. 1841

JOHN TYLER (1790-1862) Term of office: 1841-1845

JAMES K. POLK (1795-1849) Term of office: 1845-1849

ZACHARY TAYLOR (1784-1850) Term of office: 1849-1850

MILLARD FILLMORE (1800-1874) Term of office: 1850-1853

FRANKLIN PIERCE (1804-1869) Term of office: 1853-1857

JAMES BUCHANAN (1791-1868) Term of office: 1857-1861

ABRAHAM LINCOLN (1809-1865) Term of office: 1861-1865

ANDREW JOHNSON (1808-1875) Term of office: 1865-1869

ULYSSES S. GRANT (1822-1885) Term of office: 1869-1877

RUTHERFORD B. HAYES (1822-1893) Term of office: 1877-1881

JAMES A. GARFIELD (1831-1881) Term of office: Mar.-Sept. 1881

CHESTER A. ARTHUR (1830-1886) Term of office: 1881-1885

GROVER CLEVELAND (1837-1908) Term of office: 1885-1889

BENJAMIN HARRISON (1833-1901) Term of office: 1889-1893

GROVER CLEVELAND (1837-1908) Term of office: 1893-1897

WILLIAM MCKINLEY (1843-1901) Term of office: 1897-1901

THEODORE ROOSEVELT (1858-1919) Term of office: 1901-1909

WILLIAM H. TAFT (1857-1930) Term of office: 1909-1913

WOODROW WILSON (1856-1924) Term of office: 1913-1921

WARREN G. HARDING (1865-1923) Term of office: 1921-1923

CALVIN COOLIDGE (1872-1933) Term of office: 1923-1929

HERBERT HOOVER (1874-1964) Term of office: 1929-1933

FRANKLIN D. ROOSEVELT (1882-1945) Term of office: 1933-1945

HARRY S. TRUMAN (1884-1972) Term of office: 1945-1953

DWIGHT EISENHOWER (1890-1969) Term of office: 1953-1961

JOHN F. KENNEDY (1917-1963) Term of office: 1961-1963

LYNDON B. JOHNSON (1908-1973) Term of office: 1963-1969

RICHARD NIXON (Born 1913) Term of office: 1969-1974

GERALD R. FORD (Born 1913) Term of office: 1974-1977

JIMMY CARTER (Born 1924) Term of office: 1977-1981

RONALD REAGAN (Born 1911) Term of office: 1981-1989

GEORGE BUSH (Born 1924) Term of office: 1989-1993

BILL CLINTON (Born 1946) Term of office: 1993 to date

| 1800 | 1825 | 1850 | 1900 | 1925 | 1950 | 1990 |

British abolish slave trade in their empire.

European powers divide up African continent; only Ethiopia and Liberia remain independent.

Most African nations gain independence.

Famine, drought Ethiopia, Sudan

...s win ...es.

Spanish colonies fight for and gain independence.

United States involvement in Vietnam War

Japan begins trading with the rest of the world.

Japan becomes world power after defeat of Russia.

Korean War

Vietnam War

Napoleon Bonaparte dominates Europe.

Victorian Age, Britain

World War I

World War II

Cold War: world is divided into two blocs of powers, Communist and non-Communist.

Maoris rebel against British rule, New Zealand.

New Zealand becomes self-governing.

Australian and New Zealand troops enter World War I on side of Britain.

Australia offers assisted passages to Europeans; about two million people settle in Australia.

KINGS AND QUEENS OF GREAT BRITAIN

RULERS OF ENGLAND

Saxon line	REIGNED		REIGNED
EGBERT	827-839	HENRY I	1100-1135
ETHELWULF	839-858	STEPHEN	1135-1154
ETHELBALD	858-860		
ETHELBERT	860-865	**House of Plantagenet**	
ETHELRED I	865-871	HENRY II	1154-1189
ALFRED THE GREAT	871-899	RICHARD I	1189-1199
EDWARD THE ELDER	899-924	JOHN	1199-1216
ATHELSTAN	924-939	HENRY III	1216-1272
EDMUND	939-946	EDWARD I	1272-1307
EDRED	946-955	EDWARD II	1307-1327
EDWY	955-959	EDWARD III	1327-1377
EDGAR	959-975	RICHARD II	1377-1399
EDWARD THE MARTYR	975-978		
ETHELRED		**House of Lancaster**	
THE UNREADY	978-1016	HENRY IV	1399-1413
EDMUND IRONSIDE	1016	HENRY V	1413-1422
		HENRY VI	1422-1461
Danish line		(also)	1470-1471
CANUTE (CNUT)	1016-1035		
HAROLD I HAREFOOT	1035-1040	**House of York**	
HARDECANUTE	1040-1042	EDWARD IV	1461-1470
		(also)	1471-1483
Saxon line		EDWARD V	1483
EDWARD THE CONFESSOR	1042-1066	RICHARD III	1483-1485
HAROLD II			
(GODWINSON)	1066	**House of Tudor**	
		HENRY VII	1485-1509
House of Normandy		HENRY VIII	1509-1547
WILLIAM I (THE CON-		EDWARD VI	1547-1553
QUEROR)	1066-1087	MARY I	1553-1558
WILLIAM II	1087-1100	ELIZABETH I	1558-1603

MONARCHS OF SCOTLAND

MALCOLM II	1005-1034	JOHN DE BALIOL	1292-1296
DUNCAN I	1034-1040	ROBERT I (BRUCE)	1306-1329
MACBETH	1040-1057	DAVID II	1329-1371
MALCOLM III	1057-1093		
DONALD BANE	1093-1094	**House of Stuart**	
DUNCAN II	1094	ROBERT II	1371-1390
DONALD BANE	1094-1097	ROBERT III	1390-1406
EDGAR	1097-1107	JAMES I	1406-1437
ALEXANDER I	1107-1124	JAMES II	1437-1460
DAVID I	1124-1153	JAMES III	1460-1488
MALCOLM IV	1153-1165	JAMES IV	1488-1513
WILLIAM THE LION	1165-1214	JAMES V	1513-1542
ALEXANDER II	1214-1249	MARY	1542-1567
ALEXANDER III	1249-1286	JAMES VI	
MARGARET OF		(became James I of England)	1567-1625
NORWAY	1286-1290		

MONARCHS OF GREAT BRITAIN

House of Stuart		GEORGE III	1760-1820
JAMES I	1603-1625	GEORGE IV	1820-1830
CHARLES I	1625-1649	WILLIAM IV	1830-1837
Commonwealth	1649-1660	VICTORIA	1837-1901
CHARLES II	1660-1685		
JAMES II	1685-1688	**House of Saxe-Coburg-Gotha**	
WILLIAM III	1689-1702	EDWARD VII	1901-1910
MARY II	1689-1694		
ANNE	1702-1714	**House of Windsor**	
		GEORGE V	1910-1936
House of Hanover		EDWARD VIII	1936
GEORGE I	1714-1727	GEORGE VI	1936-1952
GEORGE II	1727-1760	ELIZABETH II	1952 to date

PRIME MINISTERS OF GREAT BRITAIN

Sir Robert Walpole

William Pitt

Sir Winston S. Churchill

William E. Gladstone

Benjamin Disraeli

PRIME MINISTER	TERM OF OFFICE	PRIME MINISTER	TERM OF OFFICE
SIR ROBERT WALPOLE	1721-1742	BENJAMIN DISRAELI	1868
EARL OF WILMINGTON	1742-1743	WILLIAM E. GLADSTONE	1868-1874
HENRY PELHAM	1743-1754	BENJAMIN DISRAELI	1874-1880
DUKE OF NEWCASTLE	1754-1756	WILLIAM E. GLADSTONE	1880-1885
DUKE OF DEVONSHIRE	1756-1757	MARQUESS OF	
DUKE OF NEWCASTLE	1757-1762	SALISBURY	1885-1886
EARLE OF BUTE	1762-1763	WILLIAM E. GLADSTONE	1886
GEORGE GRENVILLE	1763-1765	MARQUESS OF	
MARQUESS OF		SALISBURY	1886-1892
ROCKINGHAM	1765-1766	WILLIAM E. GLADSTONE	1892-1894
WILLIAM PITT		EARL OF ROSEBERY	1894-1895
(EARL OF CHATHAM)	1766-1767	MARQUESS OF	
DUKE OF GRAFTON	1767-1770	SALISBURY	1895-1902
LORD NORTH	1770-1782	ARTHUR J. BALFOUR	1902-1905
MARQUESS OF		SIR HENRY CAMPBELL-	
ROCKINGHAM	1782	BANNERMAN	1905-1908
EARL OF SHELBORNE	1782-1783	HERBERT HENRY	
DUKE OF PORTLAND	1783	ASQUITH	1908-1915
WILLIAM PITT (THE		HERBERT HENRY	
YOUNGER)	1783-1801	ASQUITH	1915-1916
HENRY ADDINGTON	1801-1804	DAVID LLOYD GEORGE	1916-1922
WILLIAM PITT	1804-1806	ANDREW BONAR LAW	1922-1923
BARON GRENVILLE	1806-1807	STANLEY BALDWIN	1923-1924
DUKE OF PORTLAND	1807-1809	J. RAMSAY MACDONALD	1924
SPENCER PERCEVAL	1809-1812	STANLEY BALDWIN	1924-1929
EARL OF LIVERPOOL	1812-1827	J. RAMSAY MACDONALD	1929-1931
GEORGE CANNING	1827	J. RAMSAY MACDONALD	1931-1935
VISCOUNT GODERICH	1827-1828	STANLEY BALDWIN	1935-1937
DUKE OF WELLINGTON	1828-1830	NEVILLE CHAMBERLAIN	1937-1940
EARL GREY	1830-1834	WINSTON S. CHURCHILL	1940-1945
VISCOUNT MELBOURNE	1834	CLEMENT R. ATTLEE	1945-1951
DUKE OF WELLINGTON	1834	SIR WINSTON S.	
SIR ROBERT PEEL	1834-1835	CHURCHILL	1951-1955
VISCOUNT MELBOURNE	1835-1841	SIR ANTHONY EDEN	1955-1957
SIR ROBERT PEEL	1841-1846	HAROLD MACMILLAN	1957-1963
LORD JOHN RUSSELL	1846-1852	SIR ALEC	
EARL OF DERBY	1852	DOUGLAS-HOME	1963-1964
EARL OF ABERDEEN	1852-1855	HAROLD WILSON	1964-1970
VISCOUNT PALMERSTON	1855-1858	EDWARD HEATH	1970-1974
EARL OF DERBY	1858-1859	HAROLD WILSON	1974-1976
VISCOUNT PALMERSTON	1859-1865	JAMES CALLAGHAN	1976-1979
EARL RUSSELL	1865-1866	MARGARET THATCHER	1979-1990
EARL OF DERBY	1866-1868	JOHN MAJOR	1990-1997
		TONY BLAIR	1997-

THE WORLD

LARGEST COUNTRIES

Russian Federation
17.1 million square km
6.58 million square miles

United States
9.36 million square km
3.61 million square miles

Canada
9.9 million square km
3.8 million square miles

United States of America

India
3.17 million square km
1.22 million square miles

Australia
7.68 million square km
2.97 million square miles

China
9.6 million square km
3.7 million square miles

Brazil
8.51 million square km
3.29 million square miles

BIGGEST CITIES

Population (millions)
25
20
15
10

1 Tokyo/Yokohama, Japan
2 Mexico City
3 Sao Paulo, Brazil
4 New York, USA
5 Seoul, S. Korea
6 Osaka/Kobe/ Kyoto, Japan
7 Buenos Aires, Argentina
8 Calcutta, India
9 Bombay, India
10 Rio de Janeiro, Brazil

ANTARCTICA

Seven nations claim portions of the continent.

Argentina, Chile and United Kingdom
Chile & United Kingdom
Chile
Unclaimed
New Zealand
Australia
Argentina and United Kingdom
United Kingdom
Norway
Australia
France

☐ LESSER ANTILLES

Anguilla (UK)
Antigua and Barbuda
Aruba (Neth)
Barbados
British Virgin Islands (UK)
Dominica

Grenada
Guadeloupe (Fr)
Martinique (Fr)
Montserrat (UK)
Netherlands Antilles (Neth)
St. Kitts and Nevis

St. Lucia
St. Vincent and the Grenadines
Trinidad and Tobago
Virgin Islands (US)

WORLD POPULATION

Since time began, world population has risen and fallen as health and food supplies have changed. The number of people alive at any one time rose when there was plenty of food, and fell when famine or disease killed many people. Until about A.D. 800, the population of the world stayed below 200 million. But since then it has risen dramatically. The rise was greatest in the 20th century; by the year 2000, experts predict that there will be more than six billion people living, causing enormous problems of hunger and overcrowding. The graph on the next four pages charts the world's rising population through the last 12,000 years.

LIFE EXPECTANCY

How many years can men and women expect to live in the Western world and in developing nations?

Women
Men

	Chad	India	Brazil	China	USA	Australia
Women	47	58	68	71	79	80
Men	44	58	62	68	72	73

FOOD

United States 3,600
Australia 3,300
Brazil & China 2,600
India 2,200
Chad 1,700

How many calories do most people eat each day?

Map labels

Greenland (Denmark)
Canada
United States of America
St. Pierre and Miquelon (Fr)
Bermuda (UK)
Mexico
Cuba
Bahamas
Turks and Caicos Is. (UK)
Haiti
Dominican Republic
Puerto Rico (US)
Belize
Cayman Is. (UK)
Jamaica
Lesser Antilles (see below left)
Guatemala
El Salvador
Nicaragua
Honduras
Costa Rica
Panama
Guyana
Venezuela
Surinam
French Guiana (Fr)
Colombia
Ecuador
Brazil
Peru
Bolivia
Paraguay
Chile
Uruguay
Argentina
Falkland Islands (UK)
S. Georgia and the Sandwich Is. (UK)

9,000 B.C.   8,000 B.C.   7,000 B.C.   6,000 B.C.   5,000 B.C.

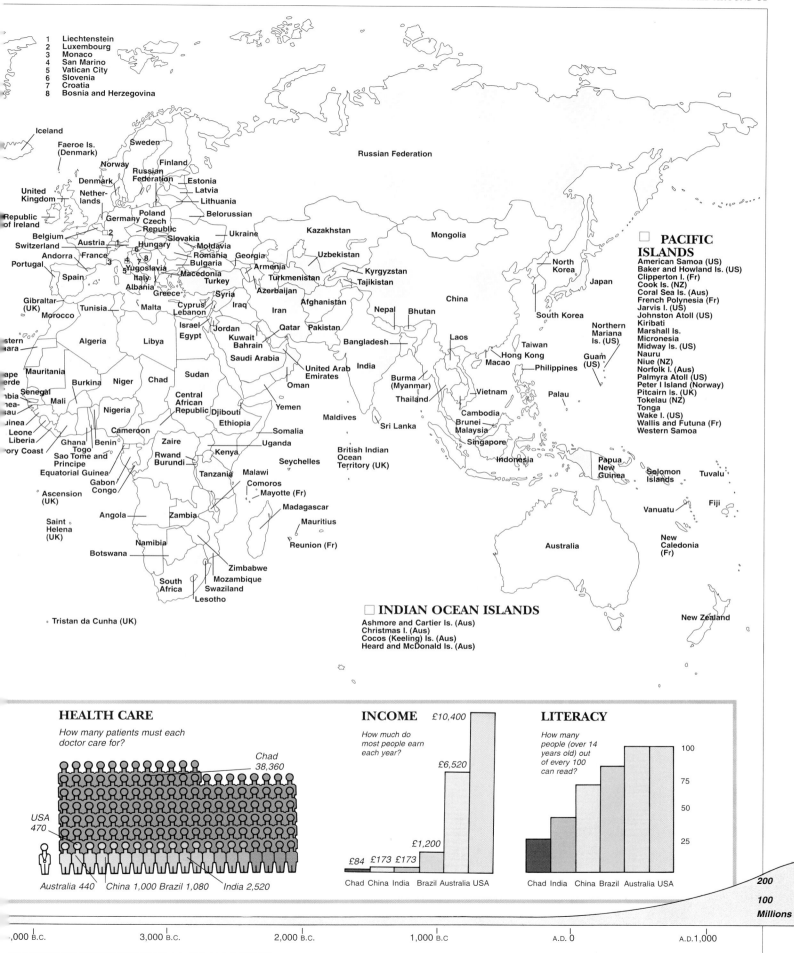

1 Liechtenstein
2 Luxembourg
3 Monaco
4 San Marino
5 Vatican City
6 Slovenia
7 Croatia
8 Bosnia and Herzegovina

Iceland
Faeroe Is. (Denmark)
Sweden
Norway
Finland
Russian Federation
Denmark
Estonia
Latvia
Netherlands
Lithuania
United Kingdom
Belorussian
Republic of Ireland
Germany
Poland
Czech Republic
Ukraine
Belgium
Slovakia
Switzerland
Austria
Hungary
Moldavia
Andorra
France
Romania
Georgia
Portugal
Yugoslavia
Bulgaria
Armenia
Spain
Italy
Macedonia
Turkey
Albania
Greece
Gibraltar (UK)
Malta
Cyprus
Syria
Iraq
Morocco
Tunisia
Lebanon
Israel
Iran
Algeria
Libya
Jordan
Egypt
Kuwait
Bahrain
Qatar
Western Sahara
Mauritania
Saudi Arabia
United Arab Emirates
Oman
Cape Verde
Senegal
Mali
Niger
Chad
Sudan
Yemen
Guinea-Bissau
Leone
Liberia
Ivory Coast
Ghana
Togo
Benin
Nigeria
Burkina
Central African Republic
Djibouti
Ethiopia
Somalia
Sao Tome and Principe
Equatorial Guinea
Gabon
Congo
Cameroon
Zaire
Rwanda
Burundi
Uganda
Kenya
Ascension (UK)
Saint Helena (UK)
Angola
Zambia
Tanzania
Malawi
Comoros
Mayotte (Fr)
Madagascar
Mauritius
Namibia
Botswana
Zimbabwe
Reunion (Fr)
South Africa
Mozambique
Swaziland
Lesotho
Seychelles
Tristan da Cunha (UK)

Russian Federation
Kazakhstan
Mongolia
Uzbekistan
Kyrgyzstan
Turkmenistan
Tajikistan
Azerbaijan
Afghanistan
Pakistan
Nepal
Bhutan
China
India
Bangladesh
Burma (Myanmar)
Thailand
Laos
North Korea
South Korea
Japan
Taiwan
Hong Kong
Macao
Philippines
Vietnam
Cambodia
Brunei
Malaysia
Singapore
Indonesia
Maldives
Sri Lanka
British Indian Ocean Territory (UK)
Palau
Northern Mariana Is. (US)
Guam (US)
Papua New Guinea
Solomon Islands
Tuvalu
Vanuatu
Fiji
New Caledonia (Fr)
Australia
New Zealand

PACIFIC ISLANDS

American Samoa (US)
Baker and Howland Is. (US)
Clipperton I. (Fr)
Cook Is. (NZ)
Coral Sea Is. (Aus)
French Polynesia (Fr)
Jarvis I. (US)
Johnston Atoll (US)
Kiribati
Marshall Is.
Micronesia
Midway Is. (US)
Nauru
Niue (NZ)
Norfolk I. (Aus)
Palmyra Atoll (US)
Peter I Island (Norway)
Pitcairn Is. (UK)
Tokelau (NZ)
Tonga
Wake I. (US)
Wallis and Futuna (Fr)
Western Samoa

INDIAN OCEAN ISLANDS

Ashmore and Cartier Is. (Aus)
Christmas I. (Aus)
Cocos (Keeling) Is. (Aus)
Heard and McDonald Is. (Aus)

HEALTH CARE

How many patients must each doctor care for?

Chad 38,360
USA 470
Australia 440
China 1,000
Brazil 1,080
India 2,520

INCOME

How much do most people earn each year?

£10,400
£6,520
£1,200
£84
£173
£173

Chad China India Brazil Australia USA

LITERACY

How many people (over 14 years old) out of every 100 can read?

100
75
50
25

Chad India China Brazil Australia USA

200
100
Millions

4,000 B.C.   3,000 B.C.   2,000 B.C.   1,000 B.C   A.D. 0   A.D. 1,000

OLYMPIC GAMES

Every Games must include at least 15 of these Olympic sports.

Archery
Athletics
Badminton
Baseball
Basketball
Boxing
Canoeing
Cycling
Equestrian sports
Fencing
Football
Gymnastics
Handball
Field hockey
Judo
Modern pentathlon
Rowing
Rhythmic gymnastics
Shooting
Swimming
Synchronized swimming
Table tennis
Tennis
Volleyball
Water polo
Weight lifting
Wrestling
Yachting

SITES

	Location of Summer Games
Athens	1896
Paris	1900
St. Louis	1904
London	1908
Stockholm	1912
Antwerp	1920
Paris	1924
Amsterdam	1928
Los Angeles	1932
Berlin	1936
London	1948
Helsinki	1952
Melbourne	1956
Rome	1960
Tokyo	1964
Mexico City	1968
Munich	1972
Montreal	1976
Moscow	1980
Los Angeles	1984
Seoul	1988
Barcelona	1992
Atlanta	1996
Sydney	2000

WRITERS

The list of writers below gives the dates of their birth and death, the country in which they were born, and one of their most famous works.

Chaucer, Geoffrey
1340?-1400 England
The Canterbury Tales

Cervantes, Miguel de
1547-1616 Spain
Don Quixote

Shakespeare, William
1564-1616 England
Romeo and Juliet

Swift, Jonathan
1667-1745 England
Gulliver's Travels

Voltaire
1694-1778 France
Candide

Wordsworth, William
1770-1850 England
"The Daffodils"

Poe, Edgar Allan
1809-49 USA
"The Raven"

Dickens, Charles
1812-70 England
Oliver Twist

Whitman, Walt
1819-1892 USA
Leaves of Grass

Dostoevsky, Fyodor
1821-81 Russia
Crime and Punishment

Ibsen, Henrik
1828-1906 Norway
Hedda Gabler

Twain, Mark
1835-1910 USA
Tom Sawyer

Stevenson, Robert Louis
1850-94 Scotland
Treasure Island

Chekhov, Anton
1860-1904 Russia
The Cherry Orchard

Colette
1873-1954 France
Chéri

Frost, Robert
1874-1963 USA
"The Road Not Taken"

Joyce, James
1882-1941 Ireland
Ulysses

Lawrence, D.H.
1885-1930 England
The Rainbow

O'Neill, Eugene
1888-1953 USA
Long Day's Journey into Night

Eliot, T.S.
1888-1965 England
The Wasteland

Faulkner, William
1897-1962 USA
Absalom, Absalom!

Hemingway, Ernest
1899-1961 USA
For Whom the Bell Tolls

CHILDREN'S WRITERS

Andersen, Hans Christian
1805-75 Denmark
The Snow Queen

White, E.B.
1899-1985 USA
Charlotte's Web

Dr. Seuss
1904-91 USA
The Cat in the Hat

ARTISTS

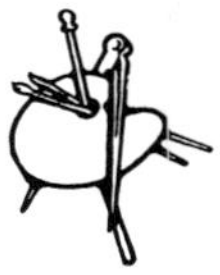

The list of artists below gives the dates of their birth and death, the country in which they were born, and one of their most famous works.

Da Vinci, Leonardo
1452-1519 Italy
Mona Lisa

Dürer, Albrecht
1471-1528 Germany
The Great Piece of Turf

Michelangelo
1475-1564 Italy
David

Raphael
1483-1520 Italy
Sistine Madonna

Rubens, Peter Paul
1577-1640 Belgium
Self-Portrait

Velázquez, Diego
1599-1660 Spain
Rokeby Venus

Rembrandt van Rijn
1606-69 Holland
The Night Watch

Goya, Francisco
1746-1828 Spain
The Gypsies

Hokusai
1760-1849 Japan
The Wave

Audubon, John James
1785-1851 USA
Birds of America

Degas, Edgar
1834-1917 France
Dancers on a Stage

Cézanne, Paul
1839-1906 France
The Card Players

Rodin, Auguste
1840-1917 France
The Burghers of Calais

Monet, Claude
1840-1926 France
Water Lilies

Renoir, Pierre Auguste
1841-1919 French
Le Jugement de Paris

Cassatt, Mary
1845-1926 USA
Morning Toilette

Gaugin, Paul
1848-1903 France
The Yellow Christ

Van Gogh, Vincent
1853-90 Holland
Sunflowers

Toulouse-Lautrec
1864-1901 France
At the Moulin Rouge

Matisse, Henri
1869-1954 France
The Dance

Picasso, Pablo
1881-1973 Spain
Guernica

O'Keeffe, Georgia
1887-1986 USA
Pelvis Series

Dali, Salvador
1904-89 Spain
Persistence of Memory

Pollock, Jackson
1912-56 USA
Full fathom five

Improvements in city sanitation in the 19th century greatly reduced death through disease, and population began to rise sharply.

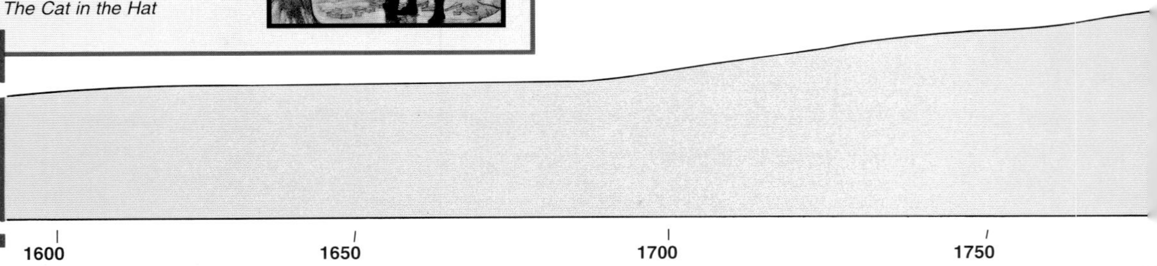

WORLD POPULATION
To show population increase after 1600, the starting point on the chart at right represents the same population as the highest point of the chart on the previous page.

1600	1650	1700	1750

COMPOSERS

The list of composers below gives the dates of their birth and death, the country in which they were born, and one of their most famous works.

Monteverdi, Claudio
1567-1643 Italy
Orfeo

Vivaldi, Antonio
1675-1741 Italy
The Four Seasons

Bach, Johann Sebastian
1685-1750 Germany
Brandenburg Concertos

Handel, George F.
1685-1759 Germany
Messiah

Haydn, Franz Joseph
1732-1809 Austria
The Creation

Mozart, Wolfgang
1756-91 Austria
Don Giovanni

Beethoven, Ludwig van
1770-1827 Germany
Fifth Symphony

Schubert, Franz Peter
1797-1828 Austria
The Trout

Mendelssohn, Felix
1809-47 Germany
Fingal's Cave

Chopin, Frédéric
1810-49 Poland
Piano Études

Verdi, Giuseppe
1813-1901 Italy
La Traviata

Wagner, Richard
1813-83 Germany
The Ring

Brahms, Johannes
1833-97 Germany
Hungarian Dances

Tchaikovsky, Peter I.
1840-93 Russia
The Nutcracker

Puccini, Giacomo
1858-1924 Italy
Madame Butterfly

Debussy, Claude
1862-1918 France
La Mer

Strauss, Richard
1864-1949 Germany
Der Rosenkavalier

Stravinsky, Igor
1882-1971 Russia
The Firebird

Prokofiev, Sergei
1891-1953 Russia
Love for Three Oranges

Gershwin, George
1898-1937 USA
Rhapsody in Blue

Ellington, Duke
1899-1974 USA
Mood Indigo

Copland, Aaron
1900-1990 USA
Appalachian Spring

Bernstein, Leonard
1918-1990 USA
West Side Story

INTERNATIONAL ORGANIZATIONS

UNESCO
United Nations Educational, Scientific, and Cultural Organization. Promotes co-operation among its 158 members in education, science, culture, and communication.

IMF
The International Monetary Fund aims to promote world trade and support countries that are having financial problems.

INTERPOL
The International Criminal Police Organization helps the police of 146 nations to co-operate in catching criminals who cross borders to escape capture.

OAU
From its headquarters in Ethiopia, the Organization of African Unity promotes unity among African states.

ILO
The International Labour Organization promotes peace by working for better economic and social conditions everywhere.

GATT

GATT
The General Agreement on Tariffs and Trade – now called the World Trade Organisation – began in 1948. It is a conference of states which aims to make international trade easier, especially for developing nations.

World population (1,000 million)

BIGGEST POPULATIONS
The height of each bar indicates the number of people living in the 10 countries with the biggest populations. The number at the top of each bar is the population in millions.

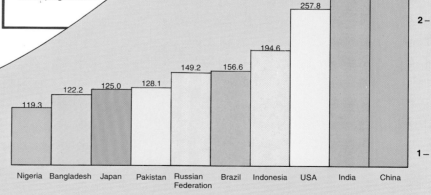

Nigeria	Bangladesh	Japan	Pakistan	Russian Federation	Brazil	Indonesia	USA	India	China
119.3	122.2	125.0	128.1	149.2	156.6	194.6	257.8	896.6	1,205.2

POPULATION GROWTH
Each figure indicates that for each 100 people in the country, the population grows by one person every year.

Australlia 1.9   Chad 2.3   India 2.9   China 2.9   Brazil 3.4

1800   1850   1900   1950   2000   2025

HOW LIVING THINGS ARE CLASSIFIED

Scientists classify living things, or organisms, into groups called kingdoms. This chart shows the five main kingdoms and the main types of organisms that belong to each one. Within a kingdom, organisms are divided into groups called phyla (singular, phylum). Scientists divide phyla into subphyla, and again into classes. Classes are divided into orders, then into suborders. Orders and their suborders are divided into families, then into genera (singular, genus), and finally into species. The human species belongs to the animal kingdom, the primate order, and the mammal class.

MONERANS

The moneran kingdom includes simple organisms such as bacteria, which live in the air, on land, and in water. There are at least 4,000 species of monerans.

PROTISTS

The protist kingdom includes simple organisms such as amoebas, which live mainly in water. There are about 50,000 species of protists.

FUNGI

The fungi kingdom includes mushrooms, toadstools, and moulds, which are neither plants nor animals. There are more than 100,000 species of fungi.

Bacteria
About 2,000 species

Blue-green algae
About 2,000 species

Amoebas
10,000 species

Diatoms
2,000 species

Euglenas
10,000 species

Slime moulds
5,000 species

True fungi
About 100,000 spe

ANIMALS

The animal kingdom includes organisms which are able to move around, and survive by eating other animals or plants. There may be more than 10 million species in the animal kingdom.

Sponges
5,000 species

Coelenterates
9,400 species

Bryozoans
4,000 species

Small phyla
5,500 species

Flatworms
10,000 species

Nematode worms
12,000 species

True worms
12,000 species

Arthropods
More than 1 million species

Mollusks
40,000 species

Echinoderm
6,000 specie

Corals
Jellyfish
Hydras
Sea anemones

Ctenophores (comb jellies)
Velvet worms
Ribbon worms
Lamp shells

Flukes
Free-living flatworms
Tapeworms

Earthworms and bloodworms
Leeches
Lugworms and other marine worms

Chitons
Clams and other bivalves
Snails and slugs
Tooth shells
Octopuses, cuttlefish, and squid

Brittle stars
Sea urchins
Sea cucumbers
Starfish
Sea lilies and feather stars

Cockroaches
Termites

Flies, mosquitoes, and gnats
Stoneflies

Earwigs
Lice

Fleas

Bees, wasps, and ants

Weevils and beetles
Mantises

Silverfish and bristletails

Dragonflies and damselflies
Thrips

Scorpionflies

Bugs such as greenfly and ladybugs

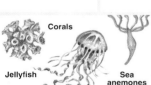

Lacewings and antlions

Stick and leaf insects

Grasshoppers, crickets, and locusts

Millipedes
7,000 species

Centipedes
1,700 species

Insects
more than 1 million species

Crustaceans
40,000 species

Arachnids
70,000 species

Barnacles
Crabs and prawns
Fish lice
Sand hoppers
Water fleas
Woodlice

Spiders
Scorpions
Daddy-longlegs
Mites and ticks
King crabs

Butterflies and moths

HOW TO USE THE CHART
These colours are a guide to the main plant and animal groupings. You can see at a glance which groups each organism belongs to.

- Kingdom
- Phylum
- Subphylum
- Class
- Subclass
- Order

PLANTS
The plant kingdom contains living organisms which can produce their own food using sunlight. Unlike animals, plants cannot move around freely. There are at least 400,000 species in the plant kingdom.

Green algae
6,000 species

Red algae
4,000 species

Brown algae
2,000 species

Mosses and liverworts
25,000 species

Ferns
12,000 species

Club mosses
400 species

Horsetails
35 species

Conifers
500 species

Flowering plants
at least 300,000 species

MONOCOTYLEDONS
These plants have one pair of leaves when they germinate. These leaves are called seed leaves, or cotyledons. They are food for the embryo plant.

Irises

Grasses and cereals

Orchids

There are at least 55,000 species in this plant group.

DICOTYLEDONS
These plants have two pairs of leaves when they germinate, also called seed leaves, or cotyledons. They are food for the embryo plant.

Daisies

Roses

Teas

Primroses

Poppies

Buttercups

Nettles

Legumes

Cabbages

Cacti

Oaks

Myrtles and gums

There are about 250,000 species in this plant group.

Elms

Lilacs

Heathers

Maples

Parsleys and carrots

Willows

Chordates
44,000 species

Mammals
4,070 species

Jawless fish
60 species

Sharks and rays
700 species

Birds
8,800 species, including

Reptiles
6,600 species

Bony fish
21,000 species

Perching birds (order includes more than half of all kinds of birds, such as crows and thrushes)	Eagles, hawks, and vultures	Owls
	Gulls, terns, and waders	Parrots, woodpeckers, and toucans
	Herons, storks, and flamingos	Pelicans, gannets, and cormorants
Albatrosses and petrels	Kingfishers, bee-eaters, and hornbills	Penguins
Cranes and coots	Nightjars, swifts, and hummingbirds	Pheasants, turkeys, and jungle fowl
Cuckoos and roadrunners		Pigeons, doves, and sand grouse
Ducks, geese, and swans	Ostriches, emus, and kiwis	

Marsupial mammals

Placental mammals

Monotreme mammals

Bowfins, garfish
Bristlemouths, viperfish, dragonfish
Carps, catfish, characins, hatchetfish
Coelacanth, birchir, lungfish
Cod, anglers, clingfish
Elephant fish, featherbacks
Eels, tarpons
Herrings, anchovies
Lanternfish, lancetfish, bombay duck
Perch, barracudas, sea horses, and swordfish
Pike, salmon, trout
Silversides, ricefish, flying fish
Sturgeons, paddlefish

Amphibians
3,100 species

Crocodiles and alligators

Lizards and snakes

Newts and salamanders

Legless amphibians (caecilians)

Tuatara

Frogs and toads

Tortoises and turtles

Lemurs, monkeys, apes, and humans

Elephants

Tree shrews

Anteaters, armadillos, and other toothless mammals

Aardvarks

Cats, dogs, and other carnivores

Camels, horses, and other hoofed mammals

Rabbits, hares, and pikas

Squirrels, mice, and other rodents

Seals, sea lions, and walruses

Bats and flying foxes

Hedgehogs and other insectivores

Whales, dolphins, and porpoises

Sea cows and dugongs

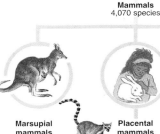

WILDLIFE FACTS

Here are dozens of useful facts about all kinds of plants and animals.

SEVERAL HOURS	SEVERAL DAYS	SEVERAL WEEKS	SEVERAL MONTHS	1 - 5 YEARS	5 - 15 YEARS	15 - 30 YEARS	30 - 45 YEARS	45 - 60 YEARS	60 - 80 YEARS	80 - 10 YEARS
SOME BACTERIA 20 minutes	MORNING-GLORY FLOWER 1 day	FOOTPRINT CARP 8 months		COMMON POPPY 1 year	COMMON STARFISH 6 years		JEWEL BEETLE 35 years	ALLIGATOR 61 years		
	FRUIT FLY 2 weeks				PITCHER PLANT 20 years		BLUE WHALE 45 years		ACTINIA ANEMON 80 year	
MAYFLY (adult) 12 hours	COMMON HOUSEFLY 3 weeks		MONARCH BUTTERFLY 1- 2 years		FRUIT BAT 25 years		ORANG-UTAN 50 years			
	FAIRY RING MUSHROOM 5 days	COMMON FIELD SPEEDWELL 6 months		RED FOX 8 years		CANARY 34 years		BLUE MACAW 64 years	EUROPE EEL 80 year	
	WATER FLEA 7 days	BEDBUG 6 months		BADGER 15 years		BROWN BEAR 40 years		ANDEAN CONDOR 70 years		
SOME KINDS OF FUNGI 18 hours	SMALL SKIPPER BUTTERFLY 3 weeks	WILD PARSNIP 2 years		GOLDFISH 30 years		GREEN TURTLE 50 years		LAKE STURGE 81 year		
	BLACK WIDOW SPIDER 3 - 9 months		QUEEN ANT 15 years		COMMON BOA 40 years		ELEPHANT 75 years			
SHEPHERD'S PURSE 6 weeks		COMMON SHREW 3 years		KOMODO DRAGON 30 years		ROYAL ALBATROSS 53 years		KILLER WHAL 90 year		

MIGRATION FACTS

Reindeer
Reindeer (caribou) walk hundreds of miles each year in search of fresh pasture.

Locust
Swarms of desert locusts migrate more than 3,000 km (2,000 miles) in less than 2 months.

Fur seal
The Northern fur seal swims 3,000 km (2,000 miles) and back again each year.

European swallow
This bird flies 11,000 km (7,000 miles) from Northern Europe to South Africa and back again each year.

Many animals migrate great distances once, and often twice a year, to find fresh pasture, a place to breed, or to escape harsh winters. Here are some animals that migrate – by land, sea, or air.

ANIMAL SPEEDS

AIR

LAND

SEA

Dragonfly
58 km/h (36 mph)

Frigate bird
153 km/h (95 mph)

Spine-tailed swift
170 km/h (106 mph) – fastest level flier

Racing pigeon
177 km/h (110 mph)

Brown hare
25 km/h (16 mph)

Ostrich
72 km/h (45 mph) – fastest bird on land

Pronghorn antelope
88.5 km/h (55 mph) – fastest runner over long distances

Cheetah
96.5 km/h (60 mph) – fastest runner over short distance

Gentoo penguin
27 km/h (17 mph) – fastest bird in water

Killer whale
55.5 km/h (34.5 mph)

Marlin
80 km/h (50 mph)

Sailfish
109 km/h (68 mph) – fastest fish

IMALS | FISH | FUNGI
BIRDS | ARTHROPODS | PLANTS
PTILES BIANS | OTHER INVERTEBRATES | SIMPLE ORGANISMS

) - 1,000 EARS	OVER 1,000 YEARS
IATARA 1 years	ENGLISH OAK 1,500 years
RTOISE 0 years	YEW 3,500 years
ROPEAN EECH 0 years	GIANT SEQUOIA 6,000 years
NDEROSA PINE 0 years	CREOSOTE BUSH 11,000 years

ctic n e greatest grator. It s 19,000 km 2,000 miles) ce a year.

regrine con 2 km/h 26 mp/h) – stest bird in dive

PLANT AND ANIMAL RECORDS

This chart gives you information about plant and animal sizes. It is divided into groups, such as mammals, fish, and birds.

HOW TO USE THE CHART
The colours in this key indicate the different habitats of each of the plants and animals on this page.

LAND
AIR
WATER

MAIN GROUP	BIGGEST	BIGGEST	SMALLEST	SMALLEST	LONGEST	TALLEST	MOST POISONOUS
MAMMALS including marsupial, monotreme, and placental mammals	**African elephant** 3.2 m (10 ft 6 in) high; weighs 5.2 tonnes (5.1 tons).	**Blue whale** 30 m (100 ft) long; weighs 120 tonnes (118 tons).	**Pygmy shrew** 40 mm (1.6 in) long; weighs 1.5 gm (0.05 oz).	**Bumblebee bat** 15 cm (6 in); weighs 1.5 gm (.05 oz).	**Finback whale** 25 m (85 ft) long. Longest mammal after blue whale.	**Giraffe** 5.2 m (17 ft) high; weighs 1.2 tonnes (1.2 tons).	Some moles and shrews can give a bite that contains poisonous saliva (spit).
BIRDS including flying and nonflying birds	**Kori bustard** weighs 18 kg (40 lb). The biggest flying bird.	**Ostrich** weighs 130 kg (280 lb). The biggest of all birds.	**Bee hummingbird** 57 mm (2.2 in) long; weighs 1.6 g (0.06 oz).	Hummingbirds use so much energy that they eat half their weight in food each day.	**Phoenix red jungle fowl** has tail feathers 10 m (33 ft) long.	Ostrich is the tallest bird on Earth, measuring 2.4 m (8 ft) in height.	No birds are poisonous, but the red-billed quelea is the most destructive bird in the world.
REPTILES, such as snakes, and AMPHIBIANS, such as frogs and newts	**Chinese giant salamander** 1.8 m (6 ft) long; weighs 0.91 tonnes (0.89 tons). The biggest amphibian.	**Saltwater crocodile** 5 m (18 ft) long; weighs 1 tonne (0.98 tons). The biggest reptile.	**Gecko** Some geckos are only 1.8 cm (0.7 in) long.	**Cuban arrow-poison frog** 1 cm (0.5 in) long.	**Reticulated python** 10 m (33 ft) long.	**Giant tortoise** 1.2 m (4 ft) high.	**Black-headed sea snake** is the most poisonous reptile.
FISH including bony fish, jawless fish, and cartil-aginous fish	**Whale shark** 18 m (60 ft) long; weighs 40 tonnes (39 tons).		**Dwarf pygmy gobi** 2.03 cm (0.8 in) long; weighs 5 mg (0.00018 oz).	Some of the smallest fish eggs are those of the ling, which lays millions of eggs during its life.	**Oarfish** 14 m (46 ft) long.	**Ocean sunfish** 4.3 m (14 ft) high;3 m (10 ft) long; weighs 2.2 tonnes (2.1 tons).	**Stonefish horrida** has spines to inject its victim with venom.
ARTHRO-PODS, such as spiders, insects, centipedes, and crabs	**Goliath beetle** 110 mm (4.3 in) long; weighs 100g (3.5 oz). The heaviest insect.	**Japanese spider crab** 3.5 m (11 ft) across.The biggest crustacean.	**Fairy fly** Only .02 mm (0.0008 in) long when adult. The smallest insect.	**Alonella water flea** Only 0.25 mm (0.0098 in) long. The smallest crustacean.	**Giant stick insect** 38 cm (15 in) long. The biggest insect.		**Sydney funnel-web spider** has a deadly poisonous bite.
OTHER INVER-TEBRATES (animals without a backbone), such as mollusks	**Giant squid** 17.4 m (57 ft) long. The biggest mollusk.	**African giant snail** weighs 907 gm (2 lb). The biggest land mollusk.	**Amoebas** are so small we cannot see them with the naked eye.		**African giant earthworm** 6.7 m (22 ft) long. Longest segmented worm.	**Arctic giant jellyfish** tentacles 36 m (120 ft). Longest coelenterate.	**Australian sea wasp** has the most painful sting of all animals.
FUNGI, such as mushrooms, toadstools, molds, and yeasts	**Bracket fungus** can measure several metres across.	**American giant puffball** 194 cm (76 in) across.	All fungi produce microscopic spores. Bracket fungi make 30 million a day.	WARNING. DO NOT TOUCH WILD FUNGI. MANY ARE EXTREMELY POISONOUS.	Fungi roots (mycelia) can stretch for hundreds of metres underground.	Some fungi, such as the bootlace fungi, grow inside trees, to the very top.	**Death cup** is the most poisonous fungi.
PLANTS, such as trees, flowering plants, and grasses	**Giant sequoia tree** 83.8 m (274.9 ft) high; weighs 2,000 tonnes (1,970 tons).	**Rafflesia** Largest flowering plant.	**Dwarf snow willow** Only a few centi-metres long. The smallest land plant.	**Lemna aquatic duckweed** Only 0.6 mm (1/42 in) long.	**Pacific giant kelp seaweed** 60 m (200 ft) long. The longest seaweed.	**Douglas fir** 126.5 m (415 ft) high; the tallest plant and the tallest tree on Earth.	**Deadly nightshade** is one of the most poisonous plants.

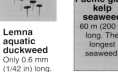

THREATS TO WILDLIFE

Every day the lives of plants and animals are increasingly in danger – mostly because of human interference. The main threat to wildlife today is loss of habitat as a result of humans' changing the natural areas where plants and animals live. The other main threats to wildlife are pollution, hunting and collecting, and competing with humans for food.

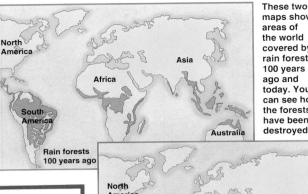

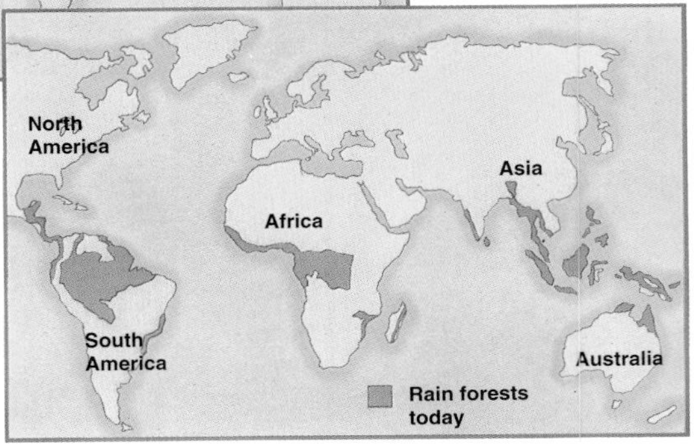

These two maps show areas of the world covered by rain forests 100 years ago and today. You can see how the forests have been destroyed.

North America
Asia
Africa
South America
Australia
Rain forests 100 years ago

North America
Asia
Africa
South America
Australia
Rain forests today

POLLUTION PYRAMID

This picture and the key (right) show how a small amount of chemical pesticide sprayed onto plants becomes concentrated in the bodies of the animals that feed on each other up the food chain.

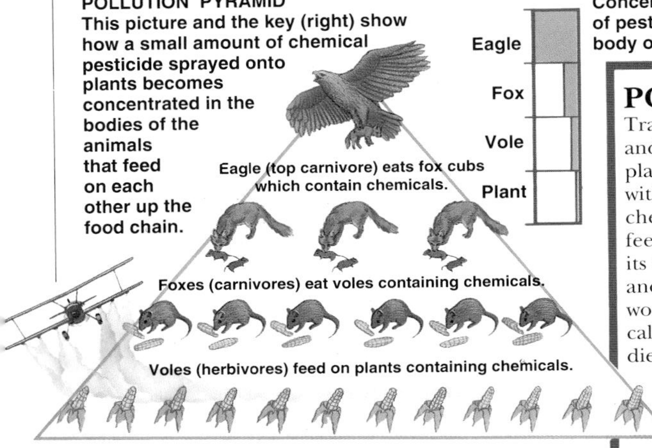

Concentrated level of pesticide in the body of each animal

Eagle
Fox
Vole
Plant

Eagle (top carnivore) eats fox cubs which contain chemicals.

Foxes (carnivores) eat voles containing chemicals.

Voles (herbivores) feed on plants containing chemicals.

Farmer sprays chemical pesticide onto each plant in a field.

POLLUTION

Traffic fumes, oil slicks, acid rain, litter, and chemicals threaten the lives of many plants and animals. When we spray crops with chemicals, a certain amount of the chemical stays on the plant. If an animal feeds on the crops, the chemical enters its body. As each creature is eaten by another, certain amounts of the chemical work their way up the food chain. This is called a pollution pyramid. Many animals die as a result of chemical crop spraying.

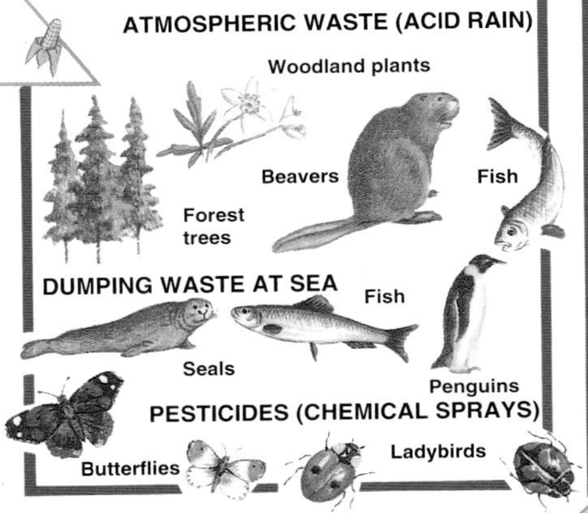

ATMOSPHERIC WASTE (ACID RAIN)

Woodland plants
Beavers
Fish
Forest trees

DUMPING WASTE AT SEA
Fish
Seals
Penguins

PESTICIDES (CHEMICAL SPRAYS)
Butterflies
Ladybirds

COMPETING WITH HUMANS

All kinds of sea creatures, including seals and dolphins, are at risk from humans because they feed on the fish that humans want. Many dolphins die each year because they become caught up in fishing nets. Other sea creatures die because they cannot get enough food.

Dolphins
Seals
Porpoises

HABITAT LOSS

Only 100 years ago, large areas of the world were covered by forests, where millions of different species of plants and animals lived. Today these forests are much smaller because people burn the forests and cut down the trees for farmland and housing. All sorts of unusual animals and plants now have nowhere to live. Today many species are rare, and scientists believe that huge numbers are already extinct.

RAIN FOREST DESTRUCTION (DEFORESTATION)

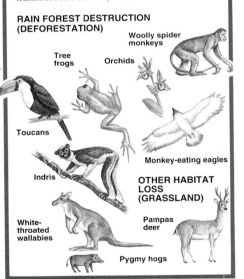

Woolly spider monkeys
Tree frogs
Orchids
Toucans
Monkey-eating eagles
Indris
White-throated wallabies

OTHER HABITAT LOSS (GRASSLAND)
Pampas deer
Pygmy hogs

RATE OF EXTINCTION

Many species of plants and animals have died out since the Earth formed. This is often due to habitat loss. In recent years, the number of extinctions has increased greatly. If this number continues to grow at the current rate, 50,000 species will die out each year by the year 2000. This graph shows some animals which have become extinct in the past few hundred years. It also shows those that are critically in danger of extinction today.

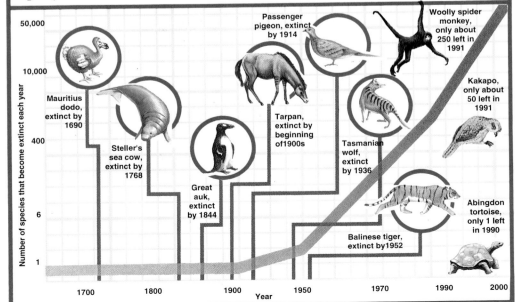

Number of species that become extinct each year

50,000
10,000
400
6
1

Mauritius dodo, extinct by 1690
Steller's sea cow, extinct by 1768
Great auk, extinct by 1844
Passenger pigeon, extinct by 1914
Tarpan, extinct by beginning of 1900s
Woolly spider monkey, only about 250 left in 1991
Tasmanian wolf, extinct by 1936
Kakapo, only about 50 left in 1991
Balinese tiger, extinct by 1952
Abingdon tortoise, only 1 left in 1990

1700   1800   1900   1950   1970   1990   2000
Year

HUNTING AND COLLECTING

Many plants and animals are on the verge of extinction because people have hunted and killed them for their fur, skin, horns, meat, and sometimes simply for their beauty. Today it is illegal to hunt whales, big cats, rhinoceroses, and many other species of animals. It is also illegal to dig up plants from the wild in many areas.

Butterflies
Polar bears
Green turtles
Rhinoceroses

CONSERVATION ACTION

Organizations such as the IUCN (International Union for the Conservation of Nature and Natural Resources) are concerned with the protection of wildlife. The IUCN collects conservation information all over the world. Campaigners work to stop the trade in animal products, and to save plants and animals from extinction. Some of the best-known international organizations are listed below.

WORLD WILDLIFE ORGANIZATIONS

FRIENDS OF THE EARTH INTERNATIONAL SECRETARIAT
P.O. Box 19199
1000 G.D.
Amsterdam
The Netherlands

Committed to the preservation and sensible use of the environment

INTERNATIONAL COUNCIL FOR BIRD PRESERVATION
32 Cambridge Rd.
Girton
Cambridge
CB3 0PJ
England

Dedicated to saving all kinds of birds and their habitats

WORLD WIDE FUND FOR NATURE (WWF U.K.)
Panda House
Weyside Park
Godalming
Surrey
GU7 1XR
England

Protects all kinds of wildlife

INTERNATIONAL FUND FOR ANIMAL WELFARE
Tubwell House
New Road
Crowborough
East Sussex
TN6 2QH
England

Aims to ensure the kind treatment of all animals

WORLD SOCIETY FOR THE PROTECTION OF ANIMALS
Park Place
10 Lawn Lane
London SW8 1UD
England

Seeks to relieve the suffering of all animal life throughout the world

INTERNATIONAL WATERFOWL AND WETLANDS RESEARCH BUREAU
Slimbridge
Gloucester
England

Helps conserve migratory water birds and their wetland habitats

GREENPEACE
Canonbury Villas
London
N1 2PN
England

Works as a pressure group against damage to the natural world

In many parts of the world people have set up special wildlife parks and reserves to help endangered plants and animals survive in their natural surroundings. In these areas, many species are able to live in their natural habitats.

This chart lists some of the national parks and wildlife reserves around the world. The information tells you how large these wildlife areas are, when they were first set up, and the animals and plants that they seek to protect.

NATIONAL WILDLIFE PARKS AND RESERVES

SALONGA RESERVE, ZAIRE, AFRICA

Forest habitat
36,417 sq km
(14,115 sq miles)
The biggest wildlife reserve in Africa

Pygmy chimps, African elephants

GREENLAND NATIONAL PARK, SCANDINAVIA

Tundra habitat
700,000 sq km
(270,271 sq miles)
The world's largest park

Polar bears, seals, walruses

FJIORDLAND NATIONAL PARK, NEW ZEALAND

Mountain and island habitat
10,232 sq km
(3,950 sq miles)

Seals, sea birds

EVERGLADES NATIONAL PARK, FLORIDA

Swamp habitat
5,661sq km
(2,185 sq miles)

Alligators, West Indian manatee

KUSHIRO PARK, HOKKAIDO, JAPAN

Wetland marsh habitat
200 sq km
(77 sq miles)

Japanese red-crowned crane

GREEK NATIONAL MARINE PARK, GREECE

Island habitat

Mediterranean monk seal

GALAPAGOS ISLANDS, SOUTH AMERICA

Island habitat
6,912 sq km
(2,668 sq miles)

Giant tortoise, finches, marine iguana

WOOD BUFFALO NATIONAL PARK, CANADA

Forest habitat
44,900 sq km
(17,335 sq miles)

Buffalo, lynx, reindeer

YELLOWSTONE PARK, NORTH AMERICA

Mountain habitat
8,945 sq km
(3,467 sq miles)

Bighorn sheep, moose

SNOWDONIA NATIONAL PARK, WALES

Mountain habitat
2,188 sq km
(845 sq miles)

Mountain plants, peregrine falcon, kite, merlin

GREAT BARRIER REEF, CAIRNS SECTION, AUSTRALIA

Sea habitat
36,000 sq km
(13,899 sq miles)

Corals, jellyfish, and other sea creatures

IGUAZU NATIONAL PARK, ARGENTINA, SOUTH AMERICA

Forest and riverbank habitat
492 sq km
(189 sq miles)

Jaguar, caiman

TAI NATIONAL PARK, IVORY COAST, AFRICA

Moist forest habitat
3,300 sq km
(1,274 sq miles)

Many rare trees

ULURU NATIONAL PARK, AUSTRALIA

Desert habitat
132,490 sq km
(51,671 sq miles)

Desert plants, thorny devil

ROYAL CHIAWAN SANCTUARY, NEPAL, ASIA

Forest habitat
932 sq km
(359 sq miles)

Tigers, rhinoceros

PYRENEES OCCIDENTALES PARK, FRANCE

Mountain habitat
457 sq km
(176 sq miles)

Bears, chamois

STAR MAPS

About 6,000 stars are visible from Earth without the aid of a telescope – roughly 3,000 in the northern sky and 3,000 in the southern sky. Certain constellations, or groups of stars, are visible depending on the season, the time of night, and whether you are on the Northern or Southern Hemisphere. The visibility of stars also depends on how dark the sky is: city streetlights light up the sky and make fainter stars impossible to see. These star maps (right) show the main stars visible from the Northern and Southern Hemispheres. You can usually see the stars in the centre of the maps at all times of the year because they are directly overhead. The visibility of stars at the edges of the maps depends on the season and the time of night.

The size of the stars on the star maps represents their brightness as seen from Earth. The larger the dot on the map, the brighter the star.

Milky Way _____

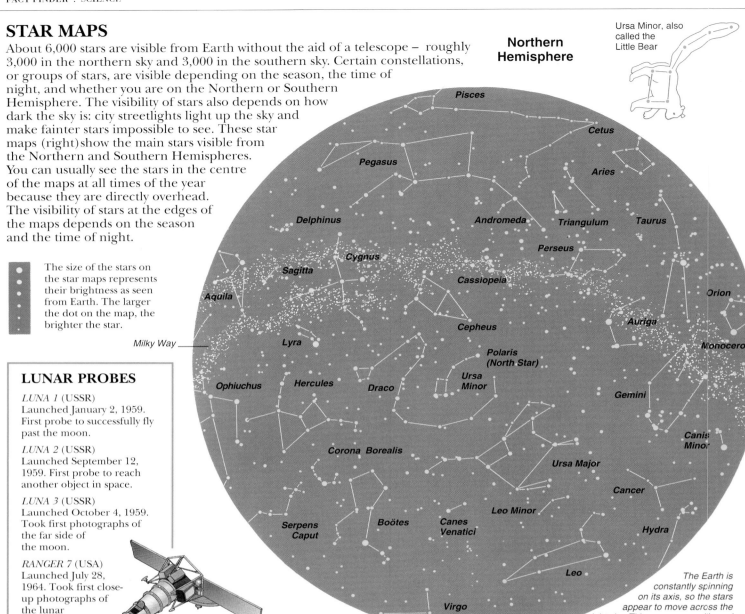

Northern Hemisphere

Ursa Minor, also called the Little Bear

The Earth is constantly spinning on its axis, so the stars appear to move across the night sky. This means you will need to rotate these star maps so that they match up with the night sky.

LUNAR PROBES

LUNA 1 (USSR)
Launched January 2, 1959. First probe to successfully fly past the moon.

LUNA 2 (USSR)
Launched September 12, 1959. First probe to reach another object in space.

LUNA 3 (USSR)
Launched October 4, 1959. Took first photographs of the far side of the moon.

RANGER 7 (USA)
Launched July 28, 1964. Took first close-up photographs of the lunar surface.

Ranger 7

LUNA 9 (USSR)
Launched January 31, 1966. First controlled landing of a probe on the lunar surface. Transmitted pictures and data over four days.

LUNA 10 (USSR)
Launched March 31, 1966. First successful orbit of the moon.

APOLLO 11 (USA)
Launched July 16, 1969. First spacecraft to carry people to the moon. On July 20, 1969, Neil Armstrong and Edwin Aldrin landed on the moon.

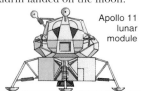

Apollo 11 lunar module

THE SOLAR SYSTEM

Planet	Diameter at equator km	miles	Distance from sun millions of km	miles	Mass (Earth = 1)	Volume (Earth = 1)	Surface temperature °C	°F
Mercury	4,879	3,033	57.9	36.0	0.055	0.056	+350	+662
Venus	12,104	7,523	108.2	67.2	0.86	0.86	+480	+896
Earth	12,756	7,928	149.6	93	1	1	+22	+72
Mars	6,794	4,222	227.9	141.5	0.107	0.15	-23	-9
Jupiter	142,884	88,784	778.3	483.3	318	1,319	-150	-238
Saturn	120,536	74,914	1,427	886.1	95	744	-180	-292
Uranus	51,118	31,770	2,869.6	1,783	15	67	-214	-353
Neptune	50,538	31,410	4,496.7	2,793	17	57	-220	-364
Pluto	2,445	1,519	5,900	3,666	0.002	<0.01	-230	-382

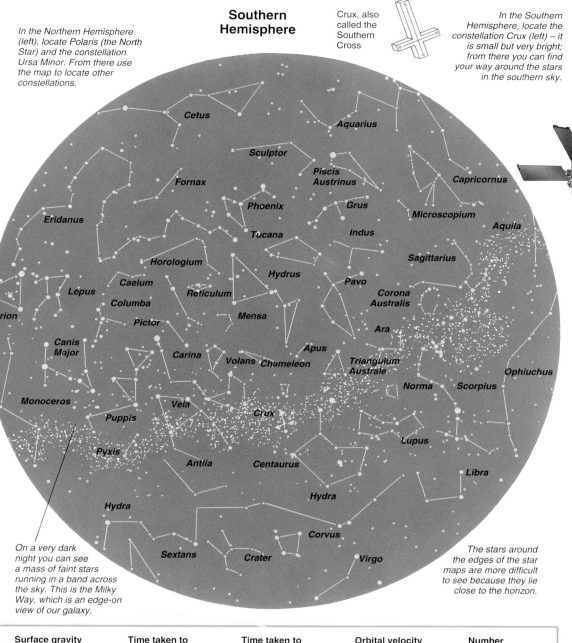

Southern Hemisphere

Crux, also called the Southern Cross

In the Northern Hemisphere (left), locate Polaris (the North Star) and the constellation Ursa Minor. From there use the map to locate other constellations.

In the Southern Hemisphere, locate the constellation Crux (left) – it is small but very bright; from there you can find your way around the stars in the southern sky.

On a very dark night you can see a mass of faint stars running in a band across the sky. This is the Milky Way, which is an edge-on view of our galaxy.

The stars around the edges of the star maps are more difficult to see because they lie close to the horizon.

Star map constellation labels: Cetus, Aquarius, Sculptor, Fornax, Piscis Austrinus, Capricornus, Eridanus, Phoenix, Grus, Microscopium, Aquila, Tucana, Indus, Horologium, Sagittarius, Caelum, Hydrus, Pavo, Corona Australis, Lepus, Reticulum, Columba, Mensa, Ara, Pictor, Canis Major, Carina, Apus, Triangulum Australe, Ophiuchus, Volans, Chameleon, Norma, Scorpius, Monoceros, Vela, Crux, Puppis, Lupus, Pyxis, Antlia, Centaurus, Libra, Hydra, Hydra, Corvus, Sextans, Crater, Virgo, Orion

Surface gravity (Earth = 1)	Time taken to orbit sun	Time taken to spin once on axis	Orbital velocity km per second	Orbital velocity miles per second	Number of moons
0.38	87.97 days	58.65 days	47.9	29.7	0
0.9	224.7 days	243.16 days	35	21.8	0
1	365.26 days	23 hr 56 min 4 sec	29.8	18.5	1
0.38	779.9 days	24 hr 37 min 23 sec	24.1	15	2
2.64	11.86 years	9 hr 50 min 30 sec	13.1	8.1	16
1.16	29.46 years	10 hr 39 min	9.6	6	23
0.93	84.01 years	17 hr 14 min	6.8	4.2	15
1.2	164.8 years	16 hr 3 min	5.4	3.4	8
0.05	247.7 years	6 days 9 hr	4.7	2.9	1

PLANETARY PROBES

These are some of the most important space probes launched to date.

PIONEER 5 (USA) Launched March 11, 1960. First probe to enter deep space. Flew to a distance of 36.5 million km (22.7 million miles) from Earth.

Mariner 9

MARINER 9 (USA) Launched May 30, 1971. First probe to successfully orbit Mars. Sent back about 7,000 pictures of Mars and its moons.

PIONEER 10 (USA) Launched March 3, 1972. First probe to make a successful flyby of Jupiter.

Pioneer 10

HELIOS 2 (W. GERMANY) Launched January 15, 1976. Solar probe that passed the sun at a distance of about 43 million km (27 million miles).

VENERA 9 (USSR) Launched June 8, 1975. Carried a lander that sent back the first pictures of the surface of Venus.

Venera 9

VOYAGER (USA) Two probes, Voyager 1 and 2, launched 1977. Between them they explored much of the solar system, including Jupiter, Saturn, Uranus, and Neptune.

Giotto

Voyager 1

GIOTTO (EUROPEAN SPACE AGENCY) Launched July 2, 1985. Probe launched to study Halley's Comet. Made the first close approach to a comet, and sent back pictures and data.

GALILEO (USA) Launched October 18, 1989. Due to enter Jupiter orbit in 1995. Carries probe that will be dropped into Jupiter's atmosphere.

WORLD'S GREATEST OCEANS AND SEAS

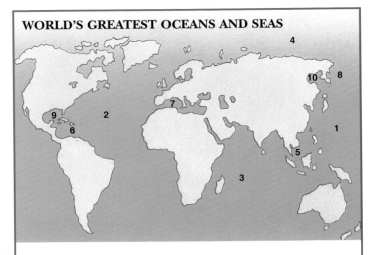

1 Pacific Ocean
166,240,000 sq km
(64,190,000 sq miles)

2 Atlantic Ocean
86,560,000 sq km
(33,420,000 sq miles)

3 Indian Ocean
73,430,000 sq km
(28,350,000 sq miles)

4 Arctic Ocean
13,230,000 sq km
(5,110,000 sq miles)

5 South China Sea
2,974,600 sq km (1,148,500 sq miles)

6 Caribbean Sea
2,753,000 sq km (1,063,000 sq miles)

7 Mediterranean Sea
2,503,000 sq km (966,750 sq miles)

8 Bering Sea
2,268,180 sq km (875,750 sq miles)

9 Gulf of Mexico
1,542,985 sq km (595,750 sq miles)

10 Sea of Okhotsk
1,527,570 sq km (589,800 sq miles)

WORLD'S GREATEST DESERTS

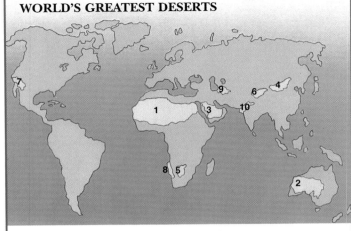

1 Sahara (N. Africa)
8,400,000 sq km (3,250,000 sq miles)

2 Australian Desert
1,550,000 sq km (600,000 sq miles)

3 Arabian Desert
1,300,000 sq km (500,000 sq miles)

4 Gobi (China - Mongolia)
1,040,000 sq km (400,000 sq miles)

5 Kalahari Desert (Southern Africa)
520,000 sq km (200,000 sq miles)

6 Takla Makan (W. China)
320,000 sq km (125,000 sq miles)

7 Sonoran Desert (USA - Mexico)
310,000 sq km (120,000 sq miles)

8 Namib Desert (Namibia)
310,000 sq km (120,000 sq miles)

9 Kara Kum (Turkmenistan)
270,000 sq km (105,000 sq miles)

10 Thar Desert (India and Pakistan)
260,000 sq km (100,000 sq miles)

WORLD'S LARGEST ISLANDS

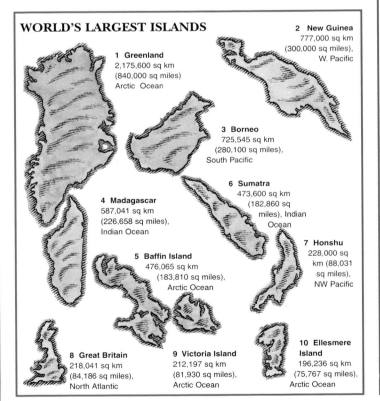

2 New Guinea
777,000 sq km
(300,000 sq miles),
W. Pacific

1 Greenland
2,175,600 sq km
(840,000 sq miles)
Arctic Ocean

3 Borneo
725,545 sq km
(280,100 sq miles),
South Pacific

6 Sumatra
473,600 sq km
(182,860 sq
miles), Indian
Ocean

4 Madagascar
587,041 sq km
(226,658 sq miles),
Indian Ocean

7 Honshu
228,000 sq
km (88,031
sq miles),
NW Pacific

5 Baffin Island
476,065 sq km
(183,810 sq miles),
Arctic Ocean

**10 Ellesmere
Island**
196,236 sq km
(75,767 sq miles),
Arctic Ocean

8 Great Britain
218,041 sq km
(84,186 sq miles),
North Atlantic

9 Victoria Island
212,197 sq km
(81,930 sq miles),
Arctic Ocean

WEATHER RECORDS

Greatest Snowfall
12 months, 31,102 mm (1,224.5 in), Paradise, Mt. Rainier, Washington State, USA, 19/2/1971 to 18/2/1972.

Greatest Rainfall
(24 hours) 1,870 mm (73.62 in), Cilaos, Réunion, Indian Ocean, 15/3 – 16/3/1952

Driest Place/Longest Drought
(Annual average) Nil, in the Atacama Desert, near Calama, Chile/ 400 years to 1971, also in Atacama Desert.

Highest Surface Wind Speed
371 km/h (231 mph), Mt. Washington (1,916 m/6,288 ft), New Hampshire, USA, 12/4/1934

Maximum Sunshine
97% (over 4,300 hours), Eastern Sahara

Minimum Sunshine
Nil, North Pole - for winter stretches of 182 days

Highest Shade Temperature
58°C (136.4°F), al'Azizyah, Libya (alt. 111m/367 ft), 13/9/1922

Hottest Place
(Annual average) 34.4°C/94°F, Dallol, Ethiopia (1960-66)

Coldest Place
(Coldest measured average) -56.6°C (-70°F), Plateau Station, Antarctica

Most Rainy Days
(Year) up to 350 per year, Mt. Waialeale (1,569 m/5,148 ft), Kauai, Hawaii

Windiest Place
Where gales reach 320 km/h (200 mph), Commonwealth Bay, George V Coast, Antarctica

WORLD'S MAJOR MOUNTAINS

All of the world's highest mountains
lie in the Himalayas.

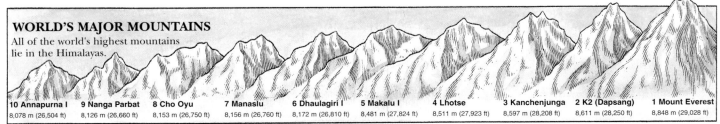

10 Annapurna I	9 Nanga Parbat	8 Cho Oyu	7 Manaslu	6 Dhaulagiri I	5 Makalu I	4 Lhotse	3 Kanchenjunga	2 K2 (Dapsang)	1 Mount Everest
8,078 m (26,504 ft)	8,126 m (26,660 ft)	8,153 m (26,750 ft)	8,156 m (26,760 ft)	8,172 m (26,810 ft)	8,481 m (27,824 ft)	8,511 m (27,923 ft)	8,597 m (28,208 ft)	8,611 m (28,250 ft)	8,848 m (29,028 ft)

EARTHQUAKES

There are two different scales for measuring earthquakes: the Richter scale and the Modified Mercalli scale.

RICHTER SCALE

The Richter scale measures the strength of an earthquake at its source and takes account of the distance from the earthquake. It is a logarithmic scale, which means that each time the magnitude increases by one unit, the ground moves 10 times more and the earthquake releases about 30 times as much energy. The scale below gives an indication of the probable effects of earthquakes of particular magnitudes.

Magnitude	Probable effects
1	Detectable only by instruments.
2-2.5	Can just be felt by people.
4-5	May cause slight damage.
6	Fairly destructive.
7	A major earthquake.
8-9	A very destructive earthquake.

MODIFIED MERCALLI SCALE

The Modified Mercalli scale measures how much an earthquake shakes the ground at a particular place. This is called the felt intensity, and the scale gives a list of descriptions of earthquake effects.

Intensity	Probable effects
1	Not felt by people.
2	May be felt by some people on upper floors.
3	Detected indoors. Hanging objects may swing.
4	Hanging objects swing. Doors and windows rattle.
5	Felt outdoors by most people. Small objects moved or upset.
6	Felt by everyone. Furniture moves. Trees and bushes shake.
7	Difficult for people to stand. Buildings damaged, loose bricks fall.
8	Major damage to buildings. Branches of trees break.
9	General panic. Large cracks form in ground. Some buildings collapse.
10	Large landslides occur. Many buildings are destroyed.
11	Major ground disturbances. Railway lines buckle.
12	Damage is nearly total. Large objects thrown into the air.

BEAUFORT SCALE OF WIND SPEED

Force	Description	Mean Speed km/h	mph
0	Calm	Less than 1	Less than 1
1	Light air	1-5	1-3
2	Light breeze	6-11	4-7
3	Gentle breeze	12-19	8-12
4	Moderate breeze	20-29	13-18
5	Fresh breeze	30-39	19-24
6	Strong breeze	40-50	25-31
7	Moderate gale	51-61	32-38
8	Fresh gale	62-74	39-46
9	Strong gale	75-87	47-54
10	Whole gale	88-101	55-63
11	Storm	102-117	64-73
12	Hurricane	Above 119	Above 74

TALLEST STRUCTURES

Towers (including those supported by guy ropes)

		Metres	Feet	Stories	Date
1	Warsaw Radio Mast, Plock, Poland	646	2,120	—	1974
2	KTHI-TV Tower, North Dakota, U.S.A.	629	2,063	—	1963
3	CN Tower, Toronto, Canada	553	1,815	—	1975

Habitable Buildings

1	Petronas Towers, Kuala Lumpur, Malaysia	449	1,483	110	1996
2	Sears Tower, Chicago, U.S.A.	443	1,454	110	1974
3	World Trade Centre, New York City, U.S.A.	412	1,350	110	1973
4	Empire State Building, New York City, U.S.A.	381	1,250	102	1931
5	Standard Oil Building, Chicago, U.S.A.	346	1,136	80	1973
6	John Hancock Centre, Chicago, U.S.A.	344	1,127	100	1968
7	Chrysler Building, New York City, U.S.A.	319	1,046	77	1930
8	Bank of China, Hong Kong, China	315	1,033	70	1989
9	Texas Commerce Tower, Houston, U.S.A.	305	1,002	75	1981
10	Allied Bank Plaza, Houston, U.S.A.	300	985	71	1983

The Petronas Towers in Malaysia, the world's tallest habitable building.

LONGEST BRIDGES

The figures given below relate to the length of the central span of each bridge. All the bridges listed are suspension bridges.

1 Akashi-Kaikyo
1,780 m (5,839 ft), Honshu-Shikoku, Japan, completed 1997

2 Humber Estuary
1,410 m (4,626 ft), Humber, England, completed 1980

3 Verrazano-Narrows
1,298 m (4,260 ft), New York City, U.S.A., completed 1964

4 Golden Gate
1,280 m (4,200 ft), San Francisco, U.S.A., completed 1937

5 Mackinac Straits
1,158 m (3,800 ft), Michigan, U.S.A., completed 1957

6 Bosporus
1,074 m (3,524 ft), Istanbul, Turkey, completed 1973

7 George Washington
1,067 m (3,500 ft) New York City, U.S.A., completed 1931

8 Tagus River Bridge
1,013 m (3,323 ft), Lisbon, Portugal, completed 1966

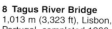

9 Forth Road Bridge
1,006 m (3,300 ft), Firth of Forth, Scotland, completed 1964

10 Severn
988 m (3,240 ft), Severn Estuary, England, completed 1966

Many geographical statistics are approximate because of factors such as seasonal changes and the method of measurement.

AREA AND VOLUME

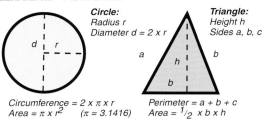

Circle:
Radius r
Diameter d = 2 x r

Circumference = 2 x π x r
Area = π x r^2 (π = 3.1416)

Triangle:
Height h
Sides a, b, c

Perimeter = a + b + c
Area = $^1/_2$ x b x h

Rectangle:
Sides a, b

Perimeter = 2 x (a + b)
Area = a x b

Cylinder:
Height h
Radius r

Surface area = 2 x π x r x h (excluding ends)
Volume = π x r^2 x h

Cone:
Height h
Radius r
Side l

Surface area = π x r x l (exclu...)
Volume = $^1/_3$ x π x r^2 x l

UNITS OF MEASUREMENT

METRIC UNIT	EQUIVALENT	IMPERIAL UNIT	EQUIVALENT
Length		**Length**	
1 centimetre (cm)	10 millimetres (mm)	1 foot (ft)	12 inches (in)
1 metre (m)	100 centimetres (cm)	1 yard (yd)	3 feet
1 kilometre (km)	1,000 metres	1 mile	1,760 yards
Mass		**Mass**	
1 kilogram (kg)	1,000 grams (g)	1 pound (lb)	16 ounces (oz)
1 tonne (t)	1,000 kilograms	1 ton	2,240 pounds
Area		**Area**	
1 square centimetre (cm^2)	100 square millimetres (mm^2)	1 square foot (ft^2)	144 square inches (in^2)
1 square metre (m^2)	10,000 square centimetres	1 square yard (yd^2)	9 square feet
1 hectare	10,00 square metres	1 acre	4,840 square yards
1 square kilometre (km^2)	1 million square metres	1 square mile	640 acres
Volume			
1 cubic centimetre (cc)	1 millilitre (ml)	1 pint	34.68 cubic inches (in^3)
1 litre (l)	1,000 millilitres	1 quart	2 pints
1 cubic metre (m^3)	1,000 litres	1 gallon	4 quarts

METRIC-IMPERIAL CONVERSIONS

Metric units into imperial units

To convert	into	multiply by
Length		
Centimetres	inches	0.39
Metres	feet	3.28
Kilometres	miles	0.62
Area		
Square cm	square inches	0.16
Square metres	square feet	10.76
Hectares	acres	2.47
Square km	square miles	0.39
Volume		
Cubic cm	cubic inches	0.061
Litres	pints	1.76
Litres	gallons	0.22
Mass		
Grams	ounces	0.04
Kilograms	pounds	2.21
Tonnes	tons	0.98

BINARY SYSTEM

The binary number system is used in computers to represent numbers and letters. The binary system uses only two symbols – 0 and 1 – which represent "On" and "Off" in computer circuits.

Decimal	Binary
1	1
2	10
3	11
4	100
5	101
6	110
7	111
8	1000
9	1001
10	1010
11	1011
12	1100

MATHEMATICAL SYMBOLS

+	plus
-	minus
±	plus or minus
x	multiplication (times)
÷	divided by
=	equal to
≠	not equal to
≈	approximately equal to
>	greater than
<	less than
≥	greater than or equal to
≤	less than or equal to
%	per cent
√	square root
π	pi (3.1416)
°	degree
'	minute, foot
"	second, inch

PERIODIC TABLE

The periodic table classifies chemical elements in order of atomic number (the number of protons in each atom of the element). The elements are arranged in horizontal rows, called periods, and vertical columns, called groups. In this way, elements with similar chemical properties (such as the alkali metals) lie in the same vertical group.

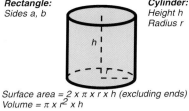

Chemical symbol
Atomic number of the element
Name of element
Atomic weight, the weight of one atom of the element compared to an atom of the element carbon. When the figure is in parentheses... refers to the most stable isotope.

26 Fe Iron 55.847

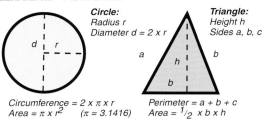

H 1 Hydrogen 1.008

Li 3 Lithium 6.941	Be 4 Beryllium 9.012
Na 11 Sodium 22.990	Mg 12 Magnesium 24.305

K 19 Potassium 39.098	Ca 20 Calcium 40.08	Sc 21 Scandium 44.956	Ti 22 Titanium 47.90	V 23 Vanadium 50.941	Cr 24 Chromium 51.996	Mn 25 Manganese 54.938	Fe 26 Iron 55.847	Co Cobalt 58.933
Rb 37 Rubidium 85.468	Sr 38 Strontium 87.62	Y 39 Yttrium 88.906	Zr 40 Zirconium 91.22	Nb 41 Niobium 92.906	Mo 42 Molybdenum 95.94	Tc 43 Technetium (97)	Ru 44 Ruthenium 101.07	Rh Rhodium 102.90
Cs 55 Caesium 132.910	Ba 56 Barium 137.34		Hf 72 Hafnium 178.49	Ta 73 Tantalum 180.948	W 74 Tungsten 183.85	Re 75 Rhenium 186.207	Os 76 Osmium 190.2	Ir Iridium 192.22
Fr 87 Francium (223)	Ra 88 Radium 226.025		Rf-Ku 104 (Rutherfordium; Kurchatovium) (261)	Ha 105 Hahnium (262)	106 (263)	107		

New elements are sometimes discovered it takes time for them to be officially recognized and named.

La 57 Lanthanum 138.906	Ce 58 Cerium 140.12	Pr 59 Praseodymium 140.908	Nd 60 Neodymium 144.24	Pm 61 Promethium (145)	Sm 62 Samarium 150.4	Eu 63 Europium 151.96	Gd Gadolinium 157.25
Ac 89 Actinium (227)	Th 90 Thorium 232.038	Pa 91 Protactinium 231.036	U 92 Uranium 238.029	Np 93 Neptunium 237.048	Pu 94 Plutonium (244)	Am 95 Americium (243)	Cm Curium (247)

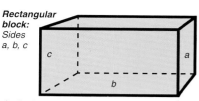

Rectangular block:
Sides
a, b, c

e) Surface area = 2 x (ab + bc + ac)
Volume = a x b x c

perial units into metric units		
convert	into	multiply by
ngth		
hes	centimetres	2.54
et	metres	0.30
es	kilometres	1.61
ea		
uare inches	square cm	6.45
uare feet	square metres	0.09
es	hectares	0.41
uare miles	square km	2.59
ume		
bic inches	cubic cm	16.39
ts	litres	0.57
lons	litres	4.55
ss		
ces	grams	28.35
unds	kilograms	0.45
s	tonnes	1.02

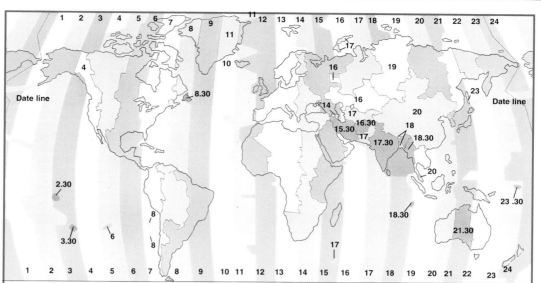

TIME ZONES

As Earth spins, the sun appears to rise and set. However, while the sun is rising at one place on the globe, it is setting at another. For instance, when it is 5 A.M. in New York, it is 8 P.M. in Australia. To take account of this, the Earth is divided into a series of time zones. In each zone, the clocks are set to a different time. These times are calculated to ensure that, in every part of the world, the time is about 12 P.M. during the middle of the day, and midnight during the middle of the night.

Alkali metals	Alkaline earth metals

Transition metals	Other metals

Nonmetals	Noble gases

Lanthanide series	Actinide series

							2 He Helium 4.003
5 B Boron 10.81	**6** C Carbon 12.011	**7** N Nitrogen 14.007	**8** O Oxygen 15.999	**9** F Fluorine 18.998	**10** Ne Neon 20.179		
13 Al Aluminium 26.982	**14** Si Silicon 28.086	**15** P Phosphorus 30.974	**16** S Sulphur 32.06	**17** Cl Chlorine 35.453	**18** Ar Argon 39.948		

28 Ni Nickel 68.70	**29** Cu Copper 63.546	**30** Zn Zinc 65.38	**31** Ga Gallium 69.72	**32** Ge Germanium 72.59	**33** As Arsenic 74.922	**34** Se Selenium 78.96	**35** Br Bromine 79.904	**36** Kr Krypton 83.80
46 Pd Palladium 106.4	**47** Ag Silver 107.868	**48** Cd Cadmium 112.40	**49** In Indium 114.82	**50** Sn Tin 118.69	**51** Sb Antimony 121.75	**52** Te Tellurium 127.60	**53** I Iodine 126.905	**54** Xe Xenon 131.30
78 Pt Platinum 195.09	**79** Au Gold 196.967	**80** Hg Mercury 200.59	**81** Tl Thallium 204.37	**82** Pb Lead 207.2	**83** Bi Bismuth 208.98	**84** Po Polonium (209)	**85** At Astatine (210)	**86** Rn Radon (222)

(117)

65 Tb Terbium 158.925	**66** Dy Dysprosium 162.50	**67** Ho Holmium 164.930	**68** Er Erbium 167.26	**69** Tm Thulium 168.934	**70** Yb Ytterbium 173.04	**71** Lu Lutetium 174.97
97 Bk Berkelium (247)	**98** Cf Californium (251)	**99** Es Einsteinium (254)	**100** Fm Fermium (257)	**101** Md Mendelevium (258)	**102** No Nobelium (255)	**103** Lr Lawrencium (260)

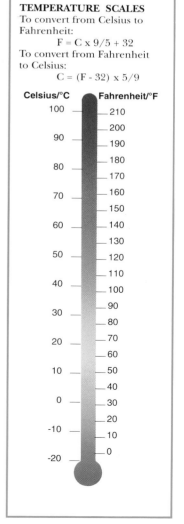

TEMPERATURE SCALES
To convert from Celsius to Fahrenheit:
$$F = C \times 9/5 + 32$$
To convert from Fahrenheit to Celsius:
$$C = (F - 32) \times 5/9$$

Celsius/°C   Fahrenheit/°F

INDEX

Page numbers in **bold** type refer to main entries. Numbers in *italics* refer to pages in the Fact Finder.

ACKNOWLEDGEMENTS

Additional editorial assistance from Jane Birdsell, Lynn Bresler, Claire Gillard,
Carl Gombrich, Caroline Murrell, Connie Novis, Louise Pritchard, Jill Somerscales
Additional design assistance from Duncan Brown, Simon Yeomans
Revisions for the second edition Liza Bruml
Index Hilary Bird
Photography Stephen Oliver

**In addition, Dorling Kindersley would like to thank the following people
and organizations for their assistance in the production of this book:**

Alan Baker; All England Tennis Club; Amateur Swimming Association; Alvis Ltd; Araine Space Ltd.; David Atwill, Hampshire Constabulary; BMW; Beech Aircraft Corp; Beaufort Air Sea Equipment; Bike UK Ltd.; Boeing Aircraft Corporation; BP Ltd; British Amateur Athletics Association; British Amateur Gymnastics Association; British Steel; British Telecom International Ltd.; British Antarctic Survey; British Canoe Union; British Coal Ltd; British Forging Industry Association; British Foundry Association; British Gas Ltd; British Paper and Board Federation; British Parachuting Association; British Ski Federation; British Sub-Aqua Club; Paul Bush; Karen Caftledine, Courtauld Fibres; Michelle Byam; Cartoon frames taken from "Spider in the Bath", Reproduced by permission from HIBBERT RALPH ENTERTAINMENT © and SILVEYJEX PARTNERSHIP ©; Citroen; Colourscan, Singapore; "Coca-Cola" and "Coke" are registered trade marks which identify the same products of The Coca-Cola Company; Commander Richard Compton-Hall; Lyn Constable-Maxwell; Cottrell & Co Ltd; Geoffrey Court; Sarah Crouch, Black & Decker Ltd; F. Darton and Co. Ltd.; Department of Energy, Energy Conservation Support Unit; DRG paper Ltd; Adrian Dixon; Patrick Duffy, IBA Museum; Earth Observation Data Centre; Electronic Arts; Embassy of Japan, Transportation Department; Esso Plc; Eurotunnel Ltd; Ford UK Ltd.; Sub Officer Jack Goble, London Fire Brigade; Julia Golding; Brian Gordon; Paul Greenwood, Pentax Cameras UK Ltd.; Patrick and Betty Gunzi; Hamleys, Regent Street, London; Helmets Ltd.; Jim Henson Productions Ltd; Hoover Ltd.; Horniman Museum; House of Vanheems Ltd.; Institute of Metals; Alan Heward, Shell UK Ltd.; John Reedman Associates; IAL Security products; ICI Ltd; Ilford Ltd.; Janes Publications Ltd.; Jonathan Kettle, Haymarket Publishing; Julia Kisch; Thorn EMI Ltd.; Sarah Kramer; Krauss-Maffei GMBH; Lambda Photometrics Ltd.; Leica GmbH; Sandy Law; Richard Lawson Ltd.; Leyland Daf Ltd.; Liz Abrahams, BBC Television; London Transport Museum; London Weather Centre; Lyndon-Dykes of London; Malcolm Saunders, Simon Gloucester Saro Ltd.; Neil MacIntyre; Marconi Electronic Devices Ltd., Lincoln.; Martin Christopher, VAG Group; Paul McCarthy, Cosser Electronics Ltd.; McDonnell Douglas Aircraft Corporation; Philip Mead; Philips Ltd.; Mercedes; A. Mondadori Editore, Verona; Joan MacDonnell, Sovreign Oil and Gas Ltd.; Ruth Milner, Comark Ltd.; Mysteries New Age Centre Covent Garden, London; National Remote Sensing Centre. Farnborough; Nautilus Ltd, London; Newcastle Hindu Temple; Nina Kara; Olympus Ltd.; Osel Ltd.; Otis PLC; Pamela Barron; Gary Palmer, Marantz Ltd.; Personal Protection Products; Pilkington glass Ltd; Pioneer Ltd.; Porter Nash Medical; Robertson research Ltd; Tony Robinson; Rockware glass Ltd; Rod Argent Music; Rolls Royce Ltd.; Liz Rosney; Royal Aircraft Establishment; Royal Astronomical Society, London; Royal Military Academy, Sandhurst; SNCF; Andrew Saphir; Apple UK Ltd.; Seagate Ltd.; Shell UK Ltd.; Skyship International Ltd.; Dennis Slay, Wessex Consultants Ltd.; Amanda Smith, Zanussi Ltd.; Sony Ltd.; Stanfords Map Shop, London; Steel casting Research and Trade Association; Stollmont Theatres Ltd.; Swatch Watches Ltd; Texaco Ltd.; The British Post Office; The Institution of Civil Engineers; The Kite Shop, London; The Lord Mayor of Westminster's New Year Parade; The Meteorological Office, London; The National Grid Company Ltd.; The National Physical Laboratory; The Ordinance Survey; The YHA Shop, London; Theatre Museum, Covent Garden, London; Toyota; Trafalgar House, Building and Civil Engineering; Trevor Hyde; Wastewatch; Jim Webb; Westland Helicopters Ltd.; Malcolm Willingale, V Ships, Monaco; Wiggins Teape Ltd.; Howard Wong, Covent Garden Records, London; Woods Hole Oceanographic Institute; Yarrow Shipbuilders Ltd.

PICTURE SOURCES

The publishers are grateful to the following individuals and picture libraries for permission to reproduce their photographs.

Abbreviations: t = top; b = below; c = centre; l = left; r = right.

A

Airship Industries: 63 bl; **Max Alexander:** 382 br; **Alvis Ltd:** 453 br; **Ancient Art & Architecture Library/ Ronald Sheridan:** 180 tr, 253 tl, 287 tl, 300 br, 354 tr, 354 bc, 384 t; 408 b, 444 c; **Animal Photography/Sally Anne Thompson:** 411 bl; **Animals Unlimited/Paddy Cutts:**101 br, 411 cr; **AP:** 304 br, 502 cl; **Arcaid/Lucinda Lambton:** 268; **Ardea London Ltd:** Liz Bomford: 210 cr; François Gohier: 140 bc; Ron and Valerie Taylor: 143 tr, 393 cl, 479 cr, 479 bc; **Neil Ardley:** 47 bl; By courtesy of the **Visitors of the Ashmolean Museum, Oxford:** 179 bc; **Catherine Ashmore:** 62 c; **Associated Press:** 192 t, 304 cl, 568 br; **Australian Overseas Information Service, London:** 10 br, 50 cl, 55 bl.

B

B.N.S. Barrett: 220 tr; **Beechcraft Aircraft Corporation:** 422 br; **BFI Stills, Posters & Designs:** 206 tr; **The Boeing Company** pp. 21 c, 339 tr; **Courtesy of de Brant, Joyce & Partners** pp. 36 bc, 37 bl; **Bridgeman Art Library:** 133 tl, 185 tr, 203 cl, 320 br, 323 bl, 406 br, 560 cr. Also: collections of Albertina, Vienna: 168 tr; Bibliotheque Nationale, Paris: 194 tl, 405 c; British Museum, London: 25 bl, 25 br, 64 b, 243 tl, 319 bl, 337 cl, 405 tl, 523 tl, 570 br; Cairo Museum/ Giraudon: 35 br; Château de Versailles: 295 cr; Chester Beatty Library & Gallery of Oriental Art: 298; Christies, London: 16 bl, 431 tr, 461 bl, 580 bl, 602 t; City of Bristol Museum & Art Gallery: 300 tl, 301 tl; Eton College, Windsor: 337 tr; Fabbri: 85 b; Forbes Magazine Collection: 371 br; Galleria Dell'Accademia, Florence: 444 bl; Hereford Cathedral: 333 tl; Kunsthistorisches Museum, Vienna: 311 tl; Louvre, Paris: 230 tc, 254 bc, 441 b; Mallett & Son Antiques, London: 235 tl; Musée des Beaux Arts, Tourcoing/Giraudon: 185 br; Musée d'Orsay, Paris: 406 cr (© DACS); National Army Museum, London: 278 t; National Gallery, London: 377 bl; National Maritime Museum, Greenwich: 373 tr; New Zealand High Commission, London: 382 cl; Prado, Madrid: 372 tl, 508 tl, 510 tr; Queensland Art Gallery, Brisbane: 10 tl; Roy Miles Gallery, London: 294 bl; Santa Maria della Grazie, Milan: 300 bl; Scott Polar Research Institute, Cambridge: 423 br; Staatliche Museen zu Berlin: 103 bc; Tate Gallery, London: 59 bc; Trade Union Congress, London: 282 bc; Vatican Museum & Art Galleries, Rome: 405 bl; Victoria & Albert Museum, London: 277 bl; William Morris Gallery, Walthamstow: 307 br. **Paul Brierley:** 491 bl; **Britain on View (BTA/ETB)/ Barry Hicks:** 549 bl; **British Airways:** 260 tr; **British Airways Archives & Museum Collection:** 542 tr; By kind permission of the **British Library:** 74 tr, 74 br, 75 tl, 320 cl, 346 bl, 346 br, 355 tl, 383 br; By courtesy of the **Trustees of the British Museum:** 58 l, 78 tl; **British Steel:** 289 c, br; **Duncan Brown:** 606 c.

C

Camera Press: 71 br; **Cannon:** 135 tr; **Peter Clayton:** 180 cr; **Coca Cola:** 11 tr, tc; **Bruce Coleman Ltd:** 173 tl, 234 tc, 307 tl, 385 r, 476 tr, 483 bl. Also: Gene Ahrens: 556 tr, 557 bl, 561 c; B. and C. Alexander: 331 bc, 465 cr; Jen and Des Bartlett: 317 br, 475 t, 586 b; Erwin and Peggy Bauer: 207 bl; Melinda Berge: 112 tl, 403 br; Mark

N. Boulton: 32 cl; E. Breeze-Jones: 401 tl; Jane Burton: 27 cr, 167 tl, 172, 177 b, 251 l, 309 r, 342 b, 365 br, 450 tl, 515 bc, 586 cr; Bob and Clara Calhoun: 66 bl; R.I.M. Campbell: 35 cr, 35 r, 224 br; Ron Cartmel: 317 br; John Caucalosi: 51 bl; Patrick Clement: 148 tl; Brian Coates: 73 bl, 143 bl, 145 bl, 403 bl; Rex Coleman: 265 bl; Alain Compost: 218 tr, 397 tr, 436 bl, 531 cr; Eric Crichton: 216 c; Gerald Cubitt: 13 tl, 40 br, 139 cr, 200 br, 246 tl, 264 br, 330 bl, 407 tl; Adrian Davies: 475 bl; David Davies: 75 bl, 451 b; A.J. Deane: 273 tr; Jack Dermid: 478 tl; Nicholas Devore: 544 br; Gerhard Egger: 532 tr; Jessica Ehlers: 170 cl; Francisco Erize: 476 b; Inigo Everson: 425 tl, r; N. Fenech: 265 br; Wedigo Ferchland: 30 b; Michael Fogden: 160 tr, 217 cr, 413 br; Jeff Foot: 271 c, 476 c; Neville Fox-Davies: 361 bl; M. Freeman: 105 cr, 116 br, 264 bl, 369 bl; C. B. Frith: 79 tl, 164 tl, 266 tr, 398 bc; Frithfoto: 109 bc; F. Greenaway: 401 l; Keith Gunner: 363 l; C. Henneghien: 123 bc, 310 tr, 470 cr, 505 br; Hans Gerde Heyer: 474 tl; Udo Hirsch: 272 tl; Cliff Hollenbeck: 237 bl, 557 tl; David C. Houston: 276 bl; David Hughes: 477 tl; Manfred Kage: 76 br; M.P. Kahl: 214 bl; Michael Klinec: 124 tr, 127 bl; Herbert Kranawetter: 228 bl, 229 cl; Stephen J. Krasemann: 67 tr, 386 tl; O. Langrand: 245 r; Wayne Lankinen: 48 bc, 263, 310 cl; Frans Lanting: 280 br; Norman R. Lightfoot: 261 c; Lee Lyon: 60 c; L.C. Marigo: 178 br, 201 tr, 235 b, 269 br, 431 b; John Markham: 74 cl; Marquez: 334 tl; Colin Molyneux: 533 br, bc; Norman Myers: 12 br, 318 tr, 359 bl, 427 tl; D. and J. McClurg: 181 tl; NASA: 173 tr, 176 tl, 360 bl; M. Timothy O'Keefe: 448 tr; Charlie Ott: 289 bl, 437 c; Alfred Pasieka: 136 r; Robert Perron: 413 cr; R. Tory Peterson: 375 bl; Douglas Pike: 13 bl; Dieter and Mary Plage: 184 bl, 591 bl, 367 bl; G.D. Plage: 171 tl, 266 cl, 316 br, 427 bl; Jaroslav Poncar: 578 tl; Dr. Eckart Pott: 51 bc, 316 br, 427 bl; Prato: 531 bl; Fritz Prenzel: 48 bl, 57 bl, 189 bl, 396 tl; Hans Reinhard: 100 tr, 182 tr, 330 cr, 421 br, 582 cl; H. Rivarola: 68 cl; Norbert Rosing: 194 tr; Leonard Lee Rue III: 386 c, 526 br; Len Rue Jr: 166 tr; Dr. Frieder Saver: 345 c; Norbert Schwirtz: 574 br; John Shaw: 174 cl, 352 bl, 440 br; Jeff Simon: 310 bl; James Simon: 167 tc; Werner Stoy: 173 br, 574 bl; Sullivan and Rogers: 167 c; Kim Taylor: 104 bl, 143 br, 183 b, 196 l, 365 cr, 489 cl, 593 tl; Bernd Thies: 478 c; Norman Tomalin: 26, 358 br, 451 tr, 536 tl, 555 tr; John Topham: 228 tr; Michel Viard: 365 tl; Carl Wallace: 217 cl; John Wallis: 375 cl; Rod Williams: 83 bc, 313 tr, 359 cl; Roger Wilmshurst: 475 r; Joseph van Wormer: 398 br, 425 bl; Jonathan T. Wright: 298 br, 391 tl, 482 tr; G. Zeisler: 86 br; Christian Zuber: 322 b, 403 bc; **Colorific/Wheeler Pictures/Joe McNally:** 246 r; *Corbusier: The Complete Architectural Works* 120 bc; **Dr. John Coates:** 254 tl; **Lupe Cunha:** 257 bl, 267 bl, 336 r; **Her Majesty's Customs & Excise:** 23 bl.

D

Douglas Dickins: 499 r; **C. M. Dixon:** 277 tl; **Zoë Dominic:** 396 c, br; **The Dutch Dairy Bureau:** 376 bc.

E

T. Malcolm English p. 262 bc; **E.T. Archive:** 107 bc, 141 bl, 332 bl, 372 br; **Mary Evans Picture Library** pp. 17 tl, 17 tr, 22 bl, 34 tl, 35 bc, 49 bl, 55 tl, 55 cl, 62 r, 63 tl, 63 cl, 64 tl, 65 tl, 70 tr, 77 r, 84 bl, 92 br, 93 cl, 97 tl, 103 tl, 108 b, 113 bl, 114 bl, 115 c, 118 tr, 122 bl, 122 tr, 136 bl, 142 brc, 149 bl, 149 c, 151 tl, 151 bl, 155 tr, 155 l, 169 tr,

174 bl, 178 bl, 182 bl, 184 tl, 185 cl, 188 br, 195 tl, 197 cr, 198 cl, 203 bl, 203 cr, 204 tl, 204 bl, 208 r, 210 tlc, 211 tr, 214 tl, 229 br, 230 cl, 231 tl, 239 bl, 243 br, 244 cr, 247 bc, 247 br, 256 bl, 257 cl, 265 cl, 267 tl, 269 tl, 272 bl, 279 tr, 282 t, 282 cl, 282 bl, 295 tl, 295 tr, 299 cl, 300 bc, 302 bc, 319 br (from *The Arabian Nights,* illustrated by Dulac, published by Hodder & Stoughton), 320 tr, 320 cr (from *Stories from Hans Andersen,* illustrated by Dulac, published by Hodder & Stoughton), 325 bl, 328 tl, 337 bl, 337 br, 338 c, 344 bl, 345 tr, 355 bl, 355 r, 370 tl, 370 cl, 370 bl (© Medici Society), 371 bl, 375 tl, 393 bl, 395 tl, 397 bl, 399 bc, 400 cl, 410 tl, 413 tr, 413 bl, 421 cr, 426 tl, 435 bl, 439 tr, 439 b, 440 tr, 443 br, 460 bl, 461 cr, 461 bc, 462 tr, 462 bc, 468 tl, 468 tr, 469 cl, 469 bl, 470 cl, 471 c, 471 b, 472 tl, 472 tc, 473 tl, 483 c, 483 b, 485 tl, 487 tr, 491 cr, 497 cl, 509 br, 510 cr, 513 tr, 527 bc, 528 tl, 531 tl, 532 bl, 534 tl, 535 tl, 537 tr, 538 bl, 540 cr, 544 cr, 544 bc, 547 tr, 553 tr, 553 cr, 554 tr, 554 tc, 561 bl, 569 tl, 570 tl, 570 cl, 570 bl, 571 br, 595 tl, 595 tc, 596 tc, 599 tr (from *Tanglewood Tales,* illustrated by Dulac, published by Hodder & Stoughton); 600 t, 600cl, 600 c, 600 br, 601 tr, 605 cr, 607 cl, 607 cl, 612 b. Also: Bruce Castle Collection: 400 bl; Explorer: 122 cl, 134 tl, 134 cl, 231 cl, 231 br, 338 bl, 510 cl; Fawcett Library: 592 c, 595 cl; Sigmund Freud Copyrights: 338 br.

F

By courtesy of the **Folio Society:** 320 tl; **Ford Motor Company:** 19 r, 96 bl; **Werner Forman Archive:** 44 tl. Also: collections of the British Museum, London: 44 blc, 370 bl; Metropolitan Museum of Art, New York: 235 tr; Mr. and Mrs. C. D. Wertheim: 299; Stateus Historika Museet, Stockholm: 573 tl; **French Railways:** 539; **John Frost Newspaper Archive:** 561bl, 597 tl.

G

General Motors: 522 bl; **Geoscience Features Picture Library:** 51 br, 102 b, 166 tl, 175 bl, 239 tr, 410 br; **German National Tourist Office:** 241 bc; **Stanley Gibbons Auctions:** 607 cr; **Giraudon:** 346 c. Also: collection of Musée Condé, Chantilly p. 229 bc; Lauros-Giraudon: 371 cl, 372 bc; **Greenpeace**/Gleizes: 138 tr; **Group Lotus Plc.:** 246 c.

H

Habitat: 161 bc; **Sonia Halliday Photographs** pp. 84 br, 306 bl, 399 tl. Also: F.H. Birch: 253 tr; Sonia Halliday and Laura Lushington: 228 br; James Wellard: 203 tl. **Hampshire County Constabulary:**. 426 tr; **Robert Harding Picture Library:** 12 tl, 13 br, 41 bl, 47 b, 110, 113 blc, 113 brc, 298 tl, 348 tr, 381, 474 tr. Also: Thierry Borredan: 225 bl; G. and P. Corrigan: 37 t, 111; Robert Francis: 226 l; Michael Jenner:. 349 br; G.R. Richardson: 240 bl; Paul van Riel: 293 bl; Nedra Westwater: 506 br; Carl Young: 474 bl; **Harland and Wolff:** 481 tl, 552 br; **Henson Associates Inc:** 436 br, c; © 1991 Alexander Wolf/Friedrich W.Heye Verlag GmbH, Munchen, Hamburg: 97 bc; frames taken from "Spider in the Bath". Reproduced by permission from **Hibbert Ralph Entertainment** © and **Silveyjex Partnership** © : 97 t; **Kaii Higashiyama:** 406 tr; **The Historical Society of Pennsylvania:** 576 bl; By courtesy of **Al Hoda:** 290 tr; **Michael Holford:** 33 bl, 59 tl, 59 bl, 107 c, 117 br, 130 br, 131 cr, 277 br, 366 tr, 410 bc, 412 blc, 417 br, 605 t, 606 tl; **Holt Studios Ltd.:** Richard Anthony: 525 tr; Nigel Cattlin: 325 r; Duncan Smith: 202 bl; **Hulton Picture Company:** 33 br, 55 c, 114 bc, 118 bl, 128 tl, 128 bl, 132 br, 157 bl, 187 t, 188 tr, 203 b, 278

(continued)

tl, 278 c, 287 bl, 295 cl, 299 bc, 301 bl, 301 bc, 423 tl, 428 tr, br, 472 bl, 472 br, 502 bl, 554 cl, 554 cr, 568 cl, 592 bc, 594 bl, 596 bl, 597 bl, 597 br, 597 c, 599 bl, 606 br; **Bettmann Archive:** 36 cl, 128 tr, 316 cl, 416 br, 608 br; UPI/Bettmann Newsphotos: 77 brc; **The Hutchison Library:** 291 bc, 408 tr, 492 bl, 488 c; Robert Aberman: 349 cr; H.R. Dorig: 496 cr, 337 tl; Sarah Errington: 109 cr, 201 bl, 202 tl, 164 br; Robert Francis: 311 br; Melanie Friend: 132 bl; Carlos Friete: 273 bc; J.G. Fuller: 76 tl; Bernard Gérard: 488 tl; Felix Greene: 11 br, 332 br; R. Ian Lloyd: 442 r; Michael MacIntyre: 442 bl; P. Moszynski:. 169 cr; P.E. Parker: 569 br; B. Regent: 412 bc; Kerstin Rodgers: 592 tl; Anna Tully: 165 bl.

I

By courtesy of **IAL·Security Products** p. 601 cr; **ICI Fibres** p. 531 cl; **ITN Ltd.** p. 530 bl; **Illustrated London News Picture Library** pp. 278 bl, 541 bl; **The Image Bank:** 43 t, 61 br, 93 bl, 206 bc, 291 br, 375 bc, 264 r, 463 bc, 498 b; Arthur d'Arazien p. 492 br; Joe Azzara p. 588 tr; Alan Becker p. 541 tc; Bernard van Berg pp. 227 tr, 378 b, 379 b; Derek Berwin: 350; Walter Bibikow p. 452 bc; Anthony A. Boccoccio: 208 l; Peter and Georgina Bowater: 52 c, 99 tr, 241 t; P. and Joseph Brignolo:. 429, 545 bl, 351; J. Brousseau: 80 tr; J. Bryson: 87 br; James H. Carmichael Jr: 106 br; Luis Castenada: 192 b, 221 tl, 509 tl; Eva Cellini: 604 tl; Kay Chernush: 178 cl, 291 bl; Alain Choisnet: 540 tr; Gianalberto Cigolini: 116 tl, 136 tl; Giuliano Colliva: 89 bl, 493 tr; Jean Claude Comminges: 297 t; DC Productions: 376 br; Hank Delespinasse: 513 tl; Lisl Dennis: 32 br; Marc Domanelli: 89 cl; Steve Drexler: 117 bl; Steve Dunwell: 356 br; Grant U. Faint: 41 tr, 89 br, 271 tr; Faustino: 61 tl; Jay Freis: 106 tr; P. Frey: 492 bc; Brett Froomer: 112 bl, 211 bl; Dr. J. Gebhardt: 212 cl; G. Giacomo: 87 bl; Gary Gladstone: 538 t; Larry Dale Gordon: 144 tlc, 495 t, 578 bl; David W. Hamilton: 99 tl, 549 tl, 557 tr; G. K. and Vicky Hart: 541 bc; Gregory Heisler: 161 br; Francisco Hidalgo: 272 bc, 137 tr; Eddie Hironaka: 91 b; David Hiser: 310 c; Robert Holland: 402 br; Alex Hubrich: 326 bc; Laurence Hughes: 15 b; C. Isy-Schwart: 204 cr; Marcel Isy-Schwart: 404 t; Lou Jawitz: 489 tl, 525 tl; Lou Jones: 490 br; Ronald R. Johnson: 296 cl, 505 c; Gunther Kaufmann: 324 tl; John P. Kelly: 579 br; Don Klumpp: 348 b, 349 tl; Kodansha Images: 481 r; Dan Landwehrle: 181 tr; Erik Leigh: 374 br; Romilly Lockyer: 150 bl; Walter Iooss Jr.: 237 br; Charles Mahaux: 246 br; David Martin: 326 tr; Burton McNeely: 547 tl; Michael Melford: 439 tl, 521 tl; Colin Molyneux: 220 bl, 259 tl; Kaz Mori: 173 tl; Toyofumi Mori: 297 b; Terry Madison: 526 tl; Fong Siu Nang: 112 br; Paul Nehrenz:. 498 br; Marvin E. Newman: 465 cl; Steve Niedorf: 165 br, 336 c; Francisco Ontanon: 508 bl; Robert Phillips: 429 bl; Jean-Pierre Pieuchot: 440 bl; Andrea Pistoles: 455 tl, 608 tc; Thomas R. Rampy: 392 br; Toby Rankin: 520 bl; Magnus Reitz: 93 tr; Co Rentmeester: 551 tr; F. Roiter: 59 br, 252 br; Ben Rose: 413 c; Guido Alberto Rossi: 52 b, 53, 91 t, 292 cr, 325 t, 505 c, 508 br, 579 l; Michael Salas: 54 tr; Steve Satushek: 43 b; Ulli Seer : 411 tl; Milan Skaryd: 23 br; Paul Slaughter: 142 bl, 606 tr; Grafton G. Smith: 144 br; Marc Solomon: 221 br; Harald Sund: 58 r, 340 tr, 556 cl; S. Sundberg: 466 b; Peter Thomann: 127 cl; Anne de Vaeren: 117 tl; Eric L. Wheater: 86 c, 494 t; C.A. Wilton: 162 tl; Sah Zarember: 535 cl; **The Trustees of the Imperial War Museum, London:** 38 tl, 592 bl, 595 c; **Innes Photographic Library:** John Blackburn: 77 bc; Ivor Innes: 77 tl, bl; **Intercity:** 187 br.

J

Japan Information & Cultural Centre p. 320 bl; **JET Joint Undertaking** p. 388 tl; **Barri Jones, University of Manchester, Department of Archaeology** p. 35 tr.

K

David King Collection: 132 tr; By kind permission of the Provost and Scholars, **King's College, Cambridge:** 320 bc; By courtesy of **Kodak:** 414 tr; **The Kobal Collection:** 50 br, 205 tr, 206 bl, 276 tr, 367 bc, 453 tr, 600 bl.

L

Frank Lane Picture Agency: 475 cl; Dick Jones: 104 tr; Robert Steinar: 520 cl; *As an Fhearan*, published by **An Lanntair, Stornaway:** 473 bl; **Leica Camera GmbH:** 240 br; **London Features International** ILPO/Musto: 369 br; SKR Photos: 366 bl; Serge Thomann: 428 bl; **Anne Lyons:** 430 tr.

M

Magic Circle/Mac Wilson: 328 bl; **Magnum:** Pinkhassov 568 bl; **Raymond Mander and Joe Mitcheson Theatre Collection:** 119 b, tlc, blc; **The Mansell Collection:** 24 b, 55 tr, 85 cl, 133 br, 468 bl, 594 tl, 604 tr, 607 tl; **Stephen Marks Collection:** 497 c; **Mercedes-Benz:** 95 cl; **The Metropolitan Museum of Art,** Rogers Fund, 1904 (04.3.241)**:** 302 c; By courtesy of **Michelin Tyre Plc.:** 588 cl; **Montana Historical Society, Helena:** 144 bl; **Museum of London:** 74 bc; **McDonnell Douglas Corp.:** 524-525 t.

N

NASA: 45 tl, 48 br, 360 bc, 402 bl, 419 br, 419 tl, 464 br, 542 cl, 542 br, 562 cl, 583 tl, 584 bl, 246 far r; **National Gallery, London:** 406 tl, 444 t; **National Maritime Museum, Greenwich:** 373 tr, 399 bl; **National Museum of Wales, Cardiff:** 552 cr; By courtesy of the **Natural History Museum, London :** 31 tl; **Netherlands Institute for War Documentation/**© 1990, Copyright by **Cosmopress Geneva & Anne Frank-Fonds:** 599 cr; **Network:** Goldwater p. 38 r, 105 br; Sturrock: 426 cr; **Peter Newark's Pictures:** 20 tl, 118 cr, 121 tl, 121 cr, 126 c, 157 c, 157 br, 279 bc, 279 br, 280 tl, 280 cl, 316 tr, 316 bl, 328 cl, 400 tl, 400 br, 417 bc, 430 b, 449 cl, 485 br, 496 br, 518 tr, 589 b, 590 tl, c, bl, br; **NHPA:** Anthony Bannister: 69 c, 104 tl; G.I. Bernard: 493 br; J.H. Carmichael: 389 tr; Stephen Dalton: 65 c; Manfred Dannegger: 362; William S. Paton: 334 c; Jany Sauvanet: 223; G.E. Schmida/ANT: 324; Philippa Scot: 322 cl; Roger Tidney: 159 tl; Dave Watts/ANT: 51 tl; Martin Wendler: 308 cl; Bill Wood: 448 tl; **The Nobel Foundation:** 469 br; **Novosti Press Agency:** 460 tl, 462 bl, 566 b, 567 t, bc, br.

O

Ordnance Survey/Crown Copyright: 333 c; **Christine Osborne Pictures:** 10 cl, 40 bl, 51 tr, 336 tl, 474 cr, 545 tl; **Osel Group** by courtesy of Quest, Marshall Cavendish: 548 cr; issued by Peter Sawell & Partners and made available by courtesy of **Otis Elevator Plc:** 189 bl; **Oxford Scientific Films:** 486 b. Also Fran Allan/Animals Animals: 266 cr; Doug Allen: 587 br; Tony Allen: 487 b; Kathie Atkinson: 56 tr, 330 tl; M. Austerman/Animals Animals: 450 bl; G.I. Bernard p. 213 c; Mike Birkhead: 322 cr; Raymond Blythe: 69 tl; J.A.L. Cooke: 31 b, 249 br, 486 l; Michael Fogden: 57 tl; David Fox: 171 cl; Laurence Gold: 210 tr; Pam and Willy Kemp: 177 tl; Richard Kirby: 308 tr; B.G. Murray Jr./Earth Scenes: 440 c; Stan Osolinski: 147 c; John Paling: 27 bl, Edward Parker: 18 tr; Ronald Toms: 591 bl; Kim Westerskov: 153 t.

P

Patten & Stroud: 262 bl; *Winstanley: The Law of Freedom* published by **Penguin Books:** 122 br; **Pickthall Picture Library/Barry Pickthall:** 463 tl; **Philips:** 529 br; **Philips Scientific:**. 344 cr; **Planet Earth:** Peter Capen 211 br; Peter David: 152 tr, bl; John Lythgoe: 602 b; Christian Petron: 35 br; David Phillips: 361 c; Flip Schulke: 548 tr; Jonathan Scott: 569 bl; William Smithey: 153 c; Marty Snyderman: 479 bl; Herwath Voigtmann: 548 bl; Warren Williams: 392 c; **Richard Platt:** 63 bc, 182 br, 327 br; **Popperfoto:** 17 c, 17 cl, 114 br, 116 bl, 118 cl, 118 br, 230 bl, 230 br, 244 cl, 249 c, 304 bl, 363 tr, 391 bl, 395 tl, 459 bl, 459 br, 472 bc, 497 bl, 497 br, 512 t, 555 tl, 561 lc, 572 br, 572 lc, 606 bl; **The Post Office, London:** 430 2nd cr; **Press Association/**Topham Picture Source: 473 bc; Crown Copyright/**Public Record Office:** 384 c.

Q

Q. A. Photos/Eurotunnel: 546 bl; By gracious permission of **Her Majesty the Queen:** 133 tr.

R

RSC Collection, Stratford/Angus McBean: 533 c; type-metal engraving by J. G. Posada, courtesy of the **Redstone Press:** 340 cl; **Rex Features:** 382 bl. Also: Frilet/Sipa: 554 bc; John Shelley: 41 tl; Sipa Press: 126 cl; Wheeler: 186 tl; **Rijksmuseum, Amsterdam:** 377 bc; **Redferns/Steve Gillet:** 367 tl; **Ann Ronan Picture Library:** 131 br, 203 c, 347 tl; **Clifford Rosney:** 326 cl, 557 bc; **Rover Group:**. 191 br; By kind permission of the **Royal Mint:** 356 tl.

S

Scala: 405 br, 471 cr (Biblioteca Reale); **Science Photo Library:** Doug Allen: 30 brc; Ken Biggs: 108 tr, 186 b; Biophoto Associates: 446 br; Dr. Jeremy Burgess: 345 tl, bl; CNRI: 164 c, 219 r; William Curtsinger: 30 trc; Martin Dohrn: 19 bc, 236 tr; Earth Satellite Corp.: 464 bc, 333 br; Prof. Harold Edgerton: 413 tc; Dr. Fred Espenak: 47 tlc, 136 cl, 335 cl, 516 tl; Simon Fraser: 123 tr, 423 bl; European Space Agency: 47 tr, 418 brc; Prof. R. Gehrz: 47 tl; Dr. George Gornacz: 515 bl; Eric Grave: 344 c; Allen Green: 557 br; T. Gull & R. Fesen, NASA GSFC: 49 br; Adam Hart-Davis: 259 br; IBM: 344 bc; Alexander Isiaras: 388 bl, 524 bl; R.E. Litchfield: 345 br; Lawrence Migoale: 164 bl; Tim Malyon: 312 tr; Astrid and Hans Frieder Michler: 524 c; Tom McHugh: 269 bl; NASA: 45 bl, 47 blc, 312 br, 418 bl, 418 blc, 419 blc, 419 bl, 419 bc, 419 br, 601 br, 45 bl, 605 br; Division of Computer Research & Technology, National Institute of Health: 49 r; NIBSC: 258 bl; NRAO: 47 c; David Parker: 46 t, 136 c, 438 l, 528 bl; David Parker/Max-Planck-Institut fur Aeronomie: 131 tr; David Parker/IMI/University of Birmingham High TC Consortium: 181 cl; David Parker/600 Group France: 453 c; Philippe Plailly: 312 bl, 336 b; Royal Greenwich Observatory: 124 br; John Sanford: 131 bl, 360 tl; Dr. Gerald Schatten: 257 br; Smithsonian Institute: 47 tc; Jim Stevenson: 156 c, 445 tl; Takeshi Takahara: 540 bl; Dr. T.E. Thompson: 165 c; U.S. Geographical Survey: 418 br; U.S. Navy: 581 br; Novosti: 45 br; M.I. Walker: 345 cl; **Shell Photo Service:** 394 br; **Silkeborg Museum, Denmark:** 35 tl; **South American Pictures/Tony Morrison:** 58 b, 497 tr; **Spectrum Colour Library:**. 150 br, 285 br, 552 cl; **Frank Spooner Pictures:** Bartholomew: 155 cr; Bennett: 604 br; Eric Bouvet/Gamma: 17 bl, 502 br; John Chiasson: 39 br; Deborah Copaken:

(continued)

ILLUSTRATORS